THE 1992 GUIDE

Contents

Les Routiers 21 Years in Britain

How to use this Guide   5

Symbols used in this Guide   7

Join Club Bon Viveur   8

The 1992 Awards   10

Key to Maps   19

Regional Maps of Britain   20

Guide Entries

   The South West and the Channel Islands   39

   Central and Southern England   143

   London   321

   Wales and The Borders   343

   Northern England and the Isle of Man   409

   Central, Lowlands and Scottish Borders

   incorporating Northumberland   531

   Scottish Highlands   595

Index of Towns   629

Club Bon Viveur Application Form   639

First published in the United Kingdom in 1992
Alan Sutton Publishing Ltd
Phoenix Mill · Far Thrupp · Stroud
Gloucestershire

British Library Cataloguing in Publication Data

Les Routiers guide to Britain.
  647.9541

  ISBN 0-7509-0084-9

Editor: Mandy Morton-Smith
Assistant Editor: Linda Bird
Maps: John Flower
Illustrations: Trudy Price

Typeset by Microgen, Welwyn Garden City, Herts
Printed and bound in Great Britain at The Bath Press, Bath, Avon.

Routiers inspectors visit each establishment
anonymously and settle the bill before
revealing their identity. Complimentary
meals and/or accommodation are not
accepted.

LES ROUTIERS
21 YEARS IN BRITAIN

In 1971 the search began for quality, value and a warm welcome at restaurants, pubs, hotels and guest houses in Britain.

Travellers in France had long associated the red and blue Les Routiers sign with good food and value for money but, in Britain, many establishments were typified by poor quality, inflated prices and indifferent service, with eating out regarded as elitist. Over the past 21 years, Les Routiers has helped to change standards and attitudes by recognising independently owned and run hotels and restaurants which provide quality and value to the customer.

Today, better quality fresh produce, improved service, and greater expectations from the public due to increased European travel, have led to a general improvement in standards. To ensure that the highest standards are met by Les Routiers recommended establishments, an anonymous inspection is carried out before inclusion in the Guide.

The Les Routiers inspectorate have enjoyed the best and endured the worst that British catering and hospitality can provide. They have visited outstandingly good establishments and survived those where 'a bad night' happens all too often. Only those that pass the strict inspection are featured in the Guide. To ensure an authentic judgement, the bill is paid before the inspector's identity is revealed and no complimentary food or accommodation is accepted. The inspection covers all aspects of the establishment from food and service to comfort and hygiene, including a full kitchen inspection.

Whether you are looking for a country house hotel, cosy bed and breakfast, village inn or cosmopolitan restaurant, consult the Les Routiers Guide and take away the element of risk involved in eating out or finding a place to stay. The Les Routiers Guide lists over 1,800 establishments where you are guaranteed good quality food and accommodation, and a warm and friendly welcome – all at a price you can afford.

THE LES ROUTIERS SIGN

Before an establishment can display the famous red and blue Les Routiers sign, it has to pass the strict Les Routiers inspection for quality and value. That is why your Les Routiers Guide takes the risk out of finding a good place to eat or stay. Although Les Routiers recommended establishments vary in style and size, every Routiers will provide quality, value and a warm welcome.

The inspection is carried out anonymously and covers all aspects of an establishment from food and service to comfort and hygiene, including a full kitchen inspection. In addition, once an establishment has been awarded the Les Routiers recommendation, they are regularly reinspected to ensure that standards are maintained.

The sign is displayed by all members demonstrating their commitment to providing quality and value for their customers. However, only if an establishment has a current certificate with the correct proprietor's or manager's name, is it a current member.

Every year, there are establishments which close down or change ownership, or occasionally places which allow their standards to drop and have to be withdrawn. Unfortunately, despite our efforts, there are establishments which continue to display the sign when they are no longer members. If you know of a Les Routiers establishment which you do not consider worthy of the Les Routiers sign, or which is displaying the sign without a current certificate, please let us know.

We receive recommendations for new appointments throughout the year, and our inspectors are always busy trying out new places, with new members joining Les Routiers each month. If you know of an establishment worthy of the Les Routiers recommendation, please let us know. An opinion form can be found on the last page of this Guide.

HOW TO USE THIS GUIDE

This Guide gives full details on 1,800 Les Routiers recommended establishments throughout Britain. These range from cosy country inns and guest houses on quiet backroads, to elegant hotels and restaurants in major resorts and on main travelling routes. The Guide has been designed to help you locate easily the Routiers that suits you.

How to Find A Routiers

If you have a specific town in mind, all you need do is refer to the index in the back pages of the Guide for a full list of towns and villages where you will find a Routiers. However, if you wish to travel across a broader area or discover areas previously unknown to you, there are detailed maps to help you plan your route.

The Guide itself has been divided into seven regional sections: South West England and the Channel Islands; Central and Southern England; London; Wales and the Borders; Northern England; Central, Lowlands and Scottish Borders; and the Scottish Highlands. In some cases, these regions may encompass fairly broad areas, or borders may overlap. This is intended to help you position your place on the map in relation to other parts of the country.

Within the regions, all entries are listed alphabetically by town with details of the type of recommendation in the margin alongside each entry. If you are uncertain of the region in which to find a specific town, refer to the key to maps, page 19, which will point you to the correct regional map. Towns or villages with a Routiers are marked on the map in blue, with the main roads in red. Towns marked in red are for reference only.

For Quick Reference

At the beginning of each section, you will also find a quick reference guide indicating the exact number of Routiers in the specified town, with a star showing whether they are recommended for food and/or accommodation, and at what price. For brief directions on how to find an establishment, turn to the particular entry.

On pages 6 and 7 you will find an explanation of the price brackets used and a list of the symbols found in this guide. We hope you will have no trouble finding the Routiers of your choice but, if in doubt, look out for the distinctive red and blue Les Routiers sign.

ROUTIERS RECOMMENDS ...

The Routiers recommendation is for quality and value. Les Routiers recognise that value for money can be found in a variety of different establishments and the costs involved in providing more elaborate menus or better facilities will be reflected in the prices. A more expensive establishment can prove to be equally good value for money as a cheaper one because of the type of food and accommodation on offer. Regional price variations have also been reflected in the prices.

Food and accommodation recommendations fall into one of four price ranges as follows:

⊗ **FOOD RECOMMENDATION:** for establishments offering a 3 course meal excluding wine and service which offers quality and value within the following price bands:

£   up to £10
££   between £10 and £15
£££   between £15 and £20
££££ between £20 and £25

▭ **ACCOMMODATION RECOMMENDATION:** is awarded to establishments providing bed and breakfast (based on 2 people sharing a room) within the following price bands:

£   up to £15 per person
££   between £15 and £22 per person
£££   between £22 and £30 per person
££££ between £30 and £40 per person

Please note:
The price bands are intended to give an indication of the style and price of meals or accommodation available. Price ranges are based on information available at the time of this Guide going to press; however, prices are set by the establishment and cannot be guaranteed. In addition, expensive selections from a menu or the choice of luxury accommodation may cost more. Where an inn or pub offers restaurant and bar meals or snacks, the bar meals are almost invariably in the lower price band. Likewise luncheons will often be in the lower price bracket when dinner is in the more expensive range. The recommendations given refer to the evening restaurant meals.

SYMBOLS USED IN THIS GUIDE

&. ACCESS FOR DISABLED

(V) VEGETARIAN MEALS

cc CREDIT CARDS

🛏 ACCOMMODATION – with the number of bedrooms

🅿 CAR PARK ON SITE

🍲 CASSEROLE AWARD – the Les Routiers mark of excellence, see pages 10 to 12.

🧀 CHEESE SYMBOL – indicates an establishment offering an outstanding cheese selection. See page 33 for further details.

w WINE SYMBOL – awarded to those establishments with an interesting and well selected wine list. See page 36 for further details.

CLUB CLUB BON VIVEUR SYMBOL – indicates an establishment offering special discounts or benefits to Club Bon Viveur members. See page 8 to join.

Note:
1. Restaurant recommendations which include accommodation details but have no suitcase symbol, may offer bed and breakfast but are outside the Routiers price range, or below the standards accepted by Les Routiers.

2. Some establishments in the Guide are recommended for accommodation only. This means that either no meals are served or that the restaurant is open to residents only. The meals will still have passed the Routiers inspection and will often be of outstanding quality and value.

3. Almost all bedrooms have washbasins in the room. Where en suite facilities are available this is indicated.

4. Children – where there is no indication that children are welcome, this does not imply an unfriendly establishment. The facilities or licensing laws may not allow for children.

5. Pets – it is always advisable to clarify whether pets are permitted. With few exceptions, Guide dogs are always welcome.

JOIN CLUB BON VIVEUR

**Have you heard of Club Bon Viveur? . . .
the club which offers superb benefits for
Les Routiers Guide users who enjoy good food,
wine and travel.**

Wouldn't you like to enjoy A FREE BOTTLE OF WINE with
your meal?

Or, how about A 20% REDUCTION ON YOUR
ACCOMMODATION BILL?

Or, taking up a COMPLIMENTARY DESSERT after a
starter and main course?

If these kinds of benefits interest you, perhaps these will
also:

- £2 off Les Routiers Guides

- Special motoring kits for travelling

- Discounts on insurance and holidays

    and more . . .

Club Bon Viveur members are offered incentives and
discounts by over 300 Les Routiers establishments. All you
have to do to obtain these discounts is to show your Club
membership card when you visit. There is a special
Discounts Booklet sent with your card, listing all the
establishments offering incentives.

CLUB BON VIVEUR BENEFIT PACKAGE

Just look at the full benefit package you are entitled to!

- Your Club Bon Viveur membership card which entitles you to special concessions at over 300 Les Routiers restaurants and hotels throughout Britain

- £2 off additional copies of either Les Routiers Guide to Britain or to France (no charge for p&p)

- Discounts off motoring services and insurance with Europ Assistance

- 10% discount off all holidays in the Paris and France brochures booked through Jet Tours and the French Travel Service

- Newsletters including promotional offers, e.g. special motoring kits for travellers

New ideas to improve club benefits and to make the club more useful are always welcome, so if you have any thoughts of your own, please let us know.

THE 1992 CASSEROLE AWARDS

The 'Casserole' is the Les Routiers mark of excellence awarded annually to hotels and restaurants, which in the opinion of our inspectors, consistently offer outstanding quality. There are no restrictions on the type of establishment that can be awarded the distinction. The list includes pubs, restaurants, hotels and bed and breakfast establishments, all of which offer something out of the ordinary. Each 'Casserole' owner displays a special certificate and the 'Casserole' symbol appears alongside their entry in the Guide and on the maps by the town name.

THE SOUTH WEST AND CHANNEL ISLANDS
CHELWOOD, Avon – Chelwood House Hotel
POLPERRO, Cornwall – The Kitchen
ST IVES BAY, Cornwall – Pedn-Olva Hotel
TRURO, Cornwall – Long's Restaurant
BAMPTON, Devon – The Swan Hotel
BARNSTAPLE, Devon – Downrew House Hotel
BOVEY TRACEY, Devon – Edgemoor Hotel
EXETER, Devon – Old Thatch Inn
PAIGNTON, Devon – Dolce Vita
PLYMOUTH, Devon – Trattoria Pescatore
WEYMOUTH, Dorset – Sea Cow Bistro
VAZON BAY, Guernsey – La Grande Mare
ST OUEN'S BAY, Jersey – Lobster Pot

CENTRAL AND SOUTHERN ENGLAND
BEDFORD, Bedfordshire – Knife and Cleaver
MAIDENHEAD, Berkshire – Boulters Lock Inn
BEACONSFIELD, Buckinghamshire – Royal Standard of England
POOLE, Dorset – Allans Seafood Restaurant
CIRENCESTER, Gloucestershire – Wild Duck Inn
STOW-ON-THE-WOLD, Gloucestershire – Grapevine Hotel
FAREHAM, Hampshire – Chives
ODIHAM, Hampshire – La Forêt
ROTHERWICK, Hampshire – Tylney Hall
SEAVIEW, Isle of Wight – Seaview Hotel and Restaurant
BOUGHTON MONCHELSEA, Kent – Tanyard
WHITSTABLE, Kent – Giovanni's Restaurant
OLD DALBY, Leicestershire – The Crown Inn
HARROW, Middlesex – Fiddler's Restaurant
PINNER, Middlesex – La Giralda
SNETTISHAM, Norfolk – Rose and Crown
SOULDERN, Oxfordshire – Fox Inn
WATLINGTON, Oxfordshire – The Well House

ARMITAGE, Staffordshire – The Old Farmhouse Restaurant
BURY ST EDMUNDS, Suffolk – The Six Bells Inn
LAVENHAM, Suffolk – The Great House Restaurant
BRIGHTON AND HOVE, East Sussex – Le Grandgousier
RYE, East Sussex – Flackley Ash Hotel and Restaurant
MIDHURST, West Sussex – Spread Eagle Hotel
CORSHAM, Wiltshire – Rudloe Park Hotel

LONDON
BATTERSEA – Jack's Place
BAYSWATER – Veronica's Restaurant
BLOOMSBURY – Academy Hotel
HERNE HILL – Jacques' Restaurant
KENSINGTON – Observatory Hotel

WALES AND THE BORDERS
CLEARWELL, Gloucestershire – Wyndham Arms
ROSS-ON-WYE, Hereford and Worcester – Pengethley Manor
NORTON, Shropshire – Hundred House Hotel
LLANDYBIE, Dyfed – Cobblers Restaurant
MONMOUTH, Gwent – The Crown at Whitbrook
BETWS-Y-COED, Gwynedd – The Ty Gwyn
CRICCIETH, Gwynedd – The Moelwyn Restaurant
DOLGELLAU, Gwynedd – Clifton House Hotel
LLANDUDNO, Gwynedd – Dunoon Hotel

NORTHERN ENGLAND
CHESTER, Cheshire – Francs Restaurant
CHESTER, Cheshire – Redland Hotel
AMBLESIDE, Cumbria – Riverside Hotel
BASSENTHWAITE LAKE, Cumbria – Pheasant Inn
BOWNESS-ON-WINDERMERE, Cumbria – Blenheim Lodge
CARLISLE, Cumbria – String of Horses Inn and Restaurant
GRANGE-OVER-SANDS, Cumbria – Netherwood Hotel
GRIZEDALE, Cumbria – Grizedale Lodge Hotel
LONGTOWN, Cumbria – Sportsman's Restaurant, March Bank Hotel
MELMERBY, Cumbria – Shepherds Inn
WITHERSLACK, Cumbria – Old Vicarage
WIRKSWORTH, Derbyshire – Le Bistro
GOOSNARGH, Lancashire – Bushells Arms
LANCASTER, Lancashire – Springfield House Hotel
LONGRIDGE, Lancashire – Corporation Arms
LONGSDON, Staffordshire – Bank End Farm Motel
GREAT AYTON, North Yorkshire – Ayton Hall
NORTON, North Yorkshire – Cornucopia
THIRSK, North Yorkshire – Nags Head Hotel and Restaurant
WHITBY, North Yorkshire – The Magpie Cafe

ROTHERHAM, South Yorkshire – The Elton Hotel
ELLAND, West Yorkshire – Berties Bistro
HUDDERSFIELD, West Yorkshire – Hey Green Hotel
LEEDS, West Yorkshire – Olive Tree Greek Restaurant

CENTRAL, LOWLANDS AND SCOTTISH BORDERS
PEEBLES, Borders – Cringlettie House Hotel
SELKIRK, Borders – Phillipburn House Hotel
BURNTISLAND, Fife – Kingswood Hotel
EDINBURGH, Lothian – The Tattler
EDINBURGH, Lothian – Verandah Tandoori Restaurant
AYR, Strathclyde – Fouters Bistro
GLASGOW, Strathclyde – La Fiorentina
KILWINNING, Strathclyde – Montgreenan Mansion House Hotel
STRACHUR, Strathclyde – The Creggans Inn

SCOTTISH HIGHLANDS
BANCHORY, Grampian – Banchory Lodge
CULLEN, Grampian – Bay View Hotel
NEWBURGH, Grampian – Udny Arms Hotel
GRANTOWN-ON-SPEY, Highland – Ravenscourt House Hotel
INVERNESS, Highland – Whinpark Hotel and Restaurant
NAIRN, Highland – The Woodland Cottage Restaurant
SHETLAND ISLES – Da Peerie Fisk Restaurant

Sélection Les Routiers
VIN DE PAYS
FRANÇAIS
GOOD QUALITY · GOOD VALUE

LES ROUTIERS AWARDS
– YOUR OPINION

Each year the Les Routiers inspectorate use their experience to decide which establishments are worthy of the Les Routiers Casserole. In addition, there are several individual awards made each year. To be considered for an award, an establishment must offer that something extra, which is difficult to define but easy to recognise.

Many thanks for all the letters nominating establishments for a Les Routiers Award. Your help and opinions are invaluable in compiling our list of award winners. On the back page of the Guide you will find an Opinion Form, allowing you to nominate your favourite Les Routiers establishment for a Casserole Award. Alternatively, tell us why you think an establishment should be considered for one of the following:

Restaurant of the Year – a restaurant that has been Les Routiers recommended for at least one year and is considered to be outstanding in terms of food and service.

Accommodation of the Year – a hotel or guest house offering comfortable accommodation and the best in hospitality. The meals served must also be of the highest standard.

Pub of the Year – a public house or free house which best illustrates the Les Routiers criteria of a warm welcome, quality and value. The quality of the food, service and atmosphere are of prime importance.

Newcomer of the Year – any establishment that is featured in the Les Routiers Guide for the first time. Each year the Les Routiers inspectors decide which establishment has most impressed inspectors at the first inspection.

Prix d'Elite – the award for the most outstanding wine list at a Les Routiers establishment.

Cheeseboard of the Year – the award for the best chosen cheeseboard at a Les Routiers establishment.

Symbol of Excellence – not an annual award but given to an establishment that has been recommended by Les Routiers for many years and has consistently impressed the Les Routiers inspectorate and Guide users. This award has only been presented to three establishments since its creation. The past winners were **Jack's Place**, **London** and **La Giralda**, **Pinner** – two restaurants well worth visiting!

ROUTIERS RESTAURANT OF THE YEAR

THE LOBSTER POT HOTEL AND RESTAURANT
L' Etacq, St Ouen's, Jersey
Tel: (0534) 82888

Proprietor: GERALD HOWE
Manager: AURELIO CARVALHO

Internationally famous for the quality of its cuisine, the Lobster Pot is claimed to be 'Jersey's most famous restaurant for over a quarter of a century'. The location and seafaring name of the restaurant are reflected in the décor and, not surprisingly, a mouth-watering selection of seafood is offered, with fresh lobster the house speciality. Consistently praised by Les Routiers inspectors for its outstanding quality and excellent value for money.

ROUTIERS ACCOMMODATION OF THE YEAR

BLENHEIM LODGE
Brantfell Road, Bowness-on-Windermere, Cumbria
Tel: (05394) 43440

Proprietors: JACKIE and FRANK SANDERSON

A beautiful Lakeland stone house with lake and mountain views, peacefully set against National Trust lands. The eleven individually furnished bedrooms and outstanding food featuring Old English recipes are complemented by the warmest of welcomes and a true home from home atmosphere. The personal service and hospitality provided by Mr and Mrs Sanderson is endorsed by the large number of repeat visits to this charming hotel.

ROUTIERS PUB OF THE YEAR

THE TATTLER
23 Commercial Street, Leith, Edinburgh, Lothian
Tel: (031) 554 9999

Proprietors: ALAN and LINDA THOMSON

A worthy winner for its combination of friendliness, good food and comfort. Beautifully appointed and furnished, The Tattler caters for most tastes, either in the relaxing restaurant or in the bar with its cosy Victorian nooks and crannies and a blazing parlour fire. Using natural Scottish produce, the menu features French, Scottish, English and Mediterranean recipes with fresh local seafood high on the menu. Enjoy good food, a welcoming atmosphere and a sense of how Leith must once have been.

ROUTIERS NEWCOMER OF THE YEAR

GRASSINGTON HOUSE HOTEL
Grassington, Skipton, North Yorkshire
Tel: (0756) 752406

Proprietors: GORDON and LINDA ELSWORTH

Chosen from almost 400 establishments new to the 1992 Les Routiers Guide, Grassington House Hotel has been a favourite with a wide variety of guests for many years. Welcoming service and imaginative, superbly cooked food made from the best of fresh local produce, are provided within the delightful surroundings of this listed Georgian hotel. A worthy winner of this award for its excellent food, comfortable accommodation and atmosphere of warmth and friendliness.

THE ROUTIERS SYMBOL OF EXCELLENCE AWARD 1992

LE GRANDGOUSIER RESTAURANT
15 Western Street, Brighton, East Sussex
Tel: (0273) 772005

Proprietor: LEWIS HARRIS

In recognition of consistently high standards over the past ten years, and in celebration of 21 years of Les Routiers in Britain, we have pleasure in presenting this award to Le Grandgousier Restaurant in Brighton. A Casserole Award winner for many years, Le Grandgousier has continued to delight Les Routiers inspectors with the excellent quality of the 6 course menu, friendly service and outstanding value for money.

Key to map pages

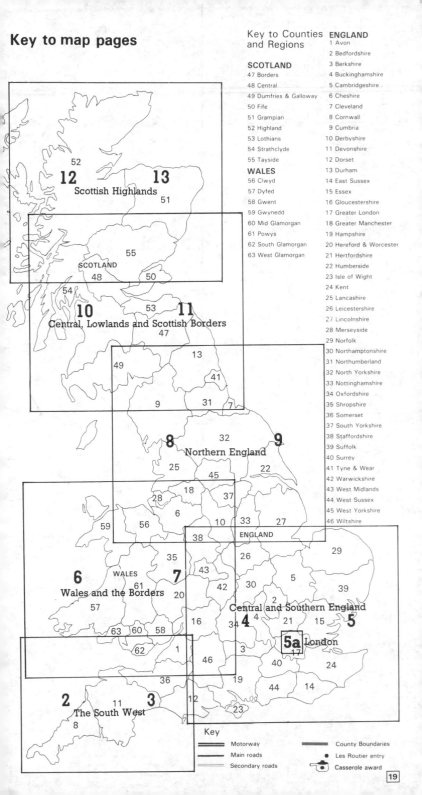

Key to Counties and Regions

SCOTLAND
47 Borders
48 Central
49 Dumfries & Galloway
50 Fife
51 Grampian
52 Highland
53 Lothians
54 Strathclyde
55 Tayside

WALES
56 Clwyd
57 Dyfed
58 Gwent
59 Gwynedd
60 Mid Glamorgan
61 Powys
62 South Glamorgan
63 West Glamorgan

ENGLAND
1 Avon
2 Bedfordshire
3 Berkshire
4 Buckinghamshire
5 Cambridgeshire
6 Cheshire
7 Cleveland
8 Cornwall
9 Cumbria
10 Derbyshire
11 Devonshire
12 Dorset
13 Durham
14 East Sussex
15 Essex
16 Gloucestershire
17 Greater London
18 Greater Manchester
19 Hampshire
20 Hereford & Worcester
21 Hertfordshire
22 Humberside
23 Isle of Wight
24 Kent
25 Lancashire
26 Leicestershire
27 Lincolnshire
28 Merseyside
29 Norfolk
30 Northamptonshire
31 Northumberland
32 North Yorkshire
33 Nottinghamshire
34 Oxfordshire
35 Shropshire
36 Somerset
37 South Yorkshire
38 Staffordshire
39 Suffolk
40 Surrey
41 Tyne & Wear
42 Warwickshire
43 West Midlands
44 West Sussex
45 West Yorkshire
46 Wiltshire

12 13 Scottish Highlands

10 11 Central, Lowlands and Scottish Borders

SCOTLAND

8 9 Northern England

6 7 Wales and the Borders

WALES

ENGLAND

Central and Southern England

5a London

2 3 The South West

Key

———— Motorway

———— Main roads

———— Secondary roads

▬▬▬▬ County Boundaries

● Les Routier entry

🍲 Casserole award

19

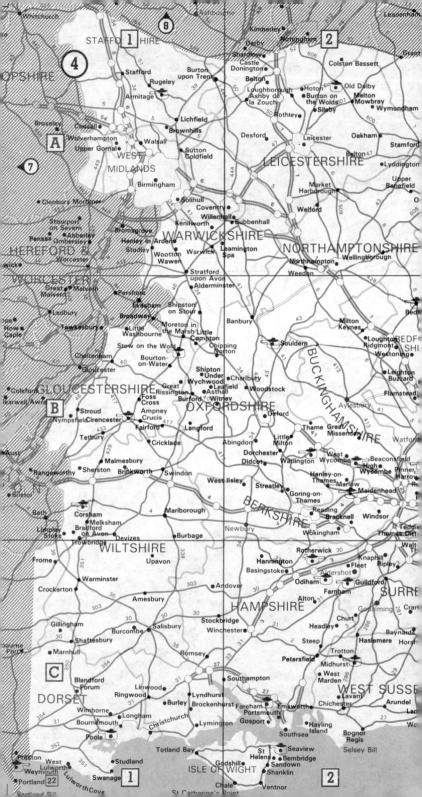

Central and Southern England

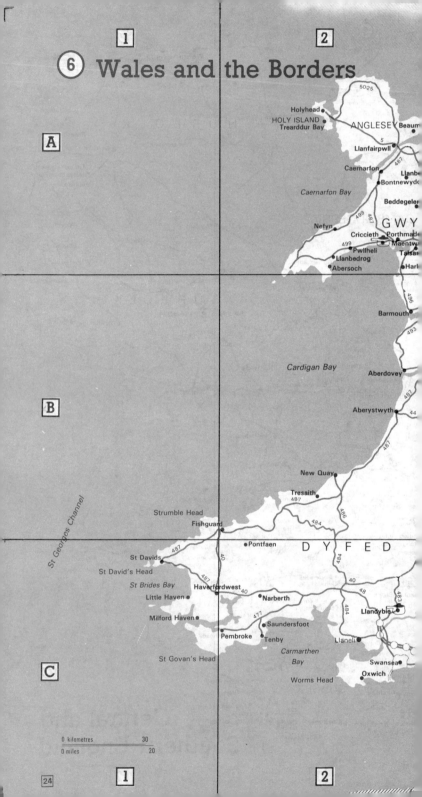

⑥ Wales and the Borders

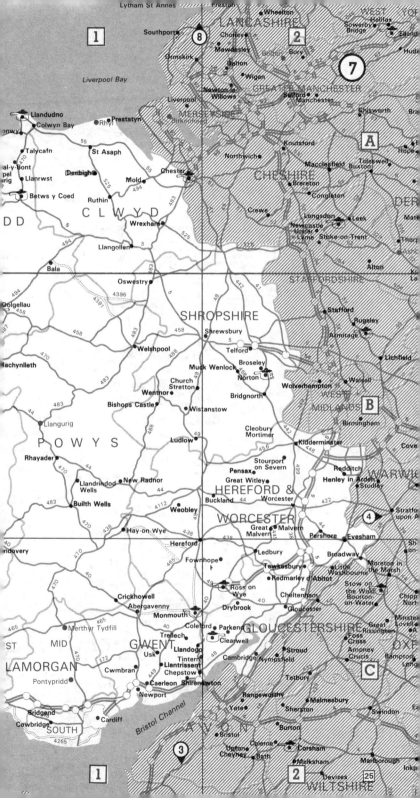

Northern England

Rothbury
Alnmouth
Longframlington
11
AND

A

Whitley Bay
Newcastle upon Tyne
TYNE
South Shields
ylam
& WEAR
Sunderland

Durham
Haswell Plough
URHAM
688 161
Bishop
Auckland
688
67

0 kilometres   30
0 miles   20

Billingham
Redcar   174
CLEVELAND

Darlington
Neasham   Yarm   Ellerby
iddleton Tyas   Stokesley   Great Ayton   Whitby
66   Scotch   Ingleby Greenhow
Corner   Great Broughton
Richmond   Osmotherley   Goathland
684   Leeming
Northallerton   Rosedale
Appleton
le Moors   171
Thirsk   East
Ayton   Scarborough
6108   57   Helmsley   170   Pickering   170
168   Thornton   Filey
1257   Dale   64   165
Ripon   Malton   Norton
ORTH   YORKSHIRE   B
6185   64
59   Langtoft   Flamborough Head
Harrogate   59   19   Bridlington
658   661   166   Driffield
Otley   65   York   164
ey   64   165
hipley   55   Market
dford   Thorganby   Weighton
Leeds   163   19   Beverley
ORKSHIRE   63   Selby   614   1079
ng   62   Fairburn   62   63   Hull
Liversedge   62
ddersfield   638   1033
Thorne   18
61   15   180
628   Barnsley   18   18
635   18
SOUTH YORKSHIRE   180   Brigg   18
630   Doncaster   46   Cleethorpes   Spurn Head
Rotherham   638   16   1031
57   631   15   1103
Bamford   Sheffield   631
625   Worksop   Market   Louth   C
61   57   Rasen
619   57   158
Bakewell   Edwinstowe   46   158
gin by   617   Lincoln   158
ington   Matlock   LINCOLNSHIRE   Skegness
NOTTINGHAMSHIRE   46   158
Wirksworth   617   Newark   1191
bourne   69   Laxton   17
52   Kimberley   Gunthorpe   Leadenham   15   16   5
Nottingham   612   46   17   52
Derby   52   17   Boston   Hunstanton

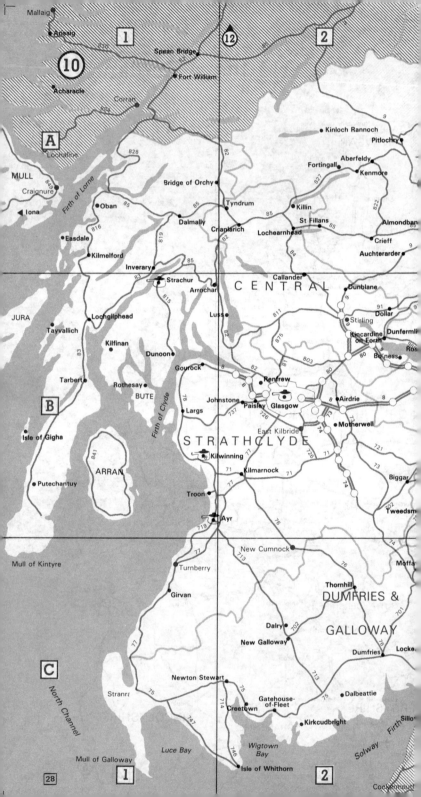

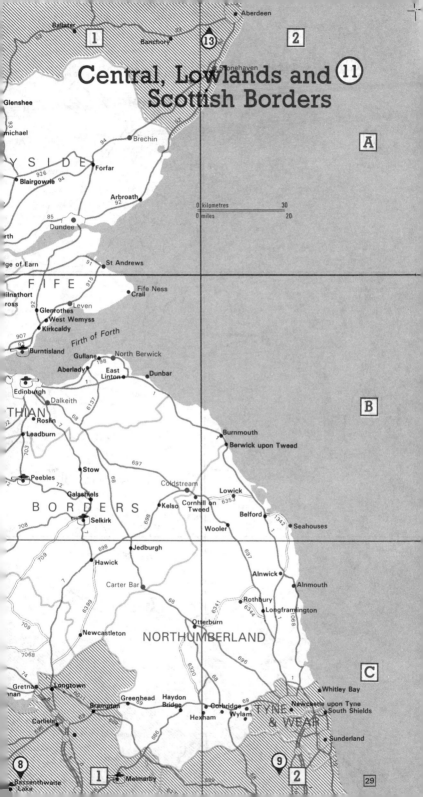

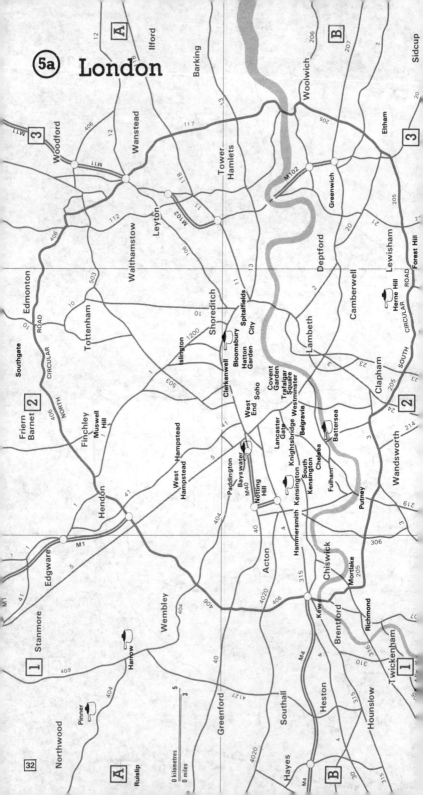

THE LES ROUTIERS CHEESEBOARD OF THE YEAR AWARD 1992

Throughout the year, Les Routiers inspectors have been identifying hotels and restaurants where the quality and presentation of the cheeses on offer are of the highest standard. The inspectorate looked for TASTE through expert selections, handling and storage; VARIETY with an imaginative use of traditional, new and local cheeses; PRESENTATION using colour, texture and shape to create a mouthwatering display; and KNOWLEDGE of the cheeses offered.

Yet again, 1991 has seen an increasing number of restaurants, pubs and hotels offering an interesting and varied cheeseboard. A greater interest and appreciation by the customer of cheese as part of a meal has also been evident.

The following establishments have all been judged worthy of inclusion in the Routiers Cheeseboard Honours list. From this list, one establishment has been chosen to receive the prestigious Les Routiers Cheeseboard of the Year Award 1992.

LES ROUTIERS CHEESEBOARD HONOURS LIST 1992

ABOYNE, Grampian – Balnacoil Hotel
ALNMOUTH, Northumberland – The Saddle Hotel & Grill
AMBLESIDE, Cumbria – Riverside Hotel
AYR, Strathclyde – Stables Restaurant
BARTLOW, Cambridgeshire – The Three Hills
BATH, Avon – Tarts Restaurant
BEACONSFIELD, Buckinghamshire – Royal Standard of England
BEDFORD, Bedfordshire – Knife & Cleaver
BIGGLESWADE, Bedfordshire – La Cachette
BRIDGNORTH, Shropshire – The Down Inn
CLITHEROE, Lancashire – The Inn at Whitewell
CORSHAM, Wiltshire – Rudloe Park Hotel
DURNESS, Highland – Far North Hotel
FALMOUTH, Cornwall – Green Lawns Hotel
GLENSHEE, Tayside – Blackwater Inn
GRANGE-OVER-SANDS, Cumbria – Abbot Hall
HAUGHLEY, Suffolk – Old Counting House Restaurant
HELMSLEY, North Yorkshire – The Feversham Arms Hotel

KENDAL, Cumbria – Riverside Hotel & Restaurant
LAVENHAM, Suffolk – The Great House Restaurant
LEADENHAM, Lincolnshire – George Hotel
LEEMING SPA, North Yorkshire – Motel Leeming
LONDON, Covent Garden, WC2 – Le Café des Amis du Vin
LONDON, Battersea, SW11 – Buchan's
LOOE, Cornwall – Allhays Country House Hotel
LOUGHBOROUGH, Leicestershire – The Cedars Hotel
MAIDENHEAD, Berkshire – Chauntry House Hotel
MALVERN, Hereford & Worcester – Sidney House
MELMERBY, Cumbria – Shepherds Inn
MONMOUTH, Gwent – Crown at Whitebrook
NEWARK, Nottinghamshire – New Ferry Restaurant
OLD DALBY, Leicestershire – The Crown Inn
ORMSKIRK, Lancashire – Beaufort Hotel
OSWESTRY, Shropshire – Bradford Arms
PINNER, Middlesex – La Giralda
REETH, North Yorkshire – Arkleside Hotel
REIGATE, Surrey – La Barbe Restaurant
SALFORD, Greater Manchester – Mark Addy Riverside Pub
SHREWSBURY, Shropshire – Sydney House Hotel
WARE, Hertfordshire – Le Rendez-vous Restaurant
WELLS, Somerset – Fountain Inn & Boxers Restaurant
WEST BEXINGTON, Dorset – The Manor Hotel

LES ROUTIERS CHEESEBOARD OF THE YEAR 1992

ALLHAYS COUNTRY HOUSE HOTEL
Talland Bay, Looe, Cornwall
Tel: (0503) 72434

Proprietors: BRIAN and LINDA SPRING

The cheeseboard at Allhays Country House was declared the overall winner due to the extensive choice of cheeses offered and for the knowledge and enthusiasm with which they have been selected.

Overlooking the beautiful Talland Bay, Allhays Country House Hotel specialises in British and local cheeses. Try Belstone which is made in Devon partly to a 17th century recipe, Cornish Yarg, hand-made in Liskeard, Cornwall, from a recipe of the Gray family, or Nutwood, a delightful mixture of cheddar, nuts and cider. A must for all cheese enthusiasts.

LES ROUTIERS CORPS D'ELITE
1992

In recent years, the consumption of wine has increased in the UK. Furthermore, the British are becoming more adventurous and more selective in their choice of wines.

In recognition of this increased awareness, Les Routiers have a special award which focuses entirely upon the range and quality of wines at Les Routiers restaurants and hotels where a good wine list is now being given the more prominent position it deserves.

Points are awarded for value, range, information, interest and presentation. More points are given for value than for looks and length is never a virtue in itself without careful selection and balance. Of prime importance in a well-balanced wine list is a clear effort to supply wines in the lower price brackets as imaginatively as in the upper. Additionally, provision of half bottles throughout the range shows consideration for the customer and is judged important in a good wine list. Last but not least is the enthusiasm and interest in wine shown by the proprietor.

The Routiers inspectorate are expert at assessing establishments for their welcome, atmosphere, food, wine and service. Each year, the inspectors exercise their palates and judgement to produce a shortlist of establishments which combine an exceptional wine list with knowledge of wine and how it should be served. These are the winners of the Les Routiers Corps d'Elite. From this list, one establishment has been chosen to receive the Les Routiers Prix d'Elite – the award for the most outstanding wine list of all.

LES ROUTIERS CORPS D'ELITE 1992

BRANCASTER STAITHE, Norfolk – Jolly Sailors
CHURCH STRETTON, Shropshire – Mynd House Hotel
CLAWTON, Devon – Court Barn Country House Hotel
CLITHEROE, Lancashire – Inn at Whitewell
CORSHAM, Wiltshire – Rudloe Park Hotel
FALMOUTH, Cornwall – Green Lawns Hotel
HELMSLEY, North Yorkshire – Feversham Arms Hotel
LLANGOLLEN, Clwyd – Gales of Llangollen
MONMOUTH, Gwent – The Crown at Whitebrook
NEWBY BRIDGE, Cumbria – Swan Hotel
PINNER, Middlesex – La Giralda
RYE, East Sussex – Flackley Ash Hotel
SELKIRK, Borders – Philipburn House Hotel
TEYNHAM, Kent – Ship Inn & Smugglers Restaurant
WELLS, Somerset – Fountain Inn & Boxers Restaurant
WEST BEXINGTON, Dorset – The Manor Hotel
WREXHAM, Clwyd – Cross Lanes Hotel

LES ROUTIERS PRIX D'ELITE

RUDLOE PARK HOTEL
Leafy Lane, Corsham, Wiltshire
Tel: (0225) 810555

Proprietors: IAN and MARION OVEREND

With a selection of over 800 wines, ports, brandies, whiskies and liqueurs, it is difficult not to feel humbled by the sheer range, depth and span of the cellar lists at Rudloe Park. However, with a sensible pricing policy, clear but informative layout, and expert help always on hand, the Rudloe Park wine list is a must for anyone interested in wine.

The 44 page, leather-bound wine list will delight connoisseurs but for quick reference there is also a 'Short Selection' of 36 wines. At the end of your meal, enjoy one of over 400 digestifs, such as a glass of port with the award-winning cheeseboard.

THE SOUTH WEST

THE SOUTH WEST

With its natural beauty and striking contrasts, the South West is quite understandably one of the most popular holiday areas. Bordered by the fierce Atlantic Ocean and the calmer waters of the English Channel, the land has been fashioned by competing forces. Every county is different: from the rugged cliffs and dramatic moors in the north, to the sheltered coves and wooded landscapes in the south. Its mild climate produces some of the richest farmland in Britain, but it also has a history of mining and ship-building.

In the South West, you are never far from the sea and it is this which has the greatest influence. The importance of the fishing industry can still be seen at places like St Ives and Mevagissey in Cornwall, and Brixham in Devon, where crab and lobster pots still line the quays. These are some of the best places to enjoy really fresh mussels, whelks, fish, crab and lobster.

The name of King Arthur appears throughout the area. He was reputed to have been an important chieftain in the South West around the 6th century AD. Legend has it that he was born at Tintagel, in Cornwall, and you can still visit his ruined clifftop castle. He lived at Camelot in the kingdom of Avalon, claimed to be Glastonbury, and the mysterious 521ft hill known as the Tor has drawn 'pilgrims' for centuries.

The best way to discover the South West is on foot, and walkers have enjoyed access to nearly all coastal paths for the past thirty years. Inland, the national parks of Exmoor and Dartmoor offer the opportunity to enjoy moments of true peace in beautiful open countryside. This is the land that inspired the tragic romance of Lorna Doone and the Cornish romances of Daphne du Maurier.

Dorset is often known as 'Hardy Country' and at Higher Brockhampton you can visit the cottage where the great writer was born. Hardy immortalised the Dorset way of life in novels such as 'Tess of the D'Urbervilles', and 'Far From the Madding Crowd', brilliantly evoking the county's lonely heaths, fertile valleys and the warmth and tradition of its people.

The county of Avon stretches north and south of the river from which it takes its name, and is home to Bristol and

Bath. The 18th century was the 'golden age' for these cities, with Bristol being the leading port outside London, playing an important part in the colonization of the 'New World' as ships sailed to Virginia, New York and Boston. The City of Bath is a monument to 18th century design, but started its popularity as a famous leisure resort for the Romans.

If the medieval era is of interest, visit Devon with its ruined castles at Okehampton, Lydford or Totnes. The South West is rich in history and legend, with examples from every age. Some of the most important prehistoric remains can be found here, with one of the earliest human dwellings being Kent's Cavern in Devon. Leisure pursuits are also plentiful, with boat trips from the harbours, surfing off the North coast, and fishing trips.

As you travel, sample some of the regional dishes and specialities. The apple orchards of Devon and Somerset produce some of the finest cider in Britain. In Dorset, you will find the county's distinctive blue-veined cheeses and, in Somerset, you will discover original Cheddar. From the South West comes a rich variety of dairy products and it would take the strongest iron will to resist the world-renowned 'clotted cream' teas.

CHANNEL ISLANDS

The Channel Islands have a distinctive character of their own. Situated 100 miles from England and just 14 miles from the coast of France, their laws, customs and food have a Gallic flavour. The islanders themselves are of Norman descent and, although they now speak English, their native tongue used to be Norman-French patois.

The Channel Islands comprise Jersey, Guernsey, Alderney and Sark and are self-governing, although they still owe allegiance to the crown. Sark, for example, has had a feudal constitution since Elizabethan times, the hereditary ruler being known as the 'Seigneur of Sark'. Cars are still not allowed and wild flowers and birdlife prosper in the wonderfully clean air.

The Islanders are known for their fine hospitality and it is easy to see why the Islands enjoy a thriving tourist industry. Although popular, it is always possible to get away from the crowds – with a choice of quiet bays to long beaches, bustling harbours and acres of countryside. In addition, the summers are long and the winters mild, making the Islands an ideal retreat all year round.

QUICK REFERENCE GUIDE

THE SOUTH WEST

	NO. OF ESTS.	⊗ £	⊗ ££	⊗ £££	⊗ ££££	🛏 £	🛏 ££	🛏 £££	🛏 ££££
MAP 2 A2									
Woolacombe	3			★				★	★
MAP 2 B1									
Cubert	1	★							
Newquay	10	★	★			★	★	★	★
Perranporth	1	★							
St Agnes	2			★		★	★		
MAP 2 B2									
Boscastle	3			★			★	★	
Bude	3		★				★		
Clawton	1		★						
Constantine Bay	1			★					★
Crackington Haven	1	★					★		
Fowey	1		★						
Gunnislake	1		★					★	
Launceston	2		★			★		★	
Lifton	1		★					★	
Liskeard	1		★					★	
Looe	6	★	★	★		★	★	★	
Lostwithiel	1			★					
Pelynt	1		★						
Pendoggett	1		★					★	
Plymouth	11	★	★	★		★	★	★	
Polperro	2		★	★					
Port Isaac	2		★			★			★
Rock	1		★				★		
St Austell	1		★				★		
Tintagel	1		★						★
Wadebridge	3	★	★					★	
MAP 2 C1									
Falmouth	4			★	★		★	★	★
Isles of Scilly	1							★	
Land's End	2						★	★	
Penzance	7	★	★		★		★	★	★
Redruth	1		★				★		
St Ives	2						★	★	
St Ives Bay	5	★	★					★	★
the Lizard	2		★				★	★	
Truro	4		★	★					★
MAP 2 C2									
Mevagissey	2	★	★				★		
Philleigh	1			★					
Portscatho	1			★					★
Tregony	1			★					
MAP 3 A1									
Barnstaple	2			★					
Bideford	3		★		★				
Combe Martin	2		★				★		★
Dulverton	3		★	★				★	
Dunster	3	★	★				★	★	
Exford	1		★					★	
Ilfracombe	5	★	★				★	★	

QUICK REFERENCE GUIDE

	NO. OF ESTS.	⊗ £	⊗ ££	⊗ £££	⊗ ££££	⌂ £	⌂ ££	⌂ £££	⌂ ££££
Lynmouth	3		★				★	★	
Lynton	3		★				★	★	★
Minehead	1							★	
Mortehoe	3						★	★	
Saunton	1		★						★
Watchet	1	★							
Woody Bay	1			★				★	
MAP 3 A2									
Bath	16	★	★	★		★	★	★	★
Brent Knoll	1		★				★		
Bridgwater	1		★						
Bristol	8	★	★				★	★	
Burnham on Sea	1		★				★		
Chelwood	1			★					
Clevedon	2		★						★
Compton Martin	1	★							
Flax Bourton	1	★							
Frome	2	★	★					★	
Glastonbury	1			★				★	
Litton	1		★					★	
North Wootton	1		★			★			
Rangeworthy	1		★						★
Upton Cheyney	1	★							
Wells	5	★	★	★			★	★	
Weston Super Mare	2	★	★				★		
Yate	1	★							
MAP 3 B1									
Bampton	1		★				★		
Bickington	1	★							
Bickleigh	1		★					★	
Bovey Tracey	1		★				★		
Brixham	2		★				★		
Chagford	1	★							
Christow	1		★				★		
Crediton	1		★					★	
Dartmoor	1		★					★	
Dawlish	1		★						★
Drewsteignton	1		★						
Dulverton	1						★		
Exebridge	1		★					★	
Exeter	5	★	★				★	★	
Exmouth	1		★						
Halwell	1		★				★		
Ivybridge	2		★			★			
Modbury	1			★			★		
Moretonhampstead	1						★		
Paignton	4	★	★				★		
Poundsgate	1	★							
Shaldon	1		★						
South Zeal	1						★		
Southerton	1		★					★	
Staverton	1		★				★		
Tavistock	1	★							
Thelbridge	1	★						★	
Throwleigh	1				★				
Tiverton	2	★					★		
Topsham	1		★						
Torquay	8	★	★			★	★	★	★

QUICK REFERENCE GUIDE

	NO. OF ESTS.	⊗ £	⊗ ££	⊗ £££	⊗ ££££	⊡ £	⊡ ££	⊡ £££	⊡ ££££
Totnes	1		★					★	
Wembworthy	1	★					★		
Whimple	1	★							
MAP 3 B2									
Axminster	2	★	★				★		
Axmouth	1	★							
Beer	1						★		
Bridport	1		★					★	
Chard	1		★					★	
Charmouth	2	★					★		
Chideock	1	★							
Crewkerne	1		★					★	
Dorchester	1	★							
Holton	1	★							
Honiton	1	★							
Langport	1		★			★			
Lyme Regis	6	★	★			★		★	★
Misterton	1	★							
Portesham	1						★		
Portland	1		★					★	
Preston	1							★	
Seavington St. Michael	1	★							
Sidford	1	★					★		
Sidmouth	3		★	★			★		★
Somerton	2	★		★			★	★	
Taunton	4	★	★			★			★
Trent	1	★							
West Bexington	1			★					★
West Stafford	1						★		
Weymouth	8	★	★			★	★	★	★
Wincanton	2		★						★
MAP 3 C1									
Bigbury on Sea	1		★					★	
Chillington	1		★					★	
Dartmouth	4	★	★	★		★			★
Kingsbridge	4	★	★				★	★	
Salcombe	1		★					★	
MAP 3 C2									
Alderney	1							★	
Beaumont	1						★		
Castel	1		★						
Gorey Harbour	2		★				★		★
St Aubin	1						★		
St Brelade	1			★					
St Clement	1							★	
St Helier	7		★				★	★	
St Martins	2	★					★	★	
St Ouen	1							★	
St Ouen's Bay	2		★			★			
St Peter Port	2			★			★		
St Sampsons	1						★		
Torteval	1		★					★	
Trinity	1			★			★		
Vazon Bay	1		★						

BAMPTON

AXMINSTER Devon **Map 3 B2**

⊗£ **THE NEW COMMERCIAL INN** Trinity Square, Axminster.

CLUB **Hours:** Breakfast 7.30am - 12 noon, Lunch 12 noon - 2pm, Dinner 6pm - 10.30pm (last orders 10pm) and Teas 2pm - 5.30pm. Restaurant closed: Sundays. **Cuisine:** Separate Breakfast, Lunch, Afternoon Tea and Childrens menu. Meal menu includes dishes such as fish, steak, chilli con carne and pizza. ⊨ None. **CC** Access, Visa. **Other Points:** Children welcome. Afternoon Tea. Bread shop. On street parking adjacent. ᗌ **(V) Directions:** In the main square in Axminster.

MR WALDEN ☎ (0297) 33225.

This restaurant is found in a natural stone Victorian building in the centre of Axminster and offers excellent service and menu variety, including a special childrens menu. The value for money is outstanding.

⊗££ **THE TUCKERS ARMS** Dalwood, Nr Axminster.

⊞££ **Hours:** Lunch 12 noon - 2pm, dinner 7pm - 10pm. **Cuisine:** Wide range of dishes including 'Tucker skins' & 'Tucker tiddies' (pies). International Cuisine. ⊨ 5 bedrooms, all en suite. **CC** Access, Visa. **Other Points:** Children welcome. Open Bank Holidays. Garden dining. ⊡ ᗌ **(V) Directions:** 2 miles north of A35, between Axminster & Honiton.

DAVID & KATE BECK ☎ (0404) 88342.

Situated in the pretty, unspoilt village of Dalwood, this traditional Inn is over 800 years old. Oak beams, old oak furniture, an open log fire and antique copper pans add to the historic feel of the Inn. The Tuckers Arms has a good reputation locally for its well cooked food and friendly atmosphere. Good, comfortable accommodation.

AXMOUTH Devon **Map 3 B2**

⊗£ **THE SHIP INN** Near Seaton.

CLUB **Hours:** Open 11am - 2.30pm and 6pm - 11pm Mondays to Saturdays in summer and 11am - 2pm and 6pm - 11pm in winter. Sundays 12 noon - 2.30pm and 7pm - 10.30pm. **Cuisine:** Deep sea surprise, baked plaice with seafood stuffing, accent on local game and seafood in season. Homegrown fruit, vegetables and herbs. ⊨ None. **CC** None. **Other Points:** Children welcome in dining area, large attractive garden and in family/games room. ⊡ ᗌ **(V) Directions:** 1 mile south of the A3052 Lyme Regis - Exeter road towards Seaton.

MR & MRS C CHAPMAN ☎ (0297) 21838.

A small pub on the road from Seaton serving an extensive range of meals in both bars and the garden at lunchtime and in the evening. Real ales.

BAMPTON Devon **Map 3 B1**

⊗££ **THE SWAN HOTEL** Station Road, Bampton, Nr Tiverton.

⊞££ **Hours:** Breakfast 8am - 9.30am, lunch 12 noon - 2pm, Dinner 7pm - 10pm (last orders). Bar meals 12 noon - 2pm and 6pm - 10pm (last orders). **Cuisine:** Home style traditional cooking, using fresh produce such as local trout and fresh vegetables. ⊨ 6 rooms, 2 en suite. **CC** Access, Visa, Diners. **Other Points:** Open Bank Holidays. Children welcome. Pets welcome. Afternoon teas served. Bar. ᗌ **(V) Directions:** On main Barnstable - Taunton Rd on B3227. Close to public car park.

THE SOUTH WEST

Bampton continued
BRIAN & PAM DUNESBY ☎ (0398) 331257.
A 15th century building which retains its old charm and character. Originally The Swan housed the stone masons who built the nearby church. Close to Exmoor, Bickley Mill and Wimbleball Lake.

BARNSTAPLE Devon **Map 3 A1**
⊗£££ **DOWNREW HOUSE HOTEL** Bishops Tawton, Barnstaple.
Hours: Breakfast 7.30am - 9.30am, Lunch 12.30pm - 2pm, Dinner 7pm - 9.30pm. Bar meals 12 noon - 1pm. Afternoon teas. **Cuisine:** French and English cuisine. Specialities include Wrapped Salmon with a Crab & Spring Onion sauce, Loin of Lamb with a Rosemary & Tomato sauce. ⋉ 12 bedrooms, all en suite. ☒ Access, Visa.
Other Points: Children over 7 welcome. Dogs allowed. No smoking area. Swimming pool. Golf course. Tennis court. Croquet lawn. Full-size Billiards table. ▯ ⅗ **(V) Directions:** A377 from Barntaple towards Exeter. Turn left up Codden Hill.
C.B. HOTELS & REST. LTD ☎ (0271) 42497.
Originally built in 1640, then enlarged during the reign of Queen Anne, Downrew stands in 12 acres of meadowland and gardens amidst beautiful countryside. Warm, courteous service, personal supervision of the resident proprietors and the charm and elegance of the furnishings and decor, combine to make Downrew the ideal place to relax and enjoy good food.

⊗£££ **LYNWOOD HOUSE** Bishops Tawton Road, Barnstaple.
Hours: Breakfast 7am - 10am, lunch 12 noon - 2pm, dinner 7pm - 10pm. **Cuisine:** A la carte menu, bar meals. ⋉ 5 twin bedrooms all en suite. ☒ Access, Visa. **Other Points:** Children welcome. No smoking in dining room. ▯ ⅗ **(V) Directions:** Junction 27 off M5. On A377.
MR & MRS ROBERTS. ☎ (0271) 43695.
Formly a Victorian gentlemans house, the 'Lynwood House' is set in a small neat garden. Decorated in keeping with the age and style of the building and comfortably furnished. Offering excellent meals accompanied by a distinguished wine list. A calm atmosphere created by the skillful staff. Visited by locals and business people.

BATH Avon **Map 3 A2**
⌂£££ **AVON HOTEL** 9 Bathwick Street, Bath.
⋉ 12 bedrooms, all en suite. All rooms have welcome tray, colour TV and radio alarm. Baby listening service. Laundry. Four poster bed. **Hours:** Breakfast 8am - 10am. ☒ All major cards. **Other Points:** Children welcome. No smoking area (some bedrooms reserved for non-smokers). Dogs allowed. Residents lounge. 6 ground floor bedrooms. Fax No: (0225) 447452. ▯ **Directions:** A4 - A36. Walking distance from centre of Bath.
FRANK THAXTER ☎ (0225) 446176.
Built in 1750, Avon Hotel is centrally situated with the Abbey and Roman Baths less than half a mile away. All the bedrooms have been newly decorated to provide comfortable, attractive accommodation. The hotel offers high standards at good value for money and has the added convenience of a large floodlit carpark - a rarity in the centre of Bath.

Bath continued

®£ **CROSS KEYS INN** Midford Road, Combe Down, Bath.
Hours: Lunch 12 noon - 2pm, Dinner 7pm - 10pm. Restaurant closed mornings and Sunday and Monday evenings but bar meals served 7 days and evenings. **Cuisine:** A la carte and bar meals. Dishes include Somerset Pork, Guinea Fowl, Salmon & Prawn Cutlets. Good choice of bar meals. Traditional Sunday lunch. ﹏ None. **CC** None. **Other Points:** Children welcome. Garden. Dogs on leads allowed. Childrens bar menu. Every assistance given to disabled guests but restaurant down steps. **P** **(V)** **Directions:** B3110 overlooking Bath. Near the American Museum.
MARK & CAROLINE PALMER ☎ (0225) 832002.
An attractive olde worlde pub with a friendly, welcoming atmosphere. Whether you choose the restaurant or bar meals, the food is well cooked and offers variety and good value for money. The B3110 is a scenic alternative to the main A36 and is worth taking even if only to visit the Cross Keys for its good food, warm welcome and friendly service.

⌂£££ **DORIAN HOUSE** 1 Upper Oldfield Park, Bath.
﹏ 1 single, 4 double/twin (zip & link beds) and 2 family rooms, all en suite. Colour TV, tea/coffee making facilities, direct dial telephones and hairdryer in all rooms. **Hours:** Breakfast served 8am - 9am (menu selected). **CC** All major cards. **Other Points:** Children welcome. No dogs allowed. Resident's lounge, small bar and garden. Vegetarian meals available. Full and varied breakfast menu. **P** **Directions:** Up A367 Wells Rd for 250m to left hand bend. Take 1st right.
IAN & DOREEN BENNETTS ☎ (0225) 426336.
A gracious Victorian home, with parking. Situated on the southern slopes overlooking Bath, yet only ten minutes stroll to the city centre. There are seven charming bedrooms, all en suite. The lounge and small licensed bar provide a pleasant atmosphere for friends to meet. There is a full English breakfast menu and a warm welcome for all guests.

®£££ **FERN COTTAGE HOTEL** 9 Northend, Batheaston, Bath.
⌂£££ **Hours:** Breakfast 8am - 9.30am, dinner 7.30pm - 10pm (last orders 9pm). Closed: January. **Cuisine:** 4 course Table d'Hote menu and extensive A La Carte menu. Dishes may include Lamb Fillet in Pastry, Coral Fish (Parrot fish in Sloe Gin sauce). ﹏ 6 bedrooms, all en suite. **CC** Visa. **Other Points:** Children welcome. No smoking area. Dogs allowed. Residents lounge. Mastercard accepted. **P** **(V)** **Directions:** A4 from Bath to Batheaston. Turn left to Northend. 400 yds on left.
SANDIE & DOUG WEBB ☎ (0225) 858190.
A small Country House Hotel set in half an acre of gardens and orchard, combining the peace and tranquility of the countryside with the nearby attractions of Bath. The restaurant and bar are lit by gas mantles adding to the old world feel. All meals are home cooked using fresh ingredients and the menus offer a wide choice of excellently cooked and served dishes.

THE SOUTH WEST

Bath continued

⊗££ **HARINGTON'S HOTEL & RESTAURANT** 8-9-10 Queen
⌶££ Street, Bath.
Hours: Breakfast 8am - 9.30am, lunch 12 noon - 2pm and dinner
6.30pm - 10pm (last orders). Teas 2pm - 5.30pm. **Cuisine:**
Harington's Dover Sole, Chateaubriand. ⊨ 12 bedrooms, 5 en
suite. **CC** Access, Visa, AmEx. **Other Points:** Children welcome.
(V) Directions: In the centre of Bath behind Queen's Square.
MR ANTHONY DODGE ☎ (0225) 461728.
*A small family run hotel and restaurant housed in a well
maintained 18th century building. Situated in the city centre in
an attractive cobbled street within easy walking distance of the
theatre and Bath's many attractions. All rooms have been
tastefully furnished to a high standard.*

⊗£££ **HINTON GRANGE HOTEL** Hinton, Nr Dyrham.
⌷CLUB⌷ **Hours:** Breakfast 7.30am - 9.30am, lunch and bar snacks
12.30pm - 2pm, dinner 7pm - 9.30pm. Open all year round.
Cuisine: Dishes may include Rack of English lamb, Lemon sole
with a Champagne sabayou, Supreme of chicken in a Tarayaki
sauce. ⊨ 16 bedrooms, all en suite. **CC** All major cards. **Other
Points:** Afternoon teas. Dogs allowed. Garden dining. Gym. Lake.
Swimming pool. Fax No. (027582) 3285. Weddings catered for.
Lawn tennis. Golf course. **P** **(V) Directions:** Off M4 Jct 18 to A46
to Bath - approx half a mile, right to Hinton.
JOHN & MAY LINDSAY-WALKER. ☎ (027582) 2916.
*A 15th century farmhouse which has been converted into a
luxurious, unique hotel. All rooms are decorated in period style
and furnished with genuine antiques and the hotel has 20 open
fires. Candlelit dinners can be enjoyed in the Inglenook
restaurant which provides the finest in cuisine, wines and silver
service. An exceptional hotel and the ideal choice for a special
occasion.*

⌶££ **LEIGHTON HOUSE** 139 Wells Road, Bath.
⊨ 7 bedrooms, 7 with en suite facilities. Tea/coffee making
facilities. Colour TV. Hairdryer. Direct dial phone. Baby listening
device. **Hours:** Breakfast 8am - 9am. Dinner by arrangement in off
peak season. **CC** Access, Visa. **Other Points:** Children welcome.
Residents lounge and dining room. Residents garden. Pets
allowed (by arrangement). Special breaks available in off peak
seasons. **P** **Directions:** Situated on the southern side of Bath on the
A367 Exeter road.
DAVE & KATHY SLAPE ☎ (0225) 420210.
*A well appointed Victorian residence that has been tastefully
furnished by Kathy and Dave Slape, who have successfully
created a warm and friendly haven for their guests. With the
emphasis on comfort, warm hospitality and attention to detail,
guests can be assured of an enjoyable stay. Situated just 10
minutes walk from the City centre, Leighton House comes
highly recommended.*

⌶£££ **OLDFIELDS HOTEL** 102 Wells Road, Bath.
⊨ 14 bedrooms, 8 en suite with tea/coffee making facilities,
colour TV and alarm. Central heating. **Hours:** Breakfast 8am -
9.30am. **CC** None. **Other Points:** Residents' lounge. Garden. No

Bath continued

dogs. 🅿 ⟡ **Directions:** Off Bristol - Warminster Road (A36). Corner of Upper Oldfield Park.
ANTHONY & NICOLE O'FLAHERTY ☎ (0225) 317984.
This large Victorian family home is set in its own grounds, elegantly furnished and superbly positioned. Full English or continental breakfasts, beautiful furnishings and comfortable, well-appointed bedrooms. Resident owners, Mr and Mrs O'Flaherty endaevour to create a welcoming, homely atmosphere - they have succeeded!

⊗££ **PRATT'S HOTEL** South Parade, Bath.
⌂££££ **Hours:** Breakfast Mon-Sat 7.30am - 9.30am. Sunday 8am - 10am. Lunch 12.30pm - 2pm, Dinner 7pm - 9.30pm (last orders). **Cuisine:** Innovative English cuisine eg. medallions of lamb en croute; Rosette of Beef Stilton; escalope of turkey filled with chestnut, apple and almonds. ⊨ 46 bedrooms, all en suite **CC** All major cards. **Other Points:** Children welcome. Pets allowed. Fax No (0225) 448807. Limited disabled access. Refund given to guests on cost of NCP parking close by. **(V) Directions:** City centre.
MR. D. MEAKIN - General Manager ☎ (0225) 460441.
A listed Georgian terraced house in central Bath with all its many attractions: Bath Abbey and Pump rooms 3 minutes walk, railway 5 minutes. Pratt's Hotel was the home of Sir Walter Scott when the building was still a private house. A comfortable, welcoming hotel in which to eat or stay. Highly recommended.

⊗££ **RAJPOOT** Rajpoot House, 4 Argyle Street, Bath.
Hours: Restaurant open 12 noon - 2.30pm and 6pm - 11pm. Closed: Christmas and Boxing Day. **Cuisine:** Northern Indian cuisine. ⊨ None. **CC** All major cards. **Other Points:** Children welcome. No dogs. Disabled access by arrangement. Fax: 0225 442462. **(V) Directions:** By the Pultney Bridge next to Great Pultney Street.
A & M CHOWDHURY ☎ (0225) 466833/464758
The restaurant is in the cellar of a Georgian building. Its layout comprises 3 large spacious halls with typically Indian decor including painted wooden images of Hindu gods. The menu offers a wide choice of well cooked Indian dishes.

⊗£££ **TARTS RESTAURANT** 8 Pierrepont Place.
⌂ **Hours:** Open Monday to Saturday. Lunch 12 noon - 2.30pm. Dinner 7pm - 10.45pm (last orders). Closed: Sundays, four days over Christmas and on New Year's Day. **Cuisine:** Grilled rib of beef in a rich red wine and shallot sauce. Desserts include Dark and white chocolate truffle cake on a Creme Anglaise. ⊨ None. **CC** Access, Visa. **Other Points:** Children welcome. No dogs. Often necessary to reserve table. Good choice of vegetarian dishes. **(V) Directions:** Off Pierrepont St. Through the stone pillars behind Compass Hotel.
JOHN EDWARDS ☎ (0225) 330280/330201
One of Bath's most popular and attractive restaurants, with the tables set in alcoves to create a warm and intimate atmosphere. Two private dining rooms. Only fresh ingredients are used and all desserts, including ice cream are made on the premises. Award winning wine list.

THE SOUTH WEST

Bath continued

⌂£££ **THE BATH TASBURGH HOTEL** Warminster Road, Bathampton, Bath.
 ⊨ 13 bedrooms, 10 en suite. Colour TV, telephone, radio, alarm and tea/coffee making facilities. Well-appointed. **Hours:** Breakfast 8.15am - 9.45am. Dinner available on request. Closed: Christmas. **CC** All major cards. **Other Points:** Children welcome. No smoking area. Residents' lounge. Garden. Croquet lawn. Fax No. (0225) 425096. Children half price if sharing parents room. **P** &. **Directions:** A36. 1 mile from City Centre in the Bathampton area of Bath, on A36.
BRIAN & AUDREY ARCHER ☎ (0225) 425096/463842
This charming and spacious Victorian house built in 1890 is set in 7 acres of lovely gardens and grounds, with canal frontage and beautiful views across the Avon Valley. Situated close to the City Centre and Tourist attractions, the accommodation is of a very high standard and is beautifully furnished. With a warm welcome from the owners and their staff, it's a delightful place to stay.

⊗£ **THE INN AT FRESHFORD** Freshford, Nr Bath.
 Hours: Lunch 12 noon - 2pm, Dinner 6pm - 10pm. Bar meals served 11am - 2pm and 6pm - 10pm. **Cuisine:** Extensive choice of predominantly traditional English cuisine. Menus and a large daily specials board. ⊨ None. **CC** Access, Visa. **Other Points:** Children welcome. Dogs allowed. Beer garden. Good wine list. Mastercard also accepted. Functions room for 50 people. **P** **(V) Directions:** Off A36, 5 miles S of Bath. Between Limpley Stoke & Bradford on Avon
JOHN THWAITES ☎ (0225) 722250.
An attractive stone-built inn with hanging baskets adding to its charm, situated in beautiful countryside. The pleasant interior is enhanced by fresh flowers and a friendly, relaxed atmosphere. There is an extensive choice of meals which are well-cooked and served by cheerful, efficient staff. A good choice for an enjoyable meal in attractive, welcoming surroundings.

⊗£££ **THE VINEYARD** Bath Road, Colerne, Chippenham.
 Hours: Lunch 12 noon - 2pm, dinner 7pm - 11pm (last orders 9.30pm). Bar meals 12 noon - 2pm. Closed: Sunday evening. **Cuisine:** A la carte, table d'hote and bar meals, featuring Dover sole, salmon, halibut, grills, poultry, spicy and vegetarian dishes. ⊨ None. **CC** All major cards. **Other Points:** No pets. No smoking area. **P** &. **(V) Directions:** From A4 follow signs to Colerne, Vineyard is on left before village.
ELIZABETH & EDGAR JONES ☎ (0225) 742491.
A charming ivy clad restaurant on the fringe of the Domesday Village of Colerne. Built in an ancient stone quarry on the site of a former monk's resting house, The Vineyard overlooks the beautiful Box Valley. An ideal touring area close to Bath, the Cotswolds, Castle Combe and local towns.

⊗£ **THE WIFE OF BATH RESTAURANT** 12 Pierrepont Street, Bath.
 Hours: Meals from 12 noon - 2.30pm and 5.30pm - 11pm. Closed: Sunday lunch. **Cuisine:** Casseroles, stuffed peppers, steaks, fresh fish, daily specials, toasted sandwiches at lunchtime.

Bath continued

⊨ None. **CC** Access, Visa. **Other Points:** Children welcome. Vegetarian dishes. No smoking area. **(V) Directions:** Close to Bath Abbey.

DICK & AINSLIE ENSOM ☎ (0225) 461745.

An attractive bar/restaurant in 3 sections at the garden level of a listed Georgian house. Private rooms. Patio garden. Good wine list.

⌂£ **WANSDYKE COTTAGE** Crosspost Lane, Marksbury Gate, Bath.

⊨ 4 bedrooms, 1 with en suite bathroom. **Hours:** Breakfast 7am - 10am, Dinner 6.30pm - 8pm. **CC** None. **Other Points:** Evening meal on request. Unlicensed but guests welcome to bring own wine. Fully centrally heated. Open fires. Lounge with colour TV. Children welcome. **P** & **Directions:** Near junction of A3116, Bath to Wells, Keynsham to Wells.

NATHALIE DAMREL ☎ (0225) 873674.

Built around 1790 in Georgian style, and set in an acre of garden, Wandsdyke Cottage is a family home, providing a relaxing atmosphere and the warmest of welcomes. An evening meal is available at extremely good value. Ideal choice for those looking for a friendly place to stay at very good value for money. Set in unspoilt countryside near Bath, Wells, Cheddar & the Cotswolds.

BEER Devon **Map 3 B2**

⌂££ **GARLANDS** Stovar Long Lane, Beer, Seaton.

⊨ 1 single, 2 double, 1 twin and 3 family bedrooms: 5 with en suite. 1 bathroom. Tea/coffee making facilities in all bedrooms. **Hours:** Breakfast 8.30am - 9.30am, dinner 6.30pm - 7.30pm (order by midday). **CC** Access, Visa. **Other Points:** Central heating. Children welcome. Licensed. Residents lounge. TV. Garden. **P** **Directions:** Turn south off A3052 at Hangmans Stone onto B3174. Signposted.

ANN & NIGEL HARDING ☎ (0297) 20958.

An Edwardian character house set in an acre of ground on the main coast road between Seaton and Beer. There are superb views from the house both of the sea and the Devon countryside and the beach is within easy walking distance. Fishing trips can be arranged - and your catch cooked for supper.

BICKINGTON Devon **Map 3 B1**

⊗£ **THE DARTMOOR HALFWAY** Bickington, nr Newton Abbot.

Hours: Open 11am - 11pm. 12 noon - 10.30pm on Sundays. (Last orders 10.30pm and 10pm respectively). Closed: Christmas Day. **Cuisine:** English home cooking. ⊨ None. **CC** All major cards. **Other Points:** Children welcome. Caravan club listed site. Open during normal pub opening hours. **P** **Directions:** On the A383, half way between Ashburton and Newton Abbot.

MESSRS BR & MD HUGGINS ☎ (0626) 821270.

A charming pub, aptly named, half way between Ashburton and Newton Abbot. The Dartmoor Halfway offers first class food and service.

THE SOUTH WEST

BICKLEIGH Devon **Map 3 B1**

⊗££ **THE FISHERMAN'S COT HOTEL** Bickleigh, Nr Tiverton.
£££ **Hours:** Breakfast 7.30am - 9.30am, lunch 12 noon - 2.30pm,
dinner 6.30pm - 10pm (last orders 10pm). **Cuisine:**
English/Continental: carvery/buffet counter - full a la carte
restaurant. Grills, seafood and speciality dishes. ⊨ 23 bedrooms,
1 single, 22 double/twin. All en suite. **CC** Access, Visa. **Other
Points:** Fax No: (0884) 855241. Mastercard accepted. **P** & **(V)**
Directions: A396 Exeter to Tiverton.
NORJUST LTD ☎ (0884) 855237/855289
*A delightful riverside hotel offering comfortable
accommodation, good food and outstanding hospitality.
Beautiful gardens stretching down to the River Exe are a must in
summer. Local features include Bickleigh Castle, Fursdon
House; Exeter is only 8 miles distant.*

BIDEFORD Devon **Map 3 A1**

⊗££ **ALL SEASONS RESTAURANT** 14 The Quay, Bideford.
Hours: Lunch 11am - 3pm, Summer open until 5pm. Sunday 12
noon - 3pm. Dinner 7pm - 11pm. Sunday 7pm - 10pm. Closed:
Wednesday evening. **Cuisine:** French. Fresh locally caught fish a
speciality. ⊨ None. **CC** Access, Visa. **Other Points:** Children
welcome. Limited disabled access. **P (V) Directions:** On the Quay
near 'Old Bridge'.
PETER AND JANICE COPELAND ☎ (0237) 477799.
*A friendly, family run restaurant beside the river, in a grade 2
Georgian listed building. The quayside is where much of the
fish cooked in the All Seasons is landed, so customers can rest
assured that the fish is definately fresh.*

⊗££ **RIVERSFORD HOTEL** Limers Lane, Bideford.
CLUB **Hours:** Hotel open from January to December. **Cuisine:**
Homemade country fare e.g. homemade sweets, Devonshire
cream teas and interesting wines. Traditional Sunday lunch.
Extensive snack meals. ⊨ 16 bedrooms, 14 en suite. **CC** All major
cards. **Other Points:** Children welcome. **P** & **(V) Directions:**
Limers Lane is on the right, 1 mile North of Bideford on the A386.
MAURICE & MERRILYN JARRAD ☎ (0237) 474239/470381
*A country house hotel in 3 acres of gardens, affording
magnificent views of the River Torridge. Ideal touring centre for
beaches and countryside or discovering the hidden charms of
Devon and Exmoor.*

⊗££££ **YEOLDON HOUSE HOTEL & RESTAURANT** Durrant
CLUB Lane, Northam, Bideford.
Hours: Breakfast 8am - 9.30am, lunch 12.30pm - 2pm (Sunday
2.30pm) and dinner 7pm - 8.30pm (last orders). **Cuisine:** English
and continental dishes, using local fresh produce wherever
possible. In season, local salmon and pheasant. Chef's homemade
sweet table. ⊨ 10 luxury bedrooms: all en suite. Honeymoon suite
available. **CC** All major cards. **Other Points:** Children welcome.
Garden. Afternoon teas. Pets allowed. Residents lounge.
Residents bar. Tea/coffee room service. **P (V) Directions:** A386 to
Northam, third right into Durrant Lane for 1/4 mile.
MR & MRS N.M. TURNER ☎ (0237) 474400.
*Set beside the River Torridge, with lawns sloping down to the
river, you will find a warm welcome at Yeoldon House. Good*

Bideford continued

cuisine, using local fresh produce wherever possible, and excellent accommodation are complemented by friendly efficent service, making this hotel a pleasure to visit.

BIGBURY ON SEA Devon **Map 3 C1**

⊗££ **HENLEY HOTEL** Folly Hill, Bigbury on Sea.

🏠££ **Hours:** Lunch 12 noon - 2.30pm. Dinner - Table d'Hote 7pm -
CLUB 8pm, A la carte/bar meals 8pm - 9pm. Restaurant reservations for table d'hote and a la carte meals advisable for non-residents by 5pm. **Cuisine:** Fresh fish and seafood. Local speciality dishes. 🛏 2 singles, 2 doubles, 2 twins and 2 family rooms, all en suite. Colour TV, radio and tea/coffee making facilities, direct dial telephone. 💳 Access, Visa. **Other Points:** Non-Smoking establishment. Children welcome. Pets welcome. Private cliff path to beach. Access for disabled to restaurant only. Residents' lounge. 🅿 **(V)** **Directions:** Follow signs for Modbury. On B3392 - Hotel on left as enter village.
MRS L BEER ☎ (0548) 810240.
Edwardian Cottage style hotel with spectacular sea views from most rooms over Bigbury Bay and Burgh Island, providing a homely and peaceful atmosphere in which to relax. Bar meals, table d'hote and a la carte menus to suit all tastes & pockets. Near superb beach, golf course, good walking.

BOSCASTLE Cornwall **Map 2 B2**

⊗££ **BOTTREAUX HOTEL** Boscastle.

🏠££ **Hours:** Meals from 8.15am - 9.15am and 7pm - 9.30pm (last orders). **Cuisine:** Dishes may include Fillet plaice in sauce aux crevettes, Barbarie duck - breast braised in sherry & orange sauce, Suprema di Pollo Cacciatora. 🛏 7 bedrooms, all en suite. 💳 Access, Visa. **Other Points:** Children over 10 years welcome. **Directions:** On the B3266 Boscastle to Camelford road at the top of the village.
CLIVE & ANNA DARVILL ☎ (084 05) 231.
The name 'Bottreaux' dates back to the Norman family who settled here shortly after 1066. The hotel enjoys commanding views over the sea and the Jordan and Valency valleys. Boscastle is on the B3263 in the middle of a protected area with many facilities for every taste.

🏠££ **MELBOURNE HOUSE** New Road, Boscastle.

🛏 1 single, 3 double, and 2 twin bedrooms. All rooms have colour TV, morning call and room service, telephones and tea/coffee making facilities. **Hours:** Breakfast 8.30am - 9.15am and dinner served 7.30pm (last orders 6pm). 💳 Access, Visa. **Other Points:** No dogs. Resident's lounge and garden. Afternoon teas served. 🅿 **(V) Directions:** From Launceston take A395 signed Camelford. Boscastle is on B3266.
MRS B LUCAS ☎ (084 05) 650.
An elegant Victorian house, with all rooms excellently furnished and most of them having views over the Jordan Valley and village. Melbourne House is set in a beautiful conservation area, within half a mile of the harbour, which is under National Trust protection. An ideal base from which to explore Cornwall and its various activities.

THE SOUTH WEST

Boscastle continued

⊗££ **THE WELLINGTON HOTEL** The Harbour, Boscastle.

⏤££ **Hours:** Breakfast 8.30am - 9.30am, dinner 7pm - 9.30pm. **Cuisine:** Table d'Hote, A la carte, Bar meals, Anglo-French cuisine. ⊨ 21 rooms: 8 single, 11 double and 2 twin bedrooms. 16 en suite. **CC** All major cards. **Other Points:** Children over 10 years welcome. Garden. 10 and half acres of woodland. Dogs allowed. Fax No. (0840) 250621. **P** **(V) Directions:** Opposite the old mill, near the harbour.
VICTOR & SOLANGE TOBUTT ☎ (08405) 250202.
You will be assured of a warm and traditional welcome at 'The Wellington Hotel', one of the oldest coaching inns in North Cornwall. While enjoying the beauty of the surrounding area your every need will be catered for.

BOVEY TRACEY Devon **Map 3 B1**

⊗££ **THE EDGEMOOR HOTEL** Lowerdown Cross, Haytor Road,

⏤££ Bovey Tracey.

CLUB **Hours:** Breakfast 8.15am - 9.30am, lunch 12 noon - 2pm, dinner 7.30pm - 9.30pm. **Cuisine:** French and English cuisine. Dishes including marinated herrings with sour cream, ducks breast a l'orange and chocolate and rum shells. ⊨ 3 single, 2 twin, 6 double and 1 family bedroom, all en suite. Four posters and bridal suite available. **CC** All major cards. **Other Points:** Children welcome. Garden. Afternoon tea. Dogs allowed. Fax No; (0626) 834760. **P** & **(V) Directions:** 7 minutes from A38, 1 mile from Bovey Tracey.
ROD & PATRICIA DAY ☎ (0626) 832466.
A 19th century country house, surrounded by extensive well tended lawns and gardens, lovingly decorated and comfortably furnished in keeping with the era. Offering good quality food, excellently cooked and presented, complemented by a distinguished wine list and attentive well trained staff. A delightful establishment not to be missed. Highly recommended.

BRENT KNOLL Somerset **Map 3 A2**

⊗££ **BATTLEBOROUGH GRANGE COUNTRY HOTEL** Bristol

⏤££ Road, Brent Knoll.

Hours: Breakfast 7.30am - 9.30am, lunch 12 noon - 2pm, dinner 7pm - 9pm (last orders). Bar meals 12 noon - 2pm only. **Cuisine:** Peking prawns, Scampi Pernod, Grange fillet steak. ⊨ 18 bedrooms, 14 en suite. **CC** All major cards. **Other Points:** No pets. Afternoon tea served. **P** & **(V) Directions:** 1 mile from M5 junction 22 on A38.
TONY & CAROL WILKINS ☎ (0278) 760208.
The hotel and restaurant nestles in its own grounds at the foot of the historic Iron Age fort known as Brent Knoll. Both the restaurant and bar offer imaginative, well presented home made food. The proprietors and their staff ensure that each guest enjoys their visit.

BRIDGWATER Somerset **Map 3 A2**

⊗££ **WALNUT TREE INN** North Petherton, nr Bridgwater.

CLUB **Hours:** Restaurant open 12 noon - 2pm and 7pm - 10pm. **Cuisine:** Local produce, fresh meat, duck, local dishes. ⊨ 28 bedrooms all en suite. **CC** All major cards. **Other Points:** Children welcome. No

Bridgwater continued

dogs. ▣ ⅄ **(V) Directions:** Off M5 exit 24, travel one mile south on the A38.

RICHARD & HILARY GOULDEN ☎ (0278) 662255.

Situated on the A38 between Bridgwater and Taunton. The menus are varied and interesting, and the quality of the food is very good.

BRIDPORT Dorset **Map 3 B2**

⊗££ **HADDON HOUSE HOTEL** West Bay, Bridport.

⊞££ **Hours:** Meals from 7.45am - 9.15am, 12 noon - 1.30pm and 7pm - 9pm (last orders 8.45pm). **Cuisine:** Fresh local fish, grills, own label wines. ⊨ 13 bedrooms, all en suite. **CC** All major cards. **Other Points:** Children welcome. Coaches welcome. ▣ ⅄ **(V) Directions:** 0.5 mile south of main A35 at Bridport. Follow signpost to West Bay.

MR & MRS P W LOUD ☎ (0308) 23626/25323.

Regency style country house hotel renowned for fine cuisine, only 500 yds from the picturesque harbour and coast of West Bay, overlooking Dorset's beautiful countryside. Amenities available to visitors include deep sea fishing, riding, tennis, and golf (18 hole course opposite hotel with reduced green fees). Ideal for touring Dorset, Devon and Somerset.

BRISTOL Avon **Map 3 A2**

⊗££ **51 PARK STREET** 51 Park Street, Bristol.

Hours: Serving full menu from 12 noon -11pm. Open Bank Holidays. Closed: Christmas Day, Boxing Day and New Year's Day. **Cuisine:** Mainly English with Chinese, French and American influences. Speciality - Modern American influenced brasserie food. ⊨ None. **CC** All major cards. **Other Points:** Children welcome. No smoking area. Afternoon teas served. Garden dining. ▣ **(V) Directions:** From City centre follow route to Bristol University.

MR GEORGE TIMMONS ☎ (0272) 268016.

Prominently positioned in Bristols shopping area, 51 Park Street is well decorated and offers a wide variety of dishes at value for money prices. Frequented by mixed ages of both holidaymakers and locals alike.

⊗££ **BOUBOULINA'S RESTAURANT & MEZE BAR** 9 Portland Street, Clifton, Bristol.

Hours: Lunch 12 noon - 2.30pm and dinner 6pm - 11.30pm. Sundays open 12 noon - 10pm. Bar also open for lunches and early evening meals. **Cuisine:** Full Greek menu. Extensive vegetarian and vegan choices. ⊨ None. **CC** Access, Visa. **Other Points:** Children welcome. No pets. No smoking area. Pavement dining in summer. ⅄ **(V) Directions:** Near the Bristol Suspension Bridge in Clifton Village.

MR K A KOUSIOUNIS ☎ (0272) 731192/738387

A popular Greek restaurant in an up-market area of Bristol. The emphasis is on traditional Greek and Cypriot cuisine and fish and game cooked on charcoals served in an intimate atmosphere by charming waiters. A regular choice for businessmen and locals of all ages.

Bristol continued

⊗££ **CHINA PALACE RESTAURANT** 18a Baldwin Street, Bristol.
Hours: Lunch 12 noon - 2.30pm, dinner 6pm - 11.30pm.
Cuisine: Chinese cuisine, with Cantonese, Szechuan and
Pekinese specialities. ⊨ None. ☒ Access, Visa, AmEx. **Other
Points:** Open Sundays. Fax No: (0272) 256168. **(V) Directions:** In
the centre of Bristol, near theatre and cathedral on Baldwin St.
KAM WONG ☎ (0272) 262719.
*The China Palace, the largest Cantonese restaurant in the West
of England, is air-conditioned, has 2 attractive bars and
facilities for dancing. Extensive menu, with all food beautifully
cooked and presented.*

⊗£ **NATRAJ TANDOORI (NEPALESE & INDIAN CUISINE)**
185 Gloucester Road, Bishopston, Bristol.
Hours: Monday to Thursday lunch 12 noon - 2pm and dinner 6pm
- 12 midnight. Friday and Saturday 12 noon - 2pm and dinner
6pm - 12.30am. Open Sunday dinner 6pm - 12 midnight.
Cuisine: Nepalese and Indian dishes. Specialities include Gurkha
chick, Momocha, Murgi Mussalam, Thuckpa. Continental dishes
also available. ⊨ None. ☒ All major cards. **Other Points:**
Children welcome. No dogs. No-smoking area. Take-aways
available. Parties catered for. ⅋ **(V) Directions:** A38, north of city
centre. Opposite Bristol North Swimming Baths.
MR D KARKI ☎ (0272) 248145.
*Natraj offers an excellent mix of traditional Tandoori with more
unusual Nepalese dishes. Try Momocha (spiced minced lamb in
pastry served with Nepalese pickle) as one of the many
Nepalese specialities on offer, or one of the set menus. Friendly,
helpful staff will help you choose from the extensive menu.
Generous helping of food in comfortable, oriental surroundings.*

⊗£ **RAINBOW CAFE** 10 Waterloo Street, Clifton, Bristol.
Hours: Open 10am - 5.30pm lunch 12 noon - 2.30pm. Closed:
Sundays and Bank Holidays and from 25 December - 1 January.
Cuisine: Fish and meat dishes. The lunch menu varies daily and all
food is fresh each day. ⊨ None. ☒ None. **Other Points:** Children
welcome. No dogs. Wine licence. ⅋ **(V) Directions:** From Bristol
City Centre follow Clifton signs. Off Princess Street.
ALISON MOORE & TIM ANSELL ☎ (0272) 738937.
*The combination of homemade meat and vegetarian dishes on
offer has made this small restaurant very popular. Quality
secondhand books on sale and monthly exhibitions of work by
local artists.*

⊗££ **THE GANGES** 368 Gloucester Road, Horfield, Bristol.
Hours: Lunch 12 noon - 2.30pm and dinner 6pm - 11.30pm (last
orders). Closed: Christmas and Boxing Day. **Cuisine:** North
Indian. ⊨ None. ☒ All major cards. **Other Points:** Children
welcome. No dogs. ⅋ **(V) Directions:** On the A38, Gloucester
Road.
MR CHOWDHURY ☎ (0272) 428505/245234
*A friendly restaurant, tastefully decorated in Indian style, with
intimate alcoves for romantic dining. The service is courteous
and efficient and the menu includes some lesser known Indian
dishes.*

Bristol continued

Ⅲ££ **THE OAKDENE HOTEL** 45 Oakfield Road, Clifton, Bristol.
⮞ 4 single, 6 double, 4 twin bedrooms, 7 en suite. Colour TV,
Tea/Coffee facilities, Shaver points in all rooms. **Hours:** Breakfast
7am - 9am. **Other Points:** Children welcome. Garden.
Directions: Off the A4018.
BRIAN & PAULINE JOHNSON JONES ☎ (0272) 735900.
A large Georgian House hotel set in a quiet tree lined avenue,
close to the university, zoo, hospitals, restaurants, shops,
cinemas, theatres and Clifton Suspension Bridge.

⊗££ **THE PARKSIDE HOTEL** 470 Bath Road, Brislington, Bristol.
Ⅲ££££ **Hours:** Breakfast 7am - 9am, lunch 12 noon - 3pm (last orders
2.30pm) and dinner 7pm - 10.30pm (last orders). Open Sunday
lunch 12 noon - 2.30pm and dinner 7pm - 10pm. **Cuisine:** A la
carte and Carvery. ⮞ 30 bedrooms, 8 en suite. **CC** Access, Visa,
AmEx. **Other Points:** Children welcome. Garden. Victorian
Conservatory. Snooker room. Club bar. Banqueting suites,
conference and function rooms. Fax:(0272) 715507. **P** & **(V)**
Directions: 1 mile from Bristol city centre on the A4 Bath road.
ADRIAN BOONE - General Manager ☎ (0272) 711461.
Only 1 mile along the A4 from Bristol city centre and only
minutes from national motorway and rail links, the Parkside
Hotel is situated in its own grounds. Recently refurbished and
upgraded, this hotel offers comfortably furnished bedrooms and
a la carte and carvery restaurant. With leisure facilities,
including Snooker room with competition quality tables.

BRIXHAM Devon Map 3 B1

⊗££ **POOPDECK RESTAURANT** 15 The Quay, Brixham.
Hours: Dinner 6.30pm - 10pm. November, December and March
open for Thursday, Friday, Saturday dinner and Sunday lunch.
Closed: January and February. **Cuisine:** Locally caught fish and
seafood and Anglo/Italian meat and fish dishes. ⮞ None. **CC** All
major cards. **Other Points:** Children welcome. No dogs. **(V)**
Directions: On the quayside, overlooking the harbour.
EDWARD C. ALLEN ☎ (08045) 7415.
Situated overlooking the harbour opposite the replica of the
Golden Hind. The building started life in 1830 as a fish shop.

Ⅲ££ **RADDICOMBE LODGE** 120 Kingswear Road, Brixham.
[CLUB] ⮞ 5 double, 1 twin and 2 family bedrooms, some en suite. 2
bathrooms. Colour TV and tea/coffee making facilities in all
rooms. **Hours:** Breakfast 8am - 9am. **CC** Access, Visa. **Other Points:**
Central heating. Children welcome. Residents lounge. TV.
Garden. Vegetarian meals available. **P Directions:** On the B3205
between Brixham and Dartmouth.
MR & MRS GLASS ☎ (0803) 882125.
The latticed windows and pitched ceilings give this country
house a cottage atmosphere. Most rooms have a fine sea or
country view. A good base for touring the Devon coast and for
Dartmoor.

BUDE Cornwall Map 2 B2

Ⅲ££££ **MAER LODGE HOTEL** Crooklets Beach, Bude.
[CLUB] ⮞ 3 single, 4 twin, 9 double and 3 family bedrooms, 15 en suite
and with colour TV and tea/coffee making facilities.

Bude continued

> **Hours:** Breakfast 8.30am - 9.15am, Lunch 12 noon - 1.45pm, Dinner 6.45pm - 7.45pm (last orders 7.30pm). Open to non-residents for lunch and dinner but please **CC** Access, Visa. **Other Points:** Children welcome. Tea served at 5.30pm for children under 5. Dogs allowed. Garden. **P** &. **Directions:** Overlooking Golf Course and close to the beach.
> MR & MRS STANLEY ☎ (0288) 353306.
> *Maer Lodge is a Hotel serving good, home cooked food. The good quality of the ingredients and the care in preparation ensures that guests receive good home cooking. The breakfasts are equally good and are varied daily. A friendly, family hotel.*

MORNISH HOTEL 20 Summerleaze Crescent, Bude.
> 5 double, 2 twin, 3 family bedrooms - all en suite. TVs in all rooms. Tea/coffee making facilities in rooms. **Hours:** Breakfast 8.30am - 9am and Dinner 6.30pm - 7pm, (order by 5.30pm). Closed: November to February. **CC** Access, Visa, AmEx. **Other Points:** Central heating. Children welcome. Licensed. Residents lounge. TV. Eurocard also accepted. **P** **Directions:** From town centre, turn left at Post Office corner, towards sea.
> JOHN & JULIA HILDER ☎ (0288) 352972.
> *The Mornish Hotel offers magnificent views from a prime location in Bude overlooking the beach. Centrally situated, with shops, golf course and beach nearby.*

THE FALCON HOTEL Breakwater Road, Bude, Cornwall.
> **Hours:** Breakfast 8.30am - 9.30am, Lunch 12 noon - 2pm and 7pm - 9pm (last orders). Closed: Christmas day. **Cuisine:** An 'international' menu offering Italian, Chinese, Indian and Mexican dishes, as well as 'Falcon grills' and fresh local fish. 12 bedrooms, all en suite. **CC** All major cards. **Other Points:** Children welcome. Dogs allowed. **P** **(V) Directions:** On western side of Bude, easily seen from the main road.
> TIM & DOROTHY BROWNING ☎ (0288) 2005.
> *The Falcon is the oldest coaching house in North Cornwall and was once headquarters for the four-horse coaches which ran along the coast. Warm hospitality still exists here today and guests can expect high quality food in the candlelit restaurant. The lobster, if available, is particularly recommended*

BURNHAM ON SEA Somerset Map 3 A2

ROYAL CLARENCE HOTEL 31 Esplanade, Burnham on Sea.
> **Hours:** Meals served 8am - 9.30am, 12 noon - 2.15pm and 7pm - 8.30pm last orders. Meals served in the bar 11.30am - 2.30pm and 6pm - 9.30pm. **Cuisine:** Traditional British cooking. 15 bedrooms, 12 en suite. 2 bathrooms. **CC** All major cards. **Other Points:** Children welcome. Coaches by appointment. &. **(V)**
> D Q & P Q DAVEY ☎ (0278) 783 138/9
> *Old coaching inn situated on the Esplanade. Convenient for town centre and the adjacent countryside. Self-contained banquet/ballroom for private functions of up to 200 people.*

CHAGFORD Devon Map 3 B1

THE THREE CROWNS HOTEL Chagford.
> **Hours:** Meals from 8.30am - 9.30am, from 12 noon - 2pm and 7pm - 9.30pm. **Cuisine:** Bar menu, eg. basket meals,

Chagford continued

ploughman's, mermaid's lunch. A la carte and table d'hote menus. ⊨ 17 bedrooms, 9 en suite. **CC** Access, Visa. **Other Points:** Children welcome. **P** **(V)**

MR & MRS J GILES ☎ (064 73) 3444/3279.

Situated in the pretty village of Chagford within the Dartmoor National Park, this 13th century inn retains its olde worlde charm with its open fires and four poster beds.

CHARD Somerset **Map 3 B2**

⊗££ **HORNSBURY MILL** Eleighwater, Nr Chard.

⊞££ **Hours:** Breakfast 8.30am - 9.30am, Lunch 12.30pm - 2.30pm, Dinner 7pm - 10pm (last orders). Bar snacks served all day. **Cuisine:** Predominantly English cuisine with all dishes homemade including bread and scones. ⊨ 5 bedrooms, all en suite. **CC** Access, Visa. **Other Points:** Children welcome. Afternoon teas. Dogs allowed. Lounge. Garden dining. **P** ₺ **(V) Directions:** Midway between Chard and Ilminster on A358.

BRYAN HOLLAND ☎ (0460) 63317.

Set in beautiful grounds and with a working mill and museum, Hornsbury Mill is highly recommended for its good, homecooked food and excellent accommodation at very reasonable prices. All visitors are warmly welcomed by friendly staff and special consideration has been given to disabled guests. Excellent cream teas. Well worth a visit.

CHARMOUTH Dorset **Map 3 B2**

⊞££ **HENSLEIGH HOTEL** Lower Sea Lane, Charmouth, nr Bridport.

⊨ 2 single, 3 double, 3 twin and 2 family bedrooms all with en suite facilities. Tea/coffee making facilities and colour TVs in all rooms. **Hours:** Breakfast 8am - 9am, lunch 12 noon - 2pm, dinner 6.45pm - 7.30pm. Closed: November to February inclusive. Open for meals to non-residents by arrangement. **CC** None. **Other Points:** Central heating. Children welcome. Dogs allowed. Licensed. Resident lounge. Garden. **P** **Directions:** Midway between the village and beach off the A35.

MALCOLM & MARY MACNAIR ☎ (0297) 60830.

A comfortable, well-equipped family run hotel in a quiet position. A friendly, homely atmosphere is complimented by good home cooking using local produce. The rolling hills of Dorset and stunning cliff walks are on the doorstep.

⊗£ **NEWLANDS HOUSE** Stonebarrow Lane, Charmouth.

⊞££ **Hours:** 8.30am - 9.15am and 7pm - 7.30pm. Open Bank Holidays. Open to non-residents by arrangement. **Cuisine:** Cordon bleu cuisine. Home-produced dishes. ⊨ 12 bedrooms, 11 of them en suite. All rooms have colour TV and tea/coffee making facilities. Smoking forbidden in bedrooms. **CC** None. **Other Points:** Children over 6 years welcome. Pets allowed by arrangement. Resident's lounges and garden. No smoking in bedrooms, dining room & one lounge. **P** **Directions:** A35, 7 miles west of Bridport at foot of Stonebarrow Lane.

ANNE & VERNON VEAR ☎ (0297) 60212.

A former 16th century farmhouse, family run and situated in approximately 2 acres of gardens and old orchards at the foot of Stonebarrow Hill, which is part of the National Trust Golden

THE SOUTH WEST

Charmouth continued

> *Cap Estate. Newlands House makes an ideal centre for walking and touring and is just minutes away from the famous fossil cliffs and beaches of Lyme Bay. 6 miles east of Axminster.*

CHELWOOD Avon **Map 3 A2**

⊗£££ **CHELWOOD HOUSE HOTEL** Chelwood.

Hours: Breakfast from 7.30am - 9.30am and dinner 7.30pm - 11.30pm (last orders 9pm). Residents only Sunday evenings 7pm - 8pm. Closed: 2 weeks Christmas/New Year. **Cuisine:** Traditional English and German cuisine. 11 bedrooms, all en suite. **CC** All major cards. **Other Points:** Children over 10 welcome. Fax as telephone number. **P** & **Directions:** Just past Chelwood Bridge on the A37 between Pensford and Clutton.
JILL & RUDI BIRK ☎ (0761) 490730.

> *A historic house of charm and character, built in 1681 with listed panelled lounges and glorious rural views in every direction. There is a delightful new 'Restaurant in a Garden' - a conservatory-type dining room with the ambiance of a garden, tastefully decorated public rooms, and each bedroom has been individually furnished. A family concern with a welcoming atmosphere.*

CHIDEOCK Dorset **Map 3 B2**

⊗£ **GEORGE INN** Chideock, nr Bridport.

CLUB **Hours:** Meals 12 noon - 2pm and 6.45pm - 10.30pm (last orders 9.30pm). Open all year. Special hours certificate available. **Cuisine:** Specialities - omelettes with various fillings. Steaks including massive mixed grill. Salads, fish, gammon. Daily specials - e.g. venison, lamb, trout. None. **CC** None. **Other Points:** Children welcome. Real local and low alcohol beers, lagers and ciders. Extensions planned for entire inn. **P** & **(V) Directions:** On the A35, 2 miles west of Bridport in the east of Chideock.
MIKE & MARILYN TUCK ☎ (0297) 89419.

> *A 16th century thatched inn offering an extensive menu with 3 daily extras and prices to suit all pockets. Restaurant, beer garden, family room with pool, darts and skittles. A true local welcome is assured in this Dorset Evening Echo 1985 Pub of the Year.*

CHILLINGTON Devon **Map 3 C1**

⊗££ **WHITE HOUSE HOTEL** Chillington, Kingsbridge, Devon.

⊞£££ **Hours:** Breakfast 8.30 - 9.30am, Lunch anytime for residents only. Dinner 7pm - - 10pm. **Cuisine:** All dishes are home made with constant change of fixed menu eg. Roast rack of lamb, fresh lemon sole. 8 bedrooms. TV and direct dial telephone in all rooms. **CC** Access, Visa. **Other Points:** Children over 5 welcome. Dogs allowed (by arrangement), Residents' lounge & bar. TV in all rooms. **P** **(V) Directions:** On A379 between Kingsbridge and Dartmouth.
MICHAEL ROBERTS & DAVID ALFORD ☎ (0548) 580580.

> *The White House Hotel is a lovely Georgian house set in an acre of lawned and terraced gardens and is just two miles from the coast. It offers excellent food and friendly service in peaceful and relaxed surroundings.*

CHRISTOW Devon **Map 3 B1**

⊗££ **THE ARTICHOKE INN** Christow, nr Exeter.

⌂££ **Hours:** Meals from 8.30am - 9.30am, 12 noon - 1.30pm and 7.30pm - 9.15pm. **Cuisine:** Stuffed trout, fresh salmon, chicken breast stuffed with lobster and prawns, whole plaice on the bone. ⊨ 3 bedrooms, 1 bathroom. ◫ Access, Visa. **Other Points:** Children welcome. ▣ **Directions:** On the B3193 (off A38) midway between Chudleigh and Dunsford.
MR & MRS M H FOX ☎ (0647) 52387.

The Artichoke is a long, low thatched inn in the friendly village of Christow, in the Teign valley. Log fires in winter and a cheerful atmosphere compliment the excellent home cooking.

CLAWTON Devon **Map 2 B2**

⊗££ **COURT BARN COUNTRY HOUSE HOTEL** Clawton, nr

W Holsworthy.

Hours: Morning coffee from 10am - 12 noon. Lunch 12 noon - 2pm. Afternoon teas 3pm - 5pm. Dinner 7.30pm - 9pm (Booking advisable). Closed: January 1st - January 7th. **Cuisine:** English/French. Cordon Bleu cuisine. 6 course candlelit dinners. Fresh local produce. Vegetarian dishes. Menu changes daily. Award winning cream teas. ⊨ 8 bedrooms, all en suite. Telephone, colour TV, hairdryer, trouser press, tea/coffee (fresh milk), books and flowers. ◫ All major cards. **Other Points:** Children & dogs welcome. 5 acres of garden. Outstanding views. Tennis Court. Croquet lawn. Chip & Putt. 2 lounges. Library. Games room. Gym. ▣ **(V) Directions:** 3 miles south of Holsworthy, off A388. Next to 12th century church.
ROBERT & SUSAN WOOD ☎ (040927) 219.

A country house of great character and charm, with antiques, pictures and flowers throughout, Court Barn is the perfect touring hotel for Dartmoor, Bodmin and Exmoor. Les Routiers/Mercier Winelist of the Year 1989, Corps d'Elite 90/91. Tea Council 'Best Teas in Britain' 87/89. National Awards for cuisine. A Devon's 'Hotel of Distinction'.

CLEVEDON Avon **Map 3 A2**

⊗££ **THE REGENT** 26 Hill Road, Clevedon.

Hours: Meals 12 noon - 2pm and 7pm - 10.15pm (last orders). Bar meals 12 noon - 2pm and 7pm - 10.15pm. Closed: Christmas day. **Cuisine:** English cuisine, including house speciality steaks. ⊨ None. ◫ Access, Visa. **Other Points:** Children welcome. No dogs. Coaches welcome. ▣ ⅙ **(V)**
MARIE HEGARTY ☎ (0272) 872460/872909

An early Victorian building with a homely atmosphere. Coffee served from 10am every morning. Very popular with the locals and tourists.

⊗££ **WALTON PARK HOTEL** Wellington Terrace, Clevedon, Nr

⌂££££ Bristol.

CLUB **Hours:** Breakfast 7.30am - 9.30am, Lunch 12.30pm - 2pm and Dinner 7.30pm - 9.30pm (last orders). Bar meals 12 noon - 2pm. **Cuisine:** An interesting and constantly changing range of English and French cuisine from both A la carte and table d'hote menus. ⊨ 37 bedrooms, all en suite. ◫ All major cards. **Other Points:** Children welcome. Dogs allowed. Open Sundays and bank holidays. Residents lounge and Channelside garden. ▣ ⅙ **(V)**

THE SOUTH WEST

Clevedon continued

Directions: Jct 20, M5. Follow signs to seafront & continue to end of Terrace.

M A BRIGGS ☎ (0272) 874253.

Situated high above the Bristol channel, this attractive Victorian hotel enjoys spectacular views, spacious rooms and a peaceful location to compliment a restaurant with a well earned repuation for excellent food and wine and professional service. Local attractions include Cheddar Gorge, Tintern Abbey, the zoo and Clevedon pier.

COMBE MARTIN Devon Map 3 A1

⊗££ **RONE HOUSE HOTEL** King Street, Combe Martin.
⌂££ **Hours:** Breakfast 8.30am - 9.15am, lunch 12.30pm - 2pm (residents only), dinner 6.30pm - 9.30pm. Last orders for lunch 2pm, dinner 9.30pm. **Cuisine:** Dishes may include Chicken Breast filled with Prawn & Lobster, Steaks with Garlic or Brandy sauce, Fresh Rainbow Trout, Venison, whole boneless Plaice. ⮞ 4 doubles, 4 family rooms, all en suite. 2 twins and 1 single. **CC** Access, Visa. **Other Points:** Garden. Children welcome (special rates). Dogs allowed. Outdoor heated swimming pool. Bargain breaks available. **P Directions:** Jct 27 on M5. Then follow 369 link road to sign for Combe Martin.

GRAHAM & ELSPETH COTTAGE ☎ (0271) 883428.

A small, privately run hotel where the emphasis is on comfort, relaxation and superb food and service. Nearby are fine sandy beaches, Exmoor, beautiful hills and valleys, such as Valley of the Rocks, Watersmeet and Doone and the famous Dartington Glass Factory.

⊗££ **SANDY COVE HOTEL** Berrynarbor, Combe Martin, nr
⌂£££££ Ilfracombe.
Hours: Meals 8.30am - 9.30am, 12.30pm - 2.30pm and 7pm - 9.30pm (last orders). Afternoon teas 3pm - 5pm. Open 11am - 11pm. **Cuisine:** Fondue, kebabs, 5 variations of lobster. Large a la carte menu. ⮞ 34 bedrooms, all en suite. **CC** None. **Other Points:** Children welcome. Coaches by appointment. **P** & **(V) Directions:** On the A399 (coast road), 1 mile from Combe Martin.

MR R GILSON ☎ (0271) 882243.

The hotel stands in 20 acres of gardens featuring woods, cliffs and coves. Other facilities include outdoor swimming pool, sauna and whirlpool.

COMPTON MARTIN Avon Map 3 A2

⊗£ **RING OF BELLS** Compton Martin, Nr Bristol.
Hours: Lunch 11.30pm - 2pm and dinner 7pm - 11pm (last orders 10pm). Bar meals 12 noon - 2pm and 7pm - 11pm. **Cuisine:** Full menu and daily blackboard specials. ⮞ None. **CC** None. **Other Points:** Children welcome. No dogs. Beer garden. Large family room with highchair, games and rocking horse. **P** & **(V) Directions:** On A364 (Bath to Weston-Super-Mare) in Compton Martin village.

MR WHITMORE ☎ (0761) 221284.

A large, character licensed house in pleasant countryside at the edge of the Mendips. A varied menu is served by friendly, efficient staff, and is complimented by a comprehensive wine list.

CONSTANTINE BAY Cornwall **Map 2 B2**

⊗£££ **TREGLOS HOTEL** Constantine Bay, nr Padstow.

⊞£££ **Hours:** Breakfast 8.30am - 9.30am, lunch 12.30pm - 1.30pm and dinner 7.45pm - 9.30pm (last orders). Bar meals 12 noon - 2.30pm. Closed: 6th November to 10th March. **Cuisine:** Selection of French cuisine. ⊨ 44 bedrooms, all en suite. **CC** Access, Visa. **Other Points:** Children welcome (over 3 years in restaurant). Non-smoking area. Afternoon tea served. Early breakfast by arrangement. Fax: (0841) 521163. ▯ ₺ **(V) Directions:** Off the B3276, east of Padstow.

TED & BARBARA BARLOW ☎ (0841) 520727.

Treglos is a country house style hotel which offers a high standard of service. The restaurant specialises in local fresh seafood and meats, fresh vegetables from their own garden, and home made desserts with Cornish cream. Good food, an extensive wine list and excellent service can be expected.

CRACKINGTON HAVEN Cornwall **Map 2 B2**

⊗£ **COOMBE BARTON INN** Crackington Haven, Nr Bude.

⊞££ **Hours:** Breakfast 8.45am - 9.30am, bar meals 11am - 2.30pm and 6.30pm - 9.45pm (last orders). **Cuisine:** A wide variety of dishes such as charcoal grilled steaks and fish of the day. Carvary. Daily specials board and childrens menu. ⊨ 6 bedrooms, all en suite. **CC** AmEx. **Other Points:** Children welcome. Dogs allowed. Family room. Terrace and patio areas for summer dining. Pool table and games room. ▯ **(V) Directions:** Off A39 Bude to Wadebridge road.

JOHN COOPER ☎ (08403) 345.

An extensive choice of excellently cooked meals can be found at this comfortable, welcoming Free House where specialities include grilled steaks and locally caught fish, crab and lobster. On the National Trust, South West Way Coastal path and by a safe, sandy beach, the Inn is an ideal place to relax in a friendly atmosphere and enjoy high quality food and service. Families welcome.

CREDITON Devon **Map 3 B1**

⊗££ **COOMBE HOUSE COUNTRY HOTEL** Coleford, Nr

⊞£££ Crediton.

Hours: Breakfast 7.30am - 9am, lunch 12 noon - 2pm and dinner 7pm - 9.30pm (last orders). Bar meals 12 noon - 2.3pm and 7pm - 9.30pm. **Cuisine:** French and English dishes including deep fried Camembert, mushrooms cooked with garlic, rack of lamb, Scotch salmon and venison. ⊨ 12 bedrooms, 11 en suite. **CC** Access, Visa, AmEx. **Other Points:** Children welcome. Dogs allowed. Afternoon teas. Dining al fresco in summer. Garden. Heated outdoor swimming pool. Tennis Court. ▯ ₺ **(V) Directions:** Through Crediton on A377 to Barnstaple. Off A377 towards Coleford.

DAVID WIRRICH & MAURICE LILLIS ☎ (0363) 84487.

A listed Georgian Manor House set in 5 acres of parkland, Coombe House provides magnificent views over open countryside. The chef is a member of Chaine des Rotisseurs and good food can be enjoyed in the relaxing surroundings of Hunters Restaurant, formally the site of the ballroom. A welcoming hotel with friendly, helpful service.

CREWKERNE Somerset **Map 3 B2**
⊗££ **THE OLD PARSONAGE HOTEL & RESTAURANT** Barn
⊞£££ Street, Crewkerne.
Hours: Breakfast 7.30am - 9am, lunch by arrangement only 12
noon - 2.30pm, Dinner 7pm - 8pm (last orders). **Cuisine:**
Anglo/French cuisine. ⊨ 10 bedrooms, all en suite. **CC** All major
cards. **Other Points:** Children welcome. Pets allowed. Garden. **P**
(V) Directions: Off the A30. From town centre take exit road to
Chard & turn left.
STEVEN BRAZIER ☎ (0460) 73516.
You can expect a high standard of care and attention from
Steven Brazier as your host. The hotel has been recently
redecorated and, with open fires and fresh flowers, has a
gracious country hotel atmosphere.

CUBERT Cornwall **Map 2 B1**
⊗£ **ANVIL GRILL** Nr Holywell Bay, Newquay.
[CLUB] **Hours:** Open 6pm - 9.30pm. Closed: November to March.
Cuisine: Charcoal-grilled steaks, steak pie, vegetarian dishes,
homemade curries. Chef's daily specials. ⊨ None. **CC** Access,
Visa. **Other Points:** Children welcome. No smoking area.
Mastercard also accepted. **P** ⅍ **(V) Directions:** Situated close to
Holywell Bay and just off the A3075.
MR W G FARROW ☎ (0637) 830631.
A busy and popular place offering good value for money and
friendly service.

DARTMOOR Devon **Map 3 B1**
⊗££ **TWO BRIDGES HOTEL** Princetown, Dartmoor.
⊞£££ **Hours:** Breakfast 8am - 9.30am, lunch 12 noon - 2pm, dinner
7.30pm - 9pm. **Cuisine:** A la carte, fixed 3 course, bar
snacks/meals. Dish of the day. ⊨ 24 rooms, 20 with en suite.
CC All major cards. **Other Points:** Children welcome. Garden
dining. Afternoon teas served. Pets allowed. Non smoking areas.
Open bank holidays and Sunday. Residents lounge. **P** ⅍ **(V)**
Directions: At crossrds of B3212 & B3357 - the 2 main rds
crossing Dartmoor.
PHILIP & LESLEY DAVIES. ☎ (082 289) 581.
This beautiful, rambling 18th century inn has a riverside
location in the heart of Dartmoor. Two Bridges is a charming
hotel in every aspect and provides an idyllic holiday retreat.
Very good accommodation, tasty food and friendly welcoming
service awaits any who visit.

DARTMOUTH Devon **Map 3 C1**
⊗£££ **ROYAL CASTLE HOTEL** The Quay, Dartmouth.
Hours: Meals from 8am - 9.30am, 12.30pm - 2.15pm and 7pm -
9.45pm (last orders). Bar meals served everday, all day from 12
noon - 9.45pm. **Cuisine:** Seafood, traditional roasts. ⊨ 26
bedrooms, all en suite, some with 4 poster beds. **CC** Access, Visa.
Other Points: Children welcome. Afternoon teas. Dogs allowed.
Satellite TV. Weekend breaks & Bargain breaks during week
available. **P** **(V) Directions:** From A38 take A384 to Totnes, A381
to Halwell, then B3207.
MR NIGEL WAY ☎ (0803) 833033.
Standing on the quayside of the River Dart, this hotel was a
coaching inn and has a fascinating history. The ceiling of the

Dartmouth continued

bar is reputed to have been constructed with timber from the wreckage of the Armada. The hotel's elegant atmosphere is reflected in the traditional English cooking and service.

⊗£ **SLOPING DECK RESTAURANT** The Butterwalk, Dartmouth. **Hours:** Meals served 9am - 5.30pm (last orders 5pm). Evening meals served during July and August. **Cuisine:** English home-cooking, including fresh fish and steak and kidney pie. ⊨ None. ◼ Access, Visa. **Other Points:** Children welcome. Pets allowed. Afternoon teas served. **(V) Directions:** In Butterwalk, centre of town. Historic building.
MR & MRS BARNES ☎ (0803) 832758.
The Sloping Deck consists of a bakery on the ground floor and a restaurant on the first floor; both offering quality food at very good value. Situated in one of Dartmouth's most famous historic buildings.

⊗££ **STOKE LODGE HOTEL** Stoke Fleming, Nr Dartmouth.
⊞£££ **Hours:** Breakfast 8.30am - 9.45am, lunch 12.30pm - 2pm, dinner 7pm - 9pm. **Cuisine:** A large variety of English/French cuisine using only the best local fresh ingredients. eg. Poached salmon with Hollandaise sauce. ⊨ 24 rooms: all en suite. 9 double, 8 twin, 3 single and 4 family bedrooms. ◼ Access, Visa. **Other Points:** Indoor/outdoor pools. Jacuzzi. Gym. Sun bed. Sauna. Fishing. River trips. Historic sites. Bird watching. Garden. Children welcome. Pets allowed. ▣ **(V) Directions:** A379. 2 miles south of Dartmouth.
STEVEN MAYER ☎ (0803) 770523.
Situated on the scenic coastal road between historic Dartmouth and Kingsbridge, this charming hotel is very popular locally and offers first class service and comfort with fresh local food, 3 acres of grounds and every facility for a truly relaxing holiday.

⊞£ **TOWNSTAL FARMHOUSE** Townstal Rd, Dartmouth.
⊨ 2 single, 4 double, 2 twin, and 2 family rooms. 2 general bathrooms. 2 showers. TV and tea/coffee making facilities in all rooms. **Hours:** Breakfast 8am - 9am, and dinner served 6.30pm. ◼ None. **Other Points:** Children welcome. Pets allowed. Resident's lounge and garden. ▣ **Directions:** 1/2m from centre of Dartmouth, close to Britannia Royal Naval College
JEAN HALL ☎ (0803) 832300.
A 16th century listed building, with oak beams and inglenook fireplaces. Townstal was once a working farm and still retains the 'lived in' atmosphere of a family home. Personally run by the owner, Jean Hall, it now provides comfortable accommodation and good country food. There are many attractive towns and villages for the visitor to explore and miles of coastal walks.

DAWLISH Devon **Map 3 B1**
⊗££ **LANGSTONE CLIFF HOTEL** Mount Pleasant Road, Dawlish.
⊞££££ **Hours:** Breakfast 7.30am - 10am, Lunch 12.30pm - 2pm, Dinner 7pm - 9pm (last orders). Bar meals available all day. **Cuisine:** Traditional English cuisine. Table d'hote dinner menu and carvery. Coffee shop offering light refreshments. ⊨ 68 bedrooms, all en suite. ◼ All major cards. **Other Points:** Children very welcome. Games room. Tennis courts. Indoor & outdoor

DULVERTON

Dawlish continued
swimming pools. Dinner dances. Conference suites. Fax No: (0626) 867166. ▣ ᴕ **(V) Directions:** 1 mile off the A379. 1 mile North of Dawlish.
GEOFFREY ROGERS ☎ (0626) 867155
Set in 19 acres of wooded grounds and only 500 yards from the beach, this hotel offers the warmest of welcomes and the best in friendly service with special consideration for families and children. Superbly decorated, the hotel provides a high standard of food and accommodation and there is a host of activities for all ages to enjoy. Set in an area of outstanding beauty.

DORCHESTER Dorset Map 3 B2
⊗£ **JUDGE JEFFREYS RESTAURANT** 6 High West Street, Dorchester.
Hours: Morning coffee served from 9.30am, lunch 12 noon - 2.30pm, dinner 7pm - 9.30pm (last orders). Open for coffee, lunch and afternoon teas Monday - Saturday. Open for dinner Friday and Saturday in winter and Tuesday, Wednesday, Friday and Saturday from Easter - end summer. **Cuisine:** Wide range of lunchtime specials which change daily. Evening a la carte menu. Morning coffee and afternoon teas. ⊨ None. ☲ Access, Visa, AmEx. **Other Points:** Children welcome. Dogs allowed. No smoking area. Afternoon teas. Morning coffee. Several public car parks in the area. ᴕ **(V) Directions:** In centre of town on main road. Public car parks nearby.
IAN AND PAT MCLELLAN ☎ (0305) 264369
In 1685 the nortorious Judge Jeffreys lodged at this famous Dorchester House during the time of 'The Bloody Assize'. Today the original beamed building houses a restaurant which provides very good food and polite, friendly service. Highly recommended for its warm welcome, good food and value for money prices.

DREWSTEIGNTON Devon Map 3 B1
⊗££ **THE ANGLERS REST** Fingle Bridge, Drewsteignton, nr Exeter.
Hours: Restaurant open 10.30am - 5.30pm and 7pm - 9pm April to October. In winter open Monday to Saturday 11.00am - 2.30pm and 7pm - 11pm on Saturdays. Sundays 12 noon - 2pm. **Cuisine:** Steak and kidney pie, Devon steaks, salmon and trout. Bar meals.Devonshire cream teas. A selection of vegetarian dishes. ⊨ None. ☲ Access, Visa. **Other Points:** Children welcome. Party and function catering. ▣ ᴕ **(V) Directions:** Next to Fingle Bridge in Drewsteignton.
THE PRICE FAMILY ☎ (064 721) 287.
A family run restaurant and lounge bar with riverside terraces. Adjoining Fingle Bridge on the banks of the River Teign deep in Fingle Gorge, The Anglers Rest provides a starting point for miles of walks, fishing and birdwatching.

DULVERTON Somerset Map 3 A1
⊗£££ **CARNARVON ARMS HOTEL** Dulverton.
Hours: Breakfast 8am - 9.30am, lunch 12.30pm - 1.30pm and dinner 7.30pm - 9pm (last orders). Bar meals 12 noon - 2pm and 7pm - 9pm. Closed for 3 weeks in February. **Cuisine:** Good wholesome English cooking - all home prepared using fresh local

Dulverton continued

produce. ⊨ 22 bedrooms all en suite. **CC** Access, Visa. **Other Points:** Children welcome. Dogs allowed. No smoking area. Afternoon tea served. **P** & **(V) Directions:** 1 mile south of Dulverton on B3222 on the edge of Brushford Village. MRS TONI JONES ☎ (0398) 23302.

An imposing Victorian hotel set in 50 acres of grounds which stands guard at one of the entrances to the Exmoor National Park near the banks of the River Barle. Billed as a 'fine English country sporting hotel', fishing, shooting and swimming are available, and 1st class English cooking guaranteed.

£££ **PARTRIDGE ARMS FARM** Yeo Mill, West Anstey, South Molton.

⊨ 2 single, 6 double and 1 family bedroom, 4 en suite. 1 bathroom. **Hours:** Breakfast 8.30am - 9am and dinner 6.45pm (order by 5pm). Open all year. Cuisine: Traditional farmhouse fare. **CC** None. **Other Points:** Central heating. Children welcome. Licensed. Residents lounge. TV. **P** & **(V) Directions:** Off A361, 8 miles west of Bampton. Follow directions for Yeo Mill. MRS H J MILTON ☎ (03984) 217.

Formerly a country inn, Partridge Arms Farm is set in over 200 acres of land. Ideally suited for touring or walking in the National Park and the many local coastal beauty spots. Trout fishing and pony trekking also available.

⊗££ **TARR STEPS HOTEL** Hawkridge, Dulverton.

Hours: Breakfast 8.30am - 9.45am, bar meals 12.15pm - 2pm, dinner 7.45pm - 8.45pm. Sunday lunch 1pm - 1.30pm. Closed: January - February. Routiers priced menu applies to bar meals and Sunday lunches. **Cuisine:** Soups, fresh local fish, game. ⊨ 14 bedrooms - 11 double/twin all en suite, and 3 singles. **CC** Access, Visa, AmEx. **Other Points:** Children welcome. & **(V)** MR & MRS KEANE ☎ (064 385) 293.

Within the hotel grounds there are ample facilities for sportsmen: the 3 miles of both banks of River Barle offer excellent salmon and trout fishing; the hotel's 500 acres offer both rough and clay pigeon shooting; and loose boxes are available for guests' horses.

⊗££ **THE LION HOTEL** Bank Square, Dulverton.
£££ **Hours:** 8.30am - 9.30am, 12 noon - 2pm, and 6.30pm - 9pm.
CLUB Sunday lunch 12 noon - 2pm, and 7pm - 9pm. **Cuisine:** Fresh Exmoor produce including salmon, trout, game birds and venison, traditionally cooked and available in the restaurants and bars. ⊨ 4 single, 4 twin, 4 double, and 1 family room, all en suite, with colour TVs, direct dial telephones and tea/coffee making facilities. **CC** Access, Visa. **Other Points:** Reductions for children. Dogs welcome at daily rate of £2. Bargain breaks: shooting, hunting, fishing, walking. **P** & **(V) Directions:** Jct 27, off M5. Then off A396, between Tiverton and Minehead. DUNCAN & JACKIE MACKINNON - Managers ☎ (0398) 23444.

Set in the heart of the Exmoor National Park, the Lion is an ideal base for exploring this beautiful, unspoilt corner of England. It offers a warm welcome, comfortable accommodation and good food at excellent value for money. The wide range of holiday

Dulverton continued

breaks cater for every interest, including those who fancy a trip in a hot air balloon.

DUNSTER Somerset **Map 3 A1**

⊗££ **DUNSTER CASTLE HOTEL** High Street, Dunster.

⬚£££ **Hours:** Breakfast served 8.30am - 9.30am, lunch 12 noon - 2.30pm, dinner 6.30pm - 9.30pm. **Cuisine:** International and English cuisine, daily specialities. Fresh Exmoor produce used whenever possible. ⊨ 9 rooms, 7 en suite. **CC** Access, Visa, AmEx. **Other Points:** Children welcome. Garden dining. Afternoon teas. Dogs allowed. No smoking area. Function suite available. **P**
Directions: In Dunster village approx 18 miles W. of Taunton & 2 E. of Minehead.
SALY KOSH - General Manager ☎ (0643) 821445
Once the private home of Lady Elizabeth Luttrel, this hotel is situated in the medieval village of Dunster. Offering a comfortable stay, good food and a cheerful, friendly atmosphere. Good home base for touring Exmoor.

⬚££ **GRABBIST HOUSE** Dunster.

⊨ 2 twin and 1 double room. Centrally heated. Shaver points, washbasins, and tea/coffee making facilities in rooms. **Hours:** Breakfast served between 8.30am - 10.30am. **CC** None. **Other Points:** Children over 8 years old welcome. Pets allowed. Residents' garden. Residents' lounge with colour TV. **P**
Directions: Off A39 - A396. Close to Dunster Castle.
MS M O DONOGHUE ☎ (0643) 821239.
18th century house set in 2 acres of grounds on Grabbist Hill, with lovely views over the thatched roofs of the village to the Deer Park. Ideal centre for exploring Exmoor, Quantocks, Brendons, and coast. Guests receive a very warm welcome and can enjoy delicious farm breakfasts, with free-range eggs, home-baked bread and honey. Very good value.

⊗£ **THE TEA SHOPPE** 3 High Street, Dunster.

Hours: Open 10am - 5.30pm in March to October, weekends only from November to December. **Cuisine:** Homemade soups and traditional recipes. ⊨ None. **CC** Access, Visa. **Other Points:** Licensed. Children welcome. Pets allowed. Non-smoking. ঙ **(V)**
Directions: Situated on the town's main road at the end nearest the castle.
NORMAN & PAM GOLDSACK ☎ (0643) 821304.
15th century tearooms in lovely medieval village close to National Trust Castle. Norman and Pam can boast 29 years experience and specialise in home cooking. A well presented tearoom offering all sorts of unusual teas, jams, coffees etc.

EXEBRIDGE Somerset **Map 3 B1**

⊗££ **ANCHOR INN HOTEL** Exebridge, Nr Dulverton.

⬚£££ **Hours:** Breakfast 8.30am - 9.30am, lunch 12 noon - 2pm and dinner 7pm - 9pm (last orders). Closed: Christmas day. **Cuisine:** Good home cooking with local produce used where possible, including Chef who bakes own bread and makes homemade desserts. ⊨ 6 bedrooms all en suite. **CC** Access, Visa. **Other Points:** Large beer garden. Booking essential. Children made

THE SOUTH WEST

Exebridge continued

welcome with their own play area. Mastercard and Eurocard also accepted. **P** **(V) Directions:** On the A396, north east of Bampton. JOHN & JUDY PHRIPP ☎ (0398) 23433.

A 300 year old residential inn on the banks of the River Exe, with fishing from the hotel grounds. Shooting by arrangement. Standing in an acre of grounds. Recently refurbished, with a stableblock restaurant serving a full a la carte menu in excellent surroundings overlooking the river.

EXETER Devon **Map 3 B1**

PARK VIEW HOTEL 8 Howell Road, Exeter.

15 bedrooms, 9 en suite. **Hours:** Breakfast served daily. Closed: Christmas only. **CC** Access, Visa. **Other Points:** Children welcome. No dogs. Residents' lounge. **P** **Directions:** B3183 to clock tower roundabout - 3rd exit. At end turn Left.
MR & MRS BATHO ☎ (0392) 71772.

A popular hotel in the centre of Exeter, which offers comfortable accommodation and excellent full breakfasts. Attractively decorated, Park View Hotel provides a comfortable, welcoming base from which to visit Exeter, whether on business or for pleasure. Very close to the University and station.

THE LORD HALDON HOTEL Dunchideock, nr Exeter.

CLUB **Hours:** Restaurant open 11.30am - 2pm and 7pm - 10.30pm. **Cuisine:** Traditional English cooking using local produce. 14 bedrooms, most en suite with TV and tea/coffee making facilities. **CC** All major cards. **Other Points:** Children welcome. Full central heating. **P** **(V) Directions:** Near Exeter in the Devonshire Hills.
MR & MRS PREECE ☎ (0392) 832483.

The hotel has a peaceful and relaxing location as it is situated in the Devonshire hills. However, it is only a few minutes drive from the centre of the Cathedral city of Exeter.

THE OLD THATCH INN Cheriton Bishop, nr Exeter.

Hours: Lunch 12 noon - 1.45pm followed by a reduced menu until 2.15pm. Dinner 6.30pm - 9.30pm (7pm - 9pm on Sunday). **Cuisine:** Homemade food using traditional recipes. Dishes may include steak & kidney pudding, Seafood Pie, Thatch Mixed Grill, Baked Stuffed Aubergine. 3 double bedrooms, all en suite. **CC** Access, Visa. **Other Points:** No children under 14 years. **P** **(V) Directions:** From the A30, 10 miles west of Exeter, take Cheriton Bishop road.
BRIAN & HAZEL BRYON-EDMOND ☎ (0647) 24204.

Traditional 16th century thatched free house, originally built as a coaching house. Just 10 miles from Exeter and inside the eastern border of Dartmoor National Park. Routiers of the Year 1985.

THE WOODLEIGH COACH HOUSE Woodleigh, Cheriton Bishop, Exeter.

Hours: Meals served in the cafe 7am - 12 midnight Monday to Saturday, 7am - 5pm on Sunday. Restaurant open Monday - Saturday 12 noon - 3pm (bookings required), and 7.30pm - 12 midnight. Sunday lunch 12 noon - 3pm. Open all year. **Cuisine:** Imaginative, predominantly English cuisine in the restaurant. Bar style meals served in the cafe. 8 bedrooms, all en suite.

Exeter continued

CC Access, Visa, AmEx. **Other Points:** Children welcome. Access for disabled for dining only. Afternoon teas. Childrens menu. Dogs allowed. Garden dining. **P** & **(V) Directions:** Just off A30 between Exeter and Okehampton.
AILEEN & STEVEN COLLINS ☎ (0647) 24228.

A converted Victorian coach house, recently refurbished to provide a hotel and restaurant with a cafe attached. Very popular with holiday makers, the Woodleigh Coach House offers a choice of restaurant and cafe meals, all served by warm and courteous staff. An ideal stop for travellers for either a meal or overnight stay.

⊗££ **WHITE HART HOTEL** South Street, Exeter.
Hours: Breakfast 7.30am - 9.30am, Lunch 12 noon - 2.30pm and Dinner 7.30pm - 10pm (last orders). **Cuisine:** A la carte and bar menu. Traditional English, Charcoal grills, Chicken & Chestnut Pie with Sage and Escalope of Veal Cordon Bleu. ⇌ 61 bedrooms, 59 en suite. Special weekend terms. **CC** All major cards. **Other Points:** Children welcome. Afternoon tea. Garden. Real Ale. **P** **(V) Directions:** Take B3192 to South Street.
MR G STONE ☎ (0392) 79897.

A historic 14th Century Hostelry, the White Hart is one of the city's most ancient Inns, 2 minutes walk from the Cathedral and town centre. Steeped in history, the hotel offers visitors traditional meals and excellent service in the same atmosphere as Henry VI and Cromwell enjoyed on their visits!

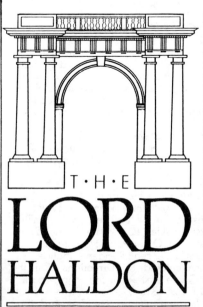

The Lord Haldon
Dunchideock, Near Exeter, Devon
Telephone: Exeter (0392) 832483
Fax: Exeter (0392) 833765

Built in 1720 as the seat of the Lords of Haldon the surviving wing was part of one of Devon's largest and finest 18th century mansions. The Lord Haldon Hotel, with its excellent reputation for good food, accommodation and interesting history, attracts visitors the world over. The hotel is fully centrally heated and most bedrooms are en-suite with T.V. and tea/coffee making facilities. Situated 5 miles SW of Exeter under the M5 in secluded mature grounds with panoramic views, under Haldon Hill, where once stood the graceful marble halls of a bygone era, one can enjoy dinner in the candlelit restaurant. In the tranquility of the gardens or in the cobbled courtyard, graced with its impressive Adam arch, one can enjoy delicious Devon cream teas, snacks or drinks alfresco. Dinner dances are held most Saturdays. Attractive colour brochure and prices on request. 3-Star RAC. RAC Merit Award for Hospitality and Comfort.

THE SOUTH WEST

EXFORD Somerset **Map 3 A1**
⊗£££ **THE EXMOOR WHITE HORSE INN** Exford.
⌂£££ **Hours:** Breakfast 8.30am - 9.30am, Lunch 12 noon - 2.30pm and
CLUB Dinner 7pm - 9pm. **Cuisine:** Steaks, seafood, venison, pub food.
🛏 18 bedrooms, all en suite. **CC** None. **Other Points:** Children
welcome. Garden. **P** **(V) Directions:** From Taunton take the
A358, then the B224 to Exford.
MR & MRS HENDRY ☎ (064 383) 229
*Your dream of an olde worlde inn with log fires, standing on the
green by the side of a trickling stream in one of Exmoors' most
beautiful villages, comes true before your eyes. Horses all
around, the blacksmith busy over the road, and rolling moors
await you at the edge of the village.*

EXMOUTH Devon **Map 3 B1**
⊗££ **DEVONCOURT HOTEL** 16 Douglas Avenue, Exmouth.
Hours: Breakfast 8am - 9.45am, Lunch and bar snacks 12 noon -
2pm, Dinner 7pm - 9.30pm (last orders). **Cuisine:** Carvery and a
la carte menus. Charcoal grill and Italian specialities. 🛏 47
bedrooms, all en suite. **CC** All major cards. **Other Points:** Children
welcome. Afternoon teas. Dogs allowed. Residents' lounge.
Garden. Full indoor and outdoor leisure facilities. Fax No: (0395)
269315. **P** **(V) Directions:** Near the seafront and Pavillion.
Opposite Rolle College.
SID & FRANCES LALANI ☎ (0395) 272277.
*A popular hotel and restaurant which enjoys a regular clientele.
A la carte and carvery menus are offered in the restaurant and
provide very good value for money. Efficient, courteous service.
The hotel has full leisure facilities including indoor and outdoor
heated swimming pools, whirlpool spa, sauna, solariums, tennis
and croquet - to name but a few. Sea views.*

FALMOUTH Cornwall **Map 2 C1**
⊗££ **GREEN LAWNS HOTEL** Western Terrace, Falmouth.
⌂££££ **Hours:** Meals from 7am - 9.30am, 12 noon - 2pm and 6.45pm -
W 10pm (last orders). Bar meals served 12 noon - 2pm and 6.45pm -
⊕ 10pm. **Cuisine:** Fresh local seafood and speciality steaks. 🛏 40
bedrooms all en suite. **CC** All major cards. **Other Points:** Children
welcome. Coaches by appointment. New honeymoon suites. **P** &
(V) Directions: On the main road into Falmouth heading towards
the main beaches.
WENDY SYMONS - Manageress. ☎ (0326) 312734.
*A chateau-style hotel - completely modernised throughout. New
indoor leisure complex and full banqueting/conference
facilities available.*

⌂££ **THE GROVE HOTEL** Grove Place, Falmouth.
🛏 2 single, 5 double,4 twin and 3/4 family bedrooms, 12 with en
suite facilities. 3 bathrooms.Colour TV and tea/coffee making
facilities in all rooms. **Hours:** Breakfast 8am - 9am. Dinner 7pm -
9pm (last orders). **CC** Access, Visa. **Other Points:** Central heating.
Children welcome. No dogs. Licensed. Residents lounge. TV.
Street parking. Vegetarians catered to. **Directions:** Off the
A39.Take harbour road to Grove Place near the Dinghy park.
PETER & JANET CORK ☎ (0326) 319 577.
*Ideally situated for the harbour, shops, beaches and train
station. There is a games room with table tennis, darts and a pool*

Falmouth continued

table. The Grove Hotel was established in 1946 and although the building itself has been changed, you will still find the same relaxed and friendly atmosphere under the 2nd generation of the Corks.

⊗£££ **THE PANDORA INN** Restronguet Creek, Mylor Bridge, Falmouth.
Hours: Bar meals 12 noon - 2.15pm and 6.30pm - 10pm. Restaurant open 7.30 - 12 midnight (last orders 9.30pm). Restaurant closed in winter. Open all day in high season. **Cuisine:** Local fresh fish and fresh produce. Cornish specialities. Afternoon teas. ⊨ None. **CC** Access, Visa. **Other Points:** Limited access for disabled. Dogs on leads. Afternoon teas served in summer. Vegetarian menu. **P** **(V) Directions:** From A39 in Falmouth take Mylor turn then down hill to Restronguet.
MR AND MRS R HOUGH ☎ (0326) 72678.
A picture book 13th century thatched inn reputedly owned by Capt. Edwards of Bounty mutiny fame. Flagstone floors, low beamed ceilings & gleaming brasswork complete the picture book setting. Come by car or by boat - yachts may be moored on the 140ft pontoon at the front, and enjoy the famous, fine cuisine.

⊞£££ **THE PARK GROVE HOTEL** Kimberley Park Road, Falmouth.
⊨ 3 single, 4 double, 6 twin and 4 family bedrooms, 15 en suite. Colour TV, Radio clock alarm, Tea/Coffee making facilities and baby listening device in all rooms. Hairdrying, shoe cleaning and ironing facilities available on request. **Hours:** Breakfast 8.30am - 9.30am, Dinner 6.30pm - 8.30pm (last orders). Packed lunches by order. **CC** Access, Visa. **Other Points:** Children welcome. Afternoon tea. Licensed bar. **P** **Directions:** Opposite Kimberley Park.
MR DEMPSEY ☎ (0326) 313276.
Overlooking the beautiful Kimberley Park, with its palms and sub-tropical species, the Park Grove hotel is within easy walking distance of the town centre, harbour and beaches. This long established family run hotel with its friendly atmosphere, is an ideal venue where activities such as golf, water skiing, windsurfing and fishing are all within easy reach.

FLAX BOURTON Avon **Map 3 A2**
⊗£ **JUBILEE INN** Flax Bourton, Bristol.
Hours: Breakfast 8.15am - 9.15am, Lunch 12 noon - 2pm, Dinner 7.30pm - 10pm (last orders). **Cuisine:** Traditional English homemade dishes. Specialities include the Special Seafood Pie (fresh salmon, white fish and prawns, topped with potato). ⊨ 4 bedrooms. **CC** None. **Other Points:** Garden. Dogs allowed. **P** **(V) Directions:** Between Bristol and Weston Super Mare.
BRIAN HAYDOCK ☎ (027583) 2741.
An olde worlde stone built inn, partly covered by creepers and hanging baskets. Fresh produce is used to provide well cooked meals and all dishes offer good value for money. Traditional English dishes are cooked with an imaginative touch. For warmer days there is an attractive garden for customers use.

THE SOUTH WEST

FOWEY Cornwall **Map 2 B2**

⊗££ **STANTON'S RESTAURANT** 11 Esplanade, Fowey.
Hours: Dinner served from 7pm daily. Closed for a short time February or March. Closed on Mondays. **Cuisine:** Local seafood & fish, char-grilled steaks. Cosmopolitan cuisine. ⊨ None. **CC** All major cards. **Other Points:** Children welcome. No dogs. Access for disabled except to toilets. Main car park off Hanson Drive. Vegan dishes. **P** **(V) Directions:** Descend hill into Fowey. Turn Rt into Esplanade. 30 yards on left.
PETER & ANN WILKES ☎ (0726) 832631.
Family owned and run restaurant with superb views over the River Fowey estuary and harbour. The emphasis is on quality, freshness and home cooking elevated to an art form. The French 'Personnes Nautique' have said that the scallops are 'meilleur qu'en France'. Stanton's is 30 yards along the Esplanade on the left hand side - almost invisible until you reach it.

FROME Somerset **Map 3 A2**

⊗££ **MENDIP LODGE HOTEL** Bath Road, Frome.
Hours: Breakfast 7.30am - 10am, lunch 12pm - 2pm, dinner 7pm - 9.30pm. **Cuisine:** A la carte menu, fixed 3 course menu. ⊨ 40 rooms, all en suite. **CC** All major cards. **Other Points:** Children welcome. Garden. Open Sunday. **P** ⅙ **(V) Directions:** Off the B3090.
MR WORZ ☎ (0373) 463223.
The Mendip Lodge is a great location for visitors to this part of the West country, with the Georgian city of Bath only a few miles away. The restaurant serves a selection of excellent dishes and offers a good value table d'Hote menu. Also available, an interesting selection of hot and cold snacks from The Mendip Bar where guests can relax in pleasant surroundings.

⊗£ **THE GEORGE HOTEL** Market Place, Frome.
⊞£££ **Hours:** Breakfast 7.30am - 9.30am, lunch 12 noon - 2pm, dinner 7pm - 9.30pm. (last orders). Bar meals 12 noon - 2pm and 6.30pm - 9.30pm. **Cuisine:** A la carte, table d'hote and bar meals. English cuisine with char grills a speciality. ⊨ 20 bedrooms, all en suite. **CC** All major cards. **Other Points:** Children welcome. Morning coffee. Afternoon teas. Dogs allowed. Residents' lounge. **P** ⅙ **(V) Directions:** In the centre of Frome overlooking the market place. A362.
MR N J BICKHAM ☎ (0373) 62584.
An old coaching inn, now completely modernised but retaining its original character. There is a choice of bars and a dining room where you can enjoy good food at very reasonable prices. The menu changes frequently to use the best of seasonal produce. The bedrooms are comfortable and attractively furnished with local wooden furniture. A cheerful, friendly hotel.

GLASTONBURY Somerset **Map 3 A2**

⊗£££ **THE RED LION HOTEL** Glastonbury Road, West Pennard,
⊞£££ Glastonbury.
Hours: Breakfast 8am - 10am, Lunch and bar snacks 12.30pm - 2.30pm, Dinner and bar snacks 6.30pm - 9.30pm (last orders). **Cuisine:** Restaurant menu and bar snacks. Dishes may include Breast of Duck with Cherry Sauce, Veal Portuguese. All dishes

Glastonbury continued

individually prepared. ⊨ 7 bedrooms, all en suite. **CC** Access, Visa, AmEx. **Other Points:** Children welcome. No dogs. Outdoor seating in summer. **⊡** **(V) Directions:** A361 between Shepton Mallet and Glastonbury in West Pennard.

BOB BUSKIN, LORRAINE JESSEMEY & PARTNERS ☎ (0458) 32941.

Built around 1678, the Red Lion has been sympathetically restored to retain the original flag stone floors, log fires and beam and stone interior. The atmosphere is relaxed and friendly, enhanced by welcoming staff, and provides an ideal setting in which to enjoy the excellent food. All dishes are individually prepared, beautifully presented and in generous portions.

GUNNISLAKE Cornwall **Map 2 B2**

⊗££ **HINGSTON HOUSE COUNTRY HOTEL** St Ann's Chapel,
⊞££ Gunnislake.

CLUB **Hours:** Breakfast 7am - 9am, dinner 7.30pm - 8pm. **Cuisine:** Varied selection of home cooked meals. ⊨ 10 bedrooms, 8 en suite. **CC** Access, Visa. **Other Points:** Children welcome. Garden dining. Pets allowed. Open Bank holidays. Residents lounge. **⊡** **(V) Directions:** On A390 between Tavistock and Callington, nr St Mellion Golf course.

MR W A SHELVEY ☎ (0822) 832468.

A charming Georgian country house, set in spacious gardens and with breathtaking views of the Tamar Valley, offering good food and accommodation in attractive relaxed surroundings. Mr and Mrs Shelvey have created a relaxed and delightful hotel where their hospitality and warm welcome extends to each and every guest. An ideal central base for touring Devon and Cornwall.

HALWELL Devon **Map 3 B1**

⊗££ **THE OLD INN** Halwell, Nr Totnes.
⊞££ **Hours:** Breakfast 8am - 10am, lunch 12 noon - 2pm, dinner 6.30pm - 10pm (last orders). Bar meals 12 noon - 2pm and 6.30pm - 10pm. **Cuisine:** A variety of local fish, steaks, salads and real Devonshire Ices. ⊨ 6 bedrooms, all en suite with tea/coffee making facilities. **CC** Access, Visa. **Other Points:** No dogs inside. Coaches by appointment. Visitors TV lounge. Beer garden. Large car park. **⊡** **& (V) Directions:** On the A381, next to the church in Halwell village.

JEREMY STARLEY ☎ (080 421) 329.

A traditional, friendly village pub, within easy reach of Totnes, Dartmouth and Kingsbridge. The Inn has recently been extended, renovated and refurbished and an extensive menu has something to suit all tastes. It is also Mr Starley's intention that no-one should leave the Inn feeling hungry!

HOLTON Somerset **Map 3 B2**

⊗£ **THE OLD INN** Holton, Nr Wincanton.
Hours: Lunch 12 noon - 2pm, dinner 7pm - 12 midnight (last orders 10pm). Bar meals 12 noon - 2pm, 7pm - 10pm. No bar meals & restaurant closed Sunday evening. Bar open 11.30am - 3pm weekdays, 11.30am - 11pm Saturdays and 12 noon - 3pm & 7pm - 10.30pm on Sundays. **Cuisine:** A la carte menu, extensive

Holton continued

wine list. 4 course Sunday lunch if booked by previous Saturday. Wide range of bar meals from sandwiches to steaks. ⊨ None. **CC** Access, Visa. **Other Points:** Beer garden. Dogs on leads allowed. Coaches by arrangement. **P** ⅄ **(V) Directions:** Just off A303 in centre of Holton, 1 mile from Wincanton.
MARTIN & LINDA LUPTON ☎ (0963) 32002.
The Old Inn is a 350 year old coaching inn with a small, intimate restaurant. The bar has an original flagstone floor and inglenook fireplace. The Inn is situated halfway between London and the West Country.

HONITON Devon Map 3 B2

⊗£ **THE WHITE COTTAGE RESTAURANT** 35 High Street, Honiton.
Hours: Open: 9.30am - 5pm Tuesday & Wednesday, 9.30am - 5pm and 7pm - 9.30pm Thursday, Friday and Saturday, 11am - 5pm Sundays. Closed: Mondays. **Cuisine:** Dishes may include curried prawns, steak, roast of the day. Fresh fish always used. Snacks such as cauliflower cheese also available. ⊨ None. **CC** Access, Visa. **Other Points:** Children welcome. Afternoon teas served. No dogs. ⅄ **Directions:** Main high street of Honiton, almost opposite the Pottery.
MRS CAROL ANN DENNIS ☎ (0404) 42814.
Concentrating on home made cooking, this establishment offers well made and presented dishes. Enjoy good food in a warm, relaxing atmosphere.

ILFRACOMBE Devon Map 3 A1

⊞£££ **BEAUFORT HOTEL** Torrs Park, Ilfracombe.
CLUB ⊨ 2 single, 6 double, 1 twin, 3 family bedrooms, 4 family suites of 2 rooms. 13 of the rooms are en suite. 2 extra bathrooms. Colour TV, radio and tea/coffee making faciities in all rooms. Four poster suites available. **Hours:** Breakfast 8.45am - 9.15am and dinner 7.15pm - 8pm. Closed: 29th December - 14th January. **CC** Access, Visa, AmEx. **Other Points:** Central heating. Children welcome. Dogs allowed. Licensed bar. Residents lounge. Garden. Laundry/drying room. Games room. Golf and clay pigeon shooting. **P** ⅄ **(V) Directions:** From High St, take Northfield Rd towards sea, Torrs Park is on left.
MR & MRS BEAGLEY ☎ (0271) 65483.
A striking, white Victorian mansion in the picturesque Torrs Park area, only minutes walk from the beach and town. The hotel caters for all tastes and has its own solarium, spa-bath, mini gym, and outdoor heated swimming pool. Famous for their food, the Beagleys have a special menu and evening meal time for children.

⊗££ **DEDES HOTEL AND WHEEL INN, PUB AND RESTAURANT** 1-3 The Promenade.
Hours: Meals from 8am - 10am, 12 noon - 2pm and 6pm - 10pm. **Cuisine:** Quality steaks and fresh, local seafood in season including fresh lobster. ⊨ 17 bedrooms some with en suite facilities. **CC** All major cards. **Other Points:** Access for disabled to restaurant only. Children welcome. **P** ⅄ **(V)**
MR & MRS C I CAWTHORNE ☎ (0271) 62545.

Ilfracombe continued

Situated on the Victorian promenade overlooking the sea, incorporating the wheel room. A delightful character restaurant and bar featuring exposed stonework, beams and old coaching wheels.

⊗££ **THE ILFRACOMBE CARLTON** Runnacleave Road,
Ⅲ££ Ilfracombe.
[CLUB] **Hours:** Beakfast 8.30am - 9.30am, lunch 12 noon - 2pm (last orders) and dinner 7pm - 8.30pm. Open Sunday. **Cuisine:** Traditional English food. ⊨ 6 single, 20 twin, 14 double and 8 family bedrooms, 40 with en suite facilities. ▣ Access, Visa, AmEx. **Other Points:** Children welcome. Afternoon teas served. ▣ **Directions:** Off the A361, close to the beach front.
DAWN MARSHALL ☎ (0271) 862446.
Situated in a central location, adjacent to the beach, this hotel offers fresh, well cooked food in pleasant surroundings. Comfortable accommodation and friendly attentive service. Ilfracombe offers its visitors a choice of recreational and sporting activities, a spectacular coastline and secluded bays.

⊗£ **TORRS HOTEL** Torrs Park, Ilfracombe.
Ⅲ££ **Hours:** Breakfast 8.30am - 9.30am, dinner 6.30pm - 7.30pm.
[CLUB] Residential licence only. Closed: November to end February. Lunches available. **Cuisine:** Roasts, grills, home cooked dishes. ⊨ 14 bedrooms all en suite and with colour TV, clock radio and tea/coffee facilities. ▣ All major cards. **Other Points:** Special diets catered for. Children over 5 years welcome. ▣ **(V) Directions:** Off the A399 or A361 at the end of the Torrs Walk.
MR R I COOK ☎ (0271) 862334.
This hotel is in a commanding position at the end of the Torrs Walk which follows the cliff along the coast. The hotel has lovely views of the surrounding countryside.

⊗££ **UPSTAIRS RESTAURANT** Mullacott Cross, Ilfracombe.
Hours: Dinner 6pm - 10pm. Closed: October - Easter. **Cuisine:** Lobster, best quality steaks, fresh fish. New Carvery (in converted coffee shop). ⊨ None. ▣ All major cards. **Other Points:** Children welcome. Childrens menu. ▣ **(V) Directions:** Found on the A361 Mullacott roundabout.
MRS C J NAPPER ☎ (0271) 863780/865500
High above Ilfracombe with unrestricted views to Lundy Isles, the Welsh coast and Exmoor.

THE BEAUFORT HOTEL

Torrs Park, Ilfracombe, Devon, EX34 8AY

A striking white Victorian mansion in the picturesque Torrs Park area. Only a few minutes walk from the beach and shops. The Hotel caters for all tastes and diets and has its own solarium, spa-bath, mini-gym and outdoor heated swimming pool, golf, clay pigeon shooting, horse riding and trout fishing arranged. Famous for its food, The Beaufort has a separate menu for the under 5's who have their own dinner time at 5.30pm allowing the adults to eat their candlelit dinners in relaxing conditions from 7.15-8.00pm. Baby listening and baby sitting available. The majority of bedrooms are en-suite and all have colour TVs, radios and tea and coffee facilities. Some suites of two rooms are available as is a beautiful 4 poster bed. Brochure and tariff available phone **0271 865483**   Credit card bookings by phone are welcome.
Superb value for the holiday you won't forget.

THE SOUTH WEST

ISLES OF SCILLY St Mary's **Map 2 C1**

⌂£££ **CARNWETHERS** Pelistry Bay, St Mary's.

🛏 4 double, 4 twin and 2 family bedrooms, all en suite. Tea/coffee making facilities and TV in all rooms. Half board only. **Hours:** Breakfast 8.30am - 9am, Dinner 6.30pm - 7.30pm. **CC** None. **Other Points:** Children over 7 years welcome. Garden. Swimming pool. Sauna. Pool table and Table tennis. Croquet. **Directions:** On the north east side of the island.
ROY & JOYCE GRAHAM ☎ (0720) 22415.
This former farmhouse stands in an acre of grounds above the Pelistry Bay, 2.5 miles from the island's only town - Hugh Town. If the leisure facilities at the hotel are not enough to exhaust you, activities such as golf, horse riding and windsurfing are within easy reach. Only half board rates are available, so why not spend a couple of hours on the secluded beach before dinner.

IVYBRIDGE Devon **Map 3 B1**

⊗££ **IMPERIAL INN** 28 Western Road, Ivybridge.

Hours: Meals from 12 noon - 2pm and 6pm - 10pm. Meals are served in the bar. **Cuisine:** Daily specials e.g. scallops, lamb kidneys, steak au poivre, mussels in cream and wine. 🛏 None. **CC** None. **Other Points:** Children welcome. No dogs. Coaches by appointment. **(V)**
PHILIP GRIMES ☎ (0752) 892269
A charming Olde Worlde village pub adorned with window boxes with a large welcoming open fire and a warm welcome to match. There is a large beer garden and a separate children's play area with play ground equipment.

⊗££ **THE CROOKED SPIRE INN** Ermington, Ivybridge.

⌂£ **Hours:** Breakfast 7am - 10am, lunch 11.30am - 2.30pm and dinner 7pm - 11pm. Closed: Christmas Day. **Cuisine:** At least 2 dozen varied main courses always available. All prepared on the premises. 🛏 3 bedrooms all with colour TV. **CC** Access, Visa. **Other Points:** Children welcome. Dogs allowed in public bar only. Vegetarian meals. Public car park. **(V) Directions:** 2 miles south of A38 at Ivybridge Junction.
JIM SHIELD & GERALDINE TAYLOR ☎ (0548) 830 202
A quiet, comfortable inn, in the middle of Ermington village square - best kept village in 1985 and 1986, where the welcome is warm and friendly. Booking advisable.

KINGSBRIDGE Devon **Map 3 C1**

⌂££ **ASHLEIGH HOUSE** Ashleigh Road, Kingsbridge.

🛏 4 double, 3 twin and 1 family bedroom. 2 showers. All 1st floor rooms have private facilities at £2.50 extra. Tea/coffee making facilities in all rooms. **Hours:** Breakfast 8.30am - 9.15am and dinner 6.45pm. Closed: 1 November to 31 March. **CC** Access, Visa. **Other Points:** Children over 5 welcome. Dogs allowed. Licensed. Residents lounge. Separate TV lounge. Garden. 2 Crowns English Tourist Board Commended. **P Directions:** Ashleigh Rd is off the A381 towards Salcombe on the edge of town.
MICHAEL & JENNIFER TAYLOR ☎ (0548) 852893.
An elegant white painted Victorian house with bright, airy rooms, tastefuly decorated and furnished and situated only a

Kingsbridge continued
short walk from the town centre. The Taylor's pride themselves on their home cooking. An ideal place to relax.

⊗£ **SLOOP INN** Bantham, nr Kingsbridge.
££££ **Hours:** Meals 12 noon - 2pm and from 7pm - 10pm. **Cuisine:** Seafood, homemade sausages and pates. 5 bedrooms, 4 en suite. Luxury self-catering cottages now available. CC None. **Other Points:** Children welcome. P (V) **Directions:** Off A379 Kingsbridge to Plymouth, through Churchstow. Signposted.
NEIL GIRLING ☎ (0548) 560215/560489
Part 16th century pub situated in the unspoilt old world village of Bantham. On the Avon estuary with the beach approximately 300 yards over the sand dunes. Large friendly bar where table skittles are played all year round.

⊗££ **THE ASHBURTON ARMS** West Charleton, Nr. Kingsbridge.
££ **Hours:** Breakfast for residents only, lunch 12 noon - 2pm, and dinner 7pm - 9.30pm (last orders). **Cuisine:** Dishes include speciality 'steak on the rocks', served on hot stones. Vegetarian dish of the day. Desserts such as pavlova & treacle tart. All homeade 2 single, 1 twin and 1 double room, all with colour TV, radio/alarm, shaver points and tea/coffee making facilities. CC Access, Visa. **Other Points:** No dogs allowed. No smoking in restaurant or bedrooms. Childrens menu. P ♿ (V) **Directions:** On A379, 1 and a half miles east of Kingsbridge - on Tor crossroads.
BRIAN & ELIZABETH SAUNDERS ☎ (0548) 531242.
A very friendly pub, serving excellent homemade food at good value for money. The steaks are particularly good, served on hot stones so they continue to cook at the table, and there is a good wine list. The pub is set on a main tourist route, in an area of outstanding natural beauty. Well worth visiting.

⊗££ **THE TOWER INN** Slapton, Near Kingsbridge.
££ **Hours:** Lunch 12 noon - 2pm (last orders). Dinner 7pm - 10pm (last orders). Restaurant closed Mondays in winter months. **Cuisine:** Italian cuisine. Seafood pasta a speciality. 4 bedrooms. CC None. **Other Points:** Children welcome. Garden. Pets allowed. P ♿ (V) **Directions:** Between Dartmouth and Kingsbridge.
J KHAN, K & K ROMP & C CASCIANELLI. ☎ (0548) 580216.
A 14th century tower used by the local monks to brew beer makes the mainstay of this hotel. Renovated into a charming restaurant with an olde worlde feel, 'The Tower Inn' provides good Italian cuisine, including a variety of seafood specialities, complemented by a choice of wines. Beamed, with open fires, the Chaucery offers an excellent relaxing atmosphere.

LAND'S END Cornwall **Map 2 C1**
⊗££ **THE LAND'S END STATE HOUSE** Sennen, Penzance,
££££ Land's End.
Hours: Breakfast 8am - 9.30am, Lunch and bar snacks 12 noon - 2pm, Dinner and bar snacks 7pm - 9.30pm (last orders). **Cuisine:** Table d'hote and gourmet menus based on high quality local produce. Fresh fish and seafood a speciality. Bar snacks also available. 34 bedrooms, all en suite. CC Access, Visa, AmEx. **Other Points:** Children welcome. No-smoking area. Afternoon

Land's End continued

teas. Weddings. Conference facilities. Fax No: (0736) 871812. **Ρ**
& **(V) Directions:** Follow A30 to the end.
PETER DE SAVARY ☎ (0736) 871844.
*Situated right on the cliff top at Land's End, the State House is a
superb hotel with awe-inspiring views across the sea to the
Scilly Isles. The all-glass observatory restaurant provides
special surroundings in which to enjoy the high quality food
and welcoming service. Comfortable accommodation and an
outstanding situation.*

⊗££ **THE OLD MANOR HOUSE** Sennen, Land's End.
⊡££ **Hours:** Main meals from 8am - 9am, 12 noon - 2.30pm and 6pm -
8.30pm. Snacks and coffee served all day. Closed: 23rd - 28th
December. **Cuisine:** Cornish seafood soup, pollock a la maison,
fresh fish, cream teas. A la carte, table d'hote and a 'quick order'
menu. ⊨ 8 bedrooms, 4 en suite. 1 WC. **CC** Access, Visa, AmEx.
Other Points: Children welcome. No dogs. **Ρ** & **(V)**
DENIS & BARBARA SEDGWICK ☎ (0736) 871280.
*17th century Manor House rebuilt in 1795 as the original
'Land's End Hotel'. It was once the headquarters for a band of
smugglers and secret tunnels still remain.*

LANGPORT Somerset **Map 3 B2**
⊗££ **THE OLD POUND INN** Aller, Langport.
⊡£ **Hours:** Breakfast 7am - 10am, Lunch 12 noon - 2pm, Dinner 7pm -
10.30pm (last orders). Bar meals 12 noon - 2pm and 7pm -
10.30pm. **Cuisine:** Predominantly fresh, local produce used. A la
carte restaurant menu and bar menu. ⊨ 7 bedrooms, all en suite.
CC Access, Visa. **Other Points:** Children welcome. No smoking
area. Residents' lounge. Garden. Garden dining. **Ρ** **(V)**
Directions: A372, main road between Langport and Bridgwater
in village of Aller.
ROGER & SUSAN PEARCE ☎ (0458) 250469.
*An attractive, old village inn, in keeping with the traditional and
unspoilt village of Aller. The dining room overlooks the garden
and provides a warm and relaxing atmosphere in which to enjoy
the well-cooked food, made from predominantly fresh, local
produce. The inn also houses 2 bars, a billiard-room and
comfortably appointed, well-furnished bedrooms. Good
service.*

LAUNCESTON Cornwall **Map 2 B2**
⊡£ **GLENCOE VILLA** 13 Race Hill, Launceston.
⊨ 1 double, 1 twin and 2 family bedrooms, 2 en suite.
Hours: Breakfast served 7.30am - 9.30am, dinner 7pm - 8.30pm.
Closed: end November - February. **CC** Access. **Other Points:**
Central heating. Children Welcome. Residents' lounge, TV.
Licensed. **Ρ Directions:** From A30 follow town centre signs under
Norman arch then 4th left.
GILLIAN ROINSON. ☎ (0566) 773012.
*This is a Victorian type house built in 1920. The rooms are large
and airy and all have lovely views across the Tamar valley
towards Dartmoor. Situated half a mile off the A30 by-pass
towards Bodmin.*

Launceston continued

⊗££ **WHITE HART HOTEL** Broad Street, Launceston.

⊞£££ **Hours:** Open 8am - 10.30pm and 8am - 11pm in the summer. **Cuisine:** Traditional cooking. ⊨ 27 bedrooms, 22 en suite. **CC** All major cards. **Other Points:** Children welcome. Snooker room. Golf packages, bargain breaks and conference facilities also available. ⅋ **(V) Directions:** In the main town square. MR B BAKER ☎ (0566) 772013.

This hotel, situated in the town square is an ideal base from which to tour Devon and Cornwall. Both its bars have log fires, and the restaurant provides good food. It is a hotel popular with golfers because of the golf course at Launceston.

LIFTON Devon **Map 2 B2**

⊗££ **LIFTON COTTAGE HOTEL** Lifton.

⊞££ **Hours:** 8am - 9am, 12 noon - 2pm and 7pm - 9pm. Bar meals 12 noon - 2pm and 7pm - 10pm (last orders for food 9.45pm). **Cuisine:** English cuisine. ⊨ 13 bedrooms, 9 of them en suite. Colour TV, alarm and tea/coffee making facilities in all rooms. **CC** All major cards. **Other Points:** Children welcome. Dogs allowed. Garden dining. Open Sundays and bank holidays. **P** ⅋ **(V) Directions:** A30, halfway through village on main road. MR & MRS N BEER, & MRS F BOSTON ☎ (0566) 84439.

A Gothic style building, parts of which are 300 years old, situated in Lifton, one of the earliest Saxon villages in Devon. Ideal for touring both Devon and Cornwall, the village being halfway between the outstanding wild country of the great moors - Dartmoor and Bodmin Moor.

LISKEARD Cornwall **Map 2 B2**

⊗££ **COUNTRY CASTLE HOTEL** Station Road, Liskeard.

⊞£££ **Hours:** Breakfast 8.15am - 9.30am, dinner 7pm - 8.30pm. **Cuisine:** Wide variety of dishes made from local, fresh produce. Daily choice of sweets and speciality dishes. ⊨ 11 rooms. 4 single, 3 twin, 3 double and 1 family bedroom. 10 en suite. **CC** Access, Visa. **Other Points:** Children welcome. Garden. Afternoon teas. Dogs allowed. Swimming pool. **P** ⅋ **(V) Directions:** Just off B3254 to Looe.

ROSEMARY WILLMOT ☎ (0579) 42694.

Originally a wool merchant's residence, this Victorian house has been tastefully converted into a hotel. Set in 2 acres of landscaped gardens overlooking the beautiful Looe valley, the hotel has been decorated in keeping with the character of the building yet is warm and inviting. Good food is made from the freshest of ingredients. The atmosphere is quiet and restful.

LITTON Somerset **Map 3 A2**

⊗££ **YE OLDE KINGS ARMS** Litton, nr Bath.

⊞£££ **Hours:** Lunch 11.30pm - 2.30pm, Dinner 6.30pm - 10.30pm (last orders). **Cuisine:** Specialises in seafood such as 'The Queen Tricot' - a selection of seafood. Specials of week shown on blackboards. ⊨ 6 bedrooms, all en suite. **CC** Access, Visa. **Other Points:** Children welcome - The 'Armoury' is planned to accommodate all the family. Garden. Afternoon teas. Malt whiskyies. Real Ales. Trout stream. **P** ⅋ **(V) Directions:** On B3114 between West Harptree and Chewton Mendip. TERENCE ANTHONY ROBINS ☎ (0761) 241301.

Litton continued

A 15th century inn, renowned for its large selection of fine ales, including several traditional beers. The long, attractive bar is open to the gardens and there are 4 lounges, all with antique tables and chairs. The restaurant offers an a la carte menu and specialises in seafood but there is a wide choice of both hot and cold dishes to suit all tastes. Ample portions.

LOOE Cornwall **Map 2 B2**

⊗£££ **ALLHAYS COUNTRY HOUSE** Talland Bay, Looe.

Hours: Breakfast 8.30am - 9am and dinner 7pm - 9.30pm (last orders 9pm). Closed: Sundays to non-residents. **Cuisine:** New English cuisine - local fish dishes, salmon, duck, steaks, tiger prawns, pork, chicken and lamb dishes with subtle sauces. British cheeses. 7 bedrooms. **CC** Access, Visa. **Other Points:** Dogs allowed. Children over 10 welcome. **P** & **(V) Directions:** Turn left 2.5 miles from Looe on A387. Follow Hotel sign.
BRIAN & LYNDA SPRING. ☎ (0503) 72434.

A period country house standing in 'an English country garden' with spectacular views over to Talland Bay. A Victorian style conservatory extends the dining room into the garden for dining al fresco whatever the weather. Allhays has an enviable reputation for its food.

£££ **COOMBE FARM** Widegates, nr Looe.

1 single, 4 double and 3 family bedrooms. 1 bathroom. 2 showers. All rooms have tea/coffee making facilities and most have colour TVs. **Hours:** Breakfast 8.30am - 9am, dinner 7pm - 7.30pm. Closed: from November until February. **CC** None. **Other Points:** Central heating. Children over 5 welcome. Licensed. Residents lounge. TV. Garden. Heated swimming pool. **P** & **(V) Directions:** Just south of Widegates on the B3253, between Looe and Hessonford.
ALEXANDER & SALLY LOW ☎ (05034) 223.

Delightful country house in ten acres of grounds with superb views to the sea, and with glorious walks and beaches nearby. Coombe Farm has a croquet lawn, heated outdoor pool and snooker and table tennis facilities, and there are many birds and animals in the grounds, including horses and peacocks. The food is superb and can be enjoyed in candlelit surroundings with real log fires.

⊗££ **FIELDHEAD HOTEL** Portuan Road, West Looe.

£££££ **Hours:** Breakfast 8.15am - 9.30am, Dinner 6.30pm - 8.30pm. Bar snacks available. Closed: December and January. **Cuisine:** Dishes may include Boeuf Bourguinon, Chicken Cordon Bleu, Savoury Crepes, Pork with a Stilton & Cream sauce, Trout Almondine, Salmon en Croute. 14 bedrooms, all en suite. **CC** Access, Visa, AmEx. **Other Points:** Afternoon teas. Residents' lounge. Garden dining. No dogs. Fax No: (0503) 264114. Terrace & patio. Heated outdoor swimming pool. Cocktail bar. **P** **(V) Directions:** From East Looe, over bridge, turn left, follow rd until overlook sea
PAT & BRYAN NORMAN ☎ (0503) 262689.

Built as a large family home, Fieldhead is still embraced by an atmosphere of comfort and tranquility. With its seaview, and flowers and candles on the tables, the restaurant provides a delightful setting in which to enjoy the homecooked food and

Looe continued

personal, friendly service. Relax with a drink by the pool or in the attractive garden with its sub tropical flowers and shrubs.

⊗££ **JUBILEE INN** Jubilee Hill, Pelynt, Nr Looe.
⏠£££ ⊡CLUB⊡ **Hours:** Breakfast 8am - 9.30am, lunch 12 noon - 2.30pm, dinner 6.30pm - 9.30pm. **Cuisine:** A la carte, fixed 3 course menu, bar meals/snacks. Barbecues every evening during summer. ⊨ 12 rooms. 3 twin, 7 double and 2 family bedrooms. All en suite. **CC** Access, Visa. **Other Points:** Children welcome. Garden. Afternoon teas. Dogs allowed. Eurocard also accepted. Fax No: (0503) 20920. ⊡ ⅃ **(V) Directions:** In Pelynt village, 4 miles from Looe.
MR & MRS WILLIAMS ☎ (0503) 20312.
Originally a 14th century farmhouse which has been converted into a charming hotel offering typical Cornish hospitality. The old world charm has been maintained while making way for modern comforts and excellent service. The attractive dining room offers an extensive choice of quality dishes, in elegant surroundings.

⊗£ **PANORAMA HOTEL** Hannafore Road, West Looe.
⏠££ **Hours:** Breakfast 8.30am - 9am, Dinner 6.30pm - 7pm. Open to non-residents for Dinner. **Cuisine:** Good homecooking using fresh produce and locally caught fish whenever available. ⊨ 1 single, 2 twin, 4 double and 3 family bedrooms, all en suite. Colour TV, intercom and baby listening, and tea/coffee/hot chocolate making facilities. **CC** Access, Visa. **Other Points:**

Coombe Farm

WIDEGATES, NR. LOOE,
CORNWALL PL13 1QN
Telephone : Widegates (05034) 223

COMMENDED

*WINNER
AA Guest
House
of the
Year Award
West of
England 1981*

*A warm
Welcome
assured by
Alexander and
Sally Low*

A delightful country house, furnished with antiques, set in ten acres of lawns, meadows, woods, streams and ponds with superb views down a wooded valley to the sea. Log Fires. Delicious home cooking. Candlelit dining. Licensed.
In the grounds - many birds, animals and flowers, a lovely heated swimming pool, a croquet lawn and stone barn for games including snooker and table tennis. Nearby - golf, fishing, tennis, horse riding and glorious walks and beaches.

RAC
Listed

The perfect centre for visiting all parts of Cornwall and Devon.
Bed and Breakfast from £16.50   Four course dinner from £10.00
Special Short Break discounts.

AA
Listed

THE SOUTH WEST

Looe continued

Children welcome. Bar. Special diets can be catered for. No pets. Stay a week and get the 7th night free. Roof garden. ▣ **(V)**
Directions: Opposite Banjo Pier in West Looe.
JACKIE & ALAN RUSSELL ☎ (0503) 262123.
Superbly situated with outstanding views over the harbour, cliffs and beaches, The Panorama is a well appointed, family run hotel. Friendly, welcoming service is just one illustration of the care shown to ensure that guests have an enjoyable stay. Good, wholesome food awaits you in the Tudor dining room and there is a lounge bar in which to relax.

⊗££ **PUNCH BOWL INN** Lanreath, Nr Looe.
▥££ **Hours:** Breakfast 8.30am - 9.30am, Lunch 12 noon - 2pm (Bar
CLUB snacks Mon - Sat and Table d'hote on Sun), Dinner 7pm - 9pm (last orders). Restaurant closed: Mon - Sat lunchtimes. **Cuisine:** Table d'Hote and a la carte. Traditional English, seasonal fish menu and ice-cream specialities. Bar snack menu. ➤ 14 bedrooms, 12 en suite. **CC** Access, Visa. **Other Points:** Children welcome. Pets allowed. Beer garden. ▣ **(V) Directions:** In the centre of Lanreath village, off the B3359.
HARVEY & SYLVIA FRITH ☎ (0503) 220218
This oak beamed inn is over 400 years old and has served as the Court House, a Coaching Inn and Smugglers' Distribution House in it's time! It now offers visitors a chance to enjoy traditional hospitality within it's historical walls.

LOSTWITHIEL Cornwall **Map 2 B2**
⊗£££ **TREWITHEN RESTAURANT** 3 Fore Street, Lostwithiel.
Hours: 7pm - 9.30pm (last orders). Closed: Sundays and Mondays and the month of May. **Cuisine:** International cuisine, including summer seafood, lobster, and winter game. ➤ None. **CC** Access, Visa, Diners. **Other Points:** Children welcome. No pets. Open Bank holidays. & **(V) Directions:** A390 midway between Liskeard and St Austell.5 miles south of Bodmin.
B F & L J ROLLS ☎ (0208) 872 373.
A personally run restaurant with a cottagey atmosphere, where all the food is home-cooked. The cuisine reflects the proprietors' international background and offers both a la carte and blackboard menus. Situated next door to the Duchy Palace, with Restormel Castle, Lanhydroch House and Bodmin all close by.

LYME REGIS Dorset **Map 3 B2**
⊗£ **BELL CLIFF RESTAURANT** 5/6 Broad Street, Lyme Regis.
Hours: Open all year round, 7 days a week for breakfasts, morning coffee, lunches and afternoon teas. Winter 9am - 5pm, Summer 8.30am - 6pm. Breakfasts served until 10am, coffe until 12 noon. Lunches 12 noon - 2.15pm, afternoon teas and snacks 2.15pm to close. **Cuisine:** English home cooking. Specialities include homemade sweets and cakes. ➤ None. **CC** None. **Other Points:** Children welcome. Limited access for disabled. Dogs allowed. Afternoon teas. Licensed. Adjacent to two public car parks. **(V) Directions:** Off A35 on A3052 or A3070. At sea end of main thoroughfare (A3052).
RICHARD & AUDREY EVANS ☎ (0297) 442459.
A small, homely restaurant, slightly Dickensian in appearance, with excellent service, quality and ambiance. The building

Lyme Regis continued

dates from the 16th century and was used in the film 'The French Lieutenants Woman' as the 'Old Fossil Depot'. Well placed in the centre of town and popular with both locals and holidaymakers.

⊗££ **BENSONS RESTAURANT** Broad Street, Lyme Regis.
Hours: Dinner served 7pm - 9.30pm, 6pm - 10pm summer. Closed: Sunday (excluding summer). **Cuisine:** Predominantly French-style cuisine. House specialities include Chicken Breast with Asparagus, Benson's Tournedos, Cod Fillet Portugaise, Pork Normandy. ⊨ None. ⬛ Access, Visa. **Other Points:** Children welcome. No dogs. ▣ **(V) Directions:** At bottom of hill on main street, next to car park, opposite sea.
ANDREW ROBERT BENSON ☎ (0297) 442049.
A small, elegantly furnished restaurant offering outstanding food at reasonable prices. The a la carte menu provides a good choice of imaginative, excellently cooked and presented dishes. Welcoming and efficient service, an excellent cheeseboard and a good wine list complement the quality of the food.

⊗££ **DEVON HOTEL** Lyme Road, Uplyme, Lyme Regis.
⌂££££ **Hours:** Breakfast 8.30am - 9.30am, dinner 7pm - 8.30pm, bar snacks 12 noon - 1.45pm. Sunday lunches served in restaurant. Closed: November - February. **Cuisine:** Local fish dishes a speciality. Table d'hote and a la carte. ⊨ 21 bedrooms, 20 en suite. ⬛ All major cards. **Other Points:** Children welcome. Afternoon teas. Dogs allowed. Fax No. (0392) 431645. ▣ ♿ **(V) Directions:** B3165 Lyme Regis. 2 miles off A35.
VINCENT & ELAINE BLACKSHAW. ☎ (0299) 443231.
In this converted old chapel you can enjoy a value for money meal, made with an emphasis on fresh food, excellently served by warm, efficient staff. You may wish to choose a wine from their extensive list or just relax in the welcoming, homely atmosphere.

⌂££ **EAGLE HOUSE** Sherborne Lane, Lyme Regis.
⊨ 2 double, 3 twin and 3 family bedrooms. 2 bathrooms. 2 showers. 4 WCs. Tea/coffee making facilities. **Hours:** Optional meal in the Pancake Restaurant 6pm - 10pm (order by 9.30pm). Eagle House closed: October - Easter (except by prior arrangement). ⬛ None. **Other Points:** Access for disabled (1 room). Teenage children welcome. Dogs allowed. Licensed. Residents lounge. TV. Garden. Sauna & jet whirlpool spa bath. ♿ **Directions:** On the A35 travelling west, turn off the Charmouth By-pass.
S TOWER & K A FITZROY ☎ (0297) 442616.
A listed building, circa 1720, renovated throughout and situated in a quiet position near the town centre. The town's claim to fame is as the location for the film 'The French Lieutenant's Woman', although Lyme Regis also has a reputation for its Cobb Harbour, and as an excellent fossil area. Golf course.

THE SOUTH WEST

Lyme Regis continued

⊗££ **KERSBROOK HOTEL & RESTAURANT** Pound Road, Lyme
⊞££££ Regis.

Hours: Breakfast 8.30am - 9.30am, lunch 12.15pm - 2.15pm and
dinner 7.30pm - 8.15pm (last orders). Closed: December and
January. **Cuisine:** Full a la carte menu and table d'hote. ⊨ 1
single, 10 double, 2 twin and 1 family bedroom, all en suite. **CC** All
major cards. **Other Points:** Licensed. Residents lounge. TV.
Garden. Intimate cocktail bar. **P** **Directions:** From main Lyme
Regis - Exeter road, turn right opp. main car park.
ERIC HALL STEPHENSON ☎ (02974) 2596.
*A thatched, 18th century listed house set in its own gardens
overlooking Lyme Bay. Carefully modernised to retain the
original character of the building and to offer a high standard of
comfort and convenience. The food is of a high standard and the
restaurant boasts an extensive wine list for every occassion.*

⊗£ **ROYAL LION HOTEL** Broad Street, Lyme Regis.

Hours: Meals from 8.30am - 9.30am, 12 noon - 2pm and 6.30pm -
9.30pm in the Grill Room, 7.30pm - 9pm in the dining room. Bar
meals 12 noon - 2pm and 6.30pm - 9.30pm. **Cuisine:** Fresh sirloin
steak. ⊨ 30 bedrooms all en suite. **CC** All major cards. **Other
Points:** Children welcome. Coaches welcome by appointment but
parking is limited. New leisure complex with swimming pool. **P (V)**
Directions: In the centre of Lyme Regis.
MR & MRS B A SIENESI ☎ (029 74) 5622/2014
*A 17th Century Coaching Inn in the centre of this attractive little
town, equipped with a large games room, with snooker and
table tennis tables. Apart from being the home town of many
writers, artists and artisans, Lyme Regis is famous for being the
location of United Artists' 'French Lieutenants' Woman'.*

LYNMOUTH Devon Map 3 A1

⊞££ **COUNTISBURY LODGE HOTEL** Tors Park, Lynmouth.

⊨ 4 double, 1 twin and 1 family room, all en suite. Tea/coffee
facilities in all rooms. **Hours:** Breakfast 8.30am - 9am and dinner
served 7pm/7.30pm. **CC** Access, Visa. **Other Points:** Children
welcome. Pets allowed. Afternoon teas served. Resident's lounge
and garden. **P (V) Directions:** Approaching on A39 via Porlock &
Countisbury. Down Countisbury Hill.
MR & MRS J HOLLINSHEAD ☎ (0598) 52388.
*A former Victorian vicarage, the hotel still retains the original
charm and character of the period. Set on the woodland slopes
of Countisbury Hill, the hotel bar is actually built into the
natural rockface. The rooms are individually furnished and most
of them have views over the Lyn valley so that guests can watch
herons and ravens from the windows. An ideal touring base for
Exmoor.*

⊗££ **RISING SUN HOTEL** Harbourside.

Hours: Meals from 8.30am - 9.30am, 12.30pm - 2pm and 7pm -
9pm (last orders). Open all year. **Cuisine:** Seafood, game in
season. ⊨ 16 bedrooms, all en suite. **CC** Access, Visa, AmEx.
Other Points: Coaches by appointment. Fax No: (0598) 53480.
(V) Directions: Exit 23 on the M5 and then the A39 to Lynmouth.
On Harbour road.
MR F. ST. H. JEUNE ☎ (0598) 53223.

Lynmouth continued

A lovely 14th century thatched smugglers inn overlooking a small picturesque harbour and Lynmouth Bay. The hotel offers free salmon fishing for residents. The buildings were once smugglers' cottages with a wealth of intriguing staircases and narrow passages.

⊗££ **ROCK HOUSE HOTEL** Lynmouth.

⌂££ **Hours:** Breakfast 8.45am - 9.45am, lunch 12 noon - 2pm (last orders), dinner 7pm - 9pm (last orders). **Cuisine:** Large and varied menu. Dishes include Crab soup, Escargots Bourguignonne, Guinea fowl, Hawaiian Duck, Peppered Steak, Steak Exmoor and a variety of sweets ⊨ 6 rooms. 2 twin and 4 double bedrooms. 4 en suite. **CC** All major cards. **Other Points:** Garden. Afternoon teas. Dogs allowed by arrangement. Packed lunches available. Bar. **P** **(V)**
MR MILLETT. ☎ (0598) 53508.
Perched on the waters edge overlooking Lynmouth's picturesque harbour, the Rock House Hotel has a backdrop of wooded trees. Tastefully decorated, the rooms are spacious and airy. Serving quality food at good value prices, the hotel is very popular with locals and holiday makers alike, with its cheerful atmosphere.

LYNTON Devon **Map 3 A1**

⊗££ **MILLSLADE COUNTRY HOUSE HOTEL** Brendon, Lynton.

⌂££ **Hours:** 8.30am - 10.30am, 12 noon - 2.30pm and 7pm - 9.30pm (last orders). Open for bar meals all day. **Cuisine:** English and continental cuisine, with fish specialities. ⊨ 4 double, 2 twin and 1 family room, 5 en suite. Also 3 four-poster suites available. All rooms have colour TV and tea making facilities. **CC** Visa, AmEx, Diners. **Other Points:** Children welcome. Pets allowed. Afternoon teas served. Open for Sunday lunch/dinner and Bank holidays. Residents' lounge and garden. **P** **&** **(V) Directions:** 2 miles from Lynton, just off the A39.
E M FREWER ☎ (05987) 322.
An 18th century country house set in 9 acres of grounds in a quiet spot on the edge of Brendon village, surrounded by the forest and River Lynn. The hotel has fishing rights (salmon and trout) for their guests to enjoy and there are plenty of local attractions including Doone valley, Barnstaple and Minehead.

⌂££ **SYLVIA HOUSE HOTEL** Lydiate Lane, Lynton.
⊨ 8 bedrooms - 6 double/twin en suite, 2 single. TV, tea/coffee making facilities. Some four poster beds. **Hours:** Breakfast 8am - 8.45am. Meals available to guests only by prior arrangement. **CC** None. **Other Points:** Children welcome. No smoking area. Dogs allowed. Residents' lounge. Garden. Residential license. Special diets catered for. Railway station collection. **(V) Directions:** Off A39. Immediately in front of Town Hall.
DAVID & MARIANNA HOLDSWORTH ☎ (0598) 52391.
A delightful Georgian hotel offering high standards and the warmest of welcomes to all guests. All bedrooms are very well decorated and furnished and there are brochures containing local information. Meals are available with prior notice as all food is bought fresh daily and cooked by traditional methods. Nothing is too much trouble.

Lynton continued

⊗££ **THE EXMOOR SANDPIPER INN** Countisbury, nr Lynton.
⌂££££ **Hours:** Breakfast 8.30am - 9.30am. Open 11am - 11pm. Meals
CLUB 11.30am - 5pm and 7pm - 10pm. **Cuisine:** A large selection table
d'hote evening meal including garlic prawns, local venison in red
wine, steaks, lobster, cold seafood platter, homemade soups. ⌖ 11
bedrooms all with en suite bathroom, colour TV, radio and
tea/coffee making facilities. **CC** None. **Other Points:** Children
welcome. Dogs by arrangement. **P Directions:** On the A39 at the
top of Countisbury Hill, outside of Lynton.
MR & MRS VICKERY ☎ (059 87) 263.

*A long, white, 13th century building of considerable charm and
character at the top of Countisbury hill with stunning views over
Exmoor. The area is distinctly rural with sheep roaming the
grounds, but the food and accommodation are sophisticated yet
homely. An excellent base for walkers.*

MEVAGISSEY Cornwall **Map 2 C2**
⊗£ **HARBOUR LIGHTS** Polkirt Hill, Mevagissey, nr St. Austell.
⌂££ **Hours:** Breakfast 8.30am - 9am, Lunch 12 noon - 2pm and Dinner
6.30pm - 9pm (last orders). **Cuisine:** Extensive bar menu served in
public bar or dining room. ⌖ 7 bedrooms, 5 en suite and all with
tea/coffee making facilities, radio, telephones and colour TVs.
CC Access, Visa. **Other Points:** No dogs. Not suitable for children
under 14 years old. Eurocard also accepted. **P Directions:** B3273
to Mevagissey from A390. Follow Gorren Haven sign post.
MR & MRS SHENTON AND MR & MRS QUINN ☎ (0726)
843249.

Mevagissey continued

A family run, fully licensed freehouse with letting accommodation, in one of the finest locations in Cornwall. Situated on the cliff top with panoramic views over Mevagissey and St Austell Bay, from all public rooms and most of the bedrooms. Comfort and atmosphere are guaranteed.

⊗££ **MR BISTRO** East Quay.
Hours: Restaurant open 12 noon - 2pm and 7pm - 10pm. Closed: November to January. **Cuisine:** Fresh fish and shellfish, sweet trolley. ⊨ None. ◪ All major cards. **Other Points:** Children welcome. ◘ (V) **Directions:** On the harbour front.
CHRIS & ROMER ROBINS ☎ (0726) 842432.
This restaurant is situated facing the harbour in a town with a long established fishing history. The menu, needless to say, specialises in fish dishes. The 'Dish of the Day' depends on the fishermen's catch of the day!

MINEHEAD Somerset Map 3 A1
⊞£££ **BEACONWOOD HOTEL** Church Road, North Hill, Minehead.
⊨ 1 single, 7 twin, 6 double and 2 family bedrooms, 14 en suite. Colour TV, tea/coffee making facilites, direct dial telephone, baby listening and clock radios. **Hours:** Breakfast 8.30am - 9.15am, Lunch 12 noon - 1pm, Dinner 6.30pm - 8pm. ◪ Access, Visa. **Other Points:** Children welcome. Garden. Dogs allowed. Bargain break weekends. Licensed. Grass tennis court. Heated swimming pool in high season. ◘ **Directions:** Close to St Michaels Church, off St Michaels Road.
MR T ROBERTS ☎ (0643) 702032.
A 16 bedroom Edwardian Country House Hotel which stands in over two acres of terraced gardens, with panoramic views over Exmoor and sea. A warm welcome awaits you and the quiet, friendly atmosphere guarantees a peaceful and relaxing stay. There is a bar decorated like an old country inn, a spacious dining room serving good food and the accommodation is of a very high standard.

MISTERTON Somerset Map 3 B2
⊗£ **THE WHITE SWAN** Misterton, Crewkerne.
Hours: Restaurant open 12 noon - 1.45pm and 7pm - 8.30pm (booking advisable). Bar snacks available from 12 noon - 1.45pm and 7pm - 10pm. **Cuisine:** Daily lunchtime specials, eg. homemade pies, flans, lasagne and omelettes, Somerset cider and Apple cake. ⊨ None. ◪ Access, Visa. **Other Points:** No dogs. Children welcome. Special family dining room. ◘
CEDRIC J TUCK ☎ (0460) 72592.
Many amenities for families including a Cygnets Restaurant which serves a special children's menu, beer garden and skittle alley. A traditional inn serving homemade English meals in a cosy atmosphere.

MODBURY Devon Map 3 B1
⊗£££ **MODBURY PIPPIN** 35 Church Street, Modbury, nr Ivybridge.
⊞££ **Hours:** Dinner 7pm - 9.30pm (last orders). Closed: Sundays and all January. Also closed Mondays (except Bank Holidays) from October to June. **Cuisine:** Fresh local produce, eg. Monkfish Thermidor, Maigret of Duck and Black- currant sauce, and Filet de

THE SOUTH WEST

Modbury continued

Boeuf en croute. ⮕ 2 bedrooms, 1 bathroom. **CC** All major cards. **Other Points**: Children welcome. No dogs. &. **(V) Directions**: Town located on A379, 12 miles east of Plymouth. MR MULLERY ☎ (0548) 830 765.

Situated on the high street of this ancient market town, Modbury Pippin is attractively decorated and is popular with discerning locals who appreciate freshly cooked food and carefully chosen, sensibly priced wines.

MORETONHAMPSTEAD Devon **Map 3 B1**

COOKSHAYES GUEST HOUSE 33 Court Street, [CLUB] Moretonhampstead.

⮕ 1 single, 4 double, 3 twin, 6 en suite. 1 bathroom, 2 showers. Colour TV and tea/coffee facilities in all rooms. **Hours**: Breakfast 8.30am - 9am, dinner 7pm (order by 5pm). Closed: November - mid-March. **CC** Access, Visa. **Other Points**: Central heating. Children welcome. Licensed. Residents lounge. Garden. Four poster suite. **P** &. **Directions**: On B3212 on the west edge of the village. MRS VERONICA HARDING ☎ (0647) 40374.

A 19th century granite villa standing in 1 acre of well-tended, south facing garden, in the heart of Dartmoor National Park. The house is tastefully furnished with antiques, china and glass. Delicious home-cooking using fresh, local produce. An ideal location for touring the Devon area.

MORTEHOE Devon **Map 3 A1**

BAYCLIFFE HOTEL Chapel Hill, Mortehoe, Woolacombe.

⮕ 2 single, 7 double and 1 family room all en suite. Colour TV, telephone, tea/coffee making facilities in bedrooms. Four poster suites available. **Hours**: Breakfast 9am - 10am, Dinner 7pm - 8pm. **CC** Access, Visa. **Other Points**: No dogs allowed. **P** **(V) Directions**: B3343 to Mortehoe village. MR & MRS MCFARLANE ☎ (0271) 870393.

Small, family run hotel offering good service, comfortable rooms and superb views of the bay. Beaches are just a few minutes away and places of interest include an 11th century church. Also, being adjacent to National Trust land, walkers will find this an ideal spot.

LUNDY HOUSE HOTEL Chapel Hill, Mortehoe, Woolacombe. [CLUB] ⮕ 2 single, 3 double, 5 family bedrooms, 6 en suite. 1 bathroom, 1 WC. **Hours**: Breakfast 8.30am - 9.30am, dinner 7.30pm. Closed: November, December and January. **CC** None. **Other Points**: Centrally heated and double glazed. Pets welcome. Reductions for children (6-13 yrs) & senior citizens. 3 night Bargain Breaks and Special Discount weeks. **P** **Directions**: Situated between Woolacombe and Mortehoe off the A361 on the B3343. ROGER & DENA SELLS ☎ (0271) 870 372.

Spectacularly situated on cliff-side opposite secluded beach, with magnificent sea views over Morte Bay to Lundy Island. Terraced gardens, comfortable licensed bar lounge, separate colour TV lounge and traditional home cooking. Vegetarian and special diets catered for.

Mortehoe continued

⌂£££ **SUNNYCLIFFE HOTEL** Chapel Hill, Mortehoe, Woolacombe.
⊨ 6 double and 2 twin bedrooms, all en suite. Colour TV, radio, hairdryers, and tea/coffee making facilities in all rooms. **Hours:** Breakfast 9am and dinner 7pm. ☒ None. **Other Points:** No children. No pets. ▣ **(V) Directions:** From Woolacombe take signs for Mortehoe.Thru' village and down hill.
MR & MRS V N BASSETT ☎ (0271) 870597.
Sunnycliffe is a quiet private hotel set above a sandy cove in an unspoilt coastal village, at a point where Mortehoe joins Woolacombe, and is surrounded by thousands of acres of open moorland and coastal walks. All rooms are spotlessly clean and comfortable and have sea views and the food is prepared by the highly qualified proprietor/chef. Highly recommended.

NEWQUAY Cornwall **Map 2 B1**

⌂£££ **CORISANDE MANOR HOTEL** Riverside Avenue, Pentire, Newquay.
⊨ 5 single, 8 double, 3 twin, 3 family bedrooms, 15 en suite. 5 bathrooms, 2 showers. **Hours:** Breakfast 8.30am - 9.30am, bar lunches 12.30pm - 1.30pm, dinner 7pm - 7.30pm. Closed: 12th October to 9th May. ☒ Access, Visa. **Other Points:** Central heating. Children over 3 years welcome. Licensed. Residents lounge. TV. Garden. ▣ **(V) Directions:** Off B3282 on the Gannel Estuary.
DAVID PAINTER, FHCIMA ☎ (0637) 872 042.
Built in 1900 of Austrian design, standing in 3 acres of grounds with private foreshore. The Painters have owned and run the hotel since 1968 and they offer many facilities,eg.rowing boats, putting green, crocquet and giant outdoor chess. Advance booking is strongly recommended.

⊗££ **HARBOUR HOTEL** North Quay Hill, Newquay.
⌂££ **Hours:** Breakfast 8.30am - 9am. Morning coffee, lunches and cream teas served all day on the sun terrace or lounge/bar. Dinner from 6.30pm. **Cuisine:** Locally caught crab and seafoods. ⊨ 7 bedrooms with sea views all en suite. TV, direct dial phone and tea/coffee facilities in all rooms. ☒ Access, Visa, AmEx. **Other Points:** Children welcome. Dogs allowed. ▣ ♿ **(V) Directions:** Situated on the cliff road above Newquay Harbour.
JOHN & JACQUI ELSOM ☎ (0637) 873040.
A friendly hotel with tasteful antique furnishing, nestled in the cliffs above Newquay Harbour and offering panoramic views of the Cornish coastline from every room. Enjoy morning coffee, lunch or afternoon tea on the sun terrace with steps to the beach. Alternatively hire a surf board from the hotel and ride on the crest of a a Cornish wave.

⊗££ **THE FALCON INN** St Mawgan Village, Nr Newquay.
⌂££ **Hours:** Breakfast 9am - 9.30am, Lunch 12 noon - 2pm, Dinner 7pm - 10pm. **Cuisine:** Dishes include crab soup, sirloin steak, seafood crepes. ⊨ 5 bedrooms, 2 en suite. ☒ Access, Visa. **Other Points:** Children welcome (over 14 years for bed & breakfast). Beer garden. Dogs allowed. Afternoon teas during summer. ▣ **(V) Directions:** Follow St Mawgan Airport signs, turn down road opp. air terminal.
ANDREW BANKS ☎ (0637) 860225.

THE SOUTH WEST

Newquay continued

Covered in wisteria and jasmine, this 15th century country inn is situated in the unspoilt vale of Lanherne. Good food is served by welcoming staff in a warm and friendly atmosphere. Those wishing to spend longer in this beautiful area will find that the accommodation is of a high standard. An idyllic retreat.

⊗£ **THE GREAT WESTERN HOTEL** Newquay.
£££ **Hours:** Breakfast 8am - 9.30am, lunch 12 noon - 2pm, dinner 7pm - 8.45pm (last orders). Bar meals 12 noon - 2pm and 6pm - 9.30pm. **Cuisine:** Homemade dishes. 67 bedrooms all en suite and with colour TV, tea/coffee making facilities and baby listening service, telephone and hair dryers. All major cards. **Other Points:** Children welcome. Coaches welcome. Fax No. 0637 874435. 🅿 ⅙ **(V) Directions:** On the cliff road near the railway station.
MR FITTER - Manager ☎ (0637) 872010.
An imposing cream building perched on the cliff above Great Western Beach with magnificent views out to sea. The hotel comprises a lawned garden, indoor swimming pool and jacuzzi and serves traditional English food with traditional hospitality.

⊗££ **THE HEADLAND HOTEL** Newquay.
££££ **Hours:** Lunch 12.30pm - 2pm, Dinner 7.30pm - 9pm. Closed: mid November - mid March but open over New Year. **Cuisine:** English and Continental dishes including local crab and lobster. Table d'hote & a la carte. Snacks, homemade cakes and scones served in coffee shop. 100 bedrooms, all en suite and with all modern facilities. Just outside Les Routiers price bracket in high season. Access, Visa. **Other Points:** Children welcome. Afternoon teas. Dogs allowed. Residents lounge. Garden. Outdoor & indoor pools. Tennis courts. Snooker & pool tables. Putting. 🅿 ⅙ **(V) Directions:** Follow directions to Fistral beach. Turn left along Headland Road.
MR & MRS ARMSTRONG ☎ (0637) 872211.
Standing on its own headland with the sea on three sides, the hotel enjoys magnificent sea views. A wide choice of meals and an extensive selection of wines and vintage port are on offer in the restaurant. Probably unique in having its own hot-air balloon but due to its superb position there are many other sports facilities available, making The Headland a sportman's paradise.

£££ **TREGURRIAN HOTEL** Watergate Bay, Newquay.
4 single, 3 twin, 13 double, 7 family bedrooms. 22 with en suite. **Hours:** Breakfast 8.30am - 9.15am, lunch 12.30pm - 1.30pm and dinner 6.45pm - 7.30pm. Access, Visa. **Other Points:** Children welcome. Garden. Afternoon teas. Pets allowed. 🅿 **Directions:** 3 miles form Newquay, on the B3276.
MR & MRS MOLLOY ☎ (0637) 860020.
A modern hotel overlooking the surf beach of Watergate Bay, offering comfortable accommodation and excellent facilities for family holidays with heated swimming pool, games room, laundry room etc. A wide range of bar meals available, with childrens early light teas. Only 100 yards from the beach, suitable for all ages and offers excellent surfing conditions.

Newquay continued

⌂££ **TREVONE HOTEL** Mount Wise, Newquay.

🛏 7 single, 13 double, 9 twin and 3 family bedrooms, 22 with en suite shower/WC, 5 with en suite bathrooms. **Hours:** Breakfast 9am - 9.30am, dinner 7pm - 7.30pm (or by arrangement). Closed: Mid October - Mid April 1992. Open Bank Holidays. **CC** None. **Other Points:** Children welcome. Non-smoking area. Licensed. Special holidays eg. bird watching, wild flowers and gardens, houses & churches. **P** **(V) Directions:** On the B3282 opposite public gardens.
PAM CHEGWIN ☎ (0637)873039/873310.
Run by the same family for 68 years, Trevone is not a grand hotel, but comfortable and friendly with plentiful delicious home-cooking and good menu choice. Picture gallery residents' bar and landscaped shrub and perennial garden, with waterfall, stream and pond. Games room. Evening entertainment.

⌂£ **TYGWYN** 107 Pentire Avenue, Newquay.

CLUB 🛏 1 single, 3 double, 1 twin and 1 family bedroom, 4 en suite. 1 bathroom and 1 shower. **Hours:** Breakfast 8.30am - 8.45pm (or by arrangement). Dinner 6pm - 8pm (last orders). 7.30pm). Closed: November to February inclusive. **CC** None. **Other Points:** Central heating. Children welcome. Lounge and garden with sun patio. TV. No smoking area. Limited access for disabled. Special diets catered for. **P** **(V) Directions:** From the centre of Newquay, take the road to Pentire headland.
MEL, CLIVE & MARK GRIFFIN ☎ (0637) 874480.
A luxury split level chalet bungalow set high on the cliff top overlooking the beach, with sea views from every room. On the food side, the emphasis is on fresh produce with a choice of menu. The Tygwyn may be small but the welcome is warm and served with true Cornish hospitality.

⊗£ **WHIPSIDERRY HOTEL** Trevelgue Road, Porth, Newquay.
⌂££ **Hours:** Breakfast 8.30am - 9am, lunch 12 noon - 2pm (bar meals) and dinner 6.30pm - 8pm. Closed: October to March. **Cuisine:** Varied table d'hote menu changes daily. 🛏 23 bedrooms, 21 en suite. All with baby listening, tea/coffee facilities, TV and radio. **CC** None. **Other Points:** Central heating. Children welcome. Dogs allowed. Heated swimming pool. Sauna. Pool room. Launderette. **P** ♿ **(V) Directions:** Trevelgue Road leads off Watergate Road (the seafront).
RICHARD & ANN DRACKFORD ☎ (0637) 874777.
The Whipsiderry commands a superb position overlooking Porth beach and bay with breathtaking views of both sea and country. Whether exploring the rugged Cornish coastland or venturing inland, the hotel provides a friendly retreat. On fine summer evenings, enjoy a barbecue on the terrace and, at night, watch the badgers feed and play only a few feet away.

⌂££ **WHITE LODGE HOTEL** Mawgan Porth, near Newquay.
🛏 17 bedrooms, 12 en suite. All rooms have colour TV, tea/coffee making facilities and are equipped with radio/intercom and child-listening facility. **Hours:** Breakfast 8am - 9am, Dinner 6pm - 8pm. Bar snacks 12 noon - 2pm. Closed: November to February. **CC** Access, Visa, AmEx. **Other Points:** Children welcome. Afternoon teas. Dogs allowed. Residents' lounge. Garden. Picnic

THE SOUTH WEST

Newquay continued

lunches available. Vegetarian meals available. Games room. **P**
Directions: B3276 coast road between Newquay & Padstow. 5
miles from Newquay.

JOHN & DIANE PARRY ☎ (0637) 860512.

Family owned and run, the hotel is beautifully situated in an
elevated position, just 100 yards from the golden sands of
Mawgan Porth. Excellent views of the sea and cliffs from the
dining room, bar and most of the bedrooms. Comments from
recent visitors highly praise the White Lodge and commend the
comfortable accommodation, good food and welcoming,
friendly service.

NORTH WOOTTON Somerset **Map 3 A2**

⊗££ **CROSSWAYS INN** North Wootton, nr. Shepton Mallet.
☐☐£ **Hours:** Meals 12 noon - 2.30pm and 7pm - 10pm (last orders).
Meals served in bar and restaurant. **Cuisine:** Sauteed trout Rob
Roy, lemon sole en Bellevue, local pheasant. In the buff bar, hot
meals, cold meats, chicken, cheese and salads. ⊨ 7 bedrooms, 2
en suite. **CC** Access, Visa. **Other Points:** Children welcome. No
dogs. Coaches by appointment. **P** & **(V) Directions:** On the A361
midway between Wells, Glastonbury, Shepton Mallet.

JOHN & CYNTHIA KIRKHAM ☎ (074 989) 237 & 476.

Located in the heart of the country, off the A361 and midway
between Wells, Glastonbury, Shepton Mallet. Overlooking the
historic Valley of Avalon and Glastonbury Tor. Advance
booking recommended.

PAIGNTON Devon **Map 3 B1**

⊗£ **BARTON PINES INN** Blagdon Road, Higher Blagdon,
Paignton.
Hours: Meals 12 noon - 2.30pm and 7pm - 10.30pm. **Cuisine:**
Home cooking, eg. steak and kidney pie, curry, and lasagne.
Extensive menu and daily specials board. Sunday lunch off
season. ⊨ 8 apartments and a touring caravan site. **CC** Visa. **Other**
Points: Children welcome. Access for disabled to restaurant and
bar. **P Directions:** From A3022, take unclassified road to Marldon
& Berry Pomeroy.

MR & MRS P B DEVONSHIRE ☎ (0803) 553350.

Elizabethan style manor in extensive grounds with superb
views, offering self catering apartments, touring caravans,
tennis court, heated pool, and solarium. Quality home cooking.
Personally run by the proprietors.

⊗££ **DOLCE VITA** Roundham Road, Paignton.
⌣ **Hours:** Lunch Monday - Friday 12 noon - 2pm, Sunday 12.30pm -
2pm. Dinner Tuesday - Sunday 7.30pm - 10pm. **Cuisine:** English
and continental cuisine, offering a selection of meat, fish and
seafood. ⊨ 29 bedrooms, all en suite. **CC** All major cards. **Other**
Points: Children welcome. Open all year including Sundays,
Bank Holidays, Christmas and New Year. **P** **(V) Directions:**
Overlooking Goodrington Bay.

MR HOWARD SHORE ☎ (0803) 529942.

The Dolce Vita, one of Torbay's premier restaurants, has
stunning sea views and a beautiful interior decor, helping to
provide a romantic, candlelit atmosphere in the evening or a
luxurious lunchtime environment for business entertaining. An

Paignton continued

ideal setting in which to enjoy the fine wines and excellent cuisine which combines the best of English and continental styles.

⌂££ **SOUTH SANDS HOTEL** 12 Alta Vista Road, Goodrington Sands, Paignton.

🛏 19 bedrooms, all en suite. Facilities include tea/coffee making, colour TV, radio, alarm, telephone, baby listening device and Video channel. **Hours:** Breakfast 8am - 9am, Dinner 6pm - 7pm. **CC** Access, Visa. **Other Points:** Children welcome. Vegetarian meals. Afternoon teas. Dogs allowed. No smoking area. Garden. Residents bar-lounge. Licensed. Sea Views. **P** & **(V) Directions:** Keep Paignton harbour on left, go to top of hill. 1st hotel on Rgt. TONY & CECILE CAHILL ☎ (0803) 557231/529947

South Sands Hotel, situated close to Goodrington Sands, enjoys outstanding views of the bay. Under the personal supervision of the proprietors, visitors are assured of a warm welcome, comfortable, well-equipped bedrooms, and superb freshly prepared food. Very good value for money. Ideally located for the beach, town centre and water adventure park.

⊗£
⌂£ **THE INN ON THE GREEN** Seafront, Paignton.
Hours: 12 noon - 3pm, and 6.30pm - 12 midnight. Sunday lunch 12 noon - 3pm, and 7pm - 10.30pm. **Cuisine:** Very extensive menu, including traditional English, Indian, and Italian dishes. Children's own menu. Desserts include Olde English puddings. 🛏 82 self-catering apartments. Maid service. **CC** None. **Other**

Paignton continued

Points: Children welcome. Pets allowed. Garden and children's playground. Heated swimming pool and children's paddling pool. Launderette. Games room. ▣ ᵹ **(V) Directions:** End of M5 to Torbay. Directly on seafront opposite the pier.
BRIAN SHONE ☎ (0803) 557841.

A holiday complex set in 2 acres right on the seafront, yet within a 2 minute walk from shops, theatre and other attractions. The menu is very extensive, offering a wide range of dishes, well-cooked and presented, and the apartments are very comfortable. An ideal place for family holidays, as children are well-catered for with sandpits, Wendy House and own discos.

PELYNT Cornwall **Map 2 B2**

⊗££ **PELYNT DAGGER RESTAURANT** Barton Meadow, Pelynt by Looe.

Hours: Open 6pm - 11.30pm (last orders 9pm), Easter to October. Bookings only from January to Easter. Closed: mid October to December. **Cuisine:** A la carte, table d'hote & bar meals. Award-winning duckling, fresh local salmon, steak Portuguese, homemade soup, Cornish cream teas, roast Sunday lunch. ⇔ None. ☒ Access, Visa. **Other Points:** Children welcome. Fully licensed. No dogs. ▣ ᵹ **Directions:** 4 miles from Looe on B3359 in Pelynt village.
JOHN & JOAN BLAKE ☎ (0503) 20386.

In a country setting, close to Looe and Polperro, this popular restaurant is under the personal supervision of the owners. Comfortable lounge bar and paved patio. English and Continental recipes.

PENDOGGETT Cornwall **Map 2 B2**

⊗££ **THE CORNISH ARMS** Pendoggett, St Isaac.

⌂£££ **Hours:** Breakfast 8.30am - 9.30am, Lunch 12.30pm - 2.30pm and
CLUB Dinner 7.15pm - 11pm (last orders 10pm). **Cuisine:** A la carte and Bar menu. Fillet Steak filled with Sauted Mushrooms and Smoked Oysters, a speciality. ⇔ 7 bedrooms, 5 en suite. ☒ All major cards. **Other Points:** Children welcome. Garden. Afternoon teas. Dogs allowed. No smoking area. Switch cards accepted. ▣ ᵹ **(V) Directions:** 1 mile E of Port Isaac. N of St Endellion, S of Delabole on B3314.
JOHN ROBINSON & MERVYN GILMOUR ☎ (0208) 880263.

This typical Cornish 16th Century Coaching Inn, located on the perimeter of the small village of Pendoggett, is indeed charming. The excellent cuisine is served in a relaxed and friendly atmosphere, and the choice of fresh seafood, from the local fishing villages, makes it well worth a visit!

PENZANCE Cornwall **Map 2 C1**

⌂£ **CARNSON HOUSE HOTEL** East Terrace, Penzance.

CLUB ⇔ 3 single and 5 double bedrooms all with tea/coffee makers and colour TV and some with en suite facilities. 1 bathroom. 1 shower. **Hours:** Breakfast 8am - 8.30am, dinner at 6.15pm (order by 4pm) Packed lunch available on request. Open at Christmas. ☒ All major cards. **Other Points:** Ground floor en suite bedroom Licensed. Central heating.No dogs. Residents lounge and garden Free glass of house wine at Dinner for Club members. ᵹ

Penzance continued

Directions: On the right side of main road entering Penzance from the A30 East.

RICHARD & TRISHA HILDER ☎ (0736) 65589.

This small, comfortable, private hotel enjoys one of Penzance's most central positions.Close to harbour and beaches, it is an ideal base for touring the Lands End Peninsula with its dramatic scenery of coves and cliffs. Tourist information and excursion booking service available. French and German spoken.

Ⓜⅅ£££ **HIGHER FAUGAN COUNTRY HOUSE HOTEL** Newlyn, Penzance.

🛏 12 bedrooms, all en suite and with tea making facilities, direct dial telephone and colour TV. **Hours:** Breakfast 7.30am - 10am, Bar snacks 12 noon - 2pm, Dinner 7.30pm - 8.30pm (order by 7pm). Non-residents welcome if book before 7pm. Open all year. **CC** All major cards. **Other Points:** Children welcome. No smoking area. Dogs allowed. Residents lounge. Bar. Garden. Billiards. Heated swimming pool. Tennis court. Fax No: (0736) 51648. **P (V)** **Directions:** Off B3315. 2 miles west of Penzance in Newlyn fishing village.

MICHAEL & CHRISTINE CHURCHMAN ☎ (0736) 62076.

A gracious Country House, built at the turn of the century, surrounded by 10 acres of lawns and woodlands. The rooms are tastefully furnished and the standard of accommodation is excellent. The dinner menu is changed daily and uses fresh, local produce including home-grown garden produce. With personal service and a warm, welcoming atmosphere, this hotel is highly recommended.

Ⓜⅅ£ **LYNWOOD GUEST HOUSE** 41 Morrab Road, Penzance.

🛏 1 single, 3 double, 2 family bedrooms all with colour TV and tea/coffee making facilities. 1 bathroom, 2 showers. **Hours:** Breakfast 8am - 8.45am, (earlier by arrangement). **CC** Access, Visa. **Other Points:** Central heating. Children welcome. No evening meal. Residents' lounge. TV. Mastercard accepted. **Directions:** Morrab Road is a turning off the Seafront. MRS JOAN WOOD ☎ (0736) 65871.

A comfortable, well-appointed family guest house built in Victorian times. Situated between the promenade and the town centre, Lynwood is convenient for all amenities, and close to the sub-tropical gardens. An ideal base for visiting Lands' End and the Lizard Peninsula, St Michael's Mount and the Isles of Scilly.

⊗£££ **MOUNT HAVEN HOTEL & RESTAURANT** Turnpike Road,
Ⓜⅅ£££ Marazion, Penzance.

Hours: Breakfast 8am - 9.15am, Lunch 12 noon - 2pm, Dinner 7pm - 9pm (last orders). **Cuisine:** A la carte and table d'hote menus. Specialities include Chicken Nell Gwyn and Trout Welsh style - stuffed with mussels & leeks, & wrapped in smoked bacon. 🛏 17 bedrooms, all en suite. **CC** Access, Visa, AmEx. **Other Points:** Children welcome. Garden. Afternoon teas. Dogs allowed. No smoking in restaurant. **P (V) Directions:** Marazion exit from A30, through village, hotel on right hand side.

JOHN & DELYTH JAMES ☎ (0736) 710249.

Situated in its own grounds on the outskirts of the ancient market town of Marazion, Mount Haven is just a few minutes walk from

Penzance continued

the sea. There are superb views over St Michael's Mount from the garden and sun terrace. With both a la carte and table d'hote menus guests have a good choice of meals in the restaurant and the service is friendly and efficient.

⊗£ **OLIVE BRANCH RESTAURANT** 3a The Terrace, Market Jew Street, Penzance.
Hours: Open from 10am - 2.30pm and 6pm - 8pm (last orders). Closed: Sundays. **Cuisine:** Semi-vegetarian restaurant offering dishes for vegetarians and non-vegetarians alike. Original Cornish recipes featured. ⊨ None. **CC** None. **Other Points:** Children welcome. Dogs must be kept under control. No-smoking room. **(V)**
Directions: Opposite the main Post Office in Penzance.
S & P MELLOR ☎ (0736) 62438.
A semi-vegetarian restaurant on the 2nd floor, above the shop where Humphrey Davy was born. Window seats are in full view of St Michael's Mount and can be booked in advance. All dishes are homecooked and there is a good choice for both vegetarians and non-vegetarians.

⊗£ **UNION HOTEL** Chapel Street, Penzance.
⊞£££ **Hours:** Breakfast 8am - 9.30am, dinner 6pm - 9.30pm (last orders), bar snacks 12 noon - 2pm and 6pm - 9pm (last orders). **Cuisine:** Full a la carte menu, table d'hote and bar snacks. ⊨ 28 bedrooms, 24 en suite. **CC** All major cards. **Other Points:** Children welcome. **P** **(V)**
MR KENNEDY - Manager. ☎ (0736) 62319.
Steeped in history, the hotel dates back to the 17th Century. It was here that news of Nelson's death and victory at the Battle of Trafalgar was first announced. Today, well-cooked and presented meals are served in a cosy atmosphere and the accommodation is comfortable. Log fires in winter add to the warm welcome extended to all guests.

⊞£ **WOODSTOCK GUEST HOUSE** 29 Morrab Road, Penzance.
⊨ 1 single, 2 double, 1 twin and 1 family bedroom, some en suite. Bathroom and shower room. Colour TV, Tea/Coffee maker, Radio clock alarms, Shaver point and hand basin in all rooms.
Hours: Breakfast 8am - 8.30am or by arrangement. **CC** All major cards. **Other Points:** Children welcome. Street parking.
Directions: Off the promenade, close to Morrab Gardens.
CHERRY HOPKINS ☎ (0736) 69049.
A large Victorian terrace house, converted into a very comfortable and friendly guest house, complimented by the delightful Morrab Gardens nearby Highly recommended and excellent value for money.

PERRANPORTH Cornwall **Map 2 B1**
⊗£ **BOLENNA COURT HOTEL** Perrancoombe Road,
⊞£££ Perranporth.
Hours: Breakfast 8am - 9.30am, Lunch 12 noon - 2pm, Dinner 6.30pm - 9.30pm. **Cuisine:** Table d'hote menu and bar meals. Predominantly fresh produce used. ⊨ 1 single, 1 twin, 3 double and 3 family bedrooms, 7 en suite. **CC** None. **Other Points:** Children welcome. Garden. Afternoon teas. Dogs allowed. Licensed. Colour TV lounge. Concession with local golf club for

Perranporth continued

guests. ◘ **(V) Directions**: In Perranporth, near the Boating Lake and St Michael's Church.

MR & MRS LOGAN ☎ (0872) 572751.

Standing in half an acre of landscaped garden, overlooking tennis courts and parkland, this is a small, licensed, family hotel. Comfortably furnished, Bolenna Court has a beamed lounge bar and restaurant providing generous portions of home cooked food. Comfortable accommodation. Only 5 minutes walk from Perranporth village and the golden sands of the 3 mile beach.

PHILLEIGH Cornwall **Map 2 C2**

⊗£££ **SMUGGLERS COTTAGE OF TOLVERNE** nr St Mawes.

Hours: Morning coffee from 10.30am, lunchtime buffet 12 noon - 2pm, cream teas 3pm - 5.30pm. Barbecues and informal suppers 7.30pm - 10pm. **Cuisine:** Home cooked food includes seafood pancakes, kebabs, breast of duck and fillet of pork. ⊨ None. ◙ None. **Other Points:** Children welcome. ◘ & **(V) Directions**: Near King Harry car ferry on Roseland Peninsula.

ELIZABETH & PETER NEWMAN ☎ (087 258) 309.

This 500 year-old thatched cottage has been run by the Newman family for over 50 years. Situated on the banks of the River Fal, near the King Harry car ferry on the Roseland Peninsula, with own landing stage and moorings.

PLYMOUTH Devon **Map 2 B2**

⌘£££ **BOWLING GREEN HOTEL** 9-10 Osborne Place, Lockyer Street, The Hoe.

⊨ 7 double, 2 twin and 3 family bedrooms, 7 en suite. TV, direct dial telephones and tea/coffee making facilities in all rooms. **Hours:** Breakfast 7.30am - 9am. Closed: Christmas week. ◙ Access, Visa. **Other Points:** Children welcome. Dogs allowed. Residents' lounge. Lock up garages. ◘ **Directions:** Off A374 near The Promenade and The Hoe.

DAVID & PADDY DAWKINS ☎ (0752) 667485.

The Bowling Green Hotel guarantees a friendly welcome and a comfortable stay. Ideally situated with views over The Hoe, the hotel is very close to the city centre and to the sea front.

⊗££ **CLOUDS RESTAURANT** 102 Tavistock Place, Plymouth.

[CLUB] **Hours:** Open for dinner Tuesday - Saturday 7.30pm - 10pm (last orders). Open for lunch Friday only 12 noon - 2pm. Private functions catered for 7 days a week, day and evening. **Cuisine:** Dishes may include Monkfish with Lime and Ginger, Herbed Rack of Lamb Soubise, Breast of Chicken Italian. Blackboard specials. Homemade puddings. ⊨ None. ◙ All major cards. **Other Points:** Children welcome. No dogs. Good vegetarian menu. **(V) Directions:** City centre close to City Library, Museum and Art College.

MICHAEL WRIGHTAM ☎ (0752) 262567.

A bistro-style interior with candlelit tables and comfortable furnishings creates an intimate atmosphere at this restaurant. The food is well-cooked, attractively presented and served in generous portions by friendly, efficient staff. Very popular with regulars, there is a welcoming atmosphere in which to enjoy the good food.

THE SOUTH WEST

Plymouth continued

CRANBOURNE HOTEL 282 Citadel Road, The Hoe, Plymouth.

2 single, 2 double, 6 twin and 3 family bedrooms, 5 en suite. Colour TV/ Video, Tea/Coffee making facilities and alarm facility. **Hours:** Breakfast 7am - 9am. **CC** Access, Visa, AmEx. **Other Points:** Children welcome. Pets allowed. Lock-up garage by prior arrangement. Fax No: (0752) 263858. **P Directions:** Close to city centre, 200 yds from Hoe Promenade.
PETER & VALERIE WILLIAMS ☎ (0752) 661400.

A clean, family run town house hotel close to the city centre with all its attractions. Cranbourne Hotel is a convenient two minute walk from the Ferry Port.

DRAKE HOTEL Lockyer Street, The Hoe, Plymouth.
Hours: Breakfast 7am - 9am, Lunch 12 noon - 2pm (last orders 1.45pm) and Dinner 6.30pm - 9pm (last orders). Closed: Christmas week only. **Cuisine:** A la carte or fixed price menu. English. Local Lemon Sole a speciality. 37 bedrooms, 28 en suite. **CC** All major cards. **Other Points:** Children welcome. **P (V) Directions:** Off Notte St, Citadel Rd or the Promenade.
MR TILLER ☎ (0752) 229730.

Situated in the attractive Hoe area of Plymouth, 300 metres from the Sound, this large detached Victorian building is also within easy reach of the city centre. A friendly, comfortable and well run hotel.

KHYBER RESTAURANT 44 Mayflower Street, Plymouth.
Hours: Meals 12 noon - 2.15pm and 5.30pm - 12 midnight (last orders 11pm). Closed: Christmas Day. **Cuisine:** Lamb kata masala, King prawn bhuna, Makhon chicken. None. **CC** All major cards. **Other Points:** Children welcome. No dogs. **P (V) Directions:** Centre of Plymouth.
ABDUL LATIF TARAFDER ☎ (0752) 266036

Unassuming from the outside, this small Indian restaurant has a cosy, intimate atmosphere. 27 years of experience have combined to earn the Khyber a good, local reputation.

KURBANI INDIAN RESTAURANT 1 Tavistock Place,
CLUB Sherwell Arcade, Plymouth.
Hours: Lunch 12 noon - 2.30pm and dinner 5.30pm - 11.30pm (last orders). **Cuisine:** Tandoori and Kurbani specialities. Set 3 and 4 course menus. None. **CC** All major cards. **Other Points:** Children welcome. **(V) Directions:** Opposite Plymouth Polytechnic, near the museum.
ABDUL MAGNI TARAFDER ☎ (0752) 266778/227615

Situated on the ground floor and basement in the centre of town. Attractive Indian decor and friendly service contribute to the informal atmosphere. No car-park, but there is ample street parking nearby in the evenings.

OLIVERS HOTEL & RESTAURANT 33 Sutherland Road, Plymouth.
Hours: Meals 7.45am - 9am, and 6pm - 8pm Monday to Thursday, 7pm to 9pm Friday to Saturday. No meals served Sunday evenings. **Cuisine:** Traditional 5 course breakfast, daily plats du jour, eg. coq au vin, beef wellington, and seafood provencal. 6

Plymouth continued

bedrooms, 4 en suite. ◙ All major cards. **Other Points:** Children over 11 years welcome. No dogs. No coaches. No smoking area. ◘ **(V) Directions:** Less than a mile from the Hoe, to the east of the railway station.
JOY & MIKE PURSER ☎ (0752) 663923.
A family-run luxury hotel in the north east corner of the city centre off the B3241. The Pursers have tastefully, and carefully, modernised the building to ensure that modern comforts can be enjoyed in Victorian splendour and ambience.

⊛£££ **PLYMOUTH MOAT HOUSE** Plymouth Hoe, Armada Way, Plymouth.
Hours: Breakfast 7am - 10am, lunch 7am - 2.30pm, dinner 6.30pm - 10.30pm (last orders). Bar snacks served all day from 7am - 11pm. **Cuisine:** Dishes may include Avocado wedges served with seafood on crispy lettuce, Roast rib of beef with Yorkshire pudding, Smoked chicken salad. ⊨ 200 bedrooms, all en suite. ◙ All major cards. **Other Points:** Children welcome. Open Bank Holidays. No smoking areas. Afternoon teas. Dogs allowed in rooms only. Residents' lounge. Fax (0752) 673816. ◘ ⅃ **(V) Directions:** Off A38 towards city centre following signs for the Hoe.
ANDREW HUCKERBY - General Manager ☎ (0752) 662866.
Lavishly decorated, this hotel is popular with both holidaymakers and locals alike. Unobtrusive classical music creates a relaxed atmosphere in which you can enjoy beautifully presented meals, cooked with care and attention. Constant care and interest is shown by the staff and chef. Comfortable accommodation.

⊛£ **SMEATONS TOWER HOTEL** 40-44 Grand Parade, The Hoe,
⊞£challenge Plymouth.
Hours: Breakfast 7am - 9am, lunch 12 noon - 2pm and dinner 6pm - 8.30pm. Bar meals 12 noon - 3pm and 6pm - 11pm. **Cuisine:** Table d'hote and full a la carte menus. ⊨ 18 bedrooms, all en suite and with colour TV, phone and tea/coffee facilities. ◙ Access, Visa. **Other Points:** Children welcome. No dogs. Afternoon tea served. ⅃ **(V) Directions:** Adjacent to Plymouth Hoe.
BRIAN & MAY MASON ☎ (0752) 221007/221664
A small, friendly, family-run hotel situated close to the seafront and 12-15 minutes walk from the city centre. A popular holiday and commercial hotel.

⊛£££ **THE WEARY FRIAR HOTEL** Pillaton, Nr Saltash, Plymouth.
⊞£££ **Hours:** Breakfast 7.30am - 10am, Lunch and bar snacks 12 noon - 2pm, dinner and bar snacks 7pm - 10pm (last orders). **Cuisine:** Dishes may include Fillets of Sole Champagne, Honey Roast Saddle of Lamb, Smokey Carpetbag Steak (with oysters), Vegetable & Nut Salousie. ⊨ 14 bedrooms, all en suite. ◙ Visa. **Other Points:** Children welcome. Afternoon teas. Residents' lounge. Garden dining. ◘ ⅃ **(V) Directions:** Between Saltash & Callington, 2 miles west of A388. Near St Mellion.
SUE & ROGER SHARMAN ☎ (0579) 50238.
A famous old 12th century inn, situated next to the Church of St. Odolphus, where you will find true character and atmosphere.

Plymouth continued

Today the Weary Friar welcomes you to imaginative food of a high standard, suberb surroundings and comfortable accommodation. Highly recommended for its high quality food and the excellent combination of modern comforts with 12th century character.

⊗££ **TRATTORIA PESCATORE** 36 Admiralty Street, Stonehouse, Plymouth.

CLUB **Hours:** Lunch 12 noon - 2pm, dinner 7pm - 11pm (last orders). Closed: Saturday lunch and Sundays. **Cuisine:** Breast of wild duck, Crayfish Thermidor, Bouillabaisse. ⊨ None. CC Access, Visa. **Other Points:** Children welcome. No dogs. Tables outside in summer. **(V) Directions:** Approx 1 mile from city centre, near Plymouth to Roscoff ferry port.
GIAN PIERO CALIGARI & RITA ATKINSON ☎ (0752) 600201.
A small Italian restaurant situated in an old Victorian building. Hand painted murals on the walls add to the truely Italian atmosphere of the restaurant. All food is freshly cooked to order and seafood is the house speciality. Delicious food and friendly, efficient service. Highly recommended.

POLPERRO Cornwall **Map 2 B2**

⊗££ **NELSON'S RESTAURANT** Big Green, Polperro.

Hours: Lunch 11.45am - 2pm and dinner 7pm - 10pm (last orders 9.45pm). Closed: all day Monday and Saturday lunchtime. Annual holiday mid-January to mid-February. **Cuisine:** Fresh seafood, roasts, braised chicken. ⊨ None. CC Access, Visa, Diners. **Other Points:** Children welcome. Dogs by arrangement. **Directions:** On the Saxon bridge in Polperro.
PETER NELSON ☎ (0503) 72366.
A large, olde worlde restaurant with a distinct nautical flavour, reflecting the proprietor's long connection with the sea. The table d'hote menu changes with the availability of fresh produce. An intimate restaurant with a friendly atmosphere.

⊗£££ **THE KITCHEN** Polperro, Cornwall.

Hours: Dinner 6.30pm until 9.30pm Closed: Sunday to Thursday from November to late March. Also closed every Tuesday during the summer. **Cuisine:** Fish, lobster, crab,duck, steak and lamb. ⊨ None. CC Access, Visa. ▯ & **(V) Directions:** On the walk down to the harbour.
IAN & VANESSA BATESON ☎ (0503) 72780.
A small, informal, licensed restaurant specialising in high quality dishes prepared by the owners who have a well deserved reputation for imaginative food.

PORT ISAAC Cornwall **Map 2 B2**

⊗££ **BAY HOTEL & RESTAURANT** 1 The Terrace, Port Isaac.

▥£ **Hours:** Breakfast 8.30am - 9.30am, bar snacks from 11am - 10pm. Table d'hote dinner 7pm - 8pm and a la carte 8pm - 10pm (last orders 9.30pm). Closed: November - Easter. **Cuisine:** Fresh local crab and lobster, home baked pies and pastries, Tournedos Rossini, scampi provencal. ⊨ 10 bedrooms, 4 en suite. CC None. **Other Points:** Children welcome. ▯ **Directions:** On the B3267 at the top of the cliff opposite main public car park.
JIM & MARY ANDREWS ☎ (0208) 880380.

Port Isaac continued

Small, friendly, family run hotel at the top of this Cornish fishing village with views out to sea and cliffs. Ideal for a quiet holiday. 3 and 4 night mini breaks available out of main season.

⊗££
⏟££££ **OLD SCHOOL HOTEL** Fore Street, Port Isaac. **Hours:** Breakfast 8am - 11am, Lunch 11am - 3pm, Dinner 7pm - 9.30pm (last orders). Bar snacks 11am - 9.30pm. Open all year round. **Cuisine:** Restaurant specialises in fish and seafood dishes such as Whole Grilled Lemon Sole, Lobster Thermidor, Mariner's Fish Pie. Bar meals. ⇌ 13 bedrooms, all en suite, including a Bridal Suite, Executive Suite and a Studio/Luxury Suite with own roof terrace overlooking harbour. **CC** Access, Visa. **Other Points:** Children welcome. Afternoon teas. Dogs allowed. Residents' lounge. Garden and terrace for meals. Clifftop barbecues. Medieval banquets. **P (V) Directions:** 9 miles N of Wadebridge on B3314 until left turn on B3267.
MICHAEL WARNER ☎ (0208) 880721.
The Old School dates from 1875 and stands sentinel on the cliff top overlooking the harbour and out to sea. The accommodation is excellent, tastefully furnished to provide a high standard of comfort yet retaining the original character of the building. The restaurant specialises in local fish and seafood. Deep-sea fishing, riding, golf and sailing are all available nearby.

THE SOUTH WEST

PORTESHAM Dorset **Map 3 B2**

££ **MILLMEAD COUNTRY HOTEL** Portesham, Nr Weymouth. 3 double and 2 twin en suite. 1 double, 1 twin and 1 single with shower. All with colour TV. **Hours:** Breakfast 8am - 9am and dinner 7pm - 7.30pm (order by 7pm). Lunches, evening meals and afternoon cream teas now served to non residents. **CC** Access, Visa. **Other Points:** Children over 10 welcome. Non-smoking. Vegetarian meals. **P** & **(V) Directions:** On the B3157 between Weymouth and Bridport.
PETER & MARION COX ☎ (0305) 871432.
A Victorian house sympathetically extended to create a period country house atmosphere. The Millmead stands in a substantial 'country garden' which produces much of the fruit and vegetables used in the cooking. Lunches and afternoon teas served to non residents in the new Victorian conservatory. Menu changes daily. An ideal location for a relaxing break.

PORTLAND Dorset **Map 3 B2**

££ **PENNSYLVANIA CASTLE HOTEL** Pennsylvania Road,
£££ Portland.
CLUB **Hours:** Breakfast 7.30am - 10.30am, Lunch 12 noon - 2.30pm (last orders 1.45pm) and Dinner 7.30pm - 10.30pm (last orders 9.30pm). **Cuisine:** Seafood specials including Paupiettes of sole stuffed with spinach and crab, Seafood fricasse. Fillet steak with tropical fruit flamed in rum. 13 bedrooms, 12 en suite. **CC** All major cards. **Other Points:** Children welcome. Dogs allowed. Afternoon teas. 6 acres of subtropical garden. **P** & **(V) Directions:** Take A354.
PAUL & INDU FRANSHAM ☎ (0305) 820561.
This 18th Century, cliff top castle is set in extensive, subtropical gardens and has splendid views of the south Dorset coast. The restaurant has an air of elegance and offers a comprehensive a la carte menu and a good table d'hote menu accompanied by a wide selection of popular wines at competitive prices.

PORTSCATHO Cornwall **Map 2 C2**

£££ **PENDOWER BEACH HOUSE HOTEL** Gerrans Bay, Ruan
££££ High Lanes, Nr Truro.
Hours: Breakfast 8.45am - 9.15am, Lunch 12 noon - 2.00pm and Dinner 7.00pm - 9.00pm (last orders). Restaurant closed Monday evenings. Hotel closed 26th Oct through to Easter. **Cuisine:** A la carte, fixed 5 course menu or bar snacks available. 13 bedrooms, all en suite. **CC** Access, Visa. **Other Points:** Children welcome. Afternoon tea. Garden. Dogs allowed. No smoking areas. **P** **(V) Directions:** A3078, turning 6 miles N of St Mawes. End of lane to 'Pink Hotel'.
PETER & CAROL BEETHAM ☎ (0872) 501241
The hotel occupies a prime position on the beautiful Roseland Peninsula. It boasts extensive grounds where peacocks and ducks roam freely. The choice of cuisine is excellent specialising in local fresh fish served in a relaxing atmosphere.

POUNDSGATE Devon **Map 3 B1**

£ **TAVISTOCK INN** Poundsgate, Newton Abbot, Devon.
Hours: Lunch 11am - 2.30pm and Dinner 6pm - 9.30pm. **Cuisine:** Wide choice of dishes such as Charcoal grill steaks, vegetarian specialities and Ploughmans. Blackboard daily

Poundsgate continued

specials. 🍴 None. 💳 Access, Visa. **Other Points:** Children welcome. Dogs allowed. Open Sundays and Bank holidays. Limited access for disabled. Eurocard and Mastercard accepted. 🅿 **(V) Directions:** 5 miles from the A38 on the B3352 between Ashburton and Tavistock.

KEN & JANICE COMER ☎ (036) 43251.

A 700 year old inn, with stone-flagged floors and open fireplace, offering good quality food at reasonable prices. In 1638, at the time of the witch trials, the Tavistock entered local legend, the story being that the Devil himself stopped here for a drink. Today you are assured of far better company! Prizewinning beer garden open May - September, weather permitting.

PRESTON Dorset **Map 3 B2**

££token **SUNNINGDALE HOTEL** Preston Road, Preston, Weymouth. CLUB 🍴 1 single, 8 double, 6 twin and 7 family bedrooms, 10 en suite. 2 bathrooms, 1 shower. **Hours:** Breakfast 8.15am - 9.15am and dinner 6.15pm - 7.15pm. Closed: mid October to March. 💳 Access, Visa. **Other Points:** Children welcome. Licensed. Residents lounge. TV. Garden. Swimming pool 6 hole putting green. Games room. 🅿 ♿ **Directions:** Off the A353, through Preston village towards the sea.

MR & MRS TONY FLUX ☎ (0305) 832 179.

Set in 1 and a half acres of grounds, all bedrooms enjoy fine views over the gardens or fields. Although only 600 yds from the sea, the heated outdoor swimming pool is always popular, especially with small children.

RANGEWORTHY Avon **Map 3 A2**

⊗££ **RANGEWORTHY COURT HOTEL** Church Lane, Wotton ££££token Road, Rangeworthy, Bristol. CLUB **Hours:** Breakfast 7.15am - 9.30am, Lunch 12 noon - 2pm, Dinner 7pm - 9pm (last orders). Sunday Lunch 12.15pm - 1.45pm, Sunday Dinner 7pm - 8.30pm. **Cuisine:** Dishes may include Devilled crab, Lamb steak in Madeira & rosemary sauce, Fresh salmon, Nut Cutlet. Vegetarian and Vegan dishes. 🍴 16 bedrooms, all en suite. 💳 All major cards. **Other Points:** Children welcome. Garden. Dogs allowed. Wedding receptions. Conferences. Fax No: (0454) 228945. Disabled access to restaurant only. 🅿 **(V) Directions:** Just off B4058. Turn opposite Rose & Crown pub in the village.

MERVYN & LUCIA GILLETT ☎ (0454) 228347.

An attractive, historic country house set in its own grounds with the church. Inside, the lounges have log fires and candles in winter, flowers all year and a relaxing atmosphere. Food is considered an important feature of the hotel and the restaurant has a strong local following. Enjoy welcoming service, well cooked food and the peace and quiet of this country house.

REDRUTH Cornwall **Map 2 C1**

⊗££ **THE INN FOR ALL SEASONS** Treleigh, Redruth. ££££token **Hours:** Restaurant open 7.30am - 9am, lunch 12 noon - 2pm (Sundays only), and dinner 7pm - 9.30pm (except Sundays). Bar food 12 noon - 2pm and 7pm - 9.30pm daily. **Cuisine:** Modern and traditional English cuisine, using fresh, local produce and

THE SOUTH WEST

Redruth continued

local fish. Menus change weekly. Sunday Lunch a speciality.
🛏 12 bedrooms, all en suite with colour TV, radio, alarm and
tea/coffee facilities. Trouser press. Direct dial phone. **CC** Access,
Visa. **Other Points:** Children welcome. Pets allowed in rooms only.
Open Sundays and bank holidays. Disabled access to bar and
restaurant only. Conference room. **P** & **(V) Directions:** On old
Redruth bypass, clearly visible from A30. Nr Cardrew Estate.
F N B ATHERLEY & R J MILAN ☎ (0209) 219511.
*A modern building, having been completely refurbished to a
high standard. Centrally situated, ideal for tourists and business
people (helicopter landing area). Friendly atmosphere.*

ROCK Cornwall **Map 2 B2**
⊗££ **ROSKARNON HOUSE HOTEL** Rock, Nr Wadebridge.
⊓££ **Hours:** Breakfast 8.30am - 9.30am, Lunch 12 noon - 1.30pm,
Dinner 7pm - 8pm. **Cuisine:** Dishes include Spaghetti Bolognaise,
Roast Chicken and poached Salmon with butter sauce. 🛏 12
bedrooms, 6 en suite. **CC** None. **Other Points:** Children welcome.
Garden. Afternoon teas. No dogs. **P** **Directions:** Overlooking
Camel Estuary. Off A39 and B3314.
IAN VEALL ☎ (0208) 862329.
*By the golden sands of Rock and the open sea of the Camel
Estuary, the Roskarnon House Hotel is an ideal place in which to
enjoy the delights of a holiday in Cornwall. This small,
unpretentious hotel offers all the essentials and amenities to
make your stay a happy one. Simple, home cooked food.*

SALCOMBE Devon **Map 3 C1**
⊗££ **THE SOUTH SANDS HOTEL & RESTAURANT** Salcombe.
⊓£££ **Hours:** 8.30am - 9.30am, 12 noon - 2pm, and 7pm - 9.30pm. Also
open Sundays. Bar meals also available in the £ Routiers price
bracket. Good wine list. **Cuisine:** Dishes may include medallions
of pork fillet flamed with Calvados, saute supreme of chicken, and
brochette of scallops, peppers, bacon and prawns. 🛏 11 twin, 10
double, and 12 family rooms, all en suite. **CC** All major cards.
Other Points: Children welcome. Pets allowed. Special interest
breaks. Hotel bar. Heated pool, sunbed, and steam room. Many
outdoor activities close by. **P** **(V) Directions:** Exeter A38. A384 to
Totnes, then A381 for Kingsbridge and Salcombe.
MR & MRS HEY ☎ (054) 884 3741.
*A modern hotel, excellently situated directly on a safe sandy
beach. The inspector reports that the hotel offers 'very good
accommodation and meals which are beautifully prepared and
presented by very friendly and efficient staff'. An ideal holiday
area, with the wild unspoilt countryside of Dartmoor, lovely
beaches, and the towns of Kingsbridge, Totnes, and Torquay
nearby.*

SAUNTON Devon **Map 3 A1**
⊗££ **PRESTON HOUSE HOTEL** Saunton, near Braunton.
⊓££££ **Hours:** Breakfast 8.30am - 9.30am, lunch 12 noon - 2pm, dinner
CLUB 7pm - 8.30pm (last orders). **Cuisine:** Table d'hote menu - changes
daily. All dishes prepared and cooked on the premises. 🛏 15
bedrooms all en suite and with colour TV, telephone, clock radio,
tea/coffee making facilities. Four poster suites available.
CC Access, Visa. **Other Points:** No dogs. Solarium, sauna & spa

Saunton continued

bath. 2 residents lounges. Garden. Terrace. Conservatory. Bar & Regency dining room. Fax: (0271) 890555. ▯ ₺ **(V) Directions:** On the coast road overlooking Saunton Beach.
ANN COOK ☎ (0271) 890472.
A grand Victorian Country House overlooking the 10 mile sweep of Barnstaple's sandy bay. Built in 1895, the stained glass windows, moulded ceilings and period furnishings, paintings and ornaments recreate the glory of the period. Golfing, riding, fishing and water sports are all available nearby and the hotel has its own heated outdoor swimming pool.

SEAVINGTON ST. MICHAEL Somerset **Map 3 B2**

⊗£ **THE VOLUNTEER INN** Seavington St. Michael, nr Ilminster.
Hours: Lunch and bar meals 12 noon - 2.30pm, dinner and bar meals 7pm - 10.30pm (last orders). Closed: Christmas Day evening. **Cuisine:** Fresh fish dishes, steaks, crepes suzette. ⊨ None. **CC** Visa. **Other Points:** Children welcome. No dogs (except in garden). Beer garden. ▯ ₺ **Directions:** On A303, 3 miles east of Ilminster.
B GEORGE & E SALZER ☎ (0460) 40126.
Believed to have originally been a Posting Inn and Cider House, the inn is now a family run Free House. A popular pub noted for good food, an extensive menu and friendly, prompt service. Ideal half way point for tourists travelling to and from Devon and Cornwall.

SHALDON Devon **Map 3 B1**

⊗££ **THE NESS HOUSE HOTEL** Marine Parade, Shaldon, Teignmouth.
Hours: Breakfast 8am - 10am, lunch 12 noon - 2pm, dinner 7pm - 10pm (last orders). Bar meals 12 noon - 2pm, 6.30pm - 10pm. **Cuisine:** A large choice of traditional French dishes. Coquille St Jacques aux safran, mignon de veau aux fraises. ⊨ 12 bedrooms all en suite. **CC** Access, Visa, AmEx. **Other Points:** Children welcome. Afternoon tea served. Garden. No dogs. Fax No. (0626) 873486. ▯ ₺ **(V) Directions:** On A379 (Teignmouth - Torquay road) in Shaldon. Parkland.
PETER & JANE REYNOLDS ☎ (0626) 873480.
Formerly a private country house, the hotel sits very happily in beautiful gardens and enjoys wonderful views of the coast and the Teign Estuary. A friendly hotel serving good food.

SIDFORD Devon **Map 3 B2**

⊗£ **THE BLUE BALL INN** Sidford, Nr Sidmouth.
⌂££ **Hours:** Breakfast 8.30am - 10am, lunch 10.30am - 2pm (last orders), dinner 6.30pm - 10pm (last orders). **Cuisine:** Home made specialities include steak and kidney pie, chicken mornay, chilli con carne and local fish. ⊨ 3 twin bedrooms. **CC** Access, Visa. **Other Points:** Children welcome. Gardens. Afternoon teas. Dogs allowed. Garden dining. Room available for Functions, Receptions. ▯ ₺ **(V) Directions:** On the A3052, just outside Sidmouth.
MR ROGER NEWTON ☎ (0395) 514062.
Dating back to 1385, 'The Blue Ball Inn' is thatched and made of cob and flint. Fresh flowers add to the tasteful decor of the building and outside customers can enjoy barbecues in the

Sidford continued

garden during summer. Run by the same family since 1912, the pub provides well cooked food in a busy but relaxed atmosphere. Excellent, friendly service.

SIDMOUTH Devon **Map 3 B2**

⊗££ **FORTFIELD HOTEL** Sidmouth.

⌂£££production **Hours:** Breakfast 8.30am - 9.30am, lunch 12 noon - 2pm, dinner 7pm - 8.30pm. Open Bank Holidays. **Cuisine:** Menu may feature - Miami Cocktail, Stuffed Pepper, Baked Crown of Lamb Garni, Braised Pheasant Casserole, Boulangaire Potatoes. ⊨ 55 bedrooms, all en suite. **CC** All major cards. **Other Points:** Children welcome. Swimming pool. Fitness centre. No smoking area. Afternoon teas. Dogs allowed. Garden dining. Fax/telephone No. (0395) 512403. ▣ & **(V) Directions:** From Exeter take A3052. Turn into Station Road.

ANDREW TORJUSSEN ☎ (0395) 512403.

Located just one block from the sea, this elegant hotel is comfortably furnished and serves good food in generous portions. With a fitness centre and swimming pool, this hotel is ideal for those wishing to keep in trim or those wishing to take in the coastal views.

⌂££ **KINGSWOOD HOTEL** Esplanade, Sidmouth, Devon.

⊨ 8 single, 6 double, 7 twin and 5 family bedrooms, all with en suite bath/ shower. 2 bathrooms. Colour TV, tea/coffee facilities and direct dial phones in all rooms. **Hours:** Breakfast 8.30am - 9.15am (earlier if required), lunch 12.30pm - 12.45pm and dinner 6.30pm - 7pm. **CC** None. **Other Points:** Central heating. Children welcome. Dogs allowed. Residents' lounge and TV. Baby listening service. Packed lunches available. ▣ & **Directions:** On the seafront.

JOY, COLIN, MARK & JOANNA SEWARD ☎ (03955) 6367/3185.

An excellent family run establishment right on the sea front with an award winning and colourful terrace garden. Fully modernised, the interior is spacious and many of the rooms look out over the Devon coast. Personally supervised by the proprietors, the food and service are excellent. The Kingswood is unlicensed but guests are invited to bring their own wine - no corkage charge.

⊗£££ **WESTCLIFF HOTEL** Manor Road, Sidmouth.

Hours: 8.30am - 9.30am, lunch 1pm - 2pm and dinner 7.30pm - 9.30 pm (last orders 8.30pm). Bar meals 12.30pm - 1.45pm. Closed: November to February. Open to non-residents for dinner. **Cuisine:** International cuisine. Sunday lunch and bar lunches. ⊨ 40 bedrooms, all en suite. **CC** Access, Visa. **Other Points:** Children welcome. Non-smoking area. Afternoon tea served. ▣ & **(V) Directions:** Off the A3052. Situated along sea front.

MRS P HARDING/MR & MRS MALLOCH BROWN ☎ (0395) 513252.

Delightful family run hotel, set in 2 acres of beautiful gardens. In a prime position for access to the town centre, Connaught Gardens, beach and golf club. Fabulous coastal views and excellent dining at affordable prices make this hotel a definite stop for tourists.

SOMERTON Somerset **Map 3 B2**

⊗£££ **RED LION HOTEL** Broad Street, Somerton.

🛏£££ **Hours:** Breakfast 7.30am - 9.30am, Lunch and bar snacks 12 noon - 2pm, Dinner and bar snacks 7.30pm - 10pm. **Cuisine:** Dishes may include Scallops Mornay, fresh Rainbow Trout, Medallions of Beef Red Lion, Grills. A good choice of bar snacks also available. 🛏 16 bedrooms, all en suite. **CC** All major cards. **Other Points:** Children welcome. Afternoon teas. Dogs allowed. Residents' lounge. Saturday night disco. **P** **(V) Directions:** B3153 in centre beside Market Sq. 15 miles from A5 via Street. THOMAS JACOBS ☎ (0458) 72339.

A traditional coaching inn, in the centre of Somerton serving a full restaurant menu and good value bar meals. Both menus offer a good choice of predominantly English cuisine with French overtones in the restaurant. The restaurant has a peaceful, relaxed atmosphere and the bars are lively. A good base for the many attractions of Somerset.

⊗£ **THE UNICORN AT SOMERTON** West Street, Somerton.

🛏££ **Hours:** Breakfast 8am - 9.30am, lunch and bar meals 12 noon - CLUB 2.30pm, dinner and bar meals 7pm - 10pm (last orders 9.45pm). **Cuisine:** English. Full menu, plus daily specials with fresh vegetables. Traditional Sunday roasts and local game. Bar snacks and morning coffee. All home cooking. 🛏 7 bedrooms, all en suite. **CC** All major cards. **Other Points:** Children welcome. Dogs allowed. Beer garden. Picturesque courtyard Skittle Alley. Boule piste for petanque. **P** ♿ **(V) Directions:** Enter from Langport, Taunton direction. On Left almost town centre. KATIE & JIM DAVIS ☎ (0458) 72101

A charming 15th century coaching inn and free house. The food is all home cooked and Katie and Jim Davis recognise the importance of good food and value for money. Efficient, friendly service can be found in both the restaurant and in the intimate bar which is dominated by a large inglenook fireplace, with log fires in the winter. Exceptionally good value meals.

SOUTH ZEAL Devon **Map 3 B1**

🛏££ **POLTIMORE COUNTRY HOTEL** Ramsley, South Zeal, Okehampton.

🛏 2 single, 2 twin, 2 double - 4 of them en suite. All rooms have wash basins, shaver points, electric blankets, drinks trays, colour TV and views of the moor. Self-catering bungalow/apartments also available. **Hours:** 8am - 9am, 1pm - 2.30pm, 7pm - 9pm. Also open for Sunday lunch/ dinner. A la carte and bar meals. **CC** Access, Visa, AmEx. **Other Points:** Garden. Dogs (by prior arrangement) are welcome. Children over 8 welcome. Special winter breaks. Licensed bar. **P** **(V) Directions:** Old A30 between Whiddon Down & Sticklepath. Behind Rising Sun Inn. P WILKENS & FAMILY ☎ (0837) 840209.

Cosy thatched cottage, set on fringe of Dartmoor, in 3 acres of grounds with breath-taking views. A lovely place to relax, with a warm and friendly atmosphere, very comfortable rooms, and good home-cooking. Surrounded by the Moors and little villages, this is a walker's paradise, and there are many National Trust properties a short drive away. Also ideal for anglers.

THE SOUTH WEST

SOUTHERTON Devon **Map 3 B1**

⊗£££ **THE COACH HOUSE HOTEL** Southerton, Ottery St Mary.
⌂£££ **Hours:** Breakfast 8.30am - 10am, dinner 7pm - 9pm (last orders).
Sunday lunch 12 noon - 2pm. Closed: January. **Cuisine:** Dishes
may include Mushrooms stuffed with stilton, Stroganoff, steaks,
ribs, curries. ⇌ 6 bedrooms, all en suite. Four poster suites
available. **CC** Access, Visa. **Other Points:** No children. No pets. No
smoking area. �**P** & **(V) Directions:** From the A3052 take the Venn
Ottery Road. Hotel is 800yds on left.
GRAHAM & BARBIE CARSON ☎ (0395) 68577.
*A small, black and white timbered country house hotel set in
2½ acres of grounds in the heart of rugged Devon. A mile from
the nearest village, the Coach House is in a tranquil location, yet
with many of Devon's famous tourist attractions on the doorstep.*

ST AGNES Cornwall **Map 2 B1**

⌂£ **PENKERRIS** Penwinnick Road (B3277), St Agnes.
⇌ 1 single, 2 double, 1 twin and 1 family bedroom, all with TV
and kettles. 2 bathrooms, 1 shower. **Hours:** Breakfast 8.30am,
cream teas 3pm - 5pm. Dinner 6.30pm (order by noon).
CC Access, Visa. **Other Points:** Partial central heating. Children
welcome. Residents' lounge with TV. Licensed. Garden. Piano.
Log fire. Vegetarian meals available. **P Directions:** Take B3277
off the A30 at the Chiverton Roundabout.
DOROTHY GILL-CAREY ☎ (0872 55) 2262
*Edwardian residence set in own grounds with large lawn.
Beaches, swimming, surfing and superb cliff walks offer
relaxing pastimes for guests. All dishes are prepared with fresh
fruit, vegetables and fresh farm eggs. Traditional roasts, fruit
tarts and home made curries are specialities.*

⊗£££ **THE DRIFTWOOD SPARS HOTEL** Trevaunance Cove, St
⌂£££ Agnes.
Hours: Breakfast 9am - 11am, lunch 12 noon - 2.30pm (last orders)
and dinner 7pm - 9.30pm. Sunday lunch 1pm - 2.30pm. Closed
for Sunday dinner to non-residents. **Cuisine:** Well presented
cuisine using local fresh produce. Variety of dishes using imported
and fresh seafood. ⇌ 1 single, 4 twin, 5 double, 1 family room, 5
with ensuite. Most have colour TV, hairdryers and tea/coffee
making facilities. **CC** Access, Visa. **Other Points:** Children
welcome (half price overnight). Pets allowed. **P** **(V) Directions:**
1/2 mile off B3285
MR G H & MRS G TRELEAVEN ☎ (87255) 2428
*Set amidst the secluded beauty of Trevaunance Cove, the
'Driftwood Spars' constructed of huge ship's timbers, makes a
wonderful retreat for an active holiday or a couple of weeks total
relaxation. Well presented, tasty food. Comprehensive selection
of single malt whiskies.*

ST AUSTELL Cornwall **Map 2 B2**

⌂£££ **THE ALEXANDRA HOTEL** 52/54 Alexandra Road, St
Austell.
⇌ 4 single, 2 double, 2 twin and 6 family bedrooms , 4 en suite. 2
bathrooms and 1 shower. Colour TV and tea making facilities in all
rooms. **Hours:** Breakfast 7.30am - 9am, dinner 6.30pm (order by
5pm). **CC** Access, Visa. **Other Points:** Central heating. Children
welcome. Licensed. Residents lounge. **P** &

St Austell continued
KATH & BRIAN BAILEY ☎ (0726) 74242.
A family-run hotel situated 5 minute's walk from the town of St Austell and the rail and coach station. The Alexandra offers clean, comfortable rooms and good food and wine. The proprietors promote a relaxed atmosphere, making the hotel a real 'home from home'.

ST IVES Cornwall **Map 2 C1**
⌂££ **BOSKERRIS HOTEL** Carbis Bay, St Ives.
🛏 2 single, 10 double (3 of which convert to family rooms), 6 twin and 1 suite. 17 rooms are en suite. All have colour TV, radio, alarm, telephones and tea/coffee facilities. Baby listening devices also available. **Hours:** 8.30am - 9.30am and 7pm - 8.30pm. Bar lunch 12.30pm - 1.30pm. **CC** Access, Visa, Diners. **Other Points:** Children welcome. Pets allowed. Afternoon teas served. Open Christmas and bank holidays. Special golfing breaks. Fax: (0736) 798632. **P (V) Directions:** Along A30 to St Ives. 3rd turning on right as enter Carbis Bay.
MR & MRS MONK ☎ (0736) 795295.
A family run hotel, set in private gardens with a heated swimming pool, noted for its fine wines and good food. Overlooks Carbis Bay, with magnificent views across to St Ives Harbour on one side and Godrevy Head on the other.

⌂££ **THURLESTONE HOTEL** St Ives Road, Carbis Bay, St Ives.
🛏 1 single, 5 double and 3 family bedrooms, 5 en suite and all with tea making facilities. **Hours:** Breakfast 8.45am - 9.30am, Dinner at 6.30pm (order by 5pm). **CC** None. **Other Points:** Children welcome (over 5 years). No pets. Central heating. 5 minutes walk to beach. **P Directions:** On main road into St Ives on the edge of Carbis Bay.
PAT & TONY LICKES ☎ (0736) 796369.
Built of Cornish granite in 1885 on the site of the old Wesleyan chapel, this is a house of character, with original beamed ceilings and attractive views of St Ives Bay. The lounge has a sea view, colour TV and a selection of books to browse through and there is a separate residents' bar. Carbis Bay sandy beach is within 5 minutes walk from this friendly, family hotel.

ST IVES BAY Cornwall **Map 2 C1**
⊗££ **CHY-AN-DOUR HOTEL** Trelyon Avenue, St Ives.
⌂£££ **Hours:** Breakfast 8.30am - 9.30am, Bar snacks 12 noon - 2pm, Dinner 7pm - 8pm. Non-residents advised to book. **Cuisine:** 6 course table d'hote dinner menu. Main course dishes include a choice of meat, fish, salad and vegetarian. 🛏 23 bedrooms, all en suite. Most bedrooms have sea views. **CC** Access, Visa. **Other Points:** Children welcome. No smoking in dining room. Residents' lounge. Garden. Bar. Fax No: (0736) 795772. **P ⅃ (V) Directions:** A3074, on main road into St Ives.
DAVID & RENEE WATSON ☎ (0736) 796436.
This 19th century, former sea captain's home has been extended to form a most attractive hotel with superb panoramic views over St Ives Bay and harbour. All bedrooms are en suite, most with breathtaking views.

THE SOUTH WEST

St Ives Bay continued
⊗££ **PEDN-OLVA HOTEL & RESTAURANT** Portminster Beach,
⬭££££ St Ives.
🍽 **Hours:** Breakfast 8am - 9.15am (continental from 7.30am), lunch
12 noon - 2pm and dinner 6.30pm - 9.30pm (a la carte from 8pm).
Cuisine: Wide selection of table d'hote or a la carte menu, using
fresh quality produce, including seafood specialities. 🛏 35
bedrooms, 33 en suite. **CC** Access, Visa. **Other Points:** Children
welcome. Afternoon teas. Pets allowed. Sheltered sun terrace with
heated swimming pool overlooking beach. Residents lounge. 🅿 ♿
(V)
KENNETH GEORGE EVANS ☎ (0736) 796222.
*'Pedn-olva' means lookout on the headland and this hotel, built
with its series of towers, is situated on a rocky promontory
overlooking the ancient town, the harbour and bay. Beautifully
presented and served, the quality of food and wine offered here
only just surpasses the restaurants seascape view. Attractive
balcony bedrooms provide guests with a relaxing holiday
setting.*

⊗££££ **PORTHMINSTER HOTEL** The Terrace, St Ives.
Hours: Meals 8am - 9.30am, 12.15pm - 2pm and 7.15pm -
8.30pm. Bar lunches 12.15pm - 2pm. **Cuisine:** Buffet lunch every
day with a daily 'special' and roasts on Sundays. Vegetarian by
prior arrangement. 🛏 49 bedrooms, all en suite. **CC** All major
cards. **Other Points:** Children welcome. Coaches by appointment.
Leisure complex with indoor pool,spa
bath,sauna,solarium,trimnasium + heated outdoor pool (Jun-Sept)
🅿 **(V) Directions:** On the A3074, the main road in St Ives.
TREVOR & ROSALIND RICHARDS ☎ (0736) 795221
*The hotel stands above the bay enjoying superb views of the
harbour and beaches. The new leisure complex will
compliment the existing hotel facilities. St Ives has always been
a prosperous town, and home to many artists and craftsmen.*

⊗££££ **SKIDDEN HOUSE HOTEL & RESTAURANT** Skidden Hill,
⬭££££ St Ives Bay.
Hours: Breakfast 8.30am - 9.30am, Lunch 12 noon - 1.30pm,
Dinner 7.30pm - 9.30pm. **Cuisine:** A la Carte and table d'hote
menus. Dishes may include Wild Salmon, poached in wine with
King Scallops, served in Scallop & cream sauce, Tornedos Rossini.
🛏 8 bedrooms, all en suite. **CC** Access, Visa. **Other Points:** Limited
access for disabled. Children welcome. Afternoon teas. Dogs
allowed. No smoking areas. 🅿 **(V) Directions:** Off A30. Pass
Railway station. 1st right with the church on corner.
MR HOOK & MR STOAKES ☎ (0736) 796899.
*Welcoming and comfortable, the Skidden House Hotel is set in
the centre of St Ives and dates back through almost 500 years of
history. Today, under the ownership of Michael and Dennis, the
hotel enjoys a fine reputation for its cuisine and comfortable
accommodation. With a peaceful, olde world atmosphere, it is
an ideal place to relax and enjoy the delights of Cornwall.*

⊗££ **THE ST UNY HOTEL** Carbis Bay, St Ives.
Hours: Breakfast 8.45am - 9.30am and dinner 7pm - 8pm. Bar
snacks 12 noon - 2pm. Afternoon teas served. Bar meals in £ price
range. **Cuisine:** Traditional English cooking, fish, roast pork, beef,

St Ives Bay continued

turkey, lamb and duck. ⊨ 30 bedrooms, 19 en suite. **CC** Access, Visa. **Other Points:** Children over 5 years welcome. **P** & **(V)** **Directions:** From A30 take the A3074, the hotel is close to Carbis Bay Station.

T & B C CARROLL ☎ (0736) 795011.

Suberb position overlooking the bay with excellent views from most rooms. Originally a private mansion, now a throroughly refurbished hotel with an atmosphere of calm and relaxation. Standing in 2 acres of sheltered gardens with semi-tropical trees and shrubs.

STAVERTON Devon **Map 3 B1**

⊗££ **THE SEA TROUT INN** Staverton, Nr Totnes.

⏉£ **Hours:** Breakfast 8am 9.30am, Lunch 12 noon - 2pm (Sundays [CLUB] 12.30pm - 2pm) and Dinner 7pm - 9.30pm (last orders). Closed: Sunday evening. **Cuisine:** A la carte and fixed 3 course menu - good selection of meat and fish dishes. Bar menu includes steak & kidney pie, steaks and mixed grill. ⊨ 10 bedrooms, all en suite. **CC** Access, Visa. **Other Points:** Children welcome. Garden. Pets allowed. **P** & **(V) Directions:** Off A38, turn at Dart Bridge, follow signs to Staverton.

ANDREW MOGFORD ☎ (080426) 274.

Attractive beamed 15th Century inn, set in a peaceful village close to the River Dart. A popular venue for families, locals and tourists offering comfortable accommodation and a varied choice of menu. Highly recommended and an ideal base for touring South Devon.

TAUNTON Somerset **Map 3 B2**

⏉£ **THE CAREW ARMS** Crowcombe, Taunton.

⊨ 4 bedrooms, 2 bathrooms. **Hours:** Breakfast 8am - 9am, bar snacks available at lunchtime, dinner 8pm - 9pm (orders taken in morning). **CC** Access, Visa. **Other Points:** Children welcome. Licensed. **P** **Directions:** Off A358 Taunton - Minehead rd. 10 miles Taunton. 4 miles Williton.

MRS C BREMNER ☎ (09848) 631.

Nestling in the Somerset countryside, yet conveniently situated for access to the South West, the Carew Arms is the ideal place to stay when exploring the West Country.

⊗££ **THE CORNER HOUSE** Park Street, Taunton.

⏉££££**Hours:** 7am - 9.30am, 12 noon - 1.30pm, and 7pm - 10pm. **Cuisine:** English and french cuisine, including trout served with almonds and chateaubriand. Good wine list. ⊨ 30 bedrooms, 28 of them en suite, all with colour TV, radio, alarm, baby listening devices, telephones and tea/coffee making facilities. **CC** Access, Visa. **Other Points:** Children welcome. No dogs allowed. Open bank holidays and Sunday evenings. **P** & **(V) Directions:** A38, on south side of Taunton Town Centre.

MR R. IRISH ☎ (0823) 284683.

A Victorian hotel of character, situated close to the centre of Taunton. Lunch and dinner is served in the Parkfield Restaurant, offering food and wine of fine quality and the staff are efficient and friendly. Close to Exmoor, Dartmoor, Quantocks, and Yeovilton Air Museum.

Taunton continued

⊗£ **THE FARMERS ARMS** West Hatch, Taunton.
Hours: Lunch and bar snacks 11.30am - 2.30pm, dinner 7pm - 9.30pm (last orders), evening bar snacks 7pm - 8.30pm (last orders). Closed: Monday lunchtimes and Christmas Day. **Cuisine:** A la carte menu and fixed priced menus. Dishes may include Chilli Con Carne, Mushrooms a la Grecque. ⊨ None. **CC** Access, Visa. **Other Points:** Children welcome. Open Bank Holidays. Dogs allowed. Garden dining. **P** & **(V) Directions:** From Taunton, follow signs, off A358.
JOHN & BRIDGET WILLIAMS ☎ (0823) 480480.
Traditional country pub, with a faithful local clientele. Well presented and cooked meals are served by friendly, helpful staff. A warm welcome is assured.

⊗££ **THE WHITE HART INN** Corfe, nr Taunton.
[CLUB] **Hours:** Lunch 11.30am - 2.30pm, Dinner 6.30pm - 10pm. **Cuisine:** International, upmarket pub food. Specialities include Sole wrapped in pastry with prawns and brie, Duck breast with pepper sauce, Rack of Lamb. ⊨ None. **CC** Access, Visa. **Other Points:** Children welcome. Beer garden. Dogs allowed. No smoking area. **P** & **(V) Directions:** B3170, 3 and a half miles south of Taunton. Only pub in Corfe.
JOHN & BEVERLEY DAVEY ☎ (082342) 388.
A friendly village pub with exposed beams and open fire place, skittle alley and garden. The White Hart offers excellently cooked meals at good value for money, served by welcoming, efficient staff. With a warm, friendly atmosphere, this Inn provides an ideal place to relax and enjoy well cooked food. 1 mile south of Taunton Racecourse, at foot of the Blackdown Hills.

TAVISTOCK Devon **Map 3 B1**

⊗£ **THE OLD PLOUGH INN** Bere Ferrers, Nr Yelverton.
Hours: Lunch and bar snacks 12 noon - 3pm, Dinner and bar snacks 7.30pm - 10.30pm (last orders). Closed: 25th December evening. **Cuisine:** Menus change daily, including, when available, fresh fish and 'Maggies Monster' homemade pies. Locally grown vegetables. All dishes homemade. ⊨ None. **CC** Access, Visa. **Other Points:** Garden dining. 4 cask-conditioned ales offered daily. **(V) Directions:** From Plymouth - A386, follow signs for Bere Alston and Bere Ferrers.
ADRIAN & MARGARET HOOPER ☎ (0822) 840358.
A 16th century Inn, situated beside the River Tavy in the scenic village of Bere Ferrers, in an unspoilt area of outstanding beauty. A wide range of homemade food and ales are offered in the bar, restaurant or beer garden. Open log fires in winter.

THE LIZARD Cornwall **Map 2 C1**

⊗££ **HOUSEL BAY HOTEL** The Lizard.
⊞£££ **Hours:** 8.30am - 10am and 7.30pm - 9.30pm. Bar meals 11.30am - 1.45pm and 7.30pm - 9.30pm (last orders). Closed: January 1st - February 8th. **Cuisine:** Traditional English cuisine, including fresh fish and seafood. ⊨ 23 bedrooms, all en suite with colour TV, radio, alarm, telephone and tea/coffee facilities. **CC** Access, Visa. **Other Points:** Children welcome. Pets allowed. Afternoon teas. Open Sundays and bank holidays. Disabled lift. **P** & **(V)**

The Lizard continued

Directions: At Lizard town signpost, take the left fork following hotel signs.

FREDA & DEREK OSWALD ☎ (0326) 290417.

An elegant Victorian hotel in a spectacular clifftop position, with a secluded sandy cove and extensive grounds. Offers well-equipped, comfortable rooms and value for money food. Kynance Cove, the Lizard and Goonhilly Downs all nearby.

⊗££   **THE CAERTHILLIAN** The Lizard, Helston.
☐☐££   **Hours:** 8.30am - 9.30am, 12 noon - 2pm and 7pm - 9pm (last
CLUB orders). Closed: In Winter - All day Wednesday and Sunday evening. Closed: In Summer - All day Monday & Tuesday and Sunday evenings. **Cuisine:** International cuisine, with a menu which changes daily. ⊨ 5 bedrooms, 2 of them en suite. All with colour TV and tea/coffee making facilities. ⬛ Access, Visa. **Other Points:** No dogs. Open Sundays and bank holidays. Garden dining. ⬛ **(V) Directions:** In the Lizard village.

P J & J B GAYTON ☎ (0326) 290019.

A Victorian building in the centre of the village, retaining much of its character with some of the original furnishings and fireplaces, yet recently refurbished to provide modern standards of comfort. Set in the beautiful surroundings of the Lizard Peninsula, with Kynance Cove and Helford river nearby.

THELBRIDGE Devon **Map 3 B1**
⊗£   **THE THELBRIDGE CROSS INN** Thelbridge, Nr Witheridge.
☐☐£££   **Hours:** Restaurant and bar meals 12 noon - 2.30pm and 7pm - 9.30pm. Including Sundays. **Cuisine:** International cuisine, traditional homemade dishes. Full a la carte menu and bar snacks. All available lunch times and evenings 7 days a week. ⊨ 8 bedrooms, all en suite, and with colour TV, tea/coffee making facilities, telephone. ⬛ Access, Visa. **Other Points:** Children welcome. No dogs. Open for Sunday lunch and bank holidays. Very popular so booking advisable at week-ends. Fax: (0884) 860316. ⬛ ♿ **(V) Directions:** 10 miles NW of Tiverton on B3042, between Witheridge & Chawleigh.

BILL & RIA BALL ☎ (0884) 860316.

A beautiful Country Inn, situated in glorious unspoilt mid-Devon with views across to Dartmoor and Exmoor. Award winning Restaurant. No live bands, juke box or pool tables - just peace and tranquility, with the enviable reputation for good food, warmth and hospitality. The only Inn left where the original Lorna Doone Stage Coach still brings passengers to enjoy the good food.

THROWLEIGH Devon **Map 3 B1**
☐☐£   **WELL FARM** Throwleigh, Okehampton.
⊨ 1 twin and 2 family bedrooms (1 on ground floor), all en suite. **Hours:** Breakfast at 9am, dinner 8pm - 9pm. Closed: Christmas. ⬛ None. **Other Points:** Partial central heating. Children welcome. Residents lounge and TV. Vegetarian meals available. Working farm. ⬛ ♿ **Directions:** 1 and a half miles from the A30 in the Dartmoor National Park.

MRS SHEELAGH KNOX ☎ (064 723) 294.

Relax in beautiful and peaceful surroundings at Well Farm - a Grade II listed medieval Dartmoor longhouse. It is a working

Throwleigh continued

family run dairy and outdoor pig farm with peacocks, ornamental pheasants, free-range poultry. Fresh produce is served in a relaxed, family atmosphere.

TINTAGEL Cornwall **Map 2 B2**

⊗££ **BOSSINEY HOUSE HOTEL & RESTAURANT** Tintagel.

⏣££££ **Hours:** Breakfast 8.45am - 9.15am, lunch 12 noon - 3pm, dinner CLUB 7pm - 10pm (last orders). **Cuisine:** Menu changes daily. Dishes include home made vegetable soup, roast leg of pork served with apple sauce, strawberry cheesecake. Table d'hote & a la carte. ⊨ 7 twin, 10 double and 1 family bedrooms. All en suite. **CC** All major cards. **Other Points:** Children welcome. Garden. Afternoon teas. Dogs allowed. Putting green. Log chalet with heated swimming pool, sauna & solarium. Fax:(0840) 770501 **P** ⅙ **(V) Directions:** M5 jct 31. On A30. R on A395 follow signs to Tintagel from Davidston

MR & MRS R L SAVAGE & MR & MRS C J SAVAGE ☎ (0840) 770240.

A large country house standing in own grounds. Tastefully decorated using light colours and comfortably furnished. The restaurant offers traditional English fayre. All rooms are very well decorated in a variety of styles. This hotel overlooking the north Cornish coast is an ideal base for those wanting to explore 'King Arthur's Country'.

TIVERTON Devon **Map 3 B1**

⏣££ **BRIDGE GUEST HOUSE** 23 Angel Hill, Tiverton.

⊨ 5 single, 3 double (2 en suite), 1 twin, 2 family bedrooms. 2 bathrooms. 2 showers. Tea/coffee making facilities in all rooms. **Hours:** Breakfast 7.30am - 9am, dinner 6.30pm - 7.30pm. Open all year. **CC** None. **Other Points:** Central heating. Children welcome. Licensed. Residents, lounge. TV. **P** **Directions:** Off M5 exit junct 27, Link Road to town centre,beside River Exe.

BOB & SUE COXALL ☎ (0884) 252804.

Situated on the main road bridge over the River Exe in the centre of the town, all rooms overlook the river. There is a pleasant riverside tea garden. Fishing rights.

⊗£ **THE MERRIEMEADE HOTEL** 1 Lower Town, Sampford

⏣££ Peverell, Nr Tiverton

Hours: Breakfast 7.30am - 9am, lunch 11.30am - 2pm, dinner 6.45pm - 10.30pm. Sunday lunch 12 noon - 2.30pm, Sunday dinner 7pm - 10pm. **Cuisine:** English/French cuisine. A la carte menu, bar meals and snacks. ⊨ 5 rooms. 1 single, 1 twin and 1 double room with 2 family rooms. All 5 en suite. **CC** Access, Visa. **Other Points:** Children welcome. Garden. Pets allowed. Garden dining. Fax No: (0884) 821614. **P** ⅙ **(V) Directions:** 1 mile from junction 27 of the M5 and North Devon Link Road. On A373

MR L J AFFLECK & MR P J P COURT ☎ (0884) 820270

Formerly a Georgian style Gentlemans Residence, The Merriemeade Hotel overlooks the Blackdown Hills. This hotel caters for all ages with a childrens play area in the rear garden. Its food is both varied and excellently cooked. The rooms are also of high standard. Great value for money.

TOPSHAM Devon **Map 3 B1**

⊗££ **DENLEYS WINE BAR & RESTAURANT** 62-64 High Street, Topsham.

Hours: Bar meals 11am - 10.30pm. Lunch 12 noon - 2.30pm (last orders 2pm) and dinner 7pm - 12pm (last orders 11pm). Open Sunday lunch 12 noon - 2.30pm and dinner 7pm - 9.30pm. **Cuisine:** A la carte and fixed price menu available. Menu changed every 3 weeks. ⊨ None. **CC** All major cards. **Other Points:** Afternoon teas. Pets allowed. **(V) Directions:** Situated on Topsham's main street.

MESSRS SMITH & MRS KING ☎ (0392) 875675.

A unique multi roomed wine bar and restaurant serving well presented tasty food in pleasant and comfortable surroundings. Excellent service and a menu which is changed every three weeks makes Denleys Wine Bar a pleasure to visit. Highly recommended.

TORQUAY Devon **Map 3 B1**

⊞££users **BLUE HAZE HOTEL** Seaway Lane, Torquay.

⊨ 4 double, 3 twin, 3 family bedrooms all en suite. Colour TV, tea/coffee making facilities, radio, fridges, hairdryers and baby-listening devices. **Hours:** Breakfast 9 - 9.30am and dinner at 7pm. **CC** Visa. **Other Points:** Vegetarian meals. Children welcome. No dogs. No smoking area in dining room. Residents, lounge and garden. **P** & **(V) Directions:** Close to Torquay railway station.

DOUG & HAZEL NEWTON. ☎ (0803) 607186.

A pleasant Victorian house in quiet, leafy grounds, situated 500 yards from the sea. Home cooking served straight from the oven. Golf grounds and riding stables nearby and fishing trips and sailing can be arranged.

⊗£
⊞££ **BOWDEN CLOSE HOTEL** Teignmouth Road, Maidencombe, Torquay.

CLUB **Hours:** Breakfast 8am - 9am, lunch 12 noon - 2pm, dinner 6.30pm - 8pm (last orders). **Cuisine:** Daily changing menu. Dishes may include Cornish shellbake, boeuf stroganoff, salads. ⊨ 20 bedrooms, 16 en suite. **CC** Access, Visa, AmEx. **Other Points:** Children welcome. Garden. Afternoon teas. Dogs allowed by prior arrangement. **P** **(V) Directions:** A379 midway between Torquay & Teignmouth.

MR & MRS J F HILL ☎ (0803) 328029

A Victorian Country House Hotel with panoramic views across Lyme Bay. The accommodation is of a high standard and the service polite and efficient.

⊞£££ **HOTEL PROTEA** Seaway Lane, Chelston, Torquay.

⊨ 11 bedrooms, all en suite and with direct dial telephone, colour TV, radio, hairdryer and mini-bar. 2 self-contained suites in hotel grounds. **Hours:** Breakfast 8am - 9.30am, Dinner 7pm - 8.30pm (last orders). Bar snacks available 12 noon - 2pm and 7pm - 11.30pm. **CC** Access, Visa. **Other Points:** Entirely non-smoking. Residents' lounge. Garden. Bar. 5 course dinner menu. Bar. Terrace. Conservatory. Heated outdoor swimming pool. Fax No: (0803) 690171. **P** **(V) Directions:** Corner of Old Mill Road & Seaway Lane.

JOHN RICHARDS & ROBERT HELLINGS ☎ (0803) 605778.

Torquay continued

An elegant Victorian Villa set in secluded, south facing grounds and decorated to exceptionally high standards. Family run, a warm welcome and total comfort awaits all guests. All rooms are spacious and comfortable and many rooms overlook the sweeping panorama of Torbay. Good food using fresh ingredients. The ideal place to unwind and relax in gracious surroundings. Highly recommended.

⊗£ **HOTEL SYDORE** Meadfoot Road, Torquay.
⌂£££ **Hours:** Breakfast 8.30am - 9.30am, Lunch 12.30pm - 2pm, Dinner 6.30pm - 8.30pm. Bar snacks served all day from 11am - 10pm. **Cuisine:** English and continental cuisine. Dishes may include poached Fillet of Salmon steak with Hollandaise sauce, Roast leg of Lamb. Vegetarian menu. ⊨ 13 bedrooms, all en suite and with colour TV, tea maker, hair dryer, trouser press and radio. **CC** Access, Visa. **Other Points:** Children welcome. No smoking area. Afternoon teas. Dogs allowed. Residents lounge. Garden. Licensed bar. Games room. Sun Terrace. **P** & **(V) Directions:** Strand, Inner harbour, left into Torwood Street, 1st right. JANE & JOHN ROWE ☎ (0803) 294758.
A Georgian villa set in 2 acres of wooded gardened grounds, only a short walk to Blue Flag awarded Meadfoot Beach and town centre. The restaurant offers good food at value for money and the accommodation is of a high standard. Personally owned and operated by the professional but jocular Jane and John Rowe. Rain or shine, you are assured of an enjoyable time at Hotel Sydore.

Torquay continued

⊗£ **JINGLE'S RESTAURANT** 34 Torwood Street, Torquay.
Hours: Lunch 12 noon - 3pm (summer only), Dinner 6pm - 11pm
(last orders). Closed: Sunday lunch. **Cuisine:** Wide choice of
dishes including chargrilled steaks, Cajun dishes, Mexican dishes,
vegetarian meals, hamburgers and deep pan pizzas. ⊨ None.
CC Access, Visa. **Other Points:** Childrens menu. No dogs.
Background music from 60s and 70s. Smoking not encouraged.
Street parking and car park close by. **(V) Directions:** 100 yards
from Clock Tower on harbourside.
JOHN & PAT GOLDER ☎ (0803) 293340.
An American themed restaurant offering a good variety of very
well cooked dishes to suit all tastes. Choice of dishes includes
chargrilled steaks, hamburgers and vegetarian meals. House
specialities are Mexican dishes such as Sizzling Fajita, a
traditional Mexican style of cooking. The good food is
complemented by generous portions and welcoming service.
International beers.

⊗££ **LIVERMEAD CLIFF HOTEL** Sea Front, Torquay TQ2 6RQ.
££££ **Hours:** Lunch 1pm - 2pm, Dinner 7pm - 8.30pm (last orders). Bar
meals served 12 noon - 2pm and 6.30pm - 8.30pm. Open all year.
Cuisine: English and Continental dishes. Locally caught fish, local
meats and poultry. ⊨ 64 bedrooms, all en suite. **CC** All major
cards. **Other Points:** Children welcome. Afternoon teas. Heated
outdoor pool, solarium. Secluded garden. Conference facilities.
Fax: (0803) 294496. Telex: 42424. ⊡ ♿ **(V) Directions:** Right at
seafront (A379 to Paignton). 600 yds on seaward (left) side

THE SOUTH WEST

Torquay continued
MR JOHN PERRY ☎ (0803) 299666.
*A comfortable family hotel situated on the seafront at waters'
edge yet only a few minutes' level walk from the centre of town
and English Riviera Centre. The hotel is tastefully decorated
and offers a high standard of comfort which is complemented by
the friendly and efficient service. All meals are cooked on the
premises using fresh ingredients.*

🏠£ **ST ANTHONY'S HOTEL** 8-10 Abbey Road, Torquay.
🛏 2 single, 2 twin, 5 double, 1 family bedroom: 7 en suite.
Hours: Breakfast 8.30am - 9.30am and dinner 6pm - 7pm. Sunday
lunch 1pm - 2pm. 💳 Access, Visa. **Other Points:** Children
welcome. Garden. Bar snacks. Residents' lounge. **Directions:** Off
the A379, near the Odeon Cinema.
MR & MRS TEAGUE ☎ (0803) 294974.
*A homely family hotel, situated in the town centre, with easy
access for shops and entertainment, offering comfortable
accommodation. Just 500 yards from the harbour and seafront,
and car parking a few minutes walking distance, 'St Anthonys'
makes an ideal stop to anyone visiting the area.*

⊗£ **TEMPLESTOWE HOTEL** Tor Church Road, Torquay.
🏠£££ **Hours:** 8.30am - 9.30am and 7pm - 8.30pm. Bar meals served 12
noon - 2pm. **Cuisine:** Mainly English cuisine, with a choice of table
d'hote, a la carte and bar meals. 🛏 87 bedrooms, all en suite.
💳 Access, Visa. **Other Points:** Pets allowed. Reduced rates for
children. 🅿 � **(V) Directions:** A380. Follow signs for town centre
passing police station on right.
A C STANDLEY ☎ (0803) 299499.
*One of Torquay's most popular holiday hotels, near the town
centre and just 600 yards from the English Riviera centre. The
hotel has excellent facilities including a games room, heated
swimming pool and ballroom and some of the rooms have sea
views.*

TOTNES Devon **Map 3 B1**
⊗££ **ROYAL SEVEN STARS HOTEL** The Plains, Totnes.
🏠£££ **Hours:** Restaurant open 8am - 9.30am, 12 noon - 2.15pm and
7pm - 9.30pm. **Cuisine:** Traditional English cooking, eg. roasts
and grills plus buffet lunch. 5 course dinners. 🛏 18 bedrooms, 12
en suite. All with colour TV, direct dial telephone, tea/coffee
making facilities and radios. 4-poster en suites available.
💳 Access, Visa, Diners. **Other Points:** Limited access for disabled.
Children welcome and family rooms available. 🅿 **Directions:**
From Newton Abbot, take the A381 to Totnes.
MR K G A STONE ☎ (0803) 862125.
*A 17th century coaching inn, recently refurbished, ideally
situated for summer holidays and Champagne weekend breaks
all the year round. There are many attractions including the
Motor Museum, Elizabethan Museum, Berry Pomeroy Castle
and Dartington Hall nearby.*

TREGONY Cornwall **Map 2 C2**

⊗£££ **KEA HOUSE RESTAURANT** 69 Fore Street, Tregony, Nr Truro.

Hours: Lunch 12 noon - 2.30pm and dinner from 7pm. Closed: Sunday and the month of November. **Cuisine:** Chicken with fresh herbs and spices fried in filo pastry served in plum sauce, also fish and cheese board. ⊨ None. **CC** Access, Visa. **P** & **(V) Directions:** On the B3287, west of Truro.

MR & MRS A NIXON ☎ (087 253) 642.

A 2 storey stone building facing the main street, tastefully decorated with a warm welcoming atmosphere. Excellent cuisine with seafood and fish specialities (in season) and special selection of malt whiskies.

TRENT Dorset **Map 3 B2**

⊗£ **THE ROSE AND CROWN** Trent, nr Sherborne.

Hours: Lunch 12 noon - 2.30pm and dinner 7pm -11pm (last orders 9.30pm). Bar meals 12 noon - 1.45pm, 7pm - 9.30pm. Closed: Christmas Day. Booking recommended at weekends. **Cuisine:** Fish and game - using local ingredients. Menu changes weekly. Specialities - Cajun and Creole Cuisine from Louisiana. ⊨ None. **CC** Access, Visa. **Other Points:** Children welcome. Dogs allowed. Open air dining. **P** & **(V) Directions:** A30 between Sherborne - Yeovil, take Trent turn, approx 1 - 2 miles.

MR C F MARION-CRAWFORD ☎ (0935) 850776.

A 16th century part thatched freehouse, which could have been plucked from a picture postcard. There are 3 open fires and stone floors - a traditional atmosphere in which to sample traditional ales and cider and tasty home cooked food, without the intrusion of juke boxes or fruit machines. Won national awards for cuisine in 1989 and 1990.

TRURO Cornwall **Map 2 C1**

⊗££ **ALVERTON MANOR** Tregolls Road, Truro.

⊞£££ **Hours:** Breakfast 7.30am - 9.45am, lunch and bar snacks 12 noon - 1.45pm (last orders), dinner 7.15pm - 9.45pm (last orders). **Cuisine:** Dishes may include Pepper Mousse with Salad, Baked Loin of Pork with an Apple and Plum Tartlet, Fresh Peaches in Champagne. ⊨ 25 bedrooms, all en suite. **CC** All major cards. **Other Points:** Children over 12 welcome. Open Bank Holidays. No smoking area. Afternoon teas. Dogs allowed. Garden dining. Fax No. (0872) 222989. **P** & **(V) Directions:** On A390 approach road to Truro from St Austell.

MR EDWARD BENCE - Manager. ☎ (0872) 76633.

Situated in the heart of Truro, this building has been in the Tweedy family for over 150 years. The interior is tastefully decorated and furnished to a high standard. In a pleasant atmosphere and delightful, elegant surroundings, you can enjoy 'superbly cooked and presented' meals. Highly recommended.

⊗££ **LONGS RESTAURANT** Blackwater, nr Truro.

Hours: Dinner Wednesday - Saturday evening 7.30pm - 9.30pm (last orders). Sunday lunch 12.30 noon - 1.45pm. **Cuisine:** English/European, specialities including marinated fillet steak in sherry and cream. ⊨ None. **CC** Access, Visa, AmEx. **Other Points:** Children over 12 welcome. No dogs allowed. **P** **(V) Directions:** On old A30 in centre of Blackwater village, close to Truro.

Truro continued
IAN LONG ☎ (0872) 561111.
Converted Victorian house situated near the beautiful Cornish coastline and countryside. Restaurant is impeccably managed, the staff being efficient and friendly and offering a superb menu which changes daily. Highly recommended. Routiers Restaurant of the Year 1991.

⊗£££ **SIMON'S RESTAURANT** The Paddlesteamer 'Compton [CLUB] Castle', Lemon Quay.
Hours: Dinner 7pm - 10pm (last orders). Closed: Sunday and Monday. **Cuisine:** Modern cuisine using fresh, local ingredients such as Cornish lamb, and a wide variety of seafood. ⊨ None. **CC** Access, Visa. **Other Points:** Limited access for disabled. Children welcome. No dogs. Public car parks close by. Eurocard also accepted. **(V) Directions:** Aboard the paddle steamer moored at Lemon Quay, in central Truro.
ROBIN & SIMON EVANS ☎ (0872) 70101.
Simon's Restaurant is uniquely situated aboard the beautiful 80 year old paddle steamer moored on Lemon Quay. The conversion to a restaurant has been made with elegance and style and the delightful surroundings form the perfect setting for the excellent food and service. The menu offers imaginative dishes, freshly cooked using the finest local produce, and beautifully presented.

⊗££ **THE GANGES INDIAN TANDOORI RESTAURANT** St Clement Street, Truro.
Hours: Lunch 12 noon - 2.15pm and dinner 6pm - 11.15pm (Friday & Saturday 11.45pm). **Cuisine:** Indian menu with English dishes. Chef's specialities, including Ganges special chicken curry cooked with king prawn & egg, tandoori king prawn masala. ⊨ None. **CC** All major cards. **Other Points:** Children welcome. 10% discount for takeaway. ▯ ♿ **(V) Directions:** Situated in the centre of Truro, near the Cathedral.
MESSRS LASKAR & UDDIN ☎ (0872) 42535.
Decorated with Indian art murals, this modern restaurant provides diners with generous portions of tasty Indian dishes, including their house speciality - Kursi lamb. Although 24 hours notice is required for this particular dish, patrons will have little problem in finding a tasty alternative. Friendly, accommodating service.

UPTON CHEYNEY Avon **Map 3 A2**
⊗£ **THE UPTON INN** Upton Cheyney, Bitton, Bristol.
Hours: Lunch and bar meals 12 noon - 2pm, dinner and bar meals 6.30pm - 10pm. Closed: Sunday evenings (restaurant and bar meals), Monday all day (restaurant). **Cuisine:** Traditional English home cooked food, steaks. Daily specials. ⊨ None. **CC** None. **Other Points:** Beer garden. No dogs. ▯ **(V) Directions:** Off A431, steep hill signposted Upton Cheyney.
WALTER JOHN HALL ☎ (0272) 324489.
A country inn with easy access to Bath and Bristol. A stone built pub attractively decorated by hanging baskets and window boxes. Nicely presented home cooked food is served in the bar and in the Village Steak Bar.

WADEBRIDGE Cornwall **Map 2 B2**

⊗££ **MALTSTERS ARMS** Chapel Amble, Wadebridge.
Hours: Lunch 12 noon - 2.30pm and dinner 7pm - 9.30pm.
Cuisine: Dishes include lamb kidneys and mushrooms in cream &
brandy sauce, fresh turbot with red wine sauce and spinach pasty,
lasagne verdi with salad. ⊨ None. **CC** Access. **Other Points:**
Children welcome. Garden dining. **P** **(V) Directions:** In centre of
Chaple Amble, sign posted 2 miles north of Wadebridge.
JEFF & VIVIENNE POLLARD ☎ (0208) 812473.
The Maltsters Arms is one of Cornwalls oldest inns, set in a
pleasant village off the main road. Imaginative and unusual
home-cooked meals are on offer accompanied by real ales, and
a wide range of malt whiskies. Retaining many of it's original
features of stonework, timbers and open fires the Maltsters
enjoys a relaxed casual atmosphere.

⊗£ **THE EARL OF ST VINCENT** Egloshayle Village, Nr
Wadebridge.
Hours: Lunch served 12 noon - 2pm, dinner 7pm - 10pm.
Cuisine: Concentrating on homemade English cuisine. Daily
specialities and vegetarian dishes. ⊨ None. **CC** None. **Other**
Points: Children welcome. Garden dining. **P** **(V) Directions:**
Centre of Egloshayle Village.
MR EDWARD CONNOLLY ☎ (0208) 814807.
Situated in the centre of a small village this Cornish stone-built
village inn is decorated in keeping with the age and charactor of
the building. The restaurant offers good value for money meals,
served by friendly and efficient staff. Frequented by
holidaymakers and locals alike.

⊗££ **THE MOLESWORTH ARMS HOTEL** Molesworth Street,
⏢£££ Wadebridge.
Hours: Breakfast 8am - 10am, Dinner 7pm - 9.30pm (last orders).
Bar meals 12 noon - 2.30pm and 6.30pm - 9.30pm. **Cuisine:**
Traditional English cuisine using local produce. Cornish produce
includes local shell fish, salmon and speciality steaks. ⊨ 14
bedrooms, 12 en suite. **CC** Access, Visa. **Other Points:** Children
welcome. Afternoon teas. Dogs allowed. Residents' lounge. Patio
dining. Small conference facilities. Fax No: (0208) 814254. **P** &
(V) Directions: A30 to Bodmin, A389 to Wadebridge. Left over
bridge. Parking at rear
NIGEL CASSIDY ☎ (0208) 812055.
True Cornish hospitality can be found at this 16th century
Coaching Inn. The traditional furnishings and old beamed
ceilings retain the character and olde worlde elegance of the
Inn whilst providing comfortable surroundings in which to
enjoy the best in fresh local produce and the friendly, caring
atmosphere.

WATCHET Somerset **Map 3 A1**

⊗£ **WEST SOMERSET HOTEL** Swain Street, Watchet.
⏢£ **Hours:** Breakfast 8.30am - 10.00am (or as requested), lunch 12
noon - 2pm and dinner 7pm - 10pm (last orders 9.45pm). **Cuisine:**
Imaginative cuisine using local produce plus standard back-up
menu and daily specials. Wine list includes interesting Russian and
Lebanese imports. ⊨ 12 bedrooms, most with en suite facilities.

Watchet continued

CC Access, Visa. **Other Points:** Dogs allowed. Children welcome.
P &. **(V) Directions:** On the A358 in Watchet.

MR & MRS CLIFFORD & VICTORIA BARBER ☎ (0984) 34434.
A two Crown town pub situated in the ancient port of Watchet.
The hotel can arrange sea, fresh water fishing and horse riding.
For fossil hunters, the local cliffs have produced some rich
pickings. Also an ideal base for cycling and walking holidays in
Somerset and Devon.

WELLS Somerset **Map 3 A2**

⊗£ **W** ⓪ CLUB **FOUNTAIN INN & BOXERS RESTAURANT** 1 St Thomas
Street, Wells.
Hours: Lunch 11.30am - 2pm and dinner 6pm - 10pm (last
orders). Bar meals 11.30am - 2pm and 6pm - 10pm (last orders).
Closed: Christmas and Boxing Day. **Cuisine:** Modern English
cooking using mainly local produce: Lamb & Redcurrant &
Rosemary Sauce. Fresh Fish daily. Interesting selection of West
Country cheeses. ⊨ None. **CC** Access, Visa, AmEx. **Other Points:**
Children welcome. Chef's specials daily blackboard menu
available. Real ales. **P** &. **(V) Directions:** In the centre of town
behind the cathedral.

ADRIAN LAWRENCE ☎ (0749) 672317.
Georgian style building, 50 yards from Wells Cathedral,
enjoying a local reputation for fine food, using the freshest
ingredients. Good selection of Spanish wines. Restaurant
decorated with pine, local prints and Laura Ashley fabrics.

⊗£ **NEW INN** Priddy, near Wells.
⊞£production£ **Hours:** Meals 12 noon - 2pm and 7pm - 10pm (9.45pm last
orders). **Cuisine:** Home cooked ham, special West Country style
jacket potatoes, with homemade toppings. Daily specials eg.
Somerset bake, liver in cider. ⊨ 6 bedrooms, 1 bathroom, 1
shower. **CC** None. **Other Points:** Children welcome. No dogs.
Skittle Alley. Childrens garden. **P** **(V) Directions:** Just off the
B3135, 3 miles from Cheddar Gorge.

MR & MRS D J WESTON ☎ (0749) 76465.
An old 14th century inn on the edge of the village green in
Priddy, where a sheep fair is held annually in August. Good
food and a friendly atmosphere have earned the New Inn a good
local and visitors trade.

⊗£££ **THE ANCIENT GATE HOUSE HOTEL** Sadler Street, Wells.
⊞£££ **Hours:** Breakfast 8am - 9.30am, Lunch 12 noon - 2pm, Dinner
7pm - 10pm (last orders). Bar meals served 12 noon - 2.15pm.
Cuisine: The Rugantino Restaurant serves a wide range of
authentic Italian dishes including pasta, fish and meat. ⊨ 9
bedrooms, 6 en suite. All have telephones. **CC** All major cards.
Other Points: Children welcome. Dogs allowed. 60 foot frontage
onto Cathedral Green (where tea is served). Public parking. **(V)**
Directions: A37 in the centre of Wells, by Wells Cathedral.

FRANCESCO ROSSI ☎ (0749) 672029.
Uniquely situated facing the West Front of Wells Cathedral, the
building dates back to before 1473. Now a hotel, much of the
original character has been preserved whilst adding modern
comforts. The Rugantino Restaurant serves excellent Italian
cuisine in a warm and friendly atmosphere. A delightful hotel

WEST BEXINGTON

Wells continued

and restaurant combining history with excellent food and accommodation.

⊗£ **THE BULL TERRIER** Croscombe, Wells.
🏠££ **Hours:** Breakfast 8.15am - 9am, lunch 12 noon - 2pm, dinner 7pm - 9.30pm. Sunday lunch 12 noon - 1.45pm, dinner 7pm - 9pm. Closed: From 1st November to 31st March the kitchen is closed Sunday evenings and all day Mondays. **Cuisine:** Dishes include Tuna and Egg Mayonnaise, Scampi, Turkey Cordon Bleu, Spiced Brazil Nut Roast, hot Butterscotch & Walnut Fudge Cake. 🛏 3 rooms. 1 single, 1 twin and 1 double bedroom. 1 en suite. **CC** Access, Visa. **Other Points:** Garden. Children welcome for meals. Pub games such as dominoes and cribbage. Real Ales. 🅿 ♿ **(V) Directions:** On A371, in the village of Croscombe, near Wells. MR & MRS LEA ☎ (0749) 343658.
An old stone built country pub with stone flagged floors, open inglenook fireplace and an attractive garden. Reputed for its good food and value for money, The Bull Terrier has an atmosphere which is warm and inviting, to locals and holiday makers alike.

⊗££ **WORTH HOUSE HOTEL** Worth, Wells.
🏠£££ **Hours:** Breakfast 8am - 9.45am, Lunch 12 noon - 2pm, Dinner
⎣CLUB⎦ 7pm - 8.30pm (last orders 8.15pm). **Cuisine:** Bresaola and pickled quail eggs, chicken skewers and yoghurt dressing, medallions of beef with raisins and peppercorn sauce. 🛏 8 bedrooms, all en suite. **CC** Access, Visa. **Other Points:** Children welcome. Garden. Croquet lawn. Limited disabled access. Vegetarian meals on request. 🅿 **Directions:** 3 miles outside Wells on B3139, in the direction of Burnham.
NICHOLAS, PENNY AND STEPHEN POTTS ☎ (0749) 672041
A quiet, sixteenth century farmhouse standing in its own grounds, which has built a justifiable local reputation for serving good value, quality meals in relaxed surroundings.

WEMBWORTHY Devon **Map 3 B1**
⊗£ **LYMINGTON ARMS** Lama Cross, Wembworthy.
🏠££ **Hours:** Meals served 12 noon - 2pm and 6pm - 11pm (last orders 10pm). Closed: Christmas Day only. **Cuisine:** Homemade soups, pate, casseroles. Interesting variety of homemade puddings, sweets etc. 🛏 1 double room with childs bed and en suite facilities. **CC** Access, Visa. **Other Points:** Beer garden. Children welcome. Dogs allowed. Limited vegetarian choice. 🅿 ♿ **Directions:** 2 miles west Eggesford Station (A377), 2 miles east Winkleigh B3220. PAMELA & ALEC ROUD ☎ (0837) 83572.
Late Georgian country Coaching Inn midway between Exmoor and Dartmoor surrounded by panoramic views and extensive forest walks. Almost equidistant from Torrington (15 miles), S.Molton (15 miles), Crediton (15 miles) and Okehampton (13 miles). High quality, freshly cooked food at good value prices.

THE SOUTH WEST

WEST BEXINGTON Dorset **Map 3 B2**
⊗£££ **THE MANOR HOTEL** Beach Road, West Bexington, nr
🏠£££ Dorchester.

W   **Hours:** Meals 8.30am - 9am, 12 noon - 2pm and 7pm - 10pm.
🍴   **Cuisine:** Local seafood and imaginative dishes. 🛏 13 bedrooms,
all en suite. 💳 All major cards. **Other Points:** Children welcome.
No dogs. 🅿 **(V) Directions:** On the B3157 Bridport to Weymouth
coast road.
RICHARD CHILDS ☎ (0308) 897616.
17th century manor house 500 yards from Chesil Beach.
Panoramic views from most bedrooms of unspoilt Dorset
coastline. Three real ales served in character cellar bar. Log
fires. Private dining room for up to 40. Facilities for conferences,
buffets, receptions.

WEST STAFFORD Dorset **Map 3 B2**
🏠££ **LOWER LEWELL FARMHOUSE** West Stafford.
🛏 1 double and 2 twin bedrooms. 1 bathroom. Tea/coffee
making facilities in all bedrooms. **Hours:** Breakfast 7.30am -
9.30am. Closed Christmas week. 💳 None. **Other Points:** Central
heating. Children welcome. No dogs. No evening meal. Residents,
lounge. TV. Garden. 🅿 **Directions:** From the A352 (Dorchester to
Wareham), take road to West Stafford.
MRS MARIAN TOMBLIN. ☎ (0305) 267169.
Set in the midst of Thomas Hardy country, this 300 year old
farmhouse is Talbothays Dairy in Hardy's novel Tess of the
D'Urbervilles. From Dorchester take the A352 to Wareham,
then secondary road to West Stafford.

WESTON SUPER MARE Avon **Map 3 A2**
⊗£ **CARRINGTON HOTEL** 28 Knightstone Road, Weston Super
🏠££ Mare.
Hours: Breakfast 8.30am - 9.30am, lunch 11.30am - 3pm and
dinner 6pm - 9.30pm (last orders). Bar meals 11am - 9.30pm.
Cuisine: In the restaurant: steaks, grills, salads, omlettes, fish. In
the bar: homemade steak and kidney pie, cottage pie, homemade
sweets. 🛏 16 bedrooms, 6 en suite. 💳 Access. **Other Points:**
Children welcome. ♿ **(V) Directions:** On the seafront between the
Grand Pier and Marine Lake.
MR & MRS ARNAOUTI ☎ (0934) 626621.
A Victorian terraced house overlooking the beach and the pier,
with a patio to the front laid with tables and umbrellas for al
fresco dining in summer. Situated near to the Winter Gardens,

Weston Super Mare continued

and with all the facilities of a British seaside town on the doorstep.

⊗££ **THE COMMODORE HOTEL** Beach Road, Sand Bay, Kewstoke, Weston Super Mare.
Hours: Breakfast 7.30am - 9.30am (8am - 10am weekends), lunch 12 noon - 2pm and dinner 6.30pm - 9.30pm (last orders). **Cuisine:** Lounge Buffet-Carvery and a la carte restaurant with International and modern English cuisine. ⊨ 20 bedrooms, 16 en suite all with tea/coffee facilities and TVs. ₢₢ All major cards. **Other Points:** Access for disabled to restaurant. Children welcome. No pets. Banqueting and conference facilities available. ₽ **(V) Directions:** Overlooking beach in Sand Bay, 1½ miles north of Weston on Toll Rd.
JOHN STOAKES, MHCIMA, MBIM ☎ (0934) 415778.
On the seafront at Sand Bay with extensive views across the Bristol Channel and the local countryside. Good access to West Country attractions and several National Trust walks. Golfing discounts and riding can be arranged.

WEYMOUTH Dorset **Map 3 B2**
⊡££ **BEECHCROFT HOTEL** 128/9 The Esplanade, Weymouth.
⊨ 6 single, 10 double, 5 twin and 8 family bedrooms, 20 en suite. 7 bathrooms, 1 shower. TVs in all bedrooms. **Hours:** Breakfast 8.30am - 9am, dinner 6pm (last orders 4.30pm). Closed: October to March inclusive. ₢₢ Access, Visa. **Other Points:** Children welcome. Dogs by prior arrangement. Licensed. Residents' lounge. ₽
MESSRS THOMPSON, CLAYDEN & EVANS-JONES ☎ (0305) 786608.
The Beechcroft Hotel is situated in a prime seafront position, only 5 minutes level walk to the city centre and the stations.

⊗££ **MOONFLEET MANOR** Moonfleet.
⊡££££ **Hours:** Trenchards Restaurant: 12.30pm - 2pm weekdays & Sunday lunch, Dinner 7pm - 9pm. Open every day. Blue Moon Restaurant: Sunday Lunch 12.30pm - 3.30pm, Dinner 7pm - 10.30pm. Blue Moon closed: Sunday evenings and Monday. **Cuisine:** Trenchards - Carvery, buffet, Sunday Roasts, Table d'hote. Blue Moon - Bistro style restaurant in hotel cellars. Dishes include seafood pancakes. ⊨ 6 single, 16 double, 6 twin and 9 family rooms - 37 en suite. ₢₢ All major cards. **Other Points:** Children welcome. No dogs allowed. ₽ ᵬ **(V) Directions:** B3157 Bridport to Weymouth, turning towards sea at Chickerell.
JAN HEMINGWAY ☎ (0305) 786948.
A complete resort hotel set in 5 acres of countryside by the sea. Many sports facilities including indoor pool, gymnasium, 4 rink indoor Bowls Hall, 9-pin automatic skittles, 2 tennis courts, 2 squash, 2 snooker tables, childrens indoor and outdoor play areas.

⊗££ **SEA COW RESTAURANT** 7 Custom House Quay.
ᵬ **Hours:** Coffee shop 10am - 4.30pm in summer (except Sundays). Restaurant all week (except Sunday evenings in winter). Smorgasbord lunch 12 noon - 2pm (except Saturday and Sunday) and for dinner Thursday, Friday, Saturday in summer. Closed:

THE SOUTH WEST

Christmas Bank Holidays. **Cuisine**: Fresh mussels and scallops in season, fresh local lobster, skate, lemon sole. Game in season, Dorset Blue Steak. Chocolate mousse. ⊨ None. **CC** Access, Visa. **Other Points**: Children welcome. No dogs. Street parking. Vegetarian meals on request and on Sunday lunchtimes. ₺ **Directions**: On the quayside.
MR & MRS T M WOOLCOCK ☎ (0305) 783524.
With a prominent quayside position this restaurant specialies in fresh fish dishes. The Swedish style hot and cold buffet (Smorgasbord) offers a wide variety of tasty and unusual dishes which are very popular with visitors to this picturesque town.

⌂££ **SOU'WEST LODGE HOTEL** Rodwell Road, Weymouth.
⊨ 2 single, 3 double, 2 twin and 2 family bedrooms: 6 with en suite. 1 bathroom. TV and tea/coffee making facilities. **Hours**: Breakfast 7.30am - 8.30am and dinner 6pm (order by 3pm same day). Closed: 2 weeks over Christmas. **CC** None. **Other Points**: Children welcome. Pets allowed. Licensed. Residents lounge with colour TV. Patio. **P** ₺ **Directions**: Situated off harbour road to Portland, over Boot Hill.
MICHAEL & JUNE MOXHAM ☎ (0305) 783749.
An extremely pleasant, well kept hotel with first class furnishings throughout. A warm friendly atmosphere is created by Michael & June Moxham, who will endeavour to make you comfortable and can offer a cosy intimate bar to relax in at the end of the day.

⌂££ **THE CHATSWORTH** 14 The Esplanade, Weymouth.
⊨ All rooms fully en suite - 2 single, 4 double , 4 twin or trebles and 1 family bedroom. Colour TV, tea/coffee making facilities, radio, direct dial telephones and central heating in all rooms. **Hours**: Breakfast 8am - 9am, dinner 6pm - 7pm. Closed: Christmas period. **CC** Access, Visa. **Other Points**: Central heating. Children welcome. Dogs allowed. Licensed. Residents' lounge. Garden/terrace. **P** **Directions**: Situated on the Esplanade, opposite Alexandra Gardens.
MR S ROBERTS ☎ (0305) 785012.
An attractive Georgian building with excellent views over Weymouth Bay and the Sands to the front and the picturesque Harbour to the rear. The Chatsworth offers a friendly and comfortable base for short breaks and family holidays. All the amenities of an English seaside town are nearby and it is an ideal centre from which to tour Hardy's Dorset.

⌂£ **THE FRENSHAM** 70 Abbotsbury Road, Weymouth.
⊨ 10 rooms. 2 twin, 4 double and 4 family rooms. 6 en suite. Tea making facilities, colour TV, radio/intercom, hair dryer & direct dial telephone available in all rooms. **Hours**: Breakfast 7am - 10am, dinner 6pm - 8pm (last orders 7.30pm). Sunday lunch 1pm - 2pm (last orders 1.30pm). **CC** None. **Other Points**: Children welcome. Dogs allowed. Licensed. Central heating. **P** ₺ **(V)** **Directions**: On B3157.
MR & MRS CONNOLLY ☎ (0305) 786827.
A family run private hotel, situated in Weymouth - an ideal base from which to tour the West country or Central Southern England. This private hotel is decorated in good taste and the

Weymouth continued

accommodation is comfortable. There is a homely and relaxing atmosphere adding to the comfort of the establishment.

⊗£ **THE ILCHESTER ARMS HOTEL** Abbotsbury, Weymouth.
££££ **Hours:** 8am - 9am, 12 noon - 2pm, and 7pm - 9pm. Also open for Sunday lunch/dinner. **Cuisine:** Dishes include chef's roast of the day, deep fried fresh farm chicken, home-made lasagne, and grilled Cumberland Sausage Lyonaisse. 🛏 3 twin, 7 double, and 1 family room, all en suite. CC Access, Visa. **Other Points:** Children welcome. Pets allowed. Afternoon teas also served. P ♿ **(V)**
MR MOORE ☎ (0305) 871243.
An old coaching inn, with tastefully decorated rooms and a relaxed atmosphere. Serves good food at value for money. Set in a rural village, close to Swannery, tropical gardens and Chesil beach.

⊗£ **WESTERS BISTRO BAR** 6 Westerhall Road, Weymouth.
CLUB **Hours:** Lunch 12 noon - 2pm (last orders), dinner 7pm - 11.30pm (last orders). Bar meals 12 noon - 2pm and 7pm - 11.30pm. Closed 25th, 26th, 27th December and 1st January only. **Cuisine:** Large selection of daily specials plus steaks, salads, baked potatoes, chillies, burgers, ice cream specials and lots more. 🛏 None. CC Access, Visa. **Other Points:** Children welcome. No dogs. Next to St Johns Church. P ♿ **(V) Directions:** Off the A354 Dorchester - Weymouth road, which splits at 'Westers'.
MR & MRS BRIDGE ☎ (0305) 784904.
Situated on the ground and lower ground floor of this attractive building. Edwardian pictures, old treadle sewing machines and open log fires enhance the cosy, informal atmosphere and melt away those winter chills.

WHIMPLE Devon **Map 3 B1**
⊗£ **THE PADDOCK INN** London Road, Whimple.
Hours: Lunch 12 noon - 2pm, Dinner 6.30pm - 9.30pm (last orders). Bar snacks 11am - 2.30pm and 6pm - 10pm. Open Saturday afternoons during summer. **Cuisine:** Daily changing menu using predominantly fresh produce. 🛏 None. CC Access, Visa. **Other Points:** Children welcome. No dogs. Beer garden. P ♿ **(V) Directions:** Halfway between Honiton & Exeter on A30. Approx. 9 miles each way.
ROBERT PUSEY ☎ (0404) 822356.
A large, country pub offering a daily changing menu in comfortable, relaxed surroundings. The service is welcoming and efficient. Places of interest nearby include Ottery St Mary (Coleridge's birthplace), Escot Aquarium, Killerton House and the attractions of Exeter.

WINCANTON Somerset **Map 3 B2**
⊗££ **HOLBROOK HOUSE HOTEL** Holbrook, Nr Wincanton.
£££££ **Hours:** Breakfast 8.15am - 9.15am, lunch 1pm - 2pm and dinner
CLUB 7.30pm - 8.30pm (last orders). Lunch bar snacks Monday - Saturday only. Closed New Year's Eve. **Cuisine:** A la carte, table d'hote, using freshest ingredients available. 🛏 5 single, 5 twin, 6 double, 3 family, 16 en suite. CC Access, Visa. **Other Points:** Children welcome. Pets allowed. Tennis. Squash. Swimming pool. Dry ski slope. Games room. Golf, riding, fishing. Croquet. Lounge

Wincanton continued

bar. Drawing room. ▣ ﾫ **(V) Directions**: 1 and a half miles off A303 on the A371 towards Castle Cary.

MR & MRS G.E. TAYLOR ☎ (0963) 32377.

A genuine country house hotel, set in 15 acres of its own grounds in unspoilt countryside. Behind the walled garden & dovecote lie the squash and tennis court. The old orchard provides a delightful setting for the outdoor heated pool. A splendid wine list complements the interesting variety of well cooked food. A lovely hotel providing a relaxing and pleasant atmosphere.

⊗££ **HORSINGTON HOUSE HOTEL** Horsington, Templecombe, ⏠££££ Wincanton.

Hours: Breakfast 7.30am - 10am, Lunch 12.30pm - 2pm, dinner 7pm - 9.30pm (last orders). Bar meals served all day until 10pm.

Cuisine: Table d'hote and a la carte featuring the best of local produce. Afternoon teas & cream teas served in the lounge or on the lawns. ⇌ 23 bedrooms, 22 en suite. ▨ Access, Visa, AmEx.

Other Points: Children welcome. Access for disabled to restaurant only. Garden. Dogs allowed. Residents' lounge. Bar. Private functions. Fax: (0963) 70554. ▣ ﾫ **(V) Directions**: Leave A303 at Wincanton, follow signs for Templecombe. A357.

ROBIN & JUDY BELCHER ☎ (0963) 70721.

A delightful country house hotel set in 8 acres of grounds near the village of Horsington. The interior offers comfort and elegance and there is a peaceful, relaxed atmosphere. Enjoy a drink in the old music room, now the bar, with its gilt vaulted ceiling and superb chandelier. A lovely environment in which to enjoy good food, comfortable accommodation and welcoming service.

WOODY BAY Devon **Map 3 A1**

⊗£££ **WOODY BAY HOTEL** Woody Bay, Parracombe.

⏠£££ **Hours**: Meals from 8.45am - 9.30am and 7.15pm - 8.30pm (last orders). Bar meals 12 noon - 2pm. Closed: January and February.

Cuisine: Local salmon, local venison, fillet steaks, eg. tournedos belle Marie, Jamaican steak (steak cooked with banana, paprika and cream flamed in rum). ⇌ 14 bedrooms, 13 en suite. 4-poster suites available. ▨ Access, Visa. **Other Points**: Children over 8 years welcome. ▣ **(V) Directions**: Well signposted off the A39 2 miles west of Barbrook.

PRUE & LAWRIE SCOTT ☎ (05983) 264.

Wincanton (Somerset)

Woody Bay continued

Well signposted off the Barnstaple-Lynton road, with superb views over National Trust woodland and the Exmoor coastline. The trees reach right down to the rocky shore. The coast may be wild and rugged but the hotel is a haven of tranquility.

WOOLACOMBE Devon **Map 2 A2**

£££ **ATLANTIC HOTEL** Sunnyside Road, Woolacombe.

16 bedrooms, 14 en suite. Radio, colour TV, tea/coffee making facilities, intercom and baby listening in all rooms. **Hours:** Breakfast 8.30am - 9am, dinner 7pm - 7.30pm. Bar meals 12 noon - 2pm and 7pm - 10pm. Open from Easter until the end of October and at Christmas. **CC** None. **Other Points:** Children welcome. Beer garden. Dogs allowed. Afternoon tea served. Games room. Central heating throughout. Fax: (0271) 870223. **P** & **(V) Directions:** Situated in the town centre off Sandy Lane. JANE & DAVID PUGH **☎** (0271) 870469.

A large Victorian mansion, magnificently situated to give superb views over the bay. The Atlantic is a family-run· hotel which caters especially for families. The interior of the hotel is attractively furnished with many antiques. The proprietors are cordon bleu cooks and offer a six course dinner for guests to enjoy.

££ **LITTLE BEACH HOTEL** The Esplanade, Woolacombe.

10 rooms: 2 single, 1 twin and 7 double bedrooms. 8 en suite. **Hours:** Breakfast 8.30am - 9.15am, dinner 7.15pm - 8pm (last orders). Sunday dinner 7.15pm - 8pm. **CC** Access, Visa. **Other Points:** Sun lounge. Bar. Residents, drawing room and separate dining room. Antique shop. **P** **(V) Directions:** Leave M5 at junction 27 and follow Tiverton by-pass to Barnstaple. BRIAN & NOLA WELLING **☎** (0271) 870398.

An Edwardian building enjoying a high position overlooking miles of sand and rockpools. All rooms are attractively decorated to a high standard of comfort and Mrs Welling is renowned for her good quality homemade food using only the freshest produce. Frequented by people of all ages the atmosphere is happy and relaxed.

££ **WOOLACOMBE BAY HOTEL** South Street, Woolacombe.

Hours: Breakfast 8.30am - 9.30am. Bistro open from 10am - 10pm in high season. Dinner 7.30pm - 10.30pm (last orders 9.45pm). Closed: January. **Cuisine:** Table d'hote menu changes daily. 59 bedrooms, all en suite. **CC** All major cards. **Other Points:** Children welcome. Self catering flats available. **P** & **(V) Directions:** On the seafront in Woolacombe. GERALD READ - Manager **☎** (0271) 870388.

A gracious, elegant hotel surrounded by rolling hills and by 3 miles of golden sands. 7 course dinners and full English breakfast. Free unlimited use of squash/tennis courts, indoor & outdoor pools, sauna, solarium, pitch & putt, snooker, short mat bowls, gym.

YATE Avon **Map 3 A2**

£ **THE SWAN AT NIBLEY** Badminton Road, Nibley, Yate.

Hours: Open for food and drink 11am - 11pm Monday to Saturday (last orders 10pm) 12 noon - 3pm, 7pm - 10.30pm

Yate continued

Sunday. **Cuisine:** Home cooked food - steak and kidney pies, curry, lasagne, chilli, scampi, steaks, roast baby leg of lamb. None. **CC** Access, Visa. **Other Points:** No dogs. Children welcome. Children's play area. Garden. Inexpensive specials board lunchtime. Booking advisable on weekends. **P** &. **(V) Directions:** On A432 Chipping Sodbury to Bristol Rd, between Coalpit Heath & Yate

GILLIAN DANGERFIELD & TONY WILLIAMS **☎** (0454) 312290.

A traditional old country pub set in an attractive garden with a barbecue area for summer months. Popular with families, the play area has real boats for children. In winter, roaring log fires maintain the warm, friendly atmosphere - an ideal environment in which to enjoy the home cooked fare.

CHANNEL ISLANDS

ALDERNEY Channel Islands **Map 3 C2**
£££ INCHALLA HOTEL St Annes, Alderney.

4 double, 4 twin and 2 family bedrooms, all en suite. Radio, colour TV, tea/coffee facilities, fridge and direct dial phones in all rooms. **Hours:** Breakfast 8.30am - 9.30am, Sunday lunch 1pm - 2pm, dinner 7pm - 8.30pm. **CC** Access, Visa, AmEx. **Other Points:** Central heating. Children welcome. No dogs. Residents lounge. Garden. **P** &. **Directions:** At the edge of St Annes overlooking the sea.

MRS VALERIE WILLS **☎** (048 182) 3220.

A modern hotel with first class facilities, eg. sauna, jacuzzi and solarium. A pleasant and relaxing atmosphere in a hotel situated in lovely grounds overlooking the sea.

BEAUMONT Jersey **Map 3 C2**
££ BRYN-Y-MOR Route de la Haule, Beaumont.

4 family, 1 single and 9 double/twin bedrooms, 11 en suite. Reductions for children sharing parents room. Intercom, direct dial telephone & colour TV in all rooms. Baby sitting service by arrangement. **Hours:** Breakfast 8.30am - 9.30am and dinner 6.30pm - 7.30pm (last orders). Lunch on request. Tariff includes bed and breakfast and evening meal. **CC** Access, Visa, AmEx. **Other Points:** Children welcome. Open throughout the year. Residents' lounge with colour TV. Garden. Packed lunches by arrangement. Pets allowed. Fax No. (0534) 24262. **P** **(V) Directions:** Off the A1. Situated on main coast road.

MISS M F TEMPLETON **☎** (0534) 20295.

A large Georgian house, set in well tended gardens, with a magnificent view of the beautiful bay of St Aubin. The combination of friendly attentive service, blended with comfortable surroundings and a fine location. Situated just two hundred yeards from three miles of golden beach makes the 'Bryn-Y-Mor' a must for all visitors - be it business or leisure. Open throughout the year.

CASTEL Guernsey **Map 3 C2**
⊗££ **HOTEL HOUGUE DU POMMIER** Castel, Guernsey.

Hours: Breakfast 8am - 9.30am and dinner 7.45pm - 9.30pm (last orders). Table d'hote served 6.45pm - 7.30pm. **Cuisine:** Seafood specialities. Afternoon tea served. ⊨ 39 Bedrooms, all en suite. TV, radio and intercom, baby listening, direct dial phone and tea/coffee making facilities. **CC** Access, Visa, AmEx. **Other Points:** Children welcome. Fax No: (0481) 56260. Pitch and putt golf course and putting green. Solar heated swimming pool. Games room and multigym. No dogs. **P (V)**
MR M J TROUTEAUD ☎ (0481) 56531/53904
Originally a 17th century farmhouse, set in 10 acres of grounds and not far from safe, sandy beaches. Friendly staff, attractive surroundings and good food at reasonable prices have made this hotel deservedly popular.

GOREY HARBOUR Jersey **Map 3 C2**
⊗££ **LES ARCHES HOTEL** Archirondel Bay, Channel Islands.
🏨££ **Hours:** Breakfast 8.15am - 9.30am, lunch 1pm - 2pm, dinner 7.15pm - 8.45pm. **Cuisine:** Fixed price 3 course menu and bar lunch. ⊨ 54 rooms. 5 single, 27 twin, 21 double and 1 family bedroom. **CC** Access, Visa. **Other Points:** Children welcome. Dogs allowed. Garden. Swimming pool. Tennis. Mini gym. Sauna. Fax (0534) 56660. **P (V)**
MR R MARTIN ☎ (0534) 53839.
Situated on Jersey's east coast, this modern hotel building with its arched verandahs has a spectacular view of the small and tranquil Archirondel Bay, with views of the French coast 15 miles away. The restaurant prides itself on the use of locally caught fish and fresh produce and the hotel offers excellent leisure facilities.

⊗££ **MOORINGS HOTEL** Gorey Pier, Gorey.
🏨££££ **Hours:** Breakfast 8am - 9.30am. Lunch 12.15pm - 2.15pm. (last orders 2pm). Dinner 7pm - 10.15pm (last orders 10pm). **Cuisine:** Traditional English/French. Speciality locally caught fruits de mer. ⊨ 7 double rooms, 4 twin, 5 single. All en suite with TV, trouser press, hair dryer, telephone, tea-making facilities. **CC** Access, Visa, AmEx. **Other Points:** Children welcome. Disco, swimming pool nearby. Fax: (0534) 56660. **(V)**
MR R MARTIN. Manager - MR E FRANCO ☎ (0534) 53633
Huddled between Gorey Castle and the harbour, the Hotel offers outstanding views over the bay. The golden beach of Grouville Bay is but a short distance from the Hotel. Local activities include golf, waterskiing and windsurfing. The restaurant offers good value and an outstanding wine list.

ST AUBIN Jersey **Map 3 C2**
🏨££ **ST MAGLOIRE** High Street, St Aubin.
⊨ 4 twin, 4 double, 4 family bedrooms, 10 with en suite. **Hours:** Breakfast 9am and dinner 6.30pm. **CC** Access, Visa, AmEx. **Other Points:** Children welcome. Vegetarian meals available. **Directions:** On main street, overlooking the bay.
DELFIN & CAROLE CERQUEIRA ☎ (0534) 41302.
A 16th century 'olde world' guest house set in the picturesque main street of St Aubin, offering clean and bright accommodation. With wonderful views of the harbour and bay,

THE SOUTH WEST

St Aubin continued
> *'St Magloire' provides a friendly, welcoming atmosphere in relaxed comfortable surroundings.*

ST BRELADE Jersey Map 3 C2

®£££ **LA PLACE HOTEL** Route Du Coin, La Haule, St Brelade.
Hours: Breakfast 8am - 9.30am, Lunch 12.30pm - 2pm, Dinner 7pm - 9.30pm (last orders). Bar meals 11am - 5pm and 7pm - 9.30pm (last orders). **Cuisine:** Classical French cuisine with seafood specialities. Table d'hote, a la carte, Pool-side and Courtyard menus. ⊨ 40 bedrooms, all en suite. **CC** All major cards. **Other Points:** Children welcome. 2 lounges. Courtyards. Swimming pool. Alfresco dining in courtyard or by pool. Gentlemen requested to wear ties at dinner **P** **(V) Directions:** 4 miles from St Helier. At the top of La Haule Hill, St Brelade. DELRICH HOTELS LTD ☎ (0534) 44261.
Dating from 1640 and farmhouse in style, this delightful hotel has two very attractive courtyards, one with swimming pool, where meals can be enjoyed alfresco. Inside, the hotel has large fireplaces and wood beams, combining charm with top comfort. Fresh, local produce and high culinary standards are found in the award-winning restaurant. Excellent service.

ST CLEMENT Jersey Map 3 C2

⑪£££ **BELLE PLAGE HOTEL** Green Island, St Clement.
CLUB ⊨ 20 bedrooms, all en suite. Rooms with private balconies and sea views available. TV rental if required. **Hours:** Breakfast 8.30am - 9.30am and dinner 7pm - 8pm (last order 7.40pm) Closed: October to March. **CC** Access, Visa, AmEx. **Other Points:** Children welcome (over 8 years). Vegetarian meals by arrangement. Swimming Pool. Fax No. (0534) 53894. **P** **(V)**
F B HOUSE & W B YATES ☎ (0534) 53750.
A small family run hotel where personal attention is paid to guests by a friendly management and staff. A genuine seaside location. Cosy bar and lounge available for guests to relax in at the end of the day. Varied menus and a selected wine list are available in the restaurant.

ST HELIER Jersey Map 3 C2

⑪££ **GLENTHORNE** Elizabeth Place, St Helier.
⊨ 1 single, 8 double, 4 twin and 5 family bedrooms, 14 en suite. All rooms have colour TV, radio, alarm, tea/coffee making facilities and baby listening. **Hours:** Breakfast 8.30am - 9am, Dinner 6.30pm - 7pm. Bar open 5.45pm - 1am. **CC** Access, Visa, AmEx. **Other Points:** Children welcome. Dogs allowed. Afternoon teas. Residents' lounge & garden. Licensed. Packed lunches available. Bar. Safe facilities. Fax No: (0534) 58002. ᴖ
MR WAYNE RHODES ☎ (0534) 22817.
A welcoming guest house situated close to the town and beach. Glenthorne is family run and offers a friendly, homely atmosphere, good home cooking and good value for money. The proprietors are always at hand to assist guests and to ensure that your stay in Jersey is enjoyable.

⑪££ **GREENWOOD LODGE** Roseville Street, St Helier.
⊨ 35 rooms, 2 single, 23 double, 6 twin and 4 family bedrooms. 21 en suite. Tea/coffee making facilities, colour TV, radio, alarm,

Glenthorne Hotel

11 Elizabeth Place, St.Helier
Tel: 0534 22817   Fax: 0534 58002

Centrally situated facing Parade Gardens. Five minutes walk from the town and beach. Comfortable lounge and bar. Colour television in all bedrooms. Tea making facilities. Radio/Intercom. Some rooms with private facilities, all with H&C. Excellent food prepared and cooked by the proprietors.

Midweek bookings accepted. No service charge. Open all year (excluding Christmas). Bed, Breakfast & Evening Meal. For brochure and tariff please phone or write enclosing s.a.e. and unaffixed stamp

Jersey Tourist Board	Les Routiers
One Sun	Approved

THE SOUTH WEST

telephone and baby listening device. **Hours:** Breakfast 8.30am - 9.30am, dinner 6.30pm - 7.30pm (last orders). Closed: December/January. **CC** Access, Visa, AmEx. **Other Points:** Children welcome. Dogs allowed. Vegetarians catered for. Residents' lounge. Open bank holidays. **P** & **(V) Directions:** From Weighbridge, through the tunnel and take second right.
HOWARD & SUE SNOW ☎ (0534) 67073.
Situated in a quieter part of St Helier, this family run hotel is decorated to a high standard. The accommodation is bright and airy and more than comfortable. Serving quality food, specialising in seafood dishes, all of which is locally caught. Staff are helpful and friendly adding to the hotels popularity with the holiday makers.

£££ KAIETEUR GUEST HOUSE 4 Ralegh Ave, St Helier.
CLUB ⊨ 1 single, 4 double, 4 twin and 1 family room. All rooms are en suite with tea/coffee making facilities, full central heating and colour TV. **Hours:** Breakfast 7.30am - 9am, and dinner 6.30pm. Closed: Christmas and New Year. **CC** Access, Visa. **Other Points:** Children welcome. Residents' lounge. No dogs. Vegetarian & special diets catered for on request. Table licence. Eurocard accepted. Fax No: (0534) 67423. **P Directions:** Off the main St Helier ring road.
NIGEL & JOAN TANGUY ☎ (0534) 37004.
The Kaieteur is a small top grade guest house where the emphasis is on comfort and good quality freshly cooked food. No 'hidden extras' - tariff is fully inclusive. No service charge. Relaxed informal atmosphere. Ideal for a short break or a longer stay. Medal and Trophy winners 1989, 1990, 1991 Salon Culinaire (part of Jersey's Annual Good Food Festival).

£££ MILLBROOK HOUSE Rue De Trachy, St Helier.
⊨ 24 bedrooms, all en suite. Tea/coffee making facilities. Colour TV. Direct dial phones. Self-catering units available. **Hours:** Breakfast 7.30am - 9.30am and dinner 6.30pm - 8.30pm (last orders 7pm). **CC** AmEx. **Other Points:** Children welcome. Residential licence and lounge bar. Lift. Vegetarian and special diets catered for. Fax No: (0534) 24317. **P Directions:** Off the A1.
Mr G. Pirouet - G.T.P. (Jersey) Ltd ☎ (0534) 33036.
Built around 1800, the combination of Georgian and Colonial architectural features and spacious gardens and grassland, gives an atmosphere of great ease and tranquility. Situated 500 yards from the beach with stupendous views overlooking St Aubin Bay, Millbrook House is an ideal setting for an 'away from it all' restful holiday. Choice of menu and comfortable accommodation.

⊗££ MONT MILLAIS HOTEL Mont Millais, St Helier.
£££ Hours: Breakfast 8.15am - 9.30am, bar snacks 12 noon - 2pm, dinner 7pm - 9pm. Closed: January to April. **Cuisine:** Dishes may include Ravioli Maison, Roast Leg of Lamb with redcurrant jelly and mint sauce, and a selection of sweets. ⊨ 44 bedrooms, all en suite. **CC** Access, Visa. **Other Points:** Children welcome. Afternoon teas served. Fax No. (0534) 66849. Coach Tours. Dry Cleaning arrangements. Picnic Lunches by arrangement. **P** & **(V)**

St Helier continued

Directions: From Howard Davis Park approx 400 metres toward Five Oaks.

COLIN KIRKHAM ☎ (0534) 30281.

Set in own attractive terraced gardens, only 5 mins away from town centre. Decorated in light shades of welcoming colours and offering accommodation of a high standard. The restaurant enjoys a friendly atmosphere, in which you can indulge in a really good meal made even more enjoyable by the excellent service. Highly recommended.

⊗££ **THE BERKSHIRE HOTEL & LILLIE LANGTRY BAR &**
⊡££££ **REST.** La Motte Street, St Helier.

Hours: Lunch 12.30pm - 2.30pm, dinner 7pm - 9pm (Thursdays, Fridays, Saturdays only). Closed: Sunday & Saturday lunch, Monday, Tuesday & Wednesday evening. **Cuisine:** Predominantly French cuisine such as Sole au Champagne, fresh Jersey Lobster, Fillet d'Agneau a la Mode de Paris. Daily specials. ⊨ 65 bedrooms, all en suite. **CC** All major cards. **Other Points:** Garden dining - enclosed courtyard/patio. Fax No. (0534) 32986. Parking available closeby. **(V) Directions:** At top of main shopping precinct.

MICHAEL BARNES ☎ (0534) 23241.

Situtated in the business district, and near the Yacht Harbour, the main Shopping Precinct, Park and Leisure complex, this is an ideal base for touring St Helier. Offering good meals, with an emphasis on fresh seafood, and comfortable accommodation. Frequented by mixed ages the hotel enjoys a convivial atmosphere.

⊡££££ **UPLANDS HOTEL** St Johns Road, St Helier.

⊨ 43 bedrooms, all en suite and with colour TV, radio, alarm, telephone, and tea/coffee making facilities. Room service. **Hours:** Breakfast 8.30am - 9.30am, Bar snacks 12 noon - 1.30pm, Dinner 6.30pm - 7.30pm (last orders). **CC** Access, Visa. **Other Points:** Children over 5 welcome. Afternoon teas. Residents' lounge. Garden. Bar. Sun lounge. Patio. Outdoor swimming pool. ▣ **(V) Directions:** Top of Queens Rd, 1st Left turn 100 yds, hotel on the right.

MORVAN FAMILY HOTELS ☎ (0534) 73006.

A spacious and well decorated hotel with a welcoming atmosphere and a high standard of accommodation. The attractive sun-lounge opens on to a patio overlooking the swimming pool and provides an ideal place to relax. English and continental cuisine is served in the restaurant and some nights entertainment can be enjoyed in the bar in the main season. A comfortable, friendly hotel.

ST MARTINS Guernsey **Map 3 C2**

⊗£ **LA QUINTA HOTEL** Rue Maze, St Martins, Guernsey.

⊡££ **Hours:** Breakfast 8.30am - 9am, lunch 12.15pm - 1.45pm (last
[CLUB] orders) and dinner 6.30pm - 10pm (last orders). Sunday dinner 6.15pm - 6.30pm. **Cuisine:** A la carte or table d'hote - baked rainbow trout with crab and almond, selection of omlettes, Coq Au Vin. Saturday evening carvery. ⊨ 15 bedrooms, 13 en suite. 2/3 bedroom apartments available. **CC** All major cards. **Other Points:** Children welcome. Garden. Dogs allowed. Packed lunches on

St Martins continued

request. Residents lounge with TV. Garden with childrens play area. Fax: (0481) 37093. ▣ **(V) Directions:** 2 miles from St Peter Port, on route towards Guernsey Airport.
RAY & JO PEACEGOOD ☎ (0481) 37973
A large country house, set in its own grounds, situated 2 miles from St Peter's Port. Bright, comfortable accommodation, good food at reasonable prices and friendly,efficent service. Excellent location for touring the island as the hotel is on most bus routes for the island's local attractions.

⌂£££ **WINDMILL HOTEL** La Rue Poudreuse, St Martins.
⊨ 18 bedrooms, all en suite and with colour TV, radio, alarm, telephone, baby listening and tea/coffee making facilities. Half-board or B and B. **Hours:** Breakfast 8.30am - 9.30am, Bar snacks 12.30pm - 1.30pm, Dinner 6.30pm - 7.30pm. Closed: November to March. ◪ All major cards. **Other Points:** Children welcome. No-smoking area. Four lounges. Garden. Heated outdoor swimming pool. Fax No. (0481) 728340. Telex No. 4191501. ▣ **Directions:** 1 mile from St Peter Port on airport road.
ERNEST GRAHAM ☎ (0481) 35383.
A warm welcome and friendly, informal atmosphere awaits you at the Windmill, just one mile from the centre of St Peter Port. The bedrooms are of a high standard with 'all the comforts of home'. Relax in one of four lounges or by the heated outdoor swimming pool before enjoying excellent homemade cuisine.

ST OUEN Jersey **Map 3 C2**
⌂£££ **HOTEL DES PIERRES (1981) LTD** Greve de Lecq Bay, St Ouen.
⊨ 14 rooms. 1 single, 10 double and 3 family bedrooms. All en suite. Colour TV, radio and tea/coffee making facilities in all rooms. **Hours:** Breakfast 7.45am - 9.15am, dinner 7pm. ◪ Access, Visa. **Other Points:** Children welcome. Garden. Mastercard and Eurocard also accepted. Hire cars and flights can be arranged by hotel. Fax No: (0534) 85273. 3 Diamond G.H. ▣ **(V)**
MR & MRS W FLATH ☎ (0534) 81858.
A privately run guest house on a gently sloping site, a few yards from Greve de Lecq beach. Pleasantly decorated in light colours, the decor of the establishment is of a high standard, the accommodation very comfortable and well maintained. Full English breakfast and 3 course evening dinner are available for guests at very reasonable prices. Delightful setting.

ST OUEN'S BAY Jersey **Map 3 C2**
⌂£ **L'ETACQUEREL** L'Etacq, St Ouen's Bay, Jersey.
⊨ 3 single, 7 double, 2 twin and 1 family bedroom, 4 en suite. 1 bathroom, 2 showers, 2 WC. **Hours:** Breakfast from 8am - 9am, dinner 6.30pm - 7pm. Closed: October to end March. ◪ None. **Other Points:** Central heating. Licensed. Residents' lounge. TV lounge. Garden. Children over 3 years welcome. ▣ **Directions:** Follow signs to L'Etacquerel, hotel opposite Lobster Pot Restaurant.
MRS MAUREEN ASHWORTH - Manageress ☎ (0534) 82492.
Small country hotel with glorious sea views and a German bunker in the grounds. Every comfort is provided including

St Ouen's Bay continued

teamakers, hairdryers, clock/radios and ironing facilities. *20 minutes' drive from St Helier overlooking a long, sweeping sandy beach.*

⊗££ **THE LOBSTER POT HOTEL & RESTAURANT** L'Etacq, St Ouens.

Hours: Breakfast 8am - 9.15am, lunch 12.30pm - 2.15pm, dinner 7.30pm - 12.30am (last orders 10.15pm). Bar meals 10.30am - 6pm. **Cuisine:** Lobster, shellfish, fish, steaks and veal dishes. ⊨ 13 bedrooms, all en suite. TV with video film channel, tea/coffee making facilities, refrigerators and direct dial telephones in all rooms. **CC** All major cards. **Other Points:** Children welcome. Afternoon tea served on request. Dining al fresco. No dogs. **P** &
(V)
GERALD HOWE ☎ (0534) 82888.

A 17th century French style granite farmhouse enjoying sweeping panoramic views of the Atlantic ocean. The restaurant is internationally famous for its cuisine and offers a mouth watering selection of seafood. The seafaring name of the restaurant is reflected in the decor and the walls are festooned with Lobster Pots. Excellent food in a friendly and comfortable atmosphere.

ST PETER PORT Guernsey **Map 3 C2**

⊗£££ **LE NAUTIQUE RESTAURANT** Quay Steps, St Peter Port.
Hours: Lunch served 12 noon, dinner 7pm. Closed: Sundays and first 2 weeks in January. Open Bank Holidays. **Cuisine:** Fish dishes a speciality. Dishes may include - Huitres de Sur Epinars au Currie, Turbot Grille Poche-Sauce Hollandaise. ⊨ None. **CC** All major cards. **Other Points:** Private dining room for parties of 8 - 30 people. **(V) Directions:** On seafront overlooking St Peter Port Yacht Marina.
CARLO GRAZIANI ☎ (0481) 721714.

Black oak beams and whitewashed walls, adorned with various fishing items all add up to create a nautical ambience. Meals of the highest quality are served by friendly, efficient staff. Frequented by business people and locals alike, Le Nautique has its fair share of regulars - a tribute to the consistenly good food and service. Established for 30 yrs, 15 under Mr Graziani.

⊞££ **MARINE HOTEL** Well Road, St Peter Port, Guernsey.
⊨ 11 bedrooms, all en suite. Optional TV, hairdryer available. Tea/coffee making facilities in all rooms. Most rooms with sea view. **Hours:** Full English breakfast 8am - 8.45am. **CC** None. **Other Points:** Children welcome. Non-smoking area. Vegetarian meals available. Packed lunches by request. **P (V) Directions:** 30 yards from sea front and new marina. Off Glategny Esplanade.
MR & MRS CLEGG ☎ (0481) 724978.

A comfortable town hotel enjoying a delightful view of the harbour and islands. Guests can relax on the attractive sun patio overlooking the sea. There are many good restaurants offering reasonably priced meals within walking distance of the hotel and the picturesque shopping centre is close by.

THE SOUTH WEST

ST SAMPSONS Guernsey **Map 3 C2**

££ **ANN-DAWN PRIVATE HOTEL** Route Des Capelles, St Sampson's.

14 rooms. 3 single, 1 twin and 10 double rooms. 12 en suite. Colour TV, radio and tea/coffee making facilities in most rooms. Central heating. **Hours:** Breakfast 8.30am - 8.45am, dinner 6.30pm - 8pm. **CC** Access, Visa. **Other Points:** Garden. No smoking area. Licensed. Vegetarian dishes by request. Packed lunches available on request. **P** **(V) Directions:** One and a half miles from the town centre towards St Sampsons.
LINDA & ROD LOVERIDGE ☎ (0481) 725606.
A Georgian style house in own well kept grounds, attractively decorated and comfortably furnished. Well prepared, generous portions of good food are served. With a mixed age of clientele the atmosphere is friendly and warm. The accommodation is comfortable and cosy.

TORTEVAL Guernsey **Map 3 C2**

££ **IMPERIAL HOTEL, BARS & RESTAURANT** Pleinmont,
££££ Torteval, Guernsey, Channel Islands.

Hours: Breakfast 8.15am - 9.15am, Lunch 12 noon - 1.30pm, Dinner 6.30pm - 9pm (last orders, 9.30pm during summer). Bar snacks 12 noon - 2pm and 7pm - 9pm. Restaurant closed: Sunday evenings, Hotel closed: Nov - March. Bar meals all year round. **Cuisine:** Traditional French haute cuisine with seafood specialities. A la carte, table d'hote and bar menus. 16 bedrooms, 14 en suite. **CC** Access, Visa. **Other Points:** Children welcome. **P** **Directions:** South western tip of the island, overlooking Rocquaine bay.
PATRICK & DIANA LINDLEY ☎ (0481) 64044/64103.
The Imperial has proved a popular rendezvous with tourists and locals alike for over 100 years, with its unequalled views of the west coast and safe, sandy beaches. The cuisine too is excellent with seafood specialities and shellfish fresh from the bay. The main restaurant offers superb cuisine for that special candle-lit dinner with fine wines and friendly service.

TRINITY Jersey **Map 3 C2**

£££ **COTE DU NORD HOTEL** Cote Du Nord, Trinity, Jersey.
££ **Hours:** Breakfast 8am - 9.30am, Lunch 12 noon - 2pm and Dinner 7pm - 10pm (last orders). Restaurant closed: Sun eves & Mons - October to March only. **Cuisine:** A la carte, Table d'hote and Bar menus. French cuisine - seafood a speciality. 12 bedrooms, all en suite. **CC** All major cards. **Other Points:** Children welcome. Afternoon teas. Fax No. (0534) 65119. **P** **(V) Directions:** Off the C93, on left towards Rozel.
MR HODSON ☎ (0534) 61171.
Standing in its own grounds on the north east coast, the Cote Du Nord has a spectacular view of the sea and surrounding country, and is within walking distance of the harbour and village of Rozel. The restaurant is known locally for the high standard of cuisine and service it offers.

VAZON BAY Guernsey **Map 3 C2**

⊗££ **LA GRANDE MARE** Vazon Bay, Guernsey, Channel Islands. **Hours:** Lunch 12.30pm - 2pm, dinner 7pm - 9.45pm (last orders). CLUB Bar meals 12 pm - 2pm. **Cuisine:** Fresh seafood, shellfish and a variety of European dishes. 36 bedrooms, all en suite. All major cards. **Other Points:** Children welcome. Non-smoking area. No dogs. Terrace for dining al fresco. Swimming pool. Fax No. (0481) 56532. **(V) Directions:** Fronts directly on to the Vazon Bay. 15 minutes from St Peter Port.

MR P M VERMEULEN ☎ (0481) 56576.

La Grande Mare, situated in its own grounds of over 100 acres, enjoys delightful views over the Atlantic Ocean. Friendly, caring and efficient service compliments the high quality food on offer at this hotel and timeshare restort. The restaurant specialises in seafood, shellfish and many European dishes. Casserole award winner 1990.

CENTRAL AND
SOUTHERN
ENGLAND

CENTRAL AND SOUTHERN ENGLAND

The South's coastline is highly popular with holiday-makers and business people alike. With a wealth of sheltered beaches, harbours and bays, and the variety of accommodation available – from luxury hotels to cosy guest houses – the coastline has something to offer everyone.

One of the best ways to appreciate the scenery is to take a walk along some of the coastal footpaths or to become part of the coastal scene yourself and try some of the many watersports available. Only a short ferry trip away lies the Isle of Wight. Blessed with safe sandy beaches and little seaside resorts, it is an ideal location for family holidays and is a paradise for those who love wind-surfing and sailing.

Back on the mainland, visit the historic maritime cities of Southampton and Portsmouth, their museums telling the story of the coast's important role in defence and seafaring. Portsmouth is home to the Royal Navy and Southampton, with its superb harbour, is an important container port.

Hampshire and East Dorset formed part of the ancient Saxon kingdom of Wessex. Winchester, Hampshire's cathedral city, was King Alfred's capital and the early Norman kings held court here. It also has strong links with the legend of King Arthur and holds the remains of the 'round table'. In the south-west of Hampshire lies the beautiful New Forest, which dates back 1,000 years. It was an ancient royal hunting preserve, originally enclosed by William the Conqueror. Today, it is a paradise at any time of the year, with its free-roaming ponies and deer. When trekking the forest, be careful to keep note of your direction as the woods can become very dense. Also, investigate the little villages located around the area, with their craft shops – and the temptation of the local cream teas are well worth giving in to.

Hampshire's rivers are famous for their salmon and trout fishing and anglers will find the rivers Test and Itchen a sheer delight. Alternatively, if your preference is for seafood – whether catching or eating it – make sure a trip to Poole harbour is on your list of things to do. Out of historical interest, travel by way of Corfe village. The castle was laid in ruins by Cromwell's men in 1645, but it is still a breath-taking sight, situated on a steep hill overlooking the countryside.

Over in East Sussex and Kent, English seaside resorts thrive alongside ancient villages and country towns. It was the Battle of Hastings that changed the course of English history and Norman castles still remain today as a reminder of the event. Similarly, Canterbury attracts visitors with its blend of medieval atmosphere and modern attractions. Famed as a great religious centre, Canterbury has drawn pilgrims throughout the ages and is, of course, the subject of Chaucer's 'Canterbury Tales'.

The county of Warwickshire is in the heart of England and it seems fitting that Shakespeare hails from these parts as his literature stands at the centre of England's cultural heritage. Stratford-upon-Avon still draws visitors from every nation, fascinated by Shakespeare's house, the Tudor architecture and the Swan Theatre. Nearby Hertfordshire and Buckinghamshire also have a wealth of historic houses and the ancient Chiltern beechwoods are a major attraction.

If rural England has particular appeal, discover the peaceful beauty of Wiltshire and the nearby Cotswolds. There are great expanses of cornfields on the uplands of Salisbury Plain and the cathedral dominates the skyline, its spire being the tallest in Britain. Alternatively, visit the eerie Druid circle of Stonehenge or the classic 'Augustan' landscaped gardens at Stourhead. In the Cotswolds, you will find the famous honey-coloured limestone villages set in gentle English countryside. The area is also renowned for its busy antique trade and excellent country inns, which still sell 'real ale'.

For architectural splendour, tour the universities of Oxford and Cambridge, where visitors can go into the college courtyards and chapels. In the summer, one of the best ways to relax and enjoy the scenery is to go punting up the river, taking with you, of course, a punnet of the local strawberries. If a relaxing trip up the river sounds particularly enticing, then the Norfolk Broads is the place to be. Boatyards offer the opportunity of exploring the Broads in a boat hired for the day and there are numerous riverside pubs providing refreshment.

Central and Southern England has a wealth of local crafts and a legacy of historical splendour which is sure to delight visitors far and wide. It is also an area rich in restaurants and pubs of all descriptions and, of course, wherever you are in this part of the country, the bustling capital of London is never far away.

QUICK REFERENCE GUIDE

CENTRAL AND SOUTHERN ENGLAND

	NO. OF ESTS.	⊗ £	⊗ ££	⊗ £££	⊗ ££££	⊞ £	⊞ ££	⊞ £££	⊞ ££££
MAP 4 A1									
Armitage	1			★					
Birmingham	8	★	★				★	★	★
Brownhills	1	★							
Burton upon Trent	1	★							
Henley in Arden	1		★						
Kenilworth	1	★							
Leamington Spa	3	★					★		
Lichfield	1		★				★		
Rugeley	1		★						
Solihull	1		★				★		
Stafford	3			★					★
Stratford upon Avon	12	★	★			★	★	★	
Sutton Coldfield	2		★				★		
Upper Gornal	1		★						
Walsall	2			★			★		
Warwick	2		★				★		
Willenhall	1		★						
Wolverhampton	2	★	★						★
Wootton Wawen	1	★							
MAP 4 A2									
Ashby de la Zouch	2		★	★					
Belton	1	★							
Belton in Rutland	1			★					
Bubbenhall	1	★							
Burton on the Wolds	1	★							
Castle Donington	2		★				★		
Colston Bassett	1		★						
Coventry	4		★					★	
Desford	1		★						
Hoton	1		★						
Leicester	10	★	★	★				★	★
Loughborough	2	★	★					★	
Lyddington	1		★						
Market Harborough	2	★		★			★		
Melton Mowbray	2		★				★		
Northampton	1			★					★
Oakham	2		★					★	
Old Dalby	1		★						
Oundle	2		★		★				
Rothley	1		★						
Sileby	1		★						
Stamford	1			★			★		
Upper Benefield	1		★						
Weedon	1	★							
Welford	1	★							
Wellingborough	2		★					★	
Wymondham	1	★							
MAP 4 B1									
Alderminster	1		★						
Ampney Crucis	1		★						★
Asthall	1		★						
Bourton on Water	3	★	★						★
Bradford on Avon	1			★					
Brinkworth	1		★						

QUICK REFERENCE GUIDE

	NO. OF ESTS.	⊗ £	⊗ ££	⊗ £££	⊗ ££££	🛏 £	🛏 ££	🛏 £££	🛏 ££££
Burbage	1		★						
Burford	2		★						
Cheltenham	8	★	★				★	★	
Chipping Norton	1	★							
Cirencester	3	★	★				★	★	★
Corsham	2			★				★	
Cricklade	1			★					
Devizes	2	★	★						
Fairford	1		★						
Foss Cross	1	★							
Great Rissington	1		★					★	
Langford	1	★							
Leafield	1		★						
Limpley Stoke	1			★					
Little Compton	1	★					★		
Little Washbourne	1		★						
Malmesbury	1						★		
Marlborough	1		★				★		
Melksham	2		★					★	
Moreton in Marsh	1						★		
Nympsfield	1	★					★		
Sherston	1	★							
Shipton on Stour	1		★				★		
Shipton under Wychwood	1		★						★
Stow on the Wold	5	★	★	★				★	★
Stroud	1		★					★	
Swindon	1		★						
Tetbury	1		★						★
Trowbridge	2		★				★	★	
Witney	1		★						
MAP 4 B2									
Abingdon	1		★						
Banbury	4		★				★	★	★
Beaconsfield	2	★	★						
Bedford	3			★				★	
Bracknell	1		★						
Charlbury	1			★					★
Didcot	1	★							
Dorchester on Thames	1				★				
Flamstead	1	★							
Goring on Thames	1		★					★	
Great Missenden	1	★							
Hampton Court	1			★					
Harrow	6		★	★				★	★
Hayes	1	★							
Henley on Thames	5	★	★					★	
High Wycombe	1	★					★		
Leighton Buzzard	1			★					
Little Milton	1	★							
Loughton	1	★							
Luton	1			★				★	
Maidenhead	3		★		★				
Marlow	1	★							
Milton Keynes	2		★					★	
Oxford	6		★	★			★	★	
Pinner	1		★						
Reading	5		★	★				★	★
Ridgmont	2	★			★				
Ruislip	1	★							

147

	NO. OF ESTS.	⊗ £	⊗ ££	⊗ £££	⊗ ££££	🛏 £	🛏 ££	🛏 £££	🛏 ££££
Souldern	1		★						
Streatley on Thames	1				★				
Teddington	1			★					
Thame	1		★					★	
Thames Ditton	1	★							
Watlington	1		★						
West Ilsley	1	★							
West Wycombe	1	★						★	
Westoning	1		★						
Windsor	1		★						
Wokingham	3		★	★	★				★
Woodstock	1					★			

MAP 4 C1

	NO. OF ESTS.	⊗ £	⊗ ££	⊗ £££	⊗ ££££	🛏 £	🛏 ££	🛏 £££	🛏 ££££
Amesbury	1			★					
Andover	3	★	★			★			
Blandford Forum	1		★						
Bournemouth	16	★	★	★		★	★	★	★
Brockenhurst	1		★						★
Burcombe	1	★							
Burley	1		★						
Christchurch	4		★	★		★	★	★	
Crockerton	1		★						
Gillingham	1	★							
Linwood	1	★							
Longham	1	★							
Lulworth	1						★		
Lulworth Cove	1	★					★		
Lymington	1						★		
Lyndhurst	2		★				★		
Marnhull	1	★					★		
Poole	5		★	★	★			★	
Ringwood	1		★						★
Romsey	2	★	★						
Salisbury	8	★	★				★	★	
Shaftesbury	2		★				★	★	
Stockbridge	2	★	★				★		
Studland	1			★					
Swanage	2		★					★	
Totland Bay	1							★	
Upavon	1		★				★		
Warminster	2	★	★				★	★	
West Lulworth	1		★						
Wimborne	2	★							

MAP 4 C2

	NO. OF ESTS.	⊗ £	⊗ ££	⊗ £££	⊗ ££££	🛏 £	🛏 ££	🛏 £££	🛏 ££££
Alton	1	★					★		
Arundel	1		★						★
Basingstoke	4	★	★	★					★
Baynards	1	★					★		
Bembridge	1	★							
Bognor Regis	2	★	★						
Chale	1		★						
Chichester	5	★	★				★		
Churt	2			★					★
Cranleigh	2		★						
Emsworth	1						★		
Fareham	2		★				★		
Farnham	2	★	★						
Fleet	1		★						★

QUICK REFERENCE GUIDE

	NO. OF ESTS.	⊗ £	⊗ ££	⊗ £££	⊗ ££££	⌂ £	⌂ ££	⌂ £££	⌂ ££££
Godshill	1		★						
Gosport	2		★	★				★	★
Guildford	2	★							
Hannington	1		★						
Haslemere	2	★		★					
Hayling Island	1		★					★	
Headley	1	★							
Horsham	1		★						
Knaphill	1		★						
Lancing	2		★	★				★	
Lavant	1	★							
Midhurst	1				★				
Odiham	1			★					
Petersfield	1		★						
Portsmouth	1		★						
Ripley	1				★				
Rotherwick	1				★				
Sandown	2	★					★		
Seaview	1		★						
Shanklin	3	★					★	★	★
Southampton	4	★	★			★			★
Southsea	2				★	★			
St Helens	1		★						
Steep	1	★							
Trotton	1	★							
Ventnor	2		★				★	★	
Walton on Thames	1		★						
West Marden	1		★						
Winchester	2	★		★					★
Worthing	7		★			★	★	★	★

MAP 5 A1

	NO. OF ESTS.	⊗ £	⊗ ££	⊗ £££	⊗ ££££	⌂ £	⌂ ££	⌂ £££	⌂ ££££
Bourne	1		★					★	
Brancaster Staithe	1		★						
Bury St Edmunds	5	★	★					★	
Castle Acre	1	★							
Cottenham	1		★						
Ely	1		★					★	
Gedney Dyke	1		★						
Great Bircham	1		★					★	
Hunstanton	1		★					★	
Huntingdon	1		★					★	
Kings Lynn	3	★	★				★	★	★
Peterborough	3	★	★	★				★	★
Snettisham	1	★					★		
Spalding	1	★						★	
St Ives	2		★					★	★
Thetford	1		★				★		
Wisbech	1	★					★		

MAP 5 A2

	NO. OF ESTS.	⊗ £	⊗ ££	⊗ £££	⊗ ££££	⌂ £	⌂ ££	⌂ £££	⌂ ££££
Blakeney	1	★							
Briston	1		★		★				
Cromer	2		★	★				★	★
Dereham	1	★							
Gorleston on Sea	2		★					★	
Great Yarmouth	3	★	★					★	
Happisburgh	1		★				★		
Hunstanton	1			★		★			
Norwich	2		★					★	

QUICK REFERENCE GUIDE

	NO. OF ESTS.	⊗ £	⊗ ££	⊗ £££	⊗ ££££	⊞ £	⊞ ££	⊞ £££	⊞ ££££
Reedham	1		★						
Rollesby	1						★		
Sheringham	1		★						
Southwold	1	★						★	
Stalham	1		★				★		
Walberswick	1	★							
Wells next the Sea	2		★			★		★	
Wolterton	1	★					★		
Wrentham	1			★					
MAP 5 B1									
Baldock	1		★					★	
Bartlow	1		★						
Biggleswade	1			★					
Billericay	1			★					
Bishops Stortford	1			★					
Braintree	1		★						
Bromley	2	★	★						
Buntingford	1		★						
Cambridge	5		★			★	★	★	
Chelmsford	5	★	★	★					★
Clare	2	★	★				★	★	
Halstead	1		★					★	
Henlow	1	★							
Kew	1	★							
Leigh on Sea	1			★			★		
Linton	1		★						
Orsett	1		★						
Puckeridge	1	★							
Richmond	3	★	★	★					
Rickling Green	1		★					★	
Romford	1	★							
Royston	1	★							
Southend	3		★						★
Southend on Sea	1					★			
St Albans	1							★	
Stevenage	1		★						
Sudbury	1	★							
Ware	1			★					
Watton at Stone	1	★							
Westcliff on Sea	1		★						
MAP 5 B2									
Aldeburgh	2		★						
Bildeston	1	★					★		
Colchester	3	★	★						★
Eyke	1			★					
Felixstowe	3	★	★					★	★
Harwich	3	★	★				★	★	
Haughley	1			★					
Kersey	1			★					
Lavenham	3		★	★				★	
Orford	1		★					★	
Saxmundham	1	★					★		
Shoeburyness	1		★						
Woodbridge	2	★	★						
MAP 5 C1									
Alfriston	2	★							
Battle	1			★					★

150

QUICK REFERENCE GUIDE

	NO. OF ESTS.	⊗ £	⊗ ££	⊗ £££	⊗ ££££	🛏 £	🛏 ££	🛏 £££	🛏 ££££
Bethersden	1		★						
Bexhill on Sea	1	★						★	
Bletchingley	1		★						★
Boughton Monchelsea	1								★
Brighton & Hove	21	★	★	★		★	★	★	★
Chiddingstone	1		★						
Crowborough	1		★						
Croydon	2		★						★
Cuckfield	1			★				★	
Ditchling	1		★				★		
Eastbourne	3	★	★					★	
Epsom	1		★					★	
Fairlight	1		★						
Hastings	1		★						
Haywards Heath	3	★	★					★	
Henfield	1			★					★
Herstmonceux	1			★					★
Hurstpierpoint	1		★						
Kenley	1	★							
Lewes	2		★						
Limpsfield	1			★					
Maidstone	1		★						
Newhaven	1	★							
Pluckley	1		★				★		
Redhill	1	★							
Reigate	1			★					
Rye	5		★				★	★	
Salehurst	1		★						
Sevenoaks	2	★		★				★	
Sittingbourne	1		★						
St Leonards on Sea	1			★					
Steyning	2		★					★	
Sutton	3		★	★				★	★
Teynham	1		★						
Tonbridge	2		★	★			★	★	
Tunbridge Wells	4		★	★					★
Uckfield	2		★		★			★	
Wadhurst	3	★	★						
Westerham	1			★					
Winchelsea	1		★				★		
MAP 5 C2									
Birchington	1		★						
Broadstairs	1		★						
Canterbury	3	★	★				★	★	
Dover	2		★			★		★	
Ickham	1			★					
Margate	4	★	★				★	★	
Ramsgate	1		★				★		
Selling	1	★							
Whitstable	1		★						

CENTRAL & SOUTHERN ENGLAND

ABINGDON Oxfordshire **Map 4 B2**
⊗££ **THE ABINGDON LODGE HOTEL** Marcham Road, Abingdon.
Hours: Breakfast 7am - 9.30am, lunch 12 noon - 2pm and dinner 7pm - 10pm (last orders. Sunday 9.30pm last orders). Bar meals 12 noon - 2pm and 6pm - 10pm. **Cuisine:** All meals prepared with fresh produce. Carvery every lunchtime and Friday & Saturday evenings. Full a la carte menu every evening. ⊨ 63 bedrooms, all en suite. **CC** All major cards. **Other Points:** Children welcome. No pets. Afternoon tea served. **P** & **(V) Directions:** At the junction of the A34 and A415.
JOHN OLDMAN ☎ (0235) 553456.
A distinctive, octagon shaped, modern hotel opened in 1986. At the heart of the hotel, overlooking the pergola patio is the Octagon restaurant and bar attractively designed in conservatory fashion with trestle ceilings and hanging ivy. Close to Oxford and the Cotswolds.

ALDEBURGH Suffolk **Map 5 B2**
⊗££ **REGATTA RESTAURANT** 171 High Street, Aldeburgh.
Hours: Lunch 12 noon - 2.30pm, dinner 6.30pm - 10.15pm. Sunday lunch 12.30pm - 2.15pm, Sunday dinner 7pm - 10.15pm. **Cuisine:** Full a la carte menu, bar snacks/meals. Specialities: local game and fish. ⊨ None. **CC** Access, Visa. **Other Points:** Garden. & **(V) Directions:** West of A12.
MR PETER HILL & MS SARA FOX ☎ (0728) 452011.
The 'Regatta' is situated on Aldburgh's high street. Decorated in a continental style and comfortably furnished, the Regatta offers excellent meals with a strong concentration on the freshest of local game and fish. The menu changes each day and with an atmosphere which is cheerful and bright, it is frequented by a mixed age group.

⊗££ **WENTWORTH HOTEL** Wentworth Road, Aldeburgh.
Hours: Meals from 8am - 9.30am, 12.30pm - 2pm and 7.30pm - 9pm (last orders). Bar lunches 12 noon - 2pm. **Cuisine:** Fresh Aldeburgh dressed crab, roasts. ⊨ 33 bedrooms, 23 en suite. **CC** AmEx, Diners. **Other Points:** Children welcome. **P** **(V) Directions:** On the seafront.
MICHAEL PRITT ☎ (072 885) 2312
A country house hotel on the beach which has been owned by the Pritts since 1920. The character is set by the elegant furnishings, antiques and log fires.

ALDERMINSTER Warwickshire **Map 4 B1**
⊗££ **THE BELL BISTRO** Alderminster.
Hours: Lunch 12 noon - 2.30pm (last orders 2pm), Dinner 7pm - 11.00pm (last orders 10pm). On Sundays open 12 noon - 2.30pm (last orders 1.45pm) and 7pm - 10.30pm (last orders 9pm). **Cuisine:** Menu written on blackboards - changes daily. Fresh fish a speciality. Slimmers & Vegetarian dishes always available. All freshly prepared. ⊨ None. **CC** Access, Visa. **Other Points:** Children welcome. Special priced quick 2 course luncheon weekdays. Fully equipped room for meetings & conferences (up to 20). Fax: (0789) 450998. **P** & **(V) Directions:** On the A3400, 4 miles south of Stratford upon Avon.
KEITH & VANESSA BREWER ☎ (0789) 450414.

Alderminster continued

Standing on the A3400, the Bell is an old Coaching Inn with flag stones, beams and fireplaces. All food is freshly prepared and cooked on the premises and because of the use of fresh produce, the menu changes daily. Traditional, predominantly English cuisine is imaginatively cooked. A friendly atmosphere prevails.

ALFRISTON East Sussex **Map 5 C1**
⊗£ **DRUSILLAS PARK** Alfriston.
Hours: Morning coffee from 10am. Full lunch menu and cream teas fron noom - 6pm. Open all year. Not open evenings. **Cuisine:** Family menu in 'Toucans' Restaurant. International pub food in 'Inn at the zoo'. ⊨ None. **CC** Access, Visa, AmEx. **Other Points:** Children welcome. Zoo, railway, playland, and 8 country style shops in award winning gardens. Pre-booked parties welcome. **P** ఈ **(V) Directions:** Off the A27 between Lewes and Polegate.
MICHAEL ANN ☎ (0323) 870656.
The attractive Toucan's thatched restaurant forms part of a leisure park which includes a zoo - known as the best small zoo in the south. Set in large well kept grounds it was established in 1924 and is still a family run business. Toucans was Egon Ronay's Family Restaurant of the Year 1991. Toy boxes & Sunday lunchtime entertainment.

⊗£ **LITLINGTON GARDENS** Litlington, Nr Alfriston.
Hours: Lunch and bar snacks 11am - 5.30pm (last orders) 7 days a week. Closed: November to March. **Cuisine:** Morning coffee. Licensed, Garden lunches, snacks, light & gourmet lunches. Traditional English Cream Teas with homemade cakes, and light refreshments. ⊨ None. **CC** None. **Other Points:** Children welcome. Open Bank Holidays. No smoking area. Afternoon teas. Dogs allowed on lead. Garden dining. Ecole de Cuisine Francaise. **P** ఈ **(V) Directions:** Between Alfriston & Seaford. 5 minutes drive from Alfriston.
CHRISTOPHE BUEY/LAINMOSS LIMITED ☎ (0323) 870222.
Set in a charming, unspoiled corner of Sussex, the Victorian Gardens and traditional cream teas were established over 150 years ago. Relax and enjoy good food surrounded by a colourful array of plants and flowers. At the weekend, the Gourmet Lunches prepared by Chef Christophe Buey and some of his students, are quite outstanding (Reservations only). A welcoming, unique establishment.

ALTON Hampshire **Map 4 C2**
⊗£ **THE WHITE HART** Holybourne, Alton.
⌂£££ **Hours:** Breakfast 7.30am - 10am, Lunch 12 noon - 3pm, Dinner 6pm - 10pm (7pm - 10pm Sundays). **Cuisine:** Dishes include Moussaka, Chilli con Carne, Grilled Rainbow Trout, Chicken Kiev, homemade Steak & Kidney Pie and a choice of prime Scotch beef steaks. ⊨ 4 bedrooms. **CC** Access, Visa. **Other Points:** Children welcome. Garden with play equipment for children. **P** ఈ **(V) Directions:** Just off the A31 on the A339 1 mile from Alton.
MERLIN INNS LTD ☎ (0420) 87654.
The White Hart is situated in the village of Holybourne, only a few hundred yards from the main A31 Guildford to Winchester road. A traditional public house boasting an A la Carte

Alton continued

restaurant, a garden with play equipment for children and letting rooms. The food is home cooked and attractively presented. A cheerful atmosphere prevails.

AMESBURY Wiltshire **Map 4 C1**

⊗£££ **THE ANTROBUS ARMS HOTEL** 15 Church Street, Amesbury.

Hours: Breakfast 8am - 9.30am, lunch 12 noon - 2pm, dinner 7pm - 10pm, bar snacks 12 noon - 2pm, 7pm - 10pm. **Cuisine:** Serving bar snacks, full a la carte menu and table d'hote. ⊨ 20 bedrooms, 14 en suite. **CC** All major cards. **Other Points:** Children welcome. Afternoon teas. Dogs allowed. Garden dining. **P** **(V) Directions:** 7 miles N of Salisbury A345. Off the A303, 11 miles W of Andover. PATRICA BARBRA STAMMERS ☎ (0980) 623163.

Situated on a quiet thoroughfare, the Antrobus Arms Hotel is decorated with old horse prints and coaching inn bricabrac. Good food and comfortable accommodation. The walled garden has a Victorian two tier fountain in the centre. Amesbury is only 2 miles from Stonehenge.

AMPNEY CRUCIS Gloucestershire **Map 4 B1**

⊗££ **THE CROWN OF CRUCIS HOTEL & RESTAURANT**

⊡£££ Ampney Crucis, nr Cirencester.

Hours: Restaurant open 12 noon - 2.30pm and 7pm - 10pm, seven days a week. **Cuisine:** Daily specials, homemade desserts, traditional English cooking including award winning steak and kidney pies. ⊨ 18 twin, 8 double, and 2 family rooms, all en suite. **CC** Access, Visa, AmEx. **Other Points:** Children welcome. Riverside garden. **P** & **(V) Directions:** On the A417 between Cirencester and Fairford.

MR R K MILLS ☎ (0285) 851806.

A well patronised and pleasant hotel and restaurant with good home cooking. On fine days the tables beside the stream are very popular with families. Facilities for private parties of up to 100 people.

ANDOVER Hampshire **Map 4 C1**

⊗£ **AMBERLEY HOTEL** 70 Weyhill Road.

Hours: Breakfast 7.30am - 9am, dinner 6.45pm - 9.15pm. Closed: 23rd December until 4th January. **Cuisine:** Lemon sole fillets in a creamy prawn, mushroom and wine sauce, lamb chops Reforme. ⊨ 17 bedrooms, 9 en suite. **CC** All major cards. **Other Points:** Children welcome. **P** **(V) Directions:** On the A343. KARL R GRIGGS ☎ (0264) 352224.

Comfortably furnished hotel with many amenities. Good centre for exploring places of interest including Stonehenge, the Cathedral cities of Winchester and Salisbury, the New Forest and Thruxton race track. Close to Southampton.

⊗£ **THE COPPER KETTLE** Shaws Walk, High Street, Andover.

Hours: Meals served all day from 8am - 5.30pm. Closed: Bank Holidays only. **Cuisine:** Wide choice of meals such as English breakfasts, filled jacket potatoes, burgers, pasta dishes, salads and afternoon cream teas. ⊨ None. **CC** Access, Visa. **Other Points:** Children welcome. No smoking area. Breakfasts, Brunch &

Andover continued

afternoon teas. Patio dining. Licensed. & **(V) Directions**: A303. Adjacent to Woolworths on the High Street.
JOHN & LYN GILL ☎ (0264) 351175.

Open for meals all day, the Copper Kettle offers a wide range of dishes to suit all tastes and times of day. The food is freshly prepared and served in generous portions. With its good food, welcoming service, a relaxed, friendly atmosphere and very reasonable prices, The Copper Kettle is very popular.

⊗££ **THE CROSS KEYS INN** Upper Chute, Chute Standen, ⏇£ Andover.

Hours: Lunch 11am - 3.30pm, dinner 7pm - midnight. Sunday lunch 12pm - 3.30pm. **Cuisine:** French/English cuisine. Game a speciality - local pheasant, local venison. Also Boeuf Stroganoff, Lobster Thermidor, Scampi Indiana. Good homemde puddings. ⊨ 2 rooms. 1 single and 1 double with en suite. ⓒⓒ Access, Visa. **Other Points:** Children welcome. Garden with play area. Dogs allowed. Hacking, fishing, walking, cycling and bird watching all nearby. 'Camra'. ▣ & **(V) Directions:** Off A34, follow signs for Chute, Upper Chute.
SIDNEY CORNISH ☎ (0264) 70295.

Outstanding views from this 16th century hilltop village free house attract many locals and foreign travelers alike. A delightful stop whether dining indoors in winter or in the garden during the summer.

ARMITAGE Staffordshire **Map 4 A1**

⊗£££ **THE OLD FARMHOUSE RESTAURANT** Armitage, nr ᵜ Rugeley.

Hours: Lunch 12.30pm - 2pm, dinner 7.30pm - 9.30pm. Closed: Saturday lunch, Sunday evening and all day Monday. Also closed 26th December to 2nd January. **Cuisine:** Extensive table d'hote menu including fish, game, poultry and meat. Traditional and innovative dishes. ⊨ None. ⓒⓒ All major cards. **Other Points:** Children welcome. No dogs. No smoking area. ▣ & **(V) Directions:** On the A513 between Armitage and Rugeley.
MR & MRS SEDDON ☎ (0543) 490179.

A 16th century farmhouse with original Tudor atmosphere set in attractive, colourful gardens. Fresh produce is used and seasonal dishes such as lobster, venison and pheasant are offered. The restaurant seats 86 and is ideally situated for a visit to the Potterys.

ARUNDEL West Sussex **Map 4 C2**

⊗££ **THE SWAN HOTEL** High Street, Arundel.

⏇££££ **Hours:** Breakfast 8am - 9am, lunch 12 noon - 2.15pm, and dinner ⎡CLUB⎤ 6.30pm - 9.30pm (last orders). Bar meals 12 noon - 2.15pm and 6.30pm - 9.30pm. **Cuisine:** English country cooking: eg. Chicken Swan Lake, filled with cream cheese, prawns & oregano, shallow fried, served with a cream sauce. Vegetarian dishes. ⊨ 2 single, 4 double, 6 twins, and 1 family room, all of them en suite. All rooms have tea/coffee facilities, colour TV, alarms and telephones. ⓒⓒ All major cards. **Other Points:** Children welcome. No smoking area. Open Sundays and bank holidays. Special weekend breaks available. No pets allowed. & **(V) Directions:** In the town centre at the bottom of High St, going up on the left.

Arundel continued

DIANA & KEN ROWSELL ☎ (0903) 882314

This friendly inn is pre-1759 and warmly decorated in Tudor style, a perfect setting from which to discover the historic, castle town of Arundel. The Swan offers an extensive menu, both in the bar and restaurant, using fresh, local produce and locally baked bread, and a well-chosen wine list compliments the meal.

ASHBY DE LA ZOUCH Leicestershire **Map 4 A2**

⊗££ **LA ZOUCH RESTAURANT** 2 Kilwardby Street, Ashby De La
CLUB Zouch.

Hours: Lunch 12 noon - 2pm and dinner 7pm - 10pm, last orders (10.30pm Saturday). High tea served during British summer time. Closed: Sunday evening and all day Monday. Also closed first 2 weeks January and first 2 weeks in July. **Cuisine:** English and continental dishes eg. Grilled Salmon & Cucumber Sauce, Rump Steak & Mustard Sauce. Homemade sweets. Speciality: Colston Bassett Stilton. ⊨ None. ☒ All major cards. **Other Points:** Children welcome. Large public car park at rear of premises. Vegetarian and special diets catered for. ⅊ **(V) Directions:** At the crossroads of the A50 and B5006 in town centre.

GEOFFREY & LYNNE UTTING ☎ (0530) 412536.

A renovated Georgian building, tastefully decorated and furnished and with a walled garden, cottage style with pebble water feature. There is a small intimate bar with a larger lounge bar upstairs and private functions and dinner parties can be arranged. The restaurant offers a large selection of English and continental dishes.

⊗£££ **THE MEWS WINE BAR & RESTAURANT** 8 Mill Lane.

Hours: Meals 12 noon - 2.30pm and 6pm - 10.30pm. Closed: Monday. **Cuisine:** Traditional English cooking, with a different menu daily using only fresh supplies. ⊨ None. ☒ Access, Visa. **Other Points:** Children welcome. No dogs. Fax No: (0530) 415111. ⊡ ⅊ **(V) Directions:** 30 yards from the junction of the A50/A453.

IAN G BRIDGE ☎ (0530) 416683.

Situated in a pedestrian mews in this historic market town, this popular Queen Anne listed building in conservation area has a reputation for excellent home cooked food in its Garden Room restaurant. Under same ownership for 10 years.

ASTHALL Oxfordshire **Map 4 B1**

⊗££ **THE MAYTIME INN** Asthall, Nr Burford

Hours: Breakfast 8am - 11am, lunch 11am - 2.30pm and dinner 6.30pm - 10.30pm. Open bank holidays. **Cuisine:** Daily specials, eg. steak & kidney pie, grilled lamb chops, medaillons of fillet steak Chinese style, fresh local trout meuniere. ⊨ 6 bedrooms, all en suite. ☒ All major cards. **Other Points:** Children welcome. ⊡ ⅊ **(V) Directions:** Down a narrow country lane on the A40 between Witney and Burford.

T M & M MORGAN ☎ (099 382) 2068.

Situated in this tiny hamlet, the Maytime Inn has retained much of its centuries-old Cotswold charm. In addition to a spacious bar, there is a dining room seating 80 where one can wine and dine in style and comfort.

BALDOCK Hertfordshire **Map 5 B1**

⊗££ **THE JESTER HOTEL** 116 Station Road, Odsey, Baldock.

⏛£££ **Hours:** Breakfast 7am - 10am, lunch 12 noon - 3pm (last orders 2.15pm), dinner 7pm - 10pm (last orders 9.45pm). Bar snacks 11.30am - 2.30pm, 6.30pm - 10pm. **Cuisine:** Serving bar snacks, table d'hote and full a la carte menu. Dishes may include Shelley salad, poached lemon sole with lobster sauce & choice of sweets. � 14 bedrooms, all en suite. **CC** Access, Visa, AmEx. **Other Points:** Children welcome. No smoking area. Afternoon teas served. Garden dining. Tele/Fax No. (046274) 2011. ☐ ⅋ **(V) Directions:** Between Royston & Baldock. Turn off Steeple Morden Ashwell St.

MR MILDENHALL-CLARKE. ☎ (046274) 2011.

Set in pleasant gardens, the Jester Hotel offers comfortable accommodation and well presented meals at value for money prices. Popular with locals, the hotel enjoys a relaxed atmosphere.

BANBURY Oxfordshire **Map 4 B2**

⊗££ **BANBURY MOAT HOUSE** 27-29 Oxford Road, Banbury.

⏛££££ **Hours:** Breakfast 7.30am - 9.30am, Lunch 12.30pm - 2pm, Dinner 7pm - 9.45pm (last orders). Bar snacks 12 noon - 2pm. Restaurant closed: Saturday lunch. Hotel closed: December 25th - 1st January. **Cuisine:** A la carte and table d'hote menus featuring imaginative, continental cuisine. Grillstones (cooking on very hot stones), a speciality. � 48 bedrooms, all en suite. Special reduced weekend tariff. **CC** All major cards. **Other Points:** Children welcome. Afternoon teas. Dogs allowed. Residents lounge. No-smoking area. Conferences and private functions. Fax No: (0295) 270954. ☐ **(V) Directions:** 200 yds up hill from Banbury Cross. A423.

QUEENS MOAT HOUSES ☎ (0295) 259361.

A hotel combining the elegance of a beautiful Georgian House with modern amenities and comfort. The restaurant with its ornate moulded ceiling and decor provides imaginative a la carte and table d'hote menus, and enjoys a good reputation. Situated on the main Oxford Road, just 200 yards from the famous Cross, this is an ideal base from which to explore the area.

⊗££ **CROMWELL LODGE HOTEL** North Bar, Banbury.

Hours: Meals from 7.30am - 9am and 7pm - 9.30pm. Bar meals from 12 noon - 2pm and 7pm - 9pm. **Cuisine:** Table d'hote & bistro menu. Summer garden barbecue restaurant - innovative homemade food: Skate wing with ginger butter, Beef fillet with orange & walnuts. � 32 bedrooms, all en suite. **CC** All major cards. **Other Points:** Children welcome. Coaches by appointment. ☐ ⅋ **(V) Directions:** On A4260, 200 yds N of Banbury Cross. 1 mile from jct. 11, M40.

KEN & CAROL SUTTON ☎ (0295) 259781.

17th century hotel offering 20th century comforts. Situated in the heart of Banbury within easy reach of many tourist attractions, eg. Blenheim Palace, Stratford upon Avon. Good vegetarian choice, excellent desserts and homemade ice creams.

Banbury continued

⊗££ **EASINGTON HOUSE HOTEL** 50 Oxford Road, Banbury.

⊞££request **Hours:** Breakfast 7.30am - 9am Monday - Friday, and 8am - 9am
CLUB Saturday, Sunday and Bank Holidays. Dinner Monday to Saturday
7pm - 8.30pm. Breakfast as well as Dinner is also served to non-
residents. **Cuisine:** French style cuisine using fresh produce.
Choice of 3 set menus including a seafood menu. Dish of the Day.
Extensive breakfast menu. ⊨ 3 single, 5 double, 4 twin and 5
family bedrooms, 10 en suite. Colour TV, tea/coffee making
facilities and direct dial telephones in all rooms. **CC** Access, Visa,
AmEx. **Other Points:** Children welcome. Garden. Dogs allowed.
Switch cards accepted. Small conference facilities. Fluent French
and Spanish spoken. **P Directions:** On A41, 300 yards south of
Banbury Cross.
MALCOLM & GWYNNETH HEARNE ☎ (0295) 270181.
*A 16th century, stone built farmhouse, decorated and
maintained to a high standard and surrounded by an award-
winning garden. Once the home of George Washington's great-
great aunt, the hotel now provides an ideal base for visits to
Blenheim Palace and Stratford upon Avon as well as Banbury
Cross! 3 set menus provide good homecooked food in the
recently extended restaurant & conservatory.*

⊗££ **ROEBUCK INN** Drayton, Banbury.

⊞££ **Hours:** Breakfast 8am - 9am, lunch 11.30am - 2pm, dinner 7pm -
11.30pm (last orders). **Cuisine:** A la carte, fish and steaks. ⊨ 2
rooms. 1 twin and 1 double bedroom. **CC** Access, Visa. **Other
Points:** Children welcome. **P** ᵟ **(V) Directions:** A422, just outside
Banbury.
MICHAEL BROWN ☎ (0295) 730542.
*The 16th century stone built village pub offers excellent value
bar meals and a good a la carte menu with fish, steak and
vegetarian specialities, served in friendly atmosphere.*

BARTLOW Cambridgeshire **Map 5 B1**

⊗££ **THE THREE HILLS** Bartlow, Cambridge.

⌂ **Hours:** Lunch 12 noon - 1.45pm and dinner 7pm - 9.30pm (last
orders). **Cuisine:** Homemade specials every day plus fine steaks
and fresh fish. ⊨ None. **CC** Access, Visa. **Other Points:**
Comprehensive vegetarian menu. **P (V) Directions:** 1 mile off the
A604 Cambridge to Haverhill Road (Linton by-pass).
SUE & STEVE DIXON ☎ (0223) 891259.
*A 16th century village inn set in glorious countryside off the
beaten track - but well worth checking out. The bar and
restaurant are a wealth of old beams, with inglenook fire in
winter. For the summer, there is a walled garden and covered
patio. A popular pub with a growing reputation.*

BASINGSTOKE Hampshire **Map 4 C2**

⊗££ **BISTRO 21** 21 London Street, Basingstoke.

Hours: Lunch 12 noon - 2.30pm, Dinner 6.30pm - 11pm (last
orders). Closed: Sundays and Bank Holidays. **Cuisine:** Frequently
changing a la carte menu and additional blackboard specials. Eg.
Duck Breast with Creme de Cassis & Black Cherries, Medallions of
Monkfish. ⊨ None. **CC** Access, Visa, AmEx. **Other Points:** No
dogs. Pedestrianised street. **(V) Directions:** Centre of old town,
opposite Red Lion Hotel. Pedestrianised street.

Basingstoke continued

KATHY FORTESCUE & BALU ANDERSON ☎ (0256) 460694.
A typical bistro-style restaurant with comfortable furnishings and a friendly, relaxed atmosphere. The menu is very varied and offers an excellent choice of well-cooked and presented food. Warm and courteous staff ensure you of a warm welcome.

⊗£ **CORKS** 25 London Street, Basingstoke.
Hours: Open 11am - 2.30pm and 6pm - 10.30pm Mondays to Saturdays. Closed: on Sundays and public holidays. **Cuisine:** Pastas, enchilladas, pies, burgers, ribs, filled jackets, salads. Chef's daily specials. Vegetarian dishes. ⊨ None. ◨ Access, Visa. **Other Points:** No dogs. **(V) Directions:** Old, pedestrianised part of town, nr Post Office, Museum & Theatre.
CHARLES & JENNIE SMITH, MARK WHATLEY ☎ (0256) 52622.
Fresh, bright decor with modern pictures. Good value wine list. Tables outside under an awning on a quiet, pedestrian street, on the outskirts of the main shopping centre and very close to the open air market.

⊗£££ **ROMANS HOTEL** Little London Road, Silchester, Near
CLUB Reading.
Hours: Breakfast 7am - 10am, lunch 12 noon - 1.30pm (last orders), dinner 7.30pm - 9pm. Sunday lunch 12.30pm - 1.30pm, dinner 7.30pm - 9pm (last orders). **Cuisine:** Dishes include Cream of courgette soup, Mullet in garlic butter, Stir-fry veal, Casserole of Seafood in white wine sauce. ⊨ 25 rooms. 14 single, 6 twin, 4 double and 1 family room. All en suite. ◨ All major cards. **Other Points:** Children welcome. Garden. Dogs allowed. Equipped meeting rooms available. Laundry service. Outdoor heated swimming pool. 2 tennis courts. ◪ **(V) Directions:** Off M4, Jct. 11. A33 to Basingstoke, follow signs to Silchester.
MICHAEL & KAY RILEY. ☎ (0734) 700421.
A privately owned, country style hotel surrounded by well kept gardens. The interior is tastefully decorated. The restaurant has a daily changing menu, serving good food with an emphasis on local fresh produce. Clientele is mainly business people.

⊗£££ **WESSEX HOUSE HOTEL** Old Reading Road, Sherfield-on-
⊡£££ Loddon, Basingstoke
Hours: Breakfast 7.30am - 9am, Lunch 12 noon - 1.45pm (last orders), Dinner 6.30pm - 9.30pm. Closed: December 25th - January 2nd. **Cuisine:** A la carte and table d'hote menus. Dishes may include Grilled whole Lemon Sole, Tournedos au poivre, Chicken Cordon Bleu, Rack of Lamb. ⊨ 17 bedrooms, all en suite. ◨ Access, Visa, AmEx. **Other Points:** Garden. Conference room accommodating 25 people. Private functions catered for. Fax No: (0256) 881131. ◪ ᶀ **(V) Directions:** Just off the A33 Reading - Basingstoke road.
PAMELA TAYLOR ☎ (0256) 882243.
The Wessex House Hotel provides its visitors with warmth, comfort, good food and wines, plus old-world courtesy and friendly, efficient service. The food is well-cooked, beautifully presented and served. The hotel is in a delightful setting and easily accessible from the M3 and M4.

CENTRAL & SOUTHERN ENGLAND

BATTLE East Sussex **Map 5 C1**
⊗£££ **POWDERMILLS HOTEL** Powdermill Lane, Battle.
⌂££££ **Hours:** Breakfast 7.30am - 9.30am, lunch and bar snacks 12 noon - 2.30pm, dinner 7pm - 9pm. Restaurant closed: Sunday night and Monday lunchtime. **Cuisine:** Full a la carte menu, table d'hote and bar snacks. Vegetarian menu. ⍩ 15 bedrooms, all en suite. **CC** Access, Visa. **Other Points:** Children welcome. Afternoon teas. Garden dining. Outdoor swimming pool. Golf and riding arrangements locally. Croquet lawn. Fax No. (04246) 4540. **P** & **(V) Directions:** Through Battle toward Hastings, 1st turn off R. Opp railway station.
DOUGLAS & JULIE COWPLAND. Chef - PAUL WEBBE ☎ (04246) 5511.
Set in 150 acres of park-like grounds and with fishing lakes and woodlands, this hotel is ideal for those wanting to return to nature. Serving an exciting range of tasty dishes and offering accommodation of a very high standard. Highly recommended.

BAYNARDS West Sussex **Map 4 C2**
⊗£ **THURLOW ARMS** Baynards, Rudgwick.
⌂£££ **Hours:** Lunch and dinner served 7 days a week during normal licensing hours. **Cuisine:** Seafood, grills, steaks and a large variety of bar snacks and home cooked sauces. ⍩ 2 bedrooms, en suite. **CC** Access, Visa. **Other Points:** Children welcome. Pleasant garden. LVs. **P** & **(V) Directions:** Situated off A281 between Guildford and Horsham.
RICHARD & MAXINE CHISHOLM ☎ (040 372) 2459
The building stands alongside the newly opened Downs Link Bridle Path. The Thurlow Arms serves a wide range of traditional beers and home cooked food.

BEACONSFIELD Buckinghamshire **Map 4 B2**
⊗££ **BUCKS TANDOORI** 7 Broadway, Penn Road, Beaconsfield.
Hours: Lunch 12 noon - 2.30pm, Dinner 6pm - 12 midnight. **Cuisine:** Nepalese and Indian cuisine including Tandoori dishes. Sunday Buffet lunch. ⍩ None. **CC** All major cards. **Other Points:** Children welcome. Take aways available. No dogs. **P** & **(V) Directions:** 2 miles from M40, 1 mile from A40. 100 yds Bekonscot Model Village.
MESSRS MAHMUD, UDDIN, MOHAMMAD & MOHAMMAD ☎ (0494) 674593/674580
A Nepalese restaurant situated in an elegant row of shops, off the main road. The menu offers a good choice of dishes which are well-cooked and served in generous portions by professional staff. Bucks Tandoori is a good choice for an enjoyable meal in a relaxed atmosphere.

⊗£ **THE ROYAL STANDARD OF ENGLAND** Forty Green,
⍩ Beaconsfield.
⌂ **Hours:** Open Mondays to Saturdays 11am - 3pm and 5.30pm - 11pm. Sundays 12 noon - 2pm and 7pm - 10.30pm. **Cuisine:** Home roast beef and baked ham, specially baked bread, brandy pate, cold buffet, cheese hostelry, hot dishes all the year round. ⍩ None. **CC** None. **Other Points:** Children welcome. Dogs allowed. **P** & **(V) Directions:** Between Beaconsfield and Forty Green.

Beaconsfield continued

MR P W ELDRIDGE. Manager - MR WAINWRIGHT ☎ (04946) 73382.

Famous old English pub boasting a beautiful country atmosphere, in character with its surroundings. Reputed to be one of the oldest public houses in England. English and continental draught beers.

BEDFORD Bedfordshire **Map 4 B2**

⌂£££ **EDWARDIAN HOUSE HOTEL** Shakespeare Road, Bedford.

🛏 19 bedrooms, all en suite. All rooms have colour TV, direct dial telephone, individually controlled heating, tea/coffee making facilities and an early morning call system. Some ground floor rooms. Reduced rates at weekends. **Hours:** Breakfast 7.30am - 9am, dinner and evening bar meals 6.30pm - 8.45pm (last orders). 🆑 Access, Visa, AmEx. **Other Points:** Children welcome. Licensed. Hotel bar & lounge. Conference facilities for up to 20 people. Good, freshly prepared food. Vegetarians catered for. 🅿 **(V) Directions:** Centrally located in Bedford, a few minutes from railway station.

JOHN & ROSSLYN ALLEN, GRAHAM & LYNDSEY WOOD ☎ (0234) 211156.

On a beautiful tree lined road in the Poets area of Bedford, just a few minutes from the town centre, this charming, family run hotel offers modern facilities, excellent service and a friendly atmosphere. The hotel is very tastefully decorated and the accommodation is of a high standard. Enjoy good, freshly

Bedford continued

prepared food in the restaurant and relax in the hotel's bar and lounge.

⊛£££ **THE KNIFE & CLEAVER** The Grove, Houghton Conquest.
⏅£££ **Hours:** 7.30am (weekends 8.30am) - 10am, 12 noon - 2.30pm, and 7pm - 10pm (last orders 9.45pm). Bar meals 12 noon - 2.30pm, and 7pm - 10pm. Closed: Sunday Closed: Sunday evenings. **Cuisine:** Modern English and French cuisine. A speciality is the 'Knife & Cleaver Hors d'Oeuvres', almost a meal in itself. ⊨ 4 double, and 5 twin bedrooms, all en suite with colour TV, radio, alarm, refrigerator and tea/coffee making facilities. **CC** Access, Visa, AmEx. **Other Points:** Children welcome. Pets allowed. Open bank holidays and Sunday Lunch. Garden dining. Private parties catered for. Fax No: (0234) 740900. **P** **(V)** **Directions:** Between A6 and B530, 5m south of Bedford and 2m north of Ampthill.
DAVID & PAULINE LOOM ☎ (0234) 740387.
In a prominent position opposite the medieval church in Houghton Conquest. The restaurant is an airy Victorian-style conservatory and the innovative menu which changes monthly incorporates seasonal specialities made from the finest fresh produce. Fresh fish, lobster & vegetarian dishes always available. List of 100 well chosen wines. Flowery terrace by the fountain.

⊛£££ **THE LAWS HOTEL** High Street, Turvey.
⏅£££ **Hours:** Breakfast 7am - 8.30am, lunch 12 noon - 2.00pm, dinner 7.00pm - 9.45pm **Cuisine:** A wide selection of dishes, may include Smoked Salmon Salad, Coq au Vin, Celestines of Lamb Oriental and Pear Belle Helene. ⊨ 19 rooms, all en suite. **CC** Access, Visa, AmEx. **Other Points:** Children welcome. Afternoon teas served. Garden dining. Dogs allowed. **P** & **(V)** **Directions:** From M1, exit 15, follow signs for A428 to Bedford.
JEROME & FRANCESCA MACK ☎ (023064) 213
Situated in the pleasant village of Turvey, this hotel offers attractive and comfortable accommodation. The restaurant serves well presented meals and provides excellent service in a light and relaxed atmosphere. Close to Woburn Abbey and Whipsnade Park Zoo.

BELTON Leicestershire **Map 4 A2**
⊛£ **THE GEORGE HOTEL** 17 Market Place, Belton, Loughborough.
Hours: Breakfast 7.30am - 9.30am, lunch 12 noon - 2.30pm and dinner 7pm - 11pm (last orders). Bar meals served 12 noon - 2.30pm and 7pm - 11pm. **Cuisine:** Homemade bar meals and very good a la carte menu available. ⊨ 20 bedrooms, 13 en suite. **CC** All major cards. **Other Points:** Vegetarian meals by arrangement. Children welcome. Pets allowed. Afternoon tea. **P** & **Directions:** 5 minutes from M1, junction 23 or 24.
MR HOUSTON ☎ (0530) 222426.
This old coaching inn dating back to 1753 is set in the rural village of Belton near the church. It offers a warm welcome and good wholesome food to travellers and locals alike. Near Castle Donington, race track and East Midland Airport.

BELTON IN RUTLAND Leicestershire **Map 4 A2**

⌂£ **THE OLD RECTORY** Belton in Rutland, Uppingham.
2 double and 5 family bedrooms all en suite. 1 bathroom, 1 shower. **Hours:** Breakfast 7.15am - 12 noon, dinner 7pm - 9pm. **CC** None. **Other Points:** Central heating. Children welcome. Residents' lounge. TV. Garden. Evening meals. **P Directions:** Just off the A47 - follow signs for the Craft Centre.
MRS DAVID RENNER ☎ (0572 86) 279.
A superb stop for B&B in this Victorian Rectory. Set in mature grounds on the outskirts of the village close to amenities. There is also a craft centre and miniature farm with Southdown sheep, Dexter cattle and Shetland ponies.

BEMBRIDGE Isle of Wight **Map 4 C2**

⊗£ **THE ROW BARGE INN** Station Road, Bembridge.
⌂£ **Hours:** Lunch 12 noon - 3pm. Dinner 7pm - 10pm (last orders).
CLUB **Cuisine:** Traditional pub fare. Speciality: pizza. 5 bedrooms. **CC** Access, Visa. **Other Points:** Children welcome and special menu offered. Garden. Fully certificated premises for food hygiene regulations. **P ⅂ (V) Directions:** Close to harbour.
CHRIS & MARY WALLIS ☎ (0983) 872874.
A pleasant traditional pub offering good value for money food and accommodation situated adjacent to Bembridge harbour and marina.

BETHERSDEN Kent **Map 5 C1**

⊗££ **THE ROYAL STANDARD** Ashford Road, Bethersden, Nr
CLUB Ashford.
Hours: Lunch 12 noon - 2pm and dinner 7pm - 9.30pm (Friday and Saturday 10pm). Open bank holidays and Sundays. **Cuisine:** Traditional featuring homemade pies. None. **CC** Access, Visa. **Other Points:** Childrens play area. Large garden where meals may be taken. No smoking area in restaurant. **P (V) Directions:** On A28 between Ashford and Tenterden.
ROGER HAMBERG ☎ (0233) 820280.
A popular freehouse with a warm and friendly atmosphere offering a very good selection of meals at reasonable prices. With the choice of dining in the restaurant or bar with the warmth of log fires in winter, or in the large garden in summer, you will enjoy your visit here at any time of the year.

BEXHILL ON SEA East Sussex **Map 5 C1**

⊗£ **THE NORTHERN HOTEL** 72-78 Sea Road, Bexhill-On-Sea.
⌂£££ **Hours:** Breakfast 8am - 9.30am, lunch 12 noon - 2pm, dinner 6pm - 8pm. **Cuisine:** Dishes include egg mayonnaise, melon boat, fillet of lemon sole, chicken chasseur, hot chocolate pudding with chocolate sauce. 21 rooms: 6 single, 7 twin, 7 double and 1 family bedroom. All en suite. **CC** Access, Visa. **Other Points:** Children welcome. Afternoon teas. Dogs allowed. ⅂ **(V) Directions:** Off the A259.
THE SIMS FAMILY ☎ (0424) 212836.
Adjacent to the Sea Front, the hotel is just one minute walk from the sea. Comfortable accommodation which has been decorated and furnished to a high standard. The Georgian style restaurant serves well prepared and well presented food at very good value for money. Quiet and relaxing atmosphere, as is the tradition of a family run hotel.

CENTRAL & SOUTHERN ENGLAND

BIGGLESWADE Bedfordshire **Map 5 B1**
⊗£££ **LA CACHETTE** 61 Hitchin Street, Biggleswade.
Ⓓ **Hours:** Dinner 7pm - 10pm (last orders). Closed: Sunday and
[CLUB] Monday. **Cuisine:** Imaginative French-style cuisine. Dishes may
include Duck breast sauteed in butter with blackcurrants, Lemon
Sole Aida. Extensive vegetarian choice. ⊨ None. **CC** All major
cards. **Other Points:** Children welcome. No dogs. On street
parking. **(V) Directions:** A1 M follow signs to town centre. 2
minutes walk from market square.
RICHARD & MARGARET POOL ☎ (0767) 313508.
A welcoming French restaurant offering an imaginative menu
and excellently cooked, fresh food. A seperate menu caters for
vegetarian guests and provides an equally good choice and
high standard of cuisine. With a warm atmosphere and
excellent service, La Cachette is definitely worth a visit.

BILDESTON Suffolk **Map 5 B2**
⊗£ **THE CROWN HOTEL** High Street, Bildeston.
Ⅲ££ **Hours:** Breakfast 7.30am - 10am, Lunch 12 noon - 2pm, Dinner
7pm - 9.30pm (last orders). Sunday lunch 12.30pm - 2.30pm.
Restaurant closed: Tues and Sun evening. **Cuisine:** Traditional
English. Victorian Diable, lamb in a spicy sauce a speciality. ⊨ 15
bedrooms, 9 en suite. **CC** Access, Visa. **Other Points:** Children
welcome. Garden. Afternoon teas. **P** **(V) Directions:** Off the
B1115.
MR HENDERSON ☎ (0449) 740510
A 15th Century coaching inn in the heart of the Suffolk
countryside. Along with excellent food and accommodation,
The Crown Hotel offers guests the chance to spot one of it's
several ghosts!

BILLERICAY Essex **Map 5 B1**
⊗£££ **DUKE OF YORK** Southend Road, South Green, Billericay.
Hours: Lunch and bar meals 12 noon - 2pm, dinner and bar meals
7pm - 10pm. Restaurant closed Saturday lunch and all day
Sunday. No bar meals served Saturday evening and all day
Sunday. **Cuisine:** French and English dishes. Choice of menus.
Large choice of bar snacks. ⊨ None. **CC** All major cards. **Other
Points:** Children welcome in restaurant. No dogs. Small patio. **P**
点 **(V) Directions:** A129 Billericay - Wickford road. 1 mile from
Billericay High Street.
MRS EDNA WHITE ☎ (0277) 651403
A pub and restaurant offering good value meals and efficient,
friendly service. The Duke of York was a beer house in 1868 and
the restaurant has since been sympathetically added to
compliment the original building. Customers will find a warm,
cosy atmosphere in which to enjoy their meal and the pub comes
complete with its own ghost in residence, 'Swanee'.

BIRCHINGTON Kent **Map 5 C2**
⊗££ **SMUGGLERS RESTAURANT** 212 Canterbury Road,
Birchington.
Hours: Lunch 12 noon - 2pm, Dinner 7pm - 10pm (last orders).
Closed: Sunday dinner and Monday lunchtime. **Cuisine:**
French/English cuisine. Table d'hote lunch and extensive
evening a la carte menu. Eg. Duckling aux Cerises,
Chateaubriand, fish dishes. ⊨ None. **CC** All major cards. **Other

Birchington continued

Points: Children welcome. Limited access for disabled. Garden dining. Private parties catered for. 🅿 (V) Directions: On road to Margate from Thanet Way, just past Birchington round'bt.
BOB & SUE SHERMAN ☎ (0843) 41185.

A comfortable, welcoming restaurant which offers a very extensive choice of well cooked food. The cuisine is predominantly French with dishes ranging from Salmon with a prawn and dill sauce to Fillet steak cooked in Brandy and French mustard. All dishes are made from fresh ingredients and attractively prsented. The quality of the food is complemented by excellent service.

BIRMINGHAM West Midlands **Map 4 A1**
🏨££ **ASHDALE HOUSE HOTEL** 39 Broad Road, Acocks Green, Birmingham.

🛏 7 single, 1 double, 2 twin or 2 family bedrooms, 4 en suite. Direct dial telephone, colour TV, tea/coffee making faciltes and radio-alarm clock in all room. Hairdryer and trouser-press available. Hours: Breakfast 7am - 9.30am. 💳 Access, Visa. Other Points: Children welcome. Pets allowed. No smoking area. Vegetarian meals. Specialist diets catered for. 🅿 Directions: Off A41, in Acocks Green village.
RICHARD MOULSON ☎ (021) 706 3598.

This comfortable family run hotel of Victorian character, overlooks the park in a quiet, yet convenient location, close to the NEC. In its tastefully decorated interior, guests will find 'green' products such as recycled paper and ecological soap,

The Duke of York

Southend Road (A129), South Green, Billericay, Essex,
Telephone No. 0277 651403

Full A La Carte Menu, Extensive Vegetarian Menu, Set Menu & Chefs Specialities: French & English Cuisine.-Extensive Wine List. Hot Food & Sandwiches in the Bar (Except Saturday evenings & all Day Sundays)-Large Car Park-Greene King Real Ales

Restaurant Opening Times

Lunches —————————— Monday - Friday ——— 12.00 - 2.00 (Last Orders)

Dinners ———————— Monday - Saturday ——— 7.00 - 10.00pm (Last Orders)

Birmingham continued

and you can be sure of a free-range, wholesome, organic breakfast.

⊗££ **FOUNTAIN COURT HOTEL** 339-343 Hagley Road,
⊞££££ Edgbaston, Birmingham.
  Hours: Breakfast 6.45am - 9am, Dinner 6.30pm - 8.30pm (last orders). **Cuisine:** Table d'hote menu. Dishes may include Roast pork, Chilli con Carne, grilled gammon. ⊨ 26 bedrooms, all en suite. **CC** Access, Visa, AmEx. **Other Points:** Children welcome. Garden. Afternoon teas. Dogs allowed. Fax No: (021) 429 1209. **◨ Directions:** A456. Corner of Hagley Rd and Fountain Rd. 2 miles from Jct 3, M5.
  GLADYS, STELLA & RICHARD SMITH ☎ (021) 429 1754.
  A friendly, family run hotel located on a main road about 3 miles from the city centre. Good location for access to M5 and the International Conference Centre. The hotel is well-maintained and has been recently refurbished. Especially popular with business travellers and weekenders.

⊗££ **HAGLEY COURT HOTEL** 229 Hagley Road, Edgbaston,
⊞££ Birmingham.
  Hours: Breakfast 7.30am - 9am, Dinner 6pm - 9.30pm (last orders). **Cuisine:** A la carte, Table d'hote and Bar menus. French/English - steaks, chicken, fish. ⊨ 28 bedrooms, all en suite. **CC** All major cards. **Other Points:** Children welcome. Conference centre nearby. Fax No.(021) 456 2722. **◨ Directions:** On A456.
  CHRISTOPHER PHILIPPIDES ☎ (021) 454 6514.
  A Georgian mansion, set back from the main road leading into the city. The Conference Centre is only one mile from the hotel, making it an ideal place for delegates to stay. The hotel is renowned for its comfortable and homely accommodation.

⊗££ **HEATH LODGE HOTEL** 117 Coleshill Road, Marston Green, Birmingham.
  Hours: Dinner is served from 6.30 - 9.00 pm (last orders). **Cuisine:** Farmhouse grill, Pork Marsala, and Chicken Kiev. ⊨ 15 rooms, some en suite. **CC** Access, Visa, AmEx. **Other Points:** Children welcome. Dogs allowed. Open for Sunday dinner and Bank holidays. ◨ **(V) Directions:** Approximately 1 mile from junction 4 off M6, near NEC and airport.
  SIMEON COLLINS ☎ (021) 779 2218/4995.
  Family run hotel, with cosy lounge and coal-effect fire, quietly situated yet just a short distance away from NEC and Birmingham International Airport. Courtesy car available for airport travellers and long-term car parking.

⊗££ **LOPEZ RESTAURANT** 73 Cornwall Street, Birmingham.
  Hours: Lunch 12 noon - 3pm, Dinner 6pm - 11pm. Closed: Sunday. **Cuisine:** Spanish dishes with Paella and King Prawns a speciality. ⊨ None. **CC** All major cards. **Other Points:** Children welcome. No dogs. **Directions:** Near Colmore Row.
  JUAN LOPEZ ☎ (021) 236 2724.
  Lopez is a small, family restaurant near the centre of Birmingham, offering well cooked Spanish dishes, live music and a warm, lively atmosphere. Spanish dishes include Paella

Birmingham continued

Valenciana, Pollo Andaluz and Scampi alo Lopez but there is also a wide choice of French dishes.

⌂££ **LYNDHURST HOTEL** 135 Kingsbury Road, Erdington, CLUB Birmingham.

🛏 8 single, 4 twin and 2 family bedrooms, 12 en suite. 2 bathrooms, 1 shower. **Hours:** Breakfast 7.30am - 8.30am, dinner 6.30pm - 8.30pm (last orders 8.15pm). Closed: Christmas. **CC** All major cards. **Other Points:** Central heating. Children welcome. No dogs. Residents lounge. TV. Garden. Restaurant and residential license. Cosy bar. Vegetarians catered for. **P** &
Directions: On the A38, half mile from M6 turn-off Junction 6.
MR & MRS R WILLIAMS ☎ (021) 3735695.
Family owned and run. Recently refurbished to a high standard but maintaining a relaxed family atmosphere. On the route of the 114 and 116 buses which go to the city centre.

⊗£££ **PINOCCHIOS RESTAURANT** Chad Square, Hawthorne Road, Harborne, Birmingham.
Hours: Lunch served 12 noon - 2.30pm, dinner 7pm - 11pm. Closed: Sunday and Bank Holidays. **Cuisine:** Italian cuisine. Extensive menu - dishes may include Filetto Farfalla, Calamari alla Livornese, Sogliola di Dover Grigliata, Pollo alla Pinocchio. 🛏 None. **CC** All major cards. **Other Points:** Children welcome. Limited access for disabled. **P** **(V) Directions:** Opp. White Swan pub, just off Harborne Road. Near Botanical Gardens.
MR SILVIO NOVELLI ☎ (021) 454 8672.
A traditional Italian decor sets the scene in which to enjoy quality Italian meals generously served. With its warm, friendly and relaxed atmosphere, it is the perfect place for a quiet or romantic dinner. Fresh fish and vegetables are bought daily. Situated just minutes from the City on the Harborne/Edgbaston border, Pinocchio is a real taste of Italy in Birmingham.

⌂££ **WESTBOURNE LODGE HOTEL** 27/29 Fountain Road, Edgbaston, Birmingham.
🛏 10 single, 2 double, 5 twin and 3 family bedrooms - 20 of them en suite. Telephones, TV, radio and tea/coffee making facilities in rooms. **Hours:** Breakfast 7am - 9am, lunch 12.30pm - 2pm and dinner 6pm - 8pm (last orders 7.30pm). Closed: Christmas. Dinner by arrangement over weekends. **CC** Access, Visa. **Other Points:** Central heating. Children welcome. Patio and garden. Residents lounge and TV. Licensed. Vegetarians catered for. Fax. No. (021) 429 7436. **P** & **Directions:** Off the A456, 200 yds from the corner of Hagley and Fountain Road.
MR & MRS J H HANSON ☎ (021) 429 1003.
Family-run hotel 2 miles from city centre offering efficient service and home cooking. The house is situated in a quiet road off the A456 within 1.5 miles of the National Exhibition Centre.

BISHOPS STORTFORD Hertfordshire **Map 5 B1**
⊗£££ **THE ORIENT EXPRESS WINE CAR & RESTAURANT** CLUB Elsenham Station, Nr Stansted Airport, Essex.
Hours: Lunch 12 noon - 2pm, Dinner 7pm - 9.30pm. Closed: Sunday dinner. **Cuisine:** Modern Anglo-French cuisine in the Restaurant Car, savoury and sweet crepes in the Wine Car.

Bishops Stortford continued

⊨ None. **CC** Access, Visa. **Other Points:** Children welcome. Patio dining. No dogs. No-smoking area. Private parties catered for. **P** **(V) Directions:** Elsenham village railway station, 2 miles from Stansted Airport.

DAVID WELLS ☎ (0279) 815880.

Three restored railway carriages, complete with Piano Salon, where the elegance, romance and intrique of the legendary Orient Express are expertly recreated. The Anglo-French cuisine is excellent and impeccably served in the Restaurant Car. For a relaxing drink or traditional French crepe, visit the Wine Car & Piano Salon. An ideal choice for first class cuisine in a superb setting.

BLAKENEY Norfolk **Map 5 A2**

⊗£ **THE KINGS ARMS** Westgate Street, Blakeney, Holt.

Hours: Licensed to serve drinks with meals all day. **Cuisine:** Local seafood. ⊨ None. **CC** Visa. **Other Points:** Children welcome. **P** ⅙ **Directions:** On the quay at Blakeney between Wells and Sheringham.

HOWARD DAVIES ☎ (0263) 740341

Situated in a beautiful coastal village, this country pub has two bars and a large sheltered beer garden and patio. A popular haunt with the sailing fraternity in summer.

BLANDFORD FORUM Dorset **Map 4 C1**

⊗££ **THE CROWN HOTEL** 1 West Street, Blandford Forum.

CLUB **Hours:** Breakfast 7.30am - 9.30am, lunch 12.30pm - 2pm, dinner 7.15pm - 9.15pm. Sunday dinner 7pm - 9pm. **Cuisine:** Dishes include chicken kiev with asparagus, saute medallions of pork, half a roast duckling, all served with a variety of sauces. ⊨ **CC** All major cards. **Other Points:** Children welcome. Garden. Afternoon Teas. Dogs allowed. Coarse fishing (in season). **P** ⅙ **(V)**

JAMES MAYO - Manager. ☎ (0258) 56626.

Offering comfortable accommodation and quality food at value for money prices, this Georgian style hotel is set in its own grounds. Frequented by mixed ages the hotel enjoys a peaceful relaxed, atmosphere in its oak-panneled restaurant.

BLETCHINGLEY Surrey **Map 5 C1**

⊗££ **THE WHYTE HARTE** 11/21 High Street, Bletchingley.

⊡£££££ **Hours:** Breakfast 7.30am - 8.30am, 8.30am - 9.30am weekends. Lunch 12 noon - 2.pm Dinner 6.30pm - 9.30pm. Closed: Christmas Day evening. **Cuisine:** Dishes may include - smoked mackerel, brie armandine, lemon salmon, cherry duckling, good selection of vegetarian dishes. ⊨ 12 bedrooms, 9 en suite. **CC** All major cards. **Other Points:** Children welcome in dining area and garden. Garden dining. **P** **(V) Directions:** On A23 off Jct 6 of M25.

DAVID & MIRIAM YARWOOD. ☎ (0883) 743 231.

This tastefully restored hostelry, dating back to 1388, offers good food and comfortable en suite accommodation. Recently refurbished to make the best of the original beams and fireplaces. Enjoying a relaxed informal atmosphere and frequented by business people and locals alike.

BOGNOR REGIS West Sussex **Map 4 C2**

⊗££ **THE ROYAL HOTEL** The Esplanade, Bognor Regis.
Hours: Meals from 7.30am - 9.30am, 12 noon - 2.30pm and 6pm - 10.30pm last orders. Bar meals from 11.30am all day. **Cuisine:** Prawns, pasta, lobster. ⊨ 40 bedrooms, all en suite. **CC** All major cards. **Other Points:** Children welcome. Coaches by appointment. **P** **(V) Directions:** Bognor Regis seafront, 50 yards west of the pier.
DAVID M COOMBS ☎ (0243) 864665/6
A Victorian Hotel situated only yards from the sea with unimpeded views from the restaurant, bars and coffee shop.

⊗£ **THE WILLIAM HARDWICKE** 12 High Street, Bognor Regis.
Hours: Lunch 12 noon - 2pm, Dinner 6.30pm - 9.30pm. Bar snacks 12 noon - 3pm and 6.30pm - 10pm. Closed for meals: Sunday evening. **Cuisine:** Carvery and daily changing blackboard menu. Honest home cooking with roasts, curries and vegetarian meals. ⊨ None. **CC** Access, Visa. **Other Points:** Children welcome. Beer garden. No dogs. No smoking area. **P** ⅋ **(V) Directions:** In Bognor High Street, diagonally opposite the main post office.
TIGGY MCNALLY ☎ (0243) 821940.
A large, attractively furbished pub with a large, airy restaurant, a patio to the front and garden at the back. During winter there are real log fires. The food is good, honest home cooking at value for money prices and is served in pleasant surroundings. Centrally located in Bognor Regis.

BOUGHTON MONCHELSEA Kent **Map 5 C1**

⊞££££ **TANYARD** Wierton Hill, Boughton Monchelsea, Nr Maidstone.
⊨ 1 suite, 1 single, 2 twin and 2 double bedrooms. All en suite and with TV, direct dial telephone, radio and tea/coffee making facilities. **Hours:** Breakfast 7.30am - 9.30am, dinner at 8pm - 8.15pm. Closed for 10 weeks mid December - early March. Residents guests are welcome for **CC** All major cards. **Other Points:** Children over 6 welcome. No dogs allowed. Licensed. **P** **Directions:** Off B2163 between Langley & Linton.
JAN DAVIES ☎ (0622) 744705.
Tanyard is a small medieval country house hotel situated in the heart of rural Kent, with the welcoming feel of a private Country Home rather than a hotel. Full of character, the accommodation and reception rooms are of a very high standard. The 4 course set menu is imaginative and well cooked using fresh local ingredients. Les Routiers Newcomer of the Year 1991.

BOURNE Lincolnshire **Map 5 A1**

⊗££ **ANGEL HOTEL** Market Place, Bourne.
⊞£££ **Hours:** Meals from 7.30am - 10am, 12 noon - 2pm and 7pm - 9.30pm (last orders). **Cuisine:** In the bar: ploughman's, soup, roast of the day. In the restaurant: extensive monthly menu includes half bottle wine per person. Plus a la carte. ⊨ 14 bedrooms, all en suite. **CC** Access, Visa, AmEx. **Other Points:** Guide dogs allowed. Children welcome. Coaches by appointment. Access for disabled to public rooms only. Fax No: (0778) 393990. **P** **(V) Directions:** In the market place. A151 and A15.
B & I SNAITH ☎ (0778) 422 346.
The former offices of a Tax Collector, this 16th century inn is reputed to have been visited by Dick Turpin. The bars bustle

Bourne continued

with locals and travellers. Recently refurbished accommodation facilities include two four-poster suites, and whirlpool bath. All types of functions catered for.

BOURNEMOUTH Dorset **Map 4 C1**

🏠££ **ALBEMARLE HOTEL** 123 West Hill Road, Bournemouth.
🛏 12 bedrooms, 5 with en suite. All with colour TVs, clock radio and tea/ coffee making facilities. **Hours:** Breakfast 8.30am - 9am and dinner served at 6pm (order by 11am). Snacks and hot drinks available 7.30pm - 10.30pm. 💳 Access, Visa. **Other Points:** Children welcome. No-smoking in dining room. Vegetarian menu. Comfortable lounge. Licensed bar. **(V) Directions:** Follow Wessex Way towards Poole, then left for Westcliff and BIC.
MR & MRS M J MOORE ☎ (0202) 551351.
A very friendly, yet efficiently run, hotel providing very clean, comfortable rooms at excellent value. All meals are home cooked and there is a choice of menu for both dinner and breakfast. 500 yds to the shops, beach and BIC.

⊗££ **BELVEDERE HOTEL - CECIL RESTAURANT** Bath Road,
🏠££££ Bournemouth.
Hours: Breakfast 7.30am - 9.30am, Lunch 12.30pm - 2pm, Dinner 6.30pm - 9pm (last orders). Bar snacks 12 noon - 2.30pm and 6pm - 9.30pm. Closed for lunch on Mondays, Tuesdays and Saturdays. **Cuisine:** Predominantly English cuisine including Carvery. 🛏 63 bedrooms, all en suite. 💳 All major cards. **Other Points:** Children welcome. No dogs. Residents' lounge. Licensed bar with live music 2 evenings a week. Full Conference facilities. Fax No: (0202) 294699. 🅿 ♿ **(V) Directions:** Centre of Bournemouth on approach road to pier.
MAUREEN PELLATT ☎ (0202) 297556.
Positioned atop Bath Hill, the Belvedere has impressive sea views from most south facing rooms and is just a short stroll from shops, beach and other amenities. The Cecil Restaurant has a long established local reputation for fine food and welcoming service. Recently refurbished, a good meal can be enjoyed in elegant, comfortable surroundings.

⊗££ **BOURNEMOUTH HEATHLANDS HOTEL** Grove Road, East Cliff, Bournemouth.
Hours: Lunch 12.30pm - 2pm. Dinner 7pm - 8.30pm. Coffee Shop 10am - 6pm. **Cuisine:** English/Continental. Daily Roast, Vegetarian Dish of the Day. 🛏 115 bedrooms all en suite. Colour TV, tea/coffee making facilities and hairdryers in all rooms. Satelite TV. 💳 Access, Visa. **Other Points:** Children welcome. Pets allowed. Residents' lounge and Garden. Swimming Pool. Extensive Conference facilities. 🅿 ♿ **(V) Directions:** 3 miles from A338-Ringwood/Bournemouth Rd.Follow signs to East Cliff
HEATHLANDS HOTELS LTD. ☎ (0202) 553336.
A large 3 star Hotel offering luxurious facilities for guests, but also offering good value for money and service in the restaurant and coffee shop. Within walking distance of the centre of town with all Bournemouth amenities, and less than 250 yards from the East Cliff top.

Bournemouth continued

⊗£ **BURLEY COURT HOTEL** Bath Road, Bournemouth.
⌂£££ **Hours:** Breakfast 8am - 9.30am, Bar snacks 12 noon - 2.30pm, Dinner 6.30pm - 8.30pm (last orders). **Cuisine:** Traditional English dishes. Snack lunches available in Lounge bar, or by the pool. ⊨ 38 bedrooms, all en suite. ▣ Access, Visa. **Other Points:** Children welcome. Afternoon teas. Dogs allowed. Residents' lounge. Lift. Games room. Heated outdoor swimming pool. Solarium. Fax No: (0202) 298514. ▣ ⅙ **Directions:** East Cliff near Bournemouth Railway Station.
MASLYN & JAN HASKER ☎ (0202) 552824.
A well-known hotel which has been in the same family for over 25 years and where the continuing aims are good quality food, courteous service and a high standard of cleanliness. The hotel is large enough to offer every luxury, yet not too large to be personally supervised throughout. A welcoming, comfortable hotel.

⊗£££ **CHINE HOTEL** Boscombe Spa Road, Bournemouth.
Hours: Breakfast 8am - 9.30am, Lunch 12.30pm - 2pm, Dinner 7pm - 8.30pm (last orders). **Cuisine:** Dishes include Fillet steak topped with mushroom and stilton, Paupiette of Plaice with Asparagus. Lunchtime cold buffet and carvery. ⊨ 97 bedrooms, all en suite. ▣ All major cards. **Other Points:** Children welcome. Garden. Afternoon teas. No dogs. ▣ ⅙ **(V) Directions:** Overlooking Poole Bay to the south.
MR J G J BUTTERWORTH ☎ (0202) 396234.

CENTRAL & SOUTHERN ENGLAND

Bournemouth continued

Constructed during 1874 on Sir Henry Drummond-Wolff's estate, The Chine overlooks Poole Bay and the beautifully landscaped Boscombe Chine Gardens. Excellent service and old world charm combine to create a warm, friendly atmosphere. The Bay Restaurant enjoys sea views and offers a high standard of freshly prepared meals for guests and non-residents.

⊗££ **CHINEHURST HOTEL** Studland Road, Alumchine, ⊡££ Westbourne, Bournemouth.
CLUB **Hours:** Breakfast 7.30am - 9.30am, lunch 12 noon - 1.45pm and dinner 6.30pm - 8.30pm (last orders). Bar meals 12.00 noon - 1.45pm. **Cuisine:** Wide selection table d'hote menu changes daily - roasts, sole in white wine, steaks, curries. A la carte menu also available. ⊨ 30 bedrooms, all en suite. Luxury suites also available, including 1 four- poster. CC All major cards. **Other Points:** Children welcome. Dogs by arrangement. No smoking area. Afternoon tea served. Cocktail bar. Garden terrace and summer barbecues. ⊡ ☒ **(V) Directions:** West of the pier overlooking Alum Chine close to the seafront.
MR C K GRIFFIN ☎ (0202) 764583.
A family run hotel overlooking the beautiful Alum Chine.Thoughtfully decorated throughout, this is a medium sized establishment with all the facilities of a large hotel. Close to the sea and shops on the West cliff. Cabaret star entertainer on Saturday nights.

⊗££ **CORIANDER RESTAURANT** 14 Richmond Hill, Bournemouth.
Hours: Meals from 12 noon - 2.15pm and 6pm - 10.30pm (last orders). Closed: Sunday lunch, Christmas Day and Boxing Day. **Cuisine:** Mexican and vegetarian dishes, eg. guacamole, nachos, coriander soup. Chicken Vesuvius, burritos, enchiladas, tacos, quesadillas. Home made sweets. ⊨ None. CC Access, Visa. **Other Points:** Coaches by appointment. Children welcome. No dogs. Cantina bar now open for drinks and/or snacks. ☒ **(V) Directions:** In the heart of Bournemouth.
CHRISTINE & ROGER MILLS ☎ (0202) 552202.
Authentic Mexican dishes, with 'Gringo Specials' for the less adventurous. The Mexican flavour is reflected in the rustic decor of the ground floor bar.

⊗£££ **CUMBERLAND HOTEL** East Overcliff Drive, Bournemouth.
Hours: Breakfast 8am - 9.30am (8.30am - 10am Sundays), Lunch 12.30pm - 1.45pm, Dinner 7pm - 8.30pm (last orders). Bar snacks 12.30pm - 2pm and 7pm - 8.30pm. **Cuisine:** 4 course Table d'Hote menu. Dishes may include Poached fillet of sole, Medalions of Pork Tenderloin with a Calvados Cream Sauce. Bar snacks. ⊨ 102 bedrooms, all en suite. CC Access, Visa. **Other Points:** Children welcome. No smoking area. Cocktail Bar. Residents lounge. Heated outdoor swimming pool. Garden patio. Conferences. Fax No: (0202) 294810. ⊡ ☒ **(V) Directions:** M3 - M27 - Wessex Way - East Cliff.
ARTHUR YOUNG ☎ (0202) 290722.
A purpose-built hotel providing luxurious accommodation and facilities. Situated in the famous East Cliff there are superb sea

Bournemouth continued

views from the Purbeck Hills to the Isle of Wight. The elegant oak-panelled restaurant offers a varied menu, carefully selected wine list and efficient, courteous service. A family run hotel which provides excellent standards.

⊗££ **DURLEY GRANGE HOTEL** 6 Durley Road, West Cliff, ⌂££££ Bournemouth.
Hours: Breakfast 8.00am - 9.30am, Dinner 6.30pm - 8pm (last orders). Bar lunches 12.30pm - 1.45pm. **Cuisine:** Seafood pancake, carbonnade of beef, selection from cold table. ▭ 50 rooms, all en suite with colour TV, telephone, radio, alarm and tea-makers. Lift. **CC** Access, Visa. **Other Points:** Children welcome over 5 years. Non-smoking area. Open Bank holidays. No dogs allowed. Heated indoor pool. Sauna, solarium, conference room. **P** & **Directions:** Near roundabout junction at top of Poole Hill, Bournemouth.
MR & MRS M KIRBY ☎ (0202) 554473/290743
Good food, comfort and hospitality are the hallmark of this lovely family owned/managed hotel. Situated only minutes from town centre and beach, it is ideal for holidays, business, golfing and bowling holidays.

⊗££ **DURLEY HALL** Durley Chine Road, Bournemouth.
⌂££££ **Hours:** Breakfast from 7.15am, buffet lunch 12 noon - 2pm
[CLUB] (12.30pm - 2pm Sunday), Dinner 7pm - 9pm. **Cuisine:** A la carte and 4 course table d'hote menus featuring dishes of the world. Vegetarian and healthy eating dishes. Afternoon teas. ▭ 81 bedrooms, all en suite. **CC** All major cards. **Other Points:** Children welcome. Garden. Outdoor swimming pool. Dogs allowed. Leisure Club - solarium, jacuzzi, gym, sauna, steam room, beauty therapist. **P** & **(V) Directions:** Off Wessex Way By-pass (A338). Nr Bournemouth International Centre.
HALLMARK HOTELS LTD ☎ (0202) 766886.
The hotel is set in 2 and a half acres of secluded gardens, close to the town centre and beach. Durley Hall offers an elegant mix of modern and traditional styles and has gained a good reputation for the quality of its food and service. The accommodation is of a high standard with each bedroom retaining an individual character.

Bournemouth continued

☐☐££ MAE-MAR HOTEL 91/93 Westhill Road, Westcliff, Bournemouth.
⊨ 11 single, 10 family, 10 double and 10 twin bedrooms, 29 en suite. 4 bathrooms, 1 shower and 3 WCs. Tea/coffee making facilities, colour TV and video channel in all rooms. **Hours:** Breakfast 8am - 9.15am and dinner 6pm - 6.30pm (order by 4.30pm). Open all year. **CC** Access, Visa. **Other Points:** Central heating. Children welcome. Dogs by arrangement. Licensed bar, lounge and TV. Lifts to all floors. ᎣᎧ **(V)**
MRS JANET CLEAVER ☎ (0202) 553167.
An attractive hotel situated in the heart of the Westcliff area. Within walking distance of both beach and town, the Mae-Mar provides a friendly family retreat at the end of the day.

☐☐£ NASEBY NYE HOTEL Byron Road, Bournemouth.
⊨ 2 single, 5 double, 4 twin and 1 family bedrooms (3 en suite). 2 bathrooms, 1 shower. **Hours:** Breakfast 8am - 9am, dinner 6pm - 7pm. **CC** None. **Other Points:** Central heating. Children over 5 years welcome. Licensed. Residents lounge. TV. Garden. **P**
Directions: Situated at the end of Boscombe Overcliff - the Coast Road.
B S & V R JENKINS ☎ (0202) 34079
A small hotel of character and charm standing in its own grounds very close to the cliff. The majority of rooms have sea views. Town centre within easy walking distance.

⊗£££ THE CLIFFSIDE HOTEL East Overcliff Drive, Bournemouth
☐☐££££ **Hours:** Breakfast 8am - 9.30am, lunch 12.45pm - 2pm, dinner
CLUB 6.45pm - 8.30pm. Sunday lunch 12.30pm - 2pm, Sunday dinner 6.45pm - 8.30pm. Last orders for lunch 2pm, for dinner 8.30pm. **Cuisine:** Dishes include grilled lamb cutlet garni and grilled whole dover sole maitre d'hotel. Cold buffet. ⊨ 62 rooms. 5 single, 25 twin and 24 double with 8 family rooms. All rooms with colour TV, telephone, radio, and tea/coffee facilities. **CC** Access, Visa. **Other Points:** Children welcome. Dogs by prior arrangement. No smoking area. Afternoon teas. Heated outdoor pool (summer). Games room. Conference facilities. **P** **(V)**
MR A D YOUNG ☎ (0202) 555724.
The Cliffside Hotel, overlooking the sea, is suitable for all ages. Well cooked food and friendly, efficient service are complemented by the comfortable furnishings throughout. In an excellent position, close to shops, theatres, the BIC, and with plenty of activities: golf, wind-surfing, tennis, and pony-trekking to name a few.

⊗£££ THE CONNAUGHT HOTEL West Hill Road, West Cliff, Bournemouth.
Hours: Breakfast 7.30am - 9.30am, Bar snacks 12.30pm - 2pm, Dinner 6.30pm - 10pm. **Cuisine:** English, Continental and Oriental cusine served in the Cameo Restaurant. Bar meals at lunchtime. ⊨ 60 bedrooms, all en suite. Includes several suites for disabled guests. **CC** All major cards. **Other Points:** Children welcome. Lift. Bars. Ballrooms & evening entertainment. Leisure Club with full facilities. Conference suite. Fax No: (0202) 298028. **P** ᎣᎧ **(V) Directions:** A338 from M27. Follow signs for B.I.C. Near the Winter Gardens.

Bournemouth continued
JON MURRAY ☎ (0202) 298020.
A delightful hotel totally rebuilt and refurbished during 1990, just 5 minutes from the town coentre, the B.I.C., pier and safe sandy beaches. The accommodation is excellent and both restaurant and bar meals are of a high standard. With professional and caring service. an excellent leisure club and comfortable, luxurious surroundings, the Connaught is highly recommended.

⊗£££ **THE QUEENS HOTEL** Meyrick Road, East Cliff, Bournemouth.
Hours: Breakfast 7.30am - 9.45am, Lunch 12.45pm - 1.45pm and Dinner 7pm - 9pm (last orders 9pm). Bar meals 12 noon - 3pm and Dinner 6pm - 10pm. **Cuisine:** English and French cuisine. 🛏 114 bedrooms, all en suite. **CC** Access, Visa. **Other Points:** Children welcome. Dogs allowed. Open Sundays and Bank holidays. Conference facilities. Fax No: (0202) 294810. **P** **(V) Directions:** A338 Wessex Way into Bournemouth, then signs to East Cliff.
MR A D YOUNG ☎ (0202) 554415.
A comfortable family-run hotel which caters for every taste, offering full a la carte, table d'hote and bar menus. Situated on the East Cliff, a minute's walk from the town centre and a host of local amenities. Other attractions like Lulworth Cove and Brownsea Island are also within easy reach.

⊗££ **TROUVILLE HOTEL** Priory Road, West Cliff, Bournemouth.
⊞£££££ **Hours:** Breakfast 8am - 9.30am, Lunch and bar snacks 12.15pm - 1.45pm, Dinner 7pm - 8.30pm (last orders). **Cuisine:** Dishes may include Cubes of Salmon, Monkfish and Scampi in a Tarragon Cream and a Flaky Pastry Case, Braised Scotch Steak, Roast Loin of Pork. 🛏 80 bedrooms, all en suite. **CC** Access, Visa. **Other Points:** Children welcome. No smoking area. Afternoon Teas. Dogs allowed. Residents lounge & bar. Leisure facilities. Conferences. Fax: (0202) 293324. **P** & **Directions:** Adjacent to Bournemouth International Centre. Very central.
DAVID ARTHUR YOUNG ☎ (0202) 552262.
Centrally situated within walking distance of all the main amenities in Bournemouth, the Trouville provides high standards of food and accommodation. The restaurant overlooks the town and offers first-class table d'hote cuisine, excellently presented and served in pleasant and relaxed surroundings. The leisure facilities include a sauna, trymnasium, jacuzzi and solarium.

BOURTON ON THE WATER Gloucestershire **Map 4 B1**
⊗£ **BO-PEEP TEA ROOMS** Riverside, Bourton-on-the-Water, Cheltenham.
Hours: Lunch 12 noon - 4.30pm, Dinner (mid July - mid September only) 4.30pm - 8pm. Closed: weekdays December to February. **Cuisine:** English dishes. Homemade. Large Cornish clotted cream teas. 🛏 None. **CC** Access, Visa. **Other Points:** Children welcome. Afternoon teas. Dogs allowed. No smoking area. Open Bank Holidays. & **(V) Directions:** Off A429 Fosse Way. Opposite side of river to village green.
JUDY & BOB HISCOKE ☎ (0451) 22005.
'Olde worlde' riverside tea rooms and licensed restaurant. The spacious interior has fitted carpets, panelling and exposed

Bourton on the Water continued
Cotswold stone walls. A homely, comfortable atmosphere prevails and the service is efficient and welcoming. All dishes are freshly cooked, well served and presented. The menu offers a good choice including vegetarian dishes. A beautiful setting.

⊗££ **OLD NEW INN** Bourton-On-Water, Cotswolds.
⬭££££ **Hours:** Breakfast 8.15am - 9.15am, lunch 12.30pm - 1.30pm and dinner 7.30pm - 8.30pm (last orders 8.15pm). Bar meals available lunchtime and evening. Closed: Christmas Day. **Cuisine:** Traditional home cooking. ⊨ 24 bedrooms, 11 en suite. **CC** Access, Visa. **Other Points:** Children welcome. Dogs allowed. Fax No: (0451) 810236. **P Directions:** Off the A429. Turn off Fosseway down to the High Street.
PETER MORRIS ☎ (0451) 20467.
A traditional country inn built in 1709, situated in the heart of the Cotswolds on the banks of the River Windrush and set in attractive gardens. Antique furnishings, warming log fires and traditional home cooking set the atmosphere. Run by the Morris family for over 50 years.

⊗££ **THE CHESTER HOUSE RESTAURANT** Chester House
⬭££££ Hotel and Motel, Victoria Street.
Hours: Open from 7pm - 10pm. No lunches in winter. **Cuisine:** Menu changed daily, using fresh produce. A la carte and table d'hote. ⊨ 22 bedrooms. Direct dial phone in all rooms. Flower arrangements by request on arrival. Reservations: Tel. (0451) 20471. **CC** All major cards. **Other Points:** Children welcome. No dogs in public rooms. **P Directions:** On the A429.
MR & MRS NORMAN JONES ☎ (0451) 21522/20192.
Bourton-on-Water is a very attractive village and popular with tourists. The restaurant is part of a motel which has been built around a converted stableyard. It is in a quiet part of the village and enjoys a thriving business all year round.

BRACKNELL Berkshire **Map 4 B2**
⊗££ **OSCARS** South Hill Park Arts Centre, Bracknell.
CLUB **Hours:** Dinner 6.30pm - 9.30pm. Bar meals from 12 noon - 2pm and 6.15pm - 7.30pm. Closed: Sunday, Monday and for 2 weeks at Christmas. **Cuisine:** Ethnic, Vegetarian, Seafood and wines. All main dishes freshly cooked to order. ⊨ None. **CC** None. **Other Points:** Children welcome. Coaches by appointment on weekdays. **P & (V) Directions:** From the A3095 or the A322 follow signs to South Hill Park.
MARK BRIDGES ☎ (0344) 59031.
Situated in a large, elegant mansion now used as an art centre. The food is excellently prepared - an ideal accompaniment to an evening at the theatre or cinema on the same site.

BRADFORD-ON-AVON Wiltshire **Map 4 B1**
⬭££££ **WIDBROOK GRANGE** Trowbridge Road, Bradford-on-Avon.
⊨ 15 bedrooms, 14 en suite. Tea/coffee facilities, telephone, colour TV in all rooms. **Hours:** Breakfast 7.30am - 9.45am, dinner by arrangement. **CC** Access, Visa, AmEx. **Other Points:** Children welcome. Residents garden and lounge. Conference room available. Fax No: (02216) 2890. **P & (V) Directions:** 1 mile from town centre, 200m past canal towards Trowbridge.

Bradford on Avon continued

JOHN & PAULINE PRICE ☎ (02216) 4750/3173.

An impressive building set in 11 acres, expertly converted to provide luxurious accommodation whilst retaining the atmosphere of a traditional English farmhouse. Inside, the decor and furnishings are elegant and provide the best in comfort. Widbrook Grange enjoys a welcoming, gracious atmosphere and is highly recommended as a delightful place to stay or as an elegant conference venue.

BRAINTREE Essex **Map 5 B1**

®££ **THE GREEN DRAGON** Upper London Road, Youngs End, CLUB Braintree.

Hours: Lunch 12 noon - 2.15pm, dinner 7pm - 9.30pm (last orders). Bar meals 12 noon - 2.15pm and 6pm - 9.30pm. **Cuisine:** English style cooking with international specialities. ⌫ None. **CC** Access, Visa, AmEx. **Other Points:** Children welcome in restaurant. No dogs. Fax No: (0245) 361030. ▣ **(V) Directions:** On the A131 between Braintree and Chelmsford.

BOB & MANDY GREYBROOK ☎ (0245) 361030.

Situated on the main road, half a mile from the Essex County Showground. Renovated to a high standard, the bar and restaurant have a friendly atmosphere. The restaurant, formerly a barn, has a wealth of original beams and hayrack. Outside there is a large garden with children's play area and aviary.

BRANCASTER STAITHE Norfolk **Map 5 A1**

®££ **THE JOLLY SAILORS** Brancaster Staithe, King's Lynn.

W **Hours:** Meals from 12 noon - 2pm and 7pm - 9pm, later on Friday and Saturday and food served all day during summer. Closed: Christmas Day. **Cuisine:** Staithe mussels, Brancaster sea trout, Norfolk duck. English cuisine - all food prepared and cooked on the premises. Bar meals in £ price range. ⌫ Bed and breakfast can be arranged in local houses. **CC** Access, Visa, Diners. **Other Points:** Dogs allowed in garden. Log fires. No music. Children welcome - special children's play area. Hard tennis court. ▣ **(V) Directions:** On A149 coast road, halfway between Hunstanton & Wells-Next-The-Sea.

ALISTER BORTHWICK ☎ (0485) 210314.

Records of The Jolly Sailors date back to 1789 - a popular haunt with locals of all types. Beer drawn by hand pump. Close to good beaches, sailing, bird reserves and many places of interest including Sandringham and Holkham Hall. Award winning wine list.

BRIGHTON & HOVE East Sussex **Map 5 C1**

⌂££££**ADELAIDE HOTEL** 51 Regency Square, Brighton.

⌫ 3 single, 7 double, 1 twin and 1 family room, all en suite. Colour TV, radio, alarm, telephone and tea/coffee facilities in all rooms. Four-poster. **Hours:** 8am - 9.15am and 6.30pm - 8.30pm. Snacks available throughout the day. **CC** All major cards. **Other Points:** Children welcome. Open bank holidays. Street parking. Fax (0273) 220904. **Directions:** Located on seafront square behind west pier.

C I & R V BUXTON ☎ (0273) 205286.

A small, quality hotel set in a beautifully restored grade II listed Regency building in the heart of Brighton, which offers a warm

Brighton & Hove continued
welcome, friendly service and quiet informality. Places of interest nearby include Brighton Royal Pavillion, Arundel Castle, Battle Abbey and Brighton Marina. Direct trains to London and Gatwick.

�£ **CAVALAIRE HOUSE** 34 Upper Rock Gardens, Brighton.
⊨ 1 single, 3 double, 2 twin and 3 family bedrooms; 3 en suite. 1 bathroom, 1 shower. Cable TV, hairdryers and tea/coffee facilities in all bedrooms. **Hours:** Breakfast 8am - 8.45am (may be varied). Closed: over Christmas. **CC** None. **Other Points:** Central heating. No evening meals. Children over 7 years welcome. Residents lounge. **P**
BARBARA & BOB JONES ☎ (0273) 696899.
The house is situated close to the Palace Pier, Conference Centre and Marina.

⌂£££ **COSMOPOLITAN HOTEL** 31 New Steine, Brighton.
CLUB ⊨ 10 single, 4 twin, 4 double and 9 family bedrooms, 19 en suite. 7 bedrooms on ground floor. All with central heating, colour TV, clock, radio, alarm, direct dial phone. **Hours:** Breakfast 8am - 9am. **CC** All major cards. **Other Points:** Children welcome. TV lounge. Residential licensed bar. **Directions:** In a garden square, just off the main seafront road.
C PAPANICHOLA ☎ (0273) 682461.
Overlooking the beach and Palace Pier, the Cosmopolitan Hotel is a friendly, comfortable place to stay and popular with holiday makers and business visitors alike. There is a cosy residential licensed bar and the hotel is very central for shopping, entertainments and conference centres.

⊗£ **CRIPES!** 7 Victoria Road, Brighton.
Hours: Breakfast 10am - 12.30pm, Lunch 12 noon - 2.30pm, Dinner 6pm - 11.30pm (last orders). Closed: Christmas Day and Boxing Day. **Cuisine:** Creperie serving Crepes, Galettes (savoury pancakes) and a wide range of meat, fish and vegetarian dishes. Real ales, French beers and ciders. ⊨ None. **CC** Access, Visa, AmEx. **Other Points:** children welcome. No dogs. **(V) Directions:** Off Montpelier Road.
JOY LEADER ☎ (0273) 27878.
The simple, attractive decor is enhanced by candles and provides the ideal setting for the high quality food. Cripes! specialises in French crepes and galettes but also offers a wide and imaginative choice of other French dishes. Helpful staff with assist in your choice of meal. A relaxing atmosphere and good value for money.

⊗£ **DONATELLO RESTAURANT** 3 Brighton Place, The Lanes, Brighton.
Hours: Open all day, seven days a week from 11.30am - 11.30pm. **Cuisine:** Extensive menu of Italian dishes including pasta, pizzas, fish and meat dishes. Italian ice cream. ⊨ None. **CC** Access, AmEx, Diners. **Other Points:** Children welcome. Open all day at weekends. **P** ċ **(V) Directions:** In centre of Brighton's Lanes.
MR PIETRO ADDIS ☎ (0273) 775477.
A popular and well run Italian restaurant specialising in pasta dishes, pizzas and Italian ice cream. The menu offers an

Brighton & Hove continued

extensive choice of dishes at good value for money. A lively restaurant with friendly service and a warm, relaxed atmosphere.

⊗£££ **ENGLISH'S OYSTER BAR & SEAFOOD RESTAURANT**
29/31 East Street, Brighton.
Hours: 12 noon - 10.15pm. Closed: 24 - 26 December and January 1st. **Cuisine:** Seafood, including 'English's oysters', and fillets of dover sole. Wild salmon served - but only when in season. ⊨ None. **CC** All major cards. **Other Points:** Children welcome. No dogs. Open bank holidays and Sunday. ⅄ **(V) Directions:** In the heart of Brighton Lanes, 2 minutes walk from Royal Pavillion.
MRS P M LEIGH-JONES ☎ (0273) 27980/25661.
The restaurant is housed in three fisherman's cottages on the edge of Brighton's historic Lanes. For more than 200 years, English's Oyster Bar has been a family business, selling oysters and fish without a break in tradition. Well worth a visit.

ⅢD£££ **KEMPTON HOUSE HOTEL** 33/34 Marine Parade, Brighton.
CLUB ⊨ 12 bedrooms, all en suite. All rooms have colour TV, radio, alarm, telephone, hairdryer and tea/coffee making facilities. Four poster suite. Rooms overlooking beach and pier available.
Hours: Breakfast 8.30am - 9am, evening meals 6pm - 6.30pm. Bar snacks available throughout the day until 8pm. **CC** All major cards **Other Points:** Children welcome. Dogs allowed. Residents' lounge. Sea facing patio garden. Vegetarian dishes. Residential bar. Free street parking within 250 yds. **Directions:** A259 Marine Parade, close to Palace Pier. Seafront.
PHILIP & VALERIE SWAINE ☎ (0273) 570248.
A friendly, family run hotel situated opposite the beach and famous Palace Pier and within minutes of all amenities. Mr & Mrs Swaine assure a warm welcome and real 'home from home' atmosphere. With a high standard of accommodation, a patio overlooking the seafront, residential bar and comfortable surroundings, an enjoyable stay is guaranteed.

ⅢD£££ **KIMBERLEY HOTEL** 17 Atlingworth Street, Brighton.
⊨ 3 single, 4 double, 5 twin and 3 family rooms, 1 of them en suite and 12 with shower only. Colour TV and tea/coffee making facilities in all rooms. **Hours:** Breakfast 8am - 9am. **CC** Access, Visa. **Other Points:** Children welcome. Open bank holidays. Resident's lounge and bar. **Directions:** Situated between Brighton Marina and Palace Pier off the A259.
MRS M LISS & MRS R ROLAND ☎ (0273) 603504.
A friendly, family hotel with clean, comfortable rooms, a resident's lounge and bar facilities. Centrally situated, being only 2 minutes from the seafront, with the Royal Pavillion, Palace Pier and Marina nearby.

⊗££ **LE GRANDGOUSIER RESTAURANT** 15 Western Street,
⌣ Brighton.
Hours: Open Monday to Friday from 12.30pm - 2.30pm and dinners, Monday to Saturday, from 7.30pm. 6-course evening menu including half bottle wine within Routiers price limit. **Cuisine:** Panier de crudites, panier de saucissons secs, terrine de foie de volaille poivre vert. ⊨ None. **CC** Access, Visa, AmEx.

Brighton & Hove continued
Other Points: Children welcome. No dogs. **Directions:** In Brighton, at the bottom of Norfolk Square.
MR LEWIS HARRIS ☎ (0273) 772 005.
A small restaurant serving authentic French cuisine in the best French tradition. The 6-course set menu is beautifully presented by friendly staff. Les Routiers Symbol of Excellence Award winner 1992 for consistently providing outstanding quality and value.

Ⓓ£££ **MELFORD HALL HOTEL** 41 Marine Parade, Brighton.
⊨ 21 bedrooms, 17 en suite. All rooms have colour TV including Satellite, and tea/coffee making facilities. **Hours:** Breakfast 8am - 9am. ⒸⒸ All major cards. **Other Points:** Children welcome. Residents' lounge. No dogs. Ⓟ **Directions:** A259 Newhaven to Brighton. A259 Marine Parade, close to Palace Pier.
IAN DIXON ☎ (0273) 681435.
A seafront hotel on a corner position of a garden square and close to all main amenities. Melford Hall also overlooks the beach. The accommodation is en suite and ground floor rooms and four poster bedrooms are available. Under the personal supervision of the resident proprietors.

Ⓓ££ **NEW STEINE HOTEL** 12a New Steine, Brighton.
⊨ 3 single, 5 double, 1 twin and 2 family bedrooms, 5 en suite. TV and tea/ coffee making facilities in all rooms. **Hours:** Breakfast 8am - 9am. ⒸⒸ None. **Other Points:** Children welcome. Pets allowed. Central heating. Residents' lounge. Street parking.
Directions: In a Regency square just off the main Promenade.
MESSRS SHAW & MILLS ☎ (0273) 681546.
A grade II listed building in a Regency square, within easy walking distance of the town centre, conference centre and the famous Royal Pavillion. Pleasantly decorated and comfortably furnished, an enjoyable stay is assured.

⊗£ **PARIS TEXAS AMERICAN BISTRO** 128 Western Road, Brighton.
Hours: Serving meals from 9am - 11pm. **Cuisine:** American Bistro serving Texan and Mexican dishes. ⊨ None. ⒸⒸ All major cards. **Other Points:** Children welcome. Open Bank Holidays. No smoking area. Afternoon teas. Parties catered for. Mexican night.
(V) Directions: Western Road at Jct with Montpellier Road.
DAVID FITZPATRICK & KARL SIMPSON ☎ (0273) 747111.
Enjoying a quietly convivial atmosphere, this bistro serves up North American dishes tempered to suit the British palate. All dishes are very well presented with a professional touch. The high quality of the food and the excellent welcoming service ensure that Paris Texas is popular with locals and holidaymakers alike.

Ⓓ£££ **PASKINS HOTEL** 19 Charlotte Street, Brighton.
CLUB ⊨ 5 single, 3 twin, 10 double and 1 family bedroom, 16 en suite. All rooms have telephone, television, trouser press, tea/coffee making facilities. **Hours:** Breakfast 8am - 9am, Dinner 6.00pm - 8.30pm. ⒸⒸ Access, Visa. **Other Points:** Dogs allowed. Bar. Vegetarian meals available. Fax (0273) 621973. **Directions:** Near A23. 2 minutes from the beach.

Brighton & Hove continued

SUE PASKINS ☎ (0273) 601203.

Paskins Hotel is part of an elegant Georgian terrace in one of Brighton's conservation areas. Centrally located, the hotel is just 2 minutes from the beach and 5 minutes from the town and conference centres. Friendly and efficient staff ensure a warm welcome and a pleasant stay and the accommodation is of a very high standard. Meals include organic produce. Highly recommended.

⊗£ **PINOCCHIO** 22 New Road, Brighton.
Hours: Lunch 12 noon - 2.30pm and dinner 5pm - 11.30pm (last orders). Saturday and Sunday open 12 noon - 11.30pm. **Cuisine:** Pizza and pasta. Selection of chicken, veal, and fish dishes. ⊨ None. ☒ All major cards. **Other Points:** Children welcome. &
(V) Directions: Easily located opposite the Pavillion Theatre.
MR PIETRO ADDIS ☎ (0273) 677676.
A traditional Italian meal at a reasonable price in pleasant, unpretentious and relaxed surroundings.

⊗£ **REGENCY RESTAURANT** 131 King's Road, Brighton.
Hours: Meals served 10am - 11pm (last orders). Closed: 23rd December to 10th January. **Cuisine:** A wide range of meals with locally caught fresh fish a speciality. Other house specialities include Steak Diane, Chicken Chasseur, King Prawns. ⊨ None. ☒ Access, Visa, Diners. **Other Points:** Children welcome. Children's menu. Morning coffee and afternoon tea. Underground car park close by. Licensed. **(V) Directions:** A259. Opposite West Pier, Brighton seafront.
ROVERTOS & EMILIO SAVVIDES ☎ (0273) 25014.
A friendly, relaxed restaurant with welcoming staff where good food can be enjoyed throughout the day. The restaurant specialises in locally caught fresh fish with a wide choice of other dishes including roasts, grills and steaks. All food is well cooked and offers good value for money. In fine weather tables are available outside on the seafront.

⊗££ **SACKVILLE HOTEL** Kingsway, Hove.
Hours: Breakfast 7.30am - 9.30am, lunch 12.30pm - 2pm, dinner 7.30pm - 9.30pm (last orders). Bar lunch 11.30am - 2pm. **Cuisine:** English cuisine including a special hors d'oeuvres selection and carving trolley. ⊨ 45 bedrooms, all en suite. Many rooms have seaview/balcony. ☒ All major cards. **Other Points:** Children welcome. Dogs allowed. No-smoking area. ◨ **(V) Directions:** A259, sea front road - west out of Brighton.
DAVID MITCHELL - Manager ☎ (0273) 736292.
The hotel has a commanding sea front position, looking out over the bowling greens and the beaches. Oak panelling, luxurious furnishings and ornamental high ceilings create the feeling of space and comfort. The restaurant menu is very English with the accent on local fresh produce such as seafood.

⊗£ **ST CATHERINES LODGE HOTEL** Kingsway, Hove.
⊞£££ **Hours:** Breakfast 7.45am - 9.30am, lunch 12.30pm - 2pm (last
CLUB orders) and 7pm - 9pm (last orders). **Cuisine:** Extensive a la carte. Dishes include roast carved at table. ⊨ 50 bedrooms, 40 en suite. Four poster suites. ☒ All major cards. **Other Points:** Children

Brighton & Hove continued

welcome. Garden. Games Room. Residents lounge. Cocktail bar. Afternoon teas. Conference facilities and function rooms. ◘ **(V) Directions:** On the A259 coast road, near King Alfred Sports Centre.

JOHN HOULTON ☎ (0273) 778181.

A 150 year old Victorian gabled hotel, centrally situated on the seafront, with full accommodation facilities. Good food at value for money prices is served by well trained attentive staff in attractive surroundings. Located nearby is the King Alfred Leisure Centre with swimming pools, water slides and ten-pin bowling.

⊗££ **THE BLUES BROTHERS** 6 Little East Street, Brighton.

Hours: 11am - 11pm, except Monday: 6pm - 11pm. **Cuisine:** French/American. Creole cooking - Blackened Bay Shark, Piquante Chicken. Speciality American beers. ► None. **CC** All major cards. **Other Points:** Children welcome. Afternoon teas. Parties up to 35. ⅙ **(V) Directions:** Adjacent to Town Hall, between Seafront & Brighton Lanes.

MICHAEL ROSS ☎ (0273) 735527

The Blues Brothers, set in a period listed building is popular with both locals and visitors. Deep mahogany furniture adds to the warm, relaxed atmosphere. Friendly staff serve fresh Cajun and Creole cusine, which is unusual and tasty. Live Jazz/Blues on Friday and Sunday evenings add to the experience The restaurant is situated near to the Lanes and Brighton Town Hall.

🛏£ **THE LANGHAM GUEST HOUSE** 16 Charlotte Street, Brighton.

► 8 bedrooms, all with colour TV and tea/coffee making facilities. **Hours:** Breakfast served only. **CC** None. **Other Points:** Children welcome. Residents' lounge. Full English breakfast. **Directions:** Off the A259 Marine Parade.

NICK & KAREN HOOPER ☎ (0273) 682843.

A warm and friendly welcome is extended to all guests at The Langham. It is a small, cosy, grade II listed guest house, situated in a quiet road just off the sea-front and close to all amenities and attractions. All bedrooms are spacious and comfortable and offer excellent value for money. Proprietors, Nick and Karen Hooper, will ensure you have an enjoyable and comfortable stay.

⊗££ **THE LATIN IN THE LANE** 10-11 King's Road, Brighton.

Hours: Meals served 12 noon - 2.15pm and 6pm - 11pm (last orders). **Cuisine:** Italian cuisine. Very extensive menu offering an excellent choice of starters, pasta, meat and fish dishes. ► None. **CC** All major cards. **Other Points:** Children welcome. Access for disabled to restaurant but toilets are upstairs. **(V) Directions:** Just off the seafront, behind the Queen's Hotel.

MR CAPPAI ☎ (0273) 28672.

A popular Italian restaurant, decorated in cool 1930's Italian designs with tiled floor, marble tables and peach and white colours. A varied menu is complemented by a good selection of wines. Situated just off the seafront close to the Palace Pier.

Brighton & Hove continued

🏨££ **TROUVILLE HOTEL** 11 New Steine, Brighton.

🛏 2 single, 3 double, 2 twin and 2 family bedrooms and 2 with en suite bath/shower. 1 bathroom. 1 shower. TV in bedrooms. Tea/coffee making facilities. 1 four poster bed. **Hours:** Breakfast 8.15am - 9am (weekdays), 8.45am - 9.15am (weekends). 🆇 Access, Visa, AmEx. **Other Points:** Central heating. Children welcome. Licensed. Residents lounge. **Directions:** Just off the seafront.

MR & MRS J P HANSELL ☎ (0273) 697384.

A spotless, white townhouse with window boxes enhancing its appearance, situated in a pleasant, grassed Regency square on the sea front. The town centre, Marina, Pavillion, Lanes and conference centre are all within walking distance.

BRINKWORTH Wiltshire **Map 4 B1**

⊗££ **THE THREE CROWNS** Brinkworth, Chippenham.

Hours: Lunch 10am - 2.30pm, Dinner 6pm - 11pm. Sunday Lunch 12 noon - 3pm, Dinner 7pm - 10.30pm. **Cuisine:** Blackboard menu - changes daily according to the availability of fresh produce. Eg. locally smoked Chicken, Rack of lamb, steaks, fresh fish. 🛏 None. 🆇 Access, Visa. **Other Points:** Children welcome. Garden. Dogs allowed. 🅿 ⅙ **(V) Directions:** On the B4042, next to the village church in Brinkworth.

MR A WINDLE ☎ (066641) 366.

A stone built, 18th century pub situated on the village green. There is an extensive menu with an emphasis on fresh produce. All dishes are cooked to order and served with a minimum of 5 fresh vegetables. The Three Crowns is justifiably proud of its award-winning cuisine. Good service and a relaxed, friendly atmosphere will add to the enjoyment of your meal.

BRISTON Norfolk **Map 5 A2**

⊗££ **THE JOHN H STRACEY** West End, Briston, Nr Melton
🏨£ Constable.

CLUB **Hours:** Lunch 12 noon - 2.15pm and dinner 7pm - 9.30pm (last orders). Bar meals served 12 noon - 2.15pm and 7pm - 10pm. **Cuisine:** Comprehensive menu including Salmon a la Stracey (fresh salmon steaks, poached in white wine, with prawns and parsley). 🛏 2 bedrooms with TV, 1 en suite. 🆇 Access, AmEx. **Other Points:** Children welcome. Vegetarian meals available on request. Afternoon tea available. 🅿 **Directions:** On B1354 close to Melton Constable and en route to Aylsham/Norwich.

MR & MRS R E FOX ☎ (0263) 860891.

Professional and friendly staff take special care to make guests feel at home. Mr Fox is at present offering Bargain Breaks. With the good food and relaxing surroundings, this promises to be a popular bargain indeed.

BROADSTAIRS Kent **Map 5 C2**

⊗££ **HARPERS WINE BAR** 8 Harbour Street, Broadstairs.

CLUB **Hours:** Meals served 7pm - 12 midnight (last orders 10.30pm). Bar meals 7pm - 10.30pm. **Cuisine:** Home cooked cuisine with fresh vegetables. 🛏 None. 🆇 Access, Visa. **Other Points:** Children welcome. 🅿 **(V) Directions:** Off the A253 north of Ramsgate. Situated near the main beach.

L J & B G BAKER ☎ (0843) 602494.

Broadstairs continued

Attractive grade 2 listed building with natural wood and flint interior creating warm and pleasant surroundings. Beautifully cooked cuisine at affordable prices makes this authentic wine bar a definite stop for those in the area.

BROCKENHURST Hampshire **Map 4 C1**

⊗££ **THE WATERSPLASH HOTEL** The Rise, Brockenhurst.
⏛££££ **Hours:** Lunch 1pm - 2pm, dinner 7.30pm - 8.30pm (last orders). Bar meals 12 noon - 2pm. **Cuisine:** English dishes. Specialities include pot roast haunch of New Forest venison. ⊨ 23 bedrooms, all en suite. Colour TV, tea/coffee making facilities and direct dial telephones in all rooms. ⃝ Access, Visa. **Other Points:** Children welcome. Garden. Dogs allowed. No-smoking area. Afternoon teas. ▣ & **(V) Directions:** Off A337 south of Lyndhurst. Turning to The Rise opp. Shell Garage.
ROBIN & JUDY FOSTER ☎ (0590) 22344.

A family run Victorian country house hotel set in 2 acres of secluded gardens. The hotel is noted for good food, friendly service and comfortable accommodation. The menu offers imaginative and well cooked food. Situated in the centre of the New Forest.

BROMLEY Kent **Map 5 B1**

⊗£ **CARIOCA RESTAURANT** 239 High Street, Bromley.
Hours: Meals from 12 noon - 2pm and 6pm - 11pm (last orders). Closed: Christmas and Boxing Day. **Cuisine:** Tandoori dishes, Karai/mango pancakes. ⊨ None. ⃝ All major cards. **Other Points:** Children welcome. No dogs. ▣ & **(V) Directions:** On the main High Street in Bromley.
MR K MODI ☎ (01) 460 7130/6486.

An authentic tandoori restaurant on Bromley High Street with an attractive frontage enhanced by window boxes. All herbs and spices are freshly ground, and combined with the finest ingredients to make delicious dishes. All breads are baked fresh to order.

⊗££ **GUESTS RESTAURANT** 18 Station Approach, Hayes, Bromley.
Hours: Lunch served Sunday only at 12 noon - 2.15pm (last orders). Dinner Tuesday to Saturday 7pm - 9.30pm (last orders). Closed: Mondays and usually 3 weeks in August. **Cuisine:** Choice of two, 4 course table d'hote menus. Dishes may include - Salmon in Brandy & Lobster sauce in flaky pastry, Rack of English Lamb. ⊨ None. ⃝ Access, Visa. **Other Points:** Children welcome. Menus change every 3 months. ▣ & **(V) Directions:** 200 yards from Hayes Station, just off the B251.
MR VINCENT SPALLINI ☎ (081) 462 8594.

An excellent restaurant offering a warm welcome, good quality and value for money. There is a good choice on both of the menus and all dishes are excellently cooked using fresh produce and attractively presented. Nothing seems too much trouble for the welcoming staff. With comfortable furnishings and a relaxed atmosphere, Guests is an ideal choice for a most enjoyable meal.

BURBAGE

BROWNHILLS West Midlands **Map 4 A1**
⊗££ **TERRACE RESTAURANT** 9 Watling Street, Newtown, Brownhills, nr Walsall.

Hours: Lunch 12 noon - 3pm, Dinner 7pm - 10pm (last orders). Closed: Sunday evening. **Cuisine:** Traditional English cuisine. Specialities include Beef Wellington and fresh fish. ⊨ None. **CC** All major cards. **Other Points:** Children welcome. Childrens portions. No dogs. Banqueting and conference facilities. Party menus. ◨ ఉ **(V) Directions:** Main A5 trunk road. 7 miles east of M6. 5 miles NE of Walsall.

MR ADSHEAD ☎ (0543) 378291/360456

A modern 150 seater restaurant which has deservedly won awards for its delightful floral gardens. The interior of the restaurant is modern and comfortable with fresh flowers in abundance. Well-cooked, attractively presented food is served in generous portions.

BUBBENHALL Warwickshire **Map 4 A2**
⊗£ **MALT SHOVEL** Lower End, Bubbenhall, nr Coventry.

Hours: Bar meals 12 noon - 2pm and 6.30pm - 9.30pm. **Cuisine:** Italian food and steaks. Wine list offers excellent value for money. ⊨ None. **CC** None. **Other Points:** Children welcome. No dogs. Patio garden. ◨ ఉ **Directions:** Off the A445, Leamington Spa to Rugby road.

ANTONIO CARDELLINO ☎ (0203) 301141.

A 17th century, tudor building, now the village pub with a charisma all of its own. Set in excellent grounds, there is a patio garden and a bowling green. Oak beams, real open fires and good home cooked food have drawn people from miles around. Excellent value for money. 10 minutes drive from Coventry.

BUNTINGFORD Hertfordshire **Map 5 B1**
⊗££ **THE FOX INN** Aspenden, Nr Buntingford.

Hours: Lunch 12 noon - 2pm and dinner 7pm - 10pm (last orders). **Cuisine:** Fresh produce country cooking with frequently changing menu, that typically includes homemade pies, steaks, fish and chicken dishes. ⊨ None. **CC** None. **Other Points:** Children welcome. Garden dining. Open bank holidays and Sunday. ◨ **(V) Directions:** Off the A10.

MR & MRS COURAGE ☎ (0763) 71886.

An old village inn, set in its own grounds with a stream running through the garden, providing a small cosy bar and dining room where guests enjoy good food and a relaxing atmosphere. Mr & Mrs Courage have brought their Routiers standards from their previous establishment and have already developed a very good local reputation for generous portions of good homecooked food.

BURBAGE Wiltshire **Map 4 B1**
⊗££ **SAVERNAKE FOREST HOTEL** Savernake Road, Burbage, nr Marlborough.

Hours: Breakfast 7.45am - 9.30am, 8.30am - 10am on Sunday, lunch 12.30pm - 2pm and dinner 7.30pm - 9.30pm (last orders 9.15pm). Bar meals 12.30pm - 2pm and 7.30pm - 9pm. Bar meals in £ price range. **Cuisine:** In the restaurant: stir fry chicken, scallops of monkfish, local Rainbow Trout. In the bar: fish, grills, prawn dips, beef goulash, pork kebab. ⊨ 14 bedrooms all en

Burbage continued

suite. **CC** All major cards. **Other Points**: Children welcome. Pets by arrangement. **P** **(V) Directions**: From the A338/A346 in Burbage village, follow signs to Savernake.

MR & MRS GRAY ☎ (0672) 810206.

Built in 1863 by the Marquis of Ailesbury on the edge of Savernake Forest, this attractive country hotel retains many original features. There are many pleasant walks in the area and shooting, horse riding and golf can be arranged locally.

BURCOMBE Wiltshire **Map 4 C1**

⊗£ **SHIP INN** Burcombe, nr Wilton, Salisbury.

Hours: Meals from 12 noon - 2pm and 6.30pm - 11pm (last orders 10pm). **Cuisine**: Grills, bar snacks. ⊨ None. **CC** Access, Visa. **Other Points**: Children welcome. No dogs. Coaches welcome. **P** &. **Directions**: Off the A30.

TONY BAXTON - Manager ☎ (0722) 743182.

A delightful country inn which is well sign posted from the A30. In the cold winter months, real log fires help to ease the chill, while in summer, the large garden running down to the river is popular.

BURFORD Oxfordshire **Map 4 B1**

⊗££ **THE ANGEL INN** Witney Street, Burford.

Hours: Lunch and bar snacks 12 noon - 2pm, Dinner and bar snacks 7pm - 9.30pm (last orders). Open all year. **Cuisine**: Imaginative dishes using high quality fresh produce. Full & light meals. Dishes may include Saute of Monkfish with a garlic, ginger & chilli cream sauce. ⊨ 2 bedrooms, both en suite - by 1992. **CC** Access, Visa. **Other Points**: Dogs allowed. Garden and dining terrace. Open all year. **(V) Directions**: A40. 50 yards off Burford High Street.

JEAN THAXTER ☎ (0993) 822438.

Situated just off Burford High Street, this traditional old Inn has been imaginatively redecorated and refurbished. Mrs Thaxter provides superb food and service to complement the new environment and the warm and friendly atmosphere is most inviting. An excellent example of a country town inn. At present, accommodation is not available but 'watch this space'!

⊗££ **THE GOLDEN PHEASANT HOTEL** The High Street, Burford.

CLUB **Hours**: Breakfast 7.30am - 9.30am, lunch 12 noon - 2pm (last orders) and dinner 7pm - 9.30pm (last orders). **Cuisine**: Variety of French and English dishes. Choice of two menus - Countryman & a la carte. ⊨ 12 bedrooms, all with private facilities. 2 four posters. **CC** Access, Visa, AmEx. **Other Points**: Children welcome. Afternoon teas. Pets allowed. No smoking areas. Fax No: (099382) 2621. **P** **(V) Directions**: Off the A40, on Burford High Street.

DANIEL HOLMES ☎ (099382) 3223/3417.

A 15th century Cotswold stone building that has been renovated to provide Burford with a small and comfortable hotel. Exposed beams, stone walling and large fireplaces with log fires provide a cosy atmosphere. Highly recommended for its excellent cuisine, attractive and comfortable bedrooms and friendly efficent service.

BURLEY Hampshire **Map 4 C1**

⊗££ **THE BURLEY MANOR HOTEL & RESTAURANT** Burley, Nr Ringwood, New Forest, Hampshire.

Hours: Monday to Saturday: breakfast 7.30am - 10am, bar snacks 12 noon - 2pm and dinner served 7pm - 10pm (last orders). Sunday: breakfast 8am - 10am, traditional lunch 12.30pm - 2pm and dinner 7pm - 9.30pm. **Cuisine:** English/French dishes. ⊨ 30 bedrooms, all en suite. **CC** All major cards. **Other Points:** Children welcome. Dogs allowed. Open for Sunday lunch and during bank holidays. Heated swimming pool for residents. Fax number 3227. Telex:41565. **P** & **(V) Directions:** Turn off A31 at Picketts Post, just before Ringwood, into village.
MISS SALLY WHITTLE - Manageress ☎ (04253) 3522.
A fine old manor house standing in its own 8 acres of beautiful grounds where horses graze. This secluded retreat is the ideal location for a relaxing meal, served by professional yet friendly staff. Well worth a visit.

BURTON ON THE WOLDS Leicestershire **Map 4 A2**

⊗£ **GREYHOUND INN** Melton Road, Burton on the Wolds.

Hours: Bar meals from 12 noon - 2pm and 7pm - 10pm. **Cuisine:** Home cooked specials. ⊨ None. **CC** All major cards. **Other Points:** Well behaved children welcome. No dogs. Coaches by appointment. LVs accepted. **P** **(V) Directions:** B676 Loughborough to Melton Mowbray road.
PHILIP & ANN ASHLEY ☎ (0509) 880860.
A traditional coaching inn renovated in 1984. All the food is home cooked and supported by a comprehensive wine list. British Institute of Innkeeping (East Midlands Section) Pub of the Year 1988 and 1989.

BURTON UPON TRENT Staffordshire **Map 4 A1**

⊗£ **THE HORSESHOE INN** Main Street, Tatenhill, Burton upon Trent.

Hours: Monday to Saturday 12 noon - 2pm, Traditional Sunday lunch 12 noon - 1.30pm (bookings only) & Sunday snacks 12 noon - 1.30pm. Evenings Tuesday to Saturday 6pm - 9pm. Bank Holiday Mondays 6pm - 9pm. **Cuisine:** Restaurant a la carte menu - steaks, fish (incl. salmon steak), duckling, chicken with stilton sauce. Bar meals include homemade steak & kidney pie. ⊨ None. **CC** Access, Visa. **Other Points:** Children welcome. No dogs. Coaches by appointment. Fax: (0283) 511314. LV's accepted. **P** & **(V) Directions:** 1 mile from A38 (Branston exit) signpost Tatenhill. Rt at crossrds.
MR & MRS M J BOULD ☎ (0283) 64913.
An attractive country inn dating back to 1600, standing in its own gardens with a large car park and childrens play area. Traditional cask ales and Sunday roasts very popular.

BURY ST EDMUNDS Suffolk **Map 5 A1**

⊗£ **BUTTERFLY HOTELS** 45a Bury East Exit, Moreton Hall, Bury ⌂££ St Edmunds.

Hours: Breakfast 7am - 9.30am, lunch 12.30pm - 2pm and dinner 7pm - 10pm. **Cuisine:** English/Continental, carvery and buffet. Fixed price menu from £7.25. ⊨ 50 rooms. 25 single, 11 twin, 10 double, 4 family rooms, all en suite. **CC** All major cards. **Other**

Bury St Edmunds continued

Points: Children welcome. No smoking areas. Conference facilities. ◘ & (V) Directions: Off A45, Bury East exit.
BUTTERFLY HOTELS LIMITED ☎ (0284) 760884.

A cosy and intimate atmosphere in a large purpose built modern hotel, the central feature being a large conservatory restaurant. The 'Bury Butterfly' offers excellent standards in both food and accommodation - all rooms equipped to a very high standard.

⊗££ **THE GRANGE HOTEL** Thurston, Bury St Edmunds.
⊞££££ Hours: 7am - 9.30am, 12 noon - 2.30pm and 7pm - 10pm (last orders 9.30pm). Bar meals 12 noon - 2.30pm and 7pm - 10pm (last orders 9.30pm). Cuisine: English and French cuisine, specialities including dover sole stuffed with mushrooms in a cream sauce. ⊨ 15 bedrooms, 10 en suite. ☒ Access, Visa. Other Points: Children welcome. Dogs allowed. Open for Sunday lunch and bank holidays. ◘ & (V) Directions: A45 to Bury St Edmunds, exit at Sugar Beet factory and follow A143.
MR & MRS E G WAGSTAFF ☎ (0359) 31260.

Attractive mock Tudor country house hotel with a large garden for al fresco dining. Very helpful and welcoming staff who are eager to please. Kilverstone Wildlife Park, Cambridge, Ickworth Hall and Anglo-Saxon village all nearby.

⊗£ **THE MASONS ARMS** Whiting Street, Bury St Edmunds.
Hours: Lunch 12 noon - 2pm, dinner 7pm - 9.30pm (last orders). Closed: Sunday evening. Cuisine: All dishes are home cooked and include Chilled carrot soup, Dover sole, Japanese prawns. ⊨ None. ☒ None. Other Points: Children welcome. Garden and courtyard. Dogs allowed. (V)
MR C WARTON ☎ (0284) 753955.

A delightful 17th century, timbered building with a typical, traditional interior. Weather permitting, bar meals can be enjoyed at tables in the courtyard. All dishes are freshly home cooked, well presented and served, and offer excellent value for money. The atmosphere is friendly and informal with welcoming staff and light background music.

⊗££ **THE SIX BELLS INN** Bardwell, Bury St Edmunds.
⊞££££ Hours: Breakfast 7.30am - 9.15am (weekends 8.30am - 9.45am). ◠ Lunch 12 noon - 2.30pm (last orders 2pm). Dinner 7pm - 11pm [CLUB] (last orders 10pm, Sunday 9.30pm). Cuisine: Extensive bar & restaurant meals. Steak & seafood specialities. Breast of chicken with apricots & brandy in cream sauce, Seafood Thermidor, Stilton steak. ⊨ 2 single, 2 twin, 2 double, 1 family, all en suite. ☒ Access, Visa. Other Points: Children welcome. Garden. ◘ (V) Directions: 1/2 mile off A143. Just off Bardwell village green, nr duck pond.
RICHARD & CAROL SALMON ☎ (0359) 50820.

A traditional 16th Century coaching inn, situated just off the village green near the duck pond in the peaceful Suffolk village of Bardwell. Offering all the delights of a country free house - good food and drink in a friendly hospitable and informal atmosphere, the Six Bells with its lovely accommodation in converted barn and stables, makes a delightful stop.

Bury St Edmunds continued

⊛£ **THE THREE KINGS** Hengrave Rd, Fornham-All-Saints, Bury St Edmunds.
Hours: Lunch 12 noon - 2pm (last orders) and dinner 7pm - 9.30pm (last orders). Closed: Sunday evening and Mondays but bar food available Monday lunchtimes. **Cuisine:** Choice of Carvery, with blackboard 'Specials of the Day' and Bar meals. ⊨ None. **CC** Access, Visa. **Other Points:** Children welcome. Garden. **P** &. **Directions:** In the Village centre on the main road, 4 m from Bury St Edmunds.
JOHN & CAROLYN CONWAY ☎ (0284) 766979.
A traditional 18th Century inn, offering very well presented, tasty food in friendly comfortable surroundings. Your hosts, John and Carolyn Conway ensure that you are promptly served and all your needs catered for.

CAMBRIDGE Cambridgeshire **Map 5 B1**

⊛££ **ARUNDEL HOUSE HOTEL** 53 Chesterton Road, Cambridge.
⌂£££ **Hours:** Restaurant open 12.15pm - 1.45pm and 6.30pm - 9.30pm. **Cuisine:** French and English cuisine, children's and vegetarian menus and extensive range of bar meals. ⊨ 88 bedrooms, 78 en suite, all with colour TV, video, radio, hairdryer, telephone, and tea/coffee making facilities. **CC** All major cards. **Other Points:** Children welcome. Limited access for disabled. Fax No: (0223) 67721. **P** **(V) Directions:** On the A1134 city centre ring-road.
MR R NORFOLK - Manager ☎ (0223) 67701.
Overlooking the River Cam and Jesus Green, the Arundel House Hotel is one of the few privately owned hotels in Cambridge. Within easy walking distance of the city centre and university colleges. An elegant conversion of fine Victorian terraced houses, with a reputation for some of the best food in the area.

⌂£ **BENSON HOUSE** 24 Huntingdon Road, Cambridge.
⊨ 2 single, 3 double, 2 twin and 2 family bedrooms, 2 en suite. 1 bathroom. 1 shower. Colour TV and tea/coffee facilities in all rooms. **Hours:** Breakfast 8am - 9am. **CC** None. **Other Points:** Central heating. Children welcome. Dogs allowed. Residents lounge. Licensed bar. **P** **Directions:** In north Cambridge on the A1307, opposite Newhall College.
MRS DOWLING & MR D MANSFIELD ☎ (0223) 311594.
A well established guest house offering comfortable accommodation only 10 minutes walk from the city centre and University. The breakfasts are hearty and a choice is offered.

⌂££ **CRISTINAS GUEST HOUSE** 47 St Andrews Road, Cambridge.
⊨ 2 twin, 2 double and 2 family bedrooms, 4 with en suite. **Hours:** Breakfast 7am - 8.30am. **CC** None. **Other Points:** Children welcome. No pets. Central heating. TV lounge. **P** **Directions:** St Andrews Road is off Elizabeth Way.
CRISTINA CELENTANO ☎ (0223) 65855/327700.
A modern building in a quiet location, only 15 minutes walk from the City centre and colleges. All bedrooms have colour TV and tea and coffee making facilities and there is also a comfortable television lounge for guests' use.

Cambridge continued

⊗££ **THE ANCIENT SHEPHERDS** High Street, Fen Ditton, Cambridge.
Hours: 12 noon - 2.15pm and 7pm - 9.30pm (last orders 9pm). Bar meals 12 noon - 2.15pm and 6.30pm - 9.30pm (last orders 9pm). Closed: Sundays and 1 week over the Christmas period. **Cuisine:** Varied a la carte menu, including moules mariniere, and fresh fish. Bar meals include Chicken Ancient Shepherds - chicken with apricots, brandy & cream. ⊨ None. ☎ Access, Visa. **Other Points:** Children over 12 welcome. Dogs allowed in garden only. Garden dining. Open bank holidays. ◨ ♿ **(V) Directions:** B1047 from A45 travelling east. Turn right into Fen Ditton High St.
HILTON ROSE ☎ (02205) 3280.
A very friendly country inn, circa 1540, serving well-cooked and presented food. Very pleasant atmosphere, with a good cross-section of business people, students and locals.

⊞££ **THE SUFFOLK HOUSE PRIVATE HOTEL** 69 Milton Road, Cambridge.
⊨ 3 double, 2 twin, 3 family bedrooms, 8 en suite. TV in all bedrooms. **Hours:** Breakfast 8am - 8.30am and 8.30am - 9am (weekends only). Lunch 12.30pm (order by 10am). ☎ Access, Visa. **Other Points:** Central heating. Children welcome. No dogs. Residents lounge. Garden. Licensed. Vegetarian meals available. ◨ **Directions:** Situated on the A1309, leave the A45 at A10 Ely and A1309 junction.
MR & MRS CUTHBERT ☎ (0223) 352016.
A large 1920s gable fronted detached house, set in a large secluded garden with an impressive array of flowers and shrubs. A high standard of comfort and cleanliness is maintained by the Cuthberts who extend a warm welcome to their guests. Less than 20 minutes walk from the city centre.

CANTERBURY Kent **Map 5 C2**

⊗££ **POINTERS HOTEL** 1 London Road, Canterbury.
⊞£££ **Hours:** Breakfast 7.30am - 9am and dinner 7.30pm - 9pm (last orders 8.15pm) **Cuisine:** Traditional. ⊨ 14 bedrooms, 10 en suite. Colour TV, Radio. Tea/coffee making facilities. Direct dial phone. ☎ All major cards. **Other Points:** Comfortable lounge and well stocked bar. Dining room open to non-residents. Children welcome. Pets allowed. ◨ **Directions:** Northside of Canterbury. On London Road opposite parish church.
MR & MRS O'BRIEN ☎ (0227) 456846.
A Grade II listed Georgian hotel situated near the City centre offering comfortable accommodation in a warm and friendly atmosphere. Enjoy good food at reasonable prices and easy access to shopping, entertainment and historical sites.

⊗£ **THE GREEN MAN** Shatterling, nr Wingham, Canterbury.
⊞££ **Hours:** Meals from 7.45am - 9am, 12 noon - 2pm and 7pm - 8.45pm (last orders). Open to non-residents all week, except Sunday evening residents only. **Cuisine:** Genuine English home cooking. ⊨ 4 bedrooms, 1 en suite. ☎ Access, Visa. **Other Points:** Children welcome. Coaches by appointment. ◨ **(V) Directions:** On the A257 between Wingham and Ash.
MESSRS FERNE & GREENWOOD ☎ (0304) 812525.

Canterbury continued
Old English country inn with garden, set in an area known for its hop growing and vineculture. 2 'bat & trap pitches'. Easy access to Dover and Ramsgate ports.

Ⓜ££ **YORKE LODGE GUEST HOUSE** 50 London Road, Canterbury.
⊨ 1 single, 2 double and 3 family bedrooms, all en suite. All rooms have tea/coffee making facilities. **Hours:** Breakfast 8am - 9am and snacks on request in the evening. **CC** None. **Other Points:** Central heating. Children welcome. Residents lounge and library. Garden. **P Directions:** Close to the A2 on London Road.
ROBIN & LINDSAY HALL ☎ (0227) 451 243.
An elegant, spacious Victorian house situated close to the city centre. With library, and a sitting room which opens onto the walled garden. Relax and enjoy a special bed and breakfast.

CASTLE ACRE Norfolk Map 5 A1
⊗£ **THE OSTRICH INN** Castle Acre, King's Lynn.
Hours: Bar meals 12 noon - 2pm and 7.30pm - 10.30pm. Closed: Christmas and Boxing Day. **Cuisine:** Bar meals ranging from sausages to caviar, cockles to T-bone steaks. Daily specials from all over the world, cooked by the chef/proprietor. ⊨ 2 bedrooms. **CC** None. **Other Points:** Children welcome - special menu available. No dogs. Coaches by appointment. **P ᴋ (V) Directions:** On the A1065 between Swaffham and Fakenham on the village green.
RAYMOND H WAKELEN ☎ (076 05) 398.
Large 16th century coaching inn with 2 big open fires in the lounge bar. On the A1065 in a typical, small Norfolk village which has the Peddars Way running through it. Many National Trust attractions nearby.

CASTLE DONINGTON Leicestershire Map 4 A2
⊗££ **DONINGTON MANOR HOTEL** High Street.
Hours: Open 7am - midnight, 9.30pm (last orders). Closed: 27th to 30th December. **Cuisine:** Melton Fillet, Encourte Dijon, game dishes in season. ⊨ 36 bedrooms, 36 en suite. **CC** All major cards. **Other Points:** No dogs. Executive suites. Four-poster rooms. French spoken. Limited access for the disabled (not to restaurant) - 3 ground-floor bedrooms. **P (V) Directions:** Off M1 at Junct. 24, 2 miles along A6 to Derby, turn left at B6540.
MR N GRIST ☎ (0332) 810253.
An 18th century Regency Coaching Inn, popular with race-goers. Donington Manor provides the epitome of traditional British hospitality.

⊗££ **LE CHEVALIER** 2 Borough St, Castle Donington.
Ⓜ££ **Hours:** 7.30am - 8.30am, 12 noon - 2pm, and 6.30pm - 11pm (last orders 11.30pm). Restaurant closed to non-residents on Sundays and Mondays. **Cuisine:** French and continental cuisine, specialities including Boudin a l'Anglaise and Filet de Boeuf Chevalier. ⊨ 4 bedrooms, all en suite, with colour TV, radio, alarm, telephone, and tea/coffee making facilities. **CC** All major cards. **Other Points:** Children welcome. No dogs allowed. Open bank holidays. Residents garden. **(V) Directions:** Just off B6540 - Jct 24 of M1. On main street of Castle Donington.

CENTRAL & SOUTHERN ENGLAND

Castle Donington continued
MR JAD OTAKI ☎ (0332) 812106/812005
A small, intimate personally-run restaurant with a well-established reputation for its good food and friendly atmosphere. It now has a number of lovely rooms around the rear courtyard and makes an ideal base for exploring the surrounding area, with Donington Park Racetrack, Nottingham, Derby and Alton Towers nearby.

CHALE Isle of Wight **Map 4 C2**
⊗££ **CLARENDON HOTEL and WIGHT MOUSE INN** Chale.
CLUB **Hours:** Open Monday to Saturday 11am - 12 midnight, Sunday 12 noon - 3pm and 7pm - 10.30pm. Restaurant open 12 noon - 10pm. Open all year round. Full menu available all afternoon Monday - Saturday, winter and summer. **Cuisine:** Wight Mouse Inn: Island steaks, local fish, crab, homemade pizzas. In the Clarendon Hotel: fresh vegetables, fresh local fish, meat and game. ⊨ 11 bedrooms, 8 en suite. 1 family suite. **CC** Access. **Other Points:** Children most welcome. Live entertainment every night throughout the year. Egon Ronay Family Pub of the Year 1990. ▣ **(V) Directions:** On B3399, 50 yds from the Military Rd B3055 in Chale. Direct access.
MR & MRS J BRADSHAW ☎ (0983) 730431.
A charming 17th century Inn overlooking Chale Bay in the south of the Island, a few minutes from Blackgang Chine. The hotel enjoys a reputation for good food, wine, comfort and hospitality. With over 365 whiskies, real ales and open fires, a warm, friendly atmosphere is assured!

CHARLBURY Oxfordshire **Map 4 B2**
⊗£££ **THE BELL HOTEL** Church Street, Charlbury.
⊞££££ **Hours:** Breakfast 7.30am - 10.30am, Lunch 12.30pm - 2pm (last orders), Dinner 7.30pm - 9pm (last orders). Bar snacks 12.30pm - 2pm and 7.30pm - 8.30pm. **Cuisine:** Classic English and French cuisine. The restaurant specialises in fresh fish and game in season. ⊨ 14 bedrooms, all en suite. **CC** All major cards. **Other Points:** Children welcome. No smoking area. Afternoon teas. Dogs allowed. Residents lounge. Garden. Conference facilites. Fax No: (0608) 811447. ▣ ⅋ **(V) Directions:** 5 miles west of Woodstock. Turning off A3400 just north of Woodstock
DAVID JACKSON ☎ (0608) 810278.
A 17th century hotel surrounded by breathtaking countryside and set in an unspoilt Cotswold village. The Bell is a privately owned, professionally run hotel offering good food and a friendly atmosphere. Only 75 minutes by rail from London and 15 minutes from Oxford.

CHELMSFORD Essex **Map 5 B1**
⊗££ **COUNTY HOTEL** Rainsford Road.
Hours: Restaurant open weekdays 7.30am - 9.15am, 12.30pm - 2pm and 6.30pm - 9pm. Sundays and Bank Holidays 8am - 9.30am, 12.45pm - 2pm and 7pm - 8.15pm. **Cuisine:** Tournedos en Croute, Escalope de Veau Marsala, Filet de porc Alaine, Supreme de volaille Bergere. ⊨ 52 bedrooms, 32 en suite. **CC** All major cards. **Other Points:** Children welcome. Fax: 0245 492762. ▣ ⅋ **(V)**
MR ANDREW HARRISON ☎ (0245) 491911.

Chelmsford continued

This is a very old established hotel where you are always assured of good food and a friendly welcome.

⊛££ **MIAMI HOTEL** Princes Road, Chelmsford.
Hours: Meals from 7.30am - 9am, 12 noon - 2.30pm and 6.30pm - 10pm. Bar meals 12 noon until 2.30pm and 6pm - 11pm. **Cuisine:** Fillet mignon, steak au poivre, beef Strogonoff. ⊨ 53 bedrooms, 50 en suite. **CC** All major cards. **Other Points:** Children welcome. No dogs in dining room. **P** & **Directions:** By the A1016 Billericay roundabout.
MR C NEWCOMBE ☎ (0245) 269603/264848
Very popular with businessmen visiting the area.

⊛£££ **SCOTT'S** The Street, Hatfield Peverel, Chelmsford.
CLUB **Hours:** Lunch by arrangement, dinner 7pm - 12 midnight (last orders 9pm). Closed: Sundays. **Cuisine:** British and Yorkshire cuisine, may include - curried parsnip soup, calves liver with gin & lime sauce, pastry shell filled with scallops, prawns & sauce. ⊨ None. **CC** Access, Visa. **Other Points:** Children welcome. Booking necessary. Exclusively non-smokers. Menus change monthly. Mastercard accepted. Public parking opposite. & **(V)** **Directions:** Take Hatfield Peverel slip road off A12 between Chelmsford & Witham.
BERYL TATE ☎ (0245) 380161.
16th century cottage decorated in keeping with the character of the establishment. Tasty dishes, attractively presented are on offer in this restaurant which enjoys a pleasantly relaxing non-smoking atmosphere. Very popular so booking essential.

⊛£ **SOLE MIO ITALIAN RESTAURANT** 11-13 Baddow Road, Chelmsford.
Hours: Meals from 12 noon - 2pm and 7pm - 11pm (last orders 10.30pm). Closed: Sundays and Bank Holidays. **Cuisine:** Grilled fresh sardines, lombatine mariapia, steak au poivre, tournedos Rossini. Vegetarian menu. ⊨ None. **CC** All major cards. **Other Points:** Children welcome. No dogs. **P** **(V) Directions:** In the town centre.
A A SOLDANI ☎ (0245) 250759.
Authentic Italian dishes in a very old building close to town centre. Catering in private room for parties. Music and dancing licence.

⊛££ **SOUTH LODGE HOTEL** 196 New London Road, Chelmsford.
⊞D££££ **Hours:** Meals served in the restaurant 7.30am - 9.30am, 12.30pm - 2.30pm and 7pm - 10pm. Meals served in the bar 12 noon - 2pm and 7pm - 10pm. **Cuisine:** International and New English cuisine. ⊨ 41 bedrooms, all en suite. **CC** All major cards. **Other Points:** Children welcome. No smoking area. **P** & **Directions:** Off the A12 close to the town centre.
MR A A SOLDANI ☎ (0245) 264 564.
A busy commercial hotel close to the town centre and County Cricket Ground. South Lodge is a converted Victorian residence standing in its own mature gardens. Full conference, function and leisure facilities available.

CHELTENHAM Gloucestershire **Map 4 B1**

⌂£££ **BEAUMONT HOUSE HOTEL** 56 Shurdington Road, Cheltenham.

⎚ 18 bedrooms, 15 en suite. All rooms have tea/coffee making facilities, telephone, radio, alarm and colour TV. **Hours:** Breakfast 7.30am - 9am, Dinner 7pm - 8pm. Bar snacks served all day until 10.30pm. Non-residents welcome for meals if book. **CC** Access, Visa. **Other Points:** Children welcome. No smoking area. Dogs allowed. Residents' lounge. Garden. **P (V) Directions:** On A46 to Stroud road in Cheltenham at start of Shurdington Road.
SUE, JOY & KEN HOLBROOK. ☎ (0242) 245986.
A warm welcome awaits guests at this attractive detached, Victorian Hotel where individual service and personal attention is a prime concern. The table d'hote dinner menu uses fresh produce and bar meals are available throughout the day. Set in peaceful gardens, Beaumont House offers comfortable accommodation and a warm atmosphere whether your stay is for business or pleasure.

⊗££ **BELOW STAIRS, THE SEAFOOD RESTAURANT** 103
CLUB Promenade, Cheltenham.
Hours: Lunch served from 12 noon Monday to Saturday, dinner from 6pm Thursday, Friday and Saturday. Closed: Sundays and Bank Holidays. **Cuisine:** Fresh seafood a speciality. Traditional cooking and fresh vegetables. Vegetarian and vegan dishes available. ⎚ None. **CC** All major cards. **Other Points:** Children welcome. No dogs. No smoking area. ⅖ **(V) Directions:** In the town centre.
MR J B LINTON ☎ (0242) 234599
Situated in the centre of town and, as its name implies, below pavement level. All the dishes are prepared under personal supervision of the chef proprietor.

⊗££ **COLESBOURNE INN** Colesbourne, Near Cheltenham.
⌂£££ **Hours:** Breakfast 8am - 10am, coffee 10am - 12 noon, bar meals
CLUB 6pm. Afternoon teas 3pm - 6pm. Restaurant 7pm - 10pm. **Cuisine:** Traditional home cooking, including fish and seafoods, steaks, and steak guiness and mushroom pies. Vegetarian meals also available. ⎚ 2 single, 6 double, 2 twin, all en suite. All rooms have tea/coffee facilities, colour TVs, radios, alarms, telephones and baby listening devices. **CC** All major cards. **Other Points:** Children welcome. Afternoon teas. Open Sundays and bank holidays. Special 'getaway' breaks. Dogs allowed in rooms only. **P** ⅖ **(V) Directions:** On A435 Cheltenham - Cirencester road.
ERIC & MARY BIRD. ☎ (0242) 87376
Set in the Cotswolds, this picturesque 200 year old coaching inn offers top quality home-cooked food, real ales, and a good selection of wines to compliment the meal. There are plenty of places of interest nearby, including the Roman villa at Chedworth, and this warm and cheerful inn is an ideal base for touring the Cotswolds.

⊗£ **COTSWOLD GRANGE HOTEL** Pittville Circus Road,
⌂£££ Cheltenham.
Hours: 7.15am - 9am, 12 noon - 2pm and 6pm - 7.30pm. Restaurant and Bar meals 12 noon - 2pm. Closed: Sundays, and from Christmas to New Year. **Cuisine:** English cuisine. ⎚ 25

Cheltenham continued

bedrooms, all en suite. **CC** Access, Visa, AmEx. **Other Points:** Children welcome. Dogs allowed. Open bank holidays. Garden dining. **P** **(V) Directions:** At roundabout on Prestbury road, take right for Pitville Circus.
MR PAUL WEAVER **☎** (0242) 515119.

Once the fine country house of a London solicitor, the mellow Cotswold stone of this attractive building is set in a tree-lined avenue forming a pleasant location close to the centre of Cheltenham. The hotel is a friendly, family run establishment and offers quality food at excellent prices.

HALLERY HOUSE 48 Shurdington Road, Cheltenham.
CLUB ⊨ 7 single, 4 double, 3 twin and 2 family: 10 en suite. 2 bathrooms and 2 showers. Colour TVs, with satellite channel, and hot drinks trays in all rooms. **Hours:** Breakfast 7.30am - 9.30am, dinner 7pm - 8pm. **CC** Access, Visa, AmEx. **Other Points:** Children welcome (under 5 free, under 12 half price). Dogs allowed. Residents lounge and garden. Special diets and vegetarians also catered for. **P** **Directions:** On the outskirts of Cheltenham on the A46 to Bath.
MRS PETKOVIC **☎** (0242) 578450.

A Victorian grade II listed building which has been restored to its former glory. Mrs Petkovic's friendly family welcome ensures guests feel at home. Only 5 minutes from the town centre, it is popular with tourists and business persons. The restaurant offers excellent meals at very good value. Winner of the Cheltenham Spa Award for food, hygiene and customer comfort. Highly recommended.

HANNAFORD'S 20 Evesham Road, Cheltenham.
CLUB ⊨ 1 single, 2 double, 5 twin and 1 family bedroom, most en suite. Colour TV. Tea/Coffee making facilities and direct dial telephones in all rooms. **Hours:** Breakfast 8am - 9am, Dinner 7pm - 7.45pm. Restaurant closed: Sat & Sun. **CC** Access, Visa. **Directions:** A435 from town centre towards race course, on left hand side.
DOROTHY CROWLEY **☎** (0242) 515181.

Built in 1833, Hannaford's is a lovely Regency house which has been carefully modernised to provide comfort, yet it still retains all the building's original features. The hotel is within walking distance of Cheltenham's famous Racecourse and the town centre.

THE GREATFIELD Caernarvon Road, Up Hatherley, Cheltenham.
Hours: Lunch 11am - 2.30pm (Sunday from 12 noon), Dinner 6pm - 9pm (Sunday from 7pm). **Cuisine:** Bar menu and daily specials. Braised Beef in Burgandy, Chicken with Mango & Ginger, Stuffed Pork Chops with Nectarine Sauce. Homemade sweets a speciality. ⊨ None. **CC** Visa. **Other Points:** Children welcome - childrens play area. Dining in garden room. **P** **と** **(V) Directions:** In Up Hatherley, close to large Safeway store.
JOHN & ANDREA CARSLAW **☎** (0242) 862902.

A modern public house, built in March 1990, offering excellent quality fresh food. With a wealth of exposed beams, open fires in winter and hundreds of gardening antiques as decoration,

Cheltenham continued

this pub offers good family hospitality. Cheltenham town and racecourse are nearby and it is also handy if you are touring the Cotswolds.

⊗£ **THE RETREAT** 10/11 Suffolk Parade, Cheltenham.
Hours: Meals from 12 noon - 2.15pm. Closed: Sundays. **Cuisine:** Menu changes daily with varied dishes, eg.Chilli with yoghurt and cucumber dressing served on rice, steak bap, todays homemade pate. ⊨ None. **CC** All major cards. **Other Points:** Children welcome. No dogs. **(V) Directions:** In the centre of Cheltenham. Antique area of town.
MIKE DEY ☎ (0242) 235436.
Lively, friendly bar with fresh food cooked daily on the premises. Its central location and distinctive atmosphere makes The Retreat a popular rendezvous.

CHICHESTER West Sussex **Map 4 C2**
⊗£ **ANGLESEY ARMS** Halnaker, nr Chichester.
Hours: Meals from 12 noon - 2pm and 7.30pm - 12 midnight, last orders 10pm. Closed: Christmas Day and New year's Eve. **Cuisine:** Peppered fillet steak, fresh Selsey lobster and crab, locally smoked salmon and ham, traditional roast Sunday lunch. ⊨ None. **CC** All major cards. **Other Points:** Children welcome. Fax No: (0243) 530034. ▯ 点 **(V) Directions:** From the A27, take the A285 to Halnaker. Pub is 2 miles up on right.
CHRISTOPHER & TESSA HOUSEMAN ☎ (0243) 773474.
A small, friendly, traditional pub serving real ales. The single bar and attractive garden are both very popular. Only 2 miles from Goodwood Racecourse and 4 miles from Chichester harbour.

⊞▯££ **EASTON HOUSE** Chidham Lane, Chidham, nr Chichester.
⊨ 1 double with en suite and 1 twin bedroom. Tea/coffee making facilities. 1 bathroom. 1 shower. **Hours:** Breakfast 8am - 9am. Closed: over Christmas. **CC** None. **Other Points:** Central heating. No evening meals. Children welcome. Dogs by arrangement. Residents lounge. TV. Garden. ▯ **Directions:** 1 mile south of the A259.
MRS C M HARTLEY ☎ (0243) 572514.
A former 16th century farmhouse situated on the Chidham peninsula. Within easy reach of Goodwood, Chichester, Portsmouth and the New Forest. Uncrowded and peaceful waterside walks within 5 minutes of the house. The bedrooms overlook either farmland, the harbour or the garden.

⊗££ **MICAWBER'S RESTAURANT** 13 South Street, Chichester.
Hours: Open 11.30am - 2.30pm, and 6pm - 10.30pm. Closed: Sunday. **Cuisine:** Wide selection of fish dishes, and shellfish, fresh meat and vegetables all from local markets. ⊨ None. **CC** All major cards. **Other Points:** Children welcome. No dogs. French spoken. 点 **(V)**
PHILIP COTTERILL & THIERRY BOISHU. ☎ (0243) 786989.
Situated just south of the Cross, this popular restaurant has a very provincial French character. The chef enjoys cooking the fruits de mer directly from the local fishermen.

Chichester continued

⊗££ **SADLERS WINE BAR & RESTAURANT** 42 East Street, Chichester.
Hours: Meals available all day until 10.30pm (last orders). **Cuisine:** Dishes include Sadlers peppercorn steak, Slice Breast of wild duck with a raspberry & honey sauce, Pasta dishes. Light snack menu available in Wine Bar. ⊨ None. **CC** All major cards. **Other Points:** Children welcome. Garden. Afternoon teas. No smoking areas. Parking available nearby. **(V) Directions:** East of the city centre, near the Clock Centre.
NICK SUTHERLAND ☎ (0243) 774765.
Sadlers is an attractive wine bar and restaurant in the centre of Chichester. The food is freshly prepared, well presented and 'could not be faulted' by the inspector. Specialities of the restaurant include steaks and a daily fish course. Friendly, efficient service adds to the pleasant atmosphere.

⊗££ **THE FOX GOES FREE** Charlton, Nr Chichester.
⊞££ **Hours:** Breakfast 7am - 12 noon, Lunch 12 noon - 2pm, Dinner 6pm - 10pm (7pm - 9pm Sundays). **Cuisine:** Traditional Old English bar meals. Separate dinner menu available during autumn and winter. ⊨ 3 bedrooms. **CC** Access, Visa, AmEx. **Other Points:** Children welcome. No smoking area. Afternoon teas/coffee and cakes (Saturday) April - September. Dogs allowed. Beer garden. **P** ⅙ **(V) Directions:** 1 mile off A286. 6 miles N of Chichester. 1st left in Singleton.
GIL BATTLEY ☎ (0243 63) 461.
Dating from the 16th century, the Fox is a traditional Sussex Inn which still retains its character and charm. There are several bar areas to choose from with open fires in winter. The meals are traditional old English and good value for money. Welcoming service. Prizewinning garden with outstanding views of Sussex Downs. Close to Goodwood Racecourse.

CHIDDINGSTONE Kent **Map 5 C1**
⊗££ **CASTLE INN** Chiddingstone, near Edenbridge.
[CLUB] **Hours:** Restaurant open 12 noon - 2pm and 7.30pm - 9.30pm. No food on Christmas evening. Routiers-priced menu applies to lunches and bar meals. **Cuisine:** Mainly British with European overtones. Roast rib of beef, roast rack of lamb, local game, fresh fish, fresh vegetables. ⊨ None. **CC** All major cards. **Other Points:** Children welcome. ⅙ **(V) Directions:** 1½ miles south of the B2027 Edenbridge to Tonbridge Road.

Charlton, Nr. Chichester, West Sussex PO18 0HU
Tel: Singleton (0243) 461

GOOD COUNTRY FARE AT FAIR PRICES

Chiddingstone continued
NIGEL D LUCAS ☎ (0892) 870247.
For centuries the centre of village life, The Castle has a justly famed restaurant as well as a wide range of bar meals which, on sunny days, may be enjoyed in the pretty courtyard garden.

CHIPPING NORTON Oxfordshire **Map 4 B1**
⊗£ **CROWN AND CUSHION** High Street, Chipping Norton.
Hours: Open from 10.30am - 2.30pm and 6pm -11pm. Meals served 12 noon - 2pm and 7pm - 9pm. No meals served Saturday evening. **Cuisine:** Individual steak and mushroom pie, fresh trout, sirloin steak, gammon and pineapple, chef's homemade pate. ⊨ 29 bedrooms all en suite and with tea/coffee making facilities and telephones. Some de-luxe rooms. **CC** All major cards. **Other Points:** Access for disabled to dining room. Children welcome. Conference facilities. Patio and beer garden. **P** & **(V) Directions:** 1 mile off the A34 midway between Oxford and Stratford.
JAMES FRASER ☎ (0608) 642533.
15th century coaching inn with excellent en suite 2 star facilities. Set amidst beautiful Cotswold scenery, the log fires and four poster bedrooms complete the idyllic setting. Convenient for Heathrow, London, the M40 and for exploring Shakespeare country.

CHRISTCHURCH Dorset **Map 4 C1**
⊞£ **BELVEDERE HOTEL** 59 Barrack Road, Christchurch.
⊨ 3 single, 4 double, 2 twin and 3 family bedrooms,1 with bath/shower. 3 bathrooms. 3 showers. TV in all bedrooms. Ground floor bedrooms. **Hours:** Breakfast 7am - 9am, dinner 6.50pm - 7.50pm (order by 4pm). **CC** None. **Other Points:** Central heating. Children welcome. Licensed. Residents lounge. TV. **P** & **Directions:** On the A35 Southampton to Bournemouth road,near the Railway bridge.
MRS L R JEFFERIS ☎ (0202) 485978.
Situated on the A35 within easy access of the 10th century priory and castle ruins. Royalty fishery for salmon, trout and all coarse fish. The hotels location also offers sailing and is close to the New Forest.

⊗£££ **LE PETIT ST TROPEZ** 3 Bridge Street, Christchurch.
Hours: Lunch from 12 noon and dinner from 7pm. **Cuisine:** Traditional French from Provence. Seasonal specialities ,such as Filet de Truite en Croute, fillet of fresh trout with crab and cooked in puff pastry. ⊨ None. **CC** Access, Visa. **Other Points:** Children welcome. Garden dining. Open bank holidays. Cater for receptions, parties and celebrations. Fax No: (0202) 470048. & **(V) Directions:** Between the two bridges, 100 metres from the Civic Offices.
MARCEL & DEBORAH DUVAL ☎ (0202) 482522.
The ambience, cuisine and service at Le Petit St Tropez combine to make dining here a special experience. This genuine French family run restaurant has a choice of fixed price or table d'hote menu, including their own seasonal specialities.

⊗££ **THE COPPER SKILLET** 17 Church Street, Christchurch.
⊞££ **Hours:** Meals 9am - 9pm. Closed: Christmas and Boxing Day.
Cuisine: Steaks and grills, and weekly fresh fish and vegetarian

Christchurch continued

specialities. ⌂ Self catering accommodation. **CC** Access, Visa. **Other Points:** No dogs. Children welcome. Coaches by appointment. ▯ & **(V) Directions:** Off main A35 into Christchurch High St,take Church St toward Priory.
MICHAEL DEVALL ☎ (0202) 485485.
A licensed steak house and family restaurant situated in the old part of Christchurch close to the town quay, priory and castle ruins. Self catering flats available.

⊗££
⌂££££ **THE FISHERMAN'S HAUNT HOTEL** Winkton, nr Christchurch.

Hours: Bar open 10am - 2.30pm and 6pm - 11pm, 12 noon - 3pm and 7pm - 10.30pm Sundays. Closed: Christmas Day. **Cuisine:** Fresh Christchurch salmon, Avon trout, steak and kidney pie. ⌂ 20 bedrooms, all en suite. Limited accommodation over Christmas week. **CC** All major cards. **Other Points:** Children welcome. ▯ & **Directions:** On the B3347 between Christchurch and Ringwood.
MR J BOCHAN ☎ (0202) 477283.
Superior 2 star/4 crowns country house hotel on the banks of the River Avon. The restaurant overlooks the river and there is an attractive beer garden with children's play area. Situated on the edge of the New Forest. A Free House serving real ales.

CHURT Surrey **Map 4 C2**

⊗£££
⌂££££ **PRIDE OF THE VALLEY HOTEL** Tilford Road, Churt, nr Farnham, Surrey.

Hours: Breakfast 7.30am - 9.30am, lunch 12 noon - 2.30pm and dinner 7.30pm - 12 midnight (last orders 10.30pm). **Cuisine:** Selection of French and English cuisine. ⌂ 12 bedrooms, all en suite. **CC** All major cards. **Other Points:** Children welcome. Pets allowed. Garden. ▯ **Directions:** Off the A3 to Farnham, half mile turn right onto Tilford Road.
MR DAVID VASEY ☎ (0428) 605799.
Set within National Trust parks, this hotel offers the cosy timeless atmosphere of a family run inn. With an intimate bar and dining room, there is a choice of French a la carte and English Table d'hote menus.

⌂£££££ **PRIDE OF THE VALLEY HOTEL** Tilford Road, Churt, nr Farnham, Surrey.

⌂ 12 bedrooms, all en suite. **Hours:** Breakfast 7.30am - 9.30am, lunch 12 noon - 2.30pm and dinner 7.30pm - 12 midnight (last orders 10.30pm). **CC** All major cards. **Other Points:** Children welcome. Pets allowed. Garden. ▯ **Directions:** Off the A3 to Farnham, half mile turn right onto Tilford Road.
MR DAVID VASEY ☎ (0428) 605799.
Set within National Trust parks, this hotel offers the cosy timeless atmosphere of a family run inn. With an intimate bar and dining room, there is a choice of French a la carte and English Table d'hote menus.

CIRENCESTER Gloucestershire **Map 4 B1**

⌂££££ **LA RONDE HOTEL** 52/54 Ashcroft Road, Cirencester.
CLUB ⌂ 5 twin, 3 double, 2 family bedrooms, all en suite. TV and tea/coffee making facilities in all rooms. **Hours:** Breakfast 8 am -

CENTRAL & SOUTHERN ENGLAND

Cirencester continued

9.15, Lunch 12.30pm - 2pm, Dinner 7pm - 9pm (last orders). Closed Saturday lunchtime and Sunday. **CC** Access, Visa. **Other Points:** Children welcome. Pets allowed, Non smoking areas. **P** **(V) Directions:** Off A419, in the town centre.
MR & MRS SHALES ☎ (0285) 654611.
A Victorian hotel, with cotswold stone facade, offering well cooked and presented food in pleasant and friendly surroundings. Attractively decorated and furnished, you can be sure of a warm welcome from the proprietors, Mr and Mrs Shales.

⊗£ **THE VILLAGE PUB** Barnsley, Cirencester.
⌂£ **Hours:** Breakfast 7.30am - 9am, Lunch 12 noon - 2pm, Dinner 7pm - 9pm/9.30pm. Closed: Christmas Day. **Cuisine:** Bar meals and A la Carte menu. Dishes include local Bibury Trout, Deep Fried Scampi, Gammon Steak, Bean and Vegetable Casserole. ⊨ 6 bedrooms, 4 en suite. **CC** Access, Visa. **Other Points:** Children welcome. Garden/Patio. Dogs allowed. Afternoon teas. **P** க **(V) Directions:** B4425 in the centre of Barnsley.
MISS S STEVENS ☎ (0285) 740421.
A Cotswold stone, traditional country pub in the middle of Barnsley village. The food is well cooked and presented and is served in generous portions. The accommodation is country style with low beams. Welcoming service and a friendly atmosphere.

⊗££ **WILD DUCK INN** Drakes Island, Ewen.
⌂££££ **Hours:** Open all day except Sunday (normal Sunday licensing hours). Breakfast 8am - 10am, Lunch 12 noon - 2pm (last orders), Dinner 7pm - 9.45pm (last orders). **Cuisine:** French/Bistro style. Extensive choice. ⊨ 20 rooms, 10 en suite. **CC** Access, Visa. **Other Points:** Children welcome. Garden. Afternoon teas. Dogs allowed. **P** க **(V) Directions:** Off the A419.
MR & MRS MUSSELL ☎ (0285) 770310.
The Wild Duck Inn is a unique 15th century inn set in its own grounds, with a delightful garden for dining al fresco and open fires in the winter. You will find very good food, piping hot and in plentiful portions complemented by a wide selection of traditional ales and wines.

CLARE Suffolk **Map 5 B1**
⊗££ **THE PLOUGH INN** Kedington Road, near Hundon.
⌂£££ **Hours:** Lunch 12 noon - 2pm, dinner 7pm - 9.30pm (last orders). Bar meals 12 noon - 2pm and 7pm - 9.30pm. **Cuisine:** Traditional country fare. Barnsley chop, Venison in red wine, Dover sole. In the bar: clam fries, Hundon ploughman's, homemade pies. Seafood speciality. ⊨ 8 bedrooms, all en suite. E.A.T.B. 4 Crowns. **CC** Access, Visa, AmEx. **Other Points:** Children welcome. Pets allowed. Beer garden. Afternoon teas. **P** க **(V) Directions:** 1½ miles east of the A143 between Hundon and Kedington.
DAVID & MARION ROWLINSON ☎ (0440) 86789.
An unpretentious, traditional country pub enjoying superb views across the countryside from its elevated position - the highest freehouse in Suffolk! The Plough has been in the family for two generations, and despite improvements, the exposed beams and brickwork retain a genuine olde atmosphere.

Clare continued

Ⓧ£
THE SEAFARER HOTEL Nethergate Street, Clare.
⌖£approx **Hours:** Breakfast 7.45am - 10am, lunch 12 noon - 2pm and dinner 7pm - 10pm (last orders). Bar meals 12 noon - 2pm and 7pm - 10.15pm. **Cuisine:** English and French cuisine: Sunday roast rib of beef, beef in red wine and lobster (when available). ⊨ 5 bedrooms: 3 with en suite facilities. **CC** Access, Visa, Diners. **Other Points:** Children welcome. Pets allowed. ⬛ **(V) Directions:** Easy to locate in the town centre.
MR & MRS ROSS ☎ (0787) 277449.
Recently renovated 17th century inn, in a picturesque market town, close to the market place, park and castle ruins. Large bar and restaurant, decorated in antiques, serving excellent cuisine accompanied by superb wine list. Beautiful landscaped garden with garden restaurant for summer evenings.

COLCHESTER Essex **Map 5 B2**

Ⓧ£
JACKLINS RESTAURANT 147 High Street, Colchester.
Hours: Meals served 9.15am - 5pm. Closed: Sundays and Bank Holidays. **Cuisine:** Breakfasts, lunches and afternoon teas. ⊨ None. **CC** Access, Visa, AmEx. **Other Points:** Children welcome. No dogs. Public car park. **Directions:** 100 yds west of the Town Hall in the High Street.
MR S H JACKLIN ☎ (0206) 572157.
A first floor restaurant, situated in the town centre on the site of the pottery shops of Roman Colchester. Delightful oak panelled rooms where breakfasts, lunches and afternoon teas are served. Also specialist shop downstairs for tobacco products, teas and confectionery.

Ⓧ££
ROSE & CROWN HOTEL East Gate, Colchester.
⌖££££ **Hours:** Breakfast 7am - 9.30am, lunch 12 noon - 2pm, dinner 7pm
CLUB - 10pm. Closed: Christmas day and Boxing day evening. **Cuisine:** A la carte, fixed price menu, French/English cuisine. ⊨ 26 rooms. 12 single, 2 twin, 10 double and 2 family bedrooms. **CC** All major cards. **Other Points:** Children welcome. Conference rooms available. ⬛ **Directions:** In town centre off A604.
MR BAGHERZADEH ☎ (0206) 866677.
The original style of this Tudor building has been retained and it is in the oldest recorded town. The restaurant has a cosy cocktail bar and offers fresh homemade food every day of the year. A delightful place for lovers of history.

Ⓧ££
THE SHEPHERD & DOG Moor Road, Langham, Colchester.
Hours: Lunch 11am - 3pm (last orders 2.30pm), bar snacks 11am - 2.30pm, dinner 5pm - midnight (last orders 10.30pm), evening bar snacks 6pm - 11pm (last orders 1.30pm). **Cuisine:** Bar and restaurant meals. Predominantly English and continental cuisine. ⊨ None. **CC** Access, Visa, AmEx. **Other Points:** Children welcome. Open Bank Holidays. Dogs allowed. Garden dining. ⬛ ♿ **(V) Directions:** 1st exit off A12 north of Colchester (signed Langham).
MESSRS BARNES & CULBERT. ☎ (0206) 272711.
Set in a small village near Colchester this pub offers tasty meals presented with care. As this is a free house there is a good selection of beers. Booking reccomended as restaurant can be busy.

CENTRAL & SOUTHERN ENGLAND

COLSTON BASSETT Nottinghamshire **Map 4 A2**

⊗££ **THE MARTINS ARMS INN** School Lane, Colston Bassett.
Hours: Lunch and bar snacks 12 noon - 2pm, Dinner and bar snacks 6pm - 9.30pm (last orders). No food Sunday evening and Monday evening. **Cuisine:** Dishes may include Roast Rack of English Lamb served with a fresh Tarragon & Cream sauce, Freshly made Tagliatelle with spicy Chicken pieces. ⊨ None.
CC None. **Other Points:** Beer garden. Colston Bassett is a Conservation village. ⊡ ⅍ **(V) Directions:** A46 Bingham Rdabout, left on A52, 1 mile 1st R for Langar & C.B.
LYNNE BRYAN & SALVATORE INGUANTA ☎ (0949) 81361.
Housed in an attractive period building, the Martins Arms offers excellent food and and a warm welcome. Only fresh produce is used and the menu offers a good choice of very well-cooked and presented dishes. During summer, drinks and meals can be enjoyed in the garden. Under the same ownership as The Crown Inn, Old Dalby - winner of the Les Routiers Pub of the Year Award 1991.

CORSHAM Wiltshire **Map 4 B1**

⊗£££ **METHUEN ARMS HOTEL** 2 High Street, Corsham.
⊞£££ **Hours:** 7.30am - 9am, 12 noon - 2pm, and 7pm - 10pm. Open for
CLUB Sunday lunch. Restaurant closed: Sunday evenings (only bar meals available). **Cuisine:** Both simple and classical cuisine, dishes including lamb and herb pie, and lasagne, using local meats and produce. Sunday lunch table d'hote. ⊨ 6 single, 7 twin, 10 double, and 2 family rooms, 24 of them en suite. All rooms have colour TV, trouser press, and tea/coffee making facilities. **CC** Access, Visa. **Other Points:** Children welcome. No dogs allowed. Garden. Skittle alley. Fax No: (0249) 712004. Coaches by appointment. ⊡ ⅍ **(V) Directions:** M4 exit 17 & 18 Chippenham or Bath. Just off A4, 3 miles W Chip'ham.
MIKE, MORWENNA & MARK LONG ☎ (0249) 714867.
The oldest part of the hotel now houses six bedrooms but is known to have been a nunnery in the early 1400s. The ancient stone walls and large oak beams still stand today. With its stone-walled charm, the restaurant is candlelit in the evening and is open for lunch and dinner. The menu offers an extensive range of both simple and classical dishes. Near Bath, Stonehenge.

⊗£££ **THE RUDLOE PARK HOTEL** Leafy Lane, Corsham.
⌣ **Hours:** Breakfast 7.30am - 9.30am. Restaurant open 12 noon -
W 2pm and 7pm - 10pm every day. **Cuisine:** A la carte and set
⊙ menus with market specials and freshly cooked food. Vegetarian
CLUB and dietary meals available. ⊨ 11 bedrooms all en suite. **CC** All major cards. **Other Points:** Children over 10 welcome. Dogs by arrangement. Fax: (0225) 811412. ⊡ ⅍ **(V) Directions:** On the A4 between Bath and Chippenham at the top of Box Hill.
IAN & MARION OVEREND - Resident Directors ☎ (0225) 810555.
A peaceful 19th century country house hotel set in 4 acres of beautiful gardens with extensive views to and beyond the Georgian city of Bath.

COTTENHAM Cambridgeshire **Map 5 A1**

⊗££ **THE WHITE HORSE** Cottenham, Cambridge.
Hours: Lunch 12 noon - 2pm, dinner 7pm - 10pm (last orders). Sunday lunch 12 noon - 2.30pm. Closed: Sunday evenings and all day Monday. **Cuisine:** Dishes include devilled whitebait, avocado pear with prawns, tournados rossini, vegetarian mushroom strogonoff, strawberry crush, homemade cheesecake. ⊨ None ⒸⒸ Access, Visa. **Other Points:** Children welcome. Children under 11 special price for Sunday Lunch. ◨ ⑰ **(V) Directions:** B1049 in the centre of the village of Cottenham.
WARREN DUNNICO ☎ (0954) 50257.
A 19th century Free House, the White Horse serves well cooked meals in a relaxed, friendly atmosphere. The menu offers an extensive choice and the restaurant is licensed until midnight. Friendly, efficient service will ensure that your meal is an enjoyable one.

COVENTRY West Midlands **Map 4 A2**

⊗££ **EATHORPE PARK HOTEL** Fosse Way, Eathorpe, Nr
⑭£££ Leamington Spa.
Hours: Breakfast 7.30am - 9.30am, lunch and bar snacks 12 noon - 2pm, (last orders 1.45pm), dinner and evening bar snacks 7pm - 10pm (last orders 9.45pm). Closed: Christmas Day. **Cuisine:** Full a la carte menu, table d'hote and bar snacks. ⊨ 15 bedrooms, all en suite. ⒸⒸ All major cards. **Other Points:** Children welcome. Open Bank Holiday. Afternoon teas. Garden. Fax No. (0926) 632481. ◨ **(V)**
MRS DOLORES DEELEY ☎ (0926) 632245.
An attractive country house situated near the River Leam in Eathorpe. Table d'hote and a la carte menus can be enjoyed in the comfortable surroundings of the restaurant and the a la carte menu includes Chateaubriand and Steak Diane which are flambed at your table. A peaceful, relaxing atmosphere prevails.

⊗££ **GODIVA HOTEL** 80/90 Holy Head Road, Coventry.
Hours: Meals from 7am - 9.30am, 12.30pm - 2.30pm and 7.30pm - 10pm (last orders). **Cuisine:** Nouvelle cuisine, eg. salmon with maltaise sauce, mille feuilles of scampi tomato, garlic, herbs. ⊨ 95 bedrooms, all en suite. ⒸⒸ All major cards. **Other Points:** Children welcome. Coaches by appointment. ◨ ⑰ **(V) Directions:** 10 minutes walk from city centre, 9 miles from NEC.
MR W N WEST - General Manager ☎ (0203) 258585.
Situated on the main Coventry/Birmingham road only 11 miles from Birmingham Airport. Good facilities for conferences and private functions of up to 350.

⊗££ **HAIGS HOTEL & RESTAURANT** Kenilworth Road, Balsall
⑭£££ Common, Nr Coventry.
⌈CLUB⌉ **Hours:** Breakfast 7.30am - 9am (9.30am weekends), Dinner 7.30pm - 9pm (last orders). Sunday lunch 12.30pm - 2pm. Closed: December 20th - January 3rd. Meals available Sunday evening by arrangement only. Snacks always available. **Cuisine:** French and English cuisine. Table d'hote and a la carte menus. ⊨ 8 single and 5 twin bedrooms, all en suite. Tea/coffe making facilities, hairdryer, trouser press and direct dial telephone in all rooms. ⒸⒸ Visa. **Other Points:** Children welcome. Garden. Dogs allowed.

Coventry continued

Mastercard also accepted. ⒫ ⅋ **(V) Directions:** A452, 6 miles from Junction 4 on the M6.
JEAN & JOHN COOPER ☎ (0676) 33004.
A family run, suburban hotel close to the Warwickshire countryside yet only 6 miles from Junction 4 of the M6. The restaurant, overlooking the garden, has a friendly atmosphere with full table d'hote or a la carte cuisine offering good English and French cooking. The accommodation is of a very high standard. A small hotel with a warm, friendly atmosphere and good service.

⊗££ **SPARROW HALL HOTEL** Brinklow Road, Coombesfield,
⏍£££ Ansty, Nr Coventry.

Hours: Breakfast 7am - 9am, Lunch 12 noon - 2pm, Dinner 7.30pm - 10pm. Bar snacks 12 noon - 2pm and 6pm - 10pm. **Cuisine:** Carvery offering a good choice of roasts and a la carte menu. Specialities include Tournedos Rossini, Scampi Provencal. Bar snacks. ⊨ 15 bedrooms, 12 en suite. All major facilities. **CC** Access, Visa, AmEx. **Other Points:** Children welcome. Afternoon teas. Residents' lounge. Garden. Conference facilites & equipment. Fax No: (0203) 602256. ⒫ ⅋ **(V) Directions:** M6, jct. 2. Follow sign for Ansty B4065, turn right to Brinklow.
A TAKIAR ☎ (0203) 611817/8/9.
Nestling on the edge of Ansty Village in the rolling Warwickshire countryside, Sparrow Hall is ideally situated for business or pleasure. The standard of service is excellent with all staff welcoming and efficient. All food is well cooked and served in generous portions. The Carvery and a la carte menu offer a wide choice of dishes at good value for money.

CRANLEIGH Surrey Map 4 C2

⊗££ **BRICKS RESTAURANT** Smithbrook Kilns, Cranleigh.

Hours: Meals from 12 noon - 2pm and Friday & Saturday 7.30pm - 9.45pm. Closed: Christmas Day, New Year's Day and Bank Holidays. **Cuisine:** Menus change daily and might include chicken Veronique, spicy Persian lamb, chocolate squidgy cake. ⊨ None. **CC** None. **Other Points:** Children welcome. No dogs. Coaches by appointment. ⒫ ⅋ **(V) Directions:** On A281 just north of crossroads with B2127.
MRS H RUSSELL-DAVIS ☎ (0483) 276780.
Situated in a multi-workshop craft centre in an old brick works. Self service from kitchen counter with table service for drinks, desserts and coffee.

⊗££ **LA SCALA RESTAURANT** High Street, Cranleigh.

Hours: Lunch 12 noon - 2pm and dinner 6.30pm - 11pm (last orders 10.45pm). Closed: Sunday and Monday and the month of August. **Cuisine:** Italian cuisine - veal escalopa a la crema, sole Isoladoro, fettucini crema, mussels. ⊨ None. **CC** Access, Visa. **Other Points:** Children welcome. ⒫ **(V) Directions:** On the A281 Guildford to Horsham road.
ROSARIO MAZZOTTA ☎ (0483) 274900.
A well established and popular restaurant under the current ownership for over 17 years. Situated on the first floor above a jeweller's shop on the high street. The menu offers an interesting selection of Italian favourites and regional cuisine.

CRICKLADE Wiltshire **Map 4 B1**

⊗£££ **RHY HOUSE RESTAURANT AT THE FORESTERS ARMS** Malmesbury Road, Leigh, Nr Cricklade.
Hours: Lunch 12 noon - 2pm, Dinner 7pm - 11.30pm (last orders 10pm). Bar meals served 12 noon - 2pm and 7pm - 9.30pm. Restaurant closed: Monday lunch. **Cuisine:** House specialities include Breast of Barbarie Duck, Garlic Mistral, Tournedos Rossini. Also fresh fish dishes & steaks all with fresh vegetables. ⊨ None. **CC** Access, Visa, AmEx. **Other Points:** Garden dining. Open Sundays and Bank Holidays. Traditional Sunday roast served. **P** & **(V) Directions:** 2 miles west of Cricklade on B4040 to Malmesbury in Leigh.
PETER & VALERIE SMITH ☎ (0793) 750901.
A large cottage-style public house and restaurant in a pleasant open situation. Both restaurant and bar meals are well cooked and presented and offer good value for money. All dishes are individually cooked to order. Friendly, helpful service and a welcoming, relaxing atmosphere.

CROCKERTON Wiltshire **Map 4 C1**

⊗£££ **BARGATE COTTAGE RESTAURANT AND TEA ROOMS**
CLUB Crockerton, Near Warminster.
Hours: Lunch from 12 noon, dinner 7pm - 11pm (last orders 10pm). Tea rooms 9.30am until dusk. **Cuisine:** Varied menu, changes fortnightly. Including deep-fried brie with raspberry sauce, pork fillet with stilton & cream sauce, spotted dick with treacle & cream ⊨ None. **CC** Access, Visa, AmEx. **Other Points:** Barbecue, garden, patio. Children welcome. Cream teas. Open every day, all year. Sunday roast. & **(V) Directions:** From A350 follow the Crockerton to Maiden Bradley road.
JANE HUMPHRIES ☎ (0985) 213255.
A particularly inviting restaurant and tea rooms set by the shore of Lake Shearwater on the famous Longleat Estate. Attention to detail, a mouth-watering and varied menu and comfortable decoration make for a pleasant experience and one worth repeating again.

CROMER Norfolk **Map 5 A2**

⊗££ **CLIFTONVILLE HOTEL** Runton Road, Cromer.
⊞£££ **Hours:** Meals from 8.15am - 9.30am, 12.30pm - 2pm and 7.15pm - 9pm. Bar meals 12 noon - 2pm and 6pm- 9pm. **Cuisine:** Local shellfish in season. ⊨ 44 bedrooms, 26 en suite. 9 bathrooms. **CC** All major cards. **Other Points:** Children welcome. No dogs in public rooms. Coaches by appointment. Fax No: (0263) 511764. **P** **(V)**
T A BOLTON ☎ (0263) 512543.
An established hotel facing the sea. Unimpeded views of the sea from most rooms. All bedrooms have telephones, radio and TV. Lift to all floors. Cromer is dominated by the stunning 14th century church.

⊗£££ **RED LION HOTEL** Brook Street, Cromer.
⊞£££££**Hours:** Breakfast 8am - 9.30am, lunch 12 noon - 2pm, dinner 7pm - 9.30pm, bar snacks 6pm - 9.30pm. Closed: 24th December - 28th December. **Cuisine:** Dishes may include Fussilli Pasta topped with Chilli Sauce, Poached Fillet of Salmon, Grilled Loin of Pork, Walnut & Caramel Meringue. ⊨ 12 bedrooms, all en suite.

Cromer continued

CC Access, Visa, AmEx. **Other Points:** Children welcome. Open Bank Holidays. Afternoon teas. Garden dining. Gym. Sauna. Snooker room. **P** **&** **(V) Directions:** On Seafront. Follow town centre signs, past Church Street.

VANESSA MEDLER **☎** (0263) 514964.

Recently refurbished and remodelled, the hotel overlooks the sea and beach. Generous portions of good food are served in the restaurant which enjoys a quiet relaxed atmosphere. With lots of picturesque places to visit, and with hotel facilities including a gym there should never be a dull moment. Comfortable accommodation.

CROWBOROUGH East Sussex **Map 5 C1**
⊗££ **BOARS HEAD INN** Boarshead, nr Crowborough.

Hours: Lunch 12 noon - 2pm, dinner 7pm - 10pm (last orders). No meals Sunday evenings. **Cuisine:** Fresh trout in season, steak, poultry. Table d'hote menu by reservation. Bar snacks. ⊨ None. **CC** Access, Visa. **Other Points:** Open air dining. **P** **&** **(V) Directions:** On the A26 in Boars Head, between Crowborough and Eridge.

JILLIENNE & GORDON McKENZIE **☎** (0892) 652412.

A real old country inn with flagstone floors and oak beams, virtually untouched by the passing of 600 years. Open fires, a warm friendly ambience and well cooked and presented food have drawn people to the Boars Head from miles around.

CROYDON Surrey **Map 5 C1**
⊗££ **BRIARLEY HOTEL** 8 Outram Road, Croydon.

⌂££££ **Hours:** Restaurant open 12 noon - 1.30pm (Sundays only) and 6.30pm - 10pm Mondays to Saturdays. **Cuisine:** Traditional homemade food with soups, steaks, Briarleyburger and fresh vegetables. ⊨ 18 bedrooms en suite. Annexe with 20 bedrooms en suite. **CC** All major cards. **Other Points:** Children welcome. Fax: (081) 656 6084. **P** **&** **(V) Directions:** Outram Rd runs between the A232 and A222, nr East Croydon station.

MRS S P MILLS FHCIMA **☎** (081) 654 1000.

A Victorian exterior but inside everything you expect from a hotel in the 90's including colour TV, teasmade and direct-dial telephone. Quietly situated but excellent for public transport.

⌂££££ **MARKINGTON HOTEL** 9 Haling Park Road, South Croydon.
CLUB ⊨ 9 single, 9 double, 3 twin and 1 family room, all en suite. Colour TV & Video channel, Radio, Tea/Coffee making facilities, Direct dial telephone, Trouser press and Hairdryer in all rooms. **Hours:** Breakfast 7.15am - 9am, Dinner 6.30pm - 8.30pm (last orders). **CC** Access, Visa, AmEx. **Other Points:** Children welcome. Garden. Pool room. Fax No. (081) 688 6530. **P** **(V) Directions:** Just off South End Rd, opposite South Croydon Bus Garage.

MR & MRS MICKELBURGH **☎** (081) 681 6494.

This comfortable, friendly hotel is situated in a quiet area, yet is very close to the commercial centre of Croydon. After a days shopping in the under- cover shopping centre, you can relax in the bar lounge or have a game of pool!

CUCKFIELD West Sussex **Map 5 C1**

⊗££££ **KINGS HEAD HOTEL** South Street, Cuckfield, nr Haywards
⏋£££ Heath.

Hours: Meals from 8am - 9am, 12.30pm - 2pm and 7.30pm -
10pm. Bar meals available at all times. Restaurant closed Saturday
and Sunday and Monday evening. **Cuisine:** Modern English
cuisine, game in season and fresh South coast fish. ⊨ 8 bedrooms,
all en suite. **CC** Access, Visa, AmEx. **Other Points:** Children
welcome. **Directions:** On the old A272 at the south western end of
the village.
MR TOLHURST ☎ (0444) 454006.
The King's Head has been one of Cuckfield's landmarks for
over a century. The village is unspoilt and the Museum
chronicles its fascinating history. Family room and children's
games room are very popular. Booking advisable.

DEREHAM Norfolk **Map 5 A2**

⊗£ **KING'S HEAD HOTEL** Norwich Street, Dereham.

Hours: Restaurant open 7.45am - 9.30am, 12.30pm - 2pm and
7pm - 9pm, 7pm - 7.45pm Sundays. **Cuisine:** Steak and kidney
pies and puddings, home-baked sweets. ⊨ 15 bedrooms, 11 en
suite. **CC** All major cards. **Other Points:** Children welcome. **P** &
(V) Directions: From the A47, follow signs to Dereham town
centre.
MR & MRS ROBERT BLACK ☎ (0362) 693283.
A 17th century hotel, modernised to a high standard,
conveniently situated for touring the Norfolk Broads and coastal
resorts. The King's Head offers courteous service and good
English cooking. A grass bowling green and grass tennis court
are attached to the hotel.

DESFORD Leicestershire **Map 4 A2**

⊗££ **OLD LANCASTER INN** Station Road, Desford.

Hours: Lunch 12 noon - 2pm and dinner 7.30pm - 9.30pm
Monday to Saturday. Bar menu available Sunday lunchtimes.
Cuisine: Steak Cafe Ootmarsum - rump or fillet steak with special
Dutch recipe sauce. ⊨ None. **CC** Access, Visa. **Other Points:**
Children welcome. Dogs at manager's discretion. **P** & **(V)**
MR PHILIP LIDDELL ☎ (045 57) 2589.
On the outskirts of Leicester, this original coaching house
dating back to the 1860's, retains much of its old world charm,
with 3 lounge bars and a cosy, intimate restaurant offering a
variety of popular homemade dishes.

DEVIZES Wiltshire **Map 4 B1**

⊗££ **THE BEAR HOTEL** Market Place, Devizes.

Hours: Open all day from 7am. Informal and a la carte dining
rooms, plus snacks bar, homemade afternoon teas. **Cuisine:**
Devizes pie, roast joints carved at your table daily, charcoal grills in
the Lawrence room. ⊨ 25 bedrooms, all en suite. **CC** Access, Visa,
AmEx. **Other Points:** Children welcome. Fax No: (0380) 2450. **P**
& **(V)**
MR W K DICKENSON ☎ (0380) 2444.
Friendly 16th century coaching inn with many historic
associations. Within easy reach of Bath, Swindon, Salisbury and
a host of stately homes and gardens. Weekend breaks.

Devizes continued

⊗£ **THE GRAPEVINE** The High Street, Devizes.
Hours: Lunch 11am - 3pm, (last orders 2.15pm), dinner 7pm - 10.15pm (last orders). Bar meals 11am - 2.30pm and 7pm - 11pm. Closed: Sunday and Monday evenings. **Cuisine:** Dishes may include Tagliatelle with smoked salmon and cream, Escalope of veal with a ginger and raspberry vinegar sauce, Coq au Vin. ⊨ None. **CC** Access, Visa. **Other Points:** Children welcome. No smoking area. Garden dining. Fax No. (0380) 725990. **(V) Directions:** Near Town Hall.
WILLIAM COOPER ☎ (0380) 726681.
Imaginative dishes served in a friendly atmosphere can be found at The Grapevine Wine Bar and Restaurant. Both restaurant and bar meals are excellently cooked and attractively presented, complemented by an interesting wine list. The service is attentive and friendly. A good choice for well-cooked, tasty meals at very reasonable prices.

DIDCOT Oxfordshire **Map 4 B2**

⊗£ **THE RED LION** Nottingham Fee, Blewbury, Nr Didcot.
Hours: Lunch 12 noon - 2pm, Dinner 6pm - 9.30pm (last orders). Closed: Sunday evening. **Cuisine:** Bar meals including daily specials. ⊨ None. **CC** Access, Visa. **Other Points:** Children welcome. Garden. ▱ **(V) Directions:** Off the A417.
ROGER SMITH ☎ (0235) 850403.
A very old, traditional country pub, tucked away in the pretty village of Blewbury. The interior has an olde worlde appearance and an informal, relaxed atmosphere in which to enjoy the good bar meals.

DITCHLING East Sussex **Map 5 C1**

⊗££ **THE BULL HOTEL** 2 High Street, Ditchling.
⊓££ **Hours:** Breakfast 7.30am - 9am, lunch 12 noon - 2pm and dinner 7pm - 9.30pm (last orders). Bar meals 12 noon - 2pm and 7pm - 9pm. **Cuisine:** Game, seafood (local) Sussex coast, local meat and produce. ⊨ 3 bedrooms, all en suite with tea/coffee making facilities and coloured TV. **CC** All major cards. **Other Points:** Children welcome. Pets allowed. ▱ **(V) Directions:** At the foot of Ditchling Beacon, on crossroads in town centre.
RONALD KEELEY BRYANT ☎ (079 18) 3147.
A 14th century coaching inn with attractive character features including inglenook wood burning fires and a wealth of oak beams. Situated in a historic village, nestling at the foot of the downs with views to Ditchling Beacon and the South Downsway.

DORCHESTER ON THAMES Oxfordshire **Map 4 B2**

⊗££££ **WHITE HART HOTEL** High Street, Dorchester On Thames.
Hours: Meals served 7am - 9.30am, 12.30pm - 2pm and 7pm - 9.30am (last orders). Bar meals 12.30pm- 2pm. **Cuisine:** Full a la carte, table d'hote & bar menus. Dishes include Scottish salmon baked in a pastry puff & served with a white wine, cream & sorrel sauce. ⊨ 20 bedrooms, all en suite. **CC** All major cards. **Other Points:** Children welcome. No dogs allowed. ▱ ♿ **(V) Directions:** 6 miles south of Oxford on the A423, between Oxford and Wallingford.
CLARE LOGUE - Manager ☎ (0865) 340074.

Dorchester on Thames continued

An old coaching inn in the Thames valley countryside, with an international reputation for comfort and fine food and wine. Places of interest nearby include Oxford university, Blenheim Palace and Dorchester Abbey.

DOVER Kent **Map 5 C2**

�£ **DELL GUEST HOUSE** 233 Folkstone Road, Dover.

🛏 2 single, 1 double, 3 family bedrooms. Tea/coffee making facilities in all rooms. 1 bathroom. 1 shower. **Hours:** Breakfast 6.30am - 8.45am. Open all year. **CC** None. **Other Points:** Central heating. Children welcome. No dogs. Residents' lounge. TV. Garden. **P Directions:** A few minutes from Dover Priory Station. MR & MRS L ROBBINS ☎ (0304) 202422.

A comfortable Victorian house close to Priory Station and convenient for docks and Hoverport. Ideal for an overnight stop or for those staying longer. Central for visiting Norman castle and many other historic sites.

⊗££ **ST MARGARET HOTEL** Reach Road, St Margarets-at-Cliffe,
⌂£££ Nr Dover.

Hours: Breakfast 8am - 9.30am, Lunch 12 noon - 2pm, Dinner 7pm - 10pm (last orders). Bar snacks 11.30am - 2pm and 6.30pm - 9.30pm. Closed: Sunday evening, all day Monday and Tuesday lunchtime. **Cuisine:** French cuisine including Coquille St Jacques, Noisettes d'Agneau Soubise, Entrecote du Boeuf a la Florentine. 🛏 24 bedrooms, all en suite. **CC** Access, Visa, AmEx. **Other Points:** Children welcome. Residents' lounge. Garden. Indoor swimming pool, gymnasium, sauna, jacuzzi & solarium. Fax No: (0304) 853434. **P (V)** OAKLEY LEISURE PARKS LTD ☎ (0304) 853262.

A superb Hotel and Country Club with an excellent restaurant. Enjoy French cusine of the highest standard and 'faultless service' within the attractive surroundings of the restaurant. The accommodation is of an equally high standard, offering excellent comfort and all major facilities. Outstanding quality and value.

EASTBOURNE East Sussex **Map 5 C1**

⊗££ **THE CHATSWORTH HOTEL** Grand Parade, Eastbourne.

Hours: Breakfast 8am - 9.45am, lunch 12 noon - 1.45pm, dinner 7pm - 8.30pm. Sunday lunch 12.30pm - 2pm (last orders 2pm). Sunday dinner 7pm - 8.30pm. Last orders for dinner 8.30pm. **Cuisine:** A wide range of food including dishes such as avocado and prawns, soup, rosset of lamb, escalope of turkey, strawberry gateaux and crepes normand. 🛏 45 rooms, 13 single, 25 twin and 7 double rooms. All ensuite. **CC** Access, Visa. **Other Points:** Children welcome. Dogs allowed but must be on lead. Cold suppers by arrangement. Conference room available. Fax: (0323) 643270 **(V) Directions:** Corner of the Grand Parade and Hartington Place. Very nr Bandstand. MRS G H BENZMANN ☎ (0323) 411016

The Chatsworth Hotel is a traditional English Hotel. The atmosphere is both pleasant and relaxing. It is ideally situated on the Grand Parade only a minute away form the beach and promanade. With the staff always ready to help in any way, the Chatsworth is a very comfortable, family hotel.

CENTRAL & SOUTHERN ENGLAND

Eastbourne continued

⊗££ **WISH TOWER HOTEL** King Edward's Parade, Eastbourne.
Hours: Breakfast 7am - 9.30am, Lunch 12 noon (12.30pm Sunday) - 2pm, Dinner 7pm - 8.45pm (last orders). **Cuisine:** Table d'hote menu. Fish is the speciality but dishes include Roast Sirloin of Scotch Beef with Burgundy Wine Sauce. Lunchtime hot and cold Buffet. ⊨ 65 bedrooms, all en suite. **CC** All major cards. **Other Points:** Children welcome. Childrens menu. Afternoon teas. Dogs allowed. No smoking area. Conference facilities. Car parking nearby. ⅄ **(V) Directions:** On the promenade overlooking 'The Wish Tower' museum and sea.
STEPHEN LEE - General Manager ☎ (0323) 22676.
Ideally situated on the seafront, the Wish Tower Hotel provides splendid views across to the Esplanade and beach beyond. There is a friendly, relaxing atmosphere in which to enjoy the well cooked food, with locally caught fish and seafood always available. With efficient, courteous service, and comfortable furnishings, the Wish Tower is a popular rendezvous.

⊗£ **YORK HOUSE HOTEL** 14-22 Royal Parade, Eastbourne.
⊞££££ **Hours:** Breakfast 8.30am - 9.30am, lunch 12.45 noon - 1.45pm, and dinner 6.30pm - 7.30pm. Also open for Sunday lunch/dinner. **Cuisine:** Dishes include hot chicken pieces with barbecue sauce, home-cooked gammon, and roast leg of Southdown lamb with apricot and mint sauce. ⊨ 26 single, 47 twin, 23 double, and 7 family rooms - 93 of them en suite. All the rooms have colour TVs, radio/intercom, and baby listening devices. **CC** Access, Visa. **Other Points:** Children welcome. Dogs allowed, but not permitted into any public room. Heated indoor swimming pool. **(V) Directions:** Road reference - A22. Nearest landmark - Beachy Head.
MR WILLIAMSON ☎ (0323) 412918.
Four generations of the Williamson family have owned and managed York House since 1896. Now a modern hotel run on traditional lines, guests benefit from the Williamson's experience, for York House offers very comfortable rooms and delicious cuisine. There is also nightly dancing and daytime activities, such as putting, bowls, table tennis, whist drives and coach trips.

ELY Cambridgeshire **Map 5 A1**
⊗££ **THE NYTON** 7 Barton Road, Ely.
⊞££££ **Hours:** Breakfast 8am - 9am, Lunch 12 noon - 2pm, Dinner 7pm - 8.30pm (last orders). **Cuisine:** Predominantly English cuisine. ⊨ 13 bedrooms, all en suite. **CC** All major cards. **Other Points:** Children welcome. Garden. No dogs. ▯ ⅄ **(V) Directions:** Off the A10 on the A142. Adjoining golf course.
MR SETCHELL ☎ (0353) 662459.
Situated in 2 acres of attractive grounds which adjoin the 18-hole golf course, guests at The Nyton can enjoy reduced green fees. For others there are the attractions of the Cathedral and city centre, only 10 minutes walk away or the river with fishing and cruising facilities. At the hotel you will be greeted with homecooked food and comfortable accommodation.

EMSWORTH Hampshire **Map 4 C2**

Ⓒ££ **JINGLES** 77 Horndean Road, Emsworth.

CLUB ⤶ 5 single, 3 twin, 5 double and 1 family bedroom, 5 en suite. Ground floor rooms available. **Hours:** Breakfast 7.15am - 9am, Sunday lunch 12 noon - 2pm, dinner 7pm - 9pm. Non-residents welcome if book in advance. Snacks available. CC Access, Visa. **Other Points:** Children welcome. Full central heating. 2 lounges. Bar. Dogs allowed. Garden. Afternoon teas. Vegetarian meals available. ☐ 🚻 **Directions:** B2148.
KIT & ANGELA CHAPMAN ☎ (0243) 373755.
A homely Victorian building flanked by open countryside. All bedrooms are individually decorated and provide comfortable accommodation. Under the personal supervision of Kit & Angela Chapman, the atmosphere and service are welcoming and friendly.

EPSOM Surrey **Map 5 C1**

⊗££ **EPSOM DOWNS HOTEL** 9 Longdown Road, Epsom.

Ⓒ£££ **Hours:** Breakfast 7.30am - 9.30am (8.30am - 10.30am Saturday & Sunday), Lunch and bar snacks 12.30pm - 2pm (bookings only), Dinner and bar snacks 7.30pm - 9.30pm (last orders). No meals on Sundays. Closed: Christmas week only. **Cuisine:** Traditional English and continental cuisine such as Lemon Sole, Rack of Lamb roasted with honey and served with a herb and garlic sauce. ⤶ 14 bedrooms, 12 en suite. Special weekend rates. CC All major cards. **Other Points:** Children welcome. No dogs. Residents' lounge, with satellite & video. Garden planned. Fax No: (0372) 723259. ☐ **(V) Directions:** Quiet, residential area on the eastern (Banstead) side of Epsom.
ANDY & JENNY CLARK - Managers ☎ (0372) 740643.
A friendly hotel with a cosy, inviting atmosphere and excellent, individual service. Comfortably furnished and attractively decorated, the hotel offers well-appointed accommodation and very good food. All dishes are tasty and served in generous portions. You are guaranteed the warmest of welcomes by new managers, Andy and Jenny Clark, and their staff.

EYKE Suffolk **Map 5 B2**

Ⓒ£ **THE OLD HOUSE** Eyke, nr Woodbridge.

⤶ 3 double bedrooms (can be let as twin, single or family rooms), 2 bathroom /showers. Colour TV and tea/coffee making facilities in all rooms. **Hours:** Breakfast 6am - 10am and dinner 6pm - 8.30pm (order by 2pm). CC None. **Other Points:** Central heating. Children welcome. No dogs. Residents lounge. Large garden. ☐ **Directions:** Situated on the A1152 in the village of Eyke.
JAN & TONY WARNOCK ☎ (0394) 460213.
A character house dating back to 1620 with oak beams and open fires. Situated in the middle of the small village of Eyke on the A1152, the heritage coast, Sutton Hoo and Aldeburgh are all close by. All food is prepared on the premises using home and locally grown produce. A friendly guest house.

FAIRFORD Gloucestershire **Map 4 B1**

⊗££ **LEO'S RESTAURANT** Market Place, Fairford.

Hours: Morning coffee from 10am - 12 noon, lunch 12 noon - 2pm and dinner 6pm - 10pm last orders. Closed: Sunday evenings. **Cuisine:** Italian dishes from the region of Naples and

Fairford continued

traditional English dishes. ⊨ None. **CC** All major cards. **Other Points:** Children welcome. No dogs. Coaches by arrangement. ⅙ **(V)**

LEO D'ELIA ☎ (0285) 712592

An authentic Italian restaurant in the heart of the Cotswolds, offering superb food and wine in a relaxed atmosphere. Live music every Saturday night.

FAIRLIGHT East Sussex **Map 5 C1**

⊗££ **CASTROS SPANISH RESTAURANT** Coastguard Lane, Fairlight.

Hours: Lunch 12 noon - 5.30pm, Dinner 6.30pm - 11pm (last orders 10pm). **Cuisine:** Spanish and Continental; house specialities being paella and shellfish. ⊨ None. **CC** All major cards. **Other Points:** Children welcome. No dogs. **P** ⅙ **(V) Directions:** Taking the road from Ore to Fairlight turn at signs for country park

J CASTRO ☎ (0424) 812387.

Small, intimate restaurant with attentive and helpful service. Fire Hill and Hastings nearby.

FAREHAM Hampshire **Map 4 C2**

⌂££ **CATISFIELD HOTEL** Catisfield Lane, Catisfield.

⊨ 10 single, 15 double and 4 family bedrooms (sleep up to 6 adults). **Hours:** Breakfast 7am - 9am weekdays, 8.30am - 10.30am weekends (at other times by arrangement). Dinner 7pm - 8pm. **CC** None. **Other Points:** Central heating. Children welcome. Licensed. TV. Fax No: (0329) 46404. **P Directions:** From M27 (jct 9) take A27 for approx 2 miles,turn into Highlands Rd.

MISS DAPHNE DOWNES ☎ (0329) 41851.

As a result of the elevated position, the rooms all have superb views of the surrounding area. The relaxing bar offers a variety of drinks and is a popular rendezvous.

⊗££ **CHIVES** 15 High Street, Fareham.

Hours: Lunch 12.15pm - 1.30pm. Dinner served 7pm (last orders 10pm). Closed: Sundays and Mondays. **Cuisine:** An extensive and varied menu, with many interesting house specialities, accompanied by a good wine list. ⊨ None. **CC** All major cards. **Other Points:** No dogs. ⅙ **Directions:** Take the Fareham central exit from M27. In centre of Fareham.

H A PALK ☎ (0329) 234170.

A long-established, family-run business, Chives is housed in a building which dates back to Saxon times. Choose from the large selection of excellently cooked dishes, all prepared from fresh, local produce. The excellent quality of the food is complimented by the attractive surroundings, faultless service and relaxing, friendly atmosphere.

FARNHAM Surrey **Map 4 C2**

⊗££ **SEVENS WINE BAR & BISTRO** 7 The Borough, Farnham.

CLUB **Hours:** Coffee 9.30am - 12 noon, Lunch 12 noon - 2.30pm, Dinner 6.30pm - 11pm. Afternoon tea served 2.30pm - 6.30pm. **Cuisine:** French style bistro, including homemade dishes, homemade sweets. ⊨ None. **CC** Access, Visa. **Other Points:** Children welcome. Garden. Afternoon teas. ⅙ **(V) Directions:** In the centre of Farnham, very close to Castle Street and market.

Farnham continued

MR A C GREEN ☎ (0252) 715345.

An 18th century beamed black and white restaurant situated in the centre of Farnham serving tasty, well prepared food. In summer you can dine in the garden but whatever the month and setting, the food is always good and the service excellent. The friendly, welcoming staff and relaxing, informal atmosphere makes this bistro a pleasure to visit.

⊗£ **THE HALFWAY HOUSE** Bucks Horn Oak, nr Farnham.
[CLUB] **Hours:** Lunch 12 noon - 3pm, Dinner 6.30pm - 11pm (last orders 1 hour before closing time). Bar meals 11am - 2.15pm, 6pm - 10.30pm. Closed: Christmas Day. **Cuisine:** Full a la carte restaurant plus traditional English pub food, daily specials and speciality coffees. ⇥ None. **CC** Access, Visa, Diners. **Other Points:** Children welcome in dining areas. Dogs allowed in bar area only. Varied childrens amusements in garden including trampolines and playhouse. **P** ⅙ **(V) Directions:** On A325 in the Alice Holt Forest. 1 mile south of Birdworld.
OLLY & LES NEIGHBOUR M.B.I.I. ☎ (0420) 22184.

An old coaching inn built from local stone and situated in the beautiful Alice Holt Forest on the Hampshire/Surrey borders. Friendly, helpful staff. Both bar and restaurant meals are available and all main courses in the restaurant include a selection of fresh vegetables.

FELIXSTOWE Suffolk **Map 5 B2**
⊗£ **FLUYDER ARMS HOTEL** Undercliff Road East, Felixstowe.
Hours: Breakfast 8am - 9am, lunch 12 noon - 2pm and dinner 7pm - 9pm (last orders). Bar meals 12 noon - 2pm, and dinner 7pm - 9pm. **Cuisine:** Home cooked bar meals. ⇥ 10 bedrooms, 4 en suite. **CC** Access, Visa. **Other Points:** Children welcome. Pets allowed. No smoking area. Family room. Open air dining. Special children's menu. Vegetarains catered to. **P** **Directions:** On the seafront.
JOHN NASH ☎ (0394) 283279.

A small family run hotel on the Beach Road which is very popular with locals for home cooked bar food. With an extensive range of wines by the glass and varied traditional beers, together with a friendly atmosphere and facilities for children, the hotel's popularity is increasing.

⊗£ **MARLBOROUGH HOTEL** Sea Front, Felixstowe.
☫££ **Hours:** 7am - 9.30am, 12 noon - 2pm, and 7pm - 10pm (last orders 9.45pm). Bar meals 12 noon - 2.30pm, and 6pm - 8pm. **Cuisine:** English and French traditional cuisine, including carvery. Good wine list. ⇥ 47 bedrooms, all en suite, with colour TV, telephone, and tea/coffee facilities. **CC** Access, Visa, AmEx. **Other Points:** Children welcome. Pets allowed. Afternoon teas served. Open bank holidays and Sundays. **P** ⅙ **(V) Directions:** 2nd turn off roundabout at end of A45,to port.At port, 1st turning.
OHI (UK) LTD ☎ (0394) 285621.

An Edwardian building facing the sea, offering panoramic views from many of the rooms. The staff are very friendly and promote a high standard of service, all the rooms being very clean and the food well-cooked and prepared. Conveniently

Felixstowe continued

situated, close to Felixstowe leisure centre and the Spa Pavillion.

⊗££ **THE WAVERLEY HOTEL** Wolsey Gardens, Felixstowe.
⬧££££ **Hours:** Restaurant open 12 noon - 2pm, and 7pm - 10pm. Bar
CLUB meals also offered throughout the day. **Cuisine:** Varied a la carte menu in the restaurant. Bar meals include grills, fresh fish, chilli, lasagne, salads and home made pies. Daily changing specials. ⊨ 20 bedrooms, all en suite and with colour TV, tea/coffee making facilities, direct dial phone, trouser press. Most with sea views or balconies. **CC** All major cards. **Other Points:** Children welcome. Fax No: (0394) 670185. Special weekend breaks available. Telex 987568 - WAVLEY G. **P** **(V) Directions:** On upper sea-cliff road, 1 minute from main street.
MR AVERY. Manager - MR FEAKES ☎ (0394) 282811.

The Waverley is a beautiful, recently refurbished Victorian Hotel standing high on the cliff offering spectacular views of the sea and promenade. The Wolsey Restaurant provides an excellent A la Carte Menu as well as specially priced changing daily menus. There is always a selection of fresh fish & seafood available. Lighter meals available in Gladstones Bar & Brasserie. Real ales.

FLAMSTEAD Hertfordshire **Map 4 B2**
⊗£ **THREE BLACKBIRDS PUBLIC HOUSE** 2 High Street,
CLUB Flamstead, nr St. Albans.
Hours: Lunch 12 noon - 2pm, dinner 7.30pm - 9.30pm. **Cuisine:** Home cooked dishes, specially made sausages, treacle tart. ⊨ None. **CC** Access, Visa. **Other Points:** Children welcome. Dogs allowed. Beer garden. **P Directions:** Off A5, just north of Junction 9 on M1. Main road in village.
ROBERT & SUSAN MELVILLE ☎ (0582) 840330.

An attractive village pub in the centre of Flamstead. Horse collars, brasses and coppers compliment the style of the interior. Good home cooking at reasonable prices. An open log fire accentuates the warm and friendly atmosphere and the service is polite and welcoming. Popular with locals.

FLEET Hampshire **Map 4 C2**
⊗££ **LISMOYNE HOTEL** Church Road, Fleet.
⬧££££ **Hours:** Breakfast 7.30am - 9.30am, lunch 12.30pm - 2pm (last orders), dinner 7.30pm - 9.30pm (last orders), bar snacks 12.30pm -2pm and 7.30pm - 9.30pm. Open Bank Holidays. **Cuisine:** Serving bar snacks, full a la carte menu, fixed three course and two course menus. ⊨ 42 bedrooms, all en suite. **CC** All major cards. **Other Points:** Children welcome. Afternoon teas. Garden. Conferences catered for. Fax No: (0252) 811761. **P** &
(V) Directions: 1st Turning on left through shopping centre.
MR R RADIA ☎ (0252) 628555.

Privately owned Country House Hotel set in over 2 acres of gardens. Happy to cater for conferences or parties, the staff are warm and friendly. Good food and comfortable accommodation.

FOSS CROSS Gloucestershire **Map 4 B1**

⊗£ **THE HARE & HOUNDS** Foss Cross, nr Chedworth, Cheltenham.

Hours: Meals from 11.30am - 2pm (last orders), and 7pm - 10pm (last orders). Closed: Christmas Day. **Cuisine:** Steak & kidney with dumplings cooked in ale, grills, selection of various home made dishes. ⊨ None. **CC** All major cards. **Other Points:** Children welcome. **Ⓟ** & **(V) Directions:** Halfway between Cirencester and Northleach on A429.

THE TURNER FAMILY ☎ (0285) 7202288.

Located in open countryside, the pub dates back to the 17th century with many original features. They now offer a new restaurant area called 'The Pantry' where all food is home made. Registered caravan site for up to 5 vehicles adjacent.

GEDNEY DYKE Lincolnshire **Map 5 A1**

⊗££ **THE CHEQUERS** Gedney Dyke, nr Spalding.

CLUB **Hours:** Lunch and bar meals 12 noon - 1.45pm, dinner and bar meals 7pm - 9.30pm (last orders). **Cuisine:** Homemade soups and pates, classic recipes using fresh produce in season. Traditional Sunday lunch. Wide choice of meat & fish dishes. ⊨ None. **CC** Access, Visa. **Other Points:** Children welcome. Garden. **Ⓟ** & **Directions:** One mile north of the A17 at Gedney Dyke. 2 miles from Holbeach.

JUDITH & ROB MARSHALL ☎ (0406) 362666.

A small, homely country freehouse with restaurant. The bar and dining room have low ceilings with exposed beams and have been attractively furnished. Good food and a friendly, welcoming atmosphere have made this pub deservingly popular.

GILLINGHAM Dorset **Map 4 C1**

⊗£ **THE DOLPHIN INN** Peacemarsh, Gillingham.

Hours: Lunch 12 noon - 2pm, Dinner 7pm - 9.30pm. **Cuisine:** Traditional English cuisine and traditional pub favourites. Eg. Gloucester Pie, Barary Duck with a black cherry & Port sauce, Long Clawson Pork. ⊨ None. **CC** All major cards. **Other Points:** Children welcome. Beer garden. No dogs. **Ⓟ** **(V) Directions:** Off A303 London to Exeter road, on the B3095.

ANN-MARIE & TIM GOULD H.C.I.M.A. ☎ (0747) 822758.

A delightful, old converted country farmhouse, clad in ivy. The menu is extensive and caters for all tastes. There are lighter bites, traditional pub favourites, English and French dishes, all of which are well and imaginatively prepared and cooked. Close to Stourhead Gardens, Longleat Gardens and Safari Park.

GODSHILL Isle of Wight **Map 4 C2**

⊗££ **ESSEX COTTAGE** Godshill, Isle of Wight.

Hours: Lunch 12 noon - 2.30pm, Dinner 7pm - 9.30pm (last orders). Bar snacks 10am - 9.30pm. **Cuisine:** Anglo/French cuisine including old English style dishes such as Pheasant in sherry with cream, apples & raisins, Lamb with Lavender. Vegetarian & vegan. ⊨ None. **CC** Access, Visa. **Other Points:** Children welcome. Afternoon teas. No-smoking area. Garden dining. No dogs. **Ⓟ** & **(V) Directions:** A3020, on the main Newport to Shanklin road in Godshill.

ROY & CHRISTINE DALBY ☎ (0983) 840232.

Godshill continued

One of the oldest buildings in Godshill and listed in the Doomesday Book, Essex Cottage now houses an excellent restaurant. The menus offer a good choice of well-cooked, imaginative dishes featuring predominantly fresh, local produce. An interesting restaurant with a good reputation for the high quality food, good value for money, and warm welcome. Booking recommended.

GORING ON THAMES Oxfordshire **Map 4 B2**

⊗££ **THE MILLER OF MANSFIELD HOTEL** High Street, Goring
⛭££££ on Thames.

Hours: Meals 7.30am - 9am, 12 noon - 2pm and 7pm - 10pm. **Cuisine:** Varied a la carte menu including grills, plus extensive bar food menu. ⊨ 10 bedrooms, 4 en suite. Special weekend rates all year except Bank Holidays. **CC** Access, Visa. **Other Points:** Children welcome. **P** ⅙ **(V) Directions:** From A329,take the B4009 at Streatley, cross river, 200yds on left.
MARTIN WILLIAMSON, FHCIMA ☎ (0491) 872829.

A beautiful 18th century building decorated in line with the period and with many antiques. The hotel is situated close to the river in the village centre. The Goring Gap is an area of outstanding natural beauty. 9 miles from Reading, 15 miles from Oxford, and with easy access from the M4.

GORLESTON ON SEA Norfolk **Map 5 A2**

⊗££ **PIER HOTEL** Harbour Mouth, Gorleston-On-Sea.
⛭££££ **Hours:** Breakfast 7.30am - 9.30am, lunch 12 noon - 2pm (last orders) and dinner 6.30pm - 9pm (last orders). Bistro closed Sundays. **Cuisine:** Selection of dishes, including meat, charcoal grill, vegetarian and fish dishes. ⊨ 19 bedrooms, all en suite. **CC** Access, Visa, AmEx. **Other Points:** Children welcome. Afternoon tea served in summer months. Pets allowed at proprietor's discretion. No smoking areas. Function rooms/catering. **P** **(V) Directions:** Overlooking head and harbour.
MR & MRS BARFIELD ☎ (0493) 662631.

A late Victorian hotel, located near the seafront overlooking the head and harbour, offering good food, well designed comfortable bedrooms and a friendly and welcoming atmosphere.

⛭££££ **SQUIRREL'S NEST** 71 Avondale Road, Gorleston On Sea.
CLUB ⊨ 1 single, 5 double, 2 twin and 1 family bedroom, 9 with en suite showers. 1 bath. Colour TV and tea/coffee making facilities in all rooms. **Hours:** Breakfast 7am - 9am and dinner 5pm - 8.30pm. **CC** Access, Visa, AmEx. **Other Points:** Central heating. Children welcome. Dogs allowed. Licensed. Resident lounge. Vegetarian meals available. **P** ⅙ **(V) Directions:** Turn Rt off A12 at 2nd traffic lights past hospital, left to end.
MR & MRS SQUIRRELL ☎ (0493) 662746.

A seaside terraced property which has been throughly renovated, refurbished and now includes 3 four poster suites. Situated a stone's throw from the beach and close to all amenities.

GOSPORT Hampshire **Map 4 C2**

⊛£££ **ALVERBANK COUNTRY HOUSE HOTEL** Stokesbay Road,
⏸£££ Alverstoke, Gosport.
Hours: Breakfast 7am - 9am, lunch 12 noon - 2.30pm, dinner 7pm
- 9.30pm. Bar snacks 12 noon - 2.30pm, 7pm - 9.30pm. **Cuisine:**
Dishes may include Coriander Pork, Peppered Steak, Beef with
Black Bean sauce, Red Snapper with Fromage Frais & Dill sauce,
Salmon Maitre d'Hotel. ⊨ 8 bedrooms, 4 en suite. **CC** All major
cards. **Other Points:** Children welcome. Afternoon teas available.
Garden dining. Fax No. (0705) 520864. **P** & **(V) Directions:** Exit
M37 to Fareham, follow A32 for 3 miles, signed Stokes Bay.
MR PATRICK DOYLE. ☎ (0705) 510005.
Victorian country house comfortably furnished and decorated.
Popular with both holidaymakers and locals, this establishment
enjoys a lively atmosphere. Offering generous portions of good
food, first class service, and accommodation of a high quality.

⊛££ **BELLE VUE HOTEL** 39 Marine Parade East, Lee-On-The-
⏸£££££ Solent, Gosport.
Hours: Breakfast 7.15am - 9.15am, lunch 12 noon - 2pm, dinner
7pm - 10.45pm. Bar snacks 12 noon - 2pm. Open bank holidays.
Cuisine: Menu may feature - breaded mushrooms filled with pate,
honey roast maigret duck breast, grilled fillet of cod. ⊨ 27
bedrooms, all en suite. **CC** Access, Visa. **Other Points:** Children
welcome. No smoking area. Seafront patio. Fax No. (0705)
552624. **P** & **(V) Directions:** M27 Junction 8 or 11, to Fareham -
to Lee on Solent, approx 8 mins.
MR T BELLASIS ☎ (0705) 550258.
Situated on the seafront, overlooking the promenade this
modern yet traditional hotel offers comfortable accommodation
for a wide range of visitors. The food in the restaurant can be
enjoyed in relaxed surroundings.

GREAT BIRCHAM Norfolk **Map 5 A1**

⊛££ **THE KINGS HEAD HOTEL** Great Bircham, Nr Kings Lynn.
⏸£££ **Hours:** Breakfast 8am - 9.30am, lunch 12 noon - 2pm and dinner
7pm - 10pm (last orders). Bar meals 12 noon - 2pm and 7pm -
9.30pm. **Cuisine:** Stuffed sardines in herbs, brodetto, duckling a
l'orange, halibut, Grenobloise, fresh Norfolk seafood and
produce. ⊨ 5 bedrooms, all en suite, with TV and tea/coffee
making facilities. **CC** Access, Visa. **Other Points:** Children
welcome. **P** & **(V) Directions:** On the edge of Royal Sandringham
Estate beside the B1153.
IRIS & ISIDORO VERRANDO ☎ (048523) 265.
A large, Norfolk flint, country hotel near the Sandringham estate
at the far end of the village. With open country on three sides,
the outlook is decidedly rural and quiet. There is a pleasant
grassed area for summer dining. An extremely popular eating
place with tourists and locals.

GREAT MISSENDEN Buckinghamshire **Map 4 B2**

⊛£ **THE GEORGE** 94 High Street, Aylesbury, Great Missenden.
Hours: Meals served 12 noon - 2pm and 7pm - 11.30pm (last
orders 9.45pm). Bar meals 12 noon - 2.15pm and 7pm - 9.45pm.
Closed evenings on Christmas Day, Boxing Day . Food served
Sunday evenings 7pm - 9.45pm. **Cuisine:** Steaks, pasta and
vegetarian selections. ⊨ None. **CC** Access, Visa. **Other Points:**

Great Missenden continued

Children welcome. Pets allowed. ▣ ㅑ **(V) Directions:** 0.25 miles from A413 between Amersham & Wendover. In town's main st. GUY & SALLY SMITH ☎ (02406) 2084.

Many levelled, old beamed and tastefully furnished pub which offers excellent food, competent service, a very pleasant atmosphere at very good value.

GREAT RISSINGTON Gloucestershire **Map 4 B1**

⊗££ **THE LAMB INN** Great Rissington, nr Bourton on the Water.

⬤£££ **Hours:** Meals from 8.30am - 9am, 12 noon - 1.45pm and 7pm - 9pm weekdays, 9.30pm on weekends, last orders. **Cuisine:** Steaks, Cotswold trout, pates, soups, casseroles. ⊨ 8 bedrooms, 5 bathrooms. ▣ Access, Visa. **Other Points:** Children welcome. MR & MRS RICHARD CLEVERLY ☎ (0451) 20388.

Situated in the heart of the Cotswolds, Great Rissington is popular with tourists. Locally there is the Cotswold Wildlife Park and slightly further afield, Oxford and Stratford-upon-Avon.

GREAT YARMOUTH Norfolk **Map 5 A2**

⬤££££ **REGENCY HOTEL** 5 North Drive, Great Yarmouth.

CLUB ⊨ 3 single, 9 double and 1 family bedroom, all en suite. **Hours:** Breakfast 8am - 9.30am, Dinner 6pm - 8.30pm (5pm - 8pm Sundays). ▣ All major cards. **Other Points:** No dogs. ▣ **Directions:** On the seafront in Great Yarmouth. J BARNETT ☎ (0493) 843759.

A modern seaside hotel offering comfortable accommodation in a good, seafront location. Guests can choose from table d'hote or A la Carte menus at dinner and there is a good choice at breakfast. The Regency Hotel is popular with holiday makers and business people alike.

⊗££ **THE CLIFF HOTEL** Cliff Hill, Gorleston on Sea, nr Great Yarmouth.

Hours: Open all year. **Cuisine:** Traditional roasts. ⊨ 34 bedrooms, all en suite. ▣ All major cards. **Other Points:** Children welcome. ▣ ㅑ MR R W SCOTT ☎ (0493) 662179.

A welcoming business and holiday hotel overlooking the harbour on the quieter side of Great Yarmouth. The chefs and their staff provide a large selection of English dishes, offering the opportunity to sample the best from the produce of Norfolk farms and market gardens.

⊗£ **THE GALLON POT** Market Place, Great Yarmouth.

Hours: Monday to Saturday - open all day. Food served 11.30am - 2pm, 7pm - 10pm. Sunday lunchtime 12 noon - 2pm and Sunday evening 7pm - 9.30pm. **Cuisine:** Traditional pub food. Special weekend and lunchtime menus. ⊨ None. ▣ None. **Other Points:** Children welcome. No dogs. Large public car park adjacent. ㅑ **(V) Directions:** In town centre, in open market square. Next to large public car park MICHAEL & MARIA SPALDING ☎ (0493) 842230.

A traditional town centre public house which has built up a reputation for good quality bar food at very reasonable prices.

Great Yarmouth continued
Popular with locals of all ages the pub also appeals to seasonal holiday makers. A relaxed and comfortable atmosphere.

GUILDFORD Surrey Map 4 C2

®£ **KINGS SHADE COFFEE HOUSE** 20 Tunsgate, Guildford.
CLUB **Hours:** Breakfast 8.30am - 11am. Meals served all day 11am - 6pm. Closed: Sundays. **Cuisine:** House specialities include Steak & Kidney Pie, Chicken & Spinach Gratin, Lasagne. Salads, toasted savouries, stuffed baked potatoes, sandwiches. ⊯ None. **CC** None. **Other Points:** Afternoon teas. No dogs. Licensed. **(V) Directions:** Off the High Street, opposite the Guild Hall.
DAVID GOLDSBY ☎ (0483) 576718.
Well situated between the famous Guildhall clock and the superb Castle gardens. Kings Shade Coffee House is open all day and is a very popular venue in which to enjoy a meal or snack. The menu is extensive, the atmosphere bustling and the service friendly and efficient. The homemade sweets are particularly recommended.

®£ **THE SPREAD EAGLE** 46 Chertsey Street, Guildford.
Hours: Lunch 12 noon - 2pm except Sundays. **Cuisine:** Bar meals - lamb provencale, moussaka, lasagne, beef and mushroom pie, asparagus quiche. ⊯ None. **CC** None. **Other Points:** Children welcome. No dogs. ▣ ♿ **Directions:** Off the main street in Guildford.
MR & MRS OLIVER ☎ (0483) 35018.
A split level older style pub, with exposed walls, specialising in real ale. The stables have been converted to a family room and children's dining area. Close to the town's shops and offices.

HALSTEAD Essex Map 5 B1

®££ **THE BULL HOTEL** Bridge Street, Halstead.
ⅢⅡ£££ **Hours:** Breakfast 6.30am - 10am, lunch 12 noon - 2.30pm, bar snacks 11.30am - 3pm and 6.30pm - 10.30pm, dinner 6.30pm - 10pm. **Cuisine:** Traditional and modern, English and International cuisine. Menu includes fish, poultry and house speciality of 'sizzling steak'. ⊯ 19 bedrooms, all en suite. **CC** All major cards. **Other Points:** Children welcome. Afternoon teas. Dogs allowed. Garden dining. Fax No: (0787) 472496. ▣ **(V) Directions:** Follow A120 to Cambridge from Colchester.
MICHAEL DAVIS ☎ (0781) 472144.
Formerly a coaching inn dating back to the 15th century, this hotel has retained all the character of its age. Tastefully decorated in keeping with the style of the establishment, the inn offers very generous portions of good food. Frequented by locals and business people alike, the non obtrusive, easy listening music adds to the pleasant atmosphere.

HAMPTON COURT Surrey Map 4 B2

®£££ **LE CAMEMBERT** Hampton Court Road, East Molesey.
Hours: Le Camembert open for dinner Friday and Saturday 7.30pm - 11pm. Bastions Restaurant (downstairs) open Monday to Saturday for lunch and dinner. **Cuisine:** French, English and Italian cuisine in both restaurants - Le Camembert and Bastions. ⊯ None. **CC** None. **Other Points:** Children welcome. Available for

Hampton Court continued
private parties. **Directions:** Opposite Hampton Court Palace, above Bastion's Restaurant.
ERIC ARMITAGE ☎ (977) 0869.
Lovely country-styled restaurant, the sister to L'Artiste Assoiffe in North Kensington, situated on the outskirts of London in a quiet tree-lined street. Le Camembert attracts a broad cross-section of people, by virtue of its excellent cuisine, good value, and its intimate yet lively atmosphere. Highly recommended. Bastions offers equally high standards of food and service.

HANNINGTON Hampshire **Map 4 C2**
⊗££ **THE VINE INN** Hannington.
Hours: Lunch from 12 noon - 2.30pm (last orders 2pm) and dinner 6.30pm - 10.30pm (last orders 10pm). **Cuisine:** Famous pies, reputable steaks, choice of vegetarian meals in the Bar and Conservatory and a seasonal changing A la Carte menu. ⍪ None.
CC All major cards. **Other Points:** Children welcome. **P** & **(V)**
Directions: Off the A339.
MR & MRS MATTHEWS ☎ (0635) 298525.
An exceptional country inn in a prime location off the A339 in this charming village. The Vine incorporates a large freehouse pub, new 42 seater Conservatory, and an a la carte restaurant, offering varied menus seven days a week. The Matthews have gained a considerable reputation locally for their food.

HAPPISBURGH Norfolk **Map 5 A2**
⊗££ **THE HILL HOUSE** Happisburgh.
⌂££ **Hours:** Lunch 12 noon - 2pm, dinner 7pm - 10pm (last orders 9.30pm). Bar meals 12 noon - 2pm and 6.30pm - 9.30pm.
Cuisine: Chargrilled steaks, mushrooms 'Amanda', giant prawns in garlic butter, and 'Hill House lifeboats'. ⍪ 1 doubleroom, en suite. **CC** Access, Visa. **Other Points:** Children welcome in pretty lawned garden with sea views. Family room. Pets allowed. Carvery bar during summer months. Functions cartered for. **P** & **(V)**
Directions: Next to church in Happisburgh.
MR & MRS RAYNER ☎ (0692) 650004.
With parts dating back to the 15th century, Hill House is clearly a building with a past! For centuries, villagers have been welcomed through the doors and fed and watered - and the Rayners are maintaining this time-honoured tradition. Close to Yarmouth, coastal resorts and the Norfolk Broads.

HARROW Middlesex **Map 4 B2**
⌂£££ **CRESCENT LODGE HOTEL** 58-62 Welldon Crescent, Harrow.
⍪ 21 bedrooms, 12 en suite. Tea/coffee making facilities, telephone, radio, alarm, Colour TV and fridge in rooms.
Hours: Full English Breakfast and evening meals available.
CC None. **Other Points:** Children welcome. Open Bank Holidays. Garden dining. Conference facilities and room available. Fax No. (081) 427 5965. Licensed bar. **P** **(V) Directions:** Off Headstone Road, on Welldon Crescent.
MR & MRS JIVRAJ ☎ (081) 863 5491.
This is a family owned and run hotel situated in Harrow, providing guests with personal service and a comfortable,

Harrow continued

carefree stay. Happy to cater for conferences. A genuine warm welcome is extended to all visitors.

⊗£££ **CUMBERLAND HOTEL** St John's Road, Harrow.

⊞££££ **Hours:** Breakfast 7am - 9.30am, lunch 12 noon - 2pm and dinner 7pm - 9.30pm. **Cuisine:** Dishes are mainly French on the a la carte menu, with various specialities on the fixed price choice menu. Eg. Sole Walewska, Magret de Canard Bigarrade. ⊨ 40 single, 13 twin, 26 double and 2 family bedrooms. All en suite. **CC** All major cards. **Other Points:** Children welcome. No smoking areas. **P** **(V)** MR I KAY - Manager ☎ (081) 863 4111.
Relax in the unrushed peaceful atmosphere of this long established hotel. Superbly decorated and furnished, the restaurant offers excellent cooking in generous portions. Every care is taken by the attentive staff to make all visitors feel relaxed and welcome. Highly recommended.

⊗££ **FIDDLER'S RESTAURANT** 221-225 High Road, Harrow Weald.

CLUB **Hours:** Lunch 12 noon - 2.30pm, Dinner 7pm - 11.30pm. Closed: Christmas Day and Boxing Day. **Cuisine:** Wide selection of Italian & French cuisine such as Duck with orange sauce; Beef al Pepe - with a crushed pepper, brandy & cream sauce; Calamari Fritti. ⊨ None. **CC** All major cards. **Other Points:** Children welcome. No dogs. No smoking area. Fiddler plays 4 days a week. Disco nightly. Meeting/Exhibition/Private functions room. Air Conditioned. **P** ১ **(V) Directions:** A409, between Harrow Wealdstone station and Uxbridge Rd roundabout.
ANTONIO BRANCA ☎ (081) 863 6066.
Part of a 1930's row of shops, 'Fiddlers' has a black and white mock Tudor frontage. Inside, Tudor decor, bric a brac and mirrors create warm, attractive surroundings in which to enjoy the excellent food. All dishes are well cooked and well presented. Everything is done to ensure that customers enjoy their meal and the service and atmosphere is warm and welcoming.

⊗££ **LINDAL HOTEL & RESTAURANT** 2 Hindes Road, Harrow.

⊞££ **Hours:** Breakfast 7.20am - 9am, dinner 7pm - 9pm. Closed:
CLUB Sundays. **Cuisine:** Dishes include homemade soups, sirloin steak with garni, and a selection of freshly made sweets. ⊨ 21 rooms. 8 single, 7 twin, 5 double and 1 family bedroom. 19 en suite. **CC** Access, Visa. **Other Points:** Children welcome. Afternoon teas available on request. No smoking. Fax No: (081) 427 5435. **P** ১ **(V) Directions:** Between Harrow on the Hill station and the Civic Centre.
MR & MRS PLUNKETT ☎ (081) 863 3164.
Located in a quiet part of Harrow the 'Lindal Hotel & Restaurant' is pleasantly decorated and comfortably furnished. The restaurant has a good a la carte menu. All rooms are well furnished with quality materials. 5 minutes walk from Harrow Town Centre and train/tube service into the centre of London. Wembley and Heathrow are within easy reach.

Harrow continued

⊗£££ **OLD ETONIAN RESTAURANT** 38 High Street, Harrow on the Hill.

Hours: Lunch 12 noon - 2.30pm, dinner 7pm - 11pm (last orders). Closed: Saturday morning, all day Sunday and bank holidays. **Cuisine:** French cuisine, featuring seafood pancake, Steak Dijon, roast duck in orange sauce, with guava, chocolate mousse, creme brulee. ⌦ None. ◪ All major cards. **Other Points:** Children welcome. Off street parking outside. ♿ **(V) Directions:** Off Uxbridge road, in the town centre near the School.
MR PELAEZ ☎ (081 422) 8482.

An 18th century French bistro-style restaurant, situated in the town centre near the famous Harrow Public School, combining the qualities of excellent food and service with comfortable and relaxed surroundings.

⊗£££ **PERCY'S RESTAURANT** 66-68 Station Road, North Harrow.
Hours: Meals served 12 noon - 3pm and 6pm - 12 midnight (last orders 10.30pm). Closed: Sunday and Monday. **Cuisine:** French/English including a good vegetarian selection plus fish & game specialities. All food created on the premises including ice creams & sorbets. ⌦ None. ◪ Access, Visa. **Other Points:** No smoking throughout. No children under 10. Fax No: (081) 427 8134. 🅿 ♿ **(V) Directions:** Opposite North Harrow Metropolitan underground station.
TONY & TINA BRICKNELL-WEBB ☎ (081) 427 2021.

A success story for this husband and wife team, this French-style 70 cover restaurant offers excellent food in warm, inviting surroundings. Only the freshest ingredients are good enough for Tony & Tina and you will find their dishes mouth watering and deliciously cooked. Homemade ice creams and sorbets tempt the diet and the smoke free atmosphere assists the palate.

HARWICH Essex **Map 5 B2**

⊗£ **CLIFF HOTEL** Marine Parade, Dovercourt, Harwich.
⌂£££ **Hours:** Breakfast 7.30am - 9.30am, lunch 12.30pm - 2pm (last orders 1.45pm), bar snacks 12 noon - 2pm, dinner 6.30pm - 9pm (last orders 8.45pm), bar snacks 6pm - 9pm. **Cuisine:** Wide choice of dishes including fresh fish. ⌦ 27 bedrooms, 25 en suite. ◪ All major cards. **Other Points:** Children welcome. Open Bank Holidays. Afternoon teas. Fax No. (0255) 240358. 🅿 **(V) Directions:** On seafront at Dovercourt.
D A HUTCHINS ☎ (0255) 50385.

Overlooking the seafront, this large Victorian hotel is decorated and furnished in keeping with the character of the building. Attractively presented meals are served by friendly, competent staff and the accommodation is very comfortable. Ideally located on the seafront for holiday makers.

⌂£££ **NEW FARM HOUSE** Spinnel's Lane, Wix, Manningtree.
⌦ 3 single, 3 twin, 1 double, 5 family bedrooms: 7 en suite.
Hours: Breakfast 8am - 10am and dinner 6.30pm - 7pm. Packed lunches by arrangement. ◪ Access, Visa. **Other Points:** Children welcome. Play area. Pets allowed. Non smoking area available. Vegetarian meals available. 🅿 ♿ **Directions:** Off A120, between Colchester and Harwich.
THE MITCHELL FAMILY ☎ (0255) 870365.

Harwich continued

A large modern farmhouse, set in its own well-tended gardens, situated on the outskirts of the quiet village of Wix. Comfortable, clean bedrooms complemented by a relaxing and friendly atmosphere.

⊗££ **TOWER HOTEL** Main Road, Dovercourt, Harwich.
⊓££ **Hours:** Breakfast 8am - 9.30am, lunch 12 noon - 2pm and dinner 6.30pm - 9.30pm (last orders). **Cuisine:** Fresh local lobster and Dover sole. ⊨ 15 bedrooms, all en suite. **CC** All major cards. **Other Points:** Children welcome. **P** & **(V) Directions:** On the left side of A136 (Harwich bound) near Dovercourt Station.
DOUGLAS HUTCHINS ☎ (0255) 504 952.
Built in 1885 the main feature of the building is a tower in the north-east corner. Inside, it retains many original architectural features with friezes, cornices and architraves. The Pattrick Suite is a magnificent function room which is available for private hire.

HASLEMERE Surrey **Map 4 C2**
⊗£££ **LYTHE HILL HOTEL & RESTAURANTS** Petworth Road, Haslemere.
Hours: Breakfast 8am - 9.30am, Lunch 12.15pm - 2.15pm and Dinner 7.15pm - 9.15pm (last orders). **Cuisine:** A la carte or table d'hote menus. ⊨ 40 bedrooms, all en suite. **CC** Access, Visa, AmEx. **Other Points:** Children welcome. Garden, Afternoon tea. Pets allowed. **P** & **(V) Directions:** On B2131.
LYTHE HILL HOTEL LIMITED ☎ (0428) 51251.
This attractive hotel and restaurant is made up of a converted 14th century farmhouse and buildings and is set on the lawn slopes of Blackdown with panoramic views over the Weald. Good food, service and a pleasant relaxing atmosphere, combine to make dining here enjoyable.

⊗£ **THE RED LION** 8 The Green, Fernhurst, Nr Haslemere.
Hours: Lunch 12 noon - 2.30pm (last orders) and dinner 7pm - 10.30pm (last orders). **Cuisine:** English/Continental, including Breast of pigeon in a blackberry sauce, Peppered chicken in a cream and Dijon sauce. ⊨ None. **CC** Access, Visa. **Other Points:** Children welcome. Garden. **P** & **(V) Directions:** Off the A286, situated in Fernhurst, 3 miles from Haslemere.
MRS BRENDA HEATH ☎ (0428) 643112/653304
One of the oldest buildings in the village, The Red Lion is an attractive stone built inn overlooking the village green. With exposed beams and open log fires to add to the cosy atmosphere, you will find the good food and Mrs Heath's hospitality hard to pass by.

HASTINGS East Sussex **Map 5 C1**
⊗££ **RESTAURANT TWENTY SEVEN** 27 George Street, Hastings Old Town, Hastings.
Hours: Dinner 7pm - 10.30pm (last orders). Closed: Monday. **Cuisine:** French dishes including Salad Maconnaise, Salmon en Croute and Steak au Poivre. Traditional Sunday lunch. ⊨ None. **CC** Access, Visa. **Directions:** East end of the seafront, pedestrianised area of the old town.
P ATTRILL & E GIBBS. Chef - C ATTRILL ☎ (0424) 420060.

CENTRAL & SOUTHERN ENGLAND

Hastings continued

> *Attractive French restaurant set in the old part of town near the seafront. All food is freshly prepared for each customer and, with its impressionist paintings and soft gallic style music, the atmosphere is both intimate and relaxing.*

HAUGHLEY Suffolk **Map 5 B2**

⊗£££ **THE OLD COUNTING HOUSE RESTAURANT** Haughley, nr Stowmarket.

CLUB **Hours:** Meals 12 noon - 2pm (except Saturday) and 7.30pm - 9.30pm. Closed: Sundays. **Cuisine:** English and French. Lunch - 2 or 3 course table d'hote plus a la carte. Dinner - 4 course table d'hote, 6 choices for each course, changed every 3 weeks None. **CC** Access, Visa. **Other Points:** Children welcome. No dogs. **P** & **(V) Directions:** 1 and a half miles from the A45, in the centre of Haughley.

MR & MRS P WOODS ☎ (0449) 673 617.

> *Typical Suffolk timber-framed house dating back to the 1500s when it was a bank. Now you may dine at tables set with damask linen, fine glass ware and classic cutlery.*

HAYES Middlesex **Map 4 B2**

⊗£ **EVEREST TANDOORI (NEPALESE STYLE CUISINE)** 53 Coldharbour Lane, Hayes.

Hours: Lunch 12 noon - 2.30pm, Dinner 6pm - 12 midnight. Closed: Christmas Day and Boxing Day. **Cuisine:** Nepalese-style cuisine including Tandoori specialities, Biryani and Karahi dishes. Special Kurzi Lamb (4 persons) available at 24 hrs notice. None. **CC** All major cards. **Other Points:** Children welcome. No dogs. Take-aways available. Street parking. **(V) Directions:** Main street in the centre of Hayes.

MUHAMMAD HUSSAIN ☎ (081) 561 1717/4134.

> *Excellent food can be enjoyed in this comfortable, attractively decorated Nepalese restaurant. The menu offers an extensive choice of dishes which are all cooked to order and to suit each individual taste. The service is welcoming and efficient, with nothing too much trouble. Highly recommended for the excellent service, good food and reasonable prices.*

HAYLING ISLAND Hampshire **Map 4 C2**

⊗££ **NEWTOWN HOUSE HOTEL** Manor Road, Hayling Island.

£££ **Hours:** Breakfast 7am - 10am, Lunch 12 noon - 2pm, Dinner 7pm - CLUB 9.30pm. **Cuisine:** Predominantly French cuisine. Specialities include File de Boeuf Diane, Tournedos Rossini, Rack of lamb roasted with honey and garlic. 28 bedrooms, 26 en suite. **CC** All major cards. **Other Points:** Children welcome. Dogs allowed. Garden. Afternoon tea. Indoor Leisure complex - heated indoor swimming pool, jacuzzi, gym and solarium. **P** & **(V) Directions:** Main road into West Hayling, close to shops and shore.

N & M PROPERTIES ☎ (0705) 466131.

> *An 18th century, converted farmhouse set in its own large gardens, Newtown House Hotel provides a cosy bar and lounge, and a la carte restaurant, comfortable accommodation and an indoor leisure complex. Well suited to families, this hotel is an ideal place to stay throughout the year due to its location near the sea and new indoor Leisure Complex.*

HAYLING ISLAND Late Entry **COCKLE WARREN** - see Page 320

HAYWARDS HEATH West Sussex **Map 5 C1**

⊗££ **BENT ARMS** Lindfield, Haywards Heath.

🏨£££ **Hours:** Breakfast 7.30am. Lunch 12 noon - 2.15pm. Dinner 6.15pm - 10.15pm. **Cuisine:** A la carte, bar meals/snacks. English cuisine. The speciality is Spit Roast Beef in bar - sliced to order, hot. 🛏 10 rooms. All en suite. **CC** All major cards. **Other Points:** Children welcome. Garden. Dogs allowed. 🅿 ♿ **(V) Directions:** 2 miles outside Haywards Heath station.
MR HOYLE. ☎ (0444) 483146.
The Bent Arms is part of a 16th century coaching inn, that sits in a typical English village with half timbered houses, a lake and swans. It is popular with locals and has a friendly and relaxed atmosphere.

⊗££ **INN THE PRIORY** Syresham Gardens, Haywards Heath.
Hours: Lunch: Monday - Saturday 12 noon - 3pm (last orders 1.30pm). Sunday lunch 11.45am - 4pm (last orders 2.45pm). Dinner Monday to Thursday 7pm - 11.30pm (last orders 9.30pm). Friday and Saturday 6.30pm - 11.30pm (last orders 9.30pm). **Cuisine:** Traditional English carvery. 🛏 None. **CC** All major cards. **Other Points:** Children welcome. No dogs allowed. 🅿 ♿ **(V) Directions:** Take Caxton Way off Sussex Square roundabout on South Road.
DAVID & MARTINA WHITE ☎ (0444) 459533.
Lovely restaurant set in the surroundings of an old priory chapel, with stained glass windows, ornate wood carvings and a turret clock; offering a freshly prepared carvery menu of high quality and good value. National Trust gardens and Bluebell steam railway located nearby.

⊗£ **THE SLOOP INN** Freshfield Lock, Nr Haywards Heath.
Hours: 10.30am - 3.pm, 6pm - 11pm. Meals served 12 noon - 2pm and 7pm - 9.30pm (last orders). **Cuisine:** Extensive menu displayed on blackboards - changes daily. 🛏 None. **CC** All major cards. **Other Points:** Children welcome. Dogs allowed in public bar. 2 beer gardens. No juke box. Separate public bar and games room. Family/Company accounts welcomed. 🅿 ♿ **(V) Directions:** Off A272, at Scaynes Hill near Haywards Heath.
DAVID MICHAEL & MARILYN MILLS ☎ (0444) 831219.
An attractive public house offering good quality bar meals in comfortable surroundings. The service is warm and courteous and the pub enjoys a friendly, welcoming atmosphere.

HEADLEY Hampshire **Map 4 C2**

⊗£ **THE CROWN INN** Arford, Headley, Nr Bordon.
CLUB **Hours:** Bar meals 12 noon - 2.30pm and 6.30pm - 10pm Monday - Saturday. 7pm - 9pm Sunday. **Cuisine:** Double decker toasted sandwiches, chilli with avocado dip, salmon steaks, steaks, homemade steak & kidney pie, trout and homemade meringues. 🛏 None. **CC** Access, Visa. **Other Points:** Beer garden. Dogs permitted. Children welcome in the garden. 🅿 **(V) Directions:** Off the A325,onto the B3002. South of Farnham.
COLIN AND JANE GREENHALGH ☎ (0428) 712150.
Situated in the picturesque village of Arford, the Crown Inn is a recently enlarged, cosy, village pub with a friendly atmosphere

Headley continued

and good food. There is a large garden leading down to a stream and there are plenty of tables for customers' use during the summer months.

HENFIELD West Sussex **Map 5 C1**
⊗£££ **TOTTINGTON MANOR HOTEL & RESTAURANT**
⌂££££ Edburton, Nr Henfield.
Hours: Breakfast 7.30am - 9.30am, Lunch 12 noon - 2.15pm and Dinner 7pm - 9.15pm (last orders). Restaurant closed: Sunday evenings and Saturday lunch. **Cuisine:** A la carte, Table d'hote and Bar menu. Traditional English, classical and international cuisine. Beef Wellington, Roast Duckling with Baked Apples. ⇌ 6 bedrooms, all en suite. **CC** All major cards. **Other Points:** Children welcome. Garden. No smoking area. 'Specials' on board. Fax No: (0903) 879331. **P (V) Directions:** Just off the 2037, which is off the 283 near Steyning.
DAVID & KATE MILLER ☎ (0903) 815757.
This typical Sussex Country Manor House, set in 4 acres of well kept grounds, dates back to the 16th Century, and commands magnificent views over the South Downs and Weald. The Chef/Proprietor, who was formerly head chef at the Ritz in London, cultivates his own herbs in the kitchen garden and guests will find the accommodation to as high a standard as the fine cuisine.

HENLEY IN ARDEN Warwickshire **Map 4 A1**
⊗££ **ARDEN TANDOORI RESTAURANT** 137 High Street, Henley In Arden.
Hours: Lunch 12 noon - 2.30pm and dinner 5.30pm - 11.30pm (last orders 11.15pm) Closed: Christmas Day. **Cuisine:** Indian. Specialities: Kurzi Lamb, lamb pasanda Nawabi, Makhon chicken. ⇌ None. **CC** All major cards. **Other Points:** Coaches by appointment. Children welcome. ⅙ **(V) Directions:** On the A34 between Solihull and Stratford upon Avon.
NANU MIAH ☎ (05642) 792503.
Situated right in the centre of the historic town of Henley in Arden. The interior has been tastefully decorated with an air of subdued elegance. The Arden offers a warm welcome and excellent food.

HENLEY ON THAMES Oxfordshire **Map 4 B2**
⊗££ **THE FIVE HORSESHOES** Maidensgrove, Henley on Thames, Oxon.
Hours: Meals served 12noon - 2pm (last orders 1.45pm) and 7pm - 10pm (last orders 9.30pm). Restaurant closed Sunday evenings. **Cuisine:** Homemade soup and pate. Chicken Kiev. Escalope of Scotch salmon. Seafood Lasagne. Grilled King Prawns. Fillet steak and grilled Scotch sirloin. ⇌ None. **CC** Access, Visa. **Other Points:** Garden with table sets. Pets allowed if on lead. **P** ⅙ **(V) Directions:** Off B480/B481.
GRAHAM CROMACK ☎ (0491) 641282.
A lovely old inn, complete with flowering creepers and well tended English garden with dining sets for the summer months. Old beamed rooms with wall mounted memorabilia sets the mood for dining and the good food (generous portions and well

Henley on Thames continued

presented), is complemented by friendly service in a relaxing comfortable atmosphere.

⊗£ **THE FIVE HORSESHOES INN** Remenham Hill, Henley on Thames.
Hours: Breakfast 7.30am - 9.30am, Lunch and bar meals 11am - 2.30pm, Dinner and bar meals 6pm - 10pm. **Cuisine:** Home cooked dishes. Blackboard specials change daily. ⊨ 3 bedrooms. **CC** Access, Visa. **Other Points:** Children welcome. Beer garden. No dogs. ▣ **(V) Directions:** A423. 1 mile out of Henley towards London.
MR P.M. STANFORD-DAVIS ☎ (0491) 574881.
A Georgian brick and flint building housing two bars and a cellar dining room. The Five Horseshoes offers a good selection of home cooked food at good value prices and the service is friendly and helpful.

⊗££ **THE FLOWER POT** Aston, Henley on Thames.
Hours: Dinner 7pm - 9pm. Bar lunches 12 noon - 2.30pm. Restaurant only closed Sunday and Monday evening. **Cuisine:** Table d'hote menu with large choice in restaurant. Dishes include panfried monkfish with a saffron sauce and duck breast with Armagnac. Bar meals. ⊨ 4 bedrooms, 1 en suite. **CC** Access, Visa. **Other Points:** Vegetarian meals by arrangement. Garden. ▣ **Directions:** Off A423 Henley/Maidenhead rd. One mile out of Henley.
J G T JONES ☎ (0491) 574721.
A Victorian pub with character, located in a secluded rural area close to the Thames. The pub houses two bars and the Flower Pot restaurant. All food is excellently presented and cooked to order only and the high standard of catering is complimented by friendly, efficient service. A relaxing atmosphere in which to enjoy a meal or simply have a drink in the pub.

⊗£ **THE GOLDEN BALL** Lower Assendon, Henley on Thames.
Hours: Lunch 11.30am - 2.15pm, dinner 6.30pm -10pm (last orders). Closed: Christmas Day and Boxing Day evening. **Cuisine:** Homemade pies, bread pudding, coffee and brandy cake. ⊨ None. **CC** None. **Other Points:** Beer garden. Dogs allowed. ▣ ♿ **Directions:** Turn right one mile north of Henley on A423.
PATRICIA BEESLEY ☎ (0491) 574157
A 400 year old building which has been a pub since the turn of this century. Olde worlde interior with a large collection of old brewery and advertising items. An ideal English country pub offering a truely warm welcome and very friendly service. Meals served outside in summer months.

⊗££ **THE WALNUT TREE** Fawley, near Henley-on-Thames.
⏤£££ **Hours:** Breakfast 7.30am - 9.30am, Lunch 12 noon - 2pm, Dinner
CLUB 7pm - 10pm (9.30pm Sundays). Traditional Sunday Lunch. **Cuisine:** A la Carte menu and bar meals. Dishes may include Sirlion Steak au Poivre, Panfried Liver, Salmon Fillet, Duck Breast with Honey & Thyme sauce. ⊨ 2 double bedrooms, en suite. **CC** Access, Visa. **Other Points:** Children welcome. No dogs. Garden. No smoking in bedrooms. Fax No: (0491) 63617. ▣ ♿ **(V) Directions:** Off the A4155 in the village of Fawley.

CENTRAL & SOUTHERN ENGLAND

Henley on Thames continued
G KNIGHT ☎ (0491) 63360.
The Walnut Tree is situated in the rural village of Fawley, set in the Chiltern Hills, 3 miles from Henley. Meals are served in an informal and relaxed atmosphere. Customers can choose from a range of bar meals or, on Thursday, Friday and Saturday nights, from the A la Carte menu in the restaurant. The accommodation is of a high standard.

HENLOW Bedfordshire **Map 5 B1**
⊛£ **THE FIVE BELLS** 101 High Street, Henlow.
Hours: Lunch 11.30am - 2pm and dinner 7pm - 10pm (last orders). Bar meals 11.30am - 2pm and 7pm - 10pm. **Cuisine:** Regularly changing selection of 6 speciality dishes created by the resident chef. ⊨ None. **CC** Access, Visa. **Other Points:** Children welcome. **P** ⅙ **(V) Directions:** Off the B6001 in the village centre.
COLIN W JOHNS ☎ (0462) 811125.
Originally three cottages, the pub is comfortably furnished with a bar and separate dining area maintained to high standards. 10 minutes drive from Letchworth and Baldock it is centrally situated for travellers in the area.

HERSTMONCEUX East Sussex **Map 5 C1**
⊛£££ **WHITE FRIARS HOTEL** Nr Herstmonceux.
⊞£££ **Hours:** Breakfast 7.15am - 9.15am, Lunch 12 noon - 2pm, Dinner 7pm - 9.30pm. Bar meals 12 noon - 2.30pm. **Cuisine:** A combination of classic and modern cuisine, featuring French and English dishes using fresh, regional produce. Bar-style meals also served at lunchtime. ⊨ 20 bedrooms, all en suite. **CC** All major cards. **Other Points:** Children welcome. Choice of restaurants. Dogs allowed. Afternoon teas. Conference facilities. Fax No: (0323) 833882. **P** **(V) Directions:** A271, just outside Herstmonceux.
LYNDA & PHILLIP WHITE ☎ (0323) 832355.
Offering a high standard of accommodation and excellent cuisine, White Friars Hotel is well worth a visit. The best fresh regional produce is used to provide outstanding French and English cuisine which has already earned the hotel an enviable reputation locally. Elegant decor, warm and courteous service and a friendly atmosphere. Conference facilities also available.

HIGH WYCOMBE Buckinghamshire **Map 4 B2**
⊛£ **DRAKE COURT HOTEL** 141 London Road, High Wycombe.
⊞££ **Hours:** Breakfast 7.30am - 8.30am, dinner 7pm - 8.30pm (last orders). Lunch by arrangement. **Cuisine:** Traditional English and continental cuisine. ⊨ 20 bedrooms, 8 en suite. **CC** All major cards. **Other Points:** Children welcome. Open Bank Holidays. Residents lounge. No dogs. Outdoor swimming pool. Fax No: (0494) 472696. **P Directions:** A40 London Road, close to High Wycombe. Approx 1 mile M40 motorway.
IAN CLARK - Resident Manager ☎ (0494) 523639.
A small, friendly hotel situated close to the centre of historic High Wycombe. The staff are welcoming and efficient. Convenient for the M40 London - Oxford motorway and for touring the Thames Valley, Oxford and the Cotswolds.

HORSHAM West Sussex **Map 4 C2**

⊗££ **COUNTRYMAN INN** Shipley, Near Horsham.
Hours: 12 noon - 2pm, and 7pm - 9.30pm (last orders). Bar meals served between 12 noon - 2pm, and 7pm - 9pm. **Cuisine:** Rural English cuisine, including speciality 'deep dish' pies and fresh fish. Good wine list. ⊨ None. ☒ Access, Visa, AmEx. **Other Points:** Children welcome. No dogs allowed. Open Sundays and bank holidays. Garden dining. Also caters for private parties. ◘ **(V) Directions:** Follow A24 to Worthing, then signs to Billingshurst. 2nd turn left.
ALAN VAUGHAN ☎ (0403) 741 383
A traditional old country pub, with a very friendly atmosphere, set in 3000 acres of Sussex farmland. Customers can enjoy delicious home-cooked meals, especially the deep dish pies which are made with fresh meat from the local farm. A very popular pub with the local community and country walkers. Places of interest nearby include Knepp Castle and Shipley Mill.

HOTON Leicestershire **Map 4 A2**

⊗££ **THE PACKE** Hoton, Loughborough.
Hours: Meals from 12 noon - 2.15pm and 7pm - 10.30pm (last orders). **Cuisine:** A predominantly Greek restaurant serving authentic Greek food, with traditional and vegetarian dishes also available. ⊨ 3 bedrooms. ☒ Access, Visa, AmEx. **Other Points:** Children welcome - play area. No dogs. Coaches by appointment. Beer garden. ◘ & **(V) Directions:** On A60 Loughborough to Nottingham road.
ANGELO & JULIO STEPHANAKIS ☎ (0509) 880 662.
The restaurant, converted from an airy loft has recently been refurbished. There are facilities to amuse all the family with a beer garden, play area, barbecue and petanque available. Private parties and receptions catered for in separate rooms.

HUNSTANTON Norfolk **Map 5 A1**

⊗££ **CALEY HALL MOTEL AND RESTAURANT** Old
⌂££ Hunstanton, Hunstanton.
Hours: Breakfast 8am - 9.30am, Lunch 12 noon - 2pm, Dinner 7pm - 9pm (last orders). **Cuisine:** Table d'hote and a la carte menus. French and British cuisine specialising in steaks and fish. Childrens portions available. ⊨ 29 bedrooms, all en suite. ☒ Access, Visa. **Other Points:** Children welcome. Dogs allowed. Residents' lounge. ◘ & **(V) Directions:** A149. Just off the coast road between Brancaster and Hunstanton.
CLIVE KING ☎ (0485) 533486.
The resident proprietors of Caley Hall have skillfully converted the outbuildings of their 17th century Manor House to provide a comfortable bar and restaurant facilities. Chalets have been sympathetically added and are closely in keeping with the overall architectural style. The restaurant serves a wide range of good food which is well presented and offers good value for money.

⌂£ **NORTHGATE HOUSE** 46 Northgate, Hunstanton.
⊨ 1 single, 2 double and 1 family bedroom, 1 en suite and all with shaver points. 1 bathroom/shower. Tea/coffee making facilities in all bedrooms. **Hours:** Breakfast 8.30am - 9am, dinner 6.30pm

Hunstanton continued

(order by 9am). Packed lunches by arrangement. **CC** None. **Other Points:** Central heating. Vegetarian menu. Children welcome. Residents lounge. TV. **(V) Directions:** Off the A149, turn right into Austin St. which leads to Northgate.

MR & MRS M R SNARE ☎ (0485) 533269.

Northgate House is a family run Guest House with comfortable, spacious accommodation, close to Hunstanton's Blue Flag beach, shops and theatre. Nearby are bird reserves, golf courses, several Stately Homes, Peddars Way, and the Norfolk Coast Path.

HUNTINGDON Cambridgeshire Map 5 A1

⊗££ **STUKELEYS COUNTRY HOTEL** Ermin Street, Great ⌂££ Stukeley.

Hours: Lunch 11.30am - 3pm. Dinner 6pm - 11pm (last orders 10pm). Bar snacks 11.30am - 3pm and 6pm - 10pm (last orders 9.30pm). **Cuisine:** Traditional English and Classic French Cuisine. Beef Wellington, Sole Veronique, Duck a l'orange. ⊨ 4 doubles, 2 twin, 1 single and 1 family room. Colour TV, radio and tea/coffee making facilities in all rooms. **CC** Access, Visa, AmEx. **Other Points:** Special weekend breaks at 40% discount. Children welcome. No pets. **P (V) Directions:** Off A1 and A604, nr to Alconbury Air Base, on Little Stukeley Road.

PAT & JACKIE McPHILLIPS ☎ (0480) 456927

A grade II listed 16th century Inn with a wealth of exposed beams and Inglenook fireplaces. Attractively furnished with antique furniture and brass beds. Recently refurbished. The weekend breaks offer exceptionally good value for money (booking recommended). Highly recommended.

HURSTPIERPOINT West Sussex Map 5 C1

⊗££ **VINYARDS RESTAURANT & WINE BAR** 42 High Street, Hurstpierpoint.

Hours: Breakfast (Saturday only) 10.30am - 3pm, lunch 11.30am - 3pm in restaurant and bar (last orders 2pm), dinner 7pm - 10pm in restaurant (last orders), bar dinners 7pm - 11pm (last orders 10pm). **Cuisine:** Wide choice including pasta, fish dishes, curry of the day, steaks, cajun chicken, Mediterranean prawns, vegetarian dishes. Light snacks. Daily specials. ⊨ None. **CC** Access, Visa. **Other Points:** Children welcome. No smoking area. Morning teas. Dogs allowed in garden. Fax No. (0273) 835041. Summer barbecues - Saturday night & Sunday lunch. ⓰ **(V) Directions:** On A23, 6 miles before Brighton at traffic lights. The new M23.

MARK & JANE COOPER. ☎ (0273) 835000.

Located just 6 miles north of Brighton this establishment offers good meals at value for money prices, accompanied by an extensive wine list. Visited by all ages, the wine bar enjoys a convivial atmosphere.

ICKHAM Kent Map 5 C2

⊗£££ **THE DUKE WILLIAM** The Street, Ickham, nr Canterbury.

Hours: Lunch 12 noon - 2pm, dinner 7pm - 10pm (last orders). Bar meals 12 noon - 2pm and 7pm - 10pm. Closed: Monday lunchtime except bank holidays. **Cuisine:** Extensive seafood menu, beef, lamb, poultry, veal. In the bar: omelettes, fish, homemade soup, chilli, home baked bread. Exciting bar meals.

Ickham continued

⊨ None. **CC** All major cards. **Other Points:** Open air dining. Children welcome. Pets allowed. Large non-smoking area. Luxury conservatory for eating and families overlooking garden. **(V)** **Directions:** In the centre of Ickham which is signposted from the A257.

MR A ROBIN & MRS C A McNEILL ☎ (0227) 721308.

A 16th century freehouse in a picturesque village, surrounded by farmlands. There is a lovely garden to the rear with ponds, a fountain and flowers, as well as swings for the children. Situated only 10 minutes from Canterbury, Ickham is central for Kent's many tourist attractions.

KENILWORTH Warwickshire **Map 4 A1**

⊗£ **CLARENDON ARMS** 44 Castle Hill, Kenilworth.

Hours: Lunch 12 noon - 2.30pm, dinner 6pm - 10.30pm (last orders), 7pm - 10.30pm on Sundays. **Cuisine:** Giant chargrilled steaks, chicken terriyaki, traditional pub meals. ⊨ None. **CC** All major cards. **Other Points:** Children welcome. No pets. ⅊ **(V)** **Directions:** Opposite the entrance to Kenilworth castle.

PATRICK McCOSKER & MAURICE KUTNER ☎ (0926) 52017.

An olde worlde inn in an historic, picture-postcard location opposite the entrance to Kenilworth castle. Dine in the small intimate bar, or in the larger restaurant area on the first floor - either way the cheerful ambiance and good home-cooked fare is sure to please.

CENTRAL & SOUTHERN ENGLAND

KENLEY Surrey **Map 5 C1**
⊗£ **WATTENDEN ARMS** Old Lodge Lane.
Hours: Restaurant open 12 noon - 2pm and 7pm - 9.30pm.
Cuisine: Fresh crab, baked ham, eggs and chips, curry. Spotted
Dick, bread pudding. ⊨ None. **CC** None. **Other Points:** No
children. �&. **Directions:** Old Lodge Lane runs from the Brighton
Road in Purley.
RON COULSTON MHCI ☎ (081) 660 8638.
*Although close to central London, the Wattenden Arms is
situated in rural surroundings. A 200 year-old inn, established
under the resident owner for 20 years. All food prepared and
cooked on premises.*

KERSEY Suffolk **Map 5 B2**
⊗£££ **THE BELL INN** The Street, Kersey, Nr Ipswich.
[CLUB] **Hours:** Meals served 11.30am - 2pm and 7pm - 10pm (last orders
9.30pm). Sunday lunch 11.30am - 2pm and dinner 7pm -
9.30pm. Closed: Christmas Day Evening and all day Boxing Day
only. **Cuisine:** Extensive menu. Good selection of steaks, Trout en
Papillote, Lobster Cardinal, Chicken Rosar, Duck Jamaican (with a
black cherry & rum sauce). ⊨ None. **CC** All major cards. **Other
Points:** Children welcome. Garden. Afternoon teas served. ▯ **(V)**
Directions: Signposted off A1141, north of Hadleigh.
ALEX & LYNNE COOTE ☎ (0473) 823229.
*A 14th century timber framed inn situated in a village that has
become know as the 'prettiest village in the world'. An extensive
selection of well presented tasty cuisine at excellent value for
money. The friendly informal atmosphere and delightful
surroundings make this a lovely place to dine.*

KEW Surrey **Map 5 B1**
⊗£ **PISSARRO'S WINE BAR** 1 Kew Green, Richmond.
Hours: Open 11.30am - 11pm Monday to Saturday. Sunday open
12 noon - 3pm and 7pm - 10.30pm. Closed: Christmas and
Boxing Day, and Easter Sunday. **Cuisine:** Homemade salmon
trout mousse, steak and kidney pie and fish pie. Daily cold buffet.
Traditional Sunday lunch. ⊨ None. **CC** Access, Visa. **Other Points:**
Limited access for disabled. No children. **(V) Directions:** On the
A205 (south circular),south of Kew Bridge just off Kew Green.
PAUL & PENNY CARVOSSO ☎ (01) 940 3987.
*A roaring open fire, oak beams, a host of antique curios, some
50 wines and a delicious selection of homemade foods are all
there to welcome and tempt you. Pissarro once painted the
buildings where this wine bar now stands.*

KINGS LYNN Norfolk **Map 5 A1**
⊗£ **BUTTERFLY HOTEL** Beveridge Way, Hardwick Narrows Est.,
⊞£££ Kings Lynn.
Hours: Breakfast 7am - 9.30am, lunch 12.30pm - 2pm and dinner
7pm - 10pm (last orders). Bar meals 12.30pm - 2pm and 7pm -
10pm. **Cuisine:** Choice of Chef's specials eg. medallions of beef.
⊨ 50 bedrooms, all en suite. **CC** All major cards. **Other Points:**
Afternoon tea served. Children welcome. ▯ &. **(V) Directions:** On
the A10/A47 roundabout, 2 miles from the centre of Kings Lynn.
BUTTERFLY HOTELS LTD. ☎ (0553) 771707.
*Situated in a region renowned for its unspoiled beauty, this
newly built hotel offers pleasant and well furnished facilities.*

Kings Lynn continued

Fixed price, a la carte and snack menus available as well as a comprehensive wine list. Newly managed by Ian and Jenny Mackenzie.

⌂££ **GUANOCK HOTEL** Southgates, Kings Lynn.
CLUB ⋿ 5 single, 4 double, 3 twin and 5 family bedrooms. 2 bathrooms, 3 showers. All rooms have colour TV, radio, tea/coffee making facilities, ironing and hairdrying facilities. **Hours:** Breakfast 7am - 8.30am. Dinner 6pm - 7pm (order by 5pm). CC Access, Visa, AmEx. **Other Points:** Central heating. Children welcome. Licensed. Residents' lounge, TV and roof garden. Pool room. ▯
Directions: On the London Road, enter Kings Lynn via Southgates.
TERRY PARCHMENT ☎ (0553) 772959.
Close to the historic Southgates and adjacent to Jubilee Gardens. Just a few minutes from the town centre in a pleasant area of town.

⊗££ **KNIGHTS HILL HOTEL** Knights Hill Village, South Wootton,
⌂££££ Kings Lynn.
CLUB **Hours:** Breakfast 7.30am - 9.30am, lunch 12 noon - 2pm and dinner 7pm - 10.30pm (last orders 10pm). Bar meals 11am - 10.30pm. **Cuisine:** Table d'hote and a la carte menu, good bar meals. ⋿ 58 bedrooms. CC All major cards. **Other Points:** Children welcome. No dogs. Coaches by appointment. Fax No: (0553) 675568. ▯ ⅙ **(V) Directions:** Situated at the intersection of the A149 and A148.
HOWARD DARKING ☎ (0553) 675566.
A sympathetically restored farm complex offering a range of restaurants, bar, accommodation and an extensive health and leisure club, in the heart of the agricultural area.

KNAPHILL Surrey Map 4 C2
⊗££ **FROGGIES WINE BAR & RESTAURANT** 42/44 High Street, Knaphill, nr Woking.
Hours: Open Monday to Friday lunch 12 noon - 2.30pm and diner 7pm - 11pm and Saturday evenings only. Closed: all day Sunday. **Cuisine:** Fresh ingredients used on a daily produced menu encompassing European and Far Eastern selected dishes. Well-known for its soup, fresh fish and puddings. ⋿ None. CC All major cards. **Other Points:** Families welcome. Private dining room available and new garden room. No dogs. ▯ ⅙ **(V) Directions:** A short drive from the main M3.
MR & MRS ROBIN AND DEBBIE de WINTON. ☎ (04867) 80835.
'Froggies' offers three seating areas for an enjoyable meeting and eating place, making it popular with locals and travellers alike. Chef patron established since 1980.

LANCING West Sussex Map 4 C2
⊗£££ **MINSTRELS GALLERY** Old Salts Farm Road, Lancing.
Hours: Lunch 11.30am - 2.30pm, dinner 7pm - 12pm (last orders 9.30pm). Closed Sunday pm and all day Monday. **Cuisine:** A la carte, fixed price menu, English-French cuisine. ⋿ None. CC Access, Visa, AmEx. **Other Points:** Children welcome. Garden. No smoking in restuaurant. ▯ ⅙ **(V) Directions:** On A257, main coast road.

Lancing continued
MR & MRS DAVIS. ☎ (0903) 766777.
This 500 year old farmhouse has been beautifully upheld and the restuarant offers an extensive French/English menu. The atmosphere is warm and service excellent, finished off with live piano music.

⊗££ **THE SUSSEX PAD HOTEL** Old Shoreham Road, Lancing.
⌂££ **Hours:** Breakfast 7.30am - 10am, lunch 12 noon - 2pm and dinner 7pm - 10pm (last orders). Open Sunday. **Cuisine:** English and French cuisine. Speciality: a seasonally-changing fish menu featuring fresh lobster. ⊨ 19 double bedrooms, all en suite. **CC** Access, Visa, AmEx. **Other Points:** Children welcome. Garden. Afternoon teas. Pets allowed. Honeymans Outlook - large, south facing conservatory restaurant. ▣ 占 **(V) Directions:** On the A27 by Lancing College.
MR PACK ☎ (0273) 454647.
The ambience, service and cuisine at The Sussex Pad combine to make dining here a special experience. Renowned for its seafood - particularly lobsters, which are kept alive in basement tanks until required for the table.

LANGFORD Oxfordshire **Map 4 B1**
⊗£ **THE CROWN AT LANGFORD** Langford, nr Lechlade.
Hours: Bar lunches served 12 noon - 2pm, lunch 7pm - 10pm, (last orders 9.45pm) Sunday lunches. **Cuisine:** English cuisine with dishes such as mixed grill and roast topside of beef with Yorkshire pudding. Homemade soup. ⊨ None. **CC** None. **Other Points:** Children Welcome. Garden dining. Near Cotswold wild life park. ▣ 占 **(V) Directions:** Langford lies off the A361.
AGNES & ERIC CRAMPTON ☎ (036786)206
A charming country pub draped in vines and flowers. A warm, comfortable, cheerful atsmophere. Serving generous quantities of well cooked tradtional English meals.

LAVANT West Sussex **Map 4 C2**
⊗£ **EARL OF MARCH** Lavant Road, Lavant, nr. Chichester.
[CLUB] **Hours:** Lunch 11.30am - 2pm and dinner 6pm - 11pm (last orders 10pm). Sunday lunch 12 noon - 2pm and Sunday dinner 7pm - 10.30pm (last orders 9.30pm). **Cuisine:** Varied selection of traditional cuisine. Special vegetarian dishes. Bar food. ⊨ None. **CC** Visa. **Other Points:** Children welcome. Dogs allowed. ▣ 占 **(V) Directions:** 2 miles from Chichester on the A286.
MR A L LAURIN ☎ (0243) 774751.
Excellent service by well-trained staff will make this a good stop for those travelling in the area. Comfortable surroundings and good food can be found here, with a special treat supplied by Mr Laurin - when in season you sample home caught and home cooked deer!

LAVENHAM Suffolk **Map 5 B2**
⊗££ **THE ANGEL** Market Place, Lavenham.
⌂££ **Hours:** Breakfast 8am - 9.30am, lunch 12 noon - 2pm, dinner 7pm [CLUB] - 9.30pm (7.30pm - 9pm Sunday). **Cuisine:** Menu changes daily. Dishes include homemade pies and casseroles, fresh fish, locally produced meat and fresh vegetables. ⊨ 7 bedrooms, all en suite. **CC** Access, Visa. **Other Points:** Children welcome. Garden.

Lavenham continued

Parking available in square and in car park at rear. **(V) Directions:** In centre of Lavenham, opposite Guild Hall.

ROY & ANNE WHITWORTH, JOHN & VAL BARRY ☎ (0787) 247388

A timbered Inn, situated in the centre of Lavenham opposite the historic Guild Hall. Well cooked meals, using fresh produce, are available at very reasonable prices and the services is warm and courteous.

⊗£££ **THE GREAT HOUSE RESTAURANT** Market Place, Lavenham.

Hours: Lunch 12 noon - 2.30pm (last orders) and 7pm - 10.30pm. Closed: Sunday evenings and Monday. Open Bank Holiday Mondays. **Cuisine:** Superb French cuisine. ⊨ 4 luxurious suites. CC Access, Visa, AmEx. **Other Points:** Children welcome. Garden. Pets allowed. ▯ **(V) Directions:** Near Sudbury. Situated in the market square of Lavenham.

REGIS CREPY ☎ (0787) 247431.

Built in the 14th and 15th centuries by the Caustons, an important weaving family in the medieval village of Lavenham, The Great House Restaurant occupies the most important house in the town. Lovingly restored to its original splendour, this outstanding building justifiably contains a most outstanding restaurant offering excellence in all things. Regional Newcomer 1991.

⊗££ **THE TIMBERS RESTAURANT** High Street, Lavenham.

Hours: Meals from 12 noon - 2pm and 7.30pm - 9.30pm (last orders). Closed Monday and Sunday. **Cuisine:** Daily specials on the blackboard at lunch. Evening: Chicken Breast cooked in Apricots and Brandy, homemade Venison Pie, Fresh pink fleshed stuffed Trout. ⊨ None. CC Access, Visa. **Other Points:** No dogs. Children welcome. ▯ **(V) Directions:** On the A1141 Sudbury to Bury St Edmunds road.

MISS B A PREECE & A M TRODD ☎ (0787) 247 218.

15th century building which, as the name suggests, has many exposed beams. Low ceilings and oak tables complete the cosy and friendly atmosphere. Full a la carte and table d'hote menus available in the evenings.

LEAFIELD Oxfordshire **Map 4 B1**

⊗££ **OLD GEORGE INN** Leafield.

Hours: Bar meals 12 noon - 2.30pm and 7pm - 9.30pm. Dinner 7pm - 9.30pm (last orders). Closed for food Tuesday evenings. **Cuisine:** Varies with the seasons. ⊨ 2 bedrooms, both en suite. CC Access, Visa. **Other Points:** Children welcome. Dogs allowed. ▯ ॐ **(V) Directions:** 5 miles north of the A40. Take Minster Lovell turn off the B4047.

CHRISTINE SEYMOUR. ☎ (099 387) 288.

Situated in Leafield village on the edge of Wychwoood forest this large sotone-built inn faces the village green. In the winter, you can gather round the log fire and forget the snow and icy winds.

CENTRAL & SOUTHERN ENGLAND

LEAMINGTON SPA Warwickshire **Map 4 A1**

⌂£€£ **COVERDALE PRIVATE HOTEL** 8 Portland Street, Leamington Spa.

🛏 2 double, 5 twin and 1 family bedroom. 4 bathrooms. Colour TV, tea/ coffee making facilities, telephones, radios, hairdryers and trouser press in all rooms. **Hours:** Breakfast 7.30am - 9am. **CC** Access, Visa. **Other Points:** Central heating. Children welcome. Dogs allowed. Residents lounge. 🅿 ⅙ **Directions:** From the parade,turn west to Warwick St, Portland St. is 3rd on left
DAVID & JEAN SELBY ☎ (0926) 30400
An attractive, double-fronted late Georgian house, skillfully modernised and tastefully decorated. Situated near the centre of Leamington within walking distance of the shops and parks. The Selbys are constantly aiming to improve their services and are clearly getting results.

⊗£ **REGENCY FARE** 86 Regent Street, Leamington Spa.
Hours: Breakfast 9am - 11.45am, lunch 12 noon - 5.30pm (last orders). Closed: Sunday and Bank Holidays. **Cuisine:** 'Home cooking'. House specialities: Steak and kidney pie and meringues with toasted almonds. 🛏 None **CC** Access, Visa, AmEx. **Other Points:** Children welcome. Afternoon teas served. **Directions:** On Regent Street, off main shopping street.
MRS S J HELM ☎ (0926) 425570
Situated near the main shopping centre, the Regency Fare offers well cooked 'Home Cooking', with delightful desserts at very good value.

⊗£ **THE GREAT WESTERN** Deppers Bridge, nr Harbury.
Hours: Lunch 12 noon - 3pm, Dinner 6pm - 10.30pm. **Cuisine:** Amongst other dishes, the Great Western presents the Burger Collection with burgers dressed in international style, such as the blue cheese Great Dane. 🛏 None **CC** Access, Visa, AmEx. **Other Points:** Children made very welcome with their own menu and play area. No dogs allowed. 🅿 ⅙ **(V) Directions:** Between Leamington Spa and Southam on the B4452.
MAURICE KUTNER & PATRICK McCOSKER ☎ (0926) 612355.
The Great Western is sure to interest adults and children alike with its creative menu, friendly service and, of course, its unique feature being the model railway system which runs overhead on the ceiling.

LEICESTER Leicestershire **Map 4 A2**

⊗££ **BARDON HALL** Beveridge Lane, Nr Coleville, Leicester.
⌂£€£££ **Hours:** Breakfast 7am - 9am, lunch 12 noon - 2.30pm (last orders), dinner 7pm - 10pm (last orders), bar meals 12 noon - 2.30pm (last orders) and 5.30pm - 11pm (last orders). **Cuisine:** Dishes may include - farmhouse pate, gammon steak, chicken chasseur, vegetable bake, raspberry pavlova, nut choc cup. 🛏 35 bedrooms, all en suite. **CC** All major cards. **Other Points:** Childrens play area. Open Bank Holidays. No smoking area. Afternoon teas. Conference room. 🅿 **(V) Directions:** A50 to Ashby, from Jct 22 M1, across 1st roundabout.
JAMES CONWAY - Manager. ☎ (0530) 813644.
Enjoying outstanding views, this hotel is tastefully decorated and houses an a la carte restaurant and traditional English pub. With its informal and welcoming atmosphere, the hotel is

Leicester continued

popular with locals, travellers and business people alike. Good food and comfortable accommodation.

⊗£££ **GIBSONS GREY LADY** Sharpley Hill, Newtown-Linford, Leicester.

Hours: Lunch (Sundays only) 12 noon - 2.30pm. Dinner 7pm - 10pm. Closed: Mondays. **Cuisine:** French and English cuisine, including fish brioche in a white wine sauce. ⊨ None. **CC** Access, Visa, AmEx. **Other Points:** Children welcome. No dogs. Garden dining. Also caters for private parties and conferences. Fax (0530) 244932. **P** ᴗ **(V) Directions:** Up A50-Leicester. Left at roundabout to Newtown. Left at T jct.

MARTIN & LIZ GIBSON ☎ (0530) 243558.

Set in 2 acres of grounds, in the heart of the Charnwood Forest, the Grey Lady, with its fresh linen, crystal and silver, makes an elegant venue for that special meal. Close to Bradgate Park and Mt St Bernards Abbey.

⌂£££ **OLD TUDOR RECTORY** Main Street, Glenfield, Leicester.

⊨ 4 single, 5 twin, 7 double, 2 family rooms, all en suite. Four posters available. Two Star 3 Crowns. **Hours:** Breakfast 7.30am - 9am weekdays and 8am - 9.45am weekends. **CC** Access, Visa. **Other Points:** Children welcome. Garden. Pets allowed. Fully equipped Beauty salon with manicure, pedicure, waxing, facials, massage, plus fitness centre. **P Directions:** Off the M1 motorway, on the outskirts of Leicester.

MRS B.A. WESTON ☎ (0533) 320220.

A Tudor hotel with Jacobean and Queen Anne additions, set in its own acre of well tended gardens, offering attractive and comfortable accommodation. The tasteful well selected interior adds to the friendly relaxed atmosphere and outstanding hospitality of Mrs Weston.

⊗££ **RESTAURANT MOZART** 63 London Road, Leicester.

CLUB **Hours:** Lunch 12 noon - 2.30pm, Dinner 6.30pm - 11pm (last orders 10.45pm). Bar meals served 10.30am - 6.30pm. Closed: Bank Holidays and Sundays except Mothers Day and Christmas. Coffee lounge open all day. **Cuisine:** Predominantly Austrian cuisine. Dishes may include Wienerschnitzel, Rack of Lamb, Monkfish topped with herb butter, Pork Hock. A la carte & table d'hote. ⊨ None. **CC** Access, Visa, AmEx. **Other Points:** Children welcome. Evening street parking. No smoking area. NCP car park. Afternoon teas. Function room for up to 45 people. Fax No: (0533) 555447. ᴗ **(V) Directions:** On main A6 from Mkt. Harborough, 50 yds before station on L.H.S.

J G THOMAS DOBLANDER ☎ (0533) 555881.

Decorated with pictures linked to Mozart, this attractive and comfortable restaurant provides a good choice of very well cooked dishes. The restaurant specialises in Austrian style cuisine and offers an interesting and varied menu. The freshly prepared food is well presented and courteously served.

⊗££ **THE COPPER BEECH RESTAURANT** 1151 Melton Road, Syston, Leicester.

Hours: Lunch 12 noon - 2.30pm, Dinner 7pm - 10.30pm (last orders). Closed: Sunday evenings and all day Monday. **Cuisine:**

Leicester continued

English and continental cuisine. House specialities include Boeuf Bourguignon & Duck aux Cerises. Charcoal grill. Traditional Sunday lunch. ⊨ None. **CC** Access, Visa. **Other Points:** Children welcome. No smoking area. Real log fires. Small Wedding Receptions, Conferences & Private Functions catered for. Chef Patron. **P** ⅋ **(V) Directions:** 3 and a half miles north of town centre on A607. Nr Railway Bridge.

L ODORICI ☎ (0533) 609861.

Named after the Copper Beech tree that stands in the garden, this Victorian property was converted into a restaurant in 1985. Many of the old features have been retained but a light, roomy conservatory has been added. The restaurant is renowned for its high class cuisine, fine wines and intimate atmosphere with candle lit tables and real log fires. Highly recommended.

⊛££ **THE COTTAGE IN THE WOOD** Maplewell Road, Woodhouse Eaves.

Hours: Wednesday - Saturday dinner 7.30pm - 9.30pm (last orders). Sunday lunch 12 noon - 2.30pm. **Cuisine:** English/Continental: steak, lamb, lasagne and Javanese chicken with a choice of homemade sweets. ⊨ None. **CC** Access, Visa. **Other Points:** Children welcome. Also caters for private parties. **P** ⅋ **(V) Directions:** Off A6 by the B591 road to Woodhouse Eaves.

ANDREW & GILL HARRIS ☎ (0509) 890318.

Situated in the heart of Charnwood forest, the cottage restaurant has a warm, local atmosphere. The menu features seasonal monthly specials and also includes a wide choice for vegetarians. Places to explore include Bradgate deer park, Beacon Hill, Broombrigs working farm and the Great Central Railway.

⊛££ **THE JOHNSCLIFFE HOTEL & RESTAURANT** 73 Main ⌂££££ Street.

Hours: Lunch 12 noon - 2pm, Dinner 7pm - 9.30pm (last orders). Closed: 6/7 days per annum. **Cuisine:** Crab, chicken, pheasant, fish and steak in interesting sauces. ⊨ 15 bedrooms, all en suite. **CC** Access, Visa, AmEx. **Other Points:** Children welcome. Dogs allowed. **P** ⅋ **(V) Directions:** 5 minutes from junction 22 off the M1.

MR & MRS DEVONPORT ☎ (0530) 242228.

The Johnscliffe provides a varied and exciting menu served by friendly and efficient staff. Set in its own wooded grounds, this elegant building has sunlit rooms and a quiet, relaxing atmosphere. Places to visit include Bradgate park the home of Lady Jane Grey, Castle Donninglow race track.

⊛££ **THE MILL ON THE SOAR HOTEL** Coventry Road, Sutton in ⌂£££ the Elms, Leicester.

Hours: Breakfast 7am - 9am, lunch 12 noon - 2pm, dinner 7pm - 10pm (last orders), bar snacks 6pm - 10.30pm (last orders). **Cuisine:** Wide and interesting menu in the a la carte restaurant. Traditional bar meals. ⊨ 20 bedrooms, all en suite. **CC** All major cards. **Other Points:** Children welcome. Open Bank Holidays. No smoking area. Conference room. Fax/telephone No. (0455) 282419. Functions marquee for Spring - Autumn. **P** ⅋ **(V)**

Leicester continued

Directions: Jct 21 M1. Approx 3 miles beyond Narborough on B581.

MRS L HENSMAN & MR M CLIFF - Managers ☎ (0455) 282419. *Converted mill, fully exploited to its greatest effect, with working mill wheel and original stone floors. Tasty, well prepared meals can be enjoyed in a cosy, unhurried atmosphere. Good selection of beers. Friendly and competent service. Comfortable accommodation.*

⊗£ **THE PLOUGH INN** Station Road, Littlethorpe, nr Leicester.
Hours: Lunch 12 noon - 2pm, Dinner 7pm - 10pm (last orders). Closed: Christmas Day and Boxing Day. **Cuisine:** Home cooked traditional British dishes such as Steak and Kidney Pie. ⊨ None. **CC** Access, Visa. **Other Points:** Children welcome. Garden. Dogs allowed. **P** & **(V) Directions:** Close to Narborough. Littlethorpe is approx 5 miles SW of Leicester.
MR & MRS STEEDMAN ☎ (0533) 862383.
The Plough Inn is a cosy thatched pub in the pretty village of Littlethorpe, near Narborough. The interior is that of a country pub with comfortable furniture and a happy, relaxed atmosphere. Highly recommended by the Routiers inspector for its excellent, beautifully cooked food, and welcoming service.

⊗££ **THE RED COW HOTEL** Hinckley Road, Leicester Forest East,
⊞£££ Leicester.
Hours: Breakfast 7am - 9am, lunch and bar snacks 12 noon - 2.30pm (last orders), dinner 7pm - 10pm (last orders), evening bar snacks 5.30pm - 10.30pm (last orders). **Cuisine:** A la carte restaurant and bar meals. House specials include Mixed Grill, Pork Fillet Dijonaise, Tournedos Mistinguette. Chef's Daily Special. ⊨ 31 bedrooms, all en suite. **CC** All major cards. **Other Points:** Children welcome. Open Bank Holidays. No smoking area. Afternoon teas. Fax/telephone No. (0533) 387878. **P** **(V) Directions:** Jct 21 M1. A563 - Leicester Forest East, A47 - Hickley.
BRYAN BEARDALL - Manager. ☎ (0533) 387878.
Thatched roof, ivy covered walls and well kept gardens greet you as you arrive at this establishement. The interior has been tastefully refurbished in keeping with the character and age of the building. Serving attractive meals made with an emphasis on fresh produce, in a friendly, relaxed atmosphere. Good service and comfortable accommodation.

LEIGH ON SEA Essex **Map 5 B1**
⊗£££ **MANOR HOUSE HOTEL & TABLE MANNERS**
⊞££ **RESTAURANT** 24-26 Nelson Drive, Leigh-On-Sea.
CLUB **Hours:** Breakfast 7am - 9.30am, lunch 12.30pm - 2.30pm (last orders 2pm), dinner 6.30pm - 10pm (last orders). Closed: Sunday evenings and Monday. **Cuisine:** A la carte menu, table d'hote and vegetarian menu. ⊨ 12 rooms. 5 single, 3 twin, 3 double and 1 family bedrooms. Most are en suite. **CC** Access, Visa, AmEx. **Other Points:** Children welcome. Garden. Dogs allowed. Bargain break weekends. **P** & **(V) Directions:** From A13, right into Old Leigh Rd (Chalkwell Pk), right to Kings Rd.
RAY & BRENDA DAVIS. ☎ (0702) 75127.
Situated in Leigh, an old fishing port close to Southend, this Victorian style hotel offers good home cooked food in pleasant

CENTRAL & SOUTHERN ENGLAND

Leigh on Sea continued

attractive surroundings. After 23 years of ownership, Mr & Mrs Davis offer their guests a warm welcome and friendly attentive service, going as far as to offer free transport to diners of 8 people or more staying within a 10 mile radius.

LEIGHTON BUZZARD Bedfordshire **Map 4 B2**

⊗£££ **SWAN HOTEL & RESTAURANT** High Street, Leighton Buzzard.
Hours: Meals 7.15am - 9.30am, 12 noon - 2pm and 7pm - 10pm (last orders 9.30pm). Bar meals 12 noon - 2.30pm (except Sundays). **Cuisine:** Local meat and game, fresh fish and vegetarian dishes. ⊨ 38 bedrooms, all en suite. **CC** All major cards. **Other Points:** Children welcome. No dogs. **P** & **(V)** **Directions:** From A5 take A4012, go straight across 1st roundabout to High St.
ERIC & FELICITY STEPHENS ☎ (0525) 372 148.
A privately owned 18th century coaching inn carefully restored and modernised and situated on the High Street of this thriving market town.

LEWES East Sussex **Map 5 C1**

⊗££ **LA CUCINA RESTAURANT** 13 Station Street, Lewes.
CLUB **Hours:** Serving lunch 12 noon - 2pm, dinner 6.30pm - 10.30pm (last orders). Closed: Sunday, Monday and 2 weeks from 24th December. **Cuisine:** Seasonal specialities may include, Fresh Mussels Marinara, Pesce Misto Marinara, Pollo alla Cacciatora, Sussex Lamb, Strawberries & Cream or Marashino. ⊨ None. **CC** Access, Visa. **Other Points:** Children welcome. No dogs. Parking nearby. **(V) Directions:** 200 metres from Station towards the High Street.
JOSE VILAS MAYO ☎ (0273) 476707.
Outstanding food and excellent service can be found at this Italian Restaurant in the centre of Lewes. The menu offers an extensive choice of authentic Italian dishes, superbly cooked and served in generous portions. Highly recommended for the high standard of cuisine and service within an atmosphere of peace and calm.

⊗££ **WHITE HART HOTEL** High Street, Lewes.
Hours: Breakfast 8am - 9.30am, Lunch 12.30pm - 2pm and Dinner 7pm - 10.15pm (last orders 10pm). **Cuisine:** A la carte, English and French. Carvery, set price with fish or vegetarian option. ⊨ 48 bedrooms, 44 en suite. **CC** All major cards. **Other Points:** Children welcome. Pets allowed. Conference facilities. Afternoon teas. **P** & **(V)**
MR AYRIS ☎ (0273) 476694.
A historic 16th century coaching house with a modern extension, tastefully blended to the original architecture. Well placed for exploring the Sussex coast, the hotel offers comfort, good food and warm hospitality.

LICHFIELD Staffordshire **Map 4 A1**

⊗££ **FRADLEY ARMS HOTEL** Rykneld Street (A38), Fradley, nr
⌂£££ Lichfield.
CLUB **Hours:** Open all day. Breakfast 7am - 9am (Sundays 8am - 9.30am), lunch 12 noon - 2.30pm (2pm Sundays), and dinner

Lichfield continued

> 7.30pm - 9.30pm (last orders, 9pm on Sundays). **Cuisine:** French cuisine. Fresh fish dishes and imaginative meat dishes. ⊨ 6 bedrooms, all en suite. **CC** All major cards. **Other Points:** Children welcome. No smoking area. Coaches by appointment. Banqueting suite for 200 for private functions or conferences. Fax: 0283 791464. **P** & **Directions:** On the A38, 3 miles north of Lichfield, on south-bound carriageway.
> MR & MRS R K TAYLOR ☎ (0283) 790 186/473
> *An outstanding white building set in 4 acres of grounds with a pleasant garden and children's play area. Despite its country setting, Fradley Arms is convenient for Lichfield, Birmingham Airport and NEC. A family-run hotel providing top class food and accommodation in a family atmosphere.*

LIMPLEY STOKE Wiltshire **Map 4 B1**

⊗£££ **THE CLIFFE HOTEL** Crowe Hill, Limpley Stoke, Wiltshire.
> **Hours:** Breakfast 8am - 9.45am, lunch 12 noon - 2.30pm (last orders) and dinner 6.45pm - 9.30pm (last orders). **Cuisine:** English/French cuisine. ⊨ 11 bedrooms, all en suite. **CC** All major cards. **Other Points:** Pets by arrangement. Children welcome. Garden. Fax No: (0225) 723871. **P** & **(V) Directions:** Off the B3108 and A36.
> BILL & TRACEY MALLINSON ☎ (0225) 723226.
> *Set in three acres of gardens overlooking, the River Avon valley, this delightful converted country house dating back 165 years provides an relaxed base in which to enjoy the best of Wiltshire. Offering comfortable accommodation, good food, well prepared and served by friendly efficient staff.*

LIMPSFIELD Surrey **Map 5 C1**

⊗£££ **THE OLD LODGE** High Street, Limpsfield, Nr Oxted.
> **Hours:** Morning coffee 10.30am - 12.30pm, Lunch 12.30pm - 2.30pm, Afternoon teas 3pm - 6pm, Dinner 7.30pm - 10.30pm. Closed: Sunday evening and all day Monday. **Cuisine:** French and English cuisine. ⊨ None. **CC** All major cards. **Other Points:** Children welcome. No dogs. **P** **(V) Directions:** Off the main A25 between Oxted and Westerham. On the High Street.
> MR CANHAM & MR MEADON ☎ (0883) 714387
> *Built in 1830, the restaurant building used to be the lodge to Hookwood Manor. Oak-panelled and with high vaulted ceilings and a beautiful fireplace, The Old Lodge provides attractive surroundings in which to dine.*

A privately owned, Grade III listed Hotel is conveniently positioned on the A38 in 4 acres of landscaped grounds. Easy access to the N.E.C. Birmingham, the airport, the Belfry Golf Course, and the beautiful counties of Staffordshire, Derbyshire and Warwickshire. Atmospheric lounge bar, delightful Olde Worlde French restaurant recommended by Egon Ronay and Les Routiers. Well equipped bedrooms, banqueting suite ideal for conferences up to 200 people, weddings and family celebrations.

★ ★ AA & RAC ♨ ♨ ♨ ETB

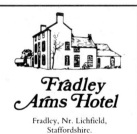

Fradley
Arms Hotel

Fradley, Nr. Lichfield,
Staffordshire.
Tel: 0283 790186/790977

LINTON Cambridgeshire **Map 5 B1**
⊗££ **THE CROWN INN** High Street, Linton.
CLUB **Hours:** Lunch 12 noon - 2pm (last orders) and dinner 6.30pm -
10pm (last orders). No food Sunday evening. Bar open 12 noon -
3pm and 6.30pm - 11pm (7pm - 10.30pm Sundays). **Cuisine:**
Home cooked food using fresh ingredients. ⊨ Four self-contained
rooms, all en suite and with TV, tea/coffee making facilities.
CC Access, Visa. **Other Points:** Children welcome. Garden. No
smoking areas. **P** & **(V) Directions:** Off A604, near the Water
tower.
JOEL PALMER ☎ (0223) 891759.
*A lime washed Georgian pub, situated in the centre of the
pleasant village of Linton, offering a choice of tasty bar meals or
an interesting a la carte menu in their restaurant. Excellent
service and a very warm welcome typical of a charming village
pub, makes a visit here well worthwhile.*

LINWOOD Hampshire **Map 4 C1**
⊗£ **HIGH CORNER INN** nr Ringwood.
Hours: Open normal licensing hours. Meals 12 noon - 2pm and
6.30pm - 10pm (Sundays 12 noon 2.15pm in the bar and 7pm -
10pm). Routiers-priced menu applies to bar meals. **Cuisine:**
Venison in season, homecooked food including steak & kidney pie
and daily specials. ⊨ Chalet - sleeps 7. 7 Bedrooms all en suite
E.T.B. 3 crowns. **CC** All major cards. **Other Points:** Children
welcome. Squash court. Forest walks. Play area. D.I.Y. stables,
Lego room and a la carte restaurant. **P** **Directions:** Between the
A31 and the A338, 6 miles north of Ringwood.
MR & MRS R KERNAN ☎ (0425) 473973.
*A 17th century inn tucked well away in the heart of the New
Forest. Situated some 6 miles north of Ringwood with indoor and
outdoor facilities for children.*

LITTLE COMPTON Gloucestershire **Map 4 B1**
⊗£ **RED LION INN** Little Compton, nr Moreton in Marsh,
⊞£token Cotswolds.
Hours: Meals in bar 12 noon - 2pm (1.15pm Sundays) and 7pm -
9pm. Booking advisable. **Cuisine:** Varying selection of
homemade dishes. Specialities: prime rump steaks cut to order
and fresh fish dishes. ⊨ 3 bedrooms, 1 bathroom. **CC** Access, Visa.
Other Points: Children over 8 welcome. No dogs. Coaches by
appointment. & **(V) Directions:** On the A44 between Moreton in
Marsh and Chipping Norton.
DAVID & SARAH SMITH ☎ (0608 74) 397.
*A charming 16th century Cotswold stone inn with a warming
open fire in the beamed lounge bar and a large garden -
popular with diners in summer months.*

LITTLE MILTON Oxfordshire **Map 4 B2**
⊗£ **THE LAMB INN** Little Milton.
Hours: Lunch 12 noon - 2pm, dinner 7pm - 10pm (last orders).
Cuisine: Steaks, salads, grilled swordfish and prawns, smoked
quail, venison in red wine. ⊨ None. **CC** AmEx, Diners. **Other
Points:** Children welcome. Garden. **P** **Directions:** On the A329,
2 miles south of the M40, junction 7.
DAVID J G BOWELL ☎ (08446) 527.

Little Milton continued

A stone built 17th century thatched inn where good food is served at reasonable prices. Popular with locals, there is a friendly atmosphere. The surrounding farmland and countryside is now a conservation area.

LITTLE WASHBOURNE Gloucestershire **Map 4 B1**

⊗££ **THE HOBNAILS INN** Little Washbourne, nr Tewkesbury.
Hours: Bar menu available every day 12 noon - 2pm and 7pm - 10pm. Full a la carte menu Friday and Saturday 7pm - 9.30pm. Closed: Christmas and Boxing Day. **Cuisine:** Hobnails Baps - soft round rolls with 52 different fillings from sausage to steak and mushrooms. Homemade gateaux and flans. ⊨ None. **CC** Access, Visa. **Other Points:** Children welcome (in dining room only). Dogs allowed in bar only. ◘ �&. **(V) Directions:** Situated on the B4077 Tewkesbury to Stowe road.
MR & MRS S FARBROTHER ☎ (0242) 620237.
Dating back to 1474, the inn has been run by the same family since 1743. A delightful location in a valley sweeping down to the River Severn at the foot of the Cotswolds.

LONGHAM Dorset **Map 4 C1**

⊗£ **ANGEL INN** Longham, Wimborne.
Hours: Meals from 12 noon - 2pm (1.45pm Sundays) and 6pm - 9.30 pm except Mondays. **Cuisine:** Dorset pate, steak and kidney pie, steaks, daily specials. ⊨ None. **CC** Access, Visa. **Other Points:** Children welcome. Large garden. ◘ ㅆ. **(V) Directions:** On the Poole to Southampton Road.
MR B SIMS ☎ (0202) 873778.
Situated on the busy road between Poole and Southampton. The menu is varied and quite extensive with the emphasis on well cooked, generous portions of food.

LOUGHBOROUGH Leicestershire **Map 4 A2**

⊗£ **PEAR TREE INN** Church Hill, Woodhouse Eaves.
Hours: Lunch 12 noon - 2pm, dinner 6.30pm - 10pm. **Cuisine:** Bar meals/snacks, bistro style. ⊨ None. **CC** Access, Visa. **Other Points:** Children welcome. Garden. Afternoon teas. Dogs allowed. ◘ **(V)**
RICHARD & BRIDGET DIMBLEBEE ☎ (0509) 890243.
The Pear Tree has been the central inn of Woodhouse Eaves for over 100 years. It is surrounded by beautiful landscape such as the Beacon Hills, a walkers paradise. Great food, all fresh and homemade at value for money prices.

⊗££ **THE CEDARS HOTEL & RESTAURANT** Cedar Road.
⌂££ **Hours:** Restaurant open 6.30pm - 9.30pm Monday to Saturday.
☺ Open Sunday lunch. **Cuisine:** Varied and interesting menus. Choice of set menus for private functions. ⊨ 37 bedrooms en suite. **CC** All major cards. **Other Points:** Children welcome. Conference facilities available. Barbecue facilities in garden for use in the summer, weather permitting. ◘ **(V) Directions:** Along the A6, after Loughborough turn left opposite cemetery.
MRS C J TOONE - Manager ☎ (0509) 214459/217834
This hotel provides many facilities for guests including a sauna, solarium and exercise room as well as a swimming pool

Loughborough continued
(residents only) in the garden. The food is good value for money and the atmosphere of the hotel friendly and welcoming.

LOUGHTON Buckinghamshire **Map 4 B2**
⊗£ **COUNTRY CARVERY AT "THE TALBOT"** London Road,
CLUB Loughton, Milton Keynes.
Hours: Lunch 12 noon - 2pm and dinner 6pm - 10pm (last orders). Bar meals 12 noon - 2pm and 6pm - 10pm. **Cuisine:** Good family meals including a choice of alternative roasts and a large selection of desserts. ⊨ None. ■ All major cards. **Other Points:** Children welcome. Non-smoking area. Separate restaurant and restaurant bar. Childrens play area. Barbeque. ▣ **(V) Directions:** On the old A5, just north of Bletchley.
MR MARC BIRCH ☎ (0908) 666420.
Country Carvery is set in a building which dates back to the 16th century and is rumoured to have a ghost which inhabits the chair in the restaurant fireplace. However, with the friendly staff, delicious roasts and desserts, the ghost can hardly fail to be a cheerful and well-fed one.

LULWORTH Dorset **Map 4 C1**
⊞££ **SHIRLEY HOTEL** West Lulworth, nr Wareham.
⊨ 5 single, 8 double, 4 twin and 2 family bedrooms, all en suite. Colour TVs, direct dial phones and tea/coffee making facilities in all rooms. **Hours:** Breakfast 8.15am - 9am, dinner 6pm - 7.30pm. Restaurant open to non- residents in summer until 9pm. ■ Access, Visa. **Other Points:** Central heating. Limited access for disabled. Children welcome. Licensed. Lounge. Garden for residents. Coin operated laundry. Outdoor heated pool. ▣ **Directions:** On the B3070 via Wareham in West Lulworth.
JESS & TONY WILLIAMS ☎ (092 941) 358.
The village shop was converted into this small hotel in the late '30s but recent modernisation has given it a complete facelift. Situated in the centre of the village amongst thatched cottages. A la carte menu and fixed price residents menu available from Spring Bank Holiday to mid-September.

LULWORTH COVE Dorset **Map 4 C1**
⊗£ **BISHOP'S COTTAGE AND HILL HOUSE HOTEL** Lulworth
⊞££ Cove.
Hours: Breakfast 8am - 9.30am, lunch 12 noon - 2.30pm and dinner 6pm - 10pm. Bar meals 12 noon - 2.30pm and 6pm - 10pm. Open all year round. **Cuisine:** Seafood, local fish, vegetarian dishes. ⊨ 25 bedrooms, 17 en suite. 4 bathrooms. ■ Access, Visa. **Other Points:** Children welcome. Heated outdoor swimming pool overlooking the cove. Pets welcome. Mastercharge also accepted. ▣ **(V) Directions:** Overlooking Lulworth Cove.
MRS PETER RUDD ☎ (092941) 261 and 404
Once the Bishop of Salisbury's home. The house stands in its own grounds on the edge of the Cove and sheltered by Bindon Hill. The grounds have direct access to coastal heritage cliffs and the Cove.

LUTON Bedfordshire **Map 4 B2**

⊗£££ **LEASIDE HOTEL** 72 New Bedford Road, Luton.

⌂£££ **Hours:** Breakfast 7am - 9am, lunch 12 noon - 2pm (last orders), dinner 7pm - 9.30pm (last orders). Closed: Saturday morning, Sunday evening, Hotel closes: Christmas Day, Boxing Day and Bank holidays. **Cuisine:** A la carte menu, fixed price 3 course menu, bar meals/snacks and vegetarian meals available. ⊨ 13 rooms. 10 single, 1 twin and 2 double bedrooms. All en suite. **CC** All major cards. **Other Points:** Children welcome. Garden. **P** **(V) Directions:** On A6 near Moor Park.

MRS C.A. GILLIES ☎ (0582) 417643.

A Victorian hotel, set in its own well tended gardens with large patio. Pleasantly decorated with comfortable furnishings and serving well cooked food, attractively presented from a comprehensive menu, the light pleasant atmosphere attracts tourists and business persons alike.

LYDDINGTON Leicestershire **Map 4 A2**

⊗££ **THE OLD WHITE HART COUNTRY INN & RESTAURANT** 51 Main Street, Lyddington, Nr Uppingham, Rutland.

Hours: Lunch 12 noon - 2pm, dinner 6.30pm - 10pm. Restaurant closed Sunday evenings. **Cuisine:** Full restaurant and bar menus, most popular dishes are mushrooms Lyddington, chicken in filo pastry with asparagus sauce and Sussex pond pudding. ⊨ None. **CC** Access, Visa. **Other Points:** Garden. Dogs allowed. Fax No: (0572) 821965. **P** **(V) Directions:** 1 mile south of Uppingham, follow 'Bede House' signs.

DIANE & BARRY BRIGHT ☎ (0572) 821703.

Situated in an unspoilt village, this stone building with its walled garden is opposite the village green. Decorated to a high standard it is furnished with good, solid yet comfortable furniture. In the restaurant you can enjoy quality food, appealingly presented and served in generous portions. The staff are skilled and helpful while the atmosphere is friendly and relaxed.

LYMINGTON Hampshire **Map 4 C1**

⊗££ **PEELER BISTRO & WINE BAR** Gosport Street, Lymington.

⌂££ **Hours:** Breakfast 8.30am - 9am (residents only), lunch 12 noon - 1.45pm and dinner 7pm - 10.15pm. **Cuisine:** Fresh fish. ⊨ 3 bedrooms with TVs. **CC** Access, Visa. **Other Points:** Children welcome. 𝄃 **(V) Directions:** 200 yds off Lymington High St in Gosport St on the left hand side.

MR & MRS W J SMITH ☎ (0590) 76165.

Built in 1700 as a Police Station, Peelers no longer dishes out law and order but rather serves a wide range of delicious food with a well deserved reputation for its fish. An extremely popular restaurant especially in the evenings. Close to the Isle of Wight ferry in a main cobbled road.

LYNDHURST Hampshire **Map 4 C1**

⊗££ **BELL INN** Brook, Nr Lyndhurst.

Hours: Restaurant: 7.30am - 9.30am, 12 noon - 2pm, and 7.30pm - 9.30pm. **Cuisine:** Dishes include Magret of Duckling, Scollops of Scottish Beef, Ragout of seafood, saddle of hare. Bar meals available, such as fresh local fish and game. ⊨ 3 single, 10 twin, 7

Lyndhurst continued

double, all en suite, with trouser press, hairdryers and tea/coffee facilities. **CC** All major cards. **Other Points:** Children welcome. Pets allowed. Garden. Fax (070)3 813958. **P** **(V) Directions:** Jct 1, M27 - B3078.

GAVIN SCOTT - General Manager **☎** (0703) 812214.

17th century building set in the New Forest, but only 1 mile from Jct 1, on the M27. The food is of an excellent standard, and beautifully presented, and the rooms are very comfortable, many with forest views. A lovely friendly atmosphere prevails.

⊗££ **THE NEW FOREST INN** Emery Down, Lyndhurst
☐D££ **Hours:** Residents breakfast 8am - 9am, Bar lunches 11.30am - 2pm and Dinner 6pm - 9.30pm (last orders - except Sundays 1.30pm and 9pm). **Cuisine:** Game in season, eg. pheasant, venison. Old English recipes. ☒ 4 bedrooms, all en suite. **CC** Access, Visa. **Other Points:** Children welcome. Coaches by appointment. **P** & **(V) Directions:** Located between A31/M27 and A35.

SUE & NICK EMBERLEY **☎** (0703) 282329.

In a delightful setting, in the heart of the New Forest, the inn dates back to the early 1700's when a caravan stood on this site claiming squatter's rights. This caravan now forms part of the porchway.

MAIDENHEAD Berkshire **Map 4 B2**
⊗££££ **BOULTERS LOCK INN** Raymead Road, Boutlers Island.
↩☐ **Hours:** Breakfast 7.30am - 10am, lunch 12.30pm - 2.30pm, dinner 7pm - 10.30pm. Sunday lunch 12.30pm - 3pm, Sunday dinner 7pm - 10pm. **Cuisine:** Highly imaginative French/English cuisine. Veal with basil, wild mushrooms asparagus in calvados, crab, spinach, rice wine parcels. ☒ 1 family room, 15 double, 3 twin, 1 single, honeymoon suite. All en suite. **CC** All major cards. **Other Points:** Children welcome. Garden. Mini-health club. Sunbed. Turkish sauna. Cruises available. Conference rooms. Fax (0628) 26048. **P** **(V) Directions:** On A4094 off A4. Junction 7 of M4.

MR ROBERT ARIF. **☎** (0628) 21291.

Standing on a small island in the River Thames, this hotel derives its name (Boulter) from the old word for miller. This is understandable as it occupies the site of a mill. Beautifully presented and cooked meals are served in the warm, soft atmosphere of the restaurant. Attractively decorated this hotel offers comfortable accommodation.

⊗££££ **CHAUNTRY HOUSE HOTEL** High Street, Bray on Thames.
☐ **Hours:** Breakfast 7.30am - 9.30am. Lunch 12 noon - 2pm. Dinner
CLUB 7.30pm - 10pm (last orders 9.30pm). Closed: Saturday lunch, all day Sunday. **Cuisine:** Imaginative French cuisine. Menu changes seasonally. House speciality - Tartlet of fresh lobster with green pepper and a sweet sherry cream sauce. ☒ 13 rooms, all en suite. **CC** All major cards. **Other Points:** Small conferences, special occasions catered for. **P** & **(V) Directions:** M4 J8/9. A308 to Windsor, B3028 to Bray. Last building on right.

ANN YOUNG **☎** (0628) 73991

An outstanding 18th century house house hotel situated in this delightful village close to Windsor and Heathrow Airport. No

Maidenhead continued

visitor can fail to be impressed by the friendly and relaxed atmosphere in this intimate restaurant.

⊗££ **CHEQUERS BRASSERIE** Dean Lane, Cookham Dean, Maidenhead.
Hours: Lunch 12 noon - 2.30pm, dinner 6.30pm - 9.45pm. Open Bank Holidays. **Cuisine:** Predominantly French with International variations. ⊨ None. **CC** Access, Visa. **Other Points:** Children welcome. Log fire. ⅋
MR PETER ROEHRIG ☎ (0628) 481232.
Set in a small village in the Thames Valley, it is hardly surprising that this pub is popular with locals and business people alike, as it offers good food at value for money prices. A good meal can be enjoyed in a lively yet relaxed atmosphere, brought about by the capable staff.

MAIDSTONE Kent **Map 5 C1**
⊗££ **RINGLESTONE INN** Twixt Harrietsham & Wormshill, Nr
CLUB Maidstone.
Hours: Hot & cold help yourself Buffet lunch 12 noon - 2pm daily, full dinner menu and evening bar snacks 7pm - 9.30pm daily. Open every day including Bank Holidays, except Christmas Day. **Cuisine:** Wide range of country dishes. Menu may feature Beef & Beer Pie, Prawn Sundae, Fresh Pink Trout, Lamb and Coconut Curry, Treacle and Nut Tart. ⊨ 9 bedrooms in adjoining farmhouse planned. **CC** All major cards. **Other Points:** Children welcome (safe garden). Log fire. Parties welcome. Garden dining. Famous for real ales and country fruit wines. Fax:(0622) 859966. **P** ⅋ **(V) Directions:** At Crossrds on B2163 above Hollingbourne, turn E towards Doddington.
MICHAEL MILLINGTON-BUCK ☎ (0622) 859900.
Built in 1533 as a hospice for monks, the Ringlestone Inn still retains the original brick and flint walls and floors, oak beams, inglenooks and centuries old English oak furniture and now has an idyllic country garden. The traditional country dishes are home created, complemented by a good selection of wines and beers. Welcoming service. Popular with visitors to Leeds Castle.

MALMESBURY Wiltshire **Map 4 B1**
⊞££ **MANOR FARM** Corston, Malmesbury.
⊨ 3 double and 1 family bedroom. 2 bathrooms. 1 shower. 1 en suite bathroom and 1 shower en suite. **Hours:** Breakfast 7am - 9am. **CC** Access, Visa, AmEx. **Other Points:** Central heating. Children welcome. Residents lounge with TV. Garden. **P Directions:** Off the A429 between jct 17 of the M4 and Malmesbury in Corston.
JOHN & ROSS EAVIS ☎ (0666) 822148.
A quaint 18th century farmhouse on a 436 acre working farm producing milk and cereals. Ideal for a retreat in the country or as a base for exploring the Cotswolds, Bath, Bristol and Cirencester or visiting the many historic houses and gardens nearby.

MARGATE Kent **Map 5 C2**
⊗£ **IVYSIDE HOTEL** 25 Sea Road, Westgate-on-Sea, Margate.
⊞£££ **Hours:** Breakfast 7.30am - 9am, lunch 12.30pm - 2pm (last orders), bar snacks 12 noon - 2pm (last orders), dinner 6.30pm -

Margate continued

8.45pm (last orders), evening bar snacks 6pm - 10pm (last orders). **Cuisine:** Traditional English cuisine. 🛏 70 bedrooms, 68 en suite. **CC** Access, Visa. **Other Points:** Childrens playroom. No-smoking area. Garden dining. Out & indoor swimming pools. Jacuzzi. Sauna. Squash courts. Laundertte. Fax as telephone no. **P** ♿ **(V)** MICHAEL WISEMAN ☎ (0843) 31082.

Two large houses successfully converted into a hotel, attractively decorated and furnished. Happy to cater for conferences, the hotels clientele ranges from locals to businesspersons. Serving traditional English cuisine at value for money prices, service and atmosphere in the restaurant cannot be faulted. Comfortable accommodation.

£££ **KINGSDOWN HOTEL** 59-61 Harold Road, Cliftonville, CLUB Margate.

🛏 6 single, 4 twin, 2 double bedrooms, 5 en suite. **Hours:** Breakfast 9am - 9.30am and dinner 6pm. Bar snacks served 12.30pm - 2pm. **CC** Access, Visa. **Other Points:** Children welcome. Afternoon teas. No smoking in dining room. Parking adjacent to hotel. MR JAMES WILLIAMS ☎ (0843) 221672.

A Victorian hotel, situated near main shopping area and seafront, offering pleasantly decorated and spotlessly clean accommodation. The warm and courteous service and welcoming atmosphere attracts business people and tourists alike.

£ **THE BEACHCOMBER HOTEL** 3-4 Royal Esplanade, £££ Westbrook, Margate.

Hours: Breakfast until 9.00am, lunch 12.30pm - 2pm and dinner 6pm. Bar meals 12 noon - 2.15pm and 7pm - 9pm. **Cuisine:** A wide variety of fresh food, prepared and cooked by the chef/proprietor. 🛏 15 bedrooms, 5 with shower. 2 bathrooms. **CC** None. **Other Points:** Children welcome. No dogs. ♿ **(V) Directions:** Close to A28. Royal Esplanade overlooks Westbrook Bay. PHILIP MCGOVERN ☎ (0843) 221616.

This quiet 15 bedroomed hotel overlooks the safe sands of Westbrook Bay with fine sea views. Inside, the hotel is tastefully decorated and the emphasis is on cleanliness, fine cuisine and personal service. Open all year.

£££ **THE FOUR LANTERNS** 6 Market Place, Margate.

Hours: Lunch 12 noon - 2pm, dinner 6pm - 11pm (last orders). Closed: Saturday, Sunday and Monday lunchtimes. **Cuisine:** Greek and continental dishes specialising in fish dishes. Fresh lobster, sea bass and red snapper. Superb fish or meat meze. 🛏 None. **CC** Access, Visa, AmEx. **Other Points:** Children welcome.Dining al fresco in summer.Special Greek evenings are organised throughout the year with live Greek music and cabaret. ♿ **Directions:** In the market place off the pier. GEORGE PTOHOPOULOS ☎ (0843) 293034.

The Four Lanterns is an attractive restaurant offering a wide variety of Greek and English food. Greek music and ornaments add to the friendly atmosphere in the restaurant. During the

Margate continued

summer, meals are served in the Market Place which is just one of Margate's tourist attractions.

MARKET HARBOROUGH Leicestershire **Map 4 A2**

⊗£   **THE FOX INN** Wilbarston, Market Harborough.
⊞£   **Hours:** Breakfast 8am - 9am, lunch 12 noon - 2pm, dinner 7pm - 10pm. **Cuisine:** A la carte menu and bar meals/snacks. ⊨ 1 Family flat, 2 twins, all en suite. ⊡ Access, Visa. **Other Points:** Children welcome. Garden. ⊡ **(V) Directions:** A427 Corby to Market Harborough.
MR & MRS MCHARG ☎ (0536) 771270.
This old iron-stone village pub dating back to the 14th century sits in the picturesque Northamptonshire countryside. The Fox Inn has a warm and friendly atmosphere and serves good home cooked food. Recently completed annexe provides guests with comfortable attractive accommodation. Recommended for providing all the warmth and value for money of a lovely village pub.

⊗£££ **THE QUEEN'S HEAD** Sutton Bassett, Nr Market Harborough.
CLUB **Hours:** Lunch 11.45am - 2pm and Dinner 7pm - 10pm. **Cuisine:** A la carte - steak on the grill and a selection of meat and fish dishes. Bar meals. ⊨ None. ⊡ Access, Visa. **Other Points:** Children welcome. Patio. **(V) Directions:** B664
MR & MRS POWELL ☎ (0858) 463530
This pretty beamed public house is situated in a small rural village and has an excellent view over the lovely surrounding countryside. You are assured of a warm welcome in this establishment which is very popular with the locals.

MARLBOROUGH Wiltshire **Map 4 B1**

⊗££   **ROYAL OAK** Wootton Rivers, nr Marlborough.
⊞££   **Hours:** (Self service breakfast available). Lunch 12 noon - 2pm and dinner 7pm - 9.30pm (last orders). Bar meals 12 noon - 2pm and 7pm - 9.30pm. **Cuisine:** Good home cooked food including steak and kidney pie. ⊨ 3 double, 1 family and 3 single bedrooms, 3 with en suite facilities and TV. ⊡ Access, Visa. **Other Points:** Children welcome. Pets allowed. Non-smoking area. Vegetarian menu available on request. Pewsey Vale charter cruises on canal at weekends. ⊡ ⅋ **Directions:** Off the A346/A345. Signposted from Pewsey to Burbage Road.
JOHN & ROSA JONES ☎ (0672) 810322.
Situated close to the Kennet and Avon canal, this is a good example of a quasi country pub with a pleasant atmosphere, good food and service. A delightful pub with its own garden that offers a wide choice for the diner.

MARLOW Buckinghamshire **Map 4 B2**

⊗£   **TWO BREWERS PUBLIC HOUSE** Saint Peter Street, Marlow.
Hours: Lunch 12 noon - 2.30pm and dinner 7pm (last orders 9.45pm). Bar meals 12 noon - 2.30pm and 7pm - 9.30pm. **Cuisine:** Grilled plaice maitre d'hotel. Regency fillet steak. ⊨ None. ⊡ Access, Visa, AmEx. **Other Points:** Children welcome. Non-smoking area. Afternoon tea served. ⊡ **(V) Directions:** Off the A4155. Situated on the river bank, near Marlow bridge.

Marlow continued

MR FREDERICK BOXALL ☎ (0628) 484140.

One of Marlow's oldest public houses situated 60 yards from the river bank with moorings. Established in 1742, this is a large comfortable pub which is well patronised.

MARNHULL Dorset **Map 4 C1**

⊗£ **CROWN HOTEL** Crown Road, Marnhull.

⌂£production **Hours:** Meals 8am - 10am, 12 noon - 2pm, and 7pm - 10pm.
Cuisine: Sandwiches, snacks, salads, traditional bar meals. Chicken supreme, Sword fish provencale. ⊨ 4 bedrooms, 3 with en suite facilities from summer 1992. ☒ Access, Visa. **Other Points:** Children welcome. No dogs. ☒ **Directions:** From A30, take B3092 south. The Crown is before Marnhull Church.

MR & MRS T O'TOOLE ☎ (0258) 820224.

An old thatched Inn, featured in Hardy's 'Tess of the D'Urbervilles' in the heart of Wessex. A full range of good homemade food is served, from sandwiches to an a la carte menu. Personally supervised by the proprietor.

MELKSHAM Wiltshire **Map 4 B1**

⊗££ **THE KING'S ARMS HOTEL AND RESTAURANT** The
⌂£££ Market Place, Melksham.
Hours: Breakfast 7.30am - 9am (Monday to Friday), 8am - 9.30am (Saturday) and 8.30am - 10am (Sundays). Lunch 12.30pm - 2.15pm and dinner 7pm - 9pm (last orders, 8.30pm Sundays.)
Cuisine: Supreme of chicken King's style - stuffed with apricots and cooked in cider. ⊨ 14 bedrooms, 10 en suite. ☒ All major cards. **Other Points:** Children welcome. Fax No. (0225) 702085.
☒ ☒ **(V) Directions:** Junction 17, M4. In Market Place in Melksham, close to the A365.

DAVID & HELEN DODD ☎ (0225) 707272.

The King's Arms is a 17th century coaching inn situated in the Market Place. The lounge bar, with its traditional open fire and oak beams serves real ale and delicious bar snacks. The dining room offers English country cooking using fresh local produce.

⊗££ **THE SHAW COUNTRY HOTEL & MULBERRY RESTAURANT** Bath Road, Shaw, Nr Melksham.
Hours: Breakfast 7.30am - 9.30am, (Mon-Fri) Lunch 12 noon - 2pm and Dinner 7pm - 9pm. Closed: 24/25/26th December.
Cuisine: Salmon poached in champagne, herbs and tomatoes and served with a champagne cream sauce. 5 course a la carte. ⊨ 13 bedrooms, all en suite.TV and tea/coffee making facilities. Fresh fruit. ☒ Access, Visa, AmEx. **Other Points:** Children welcome. Full license. Residents lounge. Garden. Outdoor heated swimming pool. Fax: 790275 ☒ **(V) Directions:** On the A365, 1 mile from Melksham and 9 miles from Bath.

MR & MRS C T BRIGGS ☎ (0225) 702836/790321

A 400 year old farmhouse which has been converted into a delightful restaurant and hotel. The menu has been imaginatively compiled to provide excellent food at reasonable prices. Enjoy your meal in a friendly, informal atmosphere. Highly reccomended.

MELTON MOWBRAY Leicestershire **Map 4 A2**
ⁿ££ **HOME FARM** Church Lane, Old Dalby, Melton Mowbray.
5 bedrooms, 2 en suite. Tea/coffee making facilities, TV, views of garden, no smoking, and washing machine on request. **Hours:** Breakfast only but light suppers available on request. **CC** None. **Other Points:** No smoking. Sitting room with TV, piano and open fire. Central heating. Small garden. Vegetarian and special diets on request. **P** **(V) Directions:** 2 miles off A606. Opposite the Church in Old Dalby.
VAL ANDERSON ☎ (0664) 822622.
Set in a delightful garden and facing the church, this charming 18th century house provides excellent accommodation and a peaceful atmosphere. Open fires and country-style furniture add to the welcoming interior. Mrs Anderson recommends the nearby Crown Inn, Les Routiers Pub of the Year 1991 for meals. Plenty to see and do in the area. Highly recommended.

⊗££ **SYSONBY KNOLL HOTEL AND RESTAURANT** Asfordby
ⁿ£££ Road, Melton Mowbray.
Hours: 7.30am - 9.30am, 12 noon - 2pm, 7pm - 10pm. Sunday lunch 12 noon - 2pm. Sunday dinner for residents only. Restaurant closed: Xmas, New Year and Sunday evening. **Cuisine:** Extensive a la carte menu which includes a vegetarian selection. 6 single, 6 twin, 11 double, and 2 family rooms, 23 of them en suite. **CC** Access, Visa. **Other Points:** Children welcome. Pets allowed. Garden. **P** **&** **(V) Directions:** M1 junction - A6006.
MRS S BOOTH ☎ (0664) 63563.
A family run hotel, set in 2 acres of grounds with river frontage, the Sysonby Knoll has beautifully decorated rooms with quality furnishings. The restaurant offers an imaginative menu which our inspector comments 'gives excellent value for money'.

MIDHURST West Sussex **Map 4 C2**
⊗££££ **THE SPREAD EAGLE HOTEL** South Street.
Hours: Meals 8am - 10am, 12.30pm - 2.15pm and 7.30pm - 9.30pm. Open 24 hours. **Cuisine:** Modern British cooking. The Fixed price menu changes every 2 weeks. 41 bedrooms, all en suite. **CC** All major cards. **Other Points:** Children welcome. Eurocard accepted. **P** **(V) Directions:** South-east outskirts of Midhurst. Off the High Street.
THE GOODMAN FAMILY & GEORGE MUDFORD ☎ (0730) 816911.
This attractive hotel started its days as a tavern in 1430 and expanded as a famous coaching inn. Excellent restaurant and bar facilities with a 17th century Jacobean Hall used for banqueting and conferences. Dine by candlelight in the beautiful restaurant, complete with huge coppered inglenook fireplace and dark oak beams. The ideal choice for that special occassion.

MILTON KEYNES Buckinghamshire **Map 4 B2**
⊗££ **LAL BAGH TANDOORI RESTAURANT** 47 Aylesbury Street, Fenny Stratford, Bletchley.
Hours: Lunch 12 noon - 2.30pm, Dinner 6pm - 11pm (last orders). Closed: Christmas Day and Boxing Day. **Cuisine:** Indian cuisine. House specialities are Mughali Chicken and Kashmiri Chicken and, at 24 hours notice, Kulchi Lamb. Good choice. None.

Milton Keynes continued

CC Access, Visa, AmEx. **Other Points:** Children welcome. No dogs. Fully licensed. Air conditioned. Take-aways available. **P** &
(V) Directions: Just off A5 (Watling Street). In a parade of shops.
RUKON UDDIN ☎ (0908) 271494/644700

An Indian Restaurant offering a good selection of very tasty dishes and a welcoming, relaxed atmosphere. The distinctive flavour and aroma of each dish comes from Indian spices, delicately prepared each day, resulting in a high standard of cuisine. The menu offers a good choice of dishes and the service is welcoming and efficient.

⊗££ **THE CARRINGTON ARMS** Cranfield Road, Moulsoe, Nr
⌂£££ Newport Pagnell.
Hours: Breakfast 7.30am - 9.30am, lunch 12 noon - 3pm (last orders 2.30pm), dinner 6pm - 11pm (last orders 9.30pm), bar snacks 12 noon - 11pm. **Cuisine:** Dishes may include supreme of chicken, mushrooms and nut fettucini, rainbow trout. ⊨ 4 bedrooms, all en suite. **CC** Access, Visa. **Other Points:** Children welcome. Open Bank Holidays. Afternoon teas. Garden dining. Fax/telephone No. (0908) 615721. **P** & **(V) Directions:** Jct 14, M1, towards Newport pagnell, approx 50yrds right to Moulsoe. KEVIN HUSH - Manager. ☎ (0908) 615721.
Set in one and a half acres of gardens, this hotel has recently been refurbished and decorated. Light background music and friendly staff help create the relaxed atmosphere in which you can enjoy generous meals presented with 'care and flair'. Comfortable accommodation.

MORETON IN MARSH Gloucestershire **Map 4 B1**
⌂££ **MORETON HOUSE** High Street, Moreton in Marsh.
⊨ 3 single, 6 double, 3 twin, 5 en suite. 2 bathrooms.
Hours: Breakfast 7.30am - 9.30am, dinner 6.30pm - 8pm.
CC Access, Visa. **Other Points:** Central heating. Children welcome. Fire certificate. Licensed restaurant. Residents' lounge. TV. **P** **Directions:** On the A429, near the junction with the A44. CHRIS & CHIC DEMPSTER ☎ (0608) 50747.
A family-run guest house and tea-room with residential and restaurant licence. The house has been in the same family for over 100 years. The Fosseway (A429) runs straight through this historic market town. Moreton-in-Marsh has a street market every Tuesday with many interesting stalls, as well as numerous antique shops.

NEWHAVEN East Sussex **Map 5 C1**
⊗£ **THE HOPE INN** West Quay, Newhaven.
[CLUB] **Hours:** Lunch 12 noon - 2pm and dinner 7pm - 9.30pm (last orders 9pm). **Cuisine:** Comprehensive menu, specialising in seafood dishes. ⊨ None. **CC** Access, Visa. **Other Points:** Children welcome. **P** **(V) Directions:** Left by police station, pass yacht club, Hope Inn is on the right.
PAULA & KEN ☎ (0273) 515389.
A superb view overlooking Newhaven Harbour, a nautical theme for decor and offering generous portions of tasty, well prepared food at reasonable prices. Friendly, efficient service and a relaxed, informal atmosphere.

NORTHAMPTON Northamptonshire **Map 4 A2**

⊗£££ **WESTONE MOAT HOUSE** Ashley Way, Weston Favell,
Ⅲ£££ Northampton.

> **Hours:** Breakfast 7.30am - 9.30am, Lunch 12.30pm - 1.45pm and
> Dinner 7pm - 9.45pm Closed: Saturday lunchtimes. **Cuisine:**
> English and French cuisine: medley of seafood pate, chicken
> boursin and lobster Martinique. ⊨ 66 bedrooms, all en suite.
> ⒸⒸ All major cards. **Other Points:** Children welcome. Dogs
> allowed in rooms. Open for Sunday lunch/ dinner and Bank
> holidays. Ⓓ **(V) Directions:** The hotel is signed off the A4500 in
> Weston Favell.
> MR G FEHLER - Manager ☎ (0604) 406262.
> *This old country house was originally owned by the Sears family
> and was used as an army brigade headquarters in the 2nd
> World War. Now it provides a haven for visitors, overlooking
> peaceful lawns, set in a quiet, residential area and offering
> facilities for croquet, mini-gym, sauna and solarium.*

NORWICH Norfolk **Map 5 A2**

⊗££ **CUMBERLAND HOTEL AND RESTAURANT** 212-216
Ⅲ£££ Thorpe Road, Norwich.

> **Hours:** Breakfast 7am - 10am, Lunch by arrangement, Dinner
> 6.30pm - 9pm (last orders). Bar snacks 12 noon - 2pm and 6.30pm
> - 10pm. **Cuisine:** Extensive table d'hote and a la carte menus.
> Specialities may include King Prawns, Peppered Steak,
> Medallions of Pork, Cumberland Mixed Grill. ⊨ 30 bedrooms, 21
> en suite. ⒸⒸ All major cards. **Other Points:** Children welcome.
> Dogs allowed. No smoking in dining room. Afternoon teas.
> Residents' lounge. Lounge bar. Fax No: (0603) 33355. Ⓓ ⅋ **(V)**
> **Directions:** Ring Rd A47 sign to Yarmouth. Hotel on left. 3/4 mile
> from City Ctr.
> MICHAEL PRICE ☎ (0603) 34550/34560.
> *A privately owned and run hotel with a warm atmosphere and
> personal, welcoming service. The candlelit restaurant provides
> a romantic setting in which to enjoy good food and wine and the
> lounge bar is a relaxing place to unwind over a pre dinner
> drink. Set in its own grounds, the Cumberland is only a short
> distance from the city centre and railway station.*

⊗££ **THE LARDER AND WEBSDALES RESTAURANT** 19
Bedford Street, Norwich.

> **Hours:** Breakfast 9am - 10.30am, lunch served all day, last orders
> 4.45pm. **Cuisine:** Three sections: sandwich bar - fresh baps &
> sandwiches to order, waitress service tea room & luncheon
> restaurant and a intimate a la carte restaurant. ⊨ None. ⒸⒸ None.
> **Other Points:** Children welcome. Afternoon teas served. No
> smoking. No dogs (Guide dogs excepted). ⅋ **(V) Directions:** Nr
> market place.
> LAURENCE DYER AND MARTYN ROBERTS ☎ (0603) 622641.
> *Good food and a warm welcome can be found at this
> establishment which is personally run by the proprietors and
> divided into 3 sections: A sandwich bar; a waitress service tea
> room and luncheon restaurant; a small and intimate a la carte
> restaurant providing quality English food at reasonable prices,
> in attractive, restful surroundings.*

NYMPSFIELD Gloucestershire **Map 4 B1**

⊗£ **ROSE & CROWN INN** Nympsfield, Stonehouse.

⊞££ **Hours:** Meals 7.30am - 9am, 12 noon - 2.00pm and bar meals 6.30pm - 9.00pm. **Cuisine:** Good bar food with sandwiches, salads, steaks, fish meals, spicy dishes. Packed lunch available. ⊨ 4 family bedrooms. 1 bathroom. **CC** Access, Visa. **Other Points:** Children welcome. No dogs. Coaches welcome. **P (V) Directions:** Off the B4066 Dursley - Stroud Road in Nympsfield village centre. BOB AND LINDA WOODMAN ☎ (0453) 860 240.

A 300 year-old coaching inn in an extremely quiet Cotswold village. Close to the Cotswold Way and Nympsfield Gliding Club. A friendly, local inn which is an ideal base for touring, and within easy access of the M4 and M5.

OAKHAM Leicestershire **Map 4 A2**

⊗££ **THE SHIRES HOTEL** Great North Road, Stretton, Oakham,
⊞££ Rutland.

Hours: Breakfast 7.30am - 9.30am, Lunch 12 noon - 3pm (2.30pm Sunday), Dinner 7pm - 11pm (last orders 10.30pm). **Cuisine:** À la carte - Classical French and English cuisine. Carvery. Bar snack menu. ⊨ 4 bedrooms. **CC** Access, Visa. **Other Points:** Children welcome. Garden. Afternoon teas. Dogs allowed. Games room. Private functions and conferences. **P** &. **(V) Directions:** A1 Stretton Junction, signposted for R.A.F Cottesmore. MRS A M BOWEN ☎ (0780) 410 332.

A blend of old worldly charm and home from home comforts await you at this 200 year old Georgian Free House. The Rutlander Bar offers a good choice of bar meals and the candlelit restaurant features genuine English and classical French cuisine. The food is excellently cooked and presented and the portions are more than adequate. A warm welcome and friendly, courteous service.

⊗££ **THE WHITE HORSE INN** 2 Main Street, Empingham, Nr
⊞££ Oakham.

Hours: Breakfast 7.30am - 9.30am, lunch and bar snacks 12 noon - 2pm, dinner 7.15pm - 9.30pm (last orders), bar snacks 7.15pm - 10pm (last orders). Restaurant closed: Sunday evenings. **Cuisine:** A la carte and fixed price menus featuring fresh produce mainly obtained direct from the local farm. Predominantly English cuisine. ⊨ 12 bedrooms, 8 en suite. **CC** All major cards **Other Points:** Children welcome. Open Bank Holidays. No smoking area. Afternoon teas served. Garden dining. Fax No. (078 086) 521. **P** &. **(V) Directions:** Main A606 Rd Between Stamford and Oakham. RODGER N BOURNE ☎ (078 086) 221/521.

This stone inn is set in a quiet village in the heart of Rutland's countryside. The food is very enjoyable and well presented and the inn enjoys a good reputation for hospitality, friendly service and comfortable accommodation. A good choice for both business and leisure travellers.

ODIHAM Hampshire **Map 4 C2**

⊗£££ **LA FORET** High Street, Odiham.

⌐☐ **Hours:** Lunch 12.30pm - 2pm and dinner 7pm - 9.45pm (last orders). **Cuisine:** Classic French cuisine, including extensive selection of fish specialities ⊨ None. **CC** All major cards. **Other**

Odiham continued

> **Points:** Children welcome. **Directions:** On the main street in Odiham.

MR & MRS HOULKER ☎ (0256) 702697.

This intimate French restaurant, situated on the main street of the delightful country town of Odiham, provides excellently cooked French cuisine in attractive comfortable surroundings. Using an imaginative menu which has obviously been devised by a creative and caring chef, you will find excellent service and candlelit surroundings complement your gastronomic delights.

OLD DALBY Leicestershire **Map 4 A2**

⊗££ **THE CROWN INN** Debdale Hill, Old Dalby, Melton Mowbray. **Hours:** Meals 12 noon - 2pm and 6pm - 9.30pm. No food available on Sunday evening. **Cuisine:** Fresh, seasonal dishes. ⊨ None. **CC** None. **Other Points:** Children welcome. **P** & **Directions:** Off the A46 and the A606 in Old Dalby.

LYNNE BRYAN & SALVATORE INGUANTA ☎ (0664) 823134.

Tucked away in a corner of the village and approached through the large car park, the Crown Inn offers the facilities of a croquet lawn, large garden and a petanque pitch. The beer is drawn straight from the wood and the bar menu is interesting and extensive. Routiers Pub of the Year 1991.

ORFORD Suffolk **Map 5 B2**

⊗££ **CROWN & CASTLE HOTEL** Orford, Woodbridge. ⊞£££ **Hours:** Breakfast 8am - 9.30am, lunch 12 noon - 2pm (last orders), dinner 7pm - 9pm (last orders). **Cuisine:** Predominantly English cuisine. ⊨ 20 bedrooms, 11 en suite. **CC** Access, Visa, Diners. **Other Points:** Children welcome. Open Bank Holidays. Afternoon teas. Garden dining. Dogs allowed. Fax No. (0394) 450176. **P** & **(V) Directions:** Turn off the A12 at Woodbridge.

SARAH MANN ☎ (0394) 450205.

Set in the Market Square and reputed to be haunted by smugglers of Tudor times, the Crown & Castle is tastefully and comfortably furnished and provides good, traditional fare. Popular with all ages, the hotel enjoys a pleasant, relaxed atmosphere.

ORSETT Essex **Map 5 B1**

⊗££ **ORSETT HALL** Prince Charles Avenue, Orsett. **Hours:** Meals 7.30am - 9am, 12 noon - 2pm and 7.30pm - 9.30pm (9.15pm last orders). **Cuisine:** Traditional English cooking, eg. roasts, steaks, steak and kidney pie. ⊨ 20 bedrooms, 17 en suite. **CC** Access, Visa, AmEx. **Other Points:** No dogs. Coaches by appointment. **P** & **(V) Directions:** Near the A13.

IVAN E GRIMWOOD ☎ (0375) 891402/891632

Situated within easy access of the A13. An elegant 17th century house in 12 acres of fine landscaped garden. Sweeping lawns, a rose garden and mature trees (including an oak, planted by King George V) help set the scene for a memorable visit.

OUNDLE Northamptonshire **Map 4 A2**

⊗££ **FITZGERALDS RESTAURANT** 26 West Street, Oundle. **Hours:** Morning coffee 10.30am - 12.30pm, Dinner 7pm - 11pm (last orders 10pm). **Closed:** All day Sunday. **Cuisine:** An English

Oundle continued

country bistro offering regional French cuisine and traditional English fayre. ⌐ None. **CC** Access, Visa. **Other Points:** Children welcome. Walled courtyard for out-door seating in summer. No dogs. & **(V) Directions:** A605. 300m beyond Oundle War Memorial, towards Corby.

NIALL FITZGERALD ☎ (0832) 273242.

A 17th century, Grade II listed building in the heart of Oundle, which has been converted to a 32 seat restaurant with walled courtyard. All dishes are homemade using fresh, seasonal produce. The Routiers inspector was impressed by the very well cooked food and welcoming service. Exposed oak beams and solid pine furniture add to the cosy, homely atmosphere. Good value.

⊗£££ **MILL AT OUNDLE** Barnwell Road, Oundle.

Hours: Meals served between 12 noon - 3pm, and 7pm - 10pm (last orders). **Cuisine:** 'Granary' Restaurant serving English fayre, and 'La Trattoria' serving continental dishes with pizzas, steaks and fish. ⌐ None. **CC** Access, Visa, AmEx. **Other Points:** Children welcome. No dogs. Garden dining. Open Sundays and Bank Holidays. **P** **(V) Directions:** Off A605 to Oundle. Signs to Barnwell Country Park.

MR N TULLEY & MRS L TULLEY ☎ (0832) 272621.

A friendly pub/restaurant, set in an 11th century restored water mill, offering a choice of eating and drinking venues on the banks of the River Nene. Mill races can be seen from the bars and it is situated close to Barnwell Country Park and Oundle Marina.

OXFORD Oxfordshire **Map 4 B2**

⊗£££ **BELFRY HOTEL** Milton Common, Oxford.

Hours: Breakfast Monday to Friday 7.30am - 9.30am, Saturday & Sunday 8.30am - 9.30am, Lunch 12.30pm - 2pm, Dinner 7.30pm - 9.30pm (last orders). Bar snacks 12.30pm - 2pm. Restaurant closed Saturday lunchtime. Hotel closed: 24th December - 31st December. **Cuisine:** Serving bar snacks, full a la carte menu and table d'hote. ⌐ 77 bedrooms, all en suite. **CC** All major cards. **Other Points:** Children welcome. Leisure complex. Conferences, exhibitions catered for. Fax as phone number. **P** & **(V) Directions:** Situated on A40 between Junction 7 and 8.

MR BARBER ☎ (0844) 279381.

Set in the Oxfordshire countryside approximately 10 minutes from Oxford. Decorated and furnished to a high standard and enjoying a friendly atmosphere. Good food and comfortable accommodation. Highly recommended.

⌂£££ **GABLES GUEST HOUSE** 6 Cumnor Hill, Oxford.

⌐ 2 double, 2 twin and 1 family bedroom, 5 en suite. 2 bathrooms and 2 showers. Tea/coffee making facilities, radio clocks and colour TVs in all rooms. **Hours:** Breakfast 7.30am - 8.45am. Closed: 4 days over Christams. **CC** None. **Other Points:** Central heating. Children welcome. Dogs allowed. Residents lounge. Garden. Vegetarian meals available. **P** **Directions:** On the A420 take the Botley exit off the ring road.

DIANNE WHITE ☎ (0865) 862153.

Oxford continued

A modern detached house in a smart residential area. Tastefully decorated, spotlessly clean and airy rooms. Ideal location for visiting the Old University city, Stratford upon Avon, Henley, Windsor and the Cotswolds.

⊗£££ **HOPCROFTS HOLT HOTEL** Steeple Aston.
🏨£££ **Hours:** Breakfast 7.30am - 9.30am, lunch 12 noon - 2pm, dinner 7pm - 9.45pm. Sunday dinner 7pm - 8.30pm. **Cuisine:** Dishes include breast of duck glazed with black grape sauce, fillets of sea bream poached in white wine and lemon sauce. 🛏 19 single, 26 twin, 42 double and 1 family bedroom. All en suite. **CC** All major cards. **Other Points:** Children welcome. Garden. Afternoon tea. Dogs allowed. **P** & **(V) Directions:** Midway between Oxford and Banbury on A4260 (formerly A423).
MR S MYLCHREEST - General Manager ☎ (0869) 40259.
A large 15th century coaching inn, which has been extensively refurbished to offer well appointed bedrooms, good food and a relaxed informal atmosphere. Situated very close to the delightful village of Steeple Aston, the hotel is an ideal base for touring North Oxfordshire and the Northern Cotswolds.

🏨££ **PICKWICKS** 17 London Road, Headington, Oxford.
🛏 3 single, 5 double, 3 twin and 3 family bedrooms: 10 with en suite. Direct dial phones, colour TV and tea/coffee making facilities in all rooms. **Hours:** Breakfast 7am - 8.30am (8am - 9am Sundays). Evening meals available on request. **CC** Access, Visa. **Other Points:** Children welcome. Pets allowed. Residents lounge and bar. Garden. Crib, high chair and baby foods available. Fax no. (0865) 742208. **P** & **Directions:** 1/4 mile from Oxford centre on London Road (A420).
G J & P MORRIS ☎ (0865) 750487/69413
A comfortable, quiet and efficiently managed hotel with 1st class decor and facilities. Large, clean, well appointed dining room and comfortable residents lounge. A welcoming and helpful attitude will be found here.

⊗££ **RESTAURANT XIAN** 197 Banbury Road, Oxford.
CLUB **Hours:** Lunch 12 noon - 2.30pm (last orders 2.15pm), dinner 6pm - 11.30pm (last orders). **Cuisine:** Cantonese cuisine. Menu indicates healthy eating and highly spiced food. 🛏 None. **CC** Access, Visa, AmEx. **Other Points:** Children welcome. Open Bank Holiday. No smoking area. **(V) Directions:** 1 mile north of city centre.
GARY TSE ☎ (0865) 54239.
Tastefully decorated in white with Chinease prints and pot plants, this restaurant offers good meals presented with flair. The friendly, efficient staff create an unhurried, tranquil atmosphere. Popular amoung locals, Restaurant Xian has many regulars - a reflection of the quality of the establishment.

🏨££ **THE RIDINGS** 280 Abingdon Road, Oxford.
🛏 3 bedrooms, 2 en suite and all with colour TV, tea/coffee making facilities and hairdryer. 2 general bathrooms. **Hours:** Breakfast 7am - 8.45am. Closed: Christmas and Boxing Day. **CC** None. **Other Points:** Central heating. Children welcome.

Oxford continued

Residents lounge. Payphone available. ▣ **Directions:** 1 mile south of the city centre.

MR & MRS TOMPKINS ☎ (0865) 248364.

A friendly, comfortable guest house situated close to the city centre and colleges, yet overlooking open fields. All rooms have been tastefully decorated and furnished and guests are always assured of a very warm welcome.

PETERBOROUGH Cambridgeshire **Map 5 A1**

⊗££ **BUTTERFLY HOTELS** Thorpe Meadows,Off Longthorpe
⊞£££ Parkway,Peterborough

Hours: Breakfast 7am - 9.30am, lunch 12.30pm - 2pm and dinner 7pm - 10pm. **Cuisine:** English/Continental dishes, carvery and buffet, plus fixed price menu. ⊨ 70 rooms. 28 single, 21 double, 17 twin, 4 family rooms, all en suite. **CC** All major cards. **Other Points:** Children welcome. No smoking areas. Conference facilities. ▣ ⅃ **(V) Directions:** From city centre, follow signs to District Hospital.

BUTTERFLY HOTELS LIMITED ☎ (0733) 64240.

A purpose built modern hotel offering well above the average welcome and a friendly family atmosphere. The restaurant is very popular with both locals and travellers and is very good value for money. All rooms are fully equipped to a very high standard.

⊗£££ **THE BELL INN** Great North Road, Stilton.
⊞£££££ **Hours:** Breakfast 7am - 9am, lunch 12 noon - 2pm, dinner 7pm - 9.30pm. **Cuisine:** A la carte. Dishes include Byron Fillet of Beef, Wild Salmon Dumpling, Vegetable Filo Parcels. ⊨ 19 rooms, all en suite. **CC** Access, Visa, AmEx. **Other Points:** Garden. No smoking areas. Conference rooms available. ▣ **(V) Directions:** 1/2 mile off A1 northbound. 5 miles south of Peterborough.

MR & MRS McGIVERN. ☎ (0733) 241066.

This hotel has been built around the courtyard of an historic inn. It offers old world charm, relaxing comfort and modern facilities. The Inn has a history dating back to 1500 and is a dream for history lovers.

⊗£ **THE WAYWARD FROG** 29 Bridge Street, Peterborough.

Hours: Wine bar open 10.30am - 11pm, serving snacks all day. Hot meals served 12 noon - 2.30pm. Closed: Sundays. **Cuisine:** A range of rolls and sandwiches served all day. Lunchtime menu includes soup, garlic bread, baked potatoes, burgers, chilli and pasta. ⊨ None. **CC** All major cards. **Other Points:** Children welcome. No dogs. **(V) Directions:** In the centre of Peterborough.

Y DEPARTE ☎ (0733) 61999.

Situated in the city centre, the Wayward Frog is a 1st floor wine bar above its parent, Ribit's. The atmosphere is set by secluded alcoves and subdued lighting. Sophisticated discotheque every Wednesday evening.

PETERSFIELD Hampshire **Map 4 C2**

⊗££ **LANGRISH HOUSE** Langrish, Petersfield.
CLUB **Hours:** Breakfast 6.45am - 10am and dinner 7.30pm - 9.30pm (last orders). Closed: Bank holidays and Sundays. **Cuisine:** Local trout. ⊨ 18 bedrooms. **CC** Access, AmEx, Diners. **Other Points:**

Petersfield continued

Children welcome. Afternoon tea served. Pets by arrangement. **P**
& **(V) Directions:** Off the A272, 3 miles west of Petersfield.
MONIQUE VON KOSPOTH **☎** (0730) 66941.
*An old English manor house, parts of which date back to the
16th century. Set in 13 acres of unspoilt countryside, it has been
restored and decorated with great flair. The restaurant is a
gourmet's delight and is not an adjunct to the hotel. Highly
recommended.*

PINNER Middlesex **Map 4 B2**

⊗££ **LA GIRALDA** 66 Pinner Green.

Hours: Open 12 noon - 2.30pm and 6pm - 10.30pm. Closed:
Sunday and Monday. **Cuisine:** Paella, fish - fixed price menus.
None. **CC** Access, Visa. **Other Points:** Children welcome.
Childrens menu. No dogs. Street parking. & **(V) Directions:**
Situated north of Pinner village.
MR D BROWN **☎** (081) 868 3429/3193.
*Situated just north of Pinner village amongst a parade of shops,
this tastefully furnished restaurant has 4 rooms of different
Spanish styles and serves authentic Spanish cuisine. Fixed
price menu using finest fresh produce. Believed to own one of
the finest lists of Spanish wine in Britain.*

PLUCKLEY Kent **Map 5 C1**

⊗££ **THE DERING ARMS** Pluckley.

£££ **Hours:** Lunch 12 noon - 3pm (last orders 2pm), Dinner 6.30pm -
11pm (last orders 10pm). Sunday Lunch 12 noon - 2pm. **Cuisine:**
Continually changing menu - Seafood specials and Daily specials.
Restaurant and bar menus. 3 rooms. 2 twin and 1 double
bedrooms. **CC** None. **Other Points:** Garden. **P** & **(V) Directions:**
On Bethersden Road, 100 yards from Pluckley railway station.
MR JAMES BUSS **☎** (023384) 371.
*Originally built as a hunting lodge for the Dering family, the inn
has some unusual features such as the curved Dutch gables and
the windows. Visitors to the Dering Arms are assured of a varied
choice of real ales and fine wines. Good homemade food is
served 7 days a week and comfortable accommodation is
available throughout the year. Friendly and welcoming.*

POOLE Dorset **Map 4 C1**

⊗£££ **ALLANS SEAFOOD RESTAURANT** 8 Bournemouth Road,
Poole.

CLUB **Hours:** Lunch 12 noon - 2pm, Dinner 6.30pm - late. Closed:
Sunday lunchtime. **Cuisine:** Fresh local fish, fresh lobster, crab -
all year. Alternative dishes include - steaks, veal, duck and
chicken. Special lunch menu. None. **CC** Access, Visa. **Other
Points:** Street parking nearby. No dogs. & **Directions:** Main road
from Bournemouth to Poole.
A D TOMLINSON **☎** (0202) 741489.
*A small seafood restaurant offering extremely fresh, perfectly
prepared seafood of all types. The exterior of the restaurant is
unpretentious and the interior has the feel of a French rural
restaurant which is in keeping with the very helpful, friendly
service. Considering the high cost of seafood, this restaurant
offers excellent value for money. Highly recommended.*

Poole continued

⊗££ **CORKERS CAFE BAR & RESTAURANT** 1 High Street, The Quay.
Hours: Restaurant open 12 noon - 2pm and 7pm - 11pm, Sunday 2pm and 10.30pm. Cafe bar open 10am - midnight daily (except Sun - 10.30pm). **Cuisine:** Seafood a speciality. ⊨ 4 bedrooms. 1 bathroom. **CC** All major cards. **Other Points:** Access for disabled to cafe bar only. Children welcome in restaurant. No dogs. Fully licensed. **Directions:** Adjacent to the quayside.
NICHOLAS CONSTANDINOS ☎ (0202) 681393.
Adjacent to Poole Quay with views overlooking the harbour, the ground floor is a cafe bar, the first floor a licensed restaurant and the second floor bed and breakfast accommodation.

⊗££ **HAVEN HOTEL** Banks Road, Sandbanks, Poole.
▥££££ **Hours:** Breakfast 7.30am - 9.45am, lunch 12.30pm - 2pm and dinner 7pm - 8.30pm (last orders). **Cuisine:** Traditional and international cuisine. ⊨ 97 bedrooms, all en suite. **CC** All major cards. **Other Points:** Vegetarians catered for. Garden. No dogs. ▣ ㄴ **(V) Directions:** On the seafront in the Sandbanks area of Poole.
BROWNSEA HAVEN PROPERTIES ☎ (0202) 707333.
An attractive building standing on the seafront with magnificent views across to the Purbeck Hills and Poole Harbour. Like its sister hotels, the Sandbanks and Chine, an informal atmosphere reigns despite its size and sophistication. The Haven Hotel has a purpose built Sports and Leisure Centre, and a newly built Business Centre Complex.

⊗£££ **SANDBANKS HOTEL** Banks Road, Sandbanks, Poole.
Hours: Breakfast 8am - 9.45am, lunch 12.30pm - 2pm and dinner 7pm - 8.30pm (last orders). **Cuisine:** Table d'hote menu changes daily - steaks, game, fish dishes. ⊨ 105 bedrooms, all en suite. **CC** All major cards. **Other Points:** Children welcome. No dogs. Garden. ▣ ㄴ **(V) Directions:** From Bournemouth follow signs to Sandbank Ferry. On the seafront.
SANDBANKS HOTEL LIMITED ☎ (0202) 707377.
Sandbanks occupies a superb position right on the beach with lovely views of the sea and Poole harbour. The beach has the coverted E.E.C. Blue Flag Award for clean beaches. A large, fully equipped hotel with the atmosphere and charm of a smaller establishment.

⊗££££ **THE MANSION HOUSE HOTEL & DINING CLUB** Thames Street, Poole.
Hours: 7am - 9.30am, 12.15pm - 2pm and 7.30pm - 10pm (last orders). Bar meals 12 noon - 2pm and 7pm - 10pm (last orders). Closed: Saturday lunch in restaurant. **Cuisine:** Fresh salmon with garlic butter and prawns, lamb with rosemary and red wine, and Chateaubriand. Fresh lobster and crab when available. ⊨ 28 bedrooms, all en suite. **CC** All major cards. **Other Points:** Children welcome. No dogs allowed. Conference facilities available. Fax No: (0202) 665709. Telex: 41495 Select G. ▣ **(V) Directions:** Thames Street is off The Quay, near St James' church
ROBERT LEONARD & CHRISTOPHER T SMITH ☎ (0202) 685666.

Poole continued
An attractive Georgian building situated in the old part of Poole, near all the local attractions. Offers professional service and an imaginative menu, using fresh produce.

PORTSMOUTH Hampshire **Map 4 C2**
⊗££ **THE SEAFARER STEAK HOUSE AND FISH RESTAURANT** 177-185 Elm Grove, Southsea, Portsmouth.
Hours: Meals served: Monday to Thursday 7pm - 10pm, Friday 6.30pm - 10.30pm and Saturday 6pm - 11pm. Closed Sunday.
Cuisine: English with strong European influence, using fresh daily market produce. ⊨ None. **CC** Access, Visa. **Other Points:** Children welcome, with special juniors menu. & **(V) Directions:** Follow M275 to Portsmouth, follow signs to Southsea.
TIM HUNT ☎ (0705) 827188.
A steak house style restaurant, situated near the central shopping centre, offering good grills, interesting fish dishes and a daily market produce board. Friendly efficient service and a welcoming pre-dinner bar.

PUCKERIDGE Hertfordshire **Map 5 B1**
⊗£ **THE WHITE HART** High Street.
Hours: Meals 12 noon - 2pm and 6pm - 9.45pm. Closed: Christmas and Boxing Day. **Cuisine:** Shellfish and seafood, eg.lobster thermidor,swordfish steaks,langoustines. Vegetarian dishes. ⊨ None. **CC** Access, Visa, Diners. **Other Points:** Childen welcome. No dogs. ▯ & **(V) Directions:** Situated at the junction of A10/A120 to Stansted airport.
COLIN & RITA BOOM ☎ (0920) 821309.
16th century coaching inn, once the legendary hideout of Dick Turpin and an overnight stop for Samuel Pepys. Renowned for its warm family atmosphere and floodlit beer garden.

RAMSGATE Kent **Map 5 C2**
⊗££ **MORTON'S FORK** 42 Station Road, Minster, Nr Ramsgate,
⌂££ Thanet.
[CLUB] **Hours:** Restaurant open from 11.30am - 2pm, and 6.30pm - 10pm (last orders). Closed: Mondays. Bar meals also served. **Cuisine:** British and continental cuisine, including salmon parcel and chicken ginger, with good vegetarian dishes available. ⊨ 3 double rooms, with en suite facilities. **CC** All major cards. **Other Points:** Children welcome. No dogs allowed. Garden dining. Open for Sunday lunch. ▯ & **(V) Directions:** Situated opposite the church in Minster just off Thanet Way (A253).
MR DAVID J SWORDER ☎ (0843) 821224.
A charming 17th century restaurant and wine bar, situated in a quiet, historical village, only 5 miles from Ramsgate. The atmsophere is relaxed and friendly and the menu offers imaginative dishes. The guest rooms have been attractively refurbished, retaining character yet providing modern conveniences.

READING Berkshire **Map 4 B2**
⌂£££ **ABBEY HOUSE HOTEL** 118 Connaught Road, Reading.
[CLUB] ⊨ 10 single, 4 double and 10 twin bedrooms, 11 of them en suite. Colour TV, radio, alarm, direct dial telephone and tea/coffee making facilities in all rooms. Reduced rates at weekends.

Reading continued

Hours: Breakfast 7.15am - 9am and dinner 7pm - 8pm. Bar snacks 6.30pm - 8.30pm. **CC** Access, Visa, AmEx. **Other Points:** Children welcome. No dogs. Open bank holidays. Fax No.(0734) 569299. Vegetarian meals available. **P (V) Directions:** From town centre, A329 under railway bridge. 3rd turning on left.
PETER & CHRISTINE PECK ☎ (0734) 590549.

The Abbey House Hotel offers remarkably good value accommodation for Reading, a notoriously expensive area. Guests receive a warm welcome, clean comfortable rooms and a good choice of evening meals. Located in a pleasant suburban road not far from the centre of Reading and convenient for London, Henley, Ascot and Windsor. Rail link to Heathrow and Gatwick.

⊗££ **CALCOT HOTEL** 98 Bath Road, Calcot, Reading.
⊞££££ **Hours:** Breakfast 7.30am - 9am, Lunch and bar meals 12 noon - 2.30pm, Dinner 7pm - 10pm (last orders). **Cuisine:** House specialities may include chargrilled steaks, Baked Chicken with Brie, Rack of Ribs with Barbecue sauce. Traditional Sunday lunch. ⇔ 78 bedrooms, 61 en suite. **CC** Access, Visa, AmEx. **Other Points:** Children welcome. Afternoon teas. Garden dining. Conference & meeting facilities for 6 - 65 delegates. No dogs. Fax No: (0734) 451223. **P** & **(V) Directions:** Less than 1 mile from Jct 12, M4. On the A4 towards Reading.
CALCOT HOTELS LTD ☎ (0734) 416423.

Although only a short distance from the M4 and Reading town centre, Calcot Hotel provides peace and quiet in relaxing, spacious surrondings. An informal atmsophere awaits diners in Restaurant Ninety Eights where there is a good choice of freshly prepared, imaginative modern dishes. Bar snacks are served in the comfortable Arch Bar at lunchtimes.

⊗££ **HONG HONG RESTAURANT** 14 West Street, Reading.
Hours: Open Monday to Thursday 12 noon - 11.30pm, Friday to Saturday from 12 noon - 12 midnight. Sunday 1pm- 11.30pm. Fully licensed. **Cuisine:** Peking, Cantonese and Szechuan food - crispy aromatic duck, Peking style imperial hors d-ouvres, Cantonese style spicy Szechuan prawn. ⇔ None. **CC** All major cards. **Other Points:** Children welcome. No dogs. Parties of more than 50 people catered for in private room. & **Directions:** In the town centre opposite the Co-op, next to Prontaprint.
NGHU CHAN & GENEVIEVE ONG ☎ (0734) 585372/507472
A friendly, traditional Chinese restaurant serving an interesting selection of regional Chinese specialities, wines and liqueurs.

⊗££ **THE SHIP HOTEL** 4/8 Duke Street, Reading.
⊞££££ **Hours:** Breakfast 7.30am - 9.30am, Lunch 12 noon - 2pm, Dinner 7pm - 10pm (last orders). Bar meals served all day until 11pm. Restaurant closed: Saturday and Bank Holiday lunch times. **Cuisine:** Bar snacks, Carvery menu and table d'hote menu. Dishes may include Scottish Venison, Fillets of Salmon, Rack of Lamb, Roast Beef. ⇔ 30 bedrooms, all en suite. **CC** All major cards. **Other Points:** Children welcome. Afternoon teas. No dogs allowed. Residents lounge. Fax No: (0734) 504450. **P (V) Directions:** M4 junction 10, A329. Follow signs to Queens Rd car park.
SPRING HOTELS LTD ☎ (0734) 583455.

Reading continued

An old coaching inn that has been well-modernised to form a comfortable hotel. The food is of a high standard and offers good value for money. There is a choice of bar snacks, a Carvery or a table d'hote dinner menu - all using predominantly fresh produce. Efficient, welcoming service.

⊗£££ **UPCROSS HOTEL** 68 Berkeley Avenue, Reading.
Hours: Open normal hotel hours. Restaurant open for lunch and dinner. **Cuisine:** Imaginative menus, herbs and vegetables from the garden whenever possible. ⊨ 26 bedrooms, 22 en suite, all with telephone, colour TV, radio and child alert. **CC** Access, Visa, AmEx. **Other Points:** Children welcome. **P** **Directions:** A4, Prospect Pk on left. Pass Beefeater mini r'about, right at next.
JESSICA & NICOLA CECIL ☎ (0734) 590796/391573
The hotel has the atmosphere of a small country house. The restaurant is in a romantic setting and overlooks the spacious garden. Conference facilities are available with their own entrance leading to the large carpark. The Town Centre, Railway Station and M4 junctions 11 and 12, are only 5 minutes away.

REDHILL Surrey Map 5 C1
⊗£ **WILLIAM IV** Little Common Lane, Bletchingley, Nr Redhill.
Hours: Lunch 12 noon - 2pm, Dinner 7pm - 9.30pm (last orders). Bar open 11am - 3pm, 6pm - 11pm. Snacks only served on Sundays. **Cuisine:** Extensive menu including grills, homemade pies, curries, pizzas, fish dishes. Daily specials and bar meals. ⊨ None. **CC** None. **Other Points:** Children welcome. Beer garden. Dogs on leads allowed. Bank Holiday barbecues. **P** **(V)** **Directions:** At the top of Bletchingley High St (A25). Signposted to Merstham.
BRIAN & SANDRA STRANGE ☎ (0883) 743278.
A traditional British village pub with compact bars and an old English garden. The pub offers an extensive a la carte & bar meals menu with dishes ranging from salmon en croute to homemade steak & kidney pie. Friendly, efficient service complements the warm, bustling atmosphere of the pub. Ideally situated for walks over the North Downs.

REEDHAM Norfolk Map 5 A2
⊗££ **REEDHAM FERRY INN** Reedham.
Hours: Meals served 11am - 3pm (12 noon Sunday) and 6.30pm - 11pm (7pm - 10.30pm Sunday). **Cuisine:** Wide selection of bar meals, including childrens meals. ⊨ None. **CC** Access, Visa. **Other Points:** Children welcome. Pets allowed. **P**
MR D.N. ARCHER ☎ (0493) 700429.
Situated on the River Yare, adjacent to the Ferry crossing, this popular old inn provides a pleasant stop for locals and tourists alike. Well presented, well served, good value meals and welcoming family atmosphere. Riverside tables and chairs with garden.

CENTRAL & SOUTHERN ENGLAND

REIGATE Surrey **Map 5 C1**
⊗££££ **LA BARBE RESTAURANT** 71 Bell Street, Reigate.
🄲🄳 **Hours:** Lunch served 12 noon - 2pm, dinner 2pm - 10pm. Closed:
CLUB Saturday & Sunday lunchtimes. **Cuisine:** Fine selection of classical and traditional, provincial French cuisine. Menu changes about every 8 weeks. Special theme evenings. ⊯ None. **CC** Access, Visa.
Other Points: Children welcome. No dogs. Vegetarian dishes available on request. Parking available opposite restaurant.
Directions: On A217, direction Gatwick Airport and Brighton.
ANTOINE JALLEY & SERGE TASSI ☎ (0737) 241966.
With its Gallic atmosphere, La Barbe serves a fine selection of classical and traditional, provincial cuisine. Head chef, Laurent Pacaud, personally selects only the highest quality and freshest produce from the market. A comfortable and intimate interior, excellent service and a good wine list complement the outstanding cuisine. Highly recommended.

RICHMOND Surrey **Map 5 B1**
⊗££ **CAFE ROUGE** 7a Petersham Road, Richmond.
Hours: Open 10am - 11pm, 7 days a week. A la carte and bar meals. **Cuisine:** Traditional French cuisine. Menu changes every 3 months, but generally offers Toulouse Sausages, Marmite Dieppoise and Plats du Jour. ⊯ None. **CC** Access, Visa. **Other Points:** Children welcome. No dogs. Afternoon teas. Open Sundays and Bank holidays. Switch cards accepted. ♿ **(V)**
Directions: Through Richmond from A3, follow one-way to Petersham, past Odeon.
CAFE ROUGE LTD ☎ (081) 332 2423.
A lively bar and restaurant, with rear conservatory, polished wood floors, chandeliers, oil paintings and posters. The food is fresh, of excellent quality and served in ample proportions. River Thames, Kew gardens, Richmond Park and Hampton Court nearby.

⊗£ **CAFFE MAMMA** 24 Hill Street, Richmond.
Hours: Meals 12 noon - 12 midnight. Closed: Christmas Day, Boxing Day and New Year's Eve. **Cuisine:** Italian, specialising in pasta dishes. ⊯ None. **CC** Access, Visa, AmEx. **Other Points:** Children welcome. No dogs. ♿ **(V) Directions:** In the centre of Richmond, near Odeon cinema.
TIM DIXON-NUTTALL ☎ (081) 940 1625.
Decorated in the style of a Neapolitan cafe with typical Italian ambience. Situated in the main shopping area of Richmond, not far from the river. Caffe Mamma enjoys a good reputation in the area and is popular with all ages.

⊗£££ **MALLARD'S WINE BAR AND RESTAURANT** Riverside House, Water Lane, Richmond Upon Thames.
Hours: Lunch 12 noon - 2.30pm, Dinner 6.30pm - 10.30pm (last orders). Bar meals 11.30am - 2.30pm and 5.30pm - 7pm. Closed: Christmas Day only. **Cuisine:** French-style cuisine. Dishes may include Medallions of Beef with a malt whisky sauce, Brochette of Scallops, Scottish Salmon with a light cream sauce. ⊯ None. **CC** Access, Visa, AmEx. **Other Points:** Children welcome. No dogs. Limited riverside dining. **(V) Directions:** On river front, next to single track lane leading from post office.
DAVID RUSSELL ☎ (081) 948 7733.

Richmond continued

In a delightful situation by Richmond's riverside development, Mallard's is a popular wine bar with a la carte restaurant. In summer, enjoy the continental atmosphere whilst relaxing over a drink by the river. The restaurant adjoins the bar and shares the same busy atmosphere. The French cuisine is of a high standard with all dishes well-cooked and presented.

RICKLING GREEN Essex **Map 5 B1**

⊗££ **CRICKETERS ARMS** Rickling Green, nr Saffron Walden. ⌂££ **Hours:** Bar meals 12 noon - 2pm and 7pm - 10pm 7 days a week. Restaurant open 7 days a week Monday to Saturday 12 noon - 2pm and 7pm - 9.45pm, Sundays 12 noon - 3.30pm and 7pm - 9pm. **Cuisine:** Bar: a range of grills and casseroles, steak and kidney pie, mussels a speciality. Restaurant: 3 table d'hote menus using English and French cuisine. ⮑ 7 Ensuite bedrooms. **CC** Access, Visa, AmEx. **Other Points:** Children welcome. Garden. Fax No. (079988) 512 **P** **(V) Directions:** Of the A11 in Rickling Green opposite the village green.
TIM & JO PROCTOR ☎ (079988) 322 & 595
A large village pub and restaurant facing the village green where cricket is played on summer weekends. This is a lively and very popular pub with an imaginative menu and within easy travelling distance of London. 10 minutes drive from Stansted Airport.

RIDGMONT Bedfordshire **Map 4 B2**

⌂£ **THE FIRS GUEST HOUSE** 85 High Street, Ridgmont.
⮑ 1 single, 1 double and 5 twin bedrooms, with H&C. 1 bathroom, 1 shower. **Hours:** Breakfast 6.30am - 9.00am. Dinner served 7.30pm to 9.00pm. **CC** None. **Other Points:** Central heating. Children welcome. No dogs. Residents lounge. TV for guests use. Garden for guests use. Closed Christmas and New Year. **P Directions:** On the A507.
SYLVIA WOOLARD ☎ (052 528) 279
A listed Georgian building close to Woburn Abbey and Wild Animal Kingdom. Situated on A507 with good access for Junction 13 of M1, the Firs Guest House is well placed for all the local attractions.

⊗£ **THE ROSE & CROWN** 89 High Street, Ridgmont, nr Woburn. ⌐CLUB⌐ **Hours:** Meals 12 noon - 2pm and 6.30pm - 10.30pm. **Cuisine:** Daily specials, grills. ⮑ None. **CC** All major cards. **Other Points:** Children welcome. **P** & **Directions:** On the main street in Ridgmont.
NEIL & ELIZABETH McGREGOR ☎ (052 5280) 245.
A 300 year old country pub with a prize-winning large garden. Patio for barbecues. Games room and conference and private party facilities. Recommended for its traditional ales and also offers an extensive wine list.

RINGWOOD Hampshire **Map 4 C1**

⊗££ **THE STRUAN HOTEL** Horton Road, Ashley Heath, Ringwood. ⌂££££ **Hours:** Breakfast 7.30am - 9.30am, Lunch and bar snacks 12 noon - 2pm, Dinner and bar snacks 7pm - 10pm (last orders). **Cuisine:** A la carte and table d'hote. Traditional Sunday Roasts. Seasonal speciality dishes. ⮑ 10 bedrooms, all en suite. **CC** All major cards.

Ringwood continued
> **Other Points:** Children welcome. Afternoon teas. Residents'
> lounge. Garden. Fully licensed bar. Fax No. (0425) 480529. ▣ 🚻
> **(V) Directions:** A31 Ashley Heath R'about to Horton Road, half a
> mile on the right.
> JOHN & WENDY HAYWOOD ☎ (0425) 473553.
> *Set in wooded surroundings, this Country Inn is ideally situated*
> *for all the beauty spots of the New Forest. The gracefully*
> *furnished accommodation is of a high standard, and good food*
> *featuring seasonal specialities can be enjoyed in the romantic*
> *candlelit restaurant. The friendly bar has traditional*
> *furnishings, oak beams and a real log fire to greet you in winter*
> *months.*

RIPLEY Surrey **Map 4 C2**
⊗£££££ **MICHELS RESTAURANT** High Street, Ripley.
> **Hours:** Lunch 12.30pm - 1.45pm (last orders), Dinner 7.30pm -
> 9pm (last orders). On Saturday dinner 7pm - 9.30pm (last orders).
> Closed: All day Monday, Saturday lunch, Sunday dinner.
> **Cuisine:** Imaginative French cuisine using the best in fresh
> produce. ⇌ None. 💳 Access, Visa. **Other Points:** Children very
> welcome for Sunday lunch. Garden. ▣ **(V) Directions:** M25 exit
> 10 to A3. Middle of the High Street in Ripley.
> ERIK & KAREN MICHEL ☎ (0483) 224777/222940
> *The spacious interior of this Georgian house provides the best in*
> *comfort and decor and is the ideal setting in which to enjoy the*
> *outstanding cuisine. The innovative French cooking is of the*
> *highest standard and is complemented by professional service.*
> *Michels Restaurant is the perfect choice for a special occasion.*
> *Very highly recommended.*

ROLLESBY Norfolk **Map 5 A2**
⬜£££ **THE OLD COURT HOUSE** Court Road, Rollesby, Great
Yarmouth.
> ⇌ 2 double en suite, 1 twin en suite, 2 family suites and 2 family
> bedrooms. 2 bathrooms. Tea/coffee making facilities.
> **Hours:** Breakfast 8am - 9am and dinner 6.30pm (summer) and
> 7pm (winter), 24 hour notice usually required. 💳 None. **Other**
> **Points:** Central heating. Children welcome. Licensed. Residents
> lounge with TV. Garden. Outdoor heated swimming pool.
> Bicycles for hire. Free tennis nearby. ▣ **Directions:** Off A149, 9
> miles from Great Yarmouth.
> MR & MRS B L MARRINER ☎ (0493) 369665.
> *Built in 1775 as a country work house, used in the late 1800s as a*
> *Court House (hence the name) and now a comfortable, well-*
> *modernised character hotel in a peaceful, rural location near*
> *the broads. The evening meals are wonderful value and will*
> *make you long to return. After a tasty home cooked meal, retire*
> *in style to the dungeons (that were), now a cosy bar.*

ROMFORD Essex **Map 5 B1**
⊗£ **THE SCHOOLHOUSE** Church Road, Noak Hill, Romford.
> **Hours:** Meals 12 noon - 2.30pm and 7pm - 11pm (last orders
> 9.30pm). Advisable to book in advance. Closed: Sunday evening
> and Bank Holidays. **Cuisine:** Traditional Sunday roast, vegetarian
> dishes, homemade desserts. ⇌ None. 💳 None. **Other Points:**

Romford continued

Children welcome. No dogs. ▣ ᝤ **(V) Directions**: From A12 at Gallow's Corner,take Straight Rd to end and turn right.
FIONA RICHARDS & TONY MERRY ☎ (04023) 49900.
As the name suggests, the building is a converted school house which has been tastefully redecorated. Comfortable bar for pre-dinner drinks. Flowers presented at table by prior order. Celebration sponge cakes made to order. Selection of paintings by local artists always available.

ROMSEY Hampshire **Map 4 C1**

⊗£ **COBWEB TEA ROOMS** 49 The Hundred, Romsey.
Hours: Morning coffee 10am - 12 noon, lunch 12 noon - 2pm, teas 2pm - 5.30pm. Closed: Sunday and Monday (except Bank Holidays). **Cuisine**: Homemade cakes and sweets. Toasted sandwiches. Light lunches. ⊨ None. **CC** None. **Other Points**: Children welcome. No dogs. Limited access for disabled. Public car park close by. **(V) Directions**: In the main street in Romsey on the A27,100yds from Broadlands Est.
MISS ANGELA WEBLEY ☎ (0794) 516434.
Situated in the centre of town, this friendly tea room has a restful atmosphere with a soft green colour scheme inside and an attractive Tea Garden. Broadlands and Romsey Abbey nearby.

⊗££ **SOUTH GARDEN CANTONESE & PEKINESE CUISINE** 9 Bell Street, Romsey.
Hours: Lunch 12.15pm - 2.15pm, Dinner 6pm - 11.30pm. **Cuisine**: Cantonese & Pekinese cusine including Sizzling dishes and a wide choice of seafood dishes. Extensive menu. Set dinners and English dishes also available. ⊨ None. **CC** Access, Visa, AmEx. **Other Points**: Children welcome. No smoking area. Parking nearby. Special monthly set menu available. **(V) Directions**: Centre of Romsey, approx 200yds from Romsey Abbey. Behind Town Hall.
JASON MAN ☎ (0794) 514428.
An elgant restaurant in the centre of Romsey offering excellent food in comfortable surroundings. All dishes are cooked from fresh ingredients and beautifully presented. Cantonese cuisine is based on freshness and stir fried cooking whilst Pekinese cuisine is more spicy and aromatic. The wine list includes Chinese wines. Excellent, welcoming service.

ROTHERWICK Hampshire **Map 4 C2**

⊗££££ **TYLNEY HALL** Rotherwick, Nr Hook.
⌣ **Hours**: Breakfast 7.30am - 10am, Lunch 12.30pm - 3pm, dinner 7.30pm - 9.30pm (last orders). **Cuisine**: A la Carte and Table d'hote menus. Haute cuisine. ⊨ 91 bedrooms, all en suite. **CC** All major cards. **Other Points**: Children welcome. Garden. Afternoon teas. No dogs. Functions, conferences, seminars. Indoor and outdoor sports facilites. ▣ ᝤ **(V) Directions**: From M3 junction 5, A287 to Basingstoke, follow signs to Rotherwick.
RITA MOONEY - General Manager ☎ (0256) 764881.
A magnificent Grade II listed mansion set in 66 acres of beautiful countryside. Respectfully restored Tylney Hall is now a gracious Country House Hotel with an atmosphere of calm and unhurried ease. The glass domed restaurant offers excellently

Rotherwick continued

cooked and presented haute cuisine which is served by highly professional staff. The ideal choice for any special occassion.

ROTHLEY Leicestershire **Map 4 A2**

⊗££ **THE RED LION INN** Rothley.

Hours: Restaurant open 12 noon - 2pm and 7pm - 10pm (last orders). Restaurant closed Saturday lunch and Sunday dinner. Bar meals 12 noon - 2pm and 6pm - 10pm. Open throughout the year. **Cuisine:** Regional French and English dishes. Traditional Sunday lunch. Extensive Bar Snacks. Vegetarian menu. Summer barbecue. ⊨ None. **CC** All major cards. **Other Points:** Children welcome. 'Dimboland' - a playground for the young. **P** & **(V) Directions:** Betw. Leicester & Loughborough at Rothley Crossrds. B5328 & old A6.

MRS IRENE DIMBLEBEE ☎ (0533) 302488.

An old farmhouse converted to a coaching inn and trading since about 1725. A la carte meals, bar platters and snacks are served every day.

ROYSTON Hertfordshire **Map 5 B1**

⊗£ **BRITISH RAJ INDIAN RESTAURANT** 55 High Street, Royston.

Hours: Meals 12 noon - 3pm and 6pm - 12 midnight. **Cuisine:** Lamb masala - a whole leg of lamb cooked for four. Tandoori, royal, karai dishes. English menu also available. Thalia dishes including wedding feast. ⊨ None. **CC** All major cards. **Other**

Royston continued

    Points: Children welcome. No dogs. Coaches by appointment. &

    (V)

    NAZIR UDDIN CHOUDHURY ☎ (0763) 241471.

    Reputed to be one of East Anglia's best Indian restaurants. All
    'Miss East Anglias' since 1977 have held press days here! With
    a varied Indian menu this restaurant has a broad appeal.

RUGELEY Staffordshire **Map 4 A1**

⊗££ **CEDAR TREE HOTEL** Main Road (A51), Rugeley.

    Hours: Meals 7am - 9am, 12 noon - 2pm and 7pm - 10pm.
    Cuisine: Flambe dishes. ⊨ 30 bedrooms, 21 en suite. **CC** All
    major cards. **Other Points:** Children welcome. No dogs. **P** &
    Directions: 5 miles from Lichfield.

    S E ROWE ☎ (0889) 584241/2

    Listed William and Mary building with furnishings in the
    restaurant to reflect the era. Located close to Cannock Chase, an
    outstanding beauty spot, the hotel is easy to spot by the vast
    cedar tree growing outside.

RUISLIP Greater London **Map 4 B2**

⊗£ **RUISLIP TANDOORI** 115 High Street, Ruislip.

    Hours: Lunch 12 noon - 2.30pm, dinner 6pm - 12 midnight
    (11.45pm last orders). Closed: Christmas and Boxing Day.
    Cuisine: Chicken Zhal Frazi, Chicken Tikka Massalla, Butter
    Chicken, Chicken Nepal, Chicken Chilly Massala, Chicken
    Katmandu and Karai dishes. Set Nepalese Thali. ⊨ None. **CC** All
    major cards. **Other Points:** Children welcome. No dogs. & **(V)**
    Directions: On the main street in Ruislip opposite MacDonalds.

    K B RAICHHETRI ☎ (0895) 632859/674890

    A 60-seater tandoori restaurant serving Nepalese cuisine. The
    atmosphere is set by subdued lighting and soft background
    music. Well patronised by the locals.

RYE East Sussex **Map 5 C1**

⊡££ **AVIEMORE GUEST HOUSE** 28-30 Fishmarket Road, Rye.

    CLUB ⊨ 8 bedrooms - 2 doubles en suite, 1 twin en suite, 2 twin, 1
    double and 1 single with shared facilities. All rooms have
    tea/coffee making facilities, shaving points, central heating.
    Hours: Breakfast 7.30am - 9am. **CC** Access, Visa, AmEx. **Other**
    Points: Children welcome. Residents' lounge with colour TV.
    Residents' dining room. All en suites luxuriously appointed. 60
    miles London, 11 miles Hastings/Battle. **Directions:** Off A259,
    beneath Rye Town.

    MRS DAWN KEAY ☎ (0797) 223052.

    A Victorian House with lovely views of the river Rother and only
    2 minutes walk from the town centre. Attractively decorated
    with East African artifacts. Comfortable accommodation. Mrs
    Keay provides a warm and friendly welcome for everyone.

⊗££ **FLACKLEY ASH HOTEL AND RESTAURANT** Peasmarsh,
ᐛ nr Rye.

    W **Hours:** Restaurant open 12.30pm - 1.45pm and 7pm - 9.45pm.
    CLUB **Cuisine:** Fresh plaice, dabs, lobster and shellfish. Carpetbagger
    steak and veal. ⊨ 32 bedrooms, all en suite. **CC** All major cards.
    Other Points: Children welcome. Indoor swimming pool and

Rye continued

leisure centre. Fax No: (079 721) 510. ◘ **(V) Directions**: Off the A21 at Flimwell, on the A268 in Peasmarsh.Set back off road. CLIVE & JEANIE BENNETT ☎ (079 721) 651.
The rooms are comfortable, the service excellent and the restaurant offers French and English cuisine. There are many points of local interest eg, Bodiam Castle, Hastings and Camber Sands.

⌖£££ **JEAKE'S HOUSE** Mermaid Street, Rye.

🛏 12 rooms, 1 single, 1 twin, 7 double and 3 family bedrooms, 10 en suite. TV and telephone in all rooms. **Hours**: Breakfast 8am - 9am. Sunday 8.30am - 9.30am. **CC** Access, Visa, AmEx. **Other Points**: Residential Bar. Fax (0797) 222623. Public car park close by. Vegetarian breakfast available. **Directions**: Old town centre. FRANCIS & JENNY HADFIELD ☎ (0797) 222828.
This beautiful listed building (1689) is set in one of Britains most picturesque medieval cobbled streets. Furnished with antiques, the bedrooms overlook the roof tops of Rye or face south across the marsh to the sea. Outstanding comfort and value for money.

⊗££ **THE HOPE AND ANCHOR HOTEL** Watchbell Street, Rye.
⌖£££ **Hours**: Breakfast 8am - 9.30am, lunch 12 noon - 2pm and dinner 7pm - 9pm (last orders, 9.30pm Friday and Saturday). Bar meals 12 noon - 2pm and 6pm - 9pm. **Cuisine**: Fresh local fish dishes, Dijon lamb, imaginative ice creams and sorbets. 🛏 15 bedrooms, 10 en suite. **CC** Access, Visa. **Other Points**: Children welcome. Afternoon teas. Parking available outside Hotel. Vegetarian dishes on request. Fax as telephone no. **Directions**: Watchbell Street is a right turn from Church Square.
LENA & DERRICK BALDOCK ☎ (0797) 222216.
The Hope & Anchor is a comfortable 17th century hotel at the end of a cobbled street in the ancient town of Rye. Overlooking the river, there are panoramic views of the surrounding countryside with Romney Marsh and the sea to the east and the historic town of Winchelsea to the west.

⊗££ **THE OLD FORGE RESTAURANT** 24 Wish Street, Rye.
Hours: Lunch 12.30pm - 2pm, dinner 6.30pm - 10pm. Closed: Tuesday and Wednesday lunchtime and all day Sunday and Monday. **Cuisine**: Specialities include fresh local fish, shellfish and chargrilled steaks. 🛏 None. **CC** Access, Visa. **Other Points**: Children welcome. No dogs. Street parking after 6pm. Public car park opposite restaurant. ♿ **(V) Directions**: On western side of Rye where Wish St. joins the main A259.
DEREK BAYNTUN ☎ (0797) 223227.
Originally a forge, the building was bought and converted by the present owner. Highly recommended for its good food within a reasonable price limit, friendly service and informal atmosphere. A large open fire adds to the character and atmosphere of the restaurant during winter.

SALEHURST East Sussex **Map 5 C1**
⊗££ **SALEHURST HALT** nr Robertsbridge.
Hours: Open 12 noon - 3pm and 7pm - 11pm (9.30pm last orders). Closed: Tuesday. **Cuisine**: Good bar and restaurant food. 🛏 None. **CC** Access, Visa. **Other Points**: Children welcome. ◘

Salehurst continued

Directions: ½ mile off the A21 adjacent to Salehurst Parish Church.

TREVOR & SHANE STEED ☎ (0580) 880620.

A small country inn in an attractive Sussex village. Good food and real ales are served in a friendly, informal atmosphere.

SALISBURY Wiltshire **Map 4 C1**

⊗£   **FINDERS KEEPERS** Southampton Road, Landford, Nr Salisbury.

Hours: Lunch Tuesday to Saturday 10.30am - 5.30pm and Dinner 6.30pm - 9.30pm. Sunday lunch 12 noon - 5.30pm. Closed: Sunday evening and Monday. **Cuisine:** A wide variety of traditional fayre and local dishes with the emphasis on fresh produce and all homemade sweets. ⊨ None. **CC** Access, Visa, AmEx. **Other Points:** Children welcome. Garden. Afternoon teas. **P** **(V) Directions:** On A36, on the left travelling west from Southampton.

KIM & SUZANNE SPROAT ☎ (0794) 390331.

This cottage style building is surrounded by well kept grounds which are lit up at night. It is decorated in a light attractive colour scheme and comfortably furnished. Serving well presented and cooked meals, the atmosphere is relaxed and is complemented by the soft tones of music in the background. Excellent value.

⊗£   **GEORGE & DRAGON** 85 Castle Street, Salisbury.

Hours: Full menu served 12 noon - 2.30pm and 6pm - 9pm (7pm - 9pm Sundays). Closed: Christmas Day. **Cuisine:** Grills, roasts, salads and daily specials. All meals prepared with fresh vegetables and produce wherever possible. ⊨ None. **CC** All major cards. **Other Points:** Dogs allowed under strict control. Barbecue area for hire for summer parties. **Directions:** By the river in Salisbury.

JOHN & WENDY WADDINGTON ☎ (0722) 333942.

A small family pub dating back to the early 16th century within 5 minutes walk of the city centre. Real ales, keg bitters, bottled beers and an extensive wine list are offered to compliment the variety of meals available. Enjoy the riverside garden - or barbecue your own meal in summer.

⊗£   **HOGS HEAD** Wilton Road.

Hours: Lunch 12 noon - 2.15pm, Dinner 6pm - 10pm. **Cuisine:** Wide range of pub food from chilli/curry to steak and kidney pies

---

Salisbury continued

and battered squid rings. Desserts include sherry trifle and pancake rolls. None. **CC** None. **Other Points:** No children. No dogs allowed. ▣ ⟨ **(V) Directions:** A36 to Wilton/Bath, just past Salisbury station.

T C BROOK ☎ (0722) 27064

Offers a wide range of food at excellent value. Very friendly pub atmosphere.

⊗£ **THE COACH AND HORSES** Winchester Street, Salisbury.
£££ **Hours:** Breakfast 8am -12 noon, serving from 10am - 10pm. Closed: Christmas Day. Open Bank Holidays. **Cuisine:** Varied menu with large selection. Dishes may include - Venison in Ruddles, Chicken Monaco, Scottish Salmon. 2 en suite bedrooms. **CC** Access, Visa. **Other Points:** Children welcome. Afternoon teas. No smoking area. Garden dining. Fax No. (0722) 414319. Off street parking. NCP parking at rear. ⟨ **(V) Directions:** 100 metres from Market Square.

MARTIN COOPER ☎ (0722) 336254.

A former Coaching Inn, the Coach and Horses offers an extensive menu of well-cooked and presented dishes at excellent value for money. Dishes range from a good choice of Ploughmans to burgers to Scotch Salmon with a choice of sauces. A busy pub and popular with all ages.

⊗£ **THE CROWN INN** Alvediston, Salisbury.
£££ **Hours:** Breakfast 7am - 11am, Lunch 12 noon - 2pm and Dinner 7pm - 10pm (last orders). Restaurant closed: Monday. **Cuisine:** A la carte and Table d'hote menus. Variations on French/English cuisine. Pork & Basil in pastry with lemon butter sauce. Bar menu also. 3 double bedrooms, all en suite, including 4 posters. **CC** Access, Visa. **Other Points:** Children welcome. Garden. Pets allowed. Afternoon teas. ▣ ⟨ **(V) Directions:** Off A30.

MARY MOXAM ☎ (0722) 780335

This is a beautifully maintained, Grade II listed, 15th Century thatched building with oaked beams. Nearby Fovant 'Badges', and scenic rolling countryside only add to the feeling of peace and contentment that surrounds this inn.

⊗£ **THE SWAN INN** Stoford, Nr Salisbury.
££ **Hours:** Breakfast 7am - 11am, lunch 11am - 3pm and dinner 6pm - 10.30pm (last orders 10.30pm). **Cuisine:** Chicken Espaniole, grilled trout with almonds, Irish stew. 8 bedrooms, 5 en suite. **CC** None. **Other Points:** Children welcome. Garden dining. Open bank holidays and Sunday. ▣ **(V) Directions:** Situated on the A36, 6 miles west of Salisbury.

AUSTIN & THERESA EMERY ☎ (0722) 790236.

Set in the beautiful Wylye Valley, fronting onto the River Wylye. This well presented old coaching inn offers a good standard of home cooked food in friendly comfortable surroundings. With well tended garden to the rear and riverside seats opposite.

££ **VICTORIA LODGE** 61 Castle Road, Salisbury.
3 single, 5 double, 6 twin and 2 family bedrooms, all en suite. 1 bathroom. 1 shower. TVs in all rooms. **Hours:** Breakfast 7am - 9am, and dinner 6pm - 9pm (order by 8.30pm). Closed: Christmas. **CC** None. **Other Points:** Central heating. Children welcome. Dogs

Salisbury continued

allowed. Lounge. Garden. Licensed bar. Fax No: (0722) 414507.
🅿 ♿ **Directions:** Off the A345, 1st right leaving Salisbury.
GRAHAM FITCH ☎ (0722) 320586.

A warm, comfortable, friendly guest house offering traditional English hospitality and food. Set away from the main streets of Salisbury, nonetheless the centre is within easy walking distance. A welcome retreat after a day of touring Wessex, Stonehenge, Wilton House or the Cathedral.

⊗££ **WHITE HORSE HOTEL** 38 Castle Street, Salisbury.
⏛££ **Hours:** 7.30am - 9.30am, 12 noon - 2.30pm and 7pm - 9.30pm
(last orders). Bar meals 12 noon - 2.30pm and 7pm - 9.30pm (last orders). **Cuisine:** Traditional English and French cuisine. ⌷ 12 bedrooms, 8 en suite, with colour TVs, radio, telephones, tea and coffee facilities. 💳 Access, Visa, Diners. **Other Points:** Children welcome. No dogs. 🅿 ♿ **(V) Directions:** In the city centre.
V LOPES ☎ (0722) 27844.

Offering comfort and a warm welcome in the heart of Salisbury, the White Horse Hotel is just a stroll from the market and the city's cathedral. There has been an inn on this site since the 13th century, and the present Victorian building has been refurbished so that guests can enjoy modern comforts.

SANDOWN Isle of Wight **Map 4 C2**
⊗£ **CULVER LODGE HOTEL & RESTAURANT** 17 Albert
⏛££ Road, Sandown, Isle Of Wight.
CLUB **Hours:** Breakfast 8.30am - 9am, Lunch 12 noon - 2pm and Dinner
6pm - 7pm (last orders). **Cuisine:** Table d'hote menu. ⌷ 20 bedrooms, all en suite. 💳 Access, Visa, AmEx. **Other Points:** Children welcome. No dogs. 🅿 **(V) Directions:** Albert Road runs off the main shopping street, parallel to seafront.
MRS LE LIEVRE ☎ (0983) 403819.

A family run hotel with glass frontage which looks out on shrubs and flower beds. Just a few minutes from beaches and entertainment for all ages, summer theatre and shops. Nightly entertainment.

⏛££ **OAKLANDS HOTEL** Yarbridge, Sandown.
CLUB ⌷ 1 single, 3 double, 1 twin and 5 family bedrooms, 9 en suite including 2 four posters. Colour TV with in-house video, hair dryer, clock radio and tea makers in all rooms. Trouser press & ironing facilities. Central heating. **Hours:** Breakfast 9am. Dinner 6.30pm - 7pm. 💳 Access, Visa. **Other Points:** Children over 5 years welcome. Garden. Dogs allowed. Heated outdoor swimming pool. Flood-lit boules. Aerospa. Vegetarian meals available. 🅿 **Directions:** On Ryde - Sandown Rd, 1 mile from Sandown in direction of Brading.
JOAN RAWLINGS & FAMILY ☎ (0983) 406197.

A friendly, family run, licensed hotel at the foot of the Brading Downs, offering cheerful service. Local activities include fishing, swimming and sailing. Ideal for walking holidays. The pool is heated to 82 degrees fahrenheit June to September.

CENTRAL & SOUTHERN ENGLAND

SAXMUNDHAM Suffolk **Map 5 B2**

⊗£ **WHITE HART HOTEL** High Street, Saxmundham.

⊞£target £ `CLUB` **Hours:** Breakfast 7am - 9am, Lunch 11.30am - 2.30pm, Dinner 6.30pm - 10pm. Sunday Lunch 12 noon - 2.30pm, Dinner 7pm - 9.30pm. **Cuisine:** Traditional home cooking. Dishes include Roast beef & Yorkshire Pudding, Steak & Kidney Pie, Deep fried Goujons of Plaice. ⊨ 8 bedrooms. **CC** All major cards. **Other Points:** Children welcome. Dogs allowed. **P Directions:** A12 mid way between Ipswich & Lowestoft.
MALCOLM & KATY BANKS ☎ (0728) 602009.
A Coaching Inn in the centre of the rural market town of Saxmundham. Good, home cooked food is well presented and served in generous portions. The table d'hote offers particularly good value for money. Friendly, welcoming service ensures that the atmosphere is friendly and relaxed. The bedrooms have been refurbished recently and offer a high standard of comfort.

SEAVIEW Isle of Wight **Map 4 C2**

⊗££ **SEAVIEW HOTEL & RESTAURANT** High Street, Seaview.

⌂ **Hours:** Meals 8am - 9.30am, 12 noon - 2pm and 7.30pm - 9.45pm (last orders). Restaurant closed Sunday evening, bar meals available all week. Booking advisable for restaurant. **Cuisine:** Local fish and shellfish. ⊨ 16 bedrooms, all en suite. **CC** Access, Visa, AmEx. **Other Points:** Children welcome. **P (V) Directions:** On the main street in centre of Seaview.
MR & MRS NICHOLAS HAYWARD ☎ (0983) 612711/612712
This Edwardian hotel is situated in the heart of the pretty village of Seaview. It is possible to while away many hours looking at the unique collection of prints of old ships and liners that once passed the hotel. Frequented by local characters and the visiting yachtsmen. Routiers Restaurant of the Year 1989.

SELLING Kent **Map 5 C2**

⊗£ **THE WHITE LION** The Street, Selling, nr Faversham.

`CLUB` **Hours:** Meals 12 noon - 2.30pm and 7pm - 10pm. Closed: Christmas Day. **Cuisine:** Traditional beef pudding, steak, kidney and mushroom pie. ⊨ None. **CC** Visa. **Other Points:** Children welcome. **P** & **(V)**
MR A C RICHARDS ☎ (0227) 752211.
This pub was originally an old coaching inn and still retains the old inglenook fireplaces, providing log fires in winter. Large garden with small pets corner and bird aviary. Jazz night every Tuesday evening.

SEVENOAKS Kent **Map 5 C1**

⊗£££ **SEVENOAKS PARK HOTEL** Seal Hollow Road, Sevenoaks.

⊞£££ **Hours:** Breakfast 7am - 9.30am, dinner 7pm - 9.30pm. Closed: Sundays. **Cuisine:** A la carte, table d'hote, dishes include Poached salmon served in lemon & mustard sauce, Breast of duck fried and served with strawberry & blackcurrant. ⊨ 27 rooms: 2 single, 14 twin, 10 double and 1 family bedroom. 18 en suite. **CC** All major cards. **Other Points:** Children welcome. Afternoon teas. Garden. Outdoor heated swimming pool. Fax (0732) 457468. & **(V) Directions:** Off A225.
MR NOBLE & MR HUNTLEY. ☎ (0732) 454245.
The Sevenoaks Park Hotel is a charming building standing in 3 acres of Elizabethan gardens overlooking superb views of Knole

Sevenoaks continued

Park. Offering well cooked and presented cuisine and attractive comfortable accommodation, the hotel provides guests with a pleasant and welcoming atmosphere. An ideal base for touring areas of interest such as Royal Tunbridge Wells and Leeds Castle.

⊗£ **THE RISING SUN** Cotmans Ash Lane, Woodlands, Kemsing, nr Sevenoaks
Hours: Lunch 11am - 2.30pm, dinner 7pm - 11pm. Sunday lunch 12 noon - 3pm, Sunday dinner 7pm - 10.30pm. **Cuisine:** A la carte menu, bar meals/snacks and vegetarian meals. Daily specialities available. ⊨ None. **CC** Access, Visa. **Other Points:** Children welcome. Garden. Dogs allowed. **P** **(V) Directions:** On M26.
MR DUNNE - Manager. ☎ (09592) 2683.
A 16th century building tastefuly decorated in keeping with the age of the establishment. Serving a good selection of value for money meals. Frequented by both locals and holiday makers as there is a caravan site on a farm 5 minutes away. The atmosphere is friendly and busy. A pub with plenty of character.

SHAFTESBURY Dorset **Map 4 C1**
⊗££ **THE BENETT ARMS** Semley, Shaftesbury.
⊞££ **Hours:** Breakfast 8.30am - 9.30am. Lunch 12 noon - 2pm, Dinner 7pm - 10pm. Restaurant closed: 25th and 26th December. **Cuisine:** Dishes in the restaurant may include steaks, Chicken Trois Frere, Traditional bar meals in the bar. ⊨ 5 bedrooms, all en suite. **CC** All major cards. **Other Points:** Children welcome. Garden. Dogs allowed. **P** ⅋ **(V) Directions:** 2 miles off the A350, north of Shaftesbury.
J C M DUTHIE ☎ (0747) 830221.
Built in the 17th century, 'The Benett Arms' overlooks the village green. With a choice of well cooked restaurant and bar meals, this pub caters for all tastes and occasions. A friendly, welcoming pub.

⊗££ **THE SUNRIDGE HOTEL** Bleke Street, Shaftesbury.
⊞£££ **Hours:** Breakfast 8am - 9am, dinner 7pm - 9pm (last orders 8.45pm). Closed: Sunday evenings. **Cuisine:** Dishes include Deep fried Camembert with apricot preserve, Lemon Chicken, Lamb & Apricot pie, 12 - 24oz T-bone steak. ⊨ 3 twin, 4 double and 3 family bedrooms, all en suite and with colour TV, radio and telephone. **CC** Access, Visa, AmEx. **Other Points:** Children welcome. Sauna. Heated indoor pool. **P** ⅋ **(V) Directions:** Between Salisbury and Yeovil on A30.
PAUL & JENNY WHITEMAN ☎ (0747) 53130.
Set in the thriving market town of Shaftesbury, and built in 1878, this character hotel is attractively decorated and the rooms are airy. One can enjoy a relaxed atmosphere and generous helpings of well presented and well cooked food. With a sauna and swimming pool, it is an ideal place to unwind.

CENTRAL & SOUTHERN ENGLAND

SHANKLIN Isle of Wight **Map 4 C2**

⊗£ **MELBOURNE ARDENLEA HOTEL** 4-6 Queens Road, ⏷£££ Shanklin.

Hours: Breakfast 8.30am - 9.30am, bar snacks 12 noon - 1.30pm, Dinner 6.30pm - 8pm (last orders). Closed: October to mid March. The restaurant is also open to non-residents. **Cuisine:** Full English breakfast, bar meals, table d'hote and a la carte menus. Homemade desserts are the speciality. ⊨ 52 bedrooms, all en suite. **CC** None. **Other Points:** Children welcome. Dogs allowed. Residents' lounge. Garden. Evening entertainment. Large indoor swimming pool. Sauna and solarium. **P** ⅄ **(V) Directions:** Take Coach Route through Shanklin.
ANNIE & WALLY CORBY, MICK & JAN DAWSON ☎ (0983) 862283.

Originally two Victorian houses, the Melbourne Ardenlea is a family run hotel set in well-tended gardens, close to the seafront and the Old Village. Decorated and furnished to a high standard, the hotel offers very comfortable accommodation. Indoor swimming pool, solarium, sauna and evening entertainment, plus all the attractions of Shanklin and the Isle of Wight.

⏷£££ **QUEENSMEAD HOTEL** Queens Road, Shanklin.
⊨ 2 single, 13 double, 10 twin and 6 family rooms, all with en suite facilities. All bedrooms have colour TV and tea/coffee making facilities. **Hours:** Breakfast 8.30am - 9am, lunch 12 noon - 2.30pm and dinner at 6.30pm. Closed: December, January and February except for Christmas. **CC** Access, Visa. **Other Points:** Children welcome. Vegetarian meals by arrangement. Garden. No dogs. Residents' lounge. No smoking area. Licensed. **P** **Directions:** Opposite the Church of St Saviour (very tall spire) on the cliff.
KEN, JEAN & JULIAN CHAPMAN ☎ (0983) 862342.

Positioned close to the famous Keats' Green area of Shanklin, just minutes from the sea, town and Old Village. An elegant Victorian villa with modern additions, the hotel has a large heated outdoor swimming pool and a sheltered rose arbor in the garden. The dining room is also open to non-residents, space allowing. Guaranteed personal all day service.

⏷££ **THE HAMBLEDON HOTEL** 11 Queens Road, Shanklin.
⊨ 11 rooms. 1 single, 1 twin, 6 double and 3 family bedrooms. All en suite. All rooms have radio, colour TV, hairdryer, shaving points and direct dial telephones. **Hours:** Breakfast 8.30am - 9am, dinner 6.30pm. **CC** Access, Visa. **Other Points:** Children welcome. Garden. Nappy washing and babysitting available. Qualified nursery nurse. Special diets catered for. Licensed bar. **P** **(V) Directions:** On the B3328.
NORMAN & BERYL BIRCH ☎ (0983) 862403.

A detached family run hotel surrounded by well kept gardens. Tastefully decorated in a traditional style to a high standard, the accommodation is very comfortable. This is an ideal place to stay if you have young children as there are special provisions for very young children including baby sitting - Mrs Birch is a trained nursery nurse.

SHERINGHAM Norfolk **Map 5 A2**

⊗££ **PRETTY CORNER CONT. CAFE & RESTAURANT** Pretty
Corner, Upper Sheringham.
Hours: Tea Garden Buttery: 10am - 5.30pm Easter - end
September (during autumn & winter the buttery meals are served
in the restaurant) Cont. Cafe-Restaurant open from 7pm and
Sunday lunchtime 12 noon (varies during high summer season
and winter months). **Cuisine:** Cream teas & continental coffees,
sandwiches, snacks in the buttery. Restaurant: Dutch and English
specialities. Special Indonesian evenings. ⊨ None. **CC** None.
Other Points: Children welcome. Dogs allowed. Outdoor seating.
Starting point for walks. Maps available. Garden parties by
appointment. Licensed. **P** & **(V) Directions:** A148, just off the
Cromer-Holt Rd. Signed at Pretty Corner Car Park.
PAUL H VAN DER HORST ☎ (0263) 822358.
*Pretty Corner is on the edge of one of Norfolk's beauty spots with
250 acres of woodlands. The Tea Garden is in 2 acres of gardens
with split level terraces and pond. The buttery serves a wide
range of refreshments and snacks and continental dishes are
served in the restaurant. A delightful place to relax whilst
visiting the Sheringham Woods. Excellent walks and riding.*

SHERSTON Wiltshire **Map 4 B1**

⊗£ **RATTLEBONE INN** Church Street, Sherston.
Hours: Lunch 12 noon - 2pm and dinner 7pm - 10pm (last orders).
Bar meals 12 noon - 2pm and dinner 7pm - 10pm. **Cuisine:**
Salmon steak with dill and lemon sauce, lamb with mustard and
rosemary, pork with stilton sauce, and homemade steak and
kidney pies. Daily specials. ⊨ None. **CC** Access, Visa. **Other
Points:** Children welcome. **P** **(V) Directions:** Acton Turville to
Malmesbury road. Past Post office.
ANNE & DAVE REES ☎ (0666) 840871.
*An old Cotswold inn with pretty gardens and boules pitch. The
lounge bar is full of nooks and crannies where every table has a
character of its own. Open fires in winter.*

SHIPTON ON STOUR Warwickshire **Map 4 B1**

⊗££ **HALFORD BRIDGE INN** Fosseway, Halford, Near Shipton On
⊓££ Stour.
Hours: Breakfast 8.30am - 9.30am (earlier by arrangement), lunch
12 noon - 2pm, Dinner 7pm - 9pm (last orders). Bar meals 12 noon
- 2pm and 6.30pm - 9.30pm (last orders). Sunday lunch 12 noon -
2pm & dinner 7pm - 8.30pm (non-residents bookings prefered).
Cuisine: Home cooking - all food is freshly prepared . Homemade
pies are especially popular. Bar snack menu. A la carte menu
available in restaurant. Sunday Roasts. ⊨ 5 bedrooms including
family room, 3 with private shower. All with colour TV. 2 Crown
E.T.B. **CC** Access, Visa. **Other Points:** Dogs allowed in the bar.
Courtyard with baskets and flower beds. Parties catered for. Real
Ale. **P** & **(V) Directions:** On the A429 in Halford, opp. Halford
Garage. 3 miles from Shipton.
TONY & GRETA WESTWOOD ☎ (0789) 740382.
*A lovely 16th century stone slate coaching inn at the edge of the
Cotswolds, 5 miles from Stratford Upon Avon. Family run, and
with log fires in winter, the atmosphere is friendly. The newly
refurbished and extended restaurant has its own bar facilities
for private functions. Lovely riverside walks nearby.*

SHIPTON UNDER WYCHWOOD Oxfordshire **Map 4 B1**

⊗££ **THE SHAVEN CROWN HOTEL** Shipton Under Wychwood.
☐££££**Hours:** Breakfast 8.30am - 9.30am and dinner 7.30pm - 9.30pm (9pm Sundays). Bar meals 12 - 2pm and 7.30pm - 9.30pm (9pm Sunday). **Cuisine:** An excellent selection of a la carte and bar meal dishes. ⊨ 9 bedrooms, all en suite. **CC** Access, Visa. **Other Points:** Children welcome. Afternoon tea served. **P** & **(V) Directions:** 4 miles north of Burford on the A361, opposite the church and green.
TREVOR & MARY BROOKES ☎ (0993) 830330.
Built in 1380 as a hospice to Bruern Abbey, The Shaven Crown is now one of the ten oldest inns in England. An attractive building of honey coloured stone around a medieval courtyard with a fountain, in the heart of the Cotswolds. In fine weather, dine al fresco in the courtyard.

SHOEBURYNESS Essex **Map 5 B2**

⊗££ **THE POLASH RESTAURANT** 86 West Road, Shoeburyness.
Hours: Meals 12 noon - 3pm and 6pm - 12 midnight. **Cuisine:** Bangladeshi food, eg. Kim's dish, Kipling's favourites, Passage to India, Sunset in Ganges. Authentic tandoori and bhoona dishes. ⊨ None. **CC** All major cards. **Other Points:** Children welcome. No dogs. Fully licensed. Air conditioned. & **(V)**
MR A KHALIQUE ☎ (0702) 293989/294721
Authentic Bangladeshi and Indian music unobtrusively relaxes diners and gives an aura of tranquility.

SILEBY Leicestershire **Map 4 A2**

⊗££ **THE WHITE SWAN** Swan Street, Sileby.
Hours: Meals 12 noon - 2pm and 7.30pm - 10pm. Restaurant closed: Sunday, Monday and 2 weeks in summer. **Cuisine:** A la carte menu in evening and self-service selection of hot and cold lunches. Fish, steaks, homemade dishes and puddings. ⊨ None. **CC** Access, Visa, AmEx. **Other Points:** Children welcome. Skittle alley for hire. Coaches by appointment. **P Directions:** On the B674 between the A6 and the A46.
MRS THERESA WALLACE ☎ (050 981) 4832.
1930's style pub with garden at rear. Large collection of ornamental frogs and bottled beers! Close to Bradgate Park and Charnwood Forest.

SITTINGBOURNE Kent **Map 5 C1**

⊗££ **CONISTON HOTEL** 70 London Road, Sittingbourne.
Hours: Meals 7.30am - 9.30am, 12 noon - 2.30pm and 7pm - 10pm (last orders). Bar lunches 12 noon - 2pm. **Cuisine:** Speciality: Dover sole. ⊨ 60 bedrooms, 52 en suite. **CC** All major cards. **Other Points:** Children welcome. Nominal charge made for dogs. Coaches by appointment. **P** & **(V) Directions:** On the A2 half a mile from town centre.
MR S KLECZKOWSKI ☎ (0795) 472131/472907
The hotel is very well placed for visiting Kent's many sights and attractions. The ballroom can seat 160 people and is available for private hire.

SNETTISHAM Norfolk **Map 5 A1**

⊗£   **THE ROSE & CROWN FREEHOUSE** Old Church Road,
⊞£££   Snettisham, King's Lynn.

⌣☺   **Hours:** Meals 12 noon - 2pm and 6.30pm - 10.30pm (last orders
10pm). Meals also served Sunday evenings. **Cuisine:** Rare roast
beef, quality steaks, good selection of vegetarian dishes, dish of the
day - good home cooking. ⊨ 1 double en suite, 1 double
standard, 1 twin standard. Listed and commended by Tourist
Board. **CC** Access, Visa. **Other Points:** Children welcome - high
chairs provided. Coaches by appointment. No dogs. Walled
garden with play area. **P** & **(V) Directions:** From A149, from
King's Lynn, turn right after Snettisham Mkt Place.
MARGARET TRAFFORD ☎ (0485) 541382
*Situated just off the A149, this 14th century pub offers good
food, real ales and a friendly welcoming atmosphere. A large
collection of old farming implements is on display. Children
have their own menu and a large, separate room, personally
supervised by the proprietor.*

SOLIHULL West Midlands **Map 4 A1**

⊗££   **FLEMINGS HOTEL** 141 Warwick Road, Olton, Solihull.
⊞£££   **Hours:** Lunch and bar meals 12 noon - 2pm, dinner and bar meals
6.30pm - 9.30pm. Closed: Christmas period. **Cuisine:** Seafood
special, steaks, beef Stroganoff. ⊨ 84 bedrooms, all en suite.
Special weekend rates. **CC** All major cards. **Other Points:** Dining al
fresco. Children welcome. Dogs allowed. Fax No. (021) 706 4494.
P **(V) Directions:** On A41, 250 yards from Olton station.
W FLEMING ☎ (021) 706 0371.
*A patron run hotel situated only 5½ miles from the centre of
Birmingham. A high standard of comfort and service are
provided at reasonable prices and the restaurant offers both a la
carte and table d'hote menus. Has the homely friendliness of a
small hotel.*

SOULDERN Oxfordshire **Map 4 B2**

⊗££   **FOX INN** Fox Lane, Souldern, nr Bicester.

⌣☺   **Hours:** Breakfast 8am - 9.30am, lunch 12 noon - 2pm and dinner
7pm - 12 midnight (last orders 9.30pm). Bar meals 12 noon - 2pm
and 7pm - 9.30pm. Closed Sunday evening. **Cuisine:** Roast
Sunday lunch, table d'hote and a la carte menu, daily specials.
⊨ 4 bedrooms, 2 en suite. Colour TV and tea/coffee facilities in
rooms. **CC** Access, Visa. **Other Points:** Children welcome. Beer
garden. Eurocard accepted. **P** **(V) Directions:** Follow Souldern
signs off the A41, situated on left in village.
IAN MACKAY ☎ (0869) 345284.
*A traditional 19th century stone-built inn, situated 7 miles north
of Bicester off the A41 in a beautiful Cotswold stone village.
Ideal for Oxford, Stratford, the Cotswolds, Warwick and
Silverstone motor racing circuit.*

SOUTHAMPTON Hampshire **Map 4 C2**

⊗£   **GOLDEN PALACE RESTAURANT** 17a Above Bar,
Southampton.
Hours: Open 11.45am to 12 midnight every day. **Cuisine:** Dim
Sum, Cantonese dishes and seafood. ⊨ None. **CC** All major cards.
Other Points: Children welcome. **(V)**
MR DAVID LAI ☎ (0703) 226636.

Southampton continued

This restaurant is popular with the student population of Southampton offering a 10% discount to those holding a National Student Card. The food is well-presented, plentiful and very good value for money.

⊗£ **LA MARGHERITA RESTAURANT** 6 Commercial Road, Southampton.
Hours: Lunch 12 noon - 2.30pm, dinner 6.30pm - 11.30pm, later on Friday and Saturday. Closed: Sunday and Bank Holiday. **Cuisine:** Langostinos, steak Diane, freshly made pizzas, and homemade lasagne. Desserts include creme caramel. ⊨ None. **CC** All major cards. **Other Points:** Access for disabled if advised in advance. Children welcome. No dogs. Eurocard, LVs and travellers cheques accepted. **(V) Directions:** From main BR station,turn right at traffic lights into Commercial Rd
FRANCESCO FANTINI ☎ (0703) 333390.
A busy, friendly bistro type restaurant near the Mayflower Theatre. Popular with theatre goers and TV stars. Repartee and good humour flow as fast as the Italian red wine.

⊗££ **NEW FOREST HEATHLANDS HOTEL** Romsey Road, Ower,
⊡£££ Romsey.
Hours: 7am - 9.30am, 12 noon - 2pm, and 7pm - 9.30pm. Bar meals also served between 12 noon - 2pm and 6pm - 9pm. Night porter service available. **Cuisine:** Classical style cuisine, made with fresh English produce. Dishes include New Forest Guinea Fowl with redcurrant and port sauce. ⊨ 53 bedrooms. All rooms

Southampton continued

en suite, with Sky TV, radio, trouser press, baby listening available, telephones and tea/coffee. Whirlpool baths in some rooms. **CC** All major cards. **Other Points:** Limited access for disabled. Open Sundays and bank holidays. Residents lounge/garden. Children welcome. Dogs allowed. Conference facilities. **P** **(V) Directions:** A31-jct 2, M27. Signs for Paultons Park.300 yds on left from r'about

MR G D FELD ☎ (0703) 814333.

Hotel built onto a 16th century inn, with mainly ground floor rooms. An ideal location for touring the south, situated close to Beaulieu, Broadlands, the New Forest and the coastline. Offers very good food in a relaxed, friendly atmosphere.

VILLA CAPRI GUEST HOUSE 52 Archers Road, Southampton.

6 single, 3 double, 6 twin bedrooms, all en suite, including a four poster and a water bed. **Hours:** Breakfast 7am - 9am, Dinner 6pm - 7pm. Closed: Sunday. **CC** Access, Visa. **Other Points:** Children welcome. Small pets allowed. Garden. Sky TV. Private steam room. **P** **&** **Directions:** Close to the cricket and football grounds, and Bedford Place.

MARY & RENE TORDO ☎ (0703) 632800.

Two semi-detached Victorian town houses have been converted into this small, friendly guest house. Ideally situated for Southampton and the New Forest, Villa Capri offers good value for money.

SOUTHEND Essex **Map 5 B1**

LA POUBELLE 50a Hamlet Court Road, Westcliff, Southend-on-Sea.

Hours: Lunch 12.30pm - 2.15pm (Sunday only, autumn & winter months), dinner 7pm - late (last orders 10.30pm). Closed: lunch times except Sunday, Sunday evening and all day Monday. **Cuisine:** Paella, chicken breast in stilton sauce, local fish, home smoked produce. A varied and interesting menu - all dishes home prepared and cooked. None. **CC** Access, Visa. **Other Points:** Children welcome. Childrens menu. Tues to Friday special low price menu. No dogs. **P** **&** **(V) Directions:** On shopping st near Westcliff railway station, 5 mins from seafront.

MR & MRS R C BERNER ☎ (0702) 351894.

A small, friendly family run restaurant with an emphasis on good, honest, fresh food in comfortable surroundings. An informal atmosphere provides the ideal ambience for pleasant dining. Very popular locally so booking advised.

ROSLIN HOTEL Thorpe Esplanade, Thorpe Bay, Southend-On-Sea.

Hours: Open all day. Meals 12.30pm - 2pm and 6.30pm - 9.30pm, snacks available. **Cuisine:** Noisette of lamb Gascoigne, Veal Millanaise, local trout with chestnut and cucumber. 44 bedrooms, all en suite. **CC** All major cards. **Other Points:** Children welcome. **P** **&** **Directions:** Close to the seafront.

MR K G OLIVER ☎ (0702) 586375

Situated on the seafront, the Roslin Hotel boasts one of the finest views of the Thames Estuary in residential Thorpe Bay. Facilities for golfing, sailing, tennis, bowling, horse riding, ten-pin

Southend continued
bowling. Weekend bargain breaks. Temporary membership of local leisure centre for residents.

⊗££ **THE ANCHOR** High Street, Canewdon, Nr Rochford, Southend.
CLUB **Hours:** 11.30am - 2.30pm, and 7pm - 10pm seven days a week. Last orders for food 2pm and 10pm. **Cuisine:** A la carte and table d'hote menu. Good choice of grills, fish, home baked and vegetarian dishes. ⊨ None. **CC** Access, Visa. **Other Points:** Children welcome. Dogs allowed. **P** **(V) Directions:** A127 or A130, near Southend airport and Wallasea marina.
RICHARD COVINGTON ☎ (0702) 258213.
Traditional old pub set in a row of fishing cottages which date back to 1624. The Anchor serves excellent food, in generous portions, in a very friendly atmosphere. Well worth a visit.

SOUTHEND ON SEA Essex **Map 5 B1**
⊡£ **THE MAYFLOWER HOTEL** 6 Royal Terrace, Southend on Sea.
⊨ 7 single, 9 double, 5 twin and 3 family bedrooms, 4 en suite. 3 showers and 4 bathrooms. TV in all bedrooms. **Hours:** Breakfast 6.45am - 9am. Closed: for a fortnight over Christmas. **CC** None. **Other Points:** Central heating. No evening meals. Limited access for the disabled. Children welcome. Residents lounge and TV.
CHRISTOPHER POWELL ☎ (0702) 340 489.
Built in 1792, this grade II listed house still retains many original Georgian features. A mass of flowers in hanging baskets are draped over the balcony and on the terrace. The hotel overlooks the Thames estuary and the Pier.

SOUTHSEA Hampshire **Map 4 C2**
⊡£ **ST ANDREWS LODGE** 65 St Andrews Road, Southsea, Portsmouth.
⊨ 1 single, 2 double, 3 twin and 3 family bedrooms. 1 bathroom, 1 shower. Colour TV and tea/coffee facilities in all bedrooms. **Hours:** Breakfast 6am - 9am. Closed: 14 days over Christmas. **CC** None. **Other Points:** Central heating. Children welcome. Residents lounge. TV. Garden. Street parking. Vegetarians catered to by request. **Directions:** Just off the B2151.
MRS D ROWLING & MRS B WATSON ☎ (0705) 827079.
A pleasant, newly renovated guest house situated minutes from the sea front and continental ferry port, and close to the motorway. All rooms have been thoughtfully furnished and are bright and clean throughout.

⊡£ **UPLANDS** 34 Granada Road, Southsea.
CLUB ⊨ 3 single, 1 double, 1 twin and 7 family bedrooms. 3 showers. Plus 1 double room which interconnects with another room, containing 1 bunk-bed and a single. Separate bathroom. Colour TVs and tea/coffee facilities in all rooms. **Hours:** Breakfast 6am - 8.30am, dinner 6pm (order in the morning). Closed: Christmas. **CC** Access, Visa. **Other Points:** Children welcome. TV. Lounge. **P** **Directions:** Off M27 to Portsea, follow the Southsea sign to South Parade Pier.
MRS H ZANELLOTTI ☎ (0705) 821 508.
2 minutes from seafront, 10 minutes from continental car ferries. Reduced rates for children sharing parent's room. Special rates

Southsea continued

> for OAPs in September. The bedrooms have all been recently refurbished in bright, modern decor.

SOUTHWOLD Suffolk **Map 5 A2**

®£ **SUTHERLAND HOUSE RESTAURANT** 56 High Street, ⑪£££ Southwold.

> **Hours:** Lunch 12 noon - 2pm, Dinner 7pm - 9pm (last orders). Closed: Wednesday during summer and Monday - Wednesday inclusive during winter. **Cuisine:** A daily menu featuring all fresh, home cooked local produce. Fresh, local fish dishes are a speciality. Informal Brasserie-style cuisine. ➤ 3 double bedrooms. **CC** Access, Visa. **Other Points:** Children welcome. No dogs. No smoking area. **(V) Directions:** 4 miles from A12. On High Street in the centre of Southwold.
> PAUL & MARGARET SAMAIN ☎ (0502) 722260.
> *Built in the 16th century, Sutherland House was once the headquarters of an Admiral who became King of England, James II. Today it carefully preserves its historic past and specialises in good food and refreshment of high quality. You can be assured of welcoming service, well presented, fresh home cooked food, and good value for money prices.*

SPALDING Lincolnshire **Map 5 A1**

® £ **THE RED LION HOTEL** Market Place.

⑪£££ **Hours:** Meals 7.30am - 9.30am, 12 noon - 2pm and 7pm - CLUB 9.30pm. **Cuisine:** Traditional home cooked fare. ➤ 15 bedrooms, all en suite. **CC** All major cards. **Other Points:** Children welcome. Specially fitted low door bell for disabled to call for assistance to gain entry. Disabled toilet. Fax No: (0775) 710074. **(V) Directions:** Centre of Spalding.
> MRS J M WILKINS & MR N J WILKINS ☎ (0775) 722869.
> *Sympathetically refurbished 18th century town centre Hotel offering en suite accommodation, real ales, real food, a warm welcome and value for money. Local facilities include beautiful gardens and nurseries, fishing, clay pigeon shooting and golf.*

ST ALBANS Hertfordshire **Map 5 B1**

⑪££ **NEWPARK HOUSE HOTEL** North Orbital Road, Nr London Colney Roundabout.

> ➤ 9 single and 5 twin bedrooms. All with tea/coffee making facilities and colour TV in most rooms. Ironing facilities available on request. **Hours:** Breakfast 6.45am - 8.45am. **CC** Access, Visa. **Other Points:** Children welcome. Garden. Packed lunches on request. Dogs allowed. Small conference facilities. Access at all times. Fax: (0727) 826700. **P Directions:** A414 dual carriageway, 400 yds from London Colney roundabout.
> DENNIS & VIOLET BYGRAVE ☎ (0727) 824839.
> *A family run, welcoming guest house offering comfortable accommodation and full English breakfast at very reasonable prices. Only 18 minutes by train from London, and close to the centre of the historic city of St. Albans. There is an excellent garden for guests use and the hotel enjoys a warm and friendly atmosphere. A good base for holiday makers, tourists and business people alike.*

ST HELENS Isle of Wight Map 4 C2

⊗££ **ST HELENS RESTAURANT** Lower Green Road, St. Helens, Nr Ryde.

Hours: Lunch 12 noon - 3pm, dinner 6.30pm - 12.30pm (last orders 10.30pm). Closed: Mondays. **Cuisine:** A la carte menu, fixed 3 course menu. Mainly traditional English with vegetarian choice. ⊨ None. **CC** Access, Visa. **Other Points:** Children welcome. ⅋ **(V) Directions:** B3330 to St. Helens, right onto Lower Green.

FRANK & ROSEMARY BALDRY ☎ (0983) 872303.

This cosy English restaurant with a big log fire in winter, has a cheerful, relaxed atmosphere and overlooks the largest green in England. The home cooking is excellent value and tastes delicious!

ST IVES Cambridgeshire Map 5 A1

⊗££ **THE DOLPHIN HOTEL** Bridge Foot, London Road, St Ives.

⊞££££ **Hours:** Breakfast 7.30am - 9.30am, Lunch 12 noon - 2pm, Dinner 7pm - 9.30pm. Last orders are at 9.30pm, except on Saturdays and Sundays when they are at 10pm and 9pm respectively. **Cuisine:** English and French cuisine, with a comprehensive wine list. Sunday lunch also served. ⊨ 47 bedrooms, all en suite. **CC** All major cards. **Other Points:** Do not go into centre of St Ives to reach Dolphin Hotel, as the bridge which leads to it is one-way. Best to follow directions outlined below. ▣ ⅋ **(V) Directions:** Ring road. At roundabout, turn for Hemingford Abbotts. Then 1st right. H R WADSWORTH ☎ (0480) 66966.

St Ives continued

The Dolphin is a small friendly hotel situated in the old town of St Ives, on the banks of the Great Ouse. Diners have a pleasant view over the river which makes for a particularly relaxed atmosphere in which to enjoy the good food. Children are welcome and charged at a reduced price.

⊗££ **THE OLD FERRYBOAT INN** Holywell, Nr St Ives, Cambridge.
⊞£££ **Hours:** 7.30am - 10am, 12 noon - 3pm and 6pm - 11pm. **Cuisine:**
CLUB International cuisine, including traditional English. Fish specials. A la carte and bar meals. ⊨ 7 bedrooms, all en suite. **CC** Access, Visa. **Other Points:** Children welcome. No dogs allowed. Open Sundays and Bank holidays. **⊡** **⅄** **(V) Directions:** Turn off A604 to St Ives.Follow by-pass to Needingworth and Holywell
RICHARD JEFFREY ☎ (0480) 63227.
Claimed to be the oldest inn in England with the spirit of over a thousand years good hospitality. Judging by the number of visitors, this reputation is still upheld today. However, one sad spirit still exists: the ghost of young Juliette whose gravestone forms part of the ancient floor in the bar. Riverside setting. Real ales.

ST LEONARDS ON SEA East Sussex **Map 5 C1**
⊗£££ **ROYAL VICTORIA HOTEL** Marina, St Leonards on Sea,
CLUB Hastings.
Hours: Breakfast 7am - 10am, lunch 12.30pm - 2pm (last orders 1.45pm) and dinner 7pm - 10pm (last orders 9.30pm). Open Sundays. **Cuisine:** Choice of English or French. ⊨ 52 bedrooms, all en suite. All major facilities. **CC** All major cards. **Other Points:** Children welcome. Afternoon tea. Pets allowed. Bargain breaks. **⊡** **⅄** **(V) Directions:** Off the A21 Hastings Road, situated on the seafront.
P.J. GOODEN ☎ (0424) 445544.
Built in 1828 by James Burton, The Royal Victoria Hotel offers superb cuisine complemented by courteous and attentive service in their Sun Terrace Restaurant. With excellent accommodation facilities and ideal seafront location - within walking distance of shopping centre, castle and old town, this hotel attracts both business people and tourists alike.

STAFFORD Staffordshire **Map 4 A1**
⊗£££ **ST GEORGE HOTEL** Castle Street, Eccleshall, Stafford.
⊞££££ **Hours:** Breakfast 7.30am - 10am, lunch 12 noon - 2pm, dinner 7pm - 9.30pm, bar snacks 11am - 2.30pm, 5.30pm - 10pm. Open Bank Holidays. **Cuisine:** Dishes may include - seafood cocktail, garlic mushrooms with stilton, scampi with whiskey & cream, steak Diane, selection of sweets or cheeseboard. ⊨ 10 bedrooms, all en suite. **CC** All major cards. **Other Points:** Children welcome. Afternoon teas. Dogs allowed. Conference room. Fax No: (0785) 851452. **⊡** **⅄** **(V) Directions:** From Jct 14 of M6, take A5013, approx 5 miles. In village centre.
GERARD & MOYRA SLATER ☎ (0785) 850300.
Set in the centre of a busy market town, this listed building serves attractive meals to be enjoyed in a quiet atmosphere. Open fires add a warmth to the bar, where traditional ales and malt whiskies are available. Offering accommodation of a high quality.

Stafford continued

⊗£££ **THE MOAT HOUSE RESTAURANT** Lower Penkridge Road, Acton Trussell, Stafford.

Hours: Lunch 12 noon - 2pm, Dinner 7pm - 9.30pm. Bar meals 12 noon - 2pm. Restaurant closed: Sunday evening and all day Monday. **Cuisine:** Traditional English cuisine. A la carte menu in evenings and table d'hote luncheon during the week. Traditional Sunday lunch. ⨦ None. **CC** Access, Visa, AmEx. **Other Points:** Children welcome. Patio. No smoking area. Ramps for wheelchair access. Functions catered for. Cocktail bar. Bar. Conservatory. **P** ⅙ **(V) Directions:** Jct 13, M6. A449 toward Stafford. 1st right to village. Near church.

JOHN & MARY LEWIS ☎ (0785) 712217.

A 13th century moated manor house set in 6 acres of landscaped grounds and overlooking the canal, yet only 1 mile from the M6. The delightful restaurant provides excellent food with all dishes homemade including the bread and petit fours. The food is of the highest quality, beautifully served in generous portions. An outstanding restaurant in all aspects.

STALHAM Norfolk **Map 5 A2**

⊗££ **SUTTON STAITHE HOTEL** Sutton Staithe, Sutton, Norwich.

⊓£££ **Hours:** Restaurant open 12 noon - 2pm (last orders) and 7pm - 9.30pm (last orders). **Cuisine:** Local game and fish in season. ⨦ 10 bedrooms, 6 en suite. **CC** All major cards. **Other Points:** Children welcome. Fishing. **P** **(V) Directions:** Just off the A149 Yarmouth to North Walsham road.

M.K. & D.P TAYLOR. ☎ (0692) 80244.

Situated by the waterside at the head of Sutton Broad, the inn is popular with boat people. The food is plentiful, well cooked and well presented.

STAMFORD Lincolnshire **Map 4 A2**

⊗££ **CANDLESTICKS HOTEL & RESTAURANT** 1 Church

⊓££ Lane, Stamford.

Hours: Continental breakfast taken in bedroom. Lunch 12 noon - 2pm, Dinner 7pm - 9.30pm (last orders), 7pm - 8.45pm Sundays. Closed: Monday. **Cuisine:** French and Continental cuisine. Specialities include Portuguese fish dishes. Menu changes monthly. ⨦ 8 bedrooms, all en suite. **CC** Access, Visa. **Other Points:** Limited access for disabled. Children welcome. No smoking area. **P** **(V) Directions:** Opposite St Martins Church.

MANUEL PINTO ☎ (0780) 64033.

Occupying the corner unit of a stone Victorian building, the Candlesticks has been established for over 12 years. During that time the restaurant has gained a fine reputation for the very high standard of food and good value prices. After an enjoyable meal it is worth taking a walk around the historic stone built town of Stamford. Highly recommended.

STEEP Hampshire **Map 4 C2**

⊗£ **CRICKETER'S INN** Steep, Petersfield.

Hours: Breakfast (residents only) when required. Bar meals 12 noon - 2pm and 6.30pm - 9.45pm. **Cuisine:** Home prepared and cooked hams, chilli, quiche, fresh cream trifle, trout, steaks, lasagne, cottage and shepherds pie, fish, omelettes, specials in evening ⨦ 3 bedrooms 2 en suite (showers), all with tea/coffee

Steep continued

facilities and clock radios. **CC** Access, Visa, AmEx. **Other Points:** Large garden where children are welcome. Dogs allowed. **P** **(V)** **Directions:** On the Alton Road.

MR W T TURNBULL ☎ (0730) 61035.

A small, good-looking pub recently refurbished in traditional style. There are two bars where patrons can enjoy anything from a light snack to a 3 course meal. All food is prepared and cooked on the premises and has earned the Cricketer's a strong local following.

STEVENAGE Hertfordshire **Map 5 B1**

⊗££ **ARCHWAYS HOTELS** 15 Hitchin Road, Stevenage.

Hours: Lunch 12 noon - 2pm and dinner 7pm - 9.30pm (last orders). **Cuisine:** Mainly British dishes including Fillet steak Archways - steak stuffed with Stilton, wrapped in bacon and served with a Madeira sauce. ⊨ 36 bedrooms, all en suite. **CC** All major cards. **Other Points:** Children welcome. Dogs allowed. Garden. **P** & **Directions:** On main A602, near Old Town Stevenage.

VIOLET BATE ☎ (0438) 316640/314537

A family run establishment offering a warm welcome and a varied, innovative menu. Stevenage Old Town is within walking distance and the New Town is only a short drive away, offering sport and leisure facilities and an excellent shopping centre.

STEYNING West Sussex **Map 5 C1**

⊗££ **CHEQUER INN** 41 High Street, Steyning.

Hours: Breakfast 10am - 11.30am, Lunch 12 noon - 2pm, dinner 6.30pm - 9pm (last orders). **Cuisine:** Traditional homemade daily specials, plus a wide selection of starters, main courses and sweets. Vegetarian dishes available. ⊨ None. **CC** None. **Other Points:** Children welcome. Dogs allowed. **P** & **Directions:** From A24 turn left on A283 to Shorham. Steyning is on right.

DOUGLAS ORD ☎ (0903) 814437.

A very old, oak beamed Coaching Inn with an attractive exterior and comfortable interior with small seating areas. The menu is displayed on blackboards and offers a good choice of excellently cooked meals at very good value prices. With its busy, friendly atmosphere and welcoming service, the Chequer Inn is well worth a visit.

⊞££users **SPRINGWELLS HOTEL** 9 High Street, Steyning.

⊨ 2 single, 4 twin, 5 double, 1 family bedroom: 6 en suite. All rooms have TV, and telephone. Coffee/tea making facilities on request. Four posters. **Hours:** Breakfast 7.15am - 10am. **CC** All major cards. **Other Points:** Children welcome. Residents' bar-lounge. Outdoor heated swimming pool. Residents' garden. **P** **Directions:** Off A283.

MRS J. HESELGRAVE ☎ (0903) 812446.

A delightful 17th century Georgian hotel, with ivy wall covering and large Georgian windows, situated on the High Street of the charming, unspoilt town of Steyning. Under the personal supervision of the owners, this hotel has been arranged and fitted to ensure maximum comfort for guests by providing attractive bedrooms and a large sunny dining room for hearty English breakfast.

STOCKBRIDGE Hampshire **Map 4 C1**
⊗£ **THE GREYHOUND HOTEL** Stockbridge.

🏠£££ | CLUB | **Hours:** Breakfast 7.30am - 9.30am, Lunch 12 noon - 2pm and
Dinner 6pm - 9.30pm (last orders). **Cuisine:** A la carte including a
range of seafood, crepes, and Ploughman's. ⊨ 10 rooms, 5 en
suite. ⓒⓒ Access, Visa, AmEx. **Other Points:** Children welcome.
Teas. Garden. Dogs allowed. & **(V)**
MR GUMBRELL ☎ (0264) 810833

*This small hotel is situated in a delightful small Hampshire town
and the restaurant offers a wide selection of seafood dishes,
including Lobster, Crepe Fruits de Mer and Smoked Trout. The
hotel has its own stretch of the famous River Test - day tickets
available. Golf day fees can also be arranged locally.*

⊗££ **THE PEAT SPADE INN** Longstock, Stockbridge.
Hours: Meals served 12.30pm - 2.30pm and 7.30pm - 10pm (last
orders). **Cuisine:** Traditional English, including homebaked ham
and fresh wild salmon. All freshly prepared. Game dishes usually
available. ⊨ None. ⓒⓒ All major cards. **Other Points:** Childrens
area. Garden. Pets allowed. 🅿 & **(V) Directions:** Off the A3057,
between Andover and Stockbridge.
JULIE TUCKETT ☎ (0264) 810612.

*An attractive Victorian inn, with ivy wall covering and red brick
facade, with gardens backing onto open countryside and the
River Test, providing a peaceful setting for visitors. There is a
varied selection of traditional English dishes using
predominantly fresh local produce. The food is complemented
by an extensive wine list.*

STOW ON THE WOLD Gloucestershire **Map 4 B1**
⊗£ **COACH & HORSES** Ganborough, Moreton in Marsh, Nr Stow
on the Wold.
Hours: Lunch 12 noon - 2pm, dinner 7pm - 9pm (9.30pm - Friday
and Saturday). Basket meals served 30 mins extra. Sunday lunch
12 noon - 2pm. Closed: Christmas Day and Boxing Day. **Cuisine:**
Dishes include game soup, garlic mushrooms, homemade steak
and kidney pie, homemade chicken kiev and fruit crumble.
⊨ None. ⓒⓒ None. **Other Points:** Children welcome. Garden.
Dogs allowed. Function room. Caravan site. No smoking area in
dining room. 🅿 & **(V) Directions:** On A424, 2 miles north of Stow
On The Wold.
ANDREW & SARAH MORRIS ☎ (0451) 830208.

*A traditional country pub with flagstone floors, situated on the
main Stow to Broadway A424 road, offering well above average
homemade pub food. In the centre of the Cotswolds, the Coach
& Horses is within easy reach of the many surrounding
picturesque villages.*

⊗£££ **GRAPEVINE HOTEL** Sheep Street, Stow on the Wold.
Hours: Breakfast 8.15am - 9.30am, dinner 7pm - 9.30pm. Bar
meals 12 noon - 2pm and 7pm - 9pm. Closed: Christmas Eve -
January 12th. **Cuisine:** Bar: Delicious selection of unusual dishes.
Restaurant: English & French haute cuisine. Daily changing menu
with fresh ingredients. ⊨ 23 bedrooms, all en suite. Getaway
breaks. ⓒⓒ All major cards. **Other Points:** Children welcome. No
dogs. Afternoon teas. Garden patio. No smoking in restaurant. Fax

Stow on the Wold continued

No: (0451) 832278. ◫ **(V) Directions:** From A429, take A436 towards Chipping Norton, 150 yds on right.
MRS SANDRA ELLIOTT ☎ (0451) 830344.

Be pampered at this welcoming, award winning hotel with its romantic vine clad conservatory restaurant, imaginative cuisine, high quality soft furnishings and caring staff, for whom nothing is too much trouble.

⊗£££ **THE FOSSE MANOR HOTEL** Fosseway, Stow on the Wold.
⊞£££ **Hours:** Breakfast 8am - 9.30am, lunch 12 noon - 2pm, dinner 7.30pm - 9.30pm. **Cuisine:** Dishes include Scottish Smoked Salmon Cups filled with Prawns, Spicy Chicken and Mushroom Crepe in a Cream Sauce. ⊨ 3 single, 3 twin, 13 double, 1 family bedroom and 1 four-poster suite. 18 en suite. **CC** All major cards. **Other Points:** Children welcome. Garden. Afternoon teas. Dogs allowed. No smoking in restaurant. ◫ ♿ **(V) Directions:** On A429 approximately one mile south of Stow On The Wold.
BOB & YVONNE JOHNSTON ☎ (0451) 830354.

Built in the style of a Cotswold manor house this hotel stands in its own grounds. Stylishly and fashionably decorated to a high standard of comfort, there is a unique collection of hats on display in the bar. The restaurant serves first class meals in beautiful surroundings. The bar is at the centre of the hotel's activity and has an informal atmosphere.

⊗££ **THE OLD STOCKS HOTEL** The Square, Stow on the Wold.
⊞£££ **Hours:** Breakfast 8.15am - 9.15am, Lunch 12 noon - 2pm Monday - Saturday, Traditional Sunday Roast 12 noon - 2pm and Dinner 7pm - 9pm Sunday - Thursday, 7pm - 9.30pm Friday - Saturday. **Cuisine:** Extensive Table d'hote and very popular Special Value Menu specialising in traditional home cooked dishes and also catering for the vegetarian. ⊨ 19 bedrooms, all en suite. **CC** Access, Visa. **Other Points:** Children welcome. Garden and patio. Dogs allowed. Limited access for disabled to Restaurant only. ◫ **(V) Directions:** Off A429 or A436 to town centre. Next to the Green in the Square.
ALAN & CAROLINE ROSE ☎ (0451) 830666

A 17th Century Grade II listed Hotel, one of the original buildings in the square, and facing the quiet village green on which the original penal stocks still stand. Refurbished to combine modern comforts with original charm and character. Friendly and caring staff make this an ideal base for exploring the beautiful Cotswolds.

⊗£ **THE WHITE HART HOTEL** Market Square, Stow on the Wold.
Hours: Meals 8.15am - 9.15am, 11.45pm - 2.15pm and 6pm - 10pm. Sunday hours 12 noon - 2pm and 7pm - 9pm. **Cuisine:** Homemade traditional pies, local grilled trout. ⊨ 7 bedrooms, 3 en suite and 2 bathrooms. **CC** Access, Visa, Diners. **Other Points:** Children welcome. ◫ ♿ **(V) Directions:** Off A429. Turn off at town centre sign, left side of main square.
MARGARET & ROY WHATELY & DES LEACH ☎ (0451) 830674.

A 17th century coaching inn which still retains much of its old character and ambience. It provides an ideal base for touring the Cotswolds and the food and service are of a high standard.

CENTRAL & SOUTHERN ENGLAND

STRATFORD UPON AVON Warwickshire **Map 4 A1**

ⁿ£365 **AMBLESIDE GUEST HOUSE** 41 Grove Road, Stratford Upon Avon.

2 single, 1 double, 1 twin and 3 family bedrooms, 2 en suite. 1 bathroom. Colour TV and tea/coffee making facilities in all rooms. **Hours:** Breakfast 7.45am - 8.45am. Closed: over Christmas. **CC** Access, Visa. **Other Points:** Central heating. Children welcome. **P**

RON & PAM BARNACLE ☎ (0789) 297239/295670

Small, homely guest house run by the Barnacles since 1961. Centrally located opposite Verdant park, only a few minutes walk from the town centre. Special off season mini breaks.

ⁿ£365 **BROOK LODGE** 192 Alcester Road, Stratford Upon Avon.

3 double, 1 twin and 3 family bedrooms - 5 with en suite showers and WCs. All rooms with showers. Also, 1 general bathroom, shower and separate toilet. **Hours:** Breakfast 8.15am - 9am. Closed: for Christmas. **CC** Access, Visa, AmEx. **Other Points:** Central heating. Children welcome. Dogs allowed. Residents' lounge and TV. **P Directions:** On the A422 to Alcester, 1/2 mile beyond railway bridge on right.

MICHAEL & ANNE BLACK ☎ (0789) 295988.

An attractive building with hanging baskets giving a welcoming appearance. The rooms are tastefully decorated and the furnishings would shame many high class hotels. There is a large car park.

ⁿ£365 **CRAIG CLEEVE HOUSE** 67-69 Shipston Road, Stratford Upon Avon.

15 bedrooms, 9 en suite and all with colour TV, radio and tea/coffee making facilities. **Hours:** Breakfast 7.30am - 9.30am. Evening meals by prior request. **CC** All major cards. **Other Points:** Children welcome. Afternoon teas. Dogs allowed. Residents' lounge. Licensed bar. Car & coach park. Smoking & non smoking areas. Fax No: (0789) 299452. **P Directions:** A3400 Stratford to Oxford Road. 5 minutes walk to town centre.

TERRY & MARGARITA PALMER ☎ (0789) 296573.

A licensed Private Hotel retaining a family atmosphere where the sole aim is to make guests feel comfortable and welcome. Good friendly service, comfortable rooms of a high standard, and a breakfast where no one is left feeling hungry! Quality, value for money and a warm welcome are guaranteed. Only 5 minutes walk from the town centre and within easy reach of the Cotswolds.

ⁿ£365 **HARDWICK GUEST HOUSE** 1 Avenue Road, Stratford-Upon-Avon.

2 single, 6 double, 3 twin and 3 family bedrooms, 6 en suite. Colour TV, Tea/Coffee making facilities, full central heating in all rooms. **Hours:** Breakfast 8am - 9.15am. **CC** Access, Visa, AmEx. **Other Points:** Children welcome. Fax No: (0789) 296760. **P Directions:** Off Warwick Road, corner of St Gregorys Road and Avenue Road.

JILL & ERNIE COULSON ☎ (0789) 204307.

A large Victorian House, in a quiet tree lined avenue, only a few minutes walk from the centre of town with all it's attractions. The Coulson family will welcome you into their comfortable home,

Stratford upon Avon continued
which is ideally situated near the Warwick Road for visitors to Warwick Castle.

⌂ℤ££ **MOONRAKER HOUSE** 40 Alcester Road, Stratford Upon Avon.
🛏 11 double, 4 twin and 4 family rooms all ensuite. TV, hairdryer and clock radio in rooms. For special occasions there are 4 luxury 4-poster suites with own garden terrace and lounge. Champagne/flowers on request **Hours:** Breakfast 8am - 9.30am. **CC** Access, Visa. **Other Points:** Central heating. Children welcome. Pets by arrangement. Residents' lounge. Garden and patio. Fax: (0789) 295504. **P Directions:** On the A422 in the centre of town, close to railway station.
MR & MRS M S SPENCER ☎ (0789) 67115/299346.
Moonraker House comprises three attractive white houses situated in a pleasant area in the north-west of the town. Very tastefully decorated and comfortably furnished throughout, the atmosphere is friendly and relaxed. An ideal location for touring Shakespeare country, the Cotswolds, and the many castles and places of interest nearby.

⌂ℤ££ **NANDO'S** 18-19 Evesham Place, Stratford Upon Avon.
🛏 6 single, 5 double and 4 family bedrooms, 7 en suite. Colour TV and Tea/ Coffee/Chocolate making facilities. **Hours:** Breakfast 8am - 9am. Dinner 6pm - 8pm. **CC** Access, Visa. **Other Points:** Children welcome. Pets allowed by arrangement. No smoking area. **P** & **Directions:** Towards the Evesham Rd.
PAT & PETER SHORT ☎ (0789) 204907.
On the south west side of town, Nando's is within easy reach of the shops, the theatre and the River Avon. A good place to stay if you have tickets for the theatre, as you can enjoy dinner here in plenty of time before the performance commences.

⌂ℤ£ **PARKFIELD GUEST HOUSE** 3 Broad Walk, Stratford Upon Avon.
🛏 1 single, 2 double, 2 twin and 1 family bedroom. 3 bedrooms en suite. 1 bathroom. 1 shower. Colour TV, tea/coffee making facilities in all bedrooms. **Hours:** Breakfast 8.15am - 8.45am (or as requested). **CC** Access, Visa. **Other Points:** Central heating. Children over 7 years welcome. Vegetarian meals available. **P Directions:** In the centre of Stratford in the old part of town.
PAULINE RUSH ☎ (0789) 293313.
An attractive Victorian house in a quiet setting about 5 minutes walk from the town and theatre. Friendly atmosphere with personal service from resident owners.

⌂ℤ££ **RAVENHURST** 2 Broad Walk, Stratford Upon Avon.
🛏 3 double, 4 twin, and 2 family bedrooms, 3 of them en suite. **Hours:** 8.15am - 8.45am. **CC** All major cards. **Other Points:** Open bank holidays. Residents' lounge. **(V) Directions:** Broad Walk is a turning off the A439 to Evesham.
R W & B E WORKMAN ☎ (0789) 292515.
Ravenhurst is a Victorian town house, quietly situated yet only a few minutes walk from the theatre and town centre. Every effort is made to ensure guests have a comfortable and enjoyable visit.

Stratford upon Avon continued
Only 15 minutes drive to Warwick Castle and 30 minutes to the Cotswolds.

ΦΦ£££ **SEQUOIA HOUSE PRIVATE HOTEL** 51-53 Shipston Road, Stratford Upon Avon.
⊨ 2 single, 7 double, 6 twin and 6 family bedrooms, 21 bedrooms en suite. 5 bathrooms. 2 showers. Colour TV in all bedrooms and direct dial telephones. **Hours:** Breakfast 7.30am - 9am. ☒ All major cards. **Other Points:** Central heating. Children welcome. No dogs. Licensed. Residents' lounge. Fully air conditioned dining room/conference facility. Vegetarian meal available ▣ ዼ **Directions:** Located on A34 approach road from the South, near Clopton Bridge.
MR P L EVANS. ☎ (0789) 268852.
Beautifully appointed, quietly run, private licensed hotel, superbly situated across the River Avon opposite the Royal Shakespeare Theatre. Large private car park. Delightful garden walk to the Theatre, Riverside Gardens and town centre. Fully air conditioned dining room and conference facility.

⊗££ **SWAN HOUSE HOTEL** The Green, Wilmcote, Stratford upon
ΦΦ£££ Avon.
Hours: Meals 7.30am - 9.30am, 12 noon - 2pm and 7.30pm - 9.30pm. Closed: Christmas Day. **Cuisine:** Extensive range of homemade bar snacks - steak and mushroom pie, lasagne. A la carte - duckling, salmon, peppered sirloin. ⊨ 12 bedrooms all en suite. ☒ Access, AmEx, Visa. **Other Points:** Children welcome. No dogs. Access for disabled on ground floor and to restaurant & bar only. Fax No: (0789) 204875. ▣ ዼ **(V) Directions:** From the A3400, 3 miles NW of Stratford take the Wilmcote turn off.
IAN & DIANA SYKES ☎ (0789) 267030.
An attractive listed building overlooking Mary Arden's House. Swan House occupies a rural setting, yet is close enough to Birmingham to be a good centre for business conferences etc.

⊗££ **THE OPPOSITION RESTAURANT** 13 Sheep Street, Stratford Upon Avon.
Hours: Breakfast 11am - 12 noon, lunch 12 noon - 2pm, dinner 5.30pm - 11pm. **Cuisine:** Continental and American Bistro. ⊨ None. ☒ Access, Visa. **Other Points:** Children welcome. Garden. No dogs. **(V) Directions:** 3 minutes from Royal Shakespeare Theatre.
MR NIGEL LAMBERT ☎ (0789) 69980.
A 500 year old, half-timbered grade II listed 16th century building, converted to a popular bistro with candle lit dining. Homemade Italian, American and continental dishes. Dine before or after the theatre - which is only 5 minutes away.

⊗£ **THE VINTNER CAFE, WINE BAR** 5 Sheep Street, Stratford upon Avon.
Hours: Meals 11am - 11.30pm (last orders 10.15pm). Closed: Christmas Day. **Cuisine:** Wide selection of sweets and salads, vegetarian dishes and steaks. The menu features homecooked dishes and changes daily. ⊨ None. ☒ Access, Visa. **Other Points:** Children welcome. Dogs at management's discretion. Coaches by

Stratford upon Avon continued

appointment. & **(V) Directions:** Off the A04, second left off the High Street. Near Town Hall.

MR N MILLS ☎ (0789) 297 259.

The Vintner's name derives from 1601 when John Smith lived at this address, working as a vintner (a wine merchant) and the Elizabethan decor reflects this association. An extensive, international wine, beer and spirits list and prompt service makes this cafe bar popular with theatre goers. Family run.

STREATLEY ON THAMES Berkshire Map 4 B2

⊗££££ **THE SWAN DIPLOMAT** Streatley on Thames, Berkshire.

Hours: Midweek breakfast 7.30am - 9.30am, lunch 12.30pm - 2pm (last orders) and dinner 7.30pm - 9.30pm (last orders). Sunday 12.30pm - 2pm and 7.30pm - 9pm. Weekends and public holidays, Breakfast 8am - 10am. **Cuisine:** Classic French cuisine. ⊨ 9 single, 12 twin, 22 double, 2 suitable for handicaped guests. All en suite. **CC** All major cards. **Other Points:** Permanently moored Magdalen College Barge for meeting and drinks receptions. Conference suites. Leisure Club. Children welcome. ▣ & **(V) Directions:** Off the A329, 200 metres on the left before the river bridge.

HOTEL DIPLOMAT OF SWEDEN ☎ (0491) 873737.

Set in beautiful Berkshire countryside on the banks of the River Thames, The Swan Diplomat has a rich tradition of providing hospitality to generation upon generation of guests. The high quality and presentation of the cuisine, ambience, unfaulted service, and superb riverside views combines to make dining here a delight. Highly recommended.

STROUD Gloucestershire Map 4 B1

⊗££ **LONDON HOTEL** 30/31 London Road, Stroud.

⌂££ **Hours:** 7.30am - 9.30am, 12 noon - 2pm, and 7pm - 9.30pm (last orders). **Cuisine:** Continental cuisine, dishes including sirloin steak Francaise, Hawaian duck, and Romany chicken. A la carte, table d'hote and bar meals. Good wine list. ⊨ 12 bedrooms, 8 of them en suite, with colour TVs, alarms, telephones, and tea/coffee making facilities. Baby listening devices available. **CC** Access, Visa, AmEx. **Other Points:** Children welcome. No dogs. Open Sunday evenings and bank holidays. Resident's lounge. Afternoon teas. Special diets also catered for. ▣ **(V) Directions:** From Stroud town centre, take A419 towards Cirencester.

MR & MRS PORTAL ☎ (0453) 759992.

A very friendly, welcoming hotel situated in the small industrial town of Stroud, where 5 valleys meet in the beautiful Cotswolds. The food in the candlelit restaurant is of excellent quality, and the accommodation is very comfortable. Places of interest nearby include Gatcombe Park, Gloucester Cathedral, and Slimbridge Wild Fowl Trust.

STUDLAND Dorset Map 4 C1

⊗£££ **THE MANOR HOUSE** Beach Road, Studland Bay, nr Swanage. **Hours:** Breakfast 8.30am - 9.30am, bar lunch 12 noon - 2pm, dinner 7pm - 8.30pm. **Closed:** 17th December to 29th January. **Cuisine:** Local venison, duckling and fresh local seafood. ⊨ 18 bedrooms, all en suite. **CC** Access, Visa. **Other Points:** Children over 5 years welcome. Dogs not permitted in public rooms.

Studland continued

Mastercard and Eurocard also accepted. 9 and 18 hole golf course 2 miles away. ▣ ⅋ **(V) Directions:** 3 miles from Swanage, 3 miles from Sandbanks Ferry.

MR RICHARD ROSE ☎ (092 944) 288

An 18th century Gothic manor in 16 acres of secluded, mature grounds with 2 tennis courts, overlooking the sea and 3 miles of sandy beach. The house has been in the Rose family since 1950 and has been fully modernised whilst retaining the original features and character. Wonderful costal walks.

SUDBURY Suffolk **Map 5 B1**

⊗£ **THE ANGEL** 43 Friar Street, Sudbury.

Hours: Breakfast 8.30am - 11am, Lunch and bar snacks 12 noon - 2pm, Dinner and bar snacks 6pm - 10pm (last orders). **Cuisine:** Traditional English and vegetarian. Homemade dish of the day speciality. ⇌ Twin rooms and 1 family room. **CC** Access, Visa. **Other Points:** Children welcome. Garden dining. No dogs. ▣ ⅋ **(V) Directions:** From town centre follow signs for Quay Theatre.

MR HOAR ☎ (0787) 79038.

Built in the 16th century and with a small walled patio, this is an attractive town pub offering good food at excellent value for money. Comfortable surroundings, welcoming service and a friendly, busy atmosphere complement the good food and ensure an enjoyable meal.

SUTTON Surrey **Map 5 C1**

⌂£££££**ASHLING TARA HOTEL** 44/50 Rose Hill, Sutton.

⇌ 16 bedrooms, 10 en suite. Colour TV, radio, hairdryer, mini bar, direct dial telephone and tea/coffee making facilities. **Hours:** Breakfast served 7.30am - 8.45am, dinner 7pm - 8.30pm (residents only). 1992: Plans to open a la carte restaurant to non-residents. **CC** Access, Visa. **Other Points:** Children welcome. Open Bank Holidays. Residents' lounge. Residents' garden. Full laundry service. Fax facilities. Fax No. (081) 644 7872. ▣ ⅋ **Directions:** Near Angel Hill.

CATHERINE HAROLD ☎ (081) 641 6142.

A family run hotel with a friendly and welcoming atmosphere situated within easy walking distance of Sutton Town centre and directly opposite the Rose Hill Tennis Centre and Sports complex. With the comfort of her guests in mind, Mrs Harold has succeeded in offering a combination of tasty homecooked meals to complement comfortable attractive accommodation. A pleasure to visit.

⊗£££ **LIAISONS** 13 Green Wrythe Lane, Carshalton, Sutton.

Hours: Lunch Monday to Friday 12 noon - 2.30pm, Dinner Monday to Saturday 6pm - 11pm (last orders). Closed: Saturday lunchtime and all day Sunday. **Cuisine:** Spanish Tapas and Continental cuisine. ⇌ None. **CC** All major cards. **Other Points:** Children welcome. No dogs. Terrace dining. Fax as phone number. 2 cocktail bars with an extensive cocktail and wine list. ⅋ **(V) Directions:** From Carshalton High St, cross over bridge. At bottom jct. turn L.

VASOS & ANDROULLA HERODOTOU ☎ (081) 647 9207.

A 25 seater tapas and cocktail bar with a 60 seater Continental Restaurant and cocktail bar to the rear. There is a pleasantly

Sutton continued

relaxed and friendly atmosphere enhanced by the welcoming, efficient staff. Whether you dine in the restaurant or enjoy the Spanish tapas, all food is freshly cooked and of a high standard. Garden patio for al fresco dining. Extensive cocktail list.

⊗££ **THATCHED HOUSE HOTEL** 135 Cheam Road, Cheam, ⏤££££ Sutton.
Hours: Breakfast 7.30am - 9am, lunch by arrangement and dinner 7pm - 9pm (last orders). **Cuisine:** English fare. Chefs specials daily. ⇤ 18 bedrooms, all en suite. Colour TV. Tea/coffee making facilities. Direct dial phone.Baby listening service. Four poster balcony room available. **CC** Access, Visa. **Other Points:** Children welcome. Afternoon teas served.Function room for weddings conferences and business meetings overlooking well-tended garden.Bar closes 12pm **P** & **(V) Directions:** On the A232, opposite Sutton Cricket and Squash Club.
MR & MR P. SELLS ☎ (081) 642 3131.
Situated a short walk from Sutton centre and Cheam village, this lovely thatched cottage has been completely modernised and offers good food, comfortable accommodation and a friendly welcome. Close proximity to Epsom Downs, Wimbledon Tennis, Hampton Court, Windsor Castle and RHS Gardens at Wisley. Golf can be arranged at Banstead Downs only a mile from the Hotel.

SUTTON COLDFIELD West Midlands **Map 4 A1**
⊗££ **GARDEN RESTAURANT at the LADY WINDSOR HOTEL** ⏤££££ Anchorage Road, Sutton Coldfield.
Hours: Restaurant open from 7.15am - 8.30am, 12.30pm - 2pm, and 6.30pm - 9pm. Bar meals served between 12.30pm - 2pm and 6.30pm - 9pm. **Cuisine:** A la carte, table d'hote and bar meals. Continental cuisine, including fish and vegetarian specialities. Good wine list. ⇤ 21 bedrooms, all en suite, with colour TV, telephones, alarms, and tea/coffee making facilities. **CC** All major cards. **Other Points:** Children welcome. Open for Sunday lunch and bank holidays. Resident's lounge and garden. Also caters for private parties. **P** & **(V) Directions:** Off the A453, close to centre of Sutton Coldfield and railway.
ANN & ROBBIE ROBERTSON ☎ (021) 354 6868.
An attractive hotel and restaurant, with friendly service and a warm ambience. The restaurant,as its name suggests, looks out onto lovely, landscaped gardens and, at night, candlelit tables add to the atmosphere. All the food is freshly prepared and there is a wide selection of imaginative dishes to choose from. Situated close to Sutton Park, the Wyndley sport complex and the N.E.C.

⊗££ **SUTTON COURT HOTEL** 66 Lichfield Road, Sutton Coldfield.
Hours: Breakfast 7.30am - 9.30am, lunch 12 noon - 2pm, dinner 7pm - midnight (last orders 10pm). Bar meals 12 noon - 2pm, 7pm - 10.30pm. Closed: Bank Holidays (restaurant). **Cuisine:** Traditional French dishes, Vegetarian meals. ⇤ 64 bedrooms, all en suite. **CC** All major cards. **Other Points:** Children welcome. No dogs. Non-smoking area. Close to NEC and Birmingham Airport. **P** & **(V) Directions:** Off A38 on corner of A5127 and A453.
PETER JOHN BENNETT ☎ (021) 355 6071.

Sutton Coldfield continued

A hotel which has succeeded in retaining its Victorian elegance yet combines to give the best of modern facilities and old fashioned hospitality. The restaurant enjoys a good reputation for dishes prepared from fresh ingredients. This popular restaurant offers efficient, friendly service.

SWANAGE Dorset **Map 4 C1**

£££ HAVENHURST HOTEL Cranborne Road, Swanage.

17 bedrooms, all en suite. 3 single, 4 twin, 8 double and 2 family bedrooms. Tea/coffee/chocolate making facilities in each bedroom. **Hours:** Breakfast 8.30am - 9.15am, Bar lunches, Dinner 7pm. **CC** None. **Other Points:** Children welcome. Garden. Afternoon teas. No smoking in restaurant. Lounge bar with snooker and darts. TV lounge. Hairdryers, iron and ironing board. **P Directions:** Close to the beach. Off Rempstone Road

MRS CHERRETT & MRS ROBSON ☎ (0929) 424224.

A comfortable hotel standing in its own grounds, just a short stroll from the shops, the safe sandy beach and all other amenities. With good home cooked food, a comfortable lounge bar and a spacious colour TV lounge, Havenhurst also offers a high standard of accommodation. The proprietors, who took over the hotel in March 1990, extend a warm and friendly welcome to all guests.

££ MOWLEM RESTAURANT Shore Road, Swanage.

Hours: Meals 12 noon - 2pm and 7pm - 10pm (last orders). Closed: Christmas Day. Morning coffee available from 10am. **Cuisine:** Seafood, steaks, salads, children's menu. None. **CC** Access, Visa. **Other Points:** Children welcome. No dogs. Coaches welcome. **(V) Directions:** On the beach road.

MR S M HOUSLEY - Manager ☎ (0929) 422 496.

Situated on the beach road with views over the beach and bay. Very popular with families as it has a special children's menu and everyone can enjoy watching their meals being prepared in front of them.

SWINDON Wiltshire **Map 4 B1**

££ BLUNSDON HOUSE HOTEL Blunsdon, nr Swindon.

Hours: Open 24 hours a day. **Cuisine:** Fillet steak Blunsdon-style. 88 bedrooms, all en suite. **CC** All major cards. **Other Points:** Children welcome. Leisure Club now open with excellent sports facilities, pools, spa, saunas, creche and beauty therapy. **P & (V) Directions:** 1 mile north of Blunsdon just off A419.

MR P CLIFFORD ☎ (0793) 721701.

Close to junction 15 on the M4, this hotel caters for every type of traveller. It is family owned and managed with a pleasant, friendly, relaxed atmosphere. The restaurant has developed a strong local following.

TEDDINGTON Middlesex **Map 4 B2**

£££ THE ITALIAN PLACE BRASSERIE 38 High Street, CLUB Teddington.

Hours: Lunch 12 noon - 2.30pm, dinner 6.30pm - 11pm. Open Bank Holidays. Sunday 11am - 3pm, 7pm - 10.30pm. **Cuisine:** Italian cuisine, dishes may include - Polenta con Funghi, Fettuccine al Salmone, Manzo alla Mostarda, Insalata Marinara.

Teddington continued

Specials change daily. ⇌ None. 💳 All major cards. **Other Points:** Children welcome. **(V) Directions:** On Teddington High Street. FEDERICO SECOLA ☎ (081) 943 2433.

An excellent Italian restaurant in the centre of Teddington. The menu offers an extensive choice of authentic Italian dishes at very reasonable prices, with all meals freshly cooked and well presented. Highly recommended for the excellent food and welcoming service in a lively yet relaxed atmosphere. Special Sunday Brunch. Live Jazz on Sunday evening.

TETBURY Gloucestershire **Map 4 B1**

⊗££ **THE PRIORY INN** London Road, Tetbury.

⊞£££ **Hours:** Breakfast 7.30am - 9.30am, lunch 12 noon - 2.30pm, dinner 7pm - 10pm (last orders). Sunday lunch 12 noon - 2pm, dinner 7pm - 9pm. **Cuisine:** Hot potted shrimps with sherry, tornedos rossini, entrecote bordelaise, honey roasted duck. Varied bar snacks. ⇌ Expanding early 1992 from 3 to 16 en suite bedrooms. Lounge and separate dining room. 💳 Access, Visa. **Other Points:** Children welcome. No smoking areas. 🅿 ⅃ **(V) Directions:** On A433 just outside town centre.
JUNE & EDDIE BUSH ☎ (0666) 502251.

Situated close to the centre of the lively market town, this 19th century Free House offers an extremely warm welcome. Nearby are historic Highgrove House, Gatcombe Park, St. Mary's with the third highest spire in England and the Arbovetum at Westonbirt.

TEYNHAM Kent **Map 5 C1**

⊗£££ **THE SHIP INN & SMUGGLERS RESTAURANT** Conyer

W Quay, Teynham, nr Sittingbourne.

Hours: Lunch and bar meals 12 noon - 2.30pm, dinner and bar meals 7pm - 10.30pm (last orders in restaurant). **Cuisine:** Moules Mariniere, King Neptunes banquet, steak au poivre. Huge choice of whiskies, rums, brandies, liqueurs, wine, real ales, draught and bottled beers. ⇌ None. 💳 Access, Visa. **Other Points:** Children welcome. Dogs allowed in main bar only. Known as the 'Whisky House of Kent' - 250 different whiskies. 150 different liqueurs. 🅿 **(V) Directions:** 2 miles off the A2 in village of Conyer. On waters edge.
ALEC HEARD ☎ (0795) 521404.

Hidden away in the picturesque village of Conyer which nestles amongst the orchards and hopfields of the marsh farms but well worth searching for. An attractive pub and restaurant offering good food and a warm and friendly atmosphere. The interior is full of character. Mercier Corps d'Elite 1991 for their excellent wine list, over 60 bottled beers, & 250 different whiskies.

THAME Oxfordshire **Map 4 B2**

⊗££ **THE PEACOCK HOTEL & RESTAURANT** Henton, Near

⊞£££ Chinnor, Thame.

Hours: 7am - 9.30am - lunch & bar snacks 12 noon - 2pm (last orders), dinner 7pm - 10pm (last orders). Open Bank Holidays. **Cuisine:** Full a la carte menu, Sunday table d'hote. Dishes may include avacado with prawns, rainbow trout with toasted almonds and a choice of sweets. ⇌ 19 bedrooms, all en suite. 💳 Access, Visa, AmEx. **Other Points:** Children welcome.

Thame continued

Dogs allowed. Garden dining. Fax No. (0844) 53891. Log fire. **P**
& **(V) Directions:** Off B4009, approx half a mile from Chinnor.
MR HERBERT GOOD. ☎ (0844) 53519.

*Dating back to the 16th century, this establishment is decorated
in keeping with the age and character of the building.
Accommodation is of a high standard. Frequented by mixed
ages, the restaurant enjoys a comfortable ambience which is
enhanced by the efficiency of the staff. Serving generous
portions of well cooked and presented meals.*

THAMES DITTON Surrey **Map 4 B2**

⊗£ **THE GREYHOUND** Hampton Court Way, Weston Green,
Thames Ditton.
Hours: Meals served 12 noon - 10pm. **Cuisine:** A la carte menu
and wide choice of dishes such as Swordfish Steak, Steaks, Steak &
Kidney Pie, Lasagne, salads & sandwiches. Sunday Roast.
Barbecues. ☒ None. **CC** All major cards. **Other Points:** Children
welcome. Meals served all day. Garden. Barbecues. **(V)**
Directions: 200 yds towards Hampton Court Palace from 'Scilly
Isles' roundabouts
ROBERT & CHRIS UPJOHN ☎ (081) 398 1155.

*Built in 1834, The Greyhound is a very popular pub serving
food. The menu offers a wide choice of dishes, all homecooked,
attractively presented and in generous portions. The pub enjoys
a cheerful, relaxed atmosphere and on Sundays there is a
barbecue in the garden. A welcoming, traditional pub with
good wholesome food at excellent value for money.*

THETFORD Norfolk **Map 5 A1**

⊗££ **WEREHAM HOUSE HOTEL** 24 White Hart Street, Thetford.
⌂££ **Hours:** Breakfast served 7am - 9am, dinner 7pm - 9.30pm.
Cuisine: Dishes may include Rainbow Trout, Salmon Steak with
Hollandaise sauce, Honey Roasted Duck, Tournedos Marseillais,
Venison in Red Wine. ☒ 8 bedrooms, 6 en suite. **CC** Access, Visa.
Other Points: Children welcome. Open Bank Holidays. Garden.
AA 1 star listing. **P** & **(V) Directions:** A134 Thetford - Bury Rd,
into Bridge St, leads to White Hart St.
COLIN RODGERS ☎ (0842) 761956.

*A small, well run, family hotel set in pleasant surroundings. In a
relaxed, friendly atmosphere you can enjoy the tasty meals
which are on offer. Comfortable accommodation.*

TONBRIDGE Kent **Map 5 C1**

⊗££ **CHIMNEYS MOTOR INN** Pembury Road, Tonbridge.
⌂££ **Hours:** Breakfast 7am - 9am (weekends 8am - 10am), lunch 12
noon - 2pm (last orders), bar snacks 12 noon - 2.15pm (last orders),
dinner 6pm - 10pm (last orders), evening bar snacks 6pm -
9.45pm (last orders). **Cuisine:** Predominantly English cuisine
including steaks, fried scampi, and traditional Sunday lunch.
Vegetarian dishes. Childrens menu. ☒ 39 bedrooms, all en suite.
CC Access, Visa. **Other Points:** Children welcome. Open Bank
Holidays. Garden dining. Residents' lounge. Guide dogs only.
Meeting rooms available. Camera security car park. **P** & **(V)**
Directions: Adjacent to the A21 and 9 miles from Jct 5 of M25.
MR SHAUN JEARY - Manager ☎ (0732) 773111

Tonbridge continued

Situated on the south side of Tonbridge in a very pleasant rural location, Chimneys is an ideal stopping place for both the business and holiday motorist. Enjoy a meal or drink within the happy atmosphere of the Steakhouse. Families are warmly welcomed by the friendly staff. Set price for single or double occupancy rooms or a family room for 2 adults and 2 children.

⊗£££ **THE CHASER INN** Stumble, Shipbourne, Nr Tonbridge.
£££ **Hours:** Breakfast 7.30am - 9.30am, Lunch 12.30pm - 2pm, Dinner 7.30pm - 9.30pm (last orders). Bar meals 12 noon - 2pm and 7pm - 9.30pm. Restaurant closed: Sunday and Monday evening. **Cuisine:** Modern English/French cuisine. Table d'hote menu in restaurant. Dishes may include Lamb fillet on a raspberry & mint sauce, Lemon sole. Also bar snacks. ⊨ 15 bedrooms, all en suite. One bedroom has been designed with facilities for the disabled. **CC** Access, Visa, AmEx. **Other Points:** Children welcome. Garden dining. Weddings and private functions catered for. Fax No: (0732) 810941. **P** & **(V) Directions:** A227, north of Tonbridge. Next to Shipbourne Church & opp. Green.
RON & CINDY NIX ☎ (0732) 810360.
Built in the 1880's, The Chaser Inn is an attractive colonial style building. An extensive and imaginative range of food is offered in the bars and a creative set menu can be enjoyed in the restaurant which features a beamed vaulted ceiling and panelled walls. Only minutes from the M25, M20 and M26 motorway networks, The Chaser Inn is well placed to greet travellers.

TOTLAND BAY Isle of Wight **Map 4 C1**
£££ **SENTRY MEAD HOTEL** Madeira Road, Totland Bay.
⊨ 14 bedrooms, all en suite. **Hours:** Breakfast 8.30am - 9.15am, Lunch 12 noon - 2pm and Dinner 7pm - 8pm. **CC** None. **Other Points:** Children welcome. Garden. Pets allowed. **P Directions:** On the Headland, opposite Turf Walk.
MIKE & JULIE HODGSON ☎ (0983) 753212.
An imposing Victorian country house on the headland, yet just a two minute walk from the beach, providing good quality, comfortable accommodation in attractive pleasant surroundings. You can be assured of a warm welcome from resident proprietors, Mike and Julie Hodgson. Ideal base for exploring Alum Bay and the Needles.

TROTTON West Sussex **Map 4 C2**
⊗£ **KEEPERS ARMS** Trotton, Rogate, Petersfield.
Hours: Open 11am - 2.30pm and 6pm - 11.00pm (last orders for food 2pm and 10pm). No meals served Monday. **Cuisine:** Menu changes from day to day, all dishes are freshly prepared. ⊨ None. **CC** Access, Visa. **Other Points:** No dogs. **P** & **(V) Directions:** On the A272 mid-way between Petersfield and Midhurst.
COLIN S MACHIN ☎ (0730) 813724.
A family run 17th century country inn, offering good food and real ale in pleasant and friendly surroundings. There is an outside patio for eating and drinking in the summer.

CENTRAL & SOUTHERN ENGLAND

TROWBRIDGE Wiltshire **Map 4 B1**

⊗££ **THE POLEBARN HOTEL** Polebarn Road, Trowbridge.

⊞££££ **Hours:** Breakfast 7.30am - 9.30am, Lunch 12 noon - 2pm (last orders 1.45pm) and Dinner 7pm - 9pm (last orders 8.45pm). **Cuisine:** A la carte, fixed price menu and bar menu. Grills a speciality. ⊨ 12 bedrooms, all en suite. **CC** Access, Visa. **Other Points:** Children welcome. Afternoon teas. **P** **(V) Directions:** Town centre, on A361.

MR & MRS BINDER ☎ (0225) 777006.

A warm welcome is offered by Mr & Mrs Binder, the chef/manager team, who until recently ran a two casserole Les Routiers restaurant in Guernsey. The hotel cellar has been converted to form a 'bistro style' bar & restaurant, beneath this large, listed Georgian Townhouse.

⊗££ **THE SOMERSET ARMS** Semington, Nr Trowbridge.

⊞££ **Hours:** Breakfast 7am - 10.30am, Lunch 11.30am - 2.30pm (last orders 2pm) and Dinner 6.30pm - 10.30pm (last orders 10pm). **Cuisine:** A la carte menu, serving steak, fish, pies. ⊨ 10 bedrooms, 7 en suite. **CC** All major cards. **Other Points:** Children welcome. Pets allowed. Garden. Teas. No smoking areas. **P** & **(V) Directions:** On A350.

JOHN DELANEY ☎ (0380) 870328.

This traditional old coaching inn offers comfortable and attractive accommodation with a warm atmosphere. In the restaurant you will find a wide choice of home made fayre, including high quality pies, friendly staff and a completely separate no smoking room - a pleasant change.

TUNBRIDGE WELLS Kent **Map 5 C1**

⊗££££ **ROYAL WELLS INN** Mount Ephraim, Tunbridge Wells.

[CLUB] **Hours:** Breakfast 7.30am - 9.30am (weekends 8am - 10am), 12.30pm - 2.15pm and dinner 7.30pm - 9.30pm/10pm. Bar snacks 12.30pm - 2.30pm and 6.30pm - 10.30pm, except Sunday. **Cuisine:** All fish dishes, fried mushrooms with Rocquefort sauce, duckling. ⊨ 22 bedrooms. **CC** All major cards. **Other Points:** Dogs allowed (except in restaurant). Children welcome. Coaches by appointment. Vegetarian meals by arrangement. Limited access for disabled. **P** **(V)**

DAVID & ROBERT SLOAN ☎ (0892) 511188.

A Victorian family run hotel, crowned with the royal crest - a reminder that Queen Victoria as a young princess stayed here. Both the restaurant and the bar have been tastefully decorated and serve a good selection of home cooked meals. Magnificent conservatory restaurant. Good value brasserie.

⊗££ **RUSSELL HOTEL** 80 London Road, Tunbridge Wells.

⊞££££ **Hours:** Breakfast 7am - 9am, dinner 7pm - 9.30pm. Sunday dinner
[CLUB] served 7pm - 9pm (last orders). **Cuisine:** A la carte menu, fixed 3 course menu, bar snacks. Dishes include stuffed mushrooms, veal cooked in marsala & cream, grilled steak in mustard sauce. ⊨ 26 rooms, 2 single, 13 twin and 11 double rooms. All en suite. **CC** All major cards. **Other Points:** Children welcome. Designated no smoking bedrooms. **P** **(V) Directions:** Exit 5 on M25 (A21). A26 London Road.

MR & MRS K A WILKINSON ☎ (0892) 544833.

Tunbridge Wells continued

The Russell Hotel is a large Victorian House furnished to a high standard. It is situated facing the common and is only a few minutes walk from the town centre. This hotel offers generous portions of appetising meals, cooked from local fresh produce. The staff are welcoming and helpful making a stay here very comfortable.

⊗£££ **THE BOTTLE HOUSE INN & RESTAURANT** Smarts Hill, Penshurst, Tunbridge Wells.
Hours: Bar meals 11am - 2.30pm. Dinner 6pm - 11pm. Closed: Sunday evening. **Cuisine:** Dishes in the restaurant may inlcude Fresh Fish, Mediterranean King Prawns, Fillet Steak Voronof. Bar meals menu and specials board. ⊨ None. **CC** Access, Visa. **Other Points:** Limited access for disabled. Dogs allowed. Garden dining. **P** (V)
GORDON & VALERIE MEER ☎ (0892) 870306.
A very popular country pub set high on a hill. The interior has an olde worlde feel with exposed beams, oak tables and chairs. The cuisine is mainly British and European with all dishes very well cooked and attractively presented. With friendly service, a relaxed atmosphere, excellent food and a garden for summer, the Bottle House is a good choice for an enjoyable meal.

⊗££ **WINSTON MANOR HOTEL** Beacon Road, Crowborough, [CLUB] Tunbridge Wells.
Hours: Breakfast 7.30am - 9.30am, Winstons Restaurant 7.30pm - 9.30pm. Coffee Shop 7.30pm - 10pm. **Cuisine:** A la carte, Table d'hote and Coffee Shop menus. French/English. Childrens menu available. Imaginative dishes for vegetarians. ⊨ 50 bedrooms, all en suite. **CC** All major cards. **Other Points:** Children welcome. Garden. Dogs allowed. Afternoon tea. No smoking area. Conference and banqueting facilities. Limited disabled access. **P** (V) **Directions:** Situated between Tunbridgewells and Uckfield on the A26.
MR FRAZIER ☎ (0892) 652772.
This large, late Victorian Hotel is set in the heart of the Ashdown Forest within easy reach of Gatwick and the South coast, offering excellent facilities including a leisure club. The atmosphere is quiet and relaxed and the food and service outstanding.

UCKFIELD East Sussex **Map 5 C1**
⊗££ **CHEQUERS INN** High Street, Maresfield, Near Uckfield.
⊞£££ **Hours:** Breakfast 7am - 9.30am, Lunch 12 noon - 2pm, Dinner [CLUB] 7pm - 10pm (9.30pm Sundays). **Cuisine:** Bar meals, A la Carte and fixed price menus. ⊨ 13 bedrooms, all en suite. **CC** Access, Visa, AmEx. **Other Points:** Children welcome. Garden. Afternoon teas. Dogs allowed. **P** ⅓ (V) **Directions:** Centre of Village by the church.
MRS M CURTIES ☎ (0825) 763843.
A 17th century Coaching Inn situated in the centre of the village of Maresfield. Recently refurbished, Chequers offers good food and accommodation with satellite TV, tea/coffee making facilities and trouser press in all rooms. The atmosphere and service are warm and friendly.

Uckfield continued

⊗££££ **HALLAND FORGE HOTEL & RESTAURANT** Halland, nr
🛏££££ Lewes.

Hours: Breakfast from 8am - 12 noon, lunch 12 noon - 2pm,
dinner 7pm - 9.30pm (last orders). Meals in Coffee Shop 8am -
6pm. Tues-Friday breakfast from 7.30 am. **Cuisine:** English,
French and Italian dishes. Only fresh ingredients. 🛏 20
bedrooms, all en suite. **CC** All major cards. **Other Points:** Children
over 5 years welcome. No dogs in public rooms. Fax No: (0825)
840773. **P** & **Directions:** At the junction of the A22 and B2192 4
miles south of Uckfield.

MR & MRS J M HOWELL ☎ (0825) 840456.

*All dishes are cooked to order for the restaurant, whilst the
coffee shop is self service. A family-run hotel in its own grounds
which include lawns, flower beds and woodlands. Its location is
ideal for the South Downs, Ashdown Forest and the coast at
Eastbourne and Brighton.*

UPAVON Wiltshire **Map 4 C1**

⊗££ **THE ANTELOPE INN** High Street, Upavon, Nr Pewsey.
🛏££ **Hours:** Lunch & bar snacks 12 noon - 2.20pm, dinner & bar
snacks 7pm - 10.25pm. **Cuisine:** English cuisine, dishes may
include - seafood & bacon mornay, stilton fritters, local pink trout &
prawns, vension steak, home made pies and sweets. 🛏 5
bedrooms. **CC** Access, Visa. **Other Points:** Children welcome.
Dogs allowed. Pets corner. **P** **(V) Directions:** Centre of Upavon -
On the junction of A345 and A342.

MR PARRISH ☎ (0980) 630206.

*Set in the pleasant village of Upavon, this former coaching inn
dates back to the 1600's. Tastefully decorated and offering
comfortable accommodation. Enjoy generous helpings of good
food in a relaxing atmosphere.*

UPPER BENEFIELD Northamptonshire **Map 4 A2**

⊗££ **THE WHEATSHEAF HOTEL & RESTAURANT** Upper
🛏£££ Benefield, Corby, Near Peterborough.

Hours: Breakfast 7.30am - 9.30am, lunch 12 noon - 3pm and
7.30pm - 12pm (last orders 9.30pm). Bar meals 12 noon - 2.30pm
and 7.30pm - 9.30pm. **Cuisine:** Above average quality bar meals
and choice from a la carte menu. 🛏 13 bedrooms, all en suite.
CC All major cards. **Other Points:** Children welcome. Garden
dining. Pets allowed. Open Bank holidays and Sundays. Residents
lounge. **P** & **(V) Directions:** Off the A427, 4 miles from Corby
and 12 miles from Peterborough.

MR & MRS LEWITT-COOKE ☎ (08325) 254.

*An attractive stone built building, set in its own well-tended
garden, offering good quality food at reasonable prices and
comfortable accommodation. With a choice of bar meals in the
welcoming stone and oak-beamed bar or a la carte menu in the
attractively decorated restaurant and both providing friendly
and efficent service.*

UPPER GORNAL West Midlands **Map 4 A1**

⊗££ **THE OLD MILL** Windmill Street, Upper Gornal.
Hours: Lunch 12 noon - 3pm (last orders 2pm) and dinner 6.30pm
- 11pm (last orders 10pm). Open Sunday lunch 12.30pm -
1.30pm. Closed:Sunday and Monday evenings. **Cuisine:**

Upper Gornal continued

Restaurant menu: Salmon in Asparagus sauce, Boeuf Bourgnon. Bar meals. Homemade Beef in local beer pie plus 15 homemade dishes. ⊨ None. **CC** Access, Visa. **Other Points:** Children welcome. Garden. Pets allowed. **P** ᠔ **(V) Directions:** On Windmill Street, off Hill Street, a mile from Sedgley bullring. JOHN MIDWOOD ☎ (0902) 887707.

A traditional oak beamed inn with restaurant above, serving good homemade food using only the freshest ingredients. Extensive menu to cater for all tastes, friendly attentive service and recently refurbished, comfortable surroundings.

VENTNOR Isle of Wight **Map 4 C2**

⊗££ **OLD PARK HOTEL** St Lawrence, Nr Ventnor.

⊞£££ **Hours:** Breakfast 8.30am - 9.30am, bar lunches, dinner 7.30pm - 8.30pm. **Cuisine:** Extensive fixed price 5 course menu (pies, pasties/traditional English). ⊨ 37 rooms. All en suite. **CC** Access, Visa. **Other Points:** Children welcome. Garden. Afternoon teas. Dogs allowed. Sauna. Solarium. Heated indoor swimming pool. Laundry. Bargain breaks. **P** ᠔ **(V)**

MR R W THORNTON ☎ (0983) 852583.

Games room, under fives supper between 4.30pm and 5.30pm, sauna, solarium, swimming pool, and no danger from traffic - all this plus comfortable accommodation, good food and a friendly atmosphere, adds up to a fantastic family holiday. Mr Thornton has created a fun safe haven for children, whilst providing all the qualities of a good hotel.

⊞££ **ST MAUR HOTEL** Castle Road, Ventnor.

CLUB ⊨ 3 single, 4 double, 4 twin and 4 family rooms, 13 of them en suite. All rooms have tea/coffee making facilities. Colour TVs in rooms can be arranged. **Hours:** Open February to December. Breakfast 8.30am - 9am, Dinner 6.30pm - 7pm. **CC** Access, Visa. **Other Points:** Children welcome. Afternoon teas served. **P** **(V) Directions:** W of Ventnor,St Maur is 100yds up Castle Rd at end of Park Ave-A3055

D J GROOCOCK ☎ (0983) 852570.

St Maur is beautifully situated on town level, only minutes from Ventnor beach and Steephill Cove. All bedrooms have views over the hotel gardens and some have sea views.

WADHURST East Sussex **Map 5 C1**

⊗£ **BEST BEECH HOTEL** Best Beech Hill, Off Wadhurst Road,
⊞£ Wadhurst.

Hours: Breakfast 8am - 9.30am, bar snacks 12 noon - 2pm, dinner 7pm - 9.30pm. Closed: Sunday & Monday evening only. **Cuisine:** Menu may feature Chicken Breast Old Vine, Chef's Steak & Kidney Pie, Prawn Curry, Pork Loin with Apricots. ⊨ 4 bedrooms. **CC** Access, Visa. **Other Points:** Children welcome. Open Bank Holidays. Garden dining. **P** ᠔ **(V) Directions:** On B2100 - Mark crossroads.

ANTHONY & JENNIE PEEL ☎ (0892) 88 2406.

A lovely old Inn, decorated in keeping with the age and character of the building. The food is of a very high standard, using only fresh ingredients, and is complemented by a good choice of wines and beers. Popular with all ages, the

Wadhurst continued

atmosphere is that of a traditional country Inn and the service is equally welcoming and friendly.

⊗££ **THE GREYHOUND** St James's Square, Wadhurst.
Hours: Meals 12 noon - 2pm and 7pm - 9.30pm. **Cuisine:** House menu contains a large range of fish, poultry, veal & beef dishes - all of a very high standard. Separate a la carte & Sunday Roast luncheon menu. ⊨ None. **CC** Access, Visa. **Other Points:** Children welcome. **P** ⅋ **(V) Directions:** Situated in the centre of Wadhurst.
ROBIN & TANNIA HEALE ☎ (089 288) 3224.
An historical coaching inn with heavily-beamed and half-panelled bar, inglenook fireplace and photographs of past eras. Variety of draught lagers and real ales, plus a fine selection of wines.

⊗££ **THE OLD VINE** Cousley Wood, Wadhurst.
Hours: Bar meals 12 noon - 2.30pm and 6pm - 9.30pm (last orders). Dinner 7pm - 11.30pm (last orders 9.30pm). **Cuisine:** Modern European cuisine with a good vegetarian selection. Dishes may include Peppered Sirloin, Chicken Caprice. ⊨ None. **CC** Access, Visa, Diners. **Other Points:** Children welcome. Dogs allowed. Garden dining. Bookings for restaurant and bar menus accepted. Live Jazz Monday nights. Switch accepted. **P** ⅋ **(V) Directions:** Off the A21 at Lamberhurst onto B2100 direction Wadhurst.
ANTHONY PEEL ☎ (089288) 2271.
The Old Vine provides an extensive choice of excellently cooked food in the bar and restaurant. All meals are freshly prepared and attractively presented whilst offering excellent value for money. The service is friendly and efficient, in keeping with the busy, friendly atmosphere. Very highly recommended by the Les Routiers inspector.

WALBERSWICK Suffolk **Map 5 A2**
⊗£ **BELL HOTEL** Walberswick, nr Southwold.
🛏£ **Hours:** Meals 9am - 9.30am, 12 noon - 2pm and 7.30pm - 9pm (last orders). **Cuisine:** Fresh, local fish, shell fish, game, vegetarian dishes. ⊨ 5 bedrooms, 2 en suite. 1 bathroom. **CC** Access, Visa. **Other Points:** Children welcome. **P** ⅋ **(V) Directions:** Very close to the beach at Walberswick.
MARK & FRANCIS STANSALL ☎ (0502) 723109.
The Bell is approximately 600 years old and still has the original stone floors, oak beams and fireplaces. The hotel is 100 yards from the beach and the large garden is very popular in the summer.

WALSALL West Midlands **Map 4 A1**
🛏£££ **ABBERLEY HOTEL** 29 Bescot Road, Walsall.
⊨ 29 bedrooms: 1 family room, 7 doubles, 5 twin and 16 single, all en suite and with TV (satellite), telephone. Laundry service. **Hours:** Breakfast 7.15am - 8.30am, Lunch 12 noon - 2pm, Dinner 6pm - 8.30pm. **CC** Access, Visa. **Other Points:** Children welcome. Garden. French, Italian & Spanish spoken. No smoking in restaurant. Fax No: (0922) 720933. **P** ⅋ **Directions:** Quarter of a mile from Junction 9 M6. Off A461 to Walsall.

Walsall continued

MR & MRS STONE ☎ (0922) 27413.

An impressive Victorian building which has been carefully modernised to complement the original craftsmanship. The accommodation is excellent value for money and the restaurant offers Vietnamese specialities, as well as traditional English food. Highly recommended by our Inspector.

⊗£££ **FAIRLAWNS HOTEL AND RESTAURANT** Little Aston Road, Aldridge, nr Walsall.
Hours: Lunch 12.30 noon - 2pm, Dinner 7pm -10pm (last orders). Closed: Saturday lunchtimes and Sunday evenings. **Cuisine:** Modern British cooking. ⊨ 36 bedrooms all en suite. ☒ All major cards. **Other Points:** Children welcome. Dogs allowed. ☐ ㅊ **(V) Directions:** From M6 junction 5 pick up A452 towards Brownhills. JOHN PETTE ☎ (0922) 55122
Staff attentive and efficient, promoting a relaxed atmosphere in this quiet hotel and restaurant with views over the countryside. Local attractions include Stratford-Upon-Avon, Warwick Castle, the Aerospace and Black country museums and Alton Towers.

WALTON ON THAMES Surrey Map 4 C2
⊗££ **SIXTIES WINE BAR** New Zealand Avenue, Walton on Thames.
Hours: Restaurant meals 12 noon - 2.15pm and 6pm - 10.15pm. Closed: Monday evening and all day Sunday. **Cuisine:** Fresh, local produce. Each dish cooked to order. No frozen foods. ⊨ None. ☒ All major cards. **Other Points:** No dogs. ㅊ **(V)** MR & MRS NEIL BARKBY ☎ (0932) 221685.
The small bar area of the 36-seater wine bar leaves plenty of room for the restaurant. The cosy atmosphere, varied wine list and good food make this a popular spot with the locals.

WARE Hertfordshire Map 5 B1
⊗£££ **LE RENDEZ-VOUS RESTAURANT** 64 High Street, Ware.
Ⓦ **Hours:** Lunch 12.15pm - 2pm Friday and Saturday only. Dinner
[CLUB] 7.30pm - 9.30pm (last orders) Tuesday to Saturday only. **Cuisine:** Traditional French Regional cooking. A different region is featured each week. ⊨ None. ☒ Access, Visa. **Other Points:** Children welcome. Evening parking available in Church Street, only a few yards away. ㅊ **(V) Directions:** On main street in Ware, almost opposite Post Office.
MICHAEL KEYTE ☎ (0920) 461021.
A 40-seat restaurant specialising in Regional French cuisine. Each week the restaurant features the dishes, cheeses and the wines of a chosen region. The food is all freshly cooked to an excellent standard and the set menu ensures good value for money. The French staff provide a warm welcome and friendly service. Highly recommended for its excellent food and service.

WARMINSTER Wiltshire Map 4 C1
⊗£ **FARMERS HOTEL** 1 Silver Street, Warminster.
⬙£ **Hours:** Meals 7am - 9.30am, 12 noon - 2pm and 6.15pm - 12 midnight (last orders 10.45pm). **Cuisine:** Fettucini alla carbonara, veal marsala, and steak and kidney pie. ⊨ 18 bedrooms, 11 en suite. ☒ All major cards. **Other Points:** Access for disabled to

Warminster continued

ground floor. Children welcome. Dogs not allowed in public rooms. Coaches welcome. ▣ **(V) Directions:** On the A36.
G BRANDANI ☎ (0985) 212068/213815
Situated on the A36 in the centre of town and very convenient for Longleat. Although the building is 400 years old and listed, the interior has contemporary decor.

⊗££ **OLD BELL HOTEL** 42 Market Place, Warminster.
⌂££££ **Hours:** Breakfast 7.30am - 9.30am, Lunch 12 noon - 3pm, Dinner 6pm - 10.30pm (last orders). Bar meals 12 noon - 2.30pm and 6pm - 9pm. Hotel closed: 24th and 25th December. **Cuisine:** English cuisine. A la carte and carvery menus, bar meals. ⊨ 20 bedrooms, 14 en suite. **CC** All major cards **Other Points:** Children welcome. Dogs allowed. Residents' lounge. Courtyard where meals can be taken. 2 bars. Private parties & receptions. Fax No: (0985) 217111. ▣ **(V) Directions:** In the centre of Warminster.
HOWARD ASTBURY ☎ (0985) 216611.
Part of the Old Bell dates from 1483 and much of the character and old English charm has been retained whilst adding modern comforts. Enjoy the high standard of English cuisine in the candlelit restaurant or good carvery and bar meals. On warm days relax in the attractive courtyard or by the open log fires in winter. Comfortable accommodation and excellent, welcoming service.

WARWICK Warwickshire **Map 4 A1**
⊗££ **LORD LEYCESTER HOTEL** Jury Street, Warwick.
Hours: Breakfast 7.30am - 9.30am, lunch 12 noon - 2pm and dinner 7pm - 8.30pm (last orders). Bar meals 12 noon - 2.30pm and 6pm - 8.30pm. **Cuisine:** Lord Leycester Grill (breakfast). ⊨ 52 bedrooms, all en suite. **CC** All major cards. **Other Points:** Children welcome. Pets allowed. Afternoon tea served. ▣ & **(V) Directions:** Off the Leamington Spa/Birmingham road, adjacent to the Castle.
MR P JOHNSON ☎ (0926) 491481.
Ideally situated for the busy executive or the tourist in search of England's historic heartland. Good food and friendly, helpful service.

⊗££ **TUDOR HOUSE INN** West Street, Warwick.
⌂££££ **Hours:** Breakfast 7am -9.30am, lunch 12 noon - 3pm and dinner 6pm - 11pm (last orders 10.45pm). **Cuisine:** Traditional English cuisine. ⊨ 11 bedrooms, 8 en suite. **CC** All major cards. **Other Points:** Children welcome. Afternoon teas. No pets. Garden. ▣ **(V) Directions:** On the A429, almost opposite the entrance to Warwick Castle.
MR P MCCOSKER & MR M KUTNER ☎ (0926) 495447
A privately owned inn of great charm and character. Dating from 1472 it still has a wealth of timbers many of which were used in old warships, and is one of the few buildings to survive the great fire of Warwick in 1694. The Inn offers good, plentiful food at reasonable prices in a very friendly and welcoming atmosphere. Good value wine.

WELFORD

WATLINGTON Oxfordshire **Map 4 B2**

®££ **THE WELL HOUSE** 34 High Street, Watlington.
Hours: Meals 12 noon - 2pm and 7.30pm - 9.30pm (last orders).
CLUB Closed: Sunday evening and Monday (except to residents), and
the first 2 weeks in February. **Cuisine:** Seasonal specials, eg
boned quail with hazelnut stuffing, salmon en croute with ginger
and herb sauce. Chocolate velvet cake and creme brulee. 🛏 9
bedrooms, all en suite. **CC** All major cards. **Other Points:** Children
welcome. No dogs. 🅿 ♿ **(V) Directions:** On the main street in
Watlington, 2 miles from junction 6 off M40.
ALAN & PAT CRAWFORD ☎ (049 161) 3333.
*An elegant 15th century house in a small picturesque town at
the foot of the Chilterns, some 40 miles from London and 30
minutes from Heathrow Airport. The Well House restaurant
comprises of an attractive cocktail bar and dining room with
inglenook fireplace. Close to National Trust woodlands.*

WATTON AT STONE Hertfordshire **Map 5 B1**

®£ **THE GEORGE & DRAGON** High Street, Watton-At-Stone.
Hours: Bar meals 12 noon - 10pm (last orders). 12 noon - 2pm
Sunday. Restaurant meals available, but in higher price range than
stated. **Cuisine:** Wide selection of bar meals using only freshest
ingredients, including lunchtime dish of the day. 🛏 None. **CC** All
major cards. **Other Points:** Small shrub-screened garden with
table sets and patio. 🅿 **Directions:** Off the A602, close to
Stevenage and Ware.
KEVIN & CHRISTINE DINNIN ☎ (0920) 830285.
*A 16th century inn, situated in attractive village handy to
Benington Lordship Gardens, offering fresh, imaginative food.
The main bar with bay windows and an interesting mix of
antique and modern prints, has country kitchen armchairs
around attractive old tables and makes a pleasant atmosphere
for sampling their excellent selection of bar meals. Friendly
efficent service.*

WEEDON Northamptonshire **Map 4 A2**

®£ **CROSSROADS** High Street, Weedon.
Hours: Breakfast and snacks served 7.15am - 6pm, lunch 12 noon
- 2pm, dinner 6.30pm - 10.30pm. Closed: Christmas Day.
Cuisine: Fine English cuisine with in-house specialities - Steak and
kidney pie and Raspberry pie. 🛏 48 bedrooms, all en suite. **CC** All
major cards. **Other Points:** Children welcome. No dogs. Fax No:
(0327) 40849. Telex 312311. 🅿 ♿ **(V) Directions:** At the junction
of the A5 and the A45, 3 miles from M1 junction 16.
RICHARD & WENDY AMOS ☎ (0327) 40354.
*Character bars, luxury rooms, a renowned restaurant and every
modern amenity combines to make this a splendid Victorian
hotel. A full descriptive wine list, together with friendly, well-
informed advice to assist in your choice. Good wine
complemented by fresh, well-presented cuisine will ensure
your next visit is a memorable one.*

WELFORD Northamptonshire **Map 4 A2**

®£ **THE SHOULDER OF MUTTON INN** 12 High Street,
Welford.
Hours: Lunch 12 noon - 2pm and dinner 7pm - 9.30pm. Closed
for meals on Thursday. **Cuisine:** Grilled steaks, seafood platter.

Welford continued

📥 None. **CC** Access, Visa. **Other Points:** Children Welcome. Mastercard also accepted. **P** & **(V) Directions:** On the A50, mid-way between Leicester and Northampton.

ARTHUR & JUDY CORLETT ☎ (0858) 575375.

Charming 17th century low beamed village inn on the A50. There is a large beer garden, and the play area will keep the liveliest children amused! Good home cooked food served with a ready smile.

WELLINGBOROUGH Northamptonshire **Map 4 A2**

⊗££ **THE COLUMBIA HOTEL** 19 Northampton Road, 🏨£££ Wellingborough.

CLUB **Hours:** Lunch: Monday to Saturday 12 noon - 2pm, and Sunday 12.30pm - 2.30pm. Dinner: Sunday to Thursday 6.30pm - 9.30pm, and Friday to Saturday 7pm - 10pm (last orders as 'closing' times stated above). **Cuisine:** Chicken kiev, pheasant, beef stroganoff and vegetarian dishes. 📥 29 bedrooms, all en suite. **CC** Access, Visa, AmEx. **Other Points:** No dogs. Children welcome. Open Sundays and Bank holidays. **P (V) Directions:** Off town centre one way system, turn left down Oxford St. for 1/2 mile

BARRIE & CAROLINE FOGERTY ☎ (0933) 229333.

A family-run hotel which promotes a relaxed, homely atmosphere in which to enjoy the good food and pleasant surroundings. Wellingborough market town is just minutes away and there are plenty of local attractions: Silverstone, Rockingham Castle, Wicksteed leisure park and Nene Valley railway.

⊗££ **THE HIND HOTEL AND RESTAURANT** Sheep Street, Wellingborough.

Hours: Breakfast 7.30am - 9.30am, lunch 12.30pm - 2pm, dinner 7.30pm - 9.30pm (last orders). Bar meals 12 noon - 2pm. Open all year. **Cuisine:** Roast beef, turkey Cromwell, scampi provencale, halibut steak Newburg, pork Mexican, beef stroganoff, steak au poivre. 📥 34 bedrooms all en suite. **CC** All major cards. **Other Points:** Children welcome. Dogs allowed. No-smoking area. **P** & **(V) Directions:** In the town centre.

ALAN JOHNSTONE ☎ (0933) 222827.

An olde worlde hotel in the heart of Wellingborough where Oliver Cromwell is reputed to have stayed prior to the Battle of Naseby. With excellent food served in a relaxed ambience, this has been a popular meeting place for over 350 years.

WELLS NEXT THE SEA Norfolk **Map 5 A2**

⊗££ **CROWN HOTEL & RESTAURANT** The Buttlands, Wells- 🏨£££ Next-The-Sea.

Hours: Bar and restaurant open 12 noon - 2pm and dinner 7pm - 9.30pm (earlier in Winter). **Cuisine:** Sea and shellfish, steak and kidney pie, homemade soups, pate and French specialities. Local produce used where possible. 📥 16 bedrooms, most en suite. **CC** All major cards. **Other Points:** Children welcome. Children's menu. **P (V) Directions:** The Buttlands is a tree-lined square in the centre of town.

MR & MRS W FOYERS ☎ (0328) 710209.

The hotel is ideally situated for visiting historic churches, priories and stately homes including Holkham Hall and

Wells next the Sea continued

Sandringham. Both table d'hote and a la carte menus are available in the restaurant.

⌂£ **EASTDENE GUEST HOUSE** Northfield Lane, Wells Next the Sea.

🛏 1 single, 1 double, 2 twin and 1 en suite. 1 bathroom. 1 shower. TV for hire in bedrooms. **Hours:** Breakfast 7am - 8.45am, dinner 6.30pm (order at breakfast). Tea/coffee always available in lounge. **CC** None. **Other Points:** Central heating. Residents lounge. TV. Garden. Pets welcome. Bicycle shed. **P Directions:** Off the A149 at the east end of Wells.
JEAN COURT ☎ (0328) 710381.

Situated just back from East Quay in a quiet area. Information on local events/attractions and a record book for bird watchers is kept in the lounge. Traditional homecooking using fresh garden produce.

WEST ILSLEY Berkshire **Map 4 B2**

⊗£ **THE HARROW** West Ilsley, Newbury.

Hours: Bar meals 12 noon - 2.15pm and 6pm - 9.15pm. 9pm on Sunday evenings. **Cuisine:** Rabbit pie with lemon, herbs and bacon. Traditional English puddings. English farmhouse cheese. 🛏 None. **CC** Access, Visa. **Other Points:** Children welcome. Coaches by appointment. **P &. (V) Directions:** 1 mile off the A34 - follow the signs to West Ilsley.
MRS HEATHER HUMPHREYS ☎ (063 528) 260.

A village pub standing on the edge of the cricket green opposite the duck pond. The village is situated on the edge of the Berkshire Downs. Beer garden and children's play area. The interior structure has been refurbished giving increased space. Visitors enjoy a high standard of home cooking using fresh ingredients with the emphasis on traditional British dishes.

WEST LULWORTH Dorset **Map 4 C1**

⊗££ **THE CASTLE INN** Main Street, West Lulworth.

Hours: Breakfast 7am - 9.30am, lunch 12 noon - 2.30pm and dinner 7.30pm - 11pm (last orders 9.45pm). Bar meals 11am - 2.30pm and 7pm - 11pm. **Cuisine:** Homemade raised pies, fillet Stilton, spicy lamb, pork in whisky. 🛏 14 bedrooms, 10 en suite. **CC** All major cards. **Other Points:** Children welcome. Coaches welcome. **P (V) Directions:** On the B3070 road from Wareham in the centre of West Lulworth.
GRAHAM & PATRICIA HALLIDAY ☎ (092 941) 311.

A charming thatched building dating back to the 1600's and close to the famous Lulworth Cove. The large garden is very popular - barbecues are held in summer.

WEST MARDEN West Sussex **Map 4 C2**

⊗££ **VICTORIA INN** West Marden, Nr Chichester, West Sussex.

Hours: Restaurant and Bar meals 12 noon - 2pm, evening 7pm - 9.30pm (last orders). **Cuisine:** All dishes home cooked. Daily blackboard menu served in both bar and restaurant. 🛏 None. **CC** Access, Visa. **Other Points:** Beer garden. Open Bank Holidays. No dogs. **P &. Directions:** On B2146 between coast and Petersfield, 9 miles west of Chichester.
JAMES NEVILLE ☎ (0705) 631330

West Marden continued

A deservedly popular pub in the heart of the Sussex countryside. The Inn is family run and enjoys a friendly atmosphere. Well cooked and presented meals are served in the bar and in the small restaurant and the emphasis is on home cooked dishes. The Inn has a well appointed garden and terrace. Draught beers available including Gibbs Mews, Bishops Tipple.

WEST WYCOMBE Buckinghamshire **Map 4 B2**

⊗£ **GEORGE & DRAGON** West Wycombe.

♕£££ **Hours:** Meals served in the bar 12 noon - 2pm (1.30pm Sundays) and 6pm - 9.30pm. No meals served Sunday evening. **Cuisine:** Home cooking, local game in season. ⊨ 10 bedrooms, all en suite, 2 with four-posters and 1 family room. **CC** Access, Visa, AmEx. **Other Points:** Limited access for disabled. Fax No: (0494) 462432. **✿ Directions:** On the A40 in West Wycombe village, 3 miles west of High Wycombe.

PHILIP TODD. Manager - SONIA HEATH ☎ (0494) 464414.

This charming country inn is situated in a National Trust village with several tourist attractions within walking distance. Renowned for traditional English home cooking, The George & Dragon offers superior accommodation for that special stay. Private room available for functions.

WESTCLIFF ON SEA Essex **Map 5 B1**

⊗££ **BISTRO 264** 264 London Road, Westcliff-on-Sea.

Hours: Dinner 7pm - 11pm (last orders, 12 midnight Friday and Saturday). Open all day Sundays. Closed: All day Tuesdays. **Cuisine:** Eclectic cuisine - dishes may include Barbary Duck Breasts with choice of sauces, Chicken Teriyaki, Pasta dishes, and a good choice of steaks. Fish menu. ⊨ None. **CC** Access, Visa. **Other Points:** Limited access for disabled. Children welcome. No dogs. Private dining room and bar for parties/functions. **(V) Directions:** Travel east on the A13. Approx 1 mile before Southend town centre.

MR SANTOMAURO & MR SHEAD ☎ (0702) 349213.

An informal Bistro serving fresh, well cooked food at reasonable prices. All food is well-cooked and obvious pride is taken in the attractive presentation of the dishes. The service is excellent and the atmosphere warm and convivial. An ideal choice for its imaginative international dishes, generous portions and friendly atmosphere. Wide range of dishes including vegetarian.

WESTERHAM Kent **Map 5 C1**

⊗£££ **THE KINGS ARMS HOTEL** Market Square, Westerham.

Hours: Breakfast 7.30am - 10am (8am - 10am at weekends), Lunch 12 noon - 2pm, Dinner 7pm - 10pm (last orders). Bar meals 12 noon - 2pm and 6pm - 10pm. **Cuisine:** Table d'hote and a la carte menus using fresh ingredients. Dishes may include Chartwell Scallops, Rack of lamb, Medallions of Veal, fresh fish of day. ⊨ 16 bedrooms, all en suite. **CC** All major cards. **Other Points:** Children welcome. Residents' lounge. Garden. Conference facilities. No dogs. Fax No: (0959) 561240. **✿ (V) Directions:** Jct 6, M25. Follow A25 into Westerham.

Westerham continued

REGUM LTD. MICHAEL CAVILLA - General Manager. ☎ (0959) 562990.

A privately owned, elegant Georgian Coaching Inn offering a relaxed, peaceful atmosphere, comfortable accommodation and professional, welcoming staff. The restaurant provides traditional but imaginative dishes, freshly prepared and cooked to order. The good food is complemented by a comprehensive wine list. Ideal location for business and pleasure.

WESTONING Bedfordshire **Map 4 B2**

⊗££ **THE CHEQUERS** Park Road, Westoning.

Hours: Restaurant: Dinner 7pm - 11pm (last orders 10.30pm) Mon - Sat & Lunch 12 noon - 2pm Sun only. Bar Food: All day 11am - 11pm (last orders 10.30pm) except Sun lunch 12 noon - 3pm & Sun eve 7pm - 10.30pm. Restaurant closed: Mon - Sat lunchtimes and Sun evening. **Cuisine:** Fixed price menu. English cuisine. Dishes include Char grilled steaks, BBQ ribs, Cajun chicken. Extensive bar food menu. Daily specials on blackboards. ⊨ None. **CC** Access, Visa, Diners. **Other Points:** Children welcome. Courtyard dining. ▣ ♿ **(V) Directions:** On A5120, in centre of village.

PAUL WALLMAN ☎ (0525) 713125

A 17th Century thatched inn, retaining all of its original character. The stables have been tastefully re-decorated to form an outstanding restaurant offering good value for money. Very highly recommended.

WHITSTABLE Kent **Map 5 C2**

⊗££ **GIOVANNIS RESTAURANT** 49-55 Canterbury Road.

➘ **Hours:** Lunch 12 noon - 2.30pm, dinner 6.30pm - 10.45pm. Closed: Monday. **Cuisine:** Italian/French cuisine. ⊨ None. **CC** All major cards. **Other Points:** Children welcome. No dogs. ▣ ♿ **(V) Directions:** On the A290 near the railway bridge.

GIOVANNI FERRARI ☎ (0227) 273034.

This fully air-conditioned cocktail bar and restaurant is very popular and booking is recommended. Established in 1968, Giovanni's is owner-managed with an enthusiastic continental staff.

WILLENHALL West Midlands **Map 4 A1**

⊗££ **YE OLDE TOLL HOUSE RESTAURANT** 40 Walsall Street, Willenhall.

Hours: Lunch 12 noon - 3pm, dinner 7pm - 9.30pm (last orders). **Cuisine:** Large, varied selection of fresh fish. Fresh vegetables, homemade desserts ⊨ None. **CC** Access, Visa. **Other Points:** Children welcome. No dogs. ▣ ♿ **(V) Directions:** Situated on A454 in the centre of Willenhall.

MR BRIAN FRENCH ☎ (0902) 605575

An 18th century toll house which has been renovated to a high standard incorporating original features, eg. oak beams. Table d'hote menu includes starter, main course, cheese and biscuits, wine and liqueur coffee.

CENTRAL & SOUTHERN ENGLAND

WIMBORNE Dorset **Map 4 C1**

⊗£ **QUINNEY'S RESTAURANT** 26 West Borough, Wimborne.
Hours: Meals 9.15am - 5.00pm. Closed: Sunday and Monday.
Cuisine: English cuisine - local trout, Dorset apple cake and
homemade desserts eg. ice cream and cheese cakes. ⊨ None.
CC None. **Other Points:** Children welcome. A bakery on premises
providing a large selection of gateaux, cream cakes and other
patisseries. **P** ⅊ **(V) Directions:** On the B3078, just off the main
town square.
MR A B SKIDMORE ☎ (0202) 883518.
An attractive 14th century building catering for locals and
visitors alike. Produce from the bakery on the premises are sold
in the shop, and in the restaurant itself. The food is interesting
and all homemade.

⊗£ **THE OLD INN** Holt Village, Nr Wimborne.
Hours: Lunch 11am - 2.30pm (last orders 1.45pm), and dinner
6.30pm - 11pm (last orders 9.30pm). **Cuisine:** Home-cooking,
including house speciality steak and kidney pie. Good selection of
'Old Inn special desserts'. ⊨ None. **CC** AmEx. **Other Points:** No
dogs allowed. Garden dining. Open Sundays and bank holidays.
Also accepts Cardnet. Children welcome. Childrens play area. **P**
(V) Directions: Turn off A31 to Holt, 2 miles outside Wimborne
towards Ringwood.
DEREK & BETTY WILLIAMS ☎ (0202) 883029.
A friendly 200 year old inn, with large log fires, offering quality
home-made food at real value for money. The inn is set in the
picturesque village of Holt and there are plenty of other places
of interest nearby, including Cranborne Chase, Horton Tower,
Kingston Lacy Country House, and Wimborne Minster.

WINCHELSEA East Sussex **Map 5 C1**

⊗££ **THE NEW INN** German Street, Winchelsea.
⊞££ **Hours:** Breakfast 8.30am - 9am, Lunch 12 noon - 2pm, Dinner
6.30pm - 9.30pm (7pm - 9.30pm Sundays). Closed: December
25th & 26th. **Cuisine:** Traditional British dishes and bar snacks.
Choose from local fish, traditional steak & kidney pie, scampi,
vegetarian dishes and many other dishes. ⊨ 6 bedrooms. **CC** All
major cards. **Other Points:** Children welcome. Garden. No
smoking area. **P (V) Directions:** A259. Facing the Church in the
town centre.
RICHARD & EILEEN JOYCE ☎ (0797) 226252.
An 18th century inn which has been attractively furnished.
Friendly, attentive service makes The New Inn the perfect
choice for all visitors seeking value for money and good, well
prepared food. The accommodation is comfortable and
centrally heated throughout.

WINCHESTER Hampshire **Map 4 C2**

⊗£ **THE ABBEY BAR** The Guildhall, The Broadway, Winchester.
Hours: Morning coffee 10am - 12 noon, Lunch 12 noon - 2pm.
Open bank holidays. **Cuisine:** Serving morning coffee, bar
snacks, salad bar and carvery. ⊨ None. **CC** None. **Other Points:**
No smoking area. Afternoon teas by arrangement. Breakfast
parties by arrangement. Public car park adjoining Guildhall. ⅊
(V) Directions: Approx 75 yards from King Alfred Statue in city
centre.

Winchester continued

MRS S A MORRISSEY. ☎ (0962) 848368.

Situated within the delightful Victorian building of Winchester Guildhall this is an ideal place to stop, meet and visit. Winchester Guildhall is an ideal venue for banqueting, promotions and conferences. Good food is provided in comfortable surroundings.

⊗£££ **THE ROYAL HOTEL** St Peter Street, Winchester.
⏠£££ **Hours:** Breakfast Monday to Friday 7am - 9.30am, Saturday and Sunday 8am - 10am. Dinner Monday to Saturday 7pm - 10pm, Sunday 7pm - 9.30pm. Bar meals 12 noon - 2.30pm. **Cuisine:** A la carte and table d'hote menus. Dishes may include Baked local Pink Trout, Navarin of Spring lamb, Medallions of Beef in a green peppercorn sauce. ⊨ 75 bedrooms, all en suite. **CC** All major cards. **Other Points:** Afternoon teas. Residents' lounge. Garden dining. Getaway breaks. Fax No: (0962) 841582. **P** **(V)** **Directions:** Follow one way system into St George St., Right into Saint Peter St.

BILL JOHNSON ☎ (0962) 840840.

Formally a Bishop's residence, the Royal Hotel was built in the 16th century and has been a hotel for about 150 years. The restaurant offers well cooked, imaginative dishes using predominantly fresh, local produce. The hotel is furnished and decorated to a very high standard, providing attractive surroundings and comfortable accommodation.

WINDSOR Berkshire **Map 4 B2**
⊗££ **CHRISTOPHER HOTEL** 110 High Street, Eton, Windsor.
Hours: Breakfast 7.15am - 9.30am, lunch 12 noon - 2pm and dinner 7pm - 10pm (last orders). **Cuisine:** Traditional English cuisine. ⊨ 23 bedrooms all en suite with tea/coffee facilities, hairdryer and telephones. **CC** All major cards. **Other Points:** Children welcome. Dogs allowed. **P** &

MICHAEL DEE ☎ (0753) 852359/857091

A former coaching inn situated in Eton High Street, close to the famous school and within walking distance of Windsor Castle. The restaurant serves an excellent selection of home cooked meals.

WISBECH Cambridgeshire **Map 5 A1**
⊗£ **CROWN LODGE COUNTRY HOTEL** Downham Road,
⏠££ Outwell, Wisbech.
Hours: Breakfast 6.30am - 9.30am, Lunch 12 noon - 2.30pm, Dinner and bar snacks 6pm - 10.30pm. Closed: Monday lunchtime. **Cuisine:** Home made dishes such as Lasagne & Chilli con carne, American style Beef Burgers. Steaks and Grills, Salad Counter & childrens menu. Blackboard specials. ⊨ 6 bedrooms, all en suite. **CC** Access, Visa, Diners. **Other Points:** Children welcome. Dogs by arrangement. Garden. Leisure & Sports Club - snooker, gymnasium, sauna, sunbeds. Bar lounge. Fax No: (0945) 773391. **P** & **(V) Directions:** Halfway between Wisbech & Downham Market. A1101/A1122.

WILLIAM JOHN MOORE ☎ (0945) 773391.

Off the beaten track yet within easy reach of London and the Midlands, Crown Lodge provides comfortable, spacious accommodation and good food at a very reasonable price.

Wisbech continued

> *Sporting facilities are available including coaching from qualified instructors. Golf, fishing and riding can be enjoyed nearby.*

WITNEY Oxfordshire **Map 4 B1**

⊗££ **THE COUNTRY PIE** 63 Corn Street, Witney.

[CLUB] **Hours:** Lunch 12 noon - 2.30pm and dinner 7pm - 9.45pm (last orders). Closed: Sunday evening and all day Monday. **Cuisine:** Traditional English and continental cuisine. Table d'hote and a la carte menus available. ⊨ None. **CC** All major cards. **Other Points:** Coaches by appointment. Children welcome. Ample 2 hour wait street parking. & **(V) Directions:** From the A40, follow signs to town centre.

JANET & ALAN DIXEY ☎ (0993) 703590.

A 16th century building of Cotswold stone, a short walk from Buttercross. Recent extensive modernisation has not detracted from the old world charm. Here, good food is served in congenial surroundings with an air of calm efficiency.

WOKINGHAM Berkshire **Map 4 B2**

⊗££££ **CANTLEY HOUSE HOTEL, MARYLINE'S BRASSERIE** Milton Road, Wokingham.

Hours: Breakfast 7.30am - 10am, lunch 12 noon - 2pm and dinner 7pm - 10pm (last orders). Bar meals in the Penguin and Vulture pub 12 noon - 2pm and 7pm - 10pm. **Cuisine:** Fine modern English cuisine. ⊨ 29 bedrooms, all en suite. **CC** All major cards. **Other Points:** Open air dining. Dogs allowed. Children welcome. **P** & **(V) Directions:** From M4, jct 10 follow signs to Wokingham. Off A321 towards Henley.

MR MAURICE MONK ☎ (0734) 789912.

A converted Victorian country house set in pleasant parklands with easy access to the M4. The Penguin & Vulture Pub and Maryline's Brasserie are situated in a converted 17th century barn in a secluded courtyard. A charming, character restaurant with old oak beams and sunken lounge around a warming log fire.

⊗£££ **EDWARD COURT HOTEL** Wellington Road, Wokingham.

⊞£££££ **Hours:** Breakfast 7.30am - 9am, lunch and bar snacks 12 noon -
[CLUB] 2pm, dinner 7.30pm - 9.30pm. Closed: Sundays and Saturday lunchtime, from 24th December - 2nd January. **Cuisine:** French cuisine. Dishes may include - smoked mackeral salad with grated apple and horseradish sauce, saute of veal strips in creamy sauce with apple. ⊨ 25 bedrooms, all en suite. **CC** All major cards. **Other Points:** Conferences and weddings catered for. Fax No. (0734) 772018. **P** & **Directions:** Leave M4 Jct 10, onto A329 towards Bracknell. Close to BR Station.

JUDITH SIMPSON ☎ (0734) 775886.

Situated in the heart of Berkshire and easily accessible by rail and road, this hotel provides comfortable accommodation and well cooked and presented meals. Local produce is used wherever possible.

Wokingham continued

⊗ff. **THE HANSOM CABINN** Lower Wokingham Road, Crowthorne, Wokingham

Hours: Open for lunch 12 noon - 2pm (last orders 2pm), dinner 7pm - 12.30pm (last orders 9.30pm). Sunday dinner 7pm - 9.30pm. Closed: Saturday and Sunday lunch. **Cuisine:** Starters range from sliced smoked trout, french soup or prawns. House specialites are duck or salmon en croute. Desserts includes crepe suzette. ⊨ None. **CC** Access, Visa. **Other Points:** No pets. **P** ᕐ **Directions:** Alongside A321.

MR JOHN HANSOM ☎ 0344 772450.

The Hansom Cabinn is an attractive cabin-like restaurant surrounded by roses. Inside, you will find pine panelling and pictoral reference to Hansom cabs. Fresh ingredients are used imaginatively to produce well cooked meals, simply and thoughtfully presented. Good, welcoming service and a happy and relaxed atmosphere prevails.

WOLTERTON Norfolk **Map 5 A2**

⊗£ **THE SARACEN'S HEAD INN AND RESTAURANT**
⊓⊓£ Wolterton, nr Aylsham, Norwich.

Hours: Breakfast from 7.30am, Sunday lunch 12 noon - 2.30pm, dinner 7pm - 10pm (last orders). Bar meals 12 noon - 2.30pm and 7pm - 10pm. **Cuisine:** Home-cooked meals using fresh, mainly local produce. ⊨ 2 bedrooms, en suite. **CC** Access, Visa, AmEx. **Other Points:** Children welcome. Garden. Dogs allowed. Sunday Roast Beef. Monthly Feasts. Party suite. **P** **(V) Directions:** 4 miles nth of Aylsham. Turn off to Erpingham, signs to Wolterton.

I BRYSON & R DAWSON-SMITH ☎ (0263) 768909.

A 19th century coaching inn, modelled on a Tuscan farmhouse and situated by Wolterton Hall in North Norfolk. The inn is open for dinner and Sunday lunch and features prime local produce and a comprehensive wine list. For lunch and dinner the inn also offers a good bar menu. Outside there is an attractive courtyard and walled garden for eating and drinking.

WOLVERHAMPTON West Midlands **Map 4 A1**

⊗£ **DILSHAD TANDOORI INTERNATIONAL INDIAN CUISINE** 40-43 Berry Street, Wolverhampton.

Hours: Lunch 12 noon - 2.30pm and dinner 6 pm - 12.30am (last orders). Closed: Sunday lunch. **Cuisine:** Kurzi Murgh. ⊨ None. **CC** Access, Visa. **Other Points:** Children welcome. No smoking area. Vegetarian menu. ᕐ **(V) Directions:** One minute from the Wolverhampton Railway Station.

MR M UDDIN ☎ (0902) 23481

A well known Indian restaurant with a strong local following, serving a variety of Indian and English dishes. Ideal for late after theatre suppers.

⊗££ **PATSHULL PARK HOTEL GOLF & COUNTRY CLUB**
⊓⊓££££ Pattingham, Nr Wolverhampton.

Hours: Breakfast 7.30am - 9.30am, Lunch 12 noon - 2pm, Dinner 7.30pm - 9.30pm. Bar snacks served all day. **Cuisine:** A la carte and table d'hote menus. Coffee shop. ⊨ 48 bedrooms, all en suite. **CC** Access, Visa, AmEx. **Other Points:** Children welcome. Afternoon teas. Dogs by arrangement. Garden dining. Conferences. Residential & Company Golf breaks. Fax No: (0902)

CENTRAL & SOUTHERN ENGLAND

Wolverhampton continued

700874. ▣ ㅌ (V) **Directions:** 4 miles from Jct 3, M54. 8 miles from Wolverhampton. Nr Pattingham.

EUROPA HOTELS ☎ (0902) 700100.

Set in 280 acres of parkland alongside 80 acres of trout & coarse fishing. The 18 hole championship golf course was designed by John Jacobs. Inside, the hotel is comfortable and spacious and the restaurant provides a pleasing variety of well presented dishes. A quiet, relaxed atmosphere prevails. In the Shropshire countryside yet only 10 minutes from the M54 and M6.

WOODBRIDGE Suffolk **Map 5 B2**

⊗£ **BULL HOTEL** Market Hill, Woodbridge.

Hours: Meals 7.30am - 9.30am, 12 noon - 2pm and 7pm - 10pm (last orders). **Cuisine:** Homemade soup, steaks, bar snacks. ⮕ 26 bedrooms, 16 en suite. ☒ All major cards. **Other Points:** Children welcome. No dogs. No smoking area. ▣ (V) **Directions:** On A12 in town centre.

NEVILLE & ANNE ALLEN ☎ (03943) 2089.

A 16th century coaching inn on A12 in the centre of town. Facilities for conferences, private hire and receptions.

⊗££ **CAPTAIN'S TABLE** 3 Quay Street, Woodbridge.

Hours: Meals 12 noon - 2pm and 6.30pm - 9.30pm. Open Sunday during the summer months. Closed: Monday. **Cuisine:** Local seafood. ⮕ None. ☒ All major cards. **Other Points:** Children welcome. No dogs. ▣ ㅌ **Directions:** Near the railway station and the quayside.

MR A J PRENTICE ☎ (03943) 3145.

This fish and seafood restaurant has a timbered interior with a distinct nautical flavour to the decor. Very close to the river and the town centre.

WOODSTOCK Oxfordshire **Map 4 B2**

⌂£ **GORSELANDS** Gorselands, Boddington Lane, Long
CLUB Hanborough.

⮕ 5 bedrooms, 2 en suite. **Hours:** Breakfast 8am - 9am, Dinner 7pm - 9pm. ☒ None. **Other Points:** Children welcome. Garden. Billiards room. Residents' lounge. French, German and some Spanish spoken. 4 course dinner. Licensed. Fax No: (0993) 882799. ▣ (V) **Directions:** Off 4095. Thro' Blandon & Long Hanborough, follow Roman Villa sign.

BARBERA NEWCOMBE-JONES ☎ (0993) 881895.

A Cotswold stone house set in one acre of lawned gardens. The building is full of period charm with its exposed beams and flagstone floors and provides an ideal base from which to explore the Cotswolds. Good home-cooked evening meals using fresh local produce are available on request in the conservatory. A warm and very friendly atmosphere prevails and the accommodation is excellent value.

WOOTTON WAWEN Warwickshire **Map 4 A1**

⊗£ **NAVIGATION INN** Stratford Road, Wootton Wawen, Nr Henley-In-Arden.

Hours: 11.30am - 3pm and 6pm - 10pm (last orders 9.50pm). Bar meals 11.30am - 3pm and 6pm - 10pm. Open for basket meals afternoons April - October. **Cuisine:** Home-made dishes, with

Wootton Wawen continued

grills, seafood casserole, lasagne and crispy chicken. Home-made sweets include apple pie and cheesecake. 🛏 None. CC All major cards. **Other Points:** Children welcome. Pets allowed. Open Sundays and bank holidays. Garden dining. Fax No. 0564 792228. P ♿ **(V) Directions:** On main A34 Birmingham - Stratford road, 6 miles north of Stratford.

MARK SMITH ☎ (0564) 792676

A friendly family pub, serving good quality food in generous portions. An excellent place to take children as it has a large garden and adventure playground and, being situated on the canalside, there are walks along the tow-path with plenty of narrow boats to look at.

WORTHING West Sussex **Map 4 C2**

⊗££ **CHAPMANS HOTEL** 27 Railway Approach, Worthing.

🛏£££ **Hours:** Breakfast 7am - 9am, Lunch 12 noon - 3pm, Dinner 6.30pm - 10.30pm (last orders). Bar meals 12 noon - 2pm. **Cuisine:** Choice of 2 restaurants: Flannagans - American Bistro Bar and Victorian Conservatory - Carvery and bar snacks. 🛏 18 bedrooms, all en suite. CC Access, Visa, AmEx. **Other Points:** Children welcome. No smoking area. Afternoon teas. Garden dining. 3 bars. 'Bensons' night club. Fax No: (0903) 204266. P ♿ **(V) Directions:** Just off the A24 and A2031, adjacent to the main railway station.

CHRISTOPHER CHAPMAN ☎ (0903) 30690.

A Victorian station hotel, recently totally refurbished but retaining its character and charm. The atmosphere is

Worthing continued

welcoming and relaxing, enhanced by the helpful, friendly staff. Relax and enjoy the home cooked food in the Victorian Conservatory or try American specialities in Flanagans Restaurant & Bar. Accommodation also refurbished to a high standard.

⊗££ **FINDON MANOR** Findon Village, Findon.

Hours: Breakfast 7.30am - 10am, lunch 12 noon - 2pm, dinner 7.30pm - 9pm (last orders). Bar meals 12 noon - 2pm and 6pm - 9.45pm. Restaurant closed Saturday and Monday lunchtime and Sunday evening. Closed: December 24th - 31st. **Cuisine:** Grilled Dover sole, venison cutlets and steaks in restuarant. Burgers, lasagne and house specialities in bar. ⊨ 10 bedrooms, all en suite. **CC** All major cards. **Other Points:** Children welcome. Garden and terrace. Dogs allowed. **P** **(V) Directions:** 4 miles north of Worthing, off A24 on the High Street.

SUSAN TYRIE ☎ (0903) 872733.

Findon Manor is an old rectory dating from the 16th century. Set in attractive gardens, the manor offers comfort and luxury. Findon is best known for its race horses. Aldaniti was trained here for Bob Champion's fairy-tale Grand National win and the main room at the manor is named after him.

⊗££ **KINGSWAY HOTEL** Marine Parade, Worthing.

⌂££££ **Hours:** Breakfast 7.45am - 9.30am, lunch 12 noon - 2pm and CLUB dinner 7pm - 9pm (last orders). Sunday lunch 12 noon - 2pm and dinner 7pm - 8.30pm. **Cuisine:** Carvery, a la carte and comprehensive bar menu. ⊨ 28 bedrooms, all en suite. **CC** All major cards. **Other Points:** Children welcome. Afternoon teas. Pets allowed. Passenger lift. Residents lounges. Sea facing patio. Function room catering for 75 persons. **P** & **(V) Directions:** On Marine Parade, near the Pier. To the west.

BRIAN & ANN HOWLETT ☎ (0903) 37542/3.

This four storey hotel, ideally situated for the promenade, town centre shopping and entertainments, has been under the personal supervision of the Howlett family for over twenty years. Offering good cuisine, with a choice of a la carte, carvery or bar meals, the Kingsway Hotel has comfotable accommodation, complemented by friendly and attentive service.

⊗££ **MARINE VIEW HOTEL** 111 Marine Parade, Worthing.

⌂££ **Hours:** Breakfast served from 8am until 9am and dinner from 6pm until 7pm. Bar snacks available at lunchtime. **Cuisine:** Compehensive menu, using freshest ingredients. ⊨ 4 Single, 1 twin and 7 family bedrooms all with H&C, 10 with en suite bath/shower, 2 bathrooms. TVs and tea/coffee facilities in all bedrooms. **CC** All major cards. **Other Points:** Children welcome. Licensed. Residents lounge. TV for guests use. **P**

JOHN & MARGARET HIGGINS. ☎ (0903) 38413/38630

A family-run guest house with a lively bar, situated on the sea front, with a small garden at the rear and a terrace leading from the bar at the front. Many of the bedrooms have uninterrupted sea views.

82/person.
110/

Worthing continued

⌂££ MOORINGS HOTEL 4 Selden Road, Worthing.

CLUB ⊨ 1 single, 3 double, 2 twin and 2 family bedrooms, all en suite. Tea/coffee facilities, colour TV and radio alarm in all bedrooms. **Hours:** Breakfast 8.30am - 9.30am, dinner 7pm - 7.30pm (last orders - later by arrangement). **CC** Access, Visa. **Other Points:** Central heating. Children welcome. No dogs. Licensed. Residents' lounge with log fire. Garden. Vegetarian meals by arrangement. **P Directions:** Off A259 Brighton Road, Selden Rd on left after swimming pool.

MRS GILL M. PRATT ☎ (0903) 208 882.

Tastefully converted mid-Victorian house close to the sea and the town centre. Fully double glazed. Gluten free and other diets a speciality. Worthing offers excellent sport and shopping facilities, and is a first class touring centre conveniently situated between the Channel Ports and the West Country and to both Gatwick Airport and London.

⌂£ THE COURT HOUSE Sea Lane, Goring by Sea, Worthing.

⊨ 1 single, 2 twin and 3 family bedrooms, 3 with en suite facilities. 1 bathroom and 1 shower. Colour TV and tea/coffee making facilities in all rooms. **Hours:** Breakfast 8.15am - 9am (earlier if requested). Evening meal only if pre-arranged. **CC** Access. **Other Points:** Reduced rates for children. Pets welcome. Residents' lounge and garden. Proprietor speaks German, Dutch and French. **P**

MRS I GOMME ☎ (0903) 48473.

Goring is just west of Worthing town. The Court House is an historic listed building within walking distance of the sea. There are train and bus services to the town centre, Sussex and London. Local attractions include yachting and wind-surfing, the National Bowls Centre and other sports facilities.

⊗££ WINDSOR HOUSE HOTEL 14-20 Windsor Road, Worthing.

⌂£££ **Hours:** Breakfast 7.30am - 9.15am, Carvery 7.30pm - 9.30pm CLUB Tuesday - Saturday and table d'hote menu 6pm - 7pm all week. A la carte menu 7pm - 9.30pm Sunday and Monday evenings. Sunday lunch 12.30pm - 2.30pm. Snacks served all day. **Cuisine:** A la carte menu, fixed price 3 course menu, bar meals/snacks and vegetarian meals. Summer sundaes. ⊨ 30 bedrooms, all en suite. **CC** Access, Visa. **Other Points:** Children welcome. Garden. Afternoon teas served. **P** & **(V) Directions:** On A24.

MR & MRS ARMSTRONG ☎ (0903) 39655.

Situated close to the sea and a short walk from the popular town centre, this well-maintained and attractively decorated hotel offers a full carvery and a selective a la carte menu in the popular Covent Garden Restaurant. With over 20 years at the hotel, Mr & Mrs Armstrong know how to offer good service and a friendly, relaxed atmosphere to both business and holiday makers.

WRENTHAM Suffolk **Map 5 A2**

⊗£££ QUIGGINS RESTAURANT 2 High Street, Wrentham, Beccles.

CLUB **Hours:** Lunch 11.30am - 2pm, dinner 7pm - 10pm (last orders). Closed: Sunday evening and Monday. Open Christmas Day. **Cuisine:** English and International cuisine, all made from fresh ingredients, including English puddings. ⊨ None. **CC** Access,

Wrentham continued

Visa. **Other Points:** Children welcome. Garden dining. No smoking area. Lunches modestly priced. Separate bar for pre-meal drinks. ◨ **(V) Directions:** Situated on crossroads in centre of Wrentham. On the A12.

DUDLEY & JILL MCNALLY ☎ (050275) 397.

An elegant, yet comfortable and relaxing, beamed restaurant, decorated with plants, family pictures and knick-knacks to create a homely atmosphere. The food is well-cooked and presented. A choice of main course may include Filet au Fromage, Hunter's Pie, and Salmon Steak, amongst others. Warm and courteous service. Wide range of wines.

WYMONDHAM Leicestershire **Map 4 A2**

⊗£ **HUNTERS ARMS HOTEL** Edmondthorpe Road, Wymondham, Melton Mowbray.

Hours: Meals served 7.30pm - 9.30pm. Bar meals 12 noon - 2pm and 7pm - 9.30pm. Closed: Monday. Restaurant open Friday & Saturday night & Sunday lunch. **Cuisine:** Medallion of fillet steak flamed with brandy, mushroom and cream. Selection of homemade desserts. ⊨ None. ☒ Access, Visa. **Other Points:** Vegetarian meals by request. Dogs allowed. Children welcome. ◨ ♿ **(V) Directions:** From the A607 onto the B676, past Wymondham.

MR & MRS M MASCARO ☎ (057 284) 633.

Old stone built country house offering beautifully cooked cuisine in the restaurant and a good snack to the traveller passing through. The hotel has a large garden at the rear, real ales and warm and friendly service.

HAYLING ISLAND Hampshire **Map 4 C2**

⊞£££ **COCKLE WARREN** 36 Seacroft, Hayling Island.

CLUB ⊨ 4 double, 1 twin, 5 en suite. Colour TV in all rooms, direct dial telephones, trouser presses, irons, hair dryers and clock radios in all rooms. **Hours:** Breakfast 7am - 9.30am, dinner 7.30pm (order by 4pm). ☒ Access, Visa. **Other Points:** Central Heating. Children over 7 welcome. Residents' lounge. Garden. Heated swimming pool. Large garden and patio. ◨

DAVID & DIANE SKELTON ☎ (0705) 464 961.

Delightful cottage hotel on the seafront in large garden with free range hens and ducks. French and English country cooking, with homemade bread and brioche, and a good selection of French wines. Lovely en suite bedrooms, some with four-poster and Victorian beds. Routiers of the Year 1987.

LONDON

QUICK REFERENCE GUIDE

	NO. OF ESTS.	⊗ £	⊗ ££	⊗ £££	⊗ ££££	⊡ £	⊡ ££	⊡ £££	⊡ ££££
LONDON									
MAP 5A A2 London	7	★	★						★
MAP 5A B1 London	2		★				★		
MAP 5A B2 London	51	★	★	★	★			★	★
MAP 5A B3 London	3	★				★	★		

LONDON

London has all the variety and vitality you would expect from a capital city: shopping in the West End and Knightsbridge, museums and art galleries, theatres, and restaurants and pubs offering every conceivable type of cuisine. Throughout the country, Britain's restaurants reflect the highly cosmopolitan nature of its population, but London offers the greatest concentration, with choices from all over the world.

Getting around London has never been easier, with the choice of British Rail, underground, and bus. For visitors new to London, the best introduction to the sights and atmosphere is via a traditional red bus tour which takes in all the major attractions, including Big Ben, Tower Bridge, the Houses of Parliament and St Paul's Cathedral.

South Kensington is a paradise for 'culture-seekers', with the famous group of museums all within walking distance of each other. Alternatively, the culture trail could take you to the Tate Gallery, with its Turner collection and modern art, or the National Gallery and National Portrait Galleries at Trafalgar Square.

Be sure to investigate London's fascinating markets, such as Petticoat Lane, Portobello Road and Camden, on the Lock. Covent Garden, with its Italian-style piazza, restaurants and street entertainers, needs little introduction.

To the newcomer, London's staggering range of evening entertainments may seem overwhelming, with its variety of theatres, nightclubs, comedy shows, opera and ballet. Take a tip from Londoners and flip through the listings magazines. The waterside concerts at Kenwood House in Hampstead offer an exciting alternative, as does open-air Shakespeare in Regent's Park.

London is hailed world-wide as a centre for arts and entertainments, business and fashion. Unfortunately, it also has a reputation for being one of the most expensive cities in the world, particularly where accommodation for the visitor is concerned. Ensure you receive value for money by referring to your Les Routiers Guide. It is still possible to find comfortable, reasonably priced accommodation, located close to many of the major attractions of this exciting city.

LONDON Map 5a B2
Battersea, SW11

⊛££ **BUCHAN'S** 62-64 Battersea Bridge Road, Battersea.
ⓒ **Hours:** Lunch 12 noon - 2.45pm, Dinner 6pm - 10.45pm (last orders). Closed: Bank Holidays only. **Cuisine:** French cuisine. Specialities include some Scottish dishes. Menu changes weekly. Master chef: Alain Jeannon. ⊨ None. **CC** All major cards. **Other Points:** Children welcome. Dogs allowed. ⅍ **(V) Directions:** 200 yds from Battersea Bridge, on the south side of River Thames. JEREMY & DENISE BOLAM ☎ (071) 228 0888.
An attractive shop fronted restaurant/wine bar which serves outstanding French cuisine in a bustling, friendly atmosphere. The service is welcoming and efficient. Although the cuisine is French, Buchan's also offers Scottish specialities such as Arbroath smokie mousse, Scotch fillet steak flambed in whisky and a Scottish based cheeseboard.

Battersea, SW11

⊛££ **JACK'S PLACE** 12 York Road.
ᵔᑌ **Hours:** Open 12 noon - 3pm, Tuesday to Friday and 6.30pm - 11pm Tuesday to Saturday. Open for Sunday lunch. Closed: Mondays. **Cuisine:** Steaks, giant scampi, gammon. ⊨ None. **CC** Access, Visa. **Other Points:** Children welcome. No dogs. MR JACK KING ☎ (071) 228 8519/1442.
This restaurant has a friendly, relaxed and informal atmosphere. The walls are covered in memorabilia which keeps the customer interested between courses. With excellent food and substantial portions, Jack's Place is very highly recommended.

LONDON Map 5a B2
Bayswater, W2

⑮£££ **MITRE HOUSE HOTEL** 178-184 Sussex Gardens, Hyde Park.
⊨ 6 single, 18 double, 26 twin and 7 family, all en suite, plus 3 junior suites. Colour TV with BSB satellite TV, Direct Dial telephone and Radio in all rooms. **Hours:** Breakfast 7.30am - 9am. **CC** All major cards. **Other Points:** Children welcome. Licensed bar. Lounge serving tea/coffee all day. Fax No. (071) 402 0990. ▯ ⅍ **Directions:** South of Paddington tube, parallel to Praed St. C. TSANGARIDES & CO. LTD ☎ (071) 723 8040.
The Mitre Hotel has been run by the same family for over 25 years, and this is reflected in it's comfortable atmosphere and ambience. Ideally located on the north side of Hyde Park, central London is easily accessible, and should you require a hired car or a sightseeing tour, the helpful staff will be happy to assist.

Bayswater, W2

⊛£££ **VERONICA'S RESTAURANT** 3 Hereford Road, Bayswater.
ᵔᑌ **Hours:** Lunch 12.30pm - 3pm (last orders). Dinner 7pm - 12
[CLUB] midnight (last orders) Closed: Saturday lunch, Sundays and Bank Holidays. **Cuisine:** The best of old British Regional, historical and seasonal dishes changed monthly. A host of fish, meat, game and vegetarian treats. ⊨ None. **CC** All major cards. **Other Points:** Children welcome. Pavement dinning. Pets welcome.

LONDON

London continued
Calorie/low fat/ high fibre advice given on dishes. ق (V)
Directions: Tube stations Queensway, Notting Hill. At South end
of Hereford Rd.
VERONICA SHAW ☎ (071) 229 5079.
Small, intimate and friendly, Veronica's looks on to a garden
square. A true and unique treatment of real British food,
drawing inspiration from historical recipes. Routiers Newcomer
of the Year 1990.

LONDON Map 5a B2
Belgravia, SW1
⊗£££ **BUMBLES RESTAURANT** 14/16 Buckingham Palace Road.
[CLUB] **Hours:** Lunch 12 noon - 2.15pm and Dinner 6pm - 10.45pm (last
orders 2.15pm and 10.45pm respectively). Closed: Saturday
lunch, all day Sunday and Bank holidays **Cuisine:**
English/International cuisine: fresh fish, savoury pancakes, lamb,
duck, homemade pies. Super puddings. Extensive wine list.
Choice of set menus. ⤟ None. **CC** All major cards. **Other Points:**
Children welcome. No dogs. Function rooms available. ▯ ق (V)
Directions: 200 yards from Victoria station going towards
Buckingham Palace.
PHILIP BARNETT ☎ (071) 828 2903
Friendly English restaurant with cartoons and old prints lining
the walls, padded bench-style seating set in alcoves and a
spacious basement which is also air-conditioned. Places of
interest nearby include Buckingham Palace, Westminister
Abbey and local theatres.

Belgravia, SW1
⊗£ **NAG'S HEAD** 53 Kinnerton Street, London.
Hours: Meals from 12 noon - 3pm and 5.30pm - 10pm Monday &
Tuesday, Sunday 12 noon - 3pm and Wednesday to Friday 12
noon - 10pm. **Cuisine:** Traditional home cooked pub food with
daily specials and daily roasts - Irish stew, various curries, chilli con
carne, homemade pies. ⤟ None. **CC** None. **Other Points:**
Children welcome lunchtimes. LVs accepted. 1930s Arcade
machines such as 'What the Butler Saw', Spangles Spin Ball.
Directions: Near to Hyde Park Corner Tube, Kinnerton St is off
Wilton Rd.
KEVIN MORAN ☎ (071) 235 1135.
Built in 1780 this has been called the smallest pub in London
and is thought to be a former gaol. In 1921 it was sold for £11 7s
6d - almost the price of couple of rounds of drinks today.

LONDON Map 5a B2
Bloomsbury, WC1
⊗££ **ACADEMY HOTEL** 17-21 Gower Street.
⊡£££££ **Hours:** Breakfast 7am - 10.30am, Lunch 12 noon - 2.30pm,
⌣ Dinner 6.30pm - 12 midnight. Also open Sundays. **Cuisine:**
Predominantly English/French cuisine using fresh ingredients.
Dishes may include Guinea Fowl in Cassis Sauce. Good wine list.
⤟ 9 single, 7 twin, 17 double, and 1 family room. 26 en suite.
Includes 2 studio suites. All rooms have TV, telephone and
tea/coffee facilities. **CC** All major cards. **Other Points:** Children
welcome. No pets. Afternoon teas. Patio Garden. Business &
Meeting facilities. Georgian Library. Fax: (071) 636 3442. Telex:

London continued

24364. **(V) Directions:** Nearest tube: Goodge St, or Tottenham Court Rd or Russell Square.

ALAN RIVERS ☎ (071) 631 4115.

The Academy Hotel provides an ideal environment for visitors who are just 'stopping over' or those who regularly travel on business. Originally three Georgian buildings, built around 1776, many original features still remain. Set in heart of publishing world, with many sights of interest nearby, including British Museum, Jewish Museum, Covent Garden, Theatreland and the West End.

Bloomsbury, WC1

⊞£££ **EURO & GEORGE HOTELS.** 51/53 Cartwright Gardens.

⊨ 2 single, 23 double, 17 twin and 11 family bedrooms. Colour TV, radio, alarm, direct dial phone, ironing and tea/coffee making facilities in all rooms. **Hours:** Breakfast 7.30am - 9am. ⊠ Access, Visa. **Other Points:** Children welcome. No dogs allowed. Residents lounge and garden. In-house films. Tennis courts. Residents lounge and garden. Fax No: (071) 383 5044. ⊡ **Directions:** Close to Kings Cross, Euston and Russell Square tube stations.

PETER EVANS ☎ (071) 387 8777/8666.

The Euro and George Hotels are situated in a quiet crescent of historically listed buildings. Both provide a high standard of service and comfort at good value prices. Its central position offers easy access to the West End and local attractions such as the British Museum.

Bloomsbury, WC1

⊞£££ **MABLEDON COURT HOTEL** 10-11 Mabledon Place, London.

⊨ 33 bedrooms, all en suite. All rooms have remote control colour TV, direct dial telephone, tea/coffee making facilities and hairdryer. **Hours:** Breakfast 7.30am - 9am. ⊠ Access, Visa. **Other Points:** Children welcome. No smoking area. Residents' lounge. Fax No: (071) 387 5686. Street parking and public car parks nearby. **Directions:** Near Euston, Kings Cross and Russell Square underground stations.

ANDREW DAVIES ☎ (071) 388 3866.

Ideally situated between the City and the West End, The Mabledon Court is an attractively decorated hotel offering a high standard of accommodation. All rooms are en suite and well-equipped. An excellent base for visiting London, with its comfortable accommodation at very reasonable prices. Full English breakfast.

LONDON Map 5a B2
Chelsea, SW1

⊗££ **LE CASINO RESTAURANT** 77 Lower Sloane Street, Chelsea. **Hours:** Lunch 11am - 3pm, Dinner 6pm - 1am. Closed: Christmas Day only. **Cuisine:** Imaginative, French-style cuisine using fresh produce. Dishes may include Duck en Croute, Malvern Pork, Scotch Salmon, Fish of the Day. ⊨ None. ⊠ Access, Visa. **Other Points:** Children welcome. No dogs. **(V) Directions:** Nearest tube: Sloane Square.

S VANKIRK ☎ (071) 730 3313.

London continued

A friendly, welcoming restaurant serving excellent food at good value for money. The menu offers a a good choice of imaginative dishes, all freshly cooked, attractively presented and served in generous portions. A lively yet relaxed atmosphere, excellent, welcoming staff, and cosy surroundings ensure that Le Casino is popular with all ages and for all occassions.

LONDON Map 5a B2
Chelsea, SW3

⊗££££ **WALTONS OF WALTON STREET** 121 Walton Street, Chelsea.
Hours: Lunch 12.30pm - 2.30pm, Dinner 7.30pm - 11.30pm (last orders). Sunday Lunch 12.30pm - 2pm and 7pm - 10pm. Closed: Christmas Day and Boxing Day. **Cuisine:** Modern British with dishes such as Chicken Supreme sauted in Grape Juice, Fillet of Salmon with Scallops, Noisette of Southdowns Lamb. ⊯ None. **CC** All major cards. **Other Points:** Air-conditioned. Post theatre suppers. Fax No: (071) 581 2848. ⅋ **(V) Directions:** Nearest underground stations: South Kensington and Knightsbridge.
ROGER WREN ☎ (071) 584 0204.
A classic London Restaurant, located in the heart of Chelsea and providing a haven of elegance and fine food. The colourful interior, enhanced by outstanding floral displays and friendly, professional staff ensures a warm welcome in which to enjoy the very best of British cuisine.

LONDON Map 5a B2
City, EC4

⊗££££ **BENTLEY'S** 11 Queen Victoria Street.
Hours: Bentley's Seafood Restaurant Monday - Friday 12 noon - 3pm. Champagne & Oyster Bars Monday - Friday 11am - 10pm (last orders 8.30pm). The Forum Bar at Bentley's Monday to Friday 11am - 10pm (last orders 8.30pm). Closed: Saturday & Sunday. **Cuisine:** Specialising in seafood and fish. Excellent wine list. ⊯ None. **CC** All major cards. **Other Points:** No dogs. Fax No: (071) 248 5145. Business luncheons and private functions catered for - phone for reservations and enquiries 9am - 9pm. ⅋ **Directions:** Entrance in Budge Row. Nearest tubes: Cannon Street & Mansion House.
MARK STEDMAN - General Manager ☎ (071) 489 8067.
A very elegant establishment, housing a Seafood Restaurant, Champagne & Oyster Bar, and the Forum Bar. The food is expertly cooked, exceptionally well presented and served by professional staff. Elegant surroundings and a peaceful atmsophere make Bentley's an ideal lunch venue for both business and pleasure.

LONDON Map 5a B2
Clerkenwell, EC1

⊗£ **CAFE ST PIERRE** 29 Clerkenwell Green, nr Farringdon Road.
[CLUB] **Hours:** Lunch 12 noon - 3pm and dinner 5.30pm - 11pm (last orders). Brasserie meals from 12 noon - 3pm and 5.30pm - 11pm. Closed: Saturday and Sunday. Routiers-priced menu applies to Brasserie. **Cuisine:** Daily fresh fish dishes. ⊯ None. **CC** All major cards. **Other Points:** Children welcome. No dogs. **(V) Directions:** Near Farringdon Tube on metropolitan and circle lines.

London continued

JIMMY LAHOUD ☎ (071) 251 6606.

A converted pub with a typical French atmosphere close to Farringdon tube. Situated alongside the Clerks Well in the historic village of Clerkenwell. Close to the Barbican and St Pauls.

Clerkenwell, EC1
⊛££ **THE HELLENIK RESTAURANT** 86 St John Street.

Hours: Open 11.45am - 3pm and 6pm - 11pm. Closed: Sundays & Bank Holidays and for 3 weeks in early August. **Cuisine:** Kleftico, moussaka, meze, souvlaki. ⊨ None. ☒ Access, Visa, AmEx. **Other Points:** Children welcome. No dogs. Street Parking. **(V) Directions:** 500 yards from Smithfield market.

MESSRS P & A KRASE ☎ (071) 253 0754

A family run, fully licensed Greek/Cypriot restaurant where good food at reasonable prices matters. Situated near Smithfield and the Barbican it is ideal for pre or post theatre meals.

Clerkenwell, EC1
⊛££ **THE THREE COMPASSES** 66 Cowcross Street, Clerkenwell, EC1.

Hours: Restaurant open Monday to Friday 12.15pm - 2.30pm (last orders). Closed: Saturdays and Sundays, but open for hire all week (minimum group 15 persons). Hot bar meals 11.30am - 3pm (Sundays 12 noon - 3pm). Cold buffet available all day. **Cuisine:** English and French, with the menu changing weekly. Includes a selection of fish, meat, pasta and home-made soups. ⊨ None. ☒ All major cards. **Other Points:** Access for disabled to bar only. Children welcome in restaurant only. No dogs allowed. N.C P carpark in Cowcross Street. ⅏ **(V) Directions:** Between Faringdon station (BR and underground) and Smithfield market

W I & E M HUTCHISON ☎ (071) 253 3368:

Traditional public house and restaurant, very popular with business people for its good food and friendly atmosphere. Ideal for Hatton Garden, the Barbican, St Bartholemew's Hospital and Clerkenwell Green.

LONDON Map 5a B2
Covent Garden, WC2
⊛£ **FOOD FOR THOUGHT** 31 Neal Street, Covent Garden.

Hours: Open Monday to Friday 8.30am - 8pm. Saturday 12 noon - 8pm & Sunday 12 noon - 4.30pm. Closed: Bank Holidays. **Cuisine:** Wide range of vegetarian dishes all prepared on premises from fresh produce - daily specials. ⊨ None. ☒ None. **Other Points:** Children welcome. No dogs. Nearest car park - NCP St Martins Lane/Drury Lane. Fax No: (071) 379 1249. **(V) Directions:** Close to Covent Garden tube.

J L DAMANT & VANESSA GARRETT ☎ (071) 836 0239.

Ideal for the hungry traveller, this busy restaurant provides a warm welcome and quick, friendly service. Menu changed twice a day. Take-away meals and snacks also available.

Covent Garden, WC2
⊛££ **FUNG-SHING** 15 Lisle Street, Covent Garden, WC2.

Hours: 12 noon - 11.30pm **Cuisine:** Cantonese: Crispy duck, Sizzling prawns. ⊨ None. ☒ All major cards. **Other Points:**

LONDON

London continued

Private dining room available. Limited disabled access (toilets upstairs). **Directions:** In Chinatown.
JIMMY CHIM ☎ (071) 437 1539
Fung-Shing is situated in a converted Victorian warehouse. Customers can enjoy a wide variety of competently served Cantonese dishes, our Inspector particularly enjoyed the crispy duck and special fried rice.

Covent Garden, WC2
⊗££ **LE CAFE DES AMIS DU VIN** 12 Hanover Place. (off Long ⌂ Acre).
[CLUB] **Hours:** Open 11.30am - 11.30pm Mondays to Saturdays. **Cuisine:** Charcuterie, plats du jour. French cheese and wines. ⊨ None. ⓒⓒ All major cards. **Other Points:** Children welcome. Fax No: (071) 379 9124. ⅋ **(V) Directions:** Nearest tube - Covent Garden on the Piccadilly Line.
MR P NOTTAGE/CAFE DES AMIS LIMITED ☎ (071) 379 3444.
This restaurant offers good value for money in that the food is well prepared, cooked and served, the service is friendly and you can enjoy your meal amidst pleasant surroundings. Popular basement wine bar for theatre goers. Adjacent to the Royal Opera House.

Covent Garden, WC2
⊗£££ **SMITH'S RESTAURANT & WINE BAR** 25 Neal Street, WC2.
Hours: Meals from 12 noon - 12 midnight Mon - Fri, 6pm - 12 midnight Saturday (last orders 11.30pm). Closed: Sundays. **Cuisine:** New English style cuisine from Head Chef, Brian O'Donoghue. ⊨ None. ⓒⓒ All major cards. **Other Points:** Children welcome. No dogs. No smoking area. Disabled access - wide stairs but no lift. **(V) Directions:** 2 minutes from Covent Garden Tube,off Neal St opposite tube station.
JAMEL BELKIR - Manager ☎ (071) 379 0310.
Situated in the basement of Smith's Art Galleries at the junction of Neal Street. Large, spacious restaurant with contemporary paintings. The restaurant, galleries and cafe Casbar are all available for private hire.

LONDON Map 5a B3
Eltham, SE9
⌂££ **THE ELTHAM HOTEL** 31 Westmount Road, Eltham.
⊨ 12 rooms. 4 single, 2 twin, 4 double and 2 family bedrooms. 10 en suite. All rooms have colour TV, tea/coffee making facilities. Most have a hairdryers and trouser press. **Hours:** Breakfast 7am - 8.30am. ⓒⓒ Access, Visa, AmEx. **Other Points:** Children welcome. Garden. Afternoon teas. �
MR N P VIRDEE ☎ (081) 850 8222.
A Victorian hotel, privately owned and set its own large garden, offering comfortable accommodation in pleasant surroundings. Easy access for touring Central London, Greenwich - with road/rail links to the Kent coast. Close to newly opened waterfront Leisure Centre and the Royal Blackheath Golf Club. Welcoming atmosphere and friendly service.

LONDON Map 5a B3
Forest Hill, SE23
⊗£ **BABUR BRASSERIE** 119 Brockley Rise.
CLUB Hours: Lunch 12 noon - 2.30pm, dinner 6pm - midnight (last orders 11.30pm). Closed: Christmas and Boxing Day. **Cuisine:** Moghlai Cuisine. ⊨ None. CC All major cards. **Other Points:** Children welcome. No dogs. **(V) Directions:** Brockley Rise is off the South circular - Stansted Road.
MR RAHMAN ☎ (081) 291 2400/4881.
An Indian style restaurant specialising in Moghlai Cuisine with an interesting selection of dishes on the menu. Soon to be extended. Free home delivery service to locals.

LONDON Map 5a B2
Fulham, SW10
⊗£ **CIAO CAFE WINE BAR** 222 Munster Road, Fulham.
Hours: Lunch 12 noon - 3.30pm, dinner 6pm - 11pm. Closed: 3 days over Christmas. **Cuisine:** Brasserie cuisine, fresh pasta dishes and daily specialities. ⊨ None. CC Access, Visa, AmEx. **Other Points:** Children welcome. Outside dining. No smoking areas. Open Bank holidays and Sundays. ♿ **(V) Directions:** Between Fulham Road and Lillie Road, north of Parsons Green.
MARK MILTON ☎ (071) 381 6137.
'Ciao', situated on Munster Road and seating 80 people, provides good food at excellent value for money in attractive surroundings and friendly, very efficent service. Offering a wide selection of tasty, well presented dishes including many fresh pasta specialities, you will find the relaxing candlelit atmosphere an excellent backdrop for business or pleasure.

LONDON Map 5a B2
Fulham, SW6
⊗££ **CAFE ROUGE** 855 Fulham Road, Fulham.
Hours: Breakfast 10am - 12 noon, lunch 1pm - 3pm (last orders), bar snacks 3pm - 7pm, dinner 7pm - 11pm (last orders). **Cuisine:** Traditional French cuisine. Menu changes every 3 months, but generally includes Marmite Dieppoise, Entrecote Bearnaise. Lighter meals also served. ⊨ None. CC Access, Visa. **Other Points:** Children welcome. Open Bank Holiday. Afternoon teas. No dogs. Switch cards accepted. Some tables on pavement in summer. ⊡ ♿ **(V) Directions:** On corner of Munster Road.
CAFE ROUGE LTD ☎ (071) 371 7600.
A cafe/restaurant with a genuine French feel and character, serving excellent traditional bistro food. Cappuccino and light meals are served all day and the restaurant offers full a la carte. The atmosphere is cosmopolitan and the French staff are very friendly yet professional. Popular with all ages.

LONDON Map 5a B3
Greenwich, SE18
⌂£ **DOVER HOUSE** 155 Shooters Hill, Greenwich.
CLUB ⊨ 6 bedrooms, all en suite and with colour TV, telephone and tea/coffee making facilities. **Hours:** Breakfast 7.30am - 9am. CC None. **Other Points:** Parking available nearby. Full English breakfast. **Directions:** A207 - Shooters Hill crosses S.Circular south of Woolwich Ferry.
JOAN ARAMIELLO ☎ (081) 856 9892.

London continued

Dover House offers home from home accommodation in an early Victorian family house. The house has been harmoniously decorated and the rooms are furnished with many period pieces. Full English breakfast is served. With a warm welcome, friendly atmosphere and excellent value for money, Dover House is an ideal place to stay, near all the attractions of Greenwich and central London.

LONDON Map 5a B1
Hammersmith, W6

⌂££ **DALMACIA HOUSE** 71 Shepherds Bush Road, Hammersmith. ⊨ 3 single, 4 double, 2 twin and 4 family bedrooms, 6 en suite. Colour TV with 8 satellite TV channels, Tea/Coffee, radio and alarm facilities. **Hours:** Breakfast 7am - 9.30am. Dinner 6pm - 8.30pm. **CC** All major cards. **Other Points:** Children welcome. No smoking area. Fax No. (071) 602 9226. **Directions:** On A219, north of Hammersmith tube.
GEORGE KRIVOSIC ☎ (071) 603 2887.
This recently refurbished Victorian terraced house offers comfortable accommodation and value for money. The family who run the hotel speak French and Serbo-Croat. Situated near to Olympia and Kensington High Street, it is ideal for visitors to London.

LONDON Map 5a A2
Hampstead, NW3

⊗££ **CAFE ROUGE** 19 High Street, Hampstead.
Hours: 10am - 11pm (last orders), 7 days a week. **Cuisine:** Traditional French cuisine. Menu changes every 3 months, but generally offers Marmite Dieppoise, Cochonaille and plats du jour. ⊨ None. **CC** Access, Visa. **Other Points:** Children welcome. No dogs allowed. Open Sundays and Bank holidays. Switch cards accepted. & **(V) Directions:** Nearest tube is Hampstead.
CAFE ROUGE LTD ☎ (071) 433 3404.
A French cafe/restaurant, serving traditional bistro food in an informal, but professional atmosphere. Serves cappuccino and light meals all day in the cafe area and the restaurant offers full a la carte.

Hampstead, NW3

⊗£ **ENTERPRISE** 2 Haverstock Hill, Hampstead.
Hours: Meals served 12 noon - 3pm Monday to Friday. Tapas Bar open 12 noon - 11pm. **Cuisine:** Roast dinners. Simple pub home cooked food and a menu that changes daily. Tapas food served all day. ⊨ None. **CC** None. **Directions:** Opposite Chalk Farm Underground. Close to Primrose Hill & Camden.
KENNETH JACKSON ☎ (071) 485 2659.
This well kept Edwardian pub is handy for those shopping in Camden Lock market. A wide selection of ales and lagers, tasty home cooked food, a very welcoming proprietor and staff, make this a very pleasant and economical stop.

LONDON Map 5a B2
Hatton Garden, EC1
⊗££ **BLEEDING HEART WINE BAR** Bleeding Heart Yard, Greville Street.
Hours: Meals from 12 noon - 3pm and 5.30pm - 10.30pm (last orders). Closed: Saturday and Sunday. **Cuisine:** Charcoal grilled meats, French regional dishes (especially Provencal). Over 120 wines, many by the glass. ⬛ None. **CC** All major cards. **Other Points:** Coaches by appointment. No dogs. ⬛ ⑆ **(V) Directions:** Nearest Tube - Farringdon.
MR R WILSON ☎ (071) 242 8238/2056.
The Bleeding Heart is well-hidden beneath historic Bleeding Heart Yard off Greville Street, near Farringdon tube. Not only does the Yard feature in Dickens' novel Little Dorrit - hence the Dickensian atmosphere and first editions - but it is said to be haunted by the ghost of Lady Hatton. Terrace for outdoor eating in summer.

LONDON Map 5a B2
Herne Hill, SE24
⊗££ **JACQUES' RESTAURANT** 272 Rosendale Road, Herne Hill, ⌣ SE24.
CLUB **Hours:** Lunch 12 noon - 2.30pm, Dinner 7pm - 10.30pm. **Cuisine:** Choice of a la carte or table d'hote menus. French cuisine with Plateau de Fruits de Mer a speciality. Les Routiers Casserole Award winner 1992. ⬛ None. **CC** Access, Visa. **Other Points:** Children welcome. Conservatory dining. No smoking area. ⬛ ⑆ **(V) Directions:** Directly off the South Circular (A205), nr Thurlow Park.
JACQUES QUEVILLON ☎ (081) 674 6060
In a tree-lined avenue, this delightful French restaurant, with its pavement conservatory is reminiscent of a Paris side-walk cafe. Among his many skills, welcoming owner and chef Jacques, is a talented saxophone player and will occasionally entertain customers. 'Gourmet Evenings' are held monthly and it is well worth joining his mailing list in order to be well informed.

LONDON Map 5a A2
Islington, N1
⊗££ **WILLOUGHBY'S CAFE-BAR** 26 Penton Street, N1.
Hours: Meals served 12 noon - 3pm, 6pm - 11pm Tuesday to Saturday, 12 noon - 3pm Monday. Closed: Monday evening, Sunday and Bank Holidays. **Cuisine:** Quarterly changing menu and a daily special menu shown on the restaurant blackboard eg. Parsley Soup, Lamb with Onion Marmalade, Seville Orange Creams. ⬛ None. **CC** Access, Visa. **Other Points:** Children welcome. **(V) Directions:** Angel Tube, right along Pentonville Road, right into Penton Street.
HUGH MORGAN & LINDA NATHAN ☎ (071) 833 1380.
An attractive, imaginatively decorated cafe-bar serving well-cooked, good quality meals. The food and atmosphere are reminiscent of a French provincial bistro and there are many regular customers in additon to the evening theatre-goers. An unpretentious establishment providing a wide choice of dishes, welcoming service and very good value for money.

LONDON

LONDON Map 5a B2
Kensington, SW5
⌒££££ **BEAVER HOTEL** 57-59 Philbeach Gardens, Kensington.
🛏 19 single, 6 double, 10 twin, and 4 family bedrooms, 20 en suite. With TV, hair dryers, telephone and radio in all rooms. **Hours:** Breakfast 7.30am - 9.30am. **CC** Access, Visa, AmEx. **Other Points:** Children welcome. Pets allowed. Fax No: (071) 373 4555. **P** **Directions:** Just off the A4 Cromwell Rd.
JAN LIS ☎ (071) 373 4553.
Situated in a quiet, tree-lined crescent of late Victorian houses, Beaver Hotel is ideally placed for Earl's Court, Olympia and central London. Car Park for hotel guests.

LONDON Map 5a B2
Kensington, W11
⊗££££ **L'ARTISTE ASSOIFFE** 122 Kensington Park Road, Kensington.
Hours: Lunch Saturday only, dinner 7pm - 12 midnight (last orders 11.30pm). Closed: Bank Holidays. **Cuisine:** Steak Dijon, creme brulee. 🛏 None. **CC** All major cards. **Other Points:** Children welcome. Dining al fresco in summer. & **(V) Directions:** Close to Portobello Antique Market.Nearest tube - Notting Hill Gate.
ERIC ARMITAGE ☎ (071) 727 4714
A three storey restaurant in a Georgian building in Kensington which provides a unique atmosphere in which to enjoy the predominantly French cuisine. Carousel horses, Cromwellian statues, washing mangles and parrots live within the beaufitully muralled walls, creating an enchanting setting.

LONDON Map 5a B2
Kensington, W8
⌒££££ **OBSERVATORY HOUSE HOTEL** Observatory Gardens, 37
⌐Ⓢ Hornton St, Kensington.
🛏 8 single, 9 double, 6 twin and 3 family, all en suite. Colour TV, Tea/ Coffee making facility, Direct dial telephone, Hair dryer and Trouser press, Mini bar and in room safes. **Hours:** Breakfast 8am - 10am. **CC** All major cards. **Other Points:** Children welcome. Fax No. (071) 938 3585. **Directions:** Off Kensington High Street near Town Hall.
MR M MEGHJI. ☎ (071) 937 1577.
An outstanding conversion of a Victorian Mansion in upper Kensington. All of the rooms are of an exceptionally high standard, with an air of restrained opulence. Although at the top of our pricing bracket, our inspector believes that this hotel offers excellent value for money for Central London.

LONDON Map 5a B2
Knightsbridge, SW3
⊗££ **LE METRO** 28 Basil Street
Hours: Breakfast 7am - 11am, lunch/dinner all day. Last orders 10pm. **Cuisine:** A la carte - French cuisine. 🛏 None. **CC** Visa, AmEx. **Other Points:** Children welcome. Afternoon teas. **(V) Directions:** Nearest tube: Knightsbridge.
DAVID LEVIN ☎ (071) 589 6286.
This is a busy French style wine bar in the heart of Knightsbridge, a stones throw from Harrods. A wide range of

London continued

top quality wines are available by the glass and by the bottle and all served in a very pleasant atmosphere.

Knightsbridge, SW3

⌂£££ **THE CLAVERLEY AT BEAUFORT GARDENS** 13-14 Beaufort Gardens, Knightsbridge.

32 bedrooms, 30 en suite. All rooms have telephone, colour TV and hairdryers. **Hours:** Full English Breakfast 7.30am - 10am. Access, Visa, Amex. **Other Points:** Children welcome. No smoking area. Fax No. (071) 584 3410. **(V) Directions:** 3rd street on left past Harrods, heading West.
MRS DEMITRA ANTONIOU ☎ (071) 589 8541.

Situated in a quiet cul-de-sac, this elegant hotel offers an excellent standard of accommodation. Completely refurbished, the Claverley provides charm, comfort, a warm welcome and personal service. A short walk to Harrods and Hyde Park, the heart of London is only a short bus, tube or taxi ride away. An ideal choice for a luxurious stay in London.

LONDON Map 5a B2
Lancaster Gate, W2

⌂£££ **AVERARD HOTEL** 10 Lancaster Gate, W2.

60 bedrooms, all en suite. All with colour TV, radio and telephone. **Hours:** Breakfast 7.30am - 9.45pm. All major cards. **Other Points:** Children welcome. Residents' lounge. No dogs. Fax No: (071) 706 0860. Bar (open until 12 midnight). Account facility available. **Directions:** Lancaster Gate Tube. Opposite Hyde Park.
ALFRED VICKERS ☎ (071) 723 8877.

A large private hotel which is ideally situated opposite Hyde Park, near Marble Arch. The accommodation, decor and furnishings are of a high standard and the cost of accommodation is reasonable, especially considering its location, so close to most of London's major attractions. Relax in the spacious lounge or enjoy a drink in the intimate bar which is open until 12 midnight.

LONDON Map 5a B1
Mortlake, SW14

⊗££ **THE DEPOT CAFE WINE BAR** Tideway Yard, Mortlake High Street, Mortlake.

Hours: Lunch 12 noon - 3pm. Dinner 6pm - 11pm. Closed for three days over Christmas. **Cuisine:** Brasserie/wine bar style: fresh pasta, lemon sole, fricassee of chicken. None. Access, Visa, AmEx **Other Points:** Children welcome. Garden dining. Afternoon teas. ▣ ₺ **(V) Directions:** Near Barnes railway bridge, just off Mortlake High Street.
MARK MILTON ☎ (081) 878 9462

Built from original Victorian stables, the Depot is an attractive 80 seat cafe offering excellent value for money. Pine tables and pitch pine flooring with the friendly bustle of customers gives the restaurant an authentic atmosphere. Stunning views of the River Thames from the terrace.

LONDON

LONDON Map 5a A2
Muswell Hill, N10

⊗££ **RAGLAN HALL HOTEL** 8-12 Queens Avenue, Muswell Hill.
⌂£££ **Hours:** Breakfast, Monday - Friday 7.30am - 9.30am, Saturday - Sunday 8am - 9am. Lunch, Monday - Saturday 12 noon - 2pm, Sunday 12 noon - 3pm. Dinner, Sunday - Thursday 7pm - 10pm, Friday - Saturday 7pm - 10.30pm. **Cuisine:** Wide and varied choice of dishes including soups, fish, pasta, steaks and house specialities such as veal, beef, chicken and duckling. ⊨ 48 rooms, all en suite. Colour TV, radio, alarm and tea/coffee making facilities in all rooms. **CC** All major cards. **Other Points:** Children welcome. Garden dining. Afternoon teas by arrangement. Open Bank Holidays. Residents' lounge. Fax (081) 883 5002. **P** & **(V)** **Directions:** Off A1 & A406. Close to Alexandra Palace in central Muswell Hill.
SPRING HOTELS LTD. ☎ (081) 883 9836.
3 Victorian houses which have been sympathetically converted into a modern hotel. Just refurbished, the accommodation offers good for money in London. Friendly and efficient staff make this an ideal place to stay, ideallly located for Hampstead Heath and Alexandra Palace.

LONDON Map 5a B2
Notting Hill, W11

⊗££ **CAFE ROUGE** 31 Kensington Park Road, Notting Hill.
Hours: Open 10am - 11pm (last orders) for breakfast, morning coffee, lunch, afternoon tea and dinner. Closed: Christmas Day and August Bank Holiday. **Cuisine:** Traditional French cuisine such as Marmite Dieppoise, Entrecote Bearnaise and Plats du Jour. Also French snacks and sandwiches. ⊨ None. **CC** Access, Visa. **Other Points:** Children welcome. No dogs. Open 7 days a week. Switch cards accepted. Downstairs room for private parties. & **(V)** **Directions:** Close to Portobello market.
CAFE ROUGE LTD ☎ (071) 221 4449.
A traditional French bistro/bar open for meals and snacks throughout the day. Whether you dine a la carte or choose a lighter snack, all dishes are very well cooked using fresh ingredients. A welcoming and relaxed atmosphere prevails and the professional but young and friendly staff will go out of their way to ensure that you enjoy your visit.

Notting Hill, W11

⊗££ **CAPS** 64 Pembridge Road, W11.
CLUB **Hours:** Dinner 6pm - 11.15pm. Closed: Sunday. **Cuisine:** Mix of English and French. Specialities include avocado salad, roast rack of lamb with rosemary and honey, fillet of beef with madeira and truffles. ⊨ None. **CC** All major cards. **Other Points:** Children welcome. No smoking area. **(V) Directions:** Close to Notting Hill tube. Located under The Pembridge Court Hotel.
PAUL CAPRA ☎ (071) 229 5177.
Close to the famous Portobello Road antique market and within easy access of the West End, Caps is an attractive restuarant with a relaxed atmosphere. The menu offers a mix of French and English dishes with daily extras. The walls are covered with school caps and 'Williams Room', named after Prince William, is available for private parties.

LONDON Map 5a B2
Paddington, W2
⌂£££ **ASHLEY HOTEL** 15 Norfolk Square.

⊨ 4 single, 8 double, 3 twin, 1 family bedroom - 10 with shower. 2 general bathrooms. Tea/coffee making facilities and colour TV in all rooms. **Hours:** Breakfast 7.30am - 9am. Closed: Christmas. ⊠ None. **Other Points:** Central heating. Children welcome. No dogs. No evening meals. Residents lounge. Colour TV in all guest rooms and in lounge. Nearest tube - Paddington. **Directions:** Situated between Praed Street & Sussex Gardens. 3 mins Paddington.
MESSRS W J & D E GEORGE ☎ (071) 723 3375.
The Ashley Hotel is flanked by its sister hotels, The Tregaron and The Oasis, and all three adjoin one another and are interconnected. Very centrally situated in a small quiet, garden square, a few minutes bus ride from Oxford St. and close to Paddington Station. The Norfolk Gardens were re-designed in 1990 to recreate the Victorian era. A lovely and quiet place to sit and take your ease.

Paddington, W2
⌂£££ **CARDIFF HOTEL** 5-9 Norfolk Square, London W2

⊨ 50 bedrooms, 32 en suite. All rooms have tea/coffee making facilities and colour TV. **Hours:** Traditional English breakfast 7am - 8.45am. ⊠ None. **Other Points:** Full English breakfast. Fax No: (071) 402 2342. **Directions:** Paddington British Rail & Underground station. Close to Hyde Park.
ELWYN DAVIES ☎ (071) 723 4500/9068.
Situated in the heart of London in a Victorian tree lined square, the Cardiff Hotel offers simple but comfortable accommodation at a very reasonable price. The generous traditional full English breakfast is included in the price and served in the bright, attractive dining room. Close to all of London's major attractions. A good base for both business and pleasure.

LONDON Map 5a B2
Putney, SW15
⊗££ **BANGLADESH CURRY MAHAL** 294 Upper Richmond Road, Putney.
Hours: Lunch 12 noon - 3pm (last orders), dinner 6pm - 12 midnight (last orders). Closed: Christmas. **Cuisine:** Bangladeshi/Indian dishes using chicken, meat, shell fish and vegetables. Tandoori specialities. Fried scampi for the less adventurous. ⊨ None. ⊠ All major cards. **Other Points:** Children welcome. Open Bank Holidays. **(V) Directions:** Opposite Putney police station, just west of Putney High Street.
NURUL ISLAM ☎ (081) 789 9763.
A Bangladeshi restaurant serving a high standard of food in a typical Indian decor. Friendly staff will advise on your choice of dishes and the service is efficient yet relaxed. With the good food, faultless service and a friendly, warm atmosphere, it is easy to understand the popularity of this restaurant. Frequented by all ages, including families.

London continued
Putney, SW15

⊗££ **CAFE ROUGE** 200-204 Putney Bridge Road, Putney.
Hours: Open 10am - 11pm (last orders), also open Bank Holidays. Closed: Christmas Day. **Cuisine:** French dishes such as Normandy Fish Stew, Entrecote Bearnaise. Snacks include Baguette du Cafe Rouge (hot steak sandwich), Croque Monsieur. ⊨ None. **CC** Access, Visa. **Other Points:** Children welcome. Dogs allowed in bar. Street parking. Terrace/pavement seating area. Fax No: (081) 789 8562. Switch cards accepted. ♿ **(V) Directions:** Left off Putney High St at Canon Cinema. Very close Putney Bridge. CAFE ROUGE LTD ☎ (081) 788 4257.
A French cafe/restaurant, serving traditional bistro food in an informal, but professional atmosphere. Cappuccino and light meals are served all day in the cafe area and the restaurant offers full a la carte. Attractively decorated in reds and dark wood and the atmosphere is busy yet relaxing. Popular with all ages.

Putney, SW15

⊗£ **GAVIN'S RESTAURANT** 5 Lacy Road, Putney.
Hours: Lunch 12 noon - 3pm, dinner 6.30pm - 11pm. **Cuisine:** A la carte menu specialising in fresh pasta dishes and brasserie style dishes. ⊨ None. **CC** Access, Visa, AmEx. **Other Points:** Children welcome. No smoking area. ♿ **(V) Directions:** Putney Bridge - South to High Street.
MR MILTON ☎ (081) 785 9151.

London continued

This lively Putney restaurant has an interesting menu based on fresh pasta with a wide selection of sauces and imaginative brasserie style dishes accompanied by a well selected wine list. A great atmosphere and a well established reputation.

Putney, SW15

⊗£££ **LA MANCHA** 32 Putney High Street, Putney.
Hours: Lunch 12 noon - 3pm, Dinner 7pm - 11pm (last orders). Tapas served 12 noon - 12 midnight. **Cuisine:** Spanish cuisine including Paella and tapas dishes. Tapas and a la carte restaurant menu. Good Spanish wine list. ⊨ None. ᴄᴄ All major cards. **Other Points:** Children welcome. Street parking in evening. Disabled access to tapas bar only. **(V) Directions:** On Putney High Street, very close to Putney Bridge & the river.
J A SKELTON & S CRICCHIO ☎ (081) 780 1022.
An excellent Spanish restaurant and Tapas bar situated close to the river Thames in Putney. The Routiers inspector had nothing but praise for the outstanding cuisine and excellent service. An ideal choice for good food in friendly, relaxed surroundings.

Putney, SW15

⊗££ **MYRA RESTAURANT** 240 Upper Richmond Road
[CLUB] **Hours:** Lunch 12pm - 2.30pm, dinner 6.30pm - 11pm. Sunday Lunch 12.30pm - 4pm. **Cuisine:** A la carte, fixed price 3 course menu. ⊨ None. ᴄᴄ All major cards. **Other Points:** Children welcome. Garden. ⑁ **(V) Directions:** South Circular, near Putney Bridge.
MISS MOLONY. ☎ (081 788) 9450.
This Victorian Terraced building is situated in a busy road close to Putney High Street and has a large number of regular local clientele. The menu includes house specialities such as roast rack of lamb and chicken midas with an imaginative variety of salads.

Putney, SW15

⊗£ **TRAPPERS** 148 Upper Richmond Road, Putney.
Hours: Restaurant open 6pm - 11.30pm, 12 noon - 11.30pm on Saturday and Sunday. Closed: Christmas and Boxing Day, Easter Sunday. **Cuisine:** Dishes include char grilled steaks, burgers and chicken. Pasta, pizza, curry and vegetarian dishes. Plus a selection of daily specials. ⊨ None. ᴄᴄ All major cards. **Other Points:** Children welcome. No dogs. ⑁ **(V) Directions:** On the south circular road, 3 minutes walk from East Putney Tube.
MR J CORY ☎ (081) 788 6324.
Decorated in the style of a Canadian log cabin close to Putney High Street. Very popular with all ages with its interesting selection of dishes, cocktail list and special children's menu.

LONDON Map 5a B2
Soho, W1

⊗£££ **BAHN THAI RESTAURANT** 21A Frith Street.
Hours: Lunch 12 noon - 2.45pm and dinner 6pm - 11.15pm (last orders) Monday to Saturday. Sunday 12.30pm - 2.30pm and 6.30pm - 10.30pm. Closed: some Bank Holidays. **Cuisine:** Thai cuisine. Extensive menu of authentic dishes. All dishes cooked to order. ⊨ None. ᴄᴄ Access, Visa, AmEx. **Other Points:** Children

LONDON

London continued

welcome. Private parties and set meals can be arranged. No dogs. Good wine and spirits list. Fax No: (071) 439 0340. **(V) Directions:** Between Tottenham Court Rd & Leicester Sq. tubes. Opp. Ronnie Scotts

PHILIP HARRIS ☎ (071) 437 8504.

An attractive restaurant in the heart of London with a relaxing atmosphere and excellently cooked Thai cuisine. Authentic Thai recipes and ingredients are used and all dishes are cooked to order and taste. The service is excellent - with all staff willing to give assistance on your choice of dishes. Good, interesting wine list.

Soho, W1

⊗££ **MING** 35 - 36 Greek Street.

Hours: Monday to Saturday 12 noon - 11.45pm (last orders). Closed: Sundays, Christmas Day and Boxing Day (open for Chinese New Year Celebration Sunday). **Cuisine:** Northern Chinese. Special menu with more unusual, innovative dishes, & seafood specialities in summer. Regional Chaozhou dishes (with 1 day's notice). ⊨ None. **CC** All major cards. **Other Points:** Children welcome. No smoking area. Private rooms available for up to 22 persons. Special menus arranged on request. Fax No: (071) 435 0812. **(V) Directions:** Corner of Greek St & Romilly St. Nearest tube: Leicester Square.

CHRISTINE YAU ☎ (071) 437 0292.

Ming offers an extensive a la carte menu of traditional and imaginative Chinese dishes and an additional 4 set menus. The food is beautifully cooked and the large choice ensures plenty of scope for exploration of new dishes for even the most regular customers. The simple decor is in keeping with the calm, relaxed atmosphere of the restaurant.

LONDON Map 5a B2
South Kensington, SW3

⊗££££ **LA BRASSERIE** 272 Brompton Road.

Hours: Open 8am - 12 midnight, Sunday 10am - 12 midnight. Closed: Christmas Day and Boxing Day. **Cuisine:** French cuisine - Crepes Brasserie, plats du jour. ⊨ None. **CC** Access, Visa, AmEx. **Other Points:** Children welcome. Afternoon tea served. ⅋ **(V) Directions:** At the junction of Pelham St and Brompton Rd near S.Kensington Tube.

PETER GODWIN ☎ (071) 581 3089/1668.

A French cafe/restaurant situated around the corner from South Kensington Tube. Large antique mirrors, plants and ceiling fans lend an elegant and Parisien atmosphere, which is compleented by good French cooking. Pavement cafe dining - weather permitting.

LONDON Map 5a A2
Southgate, N14

⊗££ **CHEZ GIANNI RESTAURANT FRANCAIS** 56 Cannon Hill, Southgate.

Hours: Lunch 12.30pm - 2.30pm, dinner 6.30pm - 11pm. Closed: Sundays. **Cuisine:** French cuisine featuring regional specialities. ⊨ None. **CC** All major cards. **Other Points:** Children welcome.

London continued

Open Bank Holidays. ◪ **(V) Directions:** In old Southgate, opposite the Green.

G CRESCENZO ☎ (081) 882 5725.

An attractive French restaurant with a typically Provencal decor. The French chef specialises in regional cuisine and all dishes are imaginative, well-cooked and presented. The food is of a very high standard, the service friendly and efficient and the restaurant offers good value for money. Highly recommended for authentic French cuisine in attractive surroundings.

LONDON Map 5a B2
Spitalfields, E1

⊗££ **CITY LIMITS RESTAURANT & WINE BAR** 16-18 Brushfield Street, Spitalfields.

Hours: Lunch served in the restaurant 12 noon - 3pm. Meals served in the bar 11.30am - 2.30pm and 5pm - 8pm. Closed Saturday and Sunday. **Cuisine:** Varied international foods; speciality starters, fresh fish, excellent gateaux. Imaginative wine list, international and unusual beers (non-draught). ⊯ None. ⚉ Access, Visa, AmEx. **Other Points:** Children welcome. No dogs. Service charge. Multi-storey car park nearby. ঙ **(V) Directions:** Situated in Spitalfields, near the Bishopsgate Institution.

DAVID HUGHES ☎ (071) 377 9877.

A buzzing, ground floor wine bar with restaurant downstairs. Situated between the market and offices with good car parking facilities very close by.

LONDON Map 5a B2
Trafalgar Square, WC2

⊗£ **CAFE IN THE CRYPT** St Martin In The Fields, Trafalgar Square.

Hours: Open 10am - 9pm Monday to Saturday, 12 noon - 6pm Sunday. **Cuisine:** English home cooking. Self-service. Menu changes daily. ⊯ None. ⚉ Access, Visa. **Other Points:** Children welcome. Afternoon teas. No dogs. Licensed. ঙ **(V) Directions:** Nearest tubes: Leicester Sq & Charing Cross. Entrance - Duncannon St

THE VICAR OF ST MARTINS IN THE FIELD ☎ (071) 839 4342.

A unique cafe, situated immediately underneath the famous Church of St Martins in the Fields, Trafalgar Square. Generous portions of wholesome food are offered at outstanding value for money. Meals can be enjoyed beneath the vaulted ceilings in what must be one of the most unusual eating places in London. Centrally situated and very close to the National Gallery.

LONDON Map 5a B2
West End, W1

⊗£££ **CAFFE VENEZIA** 15-16 New Burlington Street.

Hours: 12 noon - 11.30pm (last orders 3pm lunch, 11.30pm dinner). Closed: Sunday. **Cuisine:** Italian - Parma ham and melon, pasta, veal. ⊯ None. ⚉ All major cards. **Other Points:** Children welcome. Limited disabled access (toilets downstairs). **(V) Directions:** Off Regent Street.

LUIGI EMILIUCCI ☎ (071) 439 2378.

LONDON

London continued
A busy Italian restaurant, decorated in a clean, modern style, where customers are guaranteed a warm welcome and attentive service.

West End, W1
⌂£££ **EDWARD LEAR HOTEL** 28/30 Seymour Steet.
    🛏 14 single, 3 double, 11 twin and 4 family rooms - 4 en suite. Colour TV, radio, alarm, telephone, baby listening device and tea/coffee making facilities in bedrooms. **Hours:** Breakfast 7.30am - 9.15am. 💳 Access, Visa. **Other Points:** Children welcome. No dogs allowed. In house films and residents lounge. ♿ **Directions:** Close to Marble Arch tube and a minutes walk from Oxford Street.
PETER EVANS ☎ (071) 402 5401.
Formerly the home of the famous Victorian painter and poet, Edward Lear. The Hotel offers cheerful rooms with all the usual facilities and is in the perfect location: just minutes away from Hyde Park, Speakers Corner and Oxford Street.

West End, W1
⊗££ **PICCADILLY RESTAURANT** 31 Great Windmill Street.
    Hours: Open 12 noon - 2.30pm and 5.30pm - 11.15pm. Closed: Sunday and Bank Holidays. **Cuisine:** Italian cuisine. 🛏 None. 💳 Access, Visa, AmEx. **Other Points:** Children welcome. Guide dogs only. **(V) Directions:** Nearest Tube, Piccadilly.
CLAUDIO MUSSI ☎ (071) 734 4956.
Centrally situated in the heart of theatreland and on the fringes of Soho. The restaurant is on two levels and both have a cosy informal atmosphere. Excellent for eating either before or after the theatre.

LONDON Map 5a B2
West End, W2
⌂£££ **PARKWOOD HOTEL** 4 Stanhope Place.
    🛏 4 single, 2 double, 7 twin and 5 family rooms - 12 en suite. **Hours:** Breakfast 7.30am - 9.15am. 💳 Access, Visa. **Other Points:** Children welcome. No dogs allowed. In house films, luggage storage and ironing facilities. 🅿 **Directions:** A minutes walk from Marble Arch tube station.
PETER EVANS ☎ (071) 402 2241.
An attractive town house situated in a quiet, residential street, but just a short walk away from Oxford Street, Marble Arch and Hyde Park. The Parkwood is under excellent management, offering spotlessly clean and airy bedrooms serviced by friendly and efficient staff.

LONDON Map 5a B2
West End, WC2
⌂£££ **ROYAL ADELPHI HOTEL** 21 Villiers Street.
    🛏 54 bedrooms, 23 with en suite facilities. All rooms have direct dial telephone, colour TV, radio and hairdryer. **Hours:** Breakfast served only. 💳 All major cards. **Other Points:** Children welcome. Dogs allowed. Residents lounge and cocktail bar. Fax No: (071) 930 8735. **Directions:** Just off the Strand, between Charing Cross & Embankment stations.
MICHAEL BRIGGS ☎ (071) 930 8744.

London continued

Situated just off the Strand, two minutes from Trafalgar Square, The Royal Adelphi Hotel is perfectly situated for a visit to London with all London's major attractions within walking distance. The accommodation is of a very high standard and reasonably priced, and there is a TV lounge and Cocktail bar in which to relax. No evening meals but many good restaurants close by.

LONDON Map 5a A2
West Hampstead, NW6

⊗£ **CHARLOTTE RESTAURANT & GUEST HOUSE** 221 West
⏻£ End Lane, West Hampstead.
Hours: Breakfast 7.30am - 11.30am, lunch 12 noon - 4pm, a la carte dinner 6pm - 11pm. Closed: Sundays. **Cuisine:** English and continental cooking from liver Bavaria and deubreziner sausages to stir-fried vegetables with rice and prawn and poussin a la diable. ⤙ 40 bedrooms, 20 en suite. 8 bathrooms, 8 showers. TV. **CC** None. **Other Points:** Children welcome. No dogs. **(V)**
MR L KOCH ☎ (071) 794 6476
An old established restaurant and guest house, 2 minutes from West Hampstead Tube (Jubilee line) and direct British Rail link to Gatwick and Luton Airports. The restaurant is tastefully decorated and the ample portions are served by cheerful staff. The accommodation is unbeatable value and comfortable.

West Hampstead, NW6

⊗££ **NO 77 WINE BAR** 77 Mill Lane.
Hours: Meals from 12 noon - 3pm (last orders 2.30pm) and 6pm - 11pm (last orders 10.30pm). Closed: Bank Holidays, Good Friday and Christmas. **Cuisine:** Homemade soups, lamb Shrewsbury. ⤙ None. **CC** Access, Visa. **Other Points:** Children welcome. Dogs allowed on lead. Street parking. ⅚ **(V) Directions:** Mill Lane is off the Edgware Rd between Kilburn and Cricklewood.
DAVID BLAKEMORE ☎ (071) 435 7787
A popular wine bar decorated in pine with old film bills on the walls. International theme evenings such as Burns Night, July 4th, Greek evening. The in-house club sails, plays cricket, rugby and golf tournaments.

LONDON Map 5a B2
Westminster, SW1

⏻£££ **COLLIN HOUSE** 104 Ebury Street.
⤙ 13 bedrooms, 8 en suite. **Hours:** Breakfast 7.30am - 9am. Closed Xmas/New Year. **CC** None. **Other Points:** Children welcome. No smoking in dining room. **Directions:** Close to Victoria Station and Buckingham Palace.
DAFYDD & BERYL THOMAS ☎ (071) 7308031.
A mid-Victorian terraced house, close to Victoria Station and Buckingham Palace, offering clean, comfortable accommodation and friendly, helpful service. An ideal base from which to see the London sights.

Westminster, SW1

⊗£ **MORPETH ARMS** 58 Millbank.
Hours: 11am - 10pm. Closed: Christmas day, Boxing day and New Years day. **Cuisine:** Typical English pub food: steak and

London continued

kidney pie, sausage, beans and chips, vegetarian quiche, ploughmans,and salads. Large selection of vegetarian meals. None. **CC** Visa. **Other Points:** Children welcome. Accepts traveller's cheques, mastercard and Eurocard. **(V) Directions:** Near Tate gallery, alongside Thames. Nearest tube: Pimlico. PETER PERFECT ☎ (071) 834 6442.

Victorian pub in good condition which is under excellent management, the staff being very competent and friendly.

WALES AND THE BORDERS

WALES AND THE BORDERS

Wales is a country with its own history, heritage and culture, which is still kept very much alive today. Welsh is still spoken by one-fifth of the population and the National Eisteddfod, or competition festival, held in August, presents all aspects of music, literature, drama and art in the Welsh language.

For many centuries, leeks have been considered the national emblem of Wales, now replaced by the red dragon or daffodil. According to legend, it was the Welsh patron saint David who first encouraged Welshmen to wear leeks in their caps when they went into battle, to distinguish them from enemy Saxons. In the 18th century Caxton wrote of the Welsh passion for eating them and there are many traditional recipes for leek soups.

Today, visitors will be relieved to discover a wider range of culinary delights on offer. Traditional recipes combine with imaginative new dishes guaranteed to appeal to all tastes. Try some traditional Welsh lamb, 'cawl' (soup), or poached trout. Sample Dyfed's cheeses, Penclawdd cockles, mussels from Menai, or Cardigan Bay lobster.

The delicious food is sure to give you the energy to tackle the variety of leisure and sporting activities available. There is pony-trekking in the Brecon Beacons, hang-gliding at Rhossili, canoeing at Llangollen and, for the angler, Wales is a paradise with a choice of sea-angling, coarse fishing and game fishing.

Wales is a country of great contrasts and hill-walkers can take their choice of terrain. North Wales is dramatic and mountainous, with Snowdonia and Cader Idris being the best known peaks. Mid-Wales is a land of rolling hills and valleys, whereas the Brecon Beacons National Park in the south is a region of hills, forests and waterfalls. The coastline of South Pembrokeshire is renowned for its broad sweep of sandy beaches and the Vale of Glamorgan and the Gower Peninsula provide a green agricultural fringe, with beautiful coastal views.

Wales also has a wealth of history, with over 100 castles open to the public and a range of country mansions, ruined abbeys and museums. Caernarfon Castle's soaring defences are famous the world over and Harlech commands views across the sands, dunelands and estuaries of Cardigan and Tremadog Bays. Criccieth Castle stands on the rocky peninsula over the little seaside resort of the same name, one of its most splendid features being the high twin-towered gatehouse. In addition, prehistoric man left burial chambers at Pembrokeshire's Pentre Ifan Cromlech and tombstones can be found on the Isle of Anglesey.

In the north, the city of Bangor lies in an ancient river valley which runs parallel to the Menai Straits. The city's history dates back over fifteen hundred years and it has long been a focal point of religious and academic learning. It also offers a superb range of outdoor activities.

Whatever your taste, in both food and leisure, Wales has something to offer everyone and, wherever you go, you can be sure the people will wish you a very warm 'Croeso I Gymru' – welcome to Wales.

THE BORDERS

The beautiful hill country of Shropshire lies on the Welsh border and there are numerous castles to visit in the area, built as they were to protect the English from the marauding Welsh or, some may argue, vice versa. There are also many beautiful old towns, such as Shrewsbury and Ludlow, and many centres with exhibitions on subjects varying from farming to historic dress to modern country life.

For those who prefer a busier atmosphere, visit the cathedral city and county town of Gloucester on the River Severn. The fertile Severn valley is known for its market gardening and orchards.

Hereford and Worcester are rival cities, both with their own cathedrals, river bridges and markets. They are separated by the Malvern Hills, home to some of England's finest spring water. Between the Cotswolds and Wales are the beautiful valleys of the Severn and the Wye, and the woodlands of the Forest of Dean. On the Wye too is Tintern Abbey, one of the most romantic of ruins and an inspiration for Wordsworth. This is also the home of the world famous red and white cattle and a centre for cider making. Its hop fields, apple and cherry orchards add to the peaceful atmosphere in this part of England.

	NO. OF ESTS.	⊗ £	⊗ ££	⊗ £££	⊗ ££££	🛏 £	🛏 ££	🛏 £££	🛏 ££££

WALES AND THE BORDERS

MAP 6 A2

	NO. OF ESTS.	⊗ £	⊗ ££	⊗ £££	⊗ ££££	🛏 £	🛏 ££	🛏 £££	🛏 ££££
Abersoch	1			★				★	
Beaumaris	1		★						★
Beddgelert	1			★				★	
Bontnewydd	1					★			
Caernarfon	1	★					★		
Criccieth	5		★	★			★		
Harlech	2		★				★		
Holyhead	1	★					★		
Llanbedrog	1			★				★	
Llanberis	2		★				★		
Llanfairpwll	1			★					
Maentwrog	1	★						★	
Nefyn	1	★							
Porthmadog	2		★				★		
Pwllheli	1		★						
Talsarnau	1						★		
Trearddur Bay	1		★					★	

MAP 6 B2

	NO. OF ESTS.	⊗ £	⊗ ££	⊗ £££	⊗ ££££	🛏 £	🛏 ££	🛏 £££	🛏 ££££
Aberdovey	1		★					★	
Aberystwyth	3	★	★				★		
Barmouth	3			★			★	★	
Fishguard	1	★							
New Quay	2		★					★	
Tresaith	1		★					★	

MAP 6 C1

	NO. OF ESTS.	⊗ £	⊗ ££	⊗ £££	⊗ ££££	🛏 £	🛏 ££	🛏 £££	🛏 ££££
Haverfordwest	3		★	★				★	
Little Haven	1		★						
Milford Haven	2		★			★	★		
St Davids	4		★			★	★		

MAP 6 C2

	NO. OF ESTS.	⊗ £	⊗ ££	⊗ £££	⊗ ££££	🛏 £	🛏 ££	🛏 £££	🛏 ££££
Llandybie	1			★					
Narberth	1			★					★
Oxwich	1	★					★		
Pembroke	2	★		★					
Pontfaen	1		★					★	
Saundersfoot	2		★				★	★	
Swansea	3	★	★	★			★	★	
Tenby	3		★				★	★	

MAP 7 A1

	NO. OF ESTS.	⊗ £	⊗ ££	⊗ £££	⊗ ££££	🛏 £	🛏 ££	🛏 £££	🛏 ££££
Bala	1		★					★	
Betws y Coed	6		★	★			★	★	
Capel Curig	1		★				★		
Colwyn Bay	3	★					★		
Conwy	1		★						
Denbigh	1		★						
Llandudno	20	★	★	★	★	★	★	★	
Llangollen	1			★				★	
Llanrwst	1		★					★	
Mold	1	★							
Prestatyn	1		★				★		
Ruthin	2	★	★						
St Asaph	1		★						★

	NO. OF ESTS.	£	££	£££	££££	£	££	£££	££££
Tal y Bont	1		★						
Talycafn	1	★							
Wrexham	3	★	★				★		★
MAP 7 B1									
Bishops Castle	1	★					★		
Builth Wells	1		★					★	
Church Stretton	2		★					★	★
Dolgellau	2		★				★		
Hay on Wye	2		★				★		
Llandrindod Wells	2		★	★				★	
Ludlow	1		★						
Machynlleth	2	★		★			★	★	
New Radnor	1	★					★		
Oswestry	2		★						
Rhayader	1		★				★		
Welshpool	2		★					★	★
Wentnor	1	★					★		
Weobley	1		★				★		
Winstanstow	1	★							
MAP 7 B2									
Bridgnorth	1		★						
Broseley	1		★						
Buckland	1			★					
Cleobury Mortimer	1		★					★	
Evesham	1		★					★	
Great Malvern	1		★					★	
Great Witley	1		★					★	
Kidderminster	1		★						
Malvern	4	★	★					★	
Much Wenlock	1	★							
Norton	1			★					★
Pensax	1	★							
Pershore	1		★						
Redditch	1			★					★
Shrewsbury	3	★	★					★	
Stourport on Severn	1						★		
Telford	2		★	★			★		
Worcester	2		★					★	
MAP 7 C1									
Abergavenny	2	★				★	★		
Bridgend	1	★							
Caerleon	2		★						★
Cardiff	2		★	★				★	
Chepstow	1			★					
Cowbridge	1		★						
Crickhowell	1		★						
Cwmbran	1			★					★
Hereford	2		★					★	
Llandogo	1	★					★		
Llandovery	1	★					★		
Llantrissent	1		★						
Monmouth	2		★	★				★	
Newport	1		★						
Shirenewton	1	★					★		
Tintern	1	★							
Trellech	1	★							
Usk	1		★						

QUICK REFERENCE GUIDE

	NO. OF ESTS.	⊗ £	⊗ ££	⊗ £££	⊗ ££££	🛏 £	🛏 ££	🛏 £££	🛏 ££££
MAP 7 C2									
Broadway	1		★						
Cambridge	1	★							
Clearwell	2			★				★	★
Coleford	2		★				★		
Drybrook	1		★						
Fownhope	1	★						★	
Gloucester	1		★						
Ledbury	1		★					★	
Parkend	1		★					★	
Redmarley D'abitot	1		★						
Ross on Wye	7	★	★	★			★	★	★
Tewkesbury	2		★						

BISHOPS CASTLE Shropshire **Map 7 B1**

⊗£ **THE BOARS HEAD** Church Street, Bishops Castle.

☐£ **Hours:** Breakfast 8am - 9am, Dinner 7pm - 9.30pm. Bar meals 12 noon - 2pm and 7pm - 10pm. **Cuisine:** Bar snacks and a la carte meals. Predominantly English cuisine. ⌖ 4 bedrooms, all en suite and with colour TV and tea/coffee making facilities. **CC** Access, Visa. **Other Points:** Children welcome. Dogs allowed. ⊞ **(V) Directions:** Off A488. Pass the Livestock Market. On left before crossroads.

GRANT PERRY ☎ (0588) 638521.

A 16th century Inn and restaurant in an historic Shropshire market town. The Inn has a comfortable dining area with an extensive menu ranging from bar snacks to full a la carte meals. The stable block behind the Boars Head has been converted to provide 4 comfortable bedrooms. All food is well-cooked and provides good value for money. A relaxed, friendly atmosphere prevails.

BRIDGNORTH Shropshire **Map 7 B2**

⊗££ **THE DOWN INN** Ludlow Road, Bridgnorth.

☐ **Hours:** Lunch and bar snacks 12 noon - 2pm, Dinner and bar snacks 7pm - 9.30pm (last orders). No meals Sunday evenings. **Cuisine:** Predominantly British cuisine in restaurant such as Traditional Roast Duckling, Spatchcocked Chicken. Good choice of bar meals. Daily specials. ⌖ None. **CC** Access, Visa. **Other Points:** Children welcome. Beer garden. ⊞ & **(V) Directions:**

WALES & THE BORDERS

Bridgnorth continued

B4364, 2.5 miles from Bridgnorth town centre on the Ludlow Road.

PAUL MILLINGTON ☎ (074635) 624.

A popular, stone-built pub, set in beautiful countryside just outside Bridgnorth. The interior is spacious and comfortable and enjoys a friendly atmosphere, enhanced by very welcoming staff. Both restaurant and bar meals are of a high quality and the menus and daily specials offer a good choice of imaginative dishes using fresh produce. Well worth a visit.

BROADWAY Hereford & Worcester **Map 7 C2**
⊗££ **THE BROADWAY HOTEL** The Green, Broadway.

Hours: Lunch 12.30pm - 2.30pm on Saturday and Sunday only, Dinner 7pm - 9.30pm. Bar meals 12 noon - 2.30pm. **Cuisine:** A la carte and fixed price. Traditional British cooking. ⊨ 20 bedrooms, all en suite. **CC** All major cards. **Other Points:** Children welcome. Afternoon tea. Garden. No dogs. Non-smoking area. Fax No: (0386) 853879. **P** & **(V) Directions:** On main road through Broadway, on southern end of village Green.

IAN ALLAN HOTELS ☎ (0386) 852401.

Converted from a 16th century house, the hotel combines the half-timbers of the Vale of Evesham with the distinctive grey stone of the Cotswolds. Traditional country meals are served in the restaurant and, in the summer, drinks and teas are available in the courtyard and gardens.

BROSELEY Shropshire **Map 7 B2**
⊗££ **CUMBERLAND HOTEL** Jackson Avenue, Broseley.

Hours: Meals from 8am - 10am, 12 noon - 2.30pm and 7pm - 10pm last orders. Bar meals from 10am - 2.30pm and 7pm - 10.30pm. . **Cuisine:** Subtle salmon, chicken regal, grilled steaks. ⊨ 15 bedrooms. **CC** Visa, Diners. **Other Points:** Children welcome. Coaches welcome. **(V) Directions:** Situated on B4373 1 mile south of Iron Bridge.

IVOR & PAT SOUTHORN ☎ (0952) 882 301.

A country house built in 1720 standing in its own grounds. The interior has many interesting pictures and sketches reflecting the industrial history of the area and Coalport tiles, which are made locally.

BUCKLAND Hereford & Worcester **Map 7 B2**
⊗££££ **BUCKLAND MANOR** Buckland, Near Broadway.

Hours: Breakfast 8am - 11.30am, Lunch 12 noon - 2pm, Dinner 7.30pm - 8.45pm (last orders). Bar meals served. Open all year. **Cuisine:** Imaginative French-style cuisine using the finest ingredients including fresh vegetables grown in the hotel's vegetable garden. ⊨ 10 bedrooms, all en suite. **CC** Access, Visa, AmEx. **Other Points:** Children over 12 welcome. Garden. Croquet, putting, tennis, heated swimming pool. Own spring water. Residents' lounge. Fax: (0386) 853557. **P** & **(V) Directions:** 1.5 miles from Broadway, off the B4632 from Broadway to Cheltenham.

ROY & DAPHNE VAUGHAN. Manager - NIGEL POWER ☎ (0386) 852626.

A delightful Cotswold Manor House, dating back in part to the 13th century. The resident manager and his attentive staff

Buckland continued

ensure that guests are well looked after within these tranquil and luxurious surroundings. The food is excellent, well-cooked and beautifully presented. An outstanding country house hotel in all aspects.

CAMBRIDGE Gloucestershire **Map 7 C2**

⊗£ **THE GEORGE INN** Bristol Road, Cambridge.
Hours: Meals 12 noon - 2pm and 7pm - 11pm (last orders 10pm).
Cuisine: Traditional Gloucestershire fayre to international cuisine. ⊨ None. **CC** All major cards. **Other Points:** Special children's menu. Large riverside garden. Coaches by appointment. **P** & **(V) Directions:** On the A38, three miles south of Junction 13, M5.
ALISTAIR & JANE DEAS ☎ (0453) 890270.
Nestling on the banks of the River Cam, The George Inn is the ideal stepping stone to many of Gloucestershire's premier tourist attractions. The oak-beamed dining areas have a unique style with tables made from original Singer sewing machine treadles. Meals also available in the garden or on the patio.

CHURCH STRETTON Shropshire **Map 7 B1**

⊗££ **LONGMYND HOTEL** Cunnery Road, Church Stretton.
☐£££ **Hours:** Meals 8am - 9.30am, 12.30pm - 2pm and 7pm - 9.30pm CLUB (last orders). Bar meals 12 noon - 2pm and 6.30pm - 9.30pm.
Cuisine: Grilled fish, roasts, flambe dishes, salads. ⊨ 50 bedrooms, all en suite. Colour TV in all rooms, with satellite TV and video. **CC** All major cards. **Other Points:** Children welcome. No dogs in public rooms. Coaches by appointment. **P** & **(V) Directions:** On the A49 between Ludlow and Shrewsbury.
MISS SMITH - Director ☎ (0694) 722 244.
Longmynd Hotel stands in 10 acres of woodland commanding panoramic views of the South Shropshire hills. Amenities include a swimming pool, pitch and putt, trim gym, sauna, solarium and pavement chess. 1 bedroom cottages in the grounds and 2 bedroom apartments nearby (both self-catering).

⊗££ **MYND HOUSE HOTEL** Little Stretton, Nr Church Stretton.
☐£££ **Hours:** Breakfast 8.30am - 9.15am, light lunch 12 noon - 2pm, W dinner 7.30pm - 9.15pm last orders). Closed: January/February.
Cuisine: Four course table d'hote dinners. A la carte menu (excluding Monday). ⊨ 8 bedrooms all en suite. 2 suites, one with four poster bed and double spa bath. **CC** Access, Visa. **Other Points:** Children welcome. Dogs allowed (but not in all bedrooms). Afternoon tea served. Fax: (0694) 72180 **P (V) Directions:** Off A49 on B4370 signed Lt.Stretton Hotel in Main Village Street.
ROBERT & JANET HILL ☎ (0694) 722212.
A small Edwardian house hotel situated in the tiny village of Little Stretton and surrounded by countryside of outstanding natural beauty. Local dishes are featured on the menu and the wine list reflects the proprietor's interest in quality wines. Mercier Corps D'elite winner 1990 and overall winner 1991. Ideal for walkers and nature lovers.

WALES & THE BORDERS

CLEARWELL Gloucestershire **Map 7 C2**
⊗£££ **TUDOR FARMHOUSE HOTEL** Clearwell, nr Coleford, Forest
🏠£££ of Dean.
Hours: Breakfast 7am - 9am Tuesday - Friday, 8.30am - 9.30am
Saturday to Monday. Dinner from 7pm. Open all year. **Cuisine:**
Imaginative, freshly prepared cuisine. 🛏 5 double, 2 twin and 2
family bedrooms, all en suite. Colour TV and tea/coffee facilities &
direct dial phone. Four poster rooms available. **CC** Access, Visa,
AmEx. **Other Points:** Children welcome. Licensed. Residents
lounge and garden. Vegetarian & vegan dishes. Central heating.
Fax No: (0594) 37093. **P** & **(V) Directions:** Off A4228, follow
signs for Clearwell. Tudor Farmhouse is in centre.
MRS SHEILA REID ☎ (0594) 33046.
A beautifully restored building situated on the edge of the
Forest of Dean. The house is reputed to date back to the 13th
century and features oak beams and panelling throughout. It
has been carefully modernised and furnished to provide
excellent facilities, whilst still retaining its character. Intimate
candlelit restaurant serving both Table d'Hote and A la Carte
menus.

⊗£££ **WYNDHAM ARMS** Clearwell, Nr Coleford.
🏠£££ **Hours:** Meals 12 noon - 2pm and 7pm - 9.30pm daily. **Cuisine:**
🍳 Fresh food using home grown fruit and vegetables where possible.
Homemade puddings. 🛏 17 bedrooms, all en suite and with
colour TV, telephone, radio alarm, hairdryer, trouser press and
tea/coffee making facilities. **CC** All major cards. **Other Points:**
Children welcome. Dogs allowed. Fax No: (0594) 836450. **P** &
(V) Directions: In the centre of Clearwell village, 2 miles from
Coleford.
MR J STANFORD ☎ (0594) 833666.
Situated within easy reach of Chepstow and Lydney, yet
peaceful and secluded, off the main route. The Wyndham Arms
has beautifully decorated rooms and offers food of excellent
quality. It deservedly won the Routiers Accommodation of the
Year Award in 1990.

CLEOBURY MORTIMER Shropshire **Map 7 B2**
⊗££ **THE REDFERN HOTEL** Cleobury Mortimer, nr Kidderminster.
🏠£££ **Hours:** Open 10.30am - 2.30pm and 6pm - 10.30pm. **Cuisine:**
Shropshire chicken, stuffed loin of lamb, steak and kidney pie.
🛏 11 bedrooms all en suite. **CC** All major cards. **Other Points:**
Children welcome. Dogs welcome. Limited access for disabled. **P**
(V) Directions: On the A4117 midway between Kidderminster
and Ludlow.
MR & MRS J REDFERN ☎ (0299) 270395.
The hotel lies between Kidderminster and Ludlow within easy
reach of junctions 3 and 6 on the M5. The Redfern provides the
best in food and accommodation and there are many places of
local interest for the visitor to see including the Ironbridge
Museum and the Severn Valley Railway.

COLEFORD Gloucestershire **Map 7 C2**
⊗££ **COOPERS WINE BAR & RESTAURANT** 5-6 Market Place,
Coleford.
Hours: Lunch 12 noon - 2.30pm, Dinner 7pm - 10pm (last orders).
Closed: Sunday. Lunch bar snacks. Evening meals in bar only.

Coleford continued

Cuisine: Menu changes daily. Dishes may include Leek & Cheese Tart, King Prawns with Garlic Butter, Poulet Provencal, Salmon Fillet with Chive Hollandaise. ⊨ None. **CC** All major cards. **Other Points:** Children welcome. No smoking in dining room. No dogs. Public car park closeby and street parking available. **(V) Directions:** In the centre of Coleford, near the Clock Tower.

DAVID & FRANKIE COOPER ☎ (0594) 37559.

An excellent wine bar and restaurant set in a three storey town house with black and white tiled floor, sofas, armchairs and open fires. The attractive interior is in keeping with the friendly atmosphere and welcoming service. With all dishes excellently cooked and presented, Coopers is an ideal choice for an enjoyable meal.

⌂£££ **LAMBSQUAY HOUSE HOTEL** Perrygrove Road, Nr Coleford.

⊨ 9 bedrooms, all en suite. All rooms have colour TV, radio, direct dial telephone and beverage tray. **Hours:** Breakfast 8am - 9am. Restuarant meals 12.30pm - 1.30pm, 7pm - 8.30pm (last orders). Closed: January. **CC** Access, Visa, Diners. **Other Points:** Access for disabled to bar/restaurant only. Non-smoking area. Licensed. Full English breakfast. Garden. Afternoon tea served. Children welcome. ▪ **(V) Directions:** One mile south of Coleford on the B4228.

PETER & SERENA WAITE ☎ (0594) 33127.

An elegant Georgian Country House, family owned and run. Situated on the top of a hill, at the edge of the forest and surrounded by garden and meadows, it provides an excellent base to explore the area. All bedrooms are individually decorated and comfortably furnished and the restaurant has an a la carte menu.

DRYBROOK Gloucestershire **Map 7 C2**

⊗£££ **THE CIDER PRESS** The Cross, Drybrook.

CLUB **Hours:** Wednesday to Sunday lunch 12.30pm - 3pm (bookings only in winter) and dinner 7.30pm - 12.30am (last orders 10.30pm unless previously arranged). Closed: all day Tuesdays and Monday lunchtimes. **Cuisine:** British, French and Italian cuisine. Some dishes cooked in cider. ⊨ None. **CC** Access, Visa, AmEx. **Other Points:** Children welcome. No dogs. Non-smoking section. No cover charges. Open for afternoon tea (Spring to Autumn). ♿ **(V) Directions:** Just off the Gloucester - Monmouth road, the A4136. 3 miles off A40.

BERNADETTE FITZPATRICK ☎ (0594) 544472.

An exciting, varied menu and extensive wine list, this is a restaurant reflecting the versatility of the apple, offering a wide choice of ciders and cider brandies (calvados) as well as many sweet and savoury dishes prepared with cider and/or apples.

EVESHAM Hereford & Worcester **Map 7 B2**

⊗£££ **THE WATERSIDE HOTEL** 56 Waterside, Evesham.

⌂£££ **Hours:** Breakfast 7.30am - 9.30am, dinner 6.30pm - 8.30pm. **Cuisine:** A la carte menu, fixed price 3 course menu, bar meals/snacks. ⊨ 2 twin, 10 double and 1 family bedroom. 10 en suite. **CC** Access, Visa, AmEx. **Other Points:** Chilren welcome. Riverside garden. Afternoon teas. Dogs allowed. ▪ **(V)**

WALES & THE BORDERS

Evesham continued
DAVID & LINDA YOUNG. ☎ (0386) 442420.
*This hotel has a Victorian exterior but offers modern facilities
and service. Situated by Shakespere's river Avon and set in the
midst of the beautiful countryside, 'The Waterside' is offering
comfortable accommodation and good food in attractive
pleasant surroundings.*

FOWNHOPE Hereford & Worcester **Map 7 C2**
⊗£ **THE GREEN MAN INN** Fownhope, Hereford.
⌂£££ **Hours:** Meals from 8.15am - 9am, 12 noon - 2pm and 7.30pm -
10pm (last orders). **Cuisine:** A la carte and bar food menus. Dishes
include beef, mushroom and ale pie. ⊨ 20 bedrooms en suite.
CC Access, Visa, AmEx. **Other Points:** Children welcome. Visiting
blind masseur - one evening per week. Fax No. (0432) 860207.
Fax No: (0432) 860207. **P** ⅃ **(V) Directions:** On B4224, midway
between Ross on Wye and Hereford.
ARTHUR & MARGARET WILLIAMS ☎ (0432) 860243.
*A 15th century country inn set in the heart of the beautiful Wye
Valley, popular for businessmen, families, wedding parties or
small functions. Ideal centre for fishing with some of England's
best salmon reaches nearby.*

GLOUCESTER Gloucestershire **Map 7 C2**
⊗££ **MORAN'S EATING HOUSE** 23 Worcester Street, Gloucester.
Hours: Open 11.30am - 2pm and 6.30pm - 10.45pm. Closed:
Sunday and Monday lunchtime. **Cuisine:** Daily specials, eg.
curried parsnip soup,fillet of pork with cranberry and orange
sauce. ⊨ None. **CC** None. **Other Points:** Limited access for
disabled. Children welcome. No dogs. **P** **(V) Directions:** In the
centre of Gloucester.
BRIAN MORAN ☎ (0452) 422024.
*Centrally situated, Moran's is made up of two restaurants
seating 120 people. One in brick and pine with a large skylight,
the other with old and antique mirrors, plus a private room for
60. Blackboard menu changes daily. A variety of drinks and
cocktails.*

GREAT MALVERN Hereford & Worcester **Map 7 B2**
⊗££ **MOUNT PLEASANT HOTEL** Belle Vue Terrace, Great
⌂£££ Malvern.
Hours: Breakfast 7.45am - 9.30am, lunch 12 noon - 2pm, dinner
7pm - 9.30pm. Bar meals 12 noon - 2pm and 7pm - 9pm. Closed:
Christmas and Boxing Day. **Cuisine:** In the restaurant: Salmon
with strawberries and champagne,seafood paellas, table d'hote
menu. In the bar: an excellent variety of home-cooked meals.
⊨ 15 bedrooms all en suite and with colour TV, radio alarm,
tea/coffee facilities and direct dial telephones. **CC** All major cards.
Other Points: Children over 6 years welcome. No pets. Room
available for conferences and weddings. **P** **(V) Directions:** On the
A449 overlooking the Priory Church close to the station.
SOL AND GEOFF PAYNE ☎ (0684) 561837.
*An attractive early Georgian building and orangery set in 1½
acres of mature terraced gardens with lovely views across the
town. Close to the theatre and shops yet only seconds from the
Malvern Hills rising behind the hotel. An informal hotel with all
the facilities of a larger establishment.*

GREAT WITLEY Hereford & Worcester **Map 7 B2**

⊗££ **HUNDRED HOUSE HOTEL** Great Willey.

⊞££ **Hours:** Breakfast 7am - 9.30am, Dinner 7pm - 9.45pm (last orders). Bar meals served 11.30am - 2pm and 7pm - 9.45pm. **Cuisine:** Traditional English cuisine. Dishes may include Lamb Elizabethan, local salmon, steaks. Extensive choice of bar meals. Traditional Sunday lunch. ⊨ 18 bedrooms, all en suite. **CC** Access, Visa. **Other Points:** Children welcome. No dogs. Residents' lounge. Garden dining. 3 banqueting suites. Fax No: (0299) 896588. ◘ ఉ **(V) Directions:** On the A443 Worcester to Tenbury Wells road, in Great Witley.
DIANA JENNIFER WOOD ☎ (0299) 896888.
A family run hotel where the emphasis is on a friendly atmosphere and professional, welcoming service. The hotel is comfortable and spacious and the bedrooms afford superb views of the surrounding countryside. The restaurant provides traditional English cuisine, with all dishes well cooked and served in generous portions. A peaceful and relaxing place to stay or dine.

HAY ON WYE Hereford & Worcester **Map 7 B1**

⊗££ **THE BLACK OX INN** Painscastle, Builth Wells, Hay-On-Wye. **Hours:** Lunch and bar snacks 12 noon - 2.30pm (last orders), Dinner and bar snacks 7pm - 10.30pm (last orders). **Cuisine:** Dishes may include Fresh trout, Scampi Provencale, wild Venison, Roast Duck, a good selection of steaks, Aubergine Galleta. Bar snacks also available. ⊨ None. **CC** None. **Other Points:** Children welcome. Beer garden. ◘ ఉ **(V) Directions:** A470 to Builth Wells from Brecon. Left turn on B4594.
GIL & JAN POOLE ☎ (0497) 851279.
A welcoming, traditional country inn, serving good restaurant and bar meals. Family run, the pub enjoys a cheerful, friendly atmsosphere. A good choice of well-cooked, predominantly European dishes is offered and both food and service are of a high standard.

⊗££ **THE OLD BLACK LION** Lion Street, Hay On Wye.

⊞££ **Hours:** Breakfast 8.30am - 9.15am, Lunch 12 noon - 2.30pm, Dinner 7pm - 9pm (last orders). **Cuisine:** Home country cooking with international flair, house specials being steaks, seafood, game and vegetarian. ⊨ 10 bedrooms, most en suite. **CC** Access, Visa. **Other Points:** Children welcome. Dogs allowed. Private salmon fishing. ◘ ఉ **(V) Directions:** 50 yards off the B4352 Hereford to Hay road.
JOHN & JOAN COLLINS ☎ (0497) 820841.
Oliver Cromwell is reputed to have stayed at the Old Black Lion whilst the Roundheads besieged Hay Castle which was a Loyalist stronghold. Whether you be loyalist or roundhead, this old coaching inn extends a warm welcome to all who visit today by serving delicious country cooking. Hay is the world centre for second hand books with over 2 million books in 27 bookshops.

HEREFORD Hereford & Worcester **Map 7 C1**

⊗££ **GRAFTONBURY HOTEL** Grafton Lane, Hereford.

⊞£££ **Hours:** Breakfast 7.30am - 9.30am, Lunch and bar snacks 12.30pm - 2pm, Dinner and bar snacks 7pm - 9pm. **Cuisine:**

Hereford continued

English cuisine. A la carte and table d'hote menus. Bar snacks. Sunday lunch carvery. 🛏 29 bedrooms, 27 en suite. Weekend breaks. **CC** All major cards. **Other Points:** Children welcome. No dogs. Excellent conference facilities. Functions catered for. Health & Fitness Centre for residents only. **P** & **(V) Directions:** 2 miles from city centre off the A49 Ross-on-Wye road.

MRS E STRONER ☎ (0432) 356411.

Set in the heart of the countryside yet only 2 miles from the centre of the ancient city of Hereford, Graftonbury Hotel is an ideal base from which to visit the Wye Valley. Well run, every effort is made to ensure the comfort of guests, particularly the disabled. The accommodation is of a high standard, and the food is well cooked and very reasonably priced.

⊗££ **THE TASTE OF RAJ** 67 St Owen Street, Hereford.

Hours: Lunch 12 noon - 2.30pm, Dinner 6pm - 11.30pm (last orders). Open seven days a week. **Cuisine:** Regional Indian dishes. Specialities include Tandoori trout, mughlai mosollah, lamb pasanda. Set meals for 2 and 4 persons. 🛏 None. **CC** All major cards. **Other Points:** Children welcome. No dogs. Take-away meals with 10% discount. **P** & **(V) Directions:** On same street as Hereford Town Hall. In centre near Cathedral.

MR S RAHMAN ☎ (0432) 351075/6.

A comfortably furnished Indian restaurant providing freshly prepared and individually cooked dishes. Extensive menu with all dishes carefully explained and English meals available for the less adventurous. Good wine list with the additional choice of Indian wine, beer and liquors to compliment the food.

KIDDERMINSTER Hereford & Worcester **Map 7 B2**

⊗££ **THE COLLIERS ARMS** Clows Top, Kidderminster.

Hours: Lunch 12 noon - 2pm, dinner 7pm - 10pm. Closed: Sunday evenings during winter. **Cuisine:** A la carte menu, grills, fish and homemade specialities. 🛏 None. **CC** Access, Visa. **Other Points:** Children welcome. Garden. Dogs allowed in garden. **P** & **(V) Directions:** A456 at Clows Top. Highest point locally.

MISS SANKEY ☎ (029) 922242.

This two storey rendered country pub is set in its own gardens and is surrounded by pleasant open countryside. Providing an excellent value for money menu and excellent service.

LEDBURY Hereford & Worcester **Map 7 C2**

⊗££ **THE VERZONS COUNTRY HOUSE HOTEL** Trumpet, 🏨£££ Ledbury.

Hours: Breakfast 8am - 9.30am, lunch 12 noon - 2pm (last orders) and dinner 7pm - 9.30pm (last orders 9.30pm). Bar meals in £ price range. **Cuisine:** A la carte, Fixed 3 course menus. Bar Meals. English cuisine. 🛏 9 bedrooms, 7 en suite. **CC** Access, Visa, AmEx. **Other Points:** Children welcome. Dogs allowed. Residents lounge. Gardens. **P** & **(V) Directions:** 3 miles west of Ledbury on the A438.

MR & MRS COOMBER ☎ (0531) 670381.

Built in 1790, The Verzons is now a country house hotel, modernised in keeping with the Georgian character. Set in 3 acres of gardens, the views from many of the rooms look beyond

Ledbury continued
> *to the Malvern Hills. Diners may choose the garden restaurant or the bar restaurant for their meal.*

LUDLOW Shropshire **Map 7 B1**
⊗££ **EAGLE HOUSE RESTAURANT(Wine,food and coffee house)** 17 Corve Street, Ludlow.
Hours: Open 11am - 2.30pm and 7pm - 10pm. **Cuisine:** Interesting home made soups, pates, meat and fish dishes, sauces and sweets. Local produce, vegetarian and wholefoods. Unusual wines. ⊨ None. **CC** None. **Other Points:** Children welcome. **P** &. **(V)**
THE GREENALL FAMILY ☎ (0584) 872325.
This restaurant provides top quality food and service in pleasant surroundings, living up to its motto, 'The Eagle - house of good food and wine finds'.

MALVERN Hereford & Worcester **Map 7 B2**
⊗£ **PHEASANT INN** Welland, Malvern.
Hours: 12 noon - 2pm and 7pm - 9.30pm (last orders). **Cuisine:** English and continental. Menu changes daily. ⊨ None. **CC** Access, Visa. **Other Points:** Children welcome. No dogs. Garden dining. Open Sundays and Bank holidays. **P** &. **(V)**
Directions: On B4208/A4104 cross roads in the centre of Welland village.
A P HUXLEY ☎ (0684) 310400.
A friendly public house set in its own grounds overlooking the Malvern Hills. Extensive menu, with food of good quality and served in generous portions.

⌂££ **SIDNEY HOUSE** 40 Worcester Road, Great Malvern.
⌂ ⊨ 1 single, 3 double, 2 twin and 2 family bedrooms. 1 bathroom. 5 showers. 3 WCs. Colour TV and tea/coffee facilities in all rooms. **Hours:** Breakfast 8am - 9am, dinner 7pm (order by 3pm). **CC** All major cards. **Other Points:** Central heating. Children welcome. Dogs welcome. Licensed. Residents' lounge. TV. **P** **Directions:** Off the A449, 150 yds on right from junction with Church Street.
TOM J S & MARGARET E HAGGETT ☎ (0684) 574994.
An attractive, white Georgian listed building standing in an elevated position in Great Malvern, with stunning views over the Severn Valley towards the Vale of Evesham and the Cotswolds. The town centre, Winter gardens, Malvern Festival theatre, Priory Park and the Hills are only a few minutes walk away.

⊗££ **THE FOX & HOUNDS** Lulsley, Knightwick, Malvern.
Hours: Lunch and bar snacks 12 noon - 3pm (last orders 2.15pm), dinner and evening bar snacks 7pm - 11pm (last orders 9.30pm). Closed: Sunday evenings and all day Monday. **Cuisine:** Traditional English cuisine. Dishes may include Lamb cutlets with apricot and cumin sauce, Chargrilled steak, Dover sole. A la carte and bar meals. ⊨ None. **CC** Access, Visa. **Other Points:** Children welcome. Open Bank Holidays. Dogs allowed. Garden and terrace. Private parties and receptions. Horses can also be accommodated. **P** &. **(V) Directions:** 1 mile off A44 Worcester/Bromyard Rd, follow signs to Lulsley.
MARK & SUZANNE SHIPWAY ☎ (0886) 21228.

Malvern continued

Located in the breathtakingly beautiful area of Lulsley, this old public house has been modernised to include additional bars and public rooms. A good selection of well cooked and presented meals are served in a pleasant, friendly and unpretentious atmosphere. Entertainment and dancing. Frequented by all ages.

⊗£ **THE ROYAL MALVERN HOTEL** Graham Road, Malvern.
£££ **Hours:** Breakfast 7.30am - 9am, lunch 12 noon - 2pm and dinner 6.15pm - 9pm (last orders). Bar meals 12 noon - 2pm and 6.15pm - 9pm. **Cuisine:** Traditional English. Speciality, Herefordshire steaks, rare beef sandwiches, vegetarian meals. ⊨ 14 bedrooms, 12 en suite. Lift. TV, telephone and central heating in all rooms. **CC** All major cards. **Other Points:** Licensed bar. Real Ale. Children welcome. Run by the proprietors. Fax No: (0684) 560514. **P (V)** **Directions:** Off A449, in the town centre on Graham Road. JOHN & SUE PALLANT ☎ (0684) 563411.
An Edwardian hotel in the centre of this spa town. Malvern is within easy reach of the M5, M50, the Cotswolds, Wye Valley and the Black Mountains. The hotel is only 150 yards from the theatre and offers pre performance meals.

MUCH WENLOCK Shropshire Map 7 B2
⊗£ **THE WENLOCK EDGE INN** Hilltop, Wenlock Edge, Near Much Wenlock.
Hours: Breakfast 8am - 9am, lunch and bar snacks 12 noon - 2pm, dinner and evening bar snacks 7pm - 9pm. Closed: Mondays. **Cuisine:** Traditional English cuisine. Pies and puddings - house specialities. ⊨ 5 bedrooms, all en suite. **CC** Access, Visa. **Other Points:** Children welcome. Garden dining. Open Bank Holidays. No smoking area. Dogs allowed in Bar. **P (V) Directions:** From Much Wenlock take B4371. Approx 4 miles along on left side. THE WARING FAMILY ☎ (074 636) 403.
Stone built in the 17th century, this traditional country Inn is family run and provides a delightful rural retreat. The Inn is comfortable and the home cooking is of a high standard. Welcoming service and a relaxed atmosphere ensure an enjoyable meal or stay. Highly recommended.

NORTON Shropshire Map 7 B2
⊗£££ **THE HUNDRED HOUSE HOTEL, RESTAURANT & INN**
££££ Bridgnorth Road, Norton, Nr Shifnal, Telford.
CLUB **Hours:** Breakfast 7.30am - 11am, Lunch 11.30am - 2.30pm, Dinner 6.30pm - 10pm (last orders). Morning coffee and afternoon tea. Bar meals available throughout the day. **Cuisine:** Varied menu which changes frequently: local game, char-grilled meats, traditional roasts, homemade steak and kidney pies, lasagne and moussaka. ⊨ 9 luxury bedrooms, all en suite, with some honeymoon suites and family rooms. **CC** Access, Visa. **Other Points:** Open all day. Children welcome. Dining al fresco. Fax: 095 271 355. **P** ᕗ **(V) Directions:** Situated on the A442 Bridgenorth - Telford road, in Norton village. HENRY & SYLVIA & DAVID PHILLIPS ☎ (095) 271 353.
An award-winning, family run, country inn with character, charm and a warm atmosphere. It has patchwork themed bedrooms with antique furnishings and all facilities, and offers

Norton continued

>   *superb European and English food. Only 15 mins from Birmingham International Airport, Conference and Exhibition Centres and an ideal location to explore Ironbridge Gorge museums and the Severn Valley.*

OSWESTRY Shropshire **Map 7 B1**

⊗££ **BRADFORD ARMS AND RESTAURANT** Llanymynech, nr
ⓘ Oswestry.
Hours: Meals 12 noon - 2pm and 7pm - 10pm (Tuesday - Saturday). Sunday 12 noon - 1.45pm, 7pm - 9.45pm. Closed: Mondays (except Bank Holidays). Closed: 3 weeks mid-October/November. **Cuisine:** Brochette Jurasienne, magret of duck with a peach and brandy sauce served in the restaurant. Onion soup, chicken in mustard served in bar. ⇌ None. **CC** None. **Other Points:** Children welcome. No dogs. **P** & **(V) Directions:** Off the A483, situated on the main road in Llanymynech.
ANNE & MICHAEL MURPHY ☎ (0691) 830582.
Old coaching inn on A483 which was 'Victorianised' in 1902. The lounge bar now has a mahogany bar and a Victorian marble fireplace. The restaurant menu changes monthly, bar menus change weekly.

⊗££ **RESTAURANT SEBASTIAN** 45 Willow Street, Oswestry.
Hours: Lunch by prior arrangement for 6 or more people. Dinner 6.30pm - 10.30pm (last orders). Closed: all day Sunday and Monday. **Cuisine:** Table d'hote and a la carte menus featuring predominantly French cuisine with fresh fish a speciality. ⇌ None. **CC** Access, Visa. **Other Points:** Garden dining. **(V) Directions:** Close to the town centre.
MICHELLE & MARK SEBASTIAN FISHER ☎ (0691) 655444.
Pleasantly decorated with oak beams and panelling, Restaurant Sebastian enjoys a relaxed atmosphere. The French provincial cuisine is of the highest standard and elegantly presented. A popular restaurant and highly recommended for its outstanding food, welcoming service and attractive surroundings.

PARKEND Gloucestershire **Map 7 C2**

⊗££ **PARKEND HOUSE HOTEL** Parkend, nr Lydney.
⌂££ **Hours:** Breakfast 8.30am - 9.30am, Bar snacks 12 noon - 2pm, Dinner 7pm - 8pm (later by arrangement). **Cuisine:** Table d'hote menu with a of choice of English and Continental dishes. ⇌ 8 bedrooms, all en suite. **CC** Access, Visa. **Other Points:** Children welcome. Afternoon teas. Dogs allowed. Residents' lounge. Garden. Croquet. **P** & **(V) Directions:** A48 Chepstow/Gloucester to Lydney. In Lydney take B4234 to Parkend.
MRS ROBERTA POOLE ☎ (0594) 563666.
A small country house hotel set in three acres of parkland. Over 200 years old, the house has been tastefully converted to retain its country house atmosphere. The restaurant offers a varied menu of well-cooked dishes at good value for money, served in pleasing surroundings. A welcoming hotel where guests can relax within the peaceful surroundings of the Royal Forest of Dean.

WALES & THE BORDERS

PENSAX Hereford & Worcester **Map 7 B2**
⊗£ **THE BELL INN** Pensax, Abberley.
Hours: Lunch 12 noon - 2pm and dinner 7pm - 10pm (last orders),
7pm - 9.30pm Sundays. Closed: Christmas Day. **Cuisine:** Home
cooked dishes e.g. steak & kidney pie, lasagne, beef in Guinness.
🛏 None. **CC** None. **Other Points:** Dogs allowed. Children
welcome. Coaches by arrangement. **P** & **(V) Directions:** On the
B4202, nr Great Witley.
JOHN & CHRISTINE STROULGER ☎ (0299) 896677.
A picturesque Victorian country freehouse on the B4202 in a
beautiful location amidst rolling hills. Near the village of Great
Witley with its famous church. A variety of meals are served and
may be accompanied by one of the selection of well kept
traditional beers on tap.

PERSHORE Hereford & Worcester **Map 7 B2**
⊗££ **BENI'S RESTAURANT** 22 Bridge Street, Pershore.
Hours: Lunch 12.30pm - 2pm, Dinner 7pm - 10pm (last orders).
Closed: Sunday evening and all day Monday. **Cuisine:** Good
choice of predominantly Italian dishes. House speciality is
Tournedos Rossini. Pasta dishes also available. Special price lunch
menu. 🛏 None. **CC** All major cards. **Other Points:** Children
welcome. Limited access for disabled. Street parking and public
parking nearby. **(V) Directions:** Centre of town, next to main
square. Street leads to 14th C. bridge.
MR BENIAMINO RUFINI ☎ (0386) 553828.
A Georgian building with beamed interior and inglenook
fireplace in reception area. Beni's restaurant offers an excellent
choice of predominantly Italian dishes, all imaginatively
prepared and very well cooked by the proprietor himself. With
the high standard of food at good value for money, welcoming
service and a relaxing atmosphere, Beni's is deservedly
popular.

REDDITCH Hereford & Worcester **Map 7 B2**
⊗£££ **SOUTHCREST HOTEL** Pool Bank, Redditch.
⊞£££every**Hours:** Breakfast 7.30am - 9.30am, Lunch and bar snacks
12.30pm - 2pm, Dinner and bar snacks 7pm - 9.15pm (last
orders). Closed for lunch Saturdays and for Dinner on Sundays.
Cuisine: French style cuisine. Dishes may include Coquille St
Jacques Manhattan, Tournedos au Poivre, L'Escalope de Veau
Cordon Bleu. 🛏 58 bedrooms, all en suite. **CC** All major cards.
Other Points: Children welcome. Dogs allowed. Residents'
lounge. Garden. Special group offers. Banqueting suite and
conference facilities. Fax No: (0527) 402600. **P** & **(V) Directions:**
Avoid town centre. Follow signs 'All other directions'. Southcrest.
ROY & KAY DEVERILL ☎ (0527) 541511.
A family-run hotel, set in 7 acres of landscaped gardens framed
by woodland, yet less than a mile from the town centre and only
20 minutes from the N.E.C. The hotel enjoys a very friendly and
informal atmosphere, a high standard of accommodation and
the food and service are excellent.

REDMARLEY D'ABITOT Gloucestershire **Map 7 C2**
⊗££ **THE ROSE & CROWN** Playley Green, Redmarley d'Abitot.
Hours: Bar meals 11.30am - 2.15pm, 7pm - 10pm except Sunday
evening. Restaurant open 7pm - 10pm Tuesday to Saturday.

Redmarley D'abitot continued

Lunches by arrangement. Restaurant closed: 25th & 26th December. Restaurant available for special functions & parties. **Cuisine:** Bar food includes Camembert Pancake, fresh fish, baps and ploughmans. A la carte evening menu. House specialities are Fillet steak Balmoral & fresh salmon. ⊨ None. **CC** Access, Visa. **Other Points:** Children welcome. Dogs allowed. No easy access for disabled but staff will help all they can. **P** **(V) Directions:** 1 mile from exit 2 off M50 towards Gloucester on A417.

ROBIN & KATHY BUNNETT ☎ (0531) 650234

Very warm and friendly public house, populated by locals, tourists and businessmen. All food is freshly prepared, and every care is taken to ensure customer satisfaction.

ROSS ON WYE Hereford & Worcester **Map 7 C2**

££ **ARCHES COUNTRY HOUSE HOTEL** Walford Road, Ross on Wye.

⊨ 1 single, 2 double, 1 twin and 2 family bedrooms, 3 en suite. 2 bathrooms, 1 shower. Tea/coffee facilities in all bedrooms (optional TV). 1 ground floor luxury en suite room. **Hours:** Breakfast from 8am, dinner at 7pm (order by 5pm). Closed: Christmas. **CC** None. **Other Points:** Central heating. Children welcome. Licensed. Residents' lounge with colour TV. Garden. Dogs by arrangement. **P** **Directions:** Situated on the B4228 near the junction with the A49.

JEAN JONES ☎ (0989) 63348.

A small, family run hotel set in half an acre of lawned gardens only 10 minutes walk from the town centre. Easy access to many places of interest in the beautiful Wye Valley. All bedrooms are decorated and furnished to a high standard and overlook the gardens. Renowned for good food and a warm and friendly atmosphere with personal service.

⊗£ **LOUGHPOOL INN** Sellack, nr Ross on Wye.

Hours: Lunch served 12 noon - 2.30pm and 7pm - 9.30pm (last orders). Open all year round. **Cuisine:** Extensive range of bar food including stuffed mushrooms with garlic mayonnaise, deep fried Brie, garlic chicken and ribs in a spicy sauce. ⊨ None. **CC** None. **Other Points:** Garden. **P** ⅋ **(V) Directions:** On the A49, Sellack to Hoarwithy road.

REYFORD CATERERS/KAREN WHITFORD ☎ (0989) 87236.

A 16th century pub with oak beams, a large open fireplace and original flagstone flooring. Outside, the inn is set in a large garden, facing a pool surrounded by willows. On the main Hoarwithy road - a popular tourist route.

⊗££ **ORLES BARN HOTEL & RESTAURANT** Wilton, nr Ross on ££££ Wye.

CLUB **Hours:** Meals 8am - 9.15am, 12 noon - 2pm and 7pm - 9.30pm. Closed: November and February. **Cuisine:** Julio's chicken pate, poached Wye salmon with parsley butter, set Sunday lunch menu. Speciality - Spanish paella. ⊨ 9 bedrooms, all en suite. **CC** All major cards. **Other Points:** Children welcome. Dogs by arrangement. Fax No: (0989) 768470. **P** ⅋ **(V) Directions:** Off the A40/49.

JULIO & MARION CONTRERAS ☎ (0989) 62155.

Ross on Wye continued

Ideally situated just off the A40/49 and within easy access of the M5/M50. Serving English and continental dishes as well as catering for special diets, this hotel has a relaxed and friendly atmosphere. The Wye Valley, Forest of Dean and the Cotswolds are within easy reach.

⊗£££ **PENGETHLEY MANOR HOTEL** Nr Ross On Wye.
🍽
CLUB **Hours:** Restaurant open 7.30am - 9.30am, 12.30pm - 2pm, and 7pm - 9.30pm. Bar meals 12.30pm - 2pm (last orders 9.30pm). Routiers prices apply to table d'hote and lunch menus only. **Cuisine:** Local fresh produce, including Wye salmon, Welsh lamb and Hereford beef. Vegetables, fruit and herbs grown in hotel's own gardens. ⊨ 24 bedrooms, all en suite. **CC** All major cards. **Other Points:** Children welcome. Pets allowed. Afternoon teas. Garden. Open Sundays and bank holidays. Fax No: (0989) 87238. **P** ⅃ **(V) Directions:** 5 miles NW of Ross On Wye on A49 Ross to Hereford road.
PATRICK AND GERALDINE WISKER ☎ (0989) 87211.
Georgian country house set in 15 acres of landscaped grounds, all in exceptionally good order. The hotel also has its own 9 hole pitch and putt golf course, an outdoor swimming pool, and a croquet lawn. Staff are very friendly and professional, serving superb cuisine in style. Winner of 'Caterer & Hotelkeeper' Healthy Menu award, and Les Routiers 'Casserole' Award 1990.

⊗£££ **PETERSTOW HOUSE** Peterstow, Ross-on-Wye, Herefordshire.
🛏£££ **Hours:** 8am - 10am, 12 noon - 2pm, and 7pm - 9pm (last orders). **Cuisine:** French influence: fresh lobster with langoustine sauce, Wye salmon, and fillet of Herefordshire beef in red wine. ⊨ 9 bedrooms, all en suite, with colour TVs, telephones, trouser press. Room service and some four-poster suites available. **CC** Access, Visa. **Other Points:** Children over 7 welcome. No dogs. Open Sundays and bank holidays. Residents lounge and garden. Afternoon teas. No smoking area in restaurant. **P** ⅃ **(V) Directions:** A49 Ross-On-Wye to Hereford Road.Next to church,200yds from village.
MESSRS PINCUS & DENNE ☎ (0989) 62826.
An old Georgian rectory, refurbished to a country house hotel, offering guests very comfortable rooms and superb food in the restaurant. Set in 25 acres of magnificent pastures, woodlands and trout lakes, Peterstow House organises various activities including clay pigeon shooting, fishing and riding and, throughout the year, there are weekend courses in painting and photography.

⊗££ **THE OLD COURT HOTEL & RESTAURANT** Symonds Yat
🛏£££ West, Ross On Wye.
Hours: Breakfast 8.30am - 9.30am, dinner 7pm - 9.30pm Bar meals served 12 noon - 2pm and 6pm - 10pm. **Cuisine:** Fixed 3 course menu and bar menu. Four poster suite available. ⊨ 20 bedrooms, 14 en suite. Four poster suite available. **CC** All major cards. **Other Points:** Children welcome. Afternoon teas. Dogs allowed. No smoking area. Heated swimming pool. Conservatory with patio for garden dining. **P** ⅃ **(V)**
JOHN & ELIZABETH SLADE ☎ (0600) 890367.

WALES & THE BORDERS

Ross on Wye continued

This old 16th century manor house is situated in a most beautiful part of the Wye Valley. The carefully selected menus in the Tudor restaurant offer a wide variety of dishes and the charming Cotswold bar serves a wide choice of hot and cold bar food and a comprehensive selection of ales, lagers and wines. Excellent accommodation and service.

£££ **WOODLEA HOTEL** Symonds Yat West, Ross on Wye.
9 bedrooms, 6 en suite. **Hours:** Breakfast 8.30am - 9am. Dinner 7pm. **CC** Access, Visa, AmEx. **Other Points:** Residents bar. Vegetarian meals available on request. **Directions:** Off the A40, on the B4164 for one & a half miles to the end.
VAL & TONY BLUNT ☎ (0600) 890206.
Woodlea is a family-run Hotel, situated in a hidden corner of Symonds Yat West, close to the River Wye in the beautiful Wye Valley Gorge. Away from the noise of traffic but only one and half miles from a major trunk route. Providing well-appointed bedrooms and a relaxed atmosphere, you will find the hospitality of Mr & Mrs Blunt complements their hotel's delightful setting.

SHREWSBURY Shropshire **Map 7 B2**

££ **LION & PHEASANT HOTEL** 49/50 Wyle Cop, Shrewsbury.
£££ **Hours:** Breakfast 7.30am - 9.30am, Lunch 12 noon - 2pm, Dinner 7pm - 11pm (last orders 9.45pm). Bar meals 12 noon - 2pm and 7pm - 10.30pm. **Cuisine:** Extensive selection of bar meals. Regularly changing restaurant menu. 20 bedrooms, 17 en suite. **CC** All major cards. **Other Points:** Children welcome. Afternoon teas. Dogs allowed. Residents' lounge. Full conference facilities. Fax No: (0743) 343740. **(V) Directions:** A5112 in town centre. Town side of English Bridge.
ERNEST & DOROTHY CHIDLOW ☎ (0743) 236288.
Dating from the 17th century, the Lion & Pheasant provides an atmosphere of warmth and friendliness within its characterful surroundings. There is an excellent choice of meals and snacks in the bar areas and full meals can be enjoyed in the intimate restaurant. The bedrooms have been individually furnished and retain the character of the building. A very welcoming hotel.

££ **SHELTON HALL HOTEL** Shelton, Shrewsbury.
Hours: Meals 7.30am - 9.30am, 12.30pm - 2pm and 7.30pm - 9.30pm, Closed Boxing Day. **Cuisine:** Fixed price menus with variety of dishes, eg. rainbow trout Cleopatra, roast duck Olde Englande, steak chasseur. Popular for Sunday lunch. 9 bedrooms, 8 en suite. 1 bathroom. **CC** Access, Visa. **Other Points:** Children welcome. No dogs. **(V) Directions:** Mile and a half north west of town centre on A5.
MR GEOFFREY LARKIN ☎ (0743) 3982
A manor house set in 3 and a half acres of beautiful landscaped gardens. Extensive facilities for weddings, parties, meetings and conference. The bedrooms are comfortably furnished with TV, radio and tea/coffee facilities.

Shrewsbury continued

⊗£ **SYDNEY HOUSE HOTEL** Coton Crescent, Coton Hill,
⬚£££ Shrewsbury.

ⒻD **Hours:** Breakfast 7.30am - 9.15am, dinner 7.30pm - 9pm. Closed:
CLUB Christmas week. **Cuisine:** Fixed price menu. ⊨ 7 rooms. 2 single,
2 twin, 2 double and 1 family bedroom - some with en suite
facilities. **CC** Access, Visa, AmEx. **Other Points:** Children
welcome. No smoking in dining room. ◨ **(V) Directions:** Off the
A528 and B5067, just outside the town centre.
TERENCE & PAULINE HYDE ☎ (0743) 354681.
This Edwardian Hotel is within ten minutes walk of
Shrewsbury's historical town centre. The restaurant boasts an
extensive wine list and some excellent ports. You are assured of
a warm welcome at the restaurant as the staff aim to make all
guests feel at home.

STOURPORT ON SEVERN Hereford & Worcester **Map 7 B2**
⬚£ **OAKLEIGH GUEST HOUSE** York Street, Stourport-on-
Severn.

⊨ 2 single, 2 twin, 4 double and 2 family bedrooms. 8 en suite.
Hours: Breakfast 7.30am - 9.45am, Lunch 12.30pm - 2pm, Dinner
7pm - 9pm (last orders 8.30pm). **CC** Access, Visa. **Other Points:**
Children welcome. Garden. No dogs. ◨ ⅙ **(V) Directions:** Quiet
street, off main street. Overlooking river.
ALMA BARNES ☎ (02993) 77568.
A very well kept, Georgian house, set in a one and a half acre
walled garden and close to the river. The interior is in very good
condition and there is a relaxing, home from home atmsophere.
Comfortable accommodation and attractive decor ensure an
enjoyable stay. The set 3 course menu changes daily and all
food is freshly cooked.

TELFORD Shropshire **Map 7 B2**
⊗£££ **RAPHAELS RESTAURANT** 4 Church Street, Shifnal, Telford.
Hours: Dinner 7.30pm - 12 midnight (last orders 9.30pm). Closed:
Sunday evening and Monday. Sunday lunch 12 noon - 2.30pm.
Cuisine: Dishes may include Venison with a Game Sauce &
Apricots, Salmon in Champagne with Wild Mushrooms, Cashew &
Lemon Roast with Orange Sesame Sauce. ⊨ None. **CC** Access,
Visa. **Other Points:** Children welcome. No-smoking area. No dogs.
(V) Directions: 2 miles jct 4, M54. Off A464 in centre of Shifnal,
one-way street.
ROGER & MARY WILD ☎ (0952) 461136.
Highly recommended by the Routiers inspector, Raphaels
Restaurant offers an imaginative menu of excellently cooked
dishes to suit both vegetarians and non-vegetarians alike. The
quality of the food and service is outstanding. An ideal choice
for excellent food in attractive and comfortable surroundings.

⊗££ **THE OAKS HOTEL & RESTAURANT** Redhill, Nr St
⬚££ Georges, Telford.
Hours: Breakfast 7.30am - 9am, lunch 12 noon - 2pm and dinner
7pm - 9.30pm (last orders 9pm). Restaurant closed: Saturday
lunch and Sunday dinner. **Cuisine:** English and continental. Eg.
Chicken breast stuffed with banana with mild curry sauce, Strips of
beef sauted in herbs & garlic with white wine & cream. ⊨ 8 single,
3 double, 1 twin and 2 family bedrooms, all en suite. **CC** Access,

Telford continued

Visa. **Other Points:** Children welcome (special menu and cots available). Garden dining. Open Bank holidays. Accept Eurocard. Fax: (0952) 620257. Conference facilities. ◘ **(V) Directions:** On the A5, 2 and a half miles from Telford, 4 miles from Weston Pk. ROBERT & JILL MOORE ☎ (0952) 620126.

A family run hotel, in a secluded countryside setting on the A5, 2.5 miles from Telford, offering good home cooked food by award winning Chef Proprietor Robert Moore. The combination of good food, comfortable accommodation and a friendly, welcoming atmosphere provides guests with an enjoyable visit. Ideally situated to see all that Shropshire has to offer. Conference facilities.

TEWKESBURY Gloucestershire Map 7 C2

⊗££ **FARMERS ARMS** Apperley, Tewkesbury.

Hours: Lunch and bar meals 11am - 3pm, Dinner and bar meals 6pm - 11pm (last orders 10pm). Open every day except Christmas Day. **Cuisine:** Dishes may include Steaks, Roast Duckling, Lemon Sole. Bar snacks written on blackboards daily eg. homemade Beef & Ale Pie, Sweet & Sour Pork, Ploughmans. ⊨ None. ◙ Access, Visa. **Other Points:** Children welcome. Childrens menu available. ◘ **(V) Directions:** 1 mile south of Tewkesbury A38, turn right for Ledbury. B3213.
GEOFF & CAROLE ADAMS - Managers. ☎ (0452) 780307.

A very attractive country Inn, surrounded by open countryside. The interior is in keeping with the age of the building with exposed oak beams and an open fire. Good food, friendly service and a welcoming atmosphere complement the pleasant surroundings and the Farmers Arms enjoys a well-deserved popularity.

⊗££ **GUPSHILL MANOR** Gloucester Road, Tewkesbury.

CLUB **Hours:** Dinner 7pm - 9.30pm (last orders). Bar meals 12 noon - 2.15pm and 7pm - 9.30pm. Carvery and bar meals 7 days a week. Restaurant closed: Sunday & Monday. **Cuisine:** All home cooked and menu in carvery changes daily. ⊨ None. ◙ All major cards. **Other Points:** Children welcome. No dogs. ◘ ᇂ **(V) Directions:** On the A38 on the edge of Tewkesbury, 5 minutes from the M5. MARK & KAY RATCLIFFE ☎ (0684) 292278.

A timbered 15th century manor house and site of the 1491 Battle of Tewkesbury. Margaret of Anjou is rumoured to have watched the battle from the precarious safety of one of the bedrooms. The battles are over now, and Gupshill has been tastefully restored, offering a peaceful setting to enjoy good food.

WENTNOR Shropshire Map 7 B1

⊗£ **THE CROWN INN** Wentnor, Bishops Castle.

☐££ **Hours:** Breakfast 8.15am - 9.15am, lunch 12 noon - 2pm and CLUB dinner 7pm - 9pm Bar meals 12 noon - 2pm (evenings as above). **Cuisine:** Weekly speciality board, varied menu including steak selection. Homemade desserts. Comprehensive wine list, liqueurs and traditional ales. ⊨ 4 bedrooms. 2 bathrooms. ◙ Access, Visa. **Other Points:** Access for disabled by arrangement. Children welcome at lunchtimes. Also accepts Eurocards. ◘ **(V) Directions:** 3 miles off A489, just off unclassified Shrewsbury/Longdon road. MR & MRS G RICHARDS ☎ (058861) 613.

Wentnor continued

A wonderful old fashioned village pub, the Crown Inn is well worth visiting. It is a 16th century inn with huge log fires, friendly chatter and a very welcoming atmosphere. Set in the heart of the Shropshire countryside between the Long Mynd and the Stiperstones Hills.

WEOBLEY Hereford & Worcester **Map 7 B1**

⊗££ **UNICORN HOUSE RESTAURANT (WITH LETTING**
⏟££ **BEDROOMS)** High Street, Weobley.

Hours: Breakfast 8am - 9am, lunch 12 noon - 2pm and dinner 7pm - 10pm (last orders). **Cuisine:** Traditional English farmhouse style. Specialities include fillet steak Unicorn and homemade soups. Vegetarian menu. ⊨ 5 bedrooms, all en suite. **CC** All major cards. **Other Points:** Children welcome. Garden dining. Open Bank Holidays and Sundays. Residents lounge. **(V) Directions:** Off A4112 Leominster to Brecon Rd (on black & white village trail). MR & MRS W R PICKUP ☎ (0544) 318230.

Situated eight miles from Leominster and ten miles from Hereford, this is one of the best examples of a black and white timber-framed hotel in England. A small, friendly hotel attracting people from far and wide with its local and continental dishes. Under the personal supervision of Mr Pickup, you can be assured of a genuine welcome with log fires and friendly atmosphere.

WINSTANSTOW Shropshire **Map 7 B1**

⊗£ **PLOUGH INN** Winstanstow, Craven Arms.

Hours: Lunch 12 noon - 1.45pm and dinner 7pm - 9.30pm. **Cuisine:** Steak, grills, pheasant, pigeon in cider. Home cooking. ⊨ None. **CC** None. **Other Points:** Children welcome. No dogs. Beer garden. Games room. **P** ♿ **(V) Directions:** Off the A49 in Winstanstow.

ROBERT WEST ☎ (05882) 3251.

An inviting country inn in the centre of the tiny village of Winstantow. There is ample seating in the lounge bar for dining and the varied, inventive menu attracts visitors from miles around.

WORCESTER Hereford & Worcester **Map 7 B2**

⊗££ **KING CHARLES II RESTAURANT** King Charles House, 29 New Street.

Hours: Lunch 12.15pm - 1.45pm (last orders) dinner 7.30pm - 9.45pm (last orders) Closed: Sundays and bank holidays. **Cuisine:** High quality local seasonal meat, game, fish and vegetables comprise an international menu. ⊨ None. **CC** All major cards. **Other Points:** Children welcome. **(V)**

MRS V. BUCKLEY-WELLS ☎ (0905) 22449.

Originally built in 1577, much of the original oak timbers have survived in this delightful restaurant. Beautiful carved panelling and open fires add to the ambience and friendliness. All dishes are prepared daily using the best local and seasonal meat, game, fish and vegetables.

⊗££ **THE PEAR TREE INN** Smite, Worcester.
⏟£££ **Hours:** Breakfast 7am - 9.30am, Lunch 12 noon - 2pm (last orders), Dinner 6.30pm - 10pm (last orders). Bar snacks 12 noon - 3pm and

WALES & THE BORDERS

Worcester continued

6.30pm - 11pm. Open all year. **Cuisine:** Traditional English cuisine with daily specials of fresh fish and home cooked dishes in addition to full menu. Scottish steaks a specialitiy. 🛏 27 bedrooms, all en suite. 2 Executive rooms, en suite, and 1 Honeymoon suite. 🆑 Access, Visa, AmEx. **Other Points:** Children welcome. No dogs. Residents' lounge. Garden dining. Two small conference rooms. Luncheon vouchers accepted. 🅿 ♿ **(V) Directions:** Jct 6, M5. Droitwich Rd - 300 yds, turn right to Smite. Then 1 mile. DERRICK & JAN HILL ☎ (0905) 55003.

A traditional English country Inn with oak beams and comfortable furnishings, in a delightful countryside setting, yet just off the M5. The expertly cooked food represents excellent value, the service is friendly and efficient and the atmosphere pleasantly relaxed. Recently completed, the 27 bedrooms offer a high standard of accommodation. Very popular.

WALES

ABERDOVEY Gwynedd **Map 6 B2**

⊗££ **BODFOR HOTEL** Sea Front, Aberdovey.

🏠££££ **Hours:** Breakfast 8.15am - 9.15am, lunch 12.30pm - 2pm and dinner 7pm - 9.30pm (last orders). **Cuisine:** Excellent choice of table d'hote & a la carte menus, featuring rolled ham & banana mornay with fresly made raspberry dressing, Veal Stroganoff Julienne. 🛏 3 single, 4 twin, 6 double, 3 family bedrooms: 10 en suite. 🆑 Access, Visa. **Other Points:** Children welcome (with early suppers available). Pets allowed. Special breaks and party rates available. 🅿 **(V) Directions:** A493, opposite main village car park. DAVID & CHERYL EVANS & KAREN HUGHES ☎ (0654) 767475.

Situated in the unspoilt vilage of Aberdovey and overlooking the Dovey Esturay, Mountains and Sea, the Bodfor Hotel is an ideal place for a quiet holiday. Provides tasty, well balanced food complemented by an excellent wine list (David Evans pays particular attention to the wine selection). Warm, welcoming atmosphere and comfortable, immaculate accommodation at its best.

ABERGAVENNY Gwent **Map 7 C1**

🏠£ **SOUTH VIEW GUEST HOUSE** Llangattock Lingoed, nr Abergavenny.

🛏 2 single, 2 double, 2 family bedrooms. 1 bathroom. 1 shower. **Hours:** Breakfast at 8.30am. Open all year. 🆑 None. **Other Points:** Central heating. Children welcome. Residents lounge. TV. 🅿 **Directions:** On the B4521, 6 miles from Abergavenny. ENID JONES ☎ (0873) 821326.

Situated on the B4521, this former rectory is in a tranquil setting with attractive views and extensive own grounds. Ideal for visiting the Black Mountains, Brecon Beacons and Wye Valley.

⊗£ **THE SWAN HOTEL** Cross Street.

🏠££ **Hours:** Bar meals 12 noon - 2pm and 7pm - 9.30pm daily. **Cuisine:** Traditional home cooking, eg. Sunday lunch - roast beef with Yorkshire pud, roast lamb with mint sauce. Homemade pies, moussaka and fresh salads. 🛏 11 bedrooms, some with en suite

Abergavenny continued

shower. All with direct dial telephones, TV, radio and tea/coffee facilities. **CC** Access, Visa. **Other Points:** No dogs. **P** **(V)** **Directions:** Next to bus station in Abergavenny.

IAN S LITTLE **☎** (0873) 852829.

The hotel is situated adjacent to the bus station and within 10 minutes walk from the railway station. It is centrally placed in the town thus affording easy access to the M4. Very popular because of its excellent menu and reasonable prices.

ABERSOCH Gwynedd Map 6 A2

⊗£££ **THE WHITE HOUSE HOTEL** Abersoch.

⊞£££ **Hours:** Breakfast 8.30am - 9.30am, Dinner 7pm - 9pm (last orders). Bar snacks 12 noon - 2pm and 6pm - 9pm. **Cuisine:** Bar menu and a la carte restaurant menu (evenings). Fresh local produce used wherever possible. Local lobsters & crabs, Welsh lamb. 10 bedrooms, all en suite. **CC** Access, Visa. **Other Points:** Children welcome. Garden. Dogs allowed. Residents' lounge. Barclays Connect and Debit Cards also accepted. **P** **(V)** **Directions:** A499, 7 miles from Pwllheli.

JAYNE & DAVID SMITH **☎** (0758) 813427.

Overlooking the picturesque harbour of Abersoch, Cardigan Bay and St Tudwals Islands, this hotel is set back from the road in its own grounds. A warm welcome, comfortable accommodation and good food await you. The bedrooms have recently been modernised and the elegant dining room is comfortable and spacious. A 2 mile long sandy beach is within easy walking distance.

ABERYSTWYTH Dyfed Map 6 B2

⊗££ **COURT ROYALE HOTEL** Eastgate, Aberystwyth.

Hours: Breakfast 8am - 9.30am, lunch 12 noon - 2.30pm and dinner 7pm - 10pm (last orders). Bar meals 12 noon - 2.30pm and 7pm - 10pm. **Cuisine:** Steaks. 10 bedrooms, all en suite. **CC** Access, Visa, AmEx. **Other Points:** Children welcome. Dogs allowed. **(V)**

MR & MRS JENKINS **☎** (0970) 611722.

A hotel dating back to the early 19th century, tastefully restored and fitted with 20th century comforts. The restaurant, in mahogany finish has its own character and offers an extensive a la carte selection. Close to the beach and town centre.

⊗£ **QUEENSBRIDGE HOTEL** Promenade, Aberystwyth.

⊞££ **Hours:** Breakfast 8am - 9.30am, lunch 12 noon - 2pm and dinner 6.30pm - 8pm. Bar meals 12 noon - 2pm and 6.30pm - 8pm. **Cuisine:** A wide variety of traditional meals. 15 bedrooms all with en suite facilities, colour TVs and direct dial phone. **CC** All major cards. **Other Points:** Coaches welcome. Children welcome. No dogs (except Guide dogs). Fax No: (0970) 617452. **(V)** **Directions:** North, quiet end of Promenade, near funicular railway.

TOM & DILYS FRANCIS **☎** (0970) 612343/615025

A Victorian building, recently refurbished situated on the promenade overlooking Cardigan Bay. For residents convenience, a passenger lift has been installed. The varied amenities of Aberystwyth are all close by.

WALES & THE BORDERS

Aberystwyth continued

⊗££ **THE FOUR SEASONS HOTEL** 50/54 Portland Street, Aberystwyth.
Hours: Meals served in the restaurant 8am - 9am and 6.30pm - 8.30pm. Bar meals available lunchtime 12 noon - 2pm. Closed: Christmas and New Year. **Cuisine:** Grills, local fish, roasts. ⊨ 15 bedrooms, 11 en suite. 2 bathrooms and WCs **CC** Access, Visa. **Other Points:** Children welcome. No dogs. Coaches by appointment. **P** **(V)**
MR & MRS EMRYS JONES ☎ (0970) 612120.
A family run hotel with a homely atmosphere. Mr Jones is owner/chef and he uses freshly prepared local produce. Ideally situated for the beach and for exploring the region. Facilities locally for walking, hang gliding, pony trekking and many other activities.

BALA Gwynedd **Map 7 A1**

⊗£ **PLAS COCH HOTEL** High Street, Bala.
⊞££ **Hours:** Breakfast 8am - 9am, Lunch 12.30pm - 2pm, Dinner 7pm - CLUB 8.30pm. Closed: Christmas Day. **Cuisine:** A la carte menu, fixed 3 course menu, and Bar menu. ⊨ 1 single, 1 twin, 4 double and 4 family bedrooms. All en suite. **CC** All major cards. **Other Points:** Children welcome. Afternoon teas. Dogs allowed. No smoking areas. Fax No: (0678) 521135. **P** **(V) Directions:** Centre of Bala High Street.
MR & MRS EVANS. ☎ (0678) 520309.
This attractive stone building dating back to 1780, sits in the centre of Bala near Bala Lake, surrounded by Snowdonia National Park. The restaurant lends itself to traditional Welsh cooking with an emphasis on local produce and a choice of good wines.

BARMOUTH Gwynedd **Map 6 B2**

⊞££ **LLWYNDU FARMHOUSE** Llanaber, Barmouth.
⊨ 1 single, 3 double and 4 family bedrooms, all en suite. Some rooms have colour TVs and all have alarms and tea/coffee making facilities. **Hours:** Breakfast 8.30am - 9.15am. Dinner 6.30pm - 8.30pm. Closed: Dec/Jan. **CC** None. **Other Points:** Licensed. Central heating. Residents lounge with TV. Garden. Vegetarian meals. **P** **(V) Directions:** 2 miles north of Barmouth on the A496.
PETER & PAULA THOMPSON ☎ (0341) 280144.
17th century farmhouse of great character in a secluded position, yet giving wonderful views over Cardigan Bay and mountains. Growing reputation for freshly prepared and imaginative dishes in an atmosphere of oak beams, iglenooks, candlelight and music.

⊗£ **PANORAMA HOTEL** Panorama Road, Barmouth.
⊞££ **Hours:** Breakfast 8.30am - 9.30am, lunch 12 noon - 2.30pm and dinner 7pm - 9.30pm (last orders). Bar meals 12 noon onwards and 7pm - 9.30pm. **Cuisine:** Homemade food. ⊨ 12 bedrooms, 15 en suite. **CC** Access, Visa. **Other Points:** Dogs allowed. Children welcome. Afternoon tea served. **P** **(V) Directions:** Panorama Road is off the A496 ½ a mile east of Barmouth Harbour.
MR & MRS FLAVELL & MR & MRS MORGAN ☎ (0341) 280550.

Barmouth continued

A warm welcome awaits you at this friendly, family run hotel, set in 2 acres of wooded grounds, and overlooking the Mawddach estuary and Barmouth harbour. An excellent reputation for a la carte, table d'hote and homemade bar meals, and a comprehensive wine list.

££ **WAVECREST** 8 Marine Parade, Barmouth.
4 single, 1 double, 1 twin, 5 family bedrooms, 3 en suite. Tea/coffee facilities in all bedrooms. **Hours:** Breakfast 8.30am - 9.30am, dinner 6.30pm - 7pm (order by 5.30pm). **CC** None. **Other Points:** Partial central heating. Children welcome. Residents lounge. TV. **P** **Directions:** On the seafront in Barmouth.
MRS SHELAGH JARMAN ☎ (0341) 280330.
A family guest house with a happy family atmosphere. Situated right on the front, convenient for the beach and shops. Uninterrupted views of both the sea and the mountains. Specialising in fresh homemade food and catering for special diets can be arranged.

BEAUMARIS Gwynedd **Map 6 A2**
££ **THE BULKELEY HOTEL** Castle Street, Beaumaris, Anglesey.
££££ CLUB **Hours:** Breakfast 8am - 10am, Lunch and bar meals 12 noon - 2pm, Dinner and bar meals 7pm - 9.30pm (last orders). **Cuisine:** Predominantly British cuisine. 43 bedrooms, 39 en suite. Lift to all floors. **CC** All major cards. **Other Points:** Children welcome. Games & Snooker room. Health & beauty salon. Fax No: (0248) 810146. Weddings and Conferences. Cocktail Lounge. **P** ♿ **(V)** **Directions:** About 5 miles from Menai Bridge.
RHOBURT PLC ☎ (0248) 810415.
A grade I listed building which still exudes the luxurious ambiance of the Georgian era, whilst offering the best in modern comfort. The elegant Restaurant provides good quality cuisine as well as a resident pianist. With a variety of entertainments, a delightful seafront location and helpful, welcoming service, the Bulkeley is a good choice for an enjoyable stay.

BEDDGELERT Gwynedd **Map 6 A2**
£££ **ROYAL GOAT HOTEL** Beddgelert, Gwynedd.
££££ CLUB **Hours:** Breakfast 7.45am - 10am, lunch 12 noon - 2.30pm, dinner 7pm - 10pm. **Cuisine:** A la carte and fixed 3 course menus. Serving fish, steak, duck and veal. 34 bedrooms, all en suite. **CC** All major cards. **Other Points:** Children welcome. Garden. Afternoon teas. Dogs allowed. No smoking areas. Car hire and pony trekking by arrangement. **P** ♿ **(V)**
IRENE & EVAN ROBERTS ☎ (076 686) 224/343.
This Georgian building is situated in a charming little village in the heart of the Snowdonia National Park. The Royal Goat offers traditional Welsh hospitality in great comfort and style. The combination of excellent food, accommodation and service makes this hotel a pleasure to visit. Situated in town renowned for its 'Legend of Beddgelert'. Highly recommended.

WALES & THE BORDERS

BETWS Y COED Gwynedd **Map 7 A1**

⊗££ **FAIRY GLEN HOTEL** Betws Y Coed.

⊞££ **Hours:** Breakfast 8.45am - 9.15am, lunch 12 noon - 2pm and dinner 7pm - 7.30pm (or by arrangement). Non-residents advised to book. Closed: December & January. **Cuisine:** All dishes homecoooked using fresh produce. Dishes may include Welsh Lamb, Conwy Salmon, grilled Trout, steaks, casseroles. Traditional breakfasts. ⊨ 10 bedrooms, 6 with en suite bathroom and 2 with en suite shower. **CC** Access, Visa, Diners. **Other Points:** Children welcome. Dogs allowed. **P** **(V) Directions:** Half a mile south of the A5 by the Beaver Bridge on the A470.
JEAN & GRAHMAN BALL ☎ (0690) 710269.
Built as a coaching inn 300 year ago, the Fairy Glen is now a small, family owned and run hotel, situated in a quiet position overlooking the River Conwy. Situated only half a mile from the village centre, this is a popular hotel serving freshly prepared home cooked food in a friendly atmosphere.

⊗££ **ROYAL OAK HOTEL** Holyhead Road, Betws y Coed.

⊞££££ **Hours:** Breakfast 7.45am - 9.30am, lunch 11.45am -2pm and dinner 5.30pm - 9pm. Closed: Christmas Day and Boxing Day. **Cuisine:** Fresh fish, homemade soups, grilled steaks. ⊨ 27 bedrooms, all en suite. **CC** All major cards. **Other Points:** Children welcome. No dogs. Coaches welcome. **P** ᠖ **(V) Directions:** On the A5 in the centre of Betws y Coed.
MR F KAVANAGH - Manager ☎ (0690) 710219.
Situated in a picturesque village in the heart of Snowdonia. The hotel has recently been refurbished to provide excellen facilities.

⊗£ **SWALLOW FALLS HOTEL** Betws-Y-Coed, Gwynedd.

⊞££ **Hours:** Meals served all day untill 9.30pm. **Cuisine:** Traditiona English, featuring choice of vegetarian and childrens dishes Homemade steak and kidney pie, grilled local trout with almonds sirloin steak. ⊨ 3 separate chalets available. **CC** Access, Visa **Other Points:** Children welcome. Garden. Afternoon teas served Pets allowed. Non smoking area available. **P** ᠖ **(V) Directions** On the A5, 1.5 miles from Betws-Y-Coed.
PETER JONES ☎ (0690) 710796.
Located on a beautiful spot in Snowdonia National Park, th hotel is only 1.5 miles from Betws-Y-Coed, adjacent to th Swallow Falls. Friendly, efficient, service. Comfortabl accommodation and homecooked reasonably priced meals make the Swallow Falls an ideal place for sightseers to the area

⊗££ **TY GWYN HOTEL** Betws y Coed.

⊞££ **Hours:** Breakfast 8.15am - 10am, lunch 12 noon - 2pm and dinne
🍴 from 7pm - 9.30pm (last orders). Bar meals 12 noon - 2pm and
⌈CLUB⌉ 7pm - 9.30pm. **Cuisine:** Menu changes daily, Anglesey Oysters smoked goose breast, chicken alien, fillet steak Ty Gwyn Homemade meals using local produce where possible. ⊨ 1 bedrooms, 8 en suite. Four poster suites available. **CC** Access, Visa **Other Points:** Dogs allowed. Children welcome. **P** ᠖ **(V Directions:** On the A5 south of Betws y Coed.
JAMES & SHELAGH RATCLIFFE ☎ (06902) 383.
A delightful 16th century coaching inn which has captured th charm and character of the period with low beams, antiqu

Betws y Coed continued

furnishings and tasteful decor. An idyllic setting overlooking the river Conwy in this beautiful Welsh village. Excellent home cooking ensures a strong local following. Routiers Newcomer of the Year 1987.

TY'N-Y-CELYN HOUSE Llanrwst Road, Betws-y-Coed. 4 twin and 4 double bedrooms, all en suite. Colour TV, tea/coffee making facilities, hair dryer, radio/cassette/alarm clock in all rooms. **Hours:** Breakfast 8am - 8.45am. **CC** None. **Other Points:** Children welcome. Packed lunches by arrangement. Licensed. Limited washing and drying facilities available. Fax No: (0690) 710800. **P Directions:** A470, half a mile north of A5/A470 junction.
MAUREEN & CLIVE MUSKUS ☎ (0690) 710202.
A large Victorian house nestling in a quiet, elevated position overlooking Betws-y-coed and enjoying beautiful views of the surrounding area. A warm welcome awaits you from the proprietors, Maureen and Clive Muskus, who will ensure that your stay is a memorable one. Guests arriving by train will even be met at the station. The comfortable accommodation is of a very high standard.

TYN-Y-COED HOTEL Capel Curig, Betws y Coed. **Hours:** 8am - 9.30am and 7pm - 9.30pm (last orders) in the restaurant. 12 noon - 2.30pm and 6pm - 9.30pm (last orders) in the bar. **Cuisine:** Restaurant dishes may include trout with celery and walnut, stuffed fillet steak. Pies and pasta dishes in the bar. 13

Betws y Coed continued

bedrooms, all en suite. **CC** Access, Visa. **Other Points:** Children welcome and dogs allowed. Open for afternoon teas, Sunday dinner and Bank holidays. **P** &. **(V) Directions:** 5 mile west of Betws y Coed on main A5 road to Bangor.

G F WAINWRIGHT ☎ (06904) 331.

A friendly, informal hotel, serving good quality food in generous proportions, with freshly baked rolls and butter Ideally situated in the Snowdonia National Park.

BONTNEWYDD Gwynedd **Map 6 A2**

☎£ **BRONANT FARM GUEST HOUSE** Bontnewydd Caernarfon.

⌨ 1 double, 1 twin and 1 family bedroom. 1 bathroom, 1 shower **Hours:** Breakfast 7.30am - 9.30am. **CC** None. **Other Points** Children welcome. Residents lounge. TV. Garden. **P**

MISS MEGAN WILLIAMS ☎ (0286) 830451

Enjoy warm hospitality at Bronant, a large house of interesting character. Magnificent views of Snowdonia and the Isle of Anglesey. Farmhouse breakfasts and Welsh cream teas are served in a large spacious dining room.

BRIDGEND Mid Glamorgan **Map 7 C1**

⊗£ **ASHOKA TANDOORI** 68 Nolton Street, Bridgend.

Hours: Lunch 12 noon - 2.30pm and dinner 5.30pm- 12 midnight (last orders 11.45pm). **Cuisine:** Rogon chicken special, meat masala, sag ghosht. ⌨ None. **CC** All major cards. **Other Points** Children welcome.

MR MISPAK MIAH ☎ (0656) 50678.

Situated on the main road in Bridgend, the exterior suggests Bengali connection. The interior is pleasantly decorated, with crisp, white table cloths and unobtrusive back groundmusic. popular restaurant.

BUILTH WELLS Powys **Map 7 B1**

⊗££ **THE LION HOTEL** Broad Street, Builth Wells.

☎£££ **Hours:** Breakfast 8am - 9.30am, lunch 12 noon - 2pm, dinner 7pm - 9.30pm. Sunday lunch 12.30pm - 2.30pm. **Cuisine:** Offering la Carte menu, table d'hote dinner, bar meals/snacks and vegetarian dishes. ⌨ 3 single, 6 twin, 6 double and 5 family bedrooms. 14 en suite. **CC** Access, Visa. **Other Points:** Children welcome. Afternoon teas. Dogs allowed. **P (V) Directions:** Next the Wyeside Art Centre.

MR & MRS HOLLAND, MRS C BROWN ☎ (0982) 553670.

Commanding a prominent position on the banks of the river Wye, the Lion Hotel is the perfect place to stay for your holiday in North Wales. All visitors are assured of a warm and friendly welcome and excellent service. The comprehensive menu includes table d'hote dinner, bar snacks, traditional Sunday lunch, picnic lunch and special diets if required.

CAERLEON Gwent **Map 7 C1**

⊗££ **BAGAN TANDOORI RESTAURANT** 2 Cross Street Caerleon.

Hours: Lunch 12 noon - 2.30pm, Dinner 6pm - 11.30pm (last orders). **Cuisine:** Tandoori and Indian regional currys. Indian wine. English dishes available. Sunday Lunch buffet. ⌨ Nor

Caerleon continued

CC Access, Visa, AmEx. **Other Points:** Children welcome. Take-away meals available. Fully licensed. **P** & **(V) Directions:** Off M4, junction 25. 4 miles from Newport.

MR S RAHMAN ☎ (0633) 430086/422489

Attractively decorated with sculptured murals, this Indian restaurant provides comfortable, friendly surroundings in which to enjoy the high class Indian cuisine. The house speciality is Lobster Dilruba but all meals are very well cooked and presented. The service is excellent and, combined with the quality of the food, has ensured the popularity of the Bagan Tandoori.

⊗££ **PRIORY COUNTRY HOTEL** High Street, Caerleon.
⊞££££ **Hours:** Breakfast 7.30am - 9.45am, lunch 12.30pm - 2pm and dinner 7.30 - 9.45pm (last orders). Bar meals 12 noon - 2.30pm and 6.30pm - 10.30pm. **Cuisine:** Veal marsala: pan fried slices of veal with marsala wine served with a demi-glace and cream. Selection of traditional and continental dishes. ⊨ 23 bedrooms, all en suite. **CC** Access, Visa, AmEx. **Other Points:** Children welcome. **P** & **(V) Directions:** Off the M4 at junction 24. On the main street on the left.

JOHN O'KEEFE ☎ (0633) 421241.

A beautiful 16th century house situated in the ancient town of Caerleon on the bank of the River Usk. Close to the Roman amphitheatre and museum, and the excellent shopping facilities of Newport and Cardiff. Superb decor, comfortable atmosphere with attentive, friendly service.

CAERNARFON Gwynedd **Map 6 A2**
⊗£ **THE BLACK BOY INN** Northgate Street, Caernarton.
⊞££ **Hours:** Lunch from 12 noon - 2.30pm and dinner 6.30pm - 9pm. **Cuisine:** Traditional English cooking, eg. roast beef, roast lamb and the trimmings. ⊨ 16 bedrooms, 6 en suite. **CC** Access, Visa. **Other Points:** Children welcome. **P** **(V)**

MR ROBERT WILLIAMS ☎ (0286) 673023.

A 15th century inn situated within the walls of Caernarfon Castle. Good sea and game fishing. Ideal for yachting on inland tidal waters. Traditional home cooking.

CAPEL CURIG Gwynedd **Map 7 A1**
⊗££ **COBDEN'S HOTEL** Capel Curig.
⊞££££ **Hours:** 8am - 9.30am, 12 noon - 2.30pm and 7pm - 9.30pm. Bar
CLUB meals 12 noon - 2.30pm and 7pm - 9.30pm. **Cuisine:** Traditional English cuisine. ⊨ 16 bedrooms, all en suite, with colour TV and tea/coffee facilities. **CC** Access, Visa, AmEx. **Other Points:** Children welcome. Dogs allowed. Tea and coffee served. Open bank holidays and Sundays. Eurocard accepted. **P** **(V) Directions:** On A5, between Betws-Y-Coed and Bangor.

CRAIG GOODALL ☎ (06904) 243/308.

A 200 year old country house hotel, set in the heart of Snowdonia. Comfortable, informal and fun: perfect for total rest and relaxation. Own 200 metre clear running water rock pool for swimming, canoeing and fishing.

WALES & THE BORDERS

CARDIFF South Glamorgan **Map 7 C1**

⊗£££ **CHURCHILLS HOTEL** 3/4 Llandaff Place, Cardiff Road, Llandaff.
Hours: Breakfast 7am - 9.30am, lunch 12 noon - 2pm (last orders 1.45pm), dinner 7pm - 10pm (last orders 9.45pm), bar snacks 12 noon - 2pm (last orders). Closed: Sunday nights to non-residents.
Cuisine: Serving bar snacks, full a la carte menu and specials menu. Dishes may include - French Onion Soup, Guinea Fowl, Fresh Saudi Arabian Tuna Fish. ⊨ 35 bedrooms, all en suite. ☒ All major cards. **Other Points:** Children welcome. Open Bank Holidays. Dogs allowed. Fax No. (0222) 568347. ▣ ೬ **(V)**
Directions: Exit 29 M4, drive on - Llantrnant turning, 100 yrds on at T Jct - L.
NOEL JORDAN - Manager ☎ (0222) 562372.
Large Edwardian House with stables which have been converted into accommodation. Tastefully decorated in keeping with the charactor of the building. Enjoying a warm and friendly atmosphere, the restaurant offers meals of 'excellent' quality, beautifully presented and full of flavour. Highly recommended.

⊗££ **PHOENIX & CEDARS HOTELS** 199 Fidlas Road, Llanishen,
▥£££ Cardiff.
Hours: Breakfast 7.30am - 9am, Lunch 12 noon - 2pm, Dinner 7pm - 10pm (last orders). Bar snacks 11.45am - 2pm. Closed: Christmas Day evening. **Cuisine:** Continental cuisine in a la carte restaurant, bar meals, Carvery. Extensive choice. ⊨ 48 bedrooms, 41 en suite. ☒ Access, Visa. **Other Points:** Children welcome. Dogs allowed. Residents' lounge. Garden. 2 bars and restaurants. Banqueting facilities. Conferences. Fax No: (0222) 747812. ▣ **(V)**
Directions: Jct 32, M4 or A48. In Llanishen Village, north Cardiff.
PHILIP DAVIDSON ☎ (0222) 764615.
Two privately owned and run hotels where you can experience genuine Welsh hospitality, elegant and tasteful surroundings, and a warm atmosphere. Both the food and accommodation are of a high standard and very reasonably priced for the quality provided. Warm & courteous service. Good facilities for conferences, business meetings and wedding receptions.

CHEPSTOW Gwent **Map 7 C1**

⊗££££ **BECKFORDS RESTAURANT** 15/16 Upper Church Street Chepstow.
Hours: Lunch 12 noon - 2.30pm, Dinner 7.30pm - 10.30pm Closed: All day Monday, Sunday evenings and between Christmas and New Year. **Cuisine:** Dishes may include Fillet of Beef Bristol Blue, Wye Salmon, Barbary Duck with lime & green peppercorn sauce. Speciality: Chocolate Saint Emillion. ⊨ None ☒ Access, Visa. **Other Points:** Parking by St Marys Church Children welcome. No-smoking area. No dogs. Room for private parties. Fax No: (02912) 79200. **(V) Directions:** Upper Church Street is opp. St Marys Church gates. 150 yds on left.
JEREMY HECTOR & ANDREW BELL ☎ (02912) 6547/6665.
An excellent restaurant situated in an attractive Georgian house. All dishes are freshly prepared and presented with great care and thought. The excellence of the cuisine is complemented by welcoming service, a good wine list and comfortable surroundings. A relaxed, welcoming atmosphere prevails. Very good reputation locally.

COLWYN BAY Clwyd **Map 7 A1**

⊗£ **EDELWEISS HOTEL** Off Lawson Road, Colwyn Bay.

CLUB **Hours:** Meals from 7.45am - 9.30am, 12 noon - 2pm and 6.30pm - 9pm (or by arrangement). Open all year. On production of a current Club Routiers card accommodation available within Routiers price limit. **Cuisine:** Vegetarian meals, fresh vegetables, home cut meats. 26 en suite bedrooms, all with colour TV, video films, radio, telephone and tea/coffee tray. **CC** All major cards. **Other Points:** Pets welcome. Fax: (0492) 534707. **P** & **(V)** **Directions:** Situated off the A55 on the B5104.
IAN BURT. ☎ (0492) 532314.

A 19th century country house set in its own wooded gardens and tucked away in central Colwyn Bay. Childrens play area, games room, sauna and solarium. Private pathway leading to the Promenade, Eirias Park and the Sports and Leisure Centre.

⊞£production **NORTHWOOD HOTEL** 47 Rhos Road, Rhos-on-Sea, Colwyn Bay.

2 single, 3 double, 4 twin and 3 family bedrooms, 11 en suite. Colour TV, clock radios and tea/coffee making facilities in all rooms. 4 WCs, 1 bathroom. **Hours:** Breakfast 8.15am - 9am. Dinner 6.30pm - 7pm (last orders 6pm). **CC** Visa. **Other Points:** Central heating. Children welcome. Small dogs allowed. Residents lounge & lounge bar with TV. Patio. Ground floor rooms available. Mastercard & Eurocard. **P** & **(V) Directions:** Rhos Road, directly off the Promenade, opposite Tourist Info Centre.
GORDON & AGNES PALLISER ☎ (0492) 549931.

A family run hotel situated in a prime yet quiet position in the centre of attractive Rhos-on-Sea. Noted for its excellent cuisine with a wide choice of menu. Special dietary requirements catered for. Attractive mini-break terms and a festive Christmas programme. Golfing holidays arranged.

⊞£production **ST MARGARETS HOTEL** Princes Drive, Colwyn Bay.

CLUB 2 single, 2 twin, 6 double and 2 family bedrooms, all en suite. 1 bathroom. CTV and tea/coffee making facilities in all rooms. **Hours:** Breakfast 8am - 9am and dinner 6pm - 7pm. Closed: November. **CC** Access, Visa, AmEx. **Other Points:** Children welcome. Pets allowed. Resident's lounge and separate TV lounge. Special diets catered for, including vegetarian. Licensed. W.T.B 3 Crowns. **P** **Directions:** Off the A55. Near Colwyn Bay General Post Office.
GEOFFREY & MONICA COPLEY ☎ (0492) 532718.

Edwardian hotel, recently refurbished and upgraded, offering all one would expect from a first class establishment, yet retaining a friendly and relaxed atmosphere and continuing their policy of moderate prices and true value for money. Large reductions for children.

CONWY Gwynedd **Map 7 A1**

⊗££ **SYCHNANT PASS COUNTRY PARK HOTEL** Sychnant

CLUB Pass Road, Conwy.

Hours: Meals from 8am - 10am, 12.30pm - 2pm and 7pm - 10pm. Bar lunches 12.30pm - 2pm. Open all year. **Cuisine:** Imaginative cuisine, using fresh local produce. 14 bedrooms all en suite. **CC** All major cards. **Other Points:** Children welcome. **P** & **(V)** JEAN M JONES ☎ (049 259) 6868

Conwy continued
Renowned for its comfort, friendly atmosphere and Four Seasons Restaurant, this country house nestles in 3 acres of grounds. Adjacent to medieval Conwy where sailing boast mingle with fishing trawlers beside the world famous castle.

COWBRIDGE South Glamorgan **Map 7 C1**
⊗££ **OFF THE BEETON TRACK RESTAURANT** 1 Town Hall
CLUB Square, Cowbridge.
Hours: 10am - 12 noon, 12 noon - 2pm, 3pm - 5pm (afternoon teas) and 6.45pm - 10pm. Closed: Sunday and Monday evenings. **Cuisine:** Freshly cooked dishes on extensive a la carte menu, which includes seasonal and traditional Welsh meals. Comprehensive wine list. ⊨ None. **CC** Access, Visa, AmEx. **Other Points:** Children welcome. Courtyard. Large free car park closeby. No dogs. **(V) Directions:** Centre of Cowbridge, next to Town Hall.
DAVID & ALISON RICHARDSON ☎ (0446) 773599.
A 17th century, listed building housing a small, attractive restaurant. Mr Richardson is a highly qualified chef and provides an interesting choice of well-cooked dishes. The restaurant has gained an enviable reputation for its good food, pleasant ambience and attractive surroundings.

CRICCIETH Gwynedd **Map 6 A2**
⊗£££ **BRON EIFION COUNTRY HOUSE HOTEL** Criccieth.
⌂£££received **Hours:** Breakfast 8am - 9.30am, lunch 12 noon - 2pm, dinner 7pm - 9.15pm. (last orders lunch 2pm, dinner 9pm). Sunday lunch 12 noon - 2pm, dinner 7pm - 9pm. **Cuisine:** A la carte menu, bar snacks, bar meals, fixed 3 course menu and vegetarian meals. ⊨ 19 rooms. 8 twin, 9 double and 2 family rooms. All en suite. **CC** Access, Visa. **Other Points:** Children welcome. Garden. Afternoon teas served. Dogs allowed. Conservatory. Clock golf and croquet. Fax (0766) 522003. **P** ⅙ **(V) Directions:** From east on A497, through Criccieth, Hotel 1/4 mile on right.
MR R LILLEY ☎ (0766) 522385
Built in the 1870's, Bron Eifion is set in the heart of the tranquil Welsh countryside. The hotel is surrounded by beautifully tended rose gardens and lawns with stonewalled terraces. The decor is of tasteful pine panelling adding to the hotel's character. Meals are well prepared from fresh local produce.

⌂££ **CAERWYLAN HOTEL** Beach Bank, Criccieth.
⊨ 6 single, 4 double, 9 twin and 7 family bedrooms, many with en suite bath or shower. Colour TV and tea making facilities in all rooms. **Hours:** Breakfast 8.45am - 9.30am, dinner 6.45pm - 7.30pm. Closed: November to Easter. **CC** None. **Other Points:** Dogs allowed. Children welcome. Residents lounge with separate TV lounge. Licensed. **P** ⅙ **Directions:** Off the A497 onto B4411 to Criccieth. Hotel is on main promenade.
MR & MRS DAVIES ☎ (0766) 522547.
Caerwylan is an imposing hotel, and the only one in Criccieth situated on the promenade. The lounge and several of the bedroom windows look out across the sandy beaches to the sea, or to the castle. The food is traditional Welsh. With the welcome warm the Davies' have many repeat bookings.

Criccieth continued

GLYN Y COED HOTEL Portmadoc Road, Criccieth.

1 single, 3 double, 1 twin and 5 family bedrooms, all en suite. **Hours:** Breakfast 8.30am - 9am, lunch 12.30pm - 1.30pm, dinner 6pm - 6.30pm Closed: Christmas and New Years Eve. **CC** None. **Other Points:** Children welcome. Dogs allowed. Licensed. Residents lounge. TV. Garden. Fax No: (0766) 523341. **P** **(V)** **Directions:** On main A497, facing sea, nearest hotel to town. MRS ANN REYNOLDS ☎ (0766) 522870.

A Victorian house overlooking the sea, mountains and castle. There is an attractive garden at the front with a small stream running through it. Family run, a friendly, homely atmosphere prevails.

NEPTUN MORHELI HOTEL Min y Mor, Criccieth.

2 single, 4 double, 3 twin and 4 family bedrooms, 4 en suite. 6 bathrooms, 2 with shower. **Hours:** Breakfast 8am - 9am, dinner 6.15pm. Closed: Mid October to Easter. **CC** None. **Other Points:** Partial central heating. Children welcome. Licensed. Residents lounge. TV. **P** **Directions:** Off the A497 onto B4411 to Criccieth. Hotel located on the seafront. EIRWYN WILLIAMS ☎ (0766) 522794.

A family run, seafront hotel overlooking Cardigan Bay, Snowdonia and Llyn Peninsula. Dishes are all homemade with fresh, local produce.

THE MOELWYN RESTAURANT Mona Terrace, Criccieth. **Hours:** Open from 12.30pm - 2pm and 7pm until 9.30pm. Closed: January to March. **Cuisine:** Local salmon and lamb, interesting sauces and fresh vegetables. Homemade sweets. Lobster when available. 5 bedrooms, all en suite. All rooms have sea views. **CC** Access, Visa. **Other Points:** Children welcome. Dogs by arrangement. **Directions:** On the Seafront. MR & MRS PETER BOOTH ☎ (0766) 522500.

A Victorian, creeper clad restaurant directly overlooking Cardigan Bay, with bar/lounge and well appointed bedrooms. The restaurant serves English and French cuisine including locally caught salmon. All food is carefully prepared and complimented by a comprehensive selection of wines.

CRICKHOWELL Powys **Map 7 C1**

TY CROESO HOTEL The Dardy, Llangattock, Crickhowell. **Hours:** Breakfast 7am - 9.30am, lunch 12 noon - 2pm, dinner 7pm - 9.30pm. **Cuisine:** A la carte, table d'Hote. Traditional Welsh dishes. 8 bedrooms, 6 en suite. **CC** Access, Visa. **Other Points:** Children welcome. Garden. Afternoon teas. Dogs welcome. Conference rooms available. Weddings catered for. **P** & **(V)** **Directions:** 1/2 mile from Crickhowell Bridge. KATE & PETER JONES ☎ (0873) 810573.

Ty Croeso means 'house of welcome' and this is what you will get at this small traditional Welsh hotel above the Usk Valley - a warm welcome, good food, a large selection of malt whiskeys and lots to do in the surrounding area.

WALES & THE BORDERS

CWMBRAN Gwent **Map 7 C1**
⊗£££ **THE PARKWAY HOTEL & CONFERENCE CENTRE**
⫤£££££ Cwmbran Drive, Cwmbran.
Hours: Breakfast 7am - 9.30am, Lunch and bar meals 12.30pm -
2.30pm, Dinner 7pm - 10pm (last orders). Closed for Saturday
lunch. **Cuisine:** Extensive choice of dishes such as River Wye
Salmon, Lemon Sole Veronique, Grills, Roast Pheasant,
Tournedos Rossini. Carvery. ⇔ 70 bedrooms, all en suite.
Specially adapted ground floor bedrooms for the disabled.
Accommodation within the Routiers price bracket at weekends
only. **CC** All major cards. **Other Points:** Children welcome.
Garden. Residents' lounge. Conference Centre with full facilities.
Health and Leisure Club. Fax: (0633) 369160. **P** & **(V)**
Directions: Off junction 26 of the M4, onto A4042. Left into
Cwmbran Drive.
JOHN WOODCOCK ☎ (0633) 871199.
Outstanding in all aspects, The Parkway is ideal for
holidaymakers and business visitors alike. Designed on a
Mediterranean theme, the hotel offers accommodation of a very
high standard, first-class restaurant meals, a leisure complex
and excellent conference and banqueting facilities. Privately
owned and run, the service is excellent and a warm welcome
guaranteed. Highly recommended.

DENBIGH Clwyd **Map 7 A1**
⊗££ **BROOKHOUSE MILL TAVERN** Ruthin Road, Denbigh.
Hours: Lunch 11am - 4pm, Dinner 6pm - 10.30pm. **Cuisine:**
Traditional a la carte menu with dishes made from fresh, local
produce. Fresh, local fish is a speciality. Bar snacks also available.
⇔ None. **CC** Access, Visa, Diners. **Other Points:** Children
welcome. No smoking area. Limited access for disabled. Garden
dining. Afternoon teas. Weddings and private parties catered for.
P (V) Directions: A525, Denbigh - Ruthin road. 500 yds outside
Denbigh on L.H.S.
JOHN HALL ☎ (0745 81) 3377.
A 17th century, restored watermill next to a river, which
provides a picturesque setting in which to enjoy excellent food
and service. All dishes are well cooked using fresh, local
produce and served in generous portions. With a warm
welcome from John Hall and his staff, Brookhouse Mill is an
ideal choice for a meal, wedding, function or small conference.

DOLGELLAU Gwynedd **Map 7 B1**
⊗££ **CLIFTON HOUSE HOTEL** Smithfield Square, Dolgellau.
⫤££ **Hours:** Breakfast 8am - 9am, Lunch 12.30pm - 2pm, Dinner 7pm -
↩ 9.30pm (last orders). Closed: January. **Cuisine:** Interesting and
varied menu featuring traditional and vegetarian dishes and using
fresh, local produce. ⇔ 7 bedrooms, 4 en suite. **CC** Access, Visa.
Other Points: Limited access for disabled. Children welcome.
Garden. **P (V) Directions:** A470. Centre of Dolgellau.
ROB & PAULINE DIX ☎ (0341) 422554.
Dating from the 18th century when it was the County Gaol, the
Clifton now offers a much warmer welcome as a hotel and
restaurant. Mrs Dix, the chef, makes imaginative use of fresh,
local produce and all the dishes are excellently cooked. The
service is 'exemplary' and the warmth of the welcome is

Dolgellau continued

undoubtably genuine. Highly recommended for food and accommodation.

⊗££ **DOLSERAU HALL HOTEL** Dolgellau.
Hours: 8am - 9.15am, 12 noon - 2pm and 7pm - 9pm (last orders 8.45pm). Bar meals 12 noon - 2pm and 7pm - 8.45pm. **Cuisine:** Traditional British cuisine. ⊨ 13 bedrooms, all en suite. **CC** Access, Visa. **Other Points:** Children welcome. Pets allowed. Afternoon teas. Garden dining. Open Sundays and bank holidays. **P** ᴃ **(V) Directions:** 1 miles east of Dolgellau on the A470,then left at service station.
MARION & PETER KAYE ☎ (0341) 422 522.
The hotel, originally a Victorian mansion, stands in 4 acres of its own grounds, amidst the mountains of Snowdonia. The staff are very helpful and welcoming, the rooms are spacious and the food excellent. The hotel is popular with fishing enthusiasts as it has 8 rods on 10 miles of the nearby rivers.

FISHGUARD Dyfed **Map 6 B2**
⊗£ **THE HOPE & ANCHOR INN** Goodwick, Fishguard.
⊞£ **Hours:** Meals from 12 noon - 2.30pm and 7pm - 10pm. **Cuisine:** Pies, quiche, homemade bread, fresh crab, steaks and lobster. ⊨ 3 bedrooms. 1 bathroom and 1 shower. **CC** None. **Other Points:** Children welcome. **P** **(V) Directions:** End of A40.
MR T McDONALD ☎ (0348) 872 314.
This small family run inn overlooks the harbour and is conveniently placed for both the station and the Irish ferries. There are miles of beaches nearby with a coastal path for walkers.

HARLECH Gwynedd **Map 6 A2**
⊗££ **CASTLE COTTAGE HOTEL & RESTAURANT** Harlech.
⊞££ **Hours:** March - September opens: 7pm - 9.30pm (all week). October - March opens: 7pm - 9pm (Tuesday to Sunday). Sunday lunch 12 noon all year. **Cuisine:** Dishes include Local rack of lamb and honey & rosemary sauce. ⊨ 6 bedrooms. 4 en suite. **CC** Access, Visa. **Other Points:** Children welcome. **(V) Directions:** On B4573 road to Porthmadog.
MR ROBERTS ☎ (0766) 780479.
An oak-beamed dining room and bar in one of the oldest houses in Harlech. Only 300 yards from the Castle. International cuisine plus modestly priced wine list.

⊗££ **THE CASTLE HOTEL** Castle Square, Harlech.
Hours: Lunch 12 noon - 3pm, Dinner 7pm - 11pm (last orders 10pm). **Cuisine:** Full a la carte and pub menu, serving a range of dishes from dover sole and steak tartare to cow pie, lasagne and the Kiddies Corner selection. ⊨ 10 bedrooms, all en suite. **CC** Access, Visa. **Other Points:** Children welcome. Dogs allowed. **P** ᴃ **(V) Directions:** Opposite the castle in the centre of Harlech, which is on the A496.
R G & T M SWINSCOE ☎ (0766) 780529.
A family run hotel offering a wide menu and warm, welcoming service. Local attractions include Harlech castle, Cardigan Bay, a local golf club and Beddgelert copper mine. Nearby, Shell

WALES & THE BORDERS

Harlech continued
Island provides the opportunity for seal and bird spotting, and shell-collecting.

HAVERFORDWEST Dyfed **Map 6 C1**
⊗££ **PEMBROKE HOUSE HOTEL** Spring Gardens, Haverfordwest.
Hours: Breakfast from 7.30am - 9.30am, Lunch by arrangement and dinner from 7pm - 9.30pm (last orders). **Cuisine:** Steaks, grills and fresh fish. ⊨ 21 bedrooms, 19 en suite. ◨ All major cards. **Other Points:** Children welcome. Dogs allowed. Coaches by arrangement. ◨ **Directions:** Through the town centre, situated 2 blocks from Dew Street.
SIMON & SUZANNE DAVIES ☎ (0437) 763652.
A Virgina creeper clad, terraced Georgian house with a reputation for good food and friendly service.

⊗££ **ROCH GATE MOTEL** Roch, Haverfordwest.
▥£££ **Hours:** Breakfast 7.45am - 9.30am, lunch 12 noon - 3pm (last orders 2.30pm), dinner 6pm - 10pm (last orders). Bar snacks available all day. **Cuisine:** Menu may feature - tuna & prawn tagliatelle, cheese & walnut pasta bake, king prawns and apple pie. ⊨ 19 bedrooms, all en suite. ◨ Access, Visa, AmEx. **Other Points:** Children welcome. Open Bank Holidays. Dogs allowed. Sauna. Gym. Jacuzzi. Solarium. Indoor swimming pool. ♿ **(V) Directions:** 6 miles out of Haverfordwest towards St Davids.
JOHN SMITH ☎ (0437) 710435.
A modern motel providing excellent personal service, to both long and short term visitors. Tasty meals with an emphasis on healthy eating and comfortable accommodation. With an indoor swimming pool, family sized jacuzzi, solarium etc, there need never be a dull moment!

⊗£££ **WOLFSCASTLE COUNTRY HOTEL** Wolf's Castle,
▥£££ Haverfordwest.
Hours: Breakfast 7am - 9.30am, Dinner 7pm - 9pm (last orders). Sunday lunch only 12 noon - 2pm. Bar meals served 12 noon - 2pm and 7pm - 9pm. Closed: Some Sunday nights for dinner. **Cuisine:** A blend of nouvelle cuisine and home cooking. Predominantly fresh, local produce used. Traditional Sunday lunch. Good wine list. ⊨ 20 bedrooms, all en suite. ◨ Access, Visa. **Other Points:** children welcome. Residents' lounge. Hotel bar with log fire. Banqueting Suite. Patio. Tennis & Squash court. Fax No: (0437) 87383. ◨ **(V) Directions:** A40. 6 miles North of Haverfordwest in village of Wolf's Castle.
ANDREW STIRLING ☎ (0437) 87225/87688.
A country hotel where the traditional welcome of warmth, relaxation and friendliness has been maintained. Situated on a hillside amidst beautiful countryside, this hotel offers a high standard of accommodation. The restaurant enjoys an enviable reputation locally for its excellent food and imaginative bar meals are also available. A delightful hotel in which to stay or dine.

HOLYHEAD Gwynedd **Map 6 A2**

⊗£ **BULL HOTEL** London Road, Valley, Holyhead.

🏠£££ **Hours:** Breakfast 7.30am - 9am, lunch 12 noon - 2pm and dinner 7pm - 9.30pm (last orders). Bar meals 12 noon - 9pm. **Cuisine:** Specials change daily. 🛏 14 bedrooms, 11 en suite. **CC** Access, Visa. **Other Points:** Dogs allowed. Children welcome. Afternoon tea served. **(V) Directions:** Situated 200 yards from Holyhead side traffic lights at A5025 jct.

DAVID HALL ☎ (0407) 740 351

A pleasant, cream painted building on the main A5 road to Holyhead. There is a large, sheltered beer garden with children's play area outside, while inside the main, informal eating area is separate from the bar. For those wishing to linger a while the Bull offers comfortable accommodation.

LITTLE HAVEN Dyfed **Map 6 C1**

⊗££ **THE NEST BISTRO** 12 Grove Place, Little Haven.

Hours: Lunch 12 noon - 2.30pm (July and August only) and dinner 6.30pm - late (last orders 10pm). Closed: Mondays. **Cuisine:** An imaginative menu with all dishes homemade, featuring fresh local fish, seafood & a selection of sirloin steaks. Extended wine list. Welsh cheeseboard. 🛏 2 private flats to rent from Whitsun to end September. **CC** Access, Visa. **Other Points:** Children welcome. Afternoon teas in summer. National Parks car park 100 yds. ♿ **(V) Directions:** Off the B4341 in Little Haven.

PAUL & MARGARET MERRICK ☎ (0437) 781728.

A cosy bistro with a small cocktail bar, in an old rambling house in this unique seaside village. A wide choice of dishes such as Mexican Turkey & Breast of Duck. Fresh local fish includes Dover sole, monkfish, stuffed fillets of Lemon sole & lobster. 100 yards from the beach and coastal path. Little Haven provides a picturesque base for touring or enjoying the many water sports.

LLANBEDROG Gwynedd **Map 6 A2**

⊗£ **SHIP INN** Bryn-Y-Gro, Nr Pwllheli, Llanbedrog.

Hours: Lunch 12 noon - 3pm (last orders 2.45pm) and Dinner 5.30pm - 9.45pm. Closed: Sundays. **Cuisine:** Seafood, pizza, lasagne and special 'Ship' home-made steak and kidney pie with lean steak, sherry, fresh herbs and garlic. 🛏 None. **CC** None. **Other Points:** Children welcome. Dogs allowed. 🅿 ♿ **(V) Directions:** Approaching Llanbedrog from Pwllheli,take sharp right for Aberdaron.

MR & MRS WARD ☎ (0758) 740270.

The Ship Inn is a public house serving very tasty food at good prices. It also has open views on 3 sides with a protected outside area for diners. The 'Ship' is celebrated for its flower displays and the gardens which are attended by a professional gardener, give a particularly pleasant outlook.

LLANBERIS Gwynedd **Map 6 A2**

🏠££ **ALPINE LODGE** 1 High Street, Llanberis.

🛏 4 double and 2 family bedrooms, all en suite. **Hours:** Breakfast 8am - 9am, dinner 8pm (order by 7pm). Closed: November. **CC** All major cards. **Other Points:** Central heating. Children welcome. No dogs. Licensed. Residents lounge. TV. Garden. Vegetarians catered for. 🅿 **Directions:** Off the A4086. At the Caernarfon end of Llanberis High Street.

Llanberis continued

JAMES & RUTH GERRARD ☎ (0286) 870294.

Small family run hotel with views of Lake Padarn and Snowdonia. Situated at the quieter, Caernarfon, end of town, with easy access to the Snowdonia Railway terminus and the museum of the North in Llanberis.

⊗££ **LAKE VIEW HOTEL** Tan y pant, Llanberis.

⊞££ **Hours:** Meals from 8.30am - 9.30am, 12 noon - 2pm and 6.30pm - 9.30pm (last orders 9pm). Open all day. **Cuisine:** Homemade sauce dishes. ⊨ 10 bedrooms, 9 en suite. **CC** Access, Visa. **Other Points:** Children welcome. Coaches by appointment. **P** ᕂ **Directions:** On the A4086 on the Caernarfon side of Llanberis.

BRIAN TAYLOR ☎ (0286) 870422.

The Lake View Hotel offers exceptional views of the surrounding terrain. Close to the narrow gauge railways and Snowdonia National Park. A friendly hotel with a homely atmosphere.

LLANDOGO Gwent **Map 7 C1**

⊗£ **THE OLD FARMHOUSE INN** Llandogo, Nr Monmouth.

⊞££ **Hours:** Lunch 12 noon - 3pm, dinner 7pm - 12 midnight. Sunday lunch 12 noon - 2pm Sunday dinner 7pm - 10.30pm. **Cuisine:** Menu may feature Garlic Prawns, Swordfish Plantain, Spanish Baked Peppers, Seafood, Chicken Breast stuffed with asparagus & cream cheese. Homemade sweets. ⊨ 3 bedrooms. **CC** All major cards. **Other Points:** Children welcome. Afternoon teas. Dogs allowed. Weddings catered for. Courtesy mini bus service. **P (V) Directions:** A466.

MR R B SMITH ☎ (0594) 530095

Located near Tintern Abbey 'The Old Farmhouse Inn' is smartly decorated and has pretty flower arrangements throughout. The restaurant is comfortably furnished and spacious, offering well cooked meals made from fresh produce in generous portions. Staff are friendly and welcoming.

LLANDOVERY Dyfed **Map 7 C1**

⊗£ **THE ROYAL OAK INN** Rhandirmwyn, Llandovery.

⊞££ **Hours:** Breakfast 8am - 9.30am, Lunch 11.30am - 3.30pm, and Dinner 6pm - 10pm (last orders 10.30pm). Bar meals 11.30am - 3.30pm, 6pm - 10.30pm. **Cuisine:** Good quality country food. Excellent value bar meals. ⊨ 5 Bedrooms, 3 en suite. Tea/coffee making facilities. TV. **CC** Access, Visa. **Other Points:** Children welcome. Pets allowed. Beer garden. **P** ᕂ **(V) Directions:** From Llandovery, follow signs to 'Lyn Brainne & Rhandirmwyn.

MR & MRS L W ALEXANDER ☎ (05506) 201.

A 17th century village inn with resturant, pool room, and en suite accommodation. Near Brecon Beacons, RSPB Bird Reserve, Llyn Brianne dam and reservoir, fishing, riding and fabulous scenery. 40 minutes from the coast and 7 miles north of Llandovery.

LLANDRINDOD WELLS Powys **Map 7 B1**

⊗££ **SEVERN ARMS HOTEL** Penybont, Llandrindod Wells.

⊞£££ **Hours:** Restaurant open 7pm - 9.30pm. Hotel closed: Christmas week. **Cuisine:** Grills, Roasts, homemade steak and kidney pie, cottage pie. Full A La Carte menu and Bar snacks are always

Llandrindod Wells continued
available. ⊨ 10 bedrooms, all en suite. All rooms with tea/coffee making facilities, radio, colour TV and telephone. Central heating and double glazing. **CC** Access, Visa, AmEx. **Other Points:** Children welcome. 6 miles of fishing free to residents. Garden with seating. 3 luxury caravans & facilities for touring vans in grounds. **P** & **Directions:** On A44, Rhayader to Leominster road. GEOFF & TESSA LLOYD ☎ (059 787) 224/344.

A former coaching inn ideally situated on a popular holiday route. The Inn has an olde worlde charm with a wealth of oak beams and a log fire which burns in the Lounge Bar during winter. The Severn Arms is one of the best known unaltered coaching houses in Mid Wales but has been modernised inside to a high standard. Reduced rates on 2 golf course.

⊗£££ **THE BELL COUNTRY INN** Llanyre, Llandrindod Wells.
⊞£££ **Hours:** Breakfast 8am - 10am, lunch 12 noon - 2pm, dinner 6.30pm - 9.30pm. **Cuisine:** Traditional Welsh/Continental. ⊨ 2 single, 8 twin/double and 1 family bedroom. All en suite. **CC** All major cards. **Other Points:** Children welcome. Garden Afternoon teas. Dogs allowed. No smoking areas. Conference rooms. **P** & **(V) Directions:** One and a half miles north west of Llandrindod Wells in Powys.
CHRISTINE PRICE ☎ (0597) 823959.

A large country Inn in the centre of the village offering a very high standard of accommodation and cuisine. All rooms are very well appointed with every facility. Excellent value for money and highly recommended by our inspector.

LLANDUDNO Gwynedd **Map 7 A1**
⊞££ **AMBASSADOR HOTEL** Grand Promenade, Llandudno.
⊨ 12 single, 25 double, 18 twin and 15 family bedrooms many en suite. TV in all bedrooms. **Hours:** Breakfast 8.30am - 9.15am, bar lunches 12 noon - 1.30pm and dinner 6.30pm - 7.30pm. Closed: January. **CC** None. **Other Points:** Partial central heating. Children welcome. No dogs. Licensed. Residents lounge. 3 lifts. **P** **Directions:** Off A55 onto A470 for Llandudno, turn to Promenade then turn left.
DAVID T WILLIAMS ☎ (0492) 76886.

The Williams family have been in the hotel trade for 30 years and, in that time, have built up a regular return business. The hotel is on the Promenade and gets the sun most of the day. The two sun lounges are relaxing places to sit whatever the weather.

⊞£££ **BELLE VUE HOTEL** 26 North Parade, Llandudno.
⊨ 2 single, 5 twin, 8 double and 2 family bedrooms, all en suite. All rooms with colour TV, video player, direct dial telephone, radio, tea and coffee tray, hairdryer. **Hours:** Breakfast 8am - 9am, Lunch 12 noon - 3pm, Dinner 6.30pm - 7.30pm. **CC** All major cards. **Other Points:** Children welcome. Central heating. Lift. Dogs allowed. Sun terrace. Table tennis. Snooker. A la Carte & table d'hote menus. Vegetarian meals available. **P** **Directions:** At the end of the Promenade, near the Pier.
MR & MRS ALEX GAMEZ ☎ (0492) 879547.

A Victorian terraced hotel in a slightly elevated position affording beautiful views across the bay. Residents can enjoy the sheltered sun terrace or Fishermans's Bar, open to residents

Llandudno continued

throughout the day. The attractive restaurant has views of the bay and the fully qualified chef provides both a la carte and table d'hote menus. A welcoming hotel in a delightful setting.

⊗£££ **BRYN Y BIA LODGE HOTEL** Craigside, Llandudno
⌂£££ **Hours:** Breakfast 8.30am - 9.30am, Dinner 7pm - 8.30pm (last orders). Bar meals 12 noon - 2pm. **Cuisine:** Dishes may include Navarin of Lamb, Salmon en Croute, Chicken a la Creme. A la carte and table d'hote. Fresh, local produce used. ⊨ 13 bedrooms, all en suite. ⬛ Access, Visa, AmEx. **Other Points:** Children welcome. No-smoking area. Dogs allowed. Residents lounge. Cocktail bar. Garden. ⽥ **(V) Directions:** Along A546 (Promenade) from Llandudno towards Little Orme.
GEOFFREY GRIMWOOD ☎ (0492) 549644.
Built in the mid 1800's, the hotel stands in its own walled grounds on the Little Orme overlooking Llandudno and the sea. The hotel enjoys a relaxed and tranquil atmosphere and all guests are assured a warm welcome. The spacious yet intimate restaurant offers a high standard of freshly prepared dishes. Comfortable accommodation.

⊗££ **CASANOVA RESTAURANT** 18 Chapel Street, Llandudno.
Hours: Meals from 6pm - 10.30pm (last orders). **Cuisine:** Italian cuisine: eg. calimari fritti, insalata Casanova, filetto al funghi. ⊨ None. ⬛ Access, Visa. **Other Points:** Children welcome. No dogs. Street parking. **(V) Directions:** Off Gloddaeth Street opposite the English Presbyterian Church.
MR K R BOONHAM ☎ (0492) 78426.
Situated in the heart of town. Gingham and red tablecloths, a cedar ceiling and lively music add to the bustling atmosphere. A very popular restaurant - advance booking recommended.

⌂££ **CRICKLEIGH HOTEL** Lloyd Street, Llandudno.
⊨ 16 bedrooms, 7 en suite. Tea and coffee making facilities. **Hours:** Breakfast 8.30am - 9am, lunch 12.30pm - 2.30pm and dinner 6pm - 7pm. ⬛ Visa. **Other Points:** No dogs. TV. Lounge. Special diets catered for. W.T.B. 3 Crown Commended. ⽥ **Directions:** Off the A546. Lloyd St. is off the Promenade.
GEORGE & CAROL CLARK ☎ (0492) 75926.
A detached private licensed hotel with distinctive architecture, situated in a select area of Llandudno between the two shores - with no hills to climb. The hotel is very much a family concern and a warm welcome is assured.

⊗£ **DUNOON HOTEL** Gloddaeth Street, Llandudno.
⌂£££ **Hours:** Breakfast 9am - 10am, Lunch 1pm - 2pm, Dinner 6.30pm -
⊷ 7.30pm (last orders). **Cuisine:** Table d'hote, a la carte and bar meals. British cuisine specialising in fresh, local produce. ⊨ 56 bedrooms, all en suite. ⬛ Access, Visa. **Other Points:** Children welcome. Garden. Afternoon teas. Dogs allowed. Solarium. ⽥ ⽥ **(V) Directions:** Off Mostyn Street, close to Promenade.
MICHAEL C CHADDERTON ☎ (0492) 860787.
Lavishly appointed with great attention to detail, the Dunoon exudes charm and comfort. The hotel has been in the same family for over 40 years which accounts for the care shown in the elegant accommodation and spacious restaurant. The

Llandudno continued

Dunoon provides the ideal place to relax and enjoy the good food, civilised ambience and splendid facilities.

⊗££ **EMPIRE HOTEL** Church Walks, Llandudno.
Hours: Bar open during normal licensing hours. Snacks available. **Cuisine:** Watkins & Co serving traditional dishes and the Grill Room/Coffee Shop serving light meals, snacks and grills. ⊨ 64 bedrooms, all en suite. 🆑 All major cards. **Other Points:** Children welcome. Roof garden and sun terrace. Heated indoor pool, sauna, and steam room. 🄿 ⅍ **(V) Directions:** Church Walks leads off the Promenade.
MR & MRS MADDOCKS ☎ (0492) 860555.
A family run hotel located near the centre of this popular holiday resort. The Empire has developed a reputation for good food served in two separate restaurants, friendly service and leisure facilities.

⬙££ **EPPERSTONE HOTEL** 15 Abbey Road, Llandudno.
CLUB ⊨ 6 double or family and 2 twin bedrooms, all en suite. facilities. **Hours:** Breakfast 8.30am - 9am, Dinner 6.30pm - 7pm (later dinner until 8.30pm by arrangement). Snacks available at lunchtime for residents. 🆑 Access, Visa. **Other Points:** Children welcome. Vegetarian meals on request. Afternoon teas. Dogs allowed. Victorian conservatory. Visitors telephone no: (0492) 860681. 🄿 **Directions:** From Promenade, Abbey Rd is off Gloddeath Ave from centre of town.
MR & MRS D DREW ☎ (0492) 878746.
Epperstone is a small detached hotel surrounded by gardens. Over 100 years old, the hotel has elegant, spacious rooms, original fireplaces and a superb mahogany staircase. The hotel caters for guests seeking peace and comfort with good home cooking, a high standard of accommodation and value for money prices.

⬙£ **GRANBY GUEST HOUSE** Deganwy Avenue, Llandudno.
⊨ 2 double, 1 twin and 5 family bedrooms, all en suite. Tea/coffee making facilities and colour TV in all bedrooms. **Hours:** Breakfast 9am - 9.30am, dinner 6pm (order by 4.30pm). Closed: mid October to end of March. 🆑 Access, Visa. **Other Points:** Children welcome. No dogs. Licensed. Residents' lounge. TV. 🄿 **(V) Directions:** Located in the centre of town, 2 blocks from Mostyn St (main shops).
DAVID & JUNE ROBERTS ☎ (0492) 76095.
Situated in a popular avenue just a short distance between both shores, shops, cinemas and entertainments. Family guest house with resident proprietors. Children welcome at reduced rates if sharing room with parents. Vegetarian, diabetic, coeliac diets catered for.

⊗££ **HEADLANDS HOTEL** Hill Terrace, Llandudno.
⬙£££ **Hours:** Breakfast 8.30am - 9.15am, dinner 6.45pm - 8pm (last orders). Bar meals 12 noon - 1.30pm. Closed: January and February. **Cuisine:** A five-course table d'hote menu is offered. Wide choice of dishes, using local produce, both traditional and classical. Vegetarian meals by arrangement. ⊨ 17 bedrooms, 15 en suite. 🆑 All major cards. **Other Points:** Children over 5 years

Llandudno continued

welcome. No smoking in dining room. Dogs allowed at management's discretion. **Directions:** At top of Hill Terrace, on the Great Orme in Llandudno.

MR & MRS WOODS ☎ (0492) 77485.

Situated above the town, but only a short walk to the beach and shops, Headlands Hotel offers superb views across the bay and Conwy estuary to the mountains of Snowdonia. Friendly service and home-cooked food make this a popular choice with tourists.

⌂£☰ **HEATH HOUSE HOTEL** Central Promenade, Llandudno.

🛏 2 single, 3 double, 3 twin & and 14 family bedrooms, most en suite. Radio, teasmaid, baby listening service, telephone, & colour TV in all rooms. 2 bathrooms. 3 WCs. Central heating throughout. **Hours:** Breakfast 8am - 9am, lunch 1pm - 2pm, dinner at 6pm (order by 4pm). Snacks available to 10pm. **CC** None. **Other Points:** No dogs. Licensed bar. Residents lounge with TV. Air-conditioned,no smoking Tudor style dining room. Choice of menu. Fax: (0492) 860307. **Directions:** On the A546, 250 yards west of the Conference Centre.

JOHN & MARY HODGES ☎ (0492) 876538.

A restored seafront Victorian building, part of a listed Promenade in an unspoilt spa town. Facilities for small, residential conferences and private functions. The pine-clad Scandanavian bar has live cabaret in season. Children welcome - no charge for those under 3 years old.

⊗£££ **IMPERIAL HOTEL** Vaughan Street, Llandudno.

Hours: Lunch 12.30pm - 2pm and dinner 6.30pm - 9pm. Bar meals 12 noon - 2pm. **Cuisine:** Daily table d'hote menu and monthly speciality menu. 🛏 100 bedrooms all en suite. **CC** All major cards. **Other Points:** Children welcome. Coaches by appointment. 🅿 ₷ **(V) Directions:** On Promenade.

GEOFFREY LOFTHOUSE ☎ (0492) 877466

A large hotel with many facilities including the Speakeasy Bar - based on 1920's American gangster style, the Ivories piano bar in the basement and a formal dining room.

⌂£☰ **RAVENHURST HOTEL** West Shore, Llandudno.

🛏 6 single, 8 twin, 7 double and 3 family bedrooms, all en suite. 1 bathroom, 2 WCs. Colour TVs in all bedrooms. **Hours:** Breakfast 8.15am - 10am, lunch 12.30pm - 2pm, dinner 6.15pm - 8pm. Bar meals 12 noon - 2pm and 5.45pm - 11pm. Closed: 30th November - 1st February. **CC** Access, Visa, Diners. **Other Points:** Central heating. Children welcome. Licensed. 2 Residents' lounges. Garden. Games room. Vegetarians catered to. 🅿 ₷ **Directions:** On the seafront.

DAVID & KATHLEEN CARRINGTON ☎ (0492) 75525.

The Ravenhurst is situated on the West Shore which runs alongside the Conwy Estuary. The attractive gardens feature a water garden. Wonderful views to Snowdonia and Anglesey.

⊗£££ **RISBORO HOTEL** Clement Avenue, Llandudno.

⌂£££ **Hours:** Breakfast 8am - 9.30am, Lunch 12 noon - 2pm, Dinner

CLUB 6.30pm - 9pm (last orders 8.45pm). **Cuisine:** 4 course table d'hote menu and a la carte menu. Dishes include Fillet of Local Plaice Pan Fried and Welsh Lamb Cutlets. 🛏 67 bedrooms, all en suite.

Llandudno continued

All major cards. **Other Points:** Children welcome. Garden. Afternoon teas. Dogs allowed. Leisure facilities incl. indoor pool, jacuzzi, sauna, exercise gym - free to residents. ▣ **(V) Directions:** Llandudno town centre. A55.

COLIN A. IRVING ☎ (0492) 876343.

A privately owned, family run hotel in the centre of Llandudno, offering a combination of comfortable accommodation and all-weather leisure facilities. Relax on the roof-top sun garden, enjoy the entertainments provided by resident DJ and cabaret, or try the good food in one of the hotel's two restaurants. Four Conference Suites available.

ROSE TOR GUEST HOUSE 124 Mostyn Street, Llandudno. 15 double and 2 family bedrooms all en suite. **Hours:** Breakfast 8am - 9.30am, lunch 12 noon - 2pm, and dinner 5.30pm - 8pm (last orders 7.30pm). Access, Visa, Amex. **Other Points:** Central heating. Licensed. Residents lounge. ▣

MRS B COTTON ☎ (0492) 70433.

Family run guest house with a very relaxed atmosphere. All the bedrooms have been individually styled and have colour TVs.

SANDRINGHAM HOTEL West Parade, West Shore, Llandudno.

Hours: Meals from 8.15am - 9.15am, 12 noon - 2pm and 6.30pm - 8.30pm. Open all year. **Cuisine:** Concentration on fresh wholesome food such as home made pies, lasagne, fish and roasts. 18 bedrooms all en suite. Access, Visa. **Other Points:** Children welcome. No dogs. ▣ ⓒ **Directions:** On seafront of the quiet, sunny West Shore (not the main Promenade).

MR & MRS D KAVANAGH ☎ (0492) 876513/876447

The bar has a definite naval flavour, with the cap bands of naval vessels and seascapes on the walls. Situated in the centre of the West Shore, it is a real suntrap all day long and has unimpeded views of Anglesey and the Conwy estuary. Happy, family atmosphere.

TAN-LAN HOTEL Great Orme's Road, West Shore, [CLUB] Llandudno.

3 single, 8 twin and 7 double bedrooms, all en suite. Colour TV, tea/coffee making facilities in all rooms. **Hours:** Breakfast 8.30am - 9.30am, Lunch 12 noon - 1.30pm, Dinner 6.30pm - 7.30pm. Access, Visa. **Other Points:** Children welcome. Garden. Afternoon teas. Dogs allowed by arrangement. Bar. 2 lounges. Central heating. Restaurant and residential Licence. ▣ ⓒ **Directions:** Great Orme's Rd is parallel to the West Parade, nr Gloddaeth Ave.

ANTONIO & JENNIFER FOSSI ☎ (0492) 860221.

Situated on the West Shore of Llandudno and nestling at the foot of the majestic Great Orme, this hotel offers comfortable en suite accommodation of a high standard. Well cooked meals are served in generous portions in the pleasant dining room. Personal, welcoming service and a peaceful, relaxed atmosphere.

WALES & THE BORDERS

Llandudno continued

⊗££ **THE ORMESCLIFFE HOTEL** The Promenade, Llandudno.

⊞££ **Hours:** Breakfast 8.30am - 9.30am, Lunch 12 noon - 1pm and Dinner 6.30pm - 7.45pm (last orders). Bar meals 12 noon - 1pm. **Cuisine:** Varied international cuisine. ⊨ 60 bedrooms, all en suite. ⊠ Access, Visa. **Other Points:** Children welcome. Dogs allowed. Open Sundays and Bank holidays. ⊡ **(V) Directions:** Turn off A55 at junction and head for Llandudno on A546 onto Prom.

GRAND MARK PLC. Manager - MR J MURPHY ☎ (0492) 76012.

One of Llandudno's long established well-run hotels, situated on the seafront in the Craig Y Don area. Good quality meals served in generous proportions, in a dining room which overlooks Llandudno Bay.

⊞££ **WESTBOURNE PRIVATE HOTEL** 8 Arvon Avenue, Llandudno.

⊨ 3 single, 5 double, 2 twin and 3 family bedrooms all with colour TV and tea/coffee making facilities. 3 en suite rooms, 1 on the ground floor. 2 bathrooms. Ample toilet facilities. **Hours:** Breakfast served at 9am. Dinner at 6pm. Midday meal, sandwiches or packed lunches and evening refreshments available on request. ⊠ None. **Other Points:** Central heating. Open for Christmas. Pensioner reductions.

GEORGE & DORIS MABER-JONES ☎ (0492) 77450.

A very central and pleasantly situated hotel.

⊞£££ **WHITE COURT HOTEL** 2 North Parade, Llandudno.

[CLUB] ⊨ 14 bedrooms, all en suite and with colour TV, radio, alarm, baby listening and tea/coffee making facilities. Honeymoon/Executive suite. Room service. **Hours:** Breakfast 8am - 9am, Dinner at 6.30pm. ⊠ Access, Visa, AmEx. **Other Points:** Children welcome. Totally non-smoking. Residents' lounge. **Directions:** Near to Senataph, adjacent to pier, beach & shopping area.

NATASHA & STEPHEN GARLINGE ☎ (0492) 876719.

An attractive hotel well-situated adjacent to the pier, beach and shopping area. All bedrooms and the charming sitting room offer a very high standard of comfort, allowing guests to relax and enjoy the ambience of the hotel which is completely non-smoking. The dining room is renowned for its good food and comprehensive wine list.

LLANDYBIE Dyfed **Map 6 C2**

⊗£££ **COBBLERS RESTAURANT** 3 Church Street, Llandybie, ⌣ Ammanford.

Hours: Lunch from 12 noon - 1.30pm last orders, dinner 7pm - 9.30pm last orders. Closed: Sunday, Monday and Thursday lunch. **Cuisine:** Welsh regional dishes, wholefoods, eg. popty (salmon baked with tarragon sauce), cig oen mewn crwst (stuffed lamb in herb pastry). ⊨ None. ⊠ Access, Visa. **Other Points:** Children welcome. Coaches by appointment. ⅋ **(V) Directions:** Just off A483. Opposite church. 2 miles north of Ammanford.

HYWEL & MARGARET REES ☎ (0269) 850 540.

Margaret Rees is a trained home economist and winner of the Sunday Times Taste of Britain Award for Wales in 1987 - she passes on her award winning tips at the various cookery courses

Llandybie continued

held seasonally. Private parties and functions for up to 50 people. No second sittings in the restaurant, so booking is recommended. Welsh Lamb Entreprises Welsh Restaurant of the Year 1989-1990.

LLANFAIRPWLL Gwynedd **Map 6 A2**

⊗£££ **CARREG BRAN HOTEL** Church Lane, Llanfairpwll.

CLUB **Hours:** Breakfast 7.30am - 10am, lunch 12 noon - 2pm (last orders), dinner 7pm - 10pm (last orders). **Cuisine:** Dishes include Pain Serra, Champignon farci, Entrecote Diane, Filet du Porc Dijon and a selection of sweets from the sweet trolley. ⊨ 32 rooms. 1 single, 9 twin, 17 double and 5 family rooms. All en suite. CC All major cards. **Other Points:** Children welcome. Garden. Afternoon teas. Dogs allowed. ₽ ⅄ **(V) Directions:** On the old A5, close to Llanfair & Menai Suspension Bridge.

CAPTAIN R H EDWARDS & MRS N EDWARDS ☎ (02487) 714224

An attractive modern hotel set in 5 acres of unspoilt woodland. Decorated to a high standard, the hotel offers good food, well presented and served by experienced friendly staff. Frequented by people of all ages, the atmosphere is relaxed with light background music.

LLANGOLLEN Clwyd **Map 7 A1**

⊗£ **GALES** 18 Bridge Street.

W **Hours:** Restaurant open from 12 noon - 2.00pm and 6pm - 10.15pm. Closed: Sundays. **Cuisine:** Specialises in homemade soups and ice creams and offers a variety of dishes of the day. ⊨ 8 bedrooms, all en suite. CC Visa. **Other Points:** Children welcome. No dogs. Open air patio. Fax: 0978 861313. ₽ **(V)**

RICHARD & GILLIE GALE ☎ (0978) 860089.

An 18th century establishment, opposite the River Dee, in the town famous for the International Eisteddfod. Over 250 wines, on or off sales. Limited edition etchings and screenprints for sale. Overall winner of the Les Routiers/Mercier Wine List of the Year Award 1990.

LLANRWST Gwynedd **Map 7 A1**

⊗££ **PLAS MAENAN HOTEL** Conway Valley, Llanrwst.

⊞£££ **Hours:** Breakfast 8am - 9.30am, lunch 12 noon - 2pm, dinner 7pm - 9pm. Last orders 15 minutes prior to closing time. **Cuisine:** Dishes include smoked mackerel salad, roast lamb llandegla and a selection of sweets. Also serving a vegetarian dish of the day. ⊨ 9 double bedrooms, 4 twin and 2 family rooms. All en suite. All with radio colour TV, hairdryer, direct dial telephone and complimentary drinks tray. CC Access, Visa. **Other Points:** Children welcome. Garden dining. Afternoon teas served. Dogs allowed. Conference suite available. ₽ **(V) Directions:** Exit Llandudno Junction on A470 approx 6 miles towards Betws-y-Coed.

MRS & MRS G TURNER ☎ (0492) 69232

A Country House Hotel surounded by 12 acres of its own grounds overlooking Conwy Valley. Tastefully styled, the establishment offers comfortable accommodation and delicious meals made from fresh local produce. Frequented by all ages the Plas Maenan Hotel enjoys a warm and friendly atmosphere.

WALES & THE BORDERS

LLANTRISSENT Gwent **Map 7 C1**

⊗££ **THE ROYAL OAK** Llantrissent, nr Usk.
Hours: Breakfast 7.30am - 9.30am, dinner 7.30pm - 10pm (last orders 9.45pm). Bar meals 12 noon - 2pm and 7pm - 10pm. Closed: Sunday. **Cuisine:** Paella, beef Wellington. ⨳ 23 bedrooms all with en suite bath or shower. **CC** Access, Visa, AmEx. **Other Points:** Dogs allowed. Children welcome. Coaches by appointment. **P** **(V) Directions:** Near the A449.
MR GASCOINE. ☎ (029 13) 3317.
A 15th century residential inn situated on the A449, only 10 minutes drive from junction 24 on the M4. An attractive white painted building standing in a well kept cottage garden in the valley of the River Usk. In the summer the beer garden and the children's play area are in great demand.

MACHYNLLETH Powys **Map 7 B1**

⊗£ **THE WHITE LION COACHING INN** Heol Pentrerheydn.
⊞££ **Hours:** Restaurant open 12 noon - 2.30pm and 6pm - 9pm (last orders 8.50pm) Bar meals 12 noon - 2.30pm and 6pm - 9pm. **Cuisine:** Traditional Welsh, including Sunday lunch. Bar meals. ⨳ 9 bedrooms. **CC** All major cards. **Other Points:** Children welcome. Dogs allowed. Garden dining. Open Sundays and Bank holidays. **P** ♿ **(V) Directions:** Hotel on major T junction A487 and A489, by the Victorian clock.
M K & J F QUICK ☎ (0654) 3455.
The White Lion has been welcoming guests since the early 1800's. It was one of several coaching inns in town, and retains its original oak beams, inglenook fireplace and cobbled forecourt. Regular patrons appreciate the inn for its Dyffi salmon and traditional and innovative menus - well worth a visit.

⊗£££ **WYNNSTAY HOTEL** Machynlleth.
⊞£££ **Hours:** Breakfast 8am - 9.30am, dinner 7pm - 9.30pm. **Cuisine:** Fixed price 3 course menu, bar meals/snacks and a la carte menu. ⨳ 20 rooms. 5 single, 6 twin, 7 double and 2 family bedrooms. 20 en suite. **CC** All major cards. **Other Points:** Children welcome. Afternoon teas. Dogs allowed. No smoking areas. **P** **(V)**
PHILIP DAVIS ☎ (0654) 702941.
This old white brick hotel stands in the centre of a pretty high street. The atmosphere is relaxing yet lively as the majority of guests are holiday makers. The table d'hote menu is very good and offers an unusually wide choice.

MAENTWROG Gwynedd **Map 6 A2**

⊗£ **GRAPES HOTEL** Maentwrog.
⊞£££ **Hours:** Meals from 8am - 9.30am, 12 noon - 2.15pm and 6pm - 9.30pm. Open all year. **Cuisine:** Homemade dishes, eg. lasagne, pizza, steak pie, curry, chilli. ⨳ 3 double bedrooms and 3 single, all en suite. **CC** Access, Visa. **Other Points:** Access for disabled to bars only. Children welcome. Real ales served. **P** **Directions:** 5 miles from Blaenau Ffestiniog on the main A470 from the North.
BRIAN & GILLIAN TARBOX ☎ (076 685) 208/365.
Old, family owned coaching inn situated in the Vale of Ffestiniog - an area of outstanding beauty in the heart of Snowdonia National Park. Good fishing, walking and pony trekking country. Typical warm pub atmosphere.

MILFORD HAVEN Dyfed **Map 6 C1**

⊗££ **BELHAVEN HOUSE HOTEL** ₽ **LICENSED**
⊞££ **RESTAURANT** 29 Hamilton Terrace, Milford Haven.
CLUB **Hours:** Breakfast 6am - 10.30am, lunch 12 noon - 2pm, dinner 6.30pm - 10pm (last orders 9pm Sunday to Wednesday, Thursday to Saturday 10pm). Light meals from 5pm - 10pm. **Cuisine:** Steaks, pavlovas, vegetarian dishes. Choice of up to 40 main courses. ⊨ 12 bedrooms, 2 en suite. **CC** All major cards. **Other Points:** Children welcome. Afternoon tea served. Coaches by appointment only. ₽ **(V) Directions:** On the front street, overlooking the haven, just past the monument.
MR & MRS HENRICKSEN ☎ (0646) 695983.
A quiet hotel noted for its relaxed atmosphere. 6 of the bedrooms overlook the attractive waterway. The restaurant offers a large selection of meals to cater for most tastes.

⊗££ **THE TABERNA INN** Herbrandston, Milford Haven.
⊞£ **Hours:** Breakfast 8am - 10am, Dinner 7pm - 10pm. Bar meals 12 noon - 2pm and 7pm - 10pm. **Cuisine:** Dishes may include Shark Steaks, Lamb Shrewsbury, Italian Dish of the Day, Grilled Caribbean Gammon Steak. Local fish dishes. Bar meals lunch & evening. ⊨ 4 bedrooms. **CC** Access, Visa. **Other Points:** Children welcome. Dogs allowed. Beer garden. Mastercard and Eurocard accepted. ₽ ♿ **(V) Directions:** Off main Milford Haven to Dale road. Signposted.
NICK SKUDDER, MHCIMA, MISS KAY CROXON. ☎ (0646) 693498.
Situated in the village of Herbrandston, the Taberna Inn offers a good range of bar and restaurant meals. Popular with locals, the Inn enjoys a bustling atmosphere and is well situated for both holidaymakers and commercial visitors to the area.

MOLD Clwyd **Map 7 A1**

⊗£ **THEATR CLWYD** Rakes Lane, Mold.
Hours: Lunch 12 noon - 2.30pm, dinner 5.30pm - 10.30pm (last orders). Closed: Sundays. **Cuisine:** Dishes may include, Tagliatelle Carbonara, Tarragon and Lemon Chicken, Vegetarian Chilli and Trout Cleopatra. Menu changed monthly. ⊨ None. **CC** Access, Visa. **Other Points:** Children welcome. No smoking area. Afternoon teas served. Conference and banqueting facilities. ₽ ♿ **(V) Directions:** Situated on A494, 1/2 mile outside Mold Town. Sign-posted.
MR GORDON CARSON ☎ (0352) 756331.
Combine a meal with a visit to the Theatre at the only theatre-restaurant recommended by Les Routiers. The meals are well-cooked and provide very reasonable value for money, reason enough for visiting Theatr Clwyd at any time, lunch or dinner, whether you wish to enjoy a play or just relax over a meal.

MONMOUTH Gwent **Map 7 C1**

⊗££ **MONMOUTH PUNCH HOUSE** Agincourt Square, Monmouth.
Hours: Meals from 11.30am - 2pm and 6.30pm - 9pm (last orders). Bar meals from 11.30am - 2.30pm and 6.30pm until 9pm. **Cuisine:** Traditional British dishes using finest, fresh local produce. ⊨ None. **CC** Access, Visa. **Other Points:** Children welcome. No dogs. Coaches by appointment. ♿ **(V)**

WALES & THE BORDERS

Monmouth continued
W J L WILLS ☎ (0600) 713855.
Situated in the centre of town and so enjoying both the local and the tourist trade.

⊗£££ **THE CROWN AT WHITEBROOK** Whitebrook, Nr Monmouth.
⌂£££ **Hours:** Breakfast 8am - 9.30am, Lunch 12 noon - 2pm, Dinner
🍴 7pm - 9pm. Closed: Mondays (except Bank Holidays), Christmas
[W] Day, Boxing Day. **Cuisine:** French cuisine. Specialities include
🛏 Guinea Fowl poached in wine and herbs and Fresh Wye Salmon
[CLUB] with cream and brandy sauce. All freshly cooked to order. 🛏 12
bedrooms, all en suite. **CC** All major cards. **Other Points:** Children
welcome. Garden. Dogs allowed. Fax No: (0600) 860607. **P** ᪣
(V) Directions: Off A466, 2 miles from Bigswier Bridge. In the
Whitebrook Valley.
ROGER & SANDRA BATES ☎ (0600) 860254.
A small, intimate restaurant and hotel, remotely situated in beautiful scenery, one mile from the River Wye. The chef specialises in creating original dishes from fresh local ingredients and there is a good wine list. The cheerful hospitality of the proprietors and staff creates a relaxing, friendly atmosphere in which to dine or stay. Regional Newcomer of the Year 1991.

NARBERTH Dyfed **Map 6 C2**
⊗£££ **ROBESTON HOUSE HOTEL & RESTAURANT** Robeston
⌂£££́ Wathen, Nr Narberth.
Hours: Breakfast 8am - 9.30am and dinner 7.30pm - 9.30pm.
Cuisine: Choice of a la carte, table d'hote or buttery meals. Fresh
meat, fish and vegetables brought into kitchen daily. 🛏 2 single, 1
twin, 5 double: all en suite. **CC** All major cards. **Other Points:**
Garden. Afternoon teas. Pets allowed. Non smoking areas
available. Access for disabled to main restaurant only. Fax No:
(0834) 861195. **P** **(V) Directions:** Off the A40 on village
boundary.
PETER, PAULINE & HELEN COPEMAN ☎ ((0834) 860392.
An elegant country house hotel with spacious views, set in six acre grounds high on a hill, giving spectacular views of the countryside. Robeston House provides an atmosphere of comfort and relaxation, where good food and wine and the personal attention of the resident owners combines to make your stay a happy and memorable one.

NEFYN Gwynedd **Map 6 A2**
⊗£ **LION HOTEL** Tudweiliog, Pwllheli.
Hours: Lunch from 12 noon - 2pm and dinner from 6pm -
9.30pm. Closed: Sunday. **Cuisine:** Extensive 3-course bar menu,
outdoor cook-it-yourself barbecues. 🛏 5 bedrooms, 2 en suite.
CC None. **Other Points:** Access for disabled to ground floor.
Children welcome - family room and children's play area. Dogs by
prior arrangement. Beer garden. **P** **(V) Directions:** On the B4417,
4 miles from Nefyn on the road to Aberdaron.
IRIS LEE ☎ (075 887) 244.
The hotel is situated in pleasant surroundings on the B4417, on the North coast of the Lleym peninsula. The staff are friendly and efficient and the food good value for money.

NEW QUAY Dyfed **Map 6 B2**

⊗£ **CAMBRIAN HOTEL** New Road, New Quay.

🏠£ **Hours:** Breakfast 8.30am - 9.30am, Bar snacks 12 noon - 2pm, 6.30pm - 9pm, Dinner 6.30pm - 9.30pm. **Cuisine:** Dishes may include - poached Scotch salmon, home made chicken & mushroom pie, fillet steak, vegetarian lasagne and a selection of sweets. 🛏 6 bedrooms, all en suite. **CC** Access, Visa. **Other Points:** Children welcome. No smoking area. Dogs allowed. Garden dining. 🅿 **(V) Directions:** Turn off A487 at Llanarth, approx 2 miles further on.
MR BRIAN BLANCKENSEE ☎ (0545) 560295.

On the outskirts of the old fishing port of New Quay, this small family run hotel offers comfortable accommodation and well cooked meals. Frequented by holidaymakers it enjoys a relaxed, informal atmosphere. Within easy walking distance of several sandy beaches.

🏠£££ **TY HEN FARM HOTEL & LEISURE CENTRE**
[CLUB] Llwyndafydd, nr New Quay.

🛏 1 single, 4 double, 2 bedsits suitable for wheelchair access, all en suite. Colour TV and tea/coffee making facilities in all rooms. Cottage suites. **Hours:** Breakfast 8.30am - 9.30am, dinner 6.30pm - 9pm. **CC** Access, Visa. **Other Points:** Central heating. Children welcome. Residents lounge. Garden and garden room. Self catering cottages. Licensed. No smoking in Hotel or Leisure Centre. 🅿 **Directions:** Llangranog Rd from Llwyndafydd. 1 mile to No thru Rd on Rt. Signed.
VERONICA KELLY ☎ (0545) 560346.

Situated in beautiful wooded countryside, near the spectacular Cardigan coast, this quiet stock farm offers a choice of self-catering cottages or guest accommodation. Facilities in the area include riding, fishing and water sports. On site Leisure Centre includes large indoor heated pool, fitness room, solarium, indoor bowls etc. Restaurant & bar. Extra facilities planned for 1992.

NEW RADNOR Powys **Map 7 B1**

⊗£ **EAGLE HOTEL** Broad Street, New Radnor, Nr Presteigne.

🏠£££ **Hours:** Breakfast 8.30am - all day (earlier by arrangement), lunch and bar snacks 12 noon - 3pm, dinner and evening bar snacks 12 noon - 10pm. Closed: Monday lunchtimes. **Cuisine:** Wide selection of dishes. Daily specials may include Trout with Mushrooms, cream and Pernod, Chicken Paprika, Cottage Pie, Chilli con Carne. 🛏 8 bedrooms, 1 en suite. **CC** Access, Visa. **Other Points:** Children welcome. Open Bank Holidays. Afternoon teas. Garden dining. Dogs allowed. Patio for summer B.B.Q's. Fax No. (054421) 341. 🅿 **(V) Directions:** 6 miles west of Kington (Herefordshire) on A44 (Aberystwyth) Road.
MRS ANGELA HOY ☎ (054421) 208.

A friendly, village hostelry in wonderful walking country. The building used to house the village gaol, but guests are now free to come and go as they please! The hotel houses two bars with regular live music events, and an attractive bistro-style restaurant and coffee shop offering a wide choice of dishes at very good value for money. Simple but comfortable accommodation.

WALES & THE BORDERS

NEWPORT Gwent **Map 7 C1**

⊗££ **VILLA DINO RESTAURANT** 103 Chepstow Road, Maindee, Newport.
Hours: Dinner served 7pm - 11pm (last orders). Closed: Sunday.
Cuisine: A good choice of Italian dishes. Specialities include Chateaubriand Bouquetiere, Filletto al Stilton. Fish, veal, beef, chicken, pasta & vegetarian. ⌶ None. **CC** All major cards. **Other Points:** Children welcome. Every help given to disabled guests. Cater for wedding receptions, buffet parties etc. **(V) Directions:** On main road from Newport to Chepstow. 5 mins station & motorway.
DINO GULOTTA ☎ (0633) 251267.
This attractive Italian restaurant serves excellent food in a very relaxing and welcoming atmosphere. All dishes are freshly cooked to order and well presented. A small family business in a delightful Victorian setting. The service is outstanding - professional, efficient and very warm and courteous. Highly recommended.

OXWICH West Glamorgan **Map 6 C2**

⊗£
⌂£production **OXWICH BAY HOTEL** Oxwich, Gower.
Hours: Meals served 8am - 10.45pm. Morning coffees. Bar lunches served from midday. Afternoon teas. Evening restaurant open from 7pm. Closed: Christmas Day. **Cuisine:** Homemade sauces, eg. steak chasseur, steak with pepper sauce. ⌶ 14 bedrooms, 3 bathrooms. Closed Christmas. **CC** All major cards. **Other Points:** Children welcome. No dogs. Coaches welcome. No smoking area. ◨ ♿ **Directions:** From the A4118 take Oxwich turn then left at Oxwich crossroads.
MR IAN WILLIAMS ☎ (0792) 390329.
The hotel is situated in its own grounds just 10 yards from Oxwich Beach. Comfortable bedrooms, the majority of which have a sea view, provide an ideal base from which to explore the Gower peninsula.

PEMBROKE Dyfed **Map 6 C2**

⊗£
⌂£ **HIGH NOON GUEST HOUSE** Lower Lamphey Road, Pembroke.
Hours: Breakfast 8am - 9am, lunch 12.30pm - 2pm, and dinner 6.45pm (order by 4pm). Restaurant open to non-residents.
Cuisine: Home-cooking, all freshly prepared. ⌶ 3 single, 2 double, 2 twin, and 2 family rooms (5 rooms en suite). **CC** None.
Other Points: Children welcome. Pets allowed. ◨ **(V) Directions:** Off the one-way system in Pembroke,intersection of A4075 and A4139.
PETER & JEAN BRYANT ☎ (0646) 683736/681232
Long-established guest house, offering comfortable rooms and good food. Pembroke Castle and shops within walking distance, and many more historical buildings and places to visit. Beaches, golf course and tennis courts also nearby.

⊗£££ **THE COURT HOTEL AND RESTAURANT** Lamphey, Nr Pembroke.
Hours: Breakfast 7.15am - 9.30am, Dinner 7pm - 9.45pm (last orders). Bar meals 12 noon - 1.45pm and 7pm - 9.45pm. **Cuisine:** A la carte and table d'hote menus in the restaurant. Local produce used such as Llawhaden trout, Teifi salmon and Freshwater Bay

Pembroke continued

lobster when in season. ⊨ 31 bedrooms, all on suite. ⟨CC⟩ All major cards. **Other Points:** Children welcome. Dogs by arrangement. Leisure Centre - heated indoor swimming pool, sauna, solarium, mini-gym. Fax No: (0646) 672480. ⟨P⟩ **(V) Directions:** M4 to Carmarthen, A477 for Pembroke, turn Lt at Milton, follow signs ANTHONY LAIN ☎ (0646) 672273.

A warm Welsh welcome awaits you at this delightful mansion house, peacefully situated in its own grounds yet just a mile from the coast. The candlelit Georgian room restaurant offers excellent meals and bar snacks are served in the bar which opens on to a sheltered terrace. Outstanding food and hospitality, and enjoyment of the hotel's Leisure Centre facilities.

PONTFAEN Dyfed **Map 6 C2**

⊗££ **GELLI FAWR COUNTRY HOUSE** Pontfaen, Newport,
⬠££ Fishguard.

Hours: Breakfast 8.30am - 11am , dinner 7.30pm - 9.30pm (last orders). Bar meals served from 12.30 - 2pm. **Cuisine:** Game pie, salmon en feuillette with fennel, caraway seed and cream sauce, Welsh lamb with apricots. Homemade bread. Tipsy bread and butter pudding. ⊨ 10 bedrooms, 5 en suite. ⟨CC⟩ Access, Visa. **Other Points:** Dining al fresco. Children welcome. Dogs allowed. Afternoon tea. Cookery school - day and residential classes. Heated swimming pool. ⟨P⟩ & **(V) Directions:** Between B4329 & B4313, 5 miles from Newport Bay.

FRANCES ROUGHLEY & ANN CHURCHER ☎ (0239) 820343.

An historic Welsh hill farm house, Gelli Fawr is now a comfortable, family-run hotel. Gelli Fawr is in the middle of the countryside and worth making a journey for its idyllic setting and excellent cuisine. A friendly yet relaxing hotel for all those who enjoy the peace of the country and good food.

PORTHMADOG Gwynedd **Map 6 A2**

⊗££ **BLOSSOMS RESTAURANT** Ivy Terrace, Borth y Gest, Porthmadog.

Hours: Lunch from 12 noon - 2pm, dinner 7pm - 10.30pm (last orders). Open for coffee all day. Open Wednesday to Saturday in winter. Closed: Summer Sundays. **Cuisine:** Mediterranean cuisine, vegetarian dishes. ⊨ None. ⟨CC⟩ Access, Visa. **Other Points:** Children welcome. No dogs. No smoking area. **(V) Directions:** Half a mile from A497 in the centre of Borth y Gest. PAUL DENHAM & MEG BROOK ☎ (0766) 513500

Overlooking the bay at Borth y Gest with Snowdonia in the distance. Blossoms Restaurant is part of the 'Heartbeat Wales' programme to promote healthy eating, and also has pictures on the walls by local artists which are for sale. Log fires and classical, jazz or blues music set the atmosphere. It is a small restaurant so booking is advisable.

⬠££ **TAN YR ONNEN HOTEL** Penamser Road, Porthmadog.

⊨ 4 single, 2 double, 2 twin, 1 family room, 3 en suite. Colour TV and tea/ coffee making facilities in all rooms. **Hours:** Breakfast 8am - 9am. ⟨CC⟩ None. **Other Points:** Central heating. Children welcome. ⟨P⟩ **Directions:** At junction A497 with A487, 100 metres from Porthmadog roundabout.

WALES & THE BORDERS

Porthmadog continued
TONY & BETTY DADY ☎ (0766) 512443.
Tan yr Onnen (meaning under the ash tree) is an attractive 150 year old house standing in its own grounds, a short walk from the town centre. An ideal base for exploring Snowdonia. For the rail enthusiast, Porthmadog is the terminus for the Ffestiniog and Welsh Highland narrow gauge railways.

PRESTATYN Clwyd **Map 7 A1**
⊗£ **BRYN GWALIA INN** 17 Gronant Road, Prestatyn.
⏛££ **Hours:** Breakfast 8am - 9am, lunch 12 noon - 2pm and dinner 7pm - 9pm (last orders). Closed: 25th and 26th December. **Cuisine:** Homemade soup, pate, pies, quiche and desserts. ⊨ 8 bedrooms, 5 en suite. **CC** Access. **Other Points:** Children welcome. **P** & **(V) Directions:** On A548 from Flint, left at 'Drivers' Garage, then half a mile.
SOPHIA DREW ☎ (07456) 2442.
A black and white Georgian timbered building situated in a residential area close to the shops in Prestatyn High Street. The end of the Offa's Dyke footpath is only 100 yards away and the wealth of the Welsh countryside on the doorstep.

PWLLHELI Gwynedd **Map 6 A2**
⊗££ **DIVE INN SEAFOOD RESTAURANT** Tudweilog, Nr Pwllheli.
Hours: Lunch 12 noon - 2pm, dinner 7pm - 9pm (last orders). **Cuisine:** Specialising in seafood dishes the menu may feature Greenlip Mussels, Lobster and Kiwi Fruit Trifle. ⊨ **CC** Access, Visa. **Other Points:** Children Welcome. Vegetarian meals by arrangement. **P**
MR & MRS ENTWISTLE ☎ (0758) 87246
A stone built establishment in 8 acres of land and frequented by both holiday makers and locals. Using fresh local produce, the restaurant serves tasty home cooked meals and enjoys a relaxed atmosphere.

RHAYADER Powys **Map 7 B1**
⊗££ **ELAN HOTEL** West Street, Rhayader.
⏛££ **Hours:** Breakfast 8am - 9.30am, lunch 12 noon - 2pm (last orders), dinner 7pm - 8.30pm (Sunday 7.30pm). Closed Monday. **Cuisine:** A la carte menu, table d'hote, bar meals/snacks and vegetarian meals. ⊨ 12 rooms. 4 single, 3 twin and 5 double bedrooms. 7 en suite. **CC** Access, Visa. **Other Points:** Children welcome. Garden. Afternoon teas. Dogs allowed. **P** & **(V) Directions:** Off A470. Situated in the main street.
DAVID & JOAN JAMES ☎ (0597) 810373.
A quiet 18th century hotel, set in its own well kept gardens, offering tastefully decorated and furnished accommodation and restaurant. The well presented quality meals served in the restaurant and outstanding tableside views of the Elan Valley, compete for your attention. Friendly, attentive service. Highly recommended.

RUTHIN Clwyd **Map 7 A1**
⊗££ **RUTHIN CASTLE** Corwen Road, Ruthin.
Hours: Breakfast 8am - 9.30am, lunch 12.30pm - 2pm (Sundays only) and dinner 7pm - 9.30pm (last orders). Bar meals 12 noon - 2pm. **Cuisine:** Roasts, grills. Escalope of veal a la Suisse,

Ruthin continued

Tournedos Zurich - a speciality. ⌖ 58 bedrooms, all en suite. ☒ All major cards. **Other Points:** Children welcome. No dogs. ☒ **(V) Directions:** On the road running south of the town square. TONY WARBURTON ☎ (08242) 2664.

An 18th century castle standing in 38 acres of gardens. The ruins of a 13th century castle including the dungeons and battlements remain in the grounds. 2 princes have stayed at the castle in the aptly named Prince of Wales Suite. 20 miles from Chester in the beautiful Vale of Clwyd.

⊗£ **SIOP NAIN (GRANNY'S SHOP)** 6 Well Street, Ruthin.
Hours: Open 9.30am - 5pm. **Closed:** Sunday and Bank Holidays. **Cuisine:** Homemade steak pies and homemade cakes. ⌖ None. ☒ Access, Visa. **Other Points:** Children welcome. Licensed. Parking on Town Square. ♿ **Directions:** On the town square in the centre, by the old courthouse.
MR & MRS C DAVIES ☎ (082 42) 3572.

Small family cafe/restaurant built in 1490. Oak beams in the dining area and an olde worlde atmosphere throughout. Situated just off the town centre square, Siop Nain offers hot meals all day and specialises in home cooking.

SAUNDERSFOOT Dyfed **Map 6 C2**

⊗£ **RHODEWOOD HOUSE HOTEL** St Brides Hill, Saundersfoot.
⌂££ **Hours:** Breakfast 8.30am - 9.30am, lunch 12 noon - 2pm and dinner 6.30pm - 10.30pm (last orders 9.30pm). Bar meals 12 noon - 2pm and 6pm - 9.30pm. **Cuisine:** Excellent selection of locally caught fish dishes. Varied a la carte and table d'hote menus. ⌖ 34 bedrooms, all en suite. ☒ All major cards. **Other Points:** Children welcome. Pets allowed. No smoking area. ☒ ♿ **(V) Directions:** Off the B4136 to Tenby, few minutes from the harbour.
A.T. DOWLER ☎ (0834) 812200

Set 1.5 acres, minutes away from beautiful woodlands and Glen Beach with views of Carmarthen Bay. A varied menu and comprehensive wine list provided by friendly and attentive staff makes this a definite stop for visitors

⊗£ **ST BRIDES HOTEL** Saundersfoot.
Hours: Breakfast 8am - 10am, lunch 12 noon - 2pm and dinner 7.30pm - 9.15pm (last orders). Open 12 noon - 11pm. **Cuisine:** Specialising in locally caught fish, lobster and crab. Flambe dishes. ⌖ 45 bedrooms, all en suite. ☒ All major cards. **Other Points:** Children welcome. Coaches by appointment. ☒ ♿ **(V) Directions:** From the A40, A477 or A476, follow signposts to Saundersfoot.
IAN BELL ☎ (0834) 812 304.

Excellent location overlooking Carmarthen Bay. A very high standard is maintained in all aspects of the hotel particularly with regard to the food and service.

SHIRENEWTON Gwent **Map 7 C1**

⊗£ **THE HUNTSMAN HOTEL** Shirenewton, Chepstow, Gwent.
⌂££ **Hours:** Breakfast 7.30am - 10.30am, Lunch 12 noon - 2pm and CLUB Dinner 7pm - 10pm. **Cuisine:** Chicken in prawn and lobster sauce in the restaurant. Breaded plaice, chicken chasseur and lasagne in the bar. ⌖ 10 bedrooms, all en suite. ☒ Access, Visa, AmEx.

Shirenewton continued

Other Points: Children's play area. Dogs allowed. Catering for weddings and private functions available. ◘ **(V) Directions:** Approximately 4 miles out on the B4235 Chepstow to Usk road. MR A C MOLES ☎ (02917) 521.

A small country hotel serving well-presented food in generous portions, with polite unintrusive service. 3 miles to Chepstow racecourse and golfing facilities.

ST ASAPH Clwyd **Map 7 A1**

⊗££ **ORIEL HOUSE HOTEL** Upper Denbigh Road, St Asaph.
⟐££££**Hours:** Breakfast 7.15am - 9.30am, lunch 11.30am - 2pm (last orders) dinner 7pm - 9.30pm (last orders), bar snacks 11am - 2.30pm (last orders) and 6.15pm - 10pm (last orders). Closed: Boxing Day. **Cuisine:** Serving full a la carte menu, table d'hote and bar snacks. ⊨ 19 bedrooms, all en suite. **CC** All major cards. **Other Points:** Children welcome. Afternoon teas. Dogs allowed. Garden. fax/telephone No. (0745) 582716. Caters for conferences. ◘ ᘒ **(V) Directions:** A55 turn off for Denbigh, left at cathedral, 1 mile on right.

MR & MRS WIGGIN AND MR & MRS WOOD. ☎ (0745) 582716.
Set in own extensive grounds, this is a family owned and run hotel. In quiet, relaxed surroundings you can enjoy well prepared and presented meals. Comfortable accommodation and attractive decor. Good venue for wedding receptions and conferences.

ST DAVIDS Dyfed **Map 6 C1**

⊗££ **HARBOUR HOUSE HOTEL & RESTAURANT** The
⟐££ Harbour, Solva, nr St Davids.
Hours: Breakfast 8.30am - 10am, lunch 12 noon - 2.30pm (Sunday lunch 2pm). Dinner served until 9pm. Closed: Sunday evenings. **Cuisine:** Dishes include trout pan-fried with capers & prawns & lemon, roast breast of duck with a blackberry and orange sauce. ⊨ 1 single, 2 twin and 2 double bedrooms. 3 en suite. **CC** Access, Visa. **Other Points:** Children welcome. Afternoon teas. Dogs allowed. ◘ ᘒ **(V) Directions:** A487, 3 miles east of St Davids.

PAUL HEMMING ☎ (0437) 721267.
Nestled in the heart of the Pembrokeshire Coast National Park, yet standing at the head of a fiord. Decorated in soothing colours and comfortably furnished. Serving tastefully presented excellent meals in a quiet atmosphere.

⊗££ **OCEAN HAZE HOTEL & RESTAURANT** Haverfordwest
⟐££ Road, St Davids.
Hours: Breakfast available till 10am. Summer: lunch 11.30am - 2.30pm and 6pm - 10pm (last orders). Winter: 12 noon - 2pm and 7pm - 9pm (last orders). Bar meals available. **Cuisine:** 'Ocean Haze Special'(mixed grill). ⊨ 9 bedrooms, 6 en suite. **CC** Access, Visa. **Other Points:** Children welcome. Pets allowed. Afternoon tea by request. ◘ ᘒ **(V) Directions:** Off the A487, just outside St Davids.

B & C MORRIS ☎ (0437) 720826.
A small family run hotel on the outskirts of St Davids, next to the Marine Life Centre and within walking distance of Bishops

St Davids continued
Palace. Pleasant surroundings, attentive staff and good food, can be found here.

RAMSEY HOUSE Lower Moor, St Davids, Haverfordwest. `CLUB` ⌖ 3 twin and 4 double bedrooms, 4 en suite. **Hours:** Breakfast 8am - 8.30am and dinner 7pm (4 courses with emphasis on traditional Welsh fare). **CC** None. **Other Points:** Garden. Residents' lounge and cocktail bar. Pets allowed. Traditional Welsh fare. Vegetarians and other special diets catered for. **P (V) Directions:** Off the A487, take road from Cross Square signposted to Porthclais.
MAC & SANDRA THOMPSON ☎ (0437) 720321.
Ramsey House offers you a unique combination of professional hotel standards of accommodation and food service, coupled with the friendly relaxing atmosphere of a pleasant country guest house. Situated just 1/2 mile from St Davids, with its 12th century Cathedral, this guest house enjoys a quiet location on the road to Porthclais and is an ideal base for touring the area.

Y GLENNYDD GUEST HOUSE 51 Nun Street, St David's. ⌖ 1 single, 4 double, 2 twin and 3 family bedrooms, 3 en suite. All rooms have colour TV and tea/coffee making facilities. **Hours:** Breakfast 8am - 10am and dinner 7pm - 8.30pm. Closed: January and February. **CC** Access, Visa, Dinners. **Other Points:** Children welcome. Licensed. Residents' lounge. Packed lunches available. No dogs. Street parking and public car park close by. **Directions:** A487. Nun Street is part of the one way system from Cross Square.
TIMOTHY & TRACEY FOSTER. ☎ (0437) 720576.
A cosy guest house in the charming village city of St Davids. Y Glennydd aims to make each guest's stay relaxed and comfortable. A full English breakfast dinner, picnic baskets etc available. Guests will also enjoy exploring this attractive area.

SWANSEA West Glamorgan **Map 6 C2**
LANGROVE LODGE AND COUNTRY CLUB Parkmill, Gower, Swansea.
Hours: Breakfast 7.30am - 9.30am, dinner 7pm - 9pm (last orders 8.50pm), bar snacks 12 noon - 2pm (last orders). **Cuisine:** Dishes may include - Romany soup, roast beef with American Creole sauce, and a selection of sweets. ⌖ 28 bedrooms, all en suite. **CC** Access, Visa, Diners. **Other Points:** Children welcome. No smoking area. Afternoon teas. Garden dining. **P (V)**
BRIAN STEWART ☎ (044128) 2410/2756.
Situated in 24 acres of grounds, 12 of which have been declared a nature reserve. Serving good food and providing comfortable accommodation, this establishment is ideal for anyone wanting to get away from the hustle and bustle of everyday life.

MOGHUL BRASSERIE 81 St Helens Road, Swansea. **Hours:** Lunch from 12 noon - 2.30pm, dinner 5.30pm - 12 midnight. **Cuisine:** Tandoori and Indian dishes. ⌖ None. **CC** All major cards. **Other Points:** Children welcome. No dogs. Coaches by appointment. LVs. **(V)**
MR QUTUB UDDIN ☎ (0792) 48509.

WALES & THE BORDERS

Swansea continued

A fully air conditioned restaurant specialising in tandoori dishes. Full outside catering service and takeaway. Cocktail bar has varied selection of wines and spirits.

⊗£ **PEN-YR-AUT HOTEL** Alltwen, Pontardawe, Swansea.
⌂£££ **Hours:** Breakfast 7.30am - 9.30am, lunch 12 noon - 2.30pm,
CLUB dinner 7pm - 11pm, bar snacks 12 noon - 3pm, 7pm - 10pm. Open bank holidays. **Cuisine:** Specialising in locally reared beef steaks. ⊨ 7 bedrooms, all en suite. **CC** Access, Visa. **Other Points:** Children welcome. Dogs allowed. Garden dining. **P** &. **(V) Directions:** M4, jct 45 to Pontardawe. At Pontardawe follow signs to Alltwen.
MR DAVID HORN ☎ (0792) 863320.
Located in a quiet village in the Swansea Valley, this hotel has recently been refurbished and offers comfortable accommodation. Frequented by all ages, the hotel has a homely atmosphere, in which you can enjoy well cooked and pleasantly presented meals.

⊗£ **THE SCHOONER** 4 Prospect Place, Swansea.
Hours: Meals from 12 noon - 2pm and 7pm - 9.30pm (last orders). Bar meals 12 noon - 2pm and 6pm - 7.30pm. Closed: Sunday evening. **Cuisine:** Fresh local produce all home cooked. Traditional Sunday lunches (booking advisable). Evening special menu changes monthly. Carvery meals most evenings. ⊨ None. **CC** None. **Other Points:** Coaches by appointment. No smoking area. Vegetarian meals by request. &. **Directions:** In the east of Swansea, close to Sainsburys.
RAYMOND & CHRISTINE PARKMAN ☎ (0792) 649321.
Grade II listed building with wine bar, restaurant and function room. Situated in central Swansea on the fringe of the new Marina development and leisure centre.

⊗£ **WOODSIDE GUEST HOUSE** Oxwich, Gower, Swansea.
⌂£ **Hours:** Breakfast 8.30am - 9.30pm, lunch 12 noon - 2.30pm, dinner 7.00pm - 7.30pm. **Cuisine:** Welsh speciality meals, childrens menu. ⊨ 7 bedrooms, 3 ensuite. **CC** None. **Other Points:** Children welcome. Afternoon tea served. Licensed bar. No pets. **P** &. **(V) Directions:** From Swansea take A4118 or B4436. Oxwich is 2 miles from Penmaen.
DIANE & DAVID WORKMAN ☎ (0792) 390791.

Swansea continued

*A converted 200 year old cottage situated in a nature
conservation area. Plenty of good walking and bird watching
and the nearby beach offers wind- surfing and sailing. A warm
family welcome and good value meals are guaranteed at
Woodside.*

TAL Y BONT Gwynedd Map 7 A1
⊗££ **THE LODGE** Tal-Y-Bont.
Hours: Breakfast 8.15am - 9.30am, lunch 12 noon - 2pm, dinner
7pm - 9.30pm (last orders). **Cuisine:** Table d'hote and a la carte
menus. Fresh fish and steaks. ⊨ 10 bedrooms, all en suite.
CC Access, Visa. **Other Points:** Children welcome. Dogs by
arrangement. **P** & **Directions:** On B5106, 5 miles from Conwy.
MR & MRS BALDON ☎ (049269) 766/534.
*A pleasant hotel and restaurant nestling in the Conwy valley.
The restaurant provides a relaxed and informal setting in which
to enjoy well prepared traditional cuisine. Fresh, local produce
is used whenever possible.*

TALSARNAU Gwynedd Map 6 A2
□□£ **GWRACH YNYS COUNTRY GUEST HOUSE** Ynys,
Talsarnau, Nr Harlech.
⊨ 1 single, 1 double, 2 twin and 3 family bedrooms, 6 with en
suite facilities. **Hours:** Breakfast 8am - 9am, Dinner 6pm. **CC** None.
Other Points: Children welcome. Garden. Dogs allowed. **P** **(V)**
Directions: A496. 2 miles north of Harlech.
DEBORAH WILLIAMS ☎ (0766) 780742.
*A detached Edwardian country house which stands in its own
grounds amidst open countryside. The house has recently been
refitted to ensure standards expected by today's discerning
guests, whilst retaining the charm and homely atmosphere of a
small country house. Wholesome home cooked meals using
produce from local farms.*

TALYCAFN Gwynedd Map 7 A1
⊗£ **TALYCAFN HOTEL** Llanrwst Road, Talycafn.
□□£ **Hours:** Meals from 8.30am - 10am, 12 noon - 2.30pm and 7pm -
10.30pm. **Cuisine:** Starters, vegetarian dishes, sirloin steak,
gammon, fish dishes, and pizzas baked on the premises. Desserts
include fresh fruit nest. ⊨ 5 bedrooms, 2 bathrooms. **CC** None.
Other Points: Children welcome. No dogs. Coaches by
arrangement. **P** **(V) Directions:** Junction of A470 and B5106.
MR A G E BEARD, MBII, MCFA ☎ (049265) 0203.
*An old coaching inn of great charm and character situated
about 100 yards from the River Conwy. The intimate atmosphere
in the beamed bar is enjoyed by both visitors to Snowdonia and
the locals.*

TENBY Dyfed Map 6 C2
⊗££ **FOURCROFT HOTEL** Tenby.
□□££££ **Hours:** Open 8am - 12 midnight. Closed: November to Easter.
Cuisine: Pembrokeshire turkey, honeyed Welsh lamb, local
salmon, trout and plaice, interesting bar lunches. ⊨ 38 bedrooms
en suite, all with colour TV, radio, tea/coffee facilities, telephones.
CC Access, Visa. **Other Points:** Swimming pool. Leisure amenities.
Private garden with path to beach. Limited parking. Fax No:

WALES & THE BORDERS

Tenby continued

(0834) 2888. **(V) Directions:** Fork left after Welcome to Tenby sign, double back along seafront.

MR & MRS P L OSBORNE ☎ (0834) 2886.

Over 180 years old, the Fourcroft is situated in the most peaceful and select part of the town. It is a seafront hotel set above Tenby's North Beach with magnificent views of Carmarthen Bay and Tenby Harbour.

⌂£££ **HILDEBRAND HOTEL** Victoria Street, Tenby.

CLUB ⌸ 1 single, 3 double, 4 twin and 2 family bedrooms, (8 en suite). 1 bathroom. Colour TV, radio and tea/coffee making facilities in all rooms. **Hours:** Breakfast 8.45am - 9am, dinner 7pm (order by 5pm). Closed: December. **CC** All major cards. **Other Points:** Central heating. Children welcome. No dogs. Licensed. **P** **Directions:** From St Clears off A40 onto A477, follow South Beach signs in Tenby.

VERONICA & JIM MARTIN ☎ (0834) 842403.

The Hildebrand, conveniently situated near the beautiful South Beach, ensures a high standard of decor in your room, with colour TV, radio/intercom, complimentary beverage tray; most have private bathroom. Cellar bar and spacious lounge. Complemented by good, well prepared food served by experienced hosts, Veronica and Jim Martin. W.T.B 3 Crowns and merit graded.

⊗££ **THE IMPERIAL HOTEL** The Paragon, Tenby.

⌂£££££ **Hours:** 8am - 9.30am, 11.30am - 2.30pm and 7pm - 9pm (last orders). Bar meals 11.30am - 2.30pm and 6pm - 9pm (last orders). **Cuisine:** Traditional English cuisine, with a la carte, table d'hote and bar meals. ⌸ 45 bedrooms, all en suite. **CC** Access, Visa, AmEx. **Other Points:** Children welcome. Dogs allowed. Open Sundays and Bank holidays. Dining on cliff-top patios. Caters for private functions. Fax No: (0834) 4342. **P** 㫲 **(V) Directions:** M4, A40, A477 to Kilgetti - A478.

JAN-ROELOF EGGENS ☎ (0834) 3737.

Clifftop location overlooking the South Beach towards St Catherine's and Caldy Islands. Private steps to the beach. The Imperial offers extensive menus and a good wine list, served by courteous staff in very pleasant surroundings.

TINTERN Gwent **Map 7 C1**

⊗£ **THE FOUNTAIN INN** Trellech Grange, Tintern, nr Chepstow.

⌂£ **Hours:** Lunch 12 noon - 3pm, dinner 7pm - 10.30pm Monday to Saturday. Sunday lunch 12 noon - 2pm, Dinner 7pm - 9.30pm. Closed: Christmas evening. **Cuisine:** Dishes include Jugged hare, Tudor roast, Venison, Rack of Lamb. ⌸ 5 bedrooms. **CC** Access, Visa. **Other Points:** Children welcome. Caravan Club listed. **P** **(V) Directions:** Off B4283, 2 miles from Tintern Abbey on road to Raglan and Usk.

CHRIS & JUDITH RABBITS ☎ (0291) 689303.

A typical 17th century country Inn where the food is prepared to order. The bar provides the focal point and, on a chilly day, a log fire provides a warm welcome.

USK

TREARDDUR BAY Gwynedd **Map 6 A2**

⊗££ **THE BEACH HOTEL** Trearddur Bay, Anglesey

⏠££ **Hours:** Breakfast 7am - 9.30am, Dinner 7pm - 9pm (last orders). Bar meals 12 noon - 2pm and 7pm - 10pm. **Cuisine:** International cuisine with flambed steaks and lobster, a speciality. Fresh, local produce. ⬛ 26 bedrooms, all en suite. **CC** All major cards. **Other Points:** Children welcome. Dogs allowed. Residents' lounge. Night club. Snooker club. Conference centre. Leisure centre. Fax No: (0407) 861140. ⬛ **(V) Directions:** From mainland, A5 to Valley, left at crossroads, 2 miles on right.
PAT BLUNT ☎ (0407) 860332.
A popular and attractive hotel, ideal for conferences and as a holiday base. The restaurant is charmingly furnished and offers a high standard of food and service. Fresh, local produce is used. The Beach Hotel also provides comfortable accommodation with all major facilities, a spacious lounge for relaxing in comfort, a nightclub, bar, and sporting facilities.

TRELLECH Gwent **Map 7 C1**

⊗£ **THE LION INN** Trellech, Nr Monmouth.

⏠£ **Hours:** Lunch 12 noon - 2pm and Dinner 7pm - 11pm (last orders 9.30pm). Bar meals 12 noon - 2pm, 7pm - 11pm. **Cuisine:** Good quality home cooked meals made with local farm fresh produce. ⬛ 1 double en suite, 1 twin with vanity unit bathroom next door. **CC** None. **Other Points:** Children welcome. Pets allowed. ⬛ **(V) Directions:** B4293 Monmouth to Chepstow road, opposite church in the village.
ALAN & CHRISTINE NIXON ☎ (0600) 860322
A 17th century Inn with original beams serving home cooked meals using fresh produce - most comes from the local farm. Situated in the ancient settlement of Trellech, known for its standing stones, Norman motte and 'virtuos' well. The Lion Inn is a friendly local set in beautiful surrounding countryside.

TRESAITH Dyfed **Map 6 B2**

⊗££ **SKIPPERS** Tresaith Beach, Nr Cardigan.

⏠££ **Hours:** Breakfast 7am - 12 noon (residents only), lunch 12 noon - 3pm (last orders), dinner 6pm - 11.30pm (last orders 9pm), bar snacks 12 noon - 3pm (last orders) and 6pm - 9pm (last orders). Closed: 1st October - Easter. **Cuisine:** Extensive menu which may feature - Oysters, Fresh local Crab and Lobster, Chiken Tikka Masala, Lamb in Redcurrant Sauce. ⬛ 3 suites, all en suite. **CC** Access, Visa, AmEx. **Other Points:** Children welcome. Afternoon teas served. Garden dining. ⬛ **(V) Directions:** B4333 to Aberporth, then unclassified road to Tresaith.
IAN & JANET DARROCH ☎ (0239) 810113.
Overlooking the unspoilt bay of Tresaith, this restaurant offers meals of 'outstanding quality' in a quiet, relaxed atmosphere. Efficient and friendly staff ensure an enjoyable meal. There is a definite nautical theme in the restaurant which also has a log fire. Comfortable accommodation. Highly recommended.

USK Gwent **Map 7 C1**

⊗££ **THREE SALMONS HOTEL** Bridge Street, Usk.

Hours: Restaurant open 7am - 9.30am, 12 noon - 2pm and 7pm - 9.30pm. **Cuisine:** Fresh local produce used wherever possible - salmon and Welsh lamb, locally grown vegetables. Homemade

Usk continued

soups and desserts. ⊨ 30 bedrooms, 29 en suite. ⧯ Access, Visa, AmEx. **Other Points:** Children welcome. ▣ ⅋ **(V) Directions:** Usk is the first turning off the A40 between Newport and Monmouth. MR H P LEWIS ☎ (02913) 2133.

18th century coaching inn, pleasantly situated in a riverside town. Real ales are served in the comfortable bar lounge along with interesting bar meals. A la carte served in the cosy restaurant. Private functions catered for in the Llangibby Room.

WELSHPOOL Powys **Map 7 B1**

⊗££ **ROYAL OAK HOTEL** The Cross, Welshpool, Powys.

⏚££££ **Hours:** Breakfast 7.30am - 9am, lunch 12.30pm - 2.15pm, dinner
CLUB 7pm - 9pm. **Cuisine:** A la carte, fixed 3 course menu. Dishes include grilled trout and noodle a la pana. ⊨ 24 rooms. 7 single, 7 double, 2 family, 8 twin, all en suite. ⧯ All major cards. **Other Points:** Children welcome. Afternoon teas. Dogs allowed. Sporting Activity Package (Golf, fishing, clay pigeon shooting). Fax/telephone No: (0938) 552217. ▣ **(V) Directions:** Near the tourist information office.

MRS PRICE ☎ (0938) 552217.

The Royal Oak dates back to mid 17th century and has been privately owned by the same family since 1927. Great care has been taken to retain the character and atmosphere of the old building with the modern facilities of the 20th century. The comfortable accommodation, good food and friendly attentive service makes this hotel well worth a visit.

⊗££ **THE LION HOTEL AND RESTAURANT** Berriew, Nr
⏚££££ Welshpool.

Hours: Breakfast 8am - 9.30am, lunch 12 noon - 2pm, dinner 7.30pm - 9pm, bar snacks 12 noon - 2pm - 7pm - 9.15pm. Open Bank Holidays. **Cuisine:** English, Welsh & continental cuisine. Dishes may include prawn and salmon cocktail, roast duck with vermouth and cranberry sauce. ⊨ 7 bedrooms, all en suite. ⧯ Access, Visa. **Other Points:** Children welcome. ▣ **(V) Directions:** In village centre.

MR & MRS THOMAS ☎ (0686) 640452/640844

Situated in a quiet village on the Welsh borders surrounded by beautiful countryside, the Lion Hotel is a delightful 17th century Inn. The accommodation is of a high standard and good food is served in both the bars and restaurant.

WREXHAM Clwyd **Map 7 A1**

⊗££ **CROSS LANES HOTEL AND RESTAURANT** A525
⏚££££ Whitchurch/Wrexham Rd, Marchwiel, nr.Wrexham.

W **Hours:** Breakfast 7.30am - 9am, lunch 12.15pm - 2pm and dinner
CLUB 7.30pm - 10pm (last orders 9.30pm). Bar meals 12 noon - 2pm and 6.30pm - 10pm. **Cuisine:** Table d'hote and a la carte menus including traditional English and continental dishes - using fresh local produce wherever possible. ⊨ 18 bedrooms, all en suite. ⧯ All major cards. **Other Points:** Children welcome. Pets allowed (except in public rooms). Fax No: (0978) 780568. ▣ ⅋ **(V) Directions:** On A525 Whitchurch/ Wrexham Road, between Marchwiel & Bangor-On-Dee.

MICHAEL KAGAN ☎ (0978) 780555.

Wrexham continued

Originally a large Victorian private house, now tastefully extended and converted to a private hotel without losing its character. Cross Lanes stands in acres of beautiful grounds with lawns, shrubs, an orchard and paddock. An ideal location for visiting Erddig Hall, Chirk Castle, Chester, Llangollen, Snowdonia and the North Wales Coast.

⊗£ **MILL FARM HOUSE** Bersham, Wrexham.

Hours: Open 10am - 5pm for coffee, light lunches and afternoon teas. Lunch 12 noon - 2pm (last orders). Closed: Fridays and January and February. **Cuisine:** Traditional home cooking of a high quality. Dishes may include Seafood Bake, Cottage Pie, Meat Loaf, Pizza, Quiche, Ploughmans. ⊨ None. 🆑 Access, Visa. **Other Points:** Children welcome. Afternoon teas. No-smoking area. Garden dining. 🅿 ᵫ **(V) Directions:** B5099 2 and a half miles from Wrexham - Minera. 500 yds past bridge.
PAULINE FITZHUGH ☎ (0978) 291982.

Situated in the tranquil village of Bersham alongside the River Clywedog, Mill Farm House offers excellent home cooking at very reasonable prices. Within a peaceful and relaxed atmosphere, coffee, lunch and afternoon tea are served by cheerful and welcoming staff. The home cooking is of the highest standard. Good facilities for disabled customers.

⊗££ **TREVOR ARMS HOTEL** Marford, Nr Wrexham.
⊡££ **Hours:** Breakfast 7.30am - 9pm (later at weekends), Lunch 12 noon - 2.30pm, Dinner 6pm - 10pm (7pm - 10pm Sundays). **Cuisine:** Extensive menu available in the Restaurant and Bar Areas. Dishes may include King Scampi, Sirloin Steak, Salmon with lemon & tarragon. Daily specials ⊨ 15 bedrooms, all en suite. 🆑 Access, Visa. **Other Points:** Childrens play area. No smoking area. Afternoon teas. Dogs allowed. Beer garden. Traditional Sunday roasts. 🅿 ᵫ **(V) Directions:** Midway between Chester and Wrexham. A short distance off A483.
MARTIN & DENISE BENNETT ☎ (0244) 570436.

An old Coaching Inn which maintains traditional pub hospitality together with a wide range of modern facilities and tempting menus at affordable prices. Excellent staff team work ensures a relaxed, no fuss atmosphere in which to enjoy your meal. Comfortable accommodation, a safe childrens play area and an outdoor barbecue. Very highly recommended by the Les Routiers inspector.

NORTHERN
ENGLAND

NORTHERN ENGLAND

Northern England was the birthplace of the Industrial Revolution and this is still evident in the old cotton and wool mills, canals, railways and docks. Today, Manchester and Liverpool are fast regaining their position as cities of international importance in both the cultural and the industrial world, and Liverpool's splendid docklands have been restored.

These sprawling urban developments are perfectly contrasted with areas of outstanding natural beauty: stark moors, river valleys, wooded hills and rich pasturelands. The Shires of Middle England form one of the country's most productive farming regions and visitors will find many guest houses in the area still acting as working farms. The hills of the Derbyshire Peak District provide grazing for sheep and the rich pastures on the Leicester/Nottingham border produce the milk which makes Stilton cheese.

The Shires offer a rich variety of produce to tempt visitors' palates, including Leicester and Derby cheese, Lincolnshire sausages, Leicestershire pork pies, and the delicious Bakewell pudding. The region is also noted for its fine beer, such as Ruddles and Batemans, and the tee-totaller can enjoy pure spring and mineral water from Ashbourne and Buxton.

This country food is sure to provide you with the energy to tackle some of the outdoor activities. The Derbyshire Peak District was the first to be designated a National Park and over the years, it has become a popular location for caving, rock-climbing and gliding. For the keen hill-walker, the Pennine Way presents a real challenge: a 270 mile trip from Edale to the Scottish border.

Alternatively, walkers can investigate the pleasures of Yorkshire's National Parks – the picturesque Dales and wild heather-covered Moors that have become known as 'Herriot Country'. It is this beautiful land that also inspired the powerful novels, 'Wuthering Heights' and 'Jane Eyre' and literature enthusiasts should visit the Brontë sisters home-town of Haworth. For those more interested in food than books, Yorkshire is also home to the delicious curd tarts and of course, the famous Yorkshire puddings!

The North has many monuments to history, with reminders of the Roman occupation in Ribchester and Chester, and medieval castles at Lancaster, Beeston and Skipton. Further north, the city of York has a wealth of history within its walls with the Minster, the Viking Jorvik centre, and the 'Shambles', the buildings of which date back to the Middle Ages. Near York, at Malton, Castle Howard has excellent examples of 18th–20th century costume and paintings – and was the setting for the TV serial 'Brideshead Revisited'.

If the legend of Robin Hood interests you, then Nottinghamshire is the place to be. Although Sherwood Forest is somewhat smaller than it used to be, the visitor centre at Edwinstowe illustrates the legend of Robin and the history of the woodlands.

If you yearn for the fun and excitement of a traditional seaside holiday, visit the resorts of Blackpool, Scarborough, Skegness or Whitby. Blackpool Pleasure Beach needs no introduction and the more recent 'Sandcastle Centre' offers an inside 'seaside' all year round. Similarly, Skegness, Scarborough and Whitby, with their sand, sea and funfairs have become popular venues for family holidays.

In total contrast, the Cumbrian lakes to the north-west attract thousands of visitors with the peace and beauty of the fells and mountains. Besides the lakes, Cumbria has a coastline of cliffs and sandy beaches, many attractive villages and historical sites. The city of Carlisle includes a medieval cathedral among its historic buildings. If all this wasn't enough, Cumbria boasts some of the finest cuisine in the land. Try Cumberland ham and sausages, Herdwick lamb and Grasmere gingerbread and you won't be disappointed.

THE ISLE OF MAN

Lying midway between England and Ireland, the self-governing Isle of Man has long been a favourite venue for holiday-makers. 33 miles by 10, with mountains, glens and superb coastal views, the island is ideal for outdoor activities. The way of life is quiet and relaxing with Douglas, the capital, offering a more lively alternative. Hospitality abounds at a great variety of hotels and many interesting restaurants, some providing traditional Manx cuisine.

QUICK REFERENCE GUIDE

	NO. OF ESTS.	⊗ £	⊗ ££	⊗ £££	⊗ ££££	⊞ £	⊞ ££	⊞ £££	⊞ ££££
NORTHERN ENGLAND									
MAP 8 A1									
Bassenthwaite Lake	1			★					
Borrowdale	1		★					★	
Buttermere	1	★							
Ennerdale Bridge	1		★				★		
Silloth on Solway	1		★						
Thornthwaite	1	★						★	
MAP 8 A2									
Appleby in Westmorland	3	★	★				★		
Brampton	1						★		
Carlisle	6	★	★				★		★
Keswick	10	★	★	★		★	★	★	★
Longtown	1		★					★	
Melmerby	1	★							
Penrith	2		★				★	★	
Romaldkirk	1			★					★
Thirlmere	1			★					
MAP 8 B1									
Barrow in Furness	1				★				★
Blackpool	5		★	★		★	★	★	★
Broughton in Furness	1		★						
Calder Bridge	1	★							
Douglas	3	★							★
Eskdale Green	1	★						★	
Glen Helen	1		★						
Ramsey	2	★	★						★
Wasdale Head	1	★							★
MAP 8 B2									
Ambleside	5		★				★		★
Askrigg	1		★					★	
Austwick	1		★					★	
Bingley	1		★					★	
Bowness on Windermere	3	★						★	
Brough Sowerby	1	★							
Carnforth	2		★					★	
Clitheroe	3		★					★	
Coniston	2		★						★
Elslack	1		★					★	
Far Sawrey	1		★					★	
Garstang	1			★					
Gisburn	1		★					★	
Goosnargh	2	★	★					★	
Grange over Sands	3	★	★					★	★
Grasmere	2			★			★		
Grassington	1		★					★	
Grizedale	1		★					★	
Halifax	3	★	★	★			★	★	★
Hawkshead	2	★	★				★		
Haworth	1		★					★	
Hornby	1		★						
Kendal	2	★		★					
Kirkby Lonsdale	2	★	★					★	
Kirkby Stephen	1		★						
Lancaster	1		★					★	

412

QUICK REFERENCE GUIDE

	NO. OF ESTS.	🍴 £	🍴 ££	🍴 £££	🍴 ££££	🛏 £	🛏 ££	🛏 £££	🛏 ££££
Long Preston	1	★							
Longridge	1		★						
Lytham St Annes	4	★	★				★	★	★
Morecambe	2		★					★	
Newby Bridge	2		★						
Padiham	1		★						
Preston	4		★	★				★	
Reeth	2	★	★				★	★	
Sedbergh	2	★	★				★	★	
Settle	3	★	★				★	★	
Skipton	2	★			★				
Wensleydale	1						★		
Wigglesworth	1	★					★		
Windermere	3					★			
Witherslack	1				★				
MAP 8 C1									
Parkgate	1	★							
Southport	3		★				★	★	
Wallasey	3	★	★					★	★
MAP 8 C2									
Alton	1	★							
Altrincham	1	★							★
Ashton under Lyne	1		★						
Bolton	1		★						
Brereton	1		★						
Bury	2		★					★	
Buxton	4		★	★		★		★	★
Castleton	2		★				★		
Chester	9	★	★				★		
Chisworth	1		★						
Chorley	1		★						
Crewe	1		★						
Eccleston	1	★					★		
Frodsham	1		★						★
Holywell Green	1		★					★	
Hyde	1						★		
Knutsford	1							★	
Leek	3	★	★				★	★	
Liverpool	2		★						
Longsdon	1						★		
Manchester	7	★	★	★			★	★	★
Mawdesley	1	★							
Newcastle	1						★		
Newcastle under Lyme	2		★					★	
Newton Le Willows	1	★					★		
Northwich	1						★		
Ormskirk	1			★					
Ramsbottom	1		★						★
Salford	2	★	★				★		
St Helens	1		★					★	
Standish	1		★					★	
Stoke on Trent	1	★							
Tideswell	1	★					★		
Wigan	1		★				★		
MAP 9 A1									
Billingham	1		★						★
Bishop Auckland	1		★						

QUICK REFERENCE GUIDE

	NO. OF ESTS.	⊗ £	⊗ ££	⊗ £££	⊗ ££££	⌂ £	⌂ ££	⌂ £££	⌂ ££££
Durham	4	★	★	★			★	★	
Hartlepool	3	★	★					★	
Haswell Plough	1	★					★		
Newcastle upon Tyne	3	★	★	★				★	
Redcar	2				★				
South Shields	1	★							★
Sunderland	2		★					★	
Whitley Bay	1						★		
MAP 9 B1									
Airmyn	1	★							
Appleton Le Moors	1		★				★		
Bradford	1		★						
Darlington	1	★						★	
Ellerby	1		★				★		
Fairburn	1		★						
Goathland	2					★	★		
Great Ayton	2		★	★					
Great Broughton	1		★						
Harrogate	5		★					★	★
Helmsley	6	★	★	★			★	★	★
Ilkley	1		★						★
Ingleby Greenhow	1						★		
Leeds	4		★				★		★
Leeming	1		★				★		
Malton	1	★							
Middleton Tyas	1		★						
Neasham	2	★							
Northallerton	2	★					★		
Norton	1	★							
Osmotherley	1	★							
Otley	1			★					★
Pickering	1		★					★	
Richmond	3	★	★				★	★	
Ripon	1		★						
Rosedale Abbey	2		★						★
Shipley	1	★							
Stokesley	1		★						
Thirsk	4		★	★		★	★		★
Thorganby	1		★						
Thornton Dale	2					★	★		
West Witton	1			★					★
Yarm	1		★						
York	22	★	★	★	★	★	★	★	★
MAP 9 B2									
Beverley	2		★				★		
Bridlington	3		★			★	★		
Driffield	1		★						
East Ayton	1							★	
Filey	3	★					★		
Hull	2	★		★				★	★
Langtoft	1		★						★
Market Weighton	1		★					★	
Scarborough	9	★	★			★	★	★	★
Whitby	9	★	★	★			★	★	
MAP 9 C1									
Ashbourne	2		★	★			★	★	
Bakewell	3		★	★			★	★	

QUICK REFERENCE GUIDE

	NO OF ESTS.	£	££	£££	££££	£	££	£££	££££
Bamford	2	★					★		
Barnsley	1		★						★
Biggin By Hartington	1								★
Derby	2		★						★
Doncaster	3		★				★	★	
Edwinstowe	1		★						
Elland	1		★						
Gunthorpe	1		★						
Huddersfield	3		★	★			★	★	
Kimberley	1	★					★		
Laxton	1	★							
Liversedge	1			★					★
Matlock	3	★	★			★	★		
Newark	1		★						
Nottingham	4	★	★	★				★	
Rotherham	3		★					★	★
Shardlow	1		★						
Sheffield	4	★	★						
Thorne	1		★					★	
Wirksworth	1		★						
Worksop	1			★				★	
MAP 9 C2									
Brigg	1		★				★		
Cleethorpes	2	★							
Grantham	2	★	★				★		
Leadenham	1		★				★		
Lincoln	8		★	★		★	★	★	★
Louth	1	★							
Market Rasen	1	★							
Skegness	2		★				★		

NORTHERN ENGLAND

AIRMYN Humberside **Map 9 B1**

⊗£ **PERCY ARMS** 89 High Street, Airmyn, Nr Goole.
Hours: Monday to Saturday 11.30am - 3pm, 5.30pm (summer) - 11pm and 6.30pm (winter) - 11pm. Sunday 12 noon - 3pm, 7pm - 10.30pm. Meals served 12 noon - 2pm and until 10pm in the evening. No meals Sunday evening and Christmas Day. **Cuisine:** Traditional home-cooking with a continental flavour. ⊨ None. **CC** Access, Visa. **Other Points:** Children welcome. Open for Sunday lunch and Bank holidays. Garden dining. Quality hand pulled beers. **P** **(V) Directions:** Off M62 at junction 36 onto Rawcliffe Rd. Take road opposite garage.
DAVID A P LYON ☎ (0405) 764408.
A traditional country pub set in a rural village next to the River Aire with its own large, attractive gardens. The conservatory overlooks the gardens and makes a pleasant venue in which to enjoy the quality food. Very friendly atmosphere. Easy access to Humber Bridge, York and York wolds.

ALTON Staffordshire **Map 8 C2**

⊗£ **WILD DUCK INN** New Road, Alton, Stoke on Trent.
⊞£ **Hours:** Meals from 8.30am - 9.30am and 7pm - 8.30pm. Sundays open from 12 noon - 2pm and 7pm - 10.30pm. **Cuisine:** Traditional pub food in the bar. English style food and snacks served in the restaurant. ⊨ 6 bedrooms. **CC** Access, Visa. **Other Points:** Children welcome. No dogs. Coaches by appointment. **P Directions:** Off the B5032. Follow directions for Alton Towers.
MR & MRS KEITH MURDOCH ☎ (0538) 702218.
A country house built by Earl John. Elegant bar and family restaurant with comfortable and reasonably priced letting bedrooms. Set in Churnet Valley overlooking Alton Towers Leisure Park.

ALTRINCHAM Greater Manchester **Map 8 C2**

⊗£ **CRESTA COURT HOTEL** Church Street, Altrincham.
⊞££££ **Hours:** Breakfast 7.15am - 9.45am, Lunch 12 noon - 2.30pm, Dinner 6pm - 11pm. Bar snacks 10am - 6.30pm. **Cuisine:** 2 Restaurants: Tavern Lodge Steak Bar and the Trellis Restaurant (a la carte). Bar meals in Townfields Bar. ⊨ 139 bedrooms, all en suite and with all major facilities including in-house films, electric trouser press and baby listening. **CC** All major cards. **Other Points:** Children welcome. Afternoon teas. Dogs allowed. Conferences, Exhibitions, Wedding receptions. Fax No: (061) 926 9194. **P** &
(V) Directions: On A56 at juction of Woodlands Rd. 600 yds from Altrincham Station.
ANTHONY P BITTON - General Manager ☎ (061) 927 7272.
A unique combination of amenities and location, make the Cresta Court a perfect base whether travelling on business, taking a holiday break or looking for a venue for a private function. The hotel has been well furbished to offer comfort and a warm atmosphere prevails. There is a bar, 2 restaurants and a cocktail lounge bar where you can relax over a drink before you dine.

AMBLESIDE Cumbria **Map 8 B2**

�º££ **COMPSTON HOUSE HOTEL** Compston Road, Ambleside.

🛏 6 double, 1 twin and 1 family bedroom. 1 WC. All rooms are en suite and have colour TV and tea/coffee making facilities. Romantic 4-poster suite also available for that special break. **Hours:** Breakfast 8.30am - 9am, dinner at 7pm (order by 5pm). **CC** None. **Other Points:** Central heating. Children welcome. No dogs. Licensed. Lounge and patio. Cosy bar. Public car park 25 yds away. Vegetarian & special diets catered for. **Directions:** In the centre of Ambleside, opposite the park, by the church.
ANN & GRAHAM SMITH ☎ (05394) 32305

A family run hotel, beautifully situated opposite park and fells. Ann & Graham Smith offer excellent food and friendly service in cosy surroundings. Most rooms have views of the park where you may play tennis, croquet, bowls or test your skills on the putting green. Guided fell walking, rock climbing, pony trekking and riding can be arranged. Excellent water sports nearby.

⊗££ **FISHERBECK HOTEL** Lake Road, Ambleside.

�º££££ **Hours:** Breakfast 8.30am - 9am, bar snacks served 12 noon - 2pm and 6pm - 9pm dinner 7pm - 8pm. **Cuisine:** Dishes may include Roast Venison with Blackberry sauce, Pork Escalope Madeira, Fresh lakeland Trout Almondine. Salmon Hollandaise - house speciality. 🛏 20 bedrooms, 19 en suite. **CC** Access, Visa. **Other Points:** Children welcome. Afternoon teas. Garden. Mastercard accepted. **P (V) Directions:** From South A591 to Waterhead, bear right at Waterhead, on right.
BRIAN & KATHLEEN BARTON ☎ (05394) 33215.

Situated in the heart of the Lake District, parts of this hotel were once used as a tannery and a school. Pleasantly decorated and comfortably furnished. In the restaurant you can enjoy well presented, delicious meals, in a homely atmosphere. With a high standard of accommodation, the hotel is an ideal base for relaxing or for a climbing, fishing or sailing holiday.

⊗££ **NANNY BROW COUNTRY HOUSE HOTEL** Clappersgate, Ambleside.

Hours: Breakfast 8.30am - 9.30am, Lunch 12 noon -1.30pm, Dinner 7.30pm - 9pm. **Cuisine:** Fixed price 6 course menu and bar meals. Dishes may include Swiss Cheese Soup, Baked Halibut in Pastry, Roast Leg of Lamb. 🛏 22 bedrooms, all en suite. **CC** Access, Visa, AmEx. **Other Points:** Children welcome. Garden. Afternoon teas. Dogs allowed. No smoking in restaurant. **P & (V) Directions:** On the A593 near Clappersgate.
MICHAEL FLETCHER ☎ (05394) 32036.

Built in 1908 and set in 5 acres of peaceful gardens and woodlands, this country house has now been tastefully converted into an elegant hotel. Great care has been taken to retain the comfort and elegance of a gracious country house and to provide a high standard of accommodation. Well presented meals are served in the restaurant.

�º££ **RYSDALE HOTEL** Rothay Road, Ambleside.

🛏 9 bedrooms, 6 en suite. All rooms have colour TV, tea/coffee makers, some have a trouser press and hair dryer. **Hours:** Breakfast 8am - 8.45am. Dinner at 7.30pm. **CC** Access,

Ambleside continued

Visa. **Other Points:** Strictly no smoking. No children under 8 yrs. Ironing facilities available on request. Licensed. **(V) Directions:** 13 miles north of Kendal, 17 miles south of Keswick.

JEAN & ROY FRY. ☎ (05394) 32140.

A well run cosy hotel, set in the heart of the Lakeland. Offering good food and comfortable accommodation, accompanied by an informal atmosphere. A warm welcome awaits all guests to ensure a happy and memorable stay. Ideal base for touring.

⊗££ **THE RIVERSIDE HOTEL** Near Rothay Under Loughrigg, ⌂£££ Ambleside.

Hours: Breakfast 8.30am - 9.30am, dinner 7pm - 8pm. **Cuisine:** A la carte and table d'hote menu - changes daily. ⊨ 10 bedrooms, all en suite. ᴄᴄ Access, Visa. **Other Points:** Children welcome. No smoking area. ◘ **(V) Directions:** From A591 take A593 to Coniston, left over Rothay Bridge then right.

JIM & JEAN HAINEY ☎ (05394) 32395.

A small, family run hotel in a peaceful riverside setting in a typical English country lane. The Hainey's are Scots, with a welcome to match, in their classic hotel. Excellent food - booking highly recommended. A few minutes from the centre of Ambleside.

APPLEBY IN WESTMORLAND Cumbria **Map 8 A2**

⊗££ **COURTFIELD HOTEL** Bongate, Appleby in Westmorland. ⌂££ **Hours:** Breakfast 8am - 9am, Lunch 12.30pm - 2pm and Dinner 7pm - 8.15pm. **Cuisine:** Traditional English: specialities being roasts such as local rib of beef with Yorkshire pudding and homemade sweets such as apple pie and pavlova. ⊨ 11 bedrooms, 3 en suite. ᴄᴄ None. **Other Points:** Children welcome. Dogs allowed. Open for afternoon tea, all day Sundays and Bank holidays. Garden dining. ◘ **(V) Directions:** Signposted off main A66 onto old road. Hotel at base of hill.

A E ROBINSON ☎ (07683) 51394.

The house used to be an old vicarage, with large and airy rooms. Now the proprietors of the Courtfield offer residents and non-residents their home-cooked food and warm hospitality. Set on the outskirts of an interesting market town, with Appleby Castle and the River Eden nearby.

⊗£ **NEW INN** Brampton, nr Appleby in Westmorland. ⌂££ **Hours:** Breakfast 7.30am - 9.30am, lunch 12 noon - 2pm and dinner 7.30pm - 9.30pm (last orders). **Cuisine:** Steaks, grills, curried nut roast, pork chops in cider, Westmorland sweetbake, chocolate fudge cake. ⊨ 3 bedrooms. TV provided if required. ᴄᴄ None. **Other Points:** Children welcome. No dogs. Beer garden. No juke boxes or fruit machines. ◘ **(V) Directions:** From Appleby, follow signs to Brampton, 1½ miles away.

ROGER & ANNE CRANSWICK ☎ (076 83) 51231.

The New Inn is in fact a very old inn built around 1730 and charmingly restored with hanging baskets enhancing the appearance. Inside, low beams, open log fires and flag stone floors take you back to a bygone era. A delightful setting in the Vale of Eden - an ideal stop for the tourist.

ASHBOURNE

Appleby in Westmorland continued

ⓐ£££ ⌂£££ **THE WHITE HART HOTEL** Boroughgate, Appleby in Westmorland.

Hours: Breakfast 8am - 9am, lunch 12 noon - 2.30pm , dinner 6.30pm - 9.30pm (last orders). Bar meals 12 noon - 2.30pm, 6.30pm - 9.30pm. **Cuisine:** Cumberland brunch, steaks, fish, venison. Wide range of home made sweets ie. pavlovas, vacharines. ⊨ 9 bedrooms, most en suite. **CC** Access, Visa, AmEx. **Other Points:** Children welcome. Garden. Dogs allowed. ▯ **(V) Directions:** Off A66, down main Appleby road, cross River bridge, turn left.

THE HALL FAMILY ☎ (07683) 51598.

A warm and friendly welcome awaits all guests at this small family run hotel. Dating from the late 17th century, the hotel is surrounded by breathtaking scenery. The White Hart organises walks across the fells and provides a drop off and pick up service.

APPLETON LE MOORS North Yorkshire **Map 9 B1**

ⓧ£££ ⌂£££ **DWELDAPILTON HALL COUNTRY HOUSE HOTEL** Appleton Le Moors, York.

Hours: Breakfast 8.30am - 9.15am, and dinner 7pm - 8.15pm (last orders). **Cuisine:** English cuisine, with home-made soups and puddings. ⊨ 10 bedrooms, all en suite. All rooms have colour TV, radio, telephone and tea/coffee making facilities. Four poster suite and 2 luxury suites. **CC** Access, Visa, AmEx. **Other Points:** Pets allowed. Afternoon teas served. Open Sundays and bank holidays. Children over 12 welcome. Lifts. Fax No. (07515) 540 ▯ ⅙ **(V) Directions:** 1 and 3/4 miles from the A170. Follow signs for Appleton Le Moors.

BRENDA SMALLEY & JOHN INGLETON ☎ (07515) 227.

A delightful country house set in attractive gardens with lovely views over the Yorkshire moors. In fine weather, afternoon teas can be enjoyed on the terrace, the quality of which earned Dweldapilton Hall the place of 'Tea Council finalist' in 1989. For a more substantial meal, the dining room provides a pleasant ambience in which to enjoy the excellent cuisine.

ASHBOURNE Derbyshire **Map 9 C1**

ⓧ£££ ⌂£££ **STANSHOPE HALL** Stanshope, nr Ashbourne.

Hours: Breakfast 8.30am - 9.30am, dinner 7pm. Sunday lunch only 1pm. **Cuisine:** 3 course dinner. Home cooking and vegetables from the garden. Home made chocolates served with the coffee. Vegetarians welcome. ⊨ 3 bedrooms, 1 en suite with four poster bed. Colour TV. Tea/coffe making facilities. Telephone. **CC** None. **Other Points:** Children welcome. Dogs allowed. No smoking area. Garden. Guests drawing room. ▯ **(V) Directions:** Off A515 Ashbourne to Buxton in the hamlet of Stanshope.

NAOMI CHAMBERS & NICK LOURIE ☎ (0335) 27278.

A 17th century country house with beautiful south facing views, standing on the brow of a hill above Dovedale in the Peak National Park. The rooms are large and comfortable featuring unusual decorations such as hand painted walls. Atmosphere of a country house and family home combined with the standards and features of a hotel. Ideal for walkers. 30 mins Alton Towers.

Ashbourne continued

⊗££ **THE BENTLEY BROOK INN** Fenny Bentley, Near
🏠££ Ashbourne.

Hours: Breakfast 7am - 10am, lunch 11am - all day, dinner 7pm -
9.30pm. Sunday lunch 12 noon - 2pm. **Cuisine:** Dishes include
Savoury Derbyshire oatcake, Turkey and ham pie and a selection
of homemade sweets. ⊨ 1 single, 2 twin, 5 double and 1 family
bedroom. 4 en suite. **CC** Access, Visa. **Other Points:** Children
welcome. Garden. Dogs allowed. **P** & **(V) Directions:** On
junction of the A515 to Buxton and B5056 to Bakewell.
MR & MRS ALLINGHAM ☎ (0335) 29278.

*This traditional timbered inn, set in 2 acres of well tended
gardens provides wonderfully cooked food using only the
freshest produce - no frozen food here. With a daily changing
menu, you will find their tasty main dishes with crispy fresh
vegetables and homemade sweets a delight, especially when
teamed with their comprehensive list of wines. Good
accommodation & welcome.*

ASHTON UNDER LYNE Greater Manchester **Map 8 C2**

⊗££ **YORK HOUSE HOTEL** York Place, off Richmond Street.

Hours: Restaurant open 12 noon - 2pm Mondays to Fridays and
7pm - 9.30pm Mondays to Saturdays. **Cuisine:** Large a la carte
international menu. ⊨ 34 bedrooms, all en suite. **CC** All major
cards. **Other Points:** Children welcome. **P** & **(V) Directions:** Off
the A635.
MR KEITH ABSALOM ☎ (061) 330 5899.

*The a la carte restaurant has a reputation for good food with an
extensive menu catering to everyone's taste and pocket.
Speciality evenings and weekends are a feature of the Hotel's
restaurant.*

ASKRIGG North Yorkshire **Map 8 B2**

⊗££ **KING'S ARMS HOTEL AND RESTAURANT** Askrigg in
🏠£££ Wensleydale.

CLUB **Hours:** Breakfast 8.30am - 9.30am, dinner 7.30pm - 9pm, (last
orders 8.45pm). Bar meals 12 noon - 2pm, 6.30pm - 9pm Monday
to Saturday, 7pm - 8.30pm Sundays. Open 11am - 11pm
(10.30pm Sundays) in summer and at weekends in winter.
Cuisine: Restaurant: English and French cuisine, meat and fish
with special sauces prepared by the proprietor and using fresh
local produce wherever possible. ⊨ 10 bedrooms, all en suite and
with mini-bar, colour TV, telephone, radio tea/coffee making
facilities. Four poster and half tester beds available. **CC** Access,
Visa. **Other Points:** Mercier Corps d'Elite Winelist Award 1990.
Access to bars for disabled. Children welcome. Grill room.
Courtyard. **P** **(V) Directions:** 1 mile off the A684 at Bainbridge, in
the market square in Askrigg.
LIZ & RAY HOPWOOD ☎ (0969) 50258.

*A Grade II listed coaching inn, with atmosphere and character
which began life as the famous 18th century racing stable of
John Pratt. The bars, once the tack and harness rooms, are
familiar to many as the 'Drovers Arms' of Darrowby in the BBC
TV series of James Herriot's 'All Creatures Great and Small'.*

AUSTWICK North Yorkshire **Map 8 B2**
⊗££ **THE TRADDOCK** Austwick, Via Lancaster.
⌂££ **Hours:** Breakfast 8am - 9.30am, Lunch 12 noon - 2pm and Dinner 7.30pm - 8.30pm. Bar snacks served all day until 6pm. Open all year. **Cuisine:** All dishes homemade and may include Chicken in Calvados Cream, Halibut with Tomato & Orange sauce, Vegetable Paella. Reasonably priced wine list. ⊨ 12 bedrooms, 11 en suite. ⊠ Access, Visa. **Other Points:** Children welcome. Garden. Afternoon teas. No dogs. No smoking in dining room. Beautiful views. ⊡ & **(V) Directions:** A65. Half a mile off the main road in a very quiet situation.
FRANCES & RICHARD MICHAELIS ☎ (05242) 51224.
Situated among the breathtaking scenery of the Yorkshire Dales National Park, an area of outstanding natural beauty, the Traddock offers you the perfect base for a walking or touring holiday or break. Comfortable accommodation and a high standard of home cooking are complemented by a warm welcome. Highly recommended by the Routiers inspector and well worth a visit.

BAKEWELL Derbyshire **Map 9 C1**
⊗££ **ASHFORD HOTEL & RESTAURANT** Church Street,
⌂£££ Ashford-in-the-Water, nr Bakewell.
Hours: Breakfast 8am - 9.30am, Dinner 7pm - 9.30pm (last orders). Sunday lunch 12 noon - 2pm. Bar meals 12 noon - 2pm. **Cuisine:** French cuisine specialising in fish dishes including salmon, Dover sole and trout. A la carte and table d'hote menus. ⊨ 7 bedrooms, all en suite. ⊠ Access, Visa. **Other Points:** Children welcome. Beer garden. Afternoon teas. Dogs allowed. Residents' lounge. ⊡ **(V) Directions:** 2.5 miles outside Bakewell, off the A6 towards Buxton.
JOHN & SUE DAWSON ☎ (0629) 812725.
An 18th century grade II listed building with traditional oak beams and open fires. A family run hotel with a warm welcome and personal service. Good food is beautifully presented in the restaurant and a wide range of bar meals are also available. Behind the hotel and extending down to the River Wye is a large beer garden, a perfect place to enjoy a snack in summer.

⊗£££ **THE CROFT COUNTRY HOUSE HOTEL** Great Longstone,
⌂££££ Nr Bakewell.
Hours: Breakfast 8.30am - 9.30am, Dinner at 7.30pm. Closed: January and February. **Cuisine:** Set menu which changes daily. ⊨ 9 bedrooms, all en suite. Lift and 2 bedrooms suitable for a wheelchair. ⊠ Access, Visa. **Other Points:** Children welcome. No-smoking area. Garden. Residents' lounge. Private functions & small conferences catered for. ⊡ & **Directions:** In Great Longstone, 3 miles NE of Bakewell. Off A6 & B6465.
ALLAN & LYNNE MACASKILL ☎ (0629) 640278.
Standing in 4 acres of grounds and garden, The Croft has been tastefully converted to a comfortable hotel of great character and charm. The hotel is spacious yet intimate and provides personal service in homely, relaxed surroundings. The dinner menu is changed daily and offers good food, attractively served, in a relaxed atmosphere.

Bakewell continued

⊗££ **THE RUTLAND ARMS HOTEL** The Square, Bakewell, Derbyshire.
Hours: Breakfast 7.30 - 9.30am, Lunch 12 noon - 2pm, dinner 7pm - 9.30pm (last orders 9.15pm), Sunday 7pm - 9pm. Bar meals 12 noon - 2pm and 7pm - 9.30pm. **Cuisine:** All food prepared from fresh local produce. Speciality - Bakewell pudding. Table D'Hote dinner menu eg. Medallions of Beef with a Madeira Sauce. ⊨ 36 rooms, all en suite. **CC** All major cards. **Other Points:** Children welcome. Afternoon tea served. **P** **(V)**
MR PETER MASON ☎ (0629) 814184.
This Georgian hotel serves excellently cooked and presented food in pleasant surroundings. Located in heart of Peak National Park, close to Haddon Hall and Chatsworth House, and no visit is complete without a visit to Bakewell market held every Monday.

BAMFORD Derbyshire **Map 9 C1**

⊗£ **THE DERWENT HOTEL** Main Road, Bamford, Sheffield.
⏠££ **Hours:** Breakfast 7.30am - 9.30am, Lunch 12 noon - 2pm and Dinner 7pm - 10pm (last orders 9.30pm). **Cuisine:** English fayre, freshly prepared. Homemade sweets a speciality. ⊨ 10 bedrooms, 2 en suite. **CC** Access, Visa. **Other Points:** Children welcome. Garden. Pets allowed. **P** **(V) Directions:** Off the A57, close to town centre.
ANGELA & DAVID RYAN ☎ (0433) 51395
A stone built pub with a lively local atmosphere which is an ideal base for visiting the Peak District. The Derwent Hotel is a

Bamford continued
popular venue for Sunday lunch which can be enjoyed, weather permitting, in its large garden.

⊗£ **THE MARQUIS OF GRANBY** Hathersage Road, Bamford.
Hours: Meals 8am - 9.30am, 12 noon - 2pm and 7.30pm - 10pm.
Cuisine: Saucy cooking. A la carte. Special summer menu. ⊨ 7
bedrooms, 6 en suite. **CC** All major cards. **Other Points:** Children
welcome. **P** & **Directions:** On the main A625 between
Hathersage and Castleton.
JOHN & PATRICIA GABBARD ☎ (0433) 51206/51245.
Charming old inn surrounded by lawns and situated in the heart of the Hope Valley. Fishing rights on Derwent River. Bar with panelling from Olympic steamship - sister to the Titanic.

BARNSLEY South Yorkshire **Map 9 C1**
⊗££ **TANKERSLEY MANOR HOTEL & RESTAURANT**
⊞£££££ Church Lane, Tankersley, Barnsley.
CLUB **Hours:** Breakfast 7am - 9.30am, weekend breakfast - Satyurday
7.30am - 10am, Sunday 8am - 10am, lunch 12.30pm - 2.30pm,
dinner 7pm - 9.45pm, bar snacks 12.30pm - 2.30pm and 6pm -
9.45pm (Fridays & Saturdays 8.30pm). **Cuisine:** Serving bar
menu, table d'hote, Sunday luncheon menu and full a la carte.
Shellfish dishes and seasonal game dishes a speciality. ⊨ 20
bedrooms, all en suite. **CC** All major cards. **Other Points:** Children
welcome. Open Bank Holidays. No smoking area. Dogs allowed -
bedrooms only. Garden dining. Fax No. (0226) 745405. **P** & **(V)**
Directions: On A61, half mile west of Jct 36 of the M1.
JOHN WAINWRIGHT. ☎ (0226) 744700.
Formerly a 17th century residence, sympathetically restored to create a warm cosy atmosphere. Well presented meals of good quality and quantity, are served by friendly, efficient staff. Set in its own grounds and within easy reach of the Yorkshire Dales.

BARROW IN FURNESS Cumbria **Map 8 B1**
⊗££££ **THE ABBEY HOUSE HOTEL** Abbey Road, Barrow in Furness.
⊞£££££ **Hours:** Breakfast 7am - 10am, Lunch 12 noon - 2.30pm, Dinner
7pm - 10pm. Restaurant closed: Saturday lunch. Bar meals 12
noon - 2.30pm and 7pm - 10pm. **Cuisine:** Imaginative, French
influenced cuisine. A la carte and table d'hote menus. ⊨ 28
bedrooms, all en suite. **CC** All major cards. **Other Points:** Children
welcome. Afternoon teas. Dogs allowed. Residents lounge.
Lounge bar. Garden. Fax No: (0229) 820403. Full conference
facilities. **P** & **(V) Directions:** Leave M6 at junction 36, eastbound
for 33 miles along A590.
TIMOTHY KILROE ☎ (0229) 838282.
An elegantly appointed mansion house hotel, surrounded by lawns, fountains and an extensive private woodland park, yet only 2 miles from Barrow in Furness. The comfortable and elegant restaurant offers outstanding classical French cuisine with all dishes attractively presented and served. The service is excellent - personal and friendly without being intrusive.

BASSENTHWAITE LAKE Cumbria **Map 8 A1**
⊗£££ **THE PHEASANT INN** Bassenthwaite Lake, nr Cockermouth.
⌣ **Hours:** Restaurant open 8.30am - 9.45am, 12 noon - 2pm and
7pm - 8.30pm. Closed: Christmas Day. **Cuisine:** Roast meats -

Bassenthwaite Lake continued

pheasant, venison (in season), roast duckling with orange sauce, Silloth shrimps. 🛏 20 bedrooms, all en suite. **CC** None. **Other Points:** Non-smoking restaurant. Children welcome. No pets in bedrooms. **P** 🚻 **Directions:** Just off the A66, 7 miles west of Keswick.

MR W E BARRINGTON WILSON ☎ (076 8776) 234.

The hotel is an excellent base from which to tour the Lake District as well as the Roman Wall and Border country, the Eden Valley and Cumbrian coast. It has all the charm and character of a typical old inn and is well known for its excellent English cooking, service and friendliness.

BEVERLEY Humberside **Map 9 B2**

🏨££ **RUDSTONE WALK FARM** South Cave, Brough, Nr Beverley. 🛏 1 single, 1 double, 1 twin and 2 family bedroom, 1 en suite. 1 bathroom, 1 shower. Morning tea service. **Hours:** Breakfast 7am - 8.30am (9.30am Sundays), Dinner 7pm - 8.30pm (order previous day). Booking recommended. **CC** AmEx. **Other Points:** Central heating. Children welcome. Residents lounge with TV. Garden. No dogs. **P** 🚻 **Directions:** Situated on the B1230, off M62.

MRS PAULINE GREENWOOD ☎ (0430) 422230.

A beautiful 400 year old farmhouse mentioned in the Doomesday Book and tucked into the foot of the Yorkshire Wolds in an area steeped in history and charm. The farm offers unrivalled views across the countryside towards nearby York, Beverley and the East Riding. Luxurious, serviced, self-contained cottages in the grounds are available for hire all year round.

⊗££ **THE LAIRGATE HOTEL** Lairgate, Beverley.

Hours: Buttery and grill room opens 7.30am for breafast serving food through to 9.30pm (last orders). **Cuisine:** All dishes are homemade. Fisherman's pie, steak and kidney pie, moussaka and steaks. Flambee and fondue served in the piano bar atmosphere. 🛏 24 bedrooms, 18 en suite. **CC** Access, Visa. **Other Points:** Children welcome. Coaches by appointment. **P** 🚻 **(V) Directions:** In the centre of Beverley - Lairgate runs parallel to Market Square.

PETER WALSHAW ☎ (0482) 882141/861901

A delightful Georgian house in the centre of this busy market town, famous for its Minster, racecouse and Saturday market. This hotel has a relaxed, happy atmopshere with friendly conscientious staff.

BIGGIN BY HARTINGTON Derbyshire **Map 9 C1**

🏨£££ **BIGGIN HALL** Biggin-By-Hartington, Buxton. 🛏 15 bedrooms, all en suite, including self-contained studio apartments. Four poster suite. Room service. Dogs allowed in self-contained apartments. **Hours:** Breakfast 8.30am - 9am, Dinner at 7pm. Non-residents welcome for dinner if book in advance. **CC** Access, Visa. **Other Points:** No smoking area. Garden. 2 sitting rooms (1 with colour TV, 1 with open stone fireplace). Vegetarian and special diets can be catered for. **P** **(V) Directions:** Half a mile off A515, midway between Ashbourne and Buxton.

MR & MRS MOFFETT ☎ (0298) 84451.

A Grade II listed, 17th century house standing in 8 acres of grounds and expertly renovated to ensure the original character

Biggin By Hartington continued

has been retained. The accommodation is excellent, with all rooms spacious and individually furnished with antiques. The traditional home cooking using predominantly fresh local produce is highly recommended. A perfect choice for a relaxing holiday.

BILLINGHAM Cleveland **Map 9 A1**

⊗££ **BILLINGHAM ARMS HOTEL** The Causeway, Billingham.

££££**Hours:** Breakfast 7am - 10am, Lunch and bar snacks 12 noon - 2pm and Dinner 6pm - 11pm (last orders 10.15pm, 11pm Saturday). Sunday hours 12 noon - 3pm and 7pm - 9pm. **Cuisine:** Eg. Croissant filled with diced chicken & bacon in a cream cheese & mushroom sauce; Strips of beef cooked at your table in a sherry & oyster sauce. ⊨ 69 bedrooms, all en suite. Honeymoon suite with four poster bed. All rooms have Sky Tv, direct dial telephone, hairdryer, tea/coffee tray, trouser press. **CC** All major cards. **Other Points:** Children welcome. Coaches by appointment. Dogs allowed except in Restaurant/public area. Traditional beers. Telex: 587746. Fax: (0642) 552104. **P** & **(V) Directions:** From A19, in town square next to Forum Sports Centre and theatre. MESSRS SNAITH & HUGHES ☎ (0642) 553661/360880

A conveniently located, modern hotel, 5 minutes from Billingham railway station and 10 miles from Teesside Airport. Berties Restaurant is renowned for its good food and friendly service. An ideal hotel for tourists and business-people alike.

BINGLEY West Yorkshire **Map 8 B2**

⊗££ **OAKWOOD HALL HOTEL** Lady Lane, Bingley.

££££ **Hours:** Breakfast 7.30am - 9.30am, lunch 12 noon - 2pm, dinner 7.30pm - 9.30pm. Sunday lunch 12.30pm - 2pm, Sunday dinner 7.30pm - 9.30pm (last orders, lunch 2pm, dinner 9.30pm) **Cuisine:** A la carte menu, fixed 3 course menu, bar meals and bar snacks. ⊨ 17 rooms. 2 single, 5 twin, 9 double and 1 family room. All en suite. **CC** All major cards. **Other Points:** Children welcome. Garden. Dogs allowed. Rooms available for conferences and seminars. Weddings and parties catered for. **P** & **(V) Directions:** Off A650. MRS K BRASSINGTON ☎ (0274) 564123.

A family run hotel set in a quiet woodland. The decor of the hotel is of a very high standard with furnishings of great taste. A relaxed place to visit, serving superb food with unusual starters and sweets.

BISHOP AUCKLAND County Durham **Map 9 A1**

⊗££ **BISHOPS BISTRO** 17 Cockton Hill Road, Bishop Auckland.

Hours: Lunch 11.30am - 1.30pm, dinner 7pm - late (last orders 9.30pm). Closed: Sunday and Monday. **Cuisine:** Dishes may include Roast Lion of Lamb with fresh rosemary, sauted King Prawns in garlic butter. Daily specials displayed on blackboard. ⊨ None. **CC** Access, Visa. **Other Points:** Children welcome. No dogs. Limited access for disabled. **P** **(V) Directions:** 2 minutes from the new railway station opposite the hospital. CHARLES & KATE DAVIDSON ☎ (0388) 602462.

Old converted cottages with plenty of character situated in the main street from the town centre. Personally run by the chef/proprietor, there is a restaurant and a separate bar area

Bishop Auckland continued
*where diners may enjoy pre-dinner drinks. Efficient service and
well cooked cuisine in an informal atmosphere.*

BLACKPOOL Lancashire **Map 8 B1**
££ **HILL'S TUDOR ROSE HOTEL** 435-7 South Promenade,
Blackpool.
5 single, 5 twin, 23 double and 6 family bedrooms, 17 en suite.
Hours: Breakfast 8.30am - 9.30am, Dinner at 5.30pm. All
major cards. **Other Points:** Children welcome. Lounge bar.
Lunchtime snacks available on request. **Directions:** On the
Promenade near the South Pier.
STAN HILL ☎ (0253) 42656.
*A comfortable, medium sized family hotel overlooking the sea
and only a few minutes away from the Sandcastle. Friendly,
personal service will ensure that your stay is as enjoyable as
possible. The Lounge Bar makes a good rendez-vous for a drink
before dinner.*

£££ **MAINS HALL COUNTRY HOUSE HOTEL** Mains Lane,
££££ Little Singleton, Blackpool.
Hours: Breakfast 8am - 10am, Dinner 7.30pm - 8.30pm (last
orders, bar snacks until 10pm). Closed: Sundays. **Cuisine:** Dishes
may include Fillet Steak with red wine and mushroom sauce,
Baked Rainbow Trout, Barbecue Pork with apricots. 9
bedrooms, 7 en suite. Access, Visa. **Other Points:** Children
welcome. No smoking area. Dogs allowed. Garden dining.
Cookery courses. Conferences and private functions. Fax No:

Blackpool continued

(0253) 894132. ▣ ⅃ **(V) Directions:** Leave M55 at junction 3 for the A585. Follow signs to Fleetwood.

PAMELA & ROGER YEOMANS ☎ (0253) 885130.

A Grade II listed house, built in the 16th century by an order of monks. Mains Hall now offers excellent cuisine and accommodation in an atmosphere of elegance and tranquility. Standing in four acres of grounds, overlooking the River Wyre, there is a choice of fishing, horseriding, walking, watersports or badminton or croquet on the lawns. 7 miles from Blackpool.

▥£ **NEWLYN PRIVATE HOTEL** 31/33 Northumberland Avenue, Blackpool.

⇤ 3 single, 7 double, 2 twin, 3 family bedrooms. 2 bathrooms, 2 showers. Tea/coffee facilities in all rooms. Some en suites available. **Hours:** Breakfast 9am, and dinner 5pm. ▦ Access, Visa. **Other Points:** Children welcome. Licensed. Residents lounge. TV. ▣ Directions: Off Queens Promenade.

SHEILA HARGREAVES ☎ (0253) 53230.

Friendly private hotel personally run by owners. Adjacent to Promenade and Boating Pool. Many guests return yearly to sample the good home cooking and hospitality. Fresh produce used wherever possible.

▥£££ **SUNRAY PRIVATE HOTEL** 42 Knowle Avenue, off Queens

CLUB Promenade, Blackpool.

⇤ 3 single, 2 twin, 2 double, 2 family bedrooms, all en suite. **Hours:** Breakfast 8.30am - 9.15am and dinner at 5pm . ▦ Access, Visa. **Other Points:** Children welcome. Garden. Pets allowed. Vegetarian meals available. Eurocard also accepted. ▣ **(V) Directions:** 2 miles N Blackpool Tower, along Promenade. Turn R Uncle Toms Cabin.

JEAN & JOHN DODGSON ☎ (0253) 51937.

A cheerful and comfortable guest house that has been family run for the past 20 years under the capable hands of Mrs Jean Dodgson. With all your needs catered for by a friendly and welcoming establishment, you will find The Sunray an ideal place to stay while in the area. Providing facilities you would expect in a large hotel: direct dial telephone, TV, hairdryer and more.

⊗£££ **WHITE TOWER RESTAURANT** Balmoral Road, Blackpool.

CLUB **Hours:** 7pm - 10.45pm (last orders). Sunday lunch served 12 noon - 4pm. Restaurant closed: January. **Cuisine:** Extensive a la carte menu. Dishes may include Chateaubriand, Dover Sole. Continental dishes. Excellent wine list. ⇤ None. ▦ All major cards. **Other Points:** Children welcome. Guide dogs only. Extensive facilities for conferences and wedding receptions. ▣ ⅃ **(V) Directions:** M55. Road reference-Yeadon Way-near Pleasure Beach/Sandcastle Ctr.

BLACKPOOL PLEASURE BEACH LTD ☎ (0253) 46710/41036.

The White Tower Restaurant serves excellent food and wine in very pleasant, elegant surroundings. From its penthouse position, high in the exciting 'Wonderful World Building', the restaurant has splendid views overlooking the Promenade and the famous Illuminations.

BOLTON Lancashire **Map 8 C2**

⊗££ **GEORGIAN HOUSE HOTEL** Manchester Road, Blackrod, Bolton.

Hours: Breakfast 7am - 10am, lunch 12 noon - 2pm, bar snacks served 11am - 3pm, dinner 7pm - 10pm (last orders). **Cuisine:** Dishes may include Georgian House Pate, Egg and Prawn Marie Rose, Supreme of Chicken, Quinelles of Seafood. Flambe specialities on the a la carte menu. ⬅ 101 rooms, all en suite. Reduced rates at weekends. **CC** All major cards. **Other Points:** Children welcome. Afternoon teas served. Dogs allowed. Health and Leisure club including swimming pool, gymnasium, steam-room, and beauty therapy. **P Directions:** On the A6 one and a half miles from the M61 junction 6.

MRS DIANE NORBURY - Director ☎ (0942) 814598.

This large Georgian building is decorated to a high standard and provides a very comfortable stay. Attractive meals are presented in the relaxed atmosphere of the restaurant. With its five conference suites and banqueting facilities it is ideal for either weddings or conferences. Dinner dances on Fridays and Saturdays in the Regency Restaurant.

BORROWDALE Cumbria **Map 8 A1**

⊗£££ **THE BORROWDALE HOTEL** Nr Keswick.

🛏£££ **Hours:** Breakfast 8am - 9.30am, lunches 12 noon - 2pm and dinner 7pm - 9.15pm. Non-residents welcome. **Cuisine:** Bar meals, eg. grilled homemade Cumberland sausage, poached fresh Seathwaite trout. Lunch: traditional roast beef, escalope de veau Normandie. ⬅ 34 bedrooms, all en suite. Four poster beds available. Colour TV, radio, intercom, baby-minding system, direct dial telephone & tea/coffee facilities. **CC** Access, Visa. **Other Points:** Children welcome. Fax No: (07687) 77338. direct dial telephone and tea/coffee making facilities in all rooms. **P (V) Directions:** Off the B5289 approximately 4 miles from Keswick.

MR P FIDRMUC - Resident Manager ☎ (07687) 77224.

The Borrowdale Hotel lies in the heart of Lakeland with superb views of the surrounding lakes and mountains.

BOWNESS ON WINDERMERE Cumbria **Map 8 B2**

⊗£ **BLENHEIM LODGE** Brantfell Road, Bowness on Windermere.

🛏£££ **Hours:** Breakfast 8.30am - 9am, dinner 7pm. Booking by 4pm
⌐ㅎ would be appreciated. **Cuisine:** English - Traditional and Victorian dishes. All homemade. Fresh home grown produce. ⬅ 11 bedrooms, all en suite. **CC** Access, Visa. **Other Points:** Children welcome. No dogs. No-smoking area. Residents lounge. Eurocard accepted. **P (V) Directions:** From M6 turn left off A591 to Windermere. Opposite St Martins Church

FRANK SANDERSON ☎ (05394) 43440.

A beautiful lakeland hotel overlooking Lake Windermere, Blenheim Lodge offers peace and quiet yet is close to the Lake and shops. Jacqueline Sanderson is an expert in traditional English cuisine and guests' admiration for the food has resulted in the Sandersons own award-winning cookbook. Repeat visits vouch for the warm welcome and quality that are to be found here.

Bowness on Windermere continued

KNOLL HOTEL Lake Road, Bowness On Windermere

4 single, 4 double, 2 twin and 2 family bedrooms, 9 en suite. Colour TV, Tea/Coffee making facilities and telephones in all rooms. **Hours:** Breakfast 8.45am - 9.15am. Dinner 7pm - 7.30pm. Non residents welcome for dinner. **CC** Access, Visa. **Other Points:** Children over 3 years welcome. Garden. **P** **Directions:** Between Windermere Station and the Pier.

MRS BERRY ☎ (09662) 3756.

A large Victorian country house set in an acre of gardens and woodland, offering superb views over Lake Windermere, yet within easy reach of the shops and the bay.

RASTELLI RESTAURANT & PIZZERIA Lake Road, Bowness On Windermere.

Hours: Dinner 6pm - 10.45pm (last orders 10.40pm) Closed: Wednesdays and December to March. **Cuisine:** Pizzas, pasta and meat dishes. None. **CC** Access, Visa. **Other Points:** Booking not necessary. Eurocard also accepted. **Directions:** In the shopping centre in Bowness.

MR RASTELLI ☎ (09662) 4227

A bright, airy and modern restaurant situated in the centre of Bowness. Home baked pizzas and excellent Italian cuisine make this a firm favourite with locals, tourists - and Italians alike.

BRADFORD West Yorkshire **Map 9 B1**

FIVE FLAGS HOTEL Manywells Heights, Cullingworth.

Hours: Breakfast 7.30am - 9.30am. Lunch 12 noon - 2pm (last order 2pm). Dinner 7pm - 11pm (last orders 11pm). **Cuisine:** French cuisine. 26 rooms, all en suite. **CC** All major cards. **Other Points:** Children welcome. Open Sunday lunch and dinner. Conference facilities. **P** **(V)**

MR N KKAIS ☎ (0274) 834188.

Built in traditional Yorkshire stone blending in with the rural surroundings and offering panoramic views of the moors. The hotel is complemented by a beautiful landscaped garden (waterfall, pool) and provides two fine restaurants serving good quality, well prepared food. Attention to detail and friendly efficient staff.

BRAMPTON Cumbria **Map 8 A2**

OAKWOOD PARK HOTEL Longtown Road, Brampton.

4 twin, 4 double and 1 family bedrooms, 8 en suite. Tea/coffee making facilities. **Hours:** Breakfast 8.30am - 9.30am, Dinner 7pm - 8pm. **CC** Access, Visa. **Other Points:** Tennis court. Children welcome. Garden. Afternoon teas. No smoking in bedrooms. Lounge Bar. **P** **Directions:** A6071, 3 miles from Carlisle Airport.

MR & MRS R I PHILLIPS ☎ (06977) 2436.

A Victorian house standing off the road in its own secluded grounds with a pleasant garden and tennis court, on the edge of the historic market town of Brampton. The cuisine is mainly traditional but imaginative and the menu offers plenty of choice. Open fires are a feature of the Dining room and Drawing Room where television is available. Spacious, comfortable accommodation.

NORTHERN ENGLAND

BRERETON Cheshire **Map 8 C2**

⊗££ **THE BEAR'S HEAD HOTEL** Brereton, nr Sandbach.
Hours: Breakfast 7am - 9.30am, lunch 12.30pm - 2.30pm and dinner 7.30pm - 10pm (last orders). Closed: Sunday evening (for food only). **Cuisine:** Roast duckling, steak Roberto, chicken maison. Italian restaurant La Locanda serving homemade pasta dishes. ⊨ 24 bedrooms, all en suite. Bridal suite. **CC** All major cards. **Other Points:** Children welcome. No dogs. **P** &
Directions: On the A50 between junctions 17 and 18 on the M6.
MR R F TARQUINI ☎ (0477) 35251/2/3.
Dating back to 1615, the Bear's Head is an attractive black and white timbered building with all the original beams inside and out. Large garden with patio for summer barbecues.

BRIDLINGTON Humberside **Map 9 B2**

⊗££ **ELLIE MAES BISTRO** 55 High Street, Old Town, Bridlington.
Hours: Lunch 12 noon - 2pm, Dinner 7pm - 10pm (last orders). Closed: Sunday night, Monday lunchtime and the 1st 2 weeks of October. **Cuisine:** Dishes may include Ellie Mae's Steak with Garlic, Mushroom & Cream Sauce, Prawn Thermidor, Paella, Sole Fillet with Asparagus & Lemon. Specials on board. ⊨ None. **CC** Access, Visa. **Other Points:** Children welcome. No dogs. Garden dining. & **(V) Directions:** Well sign posted on entering Bridlington Old Town. One way Street.
PAUL BARRATT & ANGELA ALLEN ☎ (0262) 677605.
An attractive 19th century building which now houses this welcoming Bistro. The continental cuisine is well cooked and presented and the service is warm and courteous. The good food can be enjoyed in a pleasant, relaxed atmosphere. Popular with locals and holiday makers alike.

⌑££ **SOUTH BAY HOTEL** 11 Roundhay Road, Bridlington.
⊨ 1 single, 4 double, 2 twin and 2 family bedrooms, 3 en suite. Tea making facilities. Central heating. **Hours:** Breakfast 8.30am, Lunchtime sandwiches and drinks (residents only) 12 12 noon - 2pm and Dinner 5.30pm. Bar snacks 8pm - 9pm. Closed: January and **CC** Access, Visa. **Other Points:** Small, comfortable bar area. Attractive dining room & lounge. Patio area with garden tables & chairs. 2 Crown E.T.B approved. Residential license. **P**
Directions: Follow signs to South Beach,past Spa Theatre right into Mayfield Rd.
BRENDA & ALAN TAYLOR ☎ (0262) 674944.
A small family run hotel, specialising in good quality, courtesy and service. Within walking distance of one of Britain's most beautiful beaches, now holding the Blue Flag Award.

⌑£ **THE TENNYSON HOTEL** 19 Tennyson Avenue, Bridlington.
⊨ 3 double, 3 twin. 4 bedrooms en suite. Colour TV, radio, alarm, trouser press, telephone and tea/coffee making facilities. Room service. Free morning newspaper. Four poster suites available. **Hours:** Breakfast 7.30am - 9am, Lunch as required, Dinner 6pm - 8.30pm. **CC** Access, Visa. **Other Points:** Vegetarian meals. Afternoon teas. Dogs allowed. No smoking area. Residents' lounge. Garden. **P** **(V) Directions:** Off the Promenade, near Trinity Church.
LINDA STALKER ☎ (0262) 604382.

BROUGHTON IN FURNESS

Bridlington continued

A family run hotel with comfortable bedrooms and offering English cuisine and a 'healthy option' menu. Popular with holiday makers and business people alike, the Tennyson is conveniently situated close to the sea front and to Leisure World. Good value for money.

BRIGG Humberside **Map 9 C2**

⊗££ **ARTIES MILL** Wressle Road, Castlethorpe, Nr Brigg.

🛏££ **Hours:** Breakfast 7am - 9am, lunch 11.45am - 2pm, dinner 6.45pm - 10pm. Restaurant closed Sunday evening. **Cuisine:** A la carte, table d'Hote, bar meals. English cuisine. 🛏 18 bedrooms, 13 en suite. 💳 All major cards. **Other Points:** Children welcome. Garden. Function room: 90-100 people, disco or live entertainment can be arranged. Upstairs Round Room: private dinner parties. 🅿 ♿ (V) **Directions:** 1 mile from Brigg on the A18 and 5 miles from Scunthorpe.
IAN & DOREEN BRIGGS ☎ (0652) 52094.

This charming old windmill dates back to 1790 and the adjoining grain sheds have been converted into bars and restaurants with a pleasant and friendly atmosphere whilst still retaining the fascinating mill features. Good food, comfortable accommodation and the warm friendly welcome from the proprietors, Mr & Mrs Briggs, combines to make this hotel 'highly recommended'.

BROUGH SOWERBY Cumbria **Map 8 B2**

⊗£ **THE BLACK BULL INN** Brough Sowerby, Nr Kirkby Stephen, Cumbria.

Hours: Bar meals 11.30am to 2.00pm and, in the evening, 6.00pm - 9.00pm. Basket meals served 9pm until late. **Cuisine:** Barbecued spare ribs, chicken kiev, lasagne and bar snacks. 🛏 None. 💳 None. **Other Points:** Beer garden. Morning coffee 9.00am - 11.30am. Afternoon tea. Dogs allowed. Children welcome. Non-smoking area. 🅿 (V) **Directions:** On A685 between Brough and Kirkby Stephen in the Upper Eden valley.
MR G DUTTON ☎ (07683) 41413.

Country Inn where the staff are keen to make guests feel at home, the food is professionally prepared, and the steaks are served in particularly generous portions. Situated within easy reach of the Yorkshire Dales and the Lake District National Park.

BROUGHTON IN FURNESS Cumbria **Map 8 B1**

⊗£££ **BESWICKS RESTAURANT** Langholme House, The Square, Broughton in Furness.

Hours: Dinner 7.30pm - 12 midnight (last orders at approx. 9.30pm). Closed: Sunday, Monday and Tuesday unless demand allows. **Cuisine:** 5 course table d'hote menu. Main courses may include Rack of Lamb with cumberland sauce, Roast quail, Poached salmon steak with parsley sauce. 🛏 None. 💳 Access, Visa. **Other Points:** Children welcome. No dogs. No-smoking area. 🅿 (V) **Directions:** Junction of A595 & A593, in the centre of Broughton in Furness.
CHRISTINE ROE ☎ (0229) 716285.

A traditional Lakeland house facing the square in the village of Broughton, well-decorated and comfortably furnished. The 5

Broughton in Furness continued

course set menu offers a good choice of English dishes, cooked with flair. The tranquil and unhurried atmosphere, unobtrusive classical music and excellent service, ideally complement the high standard of cuisine with all dishes freshly cooked to order.

BURY Greater Manchester **Map 8 C2**

⊗££ **ROSCO'S EATING HOUSE** 173 Radcliffe Road, Bury.
Hours: Meals served Sunday, Wednesday and Thursday 7.30pm - 12 midnight and Friday and Saturday 4.30pm - 4am. Closed: Monday & Tuesday. **Cuisine:** From simple meals costing a few pounds to original dishes with imaginative sauces freshly made to order. Large selection of fresh vegetables. ⊨ None. **CC** Access, Visa. **Other Points:** Limited access for disabled. Children welcome. No dogs. Coaches by appointment. **P** **(V) Directions:** Whitfield Rd from centre, Rt at traffic lights nr Pack Horse Pub. STUART AND JACQUELINE RUSCOE ☎ (061) 797 5404.
Owned and run by 2 chefs, the atmosphere is definitely 'foody'. The unassuming frontage hides a simple and welcoming restaurant which specialises in original dishes served in a distinctive style. The charcoal grill is placed so that everyone can see their steaks cooking. Booking advisable at weekends as Rosco's is very popular with locals & other caterers - hence the late opening.

⊗££ **THE BOLHOLT** Walshaw Road, Bury.
⌂£££ **Hours:** Breakfast 7.30am - 8.45am, Lunch 12 noon - 2pm and
CLUB Dinner 7pm - 9.30pm (last orders). **Cuisine:** A la carte. Traditional English - Fillet Steak Wellington. ⊨ 47 bedrooms, some en suite. **CC** All major cards. **Other Points:** Children welcome. Garden. Pets allowed. **P** ⅖ **(V) Directions:** A58 from Bury towards Bolton, fork left at Dusty Miller pub.
STEFAN SIKORSKI ☎ (061) 764 3888
A large country house, set in 50 acres of parkland, with several modern extensions. The warm and courteous hospitality makes this hotel a joy to visit.

BUTTERMERE Cumbria **Map 8 A1**

⊗£ **BRIDGE HOTEL** Buttermere, Cumbria.
Hours: Bar meals 12 noon - 9.30pm daily. Restaurant open to non-residents. Open all year. **Cuisine:** Traditional Cumbrian dishes and French cuisine, eg. Cumberland hot pot with black pudding, Cumbrian sausages. ⊨ 22 bedrooms all with private bathroom. **CC** None. **Other Points:** Children welcome in restaurant and on patio in summer. Dogs allowed (except in public rooms). **P** ⅖ **(V) Directions:** On the B5289 Keswick to Buttermere Road.
PETER McGUIRE ☎ (059 685) 252/266.
In a beautiful and unspoiled lakeland valley with easy access to both Buttermere Lake and Crummock Water. Superb unrestricted walking country with wonderful mountain scenery.

BUXTON Derbyshire **Map 8 C2**

⌂£ **GRIFF GUEST HOUSE** 2 Compton Road, Buxton.
⊨ 1 single, 2 double, 2 twin and 1 family bedroom. 1 bathrooms, 1 shower. Tea/coffee facilities & colour TV in all bedrooms. **Hours:** Breakfast 7am - 8.30am, dinner 6pm - 6.30pm. **CC** None.

Buxton continued

Other Points: Central heating. Children welcome. Residents lounge. TV. Garden. Pets welcome. Vegetarian meals available. ▣
COLIN J. SCRUTON ☎ (0298) 23628.

Comfortable, homely accommodation situated in the heart of the Peak District. Ideal centre for touring and exploring the beautiful countryside and local attractions. Superb food prepared on the premises by the chef/proprietor who pays great attention to detail.

⊗£££ **LEE WOOD HOTEL** The Park, Buxton.

Hours: Open from 7am - 12 midnight. **Cuisine**: English and European dishes, beefsteak and kidney pie, Sunday roast, hot apple pie. ⊨ 36 bedrooms, all en suite. All with colour TV, and other modern facilities. ◪ All major cards. **Other Points**: Children welcome. Indoor garden. Dogs permitted. Telex 669848. Fax No: (0298) 23228. ▣ **(V) Directions**: Off the A5004, close to the Derbyshire Royal Hospital.
MR JOHN C MILLICAN ☎ (0298) 23002.

Pleasantly situated in its own grounds, it is only a few minutes walk from the town centre and places of entertainment. Ideal for golfers as there are two golf courses nearby. Other facilities include tennis courts, swimming pool and the new ' Garden Room' Conservatory Restaurant.

⊗££ **OLD HALL HOTEL** The Square, Buxton.

⏛£££ **Hours**: Breakfast 7.30am - 9.30am, lunch and bar snacks 12 noon - 2.30pm (last orders), dinner 6pm - 11pm (last orders 10pm), evening bar snacks 6pm - 11pm (last orders 10.30pm). Snacks served all day Saturday & Sunday. **Cuisine**: Serving bar snacks, full a la carte menu and table d'hote. ⊨ 38 bedrooms, 32 en suite. ◪ Access, Visa, AmEx. **Other Points**: Childen welcome. Afternoon teas. Garden dining. Fax No. (0298) 72437. Weddings catered for. Conference facilities. ⴱ **(V) Directions**: Centre of Buxton, past the crescent.
GEORGE & LOUISE POTTER ☎ (0298) 22841.

This historic hotel, dating back to the 16th century, has entertained thousands of visitors including Mary Queen of Scots. Overlooking the Pavillion Gardens and Opera House, this hotel is an ideal base for those wishing to take the waters, with its good food and comfortable accommodation.

⏛£££ **THE PORTLAND HOTEL** St John's Road, Buxton.

CLUB ⊨ 3 single, 8 double, 11 twin and 3 family bedrooms, all en suite. Colour TV, radio, direct dial telephone and tea/coffee making facilities in all rooms. **Hours**: Breakfast 8am - 9.30am, lunch 12.30pm - 2pm, dinner 6.45pm - 9pm (last orders). ◪ All major cards. **Other Points**: Central heating. Children welcome. Licensed. Residents lounge. Park restaurant. ▣ **Directions**: Situated on the A53 opposite the Pavillion Gardens.
MR & MRS MILLNER & MRS GILL ☎ (0298) 22462/71493.

A comfortable family run hotel in the heart of the Peak District. Central location opposite Pavillion Gardens and the swimming pool and 200 yards from the Opera House.The Portland Hotel has gained the reputation for friendliness and traditional service and offers excellent facilities for the tourist and business visitor.

NORTHERN ENGLAND

CALDER BRIDGE Cumbria **Map 8 B1**

⊗££ **THE STANLEY ARMS HOTEL** Calder Bridge, Seascale.
Hours: Lunch 11am - 2.30pm, Dinner 6pm - 10pm (last orders).
Bar meals 11am - 2.30pm and 6pm - 10pm. **Cuisine:** Mainly
traditional English cuisine including rack of lamb, steaks and
salmon. ⊨ 10 bedrooms, 6 en suite. **CC** All major cards. **Other
Points:** Children welcome. Beer garden. Dogs allowed. Special
weekend and Bank Holiday discount breaks, bed, breakfast and
dinner. ▣ ⅙ **Directions:** A595 West Cumbria coast road, 3 miles
south of Egremont.
MIKE & MOLLY PORTEOUS ☎ (0946) 84 235/760.
*This family run freehouse is housed in an 18th century coaching
inn. The hotel is set amidst beautiful West Cumbrian
countryside and the salmon and sea trout River Calder flows
through the hotel gardens, boasting deep holding pools for
game fishing. Friendly service and good home cooked food.
Close to the Western lakes and the award-winning Georgian
town of Whitehaven.*

CARLISLE Cumbria **Map 8 A2**

⅏££ **ANGUS HOTEL** 14 Scotland Road, Carlisle.
CLUB ⊨ 1 single, 4 twin, 2 double and 4 family bedrooms, 6 with en
suite facilities. **Hours:** Breakfast 7.30am - 8.45am, Dinner 6.30pm
- 8pm (7.30pm Sundays). No meals served Sundays October -
April unless prior booking. Hotel open all year. **CC** Access, Visa.
Other Points: Children welcome. Dogs allowed. Some areas non-
smoking. 3 course menu and additional bar style meals.
Residential license. TV lounge. Vegetarian meals. ▣ **Directions:**
Leave M6/A74 at Jct. 44. Hotel at 5th set of traffic lights. A7.
ELAINE & GEOFF WEBSTER ☎ (0228) 23546.
*At the Angus hotel you will find a warm welcome and an
emphasis on making guests feel at home. Good home cooked
food is available daily complimented by a residential licence.
The accommodation is comfortable and some rooms have the
added facilities of radio alarm clocks and hairdryers. A friendly
place to stay at very reasonable prices.*

⅏££ **CRAIGBURN FARMHOUSE** Catlowdy, Penton, nr Longtown,
Carlisle.
⊨ 4 family and 2 twin bedrooms all with en suite facilities.
Tea/coffee making facilities in all rooms. **Hours:** Breakfast 8am -
8.30am, dinner 7pm order by 5pm. Sunday lunch 1pm. Closed:
December. **CC** None. **Other Points:** Central heating. Children
welcome. Licensed. Residents lounge. TV. Garden. ▣ **Directions:**
Situated on B6318 3 miles from the Scottish border.
MRS JANE LAWSON ☎ (0228) 577214.
*An 18th century working farm in a quiet rural area. Only a few
miles from M6 and A7 - a perfect stopping place for
North/South travellers. However, for those staying longer there
is plenty to do both on the farm and locally. Finalist in national
cookery competition.*

⊗£ **ROYAL HOTEL** 9 Lowther Street, Carlisle.
⅏££ **Hours:** Breakfast 7.30am - 9am, lunch 11.30am - 1.30pm (last
orders 1.20pm), dinner 6.30pm - 8.30pm Tuesday - Saturday.
Sunday 6pm, Monday 6pm - 7pm. **Cuisine:** Serves high tea,
shoppers lunch, evening meals and childrens meals (under 12s).

Carlisle continued

20 rooms. 8 single, 0 twin and 4 double rooms. 11 en suite rooms. **CC** Access, Visa. **Other Points:** Children welcome. Dogs allowed. **Directions:** On A69. Nearest motorway exit is 43 (M6). MR PETER RIDLEY ☎ (0228) 22103.

Situated in centre of city the Royal Hotel is reputed by locals for its good food and value. There is a relaxed homely atmosphere due to the number of locals frequenting the hotel. The accommodation is spacious and traditional. A family run hotel.

⊗£ **THE ROYAL OAK** Scotby, Carlisle.
Hours: Bar meals 12 noon - 2pm and 6pm - 8.30pm. Sunday 12 noon - 2pm, 7pm - 8.30pm. **Cuisine:** Bar meals including Goujons of Plaice, Farmhouse Grill, Cumberland Sausage, Lasagne, Chicken in Barbecue sauce, 'T'bone steak, salads and rolls. None. **CC** None. **Other Points:** Children welcome. Dogs allowed. Beer garden. Open Bank Holidays. **Directions:** 2 miles east of Carlisle on A69. Cross M6, 1st right to Scotby. GEOFF & LINDA MITCHELL ☎ (0228) 513463.

A very popular public house in the attractive North Cumbrian village of Scotby. The Royal Oak has a good reputation locally for its well cooked bar meals. Welcoming staff and a friendly atmosphere. Only 3 miles from the historic city of Carlisle.

⊗££ **THE STRING OF HORSES INN & RESTAURANT** Faugh, ⌂£££ nr Carlisle.
Hours: Open 11.30am - 3pm and 5.30pm - 12 midnight (last orders 9.30pm). **Cuisine:** In the bar: seafood, Indian curries, steak & oyster pie, old English fish pie. In the restaurant: Salmon Elizabeth, veal scallopine. 14 bedrooms, all en suite. **CC** All major cards. **Other Points:** Children welcome. Dogs by arrangement. Fax No: (0228) 70675. **(V) Directions:** M6 exit 43. Off the A69 for Heads Nook and Faugh. MR E TASKER ☎ (0228) 70297.

Romantic 17th century inn with the luxuries of a 5 star hotel. Some four-poster suites and double baths, Whirlpool spa, sauna, solarium, outdoor pool. Ideal touring venue for northern lakes and Borders.

⊗£ **VALLUM HOUSE GARDEN HOTEL** Burgh Road, Carlisle.
⌂££ **Hours:** Breakfast 7.30am - 9.30am. Restaurant and bar meals CLUB served 12 noon - 2pm and 6pm - 9.30pm. **Cuisine:** Cumberland ham or bacon and eggs. Vegetarian menu. 9 bedrooms, 5 en suite. **CC** Access. **Other Points:** Children welcome. No smoking area. **& (V) Directions:** Situated 1.5 miles west of Carlisle off B5307. THOMAS R JENKINS - Chairman P.F.D Ltd. ☎ (0228) 21860

Vallum Garden Hotel is an ideal location for businessmen and holiday makers. On fine days bar meals are served in the magnificent gardens. The hotel is situated above the site of a 'vallum', a ditch excavated for earthworks for Hadrian's Wall, and on what was the Roman encampment. Highly recommended.

CARNFORTH Lancashire **Map 8 B2**

🏠£££ **NEW CAPERNWRAY FARM** Capernwray, Carnforth.

`CLUB` ⊨ 1 double with en suite and 2 twin with private facilities. Colour TV in all bedrooms. **Hours:** Breakfast 8.30am, dinner 7.30pm (order by 5pm). **CC** Access, Visa. **Other Points:** Central heating. Children over 10 years welcome. Residents lounge and dining room. Garden. Dogs welcome. Simple vegetarian meals by prior arrangement. **P Directions:** Exit 35, M6. Take B6254 to Over Kellet. Left at village green, 2m.

MRS SALLY TOWNEND ☎ (0524) 734284

A 17th century former farmhouse with exposed beams and stone walls. Peace and quiet, good food and elegant comfort all contribute to make this a very popular little establishment and a national prize-winner.

⊗££ **PINE LAKE** Dock Acres, Carnforth.

Hours: Breakfast 7.30am - 10am, lunch 12 noon - 2pm (last orders), dinner 6pm - 9.30pm (last orders), bar snacks 12 noon - 5pm (last orders). **Cuisine:** Menu may feature - lettuce and bacon soup with cheese scones, steamed seafood and shellfish with chablis sorrel sauce. ⊨ **CC** All major cards. **Other Points:** Children welcome. Open Bank Holidays. No smoking area. Afternoon teas. Swimming pool. Lake. Gym. Conference facilities. Fax No. (0524) 736793. **P** ও **(V) Directions:** Junction 35, M6. Follow signs to Carnforth, 1 mile away.

STEWART MORREL - Manager ☎ (0524) 736191.

Situated in the open rural countryside of North Lancashire, this hotel offers many activities to occupy all visitors. With a 70 acre watersport lake, you can try your hand at waterskiing, sailing, canoeing or windsurfing. The two restaurants offer well cooked meals served by pleasant staff and the accommodation is of a very high standard. Ideal base for touring Lake District.

CASTLETON Derbyshire **Map 8 C2**

🏠££ **RAMBLER'S REST** Back St, Millbridge, Castleton.

⊨ 5 bedrooms, 2 of them en suite, also suitable for family or twin. Some rooms let as singles. All rooms have colour TVs and tea/coffee making facilities. **Hours:** 8.30am - 9am. **CC** None. **Other Points:** Children welcome. Pets allowed. Open bank holidays. **P** ও **(V) Directions:** Off the A625.

MARY & PETER GILLOTT ☎ (0433) 620125.

The Rambler's Rest is a quietly situated, well-established 17th century guest house set in the picturesque village of Castleton.

Castleton continued

A very pleasant place to stay and explore the surrounding area, with Mam Tor and Peveril Castle in the immediate vicinity.

⊗££ **YE OLDE CHESHIRE CHEESE INN** How Lane, Castleton.
££ **Hours:** 8.30am - 9am, 12 noon - 2.30pm, and 6pm - 9pm (last orders). **Cuisine:** Imaginative dishes including smoked chicken in Stilton sauce, game, a range of pies, roast wild boar, salads & burgers. Good wine list. 1 single, 3 twin, and 2 double, all en suite. All rooms have colour TVs, hairdryers, and tea/coffee making facilities. CC Access, Visa. **(V) Directions:** In Hope Valley. MR CUNLIFFE ☎ (0433) 620330.

A 17th century, traditional black and white inn set in Castleton village. Ye Olde Cheshire Cheese Inn offers a very good range of dishes at good value for money, served by very friendly and efficient staff.

CHESTER Cheshire **Map 8 C2**

££ **CHEYNEY LODGE HOTEL** 77-79 Cheyney Road, Chester. 8 bedrooms, all en suite. All rooms have colour TV, radio and tea/coffee making facilities. **Hours:** Breakfast, Lunch 12 noon - 2pm, Dinner 6.30pm - 9pm. CC Access, Visa. **Other Points:** Children very welcome. No dogs. Licensed Bar. Drawing room for families. 3 crowns - English Tourist Board. P ♿ **(V) Directions:** From the city centre take A540 - Hoylake, left into Cheyney Rd. KEVIN DIXON - Manager ☎ (0244) 381925.

Half a mile from the City's Roman Wall, Cheyney Lodge was originally three houses. Recently completely refurbished, the hotel is now attractively decorated and provides good quality accommodation, a cosy bar, small dining room and separate lounge. A small, well-furnished hotel with a welcoming atmosphere and good, homecooked meals, offering good value for money.

⊗££ **FRANCS RESTAURANT** 14 Cuppin Street, Chester.
Hours: Plats du Jour served Monday - Saturday 12 noon - 7pm, a la carte 6pm - 11pm (last orders). **Cuisine:** Provincial French cuisine. House specialities include traditional French provincial casseroles, crepes and homemade sausages. None. CC Access, Visa, AmEx. **Other Points:** Children welcome. For parties of 4 or more, a 6-course feast, La Grande Bouffe - an alternative menu. Evening parking (free). Air conditioned. ♿ **(V) Directions:** Off Grosvenor Rd, nr main North Wales roundabout. Police Station. D JOHNSTON-CREE ☎ (0244) 317952.

A 17th century oak beamed building within the City walls serving top quality, exclusively French cuisine. Wide choice of dishes whether you are looking for 'un petit morceau' or a whole feast. The wine list has been produced to compliment their menus and there is a wide range of French aperitifs and liqueurs. A friendly, relaxing and informal atmosphere.

⊗£ **MAMMA MIA** St Werburgh Street, Chester.
Hours: Lunch 12 noon - 2.30pm, dinner 6pm - 11pm. Closed: Sundays. **Cuisine:** Authentic Italian dishes - pizzas, pasta, calamari fritti, filetto. None. CC All major cards. **Other Points:** Children welcome. No dogs. ♿ **Directions:** Next to the Cathedral. GIUSEPPE & ANNA LABELLA ☎ (0244) 314663.

Chester continued

A friendly Italian pizzeria with a lively atmosphere. Diners can watch chefs preparing and cooking the pizzas in the traditional way due to an open plan kitchen. Popular with locals and tourists alike.

⊗££ **PACINO'S TRATTORIA** Newtown Close, St Anne Street, Chester.
Hours: Meals served 6.30pm - 11.30pm (last orders). **Cuisine:** Italian, with chef's specialities. ⊨ None. 🆑 Access, Visa. **Other Points:** Children welcome. 🅿 **(V) Directions:** Off St Oswalds Way in residential area.
ALAN SPINDLER ☎ (0244) 372252.
A small modern Italian restaurant offering good food at reasonable prices in friendly and comfortable surroundings. Excellent service and well cooked dishes make this restaurant well worth the visit. Highly recommended.

⊞££ **REDLAND HOTEL** 64 Hough Green, Chester.
⊨ 2 single, 6 double and 3 twin bedrooms, all en suite. TV and tea/coffee making facilities in all rooms. Routiers Accommodation of the Year 1988. **Hours:** Breakfast 7.30am - 9.30am. 🆑 None. **Other Points:** Children welcome. Pets by arrangement. Residents' lounge. Licensed. Garden. Honeymoon suite with original Jacobean bed. 🅿 **Directions:** On the A549, 1 mile from the city centre.
MRS THERESA WHITE ☎ (0244) 671024.
An exquisite hotel with a unique Victorian ambiance recreated with genuine antiques, tasteful period furnishings and original wood panelling. Each of the rooms has been individually decorated and comprises all the facilities of a large hotel but with great character, charm and friendliness. The Redland turns a night away from home into a special experience.

⊗££ **ROWTON HALL HOTEL** Rowton Lane, Whitchurch Road.
Hours: Restaurant open 12 noon - 2pm and 7pm - 9.30pm. **Cuisine:** French and English cuisine. Game (in season), local salmon and trout. ⊨ 42 bedrooms en suite. 🆑 All major cards. **Other Points:** Children welcome. Full leisure facilities (restrictions for children). 🅿 ⅍ **Directions:** Just off the A41 Chester to Whitchurch road.
S D BEGBIE ☎ (0244) 335262.
A Georgian manor house converted to an hotel in 1955, 3 miles from Chester city. Set in 8 acres of gardens, the hall stands on Rowton Moor, site of one of the major battles in the English Civil War.

⊗££ **THE BLUE BELL RESTAURANT** 65 Northgate Street, Chester.
Hours: Lunch 12 noon - 2.30pm, Dinner 7pm - 10pm. **Cuisine:** English/French cuisine. ⊨ None. 🆑 Access, Visa. **Other Points:** Children welcome. Garden. Afternoon teas. No smoking areas. **(V)**
MRS GLENYS EVANS. ☎ (0244) 317758.
A delightful 15th century restaurant of real character including oak beams, sloping floors and resident ghost!

CHORLEY

Chester continued

⊛£ **THE SPINNING WHEEL TAVERN** The Old Warren, Broughton, Nr Chester.
Hours: Lunch and bar snacks 11.30am - 3pm (last orders 2.30pm), dinner and evening bar snacks 11pm (last orders 10.00pm, 10.30pm - Friday and Saturday). **Cuisine:** Specialities may include Sole Spinning Wheel (with white wine, mushrooms, prawns & cream), Tournedos Rossini. Blackboard specials change daily. ⊨ None. ☒ All major cards. **Other Points:** Children welcome. Open Bank Holidays. No smoking area. Garden dining. Traditional Sunday lunches. Weddings and parties catered for. ☐ & **(V) Directions:** On Old Main Rd from Broughton to Buckley, 6 miles from Chester.
MIKE & MAGGIE VERNON ☎ (0244) 531068/533637
Old roadside pub, attractively furnished and decorated with copper antiques and brass horse artifacts. Freshly prepared traditional meals are served in a convivial, welcoming atmosphere. Friendly staff and efficient service make meal complete. Good value for money.

⊛£ **THE STAFFORD HOTEL** City Road, Chester.
⊞££ **Hours:** Breakfast 7am - 9.30am. Dinner 6.30pm - 8.45pm. Closed: Lunchtimes and Sunday. **Cuisine:** Home made traditional dishes. ⊨ 4 singles, 8 doubles, 10 twins and 2 family rooms. 18 en suite. All rooms have Colour TV and tea/coffee making facilities. ☒ Access, Visa, AmEx. **Other Points:** No pets. Children welcome. Afternoon teas. Conference facilities. **(V) Directions:** Situated 2 minutes from Chester Railway Station.
MR & MRS GRAHAM ☎ (0244) 326052
A friendly family run hotel offering good food and accommodation. Five minutes walk from the historic centre of Chester.

CHISWORTH Derbyshire **Map 8 C2**
⊛££ **WOODHEYS FARM RESTAURANT** Glossop Road, Chisworth, nr Marple.
Hours: Meals 11.45am - 2pm (2.30pm on Sunday) and from 7pm - 10pm. Closed: Sunday evenings and Mondays. Routiers priced menu applies to lunches. **Cuisine:** English dishes, eg. Carvery roast. ⊨ None. ☒ Access, Visa. **Other Points:** Children welcome. No dogs. ☐ & **(V) Directions:** On the A626 between Marple and Glossop.
MRS REVINGTON ☎ (045 785) 2704.
Situated within a country park some 30 minutes from the centre of Manchester and on the edge of the Peak National Park. Lovely views through picture windows over surrounding countryside. The original farmhouse dates from the mid 1700s, but a new building now forms the major part of the dining room.

CHORLEY Lancashire **Map 8 C2**
⊛££ **HARTWOOD HALL HOTEL** Preston Road, Chorley.
[CLUB] **Hours:** Meals from 7.30am - 9am, 12 noon - 2pm and 7pm - 9pm (7pm - 8.30pm on Sunday). **Cuisine:** Steak Diane, Trout Cleopatra, Beef Strogonoff. ⊨ 22 bedrooms, most en suite. ☒ All major cards. **Other Points:** Children welcome. No dogs. Fax: (02572) 41678. ☐ & **(V) Directions:** 1 mile north of Chorley on the A6 Preston road.

Chorley continued

J E PILKINGTON ☎ (02572) 69966.

Situated 1 mile from the centre of Chorley and convenient for the M6 and M61. There are facilities for conferences, private buffets, dinners, dances or wedding receptions for up to 120 people.

CLEETHORPES Humberside **Map 9 C2**

⊗£ **AGRAH INDIAN RESTAURANT** 7-9 Sea View Street, Cleethorpes.

Hours: Lunch 12 noon - 2.30pm, dinner 6pm - 12pm. **Cuisine:** Tandoori dishes. ⊨ None. ₢ Access, Visa. **Other Points:** Children welcome. ₧ **(V)**

BASHIR MIAH ☎ (0472) 698669

The Agrah Indian Restaurant is decorated with brightly coloured pictures, illustrating a story, and with Muslim style wall panels. A broad clientele, including many thespians from the seasonal summer shows.

⊗£ **STEELS CORNER HOUSE RESTAURANT** 11-13 Market Street.

Hours: Open 9am - 10pm (Saturday until 11pm). Meals served all day, including Breakfast 9am - 11am. **Cuisine:** Fish and chips. Grills. Business lunches. ⊨ None. ₢ All major cards. **Other Points:** Children welcome. No dogs. ₧ **(V) Directions:** In the market place behind the Dolphin Hotel.

MESSRS P & K OLIVER ☎ (0472) 692644.

A popular and friendly restaurant which continues to provide excellent value for money.

CLITHEROE Lancashire **Map 8 B2**

⊗££ **CALF'S HEAD HOTEL** Worston, Clitheroe.

⊞£££ **Hours:** Breakfast 7.30am - 10am, lunch 12 noon - 2pm and dinner 7pm - 9.30pm (last orders). Bar meals 12 noon - 2pm and 7pm - 9.30pm. **Cuisine:** Full a la carte menu, bar meals, Sunday 'Hot Calvery' (12 noon - 6pm). Barbecues on request. All food homemade using fresh, local produce. ⊨ 6 bedrooms, all en suite with bath & shower. Direct dial telephone, CTV, Video, Tea/coffee/toast making, trouser press, hair dryer, baby listening. ₢ All major cards. **Other Points:** Dogs allowed. Children welcome. Weekend breaks available. Golf course nearby. ₧ ♿ **(V) Directions:** Situated just off A59.

MR & MRS DAVIS ☎ (0200) 41218/41510.

Nestling in the historic village of Worston, the hotel offers a variety of dining locations, including the beautiful walled garden with stream and rustic bridge for warm summer days. In winter, roaring fires in the a la carte dining room or intimate Tudor Room and Bar Lounge area will melt away the chill.

⊗££ **SPREAD EAGLE HOTEL (SAWLEY) LTD** Sawley, nr Clitheroe.

Hours: Restaurant open 12.30pm - 2pm and 7pm - 9pm all year round. **Cuisine:** All steaks - beef from Aberdeen Angus stock. ⊨ 10 bedrooms, all en suite. ₢ All major cards. **Other Points:** Children welcome. No dogs. ₧ ♿ **(V) Directions:** Off the A59, ½ mile down the road to Sawley Village.

PETER SPENCER - Manager ☎ (0200) 41202/41406.

Clitheroe continued

Owing to its popularity it is advisable to book for Sunday lunch, Friday and Saturday dinner. Situated on a bend of the River Ribble with lovely views across the river to the surrounding countryside. An excellent base from which to tour the Dales and the Lake District.

⊗££ **THE INN AT WHITEWELL** Whitewell, Forest of Bowland, Nr
⊡££££ Clitheroe.
[W] **Hours:** Bar open 11am - 3pm and 6pm - 11pm. Morning coffee
⊙ and afternoon tea. Dinner and bar suppers 7.30pm - 9.15pm.
Cuisine: Homemade soups. Steak, kidney and mushroom pie. Local lamb. Homemade ice cream. ⊨ 9 bedrooms, all en suite. ⟨⟩ All major cards. **Other Points:** Children welcome. ⊡ ⅃ **(V) Directions:** Follow signs to Whitewell from roundabout in Longridge centre.
RICHARD & PAM BOWMAN ☎ (02008) 222.
A lovely riverside setting with 6 miles of salmon, sea trout and trout fishing for residents. Log fires and antique furniture create a homely atmosphere. The inn has magnificent views across the trough of Bowland and provides an ideal location for exploring on foot.

CONISTON Cumbria **Map 8 B2**

⊗££ **CONISTON LODGE HOTEL** Sunny Brow, Coniston.
⊡££££ **Hours:** Breakfast 8.30am - 9.30am, Dinner 7pm - 7.30pm (last orders). Non-residents welcome but booking in advance strongly recommended. Closed: Sunday and Monday dinner and at Christmas. **Cuisine:** Traditional English and local dishes such as freshly caught Coniston Char. Full Lakeland-style breakfast. ⊨ 6 bedrooms, all en suite. ⟨⟩ Access, Visa. **Other Points:** Totally non-smoking. Residents' lounge. Mastercard and Eurocard also accepted. Vegetarian meals available on request. ⊡ **Directions:** Turn up hill at crossroads by filling station on A593.
ANTHONY & ELIZABETH ROBINSON ☎ (05394) 41201.
A family run hotel offering very high standards of comfort yet retaining a homely feel with country cottage style furnishing. The dining room serves excellent homemade cuisine, presented with originality and flair. Comfortable accommodation with beautiful views. The warm welcome and good service is vouched for by the large number of repeat bookings every year.

⊗££ **SUN HOTEL CONISTON** Coniston.
⊡££££ **Hours:** Breakfast 8am - 9.30am. dinner 7pm - 8.30pm. Bar meals 12 noon - 2pm and 6pm - 9pm. **Cuisine:** English cuisine, using fresh local produce. ⊨ 11 bedrooms, 9 en suite and 2 with private separate bathroom. ⟨⟩ Access, Visa. **Other Points:** Children welcome. Pets allowed by arrangement. Open Sunday dinner and bank holidays. ⊡ **(V) Directions:** Just off the A593 running through Coniston, signposted from main rd.
THE ELSON FAMILY ☎ (05394) 41248.
Hotel adjoining 16th century inn in own grounds at foot of Coniston Old Man, with superb views, good food and a very friendly atmosphere. Located 1 mile from Coniston Water, it was Donald Campbell's H.Q during his attempt on the world water speed record, and is a perfect spot for all water-sports.

NORTHERN ENGLAND

CREWE Cheshire **Map 8 C2**
⊗££ **THE CHESHIRE CASSEROLE** Earle Street.
[CLUB] **Hours:** Meals served Tuesday to Saturday 12 noon - 2pm and from
7.30pm. Closed Sunday and Monday. Extensive range of bar
snacks available lunches and evenings. **Cuisine:** Casseroles, black
pepper steak. ⊨ 13 bedrooms all en suite. **CC** All major cards.
Other Points: Children over 3 years welcome. Barbecues in fine
weather. No dogs. Walled garden. **P**
BRIAN & JOAN SHANNON ☎ (0270) 585479.
*As the name suggests, this restaurant specialises in hearty
home-cooked casseroles. Brian and Joan have owned and run
this restaurant for many years and its popularity is a reflection of
their high standards and hard work.*

DARLINGTON North Yorkshire **Map 9 B1**
⊗£ **GEORGE HOTEL** Cliffe, near Piercebridge, Darlington.
⊞£££ **Hours:** Breakfast 7.30am - 11am, Lunch 11.30am - 3pm, Dinner
[CLUB] 6.30pm - 10pm. **Cuisine:** A la carte menu and bar meals. ⊨ 24
rooms. All en suite. **CC** Access, Visa, AmEx. **Other Points:**
Children welcome. Riverside garden. Afternoon teas. Coach
parties catered for. **P (V) Directions:** Off the B6275.
MR WAIN ☎ (0325) 374576.
*This 17th Century Coaching Inn is set on the grassy banks of the
River Tees. The restaurant offers excellent value for money
dishes, complemented by a varied selection of good wines.
Comfortable accommodation and friendly efficient service.*

DERBY Derbyshire **Map 9 C1**
⊗££ **HOTEL RISTORANTE LA GONDOLA** 220 Osmaston Road,
⊞£££token Derby.
Hours: Breakfast 7am - 9am, lunch 12.15pm - 2pm, dinner 7pm -
10pm (last orders) Closed: Sundays. **Cuisine:** Traditional English
and Continental cuisine. dishes include Pork Cutlet Pizzaiola,
Rainbow Trout, Roast duckling. ⊨ 20 rooms. 2 twin, 11 double
and 7 family rooms. All en suite. **CC** All major cards. **Other Points:**
Children welcome. Afternoon teas served. Fax (0332) 384512.
Conference rooms available. **P** ♿ **(V) Directions:** Set back from a
dual carriageway into Derby.
MR R GIOVANNELLI ☎ (0332) 32895
*The Hotel Ristorante La Gondola is situated in the scenic beauty
of the Peak District. The hotel is elegantly decorated and very
comfortable. Meals are cooked from fresh produce and served
in generous portions which are enjoyed by locals and holiday
makers alike. Staff are friendly and pleasant, adding to the
relaxed atmosphere of the hotel.*

⊗££ **VINEYARD ON THE PARK** 432 Kedleston Road, Allestree,
Derby.
Hours: Lunch 12 noon - 3pm (last orders 2pm, Dinner 7pm - 12
midnight (last orders 10pm). Closed: Sunday night. **Cuisine:** A la
carte, fixed 3 course menu, bar snacks/meals. Wide variety of
dishes including vegetarian selection. ⊨ None. **CC** Access, Visa.
Other Points: Children welcome. Garden. **P** ♿ **(V)**
MR PATRICK. ☎ (0332) 553263.
*This attractive Hacienda style building is enhanced by a
pleasant garden with a pond and fountain. The restaurant hosts*

Derby continued

a dinner dance every Saturday night with a variety of musicians. The food is superb and beautifully presented.

DONCASTER South Yorkshire **Map 9 C1**
⊗££ **GATEWAY RESTAURANT** Station Road, Barnby Dun, Nr Doncaster.

Hours: 12 noon - 2pm, and 7.30pm - 11.30pm (last orders 10.30pm, 11.30pm at weekends). Closed: Mondays. **Cuisine:** English cuisine, including Gateway special rump steak. ⊨ None. **CC** Access, Visa. **Other Points:** Children welcome. No dogs. Open Sundays and bank holidays. **P** & **(V) Directions:** Barnby Dun is 5 miles E of Doncaster. 5 mins from junction 4 on M18.
B & L SMITH ☎ (0302) 882849.

Friendly restaurant with comfortable lounge and spacious, but intimate, dining area. Places of interest nearby include Conisboro Castle, Doncaster museum and Doncaster race course.

⊗££ **GREEN TREE INN** Tudworth Road, Hatfield, Doncaster.
⊞££ **Hours:** Meals served 12 noon - 2.30pm (Monday to Saturday) and
CLUB 6.30pm - 10pm. Sunday meals served 12 noon - 2.30pm and 7pm - 10pm. **Cuisine:** Various steaks and flambe dishes. ⊨ 4 bedrooms - 2 twin or single, 2 double, all with shower. **CC** All major cards. **Other Points:** Children welcome. No dogs. **P** & **Directions:** 1 mile from Hatfield at the junction of the A614 and A18.
TREVOR HAGAN ☎ (0302) 840305.

Situated 1 mile from Hatfield, this large public house offers excellent bar and restaurant meals. Additionally, there is a large ballroom and the inn can cater for dinner dances, weddings and conferences with a seating capacity for 120 people.

⊗££ **THE REGENT HOTEL, PARADE BAR & RESTAURANT**
⊞£££ Regent Square, Doncaster.

Hours: Restaurant open 11am - 11pm, 7 days a week. Meals served 7.30am - 9am, 12 noon - 2pm and 6pm - 10pm. **Cuisine:** Wide choice of menus and dishes includes Table d'hote, a la carte, Steak House menu, Sunday lunch, Tapas and vegetarian dishes. Giant menu. ⊨ 50 bedrooms, all en suite. **CC** All major cards. **Other Points:** Children allowed. No dogs. Coach parties welcome with prior notice. **P** **Directions:** On the main A638 road through Doncaster.
MICHAEL LONGWORTH ☎ (0302) 364180.

Established under same family ownership for 50 years, this well preserved, town centre Victorian building has the unique advantage of being situated in a small Regency Park on the A638. Close to Doncaster racecourse and an ideal stopping place when travelling north or south.

DRIFFIELD Humberside **Map 9 B2**
⊗££ **DOWNE ARMS** Little Driffield.

Hours: Lunch 12 noon - 2.30pm, Dinner 7pm - 9.30pm. Booking advised at weekends. **Cuisine:** Bar meals and a la carte menu: Dishes may include Rainbow Trout, Scampi a la Creme, Beef Wellington, Crofters Pork, Rack of Lamb. Traditional Sunday

Driffield continued

lunch 🍴 None. 💳 Access, Visa. **Other Points**: Children welcome. Garden dining. No dogs. 🚻 **(V) Directions**: Turning on right, 1 mile before Driffield on A166 from York.

STUART WOOD ☎ (0377) 42243.

A delightful 16th century public house and restaurant opposite the village green in Little Driffield. Separate lunch and dinner menus offer an extensive choice of excellently cooked dishes. The high standard of food is complemented by the comfortable, attractive decor, first class service and a warm and friendly atmosphere. Highly recommended whether for lunch or dinner.

DURHAM County Durham Map 9 A1

⊗£££ **HALLGARTH MANOR HOTEL** Pittington, Durham City.

🛏£££ **Hours**: Breakfast 7.30am - 9.30am, lunch 12 noon - 2pm, dinner 7pm - 9.15pm (last orders) bar snacks 12 noon - 2pm, 5.30pm - 9.30pm. Restaurant closed: lunchtimes except Sundays. **Cuisine**: A la carte menu, table d'hote and bar snacks. 🍴 23 bedrooms, all en suite. 💳 All major cards. **Other Points**: Children welcome. Afternoon teas served. Dogs allowed. Garden dining. Fax No. (091) 372 1249. 🅿 🚻 **(V) Directions**: 3 and a half miles from Durham city centre.

ALAN DUMIGHAM & TERENCE ROBSON. ☎ (091) 372 1188.

Located in the small village of Pittington, this hotel is brightly yet tastefully decorated. Frequented by all ages the hotel enjoys a relaxed atmosphere. First class food and accommodation of a high standard.

⊗£ **NEVILLE'S CROSS HOTEL** Darlington Road, Neville's Cross, Durham City.

Hours: Breakfast 8am - 9am Monday to Saturday, 9am - 10am Sunday and Bank Holidays. Lunch 12 noon - 2pm, dinner 7pm - 9pm (last orders 8.30pm - 8.45pm) Bar meals 12 noon - 2pm and 6.30pm - 9.30pm (approx.). **Cuisine**: Homemade steak and kidney pie, steaks grilled in red wine, veal flambe. 🍴 5 bedrooms. 💳 Access, Visa, AmEx. **Other Points**: Children welcome. Dogs allowed. Coaches by appointment. LV's accepted. **(V) Directions**: On the crossroads of the A167 and A690.

MR & MRS J B HOLLAND ☎ (091) 384 3872.

A small family run hotel on the outskirts of Durham with open fires which create a warm convivial atmosphere. ETB classification - 2 Crowns.

⊗££ **RAMSIDE HALL HOTEL** Carrville, nr. Durham.

Hours: Breakfast 7.30am - 10.30am, Lunch 12 noon - 2pm, Dinner 7pm - 9.30pm (last orders in restaurant). Last orders in Carvery 10.30pm. **Cuisine**: 3 eating areas - A La Carte Restuarant, Carvery, Grill Room. 🍴 82 bedrooms, all en suite. 💳 All major cards. **Other Points**: Children welcome. Tours/Coaches by arrangement. Fax No: (091) 386 0399. Telex No: 537681. 🅿 🚻 **(V) Directions**: On A690, just off the A1 motorway.

MR R J SMITH ☎ (091) 386 5282.

A Country House type hotel set into 280 acres of farm and parkland. Choice of 3 eating areas and musical entertainment 7 nights a week. The Ramside Hall Hotel provides an ideal venue for conferences/functions/weddings.

Durham continued

⊛££ **SEVEN STARS INN** Shincliffe Village, Durham.

⏰££ **Hours:** 8am - 9am, 12 noon - 2pm, and 7pm - 9pm. Bar meals 12
[CLUB] noon - 2pm and 7pm - 9.30pm. Bar menu within the £ Routiers
price bracket. **Cuisine:** English cuisine, with traditional roasts,
homemade lasagne, pies, and steaks. ⊨ 1 single, 6 double, and 1
twin, all en suite. All rooms have colour TV, radio, alarm,
telephone, tea/coffee facilities, trouser press adjacent to room.
CC Visa, AmEx, Diners. **Other Points:** Children welcome. No dogs
allowed. Open Sundays and bank holidays. Residents' lounge.
Hungarian spoken. Mastercard also accepted. **(V) Directions:**
From A1 take A177 to Bowburn, then main Rd into Shincliffe
village.
ANDREW & JEAN WINTERHALTER ☎ (091) 384 8454.
1725 coaching inn in charming village, in a conservation area
one mile from Durham City. The atmosphere is very relaxed and
friendly, the food is well prepared and served in generous
proportions, and the accommodation is very comfortable with all
major facilities, plus thoughtful extra touches. Close to Durham
Cathedral, castle and museums.

EAST AYTON North Yorkshire **Map 9 B2**

⏰£££ **CHURCH FARMHOUSE HOTEL AND COTTAGES** 3 Main
Street, East Ayton, nr Scarborough.
⊨ 1 single, 1 double, 1 twin and 2 family bedrooms, most en suite.
Colour TV, tea/coffee making, hairdryer etc. 3 Crowns
commended E.T.B. Holiday Cottages 5 Keys commended E.T.B.
Twin bedrooms, CH, all facilities very comfortable.
Hours: Breakfast 8.30am onwards (earlier if required), dinner
7.30pm or by request (order at breakfast). Packed lunches
available. **CC** None. **Other Points:** Central heating. Children
welcome. Licensed. Residents' lounge. TV. Garden. Games room.
Vegetarian meals by arrangement. ▣ ᕕ **Directions:** Situated on
the A170 in the North Yorks. National Park.
MRS SALLY CHAMBERLAIN ☎ (0723) 862102/863693
Listed 18th century farmhouse with many original features.
Very handy for the coast, historic houses, abbeys, York, Whitby,
Beverley and other attractions. Mrs Chamberlain creates a
homely and relaxing atmosphere. Full disabled access.
'Tourism for All' Award 1991. Y.H.T.B.

ECCLESTON Lancashire **Map 8 C2**

⊛£ **FARMERS ARMS** Towngate, Eccleston, nr Chorley.
⏰££ **Hours:** Breakfast 7am - 9am, lunch 12 noon - 2pm, dinner 5.30pm
- 10pm (last orders). Bar open all day. **Cuisine:** Wide choice of
dishes such as homemade steak & kidney pie, rack of lamb, and
mixed grill. Specials written on black board. ⊨ 4 bedrooms, 1 en
suite. **CC** None. **Other Points:** Children welcome. Childrens menu.
Beer garden. Afternoon teas. No dogs. ▣ **(V) Directions:** B5250
W. of M6 nr Chorley. 2 miles Charnock Richard service area M6.
BARRY S NEWTON ☎ (0257) 451594.
A country style pub with a warm, family atmosphere. Friendly
staff combined with a wide choice of good food served in
generous portions illustrate why the Farmers Arms enjoys such
popularity. For those wishing to stay in the area, or for travellers
on the M6, there are 4 comfortable bedrooms.

EDWINSTOWE Nottinghamshire **Map 9 C1**

⊗££ **MAID MARIAN RESTAURANT** 8 Church Street, Edwinstowe, Mansfield.

Hours: Open 9am - 10pm. **Cuisine:** Extensive grill, snack, table d'hote and a la carte menus. Excellent choice and value for money. ⊨ None. **CC** All major cards. **Other Points:** Children welcome. No dogs. Coaches by appointment. **P** & **(V) Directions:** Situated on the B6034 in the heart of Sherwood forest.

MR & MRS C A BENNETT ☎ (0623) 822266

Legend has it that Maid Marion and Robin Hood were married in the church opposite this restaurant. Still celebrating the occasion, the a la carte menu offers dishes such as Will Scarlet's Feast and Robin's Reward.

ELLAND West Yorkshire **Map 9 C1**

⊗££ **BERTIES BISTRO** 7/9 Town Hall Buildings, Elland.

Hours: Open Tuesday to Friday 7pm - 10.30pm, Saturday 6.30pm - 11pm and Sunday 5pm - 9pm. Closed: Mondays. **Cuisine:** Salad of smoked turkey and quail eggs; tartlette of mushrooms, scallops and dill; griddled lamb steak with fresh basil; and Berties bombe. ⊨ None. **CC** None. **Other Points:** Children welcome. No dogs. Advance bookings not accepted. Parking adjacent. & **(V) Directions:** Elland is 1 mile from exit 24 on the M62, next to the Town Hall.

MR G BRETT WOODWARD ☎ (0422) 371724.

All menus and wine lists are on blackboards on the walls, which change every week. Fresh produce is always used and the result is an excellent standard of well cooked and presented food.

Cottages

ACCESSIBLE

Hotel

Recommended by
'Les Routiers'
'Staying off
the beaten track'
'British Hotels Restaurant &
Catering Association'

Church Farmhouse Hotel
Horseshoe & Honeysuckle Cottages

3 Main Street, East Ayton, Scarborough, North Yorkshire YO13 9HL, England. Telephone: (0723) 862102 or 863693

Listed 18th Century village farmhouse Hotel offering all traditional comforts, large en suite bedrooms with tea & coffee making facilities and colour T.V.'s, or Self-Catering Holiday in our well equipped Horseshoe & Honeysuckle Cottages adjacent.
Dine at Sally Anne's Dining Room, 'At Home' Dinner Parties (price according to choice), Light Lunches, Business Lunches and meetings, Weddings, Parties, Anniversary's etc.

North Yorkshire Moors, National Park, Places of Interest and easy driving distance of York.

ELLERBY North Yorkshire **Map 9 B1**

⊗££   **THE ELLERBY HOTEL** Ellerby, Hinderwell, Saltburn by Sea.
⊞£££   **Hours:** Meals from 12 noon - 2pm (Sundays 1.30pm) and 7pm - 10pm (Sundays 9.30pm). **Cuisine:** An extensive range of meals including a 'special's board'. 9 course Chinese banquets on specified dates. ⊨ 10 bedrooms, all en suite and with colour TV, tea/coffee making facilities and telephone. **CC** Access, Visa. **Other Points:** Children welcome. No dogs in bar and eating areas. Coaches by arrangement. ☐ ⅋ **(V) Directions:** Off the A174, 8 miles north of Whitby - take Ellerby turn off.
D R ALDERSON ☎ (0947) 840342.
An attractive residential country inn situated in the North Yorkshire Moors National Park in the small hamlet of Ellerby. Just 1 mile from the picturesque fishing village of Runswick Bay.

ELSLACK North Yorkshire **Map 8 B2**

⊗££   **TEMPEST ARMS HOTEL & RESTAURANT** Elslack, Near
⊞£££   Skipton.
  Hours: Meals 11.30am - 2.15pm and 6.30pm - 10pm (last orders). Saturdays 11.30am - 2.15pm and 7pm - 10pm. Sundays 12 noon - 2.15pm, 7pm - 10pm. **Cuisine:** Imaginative bar snacks with fresh fish a speciality. Bonaparte Restaurant offers an inclusive price menu as well as a la carte. ⊨ 10 double bedrooms, all en suite and with tea/coffee making facilities, direct dial telephone, TV. **CC** All major cards. **Other Points:** Children welcome. Switch cards accepted. ☐ ⅋ **(V) Directions:** On the A56, 4 miles from Skipton towards Earby/Colne.
FRANCIS BOULONGNE ☎ (0282) 842450.
A 200 year old Yorkshire stone building retaining the air of a private house with its warm welcome. A delightful setting, by a brook in the middle of some lovely countryside.

ENNERDALE BRIDGE Cumbria **Map 8 A1**

⊗££   **THE SHEPHERD'S ARMS HOTEL**
⊞££   **Hours:** Restaurant open 7pm, last orders 8.30pm. Booked lunches only. Closed Mondays, and all January. **Cuisine:** All home cooked food - home smoked salmon, local game and fish. ⊨ 6 bedrooms, 3 en suite. **CC** None. **Other Points:** Access for disabled to restaurant only. Children welcome. Dogs not allowed in restaurant. ☐ **(V)**
DAVID WHITFIELD BOTT ☎ (0946) 861249.
Village centre hotel with central heating and log fires. Personal service and informal atmosphere. Walking and climbing. Children sharing with parents have free accommodation.

ESKDALE GREEN Cumbria **Map 8 B1**

⊗££   **BOWER HOUSE INN** Eskdale Green.
⊞£££   **Hours:** Breakfast 7.30am - 9.30am, lunch 12 noon - 2pm and dinner 7pm - 9pm (last orders 8.30pm). Bar meals 12 noon - 2pm and 6.30pm - 9.30pm. **Cuisine:** Freshly cooked predominantly French cuisine including game. All dishes home prepared and cooked. ⊨ 22 bedrooms, all en suite and with direct dial telephone, tea/coffee making facilities. **CC** Access, Visa. **Other Points:** Children welcome. Pets allowed. Fax No: (09467) 23308. ☐ ⅋ **(V) Directions:** Turn inland at Holmrook, from the coast road A595 for Eskdale Green.

Eskdale Green continued
MR & MRS CONNOR ☎ (09467) 23244.
An historic inn, with the ambience of a fine old Cumbrian hostelry, set in its own gardens. Good food and olde worlde charm can be found here.

FAIRBURN North Yorkshire **Map 9 B1**
⊗££ **THE BAY HORSE** Silver Street, Fairburn.
Hours: Meals from 12 noon - 2pm (last orders), and 7pm - 10pm (last orders). Restaurant closed: Saturday lunch and Sunday evening. Bar meals and carvery available at all times. **Cuisine:** Dishes may include Noisettes of lamb, Casserole of beef & Guinness, Salmon en croute. ⊨ None. **CC** Access, Visa, Diners. **Other Points:** Children welcome in the restaurant. No dogs. Fax No. (0977) 670553. Parties catered for. **P** ᴅ **(V) Directions:** On the A1 northbound at the Fairburn turn-off.
J M & P S PALFREYMAN ☎ (0977) 607265.
The Bay Horse is near the turn-off between Ferrybridge and Selby Fork, and is easily accessible from both carriageways of the A1.

FAR SAWREY Cumbria **Map 8 B2**
⊗££ **THE SAWREY HOTEL** Far Sawrey, nr Ambleside.
Ⅲ£££ **Hours:** Bar meals served 11am - 2.30pm weekdays, 12 noon - 2.30pm Sundays. Dinner 7pm - 8.45pm. Bar meals in £ price range. Closed: mid - end December. **Cuisine:** Traditional English cooking - Windermere char (in season),fresh and smoked Esthwaite trout, homemade soups and gateaux. ⊨ 17 bedrooms, 13 en suite. All with telephone, TV and tea/coffee making facilities. **CC** None. **Other Points:** Children welcome. Vegetarian food available on request. **P** ᴅ **Directions:** On the B5285 road to Hawkshead, 1 mile from Windermere car ferry.
DAVID D BRAYSHAW ☎ (05394) 43425.
This family run country hotel provides a welcoming and friendly service and excellent home cooking. Close to Windermere car ferry and Hawkshead, ideally situated for touring the Lake District.

FILEY North Yorkshire **Map 9 B2**
Ⅲ££ **ABBOTS LEIGH GUEST HOUSE** 7 Rutland Street, Filey.
⊨ 2 twin, 2 double and 2 family bedrooms, all en suite and with radio, TV and tea/coffee making facilities. One bedroom on the ground floor. **Hours:** Breakfast 8.30am - 9am, Dinner 5.30pm - 6pm (order by 4pm). **CC** Access, Visa. **Other Points:** Children over 3 welcome. No smoking in bedrooms and dining room. Vegetarian meals. Licensed. **P** **(V) Directions:** A165. Right at Church Clock Tower, then second left.
MR & MRS M P CARTER ☎ (0723) 513334.
A warm and comfortable Victorian terrace house, situated in a quiet position, close to the beach, gardens and town centre amenities. Golf, bowling and tennis courts are nearby. The accommodation is of a high standard. An ideal base for touring the Yorkshire Wolds, moors and forests. Filey itself has seven miles of golden sands.

Filey continued

⊗£ **SEA BRINK HOTEL** The Beach, Filey.
🏠££ **Hours:** Breakfast 9am - 10am, Lunch 12 noon - 2.30pm, Dinner 6pm - 7.45pm (last orders). **Cuisine:** Tradtional English cuisine such as Plaice Mornay, Roast of the Day with Yorkshire Pudding. Speciality: locally caught fish. 🛏 9 bedrooms, 7 en suite. **CC** All major cards. **Other Points:** Children welcome. Morning coffee and afternoon teas. Fully licensed. Wedding receptions. Golf, fishing or yachting weekends. **(V) Directions:** On the lower seafront, only yards from the sea.
NICK & OLGA CARTER ☎ (0723) 513257.
Ideally situated on the promenade, literally only yards from the sea, this hotel enjoys magnificent views of Filey Bay. A high standard of accommodation is offered and guest facilities include jacuzzi and satellite TV. A warm welcome is extended to all guests and traditional English cuisine can be enjoyed in the licensed restaurant & coffee shop, also open to non-residents.

🏠££ **SEAFIELD HOTEL** 9-11 Rutland Street, Filey.
CLUB 🛏 2 single, 3 double, 1 twin and 7 family bedrooms, 10 en suite and all with tea/coffee making facilities and colour TV. **Hours:** Breakfast 8.45am - 9am, dinner 6pm. **CC** Access, Visa. **Other Points:** Children welcome. No dogs. TV. Resident's lounge. Licensed. Special low season breaks. **P Directions:** Rutland Street runs off The Crescent.
JILL & DON DRISCOLL ☎ (0723) 513715.
A pleasant, family run guest house, conveniently situated for the beautiful Crescent Gardens in the traditional seaside resort of Filey. Close to the railway and bus stations. Offering good food, comfortable accommodation and a friendly, 'home from home' atmosphere.

FRODSHAM Cheshire **Map 8 C2**

⊗££ **OLD HALL** Main Street, Frodsham.
🏠££££ **Hours:** Breakfast (Mon-Fri) 6am - 10am, lunch 12 noon - 2pm, dinner 7pm - 10pm. **Cuisine:** A la carte menu. Dishes include sea bass champagne, roast duckling cerises 🛏 23 rooms. 7 single, 2 twin, 13 double and 1 family bedroom. All en suite. **CC** All major cards. **Other Points:** Children welcome. Garden. Afternoon teas. Dogs allowed. **P** ♿ **(V) Directions:** M5 junction 12.
MR & MRS WINDFIELD ☎ (0928) 32052.
This 15th century house has been beautifully renovated and modernised and is set amongst other old buildings in the centre of Frodsham. The restaurant serves an imaginative variety of dishes, all of which are beautifully presented and served by friendly attentive staff.

GARSTANG Lancashire **Map 8 B2**

⊗£££ **RESTAURANTE EL NIDO** Whinney Brow, A6 Forton, Garstang.
Hours: Open Sunday lunch throughout the year plus May to September and December 12 noon - 2pm. Dinner 7pm - 10.15pm. Closed: Mondays. **Cuisine:** Extensive Spanish and continental a la Carte, Table D'Hote lunch. 🛏 None. **CC** Access, Visa. **Other Points:** Children welcome. Gardens. Monthly Cabaret Nights. **P (V) Directions:** Conveniently situated on the A6, 1 mile south of Jct 33 of the M6.

Garstang continued

MR & MRS MOLLINGA ☎ (0524) 791254.

This popular, comfortable and atmospheric Restaurante is situated on the edge of the Gateway to the Trough of Bowland, near Garstang and is well worth a visit. It serves a variety of Spanish and continental dishes including Paella, Chicken Breast stuffed with bananas, pineapple and mushrooms, Fillet Steak in shallots, artichokes, herbs, wine and brandy sauce.

GISBURN Lancashire **Map 8 B2**

⊗££ **WHITE BULL HOTEL** Main Street, Gisburn.

Hours: Lunch 12 noon - 2.30pm, Dinner 7pm - 10pm. Bar snacks 11.30am - 2.30pm and 7pm - 9.30pm. **Cuisine:** Restaurant a la carte menu and bar meals. Dishes may include Seafood Thermidor, Chicken a la King, Steak Chasseur. Homemade puddings. ⊨ ⅭⅭ Access, Visa. **Other Points:** Children welcome. Dogs allowed. Garden dining. ⊡ ⅙ **Directions:** A59, between Skipton and Clitheroe.

MR & MRS LEE ☎ (0200) 445233.

An attractive hotel in the small village of Gisburn offering a warm welcome and well-cooked food in pleasant surroundings. The restaurant has a 'gypsy' theme with colourful tablecloths and a cheerful atmosphere. The food is of a very high standard and the service is excellent, welcoming and efficient.

GOATHLAND North Yorkshire **Map 9 B1**

⊞£ **BARNET HOUSE GUEST HOUSE** Goathland, Whitby.

⊨ 3 double, 3 twin and 1 family bedroom. 1 bathroom, 1 shower. **Hours:** Breakfast 9am, dinner 6.30pm. Closed: from December until end February. ⅭⅭ None. **Other Points:** Central heating. Children over 6 years welcome. No dogs. Residents lounge. TV. Garden. ⊡ **Directions:** Just outside Goathland on the Whitby road.

MRS CHRISTINE CHIPPINDALE ☎ (0947) 86201.

A country guest house set in its own large garden with surrounding views of the peaceful and colourful North York Moors. The combination of good food, warm comfortable accommodation and a friendly welcome offered by the proprietor, Christine Chippindale, will ensure you of a happy stay.

⊞££ **WHITFIELD HOUSE HOTEL** Darnholm, Goathland.

⊨ 2 single, 5 double, 1 twin and 1 family bedroom, all en suite. Radio alarm and tea/coffee facilities in all bedrooms. **Hours:** Breakfast 8.30am - 9am and dinner 7pm (order by 7pm). Closed: mid-November to late January. ⅭⅭ None. **Other Points:** Central heating. Children over 3 welcome. Dogs allowed. Licensed. Residents lounge. TV. Garden. ⊡ **Directions:** Off the A169, take signposted road to Goathland then onto Darnholm.

JOHN & PAULINE LUSHER ☎ (0947) 86215.

A former 17th century farmhouse, the emphasis here is on traditional country cuisine with open log fires and beamed ceilings to complete the rural scene. Situated on the edge of Goathland in the heart of the North York Moors, this is an excellent choice for a 'get away from it all' break.

GOOSNARGH Lancashire **Map 8 B2**

THE BUSHELLS ARMS Church Lane, Goosnargh, Preston.
Hours: Lunch 12 noon - 2.30pm, dinner 7pm - 10pm. Closed:
Christmas Day and occasional Mondays. **Cuisine:** Wide variety of
international dishes, such as Dublin Coddle, Kefta Tagine, and
jambalaya. 'Specials' board for food and compatible wines change
daily. None. **CC** None. **Other Points:** Children welcome for
meals. No dogs. Two non-smoking areas. Beer garden. **P** & **(V)**
Directions: Off B5269, turn into Church Lane by the Post Office.
5 mins M6.
DAVID & GLYNIS BEST ☎ (0772) 865235.
A friendly village hostelry, which offers a superb variety of
dishes. There is both a standard menu and a 'specials' board for
food and wine, the wine having been chosen to compliment the
meals of the day. All the meals are homemade and the desserts
are delicious. Visitors can enjoy all this, at very reasonable
prices, and relax in the friendly surroundings. Recommended.

YE HORN'S INN Goosnargh, nr Preston.
CLUB **Hours:** Meals from 12 noon - 2pm and 7pm - 9.15pm, last orders.
Table reservtion advisable. Closed: Mondays. **Cuisine:** English
home cooking, eg. roast duckling. None. **CC** All major cards.
Other Points: Children welcome. No dogs. **P** & **(V) Directions:**
Off the B5269, on road near Whittingham Hospital.
MRS E WOODS ☎ (0772) 865230.
This delightful oak-beamed inn offers good home cooked
English country fare, using local farm produce. Private parties
catered for. Small private rooms available.

GRANGE OVER SANDS Cumbria **Map 8 B2**

ABBOT HALL Kents Bank, Grange Over Sands.
Hours: Breakfast 9am, lunch 12 noon - 2pm (last orders 1.30pm),
dinner 6.45pm (winter 6pm). **Cuisine:** Dishes may include - cream
of mushroom and apple soup, corn on the cob, wild salmon steak,
boeuf Bourguignon, home made cherry pie, apple gateau. 56
bedrooms, 24 en suite. **CC** None. **Other Points:** Children
welcome. No-smoking area. Afternoon teas served. Table tennis.
Snooker. Bowls. Putting. Croquet. Tennis. Fax No. (05395)
35200. **P** & **(V) Directions:** Follow B5277 Rd through Grange-
Over-Sands for 2 miles.
METHODIST GUILD HOLIDAYS - MR & MRS MYCOCK.
☎ (05395) 32896.
Situated in the wooded area of Kents Bank, and run by the
Methodist Guild. Enjoying a peaceful atmosphere, perhaps
steming from the morning and evening devotions which you are
invited to join. Good food and comfortable accommodation and
welcoming, friendly staff. While the children are busy in the
play area, you can make most of the hair salon or join in the
house activities.

NETHERWOOD HOTEL Grange-over-Sands, Cumbria.
Hours: Open all year round. **Cuisine:** Imaginative home cooked
dishes using local produce eg. Breast of chicken filled with
cumberland sausagemeat, apples & cranberries, wrapped in puff
pastry 32 bedrooms, 29 en suite. Some bedrooms non-
smoking. **CC** None. **Other Points:** Children welcome. Heated
indoor swimming pool, spa bath, steam room, solarium, and fitness

Grange over Sands continued

room. No smoking in restaurant. 🅿 ౬ **(V) Directions:** 600 yards from Grange-over-Sands Railway Station.
MESSRS J D & M P FALLOWFIELD ☎ (05395) 32552.

An imposing hotel enjoying a prime position overlooking Morecambe Bay on the fringe of the Lake District. Inside, the oak panelling and log fires provide an atmosphere of old world luxury and comfort. In the restaurant, dishes include Roast Rack of Venison Caroline: Local venison roasted pink, served on a bed of tagliatelle with wild mushrooms, and a sauce Robert.

⊗££ **WOODLANDS HOTEL** Meathop Park, Grange Over Sands.
⏛££ **Hours:** Breakfast 9am - 9.30am, Sunday Lunch 12 noon - 2pm, Dinner and bar snacks 6.30pm - 9.30pm. Only open at lunchtime on Sundays. Closed Mondays & Tuesdays in November, December & February. Closed all January. **Cuisine:** Dishes may include Esthwaite Trout, Venison in red wine, Sweet & Spicy Lamb, Steaks, vegetarian dishes such as Aubergine & Red Bean Bake. ⌔ 4 bedrooms, all en suite. 2 luxury lodges to sleep 4 with spa baths. 🆑 Access, Visa. **Other Points:** Children welcome. No smoking area. Garden dining. Licensed. Sauna room. 🅿 ౬ **(V) Directions:** A590 Barrow, left at roundabout for Grange, left for Meathop Park.
DAVID & SANDRA BOYER ☎ (05395) 34128.

Nestling in the heart of a delightful wood, this hotel provides a warm welcome to all visitors whether for a meal, bar snack or overnight stay. The accommodation is of a high standard and all rooms overlook the garden and woods. Freshly prepared food can be enjoyed in the a la carte restaurant or bars and the atmosphere is informal and very friendly.

GRANTHAM Lincolnshire **Map 9 C2**
⊗££ **THE PREMIER RESTAURANT** 2-6 North Parade, Grantham.
⏛££ **Hours:** Lunch 12 noon - 2pm and dinner 6.30pm - 10.30pm (last
[CLUB] orders). Closed: Saturday lunchtime, Sunday evening, all day Monday. Last 2 weeks August and one week after Christmas. **Cuisine:** Modern English dishes including pan fried trout coated in a spicy ginger sauce. Now specialising in 14 fish dishes. Wide choice. ⌔ 3 bedrooms, 1 double en suite, 1 single en suite and 1 family room. 🆑 Access, Visa. **Other Points:** Fully licenced bar. Children welcome. No dogs. 🅿 ౬ **(V) Directions:** Junction of A52 and A1. Opposite domed Roman Catholic Church.
PAUL & MONIQUE NESBITT ☎ (0476) 77855.

The birthplace of Prime Minister Margaret Thatcher, the Premier is now a restaurant offering imaginative food a reasonable prices. Enter through number '10' to reach the tastefully decorated bar and restaurant. Excellent service, an elegant but relaxed atmosphere and high quality food.

⊗£ **THE ROYAL OAK** Swayfield, Grantham.
Hours: Lunch 11am - 2.30pm, dinner 6pm - 10.30pm. Sunday lunch 12 noon - 2pm, Sunday dinner 7pm - 10.30pm. **Cuisine:** A la carte with special Sunday lunch menu. ⌔ None. 🆑 Access Visa. **Other Points:** Children welcome. Garden. Dogs allowed. Eurocard also accepted. 🅿 ౬ **(V)**
DAVID COOKE. ☎ (047684) 247.

Grantham continued

This traditional stone built country inn has been excellently maintained and is set amidst the attractive Lincolnshire countryside. Offering well cooked and presented food, with a 'Special dish' each day, served by helpful and friendly staff. Outside dining in well tended beer garden during the summer months.

GRASMERE Cumbria **Map 8 B2**

£££ **OAK BANK HOTEL** Broadgate, Grasmere.

1 single, 8 double, 4 twin and 1 family bedroom all with en suite facilities, colour TVs and telephones. Restaurant open to non-residents with prior booking. Closed Christmas to end of January. **Hours:** Breakfast 8.30am - 9am, bar lunches 12 noon - 2.30pm, dinner 7pm - 7.30pm. **CC** Access, Visa. **Other Points:** Central heating. Children welcome. No smoking area. Licensed. Residents lounge. TV. Garden. **P Directions:** From the A591 take the Grasmere turning, hotel on this road.
MR & MRS ATTILIO SAVASI ☎ (09665) 217.

A traditional lakeland stone house, tastefully modernised to provide first class facilities. The hotel and its grounds are attractive and elegant. Mrs Savasi is a trained Cordon Bleu cook and great pride is taken with the 5-course dinner using finest, fresh produce.

£££ **THE WORDSWORTH HOTEL** Grasmere, Ambleside.

Hours: Breakfast 8am - 9.30am, Lunch 12.30pm - 2pm and Dinner 7pm - 9pm (last orders, 9.30pm Friday and Saturday). **Cuisine:** Table d'hote, 4/5 courses. High class French cuisine. Timbale of Rainbow Trout filled with Norwegian Lobster, with crisp vegetables. Bar menu for pub. 37 bedrooms, all en suite. **CC** All major cards. **Other Points:** Children welcome. Garden. Afternoon tea. Indoor heated pool with terrace, jacuzzi, mini-gym, sauna and solarium. Pub. Fax No: (05394) 35765. **P** & **(V) Directions:** A591 to Grasmere, next to village church.
ROBIN LEES - Manager ☎ (05394) 35592.

Situated in the centre of Grasmere, in the heart of beautiful lakeland Cumbria, this former Victorian gentleman's home is truly 'special' and provides the finest attention to detail, whether you dine in the 'Prelude' restaurant or in 'The Dove & Olive Branch' - the hotel's own pub.

GRASSINGTON North Yorkshire **Map 8 B2**

£££ **GRASSINGTON HOUSE HOTEL** Grassington, Skipton.

£££ **Hours:** Breakfast 8am - 9am, Dinner 7pm - 9.30pm (last orders). Bar meals 12 noon - 2pm and 7pm - 9.30pm (last orders). **Cuisine:** Monthly changing table d'hote dinner menu eg. Guinea Fowl, Venison, Medallions of Pork, Fresh Fish. Light meals/snacks lunchtime & evening. 10 bedrooms, all en suite. **CC** Visa. **Other Points:** Children welcome. Dogs allowed (except in dining room). Residents' lounge. **P (V) Directions:** B6265 from Skipton or Ripon. In Grassington Square.
GORDON & LINDA ELSWORTH ☎ (0756) 752406.

Built in the early 18th century and situated in the renowned cobbled square, the hotel enjoys an atmosphere of warmth and friendliness. The food is outstanding, imaginatively cooked from fresh ingredients and beautifully presented. The

Grassington continued

traditional decor of the dining room is delightful and forms an ideal setting for your meal. Well situated in the heart of the Yorkshire Dales.

GREAT AYTON North Yorkshire **Map 9 B1**

⊗£££ **AYTON HALL** Low Green, Great Ayton, nr Middlesbrough.
Hours: Meals from 7.30am - 9.30am, 12 noon - 2pm and 7.30pm - 9.30pm. Lunch also served in the lounge 12 noon - 1.45pm. Morning coffee 10.30am - 12 noon. Afternoon tea 3.30pm - 5pm. Lunches and teas served on lawn on fine days. **Cuisine:** Fresh local produce including homegrown vegetables. All dishes prepared & cooked to order. 4 course traditional Sunday lunch with giant Yorkshire pudd. ⌐ 9 bedrooms, all en suite. **CC** Access, Visa, AmEx. **Other Points:** No dogs. No smoking area. **P** & **(V)** MELVIN R RHODES ☎ (0642) 723595.
An elegant 19th century country house built on foundations dating back to 1281. The excellent cuisine can be accompanied by one of the 2500 bottles of wine on offer. High ceilings with mouldings, Louis XIV furniture, four-poster beds and floodli lily pond in 6 acres of park all contribute to the ambiance.

⊗££ **ROYAL OAK HOTEL** Great Ayton.
Hours: Lunch 12 noon - 2pm except Monday, dinner Monday to Saturday 7.30pm - 9pm. Sunday evening bistro menu - bar lunches available every day. **Cuisine:** Traditional English and French cuisine, eg. grilled farm trout, roast duckling, chicken mornay, stilton and walnut roulade. ⌐ 5 bedrooms, all en suite. **CC** Access, Visa. **Other Points:** Children welcome. Dogs allowed in bedrooms by prior arrangement. & **Directions:** In the centre of Great Ayton.
DEREK & LINDA MONAGHAN ☎ (0642) 722361.
An 18th century inn with a lively atmosphere. A fairly small menu but interestingly varied. Good value for money.

GREAT BROUGHTON North Yorkshire **Map 9 B1**

⊗££ **THE WAINSTONES HOTEL** 31 High Street, Great Broughton.
Hours: Meals from 7am - 9.30am, 12 noon - 2pm and 7pm - 10pm (last orders). **Cuisine:** Savoury cheese fritters, medallions of por fillet. ⌐ 16 bedrooms, all en suite. **CC** Access, Visa, AmEx. **Other Points:** Children welcome. No dogs. **P** & **(V) Directions:** Situate 2 miles South East of Stokesley on the B1257.
JAMES KEITH PIGG ☎ (0642) 712 268.
An attractive hotel with real 'village local' atmosphere in the bar. The restaurant is large and decorated in a Mediterranean style.

GRIZEDALE Cumbria **Map 8 B2**

⊗££ **GRIZEDALE LODGE HOTEL & RESTAURANT IN TH** ⊞£££ **FOREST** Grizedale, Hawkshead, Nr Ambleside.
Hours: Meals from 8.30am - 9.15am, 12.30pm - 1.45pm and 7pm - 8.30pm (last orders). Closed: January - mid February. **Cuisine:** Traditional British and French cuisine with Cumbrian specialities such as Derwentwater duck, Grizedale venison and Lak Esthwaite trout. ⌐ 6 bedrooms all en suite and 1 groundfloor room en suite. **CC** Access, Visa. **Other Points:** No dogs. No smokin

HALIFAX

Grizedale continued

restaurant. No smoking bedrooms. **D Directions:** On the road to Grizedale Visitor Centre from the Hawkshead.

JACK & MARGARET LAMB ☎ (05394) 36532

Situated 2 miles south of Hawkshead on the Satterthwaite road in the heart of Grizedale Forest, mid-way between Coniston Water and Lake Windermere. The hotel is approached down a small country road and provides an elegant and relaxing retreat in a superb, peaceful setting. Routiers Newcomer of the Year 1986.

GUNTHORPE Nottinghamshire Map 9 C1

⊛££ **THE TOLL HOUSE RESTAURANT** Riverside.

Hours: Dinner 7pm - 10pm (last orders). Closed: Sunday nights. **Cuisine:** English & French cuisine: moules Mariniere, Salmon & Smoked Salmon Mousse, fish, meat and fresh pasta dishes with a selection of desserts and cheeses. ⊨ None. **CC** Access, Visa. **Other Points:** No dogs allowed. Sunday Lunches served. **D** & **(V) Directions:** From Nottingham, turn left immediately before Gunthorpe bridge.

MR CLIVE HARRIS ☎ (0602) 663409.

First class service is upheld in this small, friendly restaurant. The building itself used to be the Toll House to the first Gunthorpe bridge built in 1875.

HALIFAX West Yorkshire Map 8 B2

⊛££ **COLLYERS HOTEL** Burnley Road, Luddendenfoot, Halifax.

☐££ **Hours:** Breakfast 7.30am - 9am (Sat/Sun 8.30am - 9.30am),
CLUB Morning coffee 10.30am - 12 noon, Lunch 12 noon - 2pm (last orders), Bar snacks 12 noon - 2pm, Afternoon tea 3.30pm - 5pm, Dinner 7pm - 12 midnight (last orders 9pm). **Cuisine:** A la carte menu includes dishes such as pork fillet in wine and coriander, roast guinea fowl and entrecote steak. Vegetarian selection.Good wine list. ⊨ 2 single, 2 twin, 2 double, 4 of them en suite. All rooms have colour TV, radio, hairdryer, and tea/coffee facilities. **CC** All major cards. **Other Points:** Children welcome. Pets allowed. Morning coffee and afternoon tea also served. Fax No: (0422) 883897. **D (V) Directions:** M62, exit 21 &22 - A646.

D F NORTHEY & N A SKELTON ☎ (0422) 882624.

A former Victorian millowners house, stone-built, beautifully refurbished, and overlooking the Calder Valley. Both accommodation and food are of a superb standard, the inspector remarking that it would be 'a pleasure to return'. Everything is beautifully clean, with pot pourri, plants and paintings adding to the charm of the furnishings. Friendly atmosphere.

⊛£ **DUKE OF YORK INN** Brighouse & Denholmegate Road, Stone
☐££ Chair Shelf.

Hours: Breakfast 7am - 9am, lunch 12 noon - 2pm, dinner 5pm - 9pm (last orders). **Cuisine:** Home cooked food, wide and varied menu. Daily specials. ⊨ 11 bedrooms, all en suite. **CC** Access, Visa, AmEx. **Other Points:** Children welcome. Garden dining. Fax No.(0422) 206618. **D (V) Directions:** Between Bradford and Halifax, 2 miles from M62 on main Howarth Road.

STEPHEN WHITAKER ☎ (422) 202056.

A former 17th Century coaching inn, this establishment lavishly displays pots and pans from the ceiling. Tasty meals at value for

terter

NORTHERN ENGLAND

Halifax continued
money prices and a wide range of ales, spirts and malt whiskies are offered. Friendly, efficient staff help create the relaxed atmosphere which is enjoyed by all ages.

⊗££ **IMPERIAL CROWN HOTEL** 42-46 Horton Street, Halifax.
£££££ **Hours:** Breakfast 7am - 9am, Dinner 7pm - 10pm (last orders). Bar snacks 5pm - 7pm. **Cuisine:** Excellent French cuisine. A la carte and table d'hote menus. 35 bedrooms, all en suite. **CC** All major cards. **Other Points:** Children welcome. No dogs. Residents' lounge. Private functions catered for. Extensive conference facilities. Fax No: (0422) 349866. 🅿 ⅊ **(V) Directions:** Jct 24, M62. Directly opposite main railway station in Halifax.
C & C H TURCZAK ☎ (0422) 342342.
The Hotel is under the personal supervision of the proprietors who, together with the local staff, take every care to look after their guests' comforts and needs. Within the atmosphere of informality and friendliness, the hotel provides an excellent standard of both food and accommodation. Well situated in the heart of historic Halifax. Extensive facilities for functions.

HARROGATE North Yorkshire **Map 9 B1**
£££ **BRITANNIA LODGE HOTEL** 16 Swan Road, Harrogate.
4 single, 3 twin, 1 double, 4 family rooms, 12 of them en suite. All rooms have colour TV, in-house films, radio/alarms, telephones, and tea/coffee. **Hours:** 7.30am - 9am, lunch by arrangement, and dinner 6.30pm - 8pm. **CC** Access, Visa, AmEx. **Other Points:** Children welcome. No dogs. No smoking in dining

T H E
DUKE
— O F —
YORK
I N N

Brighouse & Denholmgate Road, Stone Chair, Shelf, Halifax
Tel: (0422) 202056 Fax: (0422) 206618

A 17th Century coaching inn, with 11 en suite bedrooms
(5 in pub - 6 in adjacent cottages), all with colour TV's and tea & coffe
making facilities,. The pub has a well stocked bar,
boasting conditioned ales and malt whiskeys.
Famous for our good home cooked food we serve a varied
menu for lunch and evening meals.
Situated between Bradford & Halifax *(2 miles from the M62)*, Idael fc
visits to the Yorkshire Dales, with golfing only a mile away.
Weekend rates available - Horse Riding available

Harrogate continued

room. ▣ **(V) Directions:** Close to Royal Hall, Valley Gardens and Exhibition Complex.

P & E M J CULLING ☎ (0423) 508482.

A family run hotel in a very good position for all the attractions of Harrogate. Refurbished to a high standard, the hotel provides comfortable facilities for its guests and prides itself on personal service.

⊗££ **GRUNDY'S RESTAURANT** 21 Cheltenham Crescent, Harrogate.

Hours: Dinner served 6.30pm - 10pm (last orders). Closed: Sundays, Bank Holidays and 2 weeks in January and 2 weeks in July/August. **Cuisine:** Menu may feature - Baked fresh salmon with white wine, cream and chive sauce, English lamb with a rosemary & Port sauce. Table d'hote and a la carte. ⬛ None. **CC** Access, Visa, AmEx. **(V) Directions:** In town centre, approx 2 mins walk from Royal Hall/Conference Centre

VAL & CHRIS GRUNDY ☎ (0423) 502610.

An excellent restaurant serving first class meals in comfortable surroundings. The cuisine is predominantly French and all dishes are freshly cooked to order. The outstanding food is complemented by a good wine list, excellent service and a friendly, warm atmosphere. The fixed price menu offers particularly good value for money.

⌂£££ **SHANNON COURT** 65 Dragon Avenue, Harrogate.

⬛ 8 bedrooms, all en suite. Tea-coffee making facilities, colour TV. **Hours:** Breakfast 8am - 9am and dinner 7pm. **CC** None. **Other Points:** Children welcome. Residents lounge and bar. No pets. ▣ **Directions:** Off the A59 Skipton road.

TRICIA & MIKE YOUNG ☎ (0423) 509858.

A beautiful Victorian house with character and charm, bordering on the 'Stray' in High Harrogate. This family run hotel offers its guests a warm and friendly atmosphere in pleasant surroundings and your stay would be a happy one with Tricia and Mike on hand to welcome you. Within easy driving distance of the Yorkshire Dales and North Yorkshire Moors National Park.

⊗££ **STUDLEY HOTEL** Swan Road, Harrogate.

Hours: Hotel open 7.30am - midnight. Night porter on duty every night. Restaurant open 8am - 9.30am, 12.30pm - 2pm and 7.30pm - 10pm. **Cuisine:** Extensive a la carte menu, including charcoal grilled steaks, seafood kebab. Luncheon - steak and kidney pie, roasts. Bar snacks available. ⬛ 36 bedrooms, all en suite (including 2 suites). **CC** All major cards. **Other Points:** No children under 8 years old. Dogs by arrangement. Telex: 57506; Fax: (0423) 530967. Vegetarian meals by arrangement. ▣ ♿ **Directions:** Adjacent to Valley Gardens.

MR G G DILASSER ☎ (0423) 560425.

Attractively situated adjacent to the beautiful Valley Gardens but within easy walking distance of Harrogate town centre, the Studley Hotel has all amenities. All bedrooms have private facilities. The restaurant has a genuine charcoal grill and, in addition, there is a meeting room/private party room available, for up to 15 people.

Harrogate continued

⊗££ **THE LANGHAM** 21-27 Valley Drive, Harrogate.
⊞£££token **Hours:** Dinner 7.30pm - 9.30pm (last orders). Closed: Sunday and Mondays. **Cuisine:** Traditional English and French cuisine. ⊨ 50 bedrooms, all en suite. ⊠ All major cards. **Other Points:** Children welcome. Open Sundays and bank holidays. Conference facilities. ⊡ **(V) Directions:** By valley gardens, just off the town centre.
THE WARD FAMILY ☎ (0423) 502179.
Run by 3 members of the Ward family, this beautiful old hotel is in the heart of Harrogate, overlooking the renowned Valley Gardens. The Langham is a friendly comfortable establishment, offering good food, with the table d'hote menu of particularly good value. National parks, stately homes and golf courses nearby.

HARTLEPOOL Cleveland Map 9 A1

⊗££ **GRAND HOTEL** Swainson Street, Hartlepool.
CLUB **Hours:** Breakfast 7.30am - 9.30am, Lunch 12 noon - 2pm, Dinner 7.30pm - 10pm (9pm Sundays). Closed: Saturday Lunchtime. **Cuisine:** Carvery and a la carte menu. The specialities are steaks - Steak Diane, Tournedos a la Catalane etc. ⊨ 50 bedrooms, 40 en suite. ⊠ All major cards. **Other Points:** Children welcome. Afternoon teas. Dogs allowed. Conferences. Wedding Parties. Receptions. ⊡ ⅙ **(V) Directions:** Town centre by Central Library and Cenataph.
WEST HARTLEPOOL HOTELS LTD ☎ (0429) 266345.
A grade II listed, Victorian hotel situated in the town centre. Victoria's Lounge Bar serves popular bar food Monday to Saturday lunchtime whilst the New Piper's Restaurant provides a Carvery and A la Carte menus. The food is well cooked and served in generous portions. Excellent, welcoming service adds to the relaxed, friendly atmosphere of the Grand Hotel.

⊗££ **KRIMO'S** 8 The Front, Seaton Carew, Hartlepool.
Hours: Lunch 12 noon - 1.30pm and Dinner 7.30pm - 9.30pm (last orders). Closed: Sundays, Mondays and Saturday lunchtime. **Cuisine:** Mediterranean food - steaks, fish. ⊨ None. ⊠ Access, Visa. **Other Points:** Children welcome. ⅙ **(V) Directions:** On sea front, off A689.
KRIMO BOUABDA ☎ (0429) 266120
An outstanding restaurant with Mediterranean style decor, popular with both locals and visitors, offering a relaxed, welcoming atmosphere. The food is well cooked, well presented, and is highly recommended.

⊗£ **THE DALTON LODGE** Dalton Piercy, Hartlepool.
⊞£££ **Hours:** Breakfast 7.30am - 9am, Lunch 12 noon - 1.30pm, Dinner 7pm - 9.30pm. Bar meals 12 noon - 2pm, 7pm - 9.30pm. **Cuisine:** A la carte menu and special 5 star menu which is a 3 course gourmet meal (not available Saturday evening). Sunday lunch with special price for children. ⊨ 12 bedrooms, all en suite. ⊠ Access, Visa. **Other Points:** Children welcome. Afternoon teas. No dogs. Childrens play area. Meeting room for up to 16 people. ⊡ ⅙ **(V) Directions:** On main A19 trunk road. 6 miles north of Peterlee.
MR & MRS S SIMPSON ☎ (0429) 267142.
The Dalton Lodge is a bar and restaurant with hotel catering particularly well for children and families. It provides a

Hartlepool continued

convenient location for an overnight stay for business or pleasure, set in pleasant rural surroundings on the main A19 trunk road. The 5 star special menu offers particularly good value.

HASWELL PLOUGH County Durham **Map 9 A1**

⊗£ **THE GABLES** 59 Front Street, Haswell Plough.

⏢£££ **Hours:** Breakfast 7.30pm - 9pm and dinner 7pm - 10pm (last orders). Sunday lunch only 12 noon - 2pm. **Cuisine:** English a la carte. ⊨ 5 bedrooms. **CC** None. **Other Points:** Children welcome. Non smoking areas. Open Bank holidays. Residents lounge. ▣ ᕐ **(V) Directions:** 6 miles East of Durham City on the B1283.
DORCAS MILNER ☎ (091526) 2982

A very homely, comfortable and well run family restaurant and hotel, situated on the main road on the south side of the village centre. Beautifully prepared, home cooked meals complemented by fresh crispy vegeatbles and excellent homemade desserts. The Gables provides its guests with excellent value for money dining and accommodation in a warm and friendly atmosphere.

HAWKSHEAD Cumbria **Map 8 B2**

⊗£ **KINGS ARMS HOTEL** The Square.

⏢£££ **Hours:** Open 11am - 3.30pm and 6pm - 11pm, Sunday 12 noon - 2pm and 7pm - 10.30pm. **Cuisine:** Home cooking, eg. steak and kidney pie, Kings Arms chicken supreme. ⊨ 7 double rooms, 3 en suite. **CC** None. **Other Points:** Children welcome. Dogs allowed. **(V)**
MRS R JOHNSON ☎ (096 66) 372.

Situated in the picturesque village of Hawkshead, close to Beatrix Potter's house, this 16th century pub is ideally positioned for fishing and walking.

⊗££ **QUEENS HEAD HOTEL** Hawkshead, Cumbria.

⏢£££ **Hours:** Breakfast 8.30pam - 9am, lunch 12 noon - 2.30pm (last orders) and dinner 6.15pm - 9.30pm (last orders). **Cuisine:** English cuisine and local specialities. ⊨ 12 bedrooms, 6 en suite. **CC** Access, Visa, AmEx. **Other Points:** Children welcome. Afternoon teas. ᕐ **(V) Directions:** In centre of Hawkshead.
MR ANTHONY MERRICK ☎ (096 66) 271.

Situated in the picturesque village of Hawkshead, this hotel is a 17th Century Inn of character and comfort. This charming village is an ideal base for visiting all parts of the beautiful lake district and is close to Windermere and Coniston.

HAWORTH West Yorkshire **Map 8 B2**

⊗££ **OLD WHITE LION HOTEL** West Lane, Haworth, Keighley.

⏢££££ **Hours:** Breakfast 7am - 9am, 11.30am - 2.30pm and 6.30pm - 9.30pm. **Cuisine:** Dover sole, boeuf a l'Americaine, seafood pie and game in season. ⊨ 14 bedrooms, all en suite with colour TV, tea/coffee making facilities and direct dial telephone. **CC** All major cards. **Other Points:** Children welcome. Coaches by appointment. ▣ ᕐ **(V) Directions:** Off M62 take A629 through Halifax and turn off before Keighley.
MR JOHN BRADFORD ☎ (0535) 42313.

Haworth continued

An old inn at the centre of this famous village on the A629 and close to the M62 motorway. A convenient location for visitors to the Bronte Museum, parsonage and Worth Valley Steam Railway.

HELMSLEY North Yorkshire **Map 9 B1**

⊗££ **CROWN HOTEL** Market Square, Helmsley.

⊞££ **Hours:** Breakfast 8.15am - 9.15am, morning coffee 10am - 2.30pm, bar snacks 12 - 2.30pm, lunch 12 - 1.45pm, afternoon/high tea 3.30pm - 5.45pm and dinner 7.15pm - 8pm. **Cuisine:** Local roast beef and other joints, fresh fish, home baking. ⊨ 14 bedrooms, 12 en suite, all with colour TV and tea/coffee facilities, telephone. **CC** Access, Visa. **Other Points:** Winter breaks. Dogs welcome. **P Directions:** Off the A170 in Helmsley Market Square.

MR B J MANDER ☎ (0439) 70297.

A 16th century coaching inn, ideally situated for touring the North Yorkshire Moors and nearby places of interest, eg, York Minster and Castle Howard. The owner of the Crown for 30 years, Mr Mander offers traditional English cooking with many choices.

⊗£££ **PHEASANT HOTEL** Harome, nr Helmsley.

Hours: Meals 8.30am - 9.30am and 7.30pm - 8pm (last orders). Bar lunches 12 noon - 2pm all year round. Hotel closed: January and February. **Cuisine:** Steak and kidney pie, fresh local meat, fish and poultry. ⊨ 12 bedrooms all en suite. **CC** None. **Other Points:**

Helmsley continued

No smoking in dining room. ▢ & **(V)** Directions. 3 miles from Helmsley off the A170.

MR & MRS KEN & CHRISTOPHER BINKS ☎ (0439) 71241.

Near the North York Moors National Park in the charming village of Harome. The hotel was originally 2 smithy's cottages and a shop and has been carefully converted with spacious rooms and lots of character. Many of the rooms overlook the village pond.

⊗£££ **THE FEVERSHAM ARMS HOTEL** 1 High Street, Helmsley.
▥£££ **Hours:** Open 8am - 9.30pm (last orders). Bars open to non-
W residents 11am - 3pm and 6pm - 11pm. **Cuisine:** Fresh shellfish,
♋ game (in season), Spanish paella (if booked in advance). Wide range of Continental dishes complimented by impressive Spanish wine list. ⊨ 18 bedrooms, all en suite. **CC** All major cards. **Other Points:** Children welcome. Bonanza breaks. ▢ & **(V) Directions:** At the junction of the A170 and B1257 in Helmsley.

GONZALO & ROWAN ARAGUES ☎ (0439) 70766.

Attractive historic coaching Inn, modernised retaining its old charm, set in the North York Moors National Park. Accommodation includes 5 four- poster bedrooms, one suite, 6 ground floor bedrooms. Tennis court, heated outdoor swimming pool (April to October) and gardens for guests use. Golf and riding nearby.

⊗££ **THE HAWNBY HOTEL** Hawnby, Nr Helmsley, York.
▥££££ **Hours:** Breakfast 8.30am - 9.30am, lunch 12 noon - 2pm, dinner 7pm - 8.30pm (9pm last orders in bar). Closed: February. **Cuisine:** Traditional English cooking using home grown produce when possible. ⊨ 6 bedrooms, all en suite and with major facilities. **CC** Access, Visa. **Other Points:** Garden. Tennis court can be available for guests. Pony trekking centres nearby. ▢ **Directions:** Off the B125, 8 miles from Helmsley.

LADY MEXBOROUGH ☎ (04396) 202

Built in Yorkshire stone the Hawnby Hotel was originally a Drovers Inn in the 19th century. Decorated throughout to a high standard this hotel enjoys the peace of the unspoilt surrounding countryside. A high degree of personal attention is afforded to all guests.

⊗£ **THE WOMBWELL ARMS** Wass, Helmsley, York.
▥££ **Hours:** Breakfast 8.30am - 9.30am, lunch 12 noon - 2pm and dinner 7pm - 10pm. Closed Monday. **Cuisine:** English cuisine, a la carte, bar meals. ⊨ 4 bedrooms, all en suite. **CC** Access, Visa. **Other Points:** Children welcome. Open Bank holidays and Sunday. ▢ **(V) Directions:** Off A170, signposted Wass.

ALAN & LYNDA EVANS ☎ (03476) 280.

A warm welcome awaits you in this 17th century converted granary. Situated in the beautiful Yorkshire countryside, you will not be disappointed when dining here on your next visit. Serving excellent food from an interesting varied menu, you will find the homemade freshness of each dish mouth watering and the wine selection varied and unusual. Great atmosphere. Highly recommended.

Helmsley continued
⌂££ **THE WOMBWELL ARMS** Wass, Helmsley, York.
    🛏 4 bedrooms, all en suite. **Hours:** Breakfast 8.30am - 9.30am, lunch 12 noon - 2pm and dinner 7pm - 10pm. Closed Monday. 🆑 Access, Visa. **Other Points:** Children welcome. Open Bank holidays and Sunday. 🅿 **(V) Directions:** Off A170, signposted Wass.
    ALAN & LYNDA EVANS ☎ (03476) 280.
    A warm welcome awaits you in this 17th century converted granary. Situated in the beautiful Yorkshire countryside, you will not be disappointed when dining here on your next visit. Serving excellent food from an interesting varied menu, you will find the homemade freshness of each dish mouth watering and the wine selection varied and unusual. Great atmosphere. Highly recommended.

HOLYWELL GREEN West Yorkshire **Map 8 C2**
⊗££ **ROCK INN HOTEL & CHURCHILL'S RESTAURANT**
⌂£££ Holywell Green, Halifax.
    Hours: Food served daily from 12 noon - 10pm in the new Conservatory. Restaurant hours 7am - 9am, 12 noon - 2.30pm, and 7pm - 9.45pm (last orders). **Cuisine:** English and continental cuisine, including Steak a la Churchills and traditional Sunday lunch. 🛏 18 bedrooms all en suite, with full facilities. 🆑 All major cards. **Other Points:** Children welcome. Dogs allowed. Fax No. (0422) 379110. 🅿 ♿ **(V) Directions:** Situated 1.5 miles junction 24 on the M62.
    ROBERT VINSEN ☎ (0422) 379721.
    A 17th century inn set in rural surroundings, recently refurbished to include large Conservatory and Patio areas. Open all day, every day. Close to Elland and Bradley Hall Golf courses, with 'Last Of The Summer Wine' country just a few miles away. Ideal facilities for conferences and receptions, accommodating 160 people in comfort, choice of suites for smaller parties.

HORNBY Lancashire **Map 8 B2**
⊗££ **CASTLE HOTEL** Main Street, Hornby.
    Hours: Breakfast 7.30am - 10am, lunch 12 noon - 2pm, dinner 7pm - 9.30pm. Meals in bar 12 noon - 2pm and 6pm - 10pm. **Cuisine:** Fresh Lune salmon, Morecambe Bay potted shrimps, spicy lamb chops. 🛏 12 bedrooms, 8 en suite. 2 bathrooms. 🆑 Access, Visa, AmEx. **Other Points:** Children welcome. Coaches by appointment. 🅿 ♿ **(V)**
    MR S. ROBINSON ☎ (0468) 21204
    Old coaching inn in the Lune Valley about 25 miles from the Lake District and 20 miles from the Yorkshire Dales. The high standards of cuisine are complimented by a good wine list.

HUDDERSFIELD West Yorkshire **Map 9 C1**
⊗£££ **HEY GREEN HOTEL** Waters Road, Marsden, Huddersfield.
CLUB **Hours:** 7.30am - 9am, 12 noon - 2.30pm, and 7pm - 9pm. Also open Sundays. **Cuisine:** Traditional English fayre. 🛏 6 twin, 3 double, and 1 honeymoon suite. 🆑 All major cards. **Other Points:** Children welcome. No dogs allowed. Afternoon teas also served. 🅿 ♿ **(V) Directions:** Off the A62 at Marsden between Oldham and Huddersfield.

Huddersfield continued
AINA PUNINS ☎ (0484) 844235.
A country house hotel, situated in 7 acres of woodlands, with its own trout lakes, nestling in the Colne Valley. All the bedrooms are furnished to a high standard and the restaurant is renowned for its excellent traditional English fayre.

⊗££ **HUDDERSFIELD HOTEL & ROSEMARY LANE BISTRO**
⌂££££ 33 - 47 Kirkgate, Huddersfield.
Hours: Meals from 7.30am - 10am, and 7pm - 11.30pm. Bar meals 7pm - 11.30pm. Room service 24 hours a day. **Cuisine:** Grills, fish and British cooking. ⊨ 41 bedrooms, all en suite. **CC** All major cards. **Other Points:** Children welcome. Coaches by appointment. Below Parish Church. **P** **(V) Directions:** Off A62, on main ring road in town centre, opp. Sports centre.
JOE MARSDEN ☎ (0484) 512111
Hotel is made up of a bistro, formal hotel, pub, wine bar and night club all under the same roof. The pub has live music on Sundays, Mondays and Tuesdays, and Karaoke bar on other nights.

⊗££ **THE WHITE HOUSE** Slaithwaite, Huddersfield.
⌂££ **Hours:** Breakfast 7.30am - 9am. Restaurant meals 12 noon - 1.30pm (12 noon - 1.45pm on Sundays) and 7.30pm - 9.30pm. Closed: Sunday evening and Monday lunch. Bar meals everyday 12 noon - 2pm, 7.30pm - 10.30pm. **Cuisine:** Table d'hote menus both 2 course and 3 course with additional specialities Menu changes seasonally. ⊨ 8 bedrooms 6 en suite. **CC** All major cards.

Huddersfield continued
Other Points: Children welcome. Dogs allowed by arrangement.
🅿 **(V) Directions:** Off B6107. Turn off A62 in Slaithwaite Village.
MRS GILLIAN SWIFT ☎ (0484) 842245.
A 200 year old pub situated on the Lancashire-Yorkshire pack horse route, with commanding views of the local countryside. The interior has been carefully restored with original flag stone floors, wooden beams and open fires.

HULL Humberside **Map 9 B2**
⊗£££ **KINGSTOWN HOTEL** Hull Road, Hedon, Hull.
🍴££££ **Hours:** Breakfast 7am - 9.30am, Lunch 12 noon - 2.30pm, Dinner
CLUB 7pm - 10pm (last orders). **Cuisine:** English cuisine. Specialities include steaks and stir-fry dishes. A la carte menu and bar meals.
🛏 35 bedrooms, all en suite. CC Access, Visa, AmEx. **Other Points:** Children welcome. Guide dogs allowed only. No smoking area. Residents lounge. Coffee lounge. Private meeting rooms.
Fax: (0482) 890713. 🅿 ♿ **(V) Directions:** On eastern outskirts of Hull, opposite Contenential Ferry Terminal.
PETER READ ☎ (0482) 890461.
A relatively new, family run hotel which is ideally situated for the tourist, the business executive and continental traveller. An 'at home' atmosphere is encouraged, without detriment to the high standards provided. Good food is excellently served in the restaurant and bar, and the coffee lounge is open daily for light snacks.

⊗£ **PEARSON PARK HOTEL** Pearson Park, Hull.
🍴£££ **Hours:** Restaurant open for dinner. Coffee shop open for lunch.
Cuisine: French and English daily specials, fresh local produce.
🛏 35 bedrooms, 30 en suite. CC Access, Visa, AmEx. **Other Points:** Children welcome. 🅿 ♿ **(V) Directions:** Take A1079 Beverley Road from City Centre, Pearson Avenue on left.
MR & MRS D A ATKINSON ☎ (0482) 43043.
Situated within a public ornamental park, one mile north of the city centre. Very popular with families and businessman. The establishment has been under the same ownership for the last 25 years.

HYDE Cheshire **Map 8 C2**
🍴££ **NEEDHAMS FARM** Uplands Road, Werneth Low, Gee Cross, Nr Hyde.
🛏 1 single, 1 twin, 3 double, and 1 family room - 4 of them en suite. Washbasins, shaver points, colour TV, radio, and direct dial telephones in all rooms. **Hours:** Breakfast 6.30am - 11am, and dinner 7pm - 9.30pm. CC None. **Other Points:** Children welcome - under 2 years of age free. Reduced rates for more than 2 nights stay. Bar. Residents' lounge. 🅿 **Directions:** 15,M66-off A560.Between Werneth Low Country Park and Etherow Valley.
MRS WALSH ☎ (061) 368 4610.
A small working farm, dating into the 16th century, which offers very comfortable accommodation and food of an excellent standard. The inspector declared it 'a wonderful place to stay', and noted it was ideal for children as there are many friendly animals on the farm. Perfect base for walking, riding, and golf, with many local places of interest nearby. Highly recommended.

ILKLEY West Yorkshire **Map 9 B1**

⊗££ **COW & CALF HOTEL** Ilkley Moor, Ilkley.

⌂££££ **Hours:** Breakfast 7.30am - 9.30am, lunches in 'Le Jardin' 12 noon - 2pm, dinner in restaurant 7.15pm - 9.30pm. Closed: Christmas. **Cuisine:** A la carte menu in Panorama restaurant, eg. Panorama pate, chicken Panorama (chicken in chef's orange and tarragon sauce). 🛏 17 bedrooms, all en suite. **CC** All major cards. **Other Points:** Children welcome. 🅿 ⅟ **Directions:** Located one mile off A65. Follow signs for Cow & Calf Rocks.
THE NORFOLK FAMILY ☎ (0943) 607 335.
A country house on Ilkley Moor adjacent to the Cow and Calf rocks, from which it takes its name. All bedrooms are fully en suite and offer a high standard of comfort, and the well cooked food is served lunchtime and evening. The restaurant has unrivalled views of Wharfedale and the moors, immortalised by the song 'On Ilkley Moor Bahtat', are a mere 20 yards walk away.

INGLEBY GREENHOW North Yorkshire **Map 9 B1**

⌂££ **MANOR HOUSE FARM** Ingleby Greenhow, nr Great Ayton. 🛏 1 double and 2 twin bedrooms. 2 bathrooms, 1 shower. **Hours:** Breakfast 7.30am - 9am, dinner at 7pm. **CC** None. **Other Points:** Central heating. Children (over 12 years) welcome. Dogs permitted by arrangement. Residents' lounge. TV. Garden. Vegetarian meals available. 🅿 **(V) Directions:** Off B1257. From Church - entrance Rd to Manor, follow sign to farm.
DR & MRS M S BLOOM ☎ (0642) 722384.
A charming old farmhouse in idyllic surroundings and reached by a 1/2 mile private wooded drive. The accommodation is very attractive with exposed wood beams and interior stone-work. Manor House Farm provides exceptional quality and a welcoming and relaxing atmosphere. Wildlife surrounds the farmhouse. Horse riding and golf can be enjoyed nearby. Fine cuisine and excellent wines.

KENDAL Cumbria **Map 8 B2**

⊗£ **FINKLES RESTAURANT** Yard 34, Finkle Street.

CLUB **Hours:** Meals served all day 9.30am - 9.30pm. Closed: Sundays. **Cuisine:** Crepes, Pizzas, Gateaux. 🛏 None. **CC** None. **Other Points:** Dogs allowed. Coaches by appointment. Children welcome. Afternoon tea. ⅟ **(V) Directions:** Behind the main street in Kendal.
MR & MRS STANWORTH ☎ (0539) 27325

Manor House Farm

Delightful holiday accommodation in the North York Moors National Park

**Ingleby Greenhow, Great Ayton,
North Yorkshire TS9 6RB
Telephone: Great Ayton (0642) 722384**

This is a delightful stone-built farmhouse (part ca 1760) in the North York Moors National Park, idyllically set at the end of a ½-mile wooded drive, adjacent to the ancient Manor. The accommodation is of the highest standard. Fine evening dinners are served by candle-light. Residential licence. Ideal for walking, touring and relaxing and for nature-lovers. Brochure on request.

Member Les Routiers English Tourist Board

465

Kendal continued

A 300 year old building occupying one of Kendal's famous labyrinthine 'yards' behind the main street. In fine weather tables are set in the courtyard for dining al fresco. A variety of dishes are served by friendly, efficient staff.

⊗£££ **RIVERSIDE HOTEL** Stramongate Bridge, Kendal.

CLUB **Hours:** Breakfast 7am - 9.30am, lunch 12 noon - 2.15pm and dinner 7pm - 10pm (last orders). Bar meals 12 noon - 2.30pm and 6pm - 10pm. Sunday breakfast 8am - 10am. **Cuisine:** Extensive choice from a la carte and table d'hote menus including fish, shellfish, poultry and game. Speciality: Flambes. 47 bedrooms all en suite. **CC** All major cards. **Other Points:** Children welcome. No dogs (except guide dogs). **P** **(V) Directions:** By Stromongate Bridge on the riverside in Kendal.

JEREMY TREECE - General Manager ☎ (0539) 724707.

Once a thriving tannery, the Riverside has been pleasantly transformed into a hotel complex comprising restaurant, buttery, accommodation and conference centre. Good food and friendly efficient service are a major factor in this bustling hotel's success.

KESWICK Cumbria **Map 8 A2**

⌂£服 **ALLERDALE HOUSE** 1 Eskin Street, Keswick.

3 double and 3 family bedrooms, all en suite. 1 separate WC. TV, radio, hairdryer and telephone in all rooms. **Hours:** Breakfast 8.30am - 9am, dinner 6.30pm. Open all year. **CC** Access, Visa. **Other Points:** Central heating. Children welcome. Licensed. Resident's lounge and garden. The House is no-smoking. **P**

DAVID & ELLEN STEPHENSON ☎ (07687) 73891.

Quiet location only 5 minutes walk from the town centre off Ambleside Road, and only 15 minutes stroll from the lake side. David & Ellen Stephenson have built up a reputation for their good food and hospitality with people returning time after time. Advanced booking recommended.

⊗££ **APPLETHWAITE COUNTRY HOUSE HOTEL** ⌂£££ Applethwaite, Underskiddaw, Keswick.

Hours: Breakfast 8.30am - 9am, Bar snacks 12 noon - 1.45pm, Dinner 7pm (one sitting). Closed: December and January. **Cuisine:** 4 course dinner menu. Dishes may include Rump steak 'Au Poivre Vert', Poached Salmon Steak wrapped in a lettuce pouch & glazed with Hollandaise sauce. 15 bedrooms, 13 en suite. **CC** Access, Visa. **Other Points:** Children welcome. No smoking area. Afternoon teas. Residents' lounge. Garden. Putting green, croquet lawn, bowling green. No dogs. **P** **(V) Directions:** One and a half miles from Keswick, signposted Ormathwaite. A66/A591.

SUSAN & JOHN HARVEY ☎ (07687) 72413.

Magnificent views overlooking Derwentwater & Borrowdale Valley set the scene for this delightful hotel, built in 1881 and surrounded by 2 acres of woodland garden. The warmth and comfort of the Hotel is complemented by the high standard of accommodation, good food, and the professional yet friendly hospitality of the resident proprietors. A peaceful, relaxing place to stay.

Keswick continued

⏥££ GREYSTONES Ambleside Road, Keswick.

1 single, 6 double, and 2 twin bedrooms, all en suite, with colour TVs, radio/alarms, and tea/coffee making facilities. **Hours:** Breakfast 8.15am - 9am, and dinner served at 7pm. **CC** None. **Other Points:** Children over 8 welcome. No dogs allowed. Residents' lounge and garden. Vegetarian meals to order. Free golf available to guests. **P** **(V) Directions:** Directly opposite St John's Church on Ambleside Rd, Keswick. MR DAVENPORT ☎ (07687) 73108.

A comfortable guesthouse personally run by the owners, who make sure their guests have a happy, relaxed stay in a friendly atmosphere. Built in 1863, this slate lakeland house gives excellent views of the fells and is close to the town centre and all amenities. The proprietor is most helpful, offering advice on the best walks in the area and free golf is available. Recommended.

⏥££ HIGHFIELD HOTEL The Heads, Keswick.

5 single, 7 double, 4 twin and 3 family, 15 en suite. 1 bathroom. **Hours:** Breakfast 8.45am - 9.15am, dinner 7pm - 7.30pm (order by 6pm). Closed: November to end March. **CC** None. **Other Points:** Central heating. Children over 5 years welcome. Licensed. Four lounges including bar and TV lounge. Garden. **P** MR & MRS R M JORDAN ☎ (07687) 72508.

Friendly, family-run hotel with superb views of Derwentwater and the mountains. The house is opposite the miniature golf course, on a quiet road only minutes from the lake and Market Square. Bread baked on the premises and fresh produce used in all dishes.

⏥££££ IVY HOUSE HOTEL Braithwaite.

Hours: Breakfast 8.30am - 9am, Dinner 7pm - 7.30pm (last orders). Closed: All of January. **Cuisine:** Chicken stuffed with mango served with a creamy saffron sauce, Salmon with ginger & sultanas, Haunch of venison with port wine and redcurrant sauce. 12 bedrooms, all en suite. **CC** All major cards. **Other Points:** Dogs allowed on arrangement. Regret no reductions for children unless sharing with parents. No smoking in the dining room. **P (V) Directions:** NW from Keswick on A66. Braithwaite signposted after 2 miles. NICK & WENDY SHILL ☎ (07687) 78338.

Once a 17th century yeoman farmers house, this beautiful timbered building is tucked away in the corner of a typical Cumbrian village. The restaurant offers an interesting menu and both the proprietors and staff pride themselves in offering a warm welcome and personal service.

⏥£££ QUEENS HOTEL Main Street, Keswick.

Hours: Meals from 8am - 9.30am, 12 noon - 2pm and 6.30pm - 9pm. Bar meals 12 noon - 2pm and 6pm - 9pm. Bar open all day Saturday. **Cuisine:** Traditional British dishes. 36 bedrooms, all en suite. **CC** All major cards. **Other Points:** Children welcome. No dogs. Coaches by appointment. Fax No: (07687) 71144. **P** & **Directions:** In the market square in Keswick. Off the A66. PETER JAMES WILLIAMS ☎ (07687) 73333.

An old coaching inn, originally the posting house. The town is on the busy A66 to the north of the Lakes. The hayloft and

Keswick continued
stables have been converted to provide a cosy bar known as Ye Olde Queens Head.

⌂£ SPRINGS FARM Keswick.
🛏 2 single, 2 double and 2 family. 2 bathrooms, 1 shower.
Hours: Breakfast 9am - 9.30am, dinner 7pm - 8pm (order by 12 noon). Closed: December and January. **CC** None. **Other Points:** Heating in the bedrooms. Children welcome. Resident's lounge. TV. Garden. **P**
MRS ANNIE HUTTON ☎ (07687) 72144.
Large 19th century house with views of Walla Crag and Lake Derwentwater. Meals are prepared and cooked on the premises and the menus feature traditional British dishes. This is a working fell farm with over 200 sheep.

⊗£ THE RAVENSWORTH 29 Station Street, Keswick on
⌂£££ Derwentwater.
Hours: Breakfast 8am - 9am, dinner 7pm. Closed: December, January and February. **Cuisine:** Traditional English cuisine. Dishes may include Garlic Mushrooms, Cider and Cheese Pork Chop, Seathwaite Trout served with Lemon Sauce. 🛏 8 bedrooms, 7 en suite. **CC** None. **Other Points:** Children welcome. No smoking area. **P Directions:** Near centre of Keswick.
MR & MRS LOWREY. ☎ (07687) 72476.
A small, family run hotel situated close to all the amenities of Keswick. Decorated to a high standard of comfort and serving good food made from fresh quality ingredients, this hotel is an ideal base for those wishing to climb, walk, fish or play a round of golf.

⌂£££ THORNLEIGH GUEST HOUSE 23 Bank Street, Keswick.
🛏 6 bedrooms, all en suite. Colour TV and tea/coffee making facilities. **Hours:** Breakfast 8.30am - 9am and dinner at 7pm (order by 4.30pm). **CC** Access, Visa. **Other Points:** Residents lounge. Dogs allowed. Vegetarian meals available. **P (V) Directions:** On A591, opposite Bell Close car park and police station.
MR & MRS GRAHAM ☎ (07687) 72863.
A traditional lakeland stone house which enjoys magnificent views of the surrounding area. Staying at Thornleigh ensures comfortable and well decorated accommodation with light airy bedrooms, 2 being non-smoking. The food is good and the cakes and desserts are highly recommended.

⊗££ YEW TREE COUNTRY RESTAURANT Seatoller,
CLUB Borrowdale, Keswick.
Hours: Lunch 12 noon - 2.30pm and dinner from 6pm - 9pm. Closed: Friday afternoon, all day Monday and throughout January. **Cuisine:** Traditional English country fare, with speciality local dishes. 🛏 None. **CC** Access, Visa. **Other Points:** Children welcome. No dogs. Afternoon teas. ᨓ **(V) Directions:** On B5289 in Seatoller,at foot of Honister Pass in Borrowdale valley.
JAN & ANDREW LYSSER ☎ (07687) 77634.
This is a small country restaurant in Borrowdale Valley which has been converted from two 17th century Lakeland cottages with the old world charm of the mellowed oak beams, slate floor

Keswick continued

and an open fire with a display of a wealth of collectables and antiques. Booking is advisable for dinner.

KIMBERLEY Nottinghamshire **Map 9 C1**

⊛£ **THE NELSON & RAILWAY INN** Station Road, Kimberley.
⬤£ **Hours:** Breakfast as required. Lunch 12 noon - 2.30pm, dinner 5pm - 9pm. **Cuisine:** Traditional homemade pub meals. ⊨ 2 twin bedrooms. **CC** None. **Other Points:** Children welcome. Dogs allowed. Beer garden. Childrens menu. ⬤ ᕼ **(V) Directions:** 1 mile north Junction 26 on M1. On B600.
HARRY BURTON ☎ (0602) 382177.

The Nelson & Railway Inn is a traditional village pub with original beamed lounges. Good basic home cooked food and a warm welcome are guaranteed. Good beers and a Happy Hour between 5pm and 7pm. Daily specials on blackboard.

KIRKBY LONSDALE Cumbria **Map 8 B2**

⊛£ **THE COPPER KETTLE** 3-5 Market Street, Kirkby Lonsdale, via
⬤£ Carnforth.
Hours: Open 12 noon - 9pm (last orders). Breakfast served to residents only. **Cuisine:** Roasts, steaks and dishes cooked in wine. ⊨ 4 bedrooms all with TV and tea/coffee making facilities. **CC** All major cards. **Other Points:** Children welcome. ᕼ **(V) Directions:** From M6 jct 36, follow signs to Kirkby Lonsdale, Market St on left.
MR & MRS GAMBLE ☎ (05242) 71714.

A 16th century building on the main street of this busy market town. Mr Gamble is a member of the Societe Gastronomique Francaise, evident in the excellent meals produced. Kirkby Lonsdale is a charming market town, and a good base for touring the Lakes and the Yorkshire Dales.

⊛££ **WHOOP HALL & RESTAURANT** Kirkby Lonsdale,
⬤££ Carnforth.
Hours: 7.30am - 10.30am, 12 noon - 2.30pm and 6pm - 10pm. Bar meals 11.30am - 2.30pm and 6pm - 10pm (last orders). **Cuisine:** English and continental cuisine, with game (in season) and fresh fish. ⊨ 15 bedrooms, all en suite. **CC** Access, Visa. **Other Points:** Small dogs and guide dogs by arrangement. Afternoon teas served. Children welcome. Open Sundays and bank holidays. ⬤ ᕼ **(V) Directions:** Situated on A65 just outside Kirkby Lonsdale.
A JOHN PARR ☎ (05242) 71284.

An old 18th century coaching inn, which now houses a bar, serving bar meals and traditional beers; a buttery, offering a range of home-made scones, pastries and fresh coffee; and a restaurant offering a full a la carte menu. Whoop Hall is conveniently situated close to the Yorkshire Dales and the Lakes, which makes it a fine base to explore the area.

KIRKBY STEPHEN Cumbria **Map 8 B2**

⊛££ **KING'S ARMS HOTEL** Market Square, Kirkby Stephen.
Hours: Restaurant open 8am - 1.45pm and 7pm - 9pm. Bar snacks 7pm - 9.30pm. **Cuisine:** Unusual bar snacks, homemade sweets. Real ales. ⊨ 10 bedrooms, 4 en suite. **CC** Access, Visa. **Other Points:** Children welcome. ⬤ ᕼ **(V) Directions:** From M6 (jct 38) take A685 to Kirkby Stephen Market Square.

Kirkby Stephen continued
MRS J F REED & MR K SIMPSON ☎ (07683) 71378.
A 17th century posting inn in the centre of a market town, near to the lakes and dales. Bar snacks available lunchtime and evening and dinner menu in the evening, with all food home cooked. Attractive walled garden for summer dining.

KNUTSFORD Cheshire **Map 8 C2**
⌂£££ **LONGVIEW HOTEL AND RESTAURANT** Manchester Road, Knutsford, Cheshire.
🛏 5 single, 11 double, 7 twin, all with bathroom en suite facilities. Colour TV, telephone, radio, baby-listening device and tea/coffee facilities in rooms. Rollaway beds for children in parent's rooms available. Room service. **Hours:** ☐ Access, Visa. **Other Points:** Children welcome. Dogs allowed. Open Bank holidays. Fax No: (0565) 652402. ☐ **(V) Directions:** Jct 19 M6, A556 towards Chester. Left at lights. Left at roundabout.
PAULINE & STEPHEN WEST ☎ (0565) 632119.
A period hotel, recently refurbished to enhance its Victorian splendour. With many antiques, this hotel offers a relaxed and comfortable atmosphere from its open log fires to the quality of its food and welcome. Just minutes away from Junction 19, M6. Set overlooking the town common in this attractive Cheshire market town.

LANCASTER Lancashire **Map 8 B2**

⊗££ **SPRINGFIELD HOUSE HOTEL & RESTAURANT** Wheel
⊔⊔££ Lane, Pilling, nr Preston.

Hours: Lunch 12 noon - 2pm, Dinner 7pm - 9pm. Closed: Sunday
evening and Monday. **Cuisine:** Monthly changing table d'hote
menu may inlcude Trout Dundee (in a whisky & orange sauce),
duckling, steak, chicken Maryland and medallions Carribean.
⇐ 7 bedrooms, all en suite and with full facilities. Some four poster
beds. Mid-week break speciality. **CC** Access, Visa. **Other Points:**
Children welcome. Dogs allowed. Afternoon teas. Residents
lounge. Garden. Outside buffets, wedding receptions and
functions catered for. **P** ᗐ **(V) Directions:** Off A588 Blackpool -
Lancaster rd, to the west of Pilling village.
GORDON & ELIZABETH COOKSON ☎ (0253) 790301.

*A Georgian country house hotel set in extensive, attractive
grounds with walled gardens and pools. The two dining rooms,
The Corless Room and Miss Ciceleys, are sympathetically
decorated in keeping with the 1840's style of building. Very
well cooked and presented meals offering outstanding value for
money are served in a relaxed atmosphere by polite, efficient
staff.*

LANGTOFT Humberside **Map 9 B2**

⊗££ **THE OLD MILL HOTEL, RESTAURANT & BAR** Mill Lane,
⊡££££Langtoft, nr Driffield.

Hours: Lunch 12 noon - 2pm and dinner 6.30pm - 10pm. Open
every day. **Cuisine:** Dishes include Lobster tail with sauce vert and
sauce Marie-Rose, Tournedos Excelsior, Monkfish a la facon du
chef and Roast Duckling. ⇐ 9 bedrooms, all en suite. **CC** Access,
Visa. **Other Points:** No dogs. Garden. No children under 14 years.
P ᗐ **(V)**
COLIN DAWSON ☎ (0377) 87284.

*A charming hotel, restaurant and public house, once the
miller's house, stabling and cow sheds set in attractive gardens
with lawns and trees. The windmill from which the name derives
stands to the rear of the property. Mr Dawson draws his clientele
from a wide area as his reputation grows.*

LAXTON Nottinghamshire **Map 9 C1**

⊗£ **DOVECOTE INN** Laxton, nr Newark.

Hours: Meals from 12 noon - 2.30pm and 7pm - 10pm. **Cuisine:**
Daily specials. ⇐ None. **CC** None. **Other Points:** Children
welcome. No dogs. ᗐ **(V) Directions:** In the centre of Laxton
village.
JOHN & ELIZABETH WATERS ☎ (0777) 871586.

*A mellow Nottingham red-brick pub in idyllic surroundings.
Laxton is the only village which has preserved the age-old open
fields farming, which is still presided over by a 'Village jury'
and a 'Court Leet'.The Dovecote Inn provides the focal point, a
local for villagers and visitors alike.*

LEADENHAM Lincolnshire **Map 9 C2**

⊗££ **GEORGE HOTEL** High Street, Leadenham.
⊡££ **Hours:** Open 10.30am - 2.30pm and 6pm - 11pm (last orders
⟁ 10pm). **Cuisine:** Steaks, Lincolnshire duckling a l'orange,
⟁LUB Georgian trout. ⇐ 7 bedrooms, all with TV and tea/coffee
facilities. **CC** Access, Visa, AmEx. **Other Points:** Children

Leadenham continued

welcome. P ♿ (V) **Directions:** At the junction of the A17 and the A607, 8 miles from the A1.

MR G M WILLGOOSE ☎ (0400) 72251.

A family-run old coaching inn on the A17. The George is renowned for its well-stocked bar - a whisky drinkers delight with over 500 varieties of whisky and drinks from around the world.

LEEDS West Yorkshire **Map 9 B1**

£££ **ARAGON HOTEL** 250 Stainbeck Lane, Leeds.

14 bedrooms, 10 en suite. All with colour TV, telephone and tea/coffee making facilities. **Hours:** Breakfast 7.30am - 9am, Dinner 7pm. Bar snacks 6pm - 9pm. CC All major cards. **Other Points:** Children welcome. Dogs allowed. Residents' lounge and garden. Fax No: (0532) 753300. P **Directions:** A61 Scott Hall Rd from city centre. Left at 2nd roundabout.

CHRISTOPHER & SALLY HEATON ☎ (0532) 759306.

Built for a mill owner in 1893, the Aragon was converted into a hotel in 1972 and now provides a high standard of accommodation. Close to the City centre, this private hotel is comfortable, reasonably priced and quiet as it is surrounded by an acre of garden, fields and open spaces. Croquet on the lawn and mini snooker can both be enjoyed.

££ **AVALON GUEST HOUSE** 132 Woodsley Road, Leeds.

2 single, 4 twin, 3 double and 1 family bedroom, 3 with en suite facilities. **Hours:** Breakfast 7.30am - 9am. CC None. **Other Points:** Garden. Dogs allowed. P **Directions:** Half a mile from the city centre in the University area.

ELIZABETH DEARDEN ☎ (0532) 432848.

A Victorian family house situated close to the University. Comfortable and well maintained, the Avalon Guest House has a homely atmosphere. Popular with business travellers and visitors to the University.

££ **OLIVE TREE GREEK RESTAURANT** Oaklands, Rodley Lane, Rodley, Leeds.

Hours: Lunch 12 noon - 2.30pm, dinner 6.30pm - 11.30pm (last orders). Closed: Saturday lunchtime. **Cuisine:** Choice of special meze including vegetarian and seafood, blackboard specials homemade Greek pastries. None. CC Access, Visa. **Other Points:** Children welcome. No dogs. Yorkshire Post's Restaurant of Year 1986. Superloo Award Winner. World record for longest kebab. Leeds Health Award. P ♿ (V) **Directions:** By Rodley roundabout on the Leeds ring road.

GEORGE & VASOULLA PSARIAS ☎ (0532) 569283.

The awards have been pouring in for this Greek restaurant housed in an imposing Victorian building with car parks and gardens. The excellent Greek dishes are cooked to genuine recipes passed down through generations and these delicacies have even been tasted by King Constantine of the Hellenes. Undoubtably ranks as one of the top Greek Restaurants in the UK. Recommended.

Leeds continued

▥££££ THE BUTLERS HOTEL 10 Cardigan Road, Headingley,
CLUB Leeds.

🛏 8 bedrooms, all en suite. All bedrooms with colour TV, direct
dial telephone, radio/aLarm, hairdryer, welcome tray, fresh fruit
and individual toiletries. **Hours:** Breakfast 7.30am - 9am, Lunch 12
noon - 2pm, Dinner 7pm - 9pm (last orders). Bar meals 12 noon -
12 midnight. **CC** Access, Visa, AmEx. **Other Points:** Children
welcome. Dogs allowed. Residents' lounge. Licensed. Afternoon
tea. Fax: as phone number. Special weekend rates. Vegetarian
meals available. **▯ (V) Directions:** Link road betw. A65 Skipton &
A660 Otley Rd. Headingley Cricket Gd.
DAVID HARRY BUTLER ☎ (0532) 744755.
*Overlooking Headingley Cricket Ground and only 2 minutes
from the City centre, this hotel offers excellent, luxurious
accommodation and a friendly, welcoming atmosphere. The
superbly appointed licensed restaurant provides a wide choice
of well-cooked dishes such as Tournedos Rossini and Chicken
Chasseur. An elegant, comfortable and welcoming place to
stay.*

LEEK Staffordshire **Map 8 C2**

⊗£ **HOTEL RUDYARD** Lake Road, Rudyard, Leek.
▥££ **Hours:** Breakfast 7.30am - 9.30am, Dinner 7pm - 9.30pm (last
orders). Sunday Lunch 12 noon - 2pm. Bar meals 12 noon - 2pm
and 7pm - 9.30pm (last orders). **Cuisine:** Carvery and bar meals.
🛏 18 bedrooms, all en suite. **CC** Access, Visa. **Other Points:**
Children welcome. No smoking area. Access for disabled to
restaurant only. Garden dining. Residents' lounge. Fax No:
(053833) 249. **▯ ₺ Directions:** Leek to Macclesfield A523, 1 mile
turn left for Rudyard.
RONALD WILLIAM & JEAN LLOYD ☎ (053833) 208.
*An impressive Victorian building overlooking Rudyard Lake in
an attractive rural setting. The hotel enjoys a relaxed, family
atmosphere and the accommodation is of a high standard. With
friendly and efficient service, well-cooked food and generous
portions, the Carvery restaurant provides an enjoyable meal at
excellent value for money.*

⊗££ **THE JESTER AT LEEK** 81 Mill Street, Leek.
▥££ **Hours:** Open 6am - 11.30pm (last orders 10pm). Closed: Sunday
3.30pm - 7pm. **Cuisine:** All homemade dishes using fresh
produce. A la carte and bar servery. 🛏 14 bedrooms en suite, all
with colour TV and tea maker, radio and telephones. **CC** Access,
Visa. **Other Points:** Limited access for disabled. Children
welcome. Dogs allowed at management's discretion. **▯**
Directions: On the A523 Macclesfield rd, quarter of mile out of
Leek on left.
MR & MRS T BARLOW and MR & MRS D BARLOW ☎ (0538)
383997.
*A lovely renovated Victorian building with bay windows on the
outskirts of Leek. The Jester is family owned, with a relaxed,
friendly atmosphere. Within a few minutes drive of Peak Park,
Rudyard Lake, the Roaches and Alton Towers. Weekend
bargain breaks, out of season.*

Leek continued

⊗££ **THE THREE HORSESHOES INN** Blackshaw Moor, Leek.

⏰££Ɛ **Hours:** Breakfast 7.30am - 9.30am, lunch 12 noon - 2pm, and
[CLUB] dinner 7pm - 9.30pm (last orders in restaurant) or 10pm (last
orders in bar). **Cuisine:** Hot and cold table at lunch and evening a
la carte and table d'hote menus in the evening. ⌨ 6 bedrooms, 6
with showers. **CC** All major cards. **Other Points:** Children
welcome. No dogs. Large garden. Fifteen minutes drive from
Alton Towers. **P** **(V) Directions:** Located on A53 Leek-Buxton
Road.
WILLIAM KIRK ☎ (0538) 300296.
*Situated in a lovely country setting with beautiful views towards
the moors and Pennines. First class accommodation in cottage-
style bedrooms. Dinner/dance at weekends.*

LEEMING North Yorkshire **Map 9 B1**

⊗££ **MOTEL LEEMING** Great North Road, Bedale, Leeming.

⏰££ **Hours:** Open 24 hours a day. **Cuisine:** Farmhouse platter, steak
ⒸⒹ and kidney pie, traditional Sunday lunch, fresh fish dishes. ⌨ 40
[CLUB] bedrooms, all en suite. **CC** All major cards. **Other Points:** Children
welcome. **P** &. **(V) Directions:** Beside the A1 at the junction with
the A684.
CARL LES ☎ (0677) 422122/43611.
*Motel Leeming has easy access to both carriageways of the A1
and is open and serving meals 24 hours a day.*

LINCOLN Lincolnshire **Map 9 C2**

⏰££ **CARLINE GUEST HOUSE** 1-3 Carline Road, Lincoln.

⌨ 1 single, 7 double, 2 twin, 2 family bedrooms, 10 en suite. 9
bedrooms reserved for non-smokers. All rooms have TV, radio,
tea/coffee making making facilities and hair dryers.
Hours: Breakfast 7.30am - 9am. Closed: Christmas and New Year.
CC None. **Other Points:** Central heating. Children welcome.
Residents' lounge. No smoking in dining room and lounge. **P**
Directions: Travelling north on the A1102, turn right onto Carline
Road.
GILL & JOHN PRITCHARD ☎ (0522) 530422.
*Situated in a quiet location 5 minutes' walk from one of the most
historic and beautiful Cathedrals in Britain. Gill and John
Pritchard offer you a full English breakfast including free range
eggs from their own hens.*

⊗££ **CASTLE HOTEL** Westgate, Lincoln.

⏰££Ɛ **Hours:** Breakfast 7am - 10am, Lunch 12 noon - 3pm, Dinner 7pm -
9.30pm (last orders). Bar snacks 11.30am - 8pm. **Cuisine:**
Traditional British cooking. Fresh, local produce includes
Lincolnshire Duckling. ⌨ 21 bedrooms, all en suite. **CC** All major
cards. **Other Points:** Children welcome. Afternoon teas. Dogs
allowed. Fax No: (0522) 510291. **P** &. **(V) Directions:** Between
the Castle & the Cathedral. Opp official Cathedral car park.
STANCHION LTD. Manager - JAN S TOMASIK ☎ (0522)
538801.
*Conveniently situated between the Cathedral and the Castle,
this hotel was built as a school in 1852 and tastefully converted
to a hotel in 1981. The restaurant offers a wide choice of dishes
made from predominantly fresh, local produce. A good choice*

Lincoln continued
> *for an enjoyable meal with well-cooked, tastefully presented food and welcoming service.*

⊗££ **HILLCREST HOTEL** 15 Lindum Terrace, Lincoln.
⊞££££ **Hours:** Breakfast 7.15am - 9am, Lunch 12 noon - 2pm and Dinner
CLUB 7pm - 8.45pm (last orders). Closed on Sundays. **Cuisine:** Dishes may include Lamb noisettes, Gammon in peaches and honey, Steaks, Pork cutlets Swiss style, vegetarian dishes. ⊨ 17 bedrooms, all en suite. **CC** Access, Visa, AmEx. **Other Points:** Children welcome. Dogs allowed. Afternoon tea served. Childrens menu. Fax No: (0522) 510182. **P** **(V) Directions:** Off the A115 Wragby road, close to Cathedral.
JENNIFER BENNETT ☎ (0522) 510182.
A former Victorian rectory situated in a quiet avenue yet only 5 minutes walk to Cathedral, museums and shops. The Hillcrest offers a chance to relax and enjoy good food and service, in a lovely location overlooking parkland.

⊗£££ **MOOR LODGE HOTEL** Branston, Lincoln.
⊞££££ **Hours:** Breakfast 7.30am - 9.30am, Lunch and bar snacks 12.30pm - 2pm, Dinner 7pm - 9.15pm (last orders). Closed for lunch: Saturday. **Cuisine:** British and continental cuisine made from fresh, local produce. ⊨ 25 bedrooms, all en suite. **CC** All major cards. **Other Points:** Children welcome. Dogs allowed. Residents' lounge. Fax No: (0522) 794389. Ballroom. **P** ♿ **(V) Directions:** 3 miles south of the City of Lincoln on the B1188.
PETER NANNESTAD. General Manager - MR WALKER ☎ (0522) 791366.
A privately owned and run hotel in a rural Lincolnshire setting, yet only 3 miles from the centre of Lincoln. The hotel offers comfortable accommodation, welcoming, courteous service and good food. The restaurant is tastefully appointed and offers both table d'hote and a la carte menus. All food is very well cooked using entirely fresh, local prodcue.

⊞£ **PORTLAND GUEST HOUSE** 49-55 Portland Street. Lincoln.
⊨ 3 single, 8 double/twin, 1 family bedroom, all with TV. 1 bathroom, 2 showers. **Hours:** Breakfast 7.30am - 9am. Afternoon tea available. Free vending machine for coffee and chocolate. Open all year. **CC** None. **Other Points:** Central heating. No evening meal. Children welcome. Licensed. Residents lounge, games room, TV and garden. **P** **Directions:** Off the High Street, opposite the 'Ritz Theatre'.
DAVID HALLGATH ☎ (0522) 521098.
Situated 5 minutes from the city centre and close to the railway and coach stations, this guest house is ideally situated for the passing traveller or for visitors to the city. The reception is friendly and cheerful.

⊗££ **THE GRAND HOTEL AND RESTAURANT** St Mary's Street,
⊞£££ Lincoln.
Hours: Breakfast 7am - 9.30am, Lunch 12 noon - 2pm and Dinner 7pm - 9pm (last orders). Abbey Grill 10am - 10pm Monday to Saturday, 11am - 9pm Sunday. **Cuisine:** A la carte and fixed 3 course menu. English and French. ⊨ 48 bedrooms, all en suite. **CC** All major cards. **Other Points:** Children welcome. Pets allowed.

Lincoln continued

Conference facilities. Mid-week breaks also available. Fax No: (0522) 537661. **◘** **(V) Directions:** In the heart of Lincoln city centre.

MRS HUBBARD & MRS WOOTTON **☎** (0522) 524211

A family hotel of distinctive character, which has been run by the Hubbard family for over 50 years. The Grand Hotel has a strong local following for its traditional fare and good value and, situated in the heart of Lincoln, is an ideal base whether your interest is shopping, leisure or history.

⊗££ **THE PENNY FARTHING INN** Station Road, Timberland,
⊞£ Lincoln.

CLUB **Hours:** Breakfast 7am - 10am, lunch 12 noon - 2pm, Dinner 7.30pm - 9.30pm. **Cuisine:** Full restaurant & bar menus, including grilled river trout almondine and roast guinea fowl. ⊨ 6 rooms: 4 twin and 2 double bedrooms. **CC** All major cards. **Other Points:** Children welcome. Dogs allowed. **◘** **(V) Directions:** B1189.

MICHAEL DOBSON. **☎** (05267) 359/492.

Attractive hotel situated in a quiet rural village. All rooms are comfortably furnished and overlook peaceful English countryside. A very friendly and welcoming atmosphere.

⊗££ **WASHINGBOROUGH HALL COUNTRY HOUSE HOTEL**
⊞£££££Church Hill, Washingborough, Lincoln.

CLUB **Hours:** Breakfast 7.30am - 9am, Dinner 7pm - 9.30pm (last orders 9pm). **Cuisine:** Traditional cuisine. ⊨ 14 bedrooms, all en suite. **CC** All major cards. **Other Points:** Children welcome. Pets allowed.

The Grand Hotel and Restaurant — *The* **Grand Hotel** — St.Mary's Street, Lincoln LN5 7EP

Lincoln continued

Afternoon tea served. Outdoor swimming pool. No smoking in dining room. Fax No: (0522) 792936. ▣ **(V) Directions:** 200 yards off the B1190 Lincoln to Bardney road.

MARY & BRIAN SHILLAKER ☎ (0522) 790340.

Set in 3 acres of lawns and woodland, on the edge of Washingborough village. The bar serves real ales and the Wedgwood dining room serves an interesting and comprehensive menu as well as an excellent wine list.

LIVERPOOL Merseyside **Map 8 C2**

⊗££ **LA GRANDE BOUFFE RESTAURANT** 48 Castle Street, Liverpool.

Hours: Open 9am - 10.30pm (last orders). Closed: Saturday lunch all day and Bank Holidays. **Cuisine:** Fresh fish , a speciality. French orientated. ⇥ None. **CC** Access, Visa, AmEx. **Other Points:** Children welcome. Afternoon tea served. Vegetarian menu. **(V)**

MR FRANCIS NYLAND ☎ (051) 236 3375

A cosy basement level restaurant on this main road in Liverpool. Bistro style furnishings throughout complement the Brasserie style menu.

⊗££ **MAYFLOWER RESTAURANT** 48 Duke Street, Liverpool.

Hours: Open Monday to Friday 12 noon - 4am. Saturday and Sunday 6pm - 4am. Closed: Saturday and Sunday lunchtimes. **Cuisine:** Peking and Cantonese cuisine, with vegetarian and seafood specialities. ⇥ None. **CC** All major cards. **Other Points:** Children welcome. No dogs. ▣ ⅊ **(V) Directions:** 2 minutes from main shopping area. Near Pier Head and Albert Dock.

MR SIM ☎ (051) 709 6339.

A large, modern Chinese restaurant with a warm and relaxed atmosphere. The restaurant serves Pekingese, Cantonese and Schezuan dishes including crispy fragrant duck served with pancakes. As the restaurant is open until 4am, it is ideal for anyone looking for a peaceful restaurant in which to enjoy good food, but outside the more usual opening hours.

LIVERSEDGE West Yorkshire **Map 9 C1**

⊗£££ **LILLIBETS RESTAURANT & ROOMS** 64 Leeds Road, ⌂£££Liversedge.

Hours: Breakfast 7.30am - 9am, Lunch by arrangement, Dinner 7pm - 12.30am (last orders 9.30pm). Closed: Sundays, 2 weeks during August and 1 week at Christmas/New Year. **Cuisine:** Dishes may include Fillet of Sole filled with a salmon mousseline, studded with pistachio nuts, on a cream sauce; Rack of Lamb topped with herb crust. ⇥ 13 bedrooms, all en suite. **CC** Access, Visa, AmEx. **Other Points:** Children welcome. No dogs. Garden. Fax No: (0924) 404912. Light, classical background music. ▣ **(V) Directions:** 3 miles from Jct 25 & 27, M62. On A62 between Leeds & Huddersfield.

MARTIN & LIZ ROBERTS ☎ (0924) 404911.

A restaurant with rooms which provides both excellent food and comfortable accommodation. The food is modern English in style, with all dishes excellently cooked and elegantly presented. The decor is subtle and promotes a relaxing atmosphere in which to enjoy good food served by welcoming, professional staff.

LONG PRESTON North Yorkshire **Map 8 B2**

⊗£ **MAYPOLE INN** Long Preston, nr Skipton.

⌂£ **Hours:** Lunch 12 noon - 2pm, dinner 6.30pm - 9pm (Monday to
CLUB Friday), 5.30pm - 9.30pm (Saturday) and 5pm - 9pm (Sunday).
Closed: Christmas Day. **Cuisine:** Ham and eggs, lasagne, 20oz T-
bone steak, beef in beer, chicken in red wine - all home cooked.
⊨ 6 bedrooms, 2 bathrooms. **CC** None. **Other Points:** Children
welcome. No dogs in dining room. Coaches by appointment.
Residents lounge. **P** & **(V) Directions:** On the A65 between Settle
and Skipton.
ROBERT & ELSPETH PALMER ☎ (07294) 219.
*17th century inn in Yorkshire Dales National Park. Close to
Malham, the Settle/Carlisle railway and the starting point for
many beautiful walks.*

LONGRIDGE Lancashire **Map 8 B2**

⊗££ **CORPORATION ARMS** Lower Road, Longridge, nr Preston.

⌣ **Hours:** Open 12.15pm - 2pm and 7pm - 9.30pm. Closed:
Christmas Day. **Cuisine:** Eg. Pan Fried Chicken, Beef Strogonoff,
homemade Steak, Kidney & Mushroom Pie, Stuffed Mushrooms,
Hot Chocolate Fudge Cake, Hot Sticky Toffee Pudding. ⊨ None.
CC All major cards. **Other Points:** Children welcome. No dogs. Set
price Sunday Lunch now available in addition to the a la carte
menu. **P** & **(V) Directions:** On the B6245 Longridge-Blackburn
road,½ mile from Longridge Centre.
MR A GORNALL ☎ (077 478) 2644.
*Situated in the wilds of Lancashire on the borders of the Fell
country, this pub provides a warm and friendly welcome to its
customers. The food and service are excellent, making it highly
recommended.*

LONGSDON Staffordshire **Map 8 C2**

⌂££ **BANK END FARM MOTEL** Leek Old Road, Longsdon, Stoke
⌣ on Trent.
⊨ 2 single, 3 double, 3 twin and 2 family bedrooms, 8 en suite. 1
bathroom. **Hours:** Breakfast 7.30am - 9.30am, and Dinner 7pm -
8.30pm (last orders). **CC** None. **Other Points:** Central heating.
Children welcome. Licensed. Residents lounge. TV. Garden. **P** &
Directions: Situated 2 miles south-west of Leek on A53.
MRS BARBARA ROBINSON ☎ (0538) 383 638
*A 14th century stone barn converted to provide single-storey
accommodation Very convenient for the potteries, the Peak
District and Alton Towers. The motel's swimming pool and
views over Endon Brook Valley make it popular with tourists and
businessmen. Les Routiers Casserole Award winner.*

LONGTOWN Cumbria **Map 8 A2**

⊗££ **THE SPORTSMAN'S RESTAURANT, MARCH BANK**
⌂£££ **HOTEL** Scotsdyke, Longtown.
⌣ **Hours:** Breakfast 8am - 9am, Lunch 12 noon - 2pm, Dinner 6pm -
9pm (last orders). **Cuisine:** Specialities include Locally Smoked
Salmon, Whole Roast Leg of Lamb (for 4 persons at 24 hours
notice), Scotch Angus steaks, Game. ⊨ 4 bedrooms, 3 en suite.
CC Access, Visa, AmEx. **Other Points:** Children welcome. No
smoking in restaurant. **P Directions:** 3 miles north of Longtown on
the A7. 9 miles M6, Junction 44.
THE MOORE FAMILY ☎ (0228) 791325.

Longtown continued

The 'Last Hotel in England' is an old country house with beautiful views over the River Esk. Personally run by the Moore family, you are assured a warm welcome and excellent service in both the hotel and restaurant. The food is of a very high standard yet offers excellent value for money. Highly recommended.

LOUTH Lincolnshire **Map 9 C2**

⊗£ **MR CHIPS FISH RESTAURANT** 17-21 Aswell Street, Louth. **Hours:** Open Monday to Saturday 9am - 11pm, including Bank holidays. **Cuisine:** Fresh North Sea haddock, cod, plaice, halibut & scampi with chips & mushy peas. Lincolnshire sausages, Norfolk chicken, Vegetarian. Selection of sweets. ⊨ None. **CC** None. **Other Points:** Children welcome. High chairs and mother and baby room. 2 car parks 250 yds away. No smoking section. Air conditioned. Coaches welcome. ৬ **(V) Directions:** From Market Place,turn into Queen St, then 1st right into Aswell St.
THE HAGAN FAMILY ☎ (0507) 603756.
A bright and roomy restaurant which provides excellent value in both quantity and quality. Seating for 300.

LYTHAM ST ANNES Lancashire **Map 8 B2**

⊗£ **BEDFORD HOTEL** 307-311 Clifton Drive South, Lytham St
⏡£££ Annes.
Hours: Breakfast 7.30am - 9.30am, Lunch 12 noon - 5pm and Dinner 6.30pm - 8.30pm (last orders). **Cuisine:** English and continental cuisine. ⊨ 36 bedrooms, all en suite. **CC** Access, Visa. **Other Points:** Children welcome. Dogs allowed. Fax No: (0253) 729244. Leisure centre. **P** ৬ **(V) Directions:** Off M6 to M55.Turn off at junction 4, then left, following signs.
J P & T BAKER ☎ (0253) 724636.
Exclusive family run hotel, with a reputation for comfort and cuisine. Situated 200 yards from shops, beach and swimming pool with 4 golf courses nearby. Other places of nearby interest include Blackpool, Liverpool Docks, Wigan Pier and the Lake District which are all easily accessible, as the motorway is 10 mins away.

⊗£ **CHADWICK HOTEL** South Promenade.
⏡£££ **Hours:** Meals from 7.30am - 10am, 1pm - 2pm and 7pm - 8.30pm. Open all year. **Cuisine:** Traditional English cooking, local seafood specialities. ⊨ 70 bedrooms, all en suite. **CC** All major cards. **Other Points:** Children welcome. **P** ৬ **(V)**
MR CORBETT MHCIMA ☎ (0253) 720061.
Modern, family-run hotel commanding lovely sea views. Spacious lounges overlook the seafront and indoor Leisure Pool. Other facilities include a spa bath, Turkish room, sauna and solarium.

⊗££ **FERNLEA HOTEL & LEISURE COMPLEX** 15 South
⏡£££ Promenade, St Annes-on-Sea.
CLUB **Hours:** Breakfast 8am - 9.30am, Lunch 12.30pm - 1.30pm, Dinner 7pm - 8pm (last orders). **Cuisine:** Fixed price 3 course menu and bar snacks at lunchtime. ⊨ 110 bedrooms, all en suite. **CC** All major cards. **Other Points:** Children welcome. Dogs allowed. Heated indoor swimming pool. Fully equipped gymnasium.

Lytham St Annes continued

Solarium. Squash court. Disco light & laser show. **◘ (V) Directions:** 5 miles from Blackpool. Close to the Pier.
TONY P CROSTON ☎ (0253) 726726.
Situated on St. Annes' South Promenade, the Fernlea is a large comfortable family run hotel, with lots of fun things to do. They serve well prepared, generous portions of food and the accommodation is of a high standard.

⊗£ **THE LINDUM HOTEL** 63-67 South Promenade, Lytham St
⊞£££ Annes.

Hours: Breakfast 8.30am - 9.15am, Bar Lunches 12 noon - 2pm, Dinner 6pm - 7pm. Sunday Lunch 12.45pm - 1.45pm. **Cuisine:** Dishes include Sardines with saffron rice, Roast beef and Yorkshire Pudding, poached Salmon with cucumber sauce. ⤶ 80 bedrooms, all en suite. **CC** Access, Visa, AmEx. **Other Points:** Children welcome. Dogs allowed. Night porter service. Sauna, solarium and jacuzzi. **◘ (V) Directions:** Near St Annes Pier, on the seafront.
LINDUM HOTEL LTD ☎ (0253) 721534.
Open all year round, the Lindum Hotel has 80 bedrooms, all with private bath, and modern facilities. Lounge entertainment and childrens parties are held regularly throughout the season. The food is all home cooked and offers good value for money.

MALTON North Yorkshire **Map 9 B1**
⊗£ **KINGS HEAD HOTEL** 5 Market Place, Malton.

Hours: Lunch 12 noon - 2pm, dinner 7pm - 9.30pm (last orders 9pm), bar snacks 11am - 2.30pm and 7pm - 9.30pm. **Cuisine:** Menu may feature - Chinese filo rolls, Wensleydale mushrooms, home made lasagne, sizzle platters and a range of traditional home made dishes. ⤶ None. **CC** Access, Visa. **Other Points:** Children welcome. Public parking available. **(V) Directions:** Located at top of market place.
CHRISTOPHER BARLOW ☎ (0653) 692289.
A delightful welcome awaits you when you visit this establishment. Serving good food at value for money prices, in a down to earth, homely and relaxing atmosphere.

MANCHESTER Greater Manchester **Map 8 C2**
⊗£££ **BEAUJOLAIS RESTAURANT** 70 Portland Street, Manchester.

Hours: Lunch 12 noon - 2pm, Dinner 6pm - 10.30pm (last orders). **Cuisine:** Provincial French cuisine. Specialities are fresh fish and Scottish beef. A la carte and table d'hote. ⤶ None. **CC** All major cards. **Other Points:** Children welcome. No dogs. **(V) Directions:** Off Piccadilly in the City centre.
SUSAN ROBERTS & RACHEL ROBINSON ☎ (061) 236 7260.
A French Bistro-style basement restaurant in the centre of Manchester. The atmosphere is relaxed and friendly, enhanced by the welcoming staff, alcoves and candlelit tables. The menus offer a choice of excellent French dishes including medallions of fresh Monkfish tail in a red pepper sauce and a saffron sauce, or Noisetes D'Agneau. Good food, service and atmosphere.

Manchester continued

⊗£ **CRESCENT GATE HOTEL** Park Crescent, Victoria Park,
🏨£££ Manchester.

Hours: 7.30am - 9am, 12 noon - 2pm and 7pm - 8pm. Bar meals 12 noon - 2pm and 6.30pm - 10.30pm (last orders). **Cuisine:** English cuisine. 🛏 26 bedrooms, 18 en suite, with colour satellite TV, radio, alarm, telephone and tea/coffee facilities. **CC** All major cards. **Other Points:** Children welcome. Pets allowed. Open Sundays and bank holidays. Afternoon teas served. Fax No. (061) 257 2822. 🅿 **(V) Directions:** B5166,to city for 4 miles. Park Cres 3rd right after Platt Fields.
TERRY HUGHES ☎ (061) 224 0672.
The Crescent Gate is situated in Victoria Park, one of the pleasant park estates to be found near to the city centre. Set in a quiet tree-lined avenue, the hotel is an ideal place to wind down after a long journey or a hard day's work.

🏨££ **ELM GRANGE HOTEL** 561 Wilmslow Road, Withington, Manchester.

🛏 17 single, 4 double, 11 twin, 16 en suite. 3 bathrooms. Colour TV, video tea/coffee making facilities, direct dial phones, trouser presses, ironing boards and radio alarm clocks in all rooms. **Hours:** Breakfast 7.15am - 9.45am, dinner 6.30pm - 8.15pm (last orders). **CC** Access, Visa. **Other Points:** Children welcome. No dogs. Central heating. Licensed. Garden. Residents' lounge and cocktail bar. Ground floors available. 🅿 ♿ **Directions:** From A34 at W.Didsbury,take B5117 to Didsbury,hotel 1 mile on right.
GORDON W DELF ☎ (061) 445 3336.

Manchester continued

A family run commercial hotel situated approximately 20 minutes drive from the City centre, Exhibition centre and the Airport. In a main road position with a good bus service to the main shopping area and is easily located by following the signposts to Christie Hospital which is opposite the hotel. Good food from an extensive menu.

⊗£ **GAYLORD INDIA RESTAURANT** Amethyst House, Spring Gardens, Manchester.
Hours: Lunch 12 noon - 3pm, Dinner 6pm - 11.30pm. Closed: Christmas Day. **Cuisine:** North Indian Tandoori dishes, eg. kebab, tikka, pakora. Vegetarian dishes such as Saag paneer, Onion kulcha. ⊨ None. **CC** All major cards. **Other Points:** Children welcome. No dogs. No smoking area. Street parking. & **(V)** **Directions:** Centre of Manchester.
PARDEEP CHADHA ☎ (061) 832 6037/4866.
A well-known restaurant, part of an international chain. You can watch your dishes being prepared through the tandoor's window. Being situated in the heart of the city, this is a very popular lunchtime rendezvous.

⊗£ **THAT CAFE** 1031/1033 Stockport Road, South Levenshulme.
Hours: Lunch 12.30pm - 2.30pm on Sundays, Dinner 7pm - 11pm (last orders). Closed: Monday and Sunday evenings. **Cuisine:** Special £9.95 Table d'hote menu, exclusive of coffee/tea, Tuesday - Thursday evenings. Menu changes weekly. Fresh fish according to season. ⊨ None. **CC** Access, Visa, AmEx. **Other Points:** Children welcome. Private function room available for weddings etc. **(V) Directions:** On the A6 between Manchester and Stockport.
JOSEPH QUINN ☎ (061) 432 4672
Situated 3 miles from Manchester city centre, That Cafe offers a good variety of both meat and vegetarian dishes. The atmosphere and decor are unique with open fires, bric a brac and 30's and 40's music. There is live music on Sundays.

⊗££ **THE MOCK TURTLE RESTAURANT & CARROLL'S**
⊞££ **HOTEL** 256 Wilmslow Road, Fallowfield, Manchester.
Hours: Breakfast 7am - 9am, Dinner 6pm - 10.30pm (7pm - 11pm Friday & Saturday). Restaurant closed: Sunday evening. **Cuisine:** Predominantly French cuisine specialising in fish, game and vegetarian dishes. Only the finest fresh ingredients used. ⊨ 8 single, 8 double and 8 twin bedrooms, all en suite. **CC** All major cards. **Other Points:** Children welcome. No dogs. Weddings and party bookings. Fax No: (061) 257 2046. Hotel telephone no: (061) 225 2602. **P** & **(V) Directions:** Oxford Rd from City centre for 3 miles. Opp. students Residences.
MR D SANDWITH ☎ (061) 224 2340.
An intimate, candlelit, French style restaurant in a delightful old church building. The menu offers imaginative dishes, excellently cooked and presented, and served by friendly and efficient staff. The restaurant is attached to a 24-bedroom hotel complete with heated indoor swimming pool, and to the Queen of Hearts Pub.

Manchester continued

⊛££ **WILLOW BANK HOTEL** 340 Wilmslow Road, Fallowfield,
⊞££££ Manchester.
    Hours: Breakfast 7.30am - 10.15am, lunch 12.30pm - 2pm,
dinner 7pm - 10.15pm. Hotel open all day, every day of the year.
Cuisine: Extensive menu including homemade soups and sweets,
Aberdeen beef. A la carte and table d'hote. ⊨ 122 bedrooms, all
en suite. **CC** All major cards. **Other Points:** Children welcome. No
dogs. **P** **(V) Directions:** On the B5093, the main road into the city
from the south.
    MALCOLM BLACK ☎ (061) 224 0461.
Comfortable three star hotel with fully air conditioned,
international restaurant. Easy access to Manchester Airport, city
centre and major conference and exhibition sites.

MARKET RASEN Lincolnshire **Map 9 C2**

⊛£ **JOSSALS** 48-50 Queen Street, Market Rasen.
CLUB **Hours:** Restaurant: Lunch Monday to Friday bookings only.
Sunday lunch 12 noon - 2pm. Dinner Tuesday to Saturday 7pm -
9.30pm. Sunday and Monday dinner - bookings only. Coffee shop
open Monday to Saturday 9am - 4.30pm. **Cuisine:** Extensive a la
carte menu, featuring home cooking using fresh local produce.
Coffee shop: homemade hot & cold snacks, home baking.
⊨ None. **CC** All major cards. **Other Points:** Children welcome.
Afternoon teas in restaurant. ᵫ **(V) Directions:** On the A631, main
high street of Market Rasen. Below Railway bridge.
    JO PARSONS & SALLY GRAHAM ☎ (0673) 843948.
An attractive terrace-style restaurant with adjoining coffee
shop, situated on the main street of Market Rasen, offering very
good food at very reasonable prices. The combination of well
cooked and prepared food and the genuinely friendly welcome,
makes this restaurant a must for those in the area for the local
horse racing or for touring the beauty of the Lincolnshire Wolds.

MARKET WEIGHTON Humberside **Map 9 B2**

⊛££ **YE OLDE RED LION** Old Road, Holme-on-Spalding-Moor,
⊞£££ Market Weighton.
    Hours: Breakfast 7.30am - 9.30am, Dinner 7.30pm - 9.45pm (last
orders). Bar snacks 12 noon - 2pm and 7pm - 10pm. **Cuisine:**
Dishes may include Steak au Poivre, Chicken Neptune, Dover
Sole. Bar meals. ⊨ 11 bedrooms, all en suite. **CC** Access, Visa,
AmEx. **Other Points:** Children over 12 welcome. No dogs.
Conferences for up to 30 people and audio visual equipment
available. Garden dining. **P** ᵫ **(V) Directions:** A614, main road to
east coast from M62, M18 and M1.
    BRIAN & SANDRA WALSH ☎ (0430) 860220.
Nestling in the heart of the gentle Yorkshire wolds, Ye Olde Red
Lion is a distinguished and historical coaching Inn. Family run,
all guests are assured of a warm welcome, personal and homely
service. The food is traditional with a choice of a la carte menu
and bar meals. Comfortable accommodation.

MATLOCK Derbyshire **Map 9 C1**

⊛£ **THE ELIZABETHAN RESTAURANT** 4 Crown Square,
Matlock.
    Hours: Morning coffee 10am - 12 noon, lunch 12 noon - 3pm,
afternoon tea 3pm - 5pm, dinner 7.30pm - 10pm (last orders)

NORTHERN ENGLAND

Matlock continued

Thursday, Friday, Saturday and Sunday. Closed: Boxing Day. **Cuisine:** Steak and kidney pie, savoury filled pancakes. Homemade, Continental dishes. Roasts daily. ➡ None. **CC** Access, Visa. **Other Points:** Children welcome. No dogs. Coaches by appointment. **P** & **(V) Directions:** On the A6 in the centre of town.

MR G E FAULKNER ☎ (0629) 583533.

This attractive restaurant is located right in the centre of the picturesque town of Matlock on the A6. It offers a warm, friendly welcome and excellent food in idyllic surroundings.

⌂£ THE MANOR FARMHOUSE Dethick, nr Matlock.

➡ 1 twin and 1 double room, en suite with TV. 1 twin and 1 single room. 1 general bathroom. **Hours:** Breakfast 8.30am - 9am, dinner 7.30pm (order in morning). Closed: December. **CC** None. **Other Points:** Central heating. Children over 8 years welcome. No dogs. Residents lounge TV. **P** **Directions:** From the M1 jct 28, follow signs for Matlock then take Dethick turn.

NANCY GROOM ☎ (0629) 534246.

16th century part Elizabethan farmhouse near the A6, A38 and M1 in a delightful setting with open views. All meals are freshly cooked on an AGA cooker. An excellent centre for walking, riding and touring at the gateway to the Peak District, many guests returning year after year.

⊗££ THE TAVERN AT TANSLEY Nottingham Road, Tansley, nr
⌂££ Matlock.

Hours: Breakfast 7.30am - 9am, Lunch 12 noon - 2.30pm (last orders), Dinner 6.30pm - 9.30pm (last orders). Sunday Lunch 12 noon - 2.30pm, Dinner 7pm - 9pm. **Cuisine:** A la Carte & Table d'hote menus, Bar meals/snacks and vegetarian meals available. ➡ 3 double bedrooms, all en suite. **CC** Access, Visa, AmEx. **Other Points:** Children welcome. Garden. Afternoon teas. Dogs allowed but not in hotel rooms. **P** & **(V) Directions:** A615 near Riber Castle.

KEITH & JOAN COLTON ☎ (0629) 57735

17th Century olde world Country Inn. Decor and furnishings are to a very high standard. The Tavern at Tansley is popular and busy but still enjoys a relaxed atmosphere. Service is attentive and friendly.

MAWDESLEY Lancashire **Map 8 C2**

⊗£ ROBIN HOOD INN Bluestone Lane, Mawdesley, Nr Ormskirk.

Hours: Lunch 12 noon - 2pm, evening 6.30pm - 9.30pm. **Cuisine:** Traditional, varied menu available in bar. Restaurant menu: steaks, gammon. ➡ None. **CC** Access, Visa. **Other Points:** Children welcome. Open Bank holidays. Afternoon tea served Sundays. **P** **(V) Directions:** Take B5246 to Mawdesley. Through village, turn left.

DAVID CROPPER ☎ (0704) 822275.

A small family pub set in a rural area and humming with local life. Prompt friendly service and special Robin Hood dishes such as the Friar Tuck grill.

MELMERBY Cumbria **Map 8 A2**

SHEPHERDS INN Melmerby, nr Penrith.

Hours: Bar meals 11am - 2.30pm (12 noon - 2pm Sundays) and 6pm - 10pm. (7pm - 10pm Sundays). Closed: Christmas Day. **Cuisine:** Many home made dishes such as Spare ribs, Chicken Leoni, Rogan Gosht. Choice of 26 different cheeses for Ploughmans. None. **CC** Access, Visa, AmEx. **Other Points:** Children welcome. No dogs. & **(V) Directions:** On the A686 in Melmerby.

MARTIN & CHRISTINE BAUCUTT ☎ (076 881) 217.

An 18th century pub, built of traditional Cumberland stone, nestling at the foot of Hartside Pass in the Northern Pennines. Serves fine traditional beers and extensive, original, home prepared meals. Winner of the 1990 Dairy Crest Cheese Symbol of Excellence for their outstanding cheese selection. Casserole Award winner 1991.

MIDDLETON TYAS North Yorkshire **Map 9 B1**

SHOULDER OF MUTTON INN Middleton Tyas, nr Richmond.

Hours: Lunch 12 noon - 2pm, dinner 7pm - 10pm (last orders). Bar meals 12 noon - 2pm and 7pm - 10pm. **Cuisine:** Steaks, fish, poultry. Menu changes weekly. None. **CC** Access, Visa, AmEx. **Other Points:** Children welcome. No pets. **P** & **Directions:** ½ mile from the Scotch Corner roundabout on the A1.

MR & MRS TWEEDY ☎ (032 577) 271.

Built 300 years ago as a farmhouse, the Shoulder of Mutton has been tastefully restored retaining all the charm and character of a bygone era. The Shoulder of Mutton makes an ideal stopover on the route to Scotland.

MORECAMBE Lancashire **Map 8 B2**

CRAIGWELL HOTEL & LAMPLIGHT RESTAURANT 372 Marine Road East, Morecambe.

Hours: Breakfast 7.30am - 9.30am, Dinner 6pm - 10pm. **Cuisine:** A la carte and table d'hote menus. Dishes may include Salmon steak with Hollandaise sauce, Tournedos Rossini, Lamplight turkey en croute. 5 single, 5 double, 1 twin and 2 family bedrooms, all en suite. Colour TV, direct dial telephone and tea/coffee making facilities in all rooms. **CC** Access, Visa, AmEx. **Other Points:** Central heating. Children welcome. Licensed bar. Residents' lounge. 40 seater restaurant. **P** **(V) Directions:** Off the A5105, situated on the seafront in Morecambe.

PAUL & WINIFRED GRAY ☎ (0524) 410095/418399

A terraced, bay-fronted property on the sea-front with lovely views across the bay to the Lakeland Hills. The Gray's go out of their way to cater for their visitors' comfort and convenience. Recently opened, the Lamplight Restaurant provides well-cooked food, attractively presented and served by warm and courteous staff.

MIDLAND HOTEL Marine Road, Morecambe.

Hours: Breakfast 7am - 10am, Lunch 12 noon - 2pm, Dinner 7pm - 9.30pm (last orders). Bar meals 11am - 4pm. **Cuisine:** A la carte, table d'hote and bar meals. 13 single, 10 double, 21 twin and 4 family bedrooms, all en suite. All bedrooms have sea views. Special breaks. **CC** All major cards. **Other Points:** Children

Morecambe continued

welcome. Dogs allowed. Residents' lounge. Garden. Lift to all floors. Afternoon teas. Private parties & functions. ▣ ৬ **(V)** **Directions:** On the seafront adjacent to the Bobble Leisure Centre.

MR J PEARSON ☎ (0524) 417180.

A celebrated Art Deco hotel, the setting for the 'Hercule Poirot' TV series, and, under its new ownership, popular with many TV personalities for short stays. It is set in a unique beachside position directly overlooking Morecambe Bay, and close to the Lake District and Yorkshire Dales. Adjacent to Morecambe's popular all-weather family leisure complex.

⌂£££ **MIDLAND HOTEL** Marine Road, Morecambe.

🛏 13 single, 10 double, 21 twin and 4 family bedrooms, all en suite. All bedrooms have sea views. Special breaks. **Hours:** Breakfast 7am - 10am, Lunch 12 noon - 2pm, Dinner 7pm - 9.30pm (last orders). Bar meals 11am - 4pm. ☒ All major cards. **Other Points:** Children welcome. Dogs allowed. Residents' lounge. Garden. Lift to all floors. Afternoon teas. Private parties & functions. ▣ ৬ **(V) Directions:** On the seafront adjacent to the Bobble Leisure Centre.

MR J PEARSON ☎ (0524) 417180.

A celebrated Art Deco hotel, the setting for the 'Hercule Poirot' TV series, and, under its new ownership, popular with many TV personalities for short stays. It is set in a unique beachside position directly overlooking Morecambe Bay, and close to the Lake District and Yorkshire Dales. Adjacent to Morecambe's popular all-weather family leisure complex.

NEASHAM County Durham **Map 9 B1**

⊗£ **THE FOX AND HOUNDS** 24 Teesway, Neasham, nr Darlington.

Hours: Bar meals 12 noon - 2pm, and 7.30pm - 9.30pm. Family menu 5pm - 7pm (Mon - Fri), and indoor barbecue 7.30pm - 9.30pm (weekends) in new conservatory. **Cuisine:** Extensive bar meal menu. Daily specials. 🛏 None. ☒ Access. **Other Points:** Large beer garden. Children welcome. New conservatory. ▣ ৬ **(V) Directions:** From the A67 or the A167 follow signs to Neasham.

MIKE ANDERSON ☎ (0325) 720350.

This village pub is situated on the banks of the river Tees in Neasham, 2 miles south of Darlington. With a large beer garden, family room and children's play area, this is a must for the family on the move.

NEWARK Nottinghamshire **Map 9 C1**

⊗££ **NEW FERRY RESTAURANT** Riverside, Farndon, Newark.

⌂ **Hours:** Lunch 12 noon - 2pm, Dinner 7pm - 10pm (last orders). Bar snacks 12 noon - 2pm. Closed: All day Monday except Bank Holidays. **Cuisine:** Mediterranean influenced cuisine. Dishes may include fresh salmon with a fennel & cream sauce, rack of lamb with a redcurrant & port sauce. 🛏 None. ☒ All major cards. **Other Points:** Children welcome. No dogs. Garden dining. ▣ ৬ **(V Directions:** Off A46, Nottingham to Newark rd. 5 mins from Newark by River Trent.

JOSE & PAM GOMES ☎ (0636) 76578.

Newark continued

Standing attractively by the River Trent, the New Ferry Restaurant serves generous portions of well-cooked food in a relaxed and friendly atmosphere. The menus offer a wide choice of dishes and the specialities change 3 times a week to make use of the best in fresh produce. The high standard of the food is complemented by a good, varied wine list.

NEWBY BRIDGE Cumbria **Map 8 B2**

⊗££ **LAKESIDE HOTEL ON WINDERMERE** Newby Bridge, Lake Windermere.

Hours: 7.30am - 9.30am, 12 noon - 3pm, and 6pm - 9.30pm (last orders). Bar meals served between 12 noon - 3pm, and 6pm - 9pm. **Cuisine:** Traditional English fayre, including local specialities such as Cumbrian grill, and Esthwaite trout. Good wine list. Special 'children's menu'. ⊨ 2 single, 14 double, 50 twin, and 3 family rooms, all en suite. All rooms have colour TVs, telephones, and tea/coffee facilities. 4-posters available. **CC** All major cards. **Other Points:** Children welcome. Dogs allowed. Afternoon teas served. Open Sundays and bank holidays. Good conference facilities. Special 'Rain Breaks'. ▣ ⅙ **(V) Directions:** A590 for Barrow.Turn at Newby Bridge.Minor Rd on right for Hawkshead

MR N.R. TALBOT ☎ (05395) 31207

At the Lakeside hotel, guests can enjoy breathtaking views of Lake Windermere as far as the mountains in the north. The hotel has been completely refurbished to provide modern comforts, but has all the character of a traditional Lakeland hotel. New conservatory and refurbished cafe, new restaurant.

⊗££ **SWAN HOTEL** Newby Bridge, Ulverston.

[W]
[CLUB] **Hours:** Breakfast 7.30am - 9.30am (8am - 10am weekends and Bank holidays), Dinner 7pm - 9pm (7.30pm - 9.30pm Saturdays). Meals in 'The Mailcoach' Wine Bar from 11.45am - 2.45pm and 6.30pm - 9.45pm March to December. Closed: 12 days in January. **Cuisine:** English - featuring, when available, Char, Venison, Cumberland Farmhouse cheese, and French cuisine. ⊨ 36 bedrooms, all en suite. **CC** All major cards. **Other Points:** Children welcome. No dogs. Fax No: (053 95) 31917. ▣ **(V) Directions:** Overlooking Newby Bridge. The village is on the A590.

JAMES A. BERTLIN, MHCIMA, MCFA - Manager ☎ (053 95) 31681.

A 16th century coaching inn in a superb location at the southern end of Lake Windermere. The Mailcoach Wine Bar serves informal meals in a relaxed atmosphere, whilst The Tithe Barn Restaurant overlooking Newby Bridge and the River Leven offers a more extensive menu in a more traditional setting.

NEWCASTLE UNDER LYME Staffordshire **Map 8 C2**

⟐££ **GABLES HOTEL** 570-572 Etruria Road, Newcastle.

⊨ 6 double, 1 twin and 6 family bedrooms all en suite. 2 bathrooms and 1 shower. **Hours:** Breakfast 7.15am - 8.45am, dinner 6pm - 8.30pm (last orders). **CC** None. **Other Points:** Central heating. Children and pets welcome. Residents lounge. TV. Garden. ▣ ⅙ **(V) Directions:** On the A53 1/2 mile from town centre next to New Victoria Theatre.

Newcastle under Lyme continued
ROSEMARY BRASSINGTON ☎ (0782) 619748.
The Gables is a fine Edwardian townhouse set in extensive gardens. Situated next to the new Victoria Theatre and ideal for visitors to Stoke on Trent's pottery factories (e.g. Wedgwood, Spode and Royal Doulton) and to Alton Towers.

⊗££ **BRUNSWICKS RESTAURANT** 10 Brunswick Street, Newcastle-Under-Lyme
Hours: Lunch (Tuesday - Friday) 12 noon - 2pm, dinner (Tuesday - Saturday) 6.30pm onwards. Closed: Sunday and Monday. **Cuisine:** European cuisine. House specialities are steaks served with a variety of sauces, and evening blackboard specials featuring many fresh fish dishes. ⊨ None. ☒ All major cards. **Other Points:** Children most welcome. **(V) Directions:** On Brunswick Street between Rizy and Newcastle swimming baths.
MRS M ARCHER ☎ (0782) 635999.
A Victorian type building decorated brightly and tastefully decorated, only 2 minutes walk from the town centre. This restaurant serves a range of European dishes in a bright and busy atmosphere.

⊗££ **THE WHEATSHEAF INN AT ONNELEY** Barhill Road,
⊞££££ Onneley.
CLUB **Hours:** 7.30am - 10am, 12 noon - 2pm and 7pm - 9.30pm. Bar meals 12 noon - 2pm and 6pm - 10pm (last orders). **Cuisine:** English and continental cuisine. ⊨ 6 double, 2 twin and 1 family bedroom, all en suite. ☒ Access, Visa, AmEx. **Other Points:** Children welcome. Pets allowed. Open Sundays and bank holidays. Conference facilities. Fax: (0782) 751499. ▣ **(V) Directions:** A525, 6 miles W of Newcastle-Under-Lyme, between Madeley and Woore.
M A BITTNER ☎ (0782) 751581.
An 18th century country inn located in beautiful countryside, adjoining Onnerley Golf Club, but close to 'The Potteries' conurbation. The Wheatsheaf offers comfortable accommodation and food of an excellent quality in the bar and restaurant. Places of local interest include Bridgemere Garden World, Stapeley Water Gardens, The Potteries and Keele University.

NEWCASTLE UPON TYNE Tyne & Wear **Map 9 A1**
⊗££££ **COURTNEY'S RESTAURANT** 5/7 The Side, Quayside, Newcastle Upon Tyne.
Hours: Lunch Monday - Friday 12 noon - 2pm, Dinner Monday - Saturday 7pm - 10.30pm (last orders, 10.45pm Saturdays). Closed: Saturday lunch, all day Sunday and Bank Holidays except Good Friday dinner. **Cuisine:** Modern International cusine. Emphasis on fresh and quality ingredients. Daily specials and a good vegetarian choice. ⊨ None. ☒ Access, Visa, AmEx. **Other Points:** No dogs. (Except guide dogs). **(V) Directions:** Bottom of Dean St. R.H. side before roundabout at Quayside.
MICHAEL & KERENSA CARR ☎ (091) 232 5537.
A small restaurant, well decorated in a simple style to provide a restful setting in which to enjoy the good food. Only the freshest and best ingredients are used and all dishes are well cooked and presented. The service is welcoming and efficient and complements the warm, relaxed atmosphere in the restaurant.

Newcastle upon Tyne continued

⊗££ **THE ORIGINAL MASONS** Hexham Road, Walbottle, Newcastle.
Hours: Lunch 12 noon - 3pm, dinner 6.30pm - 9.45pm. Bar lunches and dinners same times. Open for Sunday lunch and dinner. **Cuisine:** English/Country style cuisine. Dishes inlcude Whitby scampi, Fillets of Chicken Princess and a wide selection of steaks. . None. CC None. **Other Points:** Children welcome. Special Senior Citizens lunch. P ♿ **(V) Directions:** Approximately 3 miles west of Newcastle. Just off A69.
KEVIN KELLY ☎ (091) 267 5563
This is a recently refurbished public house and restaurant. Located in a rural village, The Original Masons specalises in unusual well cooked food served in generous portions. A treat for all the family to visit.

⊗£ ££££ **WHITES HOTEL** 38-42 Osborne Road, Jesmond, Newcastle Upon Tyne.
Hours: Breakfast 7.30am - 9.30am, Lunch 12 noon - 2.00pm and Dinner 6.00pm - 9.30pm (last orders). Closed: Sunday evening. **Cuisine:** Table d'hote and a la carte menu, featuring fresh homemade dishes. 40 bedrooms, most en suite. CC All major cards. **Other Points:** Children welcome. Wedding and small conference facilities. P **(V) Directions:** In the Newcastle suburb of Jesmond.
MR & MRS WHITE ☎ (091) 281 5126.
An Edwardian hotel, situated in a pleasant suburb of Newcastle-Upon Tyne, providing its guests with well-cooked, tasty food, comfortable accommodation and a warm and friendly welcome by the proprietors, the White family.

NEWTON LE WILLOWS Merseyside **Map 8 C2**

⊗£ ££ **BULLS HEAD HOTEL** Southworth Road, Newton-Le-Willows.
Hours: Bar open for lunch 11.30am - 3pm and dinner 5pm - 10pm (Sundays 7pm - 10pm). **Cuisine:** Variety of specials changed daily. 7 bedrooms, 5 en suite. CC Access, Visa. **Other Points:** Children welcome (until 8pm). Childrens play area. Beer garden. Residents lounge and gym facilities. P ♿ **(V) Directions:** Outskirts of Newton-Le-Willows, close to junction M6 and M62.
TOM & CATH DARNBROUGH ☎ (0925) 221480.
The Bulls Head Hotel offers a cosy atmosphere for informal family eating, children being catered for with their own menu and a play area. The atmosphere is friendly and relaxed and the excellent food and fine Tetley beers ensure plenty of regular visitors.

NORTHALLERTON North Yorkshire **Map 9 B1**

⊗£ **DUKE OF WELLINGTON INN** Welbury, Northallerton.
Hours: Bar meals 12 noon - 2pm and 7pm - 10pm. Closed: Monday and Tuesday lunchtime. **Cuisine:** Traditional homemade cuisine. Dishes may include Duck a l'orange, Steak Diane, Goujons of Sole. Vegetarian dishes. None. CC Access, Visa. **Other Points:** Children welcome. No dogs. Beer garden. Children's play area. P ♿ **(V) Directions:** Between A19 & A167. 7 miles N of Northallerton, 3 miles W of A19.
MR & MRS THOMPSON ☎ (060982) 464.

Northallerton continued

A family run, rural village Inn with a warm, welcoming atmosphere enhanced by real log fires in winter. All food is fresh, well-cooked and attractively presented, the service warm and courteous. For a friendly, relaxed atmosphere, good food and service, the Duke of Wellington is well worth a visit.

⌂£ **THE WINDSOR GUEST HOUSE** 56 South Parade, Northallerton.

2 double en suite, 3 twin (1 with private bathroom), and 1 family bedroom. 1 bathroom, 1 shower. Colour TV and hot drink facilities in all rooms. **Hours:** Breakfast 8am - 9am and dinner 6.30pm - 7.30pm (order by lunchtime). Closed: Christmas to New Year. **CC** Access, Visa. **Other Points:** Central heating. Children welcome. Dogs allowed. Residents lounge with TV. Street parking. Eurocard accepted.

MRS CYNTHIA PEACOCK ☎ (0609) 774100.

A well-maintained Victorian town house, 5 minutes walk from the station and main street. An ideal location for touring the Dales and James Herriot Country or as a stop-over on the journey from north to south. The Peacocks aim to please and this is reflected in the friendly atmosphere in the house.

NORTHWICH Cheshire **Map 8 C2**

⌂£ **SPRINGFIELD GUEST HOUSE** Chester Road, Delamere, Northwich.

3 single, 2 double, 1 twin and 1 family bedroom, 2 en suite. 1 bathroom. 1 shower. **Hours:** Breakfast 7.30am - 9am. Dinner 6.30pm - 8pm (order by 7.30pm). **CC** None. **Other Points:** Central heating. Children welcome. Residents lounge and sun lounge. TV. Garden. **P** **Directions:** On the A556, 1 mile west of the intersection with the A49.

MR & MRS J MULHOLLAND ☎ (0606) 882538.

A family guest house built in 1863 - an impressive, white, stucco faced building surrounded by lawns. Local places of interest include Delamere Forest, Sandstone Trail and Oulton Park race track, with Chester only 12 miles away. 18 miles from the M6 motorway (exit 18). 25 minutes drive from Manchester Airport.

NORTON North Yorkshire **Map 9 B1**

⊗£ **CORNUCOPIA** 87 Commercial Street, Norton, Malton.

Hours: Lunch 12 noon - 2pm, dinner 6.30pm - 10pm (last orders 9.45pm). Bar meals 12 noon - 2pm and 6.30pm - 10pm. **Cuisine:** Halibut, salmon & prawn mornay, boned duckling, traditional Sunday lunch. braised beef simmered in ale & herb dumplings, pork casserole & apple fritters. None. **CC** Access, Visa. **Other Points:** Children welcome. No dogs. Beer garden. **P** & **(V)** **Directions:** Off the A64 in the centre of Norton.

HAROLD ST QUINTON ☎ (0653) 693456.

Set in the heart of the Horse racing capital of the North, the restaurant is appropriately adorned with horse racing memorabilia. The menu is extensive and innovative with a wine list to suite most palates. An award winning pub and a finalist in the Steak and Kidney Pie competition.

NOTTINGHAM Nottinghamshire **Map 9 C1**

⊗£ **BELL INN** Old Market Square, Nottingham.
Hours: Meals served 12 noon - 2.15pm (last orders). Closed evenings and Sundays. **Cuisine:** Good English fare at reasonable prices. ⊨ None. **CC** Access, Visa. **Other Points:** Children welcome in restaurant. Pets allowed (in bars only). On street parking. **(V) Directions:** Situated in Old Market Square in the centre of Nottingham.
DAVID R. JACKSON ☎ (0602) 475241.
A 15th century traditional inn, situated in the historic heart of Nottingham, offering well presented appetising English fare complemented by warm and courteous service. Owned and operated by the same family for over 90 years, the Bell Inn, with its original oak beams and ancient flagstones makes a pleasant lunchtime stop for locals and tourists alike.

⊗£ **THE HAVEN** Grantham Road, Whatton, Nottingham.
£££ **Hours:** Open all day for food and drinks. 7am - 9.30am, 12 noon - 2pm, and 6pm - 10pm. Bar meals and restaurant. **Cuisine:** English cuisine, including Belvoir Steak and speciality flambe. ⊨ 2 single, 17 double, 10 twin, and 4 family rooms, all en suite. All rooms have colour TV, telephone and tea/coffee facilities. 4-posters available. **CC** Access, Visa, AmEx. **Other Points:** Children welcome. Dogs allowed. Open Sundays and bank holidays. Afternoon teas. Garden dining. **P** க **(V) Directions:** Between Notts and Grantham. Corner of A52 and rd to Belvoir Castle.
LESLIE & BETTY HYDES ☎ (0949) 50800
The Haven is a pleasant, homely hotel, situated in 5 acres of grassland in the beautiful Vale of Belvoir. Offers food of fine quality, in generous proportions, at very good value for money.

⊗£££ **THE REINDEER INN** Main Street, Hoveringham, Nottingham.
Hours: Bar meals 12 noon - 2pm, Dinner 7pm - 9.30pm (last orders). Table resevations recommended for dinner. Closed: Monday lunch except Bank Holidays. **Cuisine:** Imaginative menu featuring predominantly French-style cuisine. Eg. Fillet Steak stuffed with Mushroom Pate, wrapped in Bacon, & with a rich peppery sauce. ⊨ None. **CC** Access, Visa. **Other Points:** Children welcome at lunchtime. No dogs. **P** க **(V) Directions:** Off the A612 in Hoveringham Village.
LESLEY & ASHLEY GRICE ☎ (0602) 663629.
An attractive pub and restaurant with hanging baskets and a cottage-style interior with log fire in winter. Bar meals are served at midday whilst the dinner menu offers a imaginative menu of excellently cooked dishes. The emphasis is on originality and presentation and the Routiers inspector found the quality of food to be outstanding. Friendly, welcoming service.

⊗££ **WALTON'S HOTEL** North Lodge, The Park, Nottingham.
£££ **Hours:** Breakfast 7.30am - 10am, lunch 12.30pm - 2pm and dinner 7.30pm - 9.30pm. Restaurant closed: Sunday dinner. **Cuisine:** French. Dishes include scallops in ginger sauce, chicken in hazelnut sauce, and a large selection of steaks but fish is their speciality. ⊨ 17 bedrooms, all en suite. **CC** Access, Visa. **Other Points:** Children welcome. Garden. Afternoon teas. Dogs allowed. Residents' lounge. Fax no: (0602) 475053. **P** **(V) Directions:**

Nottingham continued
A6200. From A52 follow city centre signs. 200 yards police station.

G L FLANDERS & T W K WALTON ☎ (0602) 475215

Originally the hunting lodge to the Castle Deer Park, Walton's Hotel is a Regency house furnished with antiques and offering food and accommodation of a very high standard. The atmosphere is pleasant and welcoming and guests can relax and enjoy the good food and wine in the comfort of the elegant dining room. Within walking distance of the city centre, theatres and Castle.

ORMSKIRK Lancashire Map 8 C2

⊗£££ **BEAUFORT HOTEL** High Lane, Burscough, Ormskirk.
Hours: Breakfast 7am - 9.30am, lunch and bar snacks 12 noon - 2pm, dinner 7pm - 10pm (last orders). **Cuisine:** French table d'hote and a la carte menus. ⮞ 21 bedrooms, all en suite. **CC** All major cards. **Other Points:** Children welcome. No dogs. **P** **(V)** **Directions:** 2 miles north of Ormskirk on A59, corner of Pippin St. & High Lane.

DUNCAN REICH - General Manager ☎ (0704) 892655.

A welcoming hotel offering excellent food and comfortable accommodation. These high standards are matched by friendly and efficient service and the prices, especially in the restaurant, are very reasonable. Close to M6 and M58, the hotel is within easy travelling distance of Liverpool and Southport.

OSMOTHERLEY North Yorkshire Map 9 B1

⊗£ **THREE TUNS INN** South End, Osmotherley, Nr Northallerton.
Hours: Restaurant and bar meals 12 noon - 2.30pm (last orders) and 7pm - 9.30pm (last orders). Closed: Sunday evenings. **Cuisine:** English and French cuisine, home-cooked using fresh produce,the speciality being seafood. ⮞ None. **CC** None. **Other Points:** Children welcome. Limited area for dogs. **(V) Directions:** From North A19 turn left sign Northallerton/Osmotherley.

H & J DYSON ☎ (060) 983 301.

Situated on the edge of the beautiful North Yorkshire moors, in an old village, the Three Tuns is an early 18th century inn, with a walled garden. Ideal place for a relaxing meal, at good value, especially after tackling one of the nearby walks: Lyke Wake, Hambleton Hobble and Cleveland Way.

OTLEY West Yorkshire Map 9 B1

⊗££££ **CHEVIN LODGE COUNTRY PARK HOTEL** Yorkgate,
⊞££££ Otley.
Hours: Breakfast 7am - 9.30am, lunch and bar snacks 12.30pm - 2.30pm, dinner 7pm - 9.30pm. **Cuisine:** Predominantly English cuisine using fresh, local produce. ⮞ 52 bedrooms, all en suite. **CC** Access, Visa, AmEx. **Other Points:** Children welcome. Open Bank Holidays. Afternoon teas. Garden dining. Dogs allowed. Tennis court. Games room. Sauna. Fax No. (0943) 850335. **P** **&** **(V)**

MR PETER CAULFIELD. ☎ (0943) 467818.

Delightful Scandivanian Lodge Style building, with pine furniture and a unique layout. Large windows give a good view to the abundant wildlife which can be watched from the warm and friendly atmosphere of this country hotel. Enjoying an

Otley continued

intimate, special ambience and serving excellent food at reasonable prices served by competent staff.

PADIHAM Lancashire **Map 8 B2**

⊗££ **THE CELLAR RESTAURANT** Church Street, Padiham, nr Burnley.

Hours: Dinner 7pm - 10pm (last orders). Closed: Christmas Day, Boxing Day and New Year's Day. **Cuisine:** French and English cuisine. ⊨ None. **CC** Access, Visa. **Other Points:** Children welcome. **P** & **(V)**

DAVID & ELSIE CLARKE ☎ (0282) 75888/33677.

The building dates back to the 16th century retaining many of its original features, including a stone vaulted ceiling. Warm, intimate atmosphere.

PARKGATE Cheshire **Map 8 C1**

⊗£ **THE BOATHOUSE** 1 The Parade, Parkgate.

Hours: Lunch 12 noon - 2pm, dinner 6.30pm - 9.30pm, bar snacks 11.30am - 11pm. Open Bank Holidays. **Cuisine:** Classical home cooking, which has won many awards, dishes may include Welsh trimmed lamb with elderberry suace, saddle of hare or barbary duck. ⊨ None. **CC** Access, Visa, AmEx. **Other Points:** Children welcome. Garden dining. **P** & **(V)**

KEITH PARR. ☎ (051) 336 4187.

This is an establishment which certainly has a history. First recorded on this site was The Beer House in 1664. Today, the Boathouse has been recently refurbished and pleasantly decorated. Good portions of value for money meals are served in a quiet and friendly atmosphere.

PENRITH Cumbria **Map 8 A2**

⊗££ **PROSPECT HILL HOTEL** Kirkoswald.

⌂££ **Hours:** Breakfast 8.30am - 9.30am, Business Lunches by
CLUB arrangement, dinner 7.15pm - 9pm. Closed: December 24th, 25th and 26th. **Cuisine:** Freshly prepared a la carte menu and special budget table d'hote menu. ⊨ 3 single, 3 twin and 6 double bedrooms. 5 en suite. **CC** Access, Visa, AmEx. **Other Points:** Children welcome. Garden. Disabled access to dining room only. Only 20 minutes from M6, junction 41. **P** **(V)**

Directions: A6 north to B6413. East to Kirkoswald. 1/2 mile north off B6413.

MR & MRS HENDERSON. ☎ (076883) 500.

This 18th century farm building complex is found in a beautiful rural, rich green, and unspoilt setting with panoramic views over the Eden Valley. It offers outstanding accommodation and food in a warm and friendly environment.

⊗££ **THE SWISS CHALET INN** Pooley Bridge, Penrith, Lake
⌂£££ Ullswater.

Hours: 8.30am - 9.30am, 12 noon - 2pm, 6pm - 10pm. **Cuisine:** Mainly Swiss-style cuisine, but also many Italian dishes and traditional English fayre. Children's menu. Good wine list. ⊨ 9 bedrooms - 8 double and 1 twin, all en suite. Colour TV, radio, iron, hairdryer and tea/coffee facilities. **CC** Access, Visa. **Other Points:** Dogs allowed. Open for Sunday dinner and bank holidays.

Penrith continued

    P **(V) Directions:** B5320 5 miles SW of Penrith. NE end of Ullswater.

    MR & MRS ARDLEY ☎ (07684) 86215.

This small, friendly inn is situated in a beautiful position near Lake Ullswater and only 5 miles south west of Penrith. The Swiss Chalet style restaurant offers a large selection of home cooked dishes to suit all tastes and a good selection of wines. Friendly, efficient service, very comfortable accommodation with Swiss-style furnishings and beautifully prepared meals.

PICKERING North Yorkshire **Map 9 B1**

⊗££ **BEAN SHEAF RESTAURANT AND HOTEL** Malton Road, ⊓£££ Kirby Misperton, Pickering, Malton.

    Hours: Breakfast 8am - 10am, Lunch 12 noon - 2pm, Dinner 6.30pm - 9.30pm (last orders, 9pm Sundays). Closed: Monday lunch. **Cuisine:** English and Continental cuisine. Extensive choice of menu. Recently received the 'Heartbeat Healthy Eating' Award. ⊨ 20 bedrooms, all en suite. **CC** Access, Visa. **Other Points:** Children welcome. Garden. Afternoon teas. Dogs allowed. No smoking area. Sauna & Solarium. Private parties, functions & conferences catered for. **P** **(V) Directions:** On the A169 between Malton and Pickering.

    MICHELE & ELIZABETH SARDONE ☎ (065386) 614.

An extension has been added to two old cottages to provide a restaurant, wine bar, bar and accommodation. Situated in the Vale of Pickering, the Bean Sheaf is ideally placed for touring the area. At the Bean Sheaf itself you will find good quality, comfortable accommodation, well cooked food and a friendly atmosphere.

PRESTON Lancashire **Map 8 B2**

⊗££ **CARAVELA RESTAURANT** Preston New Road, Freckleton, Preston.

    Hours: Lunch 12 noon - 2pm, Dinner 6.30pm - 10.30pm (last orders). Closed: Saturday Lunch and all day Monday. **Cuisine:** Portuguese cuisine. 3 course weekday lunch menu, Sunday lunch menu and A La Carte. Wide choice of Portuguese specialities. ⊨ None. **CC** Access, Visa. **Other Points:** Vegetarian meals by request. Children welcome. **P** & **Directions:** A584 Preston - Lytham road.

    A. FIGUEIRA & M. DE NOBREGA ☎ (0772) 632308.

A Portuguese restaurant, attractively decorated with pine wood furniture, fishing nets and old schooner paintings to create a Portuguese feel. The a la carte menu offers a wide choice of Portuguese dishes whilst the table d'hote provides a more British alternative. Excellently cooked and presented food and friendly, efficient service. Good selection of Portuguese wines.

⊗££ **DEAN COURT** Brownedge Lane, Bamber Bridge, Nr Preston. ⊓£££ **Hours:** Breakfast 7am - 9.30am, lunch 12 noon - 2pm (last orders), dinner 6.30pm - 10pm (last orders 9.45pm). **Cuisine:** House speciality: Steak Diane. Extensive menu. ⊨ 10 rooms. 1 single, 2 twin and 7 double bedrooms. 9 en suite. **CC** Access, Visa. **Other Points:** Garden. Weddings catered for. **P** & **(V) Directions:** Five minutes by car from M6 motorway junction 29.

    MR & MRS HOSKER ☎ (0772) 35114.

Preston continued

Formerly a doctors house, Dean Court is now a family run hotel. Ivy clad, the interior of the hotel is decorated to a high standard. The dining room has a good reputation locally of serving generous portions of well prepared food. Professional courtesy with warm Lancashire hospitality can be assured, whether you are staying just for one evening or for a longer period.

⊗££ **FERRARIS RESTAURANT** West End, Great Eccleston, Preston.
Hours: Dinner 6.30pm - 10.30pm (last orders). Closed: Mondays. **Cuisine:** Table d'hote, and extensive a la carte menu. English and Continental dishes. ⊨ None. **CC** Access, Visa. **Other Points:** Children welcome. No dogs. **P** & **(V) Directions:** From M55 at Kirkham, take A585 to Larbreck, then right on A586.
SUSAN & VIRGINIO FERRARI ☎ (0995) 70243.
An excellent English and Continental restaurant in the village of Great Eccleston. The interior is very Italian in style with an accent on Ferrari cars and provides attractive, comfortable surroundings in which to enjoy the first class cuisine. The meals are beautifully cooked and presented, complemented by welcoming and efficient service. Excellent food and atmosphere.

⊗£££ **PARK HALL HOTEL** Exits 27 and 28 M6, Charnock Richard.
⊞£££ **Hours:** Breakfast 7am - 10am, lunch 12 noon - 2.15pm, and
CLUB dinner 6.30pm - 10pm (9.30pm on Sundays). **Cuisine:** Table d'hote and separate a la carte restaurant. Extensive wine list. ⊨ 114 bedrooms, all en suite including 33 two bedroomed suites. **CC** All major cards. **Other Points:** Children welcome. No dogs. Open Sundays and bank holidays. Afternoon teas served. Extensive conference and banqueting facilities. **P** & **(V) Directions:** Off M6 at junctions 27 and 28 and also junction 8, M61.
FREDERICK ORCHARD ☎ (0257) 452090.
Unique complex consisting of a hotel and village within 136 acres. There are two restaurants and bars, offering food of an excellent quality, Camelot theme park, comfortable rooms with all facilities and extensive leisure equipment including a gymnasium and an indoor swimming pool.

RAMSBOTTOM Lancashire Map 8 C2
⊗££ **OLD MILL HOTEL & RESTAURANT** Springwood,
⊞££££ Ramsbottom.
Hours: Breakfast 7.30am - 9.30am, lunch 12 noon - 2.30pm, and dinner 6.30pm - 10.30pm (last orders). **Cuisine:** 2 Restaurants. French cuisine - fish, steak, shellfish, casseroles. Comprehensive wine list. Italian cuisine - pastas, pizzas. ⊨ 12 single, 12 twin, 12 double bedrooms, all en suite. All rooms have TV, tea/coffee making facilities, hairdryer, trouser press and direct dial phone. **CC** All major cards. **Other Points:** Indoor swimming pool, sauna, solarium, whirlpool and gym. Children welcome. Licensed. Residents lounge. Garden. **P** **Directions:** Off jct M66 with A56, situated on A676 north of Manchester.
KAREN & NICKY SACCO ☎ (070 682) 2991.
Originally an old mill, this hotel has been completely refurbished achieving an attractive yet comfortable atmosphere.

Ramsbottom continued

With a combination of a good choice of food and wine and attentive service both restaurants are well worth a visit.

REDCAR Cleveland **Map 9 A1**

⌂£ **WATERSIDE HOUSE** 35 Newcomen Terrace, Redcar.

⊨ 2 single, 3 double and 1 family bedroom. 2 bathrooms. TV and tea/coffee making facilities in all rooms. **Hours:** Breakfast 6.30am - 9am and dinner 5pm - 7pm (order by 12 noon). **CC** None. **Other Points:** Central heating. Children welcome. Dogs allowed. Residents lounge. TV. **Directions:** Off the A19 to A174, follow signposts to Redcar sea front.

MRS C NIXON ☎ (0642) 481062.

A red-painted terraced house on Redcar seafront overlooking the boating lake. The inside is bright and airy and meticulously clean. Close to the town centre and amenities.

⌂£ **WILLOW HOUSE** 8 Newcomen Terrace, Redcar.

⊨ 1 single, 3 double and 2 family bedrooms. 1 bathroom, 2 showers. TVs and tea/coffee making facilities in all rooms. **Hours:** Breakfast 6.30am - 9am and dinner 5pm - 7pm (order by midday). Full English breakfast. **CC** None. **Other Points:** Central heating. Children welcome. Dogs allowed. Residents lounge/TV.

MRS P NIXON ☎ (0642) 485330.

Situated on the sea front with lovely views over Coatham Bay. Comfortable accommodation at reasonable rates and true Yorkshire hospitality.

REETH North Yorkshire **Map 8 B2**

⊗££ **ARKLESIDE HOTEL** Reeth, Richmond.

⌂£££ **Hours:** Breakfast 8.30am - 9am, Dinner 7.30pm for 8pm. Booking must be made by 6pm. Non-residents welcome for dinner with advance booking, space allowing. **Cuisine:** Homemade food using fresh produce. ⊨ 3 twin and 5 double bedrooms, 7 en suite. **CC** Access, Visa. **Other Points:** Garden. Afternoon teas. Dogs allowed. No smoking in restaurant and bedrooms. Residential and restaurant licence. Packed lunches available. **🅿 (V) Directions:** In Reeth village (B6270), just off The Green.

MALCOLM & SYLVIA DARBY ☎ (0748) 84200.

A charming hotel, originally a terraced row of cottages dating from 1600 and converted during the Edwardian era to a country retreat. It became a hotel in 1904 and has since been tastefully modernised but still enjoys dramatic views of Swaledale. The hotel is noted for its fine fresh food and offers a five course evening meal. Enjoy the true Yorkshire hospitality and personal service.

⊗£ **KINGS ARMS HOTEL** High Row, Reeth, Richmond.

⌂££ **Hours:** Bar meals served daily lunchtime and evening. **Cuisine:** Home-cooking - steak and vegetable pies, shepherd's pie, chicken curry, chilli, honey roast ham and cheesecake. ⊨ 4 bedrooms all with shower and colour TV, tea and coffee making facilities. **CC** None. **Other Points:** Children welcome. Coaches by appointment. **🅿 ♿ (V) Directions:** Leave the A6108 at Richmond and take B6270 to Reeth.

ASHLEY MARKHAM & ARTHUR COOK ☎ (0748) 84259.

Reeth continued

18th century listed building situated in the heart of Swaledale. Original beams and open log fires add to the cosy and friendly atmosphere of this village 'local'.

RICHMOND North Yorkshire **Map 9 B1**

⊗££ **A66 MOTEL** Smallways, nr Richmond.

⊓⊐££ **Hours:** Breakfast 7am - 10am, lunch 12 noon - 2pm, dinner 7pm - 11pm. Bar meals 12 noon - 2.30pm, 7pm - 10.30pm. **Cuisine:** Fresh salmon salad, Aylesbury duckling, steaks with sauce Espagnole. ⊨ 6 bedrooms. **CC** All major cards. **Other Points:** Children welcome. Dogs allowed. Garden. **P** ⅙ **Directions:** On the A66 near Scotch Corner.
SONIA HALL ☎ (0833) 27334.
The A66 Motel was originally a 17th century farm. Situated close to the Dales and areas of historic interest, the motel is conveniently placed for visiting the area.

⊓⊐£££ **PEAT GATE HEAD** Low Row in Swaledale, nr Richmond.
⊨ 1 single, 2 double and 3 twin bedrooms, 3 en suite. 1 bathroom, 1 shower. 1 ground floor bedroom especially designed for disabled. **Hours:** Breakfast 8.30am, dinner 7pm. **CC** None. **Other Points:** Central heating. Children welcome. No dogs. Licensed. Residents lounge. TV and garden. Vegetarians meals available. **P** ⅙ **Directions:** Situated off B6270 on Langthwaite road.
ALAN EARL ☎ (0748) 86388
A 300 year old Dales house standing in 2 acres of grounds with magnificent and memorable view updale to the Pennines and down to Richmond. An ideal stop for travellers, to explore the bewitching countryside. All food is homemade and using fresh, seasonal produce. Special diets, likes and dislikes are catered for. A friendly, welcoming place to stay.

⊗£ **THE CROWN** Richmond Road, Brompton-on-Swale, Richmond.
Hours: Lunch 12 noon - 2pm, dinner 7pm - 9.30pm (last orders). Open bank holidays. **Cuisine:** Home made dishes, with an emphasis on fresh ingredients. ⊨ None. **CC** Access, Visa. **Other Points:** Children welcome. Garden dining. No dogs allowed. Italian night twice monthly. All meals half price to children. **(V)**
MR PASTORELLO. ☎ (0748) 811666.
Enjoying a cheerful atmosphere, The Crown is popular with locals and business people alike. This is not surprising as it offers generous helpings of appetising meals, all of which are made with an emphasis on fresh ingredients. Comfortably furnished, good value for money.

RIPON North Yorkshire **Map 9 B1**

⊗££ **RIPON SPA HOTEL** Park Street, Ripon.
Hours: Open 7.30am - 11pm. Restaurant open until 9pm. **Cuisine:** Roast beef, lamb cutlets and poached halibut. Desserts include chocolate and orange trifle, baked apple tart and fudge cake. ⊨ 40 bedrooms all en suite. **CC** All major cards. **Other Points:** Children welcome. **P** ⅙ **Directions:** From the A1 or A61 take B6265. Hotel is on the west side of Ripon.
MRS G M CURRY ☎ (0765) 2172.

Ripon continued

A country house hotel in a garden setting, some 5 minutes walk from the ancient cathedral city centre. Sunny public rooms, residents' lounges overlooking the gardens. Ideal touring centre for the Yorkshire Dales. Owned and managed by the same family for over 50 years.

ROMALDKIRK County Durham **Map 8 A2**

⊗£££ **ROSE & CROWN HOTEL** Romaldkirk, Teesdale.

⌂£££££ **Hours:** Breakfast 7.30am - 9.30am, lunch 12 noon - 1.30pm (last orders), dinner 7pm - 9pm (last orders). Closed: Sunday evenings. **Cuisine:** Full restaurant menu & and bar menu as well. Bar food includes steak, mushroom & Old Peculiar pie, fresh pasta, smoked chicken, brochette of lamb. ⊨ 11 rooms. 1 single, 5 twin, 4 double and 1 family bedroom. All en suite. **CC** Access, Visa. **Other Points:** Children welcome. Afternoon teas. Dogs allowed. **P** &. **Directions:** 6 miles northwest from Barnard Castle on B6277. MR & MRS DAVY. ☎ (0833) 50213.

An 18th century stone built coaching inn with side courtyard set on the charming village green. Decorated richly in antique furnishings to a very high standard, serving well presented and prepared meals in the panelled restaurant. Accommodation is spacious and well appointed. The atmosphere is relaxed and informal.

ROSEDALE ABBEY North Yorkshire **Map 9 B1**

⊗££ **BLACKSMITH'S ARMS HOTEL** Hartoft End, Rosedale Abbey, Pickering.

Hours: Lunch 12 noon - 2pm, dinner served from 7pm - 9.30pm (last orders 9pm). French cuisine table d'hote served 7pm - 8.30pm. Menu is changed daily. Lunch is available in restaurant every day. **Cuisine:** French/English cooking. Hot or cold meals available in bar eg. supreme of chicken filled with garlic butter. Table d'hote e.g. fresh local lobster. ⊨ 14 bedrooms. **CC** Access, Visa. **Other Points:** Children welcome. **P** &. ANTHONY & MARGARET FOOT ☎ (07515) 331.

A family run hotel at the foot of Rosedale in the North Yorkshire Moors National Park, an area renowned for its scenic beauty. The original farmhouse dates back to the 16th century and commands extensive views of the surrounding moors and dales. Ideal centre for touring and riding.

⊗££ **THE MILBURN ARMS HOTEL** Rosedale Abbey, nr

⌂£££££ Pickering.

CLUB **Hours:** Meals 8am - 9.30am, 12 noon - 2pm and 7pm - 9.30pm (last orders). **Cuisine:** English. ⊨ 11 bedrooms all en suite, with colour TV, tea/coffee making facilities and direct dial telephone. **CC** Access, Visa. **Other Points:** Children welcome. No dogs in bars. **P** **(V) Directions:** From the A170 at Wrelton follow the sign to Rosedale Abbey. TERRY & JOAN BENTLEY ☎ (07515) 312.

Set in the heart of the North York Moors National Park, this hotel is an ideal centre for walking and touring as many places of scenic and historical interest are within easy reach. The atmosphere is most convivial, with low beams, log fires and real ales.

ROTHERHAM South Yorkshire **Map 9 C1**

®££ **BRECON HOTEL** Moorgate Road, Rotherham.

⏰££ **Hours:** Breakfast 7.30am - 9.30am, Lunch and bar snacks 12 noon - 2pm, Dinner 7pm - 9.15pm (last orders). Closed: Boxing Day. **Cuisine:** Dishes may include Beef Stroganoff, Roast Chicken Grandmere, Lamb Cutlets with Rosemary, Salmon Hollandaise. Bar meals. Traditional Sunday lunch. 🛏 27 bedrooms, 22 en suite. **CC** All major cards. **Other Points:** Children welcome. Dogs allowed. Fax No: (0709) 820213. Licensed bar. **P** 🚻 **(V) Directions:** Off Jct. 33, M1. Half mile past Rotherham General Hospital on A 618.
DUNCAN CARR ☎ (0709) 828811.
A small, family run hotel where you will find true Yorkshire hospitality. The restaurant enjoys a good reputation locally for its quality, generous portions and friendliness of service. With its good food, comfortable accommodation, welcoming service and value for money, Brecon Hotel is highly recommended.

®££ **BRENTWOOD HOTEL** Moorgate Road, Rotherham.

CLUB **Hours:** Lunch 12.15pm - 2pm and dinner 7pm - 9.30pm. Bar lunches 12 noon - 2pm. Closed: some Bank Holidays. **Cuisine:** Flambe dishes, char grills, fresh fish dishes, scampi George V, rack of lamb. 🛏 43 bedrooms, all en suite. **CC** All major cards. **Other Points:** Children welcome. Coaches by appointment. Dogs allowed by arrangement. Fax No: (0709) 820289. **P** 🚻 **(V) Directions:** From M1 jct 33,follow Bawtry signs to lights,Moorgate Rd is on left.
JAMES LISTER ☎ (0709) 382772.
In a pleasant situation 1 mile from town centre in 2 acres of gardens. Gourmet wine list and restaurant with good value table d'hote menus.

®££ **THE ELTON HOTEL** Main Street, Bramley, nr Rotherham.

⏰££££ **Hours:** Meals 7.15am - 9am, 12 noon - 2pm (4pm Sundays) and 🍲 7pm - 9.30pm (last orders). **Cuisine:** English and French cuisine:
CLUB real Yorkshire pudding with onion gravy, and chicken Alexandra. 🛏 29 bedrooms, all en suite. **CC** All major cards. **Other Points:** Children welcome - cots and high chairs provided. Fax: (0709) 549100. **P** 🚻 **(V) Directions:** Jct 1, M18. From A631 in Bramley take Ravenfield turn B6093, 1st Lt.
PETER & WYNA KEARY ☎ (0709) 545681.
Situated only 4 miles from Rotherham this is a popular spot for local businessmen at lunchtime and in the evening. The M18 is only half a mile away and the M1 and A1 are nearby making this an ideal stopover for travellers. Catering also available for private functions, conferences and receptions.

SALFORD Greater Manchester **Map 8 C2**

®££ **BEAUCLIFFE HOTEL** 254 Eccles Old Road, Salford.

⏰££ **Hours:** Breakfast 7.30am - 9am, dinner 6.45pm - 8.45pm (last orders). Bar meals 12 noon - 2pm and 8pm - 10pm. Closed: 24th December to 2nd January. **Cuisine:** International cuisine. Wide choice of dishes. 🛏 21 bedrooms, 17 en suite. All bedrooms have colour TV and tea/coffee making facilities. **CC** All major cards. **Other Points:** Children welcome. Fax No: (061) 787 7739. **P** **(V) Directions:** 1/4 mile from jct 2 of the M602, opposite the Hope Hospital.

Salford continued

ANTHONY & JACINTA WHITE ☎ (061) 789 5092.

A large Victorian house in a convenient location, close to the motorway and all Manchester's amenities. The hotel has been in the family for 24 years, and the current resident proprietors pride themselves on their warm welcome, efficient service and good home cooked food.

⊗£ **MARK ADDY RIVERSIDE PUB AND WHARF** Stanley
Ⓠ Street, Salford, Manchester.

Hours: Cheese and pate served 11.30am - 8pm. **Cuisine:** Superb selection of the finest cheese and pates, served with freshly baked granary bread. ⍿ None. **CC** None. **Other Points:** Children welcome. Tables by the riverside. **(V) Directions:** Near the city centre, beside the river. Near County & Crown Courts.

JAMES RAMSBOTTOM ☎ (061) 832 4080.

A Riverside pub converted from the old boat station, the Mark Addy offers a wide selection of cheeses and pates. All food is well presented and served in very generous portions - 'doggy bags' are available. The cheeses come from all over Europe and are complemented by a good wine list. A warm welcome and excellent value for money. A must for cheese enthusiasts.

SCARBOROUGH North Yorkshire **Map 9 B2**

⊗£ **ARCHIVES BAR & RESTAURANT at VALLEY LODGE**
⍇£ **HOTEL** 51 Valley Road, Scarborough.

Hours: Meals 8am - 9am and 7pm - 10.30pm. Bar meals 12 noon - 1.45pm and 6.30pm - 10pm. Closed: Sundays. **Cuisine:** A varied menu which includes: Fondue, fillet steak Archives. ⍿ 5 bedrooms, 5 bathrooms. **CC** Access, Visa. **Other Points:** Children welcome. No dogs. Coaches by appointment. **(V) Directions:** Very close to the seafront.

NORMAN AND MARION HILL ☎ (0723) 375311.

The Archives Bar and Restaurant is situated in the Valley Lodge Hotel, only a few hundred yards from the seafront in the Edwardian part of Scarborough. Both the food and accommodation offer very good value for money.

⍇£ **ATTENBOROUGH HOTEL** 28/29 Albemarle Crescent, Scarborough.

⍿ 4 single, 5 double, 8 twin and 8 family bedrooms and 5 with en suite. 2 bathrooms. 2 showers. Tea/coffee making facilities in all bedrooms. Colour TV in all bedrooms. **Hours:** Breakfast 8.30am - 9.15am and dinner 6pm. **CC** None. **Other Points:** Central heating. Children welcome. Licensed. Residents' lounge. TV. Garden. Vegetarian meals available. **P**

MR & MRS J SNOW ☎ (0723) 360857.

A welcoming hotel set in a Victorian crescent, overlooking attractive gardens. Located in the centre of town, the train and bus station are only a short distance away.

⊗£ **BLACKSMITHS ARMS** High Street, Cloughton, Scarborough.
⍇£ **Hours:** 9am - 9.30am, 12 noon - 2pm, and 7pm - 10pm (last orders 9.45pm). Bar meals served betweeen 12 noon - 2pm, and 7pm - 10pm. Closed: Sunday evenings in the winter. **Cuisine:** House specialities include crispy duckling in a black cherry and port sauce, and trout grenbloise, fried with prawns, capers, lemon and

Scarborough continued

parsley. ⌾ 6 bedrooms, with tea/coffee facilities. Colour TV in all bedrooms. **CC** None. **Other Points:** Children welcome. Dogs allowed. Open for Sunday lunch and bank holidays. **P** **(V)** **Directions:** 5 miles north of Scarborough, on the A171 Whitby - Scarborough Road.

JEAN ANN ARNALL ☎ (0723) 870244

An old country pub, with oak beams and fires, set in a village near the North Yorkshire moors. The staff are very friendly and the food is not only excellently cooked, but also offers superb value for money. Ideal base for exploring the moors, Whitby, and for enjoying golf and pony trekking.

⊗£ **CENTRAL HOTEL** 1-3 The Crescent, Scarborough.
⊞£££ **Hours:** Meals 8.30am - 9.30am and 7.30pm - 9.30pm. Bar meals 12 noon - 2pm. No food served on Sundays. **Cuisine:** Specialities are charcoal grilled steaks and seafood. ⌾ 38 bedrooms, 25 en suite. **CC** All major cards. **Other Points:** Children welcome. **P** ⅊ **(V) Directions:** Cross Valley Bridge towards centre, right at lights, hotel on right.

JOHN & RUTH GLEDHILL & FAMILY ☎ (0723) 365 766.

A listed building forming part of an attractive Georgian Crescent overlooking the Crescent Gardens. Convenient for both bus and rail terminals, the town centre, Spa, theatres and South Bay Beach. Ideal for either holiday or business.

⊞£ **DOLPHIN HOTEL** 151 Columbus Ravine, Scarborough.
⌾ 1 single, 4 double and 2 twin bedrooms, 4 en suite. 1 bathroom, 1 shower. Colour TV and tea/coffee facilities in all rooms. **Hours:** Breakfast 9am - 9.30am (or by arrangement), lunch 12 noon - 1pm, dinner 6pm - 8pm (order at lunch). **CC** Access, Visa. **Other Points:** Central heating. No dogs. Licensed. Residents' lounge. **P** **Directions:** Situated on the A64.

MRS BERYL WILLIS ☎ (0723) 374217.

Small family run hotel situated near the beach and cricket grounds in this traditional English seaside resort. Close to North York Moors and the stately homes of Yorkshire.

⊗££ **EAST AYTON LODGE COUNTRY HOTEL** &
⊞££££ **RESTAURANT** Moor Lane, East Ayton, Scarborough.
CLUB **Hours:** Meals 12 noon - 2pm and 6pm - 9pm. Restaurant closed: Monday lunchtime. **Cuisine:** English and French cuisine using home-grown produce in season. A good selection of vegetarian meals. ⌾ 17 bedrooms, all en suite and with direct dial telephone, colour TV, tea/coffee making facilities, hairdryer and trouser press. **CC** All major cards. **Other Points:** Children welcome. Beer garden. Fax No.: (0723) 862680 ⅊ **(V) Directions:** Turn left off A170 (to Scarborough) in E.Ayton.Close to Post Office.

BRIAN GARDNER ☎ (0723) 864227.

An attractive country residence built in the early 19th century and skillfully converted to a small but luxurious hotel and restaurant. Situated 3 miles from Scarborough in a beautiful 3 acre setting in the National Park, close to the River Derwent.

Scarborough continued

MANOR HEATH HOTEL 67 Northstead Manor Drive, Scarborough.

3 single, 7 double, 2 twin and 4 family bedrooms, 13 en suite. 2 bathrooms. **Hours:** Breakfast 9pm, dinner 6pm (order by 4.30pm). Closed: Christmas and New Year's Day. **CC** None. **Other Points:** Central heating. Children welcome. Licensed bar lounge and separate TV lounge. **P** **Directions:** From Whitby, turn right just before Peasholm Park traffic lights.

MRS JANET MOORE ☎ (0723) 365720.

An attractive well appointed detached hotel overlooking Peasholm Park and North Bay. Ideally situated close to all the attractions of this English seaside resort - the beach, swimming pools, Kinderland, miniature railway, and Mr Marvels Fun Park, as well as golf links, bowling and county cricket.

RED LEA HOTEL Prince Of Wales Terrace, Scarborough. **Hours:** 8.30am - 9.30am and 6.30pm - 8pm. **Cuisine:** International cuisine, using fresh, local produce. 67 bedrooms, all en suite. Colour TV, radio, alarm and tea/coffee making facilities in all rooms. **CC** Access, Visa. **Other Points:** Children welcome. No dogs. Afternoon teas served. Indoor pool and leisure area. **(V) Directions:** On South Cliff above Spa complex.

GRAND MARK HOTELS ☎ (0723) 362431.

The Red Lea has been carefully converted from six elegant Victorian terrace houses. It is located on Scarborough's fashionable South Cliff in close proximity to the Spa and South Bay attractions, with the town centre being within walking distance.

THE FALCON INN Whitby Road, Cloughton, Nr Scarborough. **Hours:** Lunch 12 noon - 2pm and dinner 7pm - 9.30pm (last orders). Open all year, 7 days a week. **Cuisine:** Bar meals, with Carvery on Saturday evenings and Sunday lunchtimes in the restaurant. 8 bedrooms, all en suite with TV and tea/coffee making facilities. **CC** None. **Other Points:** Specially commended 'Scarborough in Bloom'. **P** **(V) Directions:** 9 miles from Scarborough on A171 to Whitby. Ravenscar turn off.

MESSRS STEWART & ROBERTS ☎ (0723) 870717.

An old coaching inn, high on the Yorkshire Moors, with open views of the sea and the Moors. Good food served by friendly attentive staff awaits the thirsty and hungry traveller. With its own well-tended gardens, The Falcon Inn makes an ideal stop

SEDBERGH Cumbria **Map 8 B2**

⊗££ **OAKDENE COUNTRY HOUSE HOTEL** Garsdale Road, ⌂££££ Sedbergh.

Hours: 8am - 9.30am and 7pm - 11pm (last orders 9pm). Bar meals 7pm - 9.30pm. Closed: lunchtimes. **Cuisine:** English and continental cuisine, including king prawns with garlic and paprika and homemade lasagne. ⊨ 6 bedrooms, all en suite with colour TV and tea/coffee in all rooms. **CC** Access, Visa. **Other Points:** Residents lounge and garden. **P** & **(V) Directions:** A684 from junction 37 on the M6. 1 mile on other side of Sedbergh.
MRS B E INGHAM ☎ (05396) 20280.
Set in the picturesque Yorkshire Dales National Park with magnificent and uninterrupted views in every direction, this imposing Victorian Country House, built in 1884, retains features of the period, including the original bathroom (the gas brackets with their engraved glass shades are still in position - now converted to electricity).

⊗£ **THE DALESMAN COUNTRY INN** Main Street, Sedbergh.
⌂££ **Hours:** Breakfast 8.30am - 9.30am, lunch 12 noon - 2pm and dinner 6.15pm - 9.30pm. Bar meals 12 noon - 2pm and 6.15pm - 9.30pm. **Cuisine:** Grills and steaks, gammon, daily specials and roasts every Sunday. ⊨ 5 bedrooms, 3 en suite all with colour TV and tea/coffee making facilities. Hair dryers and cosmetic extras. Iron facilities. **CC** Access, Visa. **Other Points:** Children welcome. Afternoon teas in summer and light lunches. **P** **(V) Directions:** 1st pub on left entering Sedbergh, 5 miles from jct 37 of the M6.
BARRY & IRENE GARNETT ☎ (05396) 21183.
An olde worlde stone-built country inn renovated by local craftsmen and situated in a village 'frozen-in-time'. Decorated in a country style throughout with traditional log fires, this is a popular retreat for locals and tourists alike. Nice place to 'get away from it all'. Winter breaks very popular.

SETTLE North Yorkshire **Map 8 B2**

⌂££ **LIVERPOOL HOUSE** Chapel Square, Settle.
⊨ 3 single, 2 twin and 2 double bedrooms. 1 bathroom, 1 shower. All rooms have razor points and tea/coffee making facilities. **Hours:** Breakfast 8.15am - 8.45am, dinner 7pm (order by 10.30am). Lunch served Monday, Tuesday and Friday 12 noon - 2pm. **CC** Access, Visa. **Other Points:** Children welcome. Fire certificate held. Licensed. Residents lounge. TV. No smoking. Eurocard also accepted. **P** **Directions:** Situated on the A65 in Ribble Valley,16 miles north west of Skipton.
MR & MRS P NOLAN ☎ (0729) 822247.
Owned and personally run by Brenda and Philip Nolan, this 18th century house is situated in a good position for exploring the Yorkshire Dales. With its warm welcome, comfortable surroundings and choice of real home-cooked food, the Liverpool House is a 'home away from home'.

⊗££ **NEW INN HOTEL** Clapham, Nr Settle.
⌂££££ **Hours:** Breakfast 8.30am - 9.30am, Lunch 12 noon - 2pm, Dinner
CLUB 7pm - 9pm. **Cuisine:** Restaurant and bar meals. Dishes include Cheese and Leek Pie, Game Pie, and Sticky Toffee Pudding. ⊨ 13 bedrooms, all en suite. **CC** Access, Visa, AmEx. **Other Points:** Children welcome. Garden. Afternoon teas. Dogs allowed.

Settle continued

Games room. Traditional real ale. Fax No: (05242) 51496. **▣ (V)**
Directions: A65. 21 miles from Lancaster and Junction 34 of the
M6 motorway.
KEITH & BARBERA MANNION ☎ (05242) 51203.
*The New Inn is over 200 years old and has provided a welcome
stop for travellers to the Lake district and Scotland and visitors to
the Yorkshire Dales since the 18th century. This coaching inn
offers a relaxing and friendly atmosphere, comfortable
accommodation and well cooked food in generous portions.
Under the personal supervision of the resident proprietors.*

⊗£ **ROYAL OAK HOTEL** Market Place, Settle.
▥£££ **Hours:** Meals 8am - 9.30am, 12 noon - 2pm and 6pm - 10pm (last
orders). Afternoon tea 3.30pm - 5.30pm. Bar meals lunchtime and
evening. Table d' hote lunch 12 noon - 2pm on Sundays. **Cuisine:**
Bar: homemade steak & kidney pie, Yorkshire fat rascals.
Restaurant: full a la carte, roast sirloin beef & Yorkshire pudding,
Fillet of steak Rothschild. ➤ 6 bedrooms, all en suite. **CC** None.
Other Points: Children welcome. No dogs. Coaches by
appointment. **▣ ᐧ (V) Directions:** On the A65 in the centre of
Settle.
BRIAN & SHEILA LONGRIGG ☎ (0729) 822561.
*In the centre of this Dales market town with easy access to caves,
walks, waterfalls and many places of historical interest. Fly
fishing available for residents.*

SHARDLOW Derbyshire **Map 9 C1**
⊗££ **CAVENDISH ARMS** London Road, Shardlow.
Hours: Lunch 12 noon - 2.30pm, dinner 7pm - 10pm (last orders).
Bar meals 12 noon - 2.30pm and 6pm - 10pm. Closed: Saturday
lunch time when Derby FC are playing at home. **Cuisine:** Soups,
rainbow trout, scampi, chicken chasseur, steaks etc. ➤ None.
CC Access, Visa. **Other Points:** Children welcome. No dogs.
Garden. **▣ ᐧ (V) Directions:** On the main A6 near to Cavendish
Bridge at Shardlow.
PETER DALTON-PRIOR ☎ (0332) 792216.
*An attractive building, enhanced by displays of fresh flowers
both inside and out. Some imaginative dishes are served in the
comfortable dining room, where the emphasis is on good food in
relaxed, informal surroundings.*

SHEFFIELD South Yorkshire **Map 9 C1**
⊗££ **LONGLAND'S EATING HOUSE** Main Road, Hathersage,
Sheffield.
Hours: Meals served all day 11.30am - 5pm. Breakfast 9am -
11.30am Saturday and Sunday only. Summer months dinner
served Wednesday to Saturday 6.45pm - 9.30pm. (Friday and
Saturday only during winter months). Closed Sunday to Tuesday.
evenings. **Cuisine:** Steak Teriyaki, cheese and spinach enchilada,
tagliatelle verde. ➤ None. **CC** Access, Visa. **Other Points:**
Children welcome. Afternoon teas. Pets allowed. **▣ (V)**
Directions: Off the A625, situated on the main road in Sheffield.
MR P.J.N. LONGLAND ☎ (0433) 51978.
*Large country style cafe/restaurant with exposed beams and
wood floor, offering well presented, generous portions of good*

Sheffield continued

> *food at excellent value for money. Situated in the main street of an attractive Peak District Village.*

⊗£ **STANHOPE ARMS** Dunford Bridge, Penistone, Nr Sheffield.
Hours: 12 noon - 3pm, (last orders 1.45pm) and 7pm - 11pm (last orders 9.45pm). Sunday teas 3.30pm - 6pm from Easter to end of September. Closed: Christmas Day. **Cuisine:** Traditional English cuisine, including T-bone steaks, gammon and egg, and chicken a la creme. Sunday lunches with choice of roasts, booking advised. ⊨ None. **CC** Access, Visa. **Other Points:** Children welcome. Dogs allowed. Garden dining. Open Sundays and bank holidays. Also caters for private parties. Sunday afternoon teas. **P** ⅃ **(V)**
Directions: A628 to Manchester.Right to Dunford at summit of Woodhead Pass(A627)
MR & MRS FOSTER ☎ (0226) 763104
The Stanhope Arms is a warm and friendly inn, formerly an old shooting lodge, which offers its guests superb home-cooked fayre. The inspector commented that it was 'well above normal bar meal standard, offering very good quality food with generous portions, at great value.' The desserts are also home-cooked, with delicious apple pies and gateaux.

⊗££ **THE OLD SIDINGS** 91 Chesterfield Road, Dronfield, Nr Sheffield.
Hours: Dinner 7pm - 12 midnight (last orders 9.30pm). Bar snacks 12 noon - 2.30pm and 6pm - 8.30pm (last orders). No meals served Sunday evening. **Cuisine:** Predominantly English cuisine. Bar meals and evening a la carte restaurant menu. House speciality: Anne's Homemade Giant Yorkshire Pudding. ⊨ None. **CC** None. **Other Points:** Children welcome. No smoking area. Dogs allowed. Beer garden. **P (V) Directions:** Off main A61 on B6057. Next to only railway bridge in Dronfield.
WILLIAM & ANNE STANAWAY ☎ (0246) 410023.
An attractive Victorian pub with railway memorabilia in the restaurant. Within the comfortable and welcoming surroundings there is a good choice of bar meals and snacks lunchtime and evening and an a la carte menu in the restaurant during the evening with the emphasis on traditional, country style, homemade fayre.

⊗££ **ZING VAA RESTAURANT** 55 The Moor, Sheffield.
Hours: Meals 12 noon - 12 midnight. Closed: Christmas and Boxing Day. **Cuisine:** Cantonese and Peking cuisine - sliced fillet with king prawns marinated and cooked in a fruity sauce, duckling dishes. ⊨ None. **CC** All major cards. **Other Points:** Children welcome. No dogs. Parking for 30 in the evening. ⅃ **(V)**
Directions: In the heart of Sheffield shopping centre opposite the bandstand.
ROGER CHEUNG ☎ (0742) 722432/729213
Genuine Cantonese dishes and atmosphere. Situated in the heart of Sheffield's busy shopping area. Very popular with both shoppers and business people.

SHIPLEY West Yorkshire **Map 9 B1**

⊗£ **THE CONNECTION** 41 Westgate, Shipley.
Hours: Dinner 6pm - 11pm from Monday to Thursday, 5pm - 11pm Friday and Saturday, and 4pm - 10pm on Sunday. **Cuisine:** Hamburgers, pizzas, steaks, pancakes and chicken. ⊨ None. **CC** Access, Visa, AmEx. **P** ⅙ **(V) Directions:** On the corner of the A657 and Westgate.
S R JENNINGS ☎ (0274) 599461
A lively, family restaurant with eye catching decor and a wide ranging menu. Much frequented by locals and tourists alike.

SILLOTH ON SOLWAY Cumbria **Map 8 A1**

⊗££ **THE GOLF HOTEL** Criffel Street, Silloth on Solway, Carlisle.
Hours: Meals 7.30am - 9.30am, 12 noon - 2pm and 7pm - 9.30pm. (9.15pm last orders). Closed: Christmas Day. **Cuisine:** Solway special, medallion Golf Hotel, Sole van den Berg. ⊨ 23 bedrooms, all en suite. **CC** All major cards. **Other Points:** Children welcome. Coaches by appointment.
FAUSTO & CHRISTINE PREVITALI ☎ (0965) 31438.
Overlooking the Solway Firth within easy reach of the Lake District and the Scottish Borders. Excellent golf course 100 yards away. Golf breaks a speciality.

SKEGNESS Lincolnshire **Map 9 C2**

⊞££ **THE CRAWFORD HOTEL** 104 South Parade, Skegness.
⊨ 3 single, 9 double, and 8 family rooms, all en suite, with colour TV, radio, alarm, and tea/coffee facilities. **Hours:** 8.30am - 9.15am, 12.30pm - 1.30pm, and 7pm. **CC** Access, Visa. **Other Points:** Children welcome. Afternoon teas. Resident's lounge. Indoor pool, sauna and sunbed. ⅙ **(V) Directions:** A52. Clock tower - right end of parade.
MR & MRS WILLIS ☎ (0754) 4215.
A very attractive and well-organised hotel, offering a high standard of service, with comfortable rooms and good food. Mr & Mrs Willis ensure their guest's have every satisfaction: a full English breakfast is provided, but vegetarian, Continental and any other dietary requirement will be catered for on request.

⊗££ **VINE HOTEL** Vine Road, Seacroft, Skegness.
Hours: Meals 8.15am - 9.15am, 12 noon - 2pm and 7pm - 9pm (last orders). Bar meals 12 noon - 2.30pm. Closed: 4 days over Christmas. **Cuisine:** Varied menu featuring traditional, British dishes. ⊨ 20 bedrooms, 17 en suite. **CC** All major cards. **Other Points:** Children welcome. Coaches by appointment. **P** ⅙ **(V) Directions:** Close to Seacroft Golf course.
HILARY & JOHN MARTIN ☎ (0754) 610611.
Built in the 17th century The Vine is the oldest hotel in Skegness. It has undergone many changes and alterations over the years but has always remained a firm favourite. Real ales served in both bars.

SKIPTON North Yorkshire **Map 8 B2**

⊗££££ **THE DEVONSHIRE ARMS COUNTRY HOUSE HOTEL**
CLUB Bolton Abbey, Skipton, North Yorkshire.
Hours: Breakfast 7.30am - 9.30am, Lunch 12.30pm - 2pm and Dinner 7pm - 10pm. Bar meals 12 noon - 2pm and Dinner 6pm - 9pm. **Cuisine:** English and continental dishes, including local

Skipton continued

game in season. Extensive wine list. ⊨ 40 bedrooms, all en suite. 6 bedrooms designated non-smoking. **CC** Access, Visa. **Other Points:** Children welcome. Dogs allowed, but not in restaurant. Conference facilities available. Fax Number (0756) 710564. **P** &
(V) Directions: On the A59 Skipton to Harrogate road at the junction with the B6160.
M HARRIS ☎ (0756) 710441.

Originally a 17th century coaching inn, the Devonshire Arms Country House Hotel has been restored under the supervision of the Duchess of Devonshire, most of the furniture and pictures coming from her house, Chatsworth. Ideal base for exploring Yorkshire dales and opportunity for golf, fishing, clay pigeon shooting, vintage car excursions and hot air ballooning.

⊛£ **THE WINE BARN** 38 Victoria Street, Skipton.
Hours: Serving full menu 11am - 11pm Monday to Saturday. Closed: Sundays and Christmas Day and Boxing Day. **Cuisine:** Mixed styles, Old English, Continental and Ethnic cuisine. ⊨ None. **CC** Access, Visa. **Other Points:** Children welcome. Afternoon teas served. Terrace dining. **(V) Directions:** Between Coach Street and Tourist Information Office.
ROGER & JOAN PROUT ☎ (0756) 794895.

Wine bar serving good food, accompanied by a good wine list. Happy, friendly atmosphere enjoyed by both holidaymakers and locals alike.

SOUTH SHIELDS Tyne & Wear **Map 9 A1**
⊛£ **SEA HOTEL** Sea Road, South Shields.
⊞£££editHours: Meals 7am - 9.30am, 12 noon - 2.30pm and 7pm - 9.30pm (last orders). **Cuisine:** Traditional English menu using local produce, and a French based a la carte menu, both offering a wide choice of dishes. ⊨ 33 bedrooms, all en suite. **CC** All major cards. **Other Points:** Children welcome. **P** & **(V) Directions:** On the sea front at A183 and A1018 junction.
MR JAMES, MR BASSETT & MR WATSON - Manager ☎ (091) 4270999.

This busy hotel is situated on the Sea Front in the heart of 'Catherine Cookson Country'. The hospitality, for which the region is renowned, is reflected in the friendly service.

SOUTHPORT Merseyside **Map 8 C1**
⊛££ **THE CRIMOND HOTEL** Knowsley Road, Southport.
⊞£££ **Hours:** Breakfast 7.30am - 9.30am, and lunch 12 noon - 2pm (residents only). Dinner 7pm - 9pm (last orders 8.30pm). Closed Sunday lunch. **Cuisine:** Grey mullet, grilled, served with a savoury filling of apple onion/herbs with lemon. Crimond steak cooked with capsicums/mushrooms blended in cream sauce ⊨ 4 single, 5 twin, 4 double, 2 family, all en suite. **CC** All major cards. **Other Points:** Garden. Pets allowed. Conference and banqueting suite. **P Directions:** Off Park Road West, near the Municipal Golf Links.
PAT & GEOFF RANDLE ☎ (0704) 36456.

A small family run hotel offering excellent facilities including indoor swimming pool and sauna. The good food, excellent service and comfortable accommodation combine to make this a

Southport continued

pleasant and relaxing stay for tourists and businessmen alike. Conference facilities, including slide projector, TV and video.

THE GILTON HOTEL 7 Leicester Street, Southport.
[CLUB] 2 single, 5 twin, 6 double and 1 family bedroom, 9 en suite. Tea/coffee making facilities and colour TV in all rooms. E.T.B 3 Crown Commended. **Hours:** Breakfast 7.30am - 9am, Lunch on request, Dinner 5.30pm. Bar meals are also available 7pm - 10pm. **CC** Access, Visa. **Other Points:** Children welcome. Garden. TV and video lounge. Tudor style bar. Reading lounge. Games room with table tennis. Golf courses and tee off times arranged. **P** **Directions:** Between main shopping area and the Promenade. MR & MRS CUNLIFFE ☎ (0704) 530646.
A Victorian house with an attractive well-kept garden, situated in the centre of Southport. Gilton Hotel is traditionally decorated to provide a comfortable place to stay for tourists and business people alike. Mrs Cunliffe extends a warm welcome to all her guests and the hotel enjoys a friendly, homely atmosphere. Particularly attractive for golfers with 5 courses nearby.

THE LOCKERBIE HOUSE HOTEL 11 Trafalgar Road, Birkdale, Southport.
12 rooms. 4 single, 5 twin, 2 double and 1 family bedroom. All en suite. Colour TV, shaver points, tea/coffee making facilities and central heating in all rooms. **Hours:** Breakfast 7am - 9am, dinner 7pm - 8pm. **CC** All major cards. **Other Points:** Children welcome. Garden. Afternoon teas. Dogs allowed. Full sized snooker table. **P** ὅ. **(V) Directions:** Nearest motorway exit M6, junction 26. Follow M58 then A570.
JOHN & ELAINE DEARY ☎ (0704) 65298.
A family run hotel, 'The Lockerbie House Hotel' is a double fronted Victorian House. Traditionally decorated the establishment has a fresh feel about it. Serving meals made from fresh produce, there is an emphasis on home- made soups and desserts. Comfortable accommodation offered. Ideally located for golfers as it is near the Royal Birkdale and Hillside Golf Courses.

ST HELENS Merseyside **Map 8 C2**
THE PRIORY HOTEL 140 Prescot Road, St Helens.
Hours: Breakfast 7am - 9am, Lunch 12 noon - 2pm, Dinner 7pm - 9pm (last orders). Bar snacks by arrangement. **Cuisine:** Freshly prepared food such as Grilled Trout with Lemon Butter, Roast of the day, Steaks, Trio of Lamb Cutlet with a Redcurrant Glaze. 21 bedrooms, 18 en suite. all with tea/coffee making facilities, direct dial telephone, colour TV and late night film. Reduced rates at weekends. **CC** All major cards. **Other Points:** Children welcome. No dogs. Private function room with conference facilities. Fax No: (0744) 453717. **P** **(V) Directions:** From A580 to A570 at BP Garage lights. Close to Pilkington Glass.
FRANK WESTHEAD ☎ (0744) 35272.
A newly converted Victorian residence of character situated just one minute from the town centre. The cosy restaurant offers freshly prepared food at very competitive prices and the accommodation is comfortable. With welcoming service and a

St Helens continued

friendly atmosphere, The Priory Hotel is a good choice for both business and pleasure. Conference facilities for up to 40 people.

STANDISH Greater Manchester **Map 8 C2**
⊗££ **THE BEECHES HOTEL & RESTAURANT** School Lane,
⊞££ Standish, Wigan.

Hours: Morning coffee 10am - 6pm, Brasserie 12 noon - 10pm Mon - Thur, Fri - Sat 12 noon - 10.30pm, Sunday 12 noon - 10pm. A la carte restaurant 7pm - 10pm Mon - Sat evenings only, Sunday 12 noon - 4.30pm. Closed: Boxing Day & New Years Day. **Cuisine:** Extensive menus including upto 13 varities of fish and seafood. Dishes may include Fillet of Scotch Beef, Roast Turbot, Sauteed Sea Scallops. ⊨ 11 bedrooms, all en suite. Colour TV, direct dial telephone, trouser press and tea/coffee making facilities. **CC** Access, Visa, AmEx. **Other Points:** Children welcome. Open Bank Holidays. Gardens. Guide dogs allowed only. Fax No: (0257) 427503. **P** & **(V) Directions:** 4 miles N of Wigan. 1.5 miles from jct 27 of the M6 on the B5239.
MR P & J MOORE ☎ (0257) 426432.
A privately owned hotel set in picturesque grounds, providing a very personal and friendly service. A high standard of cuisine can be enjoyed in the new Brasserie with its informal atmosphere, or in the corniced Victorian dining room where guests can relax within the charm and elegance of a bygone era. Comfortable accommodation.

STOKE ON TRENT Staffordshire **Map 8 C2**
⊗£ **CAPRI RISTORANTE ITALIANO** 13 Glebe Street, Stoke On Trent.

Hours: 12 noon - 2.30pm, and 6.30pm - 11pm (last orders 10.30pm). Closed: Sundays. **Cuisine:** Italian home-cooking, with specialities including lasagne, cannelloni, spaghetti, vongole, and fritto misto. ⊨ None. **CC** Access, Visa. **Other Points:** Children welcome. No dogs. **P** & **(V) Directions:** One-way for Town Hall,then immediate right into car park.
V & J CIRILLO ☎ (0782) 411889.
A friendly, family run restaurant with a great atmosphere. Serves excellent Italian cuisine at real value for money.

STOKESLEY North Yorkshire **Map 9 B1**
⊗££ **MILLERS RESTAURANT** 9 Bridge Road, Stokesley,
CLUB Middlesbrough.

Hours: Lunch 12 noon - 2pm, Dinner 7.30pm - 9.30pm (last orders). Bookings required for Dinner. Closed: Sunday and Monday all day. **Cuisine:** Dishes in the evening might include Trout with Celery and Walnut Stuffing, Lamb with Caper Sauce, Steaks. Lighter meals served on the lunchtime menu. ⊨ None. **CC** All major cards. **Other Points:** No dogs. Table reservations required for dinner. Street parking. **(V) Directions:** Off Stokesley High Street (A172), by River Leven.
KATHRYN ABBOTT ☎ (0642) 710880.
An attractive, family run restaurant with an excellent reputation locally. Bookings are required for dinner when you can enjoy dishes such as Salmon with Lemon Butter Sauce, or Pork Marsala. The lunchtime menu offers simpler meals at a very

Stokesley continued

>*reasonable price. Lunch or dinner, all meals are well-cooked and excellently served.*

SUNDERLAND Tyne & Wear **Map 9 A1**

⊗££ **MOWBRAY PARK HOTEL** Borough Road, Sunderland.

⌂£££ **Hours:** Breakfast 7am - 10am, dinner 7pm - 10pm (last orders 9.30pm). Bar meals 12 noon - 2pm. **Cuisine:** English and French cuisine, including Chateaubriand au Mowbray and breast of Duck in a port sauce with green peppercorns. Imaginative vegetarian dishes. ⊨ 58 bedrooms, 40 en suite. **CC** All major cards. **Other Points:** Children welcome. Afternoon teas. Dogs allowed. Residents' lounge. Function and small meeting rooms. **(V) Directions:** Centre of Sunderland, next to Mowbray Park, Town Museum & Library.
EDWARD HUGHES ☎ (091) 5678221.
A family run private hotel, located within five minutes walk of the Railway station, Business and Shopping areas, and backing onto one of Sunderlands most impressive parks. The restaurant offers good food, well presented and at good value for money. Ideal for either a simple business lunch or for that special occassion.

⊗££ **SHANGHAI PALACE RESTAURANT** 8-9 North Bridge Street, Sunderland.

Hours: Lunch 12 noon - 2pm (last orders), dinner 7pm - 11.30pm (last orders). Closed: Sundays 12 noon - 2pm. **Cuisine:** Extensive Chinese menu. Special set menus for groups of 2 - 8 people. ⊨ None. **CC** All major cards. **Other Points:** Children welcome. **(V) Directions:** Over Wearmouth Bridge towards Newcastle, 800 yrds on one-way system.
MICHAEL CHANG. ☎ (091) 5102477.
Soft pastel shades, armchairs and an aquarium, create a restful atmosphere in which to enjoy your meal. Professionally and carefully presented, the meals are made from fresh ingredients and served by staff who are willing to help at all times. Well worth a visit.

THIRLMERE Cumbria **Map 8 A2**

⌂££ **STYBECK FARM** Thirlmere, Keswick.

⊨ 2 double, 1 single, 1 family bedroom, all with tea/coffee making facilities. 1 bathroom. 2 showers. **Hours:** Breakfast 8.30am - 9am, dinner 7pm. Closed: Christmas Day. **CC** None. **Other Points:** Central heating. Children welcome. Residents lounge. No dogs. TV. No smoking. ▣ **Directions:** A591 near the junction with the B5322. 5 miles Keswick.
JOSEPH & JEAN HODGSON ☎ (07687) 73232.
A working mixed farm with a friendly atmosphere. Situated at the foot of Hellvellyn range of mountains, central for touring, walking, and fishing and sailing on Lake Thirlmere.

THIRSK North Yorkshire **Map 9 B1**

⊗££ **CARPENTERS ARMS** Felixkirk, Thirsk.

CLUB **Hours:** Lunch 11.30am - 3pm, Dinner 6.30pm - 9.45pm (last orders). Sunday lunch 12 noon - 3pm. **Cuisine:** A la carte menu & bar meals. Specialities include fresh lobsters delivered daily, whole Dover soles, monkfish - large variety of fresh fish. Good

Thirsk continued

steaks. ⌇ None. **CC** Access, Visa, AmEx. **Other Points:** Children welcome. No dogs. **P** ♿ **(V) Directions:** 2 miles East of Thirsk off the A170. Under Sutton Bank Escarpment.

MR & MRS DONOHOE ☎ (0845) 537369.

A 17th century country Inn set in the Hambleton Hills. Generous portions of well-cooked food are served in the restaurant and bar seven days a week. Choose from Steak Diane, Beef Stroganoff and Rainbow Trout as just some of the many dishes on offer and enjoy the friendly, relaxed atmosphere.

🏠£ **FOURWAYS GUEST HOUSE** Town End, Thirsk.

⌇ 6 bedrooms, 3 en suite. 1 single, 3 double, 2 twin. **Hours:** Breakfast 7.30am - 9.30am, Dinner at 6.30pm (order in the morning). **CC** Access, Visa. **Other Points:** Children welcome. Dogs allowed. **P**

LYNDA DOLAN ☎ (0845) 522601

Formally a pub, this large Victorian house retains much of its original hospitality and warm welcome. Two minutes walk from the centre of this Yorkshire market town, Fourways Guest House offers good value for money.

⊗££ **NAGS HEAD HOTEL & RESTAURANT** Pickhill, Nr Thirsk.
🏠££ **Hours:** 7am - 10.30am, 12 noon - 2pm, and 7pm - 9.30pm.
Sunday lunch 12 noon - 2pm and dinner 6pm - 10pm. **Cuisine:** A la carte menu, dishes including grilled duck breast with blackcherry sauce, and supreme of chicken Americano. Desserts, e.g Highland Flummery. ⌇ 3 single, 5 twin, and 7 double rooms, all en suite, with colour TVs, hairdryers, direct dial telephones, desks, and tea/coffee facilities. **CC** Access, Visa. **Other Points:** Children welcome. Pets allowed. Garden. Conference facilities. Adjoining cottage also available for holiday let. **P** ♿ **(V) Directions:** 1 mile off A1, near Thirsk.

RAYMOND & EDWARD BOYNTON ☎ (0845) 567 391.

There has been an inn on this site for over 200 years, providing food and rest for travellers and horses using the A1 which was then the only road connecting London and Edinburgh. Today, the Nag's Head has been upgraded to an excellent standard, with comfortable rooms, superb cuisine and a wide selection of real ales and wines. Highly recommended.

⊗£££ **SHEPPARD'S HOTEL, RESTAURANT & BISTRO** Front
🏠££££ Street, Sowerby, Thirsk.

Hours: Breakfast 8.30am, - 9am, lunch from 12 noon, and dinner 7pm - 9.30pm (last orders). Open all year. **Cuisine:** English and International cuisine using fresh local produce. Restaurant and Bistro. ⌇ 8 bedrooms, all en suite. All rooms have colour TV, hairdryer, direct dial telephone and tea/coffee making facilities. **CC** Access, Visa. **Other Points:** Children over 10 years welcome. No pets. Fax No: (0845) 524720. **P** **(V) Directions:** Off A19,into south west corner of Thirsk, ½ mile to Sowerby.

ROY SHEPPARD ☎ (0845) 523655.

17th century brick buildings, ideally situated in Herriot's County. Sympathetically modernised, yet still retains a comfortable, country atmosphere and is a joy to relax and

NORTHERN ENGLAND

Thirsk continued

> unwind in. *Excellent cuisine and service plus attractive surroundings.*

THORGANBY North Yorkshire **Map 9 B1**

⊗££ **THE JEFFERSON ARMS** Thorganby, nr. York.

[CLUB] **Hours:** Breakfast 7am, bar meals 12 noon - 2.30pm and 7.30pm - 10pm. Restaurant open 7.30pm - 10pm. Sunday lunch 12 noon - 2.30pm. Closed: Mondays. **Cuisine:** Traditional English, with French influence: poacher's broth, grilled dover sole and game in season. A la carte and table d'hote menus with good wine list. ⊨ 6 bedrooms, all en suite, with tea/coffee making facilities, and colour TV. **CC** All major cards. **Other Points:** Children welcome. No dogs in restaurant. Coaches welcome. **P** &. **Directions:** Turn off A19 at Crockey Hill,through Wheldrake and onto Thorganby. ROBERT MASON ☎ (0904) 89316.

Located 6 miles south of York, the building dates back some 300 years with oak beams and log fires. The bedrooms are furnished with antiques, half-tester and four poster beds and are also supplied with trouser press and hairdryers. Bars reflect sporting links with local estates.

THORNE South Yorkshire **Map 9 C1**

⊗££ **BELMONT HOTEL** Horse Fair Green, Thorne, nr Doncaster.

⌂££production £££ **Hours:** Breakfast 7am - 9am, lunch 12 noon - 2pm and 7pm -
[CLUB] 9.30pm (last orders). Bar meals 12 noon - 2pm and 7pm - 9.30pm. **Cuisine:** Best Yorkshire pudding. ⊨ 23 bedrooms, all en suite. **CC** All major cards. **Other Points:** Coaches by appointment. Dogs allowed in bedrooms. Children welcome. Afternoon tea served. Fax No: (0405) 740508. **P** &. **(V) Directions:** Situated 1 mile from the M18, off the A614 opposite market place. MURRAY & ROSEMARY STEWART ☎ (0405) 812320.

A comfortable, fully refurbished hotel in this typical Yorkshire market town. Under the personal supervision of the proprietors, the service and welcome blend in with the friendly atmosphere.

THORNTHWAITE Cumbria **Map 8 A1**

⊗£ **THWAITE HOWE HOTEL** Thornthwaite, Nr Keswick.

⌂£££ **Hours:** Breakfast 8.30am - 9.15am, dinner 7pm - 7.30pm.
[CLUB] Advance booking essential. Closed: Early November to the end of February. **Cuisine:** Set 5 course dinner menu. Non-residents are welcome if table is booked in advance. ⊨ 8 bedrooms, all en suite. All bedrooms have tea/coffee making facilities, colour TV, radio, alarm, telephone, hairdryer. Tourist Board 3 Crown commended. **CC** None. **Other Points:** Fully central heated. Children over 12 years welcome. Licensed. Pets allowed. Cocktail bar. Lounge. Garden. No smoking in dining room or lounge. **P** **Directions:** Off A66, 3 miles west of Keswick. In village, follow 'Gallery' sign. MIKE & PENNY SUTTON ☎ (07687) 78281.

A country house built of local stone, standing on an elevated site amidst 2 acres of garden and enjoying magnificent views acress the Derwent Valley to Skiddaw and the surrounding mountains. Good home cooking, comfort, value for money and a friendly yet tranquil atmosphere make this small hotel the ideal place to relax and enjoy the beauty of the Lake District.

THORNTON DALE North Yorkshire **Map 9 B1**

⌂£token **EASTHILL** Thornton Dale, nr Pickering.

1 single, 3 double, 2 twin and 2 family bedrooms, all en suite. 1 bathroom. **Hours:** Breakfast 8.30am, dinner 6.30pm (order at breakfast). **CC** None. **Other Points:** Central heating. Children welcome. No dogs. Residents lounge, TV and garden. Table licence. Vegetarian meals available. **P** & **Directions:** 1st house on left in village on A170 from Scarborough.

MARTIN GREEN ☎ (0751) 74561

A large friendly family house in 2.5 acres, with grass tennis court. Magnificent views of the surrounding countryside. On the edge of the North Yorkshire Moors and National Park, not far from coast, historic houses and other attractions.

⌂£ **WARRINGTON HOUSE** Whitbygate, Thornton Dale, Pickering.

8 bedrooms. Tea/coffee making facilities, smoke detectors and colour TV in all rooms. **Hours:** Breakfast 8.30am - 9am. Closed: December 12th to January 5th. **CC** Access, Visa. **Other Points:** Children welcome. No dogs. **Directions:** Just off the main A174.

MRS GLYNIS ASKEW ☎ (0751) 75028.

An 8 bedroomed guest house and tearoom in the centre of the quaint, picturesque village of Thornton Dale. An ideal location for touring the North York Moors, Herriot country and the coast.

TIDESWELL Derbyshire **Map 8 C2**

⊗£ **THE GEORGE HOTEL** Tideswell, nr Buxton.

⌂£token **Hours:** Bar meals 12 noon - 2pm and 7pm - 9pm. Open every day all year except Christmas Day. **Cuisine:** Pub meals, eg. homemade steak and kidney pie, steak, lasagne. 4 bedrooms. **CC** Access, Visa. **Other Points:** Children welcome. Dogs at management's discretion. **P** & **(V) Directions:** On the B6049, ¼ mile off the A623, next to Tideswell Church.

MR E D NORRIS ☎ (0298) 871382.

An 18th century coaching inn next to the Cathedral of the Peak, in the ancient market town of Tideswell, the heart of the Peak District. Olde worlde atmosphere with gleaming brass and Toby jugs to complete the picture. Recently featured in the television love story 'Yesterdays Dreams'.

WALLASEY Merseyside **Map 8 C1**

⊗££ **GROVE HOUSE HOTEL & RESTAURANT** Grove Road, ⌂£token Wallasey, Wirral.

Hours: Breakfast 7.30am - 9.30am, lunch 12 noon - 2pm and dinner 7pm - 9.30pm (last orders Sunday dinner 9pm). **Cuisine:** Comprehensive a la carte menu, featuring French and Continental dishes. 4 single, 2 twin and 8 double bedrooms, all en suite. **CC** Access, Visa. **Other Points:** Children welcome. Garden. Function rooms for weddings, parties and conferences (50-100 persons). **P** & **(V) Directions:** Off the A554.

MR N J BURN ☎ (051) 639 3947.

A well-appointed Victorian hotel and restaurant, situated in its own attractive gardens in a quiet residental area of Wallasey. Offering fine cuisine using a comprehensive menu, including an extensive selection of vegetarian dishes. Excellent accommodation and warm, courteous service.

NORTHERN ENGLAND

Wallasey continued

⊗£ **LEASOWE CASTLE** Leasowe, Moreton, Wallasey.
⌂£££££ **Hours:** Breakfast 7am - 10am, lunch 12 noon - 3pm, dinner 7pm -
CLUB 10pm. The new Stables Restaurant is open 4.30pm - 11pm.
Cuisine: A la carte and fixed 3 course menu, bar meals/snacks. A
second restaurant has recently opened serving Continental &
English dishes. ⊨ 50 bedrooms, all en suite. Four posters,
Penthouse, Family and Honeymoon suites available. 15%
discount to Club Bon Viveur members. CC All major cards. **Other
Points:** Children welcome. Garden. Afternoon teas. No smoking.
P & (V)
MR HARDING ☎ (051) 606 9191.
*This 16th Century castle has been converted to accommodate an
excellent restaurant with varied table d'hote and a la carte
menus. The Stables restaurant has recently opened and serves
continental & English dishes in a very relaxed atmosphere. Sea
views, outstanding accommodation, fine cuisine and excellent
service, combine to make Leasowe Castle a delightful place to
visit.*

⊗££ **MONROES** 45 Wallasey Road, Liscard, Wallasey.
Hours: Meals served 6.30pm - 11pm (last orders 10.30pm).
Cuisine: Specialities include over 24 steak dishes. Homemade
profiteroles and apple pie. ⊨ None. CC Access, Visa, AmEx.
Other Points: Children welcome. **(V) Directions:** Situated in
Liscard, 2 kilometres north west of Wallasey town centre
DAVID W. CULLEN ☎ (051) 638 3633.
*A Bistro style restaurant with a 'Marilyn Monroe' theme, offering
tasty and well presented food in a happy and relaxed
atmosphere. Friendly, attentive service will assist you in your
choice of over 24 steak dishes.*

WASDALE HEAD Cumbria **Map 8 B1**
⊗££ **WASDALE HEAD INN** Ritsons Bar, Wasdale Head Inn,
⌂£££££ Wasdale Head.
Hours: Meals 11am - 3pm and 6pm - 11pm. Restaurant menu at
7.30pm. Closed from 17 November until 28 December. **Cuisine:**
Cumberland sausage, locally smoked meat platter. ⊨ 10
bedrooms en suite. CC Access, Visa. **Other Points:** Children
welcome. No dogs in public rooms. No smoking in dining room. P
(V) Directions: Follow signs for Wasdale Head from Gosforth or
Holmrook (on A595).
MR J CARR ☎ (09467) 26229.
*This inn stands in an unique position at the head of Wasdale
which is one of the Lake District's most attractive and unspoilt
valleys. The deepest lake, highest mountain and smallest
church are in the area around Wasdale. Pine panelling, oak
beams and log fires all add to the mountain atmosphere.*

WENSLEYDALE North Yorkshire **Map 8 B2**
⌂££ **RIVERDALE COUNTRY HOUSE HOTEL** Bainbridge,
Leyburn.
⊨ 12 double/twin and 2 family bedrooms, 10 en suite.
Hours: Breakfast 8.30am - 9am, dinner 7.30pm. Closed:
December to February. CC None. **Other Points:** Central heating.
Children welcome. No dogs. Licensed. Residents, lounge. TV. P
Directions: Follow A684 to Bainbridge, hotel overlooks the green.

Wensleydale continued

MRS A HARRISON ☎ (0969) 50311.

Situated in the centre of a country village in Upper Wensleydale amongst hills and moors, Riverdale Country House is an ideal base for touring and walking. Used in the filming of James Heriott's novels.

WEST WITTON North Yorkshire **Map 9 B1**

⊗£££ **WENSLEYDALE HEIFER** Wensleydale, West Witton.

⌂£££師Hours: Meals 8.30am - 9.30am, 12 noon - 2pm and 7pm - 9.30pm (last orders). Open all year. **Cuisine:** Traditional Yorkshire cooking. All fresh and local produce. 🛏 19 bedrooms, all en suite. Accommodation includes four-poster bedrooms. 🆑 Access, Visa. **Other Points:** Children welcome. Fax No: (0969) 24183. 🅿 ⅃ **(V)** **Directions:** On A684 Leyburn to Hawes Road.

MAJOR & MRS J B SHARP ☎ (0969) 22322.

A 17th century Dales inn situated in the heart of James Herriot country and in the Yorkshire Dales National Park. Restaurant and bistro style bar setting. With easy access to the A684, this typical beamed coaching inn is central for walking, fishing, shooting and touring.

WHITBY North Yorkshire **Map 9 B2**

⊗££ **ANDERSONS** 3 Silver Street, Whitby.

Hours: Open 10am - 11pm every day. Lunch 11.30am - 2.15pm, dinner 6.30pm - 11pm, (9.45pm last orders). Coffee shop meals 9.30am- 6pm. **Cuisine:** Steaks with sauces, local fish dishes. 🛏 None. 🆑 All major cards. **Other Points:** Children welcome. Dogs allowed in garden.

DAVID WHISSON ☎ (0947) 605383.

Centrally located this bistro is popular for either a full meal or for a snack. Often gets very full in the evenings, booking recommended. Tables in the garden in summer.

⊗££ **INN ON THE MOOR** Goathland Hydro, Goathland.

⌂£££ **Hours:** Breakfast 8.45am - 9.30am, Lunch 12 noon - 2pm, Dinner |CLUB| 7pm - 8.15pm (last orders). **Cuisine:** English cuisine. 🛏 28 bedrooms, 24 en suite. 🆑 Access, Visa, AmEx. **Other Points:** Children welcome. Dogs allowed. Fax No: (0947) 86484. 🅿 ⅃ **Directions:** 9 miles from Whitby, 14 miles from Pickering.

MALCOLM SIMPSON ☎ (0947) 86410.

Rooms are comfortably furnished and service in the restaurant is friendly, yet prompt. The Inn overlooks the Yorkshire moors, offering the ideal opportunity to explore the countryside. Places of interest include the waterfalls and the Roman Road.

⊗££ **KIMBERLEY HOTEL** 7 Havelock Place, Whitby.

⌂££ **Hours:** Breakfast 8.30am - 9am, dinner 7pm - 9.30pm. Closed: |CLUB| Mondays. **Cuisine:** Italian cuisine. Dishes may include Risotto with wild Mushrooms, Chicken breast stuffed with Mozzarella cheese & Parma ham, Tagliatelle with salmon. 🛏 6 bedrooms, all en suite. 🆑 Access, Visa. **Other Points:** No smoking area. Street parking nearby. **(V) Directions:** Situated on west cliff close to sea front.

MR & MRS CASTOLDI ☎ (0947) 604125.

Situated in the centre of Whitby the hotel acts as an ideal base for those exploring the town. Elegantly decorated to a high degree of comfort, the hotel is very popular with locals and

Whitby continued

holidaymakers. In the restaurant you can enjoy carefully presented meals, made from the freshest of ingredients in cosy surroundings. Highly reccommended.

⊗££ **SEACLIFFE HOTEL** North Prom, West Cliff.
⏣££ **Hours**: 8am - 9.30am and 6pm - 9pm (last orders). Open all year round. **Cuisine**: English cuisine, including seafood, steaks and vegetarian dishes. ⊨ 20 bedrooms, all en suite. **CC** All major cards. **Other Points**: Children welcome. Dogs allowed. Open Sunday evenings and Bank holidays. ▣ **(V) Directions**: A171 to Whitby, then follow signs to West Cliff.
J A PURCELL ☎ (0947) 603139.

A friendly, family run hotel with a restaurant which is also open to non-residents. All food is of good quality and well-presented,at very reasonable prices. Nicely decorated bedrooms, some with sea views, and situated close to local attractions such as Whitby Abbey, the museum and the local golf course.

⊗£££ **STAKESBY MANOR** Manor Close, High Stakesby, Whitby.
⏣£££ **Hours**: Breakfast 8am - 9am and dinner 7pm - 9.30pm. **Cuisine**: 3 course a la carte menu and table d'hote including salmon & lobster mousse, lobster cardinal, veal in leek & stilton sauce. ⊨ 2 twin, 6 double. **CC** Access, Visa, AmEx. **Other Points**: Vegetarian and special diets catered for. Children welcome. Garden Packed lunches available. Function and conference facilities. Seasonal breaks. ▣ **(V) Directions**: Off the A171.

WHITBY

Whitby continued

MR & MRS HODGSON ☎ (0947) 602773

A lovely 17th century manor house, situated on the edge of Whitby, that has been owned and controlled by two generations of the Hodgson Family. Located in a quiet area approximately one mile from town centre, golf course and beach, 'Stakesby Manor' offers well cooked tasty food, friendly attentive service and comfortable accommodation in relaxed and attractive surroundings.

⊗£ **THE MAGPIE CAFE** 14 Pier Road, Whitby.
Hours: Open 11.30am - 6.30pm (last orders). Closed: end November - early March. **Cuisine:** Fresh, local fish and shellfish straight off the quayside including crab, lobster & salmon. Local ham, homemade steak pie and 30 homemade desserts. ⊨ None. **CC** Access, Visa. **Other Points:** Children welcome - special menu, baby chairs, cradles & toy boxes. No dogs. Fully licensed with reasonably priced house wines. **(V) Directions:** Pier Rd. is main road from town centre to the beach and West Pier.
S & I McKENZIE, A McKENZIE-ROBSON & I ROBSON ☎ (0947) 602058.

The McKenzie family have been serving superb fish in this historic building for nigh on 40 years. Window tables overlook the Abbey, 199 steps and picturesque harbour of Whitby. The cafe is extremely popular with holiday makers and locals alike. The food is always fresh and well cooked and the service friendly, quick and welcoming. Les Routiers Casserole Award 1991.

Whitby continued

⌂££ THE OXFORD HOTEL West Cliff Promenade, Whitby.

🛏 2 family rooms, 12 double, 1 twin, 1 single bedroom. All ensuite. TV, tea/coffee making facilities and central heating in all rooms. **Hours:** Breakfast 8am - 9.30am, dinner 6pm - 7.30 pm. Sunday Lunch 12 noon - 2.30pm **CC** All major cards. **Other Points:** Children welcome. Afternoon teas. Lift. Solarium. **P** &. **Directions:** Directly on seafront in harbour.
MR T DAY ☎ (0947) 60334.

An Edwardian hotel, situated on the sea front on the west cliff of Whitby, offering attractive comfortable accommodation in friendly relaxed surroundings. Within easy walking distance of the many historic buildings in this old Yorkshire fishing port. It is also centrally situated for shops and public transport.

⊗£ TRENCHER'S RESTAURANT New Quay Road, Whitby.

Hours: Open 11am - 6pm, dinner 6pm - 9pm (last orders), open to midnight.Closed: January and February. **Cuisine:** Fresh local fish, salad bar, freshly cut sandwiches, homemade desserts. 🛏 None. **CC** None. **Other Points:** Children welcome. **Directions:** Opposite the Harbour offices and quayside car park, off main A174.
TERRY, JUDY & NICKY FOSTER ☎ (0947) 603212.

A family run seafood restaurant in the historic fishing town of Whitby. Fresh Whitby fish and seafoods are, needless to say, a speciality and are cooked to a high standard. Terry and his sisters Judy and Nicky have received thank you letters from as far away as Europe and the USA.

⊗£ WHITE HOUSE HOTEL Upgang Lane, Whitby.
⌂£££ Hours: Meals from 8.30am - 10am, 12 noon - 2pm and 7pm - 10pm (last orders 9.30pm) Meals served in the bar. **Cuisine:** Yorkshire pudding with stew. 'Galley' 5 course dinner. 🛏 12 bedrooms, all en suite. **CC** Access, Visa. **Other Points:** Children welcome. Telephone has 3 lines. **P** & **(V) Directions:** On the A174, beside Whitby Golf Course on the West Cliff.
THOMAS CAMPBELL ☎ (0947) 600469.

The Hotel is situated adjacent to Whitby Golf Course with panoramic views of Sandsend Bay. Whitby is a charming, picturesque fishing port with a history extending back 1000 years. An ideal location for discovering an intriguing part of Yorkshire.

WHITLEY BAY Tyne & Wear **Map 9 A1**
⌂££ YORK HOUSE HOTEL 30 Park Parade, Whitley Bay.

🛏 1 single, 2 twin, 3 double and 2 family bedrooms, 7 en suite. **Hours:** Breakfast 7.30am - 9.30am, Dinner 6pm - 7pm. **CC** Access, Visa, AmEx. **Directions:** Off A193 Park Avenue.
JUDY & MICHAEL RUDDY ☎ (091) 252 8313.

A family run hotel offering comfort, home cooking and good service in a friendly atmosphere. A mid terrace Victorian building in the town centre, the hotel is ideally situated for safe, sandy beaches, parks, indoor Leisure pool and the shopping centre. Much thought has been given to the comfort of their guests whether families on holiday or business people travelling in the area.

WIGAN Greater Manchester **Map 8 C2**
⊗££ **GRAND HOTEL** Dorning Street, Wigan.
⌂££££ **Hours:** Breakfast 7am - 9.15am, (8am - 9.30am Sundays) and
[CLUB] dinner 6.30pm - 9pm (6.30pm - 9.30pm Friday & Saturday). Bar
meals 11.30am - 2.30pm and 6.30pm - 9pm (Sundays on request
only). **Cuisine:** Table d'hote and a la carte menu including scampi,
sole Veronique, medallions of veal citron, steaks, grills. ⊨ 38
bedrooms, all en suite. **CC** All major cards. **Other Points:** Beer
garden. Children welcome. Dogs by arrangement. Afternoon tea.
Fax No: (0942) 824583. **P (V) Directions:** Dorning Street turns off
A49 (Wallgate) close to BR Wigan Wallgate.
JOHN RILEY ☎ (0942) 43471.
A comfortable, Tudor style hotel situated in the town centre
close to the shops and the Wigan Pier complex. A friendly
atmosphere prevails - and ensures a loyal following.

WIGGLESWORTH North Yorkshire **Map 8 B2**
⊗£ **THE PLOUGH INN** Wigglesworth, Skipton.
⌂££ **Hours:** Meals 12 noon - 2pm and 7pm - 9.45pm (last orders).
Cuisine: Beef and Cowheel Cobbler, seafood pancakes. ⊨ 11
bedrooms, all en suite. **CC** All major cards. **Other Points:** Children
welcome. **P** & **Directions:** From the A65 at Long Preston, take the
B6478 to Wigglesworth.
BRIAN GOODALL ☎ (072 94) 243.
A residential country inn in a rural setting, 2 miles from the A65.
Dating from 1725, the Plough Inn provides comfortable
bedrooms and excellent food and service. Spectacular
conservatory restaurant.

WINDERMERE Cumbria **Map 8 B2**
⌂£ **BECKMEAD HOUSE** 5 Park Avenue, Windermere.
⊨ 1 single, 2 double, 1 twin and 1 family bedroom, 2 with shower.
1 bathroom with shower and WC. 1 separate WC. All bedrooms
have TVs, electric blankets and tea/coffee making facilities.
Hours: Breakfast 8.30am - 9am (or by arrangement). **CC** None.
Other Points: Central heating. Children welcome. No dogs.
Residents, lounge with TV. No evening meals. **Directions:** M6
junction 36, westbound on A590 for 3 miles. A591 to
Windermere.
MRS DOROTHY HEIGHTON ☎ (5394) 42757.
Delightful stone built Victorian house, with good reputation for
high standards, comfort and friendliness. The breakfasts are
famous. Convenient for lake, shops, restaurants and golf course.

⌂£ **GREEN GABLES GUEST HOUSE** 37 Broad Street,
[CLUB] Windermere.
⊨ 1 single, 2 double, 1 twin and 2 family bedrooms, 2 en suite. 1
bathroom. 2 showers. 3 WCs. Hairdryers, colour TV and
tea/coffee making facilities in all rooms. **Hours:** Breakfast 8.30am.
Closed: over Christmas and New Year. **CC** None. **Other Points:**
Central heating. Children welcome. No dogs. Residents' lounge
and TV. Special breaks October to March. No evening meals -
choice of restaurants nearby **P**
MRS SHEILA LAWLESS ☎ (05394) 43886.
A small, friendly guest house with very pretty bedrooms
providing clean, comfortable accommodation, close to local
amenities, bus and railway station. Guests are assured of a warm

Windermere continued

welcome, for the Green Gable's motto is 'Cleanliness, friendliness and a good hearty breakfast'.

⌂£ **ST JOHN'S LODGE** Lake Road, Windermere.

🛏 1 single, 6 double, 2 twin and 2 family bedrooms, 9 en suite. 1 bathroom. TVs in all bedrooms. **Hours:** Breakfast 9am, dinner 7pm (order by 6pm). Closed: December to end of January. **CC** None. **Other Points:** Central heating. Children over 2 years welcome. Residents lounge. **P Directions:** Midway between Windermere Village and Bowness on the A5074.

RAY & DOREEN GREGORY ☎ (096 62) 3078.

A small, private hotel centrally situated for touring the Lake District and only 10 minutes walk from the Lake Pier. Mini-breaks off-season. Facilities of local country sports club available to residents.

WIRKSWORTH Derbyshire **Map 9 C1**

⊗££ **LE BISTRO** 13 St John Street, Wirksworth.

⌂ **Hours:** Closed for lunch. Dinner 6.30pm - 9.30pm (last orders). [CLUB] Closed Sunday. **Cuisine:** Sauce dishes - Boeuf en Croute, Supreme de Vollaille Marsala, Medallions St Marys. Steaks, seafood and an extensive vegetarian menu. Game in season. 🛏 None. **CC** All major cards. **Other Points:** Children welcome. No dogs. Public car park nearby and street parking after 6pm outside the Bistro. Access for disabled by prior arrangement. **(V) Directions:** In the centre of Wirksworth opposite Lloyds Bank.

MARK FOX ☎ (0629) 823344.

Built in 1760, this is a candle lit cellar restaurant approached by a spiral staircase from the reception bar. Situated in the centre of this quaint market town, the freshly prepared, rural French style cuisine is very popular. The friendly efficent service complements a wonderful meal. International evenings monthly. Highly recommended.

WITHERSLACK Cumbria **Map 8 B2**

⊗££££ **THE OLD VICARAGE COUNTRY HOUSE HOTEL** Church ⌂ Road, Witherslack.

Hours: Breakfast 8.30am - 9.30am and dinner 7.30pm for 8pm (last orders). **Cuisine:** English regional cooking. 🛏 13 bedrooms, all en suite. **CC** All major cards. **Other Points:** Afternoon tea. Residents lounge and garden. Fax No:(044852) 373. Exceptional discount if stay for 2 days or more. **P (V) Directions:** Off the A590, Barrow road, Right turning to village, then first left.

BURRINGTON-BROWN & REEVE FAMILIES ☎ (044852) 381.

This outstanding establishment, a delightful Georgian period country vicarage, offers all the necessary qualities for a truly memorable evening. The ambience, cuisine and service combine to make dining here a pleasure, totally in keeping with its setting in the peaceful and unspoiled countryside where it nestles under Yewbarrow Scar. Regional Newcomer 1991.

WORKSOP Nottinghamshire **Map 9 C1**

⊗£££ **LION HOTEL** 112 Bridge Street, Worksop.

⌂£££ **Hours:** Breakfast 7am - 9.30am, Lunch 12 noon - 2pm, Dinner 7pm - 9.45pm (last orders). Bar meals 11.30am - 2.30pm and 7pm - 9.30pm. **Cuisine:** A la carte and table d'hote menus featuring

Worksop continued

traditional English and more imaginative dishes. Good vegetarian menu. Traditional Sunday lunch. ⊨ 30 bedrooms, all en suite. **CC** Access, Visa, AmEx. **Other Points:** Children welcome. Dogs allowed. Residents' lounge. Gymnasium, sauna & solarium. Private parties and functions catered for. Fax: (0909) 479038. **P** **(V) Directions:** Market Square, turn R at Eyres Furniture Store, then sharp right.

COOPLANDS DONCASTER LTD ☎ (0909) 477925.

A 16th centruy Coaching Inn situated in the centre of Worksop, offering a warm welcome and comfortable accommodation. The restaurant provides well-cooked and presented meals with a good choice of traditional and more imaginative dishes. Bar meals are served in the popular, lively bar, adjoining the restaurant. Close to Sherwood Forest, Clumber Park and Creswell Crags.

YARM Cleveland **Map 9 B1**

⊗££ **SANTORO RESTAURANT** 47 High Street, Yarm.

Hours: Restaurant open 12 noon - 2pm, and 7pm - 10.30pm. Closed: Sundays. **Cuisine:** Continental, but mainly Italian and French cuisine. Includes fish, game, meat and poultry dishes. Home-made pasta and sweets. ⊨ None. **CC** All major cards. **Other Points:** Children welcome. No dogs. Air conditioned. **P** **(V) Directions:** 2 miles from A19.

MR VINCE SERINO ☎ (0642) 781305.

Continental cuisine served in warm and colourful surroundings. Pleasantly set in a 17th century high street, within 20 miles of the coast and the Moors.

YORK North Yorkshire **Map 9 B1**

⊗£££ **ABBOTS MEWS HOTEL** 6 Marygate Lane, Bootham, York.

⊞£££ **Hours:** Breakfast 7am - 9.30am, lunch 12 noon - 2pm (bar meals only Monday - Saturday), dinner 7pm - 11pm (last orders 9.30pm). **Cuisine:** Chateaubriand Bearnaise, Canard du Poivre vert, fish and pasta. ⊨ 47 bedrooms, all en suite. **CC** All major cards. **Other Points:** Children welcome. Garden. **P** & **(V) Directions:** In centre of York. Close to Museum Gardens and Bootham Bar.

PATRICIA & NOEL DEARNLEY ☎ (0904) 622395/634866

Situated in the centre of York, only minutes away from the city's historic attractions. The hotel was an original coachman's cottage with coach-house and stables but was converted in 1976. The restaurant is renowned for its high standard of cuisine and the service is very friendly and efficient.

⊞£ **ACER HOTEL** 52 Scarcroft Hill, The Mount, York.

⊨ 5 double and 1 family bedroom, all with colour TV. 5 en suite. 1 bathroom. 1 WC. 1 four-poster suite with en suite facilities. **Hours:** Breakfast 8.30am - 9am, dinner 6.30pm - 8pm (order by 12 noon). Lunch available by arrangement. **CC** Access, Visa. **Other Points:** Central heating. Children welcome. Dogs by arrangement. Residents' lounge. All dietary requirements catered for. **P** **Directions:** Off A64 past the racecourse, turn right after traffic lights, on left.

MRS IRENE EARP ☎ (0904) 653839.

Late Victorian building, fully refurbished to the highest standards of comfort. Within walking distance of the city centre

York continued

and numerous places of interest. Easy access to Yorkshire Moors, the Dales and all coastal resorts.

⌂£ **ARNOT HOUSE** 17 Grosvenor Terrace, York.

🛏 1 single, 2 double, 1 twin and 2 family bedrooms. 1 bathroom, 2 showers and 3 WCs. Colour TV and tea/coffee making facilities in all rooms. **Hours:** Breakfast 8.15am - 9am, dinner 6.30pm - 7.30pm (order by midday). **CC** None. **Other Points:** Central heating. Children over 5 years welcome. Licensed. No evening meals on Sundays. **P** **Directions:** Off A19 to Thirsk (Bootham), 2nd on right outside Bootham Bar.

SUE & RUPERT SCOTT ☎ (0904) 641966.

Overlooking Bootham Park and York Minster, Arnot House combines period elegance with modern amenities, from the original cornicing, fireplaces and fine old staircases to the large, warm, comfortable well-appointed rooms. The welcome is exemplary, and the Scotts take pride in their guest house.

⊗££ **BARMBY MOOR HOTEL** Hull Road, Barmby Moor,
⌂£££ Pocklington, York.

Hours: Open for breakfast 7.30am - 9am, dinner 6.30pm - 8.30pm (last orders 8.30pm). Also serving Sunday Lunch 12.30pm - 1.30pm (last orders 1.30pm). Closed Sunday night except bank holidays. **Cuisine:** Dishes include Savoury pancakes, curried egg mayonaise, saucy duck, tipsy scampy. House specialities are their beef dishes. 🛏 10 rooms, 3 twins, 6 double and 1 family room, all en suite. **CC** Access, Visa, AmEx. **Other Points:** Children welcome, Garden. Swimming Pool. **P** **(V) Directions:** North along A1079 from Hull.

PETER & PAT OTTERBURN ☎ (0759) 302700

The Barmby Moor Hotel was originally a coaching inn and still has a Georgian style with flagged floors and antiques. The restaurant view is of a lovely garden and swimming pool. A peaceful and historic place to enjoy well cooked food. Barmby Moor is a picturesque village, nestled on the edge of the Yorkshire Wolds.

⊗£ **BAY HORSE INN** Murton, Nr York.

Hours: Lunch 11.45am - 1.45pm and dinner 6.45pm - 10.30pm (last orders 9.30pm). Bar meals 11.45am - 1.45pm and 6.45pm - 9.30pm. No food served Sunday evenings. **Cuisine:** Bayhorse special, Chicken Kiev, steaks, homemade pie, gammon. Sandwiches and Ploughmans. Daily specials. 🛏 None. **CC** None. **Other Points:** Children welcome. Well stocked bar, hand pulled cask conditioned beers. **P** ♿ **(V) Directions:** Off the A166 from York, follow signs to Livestock Centre.

MR & MRS RICHARD SPEIGHT ☎ (0904) 489684.

Situated very close to York, this 200 year old inn is very popular with visitors on route to the coast. Fronted by a small garden and set back from the road, you can enjoy good food, at reasonable prices, in a pleasant atmosphere.

⌂£ **CARLTON HOUSE HOTEL** 134 The Mount, York.

🛏 1 single, 7 double, 2 twin and 5 family bedrooms, all en suite. All rooms have TV, radio and tea/coffee making facilities. **Hours:** Breakfast 7.45am - 9.15am. Closed: Christmas and New

York continued

Year. **CC** None. **Other Points:** Central heating, Children welcome. 2 residents' lounges. Licensed. Light refreshments available. **P**
Directions: On the A1036 close to York station.
MALCOLM & LIZ GREAVES ☎ (0904) 622265.
A cosy family run hotel conveniently located close to the racecourse and all city centre amenities. A popular choice for many visitors to York and the surrounding countryside.

⌂£££ **CURZON LODGE AND STABLE COTTAGES** 23 Tadcaster Road, Dringhouses, York.
🛏 10 bedrooms, all en suite. Colour TV. Tea/coffee making facilities. Four poster and period brass beds. **Hours:** Breakfast 8am - 9am. **CC** None. **Other Points:** Children welcome. Open bank holidays. Residents' lounge. **P** **Directions:** On the A1036 Tadcaster road south, off the A64 York by-pass.
RICHARD AND WENDY WOOD ☎ (0904) 703157.
A charming 17th century Grade II listed house and coach house, which has been lovingly converted into 'Country Cottage' accommodation. Formerly owned by the Terry's, one of York's world renowned 'Chocolate families', Curzon Lodge welcomes its guests with a warm and friendly atmosphere in attractive surroundings. Close proximity to all York's historic attractions.

⊗£££ **DEAN COURT HOTEL** Duncombe Place, York.
Hours: Breakfast 7am - 12 noon, Lunch 12 noon - 2pm, Dinner 6.30pm - 9.30pm (last orders). Bar snacks 11.30am - 2.15pm, 6pm - 8.30pm. **Cuisine:** Fresh local produce. Dishes may include Highland Salmon with Asparagus, Fillet Steak Dijonaise, Rack of English Lamb. Light snacks in the Conservatory. 🛏 40 bedrooms, all en suite. **CC** None. **Other Points:** Children welcome. Afternoon teas. No dogs. Lounge bar, restaurant and Tea Room conservatory. Fax No: (0904) 620305. **P** **(V) Directions:** Immediately opposite York Minster.
MRS KAY MCLEOD - General Manager ☎ (0904) 625082.
Ideally situated close to York Minster, this hotel offers the highest standards of service, food and accommodation. Built in 1850 to provide houses for the clergy, the hotel has been sympathetically restored to form a very individual Victorian hotel. The restaurant is renowned locally for the quality of its cuisine, atmosphere and personal service.

⌂££ **HEDLEY HOUSE** 3 Bootham Terrace, York.
🛏 2 single, 5 double, 5 twin and 2 family bedrooms all en suite. Tea/coffee facilities, colour TVs, radio, and alarms in all bedrooms. Self catering apartments next door to hotel. **Hours:** Breakfast 8am - 9am, and dinner 6.30pm. **CC** Access, Visa, AmEx. **Other Points:** Children welcome. Dogs allowed. Licensed. Residents' lounge. Vegetarian meals available. **P** 🕭 **Directions:** Off the A19, third turning on left away from Bootham Bar.
GRAHAM & SUSAN HARRAND ☎ (0904) 637404.
A Victorian residence within walking distance of the city of York. Family run, the atmosphere is friendly and informal and complimented by good home cooking.

York continued

⊗£££ **HEWORTH COURT HOTEL** 76 Heworth Green, York.
⌂£££ **Hours:** Breakfast 8am - 9am, lunch 12 noon - 2pm, dinner 6.30pm - 9.30pm. **Cuisine:** A la carte, table d'Hote, bar meals/snacks. English and continental cuisine. ⌂ 27 rooms, all en suite. **CC** All major cards. **Other Points:** Children welcome. Garden. Afternoon teas. ◨ ⅋ **(V) Directions:** 2 minutes drive from Monk Bar, on the A1036.
TERRY & JANET SMITH ☎ (0904) 425156.
This excellently cared for Georgian town house restaurant, where 'Food is our forte', has two outstanding menus. The specialities of the house, including the desserts, are all prepared by talented chefs on the premises. The food is complemented by an extensive wine list.

⊗££ **HUDSON'S HOTEL** 60 Bootham, York.
⌂££££ **Hours:** Meals 7.30am - 9.30am, 12 noon - 2pm and 6.30pm - 9.30pm. Bar meals also available. **Cuisine:** Extensive a la carte menu served in the 'Below Stairs' Restaurant. ⌂ 30 bedrooms, all en suite. **CC** All major cards. **Other Points:** Children welcome. No dogs. Fax No: (0904) 654719. ◨ **(V) Directions:** Very close to Bootham Bar and York Minster.
C R HUDSON ☎ (0904) 621267.
A Victorian hotel in the city centre only minutes from Bootham Bar, the Minster and the Roman Walls. The hotel was converted from 2 town houses and now provides elegant accommodation and high quality cuisine.

⊗££ **KITES RESTAURANT** 13 Grape Lane, York.
Hours: Dinner 6.30pm - 10.30pm. (Mon - Sat). Lunch Saturday only. 12 noon - 1.45 pm. Closed: Sunday. **Cuisine:** Innovative international menu - Thai stuffed crab, Marinated duck breast with Chinese noodle and aubergine salad, Wood pigeon and cumberland sauce. ⌂ None. **CC** Access, Visa. **Other Points:** Children welcome - special children's menu. No dogs. **(V) Directions:** From Bootham Bar, follow Petergate to Low Petergate to Grape Lane.
MS BOO ORMAN ☎ (0904) 641 750.
Tucked away in a small street very close to the Minster and Stonegate. Access to the restaurant is up a narrow staircase to the second floor. All herbs come from the proprietor's own herb garden. Local produce used where possible including a good selection of unusual cheeses from the Dales. Well chosen but affordable wine list.

⊗£££ **KNAVESMIRE MANOR HOTEL & RESTAURANT** 302
⌂£££ Tadcaster Road, York.
CLUB **Hours:** Breakfast 7.30am - 9.30am, dinner 7pm - 9.30pm (last orders). Sunday dinner 7pm - 9pm. **Cuisine:** Dishes include prawn platter, smoked salmon salad, breast of duck. ⌂ 22 rooms. 3 single, 5 twin, 11 double and 3 family rooms. 18 en suite. **CC** All major cards. **Other Points:** Children welcome. Garden. Dogs allowed. Conservatory. Heated indoor pool. Sauna. Whirlpool. Mini Gym. ◨ **(V) Directions:** On Tadcaster Road (A1036) near the race course.
IAN & MARGARET SENIOR ☎ (0904) 702941.

HEWORTH COURT HOTEL

The Heworth Court Hotel is a family run business conveniently situated just outside the medieval bar walls on the Minster Cathedral side of the historic city. All twenty-seven bedrooms have facilities with colour TV., telephone and coffee makers with some ground floor bedrooms around a delightful courtyard. One can relax in the cosy lounge or licensed bar before dining in the renowned *"Lamplight Restaurant"*.

Heworth Court Hotel has a private enclosed car park and remains a favourite abode. Special *"Pink Elephant Breaks"* for any two days stay or longer from £38.50 per person per day which includes bed, full English breakfast and extensive three course evening meal. Christmas, bed and breakfast, and weekly rates also available.

Please telephone for a free colour brochure, menus and map.

Heworth Court Hotel
76 / 78 Heworth Green
York Y03 7TQ

Telephone 0904 425126
or 425156 / 7
Facsimile 0904 415290

Access, Visa, American Express and Diners Club are accepted.

Telephone Deposits Welcome

York continued

Home of the Rowntree Family until the 1920's, visitors to Knavesmire Manor may now dine in the same elegant surroundings where many prominent people, including Lloyd George, were entertained. With a tradition of warm hospitality you will find welcoming staff serving very good food. For those who wish to do more than just relax, there is always the mini gym.

⊗££££ **MOUNT ROYALE** The Mount, York.
🛏££££ **Hours:** 7.15am - 9.30am and 7pm onwards (last orders at around 10pm - 10.30pm). **Cuisine:** International cuisine, including rack of lamb and duckling. 🛏 23 bedrooms, all en suite with colour TV, radio, telephone, trouser press and tea/coffee facilities in rooms. Fax No: (0904) 611171. Telex 57414. 💳 All major cards. **Other Points:** Children welcome. Pets allowed by prior permission. Garden dining. Heated outdoor swimming pool in summer. Trimnasium, sauna, steam room, solarium. ⃣ **(V) Directions:** On A1036 past race course, up hill to traffic lights. On right side.
RICHARD & CHRISTINE OXTOBY ☎ (0904) 628856.
Gothic in appearance, but mainly William IV in style, the Mount Royale has been tastefully decorated and furnished to retain its character. The atmosphere is further enhanced by the presence of the old English garden, which can be seen from the restaurant. A very pleasant venue in which to enjoy good food and friendly, professional service.

⊗££ **PLUNKETS RESTAURANT LTD** 9 High Petergate.
Hours: 11am - 12 midnight. Closed: Christmas Day, Boxing Day and New Years Day. **Cuisine:** Dishes include fajitas, burritos, hamburgers, steaks, homemade pies, fresh salmon fishcakes, marinated chicken breasts, salads & various vegetarian dishes. 🛏 None. 💳 None. **Other Points:** Children welcome. No dogs. **(V) Directions:** Located on one of York's principle streets, near Bootham Bar.
TREVOR BARRINGTON WARD ☎ (0904) 637722.
Plunkets is a cheerful restaurant set in a 17th century building near York Minster. It plays music of a gentle jazz/disco kind and is full of plants, prints and polished wooden tables.

⊗£ **PUNCH BOWL HOTEL** 5 Blossom Street, York.
🛏££ **Hours:** Breakfast 7.30am - 9.30am, Lunch 12 noon - 2pm, Dinner 5.30pm - 10pm. Bar snacks 12 noon - 2pm and 5.30pm - 8pm. Closed: Christmas Day only. **Cuisine:** Bar Grill specialising in good value bar snacks. Childrens menu. 🛏 9 bedrooms, all en suite. 💳 All major cards. **Other Points:** Children welcome. No dogs. No smoking area. **(V) Directions:** On the City Wall, next to the Micklegate in Blossom St. A64.
ERIC BINGHAM ☎ (0904) 622619.
A 17th century Coaching Inn, situated below the City Wall, which provides well cooked food for tourists and day visitors. The Falstaff Grill is also popular locally and has become a lively meeting place where good food is available at good value for money. Comfortable accommodation. Well placed for all of York's tourist attractions.

York continued

⊕℔ **THE ALICE HAWTHORN** Nun Monkton, York.

CLUB **Hours:** Lunch 12 noon - 1.30pm (last orders) and dinner 7pm - 10pm (last orders). **Cuisine:** Home cooked bar meals, using freshest produce available. ⊨ None. **CC** None. **Other Points:** Children welcome. Garden. Pets allowed. No smoking in restaurant. ⊡ **Directions:** Off the main A59 at Skipbridge filling station.

MR S. WINSHIP ☎ (0423) 330303.

An old cottage style village pub, situated on the village green of the beautiful village of Nun Monkton, offering well cooked food in restaurant and bar. The welcoming and friendly atmosphere of the main bar attracts both locals and visitors to the area.

⊗££ **THE AMBASSADOR** 123-125 The Mount, York.

⊞£££ **Hours:** Breakfast 7.30am - 9.30am. Lunch 12 noon - 2pm. Dinner 6.30pm - 9.30pm. (Sunday 8.30pm). **Cuisine:** Traditional English. Bacon and asparagus served hot with salad, roast lamb. ⊨ 19 bedrooms, all en suite. **CC** Access, Visa. **Other Points:** Children welcome. Garden. Pets allowed. ⊡ & **(V) Directions:** Close to York Minster.

DAVID MILLER ☎ (0904) 641316

An elegant Georgian style hotel, built in 1842 and set in one and a half acres of superb gardens. The combination of excellent accommodation, cuisine and service has earned a 'Highly recommended' rating from the Inspector. The outstanding gardens are much in demand for weddings and Mr Miller's 'well tended' attitude to The Ambassador has been carried all the way through.

⊞££ **THE HILL HOTEL** 60 York Road, Acomb, York.

⊨ 10 bedrooms, all en suite. Radio, alarm, colour TV, direct dial telephone and tea/coffee making facilities in all rooms. **Hours:** Breakfast 8am - 9am, Dinner served 7pm - 8pm. **CC** Access, Visa, AmEx. **Other Points:** Children welcome. No dogs allowed. ⊡ **(V) Directions:** Take the B1224 York to Wetherby Road.

PETER BLACKBURN ☎ (0904) 790777.

Situated in 3/4 acre of fine, walled gardens on the highest point in York with views across the city, the Hill Hotel was once a fine Georgian residence. Now modernised, it provides a high level of comfort and promotes a warm, family atmosphere, complimented by the home-cooking.

York continued

⌂££ **THE HILL HOTEL** 60 York Road, Acomb, York.

🛏 10 bedrooms, all en suite. Radio, alarm, colour TV, direct dial telephone and tea/coffee making facilities in all rooms. **Hours:** Breakfast 8am - 9am, Dinner served 7pm - 8pm. **CC** Access, Visa, AmEx. **Other Points:** Children welcome. No dogs allowed. **P** **(V) Directions:** Take the B1224 York to Wetherby Road.

PETER BLACKBURN ☎ (0904) 790777.

Situated in 3/4 acre of fine, walled gardens on the highest point in York with views across the city, the Hill Hotel was once a fine Georgian residence. Now modernised, it provides a high level of comfort and promotes a warm, family atmosphere, complimented by the home-cooking.

⌂££ **THE HILL HOTEL** 60 York Road, Acomb, York.

🛏 10 bedrooms, all en suite. Radio, alarm, colour TV, direct dial telephone and tea/coffee making facilities in all rooms. **Hours:** Breakfast 8am - 9am, Dinner served 7pm - 8pm. **CC** Access, Visa, AmEx. **Other Points:** Children welcome. No dogs allowed. **P** **(V) Directions:** Take the B1224 York to Wetherby Road.

PETER BLACKBURN ☎ (0904) 790777.

Situated in 3/4 acre of fine, walled gardens on the highest point in York with views across the city, the Hill Hotel was once a fine Georgian residence. Now modernised, it provides a high level of comfort and promotes a warm, family atmosphere, complimented by the home-cooking.

⊗££ **WHITE SWAN INN & RESTAURANT** Deighton, Escrick, CLUB York.

Hours: Restaurant open 12 noon - 2pm (Sundays only), and 7pm - 9.30pm. Bar meals 12 noon - 2pm, and 7pm - 9.45pm. Restaurant open at lunchtime by arrangement. Restaurant closed: Mondays. **Cuisine:** British cuisine. Salmon steak with prawn sauce, and half roast duckling in restaurant. Lasagne, and steak in the bar. Game available in season. 🛏 None. **CC** Access, Visa. **Other Points:** Children welcome. No dogs allowed. Open Sundays and bank holidays. **P** ♿ **(V) Directions:** On A19, 5 miles south of York.

IAN & MARIANNE WALKER ☎ (0904) 87287.

A family run country inn, with an intimate restaurant and comfortable bar area. Offers well-prepared and presented dishes at excellent value for money - in a very pleasant, friendly atmosphere.

ISLE OF MAN

DOUGLAS Isle of Man **Map 8 B1**

⊗££ **LA BRASSERIE** Central Promenade, Douglas.

⌂££££ **Hours:** Full menu served all day from 10am - 10.45pm. Childrens menu available until 7.30pm. Open all year. **Cuisine:** Extensive menu featuring eg. Fresh Scallops wrapped in bacon with garlic

GLEN HELEN

Douglas continued

butter; Chicken Tikka; Steak, Kidney & Guiness Pie; Salmon Hollandaise. ⊨ 102 en suite bedrooms in The Empress Hotel. **CC** All major cards. **Other Points:** Children welcome. Open all day. Childrens menu (10 years & under). No-smoking area. Afternoon tea. Good wine list. Fax No: (0624) 673554. & **(V)** **Directions:** Directly beneath The Empress Hotel, Douglas Promenade. Seafront.
JOHN TURNER ☎ (0624) 661155.
An excellent restaurant situated below The Empress Hotel, serving an extensive choice of meals throughout the day. All dishes are prepared from fresh produce, well-cooked and attractively presented in generous portions. The high quality food is complemented by a good wine list and excellent service. Enjoy your meal in comfortable surroundings with a pleasant, relaxed atmosphere.

⊗££ **SEFTON HOTEL** Harris Promenade, Douglas.
⊞££££**Hours:** Breakfast 7.30am - 9.45am, lunch 12.30pm - 2pm, dinner 6.15pm - 9.30pm, bar snacks 9.45am - 11pm. Open Bank Holidays. **Cuisine:** Dishes may include - mushroom crepes with sauce mornay, grilled salmon with cucumber sauce, Manx ice cream. ⊨ 80 bedrooms, all en suite. **CC** All major cards **Other Points:** Children welcome. No smoking area. Afternoon teas. Sunbed. Gym. Beauty threapy room. Coffee Shop. Conferences catered for. Fax No (0624) 676004. ▣ & **(V) Directions:** Centre of Douglas Promenade. Next to the Gaiety Theatre.
CHRIS ROBERTSHAW - Managing Director. ☎ (0624) 626011.
Attached to the Gaiety Theatre, this hotel offers special 'Island Theatre Weekends'. Whether you wish to enjoy a play or two, or simply relax, the Sefton Hotel is ideal. Good food is served in a pleasantly relaxed atmosphere. With a health club, indoor heated swimming pool, and comfortable accommodation, this is just the place to return to after discovering the island.

⊗££ **THE EMPRESS HOTEL** Central Promenade, Douglas.
⊞££££**Hours:** Breakfast 6.45am - 10am. Full meals served all day from 10am - 10.45pm. Open all year. **Cuisine:** Meals served all day in La Brasserie. Extensive choice of dishes eg. Coq au Vin, Chateaubriand, Lamb steak with stilton & pear butter. Childrens menu. ⊨ 102 bedrooms, all en suite. All with colour TV, radio, alarm, telephone, trouser press, tea/coffee making facilities. Room service. **CC** All major cards. **Other Points:** Children welcome. No-smoking area. Afternoon teas. No pets. Residents' lounge. Conference facilities. Fax: (0624) 673554. & **(V) Directions:** Centrally located on Douglas Promenade.
JOHN TURNER ☎ (0624) 661155.
A large seafront hotel, centrally situated on Douglas Promenade. The entire hotel has been recently modernised and now offers the best in comfort and attractive, tastefully decorated surroundings. With well-appointed bedrooms, excellent service and a pleasant, relaxed atmosphere, this is an ideal place to stay. Residents can enjoy the good food served in La Brasserie, below the hotel.

GLEN HELEN Isle of Man **Map 8 B1**
⊗£££ **SWISS CHALET RESTAURANT** Glen Helen.

Hours: Midweek lunches - please phone for opening times, Sunday lunch 12 noon - 2.30pm. Dinner Tuesday to Saturday 7pm - 9.30pm. Closed: Mondays. **Cuisine:** Extensive a la carte menu specialising in fresh, local fish. Other dishes may include Pork Swiss Chalet, Beef Wellington, Rack of Lamb, and Beef Oriental. ⊭ None. **CC** None. **Other Points:** Children welcome. No dogs. Parties and weddings catered for. Licensed. ▯ ᴖ **(V) Directions:** A3, between Ballacraine traffic lights & Kirk Michael. 7 mins Peel.

CHRIS LIDGETT ☎ (0624) 801657.

Also known as 'The Restaurant in the Glen', this restaurant provides excellent food in very comfortable and relaxed surroundings. The choice of food is extensive but whatever your choice, all dishes are very well cooked using fresh produce, and attractively presented. In keeping with the high quality of the cuisine, the service is excellent.

RAMSEY Isle of Man **Map 8 B1**
⊗£££ **GRAND ISLAND HOTEL** Ramsey.

⌂□££££ **Hours:** Breakfast 7.30am - 10am, Lunch 12 noon - 2pm, Dinner 7pm - 10pm (last orders). Bar meals 12 noon - 2.30pm. Open all year. **Cuisine:** Choice of 2 restaurants. Good use of local produce. Flambe dishes a speciality. ⊭ 54 bedrooms, all en suite. **CC** All major cards. **Other Points:** Children welcome. No smoking area. Garden. Leisure and Health Club - swimming pool, jacuzzi, gym, sauna, beautician etc. Fax: (0624) 815291. ▯ ᴖ **(V) Directions:** 1 mile north east of Ramsey on the coast.

HOWARD TREVOR DAVIS ☎ (0624) 812455.

An outstanding, family owned and run hotel, situated on the coast with panoramic views of Ramsey Bay and the mountains. The two restaurants offer a choice of well-cooked dishes in elegant or informal surroundings. Tastefully furnished, the hotel offers a high standard of comfort and is renowned for its efficient service and friendly staff. Sporting, health & beauty facilities.

⊗££ **HARBOUR BISTRO** 5 East Street, Ramsey.

Hours: Lunch 12.15pm - 2.30pm (last orders), dinner 6.30pm - 10.30pm (last orders). Closed for 4 days over Christmas and Good Friday. **Cuisine:** Dishes may include - avacado and crab salad, seafood chowdar, spicy duck with pineapple, steaks. Seafood and fresh fish a speciality. ⊭ None. **CC** Access, Visa. **Other Points:** Children welcome. Special diets catered for. Street parking available. ᴖ **(V) Directions:** Between Harbour and Parliament Street.

KARL MEIER ☎ (0624) 814182.

Comfortably furnished and enjoying a relaxed atmosphere, the Harbour Bistro offers an extensive menu with an emphasis on seafood. All dishes are well cooked, attractively presented and served by helpful, friendly staff. Good wine list. Popular with locals and holidaymakers alike, the atmosphere is welcoming and relaxed.

CENTRAL, LOWLANDS & SCOTTISH BORDERS
(INCORPORATING NORTHUMBERLAND)

CENTRAL, LOWLANDS AND SCOTTISH BORDERS

NORTHUMBRIA – ENGLAND'S BORDER COUNTRY

Northumberland is the most northern county in England and forms part of the Kingdom of Northumbria which, in centuries past, ruled the lands between the rivers Humber and Forth. It was a remote region, bordering the mysterious land of Scotland and separated from it by Hadrian's Wall.

Yet Northumbria has played a major role in the shaping of today's Britain. There are remarkably well-preserved remains of Hadrian's Wall along the South Tyne valley, and many medieval castles and churches. In the far north lies beautiful Holy Island, home of the Irish missionaries who made the Anglo-Saxon kingdom of Northumbria famous as the northern centre of early Christianity.

Northumbria also has an impressive legacy as a world centre of mining, shipping and engineering. The Industrial Revolution 200 years ago was extremely important to the region. Today, traditional heritage meets modern attractions. One of the largest centres for the outdoor enthusiast is Kielder Water, with facilities for windsurfing, boating and water-skiing. The fun of the seaside can also be found along the coastline at resorts like South Shields, Whitley Bay and Seaburn.

The kingdom of Northumbria also has some of the finest countryside, in such areas as the North Pennines, the Northumberland National Park and the Cleveland Hills – an ideal escape for those seeking peace and tranquility.

CENTRAL AND SOUTHERN SCOTLAND

With its marvellous beaches, excellent fishing rivers and forest parks, one of the greatest attractions of this part of Scotland is the variety of outdoor activities for everyone.

The keen pony-trekker will find ideal country in the south-east and Borders, and the hill-walker has a choice of both gentle and challenging terrain. The Ayrshire coast has about 20 golf courses, including Troon, Turnberry and Prestwick, and there is also a wide choice in Glasgow and Dumfries. Ayr itself is one of the biggest seaside resorts, with three miles of beach with safe bathing and boat trips from the harbour, a racecourse and a beautiful park.

Two miles south and you will find what is probably the most famous thatched cottage in Scotland, that being the birthplace of national poet, Robert Burns. The museum adjacent to the cottage traces his life and works. The south-west is also an area with a rich industrial heritage and there are many fascinating museums charting the history of lead-mining, and iron and steel engineering.

History and legend haunt many areas of Central and Eastern Scotland. If visiting the Trossachs or Loch Lomond, you will be enthralled by the tales of Rob Roy, Robert the Bruce and William Wallace.

Of all the interesting towns and cities in the south-west, Glasgow is the best known. A decade ago, to call Glasgow beautiful would have been regarded by most as at least an exaggeration. The changes that have taken place since then have been wonderful. Now, its classical 19th century architecture has been cleaned to reveal its full glory and there have been projects in housing and urban planning. In 1990, Glasgow was awarded the title of European City of Culture and, being home to the Scottish Opera, Scottish Ballet and National Orchestra, it is now rightly regarded as a city where there's 'a lot Glasgowing on'.

Over in the south-east lies Edinburgh, Scotland's capital. It is one of the most handsome of European cities with a magnificent setting on hills around Castle Rock. In addition to its splendid architecture, much of Edinburgh consists of beautiful open spaces, with wonderful landscaped areas like the Royal Botanical Gardens. It also offers visitors a wide range of sporting activities and entertainment, and a variety of restaurants where you can sample cuisine from all over the world. It is also renowned for its cultural life, at a peak during the Edinburgh Festival, held in August.

On your travels, be sure to look out for the Les Routiers sign to sample some of the delicious Scottish fayre. Food in Scotland reflects its natural resources: salmon from the rivers, fish from the sea and meat from the pastures. The menus are varied and imaginative, using fresh vegetables grown in the rich lowland soil, and the Scots are also excellent bakers – so those with a sweet tooth are sure to appreciate the delicious cakes.

QUICK REFERENCE GUIDE

	NO. OF ESTS.	⊗ £	⊗ ££	⊗ £££	⊗ ££££	⍩ £	⍩ ££	⍩ £££	⍩ ££££

CENTRAL, LOWLANDS & SCOTTISH BORDERS

MAP 10 A1

	NO. OF ESTS.	⊗ £	⊗ ££	⊗ £££	⊗ ££££	⍩ £	⍩ ££	⍩ £££	⍩ ££££
Bridge of Orchy	1		★				★		
Dalmally	1		★				★		
Easdale	2	★	★					★	
Inveraray	1		★						
Isle of Iona	1		★					★	
Isle of Mull	3		★	★				★	★
Kilmelford	1		★					★	
Oban	2		★					★	★

MAP 10 A2

	NO. OF ESTS.	⊗ £	⊗ ££	⊗ £££	⊗ ££££	⍩ £	⍩ ££	⍩ £££	⍩ ££££
Aberfeldy	1			★					
Almondbank	1	★							
Auchterarder	1	★						★	
Crianlarich	1	★							
Crieff	3	★	★					★	
Fortingall	1			★				★	
Kenmore	1			★				★	
Killin	2		★					★	
Kinloch Rannoch	1	★							
Lochearnhead	1		★					★	
Pitlochry	3		★	★				★	★
St Fillans	1		★					★	
Tyndrum	2	★						★	

MAP 10 B1

	NO. OF ESTS.	⊗ £	⊗ ££	⊗ £££	⊗ ££££	⍩ £	⍩ ££	⍩ £££	⍩ ££££
Arrochar	1	★							
Ayr	9	★	★					★	★
Dunoon	1		★					★	
Gourock	1	★							
Isle of Arran	2		★					★	
Isle of Gigha	1			★					★
Kilfinan	1		★						
Kilwinning	1		★						
Largs	2		★	★				★	★
Lochgilphead	2		★					★	
Putechantuy	1		★					★	
Rothesay	1		★					★	
Strachur	1			★					
Tarbert	1				★				
Tayvallich	1		★						
Troon	1		★						

MAP 10 B2

	NO. OF ESTS.	⊗ £	⊗ ££	⊗ £££	⊗ ££££	⍩ £	⍩ ££	⍩ £££	⍩ ££££
Airdrie	1		★					★	
Biggar	1		★						★
Bo'ness	2		★				★		★
Callander	3		★			★	★		
Creetown	1		★					★	
Dollar	1		★					★	
Dunblane	1		★					★	
Dunfermline	1		★					★	
Glasgow	10	★	★	★				★	★
Johnstone	1	★						★	
Kilmarnock	1		★						
Kincardine on Forth	1		★					★	
Luss	1	★							

QUICK REFERENCE GUIDE

	NO. OF ESTS.	£	££	£££	££££	£	££	£££	££££
Motherwell	1			★				★	
Paisley	2		★						★
Renfrew	2		★						
Rosyth	1		★			★			
Tweedsmuir	1		★					★	

MAP 10 C1

	NO. OF ESTS.	£	££	£££	££££	£	££	£££	££££
Girvan	1		★					★	

MAP 10 C2

	NO. OF ESTS.	£	££	£££	££££	£	££	£££	££££
Dalbeattie	1		★					★	
Dalry	1		★				★		
Dumfries	3		★	★					★
Gatehouse of Fleet	2		★	★	★				★
Isle of Whithorn	1		★				★		
Kirkcudbright	1		★					★	
Lockerbie	1		★					★	
Moffat	4	★	★					★	
New Galloway	1	★							
Newton Stewart	1	★					★		
Thornhill	1	★					★		

MAP 11 A1

	NO. OF ESTS.	£	££	£££	££££	£	££	£££	££££
Arbroath	1		★					★	
Blairgowrie	3		★					★	★
Bridge of Earn	1				★				
Dundee	1							★	
Forfar	2		★				★	★	
Glenshee	1	★					★		
Kirkmichael	1		★				★		
Perth	2		★	★				★	★
St Andrews	3	★		★			★	★	

MAP 11 B1

	NO. OF ESTS.	£	££	£££	££££	£	££	£££	££££
Aberlady	1	★					★		
Cornhill on Tweed	1			★					
Dunbar	2		★				★	★	
East Linton	1		★						★
Edinburgh	21	★	★	★		★	★	★	★
Galashiels	2	★	★					★	
Glenrothes	1		★					★	
Gullane	1			★					★
Kelso	1		★					★	
Kinross	1		★						
Kirkcaldy	1	★							
Leadburn	1		★				★		
Milnathort	1	★						★	
Peebles	6	★	★	★			★	★	★
Roslin	1		★						
Selkirk	1			★				★	
Stow	1	★					★		
West Wemyss	1		★					★	

MAP 11 B2

	NO. OF ESTS.	£	££	£££	££££	£	££	£££	££££
Belford	1		★		★				
Berwick upon Tweed	1						★		
Burnmouth	1	★							
Burntisland	1		★				★		
Crail	1	★					★		
Cowick	1	★							

QUICK REFERENCE GUIDE

	NO. OF ESTS.	⊗ £	⊗ ££	⊗ £££	⊗ ££££	⌂ £	⌂ ££	⌂ £££	⌂ ££££
Seahouses	3	★	★				★	★	★
Wooler	1		★						
MAP 11 C1									
Annan	1		★						★
Greenhead	1					★			
Gretna	1		★					★	
Hawick	2		★	★				★	★
Haydon Bridge	1		★				★		
Jedburgh	1	★					★		
Newcastleton	1		★						
Otterburn	1		★					★	
MAP 11 C2									
Alnmouth	3		★					★	
Alnwick	1		★					★	
Corbridge	1		★						
Hexham	2		★					★	
Longframlington	1		★					★	
Rothbury	1		★						
Wylam	1			★				★	

ALNMOUTH Northumberland **Map 11 C2**

MARINE HOUSE 1 Marine Road, Alnmouth.

10 bedrooms, all en suite. Self-catering cottages:'Marine House Cottage' sleeps 6, 'Begonia House' sleeps 7. **Hours:** Breakfast 8.30am - 9am and dinner 7pm. **CC** None. **Other Points:** Children welcome. Pets allowed. Residents lounge with TV. Terraced garden. Games room with pool, table tennis, darts and stereo. Golf clubs for hire. **Directions:** Situated near the seafront.
GORDON INKSTER ☎ (0665) 830349.

A listed building which began its life as a granary 200 years ago and was then converted into a vicarage in the 19th century. The hotel's atmosphere of warmth and comfort has been further enhanced by imaginative use of decor and furnishings. With the assistance of the proprietors son Iain, experienced an chef, the table d'hote menu and standard of food is superb.

SADDLE HOTEL & SADDLE GRILL RESTAURANT 24 Northumberland Street, Alnmouth.

Hours: Lunch 12 noon - 2pm, table d'hote dinner 6pm - 9pm, a la carte 6pm - 9pm. Open 11am - 11pm. **Cuisine:** Locally caught salmon, plaice, trout, cod, sole, crab, haddock. Beef strogonoff, cumberland sausage and chicken pancake. 10 bedrooms, all en suite and with TV and telephones. **CC** Access, Visa. **Other Points:** Children welcome. **(V) Directions:** On the B1338, the main street in Alnmouth.
STAN & MARY TAIT ☎ (0665) 830 476.

Alnmouth is a picturesque village perched above the mouth of the Aln. An attractive, old building recently refurbished and redecorated.

THE SCHOONER HOTEL Northumberland Street, Alnmouth.

Hours: Breakfast 7.30am - 9.30am, lunch 12 noon - 3pm (last orders 2.30pm), dinner 7pm - 11pm (last orders 10.30pm, 9.30pm Monday & Tuesday). **Cuisine:** Serves fixed price 4 course menu, bar meals/snacks and vegetarian dishes. Fish specialities. Italian Restaurant, Edro's - a la carte menu, 5 days a week. 25 rooms. 3 single, 19 double/twin and 3 family rooms. All en suite. **CC** All major cards. **Other Points:** Children welcome. Garden. Afternoon teas. Dogs allowed. Squash court. Solarium. Conservatory. 3 bars. Fax: (0665) 830216. Conferences. **(V) Directions:** Next to the 9 hole village golf course. 5 miles A1, Alnwick exit.
MR ORDE ☎ (0665) 830216

A Georgian coaching inn, ideally situated for the golf course & coast, this hotel offers very comfortable accommodation. Good food is pleasantly presented in the spacious restaurant by attentive staff. With two ships wheels hanging behind the bar there is a definate nautical feel to the establishment. A mixed group frequent this hotel and the atmosphere is convivial yet relaxed.

ALNWICK Northumberland **Map 11 C2**

HOTSPUR HOTEL Bondgate Without, Alnwick.

Hours: Bar meals 12 noon - 2pm, dinner and bar meals 7pm - 9pm. Closed: Christmas Day, Boxing Day, New Years Day.

Alnwick continued

Cuisine: English dishes, steaks, wild salmon. ⊨ 26 bedrooms, 23 en suite. **CC** All major cards. **Other Points:** Children welcome. Dogs allowed. **P** **(V) Directions:** On B6346 just outside city wall approaching from A1.

MR D COZENS ☎ (0665) 510101.

A former coaching house converted into a comfortable, family run hotel. There is a choice of dining in the restaurant or in the wine and food bar. Friendly and polite service.

BELFORD Northumberland **Map 11 B2**

⊗££ **BLUE BELL** Market Square, Belford.

□□£ **Hours:** Meals from 8am - 9am, 12 noon - 2pm and 7pm - 8.45pm (last orders). Bar meals 12 noon - 2pm and 6.30pm - 9pm. **Cuisine:** Fresh local produce, eg. fish, lamb and game. ⊨ 17 bedrooms, all en suite. **CC** All major cards. **Other Points:** Children welcome. No dogs. Coaches by appointment. **P** & **(V) Directions:** Situated on the B6349 just off the A1.

M C SHIRLEY ☎ (06683) 543.

17th century coaching inn in the heart of a peaceful Northumbrian village. An ideal stopover for North/South travellers or those exploring Northumbria's wonderful beaches and historic castles.

BERWICK UPON TWEED Northumberland **Map 11 B2**

□□££ **THE WALLS GUEST HOUSE** 8 Quay Walls, Berwick Upon Tweed.

⊨ 1 family room, 2 double, 1 twin, All en suite. 1 single. TV, trouser press hairdryer. Tea making facilities available in rooms. **Hours:** Breakfast 8am - 9am, lunch 1pm - 2pm, dinner 6.30pm - 8.30pm (order by 6.30pm). **CC** Access, Visa. **Other Points:** Children welcome. Separate lounge/bar. Family games room. Special rates available. **P** & **(V) Directions:** Marygate St, towards river on Hide Hill, right Bridge St, 1st left.

GRACE LEAMAN & DAVID MULLENDER ☎ (0289) 330140.

A very enthuastically run guest house with above the average attention given to guests comfort. All food is fresh and cooked by the proprietors using local produce. Tastefully decorated, the rooms reflect Grace Leaman's love of interior design - well worth a visit.

CORBRIDGE Northumberland **Map 11 C2**

⊗££ **RIVERSIDE HOTEL** Main Street, Corbridge.

Hours: Restaurant 7pm - 8.30pm, prior reservation only. Open to non-residents Monday to Saturday. **Cuisine:** English and French country dishes,fixed price,3-course cordon bleu dinner. ⊨ 11 bedrooms, 7 en suite. **CC** None. **Other Points:** Children welcome. Vegetarian dishes by arrangement. **P** & **Directions:** On the A68.

HARRY & JUDY FAWCETT ☎ (043 471) 2942.

Friendly, family run hotel in attractive village in unspoilt countryside. Near Roman Wall and Northumberland National Park on A68 holiday route to Scotland yet only 17 miles from Newcastle.

CORNHILL ON TWEED Northumberland **Map 11 B1**

⊛£££ **TILLMOUTH PARK HOTEL** Cornhill-on-Tweed.
Hours: Breakfast 8am - 10am,lunch 12.30pm - 2pm and dinner
7.30pm - 9.30pm. **Cuisine:** Tweed salmon, local pheasant,
Cheviot lamb. ⊨ 13 bedrooms, all en suite. ☒ Access, Visa,
AmEx. **Other Points:** Children welcome. Dogs allowed. ▣ **(V)**
Directions: On A698 Cornhill to Berwick-on-Tweed Rd. 3 miles
from main A697.
MR J C STANDERWICK - Manager ☎ (0890) 2255.
A country-house hotel set in extensive grounds, with very
comfortable surroundings and food and accommodation of a
high standard.

GREENHEAD Northumberland **Map 11 C1**

⏃£ **HOLMHEAD FARM** Hadrian's Wall, Greenhead.
CLUB ⊨ 1 double, 2 twin and 1 family bedroom, all en suite. Radio,
hairdryer and CH in all rooms. Tea/coffee making facilities
available. **Hours:** Breakfast 9am (flexible). Dinner 7.30pm (by
arrangement). ☒ Access, Visa. **Other Points:** Children welcome.
Garden. Licensed. Heartbeat Award for provision of healthy food.
Vegetarian dishes available. ▣ **(V) Directions:** On A69 and
B6318, behind Garage in Greenhead village.
PAULINE & BRIAN STAFF ☎ (06977) 47402.
Holmhead, formerly a working farm built of Roman stones &
situated on the foundations of Hadrians Wall, welcomes guests
to its cosy guest house & holiday cottage. The owners will share
their local knowledge and tours around the Wall can be
arranged. Ideal location for all those who enjoy the country life.
'Longest breakfast menu in the world'. Good home cooking &
excellent value.

HAYDON BRIDGE Northumberland **Map 11 C1**

⊛££ **THE ANCHOR HOTEL** Haydon Bridge, Hexham.
⏃££ **Hours:** Breakfast 8am - 9am, dinner 7pm - 8.30pm (last orders).
CLUB Bar meals 12 noon - 2pm and 7pm - 9pm. **Cuisine:** Traditional
British and Continental dishes. ⊨ 12 bedrooms, 10 en suite.
☒ All major cards. **Other Points:** Children welcome. Coaches by
appointment. ▣ ♿ **(V) Directions:** On the A69 midway between
Newcastle and Carlisle.
VIVIENNE & JOHN DEES ☎ (0434) 684227
A riverside coaching inn close to Hadrian's Wall,
Northumberland National Park, Kielder Water and North
Pennines. Owned and run by the Dees since 1975, the hotel has
built up an international reputation based on both its food and
atmosphere.

HEXHAM Northumberland **Map 11 C2**

⊛££ **BEAUMONT HOTEL** Beaumont Street, Hexham.
⏃£££ **Hours:** Breakfast 7.30am - 9.45am, lunch 12 noon - 2pm and
dinner 7pm - 9.45pm (last orders). Bar meals 12 noon - 2pm.
Closed: Boxing Day and New Year's Day. **Cuisine:** Steaks, Pork
Northumbria, roast guinea fowl, trout Beaumontine. ⊨ 23
bedrooms all en suite with direct dial telephones, colour TV, radio
and tea/coffee making facilities. ☒ All major cards. **Other Points:**
Children welcome. Fax No: (0434) 602331. Lift to all floors. **(V)**
Directions: On the A69 overlooking the Abbey and the park in
the town centre.

LOWLANDS & SCOTTISH BORDERS

Hexham continued

MARTIN & LINDA OWEN ☎ (0434) 602331.

A busy, family run hotel incorporating a wine bar, cocktail bar, the Park Restaurant as well as conference facilities. Close to the centre of this historic market town in the heart of Northumbria, The Beaumont is a popular hotel with tourists and businessmen.

⊗££ **COUNTY HOTEL** Priestpopple, Hexham.

⌂££££ **Hours:** Meals from 8am - 10pm. Lunch 11.45am - 2.15pm and dinner 7pm - 9.30pm (last orders). **Cuisine:** Fresh, traditional British dishes. ⊨ 9 bedrooms, 8 en suite. 1 designated bath, shower and toilet. **CC** Access, Visa, AmEx. **Other Points:** Children welcome. Coaches welcome. & **Directions:** From A69, follow signs to Hexham. Hotel is on the main street.

MR KEN WATTS ☎ (0434) 602030.

A homely, privately run hotel situated between the train and bus stations. The cocktail bar's walls are covered with hunting prints and other equine memorabilia.

LONGFRAMLINGTON Northumberland **Map 11 C2**

⊗££ **THE GRANBY INN** Longframlington, nr Morpeth.

⌂££££ **Hours:** Restaurant open daily 11am - 3pm and 6pm - 11pm. Closed: Christmas Day. **Cuisine:** Local shellfish, lobster Thermidor, grilled prawns in garlic butter, steak and kidney pie and homemade soups. ⊨ 6 bedrooms, 5 en suite. **CC** Access, Visa. **Other Points:** No dogs. ▣ & **Directions:** On the A697 north of Morpeth.

MRS ANNE BRIGHT ☎ (066 570) 228.

200 year-old coaching inn with old oak beams. Comfortably furnished rooms with central heating, colour TV, telephone and tea-making facilities. Relaxing public lounges. Restaurant seating 24. Bar meals always available.

LOWICK Northumberland **Map 11 B2**

⊗£ **BLACK BULL INN** Main Street, Lowick, Berwick upon Tweed.

CLUB **Hours:** Meals from 12 noon - 2pm and 6.30pm (7pm in winter) - 9.30pm (last orders). Closed: Mondays from October until Easter. **Cuisine:** Well known for homemade pies and local fish. ⊨ Self catering. **CC** Visa. **Other Points:** Children welcome until 8.30pm. No dogs. Coaches by appointment. Mastercard & Eurocard also accepted. Limited access for disabled. ▣ **(V) Directions:** On B6353 between Coldstream and Holy Island.

ANNE & TOM GRUNDY ☎ (0289) 88228

A 300 year old Northumbrian pub with good local trade and excellent visitor trade in summer. Due to this pub's popularity, the proprietors Anne & Tom Grundy have expanded the food side of the business and can now offer larger dining room facilities where real ales are also served. Booking is advised for evenings and weekends.

OTTERBURN Northumberland **Map 11 C1**

⊗££ **OTTERBURN TOWER HOTEL** Otterburn.

⌂££££ **Hours:** Open 7am - 11.30pm. **Cuisine:** Homemade soups, local

CLUB beef. ⊨ 12 bedrooms, 8 en suite. **CC** All major cards. **Other Points:** Children welcome. Large garden. ▣ **Directions:** The entrance to the hotel is at the junction of the A696 and B6320.

PETER HARDING ☎ (0830) 20620.

Otterburn continued

A spacious, adapted castellated country house in extensive grounds. 3-course menu and bar meals are offered in the traditionally furnished and wood-panelled dining room and lounges. Steeped in history, the hotel is reputedly haunted! Private fishing on 3.5 miles of the River Rede.

ROTHBURY Northumberland **Map 11 C2**

⊗££ **COQUET VALE HOTEL** Rothbury.
Hours: Breakfast 7.30am - 9.30am, lunch 12 noon - 2pm, 7pm - 9pm. Meals also in the bar. **Cuisine:** Northumbrian beef, Malcolm's sizzling feast. ⊨ 14 bedrooms, 10 en suite. 2 bathrooms. **CC** Access, Visa. **Other Points:** Children welcome. Coaches by appointment. **P** **(V) Directions:** On the B6341
JAMES M. CORRISH ☎ (0669) 20305.
A Victorian type building constructed for the railways, it was previously called the Station Hotel. Situated on B6341 this hotel is very well placed for North/South travellers and for those wanting to discover the delights of the area and the Borders.

SEAHOUSES Northumberland **Map 11 B2**

⊗££ **BAMBURGH CASTLE HOTEL** Seahouses.
⬠££ **Hours:** Breakfast 8am - 9am, Dinner 7pm - 8.30pm. Bar meals
CLUB 11.30am - 2.30pm and 6pm - 9pm. **Cuisine:** A range of fresh local produce including local fish, meat and game. ⊨ 20 bedrooms, all en suite. All modern facilities including colour TV with satellite channels in all bedrooms. **CC** None. **Other Points:** Children welcome. Dogs allowed. Garden. **P** & **(V) Directions:** Situated above the harbour in Seahouses.
PAUL HOPPER ☎ (0665) 720283.
A white walled, slated building set in its own grounds overlooking the charming harbour and with splendid views across the sea to Farne Islands, Holy Island and Bamburgh Castle. During the summer months, the hotel garden is popular, while the log fire in the lounge warms away the winter chills.

⊗££ **BEACH HOUSE HOTEL** Sea Front, Seahouses.
⬠££££**Hours:** Meals 8.30am - 9.30am and 6.30pm - 7.30pm. Closed: November to end March. **Cuisine:** Local produce, eg. game and fish including Craster kippers. Clootie dumpling. ⊨ 14 bedrooms all en suite. **CC** Access, Visa. **Other Points:** Children welcome. No smoking area. Fax No: (0665) 720921. **P** & **Directions:** On the Seahouses to Bamburgh Road.
MR & MRS F R CRAIGS ☎ (0665) 720337.
A small, friendly family run hotel. Pleasantly situated overlooking the beach and Farne Islands. The Beach House Hotel specialises in imaginative home cooking and baking. Particularly suited to those looking for a quiet, comfortable holiday.

⊗£ **THE LODGE** 146 Main Street, Seahouses.
⬠££ **Hours:** Breakfast 8.30am - 9.30am (residents only). Lunch 12 noon - 2pm and dinner 6.30pm - 9.30pm (last orders). **Cuisine:** Local seafood. ⊨ 5 bedrooms, all en suite and with TV and tea/coffee facilities. **CC** Access, Visa. **Other Points:** Children welcome. Dogs by arrangement. **P** & **Directions:** On the main street in Seahouses (North Sunderland).

LOWLANDS & SCOTTISH BORDERS

Seahouses continued
SELBY & JENIFER BROWN ☎ (0665) 720 158.
The falcon sign of this small hotel makes it easy to spot. Styled along Scandanavian lines with pine panelling and furniture throughout. Relaxing by the open fire in the convivial bar is a perfect end to a day exploring this historic and beautiful area.

WOOLER Northumberland **Map 11 B2**
⊗££ **THE RYECROFT HOTEL** Ryecroft Way, Wooler.
Hours: Breakfast 8.30am - 9.30am and dinner 7pm - 8pm. Bar lunches 12 noon - 2pm. Sunday lunch 12.30pm - 1.30pm. Coffee served all day. Closed: first two weeks in November and 23 to 31 December. **Cuisine:** Menu changes daily - old style French cooking and traditional English cooking. ⇌ 9 bedrooms all en suite. **CC** Access, Visa, Diners. **Other Points:** Dogs allowed. Children welcome. Afternoon tea served. Vegetarian menu by prior arrangement. **P** **Directions:** On the A697 Morpeth to Coldstream Road.
PAT & DAVID MCKECHNIE ☎ (0668) 81459.
A friendly, family run hotel in the quiet village of Wooler. Personally supervised by the proprietors, the Ryecroft offers a high standard of food, service and accommodation. Nestling at the foot of the Cheviot hills, Wooler and the surrounding area have plenty to offer the tourist.

WYLAM Northumberland **Map 11 C2**
⊗£££ **LABURNUM HOUSE RESTAURANT** Wylam,
⊞£££ Northumberland.
Hours: Breakfast 7.30am - 10am and dinner 6.30pm - 10pm (last orders). Closed 2nd week in February. **Cuisine:** French and modern cuisine, using freshest ingredients possible. ⇌ 4 en suite double bedrooms. **CC** All major cards. **Other Points:** Children welcome. Garden. Pets allowed. ⅗ **(V) Directions:** West along A69 from Newcastle, situated in Wylam main street.
KENN ELLIOTT & ROWAN MAHON ☎ (0661) 852185.
Laburnum House dates from 1716, which makes it one of the oldest houses in the village of Wylam. The restaurant serves French and modern cuisine using all fresh seafood, game, prime meats and fresh vegetables - 'all excellently done and beautifully presented and served by chef, Kenn Elliott and co-proprietor, Rowan Mahon'. Comfortable bedrooms, attractively refurbished.

SCOTLAND

ABERFELDY Tayside **Map 10 A2**
⊗££££ **FARLEYER HOUSE HOTEL** Farleyer House, Weem, Aberfeldy.
Hours: Breakfast 7.30am - 9.15am, Lunch 12 noon - 2.30pm, Dinner 7pm - 11pm (last orders 8.30pm). Bar meals 12 noon - 2pm and 6.30pm - 9.15pm (last orders). **Cuisine:** 5 course table d'hote menu featuring imaginative use of the best fresh produce. Bistro. ⇌ 11 bedrooms, 9 en suite. **CC** All major cards. **Other Points:** Children welcome. No smoking in restaurant. No dogs. Residents lounge. Sporting activities can be arranged. Fax No: (0887) 29430. **P** ⅗ **(V) Directions:** B846 towards Loch Rannoch from Aberfeldy. Near Castle Menzies.

Aberfeldy continued
BILL & FRANCES ATKINS ☎ (0887) 20332.
Dating from the 16th century, Farleyer House has been lovingly refurbished to provide a perfect backdrop for the outstanding cuisine. Claimed by many to be one of the most outstanding restaurants in Scotland. Bill and Frances ensure all guests are welcomed and provided with a taste of excellence complemented by fine wines. Well worth a visit.

ABERLADY Lothian **Map 11 B1**
⊗£ **GOLF HOTEL** 35 Main Street, Aberlady.
⌂£target£ **Hours**: 7.30am - 9am, 12 noon - 2.30pm, and 7pm - 9pm (last orders 8.45pm). Bar meals 12 noon - 2.30pm, and 7pm - 9pm. **Cuisine**: Home cooking, including home-made soups, steak pie, and sweets. Afternoon and high teas. ⊨ 6 bedrooms, 5 of them en suite, with colour TVs, radios, alarms, telephones, and tea/coffee making facilities. ▨ Access, Visa. **Other Points**: Children welcome. Dogs allowed. Open Sundays and bank holidays. Residents lounge and garden. Special golfing packages can be arranged. **(V) Directions**: A198, 4 miles off main A1 and 17 miles outside Edinburgh.
IAIN & ANNA WHYTE, & JAYNE PEACOCK ☎ (08757) 503.
Set in a pretty conservation village, this inn is over 200 years old and has a real country atmosphere. It has been refurbished to a high standard, and is popular with locals and visitors alike. Aberlady Bay is a nature reserve sporting a wide variety of resident and migratory birds and, along the coast, there are superb sandy beaches for the whole family to enjoy.

AIRDRIE Strathclyde **Map 10 B2**
⊗££ **THE STAGING POST HOTEL** 8/10 Anderson Street, Airdrie.
⌂£££ **Hours**: Breakfast 7am - 9am, Lunch and bar snacks 12 noon - 2.30pm, Dinner 6.30pm - 9.30pm (last orders). Restaurant closed on Sundays. Restaurant Closed: 24th December 1991 to 3rd January 1992. **Cuisine**: English/French cuisine specialising in steaks and fish dishes. Some dishes cooked at your table. ⊨ 8 bedrooms, all en suite. ▨ All major cards. **Other Points**: Children welcome. No dogs. Residents' lounge. Fax No: (0236) 762742. Small conferences and parties catered for. ▣ **(V) Directions**: Off the A89 and B802 in the town centre, across from Police Station.
GEORGE & JANETTE CAIRNS ☎ (0236) 767525.
Personally managed by the resident proprietors, this small and friendly hotel offers good accommodation and an excellent standard of cuisine in the Postillion Restaurant. The emphasis is on quality and first class service within a warm and friendly atmosphere. Within easy distance of Glasgow and central Scotland.

ALMONDBANK Tayside **Map 10 A2**
⊗£ **ALMONDBANK INN** Almondbank.
Hours: Restaurant open for lunch 12 noon - 2.15pm, dinner Monday - Thursday 5pm - 8.30pm, Friday and Saturday 6.30pm - 10.15pm and Sunday 5pm - 9pm. **Cuisine**: All fresh ingredients used: Fresh melon, prawn & cheese salad, steaks, plus a wide variety of special dishes. ⊨ None. ▨ Access, Visa. **Other Points**: Children welcome. Special childrens room. Beer garden. ▣ **(V)**

Almondbank continued

Directions: Middle of main street of Almondbank village, about 3 miles from Perth

MR & MRS C LINDSAY ☎ (0738) 83242.

Olde worlde inn overlooking River Almond in an attractive country village. Good food at very reasonable prices, friendly staff and a fun local atmosphere.

ANNAN Dumfries & Galloway **Map 11 C1**

⊗££ **GOLF HOTEL** Links Avenue, Powfoot, nr Annan.

⌂☐££££ CLUB **Hours:** Breakfast from 8am - 9.30am, lunch 12 noon - 2pm and dinner 7pm - 8.30pm. Open 11am - 11pm (12 midnight Friday, Saturday and Sunday). **Cuisine:** Traditional Scottish food prepared where possible using local produce eg. fresh Solway salmon, pheasant, venison, duck, prime Galloway beef. ⊨ 21 bedrooms, 11 en suite. Direct dialing telephone in all rooms. **CC** All major cards. **Other Points:** Children welcome. No dogs. Beer garden. ☐ & **(V) Directions:** On the B724 in Powfoot next to the golf course.

ADAM T GRIBBON ☎ (04617) 254.

Standing beside an 18 hole Golf Course with fishing nearby on the River Annan, the Golf Hotel is a tempting prospect for sportspersons. however with views over the unspoilt Powfoot Bay and with the countryside and history of South West Scotland on the doorstep, it is an excellent centre for touring. Excellent wildfowling from September till February.

ARBROATH Tayside **Map 11 A1**

⊗££ **HOTEL SEAFORTH** Dundee Road, Arbroath.

⌂☐£££ **Hours:** Breakfast 7.30am - 9.30am, Lunch 12 noon - 2pm, Dinner 7pm - 10pm (last orders 9.30pm). Sunday open 12.30pm - 8pm. **Cuisine:** Traditional Scottish menus, featuring local seafood. ⊨ 23 bedrooms, all en suite. **CC** All major cards. **Other Points:** Children welcome. Indoor leisure centre including swimming pool, jacuzzi and sauna, snooker room. Driving range. Ballroom. Pets allowed. ☐ & **(V) Directions:** On the promenade.

ROBERT & CHRISTINE TINDALL ☎ (0241) 72232

A nineteenth century stone manor house with modern extension offering a warm, family welcome. Hotel Seaforth is a convenient base for visiting the nearby glens and castles, or why not spend a few days relaxing in the hotel's leisure centre. Surrounded by fine Golf Courses. Sea and river angling.

ARROCHAR Strathclyde **Map 10 B1**

⊗£ **GREENBANK GUEST HOUSE & LICENSED**
⌂☐£ **RESTAURANT** Arrochar.

Hours: Open 8am - 9.30pm during summer and 9am - 8pm during winter months. A la carte menu available all day, also lunch and snacks. **Cuisine:** Meals available all day. Dishes may include Salmon steak, fresh baked Steak & Kidney Pie, Fried Loch Fyne Herring in Oatmeal, curries, vegetarian. ⊨ 1 single, 2 double and 1 family/twin bedroom, all en suite. **CC** None. **Other Points:** Children welcome - Childrens menu. Dogs allowed. Garden. Access for disabled to restaurant. ☐ & **(V) Directions:** On the A83, opposite the famous Cobbler Mountain.

MR & MRS R CLUER ☎ (03012) 305/513.

Arrochar continued

A small, family run guest house and restaurant on the Loch side. There is a good choice of meals available throughout the day and the restaurant is licensed with a selection of wines, beers and spirits. An excellent base for fishing, climbing, boating and touring. A friendly, relaxed atmosphere prevails and both food and accommodation offer good value.

AUCHTERARDER Tayside **Map 10 A2**

⊗£ **BLACKFORD HOTEL** Moray Street, Blackford, Auchterarder,
⛽£ Perthshire.

Hours: Breakfast 8am - 9am, Lunch 12 noon - 2pm, Dinner 6pm - 9pm (last orders). **Cuisine:** 2 menus - one changes daily. Dishes may include Chicken Kiev, Herring in Oatmeal, Gammon steak, T-bone steak, salads. ⬛ 4 bedrooms, all en suite. **CC** Access, Visa. **Other Points:** Children welcome. Garden. Afternoon teas. Dogs allowed. Central heating. **Directions:** Just off the A9 in village of Blackford, 4 miles from Auchterarder.
MIKE & ROSEMARY TOMCZYNSKI ☎ (076482) 246.

A small, comfortable, family run hotel, situated in the village of Blackford in the heart of Perthshire - Scotland's Golfing County. The building is a 19th century Coaching Inn, attractively and comfortably furnished. Only 2 miles from Gleneagles, Blackford Hotel provides good food, comfortable accommodation, welcoming service and a friendly atmosphere.

AYR Strathclyde **Map 10 B1**

⊗££ **CHESTNUTS HOTEL** 52 Racecourse Road.
⛽££££ **Hours:** Extended licensing hours for non-residents. Restaurant service 7.30pm - 9.45pm. Bar lunch 12 noon - 2pm daily, bar supper Sunday to Thursday 5pm - 9.45pm, Friday and Saturday 5pm - 10.45pm. **Cuisine:** Seafood, steaks and selection of sweets. Childrens menu. ⬛ 14 bedrooms, most en suite, all with colour TV, hairdryer, direct dial telephone. **CC** Access, Visa, AmEx. **Other Points:** Children welcome. Dogs allowed. Fax No: (0292) 264393. ▯ ♿ **(V) Directions:** Situated on the A719, south of Ayr town.
MRS BENDER ☎ (0292) 264393.

A comfortable, family-owned and managed hotel, standing in its own grounds, on the coast road, 1 mile south of the town centre. Overlooking the parklands, golf courses and playing fields of Belleisle Estate. The beach is only 3 minutes away and sea angling may be arranged.

⊗££ **FOUTERS BISTRO** 2a Academy Street.
Hours: Open Tuesday to Saturday 12 noon - 2pm and 6.30pm - 10.30pm. Sunday 7pm - 10pm. Closed: 4 days over Christmas and 4 days over New Year. **Cuisine:** Fine Scottish produce cooked in the French style. Vegetarians welcomed and special diets catered for. ⬛ None. **CC** All major cards. **Other Points:** Children welcome. No dogs. 24 hour answer phone.
FRAN & LAURIE BLACK ☎ (0292) 261391.

Authentic cellar restaurant serving interesting French and Italian dishes using the best of local produce. Fouters Bistro is renowned for the high quality of its cuisine and seafood is a speciality. Personally run by the proprietors.

Ayr continued

⊗££ **LA NAUTIQUE** 28 New Bridge Street, Ayr.
Hours: Lunch 11.30am - 3pm (last orders), dinner 7pm - 11pm (last orders 10pm). Evening bar snacks 5.30pm - 11pm (last orders 10pm). **Cuisine:** Dishes may include - sherried crab, quail stuffed with pork, grapes, chestnuts and brandy. ⊨ None. **CC** Access, Visa, AmEx. **Other Points:** Children welcome. Open Bank Holidays. No smoking area. **(V) Directions:** At foot of the Sandgate, opposite the Town Hall.
ANDREW KINNIBURGH ☎ (0292) 269573.
Friendly restaurant with a strong nautical theme throughout the interior. Centrally located adjacent the Town Hall, La Nautique offers good restaurant and bar meals. The menu provides a light French touch to good quality local Scottish produce.

⊗££ **OLD RACECOURSE HOTEL** 2 Victoria Park, Ayr.
⌂££ **Hours:** Breakfast from 8am - 9am, lunch 12 noon - 2pm, afternoon teas from 3pm - 5pm, high tea from 5pm - 7pm and dinner 7pm - 9pm (last orders 8.45pm) Bar meals 5pm - 9pm. **Cuisine:** Specialising in fresh local seafood, game dishes and prime Scottish steaks. ⊨ 12 bedrooms, all en suite. **CC** Visa. **Other Points:** Children welcome. Dogs allowed. Fully licensed. **P** &
JOHN & MARGARET NICOL ☎ (0292) 262873.
An attractive stone building in pleasant garden surroundings 1 mile from the town centre and minutes from the beach. The beautiful scenery of Ayrshire is nearby, making this hotel a tempting base to return. The hotel is proud of its fresh seafood and prime Scottish game.

⊗££ **STABLES RESTAURANT** Queen's Court, 41 Sandgate, Ayr.
⌘ **Hours:** Open 10am - 10pm for morning coffee, light meals,
CLUB afternoon teas and evening meals. Dinner 6.30pm - 10pm. Closed: all day Sunday and Monday evening. Closes at 5pm during November. **Cuisine:** Coffee house and restaurant. Traditional, regional and local specialities. Wine list includes English and Country such as Silver Birch and Elder Flower. ⊨ None. **CC** All major cards. **Other Points:** Children welcome. No dogs. Vegetarian dishes to order. No smoking area during the day. Street parking. & **Directions:** In the middle of Sandgate at rear of Tourist Information Centre.
EDWARD J BAINES ☎ (0292) 283704.
A traditional style coffee house by day and full Scottish restaurant in the evening. Situated at the rear of a stone built Georgian courtyard in the town centre. Interesting selection of Scottish and English country wines made from berries and flowers.

⊗££ **THE ELMS COURT HOTEL** Miller Road, Ayr.
⌂££££ **Hours:** Breakfast 7.30am - 9.30am, lunch 12 noon - 2pm and dinner 7pm - 9.30pm (last orders). Bar meals 12 noon - 2pm and 5pm - 9.30pm. High Teas 5pm - 7pm. **Cuisine:** A la carte and carte du jour menus. Quality European wines. ⊨ 20 bedrooms, all en suite. TV, radio, telephone, tea/coffee making facilities, trouser press, hairdryers, shoe polishing facilities. **CC** Access, Visa, AmEx. **Other Points:** Children welcome. Dogs allowed in bedrooms. Morning coffees. Afternoon teas. Function suite. **P** & **(V)**

Ayr continued

Directions: On a main, but residential, road between the town and the beach.

GUY & MARGARET GREGOR ☎ (0292) 264191/282332

An attractive hotel offering excellent amenities at very reasonable prices, and within easy walking distance of both Ayr's shopping centre and the seafront. The bright Elmview lounge is a popular venue for bar meals whilst the restaurant offers both table d'hote and a la carte menus. Family owned and managed.

⊗££ **THE KYLESTROME HOTEL** 11 Miller Road, Ayr.

⊞££££ **Hours:** Breakfast 7.30am - 9.30am, lunch 12.30pm - 2pm, dinner 7pm - 10pm (last orders). Bar meals 12 noon - 2.30pm and 5pm - 10.30pm. High teas 5.30pm - 7.30pm. **Cuisine:** Fresh seafood, local produce. In the bar: lamb cutlets with minted pear. In the restaurant: steak, seafood - a la carte. ⊯ 12 bedrooms, all en suite. ☒ All major cards. **Other Points:** Children welcome. No smoking area. Conference facilities. ◨ ₺ **(V) Directions:** On a main street in Ayr, near the Railway Station.

MICHAEL GUADAGNO - Manager ☎ (0292) 262474.

A large stone house in Ayr, which is in the heart of Burns Country. The seafront, railway station and town centre are a short walk away, and Prestwick Airport a few minutes drive. The stylish restaurant provides a unique atmosphere in which to enjoy fine international cuisine.

⊗£ **TUDOR RESTAURANT** 8 Beresford Terrace, Ayr.

Hours: Open from 9am - 8pm. Closed: Sundays except July and August. **Cuisine:** Traditional Scottish high teas served with cakes and scones from own bakery. ⊯ None. ☒ None. **Other Points:** Children welcome. No dogs. ₺ **Directions:** Opposite the Burn's Statue Square off the A70 in the centre of Ayr.

KENNETH ANCELL ☎ (0292) 261404.

Now in its 25th year of operation, the reasonably priced lunch, high tea menus and friendly staff make the Tudor a favourite with family parties. Children may choose from their own menus.

⊞££ **WINDSOR HOTEL** 6 Alloway Place, Ayr.

⊯ 2 single, 3 double, 1 twin and 4 family bedrooms, 8 en suite. 2 bathrooms. Colour TV and tea/coffee making facilities in all rooms. **Hours:** Breakfast 8am - 9am (earlier by arrangement), dinner at 6pm. ☒ Access, Visa. **Other Points:** Central heating. Children welcome. Pets by arrangement. Residents' lounge. TV. Vegetarian and special diets catered for by arrangement. ◨ ₺ **Directions:** Close to the railway station and bus depot, near the seafront.

MR & MRS DAVIE ☎ (0292) 264689.

A comfortable, well decorated hotel in an excellent residential district. The Davies have moved 2 doors down to this new establishment - and many of their repeat visitors have followed. Close to the beach and town centre.

BIGGAR Strathclyde **Map 10 B2**

⊗££ **TINTO HOTEL** Symington, Nr Biggar.

⊞££££ **Hours:** Breakfast 7am - 9.30am, lunch 12 noon - 3pm, dinner 4.30pm - 10pm. **Cuisine:** Dining room: A la carte menu, lunches

Biggar continued

and high teas. Bar and lounge: less formal meals and snacks. ⟞ 26 rooms: 5 single, 7 twin, 11 double and 3 family bedrooms, all en suite. Luxury suite available. **CC** All major cards. **Other Points:** Children welcome. Afternoon teas. Dogs allowed. Garden. Golf, fishing, bowls and horse riding available locally. **P** ⅀ **(V)** **Directions:** 10 miles from M74, 9 miles south-east of Lanark. JOHN FRAIOLI ☎ (08993) 454.

Set in an area of great natural beauty near the romantic Borderland, yet only an hour from Glasgow and Edinburgh, this charming country house hotel is a perfect base for relaxation or business. Offering a very high standard of cuisine and accommodation, this hotel comes 'highly recommended'.

BLAIRGOWRIE Tayside **Map 11 A1**

⊗££ **ALTAMOUNT HOUSE HOTEL** Coupar Angus Road, ⊡££££ Blairgowrie.

Hours: Breakfast 8am - 9am, lunch and bar snacks 12 noon - 2pm, dinner Monday - Saturday 7pm - 9pm, Sunday high tea served. Closed: 7th Jan - 14th Feb. **Cuisine:** Dishes may include Grilled Tay Salmon with Parsley Butter, Roast Aylesbury Duckling with Apple Sauce. ⟞ 7 bedrooms, all en suite. **CC** None. **Other Points:** Children welcome. Open Bank Holidays. Afternoon teas. **P** ⅀ **Directions:** Half mile from town centre on Coupar Angus Road. RITCHIE & SUSAN RUSSELL ☎ (0250) 3512.

A Georgian house overlooking six acres of well kept grounds which is furnished with many antiques and with pinewood panellings and corniced ceilings. The resident owners have retained the natural character of the house whilst providing guests with highly satisfying meals at modest prices. Good value for money using local produce. Well worth a visit.

⊗££ **ANGUS HOTEL** 46 Wellmeadow, Blairgowrie.

Hours: Breakfast 8am - 9.30am, dinner 7pm - 8.30pm, bar snacks 12 noon - 1.45pm, 7pm - 8.30pm. **Cuisine:** Dishes may include Capers and Lemon Wedges, Pan Fried Rainbow Trout in Almond Butter, Filo Tartlet filled with Broccoli and Mornay Sauce. ⟞ 86 bedrooms, all en suite. **CC** Access, Visa, AmEx. **Other Points:** Children welcome. Afternoon teas served. Dogs allowed. Garden dining. Fax No. (0250) 5289. Conference rooms. Swimming pool. Sauna. Squash. **P** ⅀ **(V) Directions:** A93, Perth to Braemar road. SCOTT ARNOLD. ☎ (0250) 2455/2838.

Situated in the centre of the country town of Blairowrie, the hotel is well appointed for touring the surrounding countryside. With golf and fishing nearby and a heated indoor swimming pool, sauna and squash court the hotel has something to interest most. Presenting tasty meals and offering accommodation of a high standard.

⊗££ **BRIDGE OF CALLY HOTEL** Bridge of Cally, By Blairgowrie. ⊡£££ **Hours:** Breakfast 8am - 9am, lunch 12 noon - 2pm, dinner 7.15pm - 8.45pm. Last orders, lunch 2pm, dinner 8.45pm. Sunday lunch 12 noon - 2pm, dinner 7.15pm - 8.45pm. **Cuisine:** Menu changes daily. Dishes may include Cream of Mushroom Soup, Collops of Beef in a Mustard & Cream sauce, Salmon & Dill Tart. Always home baked sweets. ⟞ 9 rooms. 1 single, 4 twin and 4 double rooms. 6 en suite. **CC** Access, Visa, Diners. **Other Points:** Garden.

Blairgowrie continued

Vegetarian meals by arrangement. Eating out area. ▣ **(V)** **Directions:** 6 miles N of Blairgowrie on A93 to Braemar. Follow ski slope signs.

MRS P TOLLAND ☎ (0250) 86231

Formerly an old coaching inn, this is now a family run hotel. Set in beautiful countryside overlooking Muir Arde. The hotel is tastefully decorated, in keeping with the peaceful and comfortable ambience of the old inn. Serving well prepared meals made from local fresh produce the Bridge Of Cally Hotel is a perfect base for anyone interested in golf, fishing, hill walking or relaxing.

BO'NESS Central **Map 10 B2**

⌂£ **HOLLYWOOD HOUSE** 25 Grahamsdyke Road.

▭ 1 single, 3 double and 1 family bedroom. 2 bathrooms. 2 showers. Colour TV in all rooms. **Hours:** Breakfast 7am - 9am, dinner 6pm - 8pm. **CC** None. **Other Points:** Central heating. Children welcome. Residents' lounge. TV. Garden. ▣ ⅊ **(V)**

HARRY & CHRISTINA ROSS ☎ (0506) 823260.

House with outstanding character and superb views of Firth of Forth. With easy access of golf courses, stately homes, palaces. Only 30 minutes drive from Edinburgh city centre and 15 minutes from Airport.

⊗££ **RICHMOND PARK HOTEL** 26 Linlithgow Road, Bo'ness.
⌂£££ **Hours:** Breakfast 7am - 9.30am, Lunch 12pm (12.30pm Sunday) - 2.15pm, Dinner 5pm - 9.30pm (last orders). **Cuisine:** Predominantly Scottish dishes. Table d'hote and a la carte menus. ▭ 24 bedrooms, all en suite. **CC** Access, Visa, AmEx. **Other Points:** Children welcome. Garden. Afternoon teas. Dogs by arrangement. ▣ ⅊ **(V) Directions:** On the outskirts of Bo'ness. Nr Junction 3 of the M9, and the A904.

MR & MRS MILLER ☎ (0506) 823213.

A family run hotel situated in an elevated position overlooking the Firth of Forth. The hotel offers excellent value for both food and accommodation. Ideally located for visiting many places of interest in central Scotland, Edinburgh is only 30 minutes drive away. Conference facilities available.

BRIDGE OF EARN Tayside **Map 11 A1**

⌂£ **ROCKDALE GUEST HOUSE** Dunning Street, Bridge of Earn.

▭ 2 single, 5 double and 2 family bedrooms. 1 bathroom. 1 shower. 1 WC. **Hours:** Breakfast 7.30am - 9am, dinner 5pm - 7pm. **CC** None. **Other Points:** Central heating. Restricted hotel licence. Evening meal by arrangement. Children welcome. Residents' lounge. TV. ▣

MRS ADELE BARRIE ☎ (0738) 812281.

This guest house is situated in a small, ancient, picturesque village on the banks of the River Earn, in easy reach of the city of Perth which caters for all interests. Principal golf courses, shooting and fishing nearby. 'Taste of Scotland' recommended.

BRIDGE OF ORCHY Strathclyde **Map 10 A1**

⊗££ **INVERORAN HOTEL** Nr Bridge Of Orchy.
⌂££ **Hours:** Breakfast 8.30am and Dinner 7.30pm - 9pm. Bar meals 12 noon - 3pm and 6pm - 8pm. Closed: Christmas Day and Boxing

LOWLANDS & SCOTTISH BORDERS

Bridge of Orchy continued

Day. **Cuisine:** Traditional cuisine, dishes including pork fillet, gammon steak, haggis and fresh salmon and trout. Bar meals include pasta, curries and chilli. ⊨ 8 bedrooms, 4 en suite. **CC** None. **Other Points:** Children welcome. Pets allowed. Afternoon teas. No-smoking in dining room. Garden dining - weather permitting. **P** & **(V) Directions:** Main A82, then off onto single track road, the A8005.

MRS JANET BLACKIE ☎ (08384) 220.

Attractive, small Highland hotel set in beautiful countryside at the head of Loch Tulla. Very good homemade food, served by staff who are keen to ensure their guests comfort and satisfaction. Situated near Glencoe and Fort William. Well worth a visit.

BURNMOUTH Borders **Map 11 B2**

⊛£ **THE FLEMINGTON INN** Burnmouth.

Hours: Lunch 12.30pm - 2.30pm, dinner 6.30pm - 9.30pm. **Cuisine:** Traditional Scottish menu. ⊨ None. **CC** None. **Other Points:** Children welcome. **P** **(V) Directions:** 6 miles north of Berwick Upon Tweed on A1.

MR & MRS SMILLIE ☎ (08907) 81277.

An attractive, well run pub directly on the A1 in the pretty fishing village of Burnmouth. This is the 'first and last' pub in Scotland. Presenting home cooked meals made from fresh local produce at value for money prices, The Flemington Inn is very popular, especially with locals.

BURNTISLAND Fife **Map 11 B2**

⊛£ **KINGSWOOD HOTEL** Kinghorn Road, Burntisland.

⊞£users **Hours:** Meals from 7.30am - 9am, 12 noon - 2.30pm and 7pm - ⌣ 9.30pm. Bar meals 12 noon - 10pm. **Cuisine:** Full a la carte and table d'hote menus available. Choices include cullen skink and fresh salmon. ⊨ 11 bedrooms 9 with en-suite. All modern facilities. 2 honeymoon suites. **CC** Access, Visa. **Other Points:** Children welcome. Dogs by arrangement. **P** & **(V) Directions:** On the A92 coast road half way between Kinghorn and Burntisland.

RANKIN & KATHRYN BELL ☎ (0592) 872329.

Set in 2 acres of grounds with outstanding views across the River Forth towards Edinburgh. The hotel's ambience, tasteful furnishings and first class cuisine all combine to make every visit an enjoyable experience.

CALLANDER Central **Map 10 B2**

⊞£ **ABBOTSFORD LODGE GUEST HOUSE** Stirling Road, Callander.

⊨ 1 single, 10 double. 8 family bedrooms, all with tea maker (private bathrooms available). 6 bathrooms, 1 shower **Hours:** Breakfast 8am - 9am, dinner at 7pm. **CC** None. **Other Points:** Central heating. Children welcome. Licensed. Residents lounge. TV. Garden. **P Directions:** East side of town, known by locals by its monkey tree in front.

MR & MRS S SIBBALD ☎ (0877) 30066.

A comfortable and friendly guest house which is surrounded by places of interest, eg. Stirling Castle, Loch Lomond, Glen Coe Doune Castle and Doune Vintage Car Museum.

Callander continued

⊗££ **ANCASTER ARMS HOTEL** Main Street.
⟐£ **Hours:** Restaurant open 8am - 10am, 12 noon - 2.30pm, and 7pm - 9pm. **Cuisine:** Fresh seafood, game and sweet trolley. 🛏 12 bedrooms, 8 en suite. **CC** None. **Other Points:** Everything produced in hotel kitchens, which use only the highest quality ingredients. **P**
NEIL & ANNE MACARTHUR ☎ (0877) 30167.
Set in the Trossachs area of Scotland this hotel offers good value for money and the staff are friendly and helpful.

⊗££ **WOLSELEY PARK HOTEL** Stirling Road, Callander.
⟐££ **Hours:** Breakfast 8am - 9am, Dinner 7pm - 9pm. **Cuisine:** A la carte menu. Dishes include smoked trout pate, mussels poached in cream and wine, chicken veloute, venison and kiwi surfboat. Bar snacks/meals. 🛏 14 rooms. 1 single, 3 twin, 8 double and 2 family rooms. 10 en suite. **CC** Access, Visa. **Other Points:** Children welcome. Garden. Ground floor room. Dogs allowed by arrangement. **P** ♿ **(V) Directions:** On A84 approximately 1/2 mile from Callander.
DOUGLAS & ANNE GUNN ☎ (0877) 30261
Family run hotel set on own grounds. High standard of decor with very comfortable furnishings. Serving generous portions of well cooked traditional Scottish food. The pleasant atmosphere and mixed age group of the hotels clientele makes this a most attractive place to visit. An ideal base for anyone touring the Central Highlands.

CRAIL Fife **Map 11 B2**
⊗£ **THE MARINE HOTEL** 54 Nethergate South, Crail.
⟐££ **Hours:** Breakfast 8.30am - 9.30am, lunch 12 noon - 2pm and dinner 7pm - 9pm (last orders). **Cuisine:** Local seafood (in season). 🛏 10 bedrooms. **CC** Access, Visa, AmEx. **Other Points:** Children welcome. Pets allowed. Afternoon tea served. **P** ♿ **(V) Directions:** On the junction B940 with A917, south east of St Andrews.
IAIN & AILEEN GREENLEES ☎ (0333) 50207.
Small family run hotel, with ten well appointed bedrooms, a residents' lounge and a restaurant serving a la carte and table d'hote menus. Beautiful views of the Firth of Forth and the Isle of May can be enjoyed in the lounge bar which has a patio leading into the garden.

CREETOWN Dumfries & Galloway **Map 10 B2**
⊗££ **ELLANGOWAN HOTEL** St John Street, Creetown.
⟐£££ **Hours:** Breakfast 8am - 9.30am, Lunch 12 noon - 2.30pm, Dinner 5pm - 8.30pm (last orders). Bar snacks served all day during summer. **Cuisine:** Fresh, predominantly local produce used such as local lamb and fish. 🛏 8 bedrooms, 5 en suite. **CC** None. **Other Points:** Children welcome. Afternoon teas. Garden dining. **P (V) Directions:** A75. On village Square. Creetown is approx. 40 miles W of Dumfries.
WILLIAM & CATHERINE CHRISTIE ☎ (067182) 201.
A family run hotel where you will be assured of a warm welcome, comfortable accommodation and well-cooked fresh food. The hotel enjoys a very friendly, relaxed atmosphere. Off the A75, in an excellent position.

LOWLANDS & SCOTTISH BORDERS

CRIANLARICH Central **Map 10 A2**

⊗£ **THE ROD & REEL** Main Street, Crianlarich.
Hours: Bar meals 12 noon - 9pm, Dinner 6pm - 9pm (last orders),
Sunday Lunch 12.30pm - 2.30pm. **Cuisine:** Bar meals and a la
carte menu. Dishes include Baked Trout with Lemon, Garlic and
Parsley Butter, Scottish Lamb, Beef and Mushroom Ragout.
⊨ None. **CC** Access, Visa. **Other Points:** Children welcome.
Afternoon teas. No dogs. **P** **(V) Directions:** In the centre of
Crianlarich.
ELSPETH & BILL PAULIN ☎ (083 83) 271.
*A family run lounge bar and restaurant which offers a wide
choice of good food at very reasonable prices. Personally run by
Elspeth and Bill Paulin, you are assured a warm welcome and
friendly service.*

CRIEFF Tayside **Map 10 A2**

⊗££ **MURRAY PARK HOTEL** Connaught Terrace, Crieff,
Perthshire.
Hours: Restaurant open 12 noon - 2pm and 7.30pm - 9.30pm.
Cuisine: Scampi Denise. ⊨ 15 bedrooms, 14 en suite. **CC** Visa,
Diners. **Other Points:** Children welcome. **P** ᕼ **(V)**
ANN & NOEL SCOTT ☎ (0764) 3731/2/3.
*The proprietors have created a friendly atmosphere in this 'wee'
hotel, including cosy log fires in the winter months.*

⊗£ **SMUGGLERS RESTAURANT** The Hosh, Crieff, Perthshire.
Hours: Lunch from 12 noon - 3pm. Open 10am - 5pm for coffees,
tea, snacks and light meals. **Cuisine:** Glenturret pate, Tay salmon,
venison in whisky sauce, gaugers - gateaux flavoured with malt
liqueur. ⊨ None. **CC** All major cards. **Other Points:** Dining al
fresco. Children welcome. Afternoon tea served. No smoking
area. Coaches by appointment. **P** ᕼ **(V) Directions:** On the A85
in north-west Crieff towards Comrie.
MR P FAIRLIE ☎ (0764) 2424.
*Previously an old warehouse, the restaurant forms part of the
visitors' Heritage Centre at the Glenturret distillery. The site
incorporates an audio-visual theatre and a 3-D exhibition.
Visitors can also take the opportunity to taste the whiskies! For
groups of up to 60 persons, try the Pagoda Room.*

⊗££ **THE CRIEFF HOTEL** 47-49 East High Street, Crieff.
⊞£££ **Hours:** Breakfast 8am - 9.30am, Dinner 7pm - 9pm (last orders).
Bar snacks 12 noon - 2.30pm and 6pm - 9pm. Closed: New Years
Day. **Cuisine:** Dishes in the restaurant may include Trout Rob Roy,
Salmon Ecossaise, Tournedos Chasseur, Filet en Croute, Lautrec's
Chicken. Bar snacks. ⊨ 10 bedrooms, 9 en suite. **CC** Access, Visa,
AmEx. **Other Points:** Access for disabled to restaurant only.
Children welcome. Dogs allowed. Residents' lounge. Garden
dining. Fax No: (0764) 5019. **P** ᕼ **(V) Directions:** 500 yds from
town square on Perth Road, A812.
GERALD QUIN ☎ (0764) 2632.
*A family run hotel offering personal attention to ensure both
guests and locals feel welcome. Their motto is 'Where service
counts!'. Comfortable accommodation and both restaurant and
bar meals are of a high standard and very good value for money.
An excellent base for the wide range of leisure activities
available locally.*

DOLLAR

DALBEATTIE Dumfries & Galloway **Map 10 C2**
⊗££ **CLONYARD HOUSE HOTEL** Colvend, Dalbeattie.
⏳££ **Hours:** Breakfast 8am - 9.30am. Bar meals 12.15pm - 2pm and
CLUB 6pm - 9.30pm. Restaurant 7pm - 9pm. **Cuisine:** International style
a la carte menu including taste of Scotland dishes, local salmon,
venison, scallops. Luscious homemade sweets. Homemade bar
meals. 🛏 15 bedrooms, all en suite. 💳 Access, Visa. **Other Points:**
Children welcome. Fully licensed. 🚶 **(V) Directions:** From A75
take A711 to Dalbeattie then left onto A710 for 4½ miles.
DAVID THOMPSON ☎ (055 663) 372.
*A typical country hotel enjoying a busy tourist and local trade.
Family run, the hotel is small and friendly and caters well for
both visitors and local guests. The 7 acres of garden are ideal for
children. There are 4 golf courses within 10 miles and available
nearby are coarse fishing, salmon and trout fishing, sailing and
sea trips.*

DALMALLY Strathclyde **Map 10 A1**
⊗££ **GLENORCHY LODGE HOTEL** Dalmally, nr Oban.
⏳££ **Hours:** Breakfast 7am - 9am, bar meals 11am - 2.30pm and 5pm -
9pm (last orders). Closed: Christmas Day and New Years Day.
Cuisine: Traditional cuisine using fresh, Scottish produce such as
Highland Venison in a red wine sauce, Local Salmon, Awe Trout,
Steaks. 🛏 4 bedrooms, all en suite. 💳 None. **Other Points:**
Children welcome. Afternoon teas. Dogs allowed. Residents'
lounge. 🅿 🚶 **(V) Directions:** A82 from Glasgow, A85 from
Tyndrum. 10 miles Inverary, 25 miles Oban
HECTOR & PATRICIA WHYTE ☎ (083 82) 312.
*A small, family run hotel in the village of Dalmally, offering
warm, comfortable accommodation. Informal, lively bar and
good bar meals served in generous portions. Ideal base for
touring the area.*

DALRY Dumfries & Galloway **Map 10 C2**
⊗££ **LOCHINVAR HOTEL** Main St, St John's Town of Dalry, Castle
⏳££ Douglas.
Hours: Breakfast 8am - 9am, lunch 12 noon - 2.30pm (last orders),
dinner 6pm - 9.30pm (last orders). Bar snacks served all day (last
orders 9.30pm). **Cuisine:** Extensive a la carte menu, high tea
menu and bar snacks. 🛏 15 bedrooms, 7 en suite. 💳 Access,
Visa, AmEx. **Other Points:** Children welcome. Open Bank
Holidays. No smoking area. Afternoon teas. Dogs allowed. 🅿 **(V)**
Directions: A713 on Water of Ken, 2 miles N of New Galloway.
Main tourist route.
LESTER PENNINGTON ☎ (06443) 210.
*Located in a small, pretty village in Kirkcudbrightshire and
with outstanding views of rolling farmland, the establishment
has a real country house feel to it. Capable staff serve well
garnished and presented meals, made with an emphasis on
fresh local produce. Comfortable accommodation. On main
scenic route from Castle Douglas to Ayr (sign of the brown
thistle).*

DOLLAR Central **Map 10 B2**
⊗££ **STRATHALLAN HOTEL** 6 Chapel Place, Dollar.
⏳££ **Hours:** Breakfast 7.30am - 10am, lunch and bar snacks 11am -
2.30pm (last orders), dinner and evening bar snacks 6pm -

Dollar continued

10.30pm (last orders). **Cuisine:** Dishes may include Beef Lasagne, Crepe Fruit de Mer, Chicken Kiev, King Prawn Korma, Pigeon breasts on an Apple & Strawberry coulis. ⊨ 4 bedrooms, 1 en suite. ▨ Access, Visa, AmEx. **Other Points:** Children welcome. Open Bank Holidays. No smoking area. Dogs allowed. Garden dining. Package weekends for golf, fishing and shooting. ▯ **(V) Directions:** Dollar is 6 miles NE of Alloa. Midway between Stirling & Kinross.

JAMES BOYD ☎ (0259) 42205.

Friendly family run hotel, with the accent on hospitality and good food. Locally brewed real ale a speciality. Ideal base for touring and sporting activities. Highly recommended.

DUMFRIES Dumfries & Galloway **Map 10 C2**

⊗££ **CAIRNDALE HOTEL & LEISURE CLUB** English Street, ⊞££££ Dumfries.

[CLUB] **Hours:** Meals 7.15am - 10am, 12 noon - 2pm and 7pm - 9.30pm (last orders). **Cuisine:** Traditonal Taste of Scotland fayre. Sawney Beans Bar & Grill: Carvery & Steaks. Forum Cafe Bar: Snacks & light meals in a continental cafe atmosphere. ⊨ 76 bedrooms, all en suite. ▨ All major cards. **Other Points:** Children welcome. Groups & conferences catered for. Telex 77530. Fax: (0387) 50555. Entertainment: Sat night dinner dances, Sun night Ceilidh. ▯ ♿ **(V) Directions:** Close to the centre of town on A75 Dumfries to Carlisle route.

MATTHEW WALLACE ☎ (0387) 54111.

This privately owned hotel offers all the comforts expected from one of the regions leading hotels. Executive rooms and suites have queen size double beds, trouser presses, minibars and jacuzzi spa baths. The recently opened Barracuda Leisure Club offers heated indoor swimming pool, sauna, steam room, spa bath, gym, health/beauty salon, toning beds, solarium. Bargain breaks.

⊞££££ **COMLONGON CASTLE** Clarencefield, Dumfries.

[CLUB] ⊨ 11 bedrooms, all en suite - 7 fourposters with one Honeymoon suite, 2 twin and 2 single bedrooms. **Hours:** Breakfast 8am - 9.30am, lunch 12 noon - 2pm and dinner 8.15pm. ▨ Access, Visa. **Other Points:** Children welcome. Candle lit tour of Castle each evening. Private walks and nature trail. Residents lounge and garden. Fax No: (038 787) 266. ▯ **(V) Directions:** On the B724, 6 miles from Annan and 9 miles from Dumfries.

ANTHONY & BRENDA PTOLOMEY ☎ (038 787) 283.

A 15th century castle and adjoining period mansion, quietly situated down a tree lined driveway, set in 50 acres of grounds. The oak panelled Great Hall with its display of medieval regalia and the candlelit dining of the Jacobean dining room is the perfect setting for a romantic occassion or for those seeking seclusion.

⊗£££ **HETLAND HALL HOTEL** Carrutherstown, Dumfries.

[CLUB] **Hours:** Breakfast from 7.30am - 9.30am, lunch 12 noon - 2pm and dinner 7pm 9.30pm (last orders). Open Sunday to Wednesday 12 noon - 11pm and Thursday to Saturday 12 noon - 12 midnight. **Cuisine:** International menu. ⊨ 27 bedrooms, all en suite. ▨ All major cards. **Other Points:** Dogs allowed. Children welcome. No

Dumfries continued

smoking area. Afternoon tea served. ▣ ♿ **(V) Directions:** On the A75, half way between Annan and Dumfries.

DAVID & MARY ALLEN ☎ (0387) 84201.

Originally built as a manor house, then converted into a boarding school, Hetland Hall is now a grand country house hotel and restaurant. Set in 45 acres of well tended parklands with fine views over the Solway Firth. The restaurant serves an international menu in relaxed, informal surroundings.

DUNBAR Lothian **Map 11 B1**

⊗££ **REDHEUGH HOTEL** Bayswell Park, Dunbar.

🏨££ **Hours:** Breakfast 7.30am - 9am, Lunch by arrangement, Dinner 7.30pm - 9pm. **Cuisine:** Predominantly British cuisine. Menu changes daily. Specialities include Sea Trout in a Cream sauce, homemade Casseroles and fresh Fruit Pies. ⊨ 10 bedrooms, all en suite. **CC** Access, Visa, AmEx. **Other Points:** Dogs allowed. Golf packages. Street parking. **(V) Directions:** On the cliff top at Dunbar.

MRS J YOUNG ☎ (0368) 62793.

A warm, friendly welcome awaits you at the Redheugh Hotel, situated on the cliff top at Dunbar and with fine views over the Firth of Forth. Traditionally furnished, the hotel has a homely atmosphere and, with good food to match, you are sure of a relaxed stay. Golf and fishing packages can be arranged.

⊗££ **THE COURTYARD HOTEL & RESTAURANT** Woodbush
🏨££ Brae, Dunbar.

Hours: Breakfast 7am - 8:30am, Lunch 12 noon - 2pm, Dinner 7pm - 9.30pm (last orders). **Cuisine:** Dishes may include Rack of Lamb, Fillet of Dunbar Trout served with a sauce Beurre Blanc, Fillet Steak with a Madeira flavoured sauce, homemade soups. ⊨ 6 bedrooms, 1 en suite **CC** Access, Visa. **Other Points:** Disabled access to rooms and restaurant only. Children welcome. ▣ ♿ **(V) Directions:** On seafront off main street, Dunbar.

MESSRS BRAMLEY & SCHAUERTE ☎ (0368) 64169.

Well-known for its friendly hospitality and excellent restaurant, The Courtyard is pleasantly situated on the water's edge. Converted from 2 fishermen's cottages, it makes a relaxing retreat for both holidaymakers and business people. Excellent value for money. Golfing and fishing can be arranged and guests can enjoy walks in the John Muir Country Park.

DUNBLANE Central **Map 10 B2**

⊗££ **STIRLING ARMS HOTEL** Stirling Road, Dunblane.

🏨££ **Hours:** Breakfast 8am - 9am, Lunch 12 noon - 2.30pm, Dinner 7pm - 9.30pm (last orders). **Cuisine:** Modern Scottish/Continental cuisine. Specialities include Gaelic Steak and fresh water prawns. Bar meals. ⊨ 7 bedrooms, 4 en suite. **CC** Access, Visa, AmEx. **Other Points:** Children welcome. Dining al fresco. Dogs allowed. No smoking area. Garden. ▣ **(V) Directions:** Off A90 Stirling - Perth road. Close to High Street.

JANE & RICHARD CASTELOW, MHCIMA ☎ (0786) 822156.

Originally a 17th century coaching inn by the bridge over the Allan Water, this family run hotel and restaurant has been extensively refurbished. The owners pride themselves in providing comfortable accommodation and excellent food in

LOWLANDS & SCOTTISH BORDERS

Dunblane continued
their Oak Room Restaurant. Good value for money. History records the patronage of Robert Burns and the Duke of Argyle to the inn.

DUNDEE Tayside **Map 11 A1**
⌂£££ **BEACH HOUSE HOTEL** Broughty Ferry, Dundee.
🛏 2 double, 2 twin, and 1 family bedroom all en suite. TVs, alarms, direct dial telephones and tea/coffee making facilities in all bedrooms. **Hours:** Breakfast 7am - 9am, dinner 6pm - 9pm. **CC** Access, Visa. **Other Points:** Central heating. Children welcome. Dogs allowed. Licensed. Residents' lounge. Garden. Fax: (0382) 480241. **Directions:** On the A930, east of Dundee town centre, opposite the sandy beach.
LYNNE GLENNIE ☎ (0382) 76614.
Terraced house overlooking the sandy beach and Firth of Tay. Convenient for Dundee, and for touring this interesting part of Scotland. Very popular all year round so booking recommended.

DUNFERMLINE Fife **Map 10 B2**
⊗££ **HALFWAY HOUSE HOTEL** Main Street, Kingseat, nr
⌂£££ Dunfermline.
Hours: Breakfast 7.30am - 9.30am, lunch 12 noon - 2.15pm, dinner 7pm - 9.30pm (last orders). Bar meals 12 noon - 2.15pm and 6.30pm - 9.30pm. **Cuisine:** Specialities include a large range of steaks such as Fillet de boeuf Diane and steak au poivre vert. 🛏 12 bedrooms, all en suite. **CC** Access, Visa, AmEx. **Other Points:** Children welcome. Residents' lounge. **P** **Directions:** B912, 2 miles N.E. Dunfermline. Exit 3 M90 motorway.
MRS & MRS W LLOYD ☎ (0383) 731661.
Scotland is renowned for its long tradition of warm hospitality and The Halfway House Hotel is no exception. Recently redecorated, the hotel is comfortable and welcoming and the food in the bar and restaurant well presented and served. Nearby Loch Fitty is famous for trout fishing, golf lovers can visit St Andrews and Gleneagles and Edinburgh is only 30 minutes away.

DUNOON Strathclyde **Map 10 B1**
⊗££ **ROYAL MARINE HOTEL** Marine Parade, Hunter's Quay,
⌂£££ Dunoon.
Hours: Breakfast 7am - 9.30am and dinner 6.30pm - 7.30pm (Thursday, Friday and Saturday 9pm). Bar meals 12 noon - 8.30pm. **Cuisine:** Escalope of pork cordon bleu, venison in red wine sauce, fillet steak in bernaise sauce. 🛏 8 single, 13 twin, 11 double, 3 family, all en suite. **CC** Access, Visa. **Other Points:** Garden. Bar. Residents lounge. Games Room. Afternoon teas served. Full accommodation facilities. **P** **Directions:** Off the A815 to Dunnon, situated on the seafront.
MESSRS ARNOLD & GREIG ☎ (0369) 5810.
A family run country style mansion with restaurant situated on the seafront, offering well presented good food, making special use of Scottish produce especially local fresh seafood. Friendly, attentive service and comfortable accommodation. Easy access from Glasgow when using Western ferries, as you will disembark immediately opposite the Royal Marine Hotel.

EASDALE Strathclyde **Map 10 A1**

⊗£ **HARBOUR TEAROOM RESTAURANT** Easdale, by Oban, Argyll.

Hours: Meals served from 10.30am - 5pm. Last orders 4.50pm. Closed November to March. Open for Sunday lunch and Bank Holidays. **Cuisine:** Homecooking and baking. Seafood Specialities. ⊨ None. 💳 Access, Visa. **Other Points:** Children welcome. Garden dining. Pets allowed. ◘ **(V) Directions:** Off the A816 south from Oban, then B844 to Seil Island and Easdale. MR M.C.F. SHAW ☎ (08523) 349.

Situated in the picturesque village and harbour of Easdale, this stone built cottage tearoom and restaurant offers delicious homebaking, locally caught seafood specialities and a warm friendly atmosphere. Wander round the adjoining 'Country Shop' and be delighted with locally made clothes and crafts. Well worth a visit.

⊗£££ **INSHAIG PARK HOTEL (FORMERLY THE EASDALE**
⌂£££ **INN)** Easdale, By Oban, Argyll.

Hours: Breakfast 8.30am - 9.30am, dinner 7.30pm - 8.30pm. **Cuisine:** A la carte menu, bar meals, bar snacks and vegetarian meals. ⊨ 7 rooms. 3 twin, 3 double and 1 family room. 5 rooms en suite. 💳 None. **Other Points:** Children welcome. Garden. Dogs allowed. ◘ **(V) Directions:** 16 miles south of Oban. BARRIE & SHEILA FLETCHER ☎ (08523) 256

Fine Victorian House standing in its own grounds overlooking the sea and the islands with truly wonderful views. This is a small, family run, comfortable hotel in an idyllic location with good food served by friendly, helpful staff.

EAST LINTON Lothian **Map 11 B1**

⊗££ **HARVESTERS HOTEL** East Linton.
⌂£££££ **Hours:** Breakfast at guests' convenience. Lunch and bar meals 12 noon - 2pm, Dinner and bar meals 7pm - 9pm (last orders). Morning coffee and afternoon tea. **Cuisine:** International dishes including Deep Fried Mushrooms in Garlic Butter, Scampi Auld Alliance, Darnes of Salmon, Venison. Steaks are a speciality. ⊨ 12 bedrooms, 9 en suite. 💳 All major cards. **Other Points:** Children welcome. Afternoon teas. Dogs allowed. Residents' lounge. Walled garden. Fishing licence for residents' use. ◘ ♿ **(V) Directions:** Off A1, 20 miles south of Edinburgh. MR LINSLEY ☎ (0620) 860395.

A Georgian house of character, in 3 acres of garden leading down to the River Tyne. A most attractive hotel offering good food, fine wines and very comfortable en suite accommodation at attractive rates. Special weekly and weekend terms. 15 famous golf courses nearby, including the internationally renowned Muirfield Championship course.

EDINBURGH Lothian **Map 11 B1**

⌂££ **ARD THOR** 10 Mentone Terrace, Newington, Edinburgh.
⊨ 1 single, 1 double, 1 twin and 2 family bedrooms, 1 en suite. 2 bathrooms. Colour TV and tea/coffee making facilities in all rooms. **Hours:** Breakfast 8am - 8.30am. 💳 None. **Other Points:** Central heating. Children welcome. Resident's telephone. **Directions:** West side of Minto St near Craigmillar Park Church Via Mentone Gdns.

Edinburgh continued
MRS A H TELFER ☎ (031) 667 1647.
A Victorian villa in unique 'terrace within a terrace' location.
Modern amenities with 19th century character and elegance.
Quiet residential area with good shopping facilities and
Queen's Park and Commonwealth pool nearby. Easy access
from main roads (A1, A68 and A7) and to city centre attractions.

£££ **BRUNSWICK HOTEL** 7 Brunswick Street, Edinburgh.
4 double, 3 twin, 2 family bedrooms and 1 single, all en suite.
TV and tea/coffee making facilities in all rooms. 2 four poster beds.
Hours: Breakfast 8.30am - 9am. **CC** Access, Visa, AmEx. **Other**
Points: Central heating. Children welcome. No dogs. No evening
meals. Residents' lounge. Unrestricted street parking. Fax as tel.
no. Vegetarian meals. **Directions:** In NE Edinburgh around the
corner from the Playhouse Theatre.
MRS FREIDA McGOVERN ☎ (031) 556 1238.
A centrally situated listed Georgian town house only a short
walk from all transport facilities. Close to town centre.

⊗££ **CHANNINGS** South Learmonth Gardens, Edinburgh.
£££££ **Hours:** Breakfast 7.30am - 9.30am, Lunch and bar snacks 12 noon
- 2pm, Dinner 6.30pm - 10pm. **Cuisine:** Main courses may
include Noissettes of Venison with lavender jelly, Scottish Wood
Pigeon with a mousse of Sea Trout, Tagliatelle with smoked
salmon. 48 bedrooms, all en suite. Accommodation within
Routiers price limit at weekends. **CC** All major cards. **Other Points:**
Residents lounge. Garden. Library. Private functions and small
conferences. Fax No: (031) 332 9631. **(V) Directions:** Just off
Queensferry Rd, at the city end.
SIMON WILLIAMS - General Manager ☎ (031) 315 2226.
A privately owned hotel with a cosy club-like atmosphere,
Channings is situated in a quiet, cobbled street close to the City
centre. The hotel provides a warm welcome, excellent
accommodation, and a popular Brasserie known for its good
food and personal service.

££ **GALLOWAY GUEST HOUSE** 22 Dean Park Crescent.
Edinburgh.
1 single, 2 double, 1 twin, 6 family bedrooms, 6 with en suite. 3
bathrooms. **Hours:** Breakfast served from 8am until 9am. **CC** None.
Other Points: Central heating. Children welcome. Residents'
lounge. TV. Garden. Free street parking. Vegetarians catered for.
Directions: Off Princes St.into Frederick,left to Circus Pl,left into
Leslie Pl.
SHEILA & ROBERT CLARK ☎ (031) 332 3672.
A Victorian town house situated in the historically and
architecturally famous New Town area of Edinburgh. Only a
few minutes' walk to Princes Street and all of Edinburgh's many
attractions.

££ **GLENERNE** 4 Hampton Terrace, West Coates, Edinburgh.
CLUB 2 twin, 2 double and 1 family bedroom, 4 en suite. Tea/coffee
making facilities, TV, ironing and drying facilities and hairdryer on
request. **Hours:** Breakfast 8am - 9am. **CC** None. **Other Points:**
Children welcome. Dogs allowed. Vegetarian meals available.

Edinburgh continued

Directions: On main A8 Glasgow/Edinburgh road, about 1 mile from city centre.
M BALLENTYNE ☎ (031) 337 1210.
A friendly, family run guest house on the main Glasgow - Edinburgh Road yet with a quiet rear aspect. A detached Victorian villa, it is only 15 minutes walk from the centre of Edinburgh. Glenerne enjoys a friendly, welcoming atmosphere and is popular with holiday makers, weekenders visiting Edinburgh and business travellers alike. Comfortable accommodation.

££ **GLENORA HOTEL** 14 Rosebery Crescent, Haymarket, Edinburgh.
2 single, 6 double, 2 family bedrooms, all en suite. TV, telephone and tea/coffee making facilities in all rooms. **Hours:** Breakfast 8am - 9.30am. CC Access, Visa. **Other Points:** No smoking in the dining room. Children welcome. Residents licence. Full central heating. Baby listening service. **Directions:** A8 towards the airport, close to Haymarket station.
VERONICA INNES ☎ (031) 337 1186.
This privately run hotel is conveniently situated near the city centre and offers a high standard of decor and furnishings following a recent refurbishment. A friendly, comfortable hotel, popular with holiday makers and business people alike. Owner, Veronica Innes also runs the Standing Stones Hotel at Stenness, Orkney.

⊗££ **JOHNSBURN HOUSE** Johnsburn Road, Balerno, Edinburgh.
Hours: Lunch and bar meals 12 noon - 3pm, Dinner and bar meals 7pm - 10pm (last orders). Closed: Mondays. **Cuisine:** Imaginative, traditional Scottish cuisine. Bar meals & restaurant menus. None. CC Access, Visa. **Other Points:** Children welcome. Dogs allowed. Excellent choice of wine by the glass. P ♿ **(V)** **Directions:** A70 Lanark - Edinburgh road. 7 miles from Edinburgh city centre.
MARTIN & LINDA MITCHELL ☎ (031) 449 3847.
A warm welcome awaits you at Johnsburn House, an interesting, historic mansion dating back to 1760. Under the personal supervision of the proprietors, this popular pub restaurant serves superb food, freshly cooked and artistically presented. Highly recommended for its excellent food, welcoming service and friendly, relaxed atmosphere.

⊗££ **LANCERS BRASSERIE** 5 Hamilton Place, Edinburgh.
Hours: Lunch 12 noon - 2.30pm and dinner 5.30pm - 11.45pm (last orders). **Cuisine:** Bengali and North Indian dishes, Kurji lamb (48 hours notice), Vegetarian Thali, Lancers assorted Tandoori, selection of French dishes. None. CC All major cards. **Other Points:** Children welcome. ♿ **(V)** **Directions:** In Stockbridge area of the city.
WALI UDDIN ☎ (031) 332 3444/9559.
Lancers Brasserie have a good selection of French and Indian dishes at reasonable prices. Their warm welcome and helpful, efficient staff, will make eating here a pleasureable experience.

LOWLANDS & SCOTTISH BORDERS

Edinburgh continued

⌖£ **MARCHHALL HOTEL** 14/16 Marchhall Crescent, Edinburgh. ⊨ 3 single and 12 double rooms, 6 en suite. All with wash basins, colour TV and tea making facilities. **Hours:** Breakfast 7.30am - 9am. Dinner served at 6pm (only if requested). **CC** Access, Visa. **Other Points:** Prestonfield Golf Club is adjacent, where non-members may play. Tennis courts also nearby. Fax No: (031) 662 0777. **Directions:** On south side of city, off Dalkeith Rd (A68), near Queen's Park.
MR G GORDON ☎ (031) 667 2743.
A family run hotel situated in a quiet residential area of Edinburgh. This stone-built hotel offers comfortable accommodation, and, in the evenings, there is a chance to meet locals and fellow guests in the attractive bar. Near main bus route and about one and a half miles from city centre.

⊗£ **OSBOURNE HOTEL & SHELBOURNE LOUNGE** 53-59 ⌖£££££ York Place, Edinburgh.
Hours: Lunch and bar meals 12 noon - 2pm, dinner and bar meals 5.30pm - 8pm. **Cuisine:** Traditional pub meals. Continental cuisine. ⊨ 40 bedrooms, 36 en suite. **CC** All major cards. **Other Points:** Children welcome. Dogs by arrangement. **Directions:** In the city centre, near the bus station.
FEROZ WADIA ☎ (031) 556 5577/2345.
A city centre hotel, ideally located near the main coach and rail stations and only a short walk from the castle, Palace, Royal Mile and Princes Street shops and gardens. The dining room offers meals to residents and groups. Visitors receive a warm welcome and the service is polite and friendly.

⊗£ **ROTHESAY HOTEL** 8 Rothesay Place, Edinburgh.
⌖£££ **Hours:** Breakfast 7am - 9.30am, Dinner 6.30pm - 9pm. Closed: November - March inclusive. **Cuisine:** Traditional British dishes. ⊨ 40 bedrooms, 32 en suite. **CC** All major cards. **Other Points:** Children welcome. Dogs allowed. **(V) Directions:** 3 minutes walk from Princes Street in quiet, residential area.
MR M T BORLAND ☎ (031) 225 4125.
A family run, comfortable hotel set in a quiet location within the heart of Georgian Edinburgh and within easy walking distance of the city centre. Catering for tourist and business people alike, the hotel offers comfortable accommodation and a warm welcome to all.

⌖£ **ROWAN GUEST HOUSE** 13 Glenorchy Terrace, Edinburgh. ⊨ 2 single, 2 double, 3 twin (1 en suite), 2 family bedrooms (1 en suite), 2 bathrooms, 1 shower. Complimentary tea/coffee. **Hours:** Breakfast 8am - 9am. Closed Christmas and New Year. **CC** None. **Other Points:** Central heating. No evening meals. Children welcome. No dogs. Residents' lounge. TV. **P**
ALAN & ANGELA VIDLER ☎ (031) 667 2463.
An elegant Victorian town house in a quiet residential area just off the A7 from the South. Easy access to city centre and all its amenities.

⊗£ **TEX MEX** 38 Hanover Street, Edinburgh.
Hours: Meals served 12 noon - 1am. Closed: Christmas and New Years Day. **Cuisine:** Mexican/American dishes: eg. huevos

Edinburgh continued

rancheros, tacos, tortillas, enchilada burritos, burgers, grilled steaks, pecan pie, Tennessee grasshopper pie. ⬛ None. ⬛ Access, Visa. **Other Points:** Children welcome. No dogs. **(V)** DONALD BURGOYNE MAVOR ☎ (031) 225 1796.

Authentic Mexican dishes prepared with fresh, quality ingredients. The restaurant is decorated with bright, strong colours and ultra modern lighting. Situated just off Princes Street there is a constant flow of people and the restaurant tends to get very full in the evenings.

⊗£££ **THE ALBANY HOTEL** 39/43 Albany Street, Edinburgh.
⊡£££ **Hours:** Breakfast 7.30am - 9.30am, Lunch 12 noon - 2pm and Dinner 6.30pm - 9.30pm (last orders). Bar snacks 12 noon - 2pm and 6.30pm - 9pm. Closed: 25th & 26th December and 1st & 2nd January. **Cuisine:** Dishes may include Noisettes of lamb, Scottish Salmon Steak, Medallions of Beef on a whisky sauce, Garlic King Prawns, Albany Trio. ⬛ 20 bedrooms, all en suite. ⬛ Access, Visa. **Other Points:** Children welcome. No dogs. Garden dining. Small conferences. Fax No: (031) 557 6633. **(V) Directions:** City centre, behind bus station and St James Centre.
PAULINE MARIDOR ☎ (031) 556 0397.

A small, friendly hotel in a quiet area yet only 5 minutes from Princes Street and the city centre. The fine Georgian exterior is matched by the elegantly refurbished interior. Under the personal supervision of the Swiss owner, all guests are assured a warm welcome. Comfortable bedrooms and excellent cuisine with a continental influence is served in the restaurant.

⊗£ **THE CANNY MAN'S** 239 Morningside Road, Edinburgh.
Hours: Meals served 12.15pm - 2pm. Sunday: bar snacks only. **Cuisine:** Homemade soup. Selection of traditionally cooked Scottish cuisine. ⬛ None. ⬛ None. **Other Points:** Children welcome. No pets. ⬛ **(V) Directions:** On main road through Morningside, south west of town centre.
JAMES W KERR ☎ (031) 447 1484.

The Canny Man's is the nickname for this 'unique' public house. The actual name of the pub is the Volunteer Arms. It has to be seen to be believed. We recommend that when you visit, you make it a priority to read their 3 page fact sheet. All meals are freshly prepared and excellently presented.

⊗£ **THE OLD BORDEAUX** 47 Old Burdiehouse Road, Edinburgh.
Hours: Bar meals served 9.30am - 10pm (last orders). Closed: Christmas and Boxing Day and 1st & 2nd January. **Cuisine:** An extensive choice of dishes such as Fresh Mussels, Roast Beef, Steak Pie, homemade Lasagne, Salads and vegetarian meals. Daily specials. ⬛ None. ⬛ All major cards. **Other Points:** Children welcome. Meals served all day. ⬛ ⬛ **(V) Directions:** A701. 5 miles south of city centre, adjacent to A720 city bypass.
LINDA & ALAN THOMSON ☎ (031) 664 1734.

The principles of good food and friendly, efficient service in comfortable surrounding can be found at this pub on Edinburgh's southern boundary. Transformed from an original abode of exiled French silk weavers into today's warm, welcoming old world Inn, the Old Bordeaux is well worth a visit for its good food and service at very good value for money.

Edinburgh continued

⊗££ **THE TATTLER** 23 Commercial Street, Leith, Edinburgh.
Hours: Lunch 12 noon - 2pm, dinner 6pm - 10pm (last orders). Bar meals 12 noon - 2pm and 6pm - 10pm. Sunday: Food served 12.30pm - 10pm. **Cuisine:** Seafood, curries, casseroles & pies, vegetarian dishes. In the restaurant: Border lamb, scampi, steaks, seafood, beef Kitchener, roast duckling. None. All major cards. **Other Points:** Children welcome. No dogs. **(V) Directions:** Across from the Leith shore, opposite the historic Customs House. LINDA & ALAN THOMSON ☎ (031) 554 9999.
A traditional pub and restaurant - originally four derelict shops in the heart of the historic port of Leith. Tastefully decorated in Victorian/ Edwardian style, The Tattler recreates the glory of that era and offers a taste of Scotland to tourists, businessmen and locals alike.

£ **THE TOWN HOUSE** 65 Gilmore Place, Edinburgh.
1 single, 2 twin, 1 double and 1 family bedroom. 1 bathroom, 1 shower. Colour TV and tea/coffee facilities in all rooms. 2 bedrooms with en suite facilities. **Hours:** Open all year. Breakfast 8am - 9am. None. **Other Points:** Central heating. No evening meals. Children welcome. Scottish Tourist Board 2 Crown commended. **Directions:** Take A702 towards city centre, turn left at the Kings Theatre. MRS SUSAN VIRTUE ☎ (031) 229 1985.
A Victorian terraced town house on three floors. Built in 1876 as the manse for the church next door. Gilmore Place is situated opposite the King's Theatre and is within easy walking distance (15 minutes) of the city centre. It is also well placed on three city centre bus routes.

⊗£££ **THE WITCHERY BY THE CASTLE** Castlehill, Royal Mile, Edinburgh.
Hours: Lunch 12 noon - 5pm and Dinner 5pm - 11pm (last orders). **Cuisine:** Selection of char grilled Aberdeen Angus steaks, local seafood, Orkney oyster, venison, wood pigeon and game. 1 luxury four-poster suite, particularly ideal for a honeymoon couple. Furnished Victorian-style mahogany and burgundy, candlelit and rooftop view. All major cards. **Other Points:** Open for Sunday lunch/dinner and for Bank holidays. **(V) Directions:** Situated at the entrance to Edinburgh Castle, at top of Royal Mile. JAMES THOMSON ☎ (031) 225 5613.
Between 1470 and 1722 the Witchery was the centre of witchcraft and the 'Old Hell-Fire Club' are reputed to have held meetings here. This witch's coven is rumoured to be haunted by 3 ghosts, but visitors still flock here in extraordinary numbers. It must be by means of the magical cookery! A second dining room is completely candlelit & has an outdoor terrace.

⊗£ **VERANDAH TANDOORI RESTAURANT** 17 Dalry Road, Edinburgh.
Hours: Meals from 12 noon - 2.15pm and 5pm - 11.45pm (last orders). **Cuisine:** Lamb pasanda, chicken tikka massalla, tandoori mixed. None. All major cards. **Other Points:** Children welcome. No dogs. **(V) Directions:** Close to Haymarket Station in Edinburgh.

Edinburgh continued

WALI TASAR UDDIN ☎ (031) 337 5828

Winner of the Casserole Award 1988, 1989 and 1990. The Verandah Restaurant is one of Edinburgh's most popular eating establishments, offering authentic Bangladeshi dishes. The light wicker chairs, and the matching timber blinds further enhance the Restaurant's already relaxed atmosphere.

⌂££ **WOODLANDS** 55 Barnton Avenue, Davidsons Mains, Edinburgh.

🛏 1 twin with en suite facilities and 2 double with shared bathroom. All bedrooms are equipped with tea/coffee making facilities, hair dryers, electric blankets, radios and colour TVs. **Hours:** Breakfast served at guests' convenience. **CC** None. **Other Points:** Central heating. No evening meals. Children welcome. Residents' lounge. TV. Garden. Dogs by arrangement. Vegetarians catered for by request. **P Directions:** Follow signs to Lauriston Castle on A90, off Cramond Road South.

MRS HELEN HALL ☎ (031) 336 1685.

A small mansion house standing in 2 acres of garden and woodlands overlooking the Royal Burgess Golf Course. Close to Princes Street and local amenities.

FORFAR Tayside **Map 11 A1**

※££ **ROYAL HOTEL** Castle Street, Forfar.

⌂££££ **Hours:** Breakfast 7.30am - 10am, lunch 12 noon - 2pm and dinner
CLUB 7pm - 9pm. (Friday and Saturday 7.30pm - 9.30pm) **Cuisine:** Specialities include light fish mousse made from Arbroath Smokies, Prime Angus Sirloin Steak, Venison and Salmon from local rivers. 🛏 5 single, 8 twin, 5 double, 1 family room, all en suite. 'Royal Suite' with four poster bed. **CC** All major cards. **Other Points:** Children welcome. Roof garden. Gymnasium. Jacuzzi. Swimming pool. Function suite. Conference facilitites. **P (V) Directions:** Off the A94, situated in the centre of Forfar.

ALISON & BRIAN BONNYMAN ☎ (0307) 62691

Fine old coaching house in the centre of historic Forfar. All rooms are tastefully appointed with en suite facilities. The proprietors, both local, take special pride in making sure their guests enjoy excellent food in comfortable surroundings.

※££ **THE STAG HOTEL** 140-144 Castle Street, Forfar.

⌂££ **Hours:** Breakfast anytime, Pizzeria open 12 noon - 11pm. Bar meals available 12 noon - 2.30pm and 6pm - 9pm. **Cuisine:** Pizzeria. Bar meals include dishes such as chilli con carne, steak pie, T-bone steaks. 🛏 4 rooms, 3 en suite. **CC** Access, Visa. **Other Points:** Children welcome. Dogs allowed. Afternoon tea served. **Directions:** At end of Castle Street, at junction of A94 and A926.

EGON FLASCHBERGER ☎ (0307) 62737.

The Stag has been a tavern since 1690 and is rumoured to be haunted by the Earl of Strathmore of Glamis Castle, who was murdered on the doorstep here in the 1700's. However, times have changed and you can now rest assured of a very friendly welcome from owners and locals alike.

LOWLANDS & SCOTTISH BORDERS

FORTINGALL Tayside **Map 10 A2**

⊗£££ **FORTINGALL HOTEL** Fortingall, by Aberfeldy.

⏠£££ **Hours:** Breakfast 7.30am - 9.30am, lunch 12 noon - 2pm, dinne
7pm - 9pm. Closed: November to February. **Cuisine:** Goo
choice using local produce ie. fresh local salmon, venison. Hom
baking and homemade jams when available. ⊨ 9 bedrooms -
family, 3 double and 3 twin. 8 en suite. **CC** Access, Visa, AmEx
Other Points: Central heating. Children welcome. Licensed
Residents lounge. Garden. TV. **⊡ Directions:** Off the A827 an
B846, 8 miles from Aberfeldy.
MR ALAN SCHOFIELD ☎ (088 73) 367.
Fortingall, where the hotel is situated, has a yew tree reputed t
be the oldest vegetation in Europe. The rooms have outstandin
views of the hills with the River Tay and Lyon in the foregroun
Widely known for its cuisine fully supported by an extensiv
wine list, this hotel provides a relaxing and enjoyable dinne.

GALASHIELS Borders **Map 11 B1**

⊗£ **ABBOTSFORD ARMS HOTEL** 63 Stirling Street, Galashiel

⏠£££ **Hours:** Meals from 8am - 10am, 12 noon - 9pm weekdays, 10pr
Friday and Saturday. Bar meals served 12 noon - 9pm. **Cuisine**
Steak, chicken dishes. ⊨ 13 bedrooms, 9 en suite. **CC** Acces
Visa. **Other Points:** Children welcome. No dogs. Coaches b
appointment. **⊡ ↺ (V) Directions:** In Galashiels, opposite the bu
station.
JAMES GORDON & CHRISTINA WILSON SCOTT ☎ (0896
2517.
A beautifully modernised family hotel 32 miles south c
Edinburgh. Completely refurbished to a high standard.

⊗££ **HERGES** 58 Island Street, Galashiels.

Hours: Lunch and bar snacks 12 noon - 2.30pm, Dinner and ba
snacks 6pm - 12 midnight (last orders 9.30pm). Closed: Tuesday
Cuisine: Dishes may include Baked Rainbow Trout, Roast Gigot c
Lamb, Supreme of Chicken Marango. Also lighter snacks such a
filled baked potatoes & croissants. ⊨ None. **CC** Visa. **Other Point**
Children welcome. No-smoking area. No dogs. Mastercard an
Eurocard also accepted. ↺ **(V) Directions:** A72 to Peebles, near
& Q superstore.
KAREN & SANDY CRAIG ☎ (0896) 50400.
Karen and Sandy Craig offer imaginative, good value cuisine i
a very friendly and relaxed atmosphere. A former yarn broker
store, Herges has been expertly converted to form this attractiv
French-style wine bar. The service is most courteous an
efficient, and all dishes freshly cooked to a high standard.

GATEHOUSE OF FLEET Dumfries & Galloway **Map 10 C2**

⊗££ **BANK OF FLEET HOTEL** Gatehouse of Fleet.

⏠£ **Hours:** 8.30am - 9.30am, 12 noon - 2pm, and 7pm - 9pm. Als
open Sundays. **Cuisine:** A la carte includes poached salmon steak
roast duckling a l'orange, and sirloin steak garni. Bar men
includes scampi, burgers and lasagne. ⊨ 2 single, 2 double, an
1 family room, all rooms with tea/coffee facilities. Colour TV i
residents' lounge. **CC** Access, Visa. **Other Points:** Childre
welcome. Pets allowed. ↺ **(V) Directions:** A75, near Cardones
Castle.
MR & MRS WRIGHT ☎ (0557) 814302.

Gatehouse of Fleet continued

Small, family run hotel in one of Scotland's scenic heritage areas. Bar and restaurant menus are excellent value and the food is beautifully prepared and presented. There are many activities for the holiday-maker, including fishing, bird-watching, golf, sailing, cycling, and walking.

⊗£££ **MURRAY ARMS HOTEL** High Street, Gatehouse-of-Fleet.
⊡£££ **Hours:** Open 24 hours a day all year round. Meals served 12 noon - 9.45pm. **Cuisine:** Galloway beef, locally caught fish and smoked salmon, Scottish lamb, homemade soups and pate. Vegetarians catered for. ⊨ 13 bedrooms, all en suite. **CC** All major cards. **Other Points:** Children welcome. Limited access for disabled. **(V) Directions:** Off A75, 60 miles west of Carlisle between Dumfries and Stranraer.
MURRAY ARMS HOTEL LTD. ☎ (055 74) 207.
A warm, welcoming inn where Robert Burns wrote 'Scots Wha Hae'. Gatehouse-of-Fleet is one of Scotland's scenic heritage areas surrounded by unspoilt countryside. Residents enjoy free golf, tennis and fishing.

GIRVAN Strathclyde **Map 10 C1**
⊗££ **KINGS ARMS HOTEL** Dalrymple Street, Girvan.
⊡££ **Hours:** Breakfast 7.30am - 9.30am, lunch 12 noon - 2pm and
CLUB dinner 7pm - 9.30pm (last orders). Bar meals 12 noon - 2pm and 6pm - 9.30pm. **Cuisine:** In the bar: lasagne, curries, fish, homemade steak and kidney pie, roasts. In the restaurant: steaks, roasts, casseroles. ⊨ 25 bedrooms all en suite. **CC** Access, Visa. **Other Points:** Children welcome. No dogs. Afternoon teas. ▣ ㊧ **Directions:** In the centre of Girvan.
JOHN, DONALD & IAN MORTON ☎ (0465) 3322.
A fine 17th century coaching inn in the centre of this picturesque harbour town. Family run, the best of Scottish hospitality is extended to all visitors. Specialising in fully inclusive golf holidays at nearby Turnberry and Royal Troon golf courses.

GLASGOW Strathclyde **Map 10 B2**
⊡£££ **ALBION HOTEL** 405-407 North Woodside Road, Glasgow.
⊨ 16 bedrooms, all en suite. Tea/coffee facilities, trouser press, radio, telephone, colour TV. **Hours:** Breakfast 7.30am - 9am, bar snacks 6.30pm - 9pm. **CC** Access, Visa. **Other Points:** Children

LOWLANDS & SCOTTISH BORDERS

Glasgow continued

welcome. Open Bank Holidays. Fax No. (041) 334 8159. **(V)**
Directions: Off Great Western Road.
MESSRS McGREGOR & McQUADE ☎ (041) 339 8620.
A small privately owned hotel, offering comfortable accommodation of a high standard. As it is located in the heart of Glasgow's west end, close to the city centre, it is an ideal base for business or pleasure trips to the city.

⌂£££ **AMBASSADOR HOTEL** 7 Kelvin Drive, Glasgow.
16 bedrooms, all en suite. Telephone, colour TV, radio, trouser press, hairdryer and tea/coffee facilities. **Hours:** Breakfast 7.30am - 9.30am, dinner 6.30pm - 9.30pm. **CC** Access, Visa. **Other Points:** Children welcome. Open Bank Holidays. Afternoon teas. Garden. Central heating. Fax No. (041) 945 5377. ⅙ **(V) Directions:** Jct 17, M8. Off Queen Margaret Drive, opposite BBC Studios.
ROBERT & IRINE McQUADE ☎ (041) 946 1018.
Located opposite the BBC studios, this newly converted hotel offers good quality bed and breakfast. Situated in the fashionable west end of Glasgow, convenient for the city centre, museums, art galleries. An ideal base for both holiday makers and business persons alike.

⊗££ **BUSBY HOTEL** Field Road, Clarkston, Glasgow.
⌂£££££ **Hours:** Breakfast 7.30am - 9.30am, lunch 12 noon - 2.15pm
CLUB dinner 6.30pm - 9.30pm. Bar snacks 12 noon - 9pm. **Cuisine:** Bar snacks, a la carte menu and table d'hote. Dishes may include prawn vol au vents, turkey breast Cordon Bleu, stir fried chicken & a selection of sweets. 32 bedrooms, all en suite. **CC** All major cards. **Other Points:** Children welcome. No smoking area. Wedding receptions and conferences. Limited access for disabled. Dogs allowed. Fax No. (041) 644 4417. **P (V) Directions:** On A726, follow sign from M74 exit 5 to Paisley through E. Kilbride.
ALEX & VIVIEN WATSON ☎ (041) 644 2661.
Located in a tree lined avenue beside the River Cart in the southern suburbs of Glasgow, this hotel is accessible from the M74 through East Kilbride, and is only 20 minutes from the airport. The Busby Hotel offers comfortable accommodation and good food which is complemented by friendly staff.

⊗£ **CAFE GANDOLFI** 64 Albion Street, Glasgow.
Hours: Meals from 9.30am - 11.30pm. Closed: Sundays and Bank Holidays. **Cuisine:** Smoked salmon quiche, gravadlax. Daily specials, e.g. goulash, stuffed aubergine. None. **CC** None. **Other Points:** Children welcome. No dogs. ⅙ **(V)**
IAIN M MacKENZIE ☎ (041) 552 6813
In a quiet street of the City's busy Argyll Street. Proximity to the shopping centre makes this popular both with the shop staff and their customers. A typically continental and informal atmosphere.

⊗££ **CUL DE SAC** 44/46 Ashton Lane, Hillhead, Glasgow.
Hours: Meals from 12 noon - 11.30pm (last orders). **Cuisine:** Crepes, eg. trout mirza, Stilton & pear, Boursin, prawn and pepper. None. **CC** All major cards. **Other Points:** Children

Glasgow continued

welcome. No dogs. No smoking area. Coaches by appointment. &
(V)
THOMAS MATHIESON ☎ (041) 334 4749/4686
A French brasserie in true Parisienne style. Standing in a cobble-stoned lane in a bright, friendly area of town. Just 2 minutes' walk from Hillhead underground station, the university, art gallery and botanic gardens.

⊗££ **EWINGTON HOTEL** 132 Queens Drive, Queens Park,
⌂££££ Glasgow.
Hours: Open for breakfast 7.30am - 9.30am, lunch 12.30pm -
2pm (last orders 2pm) dinner 5.30pm - 9pm (last orders 9pm).
Cuisine: Both Scotish and continental dishes, including sole with
avocado fan, spaghetti carbonara, desserts range from creme
caramel to orange cheesecake. ⊨ 35 rooms, 17 single rooms, 20
twin and 8 double rooms all of which are en suite. Available in the
rooms are tv, radio, telephone, trouser press. **CC** All major cards.
Other Points: Children welcome. Local attractions Art Galleries,
Glasgow Museum of Transport. **P (V) Directions:** Located on the
M8.
MR H C EDWARD ☎ (041) 423 1152
The Ewington Hotel, in a quiet Victorian terrace overlooking the Queens park, is privately owned. Whether on business or pleasure, Ewington offers a 'home from home', with good food and accommodation it's a comfortable friendly hotel to stay in.

⊗££ **LA FIORENTINA** 2 Paisley Road West, Glasgow.
Hours: Lunch 12 noon - 2.15pm, Dinner 5.30pm - 11pm. Closed:
Sundays. **Cuisine:** A la carte, Table d'Hote - Italian cuisine.
⊨ None. **CC** All major cards. **Other Points:** Children welcome. **P**
& (V)
MR PIEROTTI ☎ (041) 420 1585.
La Fiorentina guarantees an excellent meal in a genuine Italian atmosphere. The restaurant is very popular with locals and offers an extensive and imaginative menu with a huge variety of pasta dishes. If new to the area, this restaurant is well worth a visit and 'highly recommended'.

⊗£££ **LAUTREC'S WINE BAR & BRASSERIE** 14 Woodlands
Terrace, Glasgow.
Hours: Lunch 12 noon - 2.30pm (last orders), dinner 6.30pm -
11pm (last orders 10.30pm), bar snacks 11am - 11pm. Closed:
Sundays. **Cuisine:** A la carte menu may include Duck in a black
cherry & orange sauce, Vegetarian Stroganoff, Lamb en Croute.
Good bar menu and blackboard specials. ⊨ None. **CC** All major
cards. **Other Points:** Children welcome. Open Bank Holidays. **(V)**
Directions: From Charing Cross off Woodlands Road.
TONY DEELEY ☎ (041) 332 7013.
A welcoming wine bar and restaurant situated in a Victorian Terrace with lovely views overlooking the park and city. A good variety of dishes are served in a lively atmosphere. A popular eating place and wine bar.

LOWLANDS & SCOTTISH BORDERS

Glasgow continued

⊗£££ **MACDONALD THISTLE HOTEL** Mains Avenue, Giffnock,
CLUB Glasgow.
Hours: 7am - 10am, 12.30pm - 2.30pm, and 7pm - 10pm (last
orders 9pm). Bar meals served between 12 noon - 2.30pm.
Closed: Saturday lunchtimes. **Cuisine:** Modern British cuisine,
with speciality fish and beef dishes. Good wine list. ⊨ 56 rooms,
all en suite, with colour TV, radio, alarms, baby listening devices,
telephones and tea/coffee facilities. Room service and 4-poster
suites. **CC** All major cards. **Other Points:** Children welcome. Pets
allowed. Open Sundays and bank holidays. Residents lounge and
garden. Private parties also catered for. In-house videos. **P** **(V)**
Directions: 4 miles from City Centre
MR GARY BICKLEY - GENERAL MANAGER ☎ (041) 638 2225.
*A modern, well-furnished hotel, offering quality food in
generous portions - at good value for money. Located in a quiet,
residential area yet well-situated on good road access routes for
business people and tourists. Only a short drive from Glasgow -
with its famous Burrell Collection - and some of the loveliest
parts of Scotland, including the Clyde coast and Loch Lomond.*

⊗£ **TURBAN TANDOORI RESTAURANT** 2 Station Road,
Giffnock, Glasgow.
Hours: Meals served 5pm - 12 midnight. Closed: Christmas and
New Year. **Cuisine:** Tandoori dishes. ⊨ None. **CC** Access, Visa,
AmEx. **Other Points:** Children welcome. No dogs. Coaches by
appointment. **P** ఉ **(V)**
KURBIR PUREWAL ☎ (041) 638 0069
*One of Scotland's finest tandoori restaurants in a residential
suburb of Glasgow.*

GLENROTHES Fife **Map 11 B1**

⊗££ **TOWN HOUSE HOTEL** 1 High Street, Markinch, Glenrothes.
⌂£££ **Hours:** Breakfast 7am - 9am, Lunch 12 noon - 2pm, Dinner
6.15pm - 10.30pm (last orders 9pm). **Cuisine:** Dishes may include
Chicken Stir-Fry, Tay Salmon Fillet, Chicken Tikka, Chinese
Sweet & Sour Pork, grilled steaks. ⊨ 4 bedrooms, 3 en suite.
CC All major cards. **Other Points:** Children welcome. Limited
access for disabled. Dogs allowed. Special weekend breaks. No
smoking area. Public parking nearby. **(V) Directions:** B9130,
opposite railway station in Markinch.
HARRY & LESLEY BAIN ☎ (0592) 758459.
*A family run hotel bringing together traditional values and
quality. Centrally situated in the Kingdom of Fife, ideal for
sporting breaks and for family holidays. The Town House Hotel
provides a warm welcome and good value for money.*

GLENSHEE Tayside **Map 11 A1**

⊗£ **THE BLACKWATER INN** Glenshee.
⌂££ **Hours:** Full menu served 12 noon - 9pm. Childrens special menu
⊕ also available. **Cuisine:** Homemade pies, pastas, curries, char
CLUB grilled steaks, hamburgers,speciality salads, taste of Scotland and
Louisianna style dishes. Daily specials. ⊨ 8 bedrooms, 2 en suite.
Tea/coffee facilities in all rooms. **CC** Access, Visa. **Other Points:**
Children welcome. Dogs allowed. ఉ **(V) Directions:** On the A93,
10 miles north of Blairgowrie.
IVY BAILEY ☎ (025 082) 234.

Glenshee continued

Nestling at the base of a steep hill in a landscaped heather and waterfall garden, this quaint old inn gives the impression that you have stepped back in time into Brigadoon! Situated on the main road to Balmoral, there is skiing, golf, fishing, stalking and hang-gliding available nearby. .

GOUROCK Strathclyde **Map 10 B1**

⊗£ **CAFE CONTINENTAL** 38-40 Kempock Street, Gourock. **Hours:** Meals served 12 noon - 5pm (last orders). **Cuisine:** French/Italian. Specialities include homemade soups, fish and meat dishes. ⊨ None. **CC** None. **Other Points:** Children welcome. Afternoon teas. Pets allowed. Open bank holidays **P** & **(V) Directions:** 200 yards from Gourock Station and Ferry Terminal. ROLAND TOMA ☎ (0475) 32430.

An attractive restaurant with tiling, marble and mohogany, creating a continental style atmosphere. Large windows at rear provides diners with views over the River Clyde. Good food, friendly attentive service in pleasant surroundings.

GRETNA Dumfries & Galloway **Map 11 C1**

⊗££ **GRETNA CHASE HOTEL** Gretna, nr Carlisle. ⅏£££ **Hours:** Restaurant open 11am - 3pm and 5.30pm - 10pm. 12 noon CLUB - 3pm and 7pm - 10pm Sundays. **Cuisine:** Dishes prepared from locally caught salmon and sea trout. Home grown vegetables in summer. Steaks, grills, salads, cold meat platter, fish. ⊨ 9 bedrooms, all with bath or shower and 6 with private toilet. **CC** All major cards. **Other Points:** Children welcome. No dogs. **P** & **(V) Directions:** From the A74, take Gretna (Green) turning, hotel is on this road.

JOHN W HALL ☎ (0461) 37517.

A country house hotel set in beautiful, award-winning gardens. Ideal for those wishing to break their journey when travelling north or south and as a centre for touring Scottish borders, Hadrian's Wall and the English Lakes.

GULLANE Lothian **Map 11 B1**

⊗£££ **QUEENS HOTEL** Main Street, Gullane. ⅏££££ **Hours:** Breakfast 7am - 9am, Dinner 7pm - 10pm. Bar meals served all day from 12 noon - 10pm. **Cuisine:** Dinner menu may feature Beef Wellington, Baked Halibut Steak Caprice, Chicken and Mushroom Crepe au Gratin. Bar meals available all day. ⊨ 35 bedrooms, 16 en suite. **CC** All major cards. **Other Points:** Children welcome. Afternoon teas. Dogs allowed. Residents' lounge. Garden. Fax No: (0620) 842970. **P** & **(V) Directions:** Off A1. A6137 Haddington to Aberlady, A198 to Gullane. ANN ROBERTSON ☎ (0620) 842275.

A family run hotel situated in the picturesque village of Gullane. This is a welcoming and pleasant hotel with a good reputation and good standards. A relaxed atmosphere and friendly service. Golf and other packages available.

HAWICK Borders **Map 11 C1**

⊗££ **KIRKLANDS HOTEL** West Stewart Place, Hawick. ⅏££££ **Hours:** Restaurant open 12 noon - 2pm and 7pm - 9.30pm. Also CLUB open on Sundays. **Cuisine:** Venison, pheasant, guinea fowl, salmon, and duck a l'orange. ⊨ 12 bedrooms. **CC** All major cards.

Hawick continued

Other Points: Children welcome. Large garden. Snooker room. Games room. Library. Fax No: (0450) 370404. **P Directions:** 200 yards off the main A7, ½ mile north of Hawick High Street. MR B NEWLAND ☎ (0450) 72263.

A charming small hotel pleasantly situated in the beautiful Scottish borders. Ideal base for tourists and business people. Close to many attractions. Recommended by most leading hotel guides. Weekly terms and week-end breaks available. Colour brochure and tariff on request.

⊗£££ **MANSFIELD HOUSE HOTEL** Weensland Road, Hawick.
⊞£££ **Hours:** Breakfast 7.30am - 9am, Lunch 12 noon - 2pm, Dinner 7pm - 9pm (last orders). Bar meals 12 noon - 2pm and 6.30pm - 9pm. Restaurant closed Saturday and Sunday lunchtime but bar meals available. **Cuisine:** Scottish cuisine with particular emphasis on the use of fresh local products. ⊨ 10 bedrooms, all en suite. **CC** All major cards. **Other Points:** Children welcome. Dining al fresco. Dogs allowed. Residents' lounge. Garden. Fax No: (0450) 72007. **P (V) Directions:** Approx. 1 mile from town centre. On the A698 Hawick to Jedburgh.
IAN & SHEILA MACKINNON ☎ (0450) 73988.

Standing in 10 acres of wooded grounds and gardens, this charming Victorian House Hotel overlooks the Teviot Valley. Built in 1870, the house has been expertly restored retaining the fine ceilings and rich woodwork. Personally run by the proprietors, you can be assured of real Scottish hospitality and excellently prepared fresh food.

INVERARAY Strathclyde **Map 10 A1**
⊗££ **LOCH FYNE OYSTER BAR** Clachan Farm, Cairndow, Inveraray.
Hours: Open all day from 9am - 9pm (last orders). Closed: Christmas Day and New Years Day. **Cuisine:** Local sea food and game. Specialities are oysters from their own fishery and smoked fish from own smokehouse. Locally caught langoustines. ⊨ None. **CC** Access, Visa, AmEx. **Other Points:** Children welcome. Garden dining. Sea Food Shop with Home Delivery Service in UK, to Europe and U.S.A. Fax: (04996) 234. **P & (V) Directions:** At the head of Loch Fyne on the A83.
LOCH FYNE OYSTERS LTD ☎ (04996) 217/264.

An oyster bar and restaurant in an old farm building. The menu is almost entirely their own sea food and game products. The oysters are highly popular from their own oyster beds in the clean water of Loch Fyne. Their own Smokehouse provides smoked fish and venison. A warm welcome and simple, excellent food at reasonable prices whether you want a full meal or quick snack.

ISLE OF ARRAN Strathclyde **Map 10 B1**
⊗££ **BURLINGTON HOTEL** Whiting Bay, Isle of Arran.
⊞££ **Hours:** Breakfast 8.30am - 9.15am or by arrangement, Dinner
CLUB 7pm - 9pm (last orders). Restaurant open to non-residents.
Cuisine: Dishes may include Lamlash Bay Wild Salmon Steak, Lamb Gigot Steak poached in Cream, Arran Cheese Salad, choice of vegetarian dishes. ⊨ 10 bedrooms, 5 en suite. **CC** None. **Other Points:** Children welcome. Dogs allowed. Residents'

Isle of Arran continued

lounge. Garden. ▣ **(V) Directions**: 8 miles south from Brodick Ferry. Opposite Beach.

WILF & DIANE INGS. ☎ (07707) 255.

A small, family run hotel on the beautiful Isle of Arran, offering comfortable accommodation, a friendly welcome, and a wide choice of freshly cooked local produce. Both food and accommodation are excellent value for money. Bargain breaks available October to March. Ideal for walking, golf, sailing and fishing and there are splendid opportunities for both relaxing and adventure.

⊗££ **CATACOL BAY HOTEL** Catacol, Isle of Arran.

⌂££ **Hours**: Bar meals 12 noon - 10pm. Grill Room 6pm - 10pm.

CLUB **Cuisine**: Steaks, seafood, salmon, duckling. ⊨ 6 bedrooms. 2 bathrooms. ▨ All major cards. **Other Points**: Children welcome. Dogs allowed. Fax No: (0770) 83350. ▣ **Directions**: On the A841, 1.25 miles south of Lochranza Pier.

DAVID C. ASHCROFT ☎ (0770) 83231.

Small, comfortable family-run hotel. Seafront location overlooking Kilbrannan Sound and Kintyre Peninsula. Ideally based for fishing, climbing, pony-trekking, walking, golfing, bird watching. Island breaks October to June.

ISLE OF GIGHA Strathclyde **Map 10 B1**

⊗£££ **GIGHA HOTEL** Isle of Gigha

⌂££££ **Hours**: Breakfast 9am - 10am, lunch 12 noon - 2.30pm (last orders)

CLUB and dinner 7pm - 9pm (last orders). Boathouse Bistro open May - September 10am - 10pm. **Cuisine**: International cuisine. Fresh Gigha salmon and shellfish, wild duck, and locally reared lamb. ⊨ 8 double, 5 twin, 11 ensuite. 3 self-catering cottages (two sleep 4, one sleeps 8 people) available for rent all year. ▨ Access, Visa. **Other Points**: Children welcome. Residents bar. Garden. Afternoon teas. Golf course, fishing, clay pigeon shooting. Private air strip. Fax: (05835) 282. ▣ **(V) Directions**: M8 from Glasgow, A82 onto A83 until Tayinloan. 20 mins on car ferry.

STEPHEN & ALISON HYATT - Managers ☎ (05835) 254

Privately run hotel near the famous Achamore Gardens on one of Scotlands unspoilt islands. Outstanding views over the waters of Ardminish Bay to the soft hills of Kintyre. Quality food and comfortable accommodation in a relaxed friendly atmosphere.

LOWLANDS & SCOTTISH BORDERS

ISLE OF IONA Strathclyde **Map 10 A1**
⊗££ **ARGYLL HOTEL** Isle of Iona, Argyll.
⏏£££ **Hours:** Breakfast 8.30am - 9am, lunch 12.30am - 1.30pm, and dinner 7pm. Bar meals served between 12.30pm - 1.30pm. Closed: October 12th - Easter. Restaurant also open to non-residents, but booking is essential. **Cuisine:** Scottish fayre, using fresh local produce, own vegetables in season, and offering vegetarian dishes made with wholefoods. ⊨ 10 single, 3 double, 4 twin, and 2 family rooms. 10 rooms are en suite and all have tea/coffee making facilities. Baby listening devices available. ▨ Access, Visa. **Other Points:** Children welcome. Pets allowed, but dogs must be exercised on leads. Open Sundays and bank holidays. Resident lounges and garden. **(V) Directions:** Ferry Oban-Craignure. Drive/bus to Fionnphort,then ferry to Iona.
MRS FIONA MENZIES ☎ (06817) 334.
A friendly hotel, right on the Iona seashore. Cars are not allowed on this tiny unspoilt isle and must be left at Fionnphort or Oban. Iona,with its brilliant waters, clear light, and wealth of wildlife, has inspired poets and painters for centuries. When staying at the Argyll Hotel, guests are also sure to be inspired by the superb homecooking and the comfort of the rooms.

ISLE OF MULL Strathclyde **Map 10 A1**
⊗££ **GLENFORSA HOTEL** Salen, by Aros, Isle of Mull.
⏏£££ **Hours:** Breakfast 8.30am - 9.30am, Dinner 7pm - 8.30pm. Bar meals 12 noon - 2pm and 6pm - 8.30pm. Sundays: Lunch - sandwiches, rolls & soup only. Evening - bar meals as per week day evenings. Non-residents advised to book. **Cuisine:** Fixed price 3 course menu, bar snacks/meals and vegetarian meals. ⊨ 15 rooms. 7 twin, 7 double and 1 family bedroom. All en suite. ▨ Access, Visa, AmEx. **Other Points:** Children over 5 years welcome. Garden. Dogs allowed. No smoking in dining room. Fax (0680) 300535. ▣ ⅊ **(V) Directions:** Off the ferry turn right, ten miles along the road.
JEAN & PAUL PRICE ☎ (0680) 300377.
Delightfully situated in 6 acres of secluded woodland, this timber chalet style hotel offers tasty, well presented meals in a warm atmosphere. Accommodation is to a high standard. An ideal base for touring, walking, climbing or fishing.

⊗££ **HARBOUR HOUSE HOTEL** Tobermory, Isle of Mull.
⏏££ **Hours:** Breakfast 7.30am - 9.15pm, dinner 7.30pm - 9.45pm. Open to non-residents for both breakfast and dinner. **Cuisine:** Predominantly Scottish cuisine. Dishes may include Roast Beef, Lanarkshire Ham, Trout Salad, Haggis with a Wee Dram. ⊨ 12 bedrooms, 2 en suite. ▨ None. **Other Points:** Children welcome. Afternoon tea. Dogs allowed. Holiday packages. **(V) Directions:** On the seafront in Tobermory.
MR PINCHEN ☎ (0688) 2209
A family run licensed guest house, superbly situated on the seafront overlooking Tobermory Bay. The 12 bedrooms are well-appointed and offer comfortable accommodation, and the spacious restaurant is open to guests and non-residents for both lunch and dinner. An ideal centre from which to explore the Isles of Mull, Iona and Staffa. Plenty of outdoor activities.

Isle of Mull continued

⊗£££ **LINNDHU HOUSE** Tobermory, Isle of Mull.

⌂£££ **Hours:** Breakfast 8.30am - 9.30am, dinner 8pm - 10pm. **Cuisine:** Table d'hote menu changes daily, accompanied by a comprehensive wine list. ⊨ 8 bedrooms, 5 en suite. Tea/coffee making facilities in all rooms. **CC** None. **Other Points:** Children welcome. Pets allowed. **P** **(V) Directions:** 1½ miles from Tobermory on the road to Salen.

JENNIFER & IAN McLEAN ☎ (0688) 2425.

A stunning cream house set in its own beautiful gardens surrounded by mixed woodland with excellent views across the Sound of Mull. All the bedrooms and public rooms are elegantly furnished, many with antiques. Jennifer prides herself on her cuisine - with varied and delicious menus much appreciated by all visitors to the house.

ISLE OF WHITHORN Dumfries & Galloway **Map 10 C2**

⊗££ **STEAMPACKET HOTEL** Isle of Whithorn, Wigtownshire.

⌂££ **Hours:** Breakfast 8.15am - 10am, Lunch 12 noon - 2pm and Dinner 7pm - 9.30pm (last orders). **Cuisine:** English - lobster a speciality. ⊨ 5 bedrooms, all en suite. **CC** **Other Points:** Pets allowed. **(V) Directions:** On quayside.

MR SCOULAR ☎ (098) 85334

A small family run hotel with a distinct nautical atmosphere where all the bedrooms overlook the harbour. Good food served in friendly comfortable surroundings.

JEDBURGH Borders **Map 11 C1**

⊗£ **JEDFOREST HOTEL** Camptown, Jedburgh.

⌂££ **Hours:** Breakfast 8am - 9.30am, lunch 12 noon - 2pm, dinner 6.30pm - 9.30pm. Sunday lunch 12.30pm - 2pm, Sunday dinner 6.30pm - 8.30pm. **Cuisine:** Dishes include salmon mousse, guinea fowl Jedforest and homemade sweets. ⊨ 7 rooms. 1 twin, 3 double and 3 family bedrooms. 4 en suite. **CC** Access, Visa. **Other Points:** Children welcome. Garden. Dogs allowed. **P** 🚻 **(V) Directions:** On A68.

MR & MRS WILKES ☎ (08354) 274.

Former 19th century hunting lodge, converted into a hotel in the early 60's. Standing in 30 acres of wooded pastureland, Jedforest is a family run hotel offering very good food on their bar menu and comfortable accommodation. Ideal for anyone interested in fishing as the hotel has 1 mile of private fishing.

JOHNSTONE Strathclyde **Map 10 B2**

⊗£ **LYNNHURST HOTEL** Park Road, Johnstone.

⌂££ **Hours:** Meals from 12 noon - 2pm and 6.30pm - 9pm (6.30pm - 10pm Saturdays). **Cuisine:** Home baked ham, homemade soups, steaks. ⊨ 26 bedrooms, 16 en suite. **CC** Access, Visa, Diners. **Other Points:** Children welcome. **P** 🚻 **Directions:** Off the A737 in Park Road.

MR N AND MISS J MACINTRYE ☎ (0505) 24331.

An original old Scottish stone-built house now considerably modernised. Off the A737, 10 minutes from Glasgow Airport. Golf courses nearby.

KELSO Borders **Map 11 B1**

⊗£££ **CROSS KEYS HOTEL** The Square, Kelso.

⌂£££ **Hours:** Breakfast 7.30am - 9.30am, lunch 12 noon - 2pm and
[CLUB] dinner 6.30pm - 9.30pm (last orders 9.15pm). Bar meals 12 noon -
2pm and 6.30pm - 9.30pm. **Cuisine:** Fresh selection of local
produce including game and fish. ⊨ 25 bedrooms, all en suite.
CC All major cards. **Other Points:** Children welcome. Pets allowed.
Non-smoking area. Kelso - 'Britain in bloom' winner for past 5
years, Cross Keys - top business. Fax: (0573) 25792. **P** & **(V)**
Directions: Off the A68 and A698, in the town centre.

MARCELLO BECATTELI ☎ (0573) 23303.

*The hotel is one of Scotland's oldest coaching inns and has been
extensively modernised and refurbished. The intimate
restaurant offers cuisine which is both traditional and
international. Many dishes are exclusive to the Scottish Borders.
Situated in Kelso, one of the most picturesque towns in the
Scottish Borders, it is renowned for its year round sporting
activities.*

KENMORE Tayside **Map 10 A2**

⊗£££ **CROFT-NA-CABER HOTEL** Croft-Na-Caber, Kenmore,
⌂£££ Perthshire.

Hours: Breakfast 8.30am - 9.30am, Lunch 12.30pm - 2pm, Dinner
7pm - 9pm (last orders). Bar snacks served 12 noon - 10pm (last
orders). **Cuisine:** French and Scottish cuisine. Table d'hote lunch
and a la carte dinner menus. Also a good selection of bar meals.
⊨ 6 bedrooms, 2 en suite and 17 chalets (2 chalets specially
designed for disabled guests). **CC** Access, Visa. **Other Points:**
Children welcome. Afternoon teas. Dogs allowed. Watersports &
Activities centre. Special activity breaks. Fax No: (08873) 649. **P**
& **(V) Directions:** A827 to Kemore, then 500 yds along south side
of Loch Tay.

AMBROSE CHARLES BARRATT ☎ (08873) 236.

*A unique leisure village set in the beautiful hills of Perthshire
on the shores of Loch Tay. Comfortable accommodation in the
hotel and in luxury log chalets and good food with the choice of
good value bar menus or dinner in the elegant Garden
Restaurant. Relax and absorb the beauty and peace of Loch Tay
or enjoy the extensive choice of activities available on both land
and loch.*

KILFINAN Strathclyde **Map 10 B1**

⊗££ **KILFINAN HOTEL** Kilfinan, near Tighnabruaich.

Hours: Breakfast 7.30am - 9.30am, lunch 12 noon - 2.30pm,
dinner 7pm - 9.30pm. Bar meals from 12 noon - 2.30pm and 7pm
- 10pm. **Cuisine:** Local produce, fish, shellfish, game. ⊨ 11
bedrooms, all en suite. **CC** All major cards. **Other Points:** Children
welcome. No coaches. **P** **Directions:** Situated on B800 between
Strachur and Tignabruaich.

MR N K S WILLS ☎ (070 082) 201

*An ancient coaching inn, tastefully modernised. The hotel has
excellent stalking, clay pigeon shooting, golf and fishing as well
as swimming in the lochs and burns. Facilities for private
functions of up to 75.*

KILLIN Central **Map 10 A2**

⊗££ **CLACHAIG HOTEL** Gray Street, Falls of Dochart, Killin.
⌂££ **Hours:** Breakfast served from 8.15am until 9.15am, lunch from 12 noon - 2.30pm, dinner from 6.30pm - 9.30pm (last orders 9pm). Bar meals served from 12 noon - 3.30pm and from 5.30pm - 9.30pm. **Cuisine:** Trout, salmon, Highland beef steaks, venison. ⊨ 9 bedrooms, 8 ensuite. **CC** Access, Visa. **Other Points:** Access for disabled to bar & restaurant. Children welcome. Garden for guests use. Afternoon tea. Dogs allowed. **P** ⅃ **Directions:** On A827 beside Falls of Dochart.
JOHN MALLINSON ☎ (05672) 270.
A former 17th century coaching inn, overlooking the spectacular Falls of Dochart. The intimate and characterful restaurant offers a wide choice of quality food. Trout and salmon fishing is available on the hotel's private stretch of the River Dochart.

⊗££ **FALLS OF DOCHART HOTEL & RESTAURANT** Main
⌂££ Street, Killin.
Hours: Breakfast 8.30am - 9am, Dinner 7.30pm - 9pm (last orders 8.45pm). **Cuisine:** Fresh local produce including salmon, trout, steak, lamb and venison. Vegetarian meals. ⊨ 8 bedrooms, 6 en suite. Colour TV, duvets, central heating, tea/coffee facilities in all rooms. **CC** Access, Visa. **Other Points:** Children welcome. Dogs by arrangement. **P** **(V) Directions:** Off the A827 in Killin, signposted Falls of Dochart, Killin.
MR & MRS HECKINGBOTTOM & MR & MRS MARTIN ☎ (05672) 237.
A quiet, friendly hotel with a happy home from home atmosphere in an ideal touring location.

KILMARNOCK Strathclyde **Map 10 B2**

⊗££ **COFFEE CLUB** 30 Bank Street, Kilmarnock.
Hours: Open from 9.30am until 10pm (last orders 10pm). Sunday open from 12 noon - 5.30pm.rs for food 10pm. **Cuisine:** Fast food on ground floor, eg. American-style hamburgers. Downstairs, full service for special coffees, grills, omelettes, fish, pasta & vegetarian dishes. ⊨ None. **CC** Access, Visa. **Other Points:** Children welcome. No dogs. Bring your own wine (no corkage). Outside functions catered for. Small parties. **(V) Directions:** Bank St. is off John Finnie St, close to BR and Bus stations.
MESSRS S KAMMING & W MACDONALD ☎ (0563) 22048.
There is something for everyone here depending on your appetite, purse and time. There are three restaurants, with separate menus, all housed under one roof. The restaurants all have the same lively atmosphere and friendly staff. You may bring your own wine.

KILMELFORD Strathclyde **Map 10 A1**

⊗££ **CUILFAIL HOTEL** Kilmelford, Nr Oban.
⌂£££ **Hours:** Breakfast 8.30am - 9.30am, Dinner 6.30pm - 9.30pm (last orders). Bar meals 12 noon - 2.30pm and 6.30pm - 9.30pm. Open all year. **Cuisine:** Traditional Scottish cuisine. ⊨ 12 bedrooms, all en suite. **CC** Access, Visa. **Other Points:** Children welcome. Afternoon tea. No-smoking area. Dogs allowed. Residents' lounge. Garden. Fax No: (08522) 264. **P** **(V) Directions:** On the A816 in Kilmelford, 14 miles south of Oban.

Kilmelford continued
DAVID BIRRELL ☎ (08522) 274.
A former coaching inn, attractively swathed in ivy on the outside, the interior is cosy and welcoming. The menu is imaginative and offers a healthy alternative. An ideal location for touring the beautiful west coast of Scotland.

KILWINNING Strathclyde **Map 10 B1**
⊗££ **MONTGREENAN MANSION HOUSE HOTEL**
Montgreenan Estate, Kilwinning.
Hours: Breakfast from 7am - 10.30am, lunch 12 noon - 2.30pm and dinner 7pm - 9.30pm (last orders). Routiers-priced menu applies to lunches and bar meals. **Cuisine**: Fresh Scottish Fare. ⊨ 21 bedrooms, all en suite. **CC** All major cards. **Other Points**: Children welcome. **P** & **(V) Directions**: 4 miles north of Irvine on the A736.
THE DOBSON FAMILY ☎ (0294) 57733.
A magnificent 18th Century mansion with original brass and marble fireplaces and decorative plasterwork - its character carefully retained. Set in 45 acres of unspoilt parkland, there is tennis, croquet, golf, and billiards available. Excellent Scottish fare served in the restaurant.

KINCARDINE ON FORTH Fife **Map 10 B2**
⊗££ **THE UNICORN INN** 15 Excise Street, Kincardine-on-Forth.
⏍££ **Hours**: Lunch is served 12.15pm - 1.45pm (last orders 1.45pm), dinner 6pm - 9pm (last orders). Closed: Mondays and Tuesdays. **Cuisine**: Imaginative menu, shellfish a speciality, (received 1st place in the Sea Fish Industry Authority competition of 1991). ⊨ 4 bedrooms. **CC** Access, Visa. **Other Points**: Children welcome. **P** & **(V) Directions**: Just off A876(T) in the town centre.
DOUGLAS & LESLEY MITCH. ☎ (0259) 30704/30269.
An old coaching inn, located in the centre of the old town of Kincardine-On-Forth. Recently refurbished, the oak beams and low ceilings are decorated with oil paintings. Enjoying a cosy, welcoming atmosphere created by the great team work of the staff and proprietors. Serving 'excellent meals, beautifully cooked and served without fuss or flamboyance'. Highly recommended.

KINLOCH RANNOCH Tayside **Map 10 A2**
⊗£ **BUNRANNOCH HOUSE** Kinloch Rannoch, By Pitlochry.
⏍£ **Hours**: Breakfast 8am - 9am, dinner 7am - 9am. **Cuisine**: Scottish home cooking. House specialities - venison and salmon steaks. Homecooking and baking predominant. ⊨ 7 rooms. 1 single, 3 double, 1 twin and 2 family bedrooms. 2 en suite. **CC** Access, Visa. **Other Points**: Children welcome. Afternoon teas. Dogs allowed. Garden. No smoking area. Games room. **P** **(V) Directions**: Off the A9, signposted to Kinloch Rannoch.
JENNIFER SKEAPING ☎ (08822) 407.
This listed building was formerly a shooting lodge and is set in 2 acres of grounds. Providing comfortable accommodation in a warm atmosphere and serving good home cooked meals at value for money prices. A warm welcome and top quality Scottish homecooking and baking.

KINROSS Tayside **Map 11 B1**

⊗££ **BALGEDIE TOLL TAVERN** Wester Balgedie, Kinross.
Hours: Bar open 11am - 3pm and 5pm - 11pm. Lunch 12 noon - 2pm, Dinner 5.30pm - 9pm (last orders). Open 7 days a week. **Cuisine:** Comprehensive and imaginative menu with specials board - traditional dishes may include - prime Scottish steaks with various garnishes, salmon, ham. ⊨ None. **CC** Access, Visa. **Other Points:** Children welcome. Beer garden and patio area. Real ales. Fax No: (0592) 84626. **P** **(V) Directions:** 1 mile SE jct 8, M90. N shore of Loch Leven in fork of A911 & B919.
ALAN CHRISTIE ☎ (0592) 84212.
An original Toll House with open fires, wooden beams and brasses giving a pleasant old world feel. The homemade food is excellent and all guests are made to feel immediately welcome by the friendly and efficient staff. A very popular rendezvous with many visitors travelling from far afield to enjoy the good food and convivial atmosphere.

KIRKCALDY Fife **Map 11 B1**

⊗£ **CAFE CONTINENTAL** 6 Hill Place, Kirkcaldy.
Hours: Open from 10am - 11pm (last orders 10pm). **Cuisine:** Wide variety of food. Unusual menu items giving novel taste sensations, by use of good combinations of herbs and spices. ⊨ None **CC** Access, Visa. **Other Points:** Children welcome. Garden dining. Afternoon teas served. No smoking area. **P** & **(V) Directions:** Near Kirkcaldy town centre.
C STENHOUSE ☎ (0592) 641811.
French style cafe bar. Comfortably furnished in 1940's style decor. Casual dining with a la carte menu, bar snacks and meals. Large selection of dishes of well cooked and prepared meals with more than generous portions. A must for the more adventerous diner. Live entertainment e.g. Jazz Nights.

KIRKCUDBRIGHT Dumfries & Galloway **Map 10 C2**

⊗££ **SELKIRK ARMS HOTEL** Old High Street, Kirkcudbright.
⊞£££ **Hours:** 7.30am - 10am, 12 noon - 2pm, and 7pm - 9.30pm. Also open for Sunday lunch/dinner. **Cuisine:** Dishes include local seafood, mussels, beef, and a selection of cold meat, cheese and fruit platters. ⊨ 5 single, 3 twin, 5 double, and 2 family rooms, all en suite. **CC** All major cards. **Other Points:** Children welcome. Afternoon teas served. **P** & **(V)**
MR E J MORRIS ☎ (0557) 30402.
Family run hotel set in a picturesque town. Guests can enjoy friendly hospitality, with good food and comfortable accommodation. Free golf, squash, and salmon and trout fishing for residents. Short breaks also available at special rates.

KIRKMICHAEL Tayside **Map 11 A1**

⊗££ **THE LOG CABIN HOTEL** Kirkmichael, Perthshire.
⊞££ **Hours:** Breakfast 8.45am - 9.30am, lunch 12 noon - 2pm and dinner 7.30pm - 8.45pm (last orders). Open all year. **Cuisine:** Daily specials in the bar. Table d'hote evening menu, using fresh local produce. ⊨ 13 bedrooms, all en suite. **CC** All major cards. **Other Points:** Children welcome. Pets by arrangement. Garden. Ideal for disabled as the hotel is all on one level. **P** & **(V) Directions:** Off the A924.
ALAN FINCH & DAPHNE KIRK ☎ (025081) 288.

Kirkmichael continued

A large hotel built of whole Norwegian logs, set in the hills amidst a majestic pine forest. Family run, a definite apres ski atmosphere prevails in winter. A superb 5 course dinner can be enjoyed in the Edelweis restaurant, while the Viking Bar serves a comprehensive selection of bar meals. A unique base from which to explore the Perthshire area.

LARGS Strathclyde **Map 10 B1**

⊗££ **GLEN ELDON HOTEL** 2 Barr Crescent, Largs, Ayrshire.

⊡££ **Hours:** Restaurant open Monday to Friday 7pm - 7.45pm, Saturday 5pm - 9pm. Sunday 5pm - 7.45pm. High teas served at weekends. Closed: mid-January to mid-March. **Cuisine:** Scottish dishes including haggis, venison, salmon and daily specials. ⊨ 9 bedrooms, all en suite, with TVs and direct dial telephones. **CC** Access, Visa. **Other Points:** Children welcome. No dogs. Tele/Fax No: (0475) 673381. ⊡ **Directions:** On A78, mid way between Glasgow & Prestwick airports.

MARY PATON ☎ (0475) 673381/674094

Largs is a popular family seaside resort and the Glen Eldon Hotel caters for the needs of families on holiday. It is a family run establishment at the north end of Largs close to the sea front, swimming pool, sports centre and golf course and not far from the town centre.

⊗£££ **THE MANOR PARK HOTEL** Nr Largs, Skelmorlie.

⊡££££ **Hours:** Breakfast 7.30am - 10am, lunch 12.30pm - 2.30pm (2pm last orders), dinner 7pm - 10.30pm (9.30pm last orders). **Cuisine:** All menus cooked to order using only fresh ingredients. Scottish dishes a speciality. Bar meals, table d'hote plus extensive a la carte menu. ⊨ 2 single, 10 twin, 7 double, 3 suites. All en suite. **CC** All major cards. **Other Points:** Children welcome. 15 acres of well kept garden. Afternoon tea. Fax: (0475) 520832. ⊡ **(V)** **Directions:** Midway between Skelmorlie and Largs on the A78.

ALAN WILLIAMS ☎ (0475) 520832.

A well-kept, Grade B listed mansion house hotel with many architectural features, beautifully set in 15 acres of landscaped gardens on the coast overloking the islands of the Forth Clyde. Good food and accommodation make this an ideal base from which to tour, play golf or sail.

LEADBURN Lothian **Map 11 B1**

⊗££ **THE LEADBURN INN** Leadburn, West Linton.

⊡££ **Hours:** Breakfast 7am - 9am, dinner 6pm - 10pm (last orders). Bar meals served all day from 11am - 10pm. **Cuisine:** Local game dishes, spare ribs, homemade lasagne, Madras curry, pork stroganoff, halibut. ⊨ 7 bedrooms, 2 en suite. **CC** All major cards. **Other Points:** Children welcome. Pets allowed. ⊡ 占 **(V)** **Directions:** At the junction of the A701 and A703.

LINDA & ALAN THOMSON ☎ (0968) 72952.

A country style hotel set in the beautiful Borders region. The Carriage Restaurant, aptly named, is a luxurious converted railway carriage which recreates the glory of the early trains. Only 25 minutes drive from the centre of Edinburgh, the hotel is popular with business people.

LOCHEARNHEAD Central **Map 10 A2**

⊗££ **LOCHEARNHEAD HOTEL** Lochside, Lochearnhead.

⌂££ **Hours:** Breakfast 8.30am - 9.30am, Lunch 11.00am - 2.30am and Dinner 7.00pm - 9.30pm (last orders 9.00pm). **Cuisine:** A la carte and 3 course fixed menus. French. ⊨ 14 rooms, 4 en suite. **CC** All major cards. **Other Points:** Children welcome. Teas. Dogs allowed. Garden. **P** **(V)**
ANGUS CAMERON ☎ (05673) 229
This small country house beside Loch Earn forms part of a lochside watersports development offering such sports as sailing, waterskiing and wind surfing. Coupled with the friendly atmosphere of the hotel and the superb home cooking this is a perfect place for water sport enthusiasts of all ages.

LOCHGILPHEAD Strathclyde **Map 10 B1**

⊗££ **LOCHGAIR HOTEL** Lochgair, nr Lochgilphead.

⌂£££ **Hours:** Breakfast 8.30am - 9.30am, dinner 7pm - 8.30pm. Bar meals 12.15pm - 2.15pm and 6.15pm - 9pm. Morning coffee and afternoon tea. **Cuisine:** International dishes. Local game and seafood are the specialities. Good value for money table d'hote menu. ⊨ 14 bedrooms, 8 en suite. **CC** Access, Visa. **Other Points:** Children welcome. Garden dining. Afternoon teas. No dogs. No smoking area. Residents lounge. Sheltered anchorage for yachts on Loch Gair. **P** **(V) Directions:** On A83 Glasgow - Campbeltown rd. 7 miles north of Lochgilphead.
JOHN & ELSIE GALLOWAY ☎ (0546) 86333.
A family run hotel offering a warm welcome to all discerning travellers who enjoy good food in friendly, comfortable surroundings. Situated in the village of Lochgair, only 200 yds from the Loch, the hotel enjoys wonderful views. Ideal base for exploring the West Highlands & islands. Activities include trout fishing, sea angling, pony trekking, golf and sailing.

⊗££ **STAG HOTEL** Argyll Street, Lochgilphead.

⌂£££ **Hours:** Breakfast 7.30am - 9.30am, Lunch 12 noon - 2.30pm, Dinner 7pm - 9pm. Bar meals 12 noon - 2.30pm and 6pm - 8.30pm. **Cuisine:** Traditional Scottish cuisine and bar meals. ⊨ 17 bedrooms, all en suite. **CC** Access, Visa. **Other Points:** Residents' lounge. Dogs allowed. Public and lounge bars. Sauna. Solarium. Afternoon teas. ⅋ **(V) Directions:** A83, A816. Loch Lomond to Inverary - 23 miles to Lochgilphead.
JOYCE & BILL ROSS, HEATHER & DREW MCGLYNN ☎ (0546) 2496.
A family run, modern hotel, ideally situated in scenic Argyll for a touring, residential holiday or break. Good food and comfortable accommodation in a relaxed, informal atmosphere.

LOCKERBIE Dumfries & Galloway **Map 10 C2**

⊗££ **SOMERTON HOUSE HOTEL** 35 Carlisle Road, Lockerbie.

⌂£££ **Hours:** 8am - 9am, 12 noon - 2pm, and 7pm - 9pm. Sunday lunch 12 noon - 2pm, and 7pm - 9pm. **Cuisine:** Dishes such as saute of beef stroganoff, lamb cooked with yoghurt and apricots, and Scottish salmon. ⊨ 1 single, 2 twin, 2 double, and 2 family rooms, all en suite. **CC** Access, Visa, AmEx. **Other Points:** Children welcome. Pets allowed. No smoking in certain areas. **P** **(V) Directions:** On edge of Lockerbie, 1/2m from M74.
MR & MRS FERGUSON ☎ (05762) 2583/2384.

Lockerbie continued

Victorian mansion built of local stone, standing in its own grounds 300 yds from main M6/A74. It is a family run hotel and restaurant, with a well-earned reputation for good food and accommodation. International a la carte menu and 'Taste of Scotland', real ales and interesting bar meals.

LUSS Strathclyde **Map 10 B2**

⊗£ **THE INVERBEG INN** Loch Lomond, A82, near Luss.
Hours: Bar meals served 9am - 10.30pm. Dinner in the restaurant 6.30pm - 9.30pm. **Cuisine:** Chef's special Fish bowl, Fillet steak Glen Douglas (stuffed with fresh salmon), Entrecote Tam O'Shanter (whisky-based sauce). Fresh seafood daily. ⊨ 14 bedrooms, 7 en suite. ◨ Access, Visa, AmEx. **Other Points:** Limited access for disabled. No dogs in public rooms. Children welcome. Fax No: (043 686) 678. ◨ **(V) Directions:** 3 miles past Luss on A82.
MR JACK BISSET ☎ (043 686) 678.
The Inverbeg is well situated for tourists visiting the North West of Scotland. Offers good food at reasonable prices.

MILNATHORT Tayside **Map 11 B1**

⊗£ **THE THISTLE HOTEL** 25-27 New Road, Milnathort.
⟐£££ **Hours:** Breakfast 8am - 9am, Lunch 12 noon - 2pm, Dinner 6pm - 9pm (last orders). Bar meals 12 noon - 2pm, 6pm - 9pm. Closed: 1st January each year. High teas Saturday and Sunday 5pm - 6.30pm. **Cuisine:** Specialities include steaks and homemade pate. A la carte and bar meals. ⊨ 4 bedrooms, 2 en suite. ◨ Access, Visa. **Other Points:** Children welcome. Dogs allowed. ◨ ⌕ **(V) Directions:** Junction 6 M90. A91 Perth - Stirling Road in Milnathort.
MR J. HARLEY (MR A. QUINN - Manager) ☎ (0577) 63222.
A small, residential country inn in a rural setting, only one and a half miles from Kinross and M90 junction. Under the personal supervision of the managers, Mr and Mrs Quinn, The Thistle Hotel provides welcoming, friendly service and good food in the lounge bar and in the restaurant at weekends.

MOFFAT Dumfries & Galloway **Map 10 C2**

⊗£ **BALMORAL HOTEL** High Street, Moffat.
⟐£££ **Hours:** Breakfast 8am - 9.30am, dinner 6pm - 9.30pm (last orders 9pm). Bar meals 12 noon - 2pm and 6pm - 9pm. **Cuisine:** Traditional Scottish, English and French dishes. Specialities include venison, fresh salmon, fillet steak and swordfish and shark steaks. ⊨ 16 bedrooms, 6 en suite. ◨ Access, Visa. **Other Points:** Children welcome. Dogs welcome. Residents' lounge. Fax No: (0683) 20451. ◨ ⌕ **(V) Directions:** A701, main street in Moffat.
B STOKES & FAMILY ☎ (0683) 20288
Set in the picturesque Annan Valley, the Balmoral Hotel was once a Coaching Inn and frequented by Robert Burns. It is now a friendly, family owned hotel offering comfortable accommodation, fine cuisine and welcoming, friendly service. There is a wide choice of dishes and all offer very good value. Ideal place to relax in attractive surroundings and a warm, family atmosphere.

Moffat continued

⊗££ **BUCCLEUCH ARMS HOTEL** High Street, Moffat.
⏰£££ **Hours:** Breakfast 7.30am - 9am, Lunch 12 noon - 2pm, Dinner 6pm - 9pm (or later). Bar meals 12 noon - 2pm, 6pm - 9pm (or later). Closed: Christmas Day. **Cuisine:** Speciality - Charcoal grilled Scotch steaks. Other dishes may include Local trout, Scotch wild salmon, Steak Tartar. ⊨ 11 bedrooms, all en suite. **CC** Access, Visa, AmEx. **Other Points:** Children welcome. Afternoon teas. Garden. Taste of Scotland. Pets allowed. STB - 3 crowns recommended. Off street parking. **(V) Directions:** Turn right off A74 at Moffat Junction. 2 miles to Moffat. A701.
BILL & HILARY JORDON-WHITE ☎ (0683) 20003.
Built in 1760 as a Coaching Inn, the Buccleuch Arms lies in the centre of Moffat. Recently refurbished, the accommodation is of a high standard and the restaurant offers a good selection of dishes using predominantly fresh, local produce. The speciality of the restaurant is their charcoal grilled steaks. Golf, fishing, pony trekking and walking nearby.

⊗£ **THE STAR HOTEL** 44 High Street, Moffat.
⏰£££ **Hours:** Breakfast 8am - 9.30am, lunch 12 noon - 2.30pm (last orders 2.15pm). Dinner 5.30pm - 9pm (last orders 8.45pm). Closes at 10pm. **Cuisine:** Wide and varied menu, daily specials. ⊨ 9 rooms. 2 twin, 5 double and 2 family bedrooms. All en suite. **CC** Access, Visa. **Other Points:** Children welcome. Afternoon teas. Dogs allowed. Coach parties catered for. Wedding and conference facilities. **(V)**
MR HOUSE & MR LEIGHFIELD ☎ (0683) 20156.
Although this hotel is listed in the Guiness Book of Records as the narrowest detached hotel, the interior and welcome is heartwarming and wholesome. If you enjoy good food at great value prices in splendidly comfortable surroundings then this is the place for you.

⊗££ **WELL VIEW HOTEL** Ballplay Road, Moffat.
⏰£££ **Hours:** Breakfast 8am - 9am, lunch 12.30pm - 1.30pm, dinner 7pm - 8.30pm. Lunch must be booked a day in advance. **Cuisine:** Scottish and continental dishes. 5 course dinner menu. ⊨ 7 bedrooms, 5 en suite. **CC** Access, Visa. **Other Points:** Children welcome. Afternoon teas. Dogs allowed. No smoking area. Garden. Residents' lounge. ▯ **(V) Directions:** A708 out of Moffat. Pass Fire Station and take first left.
JOHN SCHUCKARDT ☎ (0683) 20184.
A small, privately owned hotel which overlooks the town and the surrounding hills. Originally built in 1864, the Well View has been beautifully converted and offers a high standard in every aspect. The 5 course dinner menu provides excellent value for money and the welcome and service are both friendly and helpful.

MOTHERWELL Strathclyde **Map 10 B2**
⊗£££ **THE MOORINGS HOUSE HOTEL** 114 Hamilton Road,
⏰£££ Motherwell.
Hours: Breakfast 7am - 9am, lunch and bar meals 12 noon - 2pm, dinner and bar meals 6.30pm - 9pm (last orders). **Cuisine:** Table d'hote and a la carte meals. Classic French cooking with an accent on the unusual. ⊨ 14 bedrooms, all en suite. 5 Executive and 9

Motherwell continued

Standard rooms. **CC** Access, Visa, AmEx. **Other Points:** Children welcome. Afternoon teas. Dogs allowed. Garden. **P** & **(V)** **Directions:** Motherwell exit off M74. 500 yards past Strathclyde Country Park.

DAVID KERR ☎ (0698) 58131.

A family run hotel dating from the 1880's, offering a warm, relaxed atmosphere. The restaurant is in keeping with the original house and guests can choose from a wide selection of international dishes. All food is prepared under the supervision of the head chef who uses fresh Scottish produce whenever possible. The meals offer good value for money, particularly at lunchtime.

NEW GALLOWAY Dumfries & Galloway **Map 10 C2**

⊗£ **THE SMITHY** The High Street, New Galloway, ⅏£ Kirkcudbrightshire.

CLUB **Hours:** Open 7 days a week from 1st March to 31st October. Opening times from 1st March to Easter 10am - 6pm, Easter to end May 10am - 8pm, 1st June - end September 10am - 9pm, 1st October - end October 10am - 7.30pm. **Cuisine:** Home baking and cooking, trout in wine with almonds, homemade oatcakes & cheese, range of Scottish pates including wild garlic, smoked salmon, venison. ⯇ 2 bedrooms, 1 bathroom. **CC** None. **Other Points:** Children welcome. Coaches by appointment. Scottish wines. **P** & **(V) Directions:** On the A762 to Kirkcudbright.

MR & MRS McPHEE ☎ (06442) 269.

As the name implies, this is a converted blacksmith's shop. It also houses a craft shop and B&B accommodation in an attached cottage. In the summer guests may dine outside by the Mill Burn that flows through the property. Official Tourist Information agency on behalf of the Dumfries & Galloway Tourist Board.

NEWCASTLETON Borders **Map 11 C1**

⊗££ **COPSHAW KITCHEN RESTAURANT** 4 North Hermitage Street, Newcastleton.

Hours: Meals served 9.30am - 6pm and 7.30pm - 9pm. Closed January, February and Tuesdays. **Cuisine:** Varied and interesting menu, featuring Chef's Daily Choice, Scotch Gravadlax with cucumber & a mustard/drill dressing (Scandinavian sugar method). ⯇ None. **CC** Access, Visa. **Other Points:** Children welcome. Afternoon teas. **P** & **(V) Directions:** Off B6357.

JANE ELLIOTT ☎ (03873) 75250/75233.

A stone built double-fronted antique shop, cafe and restaurant, offering a varied and interesting menu of well cooked tasty dishes, prepared by very well qualified and competent chef proprietor Jane Elliott. A friendly family run establishment that offers an exceptional range of facilities. Friendly attentive service in a pleasant relaxing atmosphere.

NEWTON STEWART Dumfries & Galloway **Map 10 C2**

⊗£ **CROWN HOTEL** 101 Queen Street, Newton Stewart. ⅏££ **Hours:** Breakfast 8am - 9.30am, lunch 12 noon - 2.30pm and dinner 6.30pm - 8.30pm (last orders). Bar meals 12 noon - 2.30pm and 6pm - 9pm. **Cuisine:** A wide range of bar meals - chilli, curry, roast chicken, steaks. ⯇ 10 bedrooms, 6 en suite. **CC** Access, Visa.

Newton Stewart continued

> Other Points: Children welcome. No pets. No smoking area. ▣ &
> **Directions:** On the southern outskirts of town.
> MR & MRS PRISE ☎ (0671) 2727.
> *An attractive, cream, listed building carefully modernised in keeping with the character. The Crown Hotel has two private rods on the River Cree - a prime Salmon river - and several salmon dishes on the menu as a result!*

OBAN Strathclyde **Map 10 A1**

⊗££ **FALLS OF LORA HOTEL** Connel Ferry, by Oban.

▥£££ **Hours:** Meals from 8am - 9.30am, 12.30pm - 2pm and 7pm - 8pm.
CLUB Bar/Bistro meals 12.30pm - 2pm and 5pm - 9.30pm (last orders). Closed: Christmas and New Year's Day. **Cuisine:** Sunday presentation buffet, Thursday 7 course Scottish dinner. ▭ 30 bedrooms, all en suite. 2 bathrooms. Colour TV and telephone. ▨ All major cards. **Other Points:** Children welcome. Fax No: (0631 71) 694. ▣ & **(V) Directions:** Set back from A85, 5 miles before Oban, ½ mile from Connel Bridge.
MRS C M WEBSTER ☎ (0631 71) 483.
An imposing Victorian building in its own grounds set back from the A85. 100 yards from Connel railway station and overlooks Loch Etive. The cocktail bar has a roaring log fire and over 100 whiskies to tempt you.

▥££ **LOCH ETIVE HOTEL** Connel Village, nr Oban, Argyll.

CLUB ▭ 3 double, 1 twin and 2 family bedrooms, 4 with en suite facilities. Colour TV, radio alarms and tea/coffee making facilities in all rooms. **Hours:** Breakfast 8.15am - 9am and dinner 7pm - 7.30pm. Closed: October to March inclusive. ▨ None. **Other Points:** Central heating. Children welcome. Dogs allowed. Licensed. Residents' lounge. ▣ **Directions:** 100 yds from the A85 in Connel Village.
MISS FRANCOISE WEBER ☎ (0631 71) 400.
A stone cottage style building, modernised to a high standard, and set in its own gardens bordered by a small river. The hotel derives its name from the nearby Loch Etive - and several of the rooms have views over the loch. Traditional Scottish hospitality is found here.

LOWLANDS & SCOTTISH BORDERS

PAISLEY Strathclyde **Map 10 B2**

⊗££ **BRABLOCH HOTEL** 62 Renfrew Road, Paisley.

⑪££££**Hours:** Breakfast 7am - 10am, Lunch 12 noon - 2pm and Dinner 7.30pm - 10pm (last orders). **Cuisine:** A la carte, Table d'hote and Bar menus. French/English - Duck a l'orange, Scampi Provincal. ⊨ 30 bedrooms, all en suite. **CC** Access, Visa. **Other Points:** Children welcome. Garden. Afternoon teas. No smoking area. **P** � **(V) Directions:** On A741. Less than a mile south of M8 (junction 27).

LEWIS GRANT ☎ (041) 889 5577.

This pretty mansion house is set in 4 acres of land, conveniently situated within two miles of Glasgow airport, on the outskirts of Paisley. The restaurant serves a good selection of French and English cuisine, accompanied by a wide selection of wines.

⊗££ **STAKIS PAISLEY WATERMILL HOTEL** Lonend, Paisley.

⑪££££**Hours:** Breakfast 7am - 10am, lunch 12 noon - 3pm (last orders
CLUB 2.30pm) and dinner 5pm - 10pm (last orders). **Cuisine:** Traditional English, including steak and roast specialities. ⊨ 51 rooms. 12 single, 29 twin, 8 double and 2 family bedrooms, all en suite. **CC** All major cards. **Other Points:** Children welcome. Garden. Afternoon teas. Pets allowed. No smoking areas. **P (V) Directions:** Junction 27 off M8 motorway, following signs for East Kilbride.

THOMAS GRAHAM - General Manager ☎ (041) 8893201.

A converted riverside mill house dating from 1680, this hotel provides first class comfortable accommodation with good value menus in pleasant surroundings. The original mill wheels form the centre piece of the restaurant. The hotel is situated in the centre of Paisley facing the Abbey and within easy reach of Glasgow Airport.

PEEBLES Borders **Map 11 B1**

⊗£££ **CRINGLETIE HOUSE HOTEL** Eddleston, Peebles.

⑪££££**Hours:** Meals from 8.15am - 9.15am, 1pm - 1.45pm and 7.30pm -
🍵 8.30pm. Closed: 2 January until 6 March 1992. Re-open 7th March 1992. **Cuisine:** Frequently changing menu - all home cooking. Afternoon tea including home baking. ⊨ 13 bedrooms, all en suite. **CC** Access, Visa. **Other Points:** Children welcome. Smoking discouraged in the dining room. Fax No: (07213) 244. **P (V) Directions:** On the Edinburgh/Peebles road (A703), 2.5 miles north of Peebles.

STANLEY & AILEEN MAGUIRE ☎ (07213) 233.

Cringletie is a distinguished mansion house set well back in 28 acres of gardens and woodlands. Resident proprietors provide interesting and imaginative food, with fruit and vegetables in season from the hotel's extensive kitchen garden, which is featured in The Gourmet Garden by Geraldene Holt.

⊗££ **KINGSMUIR HOTEL** Springhill Road, Peebles.

⑪££££**Hours:** Breakfast 8.30am - 9.30am, lunch 12 noon - 2pm and dinner 7pm - 9pm (last orders). Bar meals 12 noon - 2pm and 7pm - 9.30pm. Closed: Christmas and New Years Day. **Cuisine:** Homemade soups, roasts, steak pie, sea and river fish, homemade desserts. ⊨ 10 bedrooms, all en suite. **CC** Access, Visa, AmEx. **Other Points:** Children welcome. Dogs allowed. Conference facilities. **P** � **(V) Directions:** High St, then south over Tweed Bridge, Springhill Rd ½ mile on right.

Peebles continued

ELIZABETH, NORMAN & MAY KERR ☎ (0721) 20151.

A charming country house, built in the 1850s and set in leafy grounds in a quiet area, yet only 5 minutes walk through parkland to the High Street. The resident proprietors take great pride in their Taste of Scotland cuisine, to the delight of the many guests who have dined or stayed there.

⊗££ **PARK HOTEL** Innerleithen Road, Peebles.
⫏£££ **Hours:** Breakfast 8am - 10am, lunch 12 noon - 2pm, dinner 7pm - 9.30pm. Bar snacks 12 noon - 2pm and 7pm - 9pm. **Cuisine:** Traditional cuisine featuring local produce such as smoked Scottish salmon and fresh local trout. ⊨ 25 bedrooms, all en suite. ᴄᴄ All major cards. **Other Points:** Dogs allowed. Afternoon teas. Garden. Lounge. Use of facilities at the Peebles Hydro Hotel including tennis, squash, pool and sauna. ▯ ⅍ **(V) Directions:** On the A72 south of Edinburgh.

PEEBLES HOTEL HYDRO PATHIC LTD ☎ (0721) 20451

A friendly hotel on the outskirts of Peebles, overlooking the River Tweed. Guests can enjoy attractive gardens, well-appointed bedrooms and the popular hotel restaurant. When available, guests can also benefit from the facilities at the Peebles Hydro Hotel (only 700 yards away) - leisure centre with pool, saunas and jacuzzi; squash courts; tennis courts and riding.

⊗£££ **PEEBLES HOTEL HYDRO** Innerleithen Road, Peebles.
⫏££££ **Hours:** Breakfast 8am - 9.30am, Lunch 12.45pm - 2pm, Dinner 7.30pm - 9pm (last orders). Bar snacks 12 noon - 3.30pm. **Cuisine:** Table d'hote dinner menu using local produce eg. Roast leg of Border lamb with a corriander sauce. Separate vegetarian menu. ⊨ 137 bedrooms, all en suite. ᴄᴄ All major cards. **Other Points:** Children welcome. No smoking area. Garden. Bubbles Health Club. Full range of indoor & outdoor sports & leisure facilities. Fax: (0721) 22999. ▯ **(V) Directions:** On the A72, Peebles to Galashiels road.

PEEBLES HOTEL HYDRO LTD ☎ (0721) 20602.

Few hotels offer facilities comparable to the Peebles Hydro. A 'resort' hotel with a full range of indoor and outdoor recreation facilities. There is a superb range of top value holiday packages all year round. Friendly staff and a warm welcome await you and the quality of the food is excellent. Magnificent grounds of 30 acres. Sister to the Park Hotel, also in Peebles.

⊗£ **THE GEORGE HOTEL** Galashiels Road, Walkerburn, Peebles.
⫏££ **Hours:** Breakfast 7.30am - 9.15am, Lunch 12 noon - 3pm, Dinner
CLUB 6pm - 9pm (last orders). **Cuisine:** Home cooking. Dishes may include Steak Pie, Lasagne, Chlli, Steaks, Vegetarian dishes. ⊨ 8 bedrooms, all with private shower, colour TV and tea/coffee making facilities. ᴄᴄ None. **Other Points:** Children welcome. Afternoon teas. Garden dining. Dogs allowed. No smoking aea. Residents lounge and garden. ▯ ⅍ **(V) Directions:** From Peebles take the A72 towards Galashiels for about 8 - 10 miles.

LYNDA & STEWART FORSYTH ☎ (0896 87) 336.

An attractive, family run hotel with excellent accommodation and a warm and friendly welcome. The George has a good reputation for offering carefully prepared fresh food. The hotel

LOWLANDS & SCOTTISH BORDERS

Peebles continued

overlooks the River Tweed, one of Scotland's most famous salmon and trout fishing rivers. An ideal area for anglers, golfers and hill walkers.

⊗££ **VENLAW CASTLE HOTEL** Peebles, Tweeddale.
⏠££ **Hours:** Breakfast 8.30am - 9.30am, dinner 7pm - 8pm. Closed: November - March. **Cuisine:** Dishes include baked salmon served with Hollandaise sauce, aubergine bake served with green salad. ⊨ 1 single, 4 twin, 4 double and 3 family bedrooms. 9 en suite. ▣ All major cards. **Other Points:** Childen welcome. Garden. No smoking areas. Dogs allowed. Residents coctail bar and separate lounge. ▱ **(V)**
MR & MRS CUMMING ☎ (0721) 20384.

Venlaw Castle, on the slopes of the Moorfoot Hills yet within five minutes from the centre of Peebles, is a family-owned hotel run in the country manner with the accent on personal attention. Reputed for their good quality home cooked dishes, using only the freshest produce, and for providing excellent accommodation, you will find the hospitality of the Cumming Family outstanding.

PERTH Tayside **Map 11 A1**
⊗£££ **NEWTON HOUSE HOTEL** Glencarse, nr Perth.
⏠££££ **Hours:** Breakfast 7.30am - 9.30am, Lunch 12 noon - 2pm, Dinner 6.30pm - 9pm (last orders). Bar snacks 12 noon - 2pm and 5pm - 9pm. **Cuisine:** Fresh, local produce prepared with a Scottish/French flavour by chef Sandra Pollock, finalist 1991 Scottish Chef of the year Competition. ⊨ 10 bedrooms, all en suite. ▣ All major cards. **Other Points:** Children welcome. No smoking area. Afternoon teas. Meetings, seminars and functions catered for. Fax No: (073 886) 717. Garden. ▱ **(V) Directions:** Set back from the A85, 4 miles from Perth, 13 miles from Dundee.
GEOFFREY & CAROL TALLIS ☎ (073 886) 250.

The Newton House Hotel is a former Dower House (circa 1840) and an ideal location to explore the dramatic countryside or numerous places of interest such as Scone Place, Glamis Castle or World famous golf courses. 'Old fashioned hospitality' is the standard of service set by the resident proprietors whilst enjoying excellent accommodation, fine food and wines.

⊗££ **THE TAYSIDE HOTEL** Stanlely, Nr Perth.
⏠££££ **Hours:** Breakfast 8am - 9am, lunch 12.30pm - 2pm, dinner 7pm -
CLUB 9pm (8.30pm during winter). **Cuisine:** À la carte, Table d'hote. Traditional English. Bar meals/snacks. ⊨ 17 rooms: 3 single, 3 double, 9 twin and 2 family bedrooms. 14 en suite. ▣ Access, Visa. **Other Points:** Children welcome. Afternoon teas. Dogs allowed. ▱ **(V) Directions:** Perth By-Pass A9 North, first exit to Stanley B9099.
The Manager ☎ (0738) 828249.

This Edwardian Hotel offers warm and comfortable accommodation. The Restaurant has both an a la Carte and Table d'Hote menu which features a freshly Roasted 'Plat du Jour', usually a prime Scottish joint. The lounge bar boasts a selection of over 100 varieties of Scottish Malt Whiskys. Ideal centre for touring. Fishing, Shooting and Golfing can all be arranged through the hotel.

PITLOCHRY Tayside **Map 10 A2**

⊗£££ **GREEN PARK HOTEL** Clunie Bridge Road, Pitlochry.

🏠£££ **Hours:** Bar meals from 12 noon - 2pm and 7pm - 9pm. Dinner from 6.30pm - 8.30pm. Children's teas available on request. Closed: November to mid-March. **Cuisine:** Scottish cuisine, eg. salmon, venison, Highland bonnets. 🛏 37 bedrooms, all en suite. **CC** Access, Visa. **Other Points:** Children welcome. No dogs. Switch cards also accepted. **P** ᕫ **Directions:** On the A924 in north-west Pitlochry, on the left as you leave town.
MR & MRS GRAHAM BROWN ☎ (0796) 3248.
This is a country house hotel situated on the banks of the lovely Loch Faskally and although secluded it is only five minutes walk from the centre of the town. Popular with golfers because of the nearby golf course. Other facilities include fishing, sailing and walking. Casserole Award winner 1990.

⊗££ **SCOTLAND'S HOTEL** Bonnethill Road, Pitlochry.

🏠£££ **Hours:** Breakfast 7.30am - 9.30am, Lunch 12 noon - 2pm, Dinner 6.30pm - 8.30pm. **Cuisine:** A la carte and fixed 3 course menu. Speciality - salmon. 🛏 8 single, 26 twin, 13 double and 13 family bedrooms, all en suite. **CC** All major cards. **Other Points:** Children welcome. Garden. Afternoon teas. Dogs allowed. Child listening system. Washing & ironing room. Fax (0769) 3284. **P** ᕫ **(V)** **Directions:** Half mile from Pitlochry.
MR PENKER ☎ (0769) 2292.
Scotland's Hotel has a good reputation for its fine food and service. It is ideally situated close to the main town centre and other amenities such as the golf couce and curling ring. A convenient place to stay if you wish to visit the Theatre of one of the many other entertainments in the town.

⊗££ **WELLWOOD HOTEL** West Moulin Road, Pitlochry.

🏠£££ **Hours:** Breakfast 8am - 9.30am and dinner 6pm - 10pm (last orders). Meals served all day from 11am - 11pm. Bar and business lunches. **Cuisine:** Imaginative Scottish cooking using fresh produce include choice of 14 main dishes. Vegetarian dishes are a speciality. 🛏 11 bedrooms, 8 en suite. Tea/coffee making facilities, TV and video network, private telephone, early morning call and baby listening service. **CC** All major cards. **Other Points:** Children welcome. Afternoon teas served. Two lounges, cosy bar and elegant restaurant. **P** ᕫ **(V)** **Directions:** Quiet location 200 yards from town centre.
WILMA & TIM EDWARDS ☎ (0796) 2879/2247.
Set in 2 acres of private gardens, 200 yards from the town centre, this imposing stone built mansion offers quiet surroundings, comfortable accommodation and a friendly welcome by the resident owner and his wife. A good menu offers freshly cooked, attractively served food.

PUTECHANTUY Strathclyde **Map 10 B1**

⊗££ **PUTECHAN LODGE HOTEL** nr Campbeltown, Kintyre,

🏠££ Argyll.
Hours: Breakfast 8am - 10am, coffee from 10am - 12 noon, lunch from 12 noon - 2pm, teas from 3pm - 5pm, dinner 7.15pm - 9.30pm. Closed: mid-January to end February. Routiers-priced menu applies to bar meals. **Cuisine:** Fillet steak gourmet, scampi a la creme, Highland steak, lobster Thermidor almondine. 🛏 12

Putechantuy continued

bedrooms, 10 en suite. **CC** Access, Visa, Diners. **Other Points:** Well-behaved children and pets welcome. **P** &

THE MOLL FAMILY ☎ (05832) 266.

A former shooting lodge, converted to a small, comfortable hotel, facing the Atlantic on the west coast of beautiful Kintyre. An ideal centre for walking, fishing, shooting, birdwatching and for visiting the Inner Hebrides.

RENFREW Strathclyde **Map 10 B2**

⊗££ **GLYNHILL HOTEL & LEISURE CLUB** 169 Paisley Road, Renfrew.

Hours: Breakfast 7am - 10am, lunch 12 noon - 2.30pm (last orders) and dinner 6pm - 10.30pm (last orders). **Cuisine:** The Palm Court Carverie: wide selection of starters, prime roasts, altern- ative hot dishes. Le Gourmet Rest: varied daily table d'hote, full a la carte. 125 luxury bedrooms, all en suite. **CC** All major cards. **Other Points:** Children welcome. Pets by arrangement, Non smoking areas. Leisure complex: indoor swimming pool, spa, sauna, gym, steam room, solaria etc. **P (V) Directions:** Jct. 27/M8, off the A741 Paisley - Renfrew Road.

HARRY NICHOLAS ☎ (041) 8865555.

A luxurious hotel offering every facility imaginable. Situated in two and half acres, The Glynhill is ideally located being 1 mile from Glasgow Airport and 7 miles from Glasgow City Centre. Providing luxury bedrooms and excellent menus in their Palm Court Carverie or Le Gourmet Restaurant: Friday & Saturday dinner & dance, you will find the hospitality here outstanding.

⊗££ **RISTORANTE PICCOLO MONDO** 63 Hairst Street, Renfrew.

Hours: Lunch 12 noon - 2.15pm, Dinner 7pm - 11pm (last orders). Closed: Sundays and Public Holidays. **Cuisine:** Italian/French cuisine - veal, steak, chicken, pasta and shellfish dishes. None. **CC** All major cards. **Other Points:** Children welcome. No dogs. & **(V) Directions:** 5 miles from Glasgow city centre in the centre of Renfrew.

MR R J BRUCE ☎ (041) 886 3055.

This bustling Italian restaurant is fast gaining an excellent reputation for its imaginative and extensive menu which offers exceptionally good value for money. Live entertainment and dancing every Wednesday, Friday and Saturday helps this restaurant to be one of the most popular Italian restaurants in the west of Scotland. Highly recommended.

ROSLIN Lothian **Map 11 B1**

⊗££ **OLD ORIGINAL INN** Roslin.

Hours: Meals from 7.30am - 9.30am, 12 noon - 2pm and 6pm - 10pm (5pm - 10pm at weekends). **Cuisine:** Grills, daily specials such as Salmon Vol au vents, Grilled Spring Lamb, Walnut Sundae. 6 bedrooms all en suite. **CC** Access, Visa, AmEx. **Other Points:** Children welcome. Coaches by appointment. **P** & **(V) Directions:** Just off A701, just outside Edinburgh.

MR G A HARRIS ☎ (031) 440 2384.

This historic inn was first opened in 1827 and has remained open for business ever since. The village is in a rural area and the inn's old fashioned decor gives it a charming atmosphere.

ROSYTH Fife **Map 10 B2**

⊗££ **GLAYDER INN** Heath Road, Ridley Drive, Rosyth.

☐££ **Hours:** Breakfast 7am - 9.30am, lunch 12 noon - 2pm and dinner 7pm - 9.30pm (last orders 9.30pm). Bar meals 12 noon - 2pm and 7pm - 9.30pm. **Cuisine:** Table d'hote menu including traditional dishes. 🛏 21 bedrooms, all en suite. **CC** Access, Visa, AmEx. **Other Points:** Children welcome. No smoking area. Fax: (0383) 411728 Function suite also available. Dogs allowed in rooms only. **P** & **(V) Directions:** From M90 jct 1 towards Kincardine Bridge, Ridley Drive on left.

JANET & JIM INNES ☎ (0383) 419977.

A modern, purpose built hotel with up to date facilities to match. The best of Scottish hospitality is extended to all guests whether they are staying over night, dining or having a drink. Good value for money.

ROTHESAY Isle of Bute **Map 10 B1**

⊗££ **ARDMORY HOUSE HOTEL** Ardmory Road, Ardbeg, ☐££ Rothesay.

Hours: Breakfast 8.30am - 9.30am or by arrangement, Dinner 7pm - 10pm. Bar suppers also served 7pm - 10pm. **Cuisine:** Extensive and varied menus using fresh, local produce. Eg. Local fillet steak in a spicy wine sauce, topped with pate and mushrooms; Salmon Hollandaise. 🛏 5 bedrooms, all en suite. **CC** Access, Visa. **Other Points:** Children welcome. Residents' lounge. Garden. 2 lounge bars. S.T.B. 3 Crown Commended. **P Directions:** 1 mile north of Rothesay Pier overlooking the bay.

NEIL HADDON ☎ (0700) 502346.

A privately owned hotel set in a large garden with beautiful views over Rothesay and Loch Stiven. Dating from 1833, the hotel has been tastefully appointed to ensure comfort, but retain its character. The restaurant (open evenings only) has an excellent reputation locally and outstanding panoramic views. Good food and comfortable accommodation at good value for money.

SELKIRK Borders **Map 11 B1**

⊗£££ **PHILIPBURN HOUSE HOTEL & RESTAURANT** Selkirk.

☐£££ **Hours:** 8am - 9.30am, 12.15pm - 2.15pm, and 7.30pm - 9.30pm. ⌣ Bar meals 12.25pm - 2.15pm, and 7pm - 10pm. **Cuisine:** W Innovative French and Scottish cooking, including local Saddle of CLUB Roe Deer Cassis, and Rosace of Langoustines, Sachertorte. Unusual Scottish bar menu. 🛏 16 bedrooms, all en suite, with colour TV, radio, alarm, telephone, and tea/coffee making facilities. **CC** Access, Visa. **Other Points:** Children welcome. Dogs allowed by arrangement. Afternoon teas. Open bank holidays and Sundays. Resident's lounge & garden. Fax No: (0750) 21690 **P** & **(V) Directions:** Near Selkirk rugby ground.

JIM & ANNE HILL ☎ (0750) 20747.

A charming 18th century house, carefully converted into a warm hostelry, with very interesting gourmet cooking. Set in very beautiful gardens, amidst superb historical buildings, abbeys and houses.

LOWLANDS & SCOTTISH BORDERS

ST ANDREWS Fife **Map 11 A1**

♨££ **THE ALBANY** 56 North Street, St Andrews.

🛏 2 single, 2 double, 4 twin and 4 family bedrooms, 5 en suite. 1 bathroom, 2 showers. Colour TV, teamaker and direct dial telephone in all rooms. **Hours:** Breakfast 8am - 9am, dinner 6pm - 7pm. Open all year round. **CC** Access, Visa. **Other Points:** Residents lounge with open fire. Children welcome. Mini launderette. French and German spoken. Licensed. Mastercard accepted. **(V) Directions:** On A91 opposite the university, 200 yds from the cathedral ruins.

MRS F MACNAUGHTON ☎ (0334) 77737.

Situated in a residential part of one of the Royal Burgh's main streets. A small, private, licensed hotel with a homely atmosphere and efficient service.

⊗£££ **THE GRANGE INN** Grange Road, St Andrews.

♨£££ **Hours:** Lunch 12.30pm - 2pm, Dinner 7pm - 9.30pm (last orders). Bar meals served 12.30pm - 2pm and 7pm - 10pm. Restaurant closed: Mondays throughout the year and Tuesdays during November - April. **Cuisine:** Weekly changing table d'hote menu using predominantly fresh, local produce. Dishes may include local fresh fish, steaks and woodland pigeon. 🛏 1 en suite bedroom. **CC** All major cards. **Other Points:** No smoking area. Garden dining. No dogs. Fax No: (0334) 78703. **🅿 (V) Directions:** Off A917, 1 mile from jct of Lamond Drive & Crail/Anstruther Road.

ANN RUSSELL & PETER ARETZ ☎ (0334) 72670.

An old-world inn and restaurant, situated on a hillside overlooking St Andrews. Privately owned and run, the Inn serves good restaurant and bar meals using fresh, local produce. The table d'hote menu changes weekly and offers a good choice of imaginative, well-cooked dishes. Relax with a drink in the garden during summer, or by the welcoming open fires in winter.

⊗£ **THE PANCAKE PLACE** 177/9 South Street, St Andrews.

Hours: Full menu available 9.30am - 5.30pm (8.30pm July & August). Open 7 days a week. Closed: Christmas and New Year's Day. **Cuisine:** Pancakes traditional Scottish style, savoury and sweet. Also, baked potatoes, rice and monthly specials. 🛏 None. **CC** None. **Other Points:** Children welcome. No dogs allowed. Luncheon vouchers accepted. **🅿 ♿ (V) Directions:** Towards the west port along South Street, near Madras College.

C D BURHOUSE ☎ (0334) 75671.

A cheerful family restaurant serving satisfying meals at good value for money. Spacious surroundings and relaxed atmosphere. Famous golf course, university, and sea life centre nearby. Also, beaches and cathedral ruins.

ST FILLANS Tayside **Map 10 A2**

⊗££ **ACHRAY HOUSE HOTEL** St Fillans, Loch Earn.

♨£££ **Hours:** Breakfast, Bar snacks 12 noon - 2pm and 6.30pm - 9.30pm, Dinner 7pm - 9.30pm. Closed: November to February. **Cuisine:** Traditional cuisine using fresh Scottish produce such as fish and game. 🛏 10 bedrooms, 7 en suite. **CC** Access, Visa, AmEx. **Other Points:** Children welcome. No-smoking area. No dogs. Residents' lounge. Garden. Fully licensed. 3 crown

St Fillans continued

recommended. Taste of Scotland recommended. **P** **(V)**
Directions: A85 at the east end of Loch Earn in the village of St
Fillans.
TONY & JANE ROSS ☎ (0764) 85231.
*A family run hotel in a beautiful location in the picturesque
village of St Fillans. Attractive, comfortable accommodation, a
friendly atmosphere and good food make for a very pleasant
visit or longer stay. All the attractions of central Scotland within
easy reach. Well worth a visit.*

STOW Borders **Map 11 B1**

⊗£ **THE MANORHEAD HOTEL** 168 Galashiels Road, Stow.
⊞£ **Hours:** 8am - 9.30am, 12 noon - 2pm, 7pm - 10pm. Sunday lunch
12 noon - 2pm, and dinner 8pm - 10pm. **Cuisine:** Speciality
breast of chicken lightly steamed in butter and herbs, served in a
piquant sauce. Other dishes include Angus steaks, and fresh
salmon. ⊨ 7 bedrooms, 1 with en suite facilities. **CC** Access, Visa.
Other Points: Children welcome. Garden. Afternoon teas. Dogs
allowed. **P** **(V) Directions:** Stow is on the A7, 25 miles south of
Edinburgh.
MARCUS AYLING ☎ (05783) 201.
*Built as a coaching inn in 1819 and set in over an acre of
beautiful gardens in the quiet country village of Stow. The hotel
has been tastefully refurbished and is under the personal
supervision of Marcus and Beatrix Ayling. Good food is served
in the bars and restaurant. Real ales.*

STRACHUR Strathclyde **Map 10 B1**

⊗£££ **THE CREGGANS INN** Strachur.
Hours: Open 8am - 12 midnight. **Cuisine:** Homemade soups,
rainbow trout, Aberdeen Angus steaks, poached salmon, local
seafood table including native oysters, smoked salmon and
langoustines. ⊨ 22 bedrooms, 17 en suite. **CC** All major
cards **Other Points:** Children welcome. Fax (036 986) 637. **P** ⅙ **(V)**
Directions: Via Arrochar from Glasgow or via Gournock, ferry
across Clyde & A815
SIR FITZROY MACLEAN. Manager - MICHAEL GILBERT
☎ (036 986) 279.
*Stupendous views over Loch Fyne. Genuine country lodge
atmosphere of log fires and own house Malt Whisky
'McPhunns'. Private walks, deer stalking and fishing by
arrangement. All the food is based on Lady MacLeans famous
cookbook recipes.*

TARBERT Strathclyde **Map 10 B1**

⊗££££ **STONEFIELD CASTLE HOTEL** Tarbert, Loch Fyne, Argyll.
Hours: Lunch 12 noon - 2pm, Dinner 7pm - 9pm. Bar meals
served from 12 noon - 2pm. **Cuisine:** Traditional Scottish menu
using fresh local produce. ⊨ 33 rooms, all en suite. **CC** All major
cards. **Other Points:** Children welcome. No smoking areas.
Afternoon teas served. Dogs welcome. Library, bar, sauna,
solarium, children's playground, games room. **P** ⅙ **(V)**
Directions: On A83, 10 miles south of Lochgilphead, 2 miles
north of Tarbert.
JANET & KEVIN REID - Managers ☎ (0880) 820836

Tarbert continued

A 19th century country house in an elevated position overlooking Loch Fyne. The hotel offers guests good food, comfort and service in charming surroundings. Featuring the best of local produce on its menu, the hotel is popular with holidaymakers and sporting people. Ideally situated for golf, fishing and yachting (yacht moorings available).

TAYVALLICH Strathclyde **Map 10 B1**

⊗££ **TAYVALLICH INN** Tayvallich, By Lochgilphead.

Hours: Serving lunch in bar and restaurant from 12 noon - 2pm (last orders) and dinner in bar and restaurant from 6pm - 9pm (last orders). Closed: Mondays (November - March). **Cuisine:** Traditional meals. House speciality - seafood. ⊨ None. **CC** Access, Visa. **Other Points:** Children welcome. Open Bank Holidays. No smoking area. Dogs allowed. Garden dining. **P** ᕲ **(V) Directions:** Off A816 Lochgilphead to Crinan raod.

JOHN & PAT GRAFTON ☎ (05467) 282.

Tayvallich Inn is situated in one of the most beautiful and picturesque locations in Scotland. Mr Grafton and his staff offer a warm welcome and serve really good food. Steaks and locally caught mussels, prawns and lobsters are the house specialities.

THORNHILL Dumfries & Galloway **Map 10 C2**

⊗£ **GEORGE HOTEL** 103-106 Drumlanrig Street, Thornhill.

⊡££ **Hours:** 8am - 9am, 12 noon - 2pm, and 6pm - 9pm. Also open Sundays. Restaurant closed: Monday, Tuesday and Wednesday. Bar menu in £ Routiers price bracket. **Cuisine:** A la carte menu. Dishes include Monkfish in white wine with cream and chive sauce and Trout 'Au Bleu'. ⊨ 1 single, 5 twin, 3 double, and 1 family room, 8 of them en suite. All rooms have colour TVs, radio, telephone, and tea/coffee facilities. **CC** Access, Visa. **Other Points:** Children welcome. Dogs allowed. **P** **(V) Directions:** Road reference: A76. 16 miles north of Dumfries.

ROBERT & RACHEL SAVILLE ☎ (0848) 30326.

Family run hotel and restaurant, offering good food and accommodation in a warm and friendly atmosphere. Extensive bar menu and a la carte. Golf, fishing and other outdoor activities can be arranged. Plenty of historical places of interest nearby, including Drumlanrig Castle.

TROON Strathclyde **Map 10 B1**

⊗££ **SOUTH BEACH HOTEL** South Beach Road, Troon.

⊡£ **Hours:** Breakfast 7.00am - 9.30am, Lunch 12 noon - 2.00pm, Dinner 7.00pm - 9.00pm (last orders 8.45pm). **Cuisine:** A la carte, fixed 4 course menu and bar meals. ⊨ 27 bedrooms, all en suite. **CC** Access, Visa. **Other Points:** Children welcome. Teas. Garden. Dogs allowed. No smoking areas. **P** ᕲ **(V) Directions:** Close to Troon sea front.

MR & MRS WATT ☎ (0292) 312033

This family run hotel is situated on the sea front affording perfect views of the Firth of Clyde with Arran and the Ailsa Craig on the Horizon. It has a warm and friendly atmosphere and is great value for money. Perfect for a golfing holiday!

TWEEDSMUIR Borders **Map 10 B2**

⊗££ **THE CROOK INN** Tweedsmuir, By Biggar.
££££ **Hours:** Open for meals all day 8am - 9.30pm. **Cuisine:** Dishes may
CLUB include Beef Stroganoff, Roast Duck, Poached Salmon Steak. Bar meals include fish dishes and the very popular homemade steak pies. 3 twin, 4 double, and 1 family room, 6 of them en suite. CC Access, Visa. **Other Points:** Children welcome. Garden. Afternoon teas also served. Pets allowed. P **(V) Directions:** A74 Moffat. Nearest road reference A701.
STUART & MARY REID ☎ (089) 97272.
The Crook is Scotland's oldest licensed Inn, updated over the centuries. It is family run, offers good food, comfortable accommodation, and a warm welcome. Ideal centre for country pursuits and exploring the Borders.

TYNDRUM Central **Map 10 A2**

⊗£ **CLIFTON COFFEE HOUSE** Tyndrum, Perthshire.
Hours: Open from 8.30am - 5.30pm. Closed: January to end-March. **Cuisine:** Homemade soups, good country cooking including game pies, hot pots and casseroles, fresh and smoked salmon and extensive salad table. None. CC All major cards. **Other Points:** No dogs. Children welcome. P ♿ **(V)**
GOSDEN OF TYNDRUM ☎ (083 84) 271.
Spacious self-service restaurant with adjoining shops, specialising in the best Scottish dishes, whisky and confectionery. Outstanding Scottish crafts. Extensive car park and filling station facilities.

££ **INVERVEY HOTEL** Tyndrum.
3 single, 7 double, 7 twin and 4 family bedrooms, 9 en suite. 3 bathrooms. 1 shower. **Hours:** Breakfast 8am - 10am, lunch 12 noon - 2pm and dinner 5pm - 8.30pm. CC Access, Visa, AmEx. **Other Points:** Children welcome. Licensed. Residents' lounge. TV. P **Directions:** On the A82/A85.
JOHN RILEY ☎ (08384) 219/289.
Standing on the Road to the Isles in some of Scotland's most stunning scenery. The hotel is ideal for either an overnight stop or for staying a while to explore the area.

WEST WEMYSS Fife **Map 11 B1**

⊗££ **BELVEDERE HOTEL** Main St, West Wemyss, Nr Kirkcaldy.
£££ **Hours:** 7am - 9.30am, 12 noon - 2pm, and 7pm - 9pm (last orders). Bar meals 12 noon - 2pm, and 7pm - 9pm. **Cuisine:** Scottish and continental cuisine, including seafood. 21 bedrooms, all en suite. All rooms have colour TV, telephones and tea/ coffee making facilities. CC Access, Visa. **Other Points:** Children welcome. No dogs. Open bank holidays. P ♿ **(V) Directions:** Take A955 from Kirkcaldy to Leven. 3 miles from Kirkcaldy.
WEMYSS HOTELS LTD ☎ (0592) 54167.
A seaside hotel, beautifully situated on the Firth Of Forth, in the picturesque Fife village of West Wemyss. Only 10 minutes drive from Kirkcaldy, with plenty of places to visit, including a fishing museum and a golf course.

SCOTTISH
HIGHLANDS

SCOTTISH HIGHLANDS

The scenery in the Scottish Highlands can be almost unreal in its wild beauty, encompassing Britain's highest mountains, the loveliest lochs, waterfalls and glens, and a spectacular coastline. You can find beaches with the purest white sand, particularly in the far north along Sandwood Bay, set in striking contrast to the dramatic mountain ranges.

The Islands reflect these incredible contrasts, from the placidity of Bute, to the ruggedness of Arran and Skye. The Islands provide the ideal area for ornithology and archaeology, fishing and sea-angling. Orkney is separated by a mere six miles from the mainland of Scotland and presents the richest area of prehistory anywhere in Britain. As in other parts of Scotland, there are also plenty of local crafts including weaving and pottery, and be sure to sample the locally made cheeses and smoked fish.

Lying only 200 miles from the coast of Norway, the Shetland Isles have, throughout the centuries, been strongly influenced by Scandinavia. Indeed, the local accent owes more to the Viking than the Pict.

The Highlands have had a turbulent history. The most famous of Scotland's heroes, Bonnie Prince Charlie, inspired love and loyalty in the Highlanders as he raised the rebellion in 1745. Legends surround his enterprise.

Visitors go to the Highlands mainly for their natural beauty, but there are many buildings noted for their grandeur and history. No castles have finer sites than Urquhart and Eilan Donan and the cathedral and ecclesiastical buildings on Iona have drawn pilgrims for centuries.

Inverness, Fort William and Aviemore are situated in the heart of the Highlands and bustle with visitors at every time of year. Inverness acts as a natural gateway into the Highlands whereas Fort William provides a variety of opportunities for ardent shoppers. Aviemore is, of course, also famous for its skiing.

Beyond this area lies some of the most remote, wild country and some of the most beautiful glens, such as Cannick and Affric. Visit the Loch Ness exhibition at Drumnadrochit and go 'monster-hunting'. If you have no luck there, investigate Loch Morar to the far west. It is said to be haunted by a mysterious 'something'.

The highest mountains in Scotland are also within this area, not just Ben Nevis but also the tops of the Cairngorms which form a border between the Grampian and Highland regions. Alternatively, if water-sports have more appeal to you, visit the beautiful white sands of Morar or the Spey valley.

For some, the Spey valley's special attraction lies in quite another area – the Malt Whisky Trail, to the north-west. Seven distilleries are linked by a scenic route through the Grampians and there are opportunities to sample this magical product of pure water and malted barley.

The Highlands offer the visitor a range of opportunities for outdoor activities and, perhaps most of all, peace and relaxation amongst fascinating geology and wildlife. There are still seacoasts where seals swim in clean waters and seabirds gather in vast numbers – scenery which has inspired writers and poets throughout the ages.

The Highlanders themselves welcome visitors warmly for, in centuries past, it was Highland tradition to welcome strangers and give them food and shelter without question. In many ways, this tradition continues, with the Highlanders offering food and accommodation at particularly good value and usually in a very friendly, informal atmosphere. The Scot's famous hospitality is sure to make you feel at home and you may well be invited to a local ceilidh, a Highland gathering with singing and dancing.

QUICK REFERENCE GUIDE

	NO. OF ESTS.	⊗ £	⊗ ££	⊗ £££	⊗ ££££	⊡ £	⊡ ££	⊡ £££	⊡ ££££

SCOTTISH HIGHLANDS

MAP 12 A1

	NO. OF ESTS.	⊗ £	⊗ ££	⊗ £££	⊗ ££££	⊡ £	⊡ ££	⊡ £££	⊡ ££££
Isle of Harris	1							★	
Isle of Lewis	1		★						★

MAP 12 A2

	NO. OF ESTS.	⊗ £	⊗ ££	⊗ £££	⊗ ££££	⊡ £	⊡ ££	⊡ £££	⊡ ££££
Altnaharra	1		★						
Durness	1						★		
Kinlochbervie	2	★		★			★		★
Lairg	2		★	★				★	★
Rogart	1		★						★
Scourie	1		★					★	
Tongue	1		★					★	

MAP 12 B1

	NO. OF ESTS.	⊗ £	⊗ ££	⊗ £££	⊗ ££££	⊡ £	⊡ ££	⊡ £££	⊡ ££££
Ardelve	1		★				★		
Gairloch	2		★				★	★	
Isle of Barra	1		★					★	
Isle of Benbecula	1							★	
Isle of Skye	10	★	★	★	★		★	★	★
Isle of South Uist	1		★					★	
Raasay	1		★					★	

MAP 12 B2

	NO. OF ESTS.	⊗ £	⊗ ££	⊗ £££	⊗ ££££	⊡ £	⊡ ££	⊡ £££	⊡ ££££
Drumnadrochit	1			★					★
Glenmoriston	1		★					★	
Inverness	3	★					★	★	
Struy	1		★						★
Ullapool	2		★					★	

MAP 12 C1

	NO. OF ESTS.	⊗ £	⊗ ££	⊗ £££	⊗ ££££	⊡ £	⊡ ££	⊡ £££	⊡ ££££
Acharacle	1						★		
Arisaig	1		★					★	
Strontian	1		★					★	

MAP 12 C2

	NO. OF ESTS.	⊗ £	⊗ ££	⊗ £££	⊗ ££££	⊡ £	⊡ ££	⊡ £££	⊡ ££££
Fort William	2	★	★						★
Invergarry	1		★					★	
Kinlochleven	1		★					★	
Spean Bridge	1		★			★			

MAP 13 A1

	NO. OF ESTS.	⊗ £	⊗ ££	⊗ £££	⊗ ££££	⊡ £	⊡ ££	⊡ £££	⊡ ££££
Melvich	1		★					★	

MAP 13 A1

	NO. OF ESTS.	⊗ £	⊗ ££	⊗ £££	⊗ ££££	⊡ £	⊡ ££	⊡ £££	⊡ ££££
Orkney	3	★	★	★				★	★
Shetland	2		★					★	

MAP 13 B1

	NO. OF ESTS.	⊗ £	⊗ ££	⊗ £££	⊗ ££££	⊡ £	⊡ ££	⊡ £££	⊡ ££££
Aberlour	1			★				★	
Aviemore	3				★		★	★	
Buckie	1		★					★	
Craigellachie	1			★					★
Cromarty	1		★					★	
Cullen	1		★					★	
Dornoch	3		★				★	★	★
Golspie	1		★				★		
Grantown on Spey	4		★	★			★	★	

QUICK REFERENCE GUIDE

	NO. OF ESTS.	⊗ £	⊗ ££	⊗ £££	⊗ ££££	⊞ £	⊞ ££	⊞ £££	⊞ ££££
Huntly	1		★				★		
Nairn	5	★	★				★	★	
Tain	1		★						★
Tomintoul	1		★				★		
MAP 13 B2									
Balmedie	1	★							
Insch	1		★				★		
Newburgh	1			★				★	
Peterhead	1	★					★		
MAP 13 C1									
Aboyne	1			★					★
Ballater	3		★	★			★		★
Kincraig	1	★							
Kingussie	2		★				★	★	
Strathdon	1		★				★		
MAP 13 C2									
Aberdeen	2	★						★	
Banchory	1		★						

SCOTTISH HIGHLANDS

ABERDEEN Grampian **Map 13 C2**

⊗£ **BETTY BURKES** 45 Langstane Place, Aberdeen.
Hours: Breakfast 10am - 12 noon. Bar meals 12 noon - 8pm (last orders). Sundays 6.30pm - 11pm **Cuisine:** Bar meals, including deep fried mushrooms, potato skins, and home-made puddings. ⊨ None. **CC** Access, Visa, AmEx. **Other Points:** Children welcome. No dogs. Open bank holidays. Sells real ale. Champagne happy hour 5.30pm - 7pm - £10 a bottle. **(V) Directions:** In city centre, close to Union Street, Aberdeen's main street.
MIKE COOK. ☎ (0224) 210359.
Stylish and interesting bar, themed as a gentleman's club , with old portrait paintings, wood panelling and leather seats. The massive carved eagle dominating the entrance originated in America during the period of the Wars Of Independence. There are display cabinets full of old bar and glass curios. Bustling, local atmosphere.

⊗£ **ST MAGNUS COURT HOTEL** 22 Guild Street, Aberdeen.
⊞£££ **Hours:** Breakfast 5.30am - 9.30am and dinner 6pm - 9pm. Bar meals from 12 noon (last orders 10.30pm). **Cuisine:** Dishes include homemade soup of the day, rump steak garni, chicken fillet, omelettes, ice cream and fruit. ⊨ 19 rooms. 4 single, 2 double, 12 twin and 1 family room. 14 en suite. **CC** Access, Visa. **Other Points:** Children welcome. Open for Sunday lunch. **P Directions:** Adjacent to the railway and bus station.
SUSAN SHERRY ☎ (0224) 589411.
The St Magnus Court Hotel is a family run hotel situated in city centre. The accommodation is very comfortable while the food is well cooked and well prepared. Pleasant, relaxed atmosphere.

ABERLOUR Grampian **Map 13 B1**

⊗£££ **ARCHIESTOWN HOTEL** Archiestown, By Aberlour.
⊞£££ **Hours:** Breakfast 8am - 9.30am, Sunday lunch 12.30pm - 2pm,
CLUB Dinner 7.30pm - 8.30pm (last orders). Bar snacks 12 noon - 2.30pm, 6.30pm - 9.30pm. Closed: mid December - March 1st. **Cuisine:** A la carte restaurant menu and bar meals. A la carte dishes may include Baked monkfish tail with pink peppercorns, Roast chicken with honey & ginger. ⊨ 8 bedrooms, 6 en suite. **CC** Access, Visa. **Other Points:** Children welcome. Afternoon teas. Dogs allowed. Garden and garden dining. Residents' lounge. Fax No: (03406) 239. **P (V) Directions:** B9102 in the village of Archiestown. 5 miles W of Craigellachie.
JUDITH & MICHAEL BULGER ☎ (03406) 218.
A family run hotel in the small Moray village of Archiestown, a frequent winner of the best-kept-village competitions. Good comfortable accommodation, excellent cuisine and knowledgeable service. The hotel appeals to anglers, holidaymakers and locals alike for its warm welcome and relaxing atmosphere.

ABOYNE Grampian **Map 13 C1**

⊗£££ **BALNACOIL HOTEL** Rhu-Na-Haven Road, Aboyne.
⊞££££ **Hours:** Breakfast 6.30am - 10am, Lunch 12 noon - 2pm, Dinner
⊚ 7pm - 10pm (last orders). Bar meals 12 noon - 2.30pm and 6pm

Aboyne continued

10pm. **Cuisine:** Dishes may include Rack of Lamb Diablo, Chicken Rochambeau, Fillet of Salmon with sorrell and dill. Traditional Scottish cuisine. ⊨ 12 bedrooms, all en suite. **CC** All major cards. **Other Points:** Access for disabled to restaurant only. Children welcome. No dogs. No-smoking area. Residents' lounge. Garden. Fax No: (03398) 87050. ▣ ⬥ **(V) Directions:** 1 mile west of Aboyne village on the A93.
JEAN & ROGER LEIGH ☎ (03398) 86806.
A family run, country house hotel, set amidst the natural beauty of the Dee Valley. The Balnacoil is a fine example of Edwardian architecture and, set on the river bank, it is tranquil and restful yet with many local sporting activities close at hand. Extremely comfortable bedrooms and public rooms, good food and courteous service.

ACHARACLE Highland **Map 12 C1**
⌂££ **ARDSHEALACH LODGE** Acharacle, Ardnamurchan.
⊨ 7 rooms. 1 single, 2 twin, 3 double and 1 family room. 4 en suite. All with tea/coffee making facilities. Drying. Deepfreeze. **Hours:** Breakfast 8am - 9am, dinner 7pm - 8pm (last orders). **CC** None. **Other Points:** Well behaved dogs allowed. Residents license. Boat trips on Loch Shiel. ▣ **Directions:** Entering Acharacle from A861, Ardshealach is at east end of village.
MRS CHRIS YOUNG. ☎ (096785) 301.
Set in 25 acres with frontage to Loch Shiel, this is an ideal base for anyone who is interested in fishing, nature or archery. The meals are well balanced and cooked, and the menu, featuring local produce, changes daily. Rooms are tastefully decorated and clean. With a clientele of mixed ages, the atmosphere is pleasant and relaxed.

ALTNAHARRA Highland **Map 12 A2**
⊗££ **ALTNAHARRA HOTEL** Altnaharra, By Lairg.
Hours: Breakfast 7.45am - 9am, lunch 12 noon - 2pm (last orders) and dinner 7.30pm - 8.30pm (last orders 8.15pm). Closed 29th October - 24th February **Cuisine:** Prime Scottish beef and lamb, game, fresh local fish and seafood. ⊨ 3 single, 14 twin, 3 double, all en suite. **CC** Access, Visa. **Other Points:** Children welcome. Garden. Afternoon teas. Pets allowed. Local ghillies available. Tackle shop. Rod racks, deep freeze, and drying room. ▣ **Directions:** Off the A836 Lairg road, follow sign for Tongue.
PAUL & ALISON PANCHAUD ☎ (054 981) 222.

Altnaharra continued

Privately owned and managed, 'Altnaharra' offers a warm welcome and friendly atmosphere, together with good food and comfortable accommodation. With the choice of refurbished bedrooms and two annexe cottages, this hotel is ideal for families or a party of enthusiastic sportspersons in the area to enjoy superb salmon and sea-trout fishing. Winter and spring breaks available.

ARDELVE Highland **Map 12 B1**

⊛££ **LOCH DUICH HOTEL** Ardelve, by Kyle of Lochalsh.

⌂££ **Hours:** Breakfast from 8.30am - 9.30am, bar lunches 12.30pm - 1.45pm and dinner 7pm - 3pm (last orders). Closed: November to end of March. **Cuisine:** Fresh produce cooked to order, eg. sherried duck soup, poached scallops, vegetarian dish always available. Home baking. ⊨ 18 bedrooms, 6 bathrooms. **CC** Access, Visa. **Other Points:** Dogs not allowed in public rooms. Children welcome. **(V)**
ROD STENSON ☎ (059 985) 213
Overlooking 3 sea lochs, the hills of Kintail, Eilan Donan Castle and towards the Isle of Skye. All the vegetables are grown locally and the hotel keeps free-range chickens. The sun lounge is a very popular place to relax and enjoy the views.

ARISAIG Highland **Map 12 C1**

⊛££ **THE ARISAIG HOTEL** Arisaig.

⌂£££ **Hours:** Breakfast 8.30am - 10am, lunch 12.30pm - 2pm and dinner 7.30pm - 8.30pm (last orders). Open all year. **Cuisine:** Arisaig prawns, Mallaig plaice, sirloin steak, homemade ice cream. All fresh, local produce. ⊨ 15 bedrooms, 6 en suite. **CC** None. **Other Points:** Children welcome. Pets by arrangement. **P** **Directions:** On the A830 in Arisaig village near the sea.
GEORGE, JANICE AND GORDON STEWART ☎ (06875) 210.
An old coaching inn, carefully extended in keeping with the original style, situated on the coast at the edge of the village overlooking the Small Isles. Close to the White Sands of Morar and the Glenfinnan Monument.

AVIEMORE Highland **Map 13 B1**

⌂£££ **BALAVOULIN HOTEL** Main Road, Aviemore.

⊨ 7 double, 3 twin bedrooms, all en suite. Tea/coffee making facilites, colour TV, radio alarm and direct dial phone in all rooms. Double glazing throughout. **Hours:** Breakfast 8am - 9.30am. **CC** Access, Visa. **Other Points:** Central heating. Children welcome. Licensed. Lounge bar serving bar meals and snacks, restaurant serving full dinners. Dogs by arrangement only. **P** **(V)** **Directions:** On the main village road, off the A9 to Aviemore.
MR & MRS MACKENZIE ☎ (0479) 810672.
Located on the A9 well placed for ski-ing, climbing and Aviemore Centre complex. Luxury self-catering bungalows sleeping 4 are available for hire. Childrens play area. A popular area for winter sports and summer touring.

⌂£ **CRAIGLEA GUEST HOUSE** Grampian Road, Aviemore.

⊨ 11 bedrooms, 1 en suite. **Hours:** Breakfast 8am - 9am. **CC** None. **Other Points:** Children welcome. Dogs allowed. Residents'

Aviemore continued

loungo. Garden. ◘ **Directions:** 150 yards north of Railway Station on opposite side.

HUGH & ANNE NUNN ☎ (0479) 810210.

A family run guest house offering a warm welcome and comfortable accommodation at good value for money. Craiglea is very central for all of Aviemore's amenities.

⌂£££ **RAVENSCRAIG GUEST HOUSE** Main Road, Aviemore.

🛏 5 double, 4 twin, and 2 family rooms, all en suite. All rooms have TV and tea/coffee making facilities. Hairdryers and iron available. **Hours:** Breakfast 8am - 9am. ☒ None. **Other Points:** Children welcome. Pets allowed. Open bank holidays. ◘ &

Directions: A9. At North End of Main Street in Aviemore.

ROBERT & CHRISTINE THOMPSON ☎ (0479) 810278.

Ravenscraig is a family run guest house with a friendly atmosphere, offering comfortable rooms and a full Highland breakfast. Situated on Aviemore's main street close to the shops, restaurants, and the famous Aviemore centre with all the amenities it has to offer: ski-ing, ice-skating, swimming, curling, and pony-trekking.

BALLATER Grampian **Map 13 C1**

⊗££ **ALEXANDRA HOTEL** 12 Bridge Square, Ballater.

⌂££ **Hours:** Breakfast from 8am - 9.30am, lunch 12 noon - 2.15pm,
CLUB dinner 6pm - 9pm. Open from 11am - 12 midnight. Breakfast served to residents only. **Cuisine:** Traditional Scottish and French - Entrecote au poivre, fillet steak Diane, trout with almonds, salmon, whole lemon sole, venison. Selection of cheese. 🛏 6 bedrooms, 4 en suite. ☒ All major cards. **Other Points:** Central heating. Children welcome. Dogs allowed (except in restaurant). ◘ &

Directions: On the A93 Aberdeen to Braemar road, near the River Dee Bridge.

ALAIN TABUTEAU ☎ (0338) 55376.

An attractive, well-maintained exterior opens into a tastefully decorated hotel and restaurant. Table d'hote and a la carte meals are offered with a touch of French cuisine. Close to Balmoral, Crathie church and Scottish distilleries. For the anglers, there is fishing in the River Dee.

⊗££ **AULD KIRK HOTEL** Braemar Road, Ballater.

⌂££ **Hours:** Breakfast 8.30am - 9am, Lunch 12 noon - 2pm, Dinner 6.30pm - 9pm (last orders). Bar snacks 11am - 4pm and 4.30pm - 9pm. Open all year. **Cuisine:** Wide choice of meals from Royal Deeside Salmon with Hollandaise sauce to toasted sandwiches. 🛏 6 bedrooms, all en suite. ☒ Access, Visa. **Other Points:** Children welcome. Afternoon teas. Dogs allowed. Residents' lounge. Patio dining. ◘ **(V) Directions:** On main Braemar/Aberdeen rd at northern end of Ballater. A93.

MONICE CHIVAS ☎ (03397) 55762.

Converted from a church to a hotel in 1990, the original structure including the front doors, bell tower, and many of the windows have been retained. The result is fascinating and well worth a visit. The resident proprietors provide a warm welcome, well-appointed accommodation, good food and good value.

Ballater continued

⊗£££ **DARROCH LEARG HOTEL** Braemar Road, Ballater.

⊞£££ **Hours:** Breakfast 8.30am - 9.30am, Lunch 12.30pm - 2pm, Dinner 7pm - 8.30pm (last orders). Closed: December - January. **Cuisine:** Traditional Scottish/British dishes. Local produce used such as salmon, lamb and Aberdeen Angus beef. ⊨ 21 bedrooms, all en suite. **CC** Access, Visa. **Other Points:** Vegetarian dishes by arrangement. Children welcome. Afternoon teas. Dogs allowed. Residents' lounge and garden. No smoking area. ◨ **Directions:** On the Braemar Rd at the western edge of Ballater. A93.

NIGEL FRANKS ☎ (03347) 55443.

A country house hotel, superbly situated in 5 acres of garden and woodland on the slopes of the Craigendarroch. Its high position gives panoramic views over the golf course, River Dee and Balmoral Estate to the Grampian mountains. Family run, with well appointed bedrooms and 3 comfortable lounges. New conservatory dining room. Good food and a relaxed hospitable atmosphere.

BALMEDIE Grampian **Map 13 B2**

⊗£ **COACH & HORSES COUNTRY INN** Ellon Road.

Hours: Meals from 12 noon - 2.15pm and 5.30pm - 10pm. **Cuisine:** Home cooking accompanied by large selection of wines and real ale. ⊨ None. **CC** Access, Visa, AmEx. **Other Points:** Children welcome. Beer garden. No dogs. ◨ **(V) Directions:** 7 miles north of Aberdeen on the A92 Ellon/Peterhead road.

EDWARD SHAND ☎ (0358) 43249.

This old coaching inn has a wood-beamed ceiling and panelled walls with a log and peat fire in winter. Separate dining room. Popular with both travellers and business clientele.

BANCHORY Grampian **Map 13 C2**

⊗££ **BANCHORY LODGE HOTEL** Banchory.

⌂ **Hours:** Open all day, bar licensed from 11am - 2pm and 5pm - 11pm (last orders 9.30pm). Closed: 12th December to 29th January. **Cuisine:** Prime Scottish beef, Dee salmon. ⊨ 24 bedrooms, all en suite. **CC** Access, Visa, AmEx. **Other Points:** Children welcome. Carte Blanche accepted. Salmon fishing by arrangement. Fax No: (03302) 5019. Casserole Award winner 1990. ◨ ᴦ **Directions:** Off the A93, 18 miles west of Aberdeen in Banchory, off Dee Street.

DUGALD JAFFRAY ☎ (033 02) 2625/4777/8

At the confluence of the Feugh with the Dee, the Banchory Lodge is in a striking and historic setting, with the River Dee, a celebrated salmon river, running through the grounds. As well as salmon fishing, there is also ample opportunity for golfing, nearby forest walks and nature trails. An abundance of National Trust properties to visit nearby.

BUCKIE Grampian **Map 13 B1**

⊗££ **MILL HOUSE HOTEL** Tynet, by Buckie, Banffshire.

⊞£££ **Hours:** Breakfast 7.45am - 9.30am, Lunch 12 noon - 2pm and

CLUB Dinner 7.30pm - 9pm last orders). **Cuisine:** A la carte - speciality Scottish cuisine from local produce. ⊨ 15 bedrooms, all en suite and with full facilities. **CC** All major cards. **Other Points:** Full range of meals. Functions. Sporting holiday packages. Fax No: (05427)

Buckie continued

331. ▣ ⅋ **(V) Directions:** On the A98, east of Elgin. Between Buckie and Fochabers.

GILL & PHIL SILVER ☎ (05427) 233

This attractive former Meal Mill was converted into a high standard hotel in 1973, incorporating the original water wheel machinery. The surrounding area has a multitude of outdoor pursuits available and the hotel is within reasonable driving distance of other places of interest such as Elgin Cathedral. Renowned for its friendly, efficient service, excellent cusine and good value.

CRAIGELLACHIE Grampian **Map 13 B1**

⊗£££ **CRAIGELLACHIE HOTEL** Craigellachie, Speyside, ◫£££ Banffshire.

Hours: Breakfast 7.30am - 10am, Lunch 12.30pm - 1.45pm, Dinner 7.30pm - 11.30pm (last orders 9.30pm). Bar meals served 12.30pm - 1.45pm and 6.30pm - 7.30pm. **Cuisine:** Local fresh produce. ⇌ 30 bedrooms, all en suite. **CC** All major cards. **Other Points:** Children welcome. Afternoon teas. Dogs allowed. Residents' lounge. Garden. Vegetarian meals on request. Wedding parties. Fax No: (0340) 881253. ▣ **Directions:** A96, 12 miles south of Elgin.

TOMAS GRONAGER ☎ (0340) 881204.

A privately owned and run hotel offering accommodation of a very high standard and, in the restaurant, a varied and tempting menu. The excellent facilities include a library, billiards room, exercise room, sauna and solarium. Caters for fishing and

Craigellachie continued

> *golfing holidays and is on the Malt Whisky trail. The house is Victorian and located in the most beautiful Moray setting.*

CROMARTY Highland **Map 13 B1**

⊗££ **ROYAL HOTEL** Marine Terrace, Cromarty.

🍴£££ **Hours:** Meals from 8am - 9.30am, 12 noon - 2pm and 7pm - CLUB 8.30pm. Bar meals 12 noon - 2pm and 5.30pm - 9.30pm. Reservations required for restaurant meals. **Cuisine:** Local Scottish dishes and fresh sea produce - crab, trout and salmon. 🛏 10 bedrooms, all en suite. 💳 Visa, AmEx. **Other Points:** Children welcome. Coaches by appointment. 🅿 ♿ **(V) Directions:** Off the A832 in Cromarty overlooking the beach and harbour. STEWART MORRISON ☎ (03817) 217.

> *A family run hotel with attentive staff who guard their reputation for quality food and value for money with considerable pride - the best in Scottish hospitality. Cromarty is an unspoilt fishing village on the Black Isle where relaxation and peace are guaranteed.*

CULLEN Grampian **Map 13 B1**

⊗££ **BAYVIEW HOTEL** 57 Seafield Street, Cullen, Buckie.

🍴£££ **Hours:** Breakfast 8am - 9.30am, Lunch 12 noon - 1.45pm, Dinner 6.30pm - 9pm. Also open Sundays. **Cuisine:** Restaurant part of 'Taste of Scotland' scheme offering dishes such as Fillet of Salmon wrapped in Pastry with Lemon Thyme. Good range of bar meals. 🛏 1 single, 2 twin, 2 double, and 1 family room, 5 of them en suite, with colour TV, telephone, and tea/coffee facilities.

Cullen continued

CC Access, Visa. **Other Points:** Children not permitted in the bar.
(V)
DAVID & FRANCES EVANS ☎ (0542) 41031.
A small, intimate hotel commanding spectacular views over the harbour, bay and Moray Firth, renowned for excellent food and personal service. The restaurant is open daily and meals are also served in the bar at lunchtime and in the evening. The inspector declared the food 'excellently prepared and presented' and the rooms 'attractive and very comfortable'.

DORNOCH Highland **Map 13 B1**

⊗££ **DORNOCH CASTLE HOTEL** Dornoch.
⌂££££ **Hours:** Breakfast 8am - 9.30am, Lunch 12.30pm - 2pm, Dinner 7.30pm - 8.45pm. Closed: November - mid April. **Cuisine:** Scottish and French dishes. Specialities include Aberdeen Angus steaks, Salmon and Lobster. ⊨ 19 bedrooms, 17 en suite. **CC** Access, Visa, AmEx. **Other Points:** Children welcome. Afternoon teas. Dogs allowed. Residents' lounge. Garden. No smoking in the dining room. Fax No: (0862) 810981. **P** & **(V) Directions:** 2 miles off the A9. In centre of Dornoch opposite the Cathedral.
MICHAEL KETCHIN ☎ (0862) 810216.
Formerly the Palace of the Bishops of Caithness and thought to have been built in the late 15th or early 16th century, the hotel is privately owned and personally run by the Ketchin family. The elegant lounges and most of the bedrooms overlook the sheltered gardens. Non-residents are welcome for lunch and dinner but booking is advised.

⊗££ **MALLIN HOUSE HOTEL** Church Street, Dornoch.
⌂££ **Hours:** Breakfast 8.15am - 10am, Lunch and bar snacks 12 noon - 2.30pm, Dinner and bar snacks 6.30pm - 9pm (last orders). **Cuisine:** A la Carte and Table d'Hote menus. Dishes may include Rack of Spring Lamb, Lobster Thermidor. All dishes cooked to order. Good, imaginative bar meals. ⊨ 11 bedrooms, 5 en suite. **CC** Access, Visa, AmEx. **Other Points:** Children welcome. Dogs allowed. Garden. Fax No: (0862) 810810. **P** & **(V) Directions:** In centre of Dornoch near to the famous Golf Course.
MALCOLM HOLDEN ☎ (0862) 810335.
A family run hotel situated close to the famous golf course in Dornoch. Good food and a friendly atmosphere complement the high standard of accommodation. Choose from the a la carte, table d'hote or bar meals menu. All dishes are freshly cooked to order and attractively presented. Good value for money. Especially popular with golfers and anglers.

⊗££ **THE BURGHFIELD HOUSE HOTEL** Dornoch.
⌂£££ **Hours:** Breakfast 7.30am - 10am, lunch 12.30pm - 2.30pm, dinner 7.30pm - 9pm (last orders). **Cuisine:** Highland fare using local beef, game salmon and shell-fish. House speciality: rib of beef. ⊨ 40 rooms. 5 single, 23 twin, 4 double and 8 family bedrooms. 30 en suite. **CC** All major cards. **Other Points:** Children welcome. Garden. Dogs allowed. Games room. **P** **(V) Directions:** In Dornoch, only a few minutes walk from Royal Dornoch Golf Course.
MR NIALL CURRIE ☎ (0862) 810212.

Dornoch continued

Formerly a home of Lord Rothermere, the hotel stands in 5 acres of garden overlooking Dornoch, comes complete with its own round tower and has been owned by the same family since 1946. With good food, comfortable accommodation and a relaxed, friendly atmosphere, it is an ideal place for a family holiday, near a golf course, fishing lochs and beaches. Extensively refurbished June '91.

DRUMNADROCHIT Highland **Map 12 B2**

⊗£££ **LOCH NESS LODGE HOTEL** Drumnadrochit, Inverness.

☐£££ **Hours:** Breakfast 8am - 10am and dinner 7.30pm - 9.45pm (last orders 9.30pm). Bar meals 10.30am - 6pm and 6.30pm - 9.30pm. Closed: Sunday lunch. **Cuisine:** Aberdeen Angus steaks. Table d'hote and full a la carte menus available. Bar snacks served in the bar/coffee shop. ⊨ 54 bedrooms, all with en suite facilities. **CC** All major cards. **Other Points:** Vegetarian meals by request. Children welcome. Pets allowed. Afternoon tea/snacks served. Coaches welcome by appointment. **P** ⅊ **(V)**

D W SKINNER ☎ (04562) 342.

A comfortable and friendly Highland lodge set in 8 acres of woodland near Loch Ness and Urquhart Castle. An ideal touring base for the Scottish Highlands. Regular Scottish entertainment. Visitors centre for Loch Ness, gift shop, and Loch Ness cruises.

DURNESS Highland **Map 12 A2**

☐£served **FAR NORTH HOTEL** Balnakeil Craft Village, nr. Lairg.

⊞ ⊨ 10 Bedrooms. **Hours:** Breakfast 7.30am - 11am, dinner 7.30pm. Also open to non-residents. Closed: Christmas. **CC** Access, Visa. **Other Points:** Children welcome. Pets allowed. No smoking area. Afternoon tea served. Vegetarian meals available and wholesome homecooking. **P** ⅊ **(V) Directions:** Off the A838.

NICK & MARY WEATHERHEAD ☎ (097) 181 221.

Situated near the Balnakeil Craft Village, offering interesting indoor opportunities to observe crafts people at work and buy their wares. With unspoilt views of hills and cape Wrath, as well as walks and outdoor activities, the peace and beauty of the area, and the excellent facilities of the hotel have kept people coming back year after year.

FORT WILLIAM Highland **Map 12 C2**

⊗££ **ISLES OF GLENCOE HOTEL AND LEISURE CENTRE**

☐£££ Ballachulish, nr Fort William, Argyll.

CLUB **Hours:** Breakfast 8am - 9.30am, dinner 7pm - 10pm (last orders). Bar meals served all day until 10pm. **Cuisine:** Traditional Scottish cuisine using fresh local produce including local salmon, trout, seafood and venison. Restaurant and bistro bar. ⊨ 39 bedrooms, all en suite. **CC** Access, Visa. **Other Points:** Children welcome. Afternoon teas. No-smoking area. Dogs allowed. Residents' lounge. Garden. Leisure centre and pool. Fax No: (08552) 629. **P** ⅊ **(V) Directions:** A82 Glasgow - Fort William Rd. On the Loch side at Ballachulish.

MR LAURENCE YOUNG ☎ (08552) 603.

The hotel nestles on the side of a peninsula reaching into Loch Leven and affording beautiful views from the hotel and each

Fort William continued

bedroom of sky, mountain and loch. The hotel offers comfortable accommodation, good food and leisure facilities. Watersports, walking and climbing can all be enjoyed and there is an informal Bistro Bar in which to relax during the evenings.

⊗£ **NEVISPORT RESTAURANT** High Street, Fort William, Invernesshire.
Hours: Open 9am - 9pm July to September and 9am - 5pm October to June. Open most Sundays in winter. **Cuisine:** Scottish influenced dishes, eg. pan-fried Lochy trout. ⊨ None. **CC** All major cards. **Other Points:** Children welcome. No dogs. **P** **(V)** **Directions:** On the A82 within the Nevisport complex on the high street.
IAIN SYKES & IAIN SUTHERLAND ☎ (0397) 4921.
Situated in the Nevisport complex which also includes a large mountaineering/sports shop and a craft and books department featuring many local crafts. Cafeteria-style system.

GAIRLOCH Highland **Map 12 B1**
⊗££ **MILLCROFT HOTEL** Strath, Gairloch.
⊞£££ **Hours:** 8am - 9.30am, 12 noon - 2pm and 6pm - 9pm. Bar meals 12 noon - 10pm (last orders). **Cuisine:** Home-cooking, using local produce, the specialities being seafood and some Italian dishes. ⊨ 4 rooms, all en suite. **CC** Access, Visa. **Other Points:** Children welcome. No dogs. Open Sundays and Bank holidays. **P** **(V)** **Directions:** Take B8021 off main road, signposted Melvaig. Hotel 1/2 mile along.
BERNARDI HOWES ☎ (0445) 2376.
Small family-run hotel in centre of village, with magnificent views of the mountains, islands and sea. Comfortable rooms and quality cooking, with an Italian head chef. Places of interest nearby include Inverewe gardens, Gairloch Heritage museum and Peinn Eighe National Nature Reserve.

⊞££ **WHINDLEY GUEST HOUSE** Auchtercairn, Gairloch.
⊨ 4 bedrooms, all en suite. Colour TV. Special winter breaks for the elderly who require care. **Hours:** Breakfast 8.30am - 9.15am, lunch 12.30pm - 2pm and dinner 7pm - 8pm (later dining by arrangement). Breakfast in bedroom on request. Booking creams. **CC** None. **Other Points:** Children welcome. Residents lounge. Vegetarian and special diets catered for by arrangement. Packed lunches available. Garden with patio. **P** ⅋ **(V) Directions:** Up hill as you leave Gairloch on A832 towards Poolewe.
MICK & ELIZABETH PARK ☎ (0445) 2340.
A comfortable modern guest house, with glorious views over Gairloch Bay, that offers their guests fresh home baked bread, warm comfortable bedrooms and a relaxing atmosphere. Ideal holiday guest house where you can relax with breakfast in bed before your day at the golf course or on the beach, both only a few minutes drive away. Special winter breaks featuring spinning & weaving courses.

SCOTTISH HIGHLANDS

GLENMORISTON Highland Map 12 B2
⊗££ **CLUANIE INN** Glenmoriston.
⊞£££ **Hours:** Breakfast 8am - 9.30pm, lunch and bar snacks 12 noon - 2.30pm, dinner 6pm - 9pm. **Cuisine:** Good farmhouse-style cooking. ⊨ 11 bedrooms, all ensuite. **CC** Access, Visa. **Other Points:** Children welcome. Open Bank Holidays. Dogs allowed. Garden. Fitness centre. Salmon and trout fishing. **P** & **(V)**
Directions: Midway between Loch Ness and the ferry terminal to Isle of Skye.
MR JOHN DOUGLAS. ☎ (0320) 40238.
A converted coaching house, this Inn offers good farmhouse cooking, comfortable accommodation and a warm welcome. With many beautiful walks through the mountains and glens, salmon and trout fishing, this is the ideal place to return to at the end of the day with its cosy, relaxing atmosphere, fitness centre including sauna, and the very best in comfort. Highly recommended.

GOLSPIE Highland Map 13 B1
⊗££ **SUTHERLAND ARMS** Old Bank Road, Golspie.
⊞££ **Hours:** Breakfast 7am - 9.30am, lunch 12 noon - 2.30pm and dinner 7pm - 9pm (last orders). Bar meals 12 noon - 2.30pm and 5pm - 9.30pm. Closed: 1st and 2nd January. **Cuisine:** Roast lamb and mint sauce. Gammon steak and pineapple. Cold prawn platter. ⊨ 16 bedrooms, 10 en suite. **CC** Visa. **Other Points:** Children welcome. Pets allowed. Afternoon tea served. **P** & **(V)**
Directions: Near the north end of main road (A9) through Golspie.
MR C SUTHERLAND ☎ (0324) 3216.
The coaching inn was built in 1808 and is situated close to Dunrobin Castle in the village of Golspie. Good food, welcoming and attentive service and pleasant, well furnished rooms, combine to make this an excellent stop for tourists.

GRANTOWN ON SPEY Highland Map 13 B1
⊗££ **CRAGGAN MILL RESTAURANT** Grantown on Spey, Morayshire.
Hours: Dinner 6.30pm - 10pm (last orders). Closed: 2 weeks at beginning of October. **Cuisine:** Italian and British cuisine. House specialities include fillet of venison in a cream sauce. ⊨ None. **CC** Access, Visa. **Other Points:** Children welcome. **P** & **(V)**
Directions: On A95 Grantown to Aviemore rd. 1 mile on south side of Grantown.
MR & MRS B BELLENI ☎ (0479) 2288.
An old watermill, Craggan Mill has a rustic feel with candlelight, wooden tables and interesting relics from when the mill was still operational. All food is fresh and cooked to order by Mr Belleni, the owner. Well cooked food at good value prices and the very best in friendly yet efficient service.

⊗£££ **RAVENSCOURT HOUSE HOTEL** Seafield Avenue
⊞££ Grantown-on-Spey, Morayshire.
⌣ **Hours:** Breakfast 8am - 9am, Sunday Lunch 12.30pm - 2.30pm
[CLUB] Dinner 7pm - 9.30pm (last orders). Closed: October 21st November 21st and January 2nd - 31st. **Cuisine:** 4 course table d'hote menu. Specialities include fresh fish, Scottish game and casseroles. ⊨ 10 bedrooms, all en suite. **CC** None. **Other Points** Children welcome. Garden. Afternoon teas. No smoking areas. No

Grantown on Spey continued

dogs. Fax No: (0479) 3260. ▣ &. **(V) Directions:** Close to The Square in the centre of Grantown on Spey.
FREDDIE BARTLETT & SAMMY BAIN ☎ (0479) 2286.
Formerly The Manse, this hotel is a delightful 19th century house, now tastefully restored and retaining most of its original features. The Orangery Restaurant is designed in period style and has a cosy, intimate atmosphere. The food is excellent, using local and regional, fresh Scottish produce. Regional Newcomer of the Year 1991.

⊗££ **ROSEHALL HOTEL** The Square, Grantown on Spey,
▥££ Morayshire.
Hours: Breakfast served as required until 9am, Lunch 12.30pm - 2pm, Dinner 7.30pm - 9.30pm (last orders 9pm). **Cuisine:** Light lunch menu and a la carte dinner menu. Dishes include Locally Smoked Salmon, Venison, Fondue Bourguignonne, Darne of Salmon. ⊨ 10 bedrooms, 8 en suite. 3 four poster beds. ▣ Access, Visa. **Other Points:** Afternoon teas. Dogs allowed on request. ▣ &. **(V) Directions:** Main square in Grantown, by war memorial.
RORY MACLACHLAN SMITH/SCARLETT COURTNEY-SMITH ☎ (0479) 2721.
Situated in the centre of Grantown, overlooking the square, the hotel offers cheerful, helpful service together with every modern comfort and convenience. The fresh food is attractively presented and served in a comfortable dining-room. A good place to stop whether for a meal or a holiday.

⊗££ **THE BEN MHOR HOTEL** High Street, Grantown on Spey.
▥£££ **Hours:** Breakfast 8am - 9.30am, lunch 12.30pm - 2pm (last orders), dinner 7pm - 9pm (last orders 8.45pm), bar snacks 5.30pm - 9pm (last orders 8.45pm). **Cuisine:** Meals made with an emphasis on local produce whenever possible. Dishes may include chicken with lemon mayonnaise, Lossiemouth scampi Provencale. ⊨ 24 bedrooms, all en suite. ▣ Access, Visa. **Other Points:** Children welcome. Open Bank Holiday. Afternoon teas. Dogs allowed. Garden dining. Fax No. (0479) 3532. ▣ &. **(V) Directions:** On the main street in the town centre.
CLIVE & FIONA WILLIAMSON ☎ (0479) 2056.
Comfortable family run hotel in the heart of the Spey Valley. This is an ideal spot for the holidaymaker with an 18 hole golfcourse, salmon fishing, bowling green and woods nearby. Offering good food and comfortable accommodation.

HUNTLY Grampian **Map 13 B1**
⊗££ **CASTLE HOTEL** Huntly.
▥££ **Hours:** Breakfast 8am - 9.30am, lunch 12 noon - 2.30pm, dinner 7pm - 9pm, bar snacks 6pm - 9pm. **Cuisine:** Traditional meals made from local produce. ⊨ 23 bedrooms, 15 en suite. ▣ Access, Visa, AmEx. **Other Points:** Children welcome. Open Bank Holidays. No smoking area. Afternoon teas. Dogs allowed. Garden dining. Fax No: (0466) 792641. ▣ &. **(V) Directions:** Through Huntly Sq, across monument, through arch and past castle.
DAVID PLUMPTON ☎ (0466) 792696.

Huntly continued

An ideal base for the sporting type among you - fishing, deer stalking and shooting are all included in the local activities. The Hotel itself is tastefully decorated and rich in character. Serving unpretentious meals made from local produce, in a relaxed atmosphere. Comfortable accommodation.

INSCH Grampian **Map 13 B2**

⊗££ **THE LODGE** Old Rayne, Insch.

⌂££ **Hours:** Breakfast 8am - 9am, Lunch 12 noon - 2.30pm and Dinner weekdays 7pm - 8pm weekends 7pm - 9pm (last orders). **Cuisine:** A la carte - Half Duckling in Cointreau and Orange, Prawn Marie Rose. ⮑ 2 bedrooms, en suite. **CC** Access, Visa. **Other Points:** Children welcome. Dogs allowed. Teas. Vegetarian meals by arrangement. **P** & **Directions:** Off the A96, 9 miles N of Inverurie, 12 miles S of Huntly.

MR & MRS NEIL ☎ (04645) 205

This large granite dwelling house is part of a small village with views of rolling hills and nearby fields. The interior is stunning with a relaxed atmosphere finished off with vases of fresh flowers. The fixed price menu is excellent value and all food is freshly prepared.

INVERGARRY Highland **Map 12 C2**

⊗££ **INVERGARRY HOTEL** Invergarry.

⌂£££ **Hours:** Breakfast 8.15am - 9.30am, self-service restaurant open

CLUB 9am - 7pm, Dinner 7pm - 8.30pm (last orders). Bar snacks available 12 noon - 2pm and 6pm - 9pm. **Cuisine:** Bar meals, self-service restaurant meals, and dinner featuring Scottish and international dishes and using fresh, predominantly local produce. ⮑ 10 bedrooms, all en suite. **CC** Access, Visa, AmEx. **Other Points:** Children welcome. Afternoon teas. Dogs allowed. Residents' lounge. Garden. Fax No: (08093) 207. 7 miles from Loch Ness, 25 miles from Ben Nevis. **P (V) Directions:** From A82, turn onto A87, in Invergarry, hotel on right.

DAVID, JANETTA, ROBERT & DONALD MACCALLUM ☎ (08093) 206.

A family run, Highland hotel offering comfortable accommodation, good food and friendly service. The interior decor is in keeping with the distinctive and attractive Victorian building and provides comfortable and relaxed surroundings. Well placed to enjoy the beauty of the Scottish Highlands, fishing, golf, skiiing or visits to the distilleries.

INVERNESS Highland **Map 12 B2**

⌂££ **ARDMUIR HOUSE HOTEL** 16 Ness Bank, Inverness.

⮑ 1 single, 2 twin, 6 double and 2 family bedrooms, all en suite. **Hours:** Breakfast 8am - 9am, Dinner 6.30pm - 7.30pm. **CC** None. **Other Points:** Children welcome. Garden. Dogs allowed. No smoking in dining room. **P (V) Directions:** Off B862 to Loch Ness.

JEAN & TONY GATCOMBE ☎ (0463) 231151.

A small, family run hotel situated on the east bank of the river Ness a few minutes walk from both the town centre and Ness Islands. The Georgian residence has been improved to mee modern day requirements and all bedrooms have en suite facilities, tea/coffee making facilities, colour TVs and electric blankets. Traditional Scottish fare is served in the dining room

Inverness continued

℡£££ CULDUTHEL LODGE 14 Culduthel Road, Inverness.

🛏 12 bedrooms, 12 en suite. All rooms have tea/coffee making facilities, telephone, colour TV and hair dryer. **Hours:** Breakfast 8am - 9am. **CC** Access, Visa. **Other Points:** No smoking areas. Dogs allowed. Central heating. Gardens. Eurocard and Mastercard also accepted. **P** **(V) Directions:** Less than 1 mile from city centre. B861.

DAVID & MARION BONSOR ☎ (0436) 240089.

Georgian building set in its own grounds and enjoying views of the River Ness. The resident owners ensure that their guests enjoy a comfortable, relaxing stay. Tastefully decorated and furnished to a very high standard. Ideal touring base.

⊗£ ℡££ WHINPARK HOTEL & RESTAURANT 17 Ardross Street, Inverness.

Hours: Breakfast 7.30am - 9am, Lunch 12 noon - 2pm, Dinner 6.30pm - 9.30pm (9pm Sunday). Closed: Sunday lunch. **Cuisine:** A blend of modern and classical food. Smoked salmon mousse, fish soup, roast rack of lamb, steamed roulade of salmon and sole. 🛏 9 bedrooms, 4 en suite. **CC** Access, Visa. **Other Points:** Children welcome. Pets allowed (except in restaurant). Functions catered for. **Directions:** City centre.

STEPHEN MACKENZIE ☎ (0463) 232549

Our Inspector noted that this was 'a small, friendly restaurant with bedrooms'. The emphasis in this town house hotel is definitely on high quality food prepared from fresh seasonal

Inverness continued

> *ingredients. The hotel is close to central Inverness' shopping area and Eden Court Theatre.*

ISLE OF BARRA Western Isles **Map 12 B1**
⊗££ **CASTLEBAY HOTEL** Castlebay, Isle of Barra.

⍟££££ **Hours:** Breakfast 7.30pm - 9.30pm, lunch 12.30pm - 2pm, dinner 6pm - 9pm. Bar snacks 11am - 9pm. **Cuisine:** Traditional cuisine, with an emphasis on fresh fish. Dishes may include Mussels in White Wine Sauce, Lobster, Chicken Chaseur, Strawberry Gateau. ⊨ 12 bedrooms, 8 en suite. **CC** Access, Visa. **Other Points:** Children welcome. Afternoon teas served. Dogs allowed. Offering special air and car ferry packages. **P (V)**
MR GEORGE MACLEOD. ☎ (08714) 223.

> *A small family run hotel in the main village overlooking the harbour & the Isle of Vatersay. Comfortable accommodation and good food. While visiting here you can enjoy walking, fishing or sailing. If you would rather relax, there are plenty of beautiful, secluded sandy beaches to choose from.*

ISLE OF BENBECULA Western Isles **Map 12 B1**
⍟££££ **DARK ISLAND HOTEL** Liniclate, Benbecula.

⊨ 7 single, 24 double, 12 twin, and 1 family room, 37 of them en suite. Colour TV, radio, alarm, and tea/coffee making facilities. **Hours:** 7.30am - 9.30am, 12 noon - 2pm, and 6.30pm - 9.30pm. Bar meals 12 noon - 2pm and 6pm - 10pm. **CC** Access, Visa. **Other Points:** Children welcome. Pets allowed. Open Sundays and bank holidays. Resident's lounge. **P & (V) Directions:** 4m from airport, 26m from ferry terminals: Loch Boisdale/Lochmaddy.
MR STEPHEN PETERANNA ☎ (0870) 2414.

> *Privately owned hotel, offering comfortable, well-appointed accommodation, good food and service. Ideal holiday base, being well-situated for exploring adjacent islands: North Uist, Barra, Eriskay. Golf is available free of charge and there is trout fishing on over 70 lochs. This is also the perfect place to stay if you are a keen archeologist or ornitholgist.*

ISLE OF HARRIS Western Isles **Map 12 A1**
⍟££££ **THE HARRIS HOTEL** Isle of Harris.

⊨ 5 single, 7 double, 12 twin and 2 family bedrooms, 16 with en suite. 3 bathrooms, 2 showers. **Hours:** Breakfast 8.30am - 9.15am, lunch 12 noon - 2pm, dinner 7.30pm - 9pm. Restaurant open to non residents. **CC** Access, Visa. **Other Points:** Partial central heating. Children welcome. Licensed. Residents' lounge. TV. Garden. Eurocards also accepted. **Directions:** On the A859 central to village of Tarbert.
HELEN & JOHN MORRISON ☎ (0859) 2154/2425.

> *An established family run hotel. J M Barrie once stayed here and etched his initials in the dining room window. The hotel is a perfect base for touring Harris and Lewis and people return year after year to soak up the history, peace and unspoilt beauty of these dramatic islands.*

ISLE OF LEWIS Western Isles **Map 12 A1**
⊗£££ **CABARFEIDH HOTEL** Manor Park, Stornoway, Isle of Lewis.

⍟££££ **Hours:** Breakfast 7.15am - 10am, Lunch 12.15pm - 2pm, Dinner 7pm - 9.30pm (last orders). Open all year. **Cuisine:** French cuisine

Isle of Lewis continued

using predominantly fresh local produce. Fish dishes are a speciality. ⊨ 46 bedrooms, all en suite. **CC** All major cards. **Other Points:** Children welcome. Dogs allowed. Conferences, seminars & functions. Guest memebership of nearby golf course can be arranged. Fax No: (0851) 705572. **P** ₺ **(V) Directions:** A859 from Tarbert, A866 from Stornoway. 1 mile from ferry terminal. CALA HOTELS LTD. Manager - DONNIE ROSS ☎ (0851) 702604.

The Cabarfeidh Hotel offers the highest standards of comfort and luxury. Dine within the beautiful surroundings of the restaurant with its first class choice of menus, fresh fish and shell fish specialities. An ideal base for exploring the striking scenery of the island, pursuing your favourite pastime, or simply relaxing. Highly recommended.

ISLE OF SKYE Highland **Map 12 B1**

⊗£££ **DUISDALE HOTEL** Isle Ornsay, Sleat, Isle of Skye.
⊞£££ **Hours:** Breakfast 8.30am - 9.30am, lunch 12.30pm - 2pm, dinner
CLUB 7.30pm - 8.30pm. **Cuisine:** Dishes include grilled grapefruit Napoleon, venison and orange stew, strawberry and almond gateau. ⊨ 5 single, 8 twin, 2 double and 4 family bedrooms. 14 en suite. **CC** Access, Visa, AmEx. **Other Points:** Children welcome. Garden. Afternoon teas. Dogs allowed. **P** **(V) Directions:** On A851.
MARGARET COLPUS ☎ (04713) 202.

Built in a Scottish hunting lodge style, this family run hotel is set in 25 acres, overlooking Sound of Sleat. Offering good food and comfortable accommodation, Duisdale is ideal for fishing, walking or observing the wild life. Frequented by mixed ages, the atmosphere is quiet and peaceful.

⊗££ **FLODIGARRY COUNTRY HOUSE HOTEL** Staffin, Isle of
⊞££ Skye.
Hours: Breakfast served at 8.30am, bar snacks 11am - 10.30pm, dinner 7pm - 10pm (last orders 9.30pm), Sunday lunches only 12.30pm - 2.30pm. **Cuisine:** Dishes may include Collops of veal with nettles & lemon sauce, Fresh poached salmon, Gresham duck with orange sauce. ⊨ 16 bedrooms, 11 en suite. **CC** Access, Visa. **Other Points:** Children welcome. Open Bank Holidays. No smoking area. Afternoon teas. Dogs allowed. Garden dining. Fax/telephone No (047) 052 203. **P** ₺ **(V) Directions:** Follow A855 north from Portree - Staffin, hotel approx 5km north.
ANDREW & PAMELA BUTLER ☎ (047) 052 203.

Magnificently situated with panoramic views across the sea to the Torridon mountains. Family run, the hotel offers comfortable accommodation, Highland hospitality, and the best of traditional Scottish dishes and tempting specialities prepared from fresh local produce . The cottage next to the hotel was home to Flora MacDonald who helped in the escape of Bonnie Prince Charlie.

⊗££ **GRESHORNISH HOUSE HOTEL** Greshornish, Isle of Skye.
⊞£££ **Hours:** Breakfast 8am - 10am, dinner 7.30pm - 8.30pm (last orders.) Sunday dinner 7.30pm - 8.30pm. **Cuisine:** Dishes include soups, omelettes, cannelloni, Chinese prawns, salmon steak, pineapple cake, cherry flan. ⊨ 5 rooms, 2 twin, 2 double and 1

Isle of Skye continued

family room. **CC** Visa. **Other Points:** Children welcome. Garden. Afternoon teas served. Dogs allowed. Snooker table, pool table, tennis, croquet, badminton and table tennis. **P** **(V) Directions:** On A850.
MRS J DICKSON ☎ (047082) 266.
A Highland hotel situated on Lochside with views over Loch Greshornish. The hotel is surrounded by mature trees and shrubbery. Scottish fare and comfortable accommodation is on offer in this hotel. A quiet and peaceful atmosphere adds to its allure if wanting to get away from the hustle and bustle of city life.

⊗**££** **HOTEL EILEAN IARMAIN** Sleat, Isle of Skye.
££ **Hours:** Open throughout the year. **Cuisine:** Homemade soups, CLUB mussels Te Bheag, stapag (cream and oatmeal), homemade oatcakes, fresh local prawns, chocolate brandy cake. ⊨ 12 bedrooms, 6 in 'Garden House'. **CC** None. **Other Points:** Children welcome. Stalking, shooting, fishing. **(V)**
SIR IAIN NOBLE ☎ (047 13) 332.
Old fashioned Gaelic-speaking Highland inn situated in a landscaped park on a little private harbour overlooking the Sound of Sleat to the waters of Loch Hourn and mainland hills. The Hotel has been extensively modernised to provide comfort, but with its antique furniture, it still retains its character.

⊗**££££** **KINLOCH LODGE** Sleat, Isle of Skye.
££££ **Hours:** Breakfast 8.30am - 9.30am. Dinner 8pm or by arrangement. Closed: December - February inclusive. **Cuisine:** Excellent Table d'hote menu. Main courses may include Roast Loin of Pork with Mushroom & Vermouth Sauce, Smoked Haddock Roulade with Scallops. ⊨ 10 bedrooms, 8 en suite. The accommodation prices are just outside the Les Routiers price bracket during high season. **CC** Access, Visa. **Other Points:** Afternoon teas. Dogs allowed by arrangement. Residents' lounge. Garden. Fax No: (04713) 277. **P** **(V) Directions:** 1 mile from A851. 6 miles S of Broadford and 8 miles N of Armadale.
LORD & LADY MACDONALD ☎ (04713) 214/333.
Kinloch Lodge is the home of Lord & Lady MacDonald and family, who have turned their historic home into a small, comfortable hotel. The food is superb and Lady MacDonald's cooking and attention to detail has earned great praise from some of the best known gourmets and food writers. An ideal spot for a quiet, relaxing holiday and to enjoy the spectacular views.

££££ **ROSEDALE HOTEL** Portree.
⊨ 5 single, 5 double, and 13 twin rooms, all en suite. All rooms with colour TV, radio, alarm, telephones and tea/coffee making facilities. **Hours:** 8am - 9.30am, and 7pm - 8.30pm. Closed: October to April. **CC** Access, Visa. **Other Points:** Children welcome. Pets allowed. Resident's lounge and garden. Fully licensed. Fax No: (0478) 2531. **P** **(V) Directions:** Centre of village. On harbour side, facing water.
H M ANDREW ☎ (0478) 3131.
A small hotel, created from a series of 19th century fishermen's dwellings, but with all modern comforts installed. An ideal base

Isle of Skye continued

for exploring the surrounding area, with Dunnegan Castle and the Clan Donald Centre close by.

⊗£££ **SKEABOST HOUSE HOTEL** Skeabost Bridge, Isle of Skye.
⊞£££ **Hours:** Breakfast 8.30am - 9.30am, Buffet lunch 12 noon - 1.30pm (last orders), Dinner 7pm - 8.30pm. Closed: mid October - April. **Cuisine:** Traditional Scottish cuisine using fresh, local ingredients. ⊨ 26 bedrooms, 24 en suite. ⓒⓒ Access, Visa. **Other Points:** Children welcome. Dogs allowed. No smoking in dining room. Afternoon teas. Garden dining. Private salmon & trout fishing on River Snizort. ◘ **(V) Directions:** Kyle of Lochalsh - Kyleakin Ferry. 38 miles to Skeabost Bridge.
THE STUART & MCNAB FAMILIES ☎ (047 032) 202.
A former Victorian Shooting Lodge set in 12 acres of secluded woodland and gardens. It is a comfortable and relaxing, family run hotel with 3 lounges, cocktail bar and billiard room. The cuisine is excellent using fresh, local produce. The hotel has a 9 hole golf course and salmon and sea trout fishing on River Snizort - all free to guests who stay 3 days or more.

⊗£ **THE CASTLE MOIL RESTAURANT** Kyleakin, Isle of Skye.
Hours: Breakfast all day, lunch 12 noon - 5pm, dinner 5pm - 9.15pm (last orders) Bar snacks served all day. Closed: November - February. Open Bank Holidays. **Cuisine:** Self service during the day, table service in the evening. House speciality is sea food. Also salads, steaks, grills and all day breakfast. ⊨ None. ⓒⓒ Access, Visa. **Other Points:** Children welcome. No smoking area. Restaurant self service during the day. Coach parties welcome. ◘ ⅙ **(V) Directions:** On the Skye side of the ferry.
ALEXANDER J C MACDIARMID ☎ (0599) 4164.
Comfortable restaurant serving reasonably priced snacks, lunches and evening meals. Just 300 yrds from Skye ferry terminal, The Castle Moil is worthy of a visit to break your journey and to enjoy a good value meal or snack.

⊗£ **THE STABLES - CLAN DONALD CENTRE** Armadale, Sleat, Isle of Skye.
Hours: Lunch served 12 noon - 2.30pm (last orders), dinner 5.45pm - 8pm (last orders). Closed: November - Mid March. Open Bank Holidays. **Cuisine:** Dishes may include Mallaig Kippers, Roast Gigot of Lamb with mint and apricot sauce, Haddock Meuniere. ⊨ Self-catering suites and cottages. ⓒⓒ Access, Visa, AmEx. **Other Points:** Children welcome. Afternoon teas served. Garden. Self catering accommodation available. Fax No. (047) 14275. ◘ ⅙ **(V) Directions:** 5 mins from Mallaig-Armadale ferry.
MR ROB McDONALD PARKER ☎ (047) 14 305/227.
The Clan Donald Centre is set in beautiful countryside at the Southern end of Sleat peninsula. 'Stables', the licensed restaurant offers coffee, home baking and excellent meals specialising in local seafood. With craft and book shops, the Centre is an extremely interesting place to visit.

⊗££ **UIG HOTEL** Uig, Portree, Isle of Skye.
⊞£££ **Hours:** Breakfast 8am - 9am, lunch 12.30pm - 1.45pm, dinner 7.15pm - 8.30pm. Closed: mid Oct - mid April. **Cuisine:** Traditional cuisine. House specialities are peat smoked salmon,

Isle of Skye continued

venison casserole and bread & butter pudding. ⊨ 16 bedrooms, all en suite. **CC** All major cards. **Other Points:** Children over 12 welcome. Afternoon teas. Dogs allowed by arrangement. No smoking area. Garden. Fax (047 042) 308. **P** **(V) Directions:** A856. On right hand side of road approaching Uig from Portree. GRACE GRAHAM & DAVID TAYLOR ☎ (047 042) 205.

An old Coaching Inn set on a hillside overlooking Loch Snizort. It is a family run hotel offering excellent accommodation, good food and a warm welcome. The hotel has its own pony trekking and a self catering apartment. Bargain breaks available.

ISLE OF SOUTH UIST Western Isles **Map 12 B1**

⊗££ **BORRODALE HOTEL** Daliburgh, South Uist.

⏠£££ **Hours:** Breakfast 7.30am - 9.30am, lunch 12.30pm - 2pm, bar snacks 6.30pm - 9pm, dinner 7pm - 9pm (last orders 8.30pm). **Cuisine:** Dishes may include Scotch Cockles in Whisky & Oatmeal, Venison with Red Wine and Mushroom Sauce, Strawberry Cheesecake. Speciality dishes - Seafood. ⊨ 14 bedrooms, all en suite. **CC** Access, Visa. **Other Points:** Children welcome. Afternoon Teas. Dogs allowed. Self-catering caravans available. **P** ⅅ **(V) Directions:** 2.5 miles from Lochboisdale ferry, on Jct of the A865 and B888.

MR DONALD PETERANNA ☎ (08784) 444.

The Borrodale Hotel is a small family run hotel famous for its shellfish dishes and friendly atmosphere. Offering comfortable accommodation. The helpful staff will arrange golfing, fishing or tell you of the best beaches or where to spot rare and splendid birds.

KINCRAIG Highland **Map 13 C1**

⊗£ **THE BOATHOUSE RESTAURANT** Loch Insh, Kincraig.

⏠£ **Hours:** Open December 28th - October 31st from 10am - 10pm (last orders for dinner 9pm). **Cuisine:** Home baking, fresh salads, Fondues, Barbecues. Bar meals served all day. A la carte evening menu. ⊨ 13 bedrooms, 7 bathrooms. 5 self-catering chalets: one 6 berth, three 4/5 berth and one 7 berth. **CC** Visa. **Other Points:** Children welcome. Ski instruction. Dry ski slope hire and instruction. Water sports equipment hire and instruction. **P** ⅅ **(V) Directions:** Off A9 at Kingussie.Follow Loch Insh Watersports sign at Kincraig.

MR & MRS C FRESHWATER ☎ (0540) 651272.

Situated by Loch Insh this restaurant is always a hub of activity because of the many sporting activities taking place, eg. sailing, skiing and canoeing. This restaurant offers a warm welcome, good well prepared food and value for money.

KINGUSSIE Highland **Map 13 C1**

⊗££ **THE ROYAL HOTEL** High Street, Kingussie.

⏠££ **Hours:** Breakfast 8am - 9.30am, Lunch 12 noon - 2pm, Dinner
CLUB 7pm - 9.30pm. **Cuisine:** 3 course lunches, 4 course table d'hote dinner, a la carte. Traditional Scottish cuisine prepared from fresh local produce. ⊨ 52 bedrooms, all en suite. **CC** All major cards. **Other Points:** Children welcome. Garden. Afternoon teas. Dogs allowed. No smoking area. **P** **(V) Directions:** Just off the A9. In the centre of Kingussie.

MR JUSTICE ☎ (0540) 661898.

Kingussie continued

The Royal Hotel is in the centre of Kingussie in the beautiful Spey Valley. An ideal base for all types of outdoor activities, including skiiing, and for touring the Highlands. The hotel is family owned and run offering good accommodation, food and a warm welcome.

⊗££ **THE SCOT HOUSE HOTEL** Newtonmore Road, Kingussie.
£££ **Hours:** Breakfast 8.30am - 9.30am, lunch, residents only, dinner and bar dinners 6pm - 9pm. **Cuisine:** A full range of Scottish produce and local dishes such as Salmon Tartar, Game Casserole, Medallions of Scotch Beef with Stilton & a Port wine sauce. ⇌ 10 rooms. All en suite. **CC** Access, Visa. **Other Points:** Children welcome. Garden. No smoking in dining room. Tourist Board 4 Crown Commended. **P** **(V) Directions:** At the south end of the main street of Kingussie.
ALASDAIR & KATHLEEN BUCHANAN ☎ (0540) 661351.
The traditional grey sandstone building is situated in picturesque village of Kingussie only 10 miles from Aviemore and provides the perfect base for touring or sporting holidays in the beautiful Spey Valley. A former church manse, now tastefully modernised as a licensed family run country house hotel offering good food, stylish en suite accommodation & personal attentive service.

KINLOCHBERVIE Highland **Map 12 A2**
⊗£ **OLD SCHOOL RESTAURANT & GUEST HOUSE** Inshegra,
££ Kinlochbervie, by Lairg.
CLUB **Hours:** Meals served from 12 noon - 2pm, 6pm - 8.30pm. Bar meals also available. **Cuisine:** Fresh fish, lobster, salmon, lamb, king prawns. ⇌ 4 self-contained twin bedrooms and 2 double bedrooms. All with radio, TV, telephone and tea making facilities. **CC** Access, Visa. **Other Points:** Children welcome. Dogs at management's discretion. Coaches by appointment. **P** & **(V) Directions:** From the A838 at Rhiconich take the B801 to Kinlochbervie.
TOM & MARGARET BURT ☎ (097182) 383.
Built as a school for the local community in 1879, it was an active school until 1972. Loch Clash has become Scotland's 3rd largest fishing port and the area is well known for its beaches and walks. Margaret's home cooking has made this restaurant very popular with locals and visitors. Highly recommended.

⊗££££ **THE KINLOCHBERVIE HOTEL** Kinlochbervie, By Lairg.
££££ **Hours:** Breakfast 8.30am - 9.30am, lunch 12 noon - 1.45pm (last orders), dinner 7.30pm - 8.30pm. Sunday lunch 12.30pm - 1.45pm, Sunday dinner 7.30pm - 8.30pm. Closed: January - February. **Cuisine:** A wide range of dishes including Smoked Salmon from own Smokehouse, Medallions of Venison with Mushroom & Port Sauce. Nightly changing 4 course menu ⇌ 14 rooms. 5 twin, 4 double, 5 family rooms. All rooms en suite. **CC** All major cards. **Other Points:** Children welcome. Garden. Afternoon teas served. Dogs allowed. Fax (097 182) 438 **P** **(V) Directions:** A836/A838/B801. Overlooking harbour in Kinlochbervie.
MRS & MRS NEAME ☎ (097 182) 275
The Kinlochbervie Hotel is a privately run modern hotel. It is well situated with suberb views of Kinlochbervie harbour and

Kinlochbervie continued
Lock Clash. The rugged hills, spectacular sunset and the varying mood of the Atlantic creates a lasting memory. Whether you stay a single night or a complete holiday you will enjoy good food in comfortable surroundings.

KINLOCHLEVEN Highland **Map 12 C2**

⊗££ **MACDONALD HOTEL** Wades Road, Kinlochleven.
⌂£££ **Hours:** Breakfast 8am - 9am, dinner 7pm - 9pm (last orders), bar snacks 12 noon - 9pm (last orders). Open Bank Holidays. Open all year. **Cuisine:** Menu may feature - Rack of Scottish Lamb glazed with Honey and Rosemary, Medallions of local Venison with a red wine sauce. ⊨ 10 bedrooms, 8 en suite. All rooms have colour TV, and tea/coffee making facilities. **CC** Visa. **Other Points:** Children welcome. Garden dining. Waterside location. Fax/Telephone No. (08554) 539. **P** ⅁ **(V) Directions:** Going North on A82 take turning at Glencoe Village.
PETER & SUSAN MACDONALD ☎ (08554) 539.
This is a small, new, comfortable hotel, built in a traditional West Highland style, where the resident proprietors and staff pride themselves on a warm welcome and personal service. Good food and accommodation at value for money.

LAIRG Highland **Map 12 A2**

⊗££££ **AULTNAGAR LODGE** Near Lairg.
⌂££££ **Hours:** Breakfast 8am - 9.30am, lunch 12 noon - 2.30pm (last orders 2pm) and dinner 6.30pm - 10pm (last orders). **Cuisine:** A la carte and table d'hote, including fish specialities. Light snacks and bar meals available. ⊨ 24 rooms. 8 single, 6 twin, 8 double rooms and 2 family rooms. **CC** All major cards. **Other Points:** Garden. Afternoon teas. Dogs allowed. Golf, fishing, clay pigeon shooting, hill walking and pony trekking arrangements. **P** ⅁ **(V) Directions:** A836, approximately 2 miles from the Shin Falls.
MR G F ROBERTSON ☎ (054 982) 245
Built in 1904 and set in 22 acres of beautiful, unspoilt countryside this hunting lodge has a character all its own. The combination of well prepared food - with an emphasis on fresh local produce, elegant surroundings and friendly, efficient, staff, makes The Aultnagar a delight to visit. Attractive to holidaymakers because of its warm and friendly atmosphere.

⊗££ **INCHNADAMPH HOTEL** Assynt, By Lairg, Sutherland.
⌂£££ **Hours:** 8.30am - 9am, 1pm - 1.45pm, and 7pm - 7.30pm. Restaurant closed: November - mid-March. **Cuisine:** Traditional home-cooking, dishes including poached Assynt salmon, honey glazed grilled gammon steak,and roast loin of pork served with an apricot sauce. ⊨ 11 single, 8 twin, 3 double, and 5 family rooms, 10 of them en suite. **CC** Access, Visa, Diners. **Other Points:** Children welcome. Dogs allowed. Fishing tackle suitable for the area on sale on premises. **P (V) Directions:** A837, near Ben More Assynt.
J S & E MORRISON ☎ (05712) 202.
This hotel is well-known to anglers, for it offers free fishing for salmon, grilse and brown trout. The hotel is also an ideal base for those interested in geology, botany and ornitholgy - and climbers will be delighted to to discover Ben More Assynt - the

Lairg continued

highest mountain in Sutherland - so nearby. The hotel is a cheerful place to stay, offering good food and bright rooms.

MELVICH Highland **Map 13 A1**

⊗££ **MELVICH HOTEL** Melvich, by Thurso, Sutherland.

⌂££ **Hours:** Breakfast 7am - 9am, lunch 12 noon - 2pm, dinner 7pm - [CLUB] 8.30pm (last orders). **Cuisine:** Specialities are local seafood and game. ⌣ 14 rooms. 6 single and 8 double. All en suite. ▣ Access, Visa. **Other Points:** Children welcome. Garden. Afternoon teas. Dogs allowed. French, German and Dutch spoken. ▣ &. **(V) Directions:** Approach by A9 from Inverness - Helmsdale then by A897 - Melvich.

P K & M E SCHOONENBERG. ☎ (06413) 206.

Family run country hotel with superb views over the Halladale estuary and Pentland Firth to the Orkneys. Comfortable en suite rooms, good fresh local food and friendly service make this an ideal base for fishing, hill walking, bird watching, pony trekking and relaxing. Near to fine sandy beaches. The lounge has open peat fires, lovely views & superb range of malt whiskies.

NAIRN Highland **Map 13 B1**

⌂££ **GREENLAWNS HOTEL** Seafield Street, Nairn.

⌣ 2 twin and 4 double bedrooms, 2 en suite. **Hours:** Breakfast 8am - 9am. ▣ Access, Visa. **Other Points:** Children welcome. Dogs allowed. Garden. ▣ **Directions:** About half a mile from the Elgin/Inverness Road.

WILLIAM & ISABEL CALDWELL ☎ (0667) 52738.

A Victorian villa offering comfortable accommodation of a high standard and friendly, welcoming service. Situated close to beaches, bowling greens, golf courses, tennis courts, riding stables and a swimming pool. Greenlawns is also an ideal centre for touring northern Scotland and is in easy reach of Loch Ness, Cawdor and Brodie Castles.

⊗££ **RAMLEH HOTEL & FINGAL'S RESTAURANT** Ramlet ⌂£££ House, 2 Academy Street, Nairn.

Hours: Breakfast 7.30am - 9am, Lunch 12 noon - 2pm. Last orders for dinner at 9pm. **Cuisine:** A wide variety of dishes served including, fish and seafood, poultry and game, meat and also vegetarian meals. Desserts and a cheeseboard also on menu. ⌣ 10 rooms, 3 single, 2 twin and 2 double rooms, 3 family rooms. 7 en suite. TV, shaver points, heating, tea/coffee making facilities in all rooms. ▣ Access, Visa, AmEx. **Other Points:** Children welcome. No pets. Garden. Afternoon teas served. ▣ &. **(V) Directions:** In Nairn's West End.

GEORGE & CAROL WOODHOUSE ☎ (0667) 53551.

This is a family run hotel and restaurant offering good food and comfortable accommodation. The restaurant features a new conservatory for that relaxed, friendly atmosphere. Close to the High Street, beach, 2 golf courses, harbour, and all amenities.

⊗£ **THE ALBERT INN & LAMPLIGHTER RESTAURANT** 1 ⌂££ Albert Street, Nairn.

Hours: Lunch 12 noon - 2pm (in the bar). Dinner 5pm - 9.30 pm (bar and restaurant) later in summer months. **Cuisine:** Traditional,

SCOTTISH HIGHLANDS

Nairn continued

a la carte and bar snack menus. ⊨ 8 bedrooms, all en suite. **CC** Access, Visa. **Other Points:** Children welcome. Garden. Disabled access to restaurant only. **P** **(V) Directions:** Beside the bus station, on A96.

ROBERT MACKINTOSH ☎ (0667) 54474

An attractive Inn blending old with the new, and decorated to a high standard throughout. This inn offers excellent value for money which, together with the warm friendly atmosphere and good home cooking, makes it a popular choice for locals and tourists alike. Close to golf course.

⊗££ **THE LINKS HOTEL** 1 Seafield Street, Nairn.
£££ **Hours:** Breakfast 7.45am - 9.15am, lunch 12.30pm - 2.30pm, dinner 7pm - 9pm. Bar snacks 6.30pm - 9.30pm. **Cuisine:** Menu may feature salmon en croute, local breast of wood pigeon Languedoc, fresh pink trout fillets with prawn and pernod sauce, sirloin steak. ⊨ 10 bedrooms, all en suite. **CC** Access, Visa. **Other Points:** Children welcome. Open Bank Holidays. Afternoon teas. Dogs allowed. Garden dining. **P** **(V) Directions:** Jct Marine Rd, turn down Marine Road or Albert St from A9.

IAN & CAROL COOPER ☎ (0667) 53321.

A large stone villa with lovely views of the Moray Firth, decorated in warm colours and providing real country house comfort. Generous helpings of tasty meals made from fresh ingredients can be enjoyed in the relaxed atmosphere of the restaurant. Comfortable accommodation available at a reasonable price. Ideal base for touring or a golfing break.

⊗££ **THE WOODLAND COTTAGE RESTAURANT** Geddes Village, Nairn.
CLUB **Hours:** Sunday Lunch 12.30pm - 2pm and Dinner Wednesday to Saturday 7.30pm - 9.00pm (last orders). Closed: Lunchtimes except Sun, Sunday - Tuesday evenings. **Cuisine:** Set price menu. Roast lamb with garlic & kiwi fruit, Chicken with vermouth & noodles - all dishes served with a platter of 6 fresh vegetables. ⊨ None. **CC** Access, Visa. **Other Points:** Children welcome. Pets allowed. **P** **& (V) Directions:** Off the B9090/B9091 from Nairn. Half a mile from Geddes Village.

DIANE & IAIN SCALLY ☎ (06677) 634

Booking is essential at this small but efficient restaurant, run by a husband and wife team. Diane uses only the finest fresh ingredients in imaginative dishes, served in charming surroundings, with warmth and care.

NEWBURGH Grampian **Map 13 B2**
⊗£££ **UDNY ARMS HOTEL** Newburgh, Ellon, Aberdeenshire.
£££ **Hours:** Breakfast 7am - 10am, 12 noon - 2.30pm and Dinner 6.30pm -12 midnight (last orders 9.30pm). Bar meals 12 noon - 2.30pm. **Cuisine:** Traditional: roast rib of Aberdeenshire beef, casserole of woodpigeon and pan-fried chicken breast. Fresh seafood daily. ⊨ 26 bedrooms, all en suite. **CC** Access, Visa, AmEx. **Other Points:** Children welcome. Dogs allowed. Conference facilities. **P** **(V) Directions:** Off the A92 Aberdeen to Peterhead road.

MR DENIS CRAIG ☎ (03586) 89444.

Newburgh continued

The hotel overlooks the peaceful Ythan Estuary, renowned for its colonies of birds. Within these beautiful surroundings, the Udny Arms charms its guests with its relaxed atmosphere. Excellent menu which changes daily, but sticky toffee pudding is always available as it has gained an international reputation. Recommended.

ORKNEY Kirkwall **Map 13 A1**

⊗£££ **ALBERT HOTEL** Mounthoolie Lane, Kirkwall, Orkney.
⊞££££ **Hours:** Breakfast 7.30am - 9.30am, Lunch 12 noon - 2pm, Dinner 7pm - 10pm. Bar meals 12 noon - 2pm and 6pm - 10pm. Closed: Christmas Day and New Years Day. **Cuisine:** A la carte restaurnt meals and bar meals made from fresh, local produce. House speciality is the Seafood Platter. ⊨ 19 bedrooms, all en suite. **CC** Access, Visa. **Other Points:** Children welcome. No dogs. Fax No: (0856) 5397. **Directions:** In centre of Kirkwall, off Junction Rd. Close to harbour.
ANJO CASEY ☎ (0856) 6000.
A comfortable, family run hotel in the centre of Kirkwall. Recently refurbished, the Albert Hotel is noted for its good food made from fresh, local produce. An ideal place to stay when exploring these unique islands.

⊗££ **WEST END HOTEL** 14 Main Street, Kirkwall, Orkney.
⊞££ **Hours:** Breakfast 7.30am - 9am, Dinner 6.30pm - 10pm. Bar meals 12 noon - 1.45pm and 6pm - 9.30pm. **Cuisine:** Traditional Scottish cuisine using fresh, local produce. Charcoal grilled steak a speciality. ⊨ 10 bedrooms, all en suite. **CC** Access, Visa. **Other Points:** Children welcome. Dogs allowed. Vegetarian meals on request. Fax No: (0856) 6181. **🅿 � Directions:** In Kirkwall, close to the entrance to St Magnus Cathedral.
JAMES CURRIE ☎ (0856) 2368.
A family run hotel built in 1824 which has recently undergone complete refurbishment. The bedrooms are comfortable and fully equipped and the food is well cooked using fresh, local produce. The West End Hotel is an ideal touring base for an enjoyable holiday in the Orkney Islands.

ORKNEY Stenness **Map 13 A1**

⊗£ **TORMISTON MILL RESTAURANT** Stenness, Orkney Islands.
Hours: Meals served 10am - 6pm and 7pm - 9pm (last orders). Closed: Monday - Wednesday inclusive during October to December & March to April. Closed during January and February. **Cuisine:** Dishes may include Scottish Scampi, open sandwiches, home bakes. Steak suppers Fri - Sat evenings. Speciality: Orkney T-bone steak. All day menu. ⊨ None. **CC** Access, Visa. **Other Points:** Children welcome. Smoking not permitted. No dogs. Afternoon teas. Building under the care of the Historic Buildings & Monuments Scotland. **🅿 Directions:** On main A965 Stromness/Kirkwall road, near village of Stenness.
DENNIS BULLEN ☎ (085 676) 372.
Built in 1882, this historic water-powered mill has been run as a restaurant by the Bullen family since 1977. Relax and enjoy a meal and a drink in this popular eating place which provides excellent value for money. The prehistoric chambered tomb of

Orkney continued

Maeshowe is just a few minutes walk away and the Mill has gained several European Architectural Heritage Awards.

PETERHEAD Grampian **Map 13 B2**

⊗£ **BAYVIEW HOTEL** 3 St Peter Street, Peterhead.

⌂££ **Hours:** Breakfast 7am - 9.30am, Lunch 12 noon - 2pm and Dinner 5pm - 8.30pm. **Cuisine:** Traditional Scottish cuisine using fresh fish and seafood, chicken, beef, pork and duck. ⊨ 19 bedrooms, most en suite. **CC** Access, Visa. **Other Points:** Children welcome. Dogs allowed. Fax No: (0779) 79495. **P** **(V) Directions:** Off the A952 between Aberdeen and Fraserburgh.
MR JAMES ELDER ☎ (0779) 72523.

Pleasant family run hotel situated on the coastline of Scotland. Peterhead is the home of the largest fishing fleet in Europe, and during your visit, you may have the opportuntiy to see the fish being landed. There is also a golf course nearby and Aviemore and Inverness are just a short drive away.

RAASAY Highland **Map 12 B1**

⊗££ **ISLE OF RAASAY HOTEL** Raasay, By Kyle of Lochalsh.

⌂£££ **Hours:** Breakfast, bar lunch 12.30pm - 2pm, Dinner from 7pm. Closed: October to March inclusive. **Cuisine:** Fresh Raasay Salmon, Scottish Beef, local fish, cranachan, Strathbogie mist, Raasay wild brambles, peach brulee. Homemade soups & desserts a speciality ⊨ 12 bedrooms, all en suite. **CC** None. **Other Points:** Children welcome. No smoking in restaurant. Non-residents welcome. Afternoon teas. Residents' lounge. Garden. S.T.B. 3 Crown Commended. **P** ⅙ **(V) Directions:** Between Skye & mainland. Easy access by car ferry from Sconser, Skye
ISOBEL NICOLSON ☎ (047862) 222/226

A small, comfortable, family run hotel, situated on the totally unspoilt, beautiful Isle of Raasay with views to the spectacular Cuillin mountains of Skye. The hotel offers an atmosphere of tranquility and total relaxation in an area of outstanding beauty. Good food and accommodation. Ideal for naturalists, hill-walkers and all those who wish to 'get away from it all'.

ROGART Highland **Map 12 A2**

⊗££££ **SCIBERSCROSS LODGE** Strath Brora, Rogart, Sutherland.

⌂££££ **Hours:** All meals are entirely by arrangement with guests (residents and non-residents alike). Closed: November to Janurary inclusive. **Cuisine:** Full Scottish breakfast, 'Sporting Lunch' and 5 course dinner. All wines and spirits are included. ⊨ 6 bedrooms, all en suite. **CC** None. **Other Points:** Residents' lounge. Fishing on Loch Brora & 2 private trout lochs. Stalking. Clay shoot. Not suitable for young children. Fax: (0408) 641465. **P** **(V) Directions:** At mound tn L off A9 onto A839. In Rogart tn R opp. War Memorial.
PETER & KATE HAMMOND ☎ (0408) 641246.

Built in 1876, the Lodge is now a luxurious, classic Highland fishing retreat with the atmosphere of a private house party. All meals are freshly prepared from locally grown and caught produce, cooked in traditional country-house style. A wide range of sport is offered including salmon and sea trout fishing. A luxurious place to truly 'get away from it all'.

SCOURIE Highland **Map 12 A2**

⊗££ **EDDRACHILLES HOTEL** Badcall Bay, Scourie.

⑆££ff **Hours:** Breakfast 8am - 9am, Dinner 6.30pm - 8.30pm. (last orders 8pm). Sunday dinner also served 6.30pm - 8.30pm. **Cuisine:** Dishes include salmon pate, pepper steak, lemon sole meuniere, and desserts such as blackberry & apple pie, rhum baba and pear belle helen. ⇔ 11 rooms. 7 twinbeds, 3 double and 1 family room, all en suite. TV, radio, telephone, trouser press, iron & tea making facilities in all rooms. **CC** Access, Visa. **Other Points:** Fully licenced. Local attractions include Handa Island the famous bird sanctuary, rugged scenery for the walker or climber. **P** **(V)** **Directions:** On A894 it is approximately 6 miles north of Kylesku Bridge.

MR & MRS A C M WOOD ☎ (0971) 502080/502211

Eddrachilles Hotel stands in its own 320 acre estate in a magnificient situation at the head of the Island studded Badcall Bay. This is a family run, comfortable hotel offering good food in friendly relaxing surroundings. If you are looking for a peaceful, tranquil holiday this hotel is well worth a visit.

SHETLAND Brae **Map 13 A2**

⊗££ **DA PEERIE FISK LICENSED RESTAURANT** Busta, Brae,
⌣ Shetland Isles.

Hours: From Easter to mid-October, open all day, every day, 10am - 12 midnight for morning coffee, lunches & snacks, afternoon & high teas, and a full a la carte dinner menu from 6.30pm - 12 midnight (last orders 10pm). **Cuisine:** Locally caught fish and shellfish, prime Aberdeen Angus steaks, a variety of game and a selection of vegetarian dishes. Extensive wine list. ⇔ None. **CC** All major cards. **Other Points:** Special menus for children who are welcome. Safe private beach. Smoking reserved to bar area. Facilities for disabled. Afternoon teas (summer). **P** **&** **(V)** **Directions:** Signposted from A970 west of Brae & down to harbour & jetty.

MAJOR AND MRS E. WISE ☎ (080622) 679.

The most northerly seafood restaurant in Great Britain! At 60 degrees North, Da Peerie Fisk has been recently restored to provide outstanding comfort and cuisine. There are panoramic views of the adjacent Voe where otters breed, and of the surrounding hills, the habitat of sea birds.

SHETLAND Hillswick **Map 13 A2**

⊗££ **ST MAGNUS BAY HOTEL** Hillswick, Shetland Isles.

⑆££ff **Hours:** Breakfast 6am - 9am, Dinner 7.30pm - 9pm (last orders). Bar meals 12.30pm - 2pm and 6.30pm - 9pm. **Cuisine:** Traditional Scottish cuisine with local seafood a speciality. ⇔ 27 bedrooms, all en suite. **CC** Access, Visa. **Other Points:** Children welcome. Afternoon teas. Dogs allowed. Residents' lounge. Fax No: (080 623) 373. **P** **(V) Directions:** A970 - end of road at Hillswick. 40 mins drive from Lerwick.

PETER TITCOMB ☎ (080 623) 372.

A Norwegian Mansion set amidst the unspoiled coastal scenery of the Northmavine region of Shetland and overlooking St Magnus Bay. The accommodation is comfortable and the restaurant provides good meals, with particular emphasis on local seafood. An ideal hotel for families.

SPEAN BRIDGE Highland **Map 12 C2**

⊗££   **OLD PINES** Gairlochy Road, Spean Bridge.

⌂⌖£   **Hours:** Breakfast 8.30am and Dinner 8pm (but both meals can be
CLUB arranged to suit guests). Unlicensed but guests may bring their
own wine. No corkage charge. Non-residents welcome. **Cuisine:**
Table d'hote menu, alternative available. Menu may feature fruit &
cheese salad with raspberry vineger dressing, Stuffed Trout. All
fresh ingredients. ⇤ 2 single, 2 twin, 2 double and 2 family
bedrooms, 6 en suite. Specially adapted bathrooms for disabled.
All bedrooms on ground floor. **CC** Access, Visa. **Other Points:**
Children welcome. Dogs allowed. Afternoon tea - complimentary
scones. Central heating. Log fires. S.T.B 3 Crowns Commended.
P & **(V) Directions:** 300 yards from Commando Memorial above
Spean Bridge, Gairlochy Rd.
NIALL AND SUKIE SCOTT. ☎ (039 781) 324.
A happy family home of great character built in Scandinavian
style. Set in 30 acres of grounds with spectacular views of Ben
Nevis. Guests sit down to enjoy the excellent food together and
non-residents are welcome. The accommodation is comfortable
and shows great care and thought. A uniquely warm and
friendly atmosphere prevails.

STRATHDON Grampian **Map 13 C1**

⊗££   **COLQUHONNIE HOTEL** Strathdon, Aberdeenshire.

⌂⌖££ **Hours:** Breakfast 8.30am - 10am, Lunch 12 noon - 2pm, Dinner
7pm - 8.30pm. **Cuisine:** 5 course table d'hote menu and bar
meals. Traditional Scottish dishes. ⇤ 9 bedrooms, all en suite.
CC AmEx. **Other Points:** Children welcome. Garden. Afternoon
teas. Dogs allowed. 9 miles of salmon & trout fishing. 12 miles from
the 'Lecht' ski resort. **P** **(V) Directions:** A944. A few miles west of
Alford.
W C M MAXWELL ☎ (09756) 51210.
A small country hotel overlooking the beautiful Don Valley.
Family run, you will find a warm, relaxing atmosphere and good
food representing excellent value. The Sunday buffet is a
speciality during summer months. An ideal base for fishing,
shooting, golf, pony trekking, walking or a relaxing break. The
Lonach Highland Games take place in late August.

STRONTIAN Highland **Map 12 C1**

⊗££   **STRONTIAN HOTEL** Strontian.

⌂⌖£££ **Hours:** Breakfast 8.15am - 9.30am, Dinner 6.30pm - 9pm (last
orders). Bar snacks 12 noon - 2pm and 6.30pm - 9pm. **Cuisine:**
Traditional Scottish cuisine. Table d'hote dinner menu and bar
meals. ⇤ 7 bedrooms, 5 en suite. **CC** None. **Other Points:**
Children welcome. Afternoon teas. Dogs allowed. Residents
lounge. **P** **Directions:** A82 to Corran. Take ferry to Ardgour
A861 to Strontian.
RAYMOND STEPHENSON - Manager ☎ (0967) 2029.
A small, friendly hotel offering good food and comfortable
well-appointed accommodation. The hotel lies in a sheltered
position overlooking Loch Sunart and is an excellent base for
exploring the area, fishing, stalking, and for just getting away
from it all.

STRUY Highland **Map 12 B2**

⊗££ **CNOC HOTEL** Struy, By Beauly.

⌂££££ **Hours:** 7am - 9am, 12 noon - 2.30pm, and 7pm - 11pm. **Cuisine:**
CLUB Dinner menu changes daily. Home-cooked fayre, such as Cnoc
fish savoury, and venison dishes. Scottish menus a speciality. ⊨ 3
twin, 3 double, and 2 family rooms, all en suite, with radio/alarms,
baby listening, hairdryer, telephone & tea/coffee. Laundry service
available. ◨ Access, Visa. **Other Points:** Children welcome.
Garden. Dogs welcome. Afternoon teas served. Sky TV in
residents lounge. Vegetarian dishes by arrangement. Switch
accepted. ▯ **Directions:** From A82, turn left onto A831 at
Drumnadrochit, N through Cannick.
MARTIN & PAM CARR ☎ (046376) 264.
*A family run hotel, set in beautiful countryside and ideally
situated for river or loch fishing, walking and climbing. The
Cnoc Hotel was once part of the Erchless Castle Estate, the
former seat of the Clan Chisholm. A friendly, relaxing hotel
offering a high standard of cuisine with the dinner menu
changed daily. Relaxation suite, spa bath, tanning unit, steam
room etc.*

TAIN Highland **Map 13 B1**

⊗££ **MORANGIE HOUSE HOTEL** Morangie Road, Tain.

⌂££££ **Hours:** 7am - 10am, 12.30pm - 2.30pm and 7pm - 10pm. Bar
meals 12 noon - 2.30pm, 5pm - 10pm (last orders). **Cuisine:**
Scottish and continental cuisine, fresh seafood being the
speciality. A la carte, table d'hote and bar menus. ⊨ 11 rooms, all
en suite. ◨ All major cards. **Other Points:** There are 2 Tains in
Highland, so, when heading for Morangie House, make sure it is
the one near Dingwall. Children welcome. No dogs. ▯ **(V)**
Directions: North on A9, take last turn off into Tain on right hand
side.
AVRIL & JOHN WYNNE ☎ (0862) 892281.
*A fine old Victorian mansion, with luxurious rooms and stained
glass windows. Professionally managed yet friendly and
welcoming and offering an extensive range of menus to suit all
tastes, with food of excellent quality. Reduced price golf to
residents. Tain museum and 14th century church nearby.*

TOMINTOUL Grampian **Map 13 B1**

⊗££ **ARGYLE HOUSE** Tomintoul, Ballindalloch.

⌂££ **Hours:** Breakfast 8am - 8.30am. Lunch 12 noon - 2pm. Dinner
5pm - 10pm (last orders 9.30pm). Closed November. **Cuisine:**
Traditional. Specialities: fresh local produce, venison in red wine,
trout with celery & walnut stuffing. ⊨ 5 bedrooms, 3 en suite.
◨ Access, Visa. **Other Points:** Children welcome. Pets allowed.
Afternoon teas. Open Bank holidays and Sunday. Residents
lounge. ▯ **(V) Directions:** 31 miles north of Braemar on A939.
R. & J. FORREST ☎ (08074) 223.
*A comfortable family run guest house in the centre of the village
offering good food and a warm welcome. The surrounding
scenery is spectacular and famous for walking, fishing and
horse riding. The ski slopes of the Lecht are 6 miles away and
the village is at the centre of the 'Whisky Trail', and close to
Balmoral, Braemar and Aviemore.*

SCOTTISH HIGHLANDS

TONGUE Highland **Map 12 A2**

⊗££ **BEN LOYAL HOTEL** Tongue.

⌂£££ **Hours:** Meals from 8am - 9.15am, 6pm - 8pm. Bar meals from 12 noon - 2pm and 6pm - 8.30pm. **Cuisine:** Traditional Scottish cooking using fresh local produce. ⮞ 19 bedrooms, 6 en suite. 3 bathrooms. ▨ Access, Visa. **Other Points:** Coaches by prior appointment only. Vegetarian meals by prior arrangement. ▣ **Directions:** At the junction of the A836 and A838.

MEL & PAULINE COOK ☎ (084 755) 216.

Situated between Durness and Thurso this small crofting town enjoys some of Scotlands most spectacular coastal and mountain scenery and wonderful clean beaches. The warmth of welcome and the genuine friendliness of the staff and proprietors, add to its reputation as a mecca for fishermen and hillwalkers and a holiday/touring centre. A true sanctuary from the stress of urban living.

ULLAPOOL Highland **Map 12 B2**

⊗££ **FOUR SEASONS HOTEL** Ullapool.

⌂£££ **Hours:** Breakfast 8am - 9am, Lunch 12.30pm - 2pm and Dinner 7pm - 8.30pm (last orders). Bar meals 12 noon - 2pm. Closed: 1st November to 1st March. **Cuisine:** Local seafood - lobster (when available), prawns, sole, haddock. Also entrecote steak, chicken breast with prawn sauce and duck a l'orange. ⮞ 16 bedrooms all en suite. ▨ Access, Visa, AmEx. **Other Points:** Children welcome. Pets by arrangement. Vegetarian meals by arrangement. Eurocards accepted. ▣ ও **Directions:** On the A835 by Loch Broom.

MARGARET ERRINGTON ☎ (0854) 2905.

A family run hotel with beautiful views from the restaurant across the Loch. The hotel has its own lobster pots - lobster is a speciality on the menu - and the Errington sons dive for scallops.

⊗££ **THE HARBOUR LIGHTS HOTEL** Garve Road, Ullapool.

⌂£££ **Hours:** Breakfast 8am - 9am, Bar meals 12 noon - 2pm, Dinner 7pm - 9.30pm (last orders). Sunday lunch 12.30pm - 2pm. **Cuisine:** Specialities include local salmon, seafood, Scotch beef and venison, Turf and Surf - Fillet steak, with fresh scallops, prawn tails & shellfish sauce. ⮞ 23 bedrooms, 19 en suite. ▨ Access, Visa. **Other Points:** Children welcome. Garden. Afternoon teas. Dogs allowed. ▣ **(V) Directions:** On the outskirts of Ullapool.

MARILYN & DANNY GORDON ☎ (0854) 2222.

A family run hotel and restaurant offering excellent food, a warm welcome and comfortable accommodation. The spacious lounge has a panoramic view of the harbour, Loch Broom and the surrounding hills and the hotel is only a short walk from the centre of the old fishing port of Ullapool.

INDEX

A

ABERDEEN Grampian 600
ABERDOVEY Gwynedd 368
ABERFELDY Tayside 542
ABERGAVENNY Gwent 368
ABERLADY Lothian 543
ABERLOUR Grampian 600
ABERSOCH Gwynedd 369
ABERYSTWYTH Dyfed 370
ABINGDON Oxfordshire 152
ABOYNE Grampian 600
ACHARACLE Highland 601
AIRDRIE Strathclyde 543
AIRMYN Humberside 416
ALDEBURGH Suffolk 152
ALDERMINSTER Warwickshire 152
ALDERNEY Channel Islands 132
ALFRISTON East Sussex 153
ALMONDBANK Tayside 543
ALNMOUTH Northumberland 537
ALNWICK Northumberland 537
ALTNAHARRA Highland 601
ALTON Staffordshire 416
ALTON Hampshire 153
ALTRINCHAM Greater Manchester
  416
AMBLESIDE Cumbria 417
AMESBURY Wiltshire 154
AMPNEY CRUCIS Gloucestershire 154
ANDOVER Hampshire 154
ANNAN Dumfries & Galloway 544
APPLEBY IN WESTMORLAND
  Cumbria 418
APPLETON LE MOORS North
  Yorkshire 419
ARBROATH Tayside 544
ARDELVE Highland 602
ARISAIG Highland 602
ARMITAGE Staffordshire 155
ARROCHAR Strathclyde 544
ARUNDEL West Sussex 155
ASHBOURNE Derbyshire 419
ASHBY DE LA ZOUCH Leicestershire
  156
ASHTON UNDER LYNE Greater
  Manchester 420
ASKRIGG North Yorkshire 420
ASTHALL Oxfordshire 156
AUCHTERARDER Tayside 545
AUSTWICK North Yorkshire 421
AVIEMORE Highland 603
AXMINSTER Devon 45
AXMOUTH Devon 45
AYR Strathclyde 546

B

BAKEWELL Derbyshire 421
BALA Gwynedd 370
BALDOCK Hertfordshire 157
BALLATER Grampian 603
BALMEDIE Grampian 604
BAMFORD Derbyshire 423
BAMPTON Devon 45
BANBURY Oxfordshire 157
BANCHORY Grampian 604
BARMOUTH Gwynedd 370
BARNSLEY South Yorkshire 423
BARNSTAPLE Devon 46
BARROW IN FURNESS Cumbria 423
BARTLOW Cambridgeshire 158
BASINGSTOKE Hampshire 158
BASSENTHWAITE LAKE Cumbria 423
BATH Avon 48
BATTLE East Sussex 160
BAYNARDS West Sussex 160
BEACONSFIELD Buckinghamshire 160
BEAUMARIS Gwynedd 371
BEAUMONT Jersey 132
BEDDGELERT Gwynedd 371
BEDFORD Bedfordshire 162
BEER Devon 51
BELFORD Northumberland 538
BELTON Leicestershire 162
BELTON IN RUTLAND Leicestershire
  163
BEMBRIDGE Isle of Wight 163
BERWICK UPON TWEED
  Northumberland 538
BETHERSDEN Kent 163
BETWS Y COED Gwynedd 373
BEVERLEY Humberside 424
BEXHILL ON SEA East Sussex 163
BICKINGTON Devon 51
BICKLEIGH Devon 51
BIDEFORD Devon 52
BIGBURY ON SEA Devon 53
BIGGAR Strathclyde 547
BIGGIN BY HARTINGTON Derbyshire
  424
BIGGLESWADE Bedfordshire 163
BILDESTON Suffolk 164
BILLERICAY Essex 164
BILLINGHAM Cleveland 425
BINGLEY West Yorkshire 425
BIRCHINGTON Kent 164
BIRMINGHAM West Midlands 167
BISHOP AUCKLAND County Durham
  425
BISHOPS CASTLE Shropshire 349
BISHOPS STORTFORD Hertfordshire
  167
BLACKPOOL Lancashire 427
BLAIRGOWRIE Tayside 548
BLAKENEY Norfolk 168
BLANDFORD FORUM Dorset 168
BLETCHINGLEY Surrey 168
BOGNOR REGIS West Sussex 168
BOLTON Lancashire 428
BONESS Central 549
BONTNEWYDD Gwynedd 374
BORROWDALE Cumbria 428
BOSCASTLE Cornwall 53

INDEX

BOUGHTON MONCHELSEA Kent 169
BOURNE Lincolnshire 169
BOURNEMOUTH Dorset 170
BOURTON ON WATER Gloucestershire 175
BOVEY TRACEY Devon 54
BOWNESS ON WINDERMERE Cumbria 428
BRACKNELL Berkshire 176
BRADFORD West Yorkshire 429
BRADFORD ON AVON Wiltshire 176
BRAINTREE Essex 177
BRAMPTON Cumbria 429
BRANCASTER STAITHE Norfolk 177
BRENT KNOLL Somerset 54
BRERETON Cheshire 430
BRIDGE OF EARN Tayside 549
BRIDGE OF ORCHY Strathclyde 549
BRIDGEND Mid Glamorgan 374
BRIDGNORTH Shropshire 349
BRIDGWATER Somerset 54
BRIDLINGTON Humberside 430
BRIDPORT Dorset 55
BRIGG Humberside 431
BRIGHTON & HOVE East Sussex 181
BRINKWORTH Wiltshire 183
BRISTOL Avon 55
BRISTON Norfolk 183
BRIXHAM Devon 57
BROADSTAIRS Kent 183
BROADWAY Hereford & Worcester 350
BROCKENHURST Hampshire 184
BROMLEY Kent 184
BROSELEY Shropshire 350
BROUGH SOWERBY Cumbria 431
BROUGHTON IN FURNESS Cumbria 431
BROWNHILLS West Midlands 185
BUBBENHALL Warwickshire 185
BUCKIE Grampian 604
BUCKLAND Hereford & Worcester 350
BUDE Cornwall 57
BUILTH WELLS Powys 374
BUNTINGFORD Hertfordshire 185
BURBAGE Wiltshire 185
BURCOMBE Wiltshire 186
BURFORD Oxfordshire 186
BURLEY Hampshire 187
BURNHAM ON SEA Somerset 58
BURNMOUTH Borders 550
BURNTISLAND Fife 550
BURTON ON THE WOLDS Leicestershire 187
BURTON UPON TRENT Staffordshire 187
BURY Greater Manchester 432
BURY ST EDMUNDS Suffolk 188
BUTTERMERE Cumbria 432
BUXTON Derbyshire 432

C

CAERLEON Gwent 374
CAERNARFON Gwynedd 375
CALDER BRIDGE Cumbria 433
CALLANDER Central 550
CAMBRIDGE Gloucestershire 351
CAMBRIDGE Cambridgeshire 189
CANTERBURY Kent 191
CAPEL CURIG Gwynedd 375
CARDIFF South Glamorgan 376
CARLISLE Cumbria 435
CARNFORTH Lancashire 436
CASTEL Guernsey 133
CASTLE ACRE Norfolk 191
CASTLE DONINGTON Leicestershire 191
CASTLETON Derbyshire 437
CHAGFORD Devon 58
CHALE Isle of Wight 192
CHARD Somerset 59
CHARLBURY Oxfordshire 192
CHARMOUTH Dorset 59
CHELMSFORD Essex 192
CHELTENHAM Gloucestershire 194
CHELWOOD Avon 60
CHEPSTOW Gwent 376
CHESTER Cheshire 438
CHICHESTER West Sussex 196
CHIDDINGSTONE Kent 197
CHIDEOCK Dorset 60
CHILLINGTON Devon 60
CHIPPING NORTON Oxfordshire 198
CHISWORTH Derbyshire 439
CHORLEY Lancashire 439
CHRISTCHURCH Dorset 199
CHRISTOW Devon 61
CHURCH STRETTON Shropshire 351
CHURT Surrey 199
CIRENCESTER Gloucestershire 199
CLARE Suffolk 201
CLAWTON Devon 61
CLEARWELL Gloucestershire 352
CLEETHORPES Humberside 440
CLEOBURY MORTIMER Shropshire 352
CLEVEDON Avon 61
CLITHEROE Lancashire 440
COLCHESTER Essex 201
COLEFORD Gloucestershire 352
COLSTON BASSETT Nottinghamshire 201
COLWYN BAY Clwyd 376
COMBE MARTIN Devon 62
COMPTON MARTIN Avon 62
CONISTON Cumbria 441
CONSTANTINE BAY Cornwall 62
CONWY Gwynedd 377
CORBRIDGE Northumberland 538
CORNHILL ON TWEED Northumberland 539
CORSHAM Wiltshire 202
COTTENHAM Cambridgeshire 202

INDEX

COVENTRY West Midlands 203
COWBRIDGE South Glamorgan 378
CRACKINGTON HAVEN Cornwall 63
CRAIGELLACHIE Grampian 605
CRAIL Fife 551
CRANLEIGH Surrey 204
CREDITON Devon 63
CREETOWN Dumfries & Galloway 551
CREWE Cheshire 441
CREWKERNE Somerset 63
CRIANLARICH Central 552
CRICCIETH Gwynedd 379
CRICKHOWELL Powys 379
CRICKLADE Wiltshire 205
CRIEFF Tayside 552
CROCKERTON Wiltshire 205
CROMARTY Highland 606
CROMER Norfolk 205
CROWBOROUGH East Sussex 206
CROYDON Surrey 206
CUBERT Cornwall 64
CUCKFIELD West Sussex 207
CULLEN Grampian 606
CWMBRAN Gwent 379

D

DALBEATTIE Dumfries & Galloway
  553
DALMALLY Strathclyde 553
DALRY Dumfries & Galloway 553
DARLINGTON North Yorkshire 442
DARTMOOR Devon 64
DARTMOUTH Devon 64
DAWLISH Devon 66
DENBIGH Clwyd 380
DERBY Derbyshire 442
DEREHAM Norfolk 207
DESFORD Leicestershire 207
DEVIZES Wiltshire 207
DIDCOT Oxfordshire 208
DITCHLING East Sussex 208
DOLGELLAU Gwynedd 380
DOLLAR Central 553
DONCASTER South Yorkshire 443
DORCHESTER Dorset 67
DORCHESTER ON THAMES
  Oxfordshire 208
DORNOCH Highland 607
DOUGLAS Isle of Man 529
DOVER Kent 209
DREWSTEIGNTON Devon 67
DRIFFIELD Humberside 443
DRUMNADROCHIT Highland 608
DRYBROOK Gloucestershire 353
DULVERTON Somerset 67
DUMFRIES Dumfries & Galloway 554
DUNBAR Lothian 555
DUNBLANE Central 555
DUNDEE Tayside 556
DUNFERMLINE Fife 556
DUNOON Strathclyde 556
DUNSTER Somerset 69

DURHAM County Durham **444**
DURNESS Highland 608

E

EASDALE Strathclyde 557
EAST AYTON North Yorkshire 445
EAST LINTON Lothian 557
EASTBOURNE East Sussex 209
ECCLESTON Lancashire 445
EDINBURGH Lothian 561
EDWINSTOWE Nottinghamshire 445
ELLAND West Yorkshire 446
ELLERBY North Yorkshire 447
ELSLACK North Yorkshire 447
ELY Cambridgeshire 210
EMSWORTH Hampshire 211
ENNERDALE BRIDGE Cumbria 447
EPSOM Surrey 211
ESKDALE GREEN Cumbria 447
EVESHAM Hereford & Worcester 353
EXEBRIDGE Somerset 69
EXETER Devon 70
EXFORD Somerset 71
EXMOUTH Devon 72
EYKE Suffolk 211

F

FAIRBURN North Yorkshire 448
FAIRFORD Gloucestershire 211
FAIRLIGHT East Sussex 212
FALMOUTH Cornwall 72
FAR SAWREY Cumbria 448
FAREHAM Hampshire 212
FARNHAM Surrey 212
FELIXSTOWE Suffolk 213
FILEY North Yorkshire 448
FISHGUARD Dyfed 381
FLAMSTEAD Hertfordshire 214
FLAX BOURTON Avon 73
FLEET Hampshire 214
FORFAR Tayside 563
FORT WILLIAM Highland 609
FORTINGALL Tayside 564
FOSS CROSS Gloucestershire 215
FOWEY Cornwall 74
FOWNHOPE Hereford & Worcester
  354
FRODSHAM Cheshire 449
FROME Somerset 74

G

GAIRLOCH Highland 609
GALASHIELS Borders 564
GARSTANG Lancashire 449
GATEHOUSE OF FLEET Dumfries &
  Galloway 564
GEDNEY DYKE Lincolnshire 215
GILLINGHAM Dorset 215

INDEX

GIRVAN Strathclyde 565
GISBURN Lancashire 450
GLASGOW Strathclyde 568
GLASTONBURY Somerset 74
GLEN HELEN Isle of Man 529
GLENMORISTON Highland 609
GLENROTHES Fife 568
GLENSHEE Tayside 568
GLOUCESTER Gloucestershire 354
GOATHLAND North Yorkshire 450
GODSHILL Isle of Wight 215
GOLSPIE Highland 610
GOOSNARGH Lancashire 450
GOREY HARBOUR Jersey 133
GORING ON THAMES Oxfordshire
  216
GORLESTON ON SEA Norfolk 216
GOSPORT Hampshire 217
GOUROCK Strathclyde 569
GRANGE OVER SANDS Cumbria 451
GRANTHAM Lincolnshire 452
GRANTOWN ON SPEY Highland 610
GRASMERE Cumbria 453
GRASSINGTON North Yorkshire 453
GREAT AYTON North Yorkshire 454
GREAT BIRCHAM Norfolk 217
GREAT BROUGHTON North Yorkshire
  454
GREAT MALVERN Hereford &
  Worcester 354
GREAT MISSENDEN Buckinghamshire
  217
GREAT RISSINGTON Gloucestershire
  218
GREAT WITLEY Hereford & Worcester
  354
GREAT YARMOUTH Norfolk 218
GREENHEAD Northumberland 539
GRETNA Dumfries & Galloway 569
GRIZEDALE Cumbria 454
GUILDFORD Surrey 219
GULLANE Lothian 569
GUNNISLAKE Cornwall 75
GUNTHORPE Nottinghamshire 455

H

HALIFAX West Yorkshire 455
HALSTEAD Essex 219
HALWELL Devon 75
HAMPTON COURT Surrey 219
HANNINGTON Hampshire 220
HAPPISBURGH Norfolk 220
HARLECH Gwynedd 381
HARROGATE North Yorkshire 457
HARROW Middlesex 221
HARTLEPOOL Cleveland 458
HARWICH Essex 222
HASLEMERE Surrey 223
HASTINGS East Sussex 223
HASWELL PLOUGH County Durham
  459
HAUGHLEY Suffolk 224

HAVERFORDWEST Dyfed 382
HAWICK Borders 569
HAWKSHEAD Cumbria 459
HAWORTH West Yorkshire 459
HAY ON WYE Hereford & Worcester
  355
HAYDON BRIDGE Northumberland
  539
HAYES Middlesex 224
HAYLING ISLAND Hampshire 224 &
  320
HAYWARDS HEATH West Sussex 225
HEADLEY Hampshire 225
HELMSLEY North Yorkshire 461
HENFIELD West Sussex 226
HENLEY IN ARDEN Warwickshire 226
HENLEY ON THAMES Oxfordshire
  226
HENLOW Bedfordshire 228
HEREFORD Hereford & Worcester 355
HERSTMONCEUX East Sussex 228
HEXHAM Northumberland 539
HIGH WYCOMBE Buckinghamshire
  228
HOLTON Somerset 75
HOLYHEAD Gwynedd 383
HOLYWELL GREEN West Yorkshire
  462
HONITON Devon 76
HORNBY Lancashire 462
HORSHAM West Sussex 228
HOTON Leicestershire 229
HUDDERSFIELD West Yorkshire 463
HULL Humberside 464
HUNSTANTON Norfolk 229
HUNTINGDON Cambridgeshire 230
HUNTLY Grampian 611
HURSTPIERPOINT West Sussex 230
HYDE Cheshire 464

I

ICKHAM Kent 230
ILFRACOMBE Devon 77
ILKLEY West Yorkshire 465
INGLEBY GREENHOW North
  Yorkshire 465
INSCH Grampian 612
INVERARAY Strathclyde 570
INVERGARRY Highland 612
INVERNESS Highland 613
ISLE OF ARRAN Strathclyde 570
ISLE OF BARRA Western Isles 614
ISLE OF BENBECULA Western Isles
  614
ISLE OF GIGHA Strathclyde 571
ISLE OF HARRIS Western Isles 614
ISLE OF IONA Strathclyde 571
ISLE OF LEWIS Western Isles 614
ISLE OF MULL Strathclyde 572
ISLE OF SKYE Highland 615
ISLE OF SOUTH UIST Western Isles
  618

INDEX

ISLE OF WHITHORN Dumfries &
  Galloway 573
ISLES OF SCILLY "St Marys" 78
IVYBRIDGE Devon 78

J

JEDBURGH Borders 573
JOHNSTONE Strathclyde 573

K

KELSO Borders 574
KENDAL Cumbria 466
KENILWORTH Warwickshire 231
KENLEY Surrey 232
KENMORE Tayside 574
KERSEY Suffolk 232
KESWICK Cumbria 467
KEW Surrey 232
KIDDERMINSTER Hereford &
  Worcester 356
KILFINAN Strathclyde 574
KILLIN Central 575
KILMARNOCK Strathclyde 575
KILMELFORD Strathclyde 575
KILWINNING Strathclyde 576
KIMBERLEY Nottinghamshire 469
KINCARDINE ON FORTH Fife 576
KINCRAIG Highland 618
KINGS LYNN Norfolk 232
KINGSBRIDGE Devon 79
KINGUSSIE Highland 618
KINLOCH RANNOCH Tayside 576
KINLOCHBERVIE Highland 619
KINLOCHLEVEN Highland 620
KINROSS Tayside 577
KIRKBY LONSDALE Cumbria 469
KIRKBY STEPHEN Cumbria 469
KIRKCALDY Fife 577
KIRKCUDBRIGHT Dumfries &
  Galloway 577
KIRKMICHAEL Tayside 577
KNAPHILL Surrey 233
KNUTSFORD Cheshire 470

L

LAIRG Highland 620
LANCASTER Lancashire 471
LANCING West Sussex 233
LANDS END Cornwall 79
LANGFORD Oxfordshire 234
LANGPORT Somerset 80
LANGTOFT Humberside 471
LARGS Strathclyde 578
LAUNCESTON Cornwall 80
LAVANT West Sussex 234
LAVENHAM Suffolk 235
LAXTON Nottinghamshire 471
LEADBURN Lothian 578

LEADENHAM Lincolnshire 471
LEAFIELD Oxfordshire 235
LEAMINGTON SPA Warwickshire 236
LEDBURY Hereford & Worcester 356
LEEDS West Yorkshire 472
LEEK Staffordshire 473
LEEMING North Yorkshire 474
LEICESTER Leicestershire 237
LEIGH ON SEA Essex 239
LEIGHTON BUZZARD Bedfordshire
  240
LEWES East Sussex 240
LICHFIELD Staffordshire 240
LIFTON Devon 81
LIMPLEY STOKE Wiltshire 241
LIMPSFIELD Surrey 241
LINCOLN Lincolnshire 475
LINTON Cambridgeshire 241
LINWOOD Hampshire 242
LISKEARD Cornwall 81
LITTLE COMPTON Gloucestershire
  242
LITTLE HAVEN Dyfed 383
LITTLE MILTON Oxfordshire 242
LITTLE WASHBOURNE
  Gloucestershire 243
LITTON Somerset 81
LIVERPOOL Merseyside 477
LIVERSEDGE West Yorkshire 477
LLANBEDROG Gwynedd 383
LLANBERIS Gwynedd 383
LLANDOGO Gwent 384
LLANDOVERY Dyfed 384
LLANDRINDOD WELLS Powys 384
LLANDUDNO Gwynedd 390
LLANDYBIE Dyfed 390
LLANFAIRPWLL Gwynedd 391
LLANGOLLEN Clwyd 391
LLANRWST Gwynedd 391
LLANTRISSENT Gwent 392
LOCHEARNHEAD Central 578
LOCHGILPHEAD Strathclyde 579
LOCKERBIE Dumfries & Galloway 579
LONDON Hampstead, NW3 330
LONDON Bloomsbury, WC1 324
LONDON Covent Garden, WC2 327
LONDON Fulham, SW10 329
LONDON Knightsbridge, SW3 332
LONDON Battersea, SW11 323
LONDON Islington, N1 331
LONDON South Kensington, SW3 338
LONDON Westminster, SW1 341
LONDON West End, W1 339
LONDON West End, WC2 340
LONDON Putney, SW15 337
LONDON Greenwich, SE18 329
LONDON Clerkenwell, EC1 327
LONDON Chelsea, SW1 325
LONDON Eltham, SE9 328
LONDON City, EC4 326
LONDON Battersea, SW11 323
LONDON West End, W2 340
LONDON Trafalgar Square, WC2 339

INDEX

LONDON Westminster, SW1 341
LONDON Notting Hill, W11 334
LONDON Soho, W1 337
LONDON Putney, SW15 335
LONDON Southgate, N14 338
LONDON Forest Hill, SE23 329
LONDON Muswell Hill, N10 333
LONDON Kensington, W8 332
LONDON West Hampstead, NW6 341
LONDON Islington, N1 331
LONDON Bloomsbury, WC1 324
LONDON Covent Garden, WC2 328
LONDON Hampstead, NW3 330
LONDON City, EC4 326
LONDON Fulham, SW10 329
LONDON Knightsbridge, SW3 332
LONDON Chelsea, SW1 325
LONDON Putney, SW15 336
LONDON Notting Hill, W11 334
LONDON South Kensington, SW3 338
LONDON Hampstead, NW3 330
LONDON Bloomsbury, WC1 325
LONDON Clerkenwell, EC1 326
LONDON Bayswater, W2 323
LONDON Paddington, W2 334
LONDON Fulham, SW6 329
LONDON Knightsbridge, SW3 333
LONDON Kensington, SW5 332
LONDON Notting Hill, W11 334
LONDON Bayswater, W2 323
LONDON Kensington, SW5 331
LONDON Kensington, W11 332
LONDON Hatton Garden, EC1 330
LONDON Lancaster Gate, W2 333
LONDON Covent Garden, WC2 328
LONDON Putney, SW15 336
LONDON Bayswater, W2 323
LONDON Lancaster Gate, W2 333
LONDON Fulham, SW6 329
LONDON Bloomsbury, WC1 325
LONDON Clerkenwell, EC1 326
LONDON Hammersmith, W6 330
LONDON Covent Garden, WC2 327
LONDON Belgravia, SW1 324
LONDON Herne Hill, SE24 331
LONDON Paddington, W2 335
LONDON Chelsea, SW3 326
LONDON Putney, SW15 337
LONDON West End, W1 340
LONDON Belgravia, SW1 324
LONDON West End, W1 340
LONDON Spitalfields, E1 339
LONDON Soho, W1 337
LONDON Putney, SW15 335
LONDON Spitalfields, E1 339
LONDON West Hampstead, NW6 341
LONDON Muswell Hill, N10 334
LONDON Soho, W1 338
LONDON Westminster, SW1 341
LONDON West End, WC2 340
LONDON West End, W1 339
LONDON Clerkenwell, EC1 327
LONDON West End, W2 340

LONDON Trafalgar Square, WC2 339
LONDON Hammersmith, W6 330
LONDON Putney, SW15 337
LONDON Paddington, W2 335
LONDON Chelsea, SW3 326
LONDON Belgravia, SW1 324
LONDON Covent Garden, WC2 327
LONDON Kensington, W11 332
LONDON Hatton Garden, EC1 331
LONDON Kensington, W8 332
LONDON Forest Hill, SE23 328
LONDON Mortlake, SW14 333
LONDON Southgate, N14 338
LONDON Greenwich, SE18 329
LONDON Eltham, SE9 328
LONDON Mortlake, SW14 333
LONDON West Hampstead, NW6 341
LONDON Herne Hill, SE24 331
LONDON Battersea, SW11 323
LONG PRESTON North Yorkshire 477
LONGFRAMLINGTON
 Northumberland 540
LONGHAM Dorset 243
LONGRIDGE Lancashire 478
LONGSDON Staffordshire 478
LONGTOWN Cumbria 478
LOOE Cornwall 82
LOSTWITHIEL Cornwall 84
LOUGHBOROUGH Leicestershire 24?
LOUGHTON Buckinghamshire 244
LOUTH Lincolnshire 479
LOWICK Northumberland 540
LUDLOW Shropshire 357
LULWORTH Dorset 244
LULWORTH COVE Dorset 244
LUSS Strathclyde 580
LUTON Bedfordshire 245
LYDDINGTON Leicestershire 245
LYME REGIS Dorset 84
LYMINGTON Hampshire 245
LYNDHURST Hampshire 246
LYNMOUTH Devon 86
LYNTON Devon 87
LYTHAM ST ANNES Lancashire 479

M

MACHYNLLETH Powys 392
MAENTWROG Gwynedd 392
MAIDENHEAD Berkshire 247
MAIDSTONE Kent 247
MALMESBURY Wiltshire 247
MALTON North Yorkshire 480
MALVERN Hereford & Worcester 358
MANCHESTER Greater Manchester
 482
MARGATE Kent 248
MARKET HARBOROUGH
 Leicestershire 249
MARKET RASEN Lincolnshire 483
MARKET WEIGHTON Humberside
 483
MARLBOROUGH Wiltshire 249

INDEX

MARLOW Buckinghamshire 249
MARNHULL Dorset 250
MATLOCK Derbyshire 484
MAWDESLEY Lancashire 484
MELKSHAM Wiltshire 250
MELMERBY Cumbria 485
MELTON MOWBRAY Leicestershire 251
MELVICH Highland 621
MEVAGISSEY Cornwall 89
MIDDLETON TYAS North Yorkshire 485
MIDHURST West Sussex 251
MILFORD HAVEN Dyfed 393
MILNATHORT Tayside 580
MILTON KEYNES Buckinghamshire 252
MINEHEAD Somerset 89
MISTERTON Somerset 89
MODBURY Devon 89
MOFFAT Dumfries & Galloway 581
MOLD Clwyd 393
MONMOUTH Gwent 393
MORECAMBE Lancashire 485
MORETON IN MARSH Gloucestershire 252
MORETONHAMPSTEAD Devon 90
MORTEHOE Devon 90
MOTHERWELL Strathclyde 581
MUCH WENLOCK Shropshire 358

N

NAIRN Highland 621
NARBERTH Dyfed 394
NEASHAM County Durham 486
NEFYN Gwynedd 394
NEW GALLOWAY Dumfries & Galloway 582
NEW QUAY Dyfed 395
NEW RADNOR Powys 395
NEWARK Nottinghamshire 486
NEWBURGH Grampian 622
NEWBY BRIDGE Cumbria 487
NEWCASTLE UNDER LYME Staffordshire 487
NEWCASTLE UPON TYNE Tyne & Wear 488
NEWCASTLETON Borders 582
NEWHAVEN East Sussex 252
NEWPORT Gwent 396
NEWQUAY Cornwall 93
NEWTON LE WILLOWS Merseyside 489
NEWTON STEWART Dumfries & Galloway 582
NORTH WOOTTON Somerset 94
NORTHALLERTON North Yorkshire 489
NORTHAMPTON Northamptonshire 252
NORTHWICH Cheshire 490
NORTON North Yorkshire 490

NORTON Shropshire 358
NORTON North Yorkshire 490
NORWICH Norfolk 253
NOTTINGHAM Nottinghamshire 491
NYMPSFIELD Gloucestershire 254

O

OAKHAM Leicestershire 254
OBAN Strathclyde 583
ODIHAM Hampshire 254
OLD DALBY Leicestershire 255
ORFORD Suffolk 255
ORKNEY Kirkwall 623
ORKNEY Stenness 623
ORKNEY Kirkwall 623
ORKNEY Stenness 623
ORMSKIRK Lancashire 492
ORSETT Essex 255
OSMOTHERLEY North Yorkshire 492
OSWESTRY Shropshire 359
OTLEY West Yorkshire 492
OTTERBURN Northumberland 540
OUNDLE Northamptonshire 256
OXFORD Oxfordshire 257
OXWICH West Glamorgan 396

P

PADIHAM Lancashire 493
PAIGNTON Devon 95
PAISLEY Strathclyde 584
PARKEND Gloucestershire 359
PARKGATE Cheshire 493
PEEBLES Borders 585
PELYNT Cornwall 96
PEMBROKE Dyfed 396
PENDOGGETT Cornwall 96
PENRITH Cumbria 493
PENSAX Hereford & Worcester 359
PENZANCE Cornwall 98
PERRANPORTH Cornwall 98
PERSHORE Hereford & Worcester 360
PERTH Tayside 586
PETERBOROUGH Cambridgeshire 258
PETERHEAD Grampian 624
PETERSFIELD Hampshire 258
PHILLEIGH Cornwall 99
PICKERING North Yorkshire 494
PINNER Middlesex 259
PITLOCHRY Tayside 587
PLUCKLEY Kent 259
PLYMOUTH Devon 100
POLPERRO Cornwall 102
PONTFAEN Dyfed 397
POOLE Dorset 259
PORT ISAAC Cornwall 102
PORTESHAM Dorset 104
PORTHMADOG Gwynedd 397
PORTLAND Dorset 104
PORTSCATHO Cornwall 104

INDEX

PORTSMOUTH Hampshire 261
POUNDSGATE Devon 104
PRESTATYN Clwyd 398
PRESTON Lancashire 495
PRESTON Dorset 105
PRESTON Lancashire 495
PUCKERIDGE Hertfordshire 261
PUTECHANTUY Strathclyde 587
PWLLHELI Gwynedd 398

R

RAASAY Highland 624
RAMSBOTTOM Lancashire 495
RAMSEY Isle of Man 530
RAMSGATE Kent 261
RANGEWORTHY Avon 105
READING Berkshire 261
REDCAR Cleveland 496
REDDITCH Hereford & Worcester 360
REDHILL Surrey 263
REDMARLEY DABITOT
  Gloucestershire 360
REDRUTH Cornwall 105
REEDHAM Norfolk 263
REETH North Yorkshire 496
REIGATE Surrey 264
RENFREW Strathclyde 588
RHAYADER Powys 398
RICHMOND Surrey 264
RICHMOND North Yorkshire 497
RICHMOND Surrey 264
RICHMOND North Yorkshire 497
RICHMOND Surrey 264
RICKLING GREEN Essex 265
RIDGMONT Bedfordshire 265
RINGWOOD Hampshire 265
RIPLEY Surrey 266
RIPON North Yorkshire 497
ROCK Cornwall 106
ROGART Highland 624
ROLLESBY Norfolk 266
ROMALDKIRK County Durham 498
ROMFORD Essex 266
ROMSEY Hampshire 267
ROSEDALE ABBEY North Yorkshire
  498
ROSLIN Lothian 588
ROSS ON WYE Hereford & Worcester
  362
ROSYTH Fife 589
ROTHBURY Northumberland 541
ROTHERHAM South Yorkshire 498
ROTHERWICK Hampshire 267
ROTHESAY Isle of Bute 589
ROTHLEY Leicestershire 268
ROYSTON Hertfordshire 268
RUGELEY Staffordshire 269
RUISLIP Greater London 269
RUTHIN Clwyd 398
RYE East Sussex 269

S

SALCOMBE Devon 106
SALEHURST East Sussex 270
SALFORD Greater Manchester 500
SALISBURY Wiltshire 271
SANDOWN Isle of Wight 273
SAUNDERSFOOT Dyfed 399
SAUNTON Devon 106
SAXMUNDHAM Suffolk 273
SCARBOROUGH North Yorkshire 502
SCOURIE Highland 625
SEAHOUSES Northumberland 541
SEAVIEW Isle of Wight 274
SEAVINGTON ST. MICHAEL
  Somerset 107
SEDBERGH Cumbria 502
SELKIRK Borders 589
SELLING Kent 274
SETTLE North Yorkshire 503
SEVENOAKS Kent 274
SHAFTESBURY Dorset 275
SHALDON Devon 107
SHANKLIN Isle of Wight 275
SHARDLOW Derbyshire 504
SHEFFIELD South Yorkshire 504
SHERINGHAM Norfolk 276
SHERSTON Wiltshire 277
SHETLAND Hillswick 625
SHETLAND Brae 625
SHETLAND Hillswick 625
SHIPLEY West Yorkshire 505
SHIPTON ON STOUR Warwickshire
  277
SHIPTON UNDER WYCHWOOD
  Oxfordshire 277
SHIRENEWTON Gwent 399
SHOEBURYNESS Essex 278
SHREWSBURY Shropshire 364
SIDFORD Devon 107
SIDMOUTH Devon 108
SILEBY Leicestershire 278
SILLOTH ON SOLWAY Cumbria 506
SITTINGBOURNE Kent 278
SKEGNESS Lincolnshire 506
SKIPTON North Yorkshire 506
SNETTISHAM Norfolk 278
SOLIHULL West Midlands 279
SOMERTON Somerset 109
SOULDERN Oxfordshire 279
SOUTH SHIELDS Tyne & Wear 507
SOUTH ZEAL Devon 109
SOUTHAMPTON Hampshire 280
SOUTHEND Essex 282
SOUTHEND ON SEA Essex 282
SOUTHERTON Devon 110
SOUTHPORT Merseyside 508
SOUTHSEA Hampshire 282
SOUTHWOLD Suffolk 283
SPALDING Lincolnshire 283
SPEAN BRIDGE Highland 626
ST AGNES Cornwall 110
ST ALBANS Hertfordshire 283

INDEX

ST ANDREWS Fife 000
ST ASAPH Clwyd 400
ST AUBIN Jersey 133
ST AUSTELL Cornwall 110
ST BRELADE Jersey 134
ST CLEMENT Jersey 134
ST DAVIDS Dyfed 401
ST FILLANS Tayside 590
ST HELENS Isle of Wight 283
ST HELENS Merseyside 508
ST HELIER Jersey 134
ST IVES Cornwall 111
ST IVES Cambridgeshire 284
ST IVES Cornwall 111
ST IVES Cambridgeshire 285
ST IVES Cornwall 111
ST IVES BAY Cornwall 112
ST LEONARDS ON SEA East Sussex 285
ST MARTINS Guernsey 137
ST OUEN Jersey 138
ST OUENS BAY Jersey 138
ST PETER PORT Guernsey 139
ST SAMPSONS Guernsey 139
STAFFORD Staffordshire 285
STALHAM Norfolk 286
STAMFORD Lincolnshire 286
STANDISH Greater Manchester 509
STAVERTON Devon 113
STEEP Hampshire 286
STEVENAGE Hertfordshire 287
STEYNING West Sussex 287
STOCKBRIDGE Hampshire 288
STOKE ON TRENT Staffordshire 509
STOKESLEY North Yorkshire 509
STOURPORT ON SEVERN Hereford & Worcester 365
STOW Borders 591
STOW ON THE WOLD Gloucestershire 289
STRACHUR Strathclyde 591
STRATFORD UPON AVON Warwickshire 290
STRATHDON Grampian 626
STREATLEY ON THAMES Berkshire 293
STRONTIAN Highland 626
STROUD Gloucestershire 293
STRUY Highland 626
STUDLAND Dorset 293
SUDBURY Suffolk 294
SUNDERLAND Tyne & Wear 510
SUTTON Surrey 294
SUTTON COLDFIELD West Midlands 295
SWANAGE Dorset 296
SWANSEA West Glamorgan 401
SWINDON Wiltshire 296

TALSARNAU Gwynedd 403
TALYCAFN Gwynedd 403
TARBERT Strathclyde 591
TAUNTON Somerset 114
TAVISTOCK Devon 114
TAYVALLICH Strathclyde 592
TEDDINGTON Middlesex 296
TELFORD Shropshire 365
TENBY Dyfed 403
TETBURY Gloucestershire 297
TEWKESBURY Gloucestershire 366
TEYNHAM Kent 297
THAME Oxfordshire 297
THAMES DITTON Surrey 298
THE LIZARD Cornwall 114
THELBRIDGE Devon 115
THETFORD Norfolk 298
THIRLMERE Cumbria 510
THIRSK North Yorkshire 511
THORGANBY North Yorkshire 512
THORNE South Yorkshire 512
THORNHILL Dumfries & Galloway 592
THORNTHWAITE Cumbria 512
THORNTON DALE North Yorkshire 513
THROWLEIGH Devon 115
TIDESWELL Derbyshire 513
TINTAGEL Cornwall 116
TINTERN Gwent 404
TIVERTON Devon 116
TOMINTOUL Grampian 627
TONBRIDGE Kent 298
TONGUE Highland 627
TOPSHAM Devon 117
TORQUAY Devon 120
TORTEVAL Guernsey 140
TOTLAND BAY Isle of Wight 299
TOTNES Devon 120
TREARDDUR BAY Gwynedd 405
TREGONY Cornwall 120
TRELLECH Gwent 405
TRENT Dorset 121
TRESAITH Dyfed 405
TRINITY Jersey 140
TROON Strathclyde 592
TROTTON West Sussex 299
TROWBRIDGE Wiltshire 299
TRURO Cornwall 120
TUNBRIDGE WELLS Kent 301
TWEEDSMUIR Borders 593
TYNDRUM Central 593

U

TAIN Highland 627
TAL Y BONT Gwynedd 403

UCKFIELD East Sussex 301
ULLAPOOL Highland 628
UPAVON Wiltshire 302
UPPER BENEFIELD Northamptonshire 302
UPPER GORNAL West Midlands 302
UPTON CHEYNEY Avon 122
USK Gwent 405

INDEX

V

VAZON BAY Guernsey 141
VENTNOR Isle of Wight 303

W

WADEBRIDGE Cornwall 122
WADHURST East Sussex 304
WALBERSWICK Suffolk 304
WALLASEY Merseyside 514
WALSALL West Midlands 304
WALTON ON THAMES Surrey 305
WARE Hertfordshire 305
WARMINSTER Wiltshire 305
WARWICK Warwickshire 306
WASDALE HEAD Cumbria 514
WATCHET Somerset 123
WATLINGTON Oxfordshire 306
WATTON AT STONE Hertfordshire 307
WEEDON Northamptonshire 307
WELFORD Northamptonshire 307
WELLINGBOROUGH Northamptonshire 308
WELLS Somerset 124
WELLS NEXT THE SEA Norfolk 309
WELSHPOOL Powys 406
WEMBWORTHY Devon 125
WENSLEYDALE North Yorkshire 514
WENTNOR Shropshire 366
WEOBLEY Hereford & Worcester 367
WEST BEXINGTON Dorset 126
WEST ILSLEY Berkshire 309
WEST LULWORTH Dorset 309
WEST MARDEN West Sussex 309
WEST STAFFORD Dorset 126
WEST WEMYSS Fife 593
WEST WITTON North Yorkshire 515
WEST WYCOMBE Buckinghamshire 310
WESTCLIFF ON SEA Essex 310
WESTERHAM Kent 310
WESTON SUPER MARE Avon 126
WESTONING Bedfordshire 311

WEYMOUTH Dorset 127
WHIMPLE Devon 129
WHITBY North Yorkshire 517
WHITLEY BAY Tyne & Wear 518
WHITSTABLE Kent 311
WIGAN Greater Manchester 518
WIGGLESWORTH North Yorkshire 519
WILLENHALL West Midlands 311
WIMBORNE Dorset 312
WINCANTON Somerset 129
WINCHELSEA East Sussex 312
WINCHESTER Hampshire 312
WINDERMERE Cumbria 519
WINDSOR Berkshire 313
WINSTANSTOW Shropshire 367
WIRKSWORTH Derbyshire 520
WISBECH Cambridgeshire 313
WITHERSLACK Cumbria 520
WITNEY Oxfordshire 314
WOKINGHAM Berkshire 314
WOLTERTON Norfolk 315
WOLVERHAMPTON West Midlands 315
WOODBRIDGE Suffolk 316
WOODSTOCK Oxfordshire 316
WOODY BAY Devon 130
WOOLACOMBE Devon 131
WOOLER Northumberland 542
WOOTTON WAWEN Warwickshire 316
WORCESTER Hereford & Worcester 367
WORKSOP Nottinghamshire 520
WORTHING West Sussex 319
WRENTHAM Suffolk 319
WREXHAM Clwyd 407
WYLAM Northumberland 542
WYMONDHAM Leicestershire 320

Y

YARM Cleveland 521
YATE Avon 131
YORK North Yorkshire 524

APPLICATION FORM

If you use the Guide regularly, then it would certainly be in your interest to join Club Bon Viveur and receive the numerous benefits on offer.

Remember what they are . . .

- Discounts at over 300 Les Routiers restaurants and hotels
- £2 off additional copies of both Les Routiers Guides
- Discounts off motoring services and insurance with Europ Assistance
- Discount off holidays in the Paris and France brochures booked through Jet Tours and the French Travel Service
- Newsletter including promotional offers

We are always pleased to hear your comments on any restaurants and hotels you have visited. On the reverse of this page, there is the opportunity to give your opinion.

To join Club Bon Viveur, simply complete the form below and return it to us with the annual subscription fee of £12.00.

Name _____

Address _____

_____

_____

I enclose a cheque for £12.00 (payable to Routiers Ltd) ☐
OR
Please debit my Access/Visa Card for the amount
of £12.00. ☐

Card No. .... Expiry Date _____

Signature ....

Return to: Club Bon Viveur, 25-27 Vanston Place, London SW6 1AZ.
Please allow 28 days for delivery.

YOUR OPINION

Do you have a favourite pub, restaurant or hotel which you would like to recommend to us, which is not already Les Routiers recommended? If it is worthy of nomination, please let us know on the form below so that, with their consent, we may arrange for an inspector to call.

Alternatively, if you visit a Les Routiers establishment which you think is worthy of a Les Routiers Award or, if you are dissatisfied with an establishment, we would like to hear your comments.

With your help, we can maintain Les Routiers standards, and all correspondence will be treated in strictest confidence.

Name of Establishment: _____

Address/Location: _____

_____

Type of Establishment (please circle):

Restaurant   Public House   Wine Bar/Bistro   Hotel   B&B

Please Circle: Nomination   OR   Complaint

Comments: _____

_____

_____

_____